The
Cambridge History *of*
American Literature

EDITED BY

WILLIAM PETERFIELD TRENT

JOHN ERSKINE

STUART P. SHERMAN

CARL VAN DOREN

IN THREE VOLUMES

MACMILLAN PUBLISHING CO., INC.
New York

THE CAMBRIDGE HISTORY

OF

AMERICAN LITERATURE

Volume I

Colonial and Revolutionary Literature

Early National Literature: Part I

The Cambridge History

of

American Literature

Edited by

William Peterfield Trent

John Erskine

Stuart P. Sherman

Carl Van Doren

In Three Volumes

Colonial and Revolutionary Literature
Early National Literature: Part I

MACMILLAN PUBLISHING CO., INC.
New York

HOUSTON PUBLIC LIBRARY

40   39   38   37   36   35
ISBN 0-02-520930-2

MACMILLAN PUBLISHING CO., INC.
866 Third Avenue, New York, N.Y. 10022
PRINTED IN THE UNITED STATES OF AMERICA

PREFACE

IT was a hard saying of a Spanish aphorist of the seventeenth century that "to equal a predecessor one must have twice his worth." We should deprecate the application of that standard to *The Cambridge History of American Literature*, yet we are not without hope that the work, of which we here present the first volume, will be found to mark some progress in the right direction. We would call attention to the following as perhaps its chief distinctive features: (1) It is on a larger scale than any of its predecessors which have carried the story from colonial times to the present generation; (2) It is the first history of American literature composed with the collaboration of a numerous body of scholars from every section of the United States and from Canada; (3) It will provide for the first time an extensive bibliography for all periods and subjects treated; (4) It will be a survey of the life of the American people as expressed in their writings rather than a history of *belles-lettres* alone. The significance of these features may be emphasized by some reference to the characteristic merits and defects of previous works in this field, to which we are under obligations too extensive for detailed mention.

The earliest and the latest historians of a literature have great advantages: the earliest, that he has no predecessors; the latest, that he has many. It is a pleasure to remember Samuel L. Knapp, who in the preface to his *Lectures on American Literature*, published in 1829, easily justified the publication of that interesting and patriotic overture: "We have very good histories—narrative, political, military, and constitutional; but I know none, as yet, that can be called literary—meaning by the term, a history of our literature, and of our literary men." "You are aware," he continues, "that it has been said by foreigners, and often repeated, that there was no such thing as American literature; that it would be vain for anyone to seek for proofs of taste, mind, or information, worth possessing, in our early records; and some of our citizens, who have never examined these matters, have rested so quietly after these declarations, or so fondly denied them, that the bold asserters of these libels have gained confidence in tauntingly repeating them. The great epoch in our history—the revolution of 1775—seemed sufficient, alone, to many of the present generation, to give us, as a people, all the celebrity and rank, among the nations of the earth, we ought to aspire to, without taking the trouble to go back to the previous ages of heroick virtue and gigantick labours. Many of the present generation are willing to think that our ancestors were a pious and persevering race of men, who really did possess some strength of character, but, without further reflection, they are ready to allow that a few pages are 'ample room and verge enough' to trace their character and their history together: I have ventured to think differently'';—and the editors of the present work are at this point in accord with Knapp.

Knapp, however, illustrates a temptation which has beset investigators of American literature from his day to ours, namely, the temptation to relinquish the unremunerative project of adequate scholarly publication and to compensate oneself by producing a text-book adapted to the means and the minds of school-boys. "My plan," he says, in a passage which throws an illuminating beam down the whole pathway of American literary scholarship—"My plan when I commenced my researches was an extensive one, and I gathered copious materials to carry it into effect. For several years past I have had access to libraries rich in American literature; but when I sat down to work up the mass I had collected, the thought suggested itself to my mind, that no adequate compensation could ever be reasonably expected for my pains. . . . Still I could not be persuaded to relinquish altogether my design, and I therefore set about abridging my outlines, dispensing with many of my remarks, and giving up many elaborate finishings I had promised myself to make in the course of my work. And another thought struck me most forcibly, that a heavy publication would not be readily within the reach of all classes of youth in our country, but that a single volume of common size, in a cheap edition, might find its way into some of our schools, and be of service in giving our children a wish to pursue the subject of our literary history as they advanced in years and knowledge." The philosophic observer may here remark that our historian, like his innumerable successors, follows the way of all flesh in that when he has abandoned his ideal immediately there bolts into his mind an excellent reason for abandoning it.

A second temptation of the American historian, which appeared long before Knapp and persisted long after him, is to magnify the achievements of one's own parish at the expense of the rest of the country. In Governor Bradford's *History of Plymouth Plantation* there is hardly a trace of inflation; throughout that grave and noble narrative the Governor cleaves to his purpose to write "in a plain style, with singular regard unto the simple truth in all things." But in Cotton Mather one finds already a local pride that looks disdainfully upon the neighbour colonies and deigns only to compare the New England worthies with the prophets and apostles of Palestine. In the more temperate passages of the *Magnalia Christi Americana* he cultivates the just self-esteem of his section with considerations like these: "I will make no odious comparisons between Harvard College and other universities for the proportion of worthy men therein educated; but New England, compared with other parts of America, may certainly boast of having brought forth very many eminent men, in proportion more than any of them; and of Harvard College (herein truly a Sion College) it may be said, *this and that man were bred there;* of whom not the least was Mr. Thomas Shepard." The local pride, more or less justifiable, which renders tumid the periods of this energetic old Puritan, was a useful passion at a time when literature was obliged to develop independently in widely separated colonies. It is a useful passion still in a country of a hundred million inhabitants separated by such spatial and spiritual intervals as lie between Boston, New York, Richmond, Chicago, New Orleans, and San Francisco. It has stimulated the production of our innumerable "local-colorists" in poetry and prose fiction. It underlies many entertaining books and articles on the New England School, the Knickerbocker School, the Southern School, the Hoosier School, and the rest; but it is not conducive

to the production of a quite unbiassed history of American
literature.

Many of our historians who escaped from the colonial or
provincial illusion succumbed, especially in the period before
the Civil War, to the temptation of national pride. There
was much provocation and incitement both at home and
abroad. Transatlantic critics enquired tauntingly, " Who
reads an American book?" and challenged the American
authors to show reasons why sentence of death should not be
pronounced against them. It no longer sufficed to say with the
colonial divines of New England: We have created in the
wilderness of the western world a commonwealth for Christ,
a spiritual New Jerusalem. It no longer served to declare
with the Revolutionary Fathers: We have established the
political Promised Land, and have set up the lamp of Liberty
for a beacon light to all nations. What was demanded early in
the nineteenth century of the adolescent nation was an indigenous independent national literature. The wrong answer to
this demand was given by the enthusiastic patriots who,
after the Revolution, advocated the abrogation of English in
"these States" and the invention and adoption of a new
language; or compiled, to silence their skeptical English cousins, pretentious anthologies of all our village elegists; or offered
Dwight's *Conquest of Canaan* as an equivalent to Milton's
Paradise Lost, Barlow's *Columbiad* as an imposing national
epic, Lathrop's poem on the sachem of the Narragansett Indians,
The Speech of Caunonicus, as heralding the dawn of a genuinely
native school of poetry. Our pioneer historian Knapp discreetly hesitates to say "whether she of 'the banks of the
Connecticut' [Mrs. Sigourney], whose strains of poetic thought
are as pure and lovely as the adjacent wave touched by the
sanctity of a Sabbath's morn, be equal to her tuneful sisters,
Hemans and Landon, on the other side of the water." But
Knapp, who is a forward-looking man, anticipates the spirit
of most of our *ante-bellum* critics and historians by doing what
in him lies to give to his fellow countrymen a profound bias in
favor of the autochthonous. "What are the Tibers and
Scamanders," he cries, "measured by the Missouri and the
Amazon? Or what the loveliness of Illysus or Avon by the
Connecticut or the Potomack?—Whenever a nation wills it,

Preface vii

prodigies are born. Admiration and patronage create myriads who struggle for the mastery, and for the olympick crown. Encourage the game and the victors will come." In some measure, no doubt, *Rip Van Winkle*, the Indian romances of Cooper, the philosophy of Emerson and Thoreau, the novels of Hawthorne, Longfellow's *Evangeline*, *Miles Standish*, and *Hiawatha* were responses to this encouragement of the game— to the nation's willing an expression of its new American consciousness.

Against the full rigour of the demand for an independent national literature there was, by the middle of the last century, a wholesome reaction represented in Rufus Wilmot Griswold's introduction to his *Prose Writers of America* (1847). Since this old demand is still reasserted from year to year, it may not be amiss to reprint here Griswold's admirable reply to it. "Some critics in England," he says, "expect us who write the same language, profess the same religion, and have in our intellectual firmament the same Bacon, Sidney, and Locke, the same Spenser, Shakespeare, and Milton, to differ more from themselves than they differ from the Greeks and Romans, or from any of the moderns. This would be harmless, but that many persons in this country, whose thinking is done abroad, are constantly echoing it, and wasting their little productive energy in efforts to comply with the demand. But there never was and never can be an exclusively national literature. All nations are indebted to each other and to preceding ages for the means of advancement; and our own, which from our various origin may be said to be at the confluence of the rivers of time which have swept through every country, can with less justice than any other be looked to for mere novelties in art and fancy. The question between us and other nations is not who shall most completely discard the Past, but who shall make best use of it. It cannot be studied too deeply, for unless men know what has been accomplished, they will exhaust themselves in unfolding enigmas that have been solved, or in pursuing *ignes fatui* that have already disappointed a thousand expectations." With more intelligent conceptions than many of his predecessors possessed of what constitutes a national literature, Griswold was still a proud nationalist. His valuable collections of American

prose and poetry are mainly illustrative of writers who flourished
in the first half of the nineteenth century. Of the work of
that period he forms in general estimates tempered by his
confidence that something better is yet to come.

In 1855 something better came in the shape of the two large
volumes of the *Cyclopædia of American Literature* by Evert A.
and George L. Duyckinck, a work of extensive research, designed, in the words of the authors, "to bring together as far
as possible in one book convenient for perusal and reference,
memorials and records of the writers of the country and their
works, from the earliest period to the present day." Here
for the first time were presented, in something like adequate
measure and proportion, materials for the study of our literature in what the compliers recognized as three great periods:
"the Colonial Era," "the Revolutionary Period," and "the
Present Century." Disclaiming any severe critical preten-
tions, they exhibited the breadth of their historical interests
in the declaration that "it is important to know what books
have been produced, and by whom; whatever the books may
have been or whoever the men." A similar breadth of historical interest animated Moses Coit Tyler in the production
of his notable and still unsurpassed history of American
literature from 1607 to 1783. Free from the embarrassment
of the early historians who had advanced to their task with a
somewhat inflamed consciousness that they were defending the
Stars and Stripes, Tyler had still a clear sense that he was
engaged upon a great and rewarding enterprise. In his opening sentence he strikes the note which every historian of a
national literature should have in his ear: "There is but one
thing more interesting than the intellectual history of a man,
and that is the intellectual history of a nation." If Tyler
had been able to carry his narrative down to the present day
in the spirit and manner of the portion of his work which he
brought to completion, the need for our present undertaking
would have been less obvious.

Unhappily the next noteworthy historian, Charles F. Richardson, whose *American Literature 1607–1885* was published
in 1886–8, is rather a protest against the work of Tyler than a
supplement to it. His leading purpose is not historical enquiry
and elucidation but æsthetic judgment. "We have had

enough description," he declares; "we want analysis." He opens his account with a definition of literature well framed to exclude from his consideration most of the important writing in America before the nineteenth century: "Literature is the written record of valuable thought, having other than merely practical purpose." Under this definition he is justified in asserting that "if a certain space be devoted to the colonial literature of America, then, on the same perspective ten times as much is needed to bring the record down to our day. . . . I believe that the time has come for the student to consider American literature as calmly as he would consider the literature of another country." Under this calm consideration the seventeenth and eighteenth centuries dwindle into a sombre little vestibule before the wide edifice which contains the writers who flourished through the middle years of the nineteenth century—Hawthorne is the latest novelist who receives extended notice. Richardson was not immune from the influence of the Zeitgeist of the eighties. What he does is, in short, to create the idea of what we may call the American Victorian Age, before and after which there is little that merits the attention of the dispassionate critic.

Professor Barrett Wendell in his interesting *Literary History of America*, published in 1900, presents with even sharper emphasis than Professor Richardson his similar conception of a closed "classical" period existing through the middle years of the last century. As we view the Americans from the beginning of their history, "we can instantly perceive," he declares, "that only the last, the Americans of the nineteenth century, have produced literature of any importance. The novelists and the historians, the essayists and the poets, whose names come to mind when American literature is mentioned, have all flourished since 1800." This is the somewhat restricted point of view established in the Introduction. In the composition of the history, the survey of the field, one suspects, was still further restricted by the descent upon Professor Wendell of the spirit of Cotton Mather; for the total effect of the narrative is an impression that the literary history of America is essentially a history of the birth, the renaissance, and the decline of New England.

The *Cambridge History* marks a partial reversion to the

position of the earlier historians who looked into the past with interest and into the present and future not without hope. Following in general the plan of *The Cambridge History of English Literature* and of our encyclopædic Duyckinck, we have made it our primary purpose to represent as adequately as space allowed all the periods of our national past, and to restore the memory of writers who are neglected because they are forgotten and because they are no longer sympathetically understood. To write the intellectual history of America from the modern æsthetic standpoint is to miss precisely what makes it significant among modern literatures, namely, that for two centuries the main energy of Americans went into exploration, settlement, labour for subsistence, religion, and statecraft. For nearly two hundred years a people with the same traditions and with the same intellectual capacities as their contemporaries across the sea found themselves obliged to dispense for the most part with art for art. But the long inhibition and belated expansion of their purely æsthetic impulses, unfavourable as it was to the development of poetry and fiction, was no serious handicap to the production of a prose competently recording their practical activities and expressing their moral, religious, and political ideas. Acquaintance with the written record of these two centuries should enlarge the spirit of American literary criticism and render it more energetic and masculine. To a taste and judgment unperverted by the current finical and transitory definitions of literature, there is something absurd in a critical sifting process which preserves a Restoration comedy and rejects Bradford's *History of Plymouth;* which prizes a didactic poem in the heroic couplets and despises the work of Jonathan Edwards; which relishes the letters of some third rate English poet, but finds no gusto in the correspondence of Benjamin Franklin; which sends a student to the novels of William Godwin, but never thinks of directing him to *The Federalist.* When our American criticism treats its facile novelists and poetasters as they deserve, and heartily recognizes and values the works in which the maturest and wisest Americans have expressed themselves, its references to the period prior to 1800 will be less apologetic.

For the nineteenth century, too, without neglecting the

writers of imaginative literature who have been most emphasized by our literary historians, we have attempted to do a new service by giving a place in our record to departments of literature, such as travels, oratory, memoirs, which have lain somewhat out of the main tradition of literary history but which may be, as they are in the United States, highly significant of the national temper. In this task we have been much aided by the increasing number of monographs produced within the past quarter of a century upon aspects of American literary history. Such collections as *A Library of American Literature*, edited by Edmund Clarence Stedman and Ellen M. Hutchinson in 1889–90, and the *Library of Southern Literature* (1908–13), compiled by various Southern men of letters, have been indispensable.

In the actual preparation of the work we have been indebted for many details to the unsparing assistance of Mrs Carl Van Doren, who has also compiled the index.

1 June, 1917.

W. P. T.
J. E.
S. P. S.
C. V. D.

The bibliography mentioned in the above preface is not included in this edition.

CONTENTS

BOOK I

COLONIAL AND REVOLUTIONARY LITERATURE

CHAPTER I

TRAVELLERS AND EXPLORERS, 1583-1763

By GEORGE PARKER WINSHIP, A.M., Librarian of the Harry Elkins Widener Collection, Harvard University.

CHAPTER II

THE HISTORIANS, 1607-1783

By JOHN SPENCER BASSETT, Ph.D., Professor of American History in Smith College.

CHAPTER III

THE PURITAN DIVINES, 1620-1720

By VERNON LOUIS PARRINGTON, A.M., Professor of English in the University of Washington.

Contents

Contents

CHAPTER VIII

AMERICAN POLITICAL WRITING, 1760–1789

By WILLIAM MACDONALD, Ph.D., Professor of History in Brown University.

CHAPTER IX

THE BEGINNINGS OF VERSE, 1610–1808

By SAMUEL MARION TUCKER, Ph.D., Professor of English in the Brooklyn Polytechnic Institute.

BOOK II

EARLY NATIONAL LITERATURE

CHAPTER I

TRAVELLERS AND OBSERVERS, 1763–1846

By LANE COOPER, Ph.D., Professor of English in Cornell University.

CHAPTER II

THE EARLY DRAMA, 1756–1860

By ARTHUR HOBSON QUINN, Ph.D., Dean of the College, University of Pennsylvania.

PAGE

CHAPTER III
EARLY ESSAYISTS

By GEORGE FRISBIE WHICHER, Ph.D., Associate Professor of English in Amherst College.

CHAPTER IV
IRVING

By MAJOR GEORGE HAVEN PUTNAM, Litt.D.

CHAPTER V
BRYANT AND THE MINOR POETS

By WILLIAM ELLERY LEONARD, Ph.D., Assistant Professor of English in the University of Wisconsin.

I. BRYANT

II. MINOR POETS

CHAPTER VI
FICTION I: BROWN, COOPER

By CARL VAN DOREN, Ph.D., Head Master of The Brearley School, Associate in English in Columbia University.

The Novel in the Colonies. Influence of Richardson. Mrs. Morton. Mrs.

Contents

CHAPTER VII

FICTION II: CONTEMPORARIES OF COOPER

By CARL VAN DOREN

CHAPTER VIII

TRANSCENDENTALISM

By HAROLD CLARKE GODDARD, Ph.D., Professor of English in Swarthmore College.

CHAPTER IX

EMERSON

By PAUL ELMER MORE

Book I

CHAPTER I

Travellers and Explorers, 1583-1763

THE English folk who became Americans during the early years of the seventeenth century kept the language of the relatives and friends whom they left, and with it their share in the literary heritage of the race. They owed much to the influences surrounding them in their new homes, but such skill in writing as they possessed came with them from the other side of the Atlantic. The names of an earlier group of adventurers are associated with the New World because they made a voyage along its coastline or resided for a little while at some seaside settlement. Sir Humphrey Gilbert on his homeward voyage from the New-found-land in 1583, sitting abaft with a book in his hand, while the *Golden Hind* was tossed by "terrible seas breaking short and high pyramidwise," is the finest type of the seamen who made the English occupation of America possible. The narrative of Gilbert's fatal voyage, written by Edward Haie, found a place in the ample store-house of adventurous records which makes all who love good reading and virile English the debtors of Richard Hakluyt.

It is an accident of geography which gives American readers a valid claim upon Humphrey Gilbert and his precursors and successors who told their straightforward tales for Hakluyt or for the booksellers who issued the scores of thin pamphlets in which Londoners first read about the trans-Atlantic voyage. These were in their day only a few among the many pamphlets which entertained the frequenters of St. Paul's churchyard

with experiences in odd corners of the Mediterranean or of the
Indian Ocean, or along the Arctic route to Central Asia.   They
all shared in developing the British Empire and English
literature.   Martin Frobisher and North-West-Foxe beyond
the polar circle, Thomas Hariot inside the Carolina sandspits,
and Sir Richard Hawkins in the Gulf of Mexico are by this
chance of geography given a place at the beginning of the
annals of American literature, instead of sharing the scant
notice allotted to their equally deserving contemporaries
whom fate led elsewhere.   The same fate sent Francis Drake
to sojourn for a time on the California coast, and it likewise
set in motion the economic and political forces which two
centuries later transferred this region into the keeping of the
English race, thereby adding the great circumnavigator to
the American roll.   Later came one whom Americans have
adopted as a folk hero, Captain John Smith.[1]   He risked his
life with equal abandon in Flanders and Turkey and Poto-
watomy's land, but Virginia claims him as her own.   He
may have been, as it was once the fashion to proclaim, an
inordinate liar, but whatever the historians say, the certain
fact is that what he wrote was read in his own day and has
ever since been read by thousands who have identified him
with the first English colony.

"And this is as much as my memory can call to mind
worthie of note; which I have purposely collected, to satisfie
my friends of the true worth and qualitie of Virginia."   So John
Smith wrote at the end of his "Description" of that colony
published in 1612.

Yet some bad natures will not sticke to slander the Countrey,
that will slovenly spit at all things, especially in company where
they can find none to contradict them.   Who though they were
scarse ever 10 miles from *James* Town, or at the most but at the
falles; yet holding it a great disgrace that amongst so much action,
their actions were nothing, exclaime of all things, though they never
adventured to knowe any thing; nor ever did any thing but devoure
the fruits of other mens labours.   Being for most part of such tender
educations and small experience in martiall accidents, because
they found not English cities, nor such faire houses, nor at their

owne wishes any of their accustomed dainties, with feather beds and downe pillowes, Tavernes and alehouses in every breathing place, neither such plenty of gold and silver and dissolute liberty as they expected, [they] had little or no care of any thing, but to pamper their bellies, to fly away with our Pinnaces, or procure their means to returne for England. For the Country was to them a miserie, a ruine, a death, a hell, and their reports here, and their owne actions there according.

Straightforwardness of narrative was characteristic of the period. This quality, and the absence of literary consciousness, distinguish the accounts written by these English seafarers from the productions of the rival French and Spanish voyagers. Each adapted his style to the public which he sought to influence. They were all alike trying to start or to accelerate the stream which was to transform the Western hemisphere into a part of the European world. Consequently the English tracts rarely possess qualities which separate them from the rest of the mass of seventeenth-century travel-books. Another result is that nearly all of them are more easily read, three centuries later, than the Continental output of the same period.

The corner of the New-found-land which retained this distinctive name exerted an especial attraction in the earlier days upon the adventurers who felt a longing to express themselves in literary form. Humphrey Gilbert was accompanied thither by the learned Stephen Parmenius of Buda, whose Latin verses "Ad Thamesin" are preserved on Hakluyt's pages. One of the first Englishmen to establish an American residence was William Vaughn, a Welshman and the composer of an amazing volume called *The Golden Fleece . . . Transported from Cambrioll Colchos, out of the Southermost Part of the Iland commonly called the Newfoundland, By Orpheus Junior*, to London, where it was printed in 1626. This work has long been the butt of despairing historians, who have sought for the Ariadnean thread which should guide them through its 350 pages of puerile fancies, discursive theology, significant episodes, and rhymed prose. For the reader who skips casually from paragraph to paragraph, the volume yields an entertaining notion of what was talked about in the fishing shacks on the northern coast, and of how the leader of one band of adventurers amused himself. It contains a parody of the Litany which is said to have been sung by four of the "Fraternitie attired in long white Robes," and may have been part of an embryo pageant wherewith the days were whiled away.

Vaughn had a "deare Friende and Fellow-Planter, Master Robert Hayman, who with Pen and Person" prepared "more roome for Christians in the Newfound-World," and who published in 1628 a volume of *Quodlibets, lately come over from New Britaniola, All of them Composed and done at Harbor-Grace in Britaniola, anciently called Newfound-Land*. The verses which fill its pages passed current with the similar output of his age. A number, and by no means the least rhythmical, were inspired by his associates on the western shores of the Atlantic. One of these is addressed "To the right Honourable, Sir George Calvert, Knight, Baron of Baltamore, and Lord of Avalon in Britaniola, who came over to see his Land there, 1627"; it compares Baltimore to the Queen of Sheba.

The repayment of the drafts made upon the literature of the motherland was not long delayed. It is more than probable that Shakespeare found in the reports of some New World voyagers one of his most momentous inspirations. Hugh Peters and the younger Harry Vane were only two of the temporary Americans who returned to take a lively part in the pamphleteering conflicts of the Protectorate. Roger Williams divided his controversial activities equally between the old and New England, and his *Key into the Languages of America* was cast into shape while he was on his way from one to the other.

Robert Sedgwick, one of the worthiest of those New Englanders who were recalled to serve the mother country, obtained a place for himself in literary annals by the reports which he addressed to Cromwell from the West Indies, where he was in charge of an expedition against the Spaniards. Carlyle, wearied of "the deadly inextricable jungle of tropical confusions" through which he struggled in "the Stygian quagmires of Thurloe's Collection of the State Papers from 1638 to 1661," found Sedgwick's letters "of all others the best worth reading on this subject." Sedgwick was a prospering settler at Charlestown in Massachusetts, speculating in land

and customs duties, an organizer of the Ancient and Honourable Artillery Company, when his worldly career was diverted by a chance meeting with Cromwell. The Lord Protector recognized a man after his own model, and sent him in quick succession against the Dutch on the Hudson River, the French at Acadia, and the Spanish of the Island Colonies. In one of his reports from his last expedition to Jamaica he begs the Protector to pardon his

prolix and rude expressions. I am apt sometimes to think I shall write no more. I am sometimes sick, and think I may fall among the rest of my countrymen; and durst do no other than plainly to let your highness know our state and condition.

Plainly and simply, and most convincingly, he set forth the deplorable situation of Jamaica and of the English soldiers who were dying there.

On the North American mainland, settlement followed exploration and colonization. For half a century there was little record of travelling beyond the limits of the outlying pasture lands and adjoining home sites. Occasionally someone bolder than his neighbours pushed a canoe up-stream to the head of navigation, or wandered into the valleys beyond the surrounding ridges, but very rarely were observations or physical experiences committed to paper. The impulse to print the reports of travellers did not come until there was land to be sold. The seventeenth-century promoters of speculation carried on the practice of distributing tracts telling about the property they wished others to buy. The little pamphlets issued by the Virginia Company, by the Massachusetts Agents, by William Penn in German, Dutch, and French as well as in English, by the Scots Proprietors of the Jerseys, and by the Lords of Carolina, are today worth more money than many of the acres that they describe. Most of these early tracts were written by men who had travelled through the regions of which they wrote. Rarely is there any substantial reason for doubting the honesty of what was reported as the result of actual observation. "What I write, is what I have proved," remarks one of the frankest of these promoters of a New World settlement in which he hoped to make his fortune, Edward Bland, Merchant. On 27 August,

1650, Bland set forth from the head of "Appamattuck River" in Virginia in search of the Falls of Blandina. His journey took him across broad stretches of "very rich Champian Land," "a pleasant Country, of temperate Ayre, and fertile Soyle." The beauty of the country, the heaps of bones which led the native guides to relate tales of valorous deeds, and the preservation of the party through "information our Guide told us he had from a woman that was his Sweet-heart," offered opportunities that a later-day reader wishes might have been improved with some of the appreciation of literary possibilities which a Frenchman could hardly have neglected. Bland's narrative goes steadily forward toward the goal and home again, without digression for any merely entertaining purpose from each day's march and the nightly watch against surprise.

The natives supplied the picturesque element for most of the writing of colonial times. To them also were due a number of involuntary journeyings, the accounts of which make an important part of American literature. There is nothing in English, or in any other language, that surpasses these narratives of Indian captivities in vividness or in the bare statement of physical suffering and of mental torment. They held the attention of readers who knew the writers, and the stream of successive reprintings is still going on, to supply an unabated demand.

The first and the best known of these narratives is that of Mrs. Mary Rowlandson.[1] She was the wife of the minister at Lancaster, Massachusetts, where the natives seized her when they burned the town during King Philip's War. The record of her subsequent "Removes" has seldom been equalled as a direct appeal for human sympathy. The hours following her capture may well have been

the dolefullest night that ever my eyes saw. Oh the roaring, and singing, and dancing, and yelling of those black creatures in the night, which made the place a lively resemblance of hell . . . There remained nothing to me but one poor wounded Babe, and it seemed at present worse than death, that it was in such a pitiful condition, bespeaking Compassion, and I had no refreshing for it, nor suitable things to revive it.

[1] 2d ed. 1682. The date of the first edition is unknown.

Mrs. Rowlandson's narrative is matched by that of John Gyles of Pemaquid (1736), who collected from his minutes

these private Memoirs, at the earnest Request of my Second Consort; that we might have a Memento ever ready at Hand to excite, in our selves Gratitude & Thankfulness to GOD; and in our Offspring a due Sense of their Dependance on the SOVEREIGN of the Universe.

Gyles was captured in 1689, and spent the ensuing nine years with the Indians along the Penobscot River and with the French in Canada. The natives soon tired of the too easy amusement of seeing him suffer, and as he managed to avoid death by drowning and frost-bite, he gradually made a place for himself by the humblest usefulness.

The natives of the woods of Maine and those of the ever-glades of Florida were equally skilful in devising methods of terrifying strangers who were thrown by chance or indiscretion amongst them. The account of *God's Protecting Providence In the Remarkable Deliverance of Robert Barrow, Faithfully Related by Jonathan Dickenson* (1699), is in many respects the best of all the captivity tracts. Driven ashore by a storm on the Gulf coast of Florida, late in September, 1696, the survivors, among them Dickenson's wife with their baby at her breast, six weeks later reached St. Augustine. For most of this interval, the wanderers were in hourly expectation of death. As is frequently the case, the record of these experiences is so undemonstrative that it is unconvincing, until the whole story is reread from the beginning. It was only after the more desperate dangers were over, and the prospect began to favour their escape, that Dickenson's narrative became pathetic. When the Spanish outposts were reported to be only two marches away, the fugitives

had a great Loss; having a Quart of Berries whole, and as much pounded to mix with Water, to feed our Child with; the Fire being disturbed, the Cloth which we had our Food in was burn'd.

This was a loss which might easily have proved, to persons emaciated and weakened by suffering, the fatal last straw; but in spite of a driving storm and freezing weather, all but two of the party managed to drag their blood-caked bodies through the sand to the Spanish garrison. At St. Augustine the Commandant and the other residents divided their scanty supplies with the fugitives, and nursed them until they were fit to be sent on their way to the Carolinas. The aged Quaker, Robert Barrow, survived all these experiences just long enough to greet the Friends who were awaiting him at Philadelphia. There he died three days later, on 4 April, 1697,

having passed through great Exercises, in much Patience; and in all the times of our greatest Troubles, was ready to Counsel us to Patience, and to wait what the Lord our God would bring to pass: And he would often express, That it was his Belief, that our Lives should be spared, and not be lost in that Wilderness, and amongst those People, who would have made a Prey of us.

The same fundamental religious impulse which sustained Robert Barrow on the storm-swept Florida beaches had settled the New England Puritan colonies. This same overwhelming impulse drove into these colonies, half a century after their permanent establishment, a succession of groups of wanderers whose peregrinations left a broad and often blood-stained trail the length of the continent and seaward to the islands. The men and women who made up these groups, called in derision Quakers, wrote as freely as they discoursed, and the spirit that animated them brooked no interference with either speech or progress. The names of several, Mary Dyer, Marmaduke Stevenson, and George Fox, whom Roger Williams "digg'd out of his Burrowes," to wit Edward Burroughs, are better known, but none of them wrote more forcefully than Alice Curwen. In the year 1660, "hearing of the great Tribulation that the Servants of the Lord did suffer in *Boston*, of cruel Whippings, of Bonds and Imprisonments, yea, to the laying down of their natural Lives," Mistress Curwen felt the call to go and profess in that bloody town. "Having this Testimony sealed in my Heart," she writes, "I laboured with my Husband day and night to know his Mind, but he did not yet see it to be required of him," he having but just returned from the Lancashire gaol in which he had been confined for refusing to pay the tythe. The call reached him in season to enable him to embark on the vessel on which his wife had taken passage for America. Journeying to Boston, they missed imprisonment through a legal technicality, and went on their way to the eastward. They were more fortunate on their return, for the constables drove them "all along the Street, until they came to the Prison, whereinto they thrust us; but the Lord was with us, and our Service there was great; for many people, both rich and poor, came to look upon us."

Another traveller who did his best to scour the colonists of heretical opinions, his own opinions being as pronounced when he was directed by the Quaker spirit as when he followed the Anglican order, was George Keith. He knew the controversially-minded Americans better than anyone else at the end of the seventeenth century. The descriptions of his opponents which are scattered through his hundred-odd publications are an invaluable elucidation of the state of mind which fructified in the revivals of forty years later, when George Whitefield and Jonathan Edwards came to make plain the way to salvation. Whitefield[1] kept a diary during his constant journeyings between England and America and through the mainland colonies. These personal records were published at the close of each important stage of his wanderings, and the seven pamphlets in which they appeared were reprinted in numerous editions. They contributed largely to the success of the great revivalist's ministry. Upon the reader of two hundred years later they still leave the impression of a dominating spirit, and of a sweet nature unconscious of its power. Worn out by wordy wrestlings with a recalcitrant sinner, Whitefield would cheerfully get out of a sick bed to preach to the Free Masons, "with whom I afterwards dined, and was used with the utmost civility."

An elemental fondness for rhyme and rhythm was responsible for the preservation of a few records of travellings not in themselves as remarkable as the effusions for which they gave the occasion. Two of these were *A Monumental Memorial of A Late Voyage from Boston in New-England To London, Anno 1683. In a Poem. By Richard Steere*, and a broadside, *A Journal of the Taking of Cape-Breton, Put into Metre By L. G., One of the Soldiers of the Expedition*, in 1745.

The eighteenth century brought economic independence

[1] See also Book I, Chap. v.

and settled social conditions to the older English colonies.
With these went the leisure and comfort which prepare a
community for the conscious enjoyment of literature. These
changing circumstances are reflected in the keen observations
and amusing descriptions preserved by one of the sprightliest
of New England matrons, Madame Sarah Knight. During the
winter of 1704–5, Mrs. Knight was obliged to go to New York
to attend to some business affairs. The trip from Boston
followed the shore line, and was accomplished as expeditiously
as her energetic nature, bored by the humdrum happenings
along the way, could hurry it along, but five months elapsed
before she regained her own fireside and warming pan. From
the first stopping place, where she found the other guests
"tyed by the Lipps to a pewter engine," and the next day's
guide, whose "shade on his Hors resembled a Globe on a Gate
post," there was scarcely a stage of her journey which did not
provide its subject for entertaining comment.

An equal appreciation of the fact that mileage and food
are not the only things worth recording by those who go abroad
gives permanent value to the diaries kept by the second William
Byrd of Westover in 1732 and 1733, when he followed the
course of Edward Bland in searching for the likeliest Virginian
land-holdings. Byrd was a model for all who journey in
company, for he "broke not the Laws of Travelling by uttering
the least Complaint" at inopportune torrents or "an imperti-
nent Tooth . . . that I cou'd not grind a Biscuit but with much
deliberation and presence of mind." He "contriv'd to get
rid of this troublesome Companion by cutting a Caper," with a
stout cord connecting the tooth and the snag of a log. "This
new way of Tooth-drawing, being so silently and deliberately
perform'd, both surprized and delighted all that were present,
who cou'd not guess what I was going about."

Byrd has been made known for his "happy proficiency in
polite and varied learning." He was not peculiar, however,
among the gentlemen of his generation for a style which shows
an acquaintance with what is recognized as literature. Most of
the people who possessed inherited wealth and established position
were able to spell correctly, and they obeyed the laws of English
grammar. Many of Byrd's contemporaries in the New World
could not do either of these things, and it has come to be the

fashion among their descendants to excuse those eminently respectable and often brave and prosperous men and women, because of a belief that their short-comings were in accord with the practice, or lack thereof, of their own day. Byrd's writings, and even more clearly those of the Maryland physician Alexander Hamilton, furnish the best of evidence that illiteracy was ignorance due to a lack of education as truly in 1700 as it is two centuries later.

Dr. Hamilton, who is not known to have been related to the more eminent publicist of the same name, in 1744 followed his own advice and sought to rid himself of a persistent indisposition by a change of climate and companions. Except for this health-seeking incentive, his journey from Annapolis to Portsmouth in New Hampshire was a pleasure trip, probably the earliest recorded in America.

Reading was easily the first of Dr. Hamilton's pleasures. On his journey he picked up from the Philadelphia book stalls the latest English novels, and in New York he bought a new edition of a classical favourite. When his own supply of reading matter gave out, he rummaged through the inn or explored his host's book shelves. The tavern keeper at Kingston in Rhode Island convinced him that it was unlawful, and therefore inexpedient, to travel on the Sabbath, and so he loitered about all day, "having nothing to do and no books to read, except it was a curious History of the Nine Worthies (which we found in Case's library) a book worthy of that worthy author Mr. Burton, the diligent compiler and historian of Grub Street." The scenery, luckily, furnished a partial compensation for the dearth of literary pastime, for he noted as he approached this hostelry that it brought to his mind "some romantic descriptions of rural scenes in Spenser's *Faerie Queene.*"

The day following his arrival at Boston being Sunday, he attended meeting, where he heard "solid sense, strong connected reasoning and good language." For the rest of this day's entry in his journal he records "staid at home this night, reading a little of Homer's First Iliad." As he does not say, we can only guess whether he took his Homer in the original or through a translation. With Latin we know that he was on intimate terms, even without the evidence of his Scottish medical degree. While at Newport he writes:

I stayed at home most of the forenoon and read Murcius [Meursius], which I had of Dr. Moffatt, a most luscious piece, from whom all our modern salacious poets have borrowed their thoughts. I did not read this book upon account of its lickerish contents, but only because I knew it to be a piece of excellent good Latin, and I wanted to inform myself of the proper idiom of ye language upon that subject.

On his return to New York he notes that a day

passed away, as many of our days do, unremarked and trifling. I did little more than breakfast, dine and sup. I read some of Homer's twelfth Iliad, and went to the coffee-house in the afternoon.

Back in Philadelphia, he found the September air

very sharp and cold for the season, and a fire was very grateful. I did little but stay at home all day, and employed my time in reading of Homer's Iliad.

His next forenoon was

spent in reading of Shakespear's *Timon of Athens, or Manhater*, a play which tho' not written according to Aristotle's rules, yet abounds with inimitable beauties, peculiar to this excellent author.

With such saddle-bag friends to accompany him, Dr. Hamilton was well prepared to pass judgment upon the casual acquaintances who crossed his path. When he first looked about him in Philadelphia, he

observed several comical, grotesque Phizzes in the inn where I put up, which would have afforded variety of hints for a painter of Hogarth's turn. They talked there upon all subjects,—politicks, religion, and trade,—some tolerably well, but most of them ignorantly.

The next morning the Doctor kept his room, reading Montaigne's *Essays*, "a strange medley of subjects, and particularly entertaining." On Sunday he was asked out to dinner, but found "our table chat was so trivial and trifling that I mention it not. After dinner I read the second volume of *The Adventures of Joseph Andrews*, and thought my time well spent."

Dr. Hamilton, one of the most entertaining of American travellers, appears to advantage even beside the urbanity of Byrd and the sprightliness of Mrs. Knight. Bent upon no special errand, he observed freely, and all the more so, one suspects, because of his detachment. Such a quality was not so easy during the next generation, when the wars between the French and English in America, the beginnings of colonial, and then national, pride, the growth of natural science, and the coming of the romantic spirit of solitude and love of nature furnished new motives. Then travelling became a fad, a profession, a duty, and led to the production of an extensive literature which may more properly be discussed with the work of men who were no longer colonials but citizens of the new republic.

CHAPTER II

The Historians, 1607–1783

"I N these five moneths of my continuance here," wrote John
Pory, of Virginia, in 1619, "there have come at one time or
another eleven sails of ships into this river; but fraighted
more with ignorance, than with any other marchansize."
The writer was a Cambridge graduate, a man of good standing
in England, and had crossed the Atlantic to find that Virginia
was not the Virginia of his dreams.   Ten years earlier all the
incoming ships brought well-born adventurers to Jamestown;
now they held only those who intended to produce tobacco.
Henceforth the future of the colony was with those who could
clear the forests, establish plantations, and withstand the
agues of the mosquito-infested lowlands.   The leaves of fate
for Virginia were not to be thumbed in a book.   They stood
broad and strong over the rich bottom-lands, where the summer
sun seemed to the onlooker to deck their oily surfaces with
a coat of silver.   In the days of the gentlemen adventurers
nine men wrote about the history of the colony; in the days of
the tobacco growers a century could not show as many.

The earliest Virginians were full of enthusiasm and wished
to tell the coming generations how the colony of Virginia was
founded.   Their enterprise was popular in England, and he
who wrote about it was sure of readers.   The men who planted
tobacco were prosaic.   They were poor men become rich, or
well-born men become materialistic, and it was only after many
years that any of the forms of culture appeared among them.
One of these forms was literature, but it was ever a plant of
spindling growth.

The first historian in Virginia, the first in the British colonies,

was Captain John Smith. He was twenty-seven years old
and a soldier of fortune when he landed at Jamestown in 1607.
He was a member of the council, and the council was lawmaker,
executive, and judge under the authority of the Company
which sent the colony out. According to the enthusiasts who
preached colonization three tasks awaited the men of Jamestown: to discover mines as the Spaniards had discovered them
in Mexico, to convert the Indians to Christianity, and to
plant another England in the New World. The third only
was accomplished, and it was accomplished chiefly through
the efforts and good sense of Smith.

Of the one hundred and five colonists thirty-five were
gentleman adventurers, leaders of the enterprise but useless in
the forest. They waited in idleness while labourers built
houses and constructed a fort. Then illness came, agues and
fluxes, and it seemed that Jamestown would share the fate of
Roanoke Island. Smith saved it by turning trader. Going
to the Indians with trinkets he secured enough corn to last
through the critical years of 1607 to 1609. Some of the
high-born adventurers approved of Smith's leadership, but
others found him intolerable. He was the son of a Lincoln-
shire copyholder; and how should he give orders to his betters?
Moreover, he was boastful. From mere boyhood he had
been seeking his fortune with sword in hand, in France, Italy,
and southeastern Europe. He told many stories of what he
had done, romantically coloured and tending to proclaim his
glory. Posterity does not accept them as true, and we may not
be surprised if his companions in the colony found them unbe-
lievable. Thus he had his enemies as well as his friends. In
the shifting of parties his own friends became triumphant and
Smith was recognized as president for more than a year.

Late in 1609 he returned to England. He had lost the
confidence of the Company, and nothing he could do sufficed
to regain it. In 1614 he induced some London merchants
to send him to the northern coasts with a fishing expedition.
While the sailors sought the cod at Monhegan, he sailed along
the coast, making an excellent map, and giving names to bays
headlands, and rivers. At his request the Prince of Wales
gave the name New England to this region, and to New England Smith transferred his affections. seeking support for

a colony he wished to plant there. A large expedition was promised, and he received the title "Admirall of New England"; but nothing came of his hopes save the title, which he invariably attached to his name thereafter.

It was evidently by accident that Smith became a historian. In the spring of 1608 Wingfield, one of his opponents at Jamestown, a cousin by marriage to the Earl of Southampton, departed for England, his mind full of his wrongs. Two months later another ship departed, carrying a long letter from Smith to his friends filled with a hopeful account of the colony. This letter was handed about among the members of the Company and late in the year came into the hands of one who had it published with the title, *A True Relation of Such Occurrences and Accidents of Noate as Hath Hapned in Virginia since the First Planting of that Collony*. A preface explained: "Some what more was by him written, which being as I thought (fit to be private) I would not adventure to make it publicke." The *True Relation* is the first printed American book, and of all Smith's writings it is the one which posterity most esteems. It is not boastful, or controversial, although it is very personal. The style is direct, vivid, and generally simple. It was well received, and seems to have awakened literary ambitions in its author.

Smith's second effort was made in 1612, when he published *A Map of Virginia. With a Description of the Countrey*. It contained a good map of the shores of the Chesapeake Bay, and an account of the natural history of Virginia, together with supplementary chapters on events in the colony from June, 1608, to the end of 1609. These accounts were written by some of his friends and are in his praise. Smith calls them "examinations" and had them taken down while their authors were in London. They were evidently prepared to revive his waning fortunes. In 1616, after his return from New England, he published *A Description of New England*, and in 1620 *New Englands Trials*, a tract on the fisheries. The *Trials* was brought down to date in 1622, and an account of the colony at Plymouth was included in it.

Smith was now a confirmed hack writer. Possibly he had Purchas and Hakluyt in mind when in 1624 he gave to the world a book containing all that he knew about Virginia. It was a narrative drawn from several sources. First, he used his own works, and when they were exhausted he reproduced, or culled from, any relation he had at hand. The whole bore the title *The Generall Historie of Virginia, New-England, and the Summer Isles*. Relatively an unimportant part of it is written by Smith, but he does not pretend to have written the parts he did not write. Three other books completed his literary career. One was called *An Accidence or the Path-way to Experience*, a tract which appeared in 1626 and was reissued several times, not always with the same title. It contained a description of the most observable features of a ship of war, and was designed for young seamen. In 1630 was published *The True Travels, Adventures, and Observations of Captaine Iohn Smith;* and in 1631 came another tract, *Advertisements for the Unexperienced Planters of New-England*. In the year it was published, 21 June, he died in London and was buried in St. Saviour's Church.

Two serious charges of falsification have been brought against Smith, one in connection with the Pocahontas incident, and the other in reference to his *True Travels*. Late in 1607 he made a trading expedition among the Indians and was captured and carried before Powhatan. In the *True Relation* he says he was well treated by the great chief and sent back to Jamestown with all kindness. In the *Generall Historie*, he says that he was about to be slain by the order of Powhatan, when Pocahontas, the chieftain's daughter, threw her arms over his prostrate body and begged for his life so effectively that he was set free. The case is unpleasant for Smith. Not only is the matter omitted from his early works, but it is not mentioned by any other writer of the comparatively large group of contemporary historians of Virginia. Even Hamor, who has much to say about Pocahontas, says nothing about a rescue of Captain Smith. It is conceivable that Smith may have omitted the story from the *True Relation*, lest it should produce a bad effect in England, but he could hardly have kept it from the other settlers at Jamestown, and if the story was once current there, where Pocahontas was well known, it must have been repeated by one of the other writers. By every canon of good criticism we must reject the story. Smith has also been accused of inventing most of the incidents which reflect his glory in the *True Travels*. The charge rests on an alleged misuse of geographical names and on the alleged impossible form of a grant of a coat of arms which Smith said was given him by Sigismund of Transylvania and which was accepted as genuine at the Heralds' College in London. The criticism[1] is very sweeping. If it is well taken our historian degenerated in the latter part of his career to a literary mountebank, but the matter may still await a more judicious investigation than it has yet received.

Turning from Virginia[2] we shall not find any considerable early historian in another colony outside of New England. So far as the region south of the Hudson is concerned idealism in regard to planting colonies exhausted itself with the splendid dreams of Raleigh, Hakluyt, and Edward Sandys. Lord Baltimore and Penn, it is true, attempted to revive it in Maryland and Pennsylvania, but their colonists did not respond to their efforts. These colonies were settled by as practical a class of farmers and traders as those who brought the river bottoms of Virginia under the sway of King Tobacco. Throughout this region literature had to wait on material prosperity before it could find a home.

The New Englanders, however, were idealists from the beginning. This, of course, means that their ministers and leading men were idealists. The majority of the inhabitants were as matter of fact as the majority in any other colony. But the ruling class were committed to the defence of an idealistic theory, and they naturally wished its history preserved. Out of this impulse came several historical works which we could ill afford to lose. All things considered, the Puritans made better historians than the Virginians. It is true their writings abound in superstition, but the superstitions were honestly set down as they were honestly held by the people of the age.

[1] Its most notable champion is Mr. Lewis L. Kropf, who asserts that when he communicated a copy of Smith's patent to the Hungarian Heraldic Society it was received with an outburst of laughter. Mr. Kropf pronounces Smith "an impudent forger." See Kropf, Lewis L., *Captain John Smith of Virginia, Notes and Queries*, London, 1890, Seventh Series, vol. ix; also *American Historical Review*, vol. iii, p. 737. A series of letters by the Rev. Edward D. Neill and William Wirt Henry, beginning in the Richmond *Dispatch*, 12 July, 1877, and continuing through several weeks, threshed out this controversy without settling anything.

[2] For the works of the early minor Virginia historians see the Bibliography.

They are, therefore, a necessary part of the history of the times. Moreover, the Puritans, ministers and godly laymen alike, wrote a solid and connected kind of history, and they wrote enough of it to furnish a good picture of the times.

Two minor authors introduce the early group of New England historians. The real name of the first is not known, but his book is called, from its publisher, "Mourt's" *Relation*, a description of affairs at Plymouth from its settlement until the date of publication, 1622. The other book, which appeared in 1624 with the title *Good News from New England*, was by Edward Winslow, one of the leading colonists. They are both short accounts of the daily doings of the men who planted the first permanent New England colony; and they are comparable in style and scope to Smith's *True Relation*, and to any of the other early narrations of Virginia or Maryland. They were written to inform friends in England of the progress of the Pilgrim settlements.

After "Mourt" and Winslow we come to two historians whose excellence entitles them to first rank among the earliest writers of their kind. They wrote quite as much as Captain John Smith, and their writings are more to be esteemed. No one has cast doubts on the accuracy of William Bradford, of Plymouth, or of John Winthrop, of Massachusetts Bay. While not historical compositions as such, their books are, in vivid and sustained human interest, as well as in the power of depicting the conditions of the first settlements, a most adequate and successful kind of history. Each is a journal written by a man who stood at the head of affairs, whose life was so important in his day that we have in it a reflection of the progress of the important things of the colony in which he lived.

William Bradford was one of the *Mayflower* passengers whose sober judgment and integrity had won for him the confidence of the Pilgrims ere they sailed for America. In 1621 he was chosen governor, and he held the office by annual re-election until his death in 1657, except for five years when, as Winthrop said, "by importunity he gat off." He believed it his duty to write about what he had seen and known of the trial and success of the men who, under divine guidance, had made Plymouth a fact. He began to write about 1630 and proceeded at so leisurely a gait that in 1646 he had only reached

the year 1621. Four years later his account had come to
the year 1646, but here his efforts ceased. His work is known
as *The History of Plymouth Plantation*.

Neither Bradford nor his immediate successors made an
effort to publish the history. They seem to have considered
it a document to be kept for the use of future historians. It
was, in fact, freely used for this purpose by his nephew,
Nathaniel Morton, in a book called *New England's Memorial*,
published in 1669. It remained in the hands of the family of
the author for a hundred years and finally came into the
possession of the Rev. Thomas Prince, who used it in writing his *Chronological History*, published in 1736. Hutchinson
also used it in preparing his *History*. When Prince died he
left the manuscript, with many other valuable writings, in the
tower of the Old South Church, in Boston. During the Revolution the British troops used this church for a riding school, and
Prince's carefully collected library was dispersed. The British
gone, such books as could be found were gathered together, but
no trace of Bradford's manuscript was discovered. It was
long believed to be lost, but it found its way to London, where
it came at last to the library of the Bishop of London, and for
many years lay unnoticed at Fulham Palace. In 1844 Wilberforce published a book on the Protestant Church in America,
in which he referred to the manuscript. Four years later
appeared Anderson's *History of the Colonial Church*, an English
work, and in it also was a reference to the manuscript. Seven
years later two gentlemen of Boston came across the reference
in Anderson's book. An investigation was made, and the
identity of the Fulham manuscript with Bradford's was completely established. The Bishop of London held that only
an act of Parliament could restore it to the place whence it
had been taken. He made, however, no objection to a request
that the Massachusetts Historical Society be allowed to publish
the manuscript, and in 1856 that society gave the world the
first complete publication of Bradford's book. It was enriched
with annotations by the learned Charles Deane. In 1867
another request was made that the bishop should surrender the manuscript, but the reply was the same as in the
first instance. In 1896 the then Bishop of London relented,
and Bradford's manuscript was given up without an act

of Parliament. It was received in Boston with high honour and much joy on the part of learned men and was placed in the State Library, a chief ornament of the archives of the Commonwealth of Massachusetts. In 1912 it was published in a final and authoritative form by the Massachusetts Historical Society.

The History of Plymouth Plantation is a Puritan book in the best sense. Its author was a man of intelligence, whose moderate educational opportunities had been supplemented by earnest and industrious private studies. He knew the Latin, Greek, and Dutch languages, and in his old age taught himself Hebrew so that he might read the oracles of God in the form in which they originally appeared. His *History* is loosely annalistic, but a direct and simple style gives charm, as a sincere faith in Puritanism gives purity, to the entire book. He who would understand the spirit of old Plymouth would do well to read Bradford through.

What Bradford's *History* is to Plymouth, John Winthrop's journal is to the Massachusetts Bay Colony. The author, more than any other man, was the founder of the colony. He was an earnest Puritan, a supporter of the ideas of Hampden and Pym, and by natural ability he was a leader of men. He left Cambridge before graduation, married at seventeen, became a justice of the peace at eighteen, and was soon a man of note in his shire, Suffolk, where he was lord of the manor of Groton. In 1630 he gave up all this, as well as a lucrative position as attorney in the Court of Wards, and threw in his lot with the men who were to settle Massachusetts. He was the colony's first governor, and through annual re-elections served it for twelve years, finally dying in office in 1649. Rev. John Cotton described him as

a governour . . . who has been to us as a brother, not usurping authority over the church; often speaking his advice, and often contradicted, even by young men, and some of low degree; yet not replying, but offering satisfaction also when any supposed offences have arisen; a governour who has been to us as a mother, parent-like distributing his goods to bretheren and neighbours at his first coming; and gently bearing our infirmities without taking notice of them.

The life of John Winthrop was worthy of this tribute in all respects.

Introspection was a Puritan trait, and the first governor at Boston had his share. Early in life he kept a little diary which he called *Experiencia*, a record of very deep spirituality. His letters show that he thought God directed his love and marriage. It was in the spring of 1630 that he embarked for Massachusetts, and while aboard ship, "riding at the Cowes, near the Isle of Wight," on Easter Monday, he began a journal which he kept faithfully until a few months before his death. It is filled with colony affairs, but its title, *A History of New England*, is misleading. It says little about any other colony than that over which the writer ruled, and the form is not that of history proper. Yet it is a valuable record of the life of the time, and presents good expositions of most of the problems of the early colony. While it is not written in so interesting a style as Bradford's book, it is in a fair diary manner, rarely becoming tedious to a reader who has the taste for the fine points of a contemporary document. It is Puritan in a liberal sense. Some New England writers can never forget their peculiar type of religion; but Winthrop discusses business matters like a man of business and public affairs like a man accustomed to weigh the fortunes of state in an even scale.

Like the early Virginia historians, Bradford and Winthrop were English-bred. Their culture was English and it was superior to that which the succeeding generation, born in America, could be expected to have. Two historians, however, Captain Edward Johnson and Nathaniel Morton, stand between them and the historians who are of purely American birth and training. Both were born in England, but they arrived in Massachusetts at such an early age that they were colony-trained to all intents and purposes.

Johnson was a man of strong natural traits, self-made, and representing the middle class in colonial society. He was a ship-wright by trade, and showed ability in leadership. He was the chief founder of the town of Woburn and its representative in the General Court. He gave loyal allegiance to the ministers, and was dazzled by their piety and learning. Puritanism offered him complete satisfaction, and he willingly accepted its dogmas. "You are not set up for tolerating times!" he exclaimed in the face of certain signs that the hold of the system was weakening. To preserve the influence of the early doctrines he wrote *Wonder-Working Providences of Zion's Saviour in New England*, published in 1654. We read it to-day to learn to what degrees of credulity the early New Englanders went in their acceptance of the power of the supernatural over human affairs. To the author and his contemporaries the book was plain history, a record of the actualities of life. The chief merit of the *Providences* for those who rightly value a human document is that it is a picture of early Puritan life as seen by an average man. Winthrop and Bradford lived at the centre of things. The problems of governors and assemblies concerned them. Johnson was interested in the planting of churches, the life of the towns, and the affairs of ordinary people, and it has been well said that while he "shows little precision in anything but his creed; yet his book is one of the most curious that an inquirer into the manners and institutions of our fathers can peruse."[1]

Nathaniel Morton was a trusted nephew of Governor Bradford and became secretary of the Plymouth colony. Possessed of fair ability, he was long a man of note and a pre-server of Plymouth tradition. In 1669 he published, as we have seen, *New England's Memorial*, a history of the colony. For the early years he drew directly on his uncle's book, transcribing large portions of it. Until the discovery of the Fulham manuscript, Morton's book was the best source for Bradford's text. The part which was concerned with the years following Bradford was written by Morton himself, and is meagre and disappointing, but Johnson and he were long the standard historians for the average New Englander. They may be considered the last of the early group, and in their manner and purposes they looked forward to the second group, men who were either born in America or who arrived after the American ideals were well enough formed to master the newcomers.

The second group, then, was American in a sense unknown to the first group. Its subjects were events rooted in American life, and save as American government and conditions were

[1] Winthrop, *History of New England*, ed. Savage, vol. i, p. 100 n.

dependent on relations with the mother country, this phase of history had no relation to England. It opened, naturally, with treatments of the most striking incidents of the day, Indian wars and internal disorders. Here were struggles calling for the best efforts of the settlers, struggles in which horrors and signal victories had followed one another in dramatic swiftness. Historians arose to write about them with marked ability; and their books were read far and wide. Then a generation followed during which the colonies grew in wealth and refinement. A leisure class was developed, the struggles of the assemblies against the king's prerogative gradually caused the formation of colony parties with colony ideals and aspirations, and in due time men appeared who undertook to tell the stories of colony development. These men belong to the later colonial period. In reflection and the power of dealing with materials, they are superior to the mere depicters of episodes. If their works are less readable, it must be remembered that their tasks are more difficult. It is easier to describe the Deerfield raid and the fate of the captured inhabitants than to trace the development of a political unit.

New England did not have the only Indian wars in America, but she alone had worthy historians of them. The struggles of 1622 and 1642 in Virginia, the Tuscarora War in North Carolina, and the Yemassee War in South Carolina, to say nothing of the wars of the Iroquois in New York, were as worthy of historical description as the struggle known as King Philip's War in New England, but they found no pen to describe them for the contemporary public. Bacon's rebellion in Virginia was well narrated for posterity, but the narratives long remained in manuscript; and the important struggles between South Carolina and Georgia on the one side and Spanish Florida on the other have not to this day been made the subjects of adequate treatment in a readable form.

In New England, on the other hand, historical effort for popular information was fairly abundant. Seven men appeared to describe the horrors of savage warfare, filling their pages with thrilling stories which the public read with eagerness. The first was Captain John Mason, whose *History of the Pequot War*, based upon his own experience, was published in 1677. It is written in cold-blooded indifference to the feelings of

Indian Wars 25

compassion, and we shiver today at the vengeance of the whites; but it raised no qualms in the men of the seventeenth century, who were brought up on sterner ideas. In the same year was published the Rev. William Hubbard's *Narrative of the Troubles with the Indians of New England*. Like the author's *History of New England*, it abounds in errors, but it was widely read. It appeared as Philip's War was drawing to a close, at a time when the people were especially excited against the savages. It had a worthy companion in Benjamin Church's *Entertaining Passages Relating to Philip's War*, published in 1716, a powerful book by one who took a leading part in the struggle he describes. Another work that was widely read was Samuel Penhallow's *Wars of New England with the Eastern Indians*, 1726. The author was chief justice of New Hampshire.

With 1690, when the French and Indian wars began, a new kind of warfare fell on the colonies. Bands of Indians, sometimes accompanied by Frenchmen, came out of Canada, destroyed isolated settlements, and escaped to the north with large trains of captives. The victims suffered much from the strenuous marches of their captors, and from actual cruelty. Most of them were redeemed after years of exile, and they returned with thrilling stories in their mouths. Here was a new field for the historian, and it was well worked.[1]

A distinct place must be reserved for Daniel Gookin, a Virginia Puritan who moved to Massachusetts to escape the persecutions of Governor Berkeley. He was made superintendent of Indians in his new home and showed a humane and intelligent interest in the natives that entitles him to rank with John Eliot. The retaliation of the whites in Philip's War grieved him sorely, but the tide of wrath was so strong that his protests only made him unpopular. He wrote two books on the Indians, *Historical Collections of the Indians in New England*, written in 1674 (published 1792), and *The Doings and Sufferings of the Christian Indians*, completed in 1677 (published 1836). Gookin also wrote a *History of New England* which remained in manuscript and was unhappily destroyed without having been published. The author was a man of great breadth of mind and not deeply touched by the

[1] See also Book I, Chap. I.

narrow ecclesiasticism of the day. He was also in a position
to know about the public events of his time. His history of
New England, had it been published, must have given us an
important view of the subject.

Another historian of the Indians was Dr. Cadwallader
Colden, a man of learning and high position in Philadelphia
and New York. He settled in New York in 1710, where he
enjoyed the confidence of the authorities and was promoted
to important offices. He had a deep interest in the superior
organization of the Iroquois and wrote about them in his *History
of the Five Indian Nations* (1727–47). Through great industry
he collected a large amount of valuable information about
these Indians, and the book is still a mine of facts, although
the research of later times has rendered many of its statements
unsatisfactory. In this connection mention should be made
of John Lawson's *History of North Carolina*, published first as
New Voyage to Carolina in 1709. It was written by a man of
excellent sense who had opportunity to know the Indians and
natural resources of North Carolina, but it contains little
about civil affairs. Lawson was English born and bred, and
lived only a few years after his arrival, but he had a right to
the name "American," since he gave his life to the service of
the colony. He was murdered by the Indians in 1711.

It seems certain that most of the books on the Indians
were written in answer to a popular demand. The same could
not be said of the political histories, which began to appear in
the first half of the eighteenth century. The impulse behind
such works is perhaps best stated in the words of Stith, of
Virginia, who said that he began to write his history as "a
noble and elegant entertainment for my vacant hours, which
it is not in my power to employ more to my own satisfaction,
or the use and benefit of my country." Few of the historians
of this class had a large number of readers. Two wrote about
Virginia, Robert Beverley and the Rev. William Stith. The
former was a wealthy planter who saw while in London a poor
account of the colony by the British historian and pamphleteer,
John Oldmixon, and undertook to write a better. His book,
A History of Virginia (1705), was hastily prepared without any
study of documents or other respectable sources. Its chief
value lies in the shrewd and just observations the author

made on Virginia life and history out of his own knowledge. Stith was connected with prominent persons in the colony and had been president of William and Mary College. His *History of the First Discovery and Settlement of Virginia* was published in 1747. The volume brought the story of the colony down to the fall of the London Company, 1624. It was accurate and based on the records of the Company, and is one the most modern of our colonial histories in its method. But Stith had no sense of proportion. His book was so full of details that his subscribers found it unreadable and failed to continue their support. No second part was published.

For the middle colonies we have two histories still remembered by posterity, a *History of New York* (1757), by William Smith and a *History of New Jersey* (1765) by Samuel Smith. The author of the former was a high official in New York and had much ability. He was a tory, and the unpopularity he acquired on that account was shared by his book. Unable to read Dutch, he had an inadequate idea of the early history of the colony; but for the English period the book has maintained an honourable position to this day. It is well written and, making due allowances, it is equal to the standard of historical literature in England before Hume. Samuel Smith was an industrious and conscientious Quaker, and his history was written from the point of view of the middle class of society. It is still regarded as reliable but the style is heavy.

In New England during this period political history did not engage the attention of historians as much as Indian history. Besides Gookin, whose unpublished history has been mentioned, three men deserve notice. One was the already noticed Rev. William Hubbard, whose *General History of New England* did not find a publisher until 1815. The earlier part is taken with the slightest amount of change from Morton's *Memorial* and Winthrop's journal. After these two sources are exhausted the book becomes meagre and inaccurate.

A much better writer was the Rev. Thomas Prince, of Boston, whom we have encountered in connection with Bradford's manuscript. The preservation of documents and rare pamphlets was to him a labour of love, and by industry he collected a large library of valuable materials. Many of the books are now preserved in the Boston Public Library. Prince's devotion to history is recognized in the name of the Prince Society, of Boston, one of the most honoured of American historical organizations.   The result of his efforts at writing history was a *Chronological History of New England, in the Form of Annals,* the first volume of which appeared in 1736.   It began with the creation of man on the sixth day and proceeded rapidly to the landing of the Pilgrims at Plymouth.   Then it moved with great detail through the events of the succeeding decade, until a hint from the publisher that the book was becoming too large brought it to an end with 7 September, 1630.   The poor sale of the volume discouraged the author, who did not resume his work until 1755.   He then began a continuation in serial parts at sixpence each; but the sale was so small that he gave up the project after three numbers had been issued.

Prince's work is a delight to the genealogist and the antiquarian, for precision marks every step he took.

"I cite my vouchers to every passage," he said, "and I have done my utmost, first to find out the truth, and then to relate it in the clearest order.   I have laboured after accuracy; and yet I dare not say that I am without mistake; nor do I desire the reader to conceal any he may possibly find."

No modern scientific historian could speak better.   If Prince lacked literary ability, the want was made up in his strict sense of accuracy; and we should remember that it is rare that the world has a man who is endowed with both characteristics.

Both Hubbard and Prince were ministers and wrote with a full sense of the importance of the churches in the New England life.   Their outlook was biased, although not intentionally so. From them we turn at the very close of the colonial period to a New England historian as free from this influence as Colden or William Smith.   Thomas Hutchinson was descended from Mrs. Anne Hutchinson, who was exiled from Massachusetts in 1638 because she defied the Puritan hierarchy, and he was quite free from religious narrowness.   Born in 1711, he graduated from Harvard in 1727 and began a prosperous career as a merchant.   He won the confidence of the Boston people, who sent him to the assembly, where he distinguished himself by opposing the issue of paper money.   He was for a long time the most popular man in the colony, and he was promoted from one high office to another, becoming lieutenant-governor in 1758, chief justice in 1760, acting governor in 1769, and governor in 1771.

Hutchinson loved Massachusetts, but he was intellectually a conservative, and he did not accept the theory on which the colonists rested their resistance to the king and Parliament. He wished to preserve the Empire undivided, and hoped that some plan might be found by which America might have home rule without renouncing the name British. He was opposed in principle to the Stamp Act, but disapproved of the violence with which it was received. A Boston mob, angered by false reports against him, wrecked his house, destroyed his furniture, and scattered his books and papers through the streets. The assembly paid him for the property loss, but he never recovered the good will of Boston. He tried to reconcile king and colony, but neither was in a mood to be reconciled. Early in 1774 he went to England, giving place to General Gage. He was well received, and the king allowed him a handsome pension, while Oxford conferred upon him the degree of *Doctor Civilis Juris*. But as the months passed and the war became inevitable, Hutchinson's pleas for peace made him unpopular. King, ministers, and society generally were for punishing the disobedient colonies. The protests of the exiled governor became weaker and weaker, and he finally retired from public notice. With his family he led an unhappy existence in London until his death in 1780.

In the eighteenth century history was an honored branch of literature. Hume, who published his great history between 1754 and 1761, was made independent by the sales, while Robertson, who was just coming into his fame, found himself both flattered and wealthy. History had not yet fallen into the hands of those who were to reduce it to a dull statement of facts which nobody reads except those who wish to incorporate them in other statements of fact. Nor had the world yet been submerged by the modern deluge of imaginative literature. It was in 1764, while Hume and Robertson were at the height of their freshly won fame, that Hutchinson published the first volume of his *History of the Colony of Massachusetts Bay*. The second was in preparation when the Stamp Act mob destroyed the house of the author. Among the debris recovered from the streets was the soiled manuscript of this volume. It was completed and published in 1767. The third volume was not written until the governor had taken up his residence in London, and it was not published until 1828. Hutchinson's *History* is not faultless. He was bitterly denounced by Otis and Samuel Adams, and he did not show an ability to appreciate them. He left untouched some important phases of Massachusetts history, and was indifferent to social and industrial changes. In spite of these faults, for which excuses can be made, he was the best American historian of his time. He treated narrative history in a philosophical manner and wrote simple and natural sentences whose charm endures to this day. After he left our shore many a year passed before we had a historian who could equal him in the power to understand and narrate the story of American political life.

CHAPTER III

The Puritan Divines, 1620-1720

NEW ENGLAND Puritanism—like the greater movement of which it was so characteristic an offshoot—
is one of the fascinating puzzles in the history of the
English people. It phrased its aspirations in so strange a dialect, and interpreted its programme in such esoteric terms, that
it appears almost like an alien episode in the records of a practical race. No other phase of Anglo-Saxon civilization seems
so singularly remote from every-day reality, so little leavened
by natural human impulses and promptings. Certain generations of Englishmen, seemingly for no sufficient reason, yielded
their intellects to a rigid system of dogmatic theology, and surrendered their freedom to the letter of the Hebrew Scriptures; and
in endeavouring to conform their institutions as well as their
daily actions to self-imposed authorities, they produced a
social order that fills with amazement other generations of
Englishmen who have broken with that order. Strange,
perverted, scarce intelligible beings those old Puritans seem
to us—mere crabbed theologians disputing endlessly over
Calvinistic dogma, or chilling the marrow of honest men and
women with their tales of hell-fire. And we should be inclined
to dismiss them as curious eccentricities were it not for the
amazing fact that those old preachers were not mere accidents
or by-products, but the very heart and passion of the times.
If they were listened to gladly, it was because they uttered
what many were thinking; if they were followed through tribulation and sacrifice by multitudes, it was because the way which
they pointed out seemed to the best intelligence of their
hearers the divinely approved path, which, if faithfully followed,

must lead society out of the present welter of sin and misery and misrule into a nobler state. For the moment religion and statecraft were merged in the thought of Englishmen; and it was because the Puritan ministers were statesmen as well as theologians—the political quite as much as the religious leaders—that the difficult task of social guidance rested for those generations with the divines. How they conducted themselves in that serious business, what account they rendered of their stewardship, becomes therefore a question which the historian may not neglect.

It was to set up a Kingdom of God on earth that the Puritan leaders came to America; and the phrase should enlighten us concerning their deeper purpose. But no sooner was their work well under way than the conception of a kingdom of God tended to merge in the newer conception of a commonwealth of Christ, and this in turn found itself confronted by the still newer conception of a commonwealth of free citizens; and it is the painful wrestling with these changing ideals, with all that was implied in each to the several classes and institutions of society, that gives historical significance to the crabbed writings of the New England divines. As political thinkers they inherited a wealth of political speculation, accumulated during more than a hundred years of extraordinary intellectual activity; and if we would understand the matter as well as the manner of their disputations, we must put ourselves to the trouble of translating the obsolete phraseology into modern equivalents, and conceive of Puritanism as the expression of current English radicalism. It was the English beginning of the great modern social readjustment which goes under the name of the democratic revolution; and its total history, covering a long period of a hundred and forty years, constitutes a noble chapter in the struggle for human freedom. If the evolution of modern society falls into two broad phases, the disintegration of the old caste society into free citizens, and the regrouping of the free citizens into a new social democracy, the significance of Puritanism becomes clear—it was a disruptive force that served to destroy the cohesion of the ancient caste solidarity resolving society into its individual members. It was the rebellion of the many against the overlordship of the few; a rebellion that proposed to coerce the freedom of men by the law of God alone; a challenge of existing institutions and regnant philosophies, which if successful could not fail to bring about profound social changes.

Necessarily, therefore, the Puritan reformation was allied with political reformation, and the period of ecclesiastical reorganization was equally a period of political reorganization. Modern political parties were thrown up out of the ferment of religious dispute, and the inevitable cleavages of Puritan thought were determined broadly by the cleavages of political thought. The three parties in the ecclesiastical field, Anglican, Presbyterian, and Independent, reflected the current political ideals of tory, whig, and democrat. The first was monarchical in principle, the ecclesiastical expression of tory absolutism. It gathered to its support the hereditary masters of society, who held that there should be one authoritative church, to which every subject of the crown must belong, to the support of which all must contribute, and in the governance of which only the appointed hierarchy should share. The second party was aristocratic in principle, the expression of the rising ideal of whiggery, or government by property through the instrumentality of landed gentlemen. Country squires and prosperous London citizens desired a church system which they could control, and this system they discovered in Presbyterianism, newly brought over from Geneva, which gave the control of the parish to the eldership, composed of responsible gentlemen who should serve as trustees for the good of the whole. The third party was more or less consciously democratic in principle, the expression of the newly awakened aspirations of the social underling. The poor man wanted to be ruled neither by bishops nor by gentlemen, but preferred to club with the like-minded of his own class, and set up an independent church along democratic lines. That was the true Christian church, he believed, which withdrew from all communion with sinners and established a "Congregation of the Saints"; and so he called himself a Separatist. But whatever name he might call himself by, he was at bottom a democrat who demanded the right of self-government in the church, and who, when times were ripe, would assuredly assert the greater right of self-government in the state.

Broadly speaking, the Anglicans kept the situation pretty

well in hand up to the accession of Charles I. During the long disputes between Charles and the Parliament, the rising party of Presbyterians was organizing its forces to break the rule of the bishops, and the early years of Parliamentary sovereignty marked the culmination of the middle period, dominated by the Presbyterian ideal. But no sooner was the ruthless hand of tory absolutism struck down than the long gathering forces of social discontent came to a head and broke with the moderate party of Presbyterian reformers; whereupon there followed the real Puritan revolution which had been preparing since the days of Wyclif. The Separatists seized control of Parliament and set about the work of erecting a government that should be a commonwealth of free citizens; the voice of the democratic underling, for the first time in English history, was listened to in the national councils, and the army of the democrat stood ready to enforce his demands with the sword. But unfortunately the strong wine went to the head; unbalanced schismatics endeavoured to set up impossible Utopias; zeal outran wisdom; and the Puritan movement broke at last into a thousand sects and went to pieces. But not before its real work was done; not before the political principles, which hitherto had been obscurely entangled in theological disputation, were set free and held up to the view of Englishmen; not before the new democratic philosophy had clarified its fundamental principle, namely, that the individual both as Christian and citizen derives from nature certain inalienable rights which every church and every government is bound to respect.

It was during the decade of the thirties, at the moment when Presbyterianism was in the ascendancy, that the Puritan migration to New England took place; and the leaders of that notable movement were effectively Presbyterian in sympathies and policies. Possessed of ample means and of good social position, they were liberals rather than radicals, and they shared the common Presbyterian hope of capturing the ecclesiastical establishment as a whole instead of separating from it. But they had been preceded to America by the Plymouth congregation, a body of low-born Separatists, who had set up a church upon frankly democratic principles. In an unfortunate moment for Presbyterianism, the pioneer church at Salem came under the influence of the Plymouth example, and the following year, when the main body of Puritans came over with Winthrop, they fell in with the Salem example and set up the new churches on the Congregational principle, as seeming to provide the most suitable form for the development of a theocracy. The inconsistency of an arrangement by which an aristocratic leadership accepted a democratic church organization was obscured for the moment by the unanimity of ministers and congregation; but it was clearly perceived by the Presbyterians of the old country, and it was to prove the source of much contention in later years.

Out of this fundamental inconsistency sprang a large part of the literature with which we are concerned in the present chapter. The ministers, as the spokesmen of New England, soon found themselves embroiled in controversy. During the first ten years or more the controversy lay between New England and old England Puritans, and the burden upon the former was to prove to the satisfaction of English Presbyterianism that the "Congregational way" was not democratic Separatism, with its low stigma of Brownism, but aristocratic Presbyterianism. During the later years, when Presbyterianism had been definitely overthrown in England, the controversy lay between the theocratic hierarchy—which after the year 1637 was the dominant power—and the dissenting democracy; the former seeking to Presbyterianize the church away from its primitive Congregationalism, the latter seeking to maintain the purity of the Plymouth ideal. In dealing with the several ministers, therefore, we shall divide them into the emigrant generation and the native generations, and set the aristocratic Presbyterians over against the democratic Congregationalists, endeavouring to understand the chief points at issue between them.

The most authoritative representative of the ideals of the middle period of Puritanism—its aristocratic conservatism in the guise of theocratic polities—was the celebrated John Cotton, first Teacher to the church at Boston. Of good family and sound university training, he was both a notable theologian and a courteous gentleman. "Twelve hours in a day he commonly studied, and would call that a scholar's day," his grandson reported of him; and his learned eloquence was universally admired by a generation devoted to solid argumentative discourse. When he ascended the pulpit on Sundays and lecture days, he carried thither not only the wisdom of his beloved master Calvin but the whole Puritan theology to buttress his theses. Good men were drawn to him irresistibly by his sweetness of temper, and evil men were overawed by his venerable aspect. For all his severe learning he was a lovable man, with white hair framing a face that must have been nobly chiselled, gentle-voiced, courteous, tactful, by nature "a tolerant man," than whom none "did more placidly bear a dissentient," or more gladly discover a friend in an antagonist. If his tactful bending before opposition, or his fondness for intellectual subtleties, drew from his grandson the appellation "a most excellent casuist," we must not therefore conclude that he served the cause of truth less devotedly than the cause of party.

For in his mildly persistent way John Cotton was a revolutionist. A noble ideal haunted his thought, as Utopian as any in the long roll of Utopian dreams—the ideal of a Christian theocracy which should supersede the unchristian government which Englishmen had lived under hitherto. A devout scripturist, he accepted the Hebrew Bible as the final word of God, not to be played fast and loose with but to be received as a rule of universal application, perfect to the last word and least injunction. The sufficiency of the Scriptures to social needs was an axiom in his philosophy; "the more any law smells of man the more unprofitable," he asserted in his proposed draft of laws; and at another time he exclaimed, "*Scripturae plenitudinem adoro.*" He chose exile and the leaving of his beautiful English church rather than yield to what he regarded as the unscriptural practices of Laud, and now that he was come to a new land where a fresh beginning was to be made, was it not his Christian duty to "endeavour after a *theocracy*, as near as might be, to that which was the glory of Israel, the 'peculiar people'"? The old common law must be superseded by the Mosaic dispensation, the priest must be set above the magistrate, the citizen of the commonwealth must become the subject of Jehovah, the sovereignty of the state must yield to the sovereignty of God.

It was a frankly aristocratic world in which John Cotton was bred, and if he disliked the plebeian ways of the Plymouth democracy equally with the Brownist tendencies of Plymouth Congregationalism, it was because they smacked too much of popular sovereignty to please him. And when he found himself confronted by signs of democratic unrest in Boston his course of action seemed to him clear. The desire for liberty he regarded as the sinful prompting of the natural man, a godless denial of the righteous authority of the divinely appointed rulers. If democracy were indeed a Christian form of government, was it not strange that divine wisdom should have overlooked so significant a fact? In all the history of the chosen people nowhere did God designate the democratic as the perfect type, but the theocratic; was He now to be set right by sinful men who courted popularity by stirring the dirt in the bottom of depraved hearts? To a scripturist the logic of his argument was convincing:

It is better that the commonwealth be fashioned to the setting forth of God's house, which is his church: than to accomodate the church frame to the civill state. Democracy, I do not conceyve that ever God did ordeyne as a fit government eyther for church or commonwealth. If the people be governors, who shall be governed? As for monarchy, and aristocracy, they are both of them clearly approoved, and directed in scripture, yet so as referreth the soveraigntie to himselfe, and setteth up Theocracy in both, as the best forme of government in the commonwealth, as well as in the church.[1]

Holding to such views, the duty devolving upon him was plain—to check in every way the drift towards a more democratic organization, and to prove to old-world critics that the evil reports of the growing Brownism in New England, which were spreading among the English Presbyterians, were without foundation. The first he sought to accomplish by the strengthening of the theocratic principle in practice, busying himself in a thousand practical ways to induce the people to accept the patriarchal rulership of the ministers and elders, in accordance with the "law of Moses, his Judicials"; the second he sought to accomplish by proving, under sound scriptural authority, the orthodoxy of the New England way. His chief effort in this latter field was his celebrated work, *The Way of the Con-*

---

[1] Letter to Lord Say and Sele, Hutchinson, *Hist. of Mass. Bay Colony*, vol. I, p. 497.

gregational Churches Cleared; a treatise crammed, in the opinion of an admirer, with "most practical Soul-searching, Soul-saving, and Soul-solacing Divinitie," "not Magisterially laid down, but friendly debated by Scripture, and argumentatively disputed out to the utmost inch of ground." The partisan purpose of the book was to prove that Congregational· ism, as practised in New England, was nearer akin to aristocratic Presbyterianism than to democratic Brownism; and of this purpose he speaks frankly:

> Neither is it the Scope of my whole Book, to give the people a share in the Government of the Church. . . . Nay further, there be that blame the Book for the other Extreme, That it placeth the Government of the Church not at all in the hands of the People, but of the Presbyterie.[1]

Out of this same theocratic root sprang the well-known dispute with Roger Williams concerning toleration. Not freedom to follow the ways of sin, but freedom to follow the law of God—this was Cotton's restriction upon the "natural liberties" of the subject of Jehovah. There must be freedom of conscience if it be under no error, but not otherwise; for if freedom be permitted to all sinful errors, how shall the will of God prevail on earth? In this matter of toleration of conscience, it is clear enough today that the eyes of the great theocrat, "so *piercing* and *heavenly* (in other and precious Truths of God)"—as Roger Williams acknowledged—were for the moment sadly "over-clouded and bloud-shotten." But for this the age rather than the man was to blame. It was no fault of John Cotton's that he was the product of a generation still resting under the shadow of absolutism, unable to comprehend the more democratic philosophy of the generation of Roger Williams. He reasoned according to his light; and if he was convinced that the light which shone to him was a divine torch, he proved himself thereby a sound Puritan if not a good Christian.

The native sweetness and humanity of Cotton's character, despite his rigid theocratic principles, comes out pleasantly when the great preacher is set over against the caustic lawyer·

[1] Part II, p. 15.

minister and wit, Nathaniel Ward of Ipswich, author of the strange little book, *The Simple Cobbler of Aggawam*, and chief compiler of the celebrated *Body of Liberties*. Born nearly two-score years before Roger Williams, he was well advanced in his sixties when he set foot in the new world, and upwards of seventy when he wrote the *Simple Cobbler*. More completely than any of his emigrant brethren he belonged to the late Renaissance world, which lingered on into the reigns of James and Charles, zealously cultivating its quaint garden of letters, coddling its odd phrases, and caring more for clever conceits than for solid thought. Faithful disciple of Calvin though he was, there was in him a rich sap of mind, which, fermented by long observation and much travel, made him the raciest of wits, and doubtless the most delightful of companions over a respectable Puritan bottle. "I have only Two Comforts to Live upon," Increase Mather reported him as saying; "The one is in the Perfections of Christ; The other is in The Imperfections of all Christians."

It is the caustic criticism of female fashions, and the sharp attack upon all tolerationists who would "hang God's Bible at the Devil's girdle," that have caught the attention of later readers of the *Simple Cobbler;* but it was as a "subtile statesman" that Ward impressed himself upon his own generation, and it is certainly the political philosophy which gives significance to his brilliant essay. Trained in the law before he forsook it for the ministry, he had thought seriously upon political questions, and his conclusions hit to a nicety the principles which the moderate Presbyterians in Parliament were developing to offset the Stuart encroachments. The insufficiency of the old checks and balances to withstand the stress of partisanship was daily becoming more evident as the struggle went forward. There must be an overhauling of the fundamental law; the neutral zones must be charted and the several rights and privileges exactly delimited. What was needed was a written constitution. Hitherto God "hath taken order, that ill Prerogatives, gotten by the Sword, should in time be fetcht home by the Dagger, if nothing else will doe it: Yet I trust there is both day and means to intervent this bargaine." To preserve a just balance between rival interests, and to bring all parties to a realization of their responsibility to God, were the difficult problems with which Ward's crotchety lucubra‹ tions mainly concern themselves.

Authority must have power to make and keep people honest; People, honesty to obey Authority; both, a joynt-Councell to keep both safe. Moral Lawes, Royall Prerogatives, Popular Liberties, are not of Mans making or giving, but Gods: Man is but to measure them out by Gods Rule: which if mans wisdome cannot reach, Mans experience must mend: And these Essentials, must not be Ephorized or Tribuned by one or a few Mens discretion, but lineally sanctioned by Supreame Councels. In *pro-re-nascent* occurrences, which cannot be foreseen; Diets, Parliaments, Senates, or account-able Commissions, must have power to consult and execute against intersilient dangers and flagitious crimes prohibited by the light of Nature: Yet it were good if States would let People know so much beforehand, by some safe woven *manifesto*, that grosse Delin-quents may tell no tales of Anchors and Buoyes, nor palliate their presumptions with pretense of ignorance. I know no difference in these Essentials, between Monarchies, Aristocracies, or Demo-cracies. . . .

He is a good King that undoes not his Subjects by any one of his unlimited Prerogatives: and they are a good People, that undoe not their Prince, by any one of their unbounded Liberties, be they the very least. I am sure either may, and I am sure neither would be trusted, how good soever. Stories tell us in effect, though not in termes, that over-risen Kings, have been the next evills to the world, unto fallen Angels; and that over-franchised people, are devills with smooth snaffles in their mouthes . . . I have a long while thought it very possible, in a time of Peace . . . for disert Statesmen, to cut an exquisite thred between Kings Prerogatives, and Subjects Liberties of all sorts, so as *Caesar* might have his due and People their share, without such sharpe disputes. Good Casuists would case it, and case it, part it, and part it; now it, and then it, punctually.

Nathaniel Ward was no democrat and therefore no Con-gregationalist. "For Church work, I am neither Presbyterian, nor plebsbyterian, but an Interpendent," he said of himself. But his Interpendency was only an individualistic twist of Presbyterianism. For the new radicals who were rising out of the turmoil of revolution, he had only contempt; and for their new-fangled notion of toleration, and talk of popular liberties, he felt the righteous indignation of the conservative who desires no altering of the fundamental arrangements of society. Only the Word of God could justify change; and so when he was commissioned to write a body of liberties for the new commonwealth, he presented as harsh and rigid a code as the sternest theocrat could have wished, a strange compound of the brutalities of the old common law and the severities of the Mosaic rule. He was too old a man to fit into the new ways— a fact which he recognized by returning to England to die, leaving behind him as a warning to Congregationalism the pithy quatrain:

> The upper world shall Rule,
> While Stars will run their race:
> The nether world obey,
> While People keep their place.

The more one reads in the literature of early New England the more one feels oneself in the company of men who were led by visions, and fed upon Utopian dreams. It was a day and a world of idealists, and of this number was John Eliot, saintly apostle to the Indians, who, in the midst of his missionary dreams and the arduous labours of supplying the bread of life to his native converts, found time to fashion his brick for the erection of that temple which the Puritans of the Protectorate were dreaming of. The idols had been broken under the hammer of Cromwell; the malevolent powers that so long had held sway at last were brought low; it remained now only for the people of God to enter into a solemn covenant to establish a commonwealth after the true divine model. That no mistake should be made in so important a matter, John Eliot sent out of the American wilderness the plan of a Christian Utopia, sanctioned by Mosaic example and buttressed at every point by chapter and verse, which he urged upon the people of England as a suitable guide to their feet.

Naked theocracy is nowhere more uncompromisingly delineated than in the pages of *The Christian Commonwealth*. At the base of Eliot's political thinking were the two germinal conceptions which animated his theocratic brethren generally: the conception that Christ is King of Kings, before whom all earthly authority must bow, and the conception that the

Scriptures alone contain the law of God. "There is undoubtedly a forme of civil Government instituted by God himself in the holy Scriptures. . . . We should derogate from the sufficiency and perfection of the Scriptures, if we should deny it." From these main premises he deduced a system that is altogether remarkable for its thorough-going simplicity. Since the law has been declared once for all, perfect and complete, there is no need for a legislative branch of government; and since Christ is the sole overlord and king, there is no need for an earthly head of the state; it remains only to provide a competent magisterial system to hear causes and adjudicate differences. Society is concerned wholly with duties and not at all with rights; government therefore begins and ends with the magistrate. In order to secure an adequate magistracy, Eliot proposed to divide society into groups of tens, fifties, hundreds, and thousands, each of which should choose its rulers, who in turn should choose their representatives in the higher councils; and so there was evolved an ascending series of magistrates until the supreme council of the nation was reached, the decisions of which should be final.

> The duties of all the Rulers of the civil part of the Kingdom of Christ, are as followeth . . . to govern the people in the orderly and seasonable practice of all the Commanders of God, in actions liable to Political observations, whether of piety and love to God, or of justice, and love to man with peace.

Far removed as *The Christian Commonwealth* was from the saner thought of the Army democrats, it is the logical culmination of all theocratic dreams. The ideal of social unity, of relentless conformity, according to which the rebel is a social outlaw to be silenced at any cost, dominates this Christian Utopia as mercilessly as it dominated the policy of Laud. In setting up King Jesus for King Charles, there was to be no easing of the yoke upon the rebellious spirit; and in binding society upon the letter of the Scripture there was to be no room for the democratic aspirations of the leveller. Curious as this little work is—testifying rather to the sincerity of Eliot's Hebraism than to his political intelligence or to his knowledge of men—it is characteristic of the man who consecrated his

life to the dream of an Indian mission. How little disturbed
he was by the perversities and limitations of facts, is revealed
anew in the polity which he laid down for his Indian converts·

And this VOW I did solemnly make unto the Lord concerning
them; that they being a people without any forme of Government,
and now to chuse; I would endeavour with all my might, to bring
them to embrace such Government, both civil and Ecclesiastical,
as the Lord hath commanded in the holy Scriptures; and to deduce
all their Lawes from the holy Scriptures, that so they may be the
Lord's people, ruled by him alone in all things.

Which vow, considering the state of the Indian tribes to whom
it was to apply, may serve to throw light upon the causes of
the scant success of the Saints in dealing with the Indians.
Despite the logic of the theocrats, unanimity of opinion
among the Saints was sadly lacking; and the peace of the new
Canaan was troubled and the patience of the leaders sorely
tried by pious malcontents, who were not content that God
should rule through John Cotton, but themselves desired to
be the Lord's vicegerents. The democrats were constantly
prodding the ruling coterie of gentlemen; and the democratic
conception of a commonwealth of free citizens intruded more
and more upon the earlier conception of a kingdom of God.
Capable leaders of the new radicalism were not lacking; and
if we would comprehend the dissension and heart-burnings
of those early times, we must set the figures of Roger Williams
and Thomas Hooker over against John Cotton and the
theocrats.
Roger Williams, advocate of toleration, was the most
tempestuous soul thrown upon the American shores by the
revolution then griping England, the embodiment and
spokesman of the new radical hopes. He was an arch-rebel
in a rebellious generation, the intellectual barometer of a world
of stormy speculation and great endeavour. A generation
younger than the Boston leaders, he came to maturity at the
beginning of the wave of radicalism that was to sweep England
into civil war. Older ties of class and custom he put aside
easily, to make room for the new theories then agitating young
Englishmen; and these new theories he advocated with an
importunity disconcerting to practical men more given to

weighing times and occasions. The kernel of his radicalism was the ideal of a democratic church in a democratic society. The more closely we scrutinize the thought of the great Separatist, the more clearly we perceive that the master principle of his career was Christian—the desire to embody in his life the social as well as the spiritual teachings of Christ. He put aside tradition and went back to the foundation and original of the gospel, discovering anew the profoundly revolutionary conceptions that underlie the philosophy of Jesus. He learned to conceive of men literally as the children of God and brothers in Christ, and out of this primary conception he developed his democratic philosophy. It was to set up no Hebraic absolutism that he came to America; it was to establish a free commonwealth of Christ in which the lowest and meanest of God's children should share equally with the greatest. But before there could be a free commonwealth there must be free churches; the hand of neither bishop nor presbytery must lie upon the conscience of the individual Christian; and so Roger Williams threw himself into the work of spreading the propaganda of Separatism. Not only did he protest in New England against the tyranny of the magistrates, but he flung at the heads of all enemies of freedom the notable book on toleration in which he struck at the root of the matter by arguing that "conscience be permitted (though erroneous) to be free."

In an earlier age he would have become a disciple of St. Francis; but in the days when the religious movement was passing over into a political movement, when it was being talked openly that both in church and state "the Originall of all free Power and Government" lies in the people, he threw in his lot with the levellers to further the democratic movement. As early as 1644 he had formulated his main principles:

From this *Grant* I infer . . . that the *Soveraigne, originall,* and *foundation* of *civill power* lies in the *people* . . . And if so, that a People may erect and establish what *forme* of *Government* seemes to them most meete for their *civill condition:* It is evident that such *Governments* as are by them erected and established, have no more *power,* nor for no longer time, then the *civill power* or people consenting and agreeing shall betrust them with. This is cleere not only in *Reason,* but in the experience of all *commonweales,* where the people are not deprived of their *naturall freedome* by the power of *Tyrants*.[1]

Clearly the radical times, his own experience, and his discussions with Sir Harry Vane had carried Roger Williams far into the field of political speculation, and confirmed his prepossessions of broader political rights for the common people from whom he had sprung. In all his later thinking there stood sharply before his mind the figure of the individual citizen, endowed with certain inalienable rights, a free member of a free commonwealth; and it was this profoundly modern conception which he transported to the wilderness of Rhode Island, providing there a fit sanctuary for the ark of the democratic covenant which was soon to be roughly handled by the tory reaction of Restoration England.

A courageous and unselfish thinker was this old-time Separatist and democrat. The friendliest of souls, time has brought him the friends which his restless intellect drove from him in his own day. However hopelessly we may lose ourselves in the tangle of his writings, confused by the luxuriance of his Hebraic tropes, we can plainly discern the man, the most charitable, the most open-minded, the most modern, amongst the notable company of Puritan emigrants—the sincerest Christian among many who sincerely desired to be Christians. His own words most adequately characterize him: "*Liberavi animam meam:* I have not hid within my *breast*, my *souls* belief." Naturally such a man could not get on with the Presbyterian leaders of Boston Bay; the social philosophies which divided them were fundamentally hostile; and the fate which Roger Williams suffered was prophetic of the lot that awaited later zealots in the democratic cause—to be outcast and excommunicate from respectable society.

A man of far different mettle was old Thomas Hooker of Hartford. The sternest autocrat of them all, a leader worthy to measure swords with the redoubtable Hugh Peters himself, a man of "mighty vigour and fervour of spirit" who, to further "his Master's work, would put a king in his pocket," he would seem to be the very stuff out of which to fashion a dictator

---

[1] *Narr. Club Pub.*, III., 249.

for the snug Presbyterian Utopia. Nevertheless there was some hidden bias in the old Puritan's nature that warped him away from Presbyterianism, and made him the advocate of a democratic Congregationalism. The great schism which rent the early theocracy, carrying off three congregations into the Connecticut wilderness, was an early witness to the antagonisms which lurked in the ambitions of diverse-minded enthusiasts. The seceders had other notions of church organization, it appears, than those held by the dominant group; but they were moderates, who believed that everything should be done decently and in order, and instead of setting up a clamour and bringing confusion upon God's work, they withdrew quietly under the leadership of Thomas Hooker and set up their new church at Hartford.

Concerning the "grave and juditious Hooker" surprisingly little is known, notwithstanding the work that he did and the influence that he wielded during a masterful life. He was a man evidently regardless of fame, who took small pains to publish his virtues to the ears of posterity; nevertheless it is clear that he was a better democrat than the Boston leaders— the father of New England Congregationalism as it later came to be when the Presbyterian tendency was finally checked. For his pronounced democratic sympathies some ground may be discovered in his humble origin. He was sprung of a plain yeoman family, got his education by the aid of scholarships, married a "waiting-woman" to the wife of his patron, and lived plainly, untroubled by social ambitions. He was a self-made man who had risen by virtue of strength of character and disdained to be a climber. He was evidently one of the greatest preachers of his time in either England, and he had early been marked by Laud's spies as one of "the people's creatures" "who blew the bellows of their sedition." He drew young men to him—among others John Eliot; and even though he should be silenced, his influence would remain "His genius will still haunte all the pulpits in ye country, where any of his scholars may be admitted to preach," one of the sycophants reported of him. Such a man must be reckoned with; and when in New England he found the ways too autocratic to suit him, he threw himself into the work of quickening the democratic unrest. "After Mr. Hooker's coming over," said Hubbard, "it was observed that many of the freemen grew to be very jealous of their liberties."

He was more concerned with experimental religion than with theology, more the pastor than the teacher. Nevertheless, when the Massachusetts leaders were troubled by attacks of old-world Presbyterians directed against "the New-England way," they drafted Hooker to write a defence. This was the origin of his *Survey of the Summe of Church Discipline*, a knotty book vigorous in thought and phrase, the most important contribution of New England Congregationalism to the great disputes of the time. The old champion went straight to the heart of the matter, seizing upon the political principles involved:

But whether all Ecclesiasticall power be . . . rightly taken in to the Presbytery alone: Or that the people of the Particular Churches should come in for a share . . . This is left as the subject of the inquiry of this age, and that which occasions great thought of heart of all hands: Great thoughts of hearts in the Presbytery, as being very loth to part with that so chief priviledge, and of which they have taken possession so many years. Great thoughts of heart amongst the churches, how they may clear their right, and claim it in such pious sobriety and moderation, as becomes the Saints: being unwilling to loose their cause and comfort, meerly upon a nihil dicit: or forever to be deprived of so precious a legacy, as they conceive this is, though it hath been withheld from them, by the tyranny of the Pope, and prescription of times. Nor can they conceive it lesse, then a heedlesse betraying of their speciall liberties . . . by a carelesse silence, when the course of providence, as the juncture of things now present themselves, allows them a writt Ad melius inquirendum. . . . These are the times when people shall be fitted for such priviledges, fit I say to obtain them, and fit to use them. . . . And whereas it hath been charged upon the people, that through their ignorance and unskilfulnesse, they are not able to wield such priviledges, and therefore not fit to share in any such power, The Lord hath promised: To take away the vail from all faces in the mountain, the weak shall be as David, and David as an Angel of God.[1]

If the Presbyterianizing party found the path they were treading thorny and rough, it was due in no small part to

[1] Introd.

Thomas Hooker, who liberally bestrewed their path with impediments. Hebraist and theocrat though he professed to be, his Hebraic theocracy was grounded upon the people, and pointed straight towards the sovereignty of the individual congregation. "The Lord hath promised to take away the vail from all faces in the mountain"—and if the veil be removed and the people see, shall not the people judge concerning their own causes? In this faith Thomas Hooker lived and laboured, thereby proving his right to be numbered among the stewards of our American democracy.

The fibre of the emigrant leaders had been toughened by conflict with old-world conservatism and turned radical by the long struggle with an arrogant toryism. By a natural selective process the stoutest-hearted had been driven overseas, and the well-known words of William Stoughton, "God sifted a whole Nation that he might send choice grain over into this wildernes,"[1] were the poetic expression of a bitter reality. But seated snugly in the new world, in control of church and state, the emigrant radicalism found its ardour cooling. The Synod of 1637 set a ban upon Antinomianism and other heretical innovations, and thereafter Massachusetts settled down to a rigid orthodoxy. The fathers had planted, was it not enough for the sons to water and tend the vine, and enjoy the fruit thereof? And so the spirit of conservatism took possession of the native generation, the measure of excellence being accounted the fidelity with which the husbandmen revered the work of the emigrant pioneers. Translated into modern terms, it means that the native ministers, having inherited a system of which they were the beneficiaries, discovered little inclination to question the title deeds to their inheritance, but were mainly bent on keeping them safe. To preserve what had been gained, and as far as possible to extend the Presbyterian principle, became their settled policy; and so in all the life of New England—in the world of Samuel Sewall, as well as in that of Cotton Mather—a harsh and illiberal dogmatism succeeded to the earlier enthusiasm.

The indisputable leader of the second generation was

---

[1] From a sermon entitled, *New-Englands true interests; not to lie: Or, a Treatise declaring . . . the terms on which we stand, and the tenure by which we hold our . . . precious and pleasant things.* Cambridge, 1670.

Increase Mather, son of Richard Mather, and father of Cotton, the most vigorous and capable member of a remarkable family. After graduating at Harvard, he entered Trinity College, Dublin, where he proceeded Master of Arts. He spent some years in England, preaching there to the edification of many, until the restoration of Charles sent him back to America to become the guiding spirit of the New England hierarchy. He was by nature a politician and statesman rather than a minister, the stuff of which frocked chancellors were made; and he needed only a pliant master to have become another Wolsey or Richelieu. He liked to match his wit in diplomacy with statesmen, and he served his native land faithfully and well in the matter of wheedling Dutch William into granting a new charter to Massachusetts. A natural autocrat, he was dictatorial and domineering, bearing himself arrogantly towards all underlings, unyielding in opposition to whoever crossed his will. And in consequence he gathered about his head such fierce antagonism that in the end he failed of his ambitions, and shorn of power he sat down in old age to eat the bread of bitterness.

Skill in organization was the secret of his strength. In no sense a creative thinker, wholly lacking in intellectual curiosity and therefore not given to speculation, he built up a compact hierarchical machine, and then suffered the mortification of seeing it broken to pieces by forces that lay beyond his control. If the theocratic ideal of ecclesiastical control of secular affairs were to maintain itself against the growing opposition, the ministers must fortify their position by a closer organization. They must speak as a unit in determining church policies; above all they must guard against the wolves in sheep's clothing who were slipping into the pulpits to destroy the flocks. To effect such ends Synods were necessary, and Increase Mather was an ardent advocate of Synodical organization. He prompted the calling of the "Reforming Synod" of 1679–80, served as Moderator, dominated the debates, and drafted the report; and the purpose which underlay such work was the substitution of a Presbyterian hierarchy for the older Congregationalism. The church must dominate the state; the organized ministers must dominate the church; and Increase Mather trusted that he could dominate the ministers—such

in brief was the dream of this masterful leader of the second
generation.

The source of his power lay in the pulpit, and for sixty-
four years the Old North Church was the citadel of Mather
orthodoxy. His labours were enormous. Sixteen hours a
day he commonly studied. Among many powerful preachers
he was reckoned "the complete preacher," and he thundered
above his congregation with an authority that must have been
appalling. His personal influence carried far, and doubtless
there were many good men in Boston who believed—as Roger
Williams said of John Cotton—that "God would not suffer"
Increase Mather "to err." Those whom his voice could not
reach his pen must convince, and the busy minister set a pace
in the making and publishing of books which only his busier
son could equal. He understood thoroughly the power of the
press, and he watched over it with an eagle eye; no unauthorized
or godless work must issue thence for the pollution of the people;
and to insure that only fit matter should be published he was
at enormous pains to supply enough manuscript himself to
keep the printers busy. The press was a powerful aid to the
pulpit in shaping public opinion, and Increase Mather was too
shrewd a leader not to understand how necessary it was to
hold it in strict control. He was a calculating dictator, and
he ruled the press with the same iron hand with which he
ruled the pulpit. He was no advocate of freedom, for he was
no friend of democracy.

Of the odium which an obstinate defence of a passing
order gathered about the name of Mather, the larger share fell
to the lot of Cotton Mather, whose passionately distorted
career remains so incomprehensible to us. One may well
hesitate to describe Cotton Mather; the man is unconceivable
to one who has not read his diary. Unlike Increase, he was
provincial to the core. Born and bred in Boston, his longest
trips into the outer world carried him only a few miles from the
Old North Meeting-house, where for years he served as co-
labourer with his father. Self-centred and self-righteous, the
victim of strange asceticisms and morbid spiritual debauches,
every circumstance of his life ripened and expanded the colossal
egotism of his nature. His vanity was daily fattened by the
adulation of silly women and the praise of foolish men, until

the insularity of his thought and judgment grew into a disease. His mind was clogged with the strangest miscellany of truth and fiction; he laboured to acquire the possessions of a scholar, but he listened to old wives' tales with an amazing credulity. In all his mental processes the solidest fact fell into grotesque perspective, and confused itself with the most fantastic abortions. And yet he was prompted by a love of scientific investigation, and in the matter of inoculation for smallpox showed himself both courageous and intelligent.

Living under the shadow of his father, he was little more than a reduced copy of the Mather ambitions, inheriting a ready-made theology, a passion for the ideals of the emigrant generation, an infallible belief in the finality of the Mather conclusions. The masterfulness of old Increase degenerated in the son into an intolerable meddlesomeness; and in the years of reaction against ecclesiastical domination the position of Cotton Mather was difficult. He was exposed to attack from two sides; the tories with whom he would gladly have affiliated, and the democrats whom he held in contempt, both rejected the archaic theocracy. As his meddlesomeness increased, the attacks of his enemies multiplied, wounding his self-esteem bitterly—"having perhaps the Insults of contemptible People, the Assaults of those insignificant *Lice*, more than any man in *New-England*," as his son testifies. "These troublesome but diminutive Creatures he scorn'd to concern himself with; only to *pity* them and *pray* for them." He would die willingly, he believed, to save his erring people from their sins, but he obstinately refused to be dictated to by them.

Of the content of his innumerable writings the accompanying Bibliography will give sufficient indication. A man of incredible industry, unrestrained by any critical sense, and infatuated with printer's ink, he flung together a jumble of old saws and modern instances and called the result a book. Of the 470 odd titles, the *Magnalia* alone possesses some vitality still, the repository of much material concerning early days in Massachusetts that we should not willingly lose. "In his *Style*, indeed," according to a contemporary critic, "he was something singular, and not so agreeable to the Gust of the Age. But like his *manner of speaking*, it was very *emphatical*."

The emphasis, it must be confessed, is now gone from his pages, and the singularity remains, a singularity little agreeable to the gust of today.

The party of conservatism numbered among its adherents every prominent minister of the greater churches. The organization propaganda of the Mathers spread widely, and in 1705 a group of men put forth a series of "Proposals" looking to a closer union of the churches, and greater control of the separate congregations by the ministerial association.[1] Seven years later John Wise, pastor of the second church of Ipswich, published his *Churches Quarrel Espoused*, and in 1717, his *Vindication of the New England Churches*. The two works were a democratic counterblast to the Presbyterian propaganda, and stirred the thought of the churches so effectively as to nullify the Proposals, and put an end to all such agitation in Massachusetts.

Posterity has been too negligent of John Wise hitherto. Although possessed of the keenest mind and most trenchant pen of his generation of Americans, he was untainted by any itch of publicity, and so failed to challenge the attention of later times. Nevertheless, what we know of him is to his credit. An independent man, powerful of body, vigorous of intellect, tenacious of opinion, outspoken and fearless in debate, he seems to have understood the plain people whom he served, and he sympathized heartily with the democratic ideals then taking shape in the New England village. Some explanation of his democratic sympathies may be discovered in his antecedents. His father was a self-made man who had come over to Roxbury as an indented servant—most menial of stations in that old Carolinian world. There he doubtless taught his son independence and democratic self-respect, which stood John Wise in good stead when he later came to speak for the people against the arbitrary tax of Andros, the encroachments of the Mathers, or the schemes of the hard-money men.

When, in response to the challenge of the Presbyterians, he turned to examine critically the work of the fathers, he found in it quite another meaning than Cotton Mather found.

[1] For an account of the movement, see Walker's *History of the Congregational Churches in the United States*, pp. 201–213.

It was as a radical that he went back to the past, seeking to recover the original Congregational principle, which, since the conservative triumph in the Synod of 1637, had been greatly obscured. The theme of his two books is the same, a defence of the "venerable New-English constitution"; but the significance of them in the history of democratic America lies in the fact that he followed "an unbeaten path," justifying the principles of Congregationalism by analogy from civil polity. Seemingly alone amongst the New England clergy of his day he had grounded himself in political theory; and the doctrine upon which he erected his argument was the new conception of "natural rights," derived from a study of Puffendorf's *De Jure Naturae et Gentium*, published in 1672. This was the first effective reply in America to the old theocratic sneer that if the democratic form of government were indeed divinely sanctioned, was it not strange that God had overlooked it in providing a system for his chosen people? But Wise had broken with the literal Hebraism of earlier times, and was willing to make use of a pagan philosophy, based upon an appeal to history, a method which baffled the followers of the old school. They found difficulty in replying to such argument:

That a democracy in church or state, is a very honourable and regular government according to the dictates of right reason, And, therefore . . . That these churches of New England, in their ancient constitution of church order, it being a democracy, are manifestly justified and defended by the law and light of nature.

With the advance of the democratic movement of modern times, the life and work of John Wise take on new interest. After a spirited contest lasting for three-quarters of a century, theocratic Puritanism merged in ecclesiastical democracy. For two generations it had remained doubtful which way the church would incline. Dominated by gentlemen, it was warped toward Presbyterianism; but interpreted by commoners, it leaned towards Congregationalism. The son of a plebeian, Wise came naturally into sympathy with the spirit of radical Separatism, bred of the democratic aspirations of the old Jacobean underlings; and this radical Separatism he found justified by the new philosophy, as well as by the facts of the

New England village world. The struggle for ecclesiastical democracy was a forerunner of the struggle for political democracy, which was to be the business of the next century; and in justifying his ecclesiasticism by political principles, John Wise was an early witness to the new order of thought.

Judged by the severest standards, the Puritan ministers were a notable group of men; the English race has never bred their superiors in self-discipline and exalted ideals, and rarely their equals in consecration to duty. Their interests might be narrow and their sympathies harsh and illiberal; nevertheless men who studied ten to sixteen hours a day were neither boors nor intellectual weaklings. A petty nature would not have uttered the lament of Increase Mather:

not many years ago, I *lost* (and that's an afflictive *loss* indeed!) several moneths from study by sickness. Let every God-fearing reader joyn with me in prayer, that I may be enabled to redeem the time, and (in all wayes wherein I am capable), to serve my generation.[1]

From the long hours of reading they acquired a huge mass of learning; out of the many books they read they made still other books of like nature and purpose. The way of printer's ink was the path of celebrity and authority, and the minister who had not a goodly number of volumes to his credit was an unprofitable servant, lacking ambition to glorify his Lord. Though they denied themselves in other things, they did not stint their library. In 1686 John Dunton numbered eight book-shops in the village of Boston; and in 1702 Cotton Mather described his study, "the hangings whereof, are Boxes with between two and three thousand Books in them."

According to present taste it was an uninviting library; works of pure literature were as lacking as books of history and political philosophy and science. Nevertheless, though their reading was narrow, the ministers in many respects were in advance of their times. For all his grotesque lack of scientific method, Cotton Mather was more nearly a scientist than any other man of his day in Boston,—a weakness which laid him open to criticism. Under date of 23 December, 1714, Sewall noted in his diary:

[1] Preface to *Remarkable Providences.*

Dr. C. Mather preaches excellently from Ps. 37. Trust in the Lord, etc., only spake of the Sun being in the centre of our system. I think it inconvenient to assert such problems.

His membership in the Royal Society, to which he forwarded his *Curiosa Americana,* encouraged him to keep abreast of current scientific thought; and it was from this source that he got the idea of inoculation for smallpox, which he urged upon the people of Boston so insistently that a war of pamphlets broke out. When we remember that during ninety years only two books on medicine were published in New England— one a popular pharmacopeia and the other a hand-book on smallpox prevention—it is suggestive that within a few months sixteen papers on inoculation came from the press. In this case the minister was in advance of the physicians.

If the influence of the ministers was commanding, it was due in part to their indisputable vigour, and in part, it must be acknowledged, to their control of the means of publicity. The complete domination of the press they regarded as their perquisite; and they swayed public opinion sometimes by means not wholly to their credit. Those who opposed their policies experienced difficulties in gaining a hearing. Thus Robert Calef, who attacked the Mathers because of the witch-craft business, found it desirable to send his manuscript to London for publication, and John Wise probably sent his manuscript of *The Churches Quarrel Espoused* to New York.[1] Complaints were heard that the press was closed. In the preface to *The Gospel Order Revived,* by T. Woodbridge and other malcontents, published in New York in 1700,

The Reader is desired to take Notice that the Press in *Boston* is so much under the aw of the Reverend Author, whom we answer, and his Friends, that we could not obtain of the Printer there to print the following Sheets, which is the true Reason why we have sent the Copy so far for its Impression and where it was printed with some Difficulty.

When James Franklin spoke out roundly against the tyranny of the ministers, they induced the magistrates to teach him respect by throwing him into the common gaol. It was

[1] See Bibliography on this point.

a serious matter to offend the hierarchy, even in the days of its decline, and far more serious to attack.　But the days of its domination were numbered, and after 1720 the secular authority of the Puritan divines swiftly decayed.　The old dream of a Kingdom of God was giving way, under pressure of economic circumstance, to the new dream of a commonwealth of free citizens.　The theological age was to be followed by a political age, and in this later world of thought the Puritan divines were unfitted to remain leaders of the people.

CHAPTER IV

Edwards

JONATHAN EDWARDS was born at Windsor, Connecticut, in 1703. He belonged, unlike his great contemporary Franklin in this, to the "Brahmin families" of America, his father being a distinguished graduate of Harvard and a minister of high standing, his mother being the daughter of Solomon Stoddard, a revered pastor of Northampton, Massachusetts, and a religious author of repute. Jonathan, one of eleven children, showed extraordinary precocity. There is preserved a letter of his, written apparently in his twelfth year, in which he retorts upon certain materialistic opinions of his correspondent with an easiness of banter not common to a boy; and another document, from about the same period, an elaborate account of the habits of spiders, displays a keenness of observation and a vividness of style uncommon at any age.

He studied at Yale, receiving his bachelor's degree in 1720, before his seventeenth birthday. While at college he continued his interest in scientific observations, but his main concern was naturally with theology and moral philosophy. As a sophomore he read Locke *On the Human Understanding*, with the delight of a "greedy miser" in "some newly discovered treasure." Some time after reading Locke and before graduation he wrote down a series of reflections, preparatory to a great metaphysical treatise of his own, which can be compared only with the *Commonplace Book* kept by Berkeley a few years earlier for the same purpose. In the section of "Notes on the Mind" this entry is found: "Our perceptions or ideas, that we passively receive by our bodies, are communicated to us immediately by God." Now Berkeley's *Principles* and his *Hylas and Philonous* appeared in 1710 and 1713 respectively, and the question has been raised, and not answered, whether this Berkeleian sentiment was borrowed from one of these books or was original with Edwards. Possibly the youthful philosopher was following a line of thought suggested by the English disciples of Malebranche, possibly he reached his point of view directly from Locke; in any case his life-work was to carry on the Lockian philosophy from the point where the Berkeleian idealism left off.

After graduation Edwards remained for two years at Yale, preparing for the ministry. In 1722 he was called to a Presbyterian church in New York. Here he preached acceptably for eight months, returning then to his father's house, and later to New Haven, where he held the position of tutor in the college. In 1727 he went to Northampton as colleague, and became in due time successor, to his grandfather. Almost immediately after ordination he married Sarah Pierrepont, like himself of the Brahmin caste, whom he had known as a young girl, and whose beauty of body and soul he had described in a passage of ecstatic wonder.

"They say," he began, being himself then twenty and the object of his adoration thirteen, "there is a young lady in New Haven who is beloved of that great Being who made and rules the world, and that there are certain seasons in which this great Being, in some way or other invisible, comes to her and fills her mind with exceeding sweet delight."

The marriage, notwithstanding this romantic rapture, proved eminently wise.

Like a good many other men of his age Edwards lived his inner life, so to speak, on paper. There is therefore nothing peculiar or priggish in the fact that at the beginning of his religious career he should have written out a set of formal resolutions, which he vowed to read over, and did read over, at stated intervals in order to keep watch on his spiritual progress. A number of these resolutions have been printed, as has also a part of the diary kept at about the same time. Neither of these documents, the time of their writing considered, contains anything remarkable. But it is quite otherwise with the private reflections which he wrote out some twenty years later (about 1743) at Northampton, apparently on some occasion of reading over his youthful diary. In these we have an autobiographical fragment that, for intensity of absorption in the idea of God and for convincing power of utterance, can be likened to the *Confessions* of St. Augustine, while it unites to this religious fervour a romantic feeling for nature foreign to the Bishop of Hippo's mind and prophetic of a movement that was to sweep over the world many years after Edwards's death. A few extracts from this document (not so well known as it would have been if it had not been printed with the works of a thorny metaphysician) must be given for their biographical and literary interest:

From my childhood up, my mind had been full of objections against the doctrine of God's sovereignty, in choosing whom he would to eternal life, and rejecting whom he pleased; leaving them eternally to perish, and be everlastingly tormented in hell. It used to appear like a horrible doctrine to me. But I remember the time very well, when I seemed to be convinced, and fully satisfied, as to this sovereignty of God. . . . I have often, since that first conviction, had quite another kind of sense of God's sovereignty than I had then. I have often since had not only a conviction, but a delightful conviction. The doctrine has very often appeared exceeding pleasant, bright, and sweet. Absolute sovereignty is what I love to ascribe to God. But my first conviction was not so.

The first instance that I remember of that sort of inward, sweet delight in God and divine things that I have lived much in since, was on reading those words, *Now unto the King eternal, immortal, invisible, the only wise God, be honour and glory for ever and ever, Amen.* As I read the words, there came into my soul, and was as it were diffused through it, a sense of the glory of the Divine Being. . . .

Not long after I first began to experience these things, I gave an account to my father of some things that had passed in my mind. I was pretty much affected by the discourse we had together; and when the discourse was ended, I walked abroad alone, in a solitary place in my father's pasture, for contemplation. And as I was walking there, and looking up on the sky and clouds, there came into my mind so sweet a sense of the glorious *majesty* and *grace* of God, that I know not how to express. I seemed to see them

both in a sweet conjunction; majesty and meekness joined together;
it was a sweet and gentle, and holy majesty; and also a majestic
meekness; an awful sweetness; a high, and great, and holy gentleness.

This is not the Edwards that is commonly known, and
indeed he put little of this personal rapture of holiness into his
published works, which were almost exclusively polemical in
design. Only once, perhaps, did he adequately display this
aspect of his thought to the public; and that was in the *Dissertation on the Nature of Virtue*, wherein, starting from the
definition of virtue as "the beauty of the qualities and exercises of the heart," he proceeds to combine ethics and aesthetics
in an argument as subtle in reasoning as it is, in places, victorious in expression. One cannot avoid the feeling, when his
writings are surveyed as a whole, that in his service to a particular dogma of religion Edwards deliberately threw away the
opportunity of making for himself, despite the laxness of his
style, one of the very great names in literature.

It should seem also that he not only suppressed his personal
ecstasy in his works for the press, but waived it largely in his
more direct intercourse with men. He who himself, like an
earlier and perhaps greater Emerson, was enjoying the sweetness of walking with God in the garden of earth, was much
addicted to holding up before his people the "pleasant, bright,
and sweet" doctrine of damnation. Nor can it be denied that
he had startling ways of impressing this sweetness on others.
It is a misfortune, but one for which he is himself responsible,
that his memory in the popular mind today is almost exclusively associated with certain brimstone sermons and their
terrific effect. Best known of these is the discourse on *Sinners
in the Hands of an Angry God*, delivered at Enfield, Connecticut,
in the year 1741. His text was taken from Deuteronomy:
"Their foot shall slide in due time"; and from these words
he proceeded to prove, and "improve," the truth that "there
is nothing that keeps wicked men at any moment out of hell,
but the mere pleasure of God." He is said to have had none
of the common qualities of the orator. His regular manner of
preaching, at least in his earlier years, was to hold his "manuscript volume in his left hand, the elbow resting on the cushion
or the Bible, his right hand rarely raised but to turn the leaves,

and his person almost motionless"; but there needed no gesticulation and no modulation of voice to convey the force of his terrible conviction, when, to an audience already disposed to accept the dogma, he presented that dogma in a series of pictures like the following:

The God that holds you over the pit of hell, much as one holds a spider, or some loathesome insect, over the fire, abhors you, and is dreadfully provoked; his wrath towards you burns like fire; he looks upon you as worthy of nothing else, but to be cast into the fire; he is of purer eyes than to bear to have you in his sight.

The congregation of Enfield, we are told, was moved almost to despair; "there was such a breathing of distress and weeping" that the speaker was interrupted and had to plead for silence. Sincerity of vision may amount to cruelty, and something is due to the weakness of human nature.

The result was inevitable. The people of Northampton listened to Edwards for a time; were rapt out of themselves; suffered the relapse of natural indolence; grew resentful under the efforts to keep them in a state of exaltation; and freed themselves of the burden when it became intolerable. At first all went well. Stoddard, in whose declining years the discipline of the church had been somewhat relaxed, died in 1729, and the fervour of his successor soon began to tell on the people. In 1733, as Edwards notes in his *Narrative of Surprising Conversions*, there was a stirring in the conscience of the young, who had hitherto been prone to the awful sin of "frolicking." The next year the sudden conversion of a young woman, "who had been one of the greatest company keepers in the whole town," came upon the community "like a flash of lightning"; the Great Awakening was started, which was to run over New England like a burning fire, with consequences not yet obliterated. The usual accompaniments of moral exaltation and physical convulsions showed themselves. Edwards relates with entire approbation the morbid conversion of a child of four. The poor little thing was overheard by her mother in her closet wrestling with God in prayer, from which she came out crying aloud and "wreathing her body to and fro like one in anguish of spirit." She was afraid she was going to hell!

It was inevitable that such a wave of superheated emotion should subside in a short time. In fact the enthusiasm
had scarcely reached its height when it began to show signs
of perversion and decay. Immediately after the story of
the young convert Edwards notes that "the Spirit of God
was gradually withdrawing" and "Satan seemed to be
let loose and raged in a dreadful manner." An epidemic
of melancholy and suicidal mania swept over the community,
and multitudes seemed to hear a voice saying to them: "Cut
your own throat, now is a good opportunity." Strange delusions arose and spread, until common sense once more got the
upper hand.

It was an old tale, told in New England with peculiar fury.
The saddest thing in the whole affair is the part played by
Edwards. Other leaders saw the danger from the first, or
were soon awakened to it; but Edwards never, either at this
time or later, wavered in his belief that the Awakening, though
marred by the devil, was in itself the work of the Divine Spirit.
His *Thoughts on the Revival of Religion* and his *Marks of a
Work of the True Spirit* are both a thoroughgoing apology for
the movement, as they are also an important document in
his own psychology. The jangling and confusion he admits;
he recognizes the elements of hysteria that were almost inextricably mixed up with the moral exaltation of conversion; but his
defence is based frankly on the avowal that these things are
the universal accompaniments of inspiration—they attended
the founding of the church in the Apostolic age, they were to
be expected at the instauration of religion. Often the reader
of these treatises is struck by a curious, and by no means
accidental, resemblance between the position of Edwards and
the position of the apologists of the romantic movement in
literature. There is the same directness of appeal to the
emotions; the same laudation of sheer expansiveness, at the
cost, if need be, of judgment or measure or any other restraint.
Prudence and regularity may be desirable in the service of
God, yet it is still true that "the cry of irregularity and
imprudence" has been mainly in the mouths of those who
are enemies to the main work of redemption. Perturbation,
in truth, is not properly so called when it is the means of rousing
the cold and indifferent from their lethargy; we are bound to

suppose that not even the man "of the strongest reason and greatest learning" can remain master of himself if "strongly impressed with a sense of divine and eternal things." It comes in the end to this, that, notwithstanding his verbal reservations, Edwards had no critical canon to distinguish between the order and harmony governed by a power higher than either the imagination or the emotions, and the order and harmony that are merely stagnation.

One factor in his confidence was a belief that the discovery of America, coinciding as it did with the beginning of the Reformation, came by Providence for "the glorious renovation of the world"; nay more, that the humble town in which he was preaching might be the cradle of the new dispensation, from whence it should spread over the whole earth. His language may even seem to betray a touch of spiritual pride over the part he himself should be called upon to play as the instrument of Grace in this marvellous regeneration. That vice of the saints was indeed a subject much in his meditations, and one of the finest pieces of religious psychology in his works is the passage of the *Revival* in which he tracks it through the labyrinthine deceits of the human heart. It was a sin against which he had probably to keep particular ward in these years, but we should not say that he ever, in any proper sense of the word, lapsed from the virtue of Christian humility. If he seemed to set himself above other men as an exigent judge, this was rather due to a faulty sympathy, an inability to measure others except by the standard of his own great faculties. Thus, for all his emotionalism, he lived under the control of an iron will, and he could not comprehend how the over-stimulation of terror and joy in a weaker disposition would work moral havoc. Nor from his own constant height could he understand how brief and fitful any mood of exaltation must be among ordinary men in their ordinary condition. Hence he not only failed to see the gravity of the actual evils at the time of the Awakening, but failed also, with more grievous results for himself, to recognize the impossibility of flogging the dead emotion into new life.

The issue came on a point of church discipline. Edwards believed that religion was essentially a matter of the emotions or affections. A man might have perfect knowledge of divine

things, as indeed the devil had, but unless the love of God was
implanted in his heart by the free act of Grace he had no lot
with the faithful. To develop this theme he wrote his great
Treatise Concerning Religious Affections, a work which may
without exaggeration be said to go as far as the human intellect
can go in the perilous path of discriminating between the purely
spiritual life and the life of worldly morality. Now even the
simple statement of the difference between the condition of
Grace and the condition of nature is hard for the natural man
to follow; but when Edwards, with the acumen of a genius and
the doggedness of a scholar, imposed his distinction on all the
intricate feelings of life, the natural man was dazed; and when he
attempted to make it the criterion of admission to the Lord's
Table, the natural man who thought himself a Christian rebelled. Stoddard had held it right to admit to communion
all those who desired honestly to unite themselves with the
church. Edwards protested that only those who had undergone
a radical conversion and knew the affections of supernatural
love should enjoy this high privilege. His congregation sided
with their old guide against him.

The quarrel was further embittered by another issue. It
came to light that certain young folk of the church were reading
profane books which led to lewd conversation. Edwards
called for public discipline of the sinners; the congregation
supported him until investigation showed that the evil was
widespread and would bring discredit on most of the better
families of the town, and then they blocked further proceedings.
If tradition is correct in naming *Pamela* as one of the guilty
books, we may admire the literary taste of youthful Northampton, yet think that their pastor was justified in condemning
such reading as incendiary. However that may be, when, on
22 June, 1750, a public vote was taken whether Edwards
should be dismissed from his pastorate, a large majority was
counted against him. Northampton has the distinction of
having rejected the greatest theologian and philosopher
yet produced in this country. The behaviour of Edwards
when the crisis actually came was simple, dignified, and even
noble. His *Farewell Sermon*, with its dispassionate and
submissive appeal from the tribunal of men to that final
judgment which shall be given in knowledge and righteous-

ness, cannot be read today without a deep stirring of the heart.

At the age of forty-six Edwards was thrust upon the world, discredited, in broken health, with a large family to support, but undaunted. Then befell a strange thing. This philosopher, whose thoughts and emotions ranged beyond the ken of most educated men, was sent to the frontier town of Stockbridge as a missionary to the Indians. There for six years he laboured faithfully and, at least in the practical management of affairs, successfully. It must have been one of the memorable sights of the world to see him returning on horseback from a solitary ride into the forest, while there fluttered about him, pinned to his coat, the strips of paper on which he had scribbled the results of his meditations. His days were little troubled, and not overburdened with work, peaceful it is thought; and now it was he wrote the treatise on the *Freedom of the Will* upon which his fame chiefly depends.

In 1757 his son-in-law, the Rev. Aaron Burr, died, and Edwards was chosen by the Trustees of the College of New Jersey to succeed him as president. Edwards hesitated, stating frankly to the Trustees his disabilities of health and learning, but he finally accepted the offer. He left his family to follow him later, and arrived in Princeton in January, 1758. Small-pox was in the town, and the new president was soon infected. His death took place on 22 March, in the fifty-fifth year of his age. His last recorded words were: "Trust in God and ye need not fear."

The child was indeed father of the man, and it was peculiarly fitting that he who from youth upward had been absorbed in the idea of God should have died with the sacred word on his lips. But what shall be said of the fearlessness—and there is no reason to question the perfect sincerity of his spiritual joy —in the breast of one who had made terror the chief instrument of appeal to men and had spent his life in fighting for a dogma which the genial author of *The One-Hoss Shay* thought no decent man could hold without going crazy? To understand that charge properly we must throw ourselves back into the age in which Edwards lived.

Now the Edwardian theology was a part of the great deistic debate which took its root in the everlasting question of the origin of evil in the world. It was a three-cornered contest. The Calvinists and the infidels both believed in a kind of determinism, but differed over the nature of the determining cause. The Calvinists found this cause in a personal Creator, omnipotent and omniscient, to whom they did not scruple to carry up all the evil as well as all the good of the universe—"c'est que Dieu," as Calvin himself states categorically, "non seulement a preveu la cheute du premier homme, et en icelle la ruine de toute sa posterité, mais qu'il l'a ainsi voulu." The deists, who at this time formed the fighting line of the infidels, while verbally acknowledging the existence of God and theorizing on the nature of evil, virtually regarded the universe as a perfectly working machine in which there was no room for a personal governor or for real sin. To the Arminians, including the bulk of the orthodox churchmen, the alliance between Calvinism and deism seemed altogether to outweigh the differences. As Daniel Whitby declares in the preface to his discourses *On the Five Points of Calvinism* (1710; reprinted in America), to hold God responsible for evil is to play directly into the hands of the atheists. And so the age-old dispute between Augustinian and Pelagian, and between Calvinist and Arminian, took on a new life from the deistic controversy, and there sprang up a literature which undertook to preserve the idea of an omnipotent personal Creator and at the same time to save his face, if the expression may be tolerated, by attributing to men complete free will and accountability for their actions.

It was in answer to Whitby's book and one or two others of the kind that Edwards composed his *Freedom of the Will*. His argument has a psychological basis. In the *Treatise Concerning Religious Affections* he had divided the soul into two faculties: one called the understanding, by which it discerns, views, and judges things; the other called the heart or will, being nothing else but the inclination of the soul towards or the disinclination from what is discerned and judged by the understanding. In the *Freedom of the Will* he starts with Locke's statement that "the Will is perfectly distinguished from Desire, which in the very same action may have a quite contrary tendency from that which our Wills set us upon." This theory Edwards analyses and rejects, and then proceeds to show that a man's desire and will are virtually the same faculty of the soul. It follows from this that the will at any moment is determined by the strongest motive acting upon the soul; we are free in so far as no obstacle is presented to our willing in accordance with our inclination, but our inclination is determined by what at any moment seems to us good. In his attack on the common arguments for the freedom of the will Edwards is magnificently victorious. If the psychology by which the Arminians sought to relieve God of the burden of evil in human life is pushed into a corner, it shows itself as nothing more than this: Man's will is a faculty absolutely indeterminate in itself and entirely independent of his inclinations. When, therefore, a man errs, it is because, the choice between evil with its attendant suffering and good with its attendant happiness being presented to him, the man, having full knowledge of the consequences and being impelled by no momentary preponderance of the one or the other from his innate disposition, deliberately and freely chooses what is evil and painful. Such an account of human action is monstrous, inconceivable; it offered an easy mark for so sharp a logician as Edwards.

But whence arise the conditions by which a man's inclination is swayed in one direction or the other? Edwards carries these unflinchingly up to the first cause,—that is, as a Christian, to God. Berkeley had made the world to consist of ideas evoked in the mind of man by the mind of God; Edwards accepts the logical conclusion, and holds God responsible for the inclination of the human will which depends on these ideas. Calvin did not hesitate to attribute, in the bluntest language, the source of evil to God's will, but at the same time he warned men against intruding with their finite reason into this "sanctuary of the divine wisdom." The mind of Edwards could not rest while any problem seemed to him unsolved. Confronted with the mystery of the divine permission of evil, he undertakes to solve it by applying his psychology of man to the nature of God. (He himself would put it the other way about: "Herein does very much consist that image of God wherein he made man.") The passage in which he develops this thesis, though generally overlooked by his critics, is of the first importance:

We must conceive of Him as influenced in the highest degree, by that which, above all others, is properly a moral inducement, viz., the moral good which He sees in such and such things: and therefore He is, in the most proper sense, a moral Agent, the source of all moral ability and Agency, the fountain and rule of all virtue and moral good; though by reason of his being supreme over all, it is not possible He should be under the influence of law or command, promises or threatenings, rewards or punishments, counsels or warnings. The essential qualities of a moral Agent are in God, in the greatest possible perfection; such as understanding, to perceive the difference between moral good and evil; a capacity of discerning that moral worthiness and demerit, by which some things are praiseworthy, others deserving of blame and punishment; and also a capacity of choice, and choice guided by understanding, and a power of acting according to his choice or pleasure, and being capable of doing those things which are in the highest sense praiseworthy.

In other words, the will of God is precisely like the will of man; it is merely the inclination, or *moral inducement*, to act as he is *influenced* by external power. The fatal mystery of good and evil, the true cause, lies above and beyond him; he is, like ourselves, a channel, not the source. The only difference is that God has complete knowledge of the possibilities of being, and therefore is not moved by threats and blind commands but, immediately, by what Edwards elsewhere calls the "moral necessity" of governing in accordance with the best of the "different objects of choice that are proposed to the Divine Understanding." By such a scheme God is really placed in about such a position as in the Leibnitzian continuation of Laurentius Valla's *Dialogue on Free Will and Providence*, where he is naïvely portrayed as looking upon an infinite variety of worlds piled up, like cannon balls, in pyramidal form before him, and selecting for creation that one which combines the greatest possible amount of good with the least possible admixture of evil.

From this pretty sport of the imagination Edwards would no doubt have drawn back in contempt, and indeed in his ordinary language God is merely the supreme Cause, without further speculation. One of the Leibnitzian inferences, moreover, is utterly excluded from his philosophy. He was no optimist, was in fact the last man to infer that, because this world is the best possible conceivable, evil is therefore a small and virtually negligible part of existence. On the contrary the whole animus of his teaching springs from a deep and immediate hatred of evil in itself and apart from any consideration of its cause.

"The thing," he says, "which makes sin hateful, is that by which it deserves punishment; which is but the expression of hatred. . . . Thus, for instance, ingratitude is hateful and worthy of dispraise, according to common sense; not because something as bad, or worse than ingratitude, was the cause that produced it; but because it is hateful in itself, by its own inherent deformity."

To the charge of the Arminians that the doctrine of predestination leaves no place for the punishment of sin, this is an adequate and practical reply. But the consequences of this principle of common sense are, in another way, peculiar and even disastrous to the Edwardian theology. If we are right, as we indubitably are right, in detesting evil in itself and wherever seen, and if we hold with Edwards that the will of God, like the will of man, is merely the inclination towards the best object presented to its choice, and there is no power either in God or in man above the will, in what essential way, then, does the act of God in creating a world mixed with evil differ from the act of Judas in betraying God, and how are we relieved from hating God for the evil of his work with the same sort of hatred as that which we feel for Judas? Edwards had terrified the people of Enfield with a picture of God treading down sinners till their blood sprinkled his raiment, and exulting in his wrath. The retort is obvious, and unspeakable. Nor can he, or any other Predestinarian, escape the odium of such a retort by hiding behind the necessity of things which all men must, in one way or another, admit. There is a war between the nations, he will say, and suddenly a bomb, dropping upon a group of soldiers, themselves innocent of any crime, horribly rends and mangles them. Here is a hideous thing, and by no twisting of the reason can we avoid carrying the responsibility for this evil back to the first great cause of all. Shall we be held impious for saying metaphorically that the blood of these soldiers is sprinkled on the raiment of that

Cause?—Aye, but the difference to us morally if we leave that cause in its own vast obscurity, unapproached by our reason, untouched by our pride; or if we make it into an image of ourselves, composed only of understanding and inclination like our own, and subject to our reprobation as surely as to our love!

Edwards had riddled and forever destroyed the arguments for free will commonly employed by the Arminians; is there no alternative for the human reason save submission to his theological determinism or to fatalistic atheism?

One way of escape from that dilemma is obvious and well known. It is that which Dr. Johnson, with his superb faculty of common sense, seized upon when the Edwardian doctrine came up in conversation before him. "The only relief I had was to forget it," said Boswell, who had read the book; and Johnson closed the discussion with his epigram: "All theory is against the freedom of the will, all experience for it." That is sufficient, no doubt, for the conduct of life; yet there is perhaps another way of escape, which, if it does not entirely silence the metaphysical difficulties, at least gives them a new ethical turn. Twice in the course of his argument Edwards refers to an unnamed Arminian[1] who placed the liberty of the soul not in the will itself, but in some power of suspending volition until due time has elapsed for judging properly the various motives to action. His reply is that this suspension of activity, being itself an act of volition, merely throws back without annulling the difficulty; and as the argument came to him, this refutation is fairly complete. But a fuller consideration of the point at issue might possibly indicate a way out of the dilemma of free will and determinism into a morally satisfying form of dualism within the soul of man himself. At least it can be said that the looseness of the Arminian reasoning leaves an easier loophole of escape into a human philosophy than does the rigid logic of the Predestinarians.

Yet for all that, though we may follow Edwards's logical system to the breaking point, as we can follow every meta-

---

[1] Edwards, it should seem, had immediately in mind the *Essay on the Freedom of Will in God and the Creature* of Isaac Watts; but the notion had been discussed at length by Locke (*Essay* II, xxi), and at an earlier date had been touched on with great acumen by John Norris in his correspondence with Henry More.

physical system, and though we may feel that, in his revulsion from the optimism of the deists, he distorted the actual evil of existence into a nightmare of the imagination,—yet for all that, he remains one of the giants of the intellect and one of the enduring masters of religious emotion. He had not the legal and executive brain of Calvin, upon whose *Institutes* his scheme of theology is manifestly based, but in subtle resourcefulness of reasoning and still more in the scope of his spiritual psychology he stands above his predecessor. Few men have studied Edwards without recognizing the force and honesty of his genius.

CHAPTER V

Philosophers and Divines, 1720–1789

A N old-time classification of the human faculties will serve
to explain the development of American thought in the
eighteenth century, a development which led to the
overthrow of high Calvinism. As there were three divisions
of the human mind—intellect, sensibility, and will, so were there
three divisions among the enemies of orthodoxy. Those who
followed the intellect were the rationalists, or deists. Those
who followed sensibility were the "hot" men, or enthusiasts.
Those who followed the will were the ethical reformers, who
emphasized the conscious cultivation of morality rather than
a divinely wrought change in man's nature. This last group
constituted the Arminians, the first in order of time in leading
the assault upon embattled tradition. When Jonathan Edwards, in 1734, complained of the "great noise in this part of
the country about Arminianism," he showed his alertness to
the preliminary attack of the enemy. That attack was especially directed against the middle of the five points of Calvinism.
It was not so much against particular redemption, or the perseverance of the saints, as against irresistible grace that the
battle-cry was raised. The reason given was that such grace
was bound to destroy man's free agency and convert him into a
mere machine. This explains why Edwards threw up as a
counterscarp his massive work upon the freedom of the human
will wherein that freedom was virtually denied.

Meanwhile, the second group, the men of feeling, came into
action. Received as allies, they turned out to be anything but
a help to the cause. After the religious revival and the great
awakening of 1734, Edwards the logician became, in a measure,
Edwards the enthusiast. But calling in the aid of evangelists

like George Whitefield carried sensibility beyond the limits of sense. To argue against the Arminians that, because of irresistible grace, men lack all native moral power, was to make men altogether passive in conversion and to run the risk of being carried away in a flood of feeling. So while Edwards warmed up his system by his writings on the *Religious Affections*, Whitefield had to be cautioned by the Connecticut divine for his too great dependence upon impulse. Brought in as an ally, Whitefield thus became an unconscious underminer of high Calvinism. It was one thing to preach irresistible grace; it was another to lack the restraining grace of common sense.

It was this lack which brought in the third group, those who sought the test of intellect. Agreeing with the Arminians as to the importance of the will, and opposing the enthusiasts for their extravagance of feeling, they had behind them the whole weight of the age of reason. But here a paradox appears. While, in general, our eighteenth-century thought went through the three phases of the conventional classification of man's powers, the development of that thought was anything but conventional. Before the problems of the will and of the feelings could be determined by the orderly processes of reason, the controversy was complicated by the irruption of a foreign force. George Whitefield was the disturber of the peace, and through him the question of morals lapsed into a question of manners. It was not denied that the evangelist did some good. The fault lay in the way in which he did it. Against this inspired son of a tavern keeper the New England clergy united in using the adjective "low," and naturally, as leaders of provincial society, they damned anything that was low. This staid and proper body, priding themselves upon dignity in deportment and rationality in religion, were, moreover, outraged at the conduct of an itinerant preacher who held forth in fields and barns and preferred emotional tests to cool conviction. New England now saw revealed the old struggle between masses and classes, between town and gown. Against the enthusiasts and ranters the clergy and the college authorities were speedily arrayed. Whitefield decidedly made a tactical blunder when he brought railing accusations against divines like Charles Chauncy (1705–1787), pastor of the First Church in Boston, and Edward Wigglesworth (1693–1765), professor of divinity in Harvard College. On his first visit to the colonies, Whitefield had made some unhappy remarks about the provincial universities as "abodes of darkness, a darkness which could be felt," and about the collegians at Cambridge as "close Pharisees, resting on head knowledge." On his second visit, he added insult to injury by saying that on account of these "unguarded expressions" a few "mistaken, misinformed, good old men were publishing half-penny testimonials against the Lord's Anointed."

The reference here is, among others, to Wigglesworth. The latter, in his reply, does not deign to defend the college against the charge of being a seminary of paganism, but proceeds to attack its defamer: first, because of his manners, next, because of his ways of making money, and lastly, because of the evil fruits of enthusiasm. He grants that an itinerant, who frequently moves from place to place, may have a considerable use in awakening his hearers from a dead and carnal frame. But while such an exhorter may have a manner which is very taking with the people, and a power to raise them to any degree of warmth he pleases, yet in thrusting himself into towns and parishes he destroys peace and order, extorts money from the people, and arouses that pernicious thing—enthusiasm.

This attack was to be expected. The New England clergy, as chosen members of a close corporation, abhorred the disturbers of their professional etiquette and were alarmed at poachers upon their clerical preserves. It not only threatened their social pedestals but it touched their pockets to have these "new lights" taking the people from their work and business and leading them to despise their own ministers.

This aspect of the Whitefield controversy shows that the causes of the opposition were largely social and economic, the same causes which worked—though in the other direction—in the opposition to the establishment of English episcopacy in the land. When the New England fathers had both "pence and power," as Tom Paine would say, it was natural that they should not relish the loss of either, at the expense of high churchmen or low itinerants. But a cause deeper than the economic lay in this outraging of the spirit of the times. This was the age of reason, and the leaders of church and college prided themselves on being of a cool and logical temperament. Hence Wigglesworth's most serious charge against Whitefield is that of irrationality. Enthusiasm, he explains, is a charge of a higher nature than perhaps people are generally aware of. The nature of enthusiasm is to make a man imagine that almost any thought which bears strongly upon his mind is from the Spirit of God, when at the same time he has no proof that it is. In short, to be of an enthusiastic turn is no such innocent weakness as people imagine.

This was Wigglesworth's caveat to the public. Whitefield might have made it out a mere halfpenny testimonial had it not been succeeded by the formidable work of Charles Chauncy. This was the volume entitled *Seasonable Thoughts on the State of Religion in New England* (1743). That state, in the eyes of the pastor of the First Church in Boston, was, in one word, bad. The preaching of "disorderly walkers," especially their well-advertised preaching in other men's parishes, it was argued, would lead, should it become the general practice, to the entire dissolution of our church state. But besides the evil effect upon the body politic, there was that upon the human body. With remarkable acumen, Chauncy points out the abnormalities in the practices of revivalism. The new lights, he recounts, lay very much stress on the "extraordinaries," such as agitations, outcries, swoonings, as though they were some marks of a just conviction of sin. This is their inference, but the real fact is that the influence of awful words and fearful gestures is no other than "a mechanical impression on animal nature." And the same natural explanation holds for the joy of the new lights. It may have its rise in the animal nature, for some have made it evident, by their after lives, that their joy was only a sudden flash, a spark of their own kindling. And when this is expressed among some sorts of people by singing through the streets and in ferryboats, from whatever cause it sprang it is certainly one of the most incongruous ways of expressing religious joy.

It must not be inferred from these strictures that Chauncy was a sour Puritan, averse to people's happiness. The contrary was the truth. His objections lay in the superficial and ephemeral character of the religious emotions among the new lights. Their joy was evidently but the reaction of relief from the fearsome tenets of their preachers. The doctrines of total depravity and eternal damnation struck terror into the heart of the sinner. Now it was by a sort of incantation, by a promise of immediate assurance of salvation, that the itinerant removed this terror. It was, then, in a skilful way that Chauncy met such practices. The places where the revivalists had been at work were called the burnt-over districts. To prevent future conflagrations it was then necessary to start a back-fire. This Chauncy did by removing the unreasoning terror of the old doctrines. But it was necessary to do more. In place of the old faith, which, though a painful thing to hold, men were loath to abandon, there must be brought a new and emollient doctrine. New England's nervous diathesis called for something to soothe the system. This came to be found in the exchange of pessimism for optimism; in the replacing of a dread judge by a benevolent deity, belief in whom would give a steady and lasting satisfaction. By 1784 Chauncy, as opposer of the new lights, had learned his lesson. The heart must be appealed to as well as the head. So his argument is built up from below, benevolence being first defined as "that quality, in the human mind, without which we could not be the objects of another's esteem."

With this hint taken from the learned English divine, Samuel Clarke, his American disciple shows how the old doctrines will dissolve of themselves. Out of the five points of Calvinism two were obviously inconsistent with benevolence. One of these was irresistible grace, as the correlate of irresistible power; the other was eternal damnation, as the correlate of total depravity. One reason, therefore, why Chauncy attacked the ranters was that they were reactionaries. But the cruel old penal view was bound to pass away of itself. Men's minds had entered the deistic drift. The arguments of rationality became the telling arguments.

"Some later writers"—and the remark is evidently directed against Edwards—"might make the infinitely benevolent God, the grand and only efficient, who has so connected a chain of causes that His final result should be the everlasting damnation of a great number of the creatures His hands had formed. . . . But such metaphysical reasoning does not stand the test of experience. There is too much skill and contrivance displayed in the formation of this and other globes, too numerous the creatures formed with the capacities of enjoyment to lead to a jaundiced view of the Creator and His attributes. And so many creatures brought into existence according to a settled uniform course of nature, and with a variegated capacity for happiness, preclude the notion of an inscrutable or malevolent deity."[1]

This sort of argumentation reminds one of the discussion of Square and Thwackum on the eternal fitness of things. But with the exception of an occasional hack-writer like Thomas Paine, it was the method generally employed by scholars of the upper class. The method betrays a certain weakness in the middle of Chauncy's work, since it must have gone over the heads of men of the class reached by Whitefield, son of the innkeeper, or by Tennent, promoter of log-cabin learning.

Such an optimistic purview, embracing earth, sun, and moon, dry land and water, became stale, flat and unprofitable. The argument that things as they are, including disease and death, disclose no defect of benevolence in the deity, is not helped by the disclaimer that we "know not the intire plan of heaven and are able to see but a little way into the design of the Deity." This was naught but the old argument of a learned ignorance, much used by the upholders of the scheme of inscrutable decrees.

The strong part of Chauncy's work lies in his attack upon absolute causation. The net of necessity in which the framer of the Berkshire divinity was caught, was escaped by Chauncy through an appeal to common sense.

"The abettors of this scheme," argues the Bostonian, "must clearly and fully perceive its inconsistency with men being free agents, and that it totally destroys the idea of moral good and evil. . . . The argument may hold for beasts of the field, whose whole conduct is the effect of previous choice and pleasure; but for human beings the unbroken concatenation of causes would deprive them of free agency."

And so would it be with that other prop of Puritanism, the belief in divine intervention.

An infinitely benevolent being might interpose, as occasion required, to prevent the mischief that would otherwise take place,

[1] *Benevolence of the Deity*, pp. 32, 53, 55, 61.

but possibly the method of communicating good by general laws, uniformly adhered to, is, in the nature of things, a better adapted one to produce the greatest good, than the other method of inter. positions continually repeated.[1]

In a life that nearly spanned the eighteenth century, Chauncy affords an excellent example of the double reaction of the age of reason against the doctrines of irrationalism. His works had these two merits; they undermined the harsh doctrines of Calvinism which the new lights had utilized to strike terror into the hearts of the unthinking; and they afforded a substitute for sentimentalism, for, in place of violent joy, one could gain a placid contentment in the ways and works of Providence.

Another thinker of ability, but of a less noble and elevated style, was Chauncy's younger contemporary, Jonathan Mayhew (1720–1766), a graduate of Harvard in 1744, and best known for his lively attacks upon the Tory doctrines of passive obedience and non-resistance. Mayhew gained a reputation for bringing a new style and manner into preaching. The son of a father who argued with ingenuity in behalf of human liberty, he was reputed to be a cheerful, liberal man, opposed to the gloomy doctrines of former times. Thus he early declared total depravity both dishonourable to the character of God and a libel on human nature. Mayhew's opposition to the five points of Calvinism was considered so imprudent that, at his ordination over the West Church, the Boston clergy declined the invitation to dine with the council, and one cautious cleric advised his barber not to go and hear such a heretic. Mayhew was really that, for he violently resisted the doctrine of irresistible grace, and entirely rejected the doctrine of the Trinity as taught by the Athanasian and Nicene creeds. In this he pointed the way to the coming Unitarianism, and that almost two generations before the Unitarian manifesto of 1819.

Although on the "new side," Mayhew was opposed to the "new lights." Long before the coming of Whitefield, he had been present at a religious revival in Maine, noticed its extravagance and fanaticism, and the people's violent gestures and shrieks. From this early experience, he came to value

[1] *Benevolence of the Deity*, pp. 132, 133.

"rational religion" the more highly. The phrase is significant. Upon the arrival of Whitefield in Boston in 1749, Mayhew claimed that the evangelist's hearers were chiefly "of the more illiterate sort," and that the discourse itself was "confused, conceited and enthusiastic."

The old term of reprobation reappears. So, like Chauncy himself, Mayhew offers the same antidote. In place of a God of wrath and terror, he would put the Scriptural God who is represented "under the characters of a father and a king, the wisest and best father, the wisest and best king." This sentiment eventuated in two Thanksgiving sermons *On the Nature, Extent and Perfection of the Divine Goodness*. In these the argument is ingenious. While Chauncy held that wisdom without goodness might be good, Mayhew held that goodness without wisdom might be bad. The political writer now appears in the doctrinal and shows that his God is no easy-going monarch whose goodness is to be considered mere good nature.

"As we recall certain well intentioned governors," he argues, "who, despite their paternal affection, have wrought prodigious mischief to the State, so we may in some measure conjecture, if we are not afraid even to think, what might be the consequence of boundless power, though accompanied with universal benevolence, but not adequate wisdom, extending itself at will thro-cut the universe."[1]

But the argument must not lead to the Calvinistic *cul-de-sac*, whereby there is no other end for punishment, on the part of the king of heaven, save his own glory. As Mayhew in his *Discourse Concerning Unlimited Submission and Non-Resistance to the Higher Powers* (1750) had remonstrated against the orders from Whitehall, so here he remonstrates against the immutable decrees of the Westminster Confession. His reasoning leads to a literal *reductio ad absurdum*.

Tho' God is, in the highest sense, an absolute sovereign; yet in *that* ill-sense, he is not certainly an arbitrary Being. . . . For what glory could possibly redound to any being acting unreasonably, or contrary to the dictates of true goodness? It is peculiarly absurd to suppose that He, who accounts *goodness* his glory, should aim at advancing it by *such* a conduct.[2]

---

[1] *Divine Goodness*, p. 16.   [2] *Ibid.*, p. 26.

With the same caustic irony with which he had flavoured his celebrated *Reflections on the Resistance Made to King Charles I*, Mayhew seeks to prove that the king of heaven, though absolute, is not arbitrary.

"The Earthly Prince," he continues, "may take off the head of the traitor, robber, or murderer, not to gratify his own anger, but for the common good. Contrariwise, punitive justice may be a branch of goodness, but how far from goodness it would be to condemn the bulk of mankind to eternal misery."[1]

The amiable heretic of Massachusetts may here be contrasted with the rigid Calvinist of Connecticut. Edwards, in his dreadful Enfield sermon, implied that the majority of his hearers were in danger of hell fire. Mayhew calmly carried out that implication. He had taken as an appropriate text for his Thanksgiving sermon, "The Lord is good to all." But this, for the sake of the argument, he is willing to change to, "The Lord is good to three-fourths of His creatures, and His tender mercies are over three-fourths of all His works,"—and so on down to the smallest fraction of mankind.

Mayhew is a master of ironic attack. He discloses this in his political discourses, ranging from that against Non-Resistance to that against the Stamp Act. But when it comes to defending his views, he is weak. He declaims effectively against the terrible punishment to be meted out by the Calvinistic judge of all mankind, but, in upholding benevolence, he outdoes the most complacent deist of his day. The first of his Thanksgiving sermons contends that the nature of divine goodness admits of strict application *a priori*. The companion sermon attempts to make that goodness of universal extent, and goes to such extremes as praising December weather in the town of Boston. But though the arguments are forced, these provincial writings have a certain interest as being prototypes of those hollow documents, the Thanksgiving proclamations of governors and presidents.

Through the two Massachusetts divines, Chauncy and Mayhew, one may traverse, by parallel paths, the whole controversy between old and new lights, a controversy beginning with a narrow emotionalism and ending with a rationalistic trend

[1] *Divine Goodness*, p. 38.

towards universalism. A similar course of thought, but expressed with far higher literary skill, may be pursued in the writings of the Connecticut scholar Samuel Johnson (1696–1772), a graduate of Yale College in 1714, a disciple of George Berkeley when he came to Rhode Island in 1729 and, in 1754, the first head of King's College,[1] New York. Especially does Johnson's *Elementa Philosophica* strike a balance between extremes. Like the *Alciphron* of Berkeley, to whom the *Elements* was dedicated, Johnson's work was directed against both fatalists and enthusiasts. The author's situation was logically fortunate. He was familiar with both "predestination and fanatical principles" and avoided the excesses of each. Brought up in Yale College, under the rigid Rector Clap, he came to dislike the severities of Puritanism. Acquainted with the ways of "that strange fellow Whitefield," he was also opposed to the doctrines of grace, as preached in the revivals. Strict Calvinism, as he contended against Jonathan Dickinson, "reflects dishonour upon the best of Beings"; while this "odd and unaccountable enthusiasm," as he wrote to Berkeley, "rages like an epidemical frenzy" and, by dividing the dissenters, proves to them a source of weakness rather than of strength.

Johnson's position was that of a moderate man. Add to that his cheerful and benevolent temper, and he appears one of the most attractive of the colonial thinkers. His education in Connecticut, his trip to England, his friendship with Benjamin Franklin, were all part and parcel of his training in letters. Educated at New Haven at a time when the old lights framed the policy of the college, Johnson, as he says in his autobiography, "after many scruples and an intolerable uneasiness of mind" went over to "that excellent church, the Church of England." This change, which necessitated a public disavowal of his former faith, was due in large measure to browsing in forbidden fields. Before Johnson's graduation, some of the speculations and discoveries of Descartes, Boyle, Locke, and Newton had been heard in the Connecticut colony. But the young men were cautioned against these authors, as well as against a new philosophy which was attracting attention in England. The reason given was that the new thought would

[1] Now Columbia University.

corrupt the pure religion of the country and bring in another system of divinity.

It was characteristic of Johnson, brought up in the darkened chambers of Calvinism, to attempt to obtain a glimpse into the brighter world outside. He had partially done this in reading a rare copy of Lord Bacon's *Advancement of Learning*, with the consequence of finding himself "like one at once emerging out of the glimmer of twilight into the full sunshine of open day." For himself this result was reflected in a manuscript entitled *The Travails of the Intellect in the Microcosm and Macrocosm*. For the benefit of others who might be lost in the "palpable obscure" of scholasticism, Johnson next drafted *A General Idea of Philosophy*. In this, philosophy is artfully described as "The Study of Truth and Wisdom, *i. e.* of the Objects and Rules conducing to true Happiness." Such a definition was in marked contrast with the atmosphere of the college of Connecticut, where, as Johnson's earliest biographer put it, "the metaphysics taught was not fit for worms."

In 1731 Johnson had enlarged this "Cyclopaedia of Learning," into an *Introduction to the Study of Philosophy*. The purpose of this tract was to set before young gentlemen a general view of the whole system of learning in miniature, "as geography exhibits a general map of the whole terraqueous globe." The plan of the tract was likewise noteworthy. Instead of making man's chief end to glorify God, it made the happiness of mankind to be God's chief end. In the meantime, for the purpose of obtaining Episcopal ordination, Johnson had made a trip to England. There the young colonial had the distinction of meeting Alexander Pope at his villa, and the English Samuel Johnson. He also visited Oxford and Cambridge universities, from both of which he was later to be honoured with the doctorate of divinity. But, as he subsequently wrote to his son, who made a similar literary pilgrimage, he confessed that, though he liked "to look behind the gay curtain," he preferred "ease and independence in the tranquil vales of America." On his return home, Johnson found neither ease nor tranquillity. Coming back to the land of the blue laws, he felt obliged to preach and write against current Calvinism. Thus one parish sermon was directed against absolute predestination, "with its horror, despair, and gloomy apprehension," while one pamphlet contended that the "Doctrine of Divine Sovereignty as implying God's eternal, arbitrary and absolute determination . . . is contrary to the nature and attributes of God, because inconsistent with the very notion of His being a moral governor of the world."[1] Yet even in this discussion against the Presbyterian Jonathan Dickinson, Johnson exhibits a lightness of touch which relieves the subject of much of its soberness:

Suppose some unhappy wretch entirely in the power of some arbitrary sovereign prince. Suppose the sovereign had beforehand absolutely resolved he should be hanged, but for the fancy of the thing, or purely to please himself, and gratify a capricious humour of his, commands him to lift a weight of ten thousand pounds and heave it to the distance of a mile, and tells him if he will do this he will give him an estate of ten thousand a year, and if he will not do it he shall certainly be hanged. At the same time he promises and designs him no manner of help or means whereby he might be enabled to accomplish it. It is true he speaks very kindly to him, and gives him several great encouragements expressed just like promises. He tells him if he will be up and doing he will be with him, and that if he will try and strive and pray for help, his labour shall not be in vain. However, the truth of the matter at the bottom is that he never intends to help him, having beforehand absolutely resolved he shall be hanged, and without help he can no more stir the weight than create a world. Now I humbly conceive that this unhappy wretch is under a necessity of disobeying and being hanged.[2]

Johnson's skilfulness was shown better in his constructive than in his controversial writings. If he rendered Calvin absurd by his use of the satirical paraphrase, he rendered Berkeley plausible by the glamour of his style. He was first attracted to the Irish idealism because it supplied him with the strongest arguments against the doctrine of necessity. But when Berkeley himself came to America, the neophyte fell in love with the author and his system at the same time. It was then that Johnson, according to his best biographer, became a convert to the "new principle," which he regarded, when rightly understood, as the true philosophical support of faith. The

[1] *Letter from Aristocles*, 10 September, 1744.
[2] *Letter . . . in defence of Aristocles*, pp. 14–20.

denial of the absolute existence of matter, a whimsical paradox to the superficial thinker, he found to mean nothing more than a denial of an inconceivable substratum of sensible phenomena. The affirmation of the merely relative existence of sensible things was to him the affirmation of orderly combinations of sensible phenomena, in which our corporeal pains and pleasures were determined by divine ideas that are the archetypes of physical existence.

The correspondence between Johnson and Berkeley was the most notable in the history of early American thought. It is a great literary loss that not all of Berkeley's letters have been recovered, for in them, as Johnson wrote, one can gather "that Candour and Tenderness which are so conspicuous in both your writings and conversation." From these *disjecta membra* of Johnson, however, one can reconstruct the very form of that idealism which rescues us from the absurdity of abstract ideas and the gross notion of matter, takes away all subordinate natural causes, and accounts for all appearances by the immediate will of the Supreme Spirit. From Johnson's correspondence, then, one can gather Berkeley's own notions as to archetypes, ectypes, space, spirits and substance. The fragments throw a flood of light upon subjects of high interest to the metaphysician, but the effect upon the mind of the disciple was more important, for through such veritable Berkeleian handbooks as were Johnson's, the seeds of idealism attained a lodgment in the American mind. Fruition did not occur until the time of Emerson, but for sheer literary skill in the presentment of a system deemed impossible by most men of that day, Johnson's *Elements* was remarkable. The good bishop, to w om the volume was dedicated, did not live to see it, but, as was remarked by Berkeley's son, this little book contained the wisdom of the ages and showed the author to be very capable of spreading Berkeley's philosophy.

The spreading of that system, however, was checked by untoward circumstances. When a French critic observed that Anglo-Americans of the late eighteenth century were unfit to receive or to develop true idealism, he probably had in mind the commercialism of the day and the threatening political state of affairs between the colonies and the mother country. Indeed, in both places immaterialism found the times out of joint.

From Philadelphia, then the literary centre of the country, Franklin, the printer of the book, wrote that those parts of the *Elements of Philosophy* that savoured of what is called Berkeleianism are "not well understood here." And in London one can imagine the reception that would be given to a colonial production, from the anecdote recounted of the son of the American Samuel Johnson when he met the great lexicographer. The latter, after speaking harshly of the colonials, exclaimed, "The Americans! What do they know and what do they read?" "They read, Sir, the *Rambler*," was the quick reply.

Like son, like father. The elder Johnson was able to extricate himself from even such difficulties as those offered by the Berkeleian system. He also had the boldness to apply the principles of the new rationalism not only to all men, but to all ages of man. Intellectual light, he argues, is common to all intelligent beings, a Chinese or Japanese, a European or an American. It is also to be found in children. In contrast to such an opinion as that of Jonathan Edwards that infants were "like little vipers," Johnson asserted that we ought to think them of much more importance than we usually apprehend them to be. Considering their achievements in learning not only the mother tongue but the divine visual language, we should apply to them the good trite old saying, *Pueris maxima reverentia debetur.*

Considerations such as these were so contrary to the spirit of the times as to arouse opposition from both sides. To consider children worthy of reverence was opposed to the Puritan view of them as born in sin, and to consider that man as such is assisted by an inward intellectual light "perpetually beaming forth from the great fountain of all light" ran counter to the common sense of the day. Thus William Smith, provost of the College of Philadelphia, who held the place once offered by Franklin to Johnson, argues against these very issues as presented in the *Elements*. "Our author," he explains, "from a sincere zeal to vindicate the rights of the Deity, and a just abhorrence of the absurd system of the materialists, has gone farther towards the opposite extreme than will be justified by some philosophers."[1] The extreme here referred to was, of course, Berkeleianism, against which the Philadelphian argues

[1] Preface to the *Elements*.

in substance as follows: The Dean, while at Newport, might have been justified in putting into his *Minute Philosopher* rural descriptions exactly copied from those charming landscapes that presented themselves to his eye in the delightful island at the time he was writing,—that was all very well; but for the Dean's disciple to attempt to introduce into the schools and infant seminaries in America this unadulterated Irish idealism was another thing. Doctor Johnson, explains his critic, only pretends to teach logic and moral philosophy; his logic and his morality are very different from ours. There is no matter, by his scheme; no ground of moral obligation. Life is a dream. All is from the immediate impressions of the Deity. Metaphysical distinctions which no men, and surely no boys, can understand . . . will do much to prevent the fixing of virtue on her true bottom.[1]

Such was the ironical fate that befell Johnson. Though he had done good service against the enthusiasts, and had written the best ethical treatise of colonial times, he was nevertheless charged with being fantastical, and his work with undermining morality.

A similar fate befell the last of our colonial thinkers, John Woolman (1720–1772), the Quaker, a sort of provincial Piers Plowman, whose visions of reform were far ahead of his day. In his *Journal*, the humble tailor of New Jersey takes up, in order, the evils of war and of lotteries, of negro slavery and excessive labour, of the selling of rum to the Indians, of cruelty to animals. Moreover, like the visions of the Plowman, Woolman's work might be called a contribution to the history of English mysticism. Whittier described the *Journal* as "a classic of the inner life"; Channing, as "beyond comparison the sweetest and purest autobiography in the language"; while Charles Lamb urged his readers to get the writings of Woolman "by heart."

These writings are in marked contrast to the controversial spirit of their time. They avoid entangling alliances with either the old or new divinity, and have little to do with the endless quarrels between Calvinists and Arminians. In place of doctrine and formal creed come "silent frames" and

[1] Letter to the Rev. Richard Peters, July 18, 1754, from the original in the Pennsylvania Historical Society.

the exercises of the interior or hidden life. The contrast is like
that portrayed by Woolman himself when he said that "while
many parts of the world groaned under the heavy calamities of
war, our habitation remains quiet, and our land fruitful."

In Woolman, then, we have the fruits of quietism as contrasted with the fruits of controversy. Duties rather than
doctrine are emphasized, and all with that air of innocent
simplicity held so desirable by the Society of Friends. Because
of his candour and his fervour, Woolman might be called a
socialist unconscious of his socialism, except for the fact that his
efforts were exerted in a private capacity, and that he offended
not even those with whom he laboured—soldiers, slave owners,
dealers in goods which were to be looked upon as contraband
to Christianity. He accomplished his results upon the Quaker
principle of natural sensibility. In marked contrast to the
Calvinist principle of the depravity of the human heart, he
argues upon the possibilities of the human mind towards good:
—"that as the mind was moved, by an inward principle, to
love God as an invisible, incomprehensible being; by the same
principle it was moved to love Him in all His manifestations in
the visible world."[1]

Armed with this gentle logic, he began to set down, not his
programme of reforms, but a recital of certain "heavenly openings" in respect to the care and providence of the Almighty over
his creatures. The first of those creatures for whom Woolman
was concerned was a slave. Here there arose a conflict between
the logic of compassion and the logic of commerce, for when his
employer obliged him to write a bill of sale for a poor negro
woman, he was much afflicted in mind. As was his wont,
Woolman now began to gather reasons for his feeling of uneasiness. That which was against conscience he now finds to
be against logical conviction, especially when in a journey to
the Southern provinces he meets with slave owners. To
their arguments in favour of fetching negroes from Africa
for slaves because of the wretchedness occasioned by their
intestine wars, he replies that liberty is the natural right
of all men equally. But this general principle—a commonplace of the age of reason—is not so effective as one more
particular:

[1] *Journal*, p. 9.

There is great odds on what principle we act. If compassion on the Africans, in regard to their domestic trouble, were the real motives of our purchasing them, that spirit of tenderness being attended to, would incite us to use them kindly. But to say they live unhappy in Africa is far from being an argument in our favour; our real views in purchasing them are to advance ourselves, and, while our buying captives taken in war animates those parties to push on the war and increase desolation amongst them, we too are putting upon our shoulders a burthensome stone, a burden that will grow heavier and heavier till times change in a way disagreeable to us.[1]

Upon this argument, presented with a kindly shrewdness, many of Woolman's slave-owning hearers looked serious. It was a prophecy of the irrepressible conflict between slave-holders and free-holders, and that over a century before that conflict came. So the prospect of a road lying open to degeneracy in some parts of this newly settled land of America, now drove Woolman to publish, and at his own expense, *Some Considerations on the Keeping of Negroes Recommended to the Professors of Christianity of every Denomination* (1754–62). The author is troubled with a weight of distress because, instead of the spirit of meekness, gentleness, and heavenly wisdom, a spirit of fierceness and a love of dominion too generally prevails. Yet it is not criticism, but compassion, that furnishes Woolman with his strongest lever against that great building "raised by degrees, from small beginnings in error." In a series of indirect questions, the logician of the heart brings the matter home. Drawing upon contemporary accounts of the slave trade, he argues in this fashion:

Should we consider ourselves present as spectators, when cruel negroes privately catch innocent children, who are employed in the fields; hear their lamentable cries, under the most terrifying apprehensions; or should we look upon it as happening in our own families, having our children carried off by savages, we must needs own, that such proceedings are contrary to the nature of Christianity.[2]

In the light of such disclosures, Woolman might have attacked the accursed institution with directness and bitterness, but his method is ever indirect, ever imbued with a sweet reasonableness.

[1] *Journal*, p. 60.　　　　　　　　[2] *Keeping of Negroes*, p. 317.

"The English government," he continues, "hath been commended by candid foreigners for the disuse of racks and tortures, so much practiced in some states; but this multiplying slaves now leads to it; for where people exact hard labour of others, without a suitable reward, and are resolved to continue in that way, severity to such who oppose them becomes the consequence. . . . These things are contrary to the true order of kind providence. Admit that the first negro man and his wife did as much business as their master and mistress, and that the children of the slaves have done some more than their young masters. . . . It follows, that in equity these negroes have a right to a part of this increase. . . . Again, if we seriously consider that liberty is the right of innocent men; that the Almighty God is a refuge for the oppressed; that in reality we are indebted to them . . . to retain them in perpetual servitude, without present cause for it, will produce effects, in the event, more grievous than setting them free would do."[1]

And so in a final passage breathing the very spirit of the Society of Friends, the Quaker liberator presents the fundamental objection to the keeping of the poor blacks in servitude:

There is a principle, which is pure, placed in the human mind, which in different places and ages hath had different names; it is, however, pure and proceeds from God.—It is deep, and inward, confined to no forms of religion, nor excluded from any, where the heart stands in perfect sincerity. In whomsoever this takes root, and grows, of what nation soever, they become brethren.[2]

[1] *Keeping of Negroes*, p. 298.   [2] *Ibid.*, p. 325.

CHAPTER VI

Franklin

IN a respectful and indeed laudatory notice of Franklin for *The Edinburgh Review* of July, 1806, Lord Jeffrey employed the case of the "uneducated tradesman of America" to support his contention that "regular education is unfavourable to vigour or originality of understanding." Franklin attained his eminence, so runs the argument, without academical instruction, with only casual reading, without the benefit of association with men of letters, and "in a society where there was no relish and no encouragement for literature." This statement of Franklin's educational opportunities is manifestly inadequate; but it so pleasantly flatters our long-standing pride in our self-made men that we are loath to challenge it. The hero presented to the schoolboy and preserved in popular tradition is still an "uneducated tradesman of America": a runaway Boston printer walking up Market Street in Philadelphia with his three puffy rolls; directing his fellow shopkeepers the way to wealth; sharply inquiring of extravagant neighbours whether they have not paid too much for their whistle; flying his kite in a thunderstorm; by a happy combination of curiosity and luck making important contributions to science; and, to add the last lustre to his name, by a happy combination of industry and frugality making his fortune. This picturesque and racy figure is obviously a product of provincial America, the first great Yankee with all the strong lineaments of the type: hardness, shrewdness, ingenuity, practical sense, frugality, industry, self-reliance. The conception of the man here suggested is perhaps sound enough so far as it goes, being derived mainly from facts supplied by Franklin himself in the one book through which he has secured an eternal life in literature. But the popular notion of his personality thus derived is incomplete, because the *Autobiography*, ending at the year 1757, contains no record of the thirty-three years which developed a competent provincial into an able, cultivated, and imposing man of the world.

The Franklin now discoverable in the ten volumes of his complete works is one of the most widely and thoroughly cultivated men of his age. He had not, to be sure, a university training, but he had what serves quite as well: sharp appetite and large capacity for learning, abundance of books, extensive travel, important participation in great events, and association through a long term of years with the most eminent men of three nations. In touch as printer and publisher with the classic and current literature produced at home and imported from abroad, he becomes in Philadelphia almost as good a "Queen Anne's man" as Swift or Defoe. His scientific investigations bring him into correspondence with fellow-workers in England, France, Germany, Italy, Holland, and Spain. Entering upon public life, he is forced into co-operation or conflict with the leading politicians, diplomats, and statesmen of Europe. In his native land he has known men like Cotton Mather, Whitefield, Benjamin Rush, Benjamin West, Ezra Stiles, Noah Webster, Jay, Adams, Jefferson, and Washington. In England, where his affections strike such deep root that he considers establishing there his permanent abode, he is in relationship, more or less intimate, with Mandeville, Paine, Priestley, Price, Adam Smith, Robertson, Hume, Joseph Banks, Bishop Watson, Bishop Shipley, Lord Kames, Lord Shelburne, Lord Howe, Burke, and Chatham. Among Frenchmen he numbers on his list of admiring friends Vergennes, Lafayette, Mirabeau, Turgot, Quesnay, La Rochefoucauld-Liancourt, Condorcet, Lavoisier, Buffon, D'Alembert, Robespierre, and Voltaire. It is absurd to speak of one who has been subjected to the moulding of such forces as a product of the provinces. All Europe has wrought upon and metamorphosed the Yankee printer. The man whom Voltaire kisses is a statesman, a philosopher, a friend of mankind, and a favourite son of the eighteenth century. With no softening of his patriotic fibre or loss of his Yankee tang, he has acquired all the common culture and most of the master characteristics of the Age of Enlightenment—up to

the point where the French Revolution injected into it a drop
of madness: its emancipation from authority, its regard for
reason and nature, its social consciousness, its progressiveness,
its tolerance, its cosmopolitanism, and its bland philanthropy.
Now this man deserves his large place in our literary history
not so much by virtue of his writings, which had little immediate influence upon *belles-lettres*, as by virtue of his acts and
ideas, which helped liberate and liberalize America.   To describe his most important work is to recite the story of his life.

   In reviewing his own career Franklin does not dwell on
the fact that he who was to stand before kings had emerged
from a tallow chandler's shop.   To his retrospective eye there
was nothing miraculous nor inexplicable in his origin.   On
the contrary he saw and indicated very clearly the sources of
his talents and the external impulses that gave them direction.
Born in Boston on 6 January, 1706, he inherited from his
long-lived parents, Josiah and Abiah Folger Franklin, a rugged
physical and mental constitution which hardly faltered through
the hard usage of eighty-four years.   He recognized and
profited by his father's skill in drawing and music, his "mechanical genius," his "understanding and solid judgment in
prudential matters, both in private and publick affairs," his
admirable custom of having at his table, "as often as he could,
some sensible friend or neighbour to converse with," always taking care "to start some ingenious or useful topic for discourse,
which might tend to improve the minds of his children."
Benjamin's formal schooling was begun when he was eight
years old and abandoned, together with the design of making
him a clergyman, when he was ten.   He significantly remarks,
however, that he does not remember a time when he could
not read; and the subsequent owner of one of the best private
libraries in America was as a mere child an eager collector
of books.   For the two years following his removal from
school he was employed in his father's business.   When he
expressed a firm disinclination to become a tallow chandler,
his father attempted to discover his natural bent by taking
him about to see various artisans at their work.   Everything
that Franklin touched taught him something; and everything
that he learned, he used.   Though his tour of the trades
failed to win him to any mechanical occupation,

it has ever since been a pleasure to me [he says] to see good workmen handle their tools; and it has been useful to me, having learnt
so much by it as to be able to do little odd jobs myself in my
house . . . and to construct little machines for my experiments,
while the intention of making the experiment was fresh and warm
in my mind.

Throughout his boyhood and youth he apparently devoured
every book that he could lay hands upon. He went through
his father's shelves of "polemic divinity"; read abundantly in
Plutarch's *Lives;* acquired Bunyan's works "in separate little
volumes," which he later sold to buy Burton's *Historical
Collections;* received an impetus towards practical improvements from Defoe's *Essay upon Projects* and an impetus
towards virtue from Mather's *Essays to do Good.* Before he
left Boston he had his mind opened to free speculation and
equipped for logical reasoning by Locke's *Essay Concerning
Human Understanding,* the Port Royal *Art of Thinking,*
Xenophon's *Memorabilia,* and the works of Shaftesbury and
Collins.

Franklin found the right avenue for a person of his "bookish
inclination" when his brother James, returning from England
in 1717 with a press and letters, set up in Boston as a printer,
and proceeded to the publication of *The Boston Gazette,* 1719,
and *The New England Courant,* 1721. Benjamin, aged twelve,
became his apprentice. It can hardly be too much emphasized
that this was really an inspiring "job." It made him stand
at a very early age full in the wind of local political and theological controversy. It forced him to use all his childish stock
of learning and daily stimulated him to new acquisitions. It
put him in touch with other persons, young and old, of
bookish inclination. They lent him books which kindled his
poetic fancy to the pitch of composing occasional ballads
in the Grub Street style, which his brother printed, and had
him hawk about town. His father discountenanced these
effusions, declaring that "verse-makers were generally beggars"; but coming upon his son's private experiments in
prose, he applied the right incentive by pointing out where the
work "fell short in elegance of expression, in method, and in
perspicuity." "About this time," says Franklin in a familiar
paragraph, "I met with an odd volume of the *Spectator.*"

Anticipating Dr. Johnson's advice by half a century, he gave
his days and nights to painstaking study and imitation of
Addison till he had mastered that style—"familiar but not
coarse, and elegant but not ostentatious"—which several
generations of English essayists have sought to attain.   All the
world has heard how Franklin's career as a writer began
with an anonymous contribution stealthily slipped under the
door of his brother's printing-house at night, and in the morning
approved for publication by his brother's circle of "writing
friends."   Professor Smyth[1] inclined to identify this contribution with the first of fourteen humorous papers with Latin
mottoes signed "Silence Dogood," which appeared fortnightly
in *The New England Courant* from March to October, 1722.
In this year Benjamin was in charge of the *Courant* during his
brother's imprisonment for printing matter offensive to the
Assembly; and when, on repetition of the offence, the master
was forbidden to publish his journal, it was continued in the
name of the apprentice.   In this situation James became
jealous and overbearing, and Benjamin became insubordinate.
When it grew evident that there was not room enough in Boston
for them both, the younger brother left his indentures behind,
and in 1723 made his memorable flight to Philadelphia.

Shortly after his arrival in the Quaker city, he found employment with the second printer in Philadelphia, Samuel Keimer,
a curious person who kept the Mosaic law.   In 1724, encouraged
by the facile promises of Governor Keith, Franklin went to
England in the expectation that letters of credit and recommendation from his patron would enable him to procure a
printing outfit.   Left in the lurch by the governor, he served
for something over a year in two great London printing-houses,
kept free-thinking and rather loose company, and, in refutation
of Wollaston's *Religion of Nature*, upon which he happened to
be engaged in the composing-room, published in 1725 his
suppressed tract *On Liberty and Necessity*.   Returning to
Philadelphia in 1726, he re-entered the employ of Keimer; in

---

[1] *The Writings of Benjamin Franklin*.   Collected and edited by Albert Henry
Smyth.   New York, 1907.   Vol. II, p. 1.   The Dogood Papers were claimed by
Franklin in the first draft of his *Autobiography*, and they have been long ac-
credited to him; but they were first included in his collected works by Professor
Smyth.

1728 formed a brief partnership with Hugh Meredith; and in 1730 married and set up for himself. In 1728 he founded the famous Junto Club for reading, debating, and reforming the world—an institution which developed into a powerful organ of political influence. Shortage of money in the province prompted him to the composition of his *Modest Inquiry into the Nature and Necessity of Paper Currency* (1729), a service for which his friends in the Assembly rewarded him by employing him to print the money—"a very profitable job and a great help to me." Forestalled by Keimer in a project for launching a newspaper, Franklin contributed in 1728-9 to the rival journal, published by Bradford, a series of sprightly "Busy-Body" papers in the vein of the periodical essayists. Keimer was forced to sell out; and Franklin acquired from him the paper known from 2 October, 1729, as *The Pennsylvania Gazette*. To this he contributed, besides much miscellaneous matter, such pieces as the *Dialogue between Philocles and Horatio concerning Virtue and Pleasure*, the letters of "Anthony Afterwit" and "Alice Addertongue," *A Meditation on a Quart Mug*, and *A Witch Trial at Mount Holly*. In 1732 he began to issue the almanacs containing the wit and wisdom of "Poor Richard," a homely popular philosopher, who is only the incarnation of common sense, and who is consequently not, as has been carelessly assumed, to be identified with his creator.

By the time he was thirty Franklin gave promise of becoming, by a gradual expansion of his useful activities, the leading Pennsylvanian. In 1736 he was chosen clerk of the General Assembly, and in the following year was appointed postmaster of Philadelphia. He made both these offices useful to his printing business and to his newspaper. In compensation, he used his newspaper and his business influence to support his measures for municipal improvements, among the objects of which may be mentioned street-sweeping, paving, a regular police force, a fire company, a hospital, and a public library. As his business prospered, he expanded it by forming partnerships with his promising workmen and sending them with printing-presses into other colonies. In 1741 he experimented with a monthly publication, *The General Magazine and Historical Chronicle for all the British Colonies in America;* this monthly, notable as the second issued in America, expired with the sixth number. In 1742 he invented the stove of which he published a description in 1744 as *An Account of the New Invented Pennsylvanian Fire Places.* In 1743 he drew up proposals for an academy which eventually became the University of Pennsylvania, and in 1744 he founded the American Philosophical Society. In 1746 he witnessed Spence's electrical experiments in Boston, bought the apparatus, and repeated the experiments in Philadelphia, where interest in the new science was further stimulated that year by a present of a Leyden jar given to the Library Company by the English experimenter Peter Collinson. To this English friend Franklin made extended reports of his earlier electrical investigations in the form of letters which Collinson published in London in 1751 with the title *Experiments and Observations in Electricity, made at Philadelphia in America, by Mr. Benjamin Franklin.* In 1752 he showed the identity of lightning and electricity by his kite experiment, and invented the lightning rod. In 1748, being assured of a competency, he had turned over his business to his foreman David Hall, and purposed devoting the rest of his life to philosophical inquiries. But he had inextricably involved himself in the affairs of his community, which, as soon as it found him at leisure, "laid hold" of him, as he says, for its own purposes—"every part of the civil government, and almost at the same time, imposing some duty upon me." He was made a justice of the peace, member of the common council, and alderman, and was chosen burgess to represent the city of Philadelphia in the General Assembly. In 1753 he was appointed jointly with William Hunter to exercise the office of postmaster-general of America. In 1754 as a member of the Pennsylvania commission he laid before the colonial congress at Albany the "Plan of Union" adopted by the commissioners. In 1755 he displayed remarkable energy, ability, and public spirit in providing transportation for General Braddock's ill-fated expedition against the French; and in the following year he himself took command of a volunteer military organization for the protection of the north-west frontier. In 1757 he was sent to England to present the long-standing grievances of the Pennsylvania Assembly against the proprietors for obstructing legislation designed to throw upon them a fair share of the expense of government.

Though Franklin's political mission was not wholly successful, his residence in England from 1757 to 1762 was highly
profitable to him. It developed his talent as a negotiator of
public business with strangers; it enabled him to consider
British colonial policies from English points of view; and it
afforded him many opportunities for general self-improvement.
After a fruitless effort to obtain satisfaction from the representatives of the Penn family, dismissing as impractical the
hope of procuring for Pennsylvania a royal charter, he appealed
to the Crown to exempt the Assembly from the influence of
proprietary instructions and to make the proprietary estates
bear a more equitable proportion of the taxes. To get the
Assembly's case before the public, he collaborated with an
unknown hand on *An Historical Review of the Constitution and
Government of Pennsylvania*, published in 1759. The result
was a compromise which in the circumstances he regarded as
a victory. His interest in the wider questions of imperial
policy he exhibited in 1760 by aspersing the advocates of a
hasty and inconclusive peace with France in his stinging little
skit, *Of the Meanes of disposing the Enemies to Peace*,[1] which he
presented as an extract from the work of a Jesuit historian.
In 1760, also, he was joint author with Richard Jackson of a
notably influential argument for the retention of Canada,
*The Interest of Great Britain Considered with Regard to Her
Colonies;* to which was appended his *Observations Concerning
the Increase of Mankind, Peopling of Countries*, etc. In the
intervals of business, he sat for his portrait, attended the
theatre, played upon the harmonica, experimented with electricity and heat, made a tour of the Low Countries, visited the
principal cities of England and Scotland, received honorary
degrees from the universities, and enjoyed the society of Collinson, Priestley, Price, Hume, Adam Smith, Robertson, and
Kames. He returned to America in the latter part of 1762.
In 1763 he made a 1600-mile tour of the northern provinces
to inspect the postoffices. In the following year he was
again in the thick of Pennsylvania politics, working with the
party in the Assembly which sought to have the proprietary
government of the province replaced by a royal charter. In
support of this movement he published in 1764 his *Cool Thoughts*

[1] See *Writings*, ed. Smyth, Vol. IV, pp. 89–95.

on the Present Situation of our Public Affairs and his *Preface
to the Speech of Joseph Galloway*, a brilliant and blasting indictment of the proprietors, Thomas and Richard Penn.

In the fall of 1764 Franklin was sent again to England by
the Assembly to petition for a royal charter and to express the
Assembly's views with regard to Grenville's Stamp Act, then
impending.   On 11 July, 1765, after the obnoxious measure
had been passed by an overwhelming majority, Franklin wrote
to Charles Thomson:

Depend upon it, my good neighbour, I took every step in my
power to prevent the passing of the Stamp Act. . . . But the Tide
was too strong against us.   The nation was provoked by American
Claims of Independence, and all Parties joined in resolving by this
act to settle the point.   We might as well have hindered the sun's
setting.

This letter and one or two others of about the same date
express a patient submission to the inevitable.   As soon,
however, as Franklin was fully apprised of the fierce flame of
opposition which the passage of the act had kindled in the
colonies, he caught the spirit of his constituents and threw
himself sternly into the struggle for its repeal.   In 1766 he
underwent his famous examination before the House of Commons on the attitude of the colonies towards the collection
of the new taxes.   The report of this examination, which
was promptly published, is one of the most interesting and
impressive pieces of dramatic dialogue produced in the eighteenth century.   After the repeal, Franklin received recognition
at home in the shape of new duties: in 1768 he was appointed agent for Georgia; in 1769, for New Jersey; in 1770, for
Massachusetts.   In the summer of 1766 he visited Germany;
the following summer he visited Paris; and he was in France
again for a month in 1769.   His pen in these years was employed mainly in correspondence and in communications to the
newspapers, in which he pointedly set forth the causes which
threatened a permanent breach between the mother country
and the colonies.   In 1773 he published in *The Gentleman's
Magazine* two little masterpieces of irony which Swift might
have been pleased to sign: *An Edict by the King of Prussia*
and *Rules by which a Great Empire may be Reduced to a Small*

One. In 1774, in consequence of his activity in exposing Governor Hutchinson's proposals for the military intimidation of Massachusetts, Franklin was subjected before the Privy Council to virulent and scurrilous abuse from Attorney-General Wedderburn. This onslaught it was, accentuated by his dismissal from the office of postmaster-general, which began to curdle in Franklin his sincere long-cherished hope of an ultimate reconciliation. It is a curiously ominous coincidence that in this year of his great humiliation he sent with a letter of recommendation to his son-in-law in Philadelphia one Thomas Paine, an obscure Englishman of whiggish temper, two years later to become the fieriest advocate of American independence. In disgrace with the Court, Franklin lingered in England to exhaust the last possibilities of amicable adjustment: petitioning the king, conferring with Burke and Chatham, and curiously arranging for secret negotiations with the go-betweens of the Ministry over the chessboard of Lord Howe's sister. He sailed from England in March, 1775, half-convinced that the Ministry were bent upon provoking an open rebellion. When he arrived in Philadelphia, he heard what had happened at Lexington and Concord. On 5 July, 1775, he wrote a letter to an English friend of thirty years' standing, William Strahan, then a member of Parliament; it was shortened like a Roman sword and sharpened to this point:

You and I were long Friends:—You are now my Enemy,—and I am

Yours,

B. FRANKLIN.

As Franklin was sixty-nine years old in 1775, he might fairly have retreated to his library, and have left the burden of the future state to younger hands. He had hardly set foot on shore, however, before the Pennsylvania Assembly elected him delegate to the first Continental Congress, where his tried sagacity was enlisted in organizing the country's political, economic, and military resources for the great conflict. On 7 July, 1775, the old man wrote to Priestley:

My time was never more fully employed. In the morning at six, I am at the Committee of Safety, appointed by the Assembly to put the province in a state of defence; which committee holds till near nine, when I am at the Congress, and that sits till after four in the afternoon.

In the period slightly exceeding a year previous to his departure for France, he served on innumerable committees of the Congress, was made Postmaster-General of the colonies, presided over the Constitutional Convention of Pennsylvania, was sent on a mission to Canada, assisted in drafting the Declaration of Independence, and signed it.

In October, 1776, he sailed for France on a commission of the Congress to negotiate a treaty of alliance, which was concluded in February, 1778, after the surrender of Burgoyne had inspired confidence in the prospects of the American arms. In September, 1778, he was appointed plenipotentiary to the Court of France. Clothed with large powers, he transacted in the next few years an almost incredible amount of difficult business for his country. He obtained from the French government the repeated loans which made possible the carrying on of a long war; he made contracts for clothing and ammunition; he dissuaded or recommended to Congress foreign applicants for commissions in the colonial army; he arranged exchanges of prisoners-of-war; he equipped and to some extent directed the operations of privateers; he supplied information to many Europeans emigrating to America; he negotiated treaties of amity and commerce with Sweden and Prussia. With all this engrossing business on his hands, he found time to achieve an immense personal popularity. He was not merely respected as a masterly diplomat; he was lionized and idolized as the great natural philosopher, the august champion of liberty, and the friend of humanity. In the press of public affairs, never losing interest in scientific matters, he served on a royal French commission to investigate Mesmerism; sent to his foreign correspondents ingenious geological and meteorological conjectures; and transmitted to the Royal Society reports on French experiments in aeronautics. He entertained with a certain lavishness at his house in Passy; and he was a frequent diner-out, adored for his wit and good humour in the intimate coteries of Mme. Helvetius and Mme. Brillon. He set up for the amusement of himself and his friends a private press in Passy, on which he printed a number of *bagatelles* of an accomplished and charming levity: *The Ephemera* (1778), *The Morals of Chess* (1779), *The Whistle* (1779), *The Dialogue between Franklin and the Gout* (1780.) In 1784 he resumed work on his unfinished autobiography, and published *Advice to such as would remove to America* and *Remarks Concerning the Savages of North America*. In his residence in France he began seriously to feel the siege of gout, the stone, and old age. In 1781, in reply to repeated supplications for leave to go home and die, Congress had appointed him a member of the commission to negotiate a treaty of peace between England and the United States. This last great task was completed in 1785. In midsummer of that year he said a regretful farewell to his affectionate French friends, received the king's portrait set in four hundred diamonds, and in one of the royal litters was carried down to his point of embarkation at Havre de Grace.

Franklin arrived in Philadelphia in September, 1785, resolved to set his house in order. He was soon made aware that, like the hero in *The Conquest of Granada*, he had not "leisure yet to die." He was overwhelmed with congratulations; or, as he put it with characteristic modesty of phrase in a letter to his English friend Mrs. Hewson: "I had the happiness of finding my family well, and of being very kindly received by my Country folk." In the month after his arrival he was elected President of the State of Pennsylvania; and the honour was thrust upon him again in 1786 and in 1787. In a letter of 14 November, 1785, he says:

I had not firmness enough to resist the unanimous desire of my country folks; and I find myself harnessed again in their service for another year. They engrossed the prime of my life. They have eaten my flesh, and seem resolved now to pick my bones.

In 1787 he was chosen a delegate to the convention to frame the Constitution of the United States—an instrument which he deemed not perfect, yet as near perfection as the joint wisdom of any numerous body of men could bring it, handicapped by "their prejudices, their passions, their local interests, and their selfish views." In 1789, as President of the Abolition Society, Franklin signed a memorial against slavery which was laid before the House of Representatives; and on 23 March, 1790, less than a month before his death, he wrote for *The Federal Gazette* an ironical justification of the enslaving of Christians by African Mohammedans—quite in the vein of the celebrated *Edict of the King of Prussia*. As the shadows thickened about him, he settled his estate, paid his compliments to his friends, and departed, on the seventeenth day of April, 1790, in his eighty-fifth year.

In the matter of religion Franklin was distinctly a product of the eighteenth-century enlightenment. He took his direction in boyhood and early manhood from deistical writers like Pope, Collins, and Shaftesbury. At various periods of his life he drew up articles of belief, which generally included recognition of one God, the providential government of the world, the immortality of the soul, and divine justice. To profess faith in as much religion as this he found emotionally gratifying, socially expedient, and conformable to the common sense of mankind. He would have subscribed without hesitation to both the positive and negative dogmas of the *religion civile* formulated by Rousseau in the *Contrat Social*. In his later years he was in sympathetic relations with Paine, Price, and Priestley. He was, however, of a fortunately earlier generation than these English "heretics," and certain other circumstances enabled him to keep the temper of his heterodoxy sweet while theirs grew acidulous, and to walk serenely in ways which for them were embittered by the *odium theologicum*. His earlier advent upon the eighteenth-century scene made possible the unfolding and comfortable settlement of his religious ideas before deism had clearly allied itself with political radicalism and edged its sword for assault upon inspired Bible and established church as powers federate with political orthodoxy in upholding the ancient régime. Among the diverse denominational bodies in Pennsylvania his perfectly genuine tolerance and his unfailing tact helped him to maintain a friendly neutrality between parties which were far from friendly. Like Lord Chesterfield, he sincerely believed in the decency and propriety of going to church; and he went himself when he could endure the preachers. He advised his daughter to go constantly, "whoever preaches." He made pecuniary contributions to all the leading denominations in Philadelphia; respectfully acknowledged the good features of each; and undertook to unite in his own creed the common and, as he thought, the essential features of all. Man of the world as he was, he enjoyed the warm friendship of good Quakers, good Presbyterians, Whitefield, the Bishop of St. Asaph, and his French abbés. His abstention from theological controversy was doubtless due in part to a shrewd regard for his own interest and influence as a business man and a public servant; but it was due in perhaps equal measure to his profound indifference to metaphysical questions unrelated to practical conduct. "Emancipated" in childhood and unmolested in the independence of his mind, he reached maturity without that acrimony of free thought incident to those who attain independence late and have revenges to take. He was consistently opposed to the imposition of religious tests by constitutional authority. But in the Constitutional Convention of 1787 he offered a motion in favour of holding daily prayers before the deliberations of the assembly, for, as he declared, "the longer I live, the more convincing proofs I see of this Truth, *that* God *governs in the Affairs of Men*." With his progress in eminence and years, he seems to have been somewhat strengthened in Cicero's conviction that so puissant a personality as his own could not utterly perish, and he derived a kind of classical satisfaction from the reflection that this feeling was in concurrence with the common opinions of mankind. A few weeks before his death he admitted, in a remarkable letter to Ezra Stiles, a doubt as to the divinity of Jesus; but he remarked with his characteristic tranquillity that he thought it "needless to busy myself with it now, when I expect soon an Opportunity of knowing the Truth with less Trouble." Not elate, like Emerson, yet quite unawed, this imitator of Jesus and Socrates walked in this world and prepared for his ease in Zion.

Franklin set himself in youth to the study of "moral perfection," and the work which only great public business prevented his leaving as his literary monument was to have been a treatise on the "art of virtue." His merits, however, in both the theory and practice of the moral life have been seriously called in question. It is alleged that his standards were low and that he did not live up to them. It must be conceded on the one hand that he had a natural son who became governor of New Jersey, and on the other hand that industry and frugality, which most of us place among the minor, he placed among the major virtues. When one has referred the *"errata"* of his adolescence to animal spirits, "free thinking," and bad company; and when one has explained certain laxities of his maturity by alluding to the indulgent temper of the French society in which he then lived; one may as well candidly admit that St. Francis made chastity a more conspicuous jewel in his crown of virtues than did Dr. Franklin. And when one has pointed out that the prudential philosophy of *Poor Richard's Almanac* was rather a collection of popular wisdom than an original contribution; and when one has called attention to the special reasons for magnifying economic virtues in a community of impecunious colonists and pioneers; one may as well frankly acknowledge that there is nothing in the precepts of the great printer to shake a man's egotism like the shattering paradoxes of the Beatitudes nor like the *Christian Morals* of Sir Thomas Browne to make his heart elate. Franklin had nothing of what pietists call a "realizing sense" of sin or of the need for mystical regeneration and justification—faculties so richly present in his contemporary Jonathan Edwards. His cool calculating reason, having surveyed the fiery battleground of the Puritan conscience, reported that things are properly forbidden because hurtful, not hurtful because forbidden. Guided by this utilitarian principle, he simplified his religion and elaborated his morality. His system included much more than maxims of thrift and prudent self-regard, and to insinuate that he set up wealth as the *summum bonum* is a sheer libel. He commended diligence in business as the means to a competency; he commended a competency as a safeguard to virtue; and he commended virtue as the prerequisite to happiness. The temple that he reared to Moral Perfection was built of thirteen stones: temperance, silence, order, resolution, frugality, industry, sincerity, justice, moderation, cleanliness, tranquillity, chastity, and humility—the last added on the advice of a Quaker. He wrought upon the structure with the method of a monk and he recorded his progress with the regularity of a bookkeeper. The presiding spirit in the edifice, which made it something more than a private oratory, was a rational and active benevolence towards his fellow-mortals in every quarter of the earth. The wide-reaching friendliness in Franklin may be distinguished in two ways from the roseate humanitarian enthusiasm in the Savoyard Vicar. It was not begotten by a theory of "natural goodness" nor fostered by millennial expectations, but was born of sober experience with the utility of good will in establishing satisfactory and fruitful relations among men. It found expression not in rhetorical periods but in numberless practical means and measures for ameliorating the human lot. By no mystical intuition but by the common light of reason the "prudential philosopher" discovered and acted upon the truth that the greatest happiness that can come to a man in this world is to devote the full strength of body and mind to the service of his fellow-men. Judged either by his principles or by his performance, Franklin's moral breadth and moral elevation have been absurdly underestimated.

It is perhaps in the field of politics that Franklin exhibits the most marked development of his power and his vision. A realistic inductive thinker, well versed in the rudiments of his subject long before the revolutionary theorists handled it, he was not rendered by any preconception of abstract rights indocile to the lessons of his immense political experience. He formulated his conceptions in the thick of existing conditions, and always with reference to what was expedient and possible as well as to what was desirable. He served his apprenticeship in the Philadelphia Junto Club, which at its inception was little more than a village improvement society, but which threw out branches till it became a power in the province, and a considerable factor in the affairs of the colonies. In this association he learned the importance of co-operation, mastered the tactics of organization, practised the art of getting propaganda afoot, and discovered the great secret of converting private desires into public demands. In proposing in 1754 his plan for a union of the colonies he was applying to larger units the principle of co-operative action by which he had built up what we might call to-day his "machine" in Pennsylvania. Writers like Milton and Algernon Sidney had reenforced his natural inclination towards liberal forms of government. But he had in too large measure the instincts and the ideas of a leader, and he had too much experience with the conflicting prejudices and the resultant compromises of popular assemblies, to feel any profound reverence for the "collective wisdom" of the people. "If all officers appointed by governors were always men of merit," he wrote in his *Dialogue Concerning the Present State of Affairs in Pennsylvania,* "it would be wrong ever to hazard a popular election." That his belief in popular representation was due as much to his sense of its political expediency as to his sense of its political justice is suggested by a passage in his letter on the imposition of direct taxes addressed to Governor Shirley, 18 December, 1754: "In matters of general concern to the people, and especially where burthens are to be laid upon them, it is of use to consider, as well what they will be apt to think and say, as what they ought to think." His sojourn in England widened his horizons, but not beyond the bounds of his nationality. As agent, he felt himself essentially a colonial Englishman pleading for the extension of English laws to British subjects across the sea, and playing up to the Imperial policy of crushing out the colonizing and commercial rivalry of France. The ultimate failure of his mission of reconciliation effected no sudden transformation of his political ideas; it rather overwhelmed him with disgust at the folly, the obstinacy, and the corruption rampant among English politicians of the period. He returned to the arms of the people because he had been hurled from the arms of the king; and he embraced their new principles because he was sure that they could not be worse applied than his old ones. His respect for the popular will was inevitably heightened by his share in executing it in the thrilling days when he was helping his fellow-countrymen to declare their independence, and was earning the superb epigraph of Turgot: *Eripuit fulmen coelo, sceptrumque tyrannis.* His official residence in France completely dissolved his former antagonism to that country. In the early stages of the conflict his wrath was bitter enough towards England, but long before it was over he had taken the ground of radical pacifism, reiterating his conviction that "there is no good war and no bad peace." He who had financed the Revolution had seen too much non-productive expenditure of moral and physical capital to believe in the appeal to arms. If nations required enlargement of their territories, it was a mere matter of arithmetic, he contended, to show that the cheapest way was purchase. "Justice," he

declared, "is as strictly due between neighbour Nations as
between neighbour Citizens, . . . and a Nation that makes
an unjust War, is only a *great Gang*." So far as he was able, he
mitigated the afflictions of noncombatants. He proposed by
international law to exempt from peril fishermen and farmers
and the productive workers of the world. He ordered the
privateersmen under his control to safeguard the lives and
property of explorers and men of science belonging to the enemy
country; and he advocated for the future the abolition of the
custom of commissioning privateers. In the treaty which he
negotiated with Prussia he actually obtained the incorporation
of an article so restricting the "zone of war" as to make a war
between Prussia and the United States under its terms virtually
impossible. His diplomatic intercourse in Europe and his
association with the Physiocrats had opened his eyes to the
common interests of all pacific peoples and to the inestimable
advantages of a general amity among the nations. His ultimate political ideal included nothing short of the welfare and the
commercial federation of the world. To that extent he was a
believer in "majority interests." It may be further said that
his political development was marked by a growing mastery
of the art of dealing with men and by a steady approximation
of his political to his personal morality.

For the broad humanity of Franklin's political conceptions
undoubtedly his interest in the extension of science was partly
responsible. As a scientific investigator he had long been a
citizen of the world; and for him not the least bitter consequence
of the war was that it made a break in the intellectual brotherhood of man. If he had not been obliged to supply the army
of Washington with guns and ammunition, he might have been
engaged in the far more congenial task of supplying the British
Academy with food for philosophical discussion. He could
not but resent the brutal antagonisms which had rendered
intellectual co-operation with his English friends impossible,
and which had frustrated his cherished hope of devoting his
ripest years to philosophical researches. A natural endowment he certainly possessed which would have qualified him
in happier circumstances for even more distinguished service
than he actually performed in extending the frontiers of
knowledge. He had the powerfully developed curiosity of the

explorer and the inventor, ever busily prying into the causes
of things, ever speculating upon the consequences of novel
combinations. His native inquisitiveness had been stimulated
by a young civilization's manifold necessities, mothering manifold inventions, and had been supplemented by a certain moral
and idealizing passion for improvement. The practical nature
of many of his devices, his interest in agriculture and navigation, his preoccupation with stoves and chimneys, the image
of him firing the gas of ditch water or pouring oil on troubled
waves, and the celebrity of the kite incident, rather tend to
fix an impression that he was but a tactful empiricist and a
lucky dilettante of discovery. It is interesting in this connection
to note that he confesses his lack of patience for verification.
His prime scientific faculty, as he himself felt, was the imagination which bodies forth the shapes and relations of things
unknown—which constructs the theory and the hypothesis.
His mind was a teeming warren of hints and suggestions. He
loved rather to start than to pursue the hare. Happily what
he deemed his excessive penchant for forming hypotheses was
safeguarded by his perfect readiness to hear all that could
be urged against them. He wished not his view but truth
to prevail—which explains the winsome cordiality of his
demeanour towards other savants. His unflagging correspondence with investigators, his subscription to learned publications, his active membership in philosophical societies, and his
enterprise in founding schools and academies all betoken his
prescience of the wide domain which science had to conquer
and of the necessity for co-operation in the task of subduing
it. Franklin was so far a Baconian that he sought to avoid
unfruitful speculation and to unite contemplation and action
in a stricter embrace for the generation of knowledge useful to
man. But in refutation of any charge that he was a narrow-
minded utilitarian and lacked the liberal views and long faith
of the modern scientific spirit may be adduced his stunning
retort to a query as to the usefulness of the balloons then on
trial in France: "What is the use of a new-born baby?"

Of Franklin's style the highest praise is to declare that it
reveals the mental and moral qualities of the man himself.
It is the flexible style of a writer who has learned the craft of
expression by studying and imitating the virtues of many

masters: the playful charm of Addison, the trenchancy of Swift, the concreteness of Defoe, the urbanity of Shaftesbury, the homely directness of Bunyan's dialogue, the unadorned vigour of Tillotson, and the epigrammatic force of Pope. His mature manner, however, is imitative of nothing but the thoroughly disciplined movement of a versatile mind which has never known a moment of languor or a moment of uncontrollable excitement. Next to his omnipresent vitality, his most notable characteristic is the clearness which results from a complete preliminary vision of what is to be said, and which in a young hand demands deliberate preconsideration. To Franklin, the ordering of his matter must have become eventually a light task as, with incessant passing to and fro in his experience and with the daily habit of epistolary communication, he grew as familiar with his intellectual terrain as an old field marshal with the map of Europe. For the writing of his later years is marked not merely by clearness and force but also by the sovereign ease of a man who has long understood the interrelations of his ideas and has ceased to make revolutionary discoveries in any portion of his own nature. His occasional wrath does not fluster him but rather intensifies his lucidity, clarifies his logic, and brightens the ironical smile which accompanies the thrust of his wit. The "decent plainness and manly freedom" of his ordinary tone—notes which he admired in the writings of his maternal grandfather Peter Folger—rise in parts of his official correspondence to a severity of decorum; for there is a trace of the senatorial in the man, the dignity of antique Rome. He is seldom too hurried, even in a private letter, to gratify the ear by the turning and cadence of sentence and phrase; and one feels that the harmony of his periods is the right and predestined vesture of his essential blandness and suavity of temper. His stylistic drapery, however, is never so smoothed and adjusted as to obscure the sinewy vigour of his thought. His manner is steadily in the service of his matter. He is adequate, not copious; for his moral "frugality and industry" prompt him to eschew surplusage and to make his texture firm. His regard for purity of diction is classical; he avoids vulgarity; he despises the jargon of scientific pedants; but like Montaigne he loves frank and masculine speech, and he likes to enrich the language of the well bred by discreet drafts upon the burry, homely, sententious, proverbial language of the people. Like Lord Bacon and like many other grave men among his fellow-countrymen, he found it difficult to avoid an opportunity for a jest even when the occasion was unpropitious; and he never sat below the Attic salt. When his fortune was made, he put by the pewter spoon and bowl of his apprenticeship; his biographers remind us that he kept a well stocked cellar at Passy and enjoyed the distinction of suffering from the gout. With affluence and years he acquired a "palate," and gave a little play to the long repressed tastes of an Epicurean whom early destiny had cast upon a rock-bound coast. The literary expression of his autumnal festivity is to be found in the *bagatelles*. *The Ephemera* proves that this great eighteenth-century rationalist had a fancy. It is no relative, indeed, of that romantic spirit which pipes to the whistling winds on the enchanted greens of Shakespeare. It is rather the classic Muse of eighteenth-century art which summons the rosy Loves and Desires to sport among the courtiers and philosophers and the wasp-waisted ladies in a *fête champêtre* or an *Embarkment for Cythera* of Watteau. The tallow chandler's son who enters on the cycle of his development by cultivating thrift with Defoe, continues it by cultivating tolerance and philanthropy with Voltaire, and completes it with Lord Chesterfield by cultivating "the graces."

CHAPTER VII

Colonial Newspapers and Magazines, 1704-1775

THE development of the colonial press coincides with a period often regarded as narrowly provincial in American literature. That spirit of adventure which enlivens the early historical narratives had settled into a thrifty concern with practical affairs, combined with an exaggerated interest in fine-spun doctrinal reasoning. The echoes of Spenser and other Elizabethans to be heard in some few Puritan elegies and in Anne Bradstreet's quaint imagery, had died away. Knowledge of Europe had become so casual that the colonial newspaper often found it necessary to describe Dresden or Berlin as "a fair, large, and strong city of Germany," and to insert other geographical notes of the simplest sort.

These limitations in the colonial point of view, however, had several striking effects on the early journalism between 1704 and 1750, or thereabouts. The reader who examines the small, ill-printed, half illegible news sheets is surprised to find them more varied in many ways, and more distinctly literary than modern journalism aims to be. The simple fact of the matter is that the dearth of news at length forced the editorial mind to become inventive and even, in some instances, creative. When we remember that European news failed entirely during the long winters; that intercolonial communication was irregular and unsystematic; that criticism of the government in political editorials meant an official inquiry followed by the forced discontinuance of the paper, if not by a trial for libel; that the public already had enough religious exhortation from the pulpit and from pam-

phlets on *The Fatal Consequences of Unscriptural Doctrine*
or *Twenty Considerations against Sin,*—remembering these
things it will not seem so extraordinary that the newspapers
turned to the spectacle of the actual life about them, and, to
convey it, sought their models in the world of letters so little
known in the colonies.

It was James Franklin, Benjamin Franklin's older brother,
who first made a news sheet something more than a garbled
mass of stale items, "taken from the Gazetts and other Publick
Prints of London" some six months late. Franklin, "encouraged by a number of respectable characters, who were
desirous of having a paper of a different cast from those then
published, . . . began the publication, at his own risk, of a
third newspaper, entitled *The New England Courant.*"[1] These
respectable characters were known as the Hell-Fire Club;
they succeeded in publishing a paper "of a different cast,"
which, although it shocked New England orthodoxy pretty
thoroughly, nevertheless proved vastly entertaining and established a kind of literary precedent.

For instead of filling the first page of the *Courant* with the
tedious conventionalities of governors' addresses to provincial
legislatures, James Franklin's club wrote essays and satirical
letters after the manner of *The Spectator* just ten years after the
first appearance of *The Spectator* in London. How novel the
whole method would be to New England readers may be inferred from the fact that even the Harvard library had no
copies of Addison or Steele at this period. Swift, Pope,
Prior, and Dryden would also have been looked for in vain.
Milton himself was little known in the stronghold of Puritanism.
But the printing office of James Franklin had Shakespeare,
Milton, Addison, Steele, Cowley, Butler's *Hudibras,* and "*The
Tail of the Tub*"[2] on its shelves. All these were read and used
in the editor's office, but *The Spectator* and its kind became
the actual model for the new journalism.

As a result, the very look of an ordinary first page of the
Courant is like that of a *Spectator* page. After the more formal
introductory paper on some general topic, such as zeal or

---

[1] Isaiah Thomas, *History of Printing in America.* In *Transactions and Collections of the American Antiquarian Society,* vol. v, p. 110.

[2] The spelling of the *Courant.*

hypocrisy or honour or contentment, the facetious letters of imaginary correspondents commonly fill the remainder of the *Courant's* first page. Timothy Turnstone addresses flippant jibes to Justice Nicholas Clodpate in the first extant number of the *Courant*. Tom Pen-Shallow quickly follows, with his mischievous little postscript: "Pray inform me whether in your Province Criminals have the Privilege of a Jury." Tom Tram writes from the moon about a certain "villainous Post-master" he has heard rumours of. (The *Courant* was always perilously close to legal difficulties and had, besides, a lasting feud with the town postmaster.) Ichabod Henroost complains of a gadding wife. Abigail Afterwit would like to know when the editor of the rival paper, the *Gazette*, "intends to have done printing the Carolina Addresses to their Governour, and give his Readers Something in the Room of them, that will be more entertaining." Homespun Jack deplores the fashions in general, and small waists in particular. Some of these papers represent native wit, with only a general approach to the model; others are little more than paraphrases of *The Spectator*. And sometimes a *Spectator* paper is inserted bodily, with no attempt at paraphrase whatever.

Benjamin Franklin, a mere boy at this time, contributed to the *Courant* the first fruits of his days and nights with Addison. The fourteen little essays from Silence Dogood to the editor are among the most readable and charming of Franklin's early imitations, clearly following *The Spectator*, yet at rather long range and with considerable adaptation to the New England environment. Silence rambles on amiably enough except for occasional slurs on the New England clergy, in regard to whom the *Courant* was always bitter, and often scurrilous. For the Hell-Fire Club never grasped the inner secret of Mr. Spectator, his urbane, imperturbable, impersonal kindliness of manner. Instead, they vented their hatred of dogmatism and intolerance in personalities so insolent as to become in themselves intolerant. Entertaining, however, the *Courant* is, from first to last, and full of a genuine humour and a shrewd satiric truth to life.

Offensive as the *Courant* certainly was to New England orthodoxy, its literary method was seized upon and used in the new paper established under the influence of the Boston clergy-men Mather Byles and Thomas Prince. This was *The New*

England Weekly Journal, and Mather Byles, hailed at the time as "Harvard's honour and New England's hope," who "bids fair to rise, and sing, and rival Pope"[1] contributed largely to the verse and prose on the first page of the paper. A series of "Speculations" is announced, in exact and close imitation of *The Spectator;* even a fictitious author, Proteus Echo, appears as a new Spectator of men and manners, to banter a folly by representing it in a glass. He forms a club, and sketches the members for us in his second essay, which proceeds exactly as the second number of *The Spectator.*

These characters of Proteus Echo's "Society" show some good strokes. There is Mr. Timothy Blunt, an amusing New England version of Sir Roger de Coverley. He lives at some distance from the town of Boston, but rides in every week, often bringing his "Wallet ballanced with two Bottles of Milk, to defray his necessary Expenses. . . . His Periwigg has been out of the Curl ever since the Revolution and his Dagger and Doublet are supposed to be the rarest Pieces of Antiquity in the Country." If it had not been for an unlucky stroke to his "Intellectuals" in his infancy, "he would have stood the fairest of any of his Contemporarys to have found out the Philosopher's Stone." The "wonderful Mr. Honeysuckle, the Blossom of our Society, and the beautiful Ornament of Litterature," is nothing less than Will Honeycomb translated into a poet.

On the whole, however, such work is rare in the *Journal.* Strictly moral essays, of which even *The Spectator* has its full share, soon follow the more creative touches, and we find the ordinary eighteenth-century treatment of merit, covetousness, idleness, the vapours, and so on. Such essays came to be the accepted "filling" for the first page of many newspapers up to 1740 and sometimes after that date. Jeremy Gridley's *Rehearsal* (1743–6), for instance, has a series of speculations rather above the common order, yet requiring no especial notice for their originality or their importance except as a type.

Benjamin Franklin's later journalism amply fulfilled the promise contained in the Silence Dogood papers. When he finally established himself in Philadelphia, shortly before

[1] See Book I, Chap. IX.

1730, the town boasted two wretched little news sheets, Andrew Bradford's *American Mercury*, and Keimer's *Universal Instructor in all Arts and Sciences, and Pennsylvania Gazette.* This instruction in all arts and sciences consisted of weekly extracts from Chambers's *Universal Dictionary*, actually commencing with A, and going steadily on towards Z, followed by instalments of Defoe's *Religious Courtship*, called by the editor "a scarce and delightful piece of History." Franklin quickly did away with all this when he took over the *Instructor*, and made it *The Pennsylvania Gazette*. The *Gazette* soon became Franklin's characteristic organ, which he freely used for satire, for the play of his wit, even for sheer excess of mischief or of fun.

From the first he had a way of adapting his models to his own uses. The series of essays called *The Busy-Body*, which he wrote for Bradford's *American Mercury* in 1729, followed the general Addisonian form, modified already to suit homelier conditions. The thrifty Patience, in her busy little shop, complaining of the useless visitors who waste her valuable time, is related to the ladies who address Mr. Spectator. The Busy-Body himself is a true Censor Morum, as Isaac Bickerstaff had been in the *Tatler*. And a number of the fictitious characters, Ridentius, Eugenius, Cato, and Cretico, represent traditional eighteenth-century classicism. Even this Franklin could use for contemporary satire, since Cretico, the "sowre Philosopher," is evidently a portrait of Franklin's rival, Samuel Keimer.

As time went on, Franklin depended less on his literary conventions, and more on his own native humour. In this there is a new spirit,—not suggested to him by the fine breeding of Addison, or the bitter irony of Swift, or the stinging completeness of Pope. The brilliant little pieces Franklin wrote for his *Pennsylvania Gazette* have an imperishable place in American literature. It is none the less true that they belong to colonial journalism.

The Pennsylvania Gazette, like most other newspapers of the period, was often poorly printed. Franklin was busy with a hundred matters outside of his printing office, and never seriously attempted to raise the standards of his trade. Nor did he ever properly edit or collate the chance medley of stale items which passed for news in the *Gazette*. His influence on the practical side of journalism was very small. On the other hand, his advertisements of books show his very great interest in popularizing secular literature. Undoubtedly his paper contributed to the broader culture which distinguished Pennsylvania from her neighbours before the Revolution. Starting with the custom of importing a stray volume or two along with stationer's supplies, Franklin gradually developed a book shop in his printing office. There was nothing unusual in this fact, by itself. His rival, Andrew Bradford, and many other printers in the colonies had odd collections for sale. But while Bradford was advertising the *Catechistical Guide to Sinners*, or *The Plain Man's Path-way to Heaven*, along with an occasional *Spectator*, Franklin's importations, listed in the *Gazette* for sale, included works of Bacon, Dryden, Locke, Milton, Otway, Pope, Prior, Swift, Rowe, Defoe, Addison, Steele, Arbuthnot, Congreve, Rabelais, Seneca, Ovid, and various novels, all before 1740. The first catalogue of his Library Company shows substantially the same list, with the addition of Don Quixote, and the works of Shaftesbury, of Gay, of Spenser, and of Voltaire. These latter were probably for sale in the printing office as well.

Advertisements of merchandise in all the colonies throw a good deal of light on the customs of the time, and, incidentally, also on the popular taste in reading. We find that Peter Turner has "Superfine Scarlet Cloth, Hat Linings, *Tatlers*, *Spectators*, and Barclay's *Apology*"[1]; that Peter Harry imports "Head Flowers in Boxes, Laces and Edgings, Psalm-books, Play-books, the *Guardians* in 2 vol., Women's Short Cloaks, Men's Scarlet Great Coats"[2] and other apparel. The ship *Samuel*, from London, brings over "sundry goods, particularly a very choice collection of printed Books, Pictures, Maps and Pickles, to be Sold very reasonable by Robert Pringle."[3]

Franklin's influence in journalism was not confined to Pennsylvania. He often assisted young journeymen in the establishment of newspapers in distant towns. Thomas Whitemarsh, for instance, went to Charleston, South Carolina,

---

[1] See *The American Mercury*, No. 1010, 3 May, 1739.
[2] See *The South Carolina Gazette*, February, 1734.
[3] *Ibid.*, No. 511, 9 January, 1744.

in 1731, as Franklin's partner in a new enterprise, which soon included a new paper, *The South Carolina Gazette*.   Naturally, Whitemarsh filled his front page with essays, sometimes reprinted from *The Spectator*, but often original, with a facetious quality suggesting Franklin.   A few burlesques such as the papers of a certain Meddlers' Club are little better than nonsense, rarely enlivened by a flash of wit.   Once we find an odd bit of local colour, when a member of this club criticizes the fair ones of Charleston for promenading too much along the bay.   "I have heard," he says, "that in Great Britain the Ladies and Gentlemen choose the Parks and such like Places to walk and take the Air in, but I never heard of any Places making use of the Wharfs for such Purpose except this."   Essays of one sort or another were always popular in *The South Carolina Gazette*.   Here may be found interesting notices of the various performances (probably professional) of Otway's *Orphan*, Farquhar's *Recruiting Officer*, and other popular plays of the period which were given at the Charleston theatres for twenty or thirty years before the first wandering professional companies began to play in the Northern colonies.   Here, too, we find in the issue of 8 February, 1735, what is probably the first recorded prologue composed in the colonies.

Early theatrical notices may also be followed in *The Virginia Gazette*, a paper of unusual excellence, edited by William Parks in Williamsburg, the old capital of Virginia.   Here *The Busy-Body*, *The Recruiting Officer*, and *The Beaux-Stratagem* were all performed, often by amateurs, though professionals were known as early as 1716 in Williamsburg.   Life in Williamsburg in 1736 had a more cosmopolitan quality than in other towns.   A sprightly essay-serial called *The Monitor*, which fills the first page of *The Virginia Gazette* for twenty-two numbers, probably reflects not only the social life of the capital, but also the newer fashion in such periodical work.   It is dramatic in method, with vividly realized characters who gossip and chat over games of piquet or at the theatre.   *The Beaux-Stratagem*, which had been played in Williamsburg three weeks before, is mentioned as delightful enough to make one of the ladies commit the indiscretion of giggling.   *The Monitor* represents a kind of light social satire unusual in the colonies.

Satire of a heavier sort when attempted by newspaper

writers was never long sustained above mere invective, though it sometimes began with tolerable Hudibrastic or Popean couplets. *The Dunciad* and *Hudibras* were well known and often quoted in such bitter controversies as the famous Whitefield warfare in Charleston between 1740 and 1745. *A Tale of a Tub* and *Gulliver's Travels* also furnished admirable epithets for one's foes. Occasionally some journalist tried to moderate the heat of battle by recurring to the dignity of Addison. In political controversy, especially if he happened to be a liberal, he preferred *Cato's Letters*,[1] Locke, or Algernon Sidney, throughout the early period. Thus it was that the colonists from Boston to Savannah were constantly imbibing advanced British constitutional theories.

After 1750, general news became accessible, and the newspapers show more and more interest in public affairs. The literary first page was no longer necessary, though occasionally used to cover a dull period. A new type of vigorous polemic gradually superseded the older essay. A few of the well-known conventions were retained, however. We still find the fictitious letter, with the fanciful signature, or a series of papers under a common title, such as *The Virginia-Centinel*, or Livingston's *Watch-Tower*. The former is a flaming appeal to arms, running through *The Virginia Gazette* in 1756, and copied into Northern papers to rouse patriotism against the French enemy. The expression of the sentiment, even thus early, seems national. This whole series, though somewhat florid in style, shows the familiarity of the cultivated Southerner with his favourite English poets,—Young, Pope, Shakespeare. Livingston's well-known *Watch-Tower*,[2] a continuation of his pamphlet-magazine *The Independent Reflector*, has already the keen edge of the Revolutionary writings of fifteen and twenty years later. The fifty-second number even has one of the popular phrases of the Revolution: "Had I not sounded the Alarm, Bigotry would e'er now have triumphed over the *natural Rights of British Subjects*."[3]

This expression "natural rights," occurring so early as 1755

---

[1] *Cato's Letters* or *The British Cato*, a series of political papers by Thomas Gordon and John Trenchard, published in London from 1720 to 1723.

[2] Appearing in Gaine's *Mercury* in 1754–1755.

[3] The italics are not in the original.

in Livingston's paper, is probably accidental or vague, but the full political theory of Rousseau, with all its abstractions regarding mankind in general, was soon added to the definite and always cherished belief in the constitutional privileges of Englishmen. The ideas of the French philosophers were in the air, and there is plenty of evidence in the colonial newspapers for fifteen or twenty years before the Revolution that the French influence was increasing. Even during the French and Indian war, booksellers advertised French texts, grammars, and dictionaries in the papers, while courses in French were often announced. Before the close of the war, we find *The Boston Gazette* printing extracts from Montesquieu's *Spirit of Laws*, with an apology and the expressed hope that it may not be "political Heresey" to suppose that "a Frenchman may have juster Notions of Civil Liberty than some among ourselves." This was in the days when "Gallic perfidy" was the popular note.

After 1760 all the important works of Rousseau, Montesquieu, and the Encyclopedists as well as many other French books were advertised for sale in the colonial press. Such advertisements indicate the taste of the reading public more accurately than do catalogues of private libraries, which represent individual preferences. Voltaire had long been known in the colonies. Rousseau's *Social Contract* was advertised as a *Treatise on the Social Compact, or The Principles of Political Law*. He himself is referred to again and again as "the ingenious Rousseau," or "the celebrated Rousseau." And *Émile* and *La Nouvelle Héloïse* were evidently in demand. The famous *Letters of a Farmer in Pennsylvania* by John Dickinson belong to the colonial press in a very special way, since not only did they first appear in *The Pennsylvania Chronicle*, *The Pennsylvania Journal*, and *The Pennsylvania Gazette* almost simultaneously in the winter of 1767–1768, but they were reprinted in nearly every newspaper on the continent, from Nova Scotia to Georgia.[1] The *Letters* were soon known in France, where they were translated by Jacques Barbeu Dubourg, with a preface of glowing compliment.

Reports of French interest in America inclined the colonists still more to the French philosophy of government. As a

[1] See also Book I, Chap. VIII.

matter of fact, from the time of the Stamp Act, political essays of every description filled the newspapers, and what one paper published was soon reprinted in others. Thus the influence of the press in this critical period can hardly be overrated. If the "pumpkin Gentry" of New England (to use a tory phrase) took offence at some encroachment, gentlemen planters of the South were sure to read the whole case in a few weeks and, in spite of their differing civilization, to sympathize with the Northern firebrands. When Dr. Arthur Lee sent home to *The Virginia Gazette* his *Monitor*, a series of essays describing hostile conditions in London, and urging his countrymen to non-importation, it was not by any means his countrymen of Virginia alone who heard the call. The *Monitor* has something of the distinguished style of the *Farmer*, and it is natural that the two should have been published together in a Williamsburg edition. Revolutionary Virginia burgesses always toasted the *Farmer's* and *Monitor's* letters together. But essays of an entirely different type also appeared constantly. Republicans and Loyalists fought violent battles under assumed classical names. Constitutionalis, Massachusettensis, Senex, Novanglus, Pacificus, Caesariensis, Amicus Publico, Cunctator, Virginius, Mucius Scaevola, Cato, Scipio, Leonidas, Brutus, and many more argued hotly and often powerfully the whole question of allegiance, on abstract grounds.

Isaiah Thomas's *Massachusetts Spy* shows the course of this long battle. Constantly on the verge of being suppressed, from its establishment in 1770 to the Revolution, it carried radicalism to its logical conclusion. When the *Spy* began to be reprinted in other papers, as "the most daring production ever published in America," the country as a whole was ready for Tom Paine's *Common Sense*.

In regard to other forms of periodical literature before the Revolution, it is often difficult to draw precise distinctions.[1] Newspapers are easily enough distinguished in general by the attempt to give items of current news. Outside the regular news sheets, there is a strange assortment of colonial productions usually classed as magazines, but in many cases hardly

[1] Mr. Albert Matthews notes this difficulty in his bibliography of New England magazines. See his *Lists of New England Magazines*, in *Publications of the Colonial Society of Massachusetts*, vol. XIII, pp. 69–74.

recognizable as such. For instance, William Livingston's *Independent Reflector, or Weekly Essays* and also Andrew Oliver's *Censor*, are nothing more than single essays published serially. The *Censor* was published in weekly reply to "Mucius Scaevola" and other writers of the *Spy*. The very meaning of the word "magazine" in the eighteenth century makes classification difficult. It was literally a "storehouse," being applied to literature as a "collection"; almost any assemblage of writings, especially if published serially, could be referred to as a "magazine." Even the regular London magazines of the period were made up largely of excerpts from weekly reviews and periodicals, along with a summary of the news of the month. A department called "Poetical Essays" was usually more original, but on the whole both *The Gentleman's Magazine* and *The London Magazine* could be described fairly enough as collections of material from various sources.

There were a few magazines of this standard English type in America before the Revolution. Franklin, as usual, led the way, though it happened that his rival Andrew Bradford actually published the first magazine in the colonies. Franklin's soon followed, and these two little periodicals brought out the same month in Philadelphia, 1741, clearly indicate the attempt to transplant the English type, with some adaptations, for colonial readers. Franklin's title, *The General Magazine and Historical Chronicle for all the British Plantations in America*, shows his intention of giving a review of colonial news rather than of British. He did, as a matter of fact, use *The Virginia Gazette* and other weeklies for articles and verse, but he also took European items whenever he could get them. Both magazines were evidently premature, however, for Bradford's existed only three months, and Franklin's only six.

The next attempt at this sort of periodical came from Boston two years later. Jeremy Gridley was the able editor of *The American Magazine and Historical Chronicle*. It is an excellent piece of work for that date, both in general arrangement and in details of printing. There is very little original material, however, since the editor not only imitated *The London Magazine* very closely in plan, but boldly copied most of the essays, articles, and verse from it or from *The Gentleman's Magazine*. An occasional translation from the classics by a Harvard student, a burlesque by "Jonathan Weatherwise" on the absurd weather signs of the country folk, or perhaps a timely article from a "neighbouring colony" does not suffice to impart a native flavour to the magazine as a whole. It is distinctly "imported." The attempt was nevertheless creditable, and certainly kept readers in touch with the best English reviews. The magazine continued for three years.

A dozen years later *The New England Magazine of Knowledge and Pleasure* announced its motto, "Alluring Profit with Delight we blend," but it confined itself to hackneyed essays on old models. In the same year, however, at Philadelphia, a magazine of decided originality and of genuine importance in colonial literature was coming out month by month with the first provost of the new college as its editor and guiding spirit. The Rev. William Smith, called to America from Aberdeen in 1752, brought a great love of letters to his new work and soon succeeded in imparting his own literary enthusiasms to a group of young students. It is largely due to his constant encouragement that a strain of lyric poetry at length sounded in clear, welcome notes, a strain all too short and slight, but of real beauty. These young poets belonged to the generation after that of Franklin's famous Junto, one of the college group being a son of Franklin's friend Thomas Godfrey, the mathematician. Thomas Godfrey, Jr., needed all the active help of the provost, since poetical gifts did not meet with favour in the Godfrey household. Francis Hopkinson, Joseph Shippen, and Nathaniel Evans were also introduced to the public by Smith.

The interesting thing about William Smith's own literary enthusiasms is his love of eighteenth-century romanticism. In a thoroughly romantic temper he made himself a retreat by the falls of the Schuylkill, which he describes under the guise of Theodore, the Hermit, in his *American Magazine*, noting "the singular gloom of its situation," hidden by "a romantic tuft of trees," and made more lonely by surrounding waters. He could soon announce in his magazine that he had almost too many poems to draw from. Practically all the verse in its thirteen numbers is original, although at times, especially in the long poems of James Sterling, the most conventional eighteenth-century manner is amusingly evident. The essays, with very few exceptions, were not only written in the colonies but were often well adapted to the problems of the day, the war on the border, the Indians, the public policies of the government. The pride in "this young country" is everywhere evident, combined with perfect loyalty to Great Britain. In this year 1758 the successor of *The American Magazine*, called *The New American Magazine*, continued the same general policy, without securing the same originality. William Smith had been called to England, and the new venture lacked his power. It had the honour of publishing Nathaniel Evans's fine *Ode on the late General Wolfe*, however, in probably its earliest and simplest form.

With the next magazines we are again on the eve of the revolution. "The town has met," and we read instructions, articles, orations, odes, and satires on the situation, sometimes reprinted from the newspapers, sometimes written for the magazine, but always inflammatory, since the two noteworthy periodicals of this period, *The Pennsylvania Magazine* and *The Royal American Magazine*, were edited respectively by the two firebrands, Thomas Paine and Isaiah Thomas. Paine's magazine did not lack pungent wit of one kind or another, although for the more strictly literary sections both he and Isaiah Thomas drew freely on conventional English sources which, in theory, they should have rejected. Thomas's *Royal American Magazine* is enlivened by the famous Paul Revere engravings and is otherwise interesting, particularly for its confident belief in the new country soon to be the United States.

CHAPTER VIII

American Political Writing, 1760–1789

A MERICAN history between 1760 and 1789—from the end, that is, so far as military operations were concerned, of the Seven Years' War to the inauguration of the new government under the Federal Constitution—falls naturally into three well-marked periods. The first, comprising the development of the constitutional struggle with Great Britain over taxation and imperial control, reaches its culmination in the armed collision between the British and the patriot forces at Lexington, 19 April, 1775. The second period covers the eight years of war, ending with the peace treaty of September, 1783; while the third embraces the so-called "critical period" of the Confederation, and the formation and adoption of the Constitution.

Such a time of storm and stress, of revolution and evolution, is pretty certain, especially in a new country, if it bring forth literature at all, to bring forth such as is predominantly political in content, style, and purpose. The Revolutionary leaders who have left a large and permanent impress upon American literature were concerned chiefly with such weighty matters as the nature of the British constitution, the formulation of colonial rights, and the elaboration of schemes of government and administration; and it was of these things that they chiefly wrote. It is a striking tribute to the classical education of the age, to the moulding power of closely-reasoned theological and legal treatises on which ministers and lawyers fed,[1] and to the subtle, pervasive influence of the English Bible, that the best political writing of the Revolutionary period attained a dignity and

[1] See Book I, Chap. VII, for evidence as to the knowledge of French radical books in the colonies after 1760.

impressiveness of style, a noble power of rhetorical form, and a telling incisiveness of phrase which won the instant admiration of English critics, and which stamp the political literature of American national beginnings as superior to the similar literature of any other people anywhere.

Of the first notable contribution to the literary history of the Revolution we have, unfortunately, only a second-hand report. When, in 1761, following the death of George II and the accession of George III, the surveyor-general of customs at Boston applied to the Superior Court of Massachusetts for the reissuance of writs of assistance,[1] granting authority to search for and seize uncustomed goods, some merchants of Boston and others combined to oppose the application. James Otis the younger, for ten years past one of the leaders of the Massachusetts bar, and lately advocate-general, who, unable to support the application for the writs, had resigned his office, made the leading argument for the petitioners. In a great speech, the substance of which has survived only in notes taken at the time by John Adams,[2] then a young lawyer, and more fully written out many years later, Otis challenged the writs as "the worst instrument of arbitrary power, the most destructive of English liberty and the fundamental principles of law, that ever was found in an English law-book." At once general in its terms and perpetual in its operation, lacking the exact specification of place and circumstance which a search-warrant ought to contain, such a writ was on both accounts illegal. The freedom of one's house was violated by it; the only precedent for it belonged to the days of arbitrary power under Charles II. "No acts of Parliament can establish such a writ. . . . An act against the constitution is void."

Otis could impede, but he could not defeat, the application, and the writs were eventually issued. He had, however, raised the important question of the application of English law to the colonies, and the nature and extent of the "rights of Englishmen" which the colonial charters, in express terms, had guaranteed. Elected a member of the House of Representatives, he presently led an attack upon Governor Bernard for fitting

---

[1] A form of writ is given in W. MacDonald, *Select Charters*, 259–261. The best account of the subject is in Quincy, *Massachusetts Reports*, 395–540.

[2] *Works*, II, 124 note, 521–525; X, 246–249, 274–276.

out an armed vessel without the approval of the House; drafted a communication in which the governor was charged with "taking from the House their most darling privilege, the right of originating all taxes"; and late in 1762 published his first political pamphlet, *A Vindication of the Conduct of the House of Representatives of the Province of the Massachusetts-Bay*, in which, mixed with extreme praise of the King of Great Britain and denunciation of the King of France, and vague suggestions as to the nature of human rights, the privileges of the colonies under the British constitution were stoutly maintained. Neither historically nor legally was the argument beyond question, and the claim of right was a call to the future rather than an interpretation of the past. What was said, however, was said with vigour and incisiveness, and to Otis's provincial audience carried weight.

The treaty of Paris, ceding to Great Britain all the vast possessions of France on the mainland of North America, together with Florida and other Spanish territory east of the Mississippi, was concluded 10 February, 1763. On the 23d of that month, Charles Townshend became first lord of trade, with the oversight of colonial administration, in the short-lived ministry of Bute, and some far-reaching changes in the colonial system were presently announced. The salaries of governors and judges, hitherto paid by the colonial assemblies, were now to be paid by the crown, thus insuring, it was believed, a better enforcement of the trade laws and a proper revenue from customs; and a standing army of ten thousand men was to be maintained in America, in anticipation of an attempt by France to recover what it had lost, the expense of the troops to be met by parliamentary taxation of the colonies. Grenville, who became prime minister in June, supported the plan. In March, 1764, Grenville gave notice of his intention to impose stamp duties; laying the matter over for a year, however, in order that the colonies might be consulted. In April a Sugar Act imposed new colonial customs duties.

The prospect of direct taxation by Parliament aroused widespread apprehension in America, and called forth in July the ablest and best-known of Otis's pamphlets, *The Rights of the British Colonies Asserted and Proved*. With notable moderation and restraint, and in a tone pervadingly judicial rather than partisan, Otis argued the case for the colonies, appealing as before to the British constitution as he understood it, and to the logic of right, liberty, and justice. A colony being an integral part of the mother country, though territorially separated from it, its people are, "by the law of God and nature, by the common law, and by act of Parliament . . . entitled to all the natural, essential, inherent, and inseparable rights of our fellow-subjects in Great Britain." Among these rights was that of freedom from taxation save with their own consent, and of representation in the supreme or some subordinate legislature. Parliament admittedly possessed a general supervisory authority over the colonies, but if, under the guise of regulation, it were to infringe upon the right of taxation through duly elected representatives, it would be guilty of an arbitrary violation of the constitution. Forcible resistance, however, even to an unconstitutional act, was not to be thought of.

There would be an end of all government, if one or a number of subjects or subordinate provinces should take upon them so far to judge of the justice of an act of Parliament, as to refuse obedience to it. . . . Therefore let the Parliament lay what burdens they please on us, we must, it is our duty to submit and patiently bear them, till they will be pleased to relieve us.

Otis voiced effectively the first impulse of thoughtful, patriotic Americans as they contemplated the prospect of parliamentary taxation. The proposed act violated the constitution whose benefits the colonists claimed, but forcible resistance would be treason. The same line of argument, more systematically and cogently put, characterized Oxenbridge Thacher's *Sentiments of a British American* (1764). Thacher was a fellow townsman of Otis, and the two had been associated in the case of the writs of assistance. Like Otis, Thacher's legal argument closes with a strong profession of loyalty to the crown, and there is no good ground for thinking that in either case the profession was insincere. Argument and dissent were an Englishman's right, and the constitution had grown by protest against abuses.

An even more effective statement of the American case is found in *The Rights of Colonies Examined*, a pamphlet written by Stephen Hopkins, governor of Rhode Island, and published at Providence in 1765. Admitting the right of Parliament to regulate the affairs of the whole empire, Hopkins not only claims for the colonies "as much freedom as the mother state from which they went out," but dwells forcibly upon the dangerous tendency of the new policy, the widespread apprehension which it has already aroused, and the absence of any clear necessity for raising an American revenue by parliamentary fiat.

What motive . . . can remain, to induce the parliament to abridge the privileges, and lessen the rights of the most loyal and dutiful subjects; subjects justly intituled to ample freedom, who have long enjoyed, and not abused or forfeited their liberties, who have used them to their own advantage, in dutiful subserviency to the orders and interests of Great-Britain?

Such reasoning as that of Otis, Thacher, and Hopkins, however convincing to the popular mind, avoided, but did not settle, the important and difficult constitutional question of the ultimate authority of Parliament over the colonies. On that question the wisest were certain to differ, and a presentation of the other side of the case was speedily forthcoming. In February, 1765, there appeared at Newport *A Letter from a Gentleman at Halifax, to his Friend in Rhode-Island*, published anonymously, but written by Martin Howard, a Newport lawyer of repute. In this temperate, logical, and readable pamphlet, the "Gentleman at Halifax," replying to Hopkins's "labored, ostentatious piece," puts his finger on the primary defect in the whole colonial argument, namely, the claim "that the colonies have rights independent of, and not controulable by the authority of parliament." If they derived their political rights from Parliament, were not those rights subject to interpretation or abridgement by Parliament? A lively controversy ensued. Hopkins defended himself in a series of articles in the Providence *Gazette*, while Otis, his zeal for debate knowing no provincial bounds, printed *A Vindication of the British Colonies against the Aspersions of the Halifax Gentleman.* Howard retorted with *A Defence of the Letter from a Gentleman at Halifax, to his Friend in Rhode-Island*, to which Otis responded with *Brief Remarks on the Defence of the Halifax Libel on the British-American-Colonies.* The tide of patriotism was rising, however, and the populace presently took a hand. Before the summer was over Howard, after being hanged and burned in effigy at Newport, fled to England, and the "rights of the colonies" were both "asserted and proved."

No substitute for the stamp tax having been agreed upon by the colonial assemblies, the Stamp Act became a law (March, 1765). In the interval between the approval of the act and the date (1 November) at which it was to go into effect, disorderly bodies calling themselves "Sons of Liberty" organized a campaign of forcible resistance; with the result that, when the first of November arrived, stamps and stamped paper were not to be had. Meantime, the newspaper and pamphlet controversy continued. To a pamphlet written by Soame Jenyns, a member of Parliament, published in 1765, entitled *The Objections to the Taxation of Our American Colonies, by the Legislature of Great Britain, Briefly Considered*, Otis replied with *Considerations on Behalf of the Colonies, in a Letter to a Noble Lord*, the argument of which, save in its plea for leniency and consideration on the part of Great Britain in view of the extent and importance of the colonies, does not differ materially from that which the author had previously advanced. John Adams, "with the exception of Jefferson . . . the most readable of the statesmen of the Revolutionary period," now entered the lists with a series of four essays, published anonymously and without title in the Boston *Gazette* in August, 1765. Beginning with an examination of the "ecclesiatical and civil tyranny" which he found exemplified in the canon and feudal law, and of which the Stamp Act was held up as the consummate illustration, Adams traced the course of the historical struggle between corporate oppression and individual liberty and self-assertion. "Admitting we are children, have not children a right to complain when their parents are attempting to break their limbs, to administer poison, or to sell them to enemies for slaves?" Adams had read his history with a Puritan obsession, and neither his interpretation of facts nor his reasoning did him here much credit. The essays had influence, however. Reprinted in *The London Chronicle*, they were finally published in 1768, in revised form, under the misleading title of *A Dissertation on the Canon and the Feudal Law*.[1]

[1] *Works*, III, 445–464.

With the resolutions,[1] memorials, and petitions of the Stamp
Act Congress (October, 1765), we reach the first of the series of
great state papers which, while of supreme value for the proper
understanding of the constitutional position of the colonies, are
also, in some respects, the most characteristic literary product
of the Revolutionary period. Nowhere else in American
literature does the peculiar gift of formal expression and logical
exposition in politics show itself on so large a scale or in so great
a cause, and in no country in the world has such expression
moved so long and so consistently on a high plane, or voiced
itself with so much dignity, condensed forcefulness, or formal
beauty. For the most part the work of a few hands, and in
some cases of composite authorship, the state papers of the
American Revolution became, through their force of argument
and sweep of phrase, the accepted statements of political
faith, first for the patriot party, and then for the American
people.

Of the important papers agreed to by the Stamp Act Congress, two—a declaration of rights and grievances and a petition to the king—were mainly the work of John Dickinson of
Pennsylvania, whose notable career as a political writer, already
begun in the controversial atmosphere of his own colony, was
to earn for him the title of "the penman of the Revolution."
At the end of the year 1765 Dickinson also published at Philadelphia a pamphlet entitled *The Late Regulations respecting
the British Colonies on the Continent of America Considered,
in a Letter from a Gentleman in Philadelphia to his Friend in
London*,[2] which was reprinted in London and attracted favourable notice. A notable pamphlet, published anonymously,
by Daniel Dulany of Maryland, one of the ablest of colonial
lawyers, entitled *Considerations on the Propriety of Imposing
Taxes in the British Colonies, for the Purpose of Raising a
Revenue, by Act of Parliament*, in which the notion of the "virtual representation" of the colonies in Parliament was conclusively denied, appeared while the Stamp Act Congress was in
session, and was also republished in London.

The repeal of the Stamp Act (March, 1766) caused a sudden
cessation of the agitation in America; and the ominous Declara-

[1] Text in W. MacDonald, *Select Charters*, 314, 315.
[2] *Writings*, ed. Ford, I, 211–245.

tory Act, asserting for the first time the right of Parliament "to bind the colonies and people of America, subjects of the crown of Great Britain, in all cases whatsoever," received little attention. In June, 1767, however, the New York assembly was suspended by act of Parliament for its refusal to comply with the requirements of an act for the quartering of troops; while the Townshend acts, which followed immediately, laid duties upon a number of colonial imports, established resident customs commissioners in America, legalized writs of assistance, and readjusted the tea duties in the interest of the hard-pressed East India Company. The colonies, in resisting the Stamp Act, had dwelt upon the unconstitutionality of internal taxation by a Parliament in which they were not represented. Townshend now sought to turn the tables by imposing the external taxes which he professed to think the colonies, by inference, had conceded the right of Parliament to impose.

The passage of the Townshend acts revived, though to a. less wide extent, the controversy over colonial rights. Of the writings which attended this phase of the discussion, easily the most important is John Dickinson's *Letters from a Farmer in Pennsylvania to the Inhabitants of the British Colonies.*[1] First published in a Philadelphia newspaper in 1767–68,[2] and reproduced from thence in most of the newspapers then issued in the colonies, they were in 1768 collected in a pamphlet, of which some eight editions appeared in America, two in London, one in Dublin, and a French version in Amsterdam. Without the legal mastery of Thacher or Dulany, but, fortunately, also without the discursiveness and extravagance of Otis or the intellectual and religious bias of John Adams, Dickinson reviewed, earnestly and directly, the colonial case; warned the colonies of the grave danger of admitting any form of parliamentary taxation, external or internal; sustained the right of protest and petition, and urged economy, thrift, and the development of American industry. Forcible resistance, indeed, is with him not to be thought of, and the idea of independence is spurned; yet at the same time Dickinson insists

that we cannot be happy, without being free; that we cannot be free, without being secure in our property; that we cannot be secure

---

[1] *Writings*, ed. Ford, I, 307–406. [2] See also Book I, Chap. VII.

in our property, if, without our consent, others may, as by right, take it away; that taxes imposed on us by parliament, do thus take it away.

On the whole, it is the form rather than the substance of the *Letters from a Farmer* that is most original.   Dickinson wrote as a cultivated, prosperous gentleman, addressing an audience of intelligent, but plain, people the soil of whose minds had been already somewhat prepared.   What Dickinson did, and did with effective skill, was to present in attractive literary form the best of what had already been said and thought on behalf of the colonial claims, and to adapt the argument to the new crisis presented by the Townshend programme.   Too patriotic to submit without a protest, and too thoughtful to rebel, he voiced more successfully, perhaps, than any other American publicist of his day, the sober second-thought of the great body of colonists who were ready to carry resistance to any point short of separation and war.

The Massachusetts Circular Letter[1] (11 February, 1768), prepared by Samuel Adams for a committee of the House of Representatives, and addressed to the speakers of other representative houses throughout the colonies, introduces to us the man who, more zealously and persistently than anyone else, devoted himself to achieving American independence.   Holding the humble office of tax-collector in Boston, Adams's devotion to public causes, joined to a rare talent for political organization, had already made him the master of the Boston town-meeting and the leading spirit in the provincial House of Representatives.   In the course of the bitter fight which he waged against Governor Bernard and Governor Hutchinson, and in furtherance of his relentless insistence upon the right of complete local self-government for the colonies, Adams drafted, in whole or in part, most of the resolutions and reports which made Massachusetts the leader in the constitutional struggle, and which also marked it for special punishment later at the hands of Parliament.

The Circular Letter, studiously dignified and respectful in tone, is the best summary statement of the colonial argument which had thus far been put forward.   Admitting the supreme

---

[1] Text in W. MacDonald, *Select Charters*, 331–334.

legislative authority of Parliament over the whole empire, it
rests its case on the

essential, unalterable right, in nature, engrafted into the British
constitution, as a fundamental law, and ever held sacred and ir-
revocable by the subjects within the realm, that what a man has
honestly acquired is absolutely his own, which he may freely give,
but cannot be taken from him without his consent.

So precious is the right of representation, and so great the
"utter impracticability" of actually being represented in
Parliament, that

this House think that a taxation of their constituents, even without
their consent, grievous as it is, would be preferable to any representation that could be admitted for them there.

Devotion to naked principle could go no farther, nor indicate
more clearly the desired goal of independence.

The Townshend Revenue Act remained in force until April,
1770. The act produced an inappreciable revenue, necessitated
extraordinary expenditures for its enforcement, and had no
other effect upon the situation in America than to reawaken
and solidify the colonial opposition to parliamentary taxation,
and stimulate interest in the development of colonial manufactures and in the concerted non-importation and non-con-
sumption of British goods. One of the first steps of the North
ministry was to repeal it (1770), except the tax of three pence a
pound on tea, retained to assert the principle of the Declaratory
Act of 1766. For the next two years and more the agitation
was not actively kept up, and even such violent disorders as
the Boston Massacre (March, 1770) and the burning of the
revenue schooner *Gaspée* (1772) occasioned hardly more than
local excitement. Colonial newspapers continued to print
essays on American rights, and houses of assembly embodied
their views in resolutions; but these occasional writings, while
doubtless not without their influence upon public opinion,
hardly constitute a political literature of importance.

To this early period of revolutionary agitation belong also
the first two volumes of Thomas Hutchinson's *History of the
Colony of Massachusetts Bay* (1764–67)[1] and the famous Hut-

[1] See also Book I, Chap. II.

chinson "Letters," which, although not made public until 1773,
date from 1768–69. Written by Hutchinson, previous to his
governorship, to a friend in England, the "Letters" discuss
events in Massachusetts from the point of view of a loyalist
official who, deeply attached to the colony, was also deeply concerned at the grave course which affairs were taking, and who
could honestly declare:

I wish the good of the colony when I wish to see some further
restraint of liberty rather than the connexion with the parent state
should be broken; for I am sure such a breach must prove the ruin
of the colony.

By means never divulged, Franklin, in 1773, got possession of
the letters and sent them to friends in Boston, where their
publication greatly intensified the hostility to Hutchinson and
precipitated his recall.

With the destruction of the tea at Boston (16 December,
1773), the controversy between the colonies and the mother
country entered upon the stage which was to lead to a declaration of independence and to war. In February, 1774, at a
hearing before the Privy Council on a petition from Massachusetts for Hutchinson's removal, Franklin was bitterly denounced for his connection with the Hutchinson letters, and
was presently removed from his office of deputy postmaster-
general for North America. In March, the port of Boston was
by statute closed to commerce, except in food, after 1 June,
until compensation should be made to the East India Company
for the loss of the tea. In May, the charter of Massachusetts
was so altered by act of Parliament as largely to deprive the
colony of self-government, while by another statute provision
was made for the trial in England, or in another colony, of
persons accused of murder or other capital offence because of
anything done by them in suppressing riots or enforcing the
revenue laws. In June, more stringent regulations were enacted for the quartering of troops. General Gage had already
arrived at Boston as military governor, and the coercion of the
colony began.

　　The first Continental Congress, which met at Philadelphia
5 September, adopted a set of "Declarations and Resolves,"[1]

　　[1] Text in W. MacDonald, *Select Charters*, 357–361.

similar in tone and general argument to those of the Stamp
Act Congress, but containing a significant admission of the
right of Parliament to regulate the external trade of the colonies,
provided the aim were regulation and not taxation.   A petition
to the king and an address to the inhabitants of Canada, both
drafted by Dickinson, were also adopted, together with a
memorial to the inhabitants of British America, drawn by
Richard Henry Lee of Virginia, and an eloquent address to the
people of Great Britain, the work of John Jay of New York,
later the first chief-justice of the United States Supreme Court.
An agreement known as the "Association"[1] pledged the people
of the colonies to commercial non-intercourse with Great
Britain, and to the encouragement of industry, economy, and
neighbourly kindness.   Copies of these various state papers
were separately printed and widely circulated.

The passage of the coercive acts, and the assembling of a
Congress to consider plans of united resistance, stirred anew
the fires of literary controversy.   In May, 1774, the same
month that saw the arrival of Gage and the British troops at
Boston, Josiah Quincy published at that place his *Observations
on the Act of Parliament, commonly called the Boston Port-Bill;
with Thoughts on Civil Society and Standing Armies.*   Quincy
was a brilliant young lawyer, who, in company with John
Adams, had chivalrously defended the British soldiers indicted
for participation in the Boston Massacre, in 1770.   A competent
critic[2] has suggested that the larger part of the pamphlet, dealing with "civil society and standing armies," had been
carefully prepared some time before, advantage being taken of
the Port Act to publish the work with an expanded title.
Quincy's pamphlet was shortly followed by James Wilson's
*Considerations on the Nature and the Extent of the Legislative
Authority of the British Parliament*, an ingenious rejection of
such authority in favour of allegiance to the king alone.   The
writer, a young lawyer of Philadelphia, was later to contribute
powerfully to the acceptance of the Federal Constitution by
Pennsylvania.

Not all who entered the lists, however, agreed so unreservedly with the sentiments of Congress or of the patriot

---

[1] Text in W. MacDonald.   *Select Charters*, 362–367.
[2] Tyler, *Literary History of the American Revolution*, I, 272 note.

leaders. A series of papers in *The Pennsylvania Packet*, re-printed in a pamphlet with the title *A Few Political Reflections Submitted to the Consideration of the British Colonies, by a Citizen of Philadelphia*, and attributed to Richard Wells, urged com-pensation for the tea and the abandonment of violent protest, at the same time arguing for united rejection of the claim to taxation on the ground that the colonies were too old and too strong to be kept in leading-strings. An anonymous *Letter from a Virginian*, addressed to the Congress at Philadelphia, went further and frankly questioned the constitutional sound-ness and political wisdom of the arguments put forth by the Congress.

No history of the American Revolution, or of the political literature to which it gave birth, would be complete without consideration of the loyalists. That independence was in fact the work of a minority, and that the methods by which the loyal majority was overawed and, in part, expelled were as high-handed and cruel as they were active and vigorous, must be freely conceded. Weighty as was the colonial argument, force and violence were freely employed to give effect to it. But the great loyalist party, numbering among its leaders many of the ablest, most devoted, and wealthiest men in colonial life, was not crushed without a struggle; and the arguments with which its adherents defended their cause and sought to defeat that of their opponents were not less ably put or trenchantly phrased than those of the patriots themselves.

Soon after the "Association" agreement of the Continental Congress was adopted (October, 1774), there was published in New York the first of four pamphlets by a "Westchester Farmer." The author was the Rev. Samuel Seabury, then and for some time rector of St. Peter's Church, Westchester, and later, by time's curious working, first bishop of the Protes-tant Episcopal Church in the United States. The four pam-phlets, entitled respectively *Free Thoughts on the Proceedings of the Continental Congress*, *The Congress Canvassed*, *A View of the Controversy between Great-Britain and her Colonies*, and *An Alarm to the Legislature of the Province of New-York*, were a powerful attack upon the aims and policy of the Congress and the patriot leaders, and a plea for such adjustment as would assure to the colonies local self-government, on the one hand, with full recognition of parliamentary authority on the other. For writing the pamphlets Seabury was mobbed, imprisoned, and hounded until in 1776 he took refuge within the British lines.

It was in reply to the first of Seabury's pamphlets that Alexander Hamilton, then a college student of seventeen, made anonymously his first essay in authorship with *A Full Vindication of the Measures of the Congress, from the Calumnies of their Enemies* (1774) and *A Farmer Refuted* (1775). None of the pamphleteers of the Revolutionary period excels Hamilton in the logical acumen and expository power which he here displays, and none approached him in his clear discernment of the theatre and character of the war, if war must be. Yet even Hamilton, with all his precocious intellectual power, failed to point out beyond peradventure how union with the Empire under allegiance to the king comported with a denial of the legislative power of Parliament. The only outcome for the colonies was independence, and independence was the word which, as yet, most colonial leaders appeared anxious to avoid.

Before the attacks of the "Westchester Farmer" had ceased, Daniel Leonard, a Boston lawyer of social prominence, began the publication in a loyalist newspaper, over the pen-name of "Massachusettensis," of a series of seventeen letters, *To the Inhabitants of the Province of the Massachusetts-Bay* (1774–75). Seabury had emphasized the impracticability and political unwisdom of the recommendations of the Congress. Leonard assailed the unconstitutional arguments of the patriots, and the revolutionary character of their attacks upon parliamentary enactments and crown officers.

The task of combating the influence of "Massachusettensis" was undertaken by John Adams, who, early in 1775, published in the Boston *Gazette*, over the signature of "Novanglus," a series of letters traversing Leonard's argument. Twelve articles had appeared when the battle of Lexington (19 April, 1775) intervened. Adams did not lack legal knowledge or logical proficiency, but he was no match for Leonard in debate, nor could he keep to the point; and although the republication of the letters in London, and a reprint many years later in the United States, gave some vogue to the name "Novanglus," the essays won no permanent distinction either for themselves or for their author. It was as a hard-working member of the Continental Congress, and not as a writer or political philosopher, that Adams made his worthiest contribution to the American cause.

To a different class belong the numerous writings of Joseph Galloway, a delegate from Pennsylvania to the first Continental Congress. Already prominent in the politics of his colony, Galloway submitted to the Congress a *Plan of a Proposed Union between Great Britain and the Colonies*. Read in the light of the present day, the scheme seems like a suggestive anticipation of later British colonial policy; but the Congress, after debating it at length, and rejecting it by the narrow majority of a single vote, trampled it under foot, and ordered all reference to it expunged from the printed journal. Galloway later published the plan in *A Candid Examination of the Mutual Claims of Great Britain and the Colonies* (New York, 1775). In 1778, after two years spent with the British forces, Galloway went to England, where he was thought sufficiently important to be examined before the House of Commons, and where he continued to publish pamphlets on America until the end of the war.

Another New York loyalist, President Myles Cooper of King's College (now Columbia), gifted with wit and sarcasm above most of his fellows, entered the lists in 1774 with two anonymous pamphlets—*The American Querist: or, Some Questions Proposed relative to the Present Disputes between Great Britain and her American Colonies*, and *A Friendly Address to all Reasonable Americans*. In August, 1775, a mob stripped and mutilated him, but he contrived to escape to a British ship-of-war, and thence to England, where he obtained ecclesiastical preferment. Charles Lee, soon to be numbered among the renegades and traitors, but at the moment in the enjoyment of a repute as a military expert which he had done little to earn, replied to Cooper with some cleverness in *Structures on a Pamphlet, entitled a 'Friendly Address to all Reasonable Americans'* (1775)—the only contribution of Lee's to the patriot cause for which he may be appreciatively remembered.

Although not published until 1797, by which time the author had been for more than twenty years resident in England, Jonathan Boucher's *A View of the Causes and Consequences*

of the American Revolution may perhaps be included in our
enumeration of loyalist writings. From 1762 to 1775 Boucher
was rector of parishes in Maryland and Virginia, finding time,
however, to take an active part in colonial politics. The
volume referred to, dedicated to Washington and prefaced by an
extended introduction, consists of thirteen sermons preached to
his American congregations, and forms as a whole the best presentation of the loyalist cause as embraced and championed
by an Anglican minister. For his boldness, however, his parishioners drove him into exile, in common with many another
clergyman who held similar views.

Mention should also be made here of the poems of Philip
Freneau and John Trumbull, although the fuller discussion of
their literary significance belongs elsewhere in this work.[1] The
first of Freneau's poems of the Revolution, *On the Conqueror of
America Shut up in Boston* and *General Gage's Soliloquy*, were
published in the summer of 1775, while the siege of Boston was
in progress. Trumbull, whose muse had already responded
to some of the earlier incidents of the war, published the first
canto of *McFingal* in January, 1776. Grounded, as were the
writings of both of these authors, in a clear, popular understanding of the points at issue, and foreshadowing, in Freneau's
case, the ultimate attainment of independence, the satirical
humour of the poems confirmed the faithful and strengthened
the wavering quite as effectively as state papers or pamphlet
treatises.

The great influence of Benjamin Franklin, covering the
entire period of the revolutionary struggle, was exerted chiefly
through the customary channels of diplomacy, and in a
voluminous correspondence with friends and public men on
both sides of the Atlantic; and his contemporary publications,
comparatively few in number, carried weight because of their
directness and sturdy common sense, and of the fame of their
writer as a scientist or as the author of *Poor Richard's Almanac*
or as the skilful champion of the colonial cause in England,
rather than because of their literary merit or their substantive
contribution to the American argument. The report of his
Examination[2] before the House of Commons (1766), while the
repeal of the Stamp Act was under discussion, showed a states-

[1] See Book I, Chap. IX.   [2] *Writings*, ed. Smyth, IV, 412–448.

manlike knowledge of American conditions, and dexterity and boldness in defending the patriot cause. In January, 1768, he contributed to *The London Chronicle* an article entitled *Causes of the American Discontents before 1768*, and later in the year he wrote a short preface for a London reprint of Dickinson's *Letters from a Farmer*.

For the next five years Franklin was occupied with his duties as colonial agent of Massachusetts, Georgia, and other colonies. His writings during that period consist almost wholly of letters, and of articles on electricity and economic subjects. Then, in September, 1773, he attacked the colonial policy of Hillsborough in *Rules by which a Great Empire may be reduced to a Small One*, following this, early in 1774, with an article *On the Rise and Progress of the Differences between Great Britain and Her American Colonies*. The publication of the Hutchinson letters, although it brought official censure and cost Franklin the loss of a remunerative office, did not materially affect his reputation or weaken his influence; but a *Tract relative to the Affair of Hutchinson's Letters*, written in 1774, was, possibly from prudential reasons, not published.[1]

That persistent opposition to Parliament, whether through elaborated constitutional arguments or by such practical devices as commercial non-intercourse, might in the end raise the issue of independence, had early been perceived; and the earnest protestations of loyalty to the crown which are found in the resolutions of the Stamp Act Congress or the declaration and resolves of the First Continental Congress, if read chiefly in the light of subsequent events, do not seem entirely unequivocal. Not until late in 1775, however, after armed collisions had occurred at Lexington, Concord, and Bunker Hill, after Gage had been hopelessly besieged at Boston, and after a second Continental Congress, assuming the general direction of affairs, had begun the organization of a revolutionary government, appointed Washington commander-in-chief, and taken the first steps toward obtaining foreign aid, did the demand for independence, or even the disposition seriously to consider it, become general.

Of the writings which contributed immediately to the final break, the foremost place must be given to Thomas Paine's

[1] For Franklin, see also Book I, Chap. VI.

Common Sense (1776). Paine, after an unimportant and not wholly respectable career in England, came to America in 1774, in his thirty-eighth year, armed with introductions from Franklin, and settled at Philadelphia. His pamphlet *Common Sense*, published in January, 1776, seized the psychological moment. Brushing aside all legal and historical argument as no longer to the point, and resorting to the wildest exaggeration and misrepresentation for the purpose of discrediting England and its people, Paine laid his finger on the heart of the situation. The colonies had gone too far to turn back. They were already alienated. The British connection was no longer valuable to them, and reconciliation would be an evil rather than a good. Common sense dictated that they should be free. Enthusiastic acclaim from leaders and public, and a sale of over 100,000 copies within three months, attested the success and power of Paine's first essay in political pamphleteering.

Sweeping as Paine's success was, the course of events had nevertheless prepared the way. In February, 1775, Lord North had startled the House of Commons by introducing and passing a conciliatory resolution; but the offer, unsatisfactory less because of its terms than because of want of confidence in the ministry and the king, had been effectually prejudiced by the passage, in March and April, of bills restraining the trade of the colonies to Great Britain and the British West Indies, and by further provisions for the prosecution of the war. It was on the first of the restraining bills, that relating to New England, that Burke made his great speech on conciliation. In June came the battle of Bunker Hill and the appointment of Washington as commander-in-chief. On 6 July Congress adopted a *Declaration of the Causes and Necessity of Taking Up Arms*,[1] the joint work of Dickinson and Jefferson, and one of the greatest of the state papers of the Revolution. Still protesting that "we have not raised armies with ambitious designs of separating from Great Britain, and establishing independent states," the declaration reviewed, vigorously but with dignity, the course of recent events, protested in the name of liberty against a policy that would enslave the colonies, and proclaimed solemnly the intention of fighting until freedom was assured.

[1] Text in W. MacDonald, *Select Charters*, 374-381.

In our own native land, in defence of the freedom that is our birthright, and which we ever enjoyed till the late violation of it—for the protection of our property, acquired solely by the honest industry of our fore-fathers and ourselves, against violence actually offered, we have taken up arms. We shall lay them down when hostilities shall cease on the part of the aggressors, and all danger of their being renewed shall be removed, and not before.

Two days later (8 July) a last petition to the king once more protested loyalty and devotion, and prayed the interposition of the crown to bring about reconciliation. At the end of the month, however, in an elaborate report drawn by Jefferson, Lord North's offer of conciliation was emphatically, almost contemptuously, rejected. In August a royal proclamation declared the colonies in rebellion. Franklin, meantime, had quietly slipped out of England and returned to America, where he was at once elected to Congress. He had withstood to the last the encroachments of parliamentary authority in England, and was now to witness the passing of royal authority in America. With the rejection of petitions on the one side and of compromise on the other, Paine could well urge that the time had come to act.

For the writing of the Declaration of Independence (4 July, 1776) Jefferson had had some preparation, in a way, through two publications already favourably known to members of the Congress. In 1774 he had published at Williamsburg *A Summary View of the Rights of British America, Set Forth in Some Resolutions Intended for the Instruction of the Present Delegates of the People of Virginia now in Convention*, in which, with somewhat flamboyant boldness of phrase, he had offered to the king "the advice of your great American council," and had appealed to him to open his breast "to liberal and expanded thought," that the name of George the Third might not be "a blot in the page of history." In June, 1775, he had framed an *Address of the House of Burgesses*, on the subject of Lord North's conciliatory resolution, which was adopted by the house and served as the model for the report on the same resolution which was approved by the Congress in July. He had also, as we have seen, collaborated with Dickinson in the preparation of the *Declaration of the Causes and Necessity of Taking Up Arms*.

The real preparation, however, lay, not in Jefferson's training or skill as a writer, nor in the possession by him of extraordinary insight or prophetic vision, but in the succession of events for the fifteen years past and in the innumerable pamphlets and essays which those had called out. The conduct of the king, the ministry, and the Parliament, the history and necessities of the colonies, and the constitutional foundations of empire had all been repeatedly and ably examined by lawyers and publicists, and the findings set forth by accomplished writers, long before Jefferson was called upon to say the final word. Of all the criticisms that have been passed upon the *Declaration of Independence*, the least to the point is that it is not original. The material was at hand, the argument had been elaborated, the conclusions had been drawn. For originality there was as little opportunity as there was need. What was required now was a concise summing up of the whole matter, full enough to give a clear impression of completeness, vigorous and bold enough to serve as a national manifesto, and polished, dignified, and incisive enough to catch the ear, to linger in the memory, and to bear endless repetition. That Jefferson met this need with consummate success, working into one brief statement doctrine, accusation, argument, and declaration of freedom, was a demonstration that the hour and the man had met.

The period of active hostilities (1775–1781), which had already begun when the Declaration of Independence was adopted, was not characterized by literary activity. On the American side, at least, the case had been fully stated, and with the decision of the Congress to accept no terms of conciliation that did not recognize independence, there was no longer an English-speaking audience to which to appeal; while to France and Holland, whose aid was sought, the appeal was necessarily diplomatic rather than literary. With the recourse to arms, pamphleteers and essayists entered the army, or busied themselves with public service in Congress, state, or local community. Dickinson, who had drawn back when independence severed allegiance to the crown, nevertheless shouldered a musket. The loyalists were overawed or driven out, and their writings belong thereafter to the countries of their exile. Newspapers were few, paper was scarce, mails were infrequent and precarious, schools and colleges were interrupted or suspended altogether.

Of publication and writing of certain sorts, on the other hand, there was a considerable volume. The *Journal of the Continental Congress*, published from time to time, with the exception of such parts as were thought to require secrecy,[1] is an invaluable record of proceedings, although it contains no report of debates. Numerous reports, resolutions, and other state papers of importance were, however, printed separately in broadside or pamphlet form for the use of members of Congress or for wider distribution. The acts and resolutions of the state legislatures, so far as such bodies were able to meet, were also printed, together with occasional proclamations and other public documents.

The letters of American statesmen, particularly Washington, Franklin, John Adams, Samuel Adams, John Jay, and Patrick Henry, published long afterwards in collected editions, existed for the most part only in manuscript; but their quasi-public character, together with their circulation from hand to hand, often gave to them, to an extent much greater than would be the case today, though within limited circles, the essential character of publications. Larger audiences, but still local, were reached by sermons, many of which, especially those of the New England clergy, dealt much with the war and the political issues of the time. Comparatively few of these, however, were printed contemporaneously. Of great importance to an understanding of the revolutionary struggle are the journals and letter-books of soldiers and officers, both American and British, and the controversial narratives and defences of Burgoyne, Cornwallis, Clinton, and others regarding the conduct of military affairs; but few of these are predominantly political in character, almost none were printed in America at the time, and the publication of nearly all of those by American authors dates from years long subsequent to the war.

Of the war-time pamphlets, the most important are the series to which the author, Thomas Paine, gave the title of *The Crisis*. The first issue of the series had its origin in the gloom and despondency occasioned by Washington's famous

---

[1] The material in the *Secret Journals*, 4 vols., Boston, 1821, is included in the Ford and Hunt edition of the *Journals* (see Bibliography).

retreat across New Jersey, in the fall and early winter of 1776; a retreat which to many seemed to presage the speedy collapse of the American cause. On 18 December, Washington, irritated and alarmed at the rapid dwindling of his army under the operation of short-term enlistment, wrote to his brother:

Between you and me, I think our affairs are in a very bad situation; not so much from the apprehension of General Howe's army, as from the defection of New York, Jerseys, and Pennsylvania . . . In a word, my dear Sir, if every nerve is not strained to recruit the new army with all possible expedition, I think the game is pretty near up.

The next day there issued from the press the first number of *The Crisis*, with its ringing call:

These are the times that try men's souls. The summer soldier and the sunshine patriot will, in this crisis, shrink from the service of his country; but he that stands it now, deserves the love and thanks of man and woman. . . . Up and help us; lay your shoulders to the wheel; better have too much force than too little, when so great an object is at stake. . . . The heart that feels not now, is dead.

Sixteen of these stirring pamphlets, produced as the hopes and fears, the successes and failures of the war gave occasion, were issued down to the end of 1783, when the series ended.

With the surrender of Cornwallis (October, 1781), the active military and naval operations of the war practically ceased. Nearly two years were to elapse before the treaty of peace (September, 1783) formally recognized the independence of the United States; but independence had been achieved in fact, and the way was now open for the discussion of new political problems. A frame of government, the *Articles of Confederation*, had gone into effect in March, 1781; and when fighting ended, Congress and the country turned their attention to the pressing questions of finance, the development and administration of the West, the restoration of normal conditions in industry, commerce, and social life, and the perfection of the Federal union. It is not without significance that, among the statesmen whose defence of colonial rights had developed both the theory and the practice of revolution, there were many who were now to set the United States forward in the next stage of its career.

For the replacement of the Articles of Confederation by the "more perfect" union of the Federal Constitution, private correspondence, as in the case of the Revolution, did much to prepare the way. Jefferson and John Adams were absent from the country on diplomatic service, the former in France, the latter at the Court of St. James; and Franklin, prince of American diplomatists, was not, in the larger field of government, a constructive statesman. But Washington, Madison, Jay, Hamilton, Patrick Henry, and other leaders were busy with their pens, discussing with one another, particularly in the interval from 1785 to 1787, the defects of the Articles, the need of a firmer national organization, and the practical possibilities of united action. Prominent in this epistolary discussion were such questions as the protection and encouragement of American commerce, retaliation against England for its imperfect observance of the terms of peace, the adjustment of the opposing interests of large and small states, and the provision of an adequate revenue for the payment of the revolutionary debt and the maintenance of the Federal establishment.

In May, 1787, the Federal Convention met at Philadelphia. In anticipation of its deliberations, Madison set down his opinion as to the *Vices of the Political System of the United States*,[1] and prepared a summary view *Of Ancient and Modern Confederacies*.[2] The former noted most of the important points around which the debate later turned, but there is nothing in the Constitution to show that the latter had influence with the convention. The convention was preëminently a practical body. The sources of the Federal Constitution are in the government of England, the constitutions of the states, the Articles of Confederation, and the experience of the country and of Congress under the Articles. The *Journal* of the convention comprises only a bare record of proceedings, and does not report debates; the proceedings, moreover, were behind closed doors. For our knowledge of what was said, as distinguished from what was voted, we are dependent upon Madison's elaborate *Notes*, taken down at the time and corrected and

[1] *Writings*, ed. Hunt, II, 361–369.   [2] *Ibid.*, II, 369–390.

supplemented by the journal; some *Minutes* of Yates, a New York delegate; a *Report* by Luther Martin to the Maryland assembly[1]; and the letters, many of them still unpublished, of members of the convention. The elaborate publication of documents, debates, and reports which commonly attends a modern state constitutional convention was conspicuously lacking.

While the convention was in session, there was published at Boston, New York, and Philadelphia, in separate editions, the first volume of John Adams's *Defence of the Constitutions of Government of the United States of America.* This work, written and first published in London, was occasioned, the author states, by Turgot's sweeping attack upon the American theory of government, contained in a letter to Dr. Richard Price, in 1778, and published by Price in his *Observations on the Importance of the American Revolution, and the Means of Making it a Benefit to the World* (1785). Two additional volumes appeared in 1788.[2] The prominence of the author gave the work, especially the first volume, some vogue; but the disorderly arrangement, the verbose and careless style, the many glaring inaccuracies and inconsistencies due to hasty writing and negligent proof-reading, a political philosophy nowhere profound, and the characteristic temper of the advocate rather than of the expositor, did Adams no credit; while his frank criticisms of some features of American government opened the way for attacks upon his sincerity and loyalty which followed him throughout his life. To this disfavour the "worship of the Constitution" as a perfect instrument, which began soon after the successful establishment of the government under it, undoubtedly contributed.

With the adjournment of the Convention in September, and the submission of the Constitution to ratifying conventions in the states, the public became for the first time acquainted with the pending scheme of government; and the great debate on ratification began. The newspapers teemed with political essays, and pamphlets multiplied. The Constitution lacked neither friends nor foes. On the side of the Constitution were

[1] The foregoing are included in Elliott's *Debates* and Farrand's *Records of the Federal Convention* (see Bibliography).
[2] *Works,* IV, V.

James Sullivan of Massachusetts, with his eleven letters of *Cassius*; Oliver Ellsworth of Connecticut, with thirteen letters of *A Landholder;* Roger Sherman of the same state, who contributed five letters of *A Countryman* and two of *A Citizen of New Haven*; and John Dickinson, in his *Letters of Fabius*. The opposing views of the Anti-federalists were vigorously set forth by *Agrippa*, whose eighteen letters are probably to be ascribed to James Winthrop of Massachusetts; by George Clinton of New York, who published seven letters under the name of *Cato*; by Robert Yates, in two letters of *Sydney*; and in seven letters by Luther Martin.[1]

The pamphlet literature was equally important. Noah Webster, best known to later generations as a lexicographer, came to the support of the new instrument in *An Examination into the Leading Principles of the Federal Constitution;* as did John Jay, in *An Address to the People of the State of New York;* Pelatiah Webster of Philadelphia, in *The Weakness of Brutus Exposed*, a reply to the first of a series of sixteen essays ascribed to Thomas Treadwell of New York; Tench Coxe, in *An Examination of the Constitution*, written over the pseudonym of "An American Citizen"; and David Ramsay, in *An Address to the Freemen of South Carolina*. The opposition was represented by Elbridge Gerry's *Observations on the New Constitution;* Melanchthon Smith's *Address to the People of the State of New York*, and preëminently by Richard Henry Lee, in his *Observations leading to a Fair Examination of the System of Government proposed by the late Convention*, and by George Mason of Virginia, in his *Objections to the proposed Federal Constitution*, to the latter of whom James Iredell of North Carolina made an elaborate rejoinder.[2]

Incomparably superior, whether in content, or in form, or in permanent influence, to all the other political writing of the period are the eighty-five essays known collectively as *The Federalist*. The essays, the joint work of Hamilton, Madison, and Jay, appeared in the New York *Independent Journal* during the seven months beginning October, 1787. They had been preceded, and to a considerable extent called out, by a series of attacks upon the new Constitution contributed by Governor

[1] All the foregoing are reprinted in P. L. Ford, *Essays on the Constitution*.

[2] The foregoing are collected in P. L. Ford, *Pamphlets on the Constitution*.

George Clinton and Robert Yates to the New York *Journal,* over the pen-names of "Cato" and "Brutus" respectively. The authorship of a few of the essays has been an interesting problem of historical criticism, but four were the work of Jay, fourteen were certainly written by Madison, three are probably to be ascribed to Madison, nine are probably Hamilton's, three are the work of Hamilton and Madison jointly, and the remaining fifty-one are the work of Hamilton.[1] The plan was Hamilton's, moreover, and his influence undoubtedly dominated all the numbers of the series, whoever the particular author.

The papers of *The Federalist* are in part an account of the merits and defects of confederacies, and a discussion of the difficulties and advantages of union, and in part an examination of the weaknesses of the Articles of Confederation and a defence of the provisions of the proposed Constitution. Their actual influence upon the ratification of the Constitution in New York, which was the chief reason for writing them, has probably been overrated, nor are they free from partisan bias and the kind of popular argument likely to be effective in political debate. As the earliest contemporary exposition, in extended form, of the Constitution, however, they occupy a unique position. Written in the heat of controversy, and before the great structure of American constitutional law had even been begun, they forecast with extraordinary acuteness some of the most fundamental principles of constitutional interpretation which the federal courts were later to adopt, as well as some of the grave political issues on which party lines were to form. Judicial reference and quotation have given to *The Federalist* a weight of authority second only to that of the Constitution itself, and upon the authorship of the larger part of its pages the reputation of Hamilton as a publicist mainly rests.

[1] This follows the classification in Ford's edition.

CHAPTER IX

The Beginnings of Verse, 1610–1808

THE two centuries that cover the beginnings of American poetry may be divided into three periods. The first period is that of the early colonial verse which begins in 1610 with the publication of Rich's ballad on the settlement of Jamestown and ends with the seventeenth century. With 1700 begins the second period, which is one of transition in purpose, subject, and style. The third period, which is marked by the beginnings of nationalism, opens with the passage of the Stamp Act in 1765 and closes with the publication of Bryant's *Embargo* in 1808.

Even in the light of the unliterary conditions that prevailed in the Southern and Middle colonies it is surprising to find how little verse was produced south of New England before the middle of the eighteenth century. The Southern colonists were not of a literary class, and probably would have written little or nothing under any conditions; in the Southern colonies and, to a less degree, in the Middle colonies, conditions were distinctly unfavourable to literature; and in Virginia, especially, there were no schools, no printing presses, no literary centres, and few people who cared to write books or, apparently, to read them. Yet, though the New England of the seventeenth century left us many thousands of lines of verse of various kinds, as against the less than one thousand lines left by all the colonies to the south of that region, it was Virginia that produced what is perhaps the one real American poem of the seventeenth century. This is the epitaph on the insurrectionary leader Nathaniel Bacon, written "by his Man." The "Man" clearly was no menial but a reader and a poet. His brief elegy of forty-four lines is worthy of Ben

Jonson himself, and is indeed written in that great elegist's, dignified, direct, and manly style:

> In a word
> *Marss* and *Minerva*, both in him Concurd
> For arts, for arms, whose pen and sword alike
> As *Catos* did, may admireation strike
> In to his foes; while they confess with all
> It was their guilt stil'd him a Criminall.

Maryland has even less to show than Virginia. The rhyming tags of verse appended to the chapters of George Alsop's *Character of the Province of Maryland* (1666) cannot be taken seriously. The description of Maryland contained in the *Carmen Seculare* of a certain Mr. Lewis shows that Pope had not yet reached Baltimore in 1732, however at home he may have been in Boston and Philadelphia. Of the same type is a *True Relation of the Flourishing State of Pennsylvania* (1686), by John Holme, a resident of that colony. The *True Relation* is utilitarian in purpose and homely in style, but on the whole its five hundred lines in various metres, with their catalogues of native animals and plants in the manner of William Wood's verses in his *New England's Prospect*, are rather pleasing. New York produced practically no English verse until the Revolution; and the Carolinas and Georgia continued barren until near the close of the eighteenth century, when Charleston became something of a literary centre. But Pennsylvania came to be fairly prolific early in the transition period, and continued so for almost a century until New York and Boston, as literary centres, finally displaced Philadelphia.

The earliest New England verse was as utilitarian and matter-of-fact as any prose. Narratives of the voyages, annals of the colonies, descriptions of flora, fauna, and scenery, written in the main for readers in the mother country, were versified merely for the sake of the jingle. Altogether this descriptive and historical verse amounts to less than a thousand lines. *A Looking Glass for the Times* (1677), by Peter Folger of Nantucket, derives interest from the fact that it was written by the maternal grandfather of Benjamin Franklin. Its four hundred lines in ballad quatrains are very bad verse, however, and, though it has been termed "A manly plea for toleration in an age of intolerance," there is still question as to whether it was actually published in the author's lifetime and, consequently, whether Folger ran any risk.   The most important piece of historical verse in this period was the work of the first native-born American poet, Benjamin Tompson (1644–1714), who, as his tombstone at Roxbury informs us, was a "learned schoolmaster and physician and the renowned poet of New England," and is "mortuus sed immortalis."   His chief production, *New England's Crises*, is a formal attempt at an epic on King Philip's War.   The prologue pictures early society in New England and recounts the decadence in manners and morals that has brought about the crisis,—the war as God's punishment.   The six hundred and fifty lines of pentameter couplets are somewhat more polished than those of the poet's contemporaries, and might suggest the influence of Dryden if there were any external reason for supposing that the Restoration poets gained admission to early New England.   Tompson's classical allusions, part of his epic attempt, are in amusing contrast to his rugged and homely diction, but his poem as a whole has at least the virtue of simplicity, and is interesting as the first of a long line of narratives in verse which recount the events of the wars fought on American soil.

A Brief Account of the Agency of the Honorable John Winthrop [in obtaining a charter for Connecticut], though not published until 1725, belongs in purpose and style to the seventeenth century.   The author, Roger Wolcott, afterwards governor of Connecticut, was little more of a poet than Governor Bradford, but his literary pretensions ally him with Benjamin Tompson.   His couplets are rugged and his diction prosaic, in the main, but the heroic style of the battle scenes and the lofty similes employed by the hero as he recounts to Charles II the settlement and the history of the Colony, show that Wolcott too was consciously attempting an epic.   His poem is a link between the unliterary historical and descriptive verse of early New England and the more pretentious epics that appeared so abundantly during the latter half of the eighteenth century.

The most characteristic poetic products of early New England are the memorial poems.   Subsequent generations have made merry over their matter and style, and indeed little can be said in their favour if they are to be taken as an index to the poetic taste of the time and not simply as conventional tributes to the dead. If, however, the New England elegy is to be judged on its literary merits, we should remember that it was not an isolated type, unique in the poverty of its matter and style, but that it simply reflected its English origin and was closely related to its English counterparts. Unlike the English, though, the writers of New England did not evolve a better style of their own, the elegies at the close of the century being, if anything, worse than those at the beginning. Perhaps Quarles was chiefly responsible for their pentameter couplets, rough with run-on lines and imperfect rhymes. Despite occasional variety of form in six-line stanza or quatrain, there is little variety of tone or style; and in all these thousands of lines scarcely a line of genuine poetry, or a single poem worth preservation in its entirety.

The succession of these elegies is surprisingly unbroken for at least forty years. Both authors and subjects are in the main the divines who controlled the destinies of New England and who provided its literature. When such an elegy as that on the Rev. Thomas Shepard by the Rev. Urian Oakes, president of Harvard, is discovered amid this dreary elegiac waste, its merits are sure to be exaggerated. This poem in fifty six-line stanzas, though commonplace in thought and style, is not without pathos, and gives an impression of sincerity. But the Rev. Urian Oakes himself was not so fortunate in his elegist, no less a person than the Rev. Cotton Mather, the most prolific elegist of his time. His elegy on Oakes reaches a length of over four hundred lines. To adorn his subject he "ransacks the ages, spoils the climes"; his pentameters and his quatrains are mere doggerel, his rhymes are atrocious, and his lines rife with conceits and puns and classical and biblical allusions. John Cleveland at his best could do no worse. The real feeling that probably inspired Mather's writing is obscured by the laboured insincerity of his style. But the nadir is reached by the Rev. Nicholas Noyes (1647–1717), who in his elegies on the Rev. John Higginson and the Rev. Joseph Green shows promising possibilities of bathos, but who in his poem on the Rev. James Brayley's attack of the stone revels in such a plethora of conceits and puns as to put to the blush his most gifted English contemporaries. The one elegiac poem of early New England that may be worth preserving is the *Funeral Song* (1709), written by the Rev. Samuel Wigglesworth, son of Michael, on the death of his friend Nathaniel Clarke. Together with its real feeling, it exhibits a certain felicity of diction that bespeaks Elizabethan models; and such phrases as "where increate eternity's concealed," "solemn music," and "warbling divinest airs," seem to show that Milton had reached New England. As a genre the elegy died with the decline of the clergy, and passed as a fashion passes with changed conditions.

The most interesting as well as the most pleasing figure in early New England verse is that of Anne Bradstreet, who was "fathered and husbanded" respectively by Thomas Dudley and Simon Bradstreet, both in their time governors of Massachusetts. Born in London in 1612, she emigrated in 1630 with her husband and died in 1672. Although the mother of eight children, she found time to write over seven thousand lines of verse in what must have been, to her, peculiarly uncongenial surroundings. Her brother-in-law, the Rev. John Woodbridge, when on a visit to London in 1650, published without her knowledge her poems under the title of *The Tenth Muse, Lately Sprung Up in America*, and a second edition followed in Boston in 1678. That her poems were read and admired is attested by such poetic tributes as that of Nathaniel Ward, who affirms that she was "a right Du Bartas girle," and represents Apollo as unable to decide whether Du Bartas or the New England Muse was the more excellent poet. But Anne Bradstreet was not a poet; she was a winsome personality in an unlovely age. That she should have written verse at all was phenomenal, but that it should have been poor verse was inevitable. Her *Exact Epitome of the Four Monarchies*, in several thousand lines of bad pentameter couplets, is simply a rhyming chronicle of the medieval type, the matter of which was supplied by Raleigh's *History of the World*. Her *Four Elements, Constitutions, Ages of Man, and Seasons of the Year*, almost equally worthless as poetry, is an interesting adaptation of Sylvester's translation of the *Divine Weeks*. She repeatedly states her admiration for Du Bartas and her indebtedness to him. Thirteen lines in the second day of the first week of his poem suggested her theme, and this she expands in the form of a medieval *debat*; other

passages from Du Bartas she condenses, expands, or merely
paraphrases. She gives only about 1800 lines to the entire
exposition of her elements, humours, ages, and seasons; hence
she uses but a small part of the encyclopædic material of the
French poem. The feeble New England imitation cannot
compare with the original. Du Bartas, though often flat and
prosaic, is immense in his range, and is at times even a poet;
Anne Bradstreet's range is narrow; her allusions are merely to
the best known historical and mythological characters; her
descriptions of natural phenomena, though she might be expected to find original inspiration in her New England environment, are vague and conventional. In occasional lines of
Sylvester's translation occurs something of Elizabethan
spaciousness; the only meritorious lines of Anne Bradstreet's
poem occur in the *Spring;*

> The fearfull bird his little house now builds
> In trees and walls, in Cities and in fields.
> The outside strong, the inside warm and neat,
> A natural Artificer compleat.

The verse of all her longer poems is precisely that of Sylvester—
a couplet, not quite loose, but less compact than the heroic
couplet, with the characteristic Elizabethan freedom in rhyme
and with the shifting caesura. It is not, however, in these long,
dreary, and purely didactic poems that Anne Bradstreet shows
her real capacity. When she walks in happier paths, with a
song in her heart, remembering Spenser and Giles Fletcher, she
shows that perhaps in more fortunate times she might have
written poetry. Her *Contemplations* is a meditative and descriptive poem in thirty-three seven-line stanzas, in which occur
passages at least pleasing in suggestion and rhythm, however
reminiscent of greater times and talents:

> When I behold the heavens as in their prime,
> And then the earth (though old) stil clad in green,
> The stones and trees, insensible to time,
> Nor age nor wrinkle on their front are seen;
> If winter come, and greeness then do fade,
> A Spring returns, and they more youthfull made;
> But Man grows old, lies down, remains where once he's laid.

Her lines to her husband, though not great poetry, are perhaps the most sincere, and are certainly the most human and touching she ever wrote; and her poem on the rearing of her eight children, while infelicitous in its barnyard metaphor, presents a happy and lovable picture.   So lovely and pathetic is the figure of the woman herself, and so remarkable are her achievements in the light of her environment, that one finds it ungracious to speak harshly of her verse.

It is rather remarkable that so little purely religious verse was produced in early New England.   Quarles, himself a Puritan, was prolific in hymns, divine songs, and paraphrases from the Bible.   New England boasted a distinct literary class, not unfamiliar with great religious poetry; but its one biblical paraphrase and its one effort at writing religious song was *The Bay Psalm Book*.   To meet the need for divine songs to sing in the churches, Richard Mather, Thomas Welde, and John Eliot supervised the preparation of a new metrical version of the Psalms.   *The Bay Psalm Book*, as it came to be called, was the first book published on American soil, and passed through twenty-seven editions between 1640 and 1752, when it was superseded by John Barnard's *New Version of the Psalms of David*. It surpasses even Sternhold and Hopkins in uncouthness, and as a monument of bad taste has furnished an easy target for the ridicule of subsequent and less devout generations. It is unfair, however, to take *The Bay Psalm Book* as an index to the poetic taste of its period, or its subsequent popularity as indicating anything more than its usefulness.   It was a makeshift, and they knew it was a poor one; an edition "revised and refined" by John Dunster and Richard Lyon followed in 1647.   If these were "refined," then, as Timothy Dwight remarks, "a modern reader would almost instinctively ask, 'What were they before?'"

We still possess in its original crudity the "epic of New England puritanism," *The Day of Doom; or, a Poetical Description of the Great and Last Judgment*.   This was the masterpiece of the Rev. Michael Wigglesworth (1631–1705), who was born in England, but emigrated to America, and graduated from Harvard at the age of twenty.   He was a physician as well as a theologian and a poet, amiable and humane in character, and greatly beloved.   The most widely read and perhaps the most representative poet of early New England, he was also, with the exception of Anne Bradstreet, the most prolific. In both subject-matter and style he is only too representative of his times. His *Day of Doom*, first published in 1662, versifies the scriptural passages concerning the last judgment, and adds to these a statement of the Calvinistic dogmas of eternal punishment. Its two hundred eight-line stanzas tell a story which still entertains the reader, even if it has lost its power to terrify. Relatively, no poem was ever more popular; the first edition of eighteen hundred copies was sold within a year; within the century after, ten subsequent editions were published; and its final passing was coincident only with the passing of the theology that gave it birth and rendered it tolerable. The opening stanzas of the poem show some imagination and power of description; but these are borrowed plumes; all that is good in *The Day of Doom* comes from the Bible. Wigglesworth had no real poetry in him; at no period and under no conditions would he have been a poet. His *God's Controversy with New England*, inspired by the great drought of 1662, deserves no consideration as poetry; but the poem that followed in 1669 is of greater interest. This is *Meat out of the Eater; or, Meditations concerning the Necessity, End, and Usefulness of Affliction unto God's Children*, a theological treatise in rhyme, over two thousand lines in length, in various metres and divided into many different sections. The reflections, with their references to biblical prototypes, the quaint and often fantastic style, point to Quarles's *Emblems* as their inspiration. Though even less poetic than *The Day of Doom*, the poem contains the only two good lines that Wigglesworth ever wrote:

> War ends in peace, and morning light
> Mounts upon Midnight's wing.

In his *Vanity of Vanities*, which was appended to the third edition of *The Day of Doom* in 1673, certain rather polished heroic quatrains suggest Davenant or Dryden as possible models. But, as Wigglesworth's library contained not one volume of English poetry, the poet must have found his model outside of his library; it is beyond belief that either he or any

other New England versifier of his period could have originated or even improved any form of verse.

The years between the close of the seventeenth century and
the passage of the Stamp Act in 1765 form a transition period
in the development of American verse. It is interesting
to note that the passing of the old century coincided almost
exactly with the passing of the old models. About 1700
new literary influences came from England; the old forms of
verse were discarded for others more polished; Quarles and
Sylvester gave way, first to Waller, then to Pope. But the
change was not one of form alone. The decline of clerical
influence, the increase of security and comfort in the conditions
of life, the more frequent intercourse with England—all these
and other changes were reflected also in the subject-matter,
the purpose, and the spirit of the new verse.
New England poets before 1700 learned nothing from the
English poets of the latter half of the seventeenth century;
for New England seems to have placed all the literature of
the Restoration period under a rigorous embargo. There is
no sufficient evidence that Dryden was known in America
before 1700, in spite of some fairly regular quatrains by Michael
Wigglesworth and an occasional polished couplet by Cotton
Mather and Benjamin Tompson. If they knew even Milton
they perhaps saw in him only the champion of divorce and of
other heresies. But there are other and obvious reasons for this
ignorance or neglect of Dryden and Milton. Although John
Cotton had some correspondence with Quarles, there was
not much literary communication of any kind between the
colonies and England before the eighteenth century. New
England was complete in itself.
Dr. Benjamin Colman (1673-1747), upon his return from
England in 1699, brought with him both Blackmore and Waller.
This decisive event in the history of American verse marked
the beginning of a new era, that of the heroic couplet. But
though Colman praises Waller and Blackmore and recom-
mends both to his daughter Jane Turell, he himself, when he
wrote his *Elijah's Translation* (1707) on the death of the Rev.
Samuel Willard, imitated Dryden in his heroic couplets and
his method of applying a Bible story as in *Absalom and Achito-*

phel. Jane Turell (1708-1735), whose literary tastes were formed by her father, admired the "Matchless Orinda," Blackmore, and Waller; but she wrote the couplet of Pope. Another and even earlier evidence of the influence of Pope is a poem by Francis Knapp, who was born in England in 1672, and at an uncertain date emigrated to America and settled as a country gentleman near Boston. In 1715 he addressed a poetical epistle to Pope beginning

> Hail! sacred bard! a muse unknown before
> Salutes thee from the bleak Atlantic shore,

which was included among the prefatory poems in a subsequent edition of Windsor Forest (first published in 1713). Thus promptly Pope crossed the Atlantic to begin his undisputed reign of almost a century. Knapp's heroic poem *Cloria Brittannorum* (1723), an obvious imitation of Addison's *Campaign*, celebrates "The most illustrious persons in camp and cabinet since the glorious revolution to the recent time," and is perhaps the earliest example of the patriotic narrative poem that was to become so common in American after the Revolution.

But a far more distinguished exponent of the style of Pope was the Rev. Mather Byles. "To let you see a little of the reputation which you bear in these unknown climates—I transmit to you the enclosed poems," Byles wrote to Pope in 1727. It was perhaps these poems that Byles published in a volume in 1736, and which were published anonymously in the somewhat celebrated volume of 1744, *Poems by Several Hands*. Mather Byles is a more eminent figure in the annals of American poetry than is at all warranted by his poems, which are few and altogether imitative. His reputation is due in part to the general poverty of the transition period—the barest era in our verse—and in part to his fame as a preacher and a wit. He was born in 1707, was educated at Harvard, and served as pastor of the Hollis Street church in Boston through the greater part of his ministerial life. After the Declaration, he became a staunch and vehement Tory, lost his former popularity, and died embittered and broken in 1788. He corresponded with Lansdowne, Pope, and Watts, took himself seriously as a poet, at least in his younger days; and in his attention to contemporary English literature and his setting up of something approaching an æsthetic standard in verse, represents a definite change from the point of view of the generation before him. But the Puritan is still at work in him, however modern may be his style. His most ambitious poem, *The Conflagration*, a description of the physical phenomena of the last day, and a shorter poem, *The Comet*, are both in the spirit of Wigglesworth, for all their heroic couplets and artificial diction. His elegies are unadulterated Pope; and his hymns are in imitation of Watts.

One of the first volumes of miscellaneous verse published in America was the *Poems by Several Hands* (Boston, 1744). All the poems are anonymous; and aside from humorous ballads probably by Joseph Green, they merely echo Pope, with a plethora of "amorous swains" and "blushing charms." Some were certainly written by Byles, and others are tributes to his genius. Indeed, the purpose of the volume was to extol Byles as a poet worthy to be mentioned with Homer and with his only modern rival, Pope. Already America was looking for its Homer, a search that was to continue with increasing assiduity throughout the century—and Boston found him in Byles.

More original and interesting than the poems of Byles are the humorous verses of his friend Joseph Green (1706–1780), a Boston distiller possessed of literary tastes, who ranked with Byles as a wit and social favourite. After the outbreak of the Revolution he too became a Tory, and finally found refuge in London, where he died. Though his poems seem to have been written for his own amusement and that of his friends, they are important as the first attempt to lighten the heavy Puritanism of early New England with some leaven of humour and wit. *An Entertainment for a Winter's Evening* is perhaps the earliest piece of Hudibrastic verse written in America. We have travelled far from Puritan New England when a Bostonian can find amusement in the godless spectacle of a drunken parson and his tipsy companions, and can edify his fellow townsmen with a burlesque account of their nocturnal adventures.

Associated with Byles and Green in *Poems by Several Hands* was the Rev. John Adams, a young clergyman of Boston who died in 1740 at the age of thirty-five. Five years after his death his friends published his *Poems on Several Occasions;*

Original and Translated, which contains among other pieces paraphrases from the Bible, translations from Horace, and half a dozen elegies, including one on Cotton Mather and one on Jane Turell. All these are written in the heroic couplet but in a diction more natural than Pope's. That Adams knew Milton's poems is apparent in his *Address to the Supreme Being*. Indeed these poems, though pervaded by the Puritan spirit, yet reveal a more purely æsthetic purpose and a more careful style than can generally be found before the later years of the century.

The almanacs of Nathaniel Ames, father and son, of Dedham, Massachusetts, had their part in disseminating throughout New England a knowledge of the English poets and perhaps also in fostering a taste for humorous poetry. The brief passages from Dryden, Pope, and James Thomson (yes, and Blackmore!), prefixed to the astronomical data, and the unpretentious humorous verses scattered through the other matter, were far more widely read than the laboured and ambitious poems of the literary group in Boston. An *Essay upon the Microscope* is an elaborate poem, by the elder Ames, which, if not poetic, is interesting as perhaps our first ode in irregular verse.

Boston was not the only literary centre of this transition period. Franklin tells us in his *Autobiography* that when he first entered the printing office of Samuel Keimer in Philadelphia in 1723, he found the printer laboriously composing in type an elegy on Aquila Rose, a young poet who had just died in that city—perhaps the worst elegy ever written. The poet elegized died in 1723 at the age of twenty-eight. Within the few years preceding his death he wrote the slight occasional poems in heroic couplets that were in 1740 published in a volume by his son. Probably at no time would Aquila Rose have been a poet, but his verses were quite the best that Philadelphia had yet produced, and were to remain so until Thomas Godfrey surpassed them a generation later. Furthermore, they show that the new influences from England had reached Philadelphia as well as Boston. George Webb, a member of Franklin's "Junto," wrote *Batchelors' Hall* in defence of the life led by himself and other young bachelors at their club near the city. Unconventional as that life may have been, Webb's heroic

couplets are as conventional as could be desired, and, together
with the verses written by other members of his circle, they recall
the dominant hand of Pope.   Intrinsically unimportant as was
all the verse written in Philadelphia in this early period, it must
have done its work in creating a literary atmosphere and in
establishing traditions; for this city remained throughout the
entire century the centre both for the writing and the publishing
of American poetry.

During the whole of the eighteenth century the long poem,
didactic, descriptive, and philosophic, flourished in England,
and during the latter half of the same century its imitative
progeny flourished in America.   There could be no justification
for cataloguing these imitative efforts, since not one of them
still lives in our literature, and very few of them show any
distinctive American traits.   In the main, their method, their
ideas, their imagery are as English as those of their prototypes;
their heroic couplet is that of Pope or Goldsmith; their blank
verse is that of Thomson or Young.

The tide set in with imitations of Pomfret, whose *Choice*
(1700) appeared in at least four editions in America between
1751 and 1792.   In 1747 William Livingston, who was to become
the famous governor of New Jersey, expressed his ideal of existence in a direct imitation of Pomfret which he called *Philosophic Solitude, or the Choice of a Rural Life*.   Ten years later a
second imitation of Pomfret followed in *The Choice* by Dr.
Benjamin Church of Boston, who longs for a home in the
country, the right kind of wife, congenial friends, and leisure
to read his favourite poets—Milton, Dryden, Gay, "awful
Pope, unequalled bard," and "nature-limning Thomson."
Though dwelling in a small American town, he sighs for solitude as longingly as he might have done in the midst of a world
capital.   Livingston and Church are half a century late in their
sporadic imitations; and for a while Americans were simply
catching up with almost a hundred years of English didactic
poetry; but after the tide once turned, about the middle of the
century, imitation was much more prompt and general and,
after the Revolution, immediate and universal.

Goldsmith reached Americans almost at once, and appeared
in nine editions between 1768 and 1791. His numerous
imitators are all alike in using his method, his style, and

even his very subject-matter. Among imitations of *The Deserted Village* may be mentioned Thomas Coombe's *Peasant of Auburn* (1775), which contains lines fine enough to save it from oblivion. Imitations of Thomson's *Seasons* began to appear soon after the first American edition was published in 1777, increased in number with the five successive editions up to 1792, and continued through at least the first decade of the nineteenth century. To read one of these is to know all, with their very fair verse, and their conventional and generalized descriptions of scenery that might as well be English as American. It is interesting to note, however, that the native element in our descriptive verse grows more pronounced in the decade preceding the first work of Bryant. The form is still that of Thomson, but the poet has at last opened his eyes to the distinctive beauty of American nature. In his *Descriptive Poems* (1802) John D. McKinnon wrote of the Hudson and the Mohawk Rivers and our own October landscape, as well as of

> th' illimitable plain
> Depastured by erratic buffaloes;

and some "Untaught Bard," writing under the influence of both Thomson and Young, in his *Spring* clearly foretells the coming of *Thanatopsis*. John Hayes, professor at Dickinson College, in the 2500 lines of blank verse of his *Rural Poems* (1807) celebrates American birds and flowers in spite of his imitation of Milton and Thomson. Still more interesting in this respect is *The Foresters* (1804) of the ornithologist Alexander Wilson, a poem in 2200 lines of heroic couplets which tell the story of a journey through New York and Pennsylvania to Niagara Falls. Wilson is a scientist rather than a poet, but he sees nature sympathetically and gives what he sees in a simple and direct style. At last the poet writes with his eye on American nature and not on conventional descriptions by English poets.

The one poem that sums up all the direct imitations of Goldsmith, and Thomson, and of Denham, Milton, Pope, and Beattie as well, is *Greenfield Hill*. Timothy Dwight (1752–1817), a grandson of Jonathan Edwards, at the age of nineteen graduated from Yale, where he then became a tutor. In 1777–1778 he served as chaplain in the army, and varied his duties by

writing patriotic songs for the soldiers. In 1783 he became
pastor of the church at Greenfield, Connecticut, and in 1795 was
made president of Yale. He was the first of our great college
presidents, and as theologian, scholar, patriot, and writer was
one of the eminent personalities of his time. As a poet he
belongs to a group of writers who during the last two decades
of the eighteenth century formed a literary centre at New
Haven and Hartford. The chief "Hartford Wits" were
Timothy Dwight, John Trumbull, Joel Barlow, David Humphreys, Richard Alsop, Lemuel Hopkins, and Theodore Dwight, a
brother of Timothy, all either graduates of Yale or associated
with that college. Their contemporary reputation was
immense. Dwight, Barlow, and Humphreys, indeed, were
practical men of affairs, and all were more or less versatile.
But the reading public looked upon them as geniuses; and
Freneau was the only poet aside from the Hartford group who
was ever mentioned in connection with them. Yet even as
they were issuing their declaration of literary independence,
they were in every line betraying their dependence upon
English poetic style, ideas, and imagery. Their more ambitious and laboured poems, including almost all those by Dwight,
Barlow, and Humphreys, are to the modern reader the least
successful. Their best work, which they themselves and
the public took less seriously, is in the form of satire, and was
mainly written, singly or in collaboration, by Trumbull, Theodore Dwight, Alsop, and Hopkins. Yet the work of the
"Hartford Wits" in fostering poetry in a period of political
and social struggle and change deserves grateful recognition
from the student of American literature.

Timothy Dwight's *Greenfield Hill* is a medley of echoes.
The poet stands upon a hill in his Connecticut parish, and, like
his English predecessors, describes the view, paints the social
conditions of the country, recounts its history, and prophesies
its future. The 4300 lines of the poem are divided into seven
parts, written variously in heroic couplet, Spenserian stanza,
blank verse, and octosyllabics. The poet's desire "to contribute to the innocent amusement of his countrymen and to
their improvement in manners and in economic, political, and
moral sentiments" results in a history, guide-book, and treatise
on manners, morals, and government, but not in a poem. To

say that *Greenfield Hill* is made to order and is inspired by morality and patriotism, is to state the genesis of all the serious work of the Hartford group.

Outrageously long poems on æsthetic subjects were rife in America toward the close of the century. At a time when society and politics were in a state of upheaval, when neither the domestic nor the foreign policy of the country had been settled, and when consequently there was so much of native interest to write about, it is incongruous to find so many poems suggested by Akenside's *Pleasures of the Imagination* and Brooke's *Universal Beauty*. Richard Alsop's *Charms of Fancy* in all its 2300 lines of heroic couplets contains not a fresh image or an original idea; but *The Powers of Genius* by John Blair Linn is at least the work of a man of taste and scholarship and compares favourably with all but the very best of its British counterparts. The extreme of dulness and futility is reached in the many poems on philosophy and religion for which Pope and Young were largely responsible. Somewhat stronger and more interesting than most of these is Timothy Dwight's *Triumph of Infidelity*, which purports to be a satire, and which with irony and abuse rather than logic attempts to refute the arguments of the eighteenth century "infidels," Voltaire included. Biblical paraphrases, too, multiplied after the Revolution, and appeared in large numbers between 1780 and 1810. These are supplemented by epics on biblical themes, the most celebrated of which is again the work of the indefatigable Timothy Dwight, written by the time he was twenty-two, but published when he was thirty-three and should have known better. *The Conquest of Canaan* (1785), in ten thousand lines of heroic couplets, owes its style to Pope's Homer and much of its method and imagery to Virgil and Milton. The epic as a whole is what might be expected when the poet's purpose is "to represent such manners as are removed from the peculiarities of any age or country, and might belong to the amiable and virtuous of any period, elevated without design, refined without ceremony, elegant without fashion, and agreeable because they are ornamented with sincerity, dignity, and religion." Into the heroic biblical narrative are woven the loves of Irad and Selima and of Iram and Mira, who take their evening strolls through the lanes and meadows of Connecticut. Though intolerably verbose, the poem contains purple passages which lift it to the level of the average eighteenth-century epic and which perhaps led Cowper to review it favourably. With a noble disregard of congruity, *The Conquest of Canaan* is, withal, distinctly patriotic, with its union of "Canaan and Connecticut" and its allusions to contemporary persons and events.

The third period of early American verse, which begins with 1765 and ends with 1808, is characterized by two remarkably coincident phenomena, one political, the other æsthetic. One of these is the beginning of the nationalism that produced our early patriotic poems and satires, and is marked by the passage of the Stamp Act. The other, also beginning about 1765, is the wholesale importation and reprinting of English poetry which worked with the growth of native culture to produce a great quantity of verse all more or less imitative of English models and largely independent of political conditions. All the poems of this period, whether springing from political or from purely æsthetic influences, are most conveniently treated under their various genres without regard to individual writers, though one poet, Philip Freneau, demands separate consideration.

The first ballad springing from American soil recounts a battle fought in 1725 between whites and Indians near Love-well's Pond in Maine. Composed at the time of the event, it was for generations preserved only by word of mouth, and was not published for almost a century. Though unliterary, it tells its story with vigour and directness, and is of additional interest in that Longfellow in 1820 chose the same fight as the subject of his first poem, *The Battle of Lovell's Pond*.

Many fugitive verses on the French and Indian War[1] were published anonymously in the newspapers, the best of which are perhaps *The Song of Braddock's Men*, and the lines on Wolfe—

Thy merits, Wolfe, transcend all human praise.

Anti-British ballads began to appear immediately upon the

[1] The French and Indian War gave birth to a curious volume of *Miscellaneous Poems on Divers Occasions, Chiefly to Animate and Rouse the Soldiers* (1756), by Stephen Tilden, which, in spite of its wretched verse, is of some interest as the first of its kind in America.

passage of the Stamp Act, to continue until the close of the Revolution. These spring from the heat of the conflict, and are as replete with patriotism as they are deficient in literary merit. Yet they admirably fulfilled their purpose of arousing public spirit, and many of them were known and sung everywhere. John Dickinson's *Patriot's Appeal*, which begins

> Then join hand in hand, brave Americans all,
> By uniting we stand, by dividing we fall,

gave rise to a parody which was in turn parodied in the famous *Massachusetts Liberty Song*. Almost equally popular were John Mason's *Liberty's Call*, Thomas Paine's *Liberty Tree*, and Timothy Dwight's *Columbia*, with its refrain

> Columbia, Columbia, to glory arise,
> The queen of the world and the child of the skies.

But the one ballad that shows a spark of poetry is *Nathan Hale*, which commemorates the capture and death of the young American spy. It opens with a promise that is scarcely sustained throughout the poem:

> The breezes went steadily thro the tall pines,
>   A saying "Oh! hu-sh," a saying "Oh! hu-sh,"
> As stilly stole by a bold legion of horse,
>   For Hale in the bush, for Hale in the bush.

Best known of the purely humorous ballads is Francis Hopkinson's *Battle of the Kegs* (1778), which tells of the alarm felt by the British over some kegs that the Americans had charged with powder and had set floating in the Delaware River.

The hundreds of patriotic ballads, songs, and odes that appeared after the Revolution, though more ambitious and "literary," seem less spontaneous and sincere than the earlier verse, which called a nation to arms; and for all their flaunting of the stars and stripes, they leave the reader cold. Scarcely a poet who wrote between 1780 and 1807 failed to compose at least one such poem; but, it is safe to say, the only patriotic ballads of permanent merit written between 1725 and 1807 are the sea poems of Freneau.

The longer American patriotic poems of the later eighteenth century may take the form of narratives of battle, of personal eulogies, or, perhaps most characteristically, of philosophic statements of what today is called "Americanism." They increase in number toward the close of the century, when the air was full of American principles and ideals, and finally, in spite of their imitative style, they become in spirit at least a distinctive product without exact parallel in England. The best of them express a national aspiration that can still appeal to the patriotic reader. There is little of all this, however, in the early outbursts evoked by the French and Indian War when the poets were generally loyal to Great Britain. On the accession of George the Third in 1761 the faculty and graduates of Harvard published a curious volume of congratulatory poems entitled *Pietas et Gratulatio Collegii Cantabrigiensis Apud Nov-Anglos*. The volume of one hundred and six pages includes thirty-one poems, three of which are in Greek, sixteen in Latin, and twelve in English. The poems in English are in the form of irregular odes or heroic couplets stilted and commonplace in subject and style. The modern reader may find amusement in such loyal lines as

> Bourbons to humble, Brunswicks were ordained:
> Those mankind's rights destroyed, but these regained.

But the patriotic poem was soon to transfer its allegiance. A truly remarkable quantity of narrative verse tells the story of the Revolution and celebrates its civil and military leaders. Almost everyone who wrote verse in America after the Revolution produced an ode or an epic to vindicate his patriotism. Literature was now democratic; nothing was needed but inspiration, and the air was full of that. Far above the average is the rather fine *Eulogium on Major-General Joseph Warren*, written by "A Columbian"; but the vast majority of these historic and eulogistic narratives serve but to exemplify the heights of patriotism and the depths of bathos. The elaborate and laboured elegies on Washington are as numerous and as futile as might be expected. The finest eulogy on Washington was written prior to his death by Dr. Benjamin Young Prime in a pindaric ode of 1400 lines entitled *Columbia's Glory, or*

British Pride Humbled, which, in spite of its conventional form and style and lack of imagination, contains passages of admirable rhetoric.

Closely related to the narratives and eulogies are the many and lengthy poems belonging to the philosophic and didactic "glory of America" type, of which Freneau seems to have been the originator. The most prolific poet of this school was Colonel David Humphreys (1753–1818), who graduated from Yale in 1771, served as aide-de-camp to Washington, and became a frequent guest at Mount Vernon. He was associated with the Hartford Wits after 1786; served as minister to Portugal in 1791, and as minister to Spain from 1797 to 1802. A versatile man like others of the Hartford group, he was not only soldier, diplomat, and poet, but also an experimenter in sheep-raising and wool-manufacture. His six patriotic poems vary in length from four hundred to one thousand lines of heroic couplets. "Every poet who aspires to celebrity strives to approach the perfection of Pope and the sweetness of his versification," says Humphreys. All his patriotic poems are the work of an experienced versifier with full command of his subject and with little poetic inspiration. The *Poem on the Happiness of America* celebrates liberty and democracy, American scenery, resources, achievements, and prospects, with a boundless belief in the possibilities of America and her divine mission.

No other member of the Hartford group, indeed no other man of letters of his time, lived a life so active and varied as Joel Barlow (1754–1812). After his graduation from Yale, he served as chaplain in the army, and in 1781 married and settled in Hartford as lawyer and editor. His philosophic poem *The Vision of Columbus*, published in 1787, was read and admired in France and England. Barlow later went to France as agent of the notorious Scioto Land Company, apparently in ignorance of its fraudulent character. In Paris he became a strong partisan of democracy, and for several years divided his time between France and England, writing political pamphlets and books, and making a fortune through commerce and speculation. While resident in Savoy in 1792, he wrote what is certainly his most original and enduring poem and also one of the best pieces of humorous verse in our early literature.

Hasty Pudding is a mock-heroic of the conventional eighteenth-century type, in four hundred lines of heroic couplets. Its three cantos describe the making of the famous New England dish, the eating of it, and the traits that render it delectable and worthy of eulogy. The pastoral scenes are native, not imitated, the diction is simple and natural, and the humour, though rather thin, is sufficiently amusing. Barlow rendered valuable service to his native land in 1795, when he went to Algiers and secured the release of American prisoners; and again in 1798 when he helped to avert war between France and America. He returned home in 1805, and two years later published his *Columbiad*. He again served his country well in 1811, when he was sent by President Madison as an envoy to Europe; but in journeying to meet Napoleon he was caught in the retreat from Moscow, and died and was buried in Poland. Though democrats in America celebrated his memory, he perhaps has never had justice done him as a patriot and typical American.

When *The Vision of Columbus* was published in 1787 it suited the taste of the time, and its author was hailed as a genius, not only by his fellow Hartford Wits but also by the public at large. Its subject and style gave it a reputation that it could not have attained even a decade later. Barlow was misled by his temporary success into the fatal error of expanding the 4700 lines into the 8350 lines of *The Columbiad*. But when the latter appeared in 1807, it failed to please the very public that had welcomed its predecessor. Its failure was due less to the changes in the poem than to the development of public taste during the poet's absence in Europe. Pope's dominance had been successfully contested, and the long philosophic poem itself was in its decline. Barlow's failure was all the more striking on account of his very audacity. His *Vision of Columbus* was simply a philosophic poem; his *Columbiad* was avowedly an epic, meant to have a vaster theme, a more refined style, and a higher moral purpose than Homer's. *The Columbiad*, however, remains merely a "geographical, historical, political, and philosophical disquisition." To Columbus, as he lies sick and in prison, there appears Hesper, the genius of the western world, and, with the purpose of setting forth all that Columbus and America have contributed to the welfare of the world, reviews the state of Europe in the middle ages, the voyages of discovery, conquests, and colonisation, and the war of the Revolution, with references to contemporary persons and events. He concludes with a prophecy of the future glories of America. This literary drag-net has drawn into itself nothing delicate or tender and little that is truly human, for such qualities are not compatible with its forced sublimity and its declamatory and gaudy rhetoric. To the worst vices of the conventional poetic diction, Barlow in a painful effort to achieve the grandiose, has added vile phrases of his own peculiar coinage. And yet, hidden away among these thousands of lines of laboured rhetoric, are passages really fine and free in both conception and execution. Atlas, genius of Africa, prophesies to Hesper the ruin that must follow American slavery. In the chaos

> His own bald eagle skims alone the sky,
> Darts from all points of heaven her searching eye,
> Kens thro the gloom her ancient rock of rest,
> And finds her cavern'd crag, her solitary nest.

The most vigorous poems produced in America between 1765 and 1807 were the numberless satires that marked every stage of the fight with England and of the internal strife between Whigs and Tories and, later, between Republicans and Federalists. *Hudibras*, *The Dunciad*, *The Rolliad*, *The Anti-Jacobin*, and the satires of Churchill, of Gifford, and of "Peter Pindar" bred in America songs, mock-heroics, burlesques, and satires of direct attack, in lyric measures, heroic couplets, and octosyllabics.

American political satire began with the Stamp Act. *The Times* (1765) by the Rev. Benjamin Church of Boston, which vigorously defends the colonists, imitates Churchill, who for four years had been famous in England as the most relentless satirist of the day, and is doubly interesting in that its author later changed his attitude and was expelled from Boston as a traitor. The Boston Port Bill evoked from John Trumbull an *Elegy on the Times* (1775), which uses the elegiac quartrains of Gray for satiric invective; but far more important is the same author's *McFingal*, the most effective satire of its time. Trumbull was born in what is now Watertown, Connecticut, in 1750, and graduated from Yale in 1767 in the same class with Timothy Dwight. In 1772 he published his *Progress of Dullness*, a satire in Hudibrastic verse on the current educational system and the ignorance of the clergy which is still interesting. After studying law in the office of John Adams in Boston, he returned to New Haven to practise, and in 1776 published the first two cantos of *McFingal*.[1] In 1781 he published the third and fourth cantos, and in the same year removed to Hartford, where he became associated with the Hartford Wits and joined in writing *The Anarchiad*. After serving as State's attorney, he became a judge of the Superior Court of Connecticut, and finally judge of the Supreme Court of Errors, a position which he held until 1819. For some years he was the treasurer of Yale, from which he received the degree of LL.D. in 1818. He removed to Detroit in 1825, and died there in 1831.

McFingal, Trumbull's chief work, is a political satire in favour of the whigs. As much the guide as the child of public sentiment, the piece had thirty editions. It is a burlesque epic in 3800 lines of Hudibrastic verse in four cantos, which parodies epic speeches in council, heroic encounters, and prophecy. At a town meeting held in a New England village to discuss the question of rebellion against the mother country, the whigs, led by the impassioned Honorius, and the tories, headed by Squire McFingal, an officeholder under the Crown, engage in furious argument. The whigs are finally victorious in speech and also in the battle which terminates the discussion. Under threats, McFingal's tory constable recants, but the obdurate Squire is tarred and feathered and glued to the liberty pole, where he is left to meditate his misdeeds. Escaping in the night, he convenes a meeting of fellow tories in the cellar, and relates to them the vision which he has gained through his gift of second sight, and which prophesies final victory for the whigs. The meeting breaks up at the approach of the whigs and McFingal deserts his followers and escapes to the British. The verse runs swiftly, with considerable comic force, and contains epigrammatic couplets that might have come from *Hudibras*:

[1] Published as Canto I, but since divided into two cantos.

> No man e'er felt the halter draw,
> With good opinion of the law,

and

> But optics sharp it needs, I ween,
> To see what is not to be seen.

The burlesque contrasts, the absurd figures of speech, the far-fetched allusions, are learned from Butler; and the verse, with its frequent elisions, its feminine rhymes, and its homely diction, is more nearly that of *Hudibras* than of any other satire. Churchill is responsible for such serious passages in the speeches as

> For ages blest thus Britain rose
> The terror of encircling foes;
> Her heroes ruled the bloody plain;
> Her conq'ring standard aw'd the main,

as also for the use of personifications and of the terrible:

> Around all stained with rebel blood,
> Like Milton's lazar house it stood,
> Where grim Despair attended nurse,
> And Death was gov'rnor of the house.

For all its indebtednesses *McFingal* remains the most entertaining satire in our early literature, and the only surviving poem by any member of the Hartford group.

The two most vigorous and prolific tory satirists were Joseph Stansbury (1750–1809), a merchant of Philadelphia, and the Rev. Jonathan Odell (1737–1818), of New Jersey. Their satires and satirical songs, odes, and ballads are generally alike both in matter and style, but Stansbury is the better poet, and has to his credit several satirical lyrics, quite as good as any of their time on either side of the water. He turns off an ode to the king, a comic ballad recounting an American reverse, or a loyal song, all with equal facility and with little of the invective characteristic of Odell. His *Town Meeting*, a satirical ballad of over one hundred and fifty lines, is typical, but his lyric, *To Cordelia*, addressed to his wife from Nova Scotia at the close of the Revolution, shows that he could also write a true poem. Odell, whose satires were not only in the main longer and less original, but also more virulent, was the Freneau of the tory side. Though possessed of little humour and less wit, he is at least vigorous and incisive and can give Freneau as good as he sends:

> Back to his mountains Washington may trot.
> He take this city? Yes—when ice is hot.

That Churchill was his model appears in his *Feu de Joie;* his *Word of Congress* (1779), four hundred lines of politico-personal invective against the Continental Congress; and in the still longer *American Times* (1780), which attacked the leaders of the American cause with extreme bitterness and scurrility.

After the Revolution and before the adoption of the Constitution, social and political unrest produced *The Anarchiad, a Poem on the Restoration of Chaos and Substantial Night* (1786–1787), in which four of the Hartford group, Joel Barlow, John Trumbull, David Humphreys, and Lemuel Hopkins cleverly adapted their English original *The Rolliad* to the conditions that gave rise to Shays's Rebellion, paper money, demagogy, and other evils of the time. *The Anarchiad* is in 1200 lines of heroic couplets, and is divided into fourteen parts that purport to be extracts from an ancient epic, lately discovered, which foretell conditions in the decade following the Revolution. The verse is that of Pope and Goldsmith, from whom many passages are paraphrased; the style is a parody of Homer, Dante, Milton, and Pope; and the mock-heroic method is conventional; yet the satire through its wit and good sense deserved its immense popularity. The speech of Hesper in favour of a firm union of the states is fine and eloquent; and the brilliant satirical picture of the Land of Annihilation, though obviously suggested by *The Dunciad*, is not unworthy of its original.

The entire story of the strife between federalist and republican, Hamiltonian and Jeffersonian, can be read in the verse satire of the time. No American shows this bitter partisanship more than Thomas Green Fessenden (1771–1837). His *Terrible Tractoration*, written in England about English conditions, is not political but is chiefly aimed at the critics of

Perkins's "metallic tractors," an invention of which Fessenden was the agent. Its 1800 lines of Hudibrastic verse, full of references to contemporary persons and scientific matters, form a fair example of a not very admirable type of satire. Fessenden again displays his mental alertness and his indebtedness to "Peter Pindar" in *Democracy Unveiled, or Tyranny Stripped of the Garb of Patriotism.* This surprising production, in which he reaches the nadir of indecent personalities, attacks Jacobinism, democracy, and Jefferson in particular, with a virulence that disregards both good sense and good taste.

The political mock-epic appears in the anonymous *Aristocracy* (1795), which ridicules the alleged aristocratic notions of the federalists. Also political in a sense is *The Group* (1795), by William Cliffton, a satire on the men who hid from danger during the Revolution but who now claim the reward of patriots. Though its series of portraits in the mock-heroic style of Pope is not without vigour, it is less original and amusing than Cliffton's *Rhapsody on the Times*, several hundred lines of octosyllabics in the style of Prior, which contains narrative and descriptive satire against unrestricted immigration.

Before the nineteenth century our social and literary satires are amusing only as futile attempts to make something out of nothing. The society and literary productions of Philadelphia are satirized in a series of poems beginning in 1762 and extending on into the next century; such as *The Manners of the Times* (1762) by "Philadelphiensis"; the anonymous *Philadelphiad;* and the more vigorous but still conventional *Times* (1788) by Peter Markoe. Other Philadelphia satires of this type might be named without raising the average of merit. Fortunately, New York and Boston seem to have been somewhat less analytic in their attitude; though both cities were guilty of such conventional social and literary satires as Winthrop Sargent's *Boston* (1803). The inflated journalistic style of the last decade of the century suggested the one really clever and original literary satire of its time in America. *The Echo* was begun in 1791, was published serially, and appeared complete as a volume of three hundred pages in 1807. Its authors, who seem to have been Richard Alsop and Timothy Dwight, select some particularly bombastic passage from a current newspaper and travesty its style in heroic couplets with a result that has not yet quite lost its flavour. The satire probably owed something to the parodies of *The Anti-Jacobin*, though in this case the matter and not the form is burlesqued.

At the close of the century the long satiric poem in Hudibrastic verse or heroic couplet was already passing away in England, though American versifiers continued to imitate the outworn models. In the light of *The Biglow Papers* all these early beginnings seem faint and pale; but they are still significant as indications of the growth of national consciousness. It should also be noted that in average merit our early verse satire is probably not inferior to its counterpart in England. There is little to be said for the genre on either side of the water.

Volumes of miscellaneous short poems began to appear in 1765, but, owing to the Revolution and its attendant changes, ceased almost entirely between 1770 and 1790, and revived only during the last decade of the century. Though intrinsically of little merit, they show in the main that Pope and the long poem were not absolutely dominant and that Americans were reading English lyrical poetry and were learning to write graceful verse which certain of the public were ready to read. This public was small enough, however, for most of the volumes were published by subscription; and a remarkable number were issued by pious friends as memorials to young poets, and hence show little except that friendship may make unreasonable demands.

The poems of Thomas Godfrey (1736–1763) of Philadelphia were published two years after his death by his friend and fellow poet Nathaniel Evans. His work is highly imitative; pastorals in heroic couplet, after Pope; an *Ode to Friendship* and a *Dithyrambic on Wine* in the manner of Dryden's occasional odes; a *Night Piece* in elegiac quatrains, which shows the influence of Gray and Young; songs in the manner of Shenstone and Prior; and here and there a touch of Collins. His best as well as his most ambitious poem is *The Court of Fancy*, an allegory in heroic couplets, suggested by Chaucer's *House of Fame*. Though conventional in style, it is not without originality, and as the first truly imaginative poem written in America is of more than passing interest. Godfrey's imitative habit could not quite cloak his spontaneity, and had he come only a generation later he might have contributed more permanently to our poetry.

The poems of his friend and editor the Rev. Nathaniel Evans (1742–1767), also of Philadelphia, were issued five years after his death in a volume entitled *Poems on Several Occasions* which contains a number of unimportant occasional poems, and others imitative of Milton, Cowley, Prior, Gray, and Collins. Evans's most ambitious effort is his *Ode on the Prospect of Peace;* but more interesting is his tribute to Benjamin Franklin in praise of physical science. On the whole his poems show less native ability than Godfrey's and are equally imitative; but the work of both is significant as the beginning of our more purely lyrical verse.

Had not the Revolution interfered,[1] the publication of volumes of miscellaneous poems would probably have continued unbroken. When about 1790 it began again, to continue indefinitely, the awakening of national consciousness had produced no change in the matter and style of the short poem; it was still an echo. And Philadephia was still the centre for writing and publication. But new influences—such as Mrs. Radcliffe, Ossian, and the contemporary romantic ballads—are often apparent in the last decade of the century. The sentimental, the mysterious, the horrible, environed with appropriate scenery, appear here and there in the work of such poets as William Moore Smith (1759–1821), of Philadelphia, who gives evidence of this imported "romanticism" in *The Wizard of the Rock*, a blend of Parnell, Percy, and Goldsmith; and *Maria's Grave*, which is placed amid the romantic scenery pictured by the poet's originals across the Atlantic. Most distinguished personally of the Philadelphia poets was Judge Francis Hopkinson (1737–1791),[2] signer of the Declaration of Independence, whose many occasional poems are merely as good as the average of their kind, but whose songs, some of which are suggestive of Gay and Prior, are distinctly musical and pleasing. The Rev. John Blair Linn (1777–1804), who, like Godfrey and Evans, died young and left his work unfinished, wrote odes to solitude

---

[1] Aside from patriotic songs and ballads, not much lyrical verse was published between 1770 and 1786, and that little appeared in newspapers and magazines.

[2] See also Book II., Chap. II.

and melancholy, pastorals and elegies, and other echoes of
Shenstone, Gray, and even Mason. It is noticeable that the
songs and light social lyrics of the close of the century come from
Philadelphia, the social capital. The gifted and original
William Cliffton (1772-1799) was both a satirist and a lyrist.
His half-dozen lyrics, quite the two best of which are *To Fancy*
and *To a Robin*,[1] are not without grace and delicacy, which
he owes largely to his models, Gay, Prior, and Collins. Like
Freneau and other poets of the time, Cliffton found his surroundings unsympathetic:

> In these cold shades, beneath these shifting skies,
> Where Fancy sickens, and where Genius dies;
> Where few and feeble are the Muse's strains,
> And no fine frenzy riots in the veins.

So he characterizes his environment in his epistle to William
Gifford, which was prefixed to the American edition of the
Baviad and *Maeviad* in 1799. Gifford's stinging satire on the
"Della Cruscan" school of poetry was welcomed in America
by Cliffton, whose verse was at least manly and sincere.

It is not certain that Joseph Brown Ladd (1764-1786) wrote
his *Poems of Arouet* under Della Cruscan influence, for they
were published in the year in which the school took its rise in
Florence; they are at least an anticipation of its more languishing side. But whether or not the Della Cruscan mania had
reached Charleston, where Ladd was killed in a duel, in 1786, it
was certainly widespread in Boston less than a decade later.
Mrs. Sarah Wentworth Morton (1759-1846),[2] termed by her
admirers "The American Sappho," praises Della Crusca in a
fervid address prefixed to her narrative poem *Ouabi, or the Virtues of Nature* (1790), and as "Philenia" exchanged poetical
tributes with her "Menander," no less a celebrity than Robert
Treat Paine, Jr. (1773-1811).

Boston's craving for a native poet, the bad taste of the time,
and the poet's own wayward life combined to give Paine a
reputation surpassing that of any of his contemporaries. At
Harvard he was known by his occasional poems, and his

---

[1] The latter is written in the eight-line anapestic stanza greatly favoured
by Shenstone and later used by Cowper in his *Alexander Selkirk*, which occurs
with notable frequency in the lyrics of this period.

[2] See also Book II, Chap. VI.

Robert Treat Paine 179

he practised law, he gave most of his time to the theatre and to
poetry. Soon his reputation was such that he could command
five dollars a line for his verse, a price never before approached
in America and perhaps never since equalled. His marriage
with an actress estranged him from his family, and after this
event his life was that of a wastrel. His services, however, were
in request upon all public occasions, from the opening of
theatres to meetings of the Phi Beta Kappa. For such occasions he wrote the didactic poems, prologues, and odes in conventional but vigorous heroic couplets that form the greater
part of his work. *The Ruling Passion*, for Phi Beta Kappa, and
The Invention of Letters, for a Harvard commencement, were
hailed as the spontaneous and original outbursts of genius,
though both are merely laboured and conventional didactic
poems of a type that was even then in its decline. In these
and a few other of Paine's poems one finds rhetorical passages
of some merit amid a waste of bombast and affectation but
looks in vain for any imagination or real feeling. The diction
embodies all the vices against which the new poetry rebelled.
Della Crusca plus Pope would have crushed a more genuine
talent than Paine's. His reputation is a curious evidence
of the pathetic craving for a national poet and of the determination to force the birth of a genius. His *Works in Prose and
Verse*, an octavo volume of over five hundred pages, was
published one year after his death, with all the reverence due
to a classic.

"The American Sappho" was not the only woman singer
of Boston. Mrs. Susanna Rowson,[1] besides her plays and
novels, wrote poems which unite "sensibility" and didacticism.
Her odes, hymns, elegies, nature lyrics, and songs show little
observation of life or nature, and scarcely any distinctive
American quality. Of all these, the patriotic lyric *America,
Commerce, and Freedom*, which is commonplace but not without spirit, alone has survived. The *Poems, Dramatic and
Miscellaneous*, of Mrs. Mercy Warren (1728-1814)[2] include
ponderous and solemn epistles and elegies that are merely
belated echoes of Pope. New York also had its woman poet
in Mrs. Ann Eliza Bleecker (1752-1783), whose melancholy

[1] See also Book II, Chaps. II and VI.   [2] See also Book II. Chap. II.

life is reflected in the tone of her sentimental elegies, epistles, descriptive poems, and religious lyrics, in the style of the English poets of the first half of the century. Her daughter, Mrs. Margaretta Faugeres, who published her own poems with those of her mother in 1793, shows in her poem on the Hudson the growing attention to native scenery. The inquiring reader may find all the imitative qualities of our early lyric poets if he will consult the very inclusive *Original Poems, Serious and Entertaining*, of Paul Allen (1775–1826), whose facile and graceful verse is indicative of English influences all the way from Prior to Cowper.

Aside from the lyrics of Freneau, the two original strains in our early lighter verse are the humorous poems of Thomas Green Fessenden and of Royall Tyler,[1] and the nature lyrics of Alexander Wilson. Fessenden contributed humorous poems of New England country life to Dennie's *Farmer's Weekly Museum*, and these were afterwards published in his *Original Poems*. To this same magazine and also to Dennie's *Port Folio*, Royall Tyler contributed pictures and studies in verse of American environment and character which are worth all the pretentious imitations of his contemporaries. The lyrics scattered throughout the pages of Alexander Wilson's *Ornithology* and afterwards printed in his collected poems merit more attention than they have heretofore received. Wilson was scientist and poet enough to celebrate the osprey, the Baltimore bird, the hummingbird, and the bluebird in true nature lyrics which, together with those of Freneau, are not unworthy forerunners of Bryant's.

Philip Freneau was born in New York of Huguenot ancestry in 1752, and died near Freehold, New Jersey, in 1832. His long and eventful life was spent in a variety of pursuits. After he graduated from Princeton in 1771, he was author, editor, government official, trader, and farmer. As regards the genesis of his poems, two facts in his life are especially important. His newspaper work encouraged a fatal production of the satirical and humorous verse that gave him reputation; and his trading voyages inspired poems descriptive of the scenery of the southern islands, and made possible what is perhaps his most original and distinctive work, his naval ballads.

[1] See also Book II, Chaps. II, III, and VI.

From the volumes of the most recent edition of Freneau's poems, aggregating 1200 pages, the reader gains the impression that had this poet written half as much he might have written twice as well.   That he was something of the artist is shown by the care with which he revised his poems for five successive editions; but his revisions are sometimes actually for the worse. Yet Freneau surpassed all his contemporaries not only in quality but also in sheer quantity and in variety of subject and form. Furthermore, his work presents an almost unique combination of satiric power, romantic imagination, and feeling for nature. At one extreme is the bitter invective of his satires; at the other, the delicate fancy of his best lyrics.   His early poems show the influence of Milton, as in *The Power of Fancy;* of Gray, as in *The Monument of Phaon* and *The Deserted Farm House;* and of Goldsmith, as in *The American Village*—all of which contain lines of original power and beauty; but in his *Pictures of Columbus,* he reaches complete originality.   When the poet has Columbus exclaim in the face of death,

> The winds blow high; one other world remains;
> Once more without a guide I find the way,

he shows that at last the new world has produced a poet.

In his voyages Freneau found the tropical scenery of his descriptive poems.   *The Beauties of Santa Cruz,* though unequal and crude, has a definiteness of imagery and a simplicity of diction that set it apart from the conventional school of Thomson.   *The House of Night,* which combines description and narrative, is the most remarkable poem written in America up to its time.   In the use of "romantic" scenery and of death as a theme, Freneau was not a pioneer; but in his supernaturalism and in the strange and haunting music of his lines, he stood alone, and, as has often been remarked, anticipated Coleridge and Poe.   Although Freneau was known in England, it may be doubted whether he influenced the English romantic poets. More probably, both he and they were influenced by the same general tendencies; for the romantic movement was already well under way when he wrote the *The House of Night.*   The poem is overlong, lacks unity of tone and matter, and altogether is disappointingly crude; but it contains such lines as

so loud and sad it play'd
As though all music were to breathe its last,

I saw the infernal windows flaming red,

and

Trim the dull tapers, for I see no dawn,

which are a source of astonishment to one who has followed the course of American poetry up to this point.   But unfortunately the romantic strain which promised so richly was soon lost.
Freneau's poems of the "glory of America" type, such as his *Rising Glory of America*, written in collaboration with H. H. Brackenridge[1] when the two were seniors at Princeton, were inspired by a great vision and still retain a certain eloquence. His burlesques of American scenes and characters, such as *Slender's Journey*, are less successful; but his satires in both quantity and variety surpassed all but *McFingal* in their day. "Poet of the American Revolution" is no misnomer, if the term is to include political events up to 1815.   Freneau's masters in satire are Dryden, Churchill, and "Peter Pindar"; and his tone ranges from burlesque to invective.   *The Political Balance* and *The British Prison Ship* are the most powerful and original satires of their time.   The royalist printers Rivington and Gaine were his chief targets during the last years of the Revolution. In his personal satires he uses the anapest, which he was the first to popularize in America.   His later satires, usually in lyrical stanzas, were suggested by "Peter Pindar"; the phrase "Peter Pindar of America" gives the key to his contemporary reputation.   That his finer work received no praise was to Freneau a source of discouragement and even of bitterness. His aspiration was lyrical; but he had fallen on evil days:

On these bleak climes by fortune thrown,
Where rigid reason reigns alone,
Where lovely fancy has no sway,
Nor magic forms about us play—
Nor nature takes her summer hue,
Tell me, what has the muse to do?[2]

Freneau's newspaper work, his political affiliations, and his business ventures operated unfavourably upon his lyrical poetry.

[1] For whom see also Book II, Chap. VI.   [2] *To an Author.*

Although his fervour was reawakened by the French Revolution and again by the War of 1812, almost all his best lyrics were written between 1775 and 1790. In the main these concern the American Indian, the smaller objects of nature, and the sea, and in subject at least are altogether original. *The Indian Burying Ground* is well known; *The Indian Student*, which curiously anticipates some phases of Wordsworth's *Ruth*, and *The Dying Indian*, are scarcely less fine. His nature lyrics, such as *The Wild Honeysuckle*, *The Caty-Did*, and *On the Sleep of Plants*, are the first to give lyrical expression to American nature. Their simplicity and restraint suggest Collins and Gray, but they are not imitative, and it is probable that Freneau is more original in even the style of his lyrics than has generally been acknowledged. *To a Man of Ninety* would at once be lighted upon as an imitation of Wordsworth had it not actually anticipated the *Lyrical Ballads*. The elegiac lyric *Eutaw Springs*, which Scott pronounced the best thing of its kind in the language, may have been suggested by Collins, but is still strongly original. However this may be, Freneau seems to merit all that his latest editor claims for him as a pioneer in the lyric of the sea. *On the Death of Captain Nicholas Biddle* (1779) has much of Campbell's spirit and power; *The Paul Jones* and *Captain Barney's Victory over the General Monk* deserve more than the mere credit given to the pioneer, for they are intrinsically fine.

There remains, then, out of Freneau's voluminous product, a small body of work of permanent interest. *The House of Night* deserves remembrance, not only for its pioneer romanticism but also for passages of intrinsic beauty and power; and a score of his lyrics, while far from perfect, are fine enough to deserve a permanent place in our anthologies. What his slender but genuine talent might have produced under more favourable conditions, even a generation later, can only be surmised, but even as it is we have in Freneau the only American poet before Bryant who possessed both imaginative insight and felicity of style.

A few general conclusions concerning early American poetry may be stated briefly. First, the sheer quantity of it is surprisingly large in proportion to the population. Again, it is not the product of a new civilization, but as a whole is the extremely sophisticated result of English literary traditions.   In style at least it is highly imitative of English models, and in many instances it shows an immediate transmission of literary influences.   Finally, in the average merit of its style, it is, at least in the eighteenth century, quite equal to all but the very best of its time in the mother country.   Altogether, the first two centuries of American poetry prepared the soil for the truly native growth that was to come after 1812—a growth that was no sudden phenomenon but simply the inevitable result of the cumulative forces of two hundred years.

Book II

CHAPTER I

Travellers and Observers, 1763-1846

THE literature of travel, fresh, varied, and cosmopolitan, doubtless owes its principal charm to its effect upon the sense of wonder, and hence in the last analysis is to be understood in its bearing upon imagination and poetic art; but its relation to history and geography is not superficial. Accordingly, we may first recall such dates and events as will suggest in outline the expanding region in which the second great division of American travellers range. With the close of the French and Indian War begins the supremacy of the English-speaking race in North America. Before twenty years had passed, the Colonies, no longer a mere fringe of population along the Atlantic, have achieved their independence, and possess a territory reaching inland to the Mississippi. Twenty years later, in 1803, comes the Louisiana Purchase, when the wily Napoleon, for a consideration, and to thwart his colonizing foe across the Channel, endowed the Americans with a tract of land extending from that great river north-west to the Rocky Mountains, the importance of which even Jefferson, with his westward-looking eyes, was unable to grasp in full. Another eight years, and there is a temporary check in the Astoria Settlement, later recorded by Irving. Then comes the War of 1812-14, and after it a rapid inrush of immigration. Of the native citizens, two generations have been born since the War of Independence; Revolutionary heroes are passing; and the new leaders are alien to England. The nation has become distinct. In 1819 Spain relaxes her feeble hold upon Florida.

In 1823, twenty years after the Louisiana Purchase, the utterance of the Monroe Doctrine announces to the world the position of the United States in the Occident. Meantime internal waterways and highroads have been developed; and subsequently, during the presidency of Jackson, the steam locomotive is introduced. The year 1845 marks the annexation of Texas; and with the cession of New Mexico and California in 1848, the country virtually assumes its present proportions. Almost a century has passed since the nondescript Captain Carver, immediately after the French and Indian War, conceived the idea of opening up the vast north-western tract to the enterprise of Great Britain. The interest of travellers has shifted from the character and habits of the roving Indian to the domestic manners of East and West, North and South; and science has moved from a less impersonal, yet fairly exact, observation of plants and animals, or of subterranean rivers in a terrestrial paradise, to the precise geology of a Featherstonhaugh or a Lyell.

This period of travel saw the rise of modern geography as an exact science, and the development of the ancillary sciences, geology, botany, zoology, and anthropology. If the great epoch of modern geographical discovery began with 1768 and the voyages of the Englishman Captain Cook, the scientific elaboration of results by Continental investigators also mainly occupied the second half of the eighteenth century. Linnæus was still alive, and had followers collecting specimens in America. Zimmermann, who translated the *Travels* of William Bartram into German, likewise ushered in the study of the geographical distribution of plants and animals as well as of mankind; while Blumenbach the anthropologist was making his famous collection of human skulls at Göttingen. The first work on physical geography ever published, that of the Swede Bergman, appeared in 1766, shortly before the time when books of American travel began to grow numerous. The influence of Continental science upon American observers is often obvious, as in the case of Linnæus, to which Zimmermann refers in his translation of Bartram. Indeed, a pupil of Linnæus, Pehr Kalm, who has been included among the botanists of Philadelphia, is remembered for his description of Niagara Falls. But the influence was pervasive and general, so that geography proper soon became domesticated in this country.   The *Geography Made Easy* of Jedidiah Morse, first published at New Haven in 1784, quickly went through a number of editions and transformations.   About 1796 President Dwight of Yale, in his *Travels*, records that a work of Morse is studied by both freshmen and sophomores, probably referring to a revision of the more extensive *American Geography* of 1789.   Dwight himself made judicious use of it.   The indefatigable Morse, though not a Humboldt, a Ritter, or a Leopold von Buch, was a lowly precursor of the European scientists who furnished the next generation with ideals in geography and travel.

If territorial expansion and the development of geographical science are to be noted in studying the literature of travel, the general background of eighteenth-century thought must not be forgotten.   The so-called rationalism of the French, with its tendency to destroy traditional distinctions, to suppress imagination, and yet to end in a kind of deism, is too large a subject for more than passing notice.   On the other hand, we may dwell for a moment upon the sentimental treatment of external nature in Rousseau, and upon his conception, in part derived from early American travellers, of the "natural" man in a terrestrial paradise.   Such a being could, in fact, exist only in a tropical or sub-tropical environment such as the favoured regions in which the first American explorers and missionaries encountered the natives.   Yet the transference of the idea to the Indians of North America was easy in an age when popular geography was vague; and the faith of the Jesuits in the potential goodness of the savage doubtless helped to propagate a general belief that the aborigines were noble.   The idea, which seems rather to have come from the travellers than from Rousseau, but possibly is dormant in almost every educated mind, is well established in American literature from William Bartram to Fenimore Cooper.   The related notion of social equality in a state of nature has a more solid basis.   As in Crèvecœur's *American Farmer*, it grows out of the facts of life in a new agricultural settlement.

An opposite conception was also prevalent.   Side by side with the ideal of an eloquent stoic, artless, magnanimous by nature, we find—often in the same book of travels—the cruel savage as he is, vengeful and impure.   Montaigne, indeed, a predecessor of Rousseau in admiring the unlettered aborigines, had held that the European surpassed the savage in barbarity; yet when he turns from the ideal to the actual, there is but a step between Montaigne and Hobbes, who declares the life of nature to be "nasty, solitary, brutish, and short." And Hobbes merely anticipates Voltaire and Pauw, whose unedifying pictures of American natives were put together from the accounts of travellers. We have, then, in the literature of Europe the same opposition between observed fact and preconceived notion that we meet in Bartram or Carver. On the one hand, we have *La Jeune Indienne* of Chamfort, presented at the Théâtre Français in 1764, or Rousseau's *Chanson des Sauvages* and *Danse Canadienne*; on the other, a debate among the learned on the question whether the villainy of the Indians was original, or had been acquired through contact with civilization. In *De l'Amérique et des Américains*, published at Berlin in 1771, the anonymous author attacks the theories of Pauw, and vigorously contends that the savages were evil enough to begin with.

Man in a state of nature suggests solitude; and solitude, with its charms for the eighteenth-century poet, suggests the so-called "feeling for nature" that of late has been much discussed by literary students in dealing with that period. Though the point is not always made clear, the actual topic under discussion is the Neoplatonic doctrine of divine immanence. To a man who believes in this, the world, with its plants and animals, is no longer a work of art, shaped by the fingers of a Master-Artist; it is filled with a subtle spirit which is interfused in all material and living things, "rolls" through them, and is their principle of movement and pulsation. In one form or another, this notion of immanence, familiar in the earlier poems of Wordsworth, characterizes the reaction against the age of reason, and may be found in many observers of nature in America. Its origin is obscure; nor can one readily see why Neoplatonic ideas should cast a spell over minds so diverse as those of Rousseau, Goethe, Wordsworth, and the Quaker Bartram. The suggestion has been made that the writings of the mystic Boehme had an influence upon the Society of Friends. But the sources of the "feeling for nature" are likely to have been as various as the evidences of it in American travellers.

Against the background thus rapidly sketched we are to project a hundred years of travel and observation. The wealth and variety of material are very great. For the period in question, one bibliographer has recorded 413 titles of works bearing upon the single state of Illinois; for the same region between 1818 and 1865, he notes 69 British travellers, 53 American, and 31 German. For the country as a whole, a second writer has listed forty-five books of the sort by foreigners between 1789 and 1820. Whether of American or foreign origin, such books were not restricted to one volume; gradually there came to be two or three, and sometimes four. And commonly the route described was one of these: from New York to Albany, and thence across to Niagara Falls; from an eastern port south to Savannah by boat, then overland to Mobile and New Orleans, and up the Mississippi; from Philadelphia to Pittsburgh, down the Ohio to the Mississippi, and from the Mississippi up the Missouri to the North-west. Canadian travellers followed the St. Lawrence.

As the lists would indicate, the literature is cosmopolitan— an inference that is confirmed in other ways. Not only were the works of foreigners turned into English, but British and American observers were translated on the Continent: Bartram into French, German, and Dutch; Crèvecœur into French (by himself) and German; Weld into Italian, Dutch, and German; and so on. Again, the same work, as, for example, Bartram's, might be published in the same year at Philadelphia and at London or Dublin, or first in this country, and then abroad, or *vice versa*. And finally, the borrowings from earlier by later travellers, irrespective of tongues, are endless.

Confining ourselves as far as possible to British and American travellers, we may say that their motives were as various as their callings and station, and ran from the lust of a Daniel Boone for new solitudes, through the desire to promote the fur trade or immigration, and through semi-scientific or scientific curiosity, to the impulses of the literary artist or to the religious aims of the missionary. George Rogers Clark, Logan, and Boone were pioneers. Fearon, Darby, and Faux came to study conditions for emigrants. Bernard, Tyrone Power, and Fanny Kemble were actors. Wilson, Nuttall, and Audubon were professed ornithologists; the Bartrams and Michaux, botanists.

Schoolcraft was an ethnologist, Chevalier a student of political economy, Fanny Wright a social reformer. Grund, Combe the phrenologist, and Miss Martineau had a special interest in humanitarian projects. Richard Weston was a bookseller, John M. Peck a Baptist missionary, DeWitt Clinton, who explored the route of the future Erie Canal, a statesman. Many others had eyes trained in surveying. Boone was a surveyor, like Washington himself—and Washington may be classed with the observers and diarists. Buckingham, a traveller by vocation, had journeyed about the world for thirty years before visiting America; nor did he feel his obligation ended when he had published the customary three stout volumes. Crèvecœur actually was a farmer, though he was more, and Richard Parkinson, very definitely, a student of agriculture. The abusive Ashe came to examine the "western" rivers, and to observe the products and actual state of the adjacent country. Among transients from the Continent were Chastellux, the friend of Washington, Chateaubriand, with his youthful plan of helping Washington to discover the Northwest Passage, the Duc de la Rochefoucauld, a fair observer, and De Tocqueville, who wrote his classic treatise on America after a brief visit for the purpose of studying prisons. "Charles Sealsfield" (Karl Postl), whose several periods of residence were longer, who wrote in English, yet more in German, and whose tombstone in Switzerland calls him *ein Buerger von Nordamerika*," is hard to classify.

The commonest type among these works seems to be the journal, which is the form used by William Bartram; but the epistolary type, represented by Crèvecœur, by Dwight, and by Wirt in his *Letters of the British Spy*, is very common. The general range of substance is displayed by circumstantial titles in the Bibliography. Among objects of interest to many were, in the early years of the Republic, the persons of Washington and Jefferson, and, in his time, the picturesque figure of Jackson; and among natural wonders, Niagara Falls, the "Rock Bridge" of Virginia, and the Mammoth Cave. This, after its discovery by Hutchins in 1809, took its place in the attractions of Kentucky with the furry cap of Boone. The Indians, of course, supplied an unfailing interest. Their habits, as in Bartram, speculation concerning their origin, as in Timothy

Dwight, and remarks upon their language, as in Carver, are stock material; so, too, such lists as Carver's of plants and animals. Another topic is seen in Gilbert Imlay's anticipations of states to be formed from the land to the north and west of the Ohio. Or an occasional enthusiast, possibly remembering Berkeley's project for educating the natives, will found an imaginary school of letters in a suitable landscape. Thus Stansbury in central New York, almost fifty years before the opening of Cornell University, deems the site of Ithaca most fitting for a college: "Inexhaustible stores for the study of natural history will always be at hand, and for all other sciences the scholar will be secluded in a romantic retirement which will give additional zest to his researches." The attention of others, as Fanny Kemble and Harriet Martineau, is drawn to the negro and his master in the South, more than ever, perhaps, after the anti-slavery agitation in England.

But the interest in slavery, in frontier life, and indeed in all the main topics of the later travellers, is not peculiar to them, partly because essentials are necessarily repeated, partly because subsequent observers have read, and often consciously imitate, their predecessors. Crèvecœur's ghastly picture of the slave in chains would impress any sensitive reader. But nowhere could imitation be clearer than in respect to impossible marvels, which even the steadiest early observers like Bartram are impelled to relate. We read in his description of an enraged alligator: "The waters like a cataract descend from his opening jaws; clouds of smoke issue from his dilated nostrils"; and, aware that this guileless traveller was merely yielding to custom, we are not led to undervalue his notes on sub-tropical fauna. Nor are we forced to discredit an entire later work, wherein adventures, like some of those in Ashe, may be altogether imaginary. Further, when unconscious imitation passes into extensive borrowing, as in Carver, we must recall the tolerance which the eighteenth century showed to this sort of indebtedness, and not condemn the debtor out of hand. So late as the year 1836, Irving could employ good sources in his own way, with a general acknowledgment of the fact in his Introduction.

For various reasons the earlier travels are more interesting; and it may be said that the best of them appeared, or were written, between 1775 and 1800. We may select as typical the

Travels of Carver (1778), the *Travels* of William Bartram (1791), and the *Letters from an American Farmer* of Crèvecœur (1782).

The dubious personal history of Carver, and questions as to the authenticity of his book, will excuse the introduction of certain details in his biography. Jonathan Carver, the ostensible author of *Travels through the Interior Parts of North America in the Years 1766, 1767, and 1768*, was not the great-grandson of the first colonial Governor of Connecticut, but was probably born in humble circumstances at Canterbury in that state. In 1746 he married Abigail Robbins, by whom he had seven children; he later contracted a bigamous marriage in England. The extent of his education has been disputed; but he seems to have had some knowledge of surveying and map-making, with perhaps a smattering of medicine. His title-page calls him "J. Carver, Esq., Captain of a Company of Provincial Troops during the Late War with France"; and he probably was captured with Burk's company of rangers in 1757, when he was "wounded in his Leg at the bloody Massacree of the unhappy Garrison of Fort William Henry at Lake George." The war over, he says he began to think of exploring the most unknown parts of England's new territory. In the opinion of a severe critic, Professor Edward G. Bourne, Carver's actual journey was limited to this: he went from Boston to Michilimackinac, thence by way of the Fox River and the Wisconsin to the Mississippi, and thence up the Minnesota; returning, he explored northern Wisconsin and the northern shore of Lake Superior. Failing in Boston to publish an account of his discoveries, in 1769 he went to England with a project for further exploration in the North-west. The pecuniary aid accorded him as a needy person by the Government would argue some recognition of his services. He evidently enlisted the sympathy of Dr. Lettsom and others who took an interest in his schemes, and, like many another, no doubt received help with the manuscript before his *Travels* were published in 1778. But he failed in his main endeavour, and is said to have "died in misery, in 1780, at the age of 48."

His book instantly became popular, and it so remained, as twenty-three editions and translations bear witness. The author or compiler, whoever he was, understood the public, was a man of some imagination, and knew how to combine

Carver's own material with observations from previous writers; nor does he fail to mention, in the casual way of the time, authorities like Charlevoix and Adair, from whom, as we now look at things, we must say he unblushingly filches. Here is one of the examples pointed out by Professor Bourne. Charlevoix had said of the Indians in the English translation:

> On the smoothest grass, or the hardest earth, even on the very stones, they will discover the traces of an enemy, and by their shape and figure of the footsteps, and the distance between their prints, they will, it is said, distinguish not only different nations, but also tell whether they were men or women who have gone that way.

And in Carver we read:

> On the smoothest grass, on the hardest earth, and even on the very stones, will they discover the traces of an enemy, and by the shape of the footsteps, and the distance between the prints, distinguish not only whether it is a man or woman who has passed that way, but even the nation to which they belong.

In spite of his borrowings, and in spite of incredible and monstrous stories, even worse than the sordid actualities of savage life, Carver maintains that he is strictly veracious:

> I shall in no instance exceed the bounds of truth, or have recourse to those useless and extravagant exaggerations too often made use of by travellers, to excite the curiosity of the public, or to increase their own importance. Nor shall I insert any observations but such as I have made myself, or, from the credibility of those by whom they were related, am enabled to vouch for their authenticity.

These false pretensions easily lead one to underestimate the element of truth in the narrative, and Carver's share in its production. Carver was not too uneducated to make notes and gather materials for a book. He could write a long coherent letter to his first wife, and specimens of his writing are not in the hand of an ignorant man. He, not less than his assistant or assistants in publication, could have met with the works of Charlevoix, Adair, and Lahontan in London book-stalls. But it was hardly his pen that made reference to Plato and Grotius. The volume is dedicated "To Joseph Banks, President of the Royal Society." Then follows, in the second edition, a

magniloquent Address to the Public. The journal proper
occupies but a third of the volume. Next come seventeen
chapters on the origin, physique, and dress of the Indians, their
manners and customs, their government, their food, dances,
methods of warfare and games, and their language. The
eighteenth deals with animals, birds—as, for example, "the
Whipperwill, or, as it is termed by the Indians, the Muckawiss"
—fishes, reptiles, and insects; the nineteenth, with the vegetable
kingdom. There is an Appendix on the future of discovery,
settlement, and commerce. In his Introduction Carver says:

What I chiefly had in view, after gaining a knowledge of the
Manners, Customs, Languages, Soil, and natural Productions of the
different nations that inhabit the back of the Mississippi, was to
ascertain the Breadth of that vast continent which extends from the
Atlantic to the Pacific Ocean, in its broadest part between 43 and
46 Degrees Northern Latitude. Had I been able to accomplish this,
I intended to have proposed to Government to establish a Post in
some of those parts about the Straits of Annian, which, having
been first discovered by Sir Francis Drake, of course belong to the
English. This I am convinced would greatly facilitate the discovery
of a North-West Passage, or a communication between Hudson's
Bay and the Pacific Ocean. . . . A settlement on that extremity of
America . . . would open a passage for conveying intelligence to
China and the English settlements in the East Indies, with greater
expedition than a tedious voyage by the Cape of Good Hope or the
Straits of Magellan will allow of.

This was the dream that foreshadowed the present development of the entire North-west. It worked in the mind of
Jefferson, took shape in the Lewis and Clark expedition and
in the enterprise of John Jacob Astor, and reappeared in
Irving's *Astoria*. Carver's volume still fastens upon the imagination, as it did in the time of Schiller, Wordsworth, and
Chateaubriand.

Coleridge, who found pleasure in Carver's descriptions,
doubtless set a higher value upon Bartram; he says in *Table
Talk*: "The latest book of travels I know, written in the spirit
of the old travellers, is Bartram's account of his tour in the
Floridas. It is a work of high merit every way." The poet
almost certainly refers, not to *A Journal Kept by John Bartram*

of Philadelphia, Botanist to His Majesty for the Floridas; but to the volume of *Travels* by his son, William Bartram. Yet it is difficult to mention the son without reference to the father, whom Linnæus called the greatest self-taught botanist in the world. John Bartram, born in 1699, when almost seventy years old explored the St. John's River in Florida, accompanied by William, who in turn made a second journey to the region in 1773, "at the request of Dr. Fothergill, of London," the English naturalist being zealous "for the discovery of rare and useful productions . . . chiefly in the vegetable kingdom." Both father and son corresponded with European scientists, including Gronov and Dillen, but more particularly with Peter Collinson, through whom the elder Bartram came into relations with virtually all the distinguished naturalists of his time. The botanic garden for which the father began to collect in 1730, and which is now within the limits of Philadelphia, was justly famous. Here, it is said, Washington and Franklin were wont to sit and talk just prior to the Revolution; and Bartram's Garden is still an object of interest as the first establishment of its kind on this continent. From a local guide is extracted this description of its founder:

He was one of an early incorporated company to bank the Schuylkill and the Delaware, by which means he rescued, out of extensive swamps, arable land, and pasture for many cattle and horses; his crops of wheat challenge the farmer of to-day; he fertilized his orchard in an ingenious way that was a "miracle in husbandry." Besides, he was stone-mason; his interesting old house he built with his own hands, quarrying the stone on his estate in a remarkable manner; see, also, in the Garden the watering-trough and the cider-press, cut out of solid rock. And his record is fuller yet; he had to study Latin for his botany; he was enough acquainted with medicine and surgery to be of great help to his poorer neighbors; he delineated a plan for deep-sea soundings more than a hundred years before the *Challenger* expedition. His thirst for knowledge was insatiable. His joy in the revelations of nature was unbounded. What wonder that he was astonished when people complained that they were tired of time!

His son William, called by the Seminoles "Puc-Puggy" (Flower-Hunter), was born at Kingsessing, Pennsylvania, 1739, he and his twin-sister taking fifth place in the succession of children. He grew up with the Garden, accompanied his father on collecting tours, travelled himself, and published his *Travels through North and South Carolina, Georgia, East and West Florida, the Cherokee Country, the Extensive Territories of the Muscogulges, or Creek Confederacy, and the Country of the Chactaws*, as well as "the most complete and correct list of American birds prior to the work of Alexander Wilson"; he lived in Philadelphia, unmarried, a student of science, caring for the Garden until his death in 1823. A professorship was offered him in 1782 by the University of Pennsylvania, but failing health led him to decline it. His manuscript work on the Indians was published by the American Ethnological Society in 1853.

The *Travels* reveal the enthusiasm of a man still young, with an eye that nothing escapes, not without poetical imagination or philosophical vision, and with a deep reverence for the Creative Spirit which he feels in all about him. The volume is divided into four Parts. In the first, the Introduction, he recounts the voyage by packet from Philadelphia to Savannah, whence he proceeds to the "Alatamaha" River. The second describes East Florida, and the ascent of St. John's River in a small canoe. On reaching Lake George, "which is a dilatation of the River St. Juan," his vessel "at once diminished to a nutshell on the swelling seas." The Indian whom he engaged to assist him on the upper river becoming weary, Bartram continues on alone, to encamp at an orange grove, to battle with alligators, and to observe "a large sulphureous fountain." Descending again, he is robbed by a wolf, and so, after sundry adventures, arrives at the lower trading-house. He then "proceeds on a journey to Cuscowilla," where he meets with a friendly reception from the "Siminoles," and from there goes to view the "great bason" or sink, whose subterranean waters swarm with fish. In Part III, having returned to Charleston, he sets out for the Cherokee territories and the "Chactaw" country, going as far as Mobile, from which, turning back, he accompanies a band of traders to visit the Creeks. Again in the company of traders, he sets off for Georgia; from Augusta he revisits Savannah, whence he makes a "short excursion in the South of Georgia," adding to his collection, and gathering seeds of "two new and very curious shrubs." At Charleston he began the overland journey northward through Virginia; he crossed the River Susquehanna on the ice, "next morning sat forward again towards Philadelphia," and in two days more arrived at his father's house on the banks of the River Schuylkill, having been absent nearly five years.

Though collecting as a botanist and observing as an ornithologist, Bartram thus far has mainly been occupied with the Indians. In Part IV he discusses their persons, character, and qualifications, noting that they have the "most perfect human figure," their government and civil society, their dress and amusements, property and occupations, marriage and funeral rites, and their language and monuments. The ready pencil of the naturalist provided the engraver with drawings of botanical and zoological subjects throughout the volume. The frontispiece represents "Mico Chlucco the Long Warrior, or King of the Siminoles," whose dancing crest of splendid feathers flashes again in Wordsworth's *Ruth*.

A bare survey does scant justice to the richness of form and colour in Bartram's pages. At one time he is struck with "the tall aspiring Gordonia lasianthus." "Its thick foliage, of a dark green colour, is flowered over with large milk-white fragrant blossoms, on long slender elastic peduncles, at the extremities of its numerous branches, from the bosom of the leaves, and renewed every morning"—the "budding, fading, faded flowers" of *Ruth*. Or again we see the solitary dejected "wood-pelican," alone on the topmost limb of a dead cypress; "it looks extremely grave, sorrowful, and melancholy, as if in the deepest thought"—an image used by Wordsworth in Book Third of *The Prelude*. Of the "Alatamaha" Bartram says: "I ascended this beautiful river, on whose fruitful banks the generous and true sons of liberty securely dwell, fifty miles above the white settlements." Allured by the "sublime enchanting scenes of primitive nature," and by "visions of terrestrial happiness," he wandered away to a grove at the edge of a luxuriant savannah:

How happily situated is this retired spot of earth! What an elysium it is! where the wandering Siminole, the naked red warrior, roams at large, and after the vigorous chase retires from the scorching heat of the meridian sun. Here he reclines and reposes under the odoriferous shades of Zanthoxylon, his verdant couch guarded by the Deity; Liberty, and the Muses, inspiring him with wisdom and valour, whilst the balmy zephyrs fan him to sleep.

The apostrophes and redundant descriptions, which the rigorous German translator pruned away, did not prevent Zimmermann from calling Bartram's volume one of the most instructive works of the time. The faults of an unpractised writer are relieved by a constant cheerfulness, candour, and animation; "cheerful," "cheering," and "social" are favourite epithets. The words "animate," "animating," "vibration," and the like, give a clue to his Neoplatonic and Hartleian philosophy, which subtly recommended him to contemporary European poets:

If, then, the visible, the mechanical part of the animal creation, the mere material part, is so admirably beautiful, harmonious, and incomprehensible, what must be the intellectual system? that inexpressibly more essential principle, which secretly operates within? that which animates the inimitable machines, which gives them motion, impowers them to act, speak, and perform, this must be divine and immortal?

There is a motion and a spirit in the environment itself: "At the reanimating appearance of the rising sun, nature again revives"; "the atmosphere was now animated with the efficient principle of vegetative life"; "the balmy winds breathed the animating odours of the groves around me." "At the return of the morning, by the powerful influence of light, the pulse of nature becomes more active, and the universal vibration of life insensibly and irresistibly moves the wondrous machine. How cheerful and gay all nature appears." In Bartram the "feeling for nature" is quite as distinct as the idea of the "natural" man. The social philosophy of the time is more apparent in Crèveœur.

In a letter to Richard Henderson on the subject of immigrants, Washington writes (19 June, 1788):

The author of the queries may then be referred to the *Information for those who would wish to remove to America*, and [sic] published in Europe in the year 1784, by the great philosopher Dr. Franklin. Short as it is, it contains almost everything that needs to be known on the subject of migrating to this country. . . .

Of books at present existing, Mr. Jefferson's *Notes on Virginia* will give the best idea of this part of the continent to a foreigner; and the *American Farmer's Letters*, written by Mr. Crèvecœur (commonly called Mr. St. John), the French consul in New York, who actually resided twenty years as a farmer in that State, will afford a great deal of profitable and amusive information, respecting the private life of the Americans, as well as the progress of agriculture, manufactures, and arts in their country. Perhaps the picture he gives, though founded on fact, is in some instances embellished with rather too flattering circumstances.

"The name of our Family is St. Jean, in English St. John, a name as Antient as the Conquest of England by William the Bastard." So writes St. Jean de Crèvecœur, but he puts "J. Hector St. John" on the title-page of his imaginary *Letters from an American Farmer*. Born at Caen, 31 January, 1735, at the age of sixteen he went to England. A seven years' education there may explain the superiority of his English style over his French. Emigrating to Canada, he subsequently was resident in Pennsylvania, and in 1764 became a citizen of New York. After five years he settled as a farmer in Ulster County; at a mature age for the colonies he married Mehetable Tippet of Yonkers. He made journeys in New York and Pennsylvania, and to the west, to the south as far as Charleston—possibly to Jamaica, and into New England. In 1779, on attempting to return to France, he was imprisoned in New York City as a spy. When released, he went to England, sold his *Letters* for thirty guineas, and crossed to Normandy; we find him writing from Caen in 1781. Through the Countess de Houdetot of Rousseau's *Confessions* he was enabled to send a copy of his book to Franklin, then (1782) on a mission abroad. Instrumental in helping Americans in England to return to this country, when Crèvecœur himself came back, in 1783, it was to find his wife just dead, and his children in the care of strangers. Meanwhile he had been appointed French consul in New York. His travels with Franklin gave rise to a three-volume work, not so interesting as the *Letters*, entitled *Voyage dans la Haute Pennsylvanie*. From 1790 until his death at Sarcelles, 12 November, 1813, he lived in France.

The *Letters* of this "farmer of feelings" to a doubtless hypothetical "W. S. Ecuyer" are dedicated "to the Abbé Raynal, F.R.S.":

Behold, Sir, an humble American Planter, a simple cultivator of the earth, addressing you from the farther side of the Atlantic. . . . As an eloquent and powerful advocate, you have pleaded the cause of humanity in espousing that of the poor Africans; you viewed these provinces of North America in their true light, as the asylum of freedom, as the cradle of future nations, and the refuge of distressed Europeans.

Of the twelve, the Introductory Letter is intentionally rambling. A former European guest having asked for a detailed account of colonial life, "neighbour James" seeks counsel of the minister, who tells him: "He that shall write a letter every day of the week will on Saturday perceive the sixth flowing from his pen much more readily than the first." But the Farmer's wife dissuades him, unless the plan be followed secretly, so as not to arouse gossip. A chance allusion to the speeches of "friend Edmund," that is, of Burke, accords with the attention to style in the letters that follow. "If they be not elegant," says the minister, "they will smell of the woods, and be a little wild"; but he also assures the Farmer: "Nature hath given you a tolerable share of good sense . . . some perspicuity," and "a warmth of imagination which enables you to think with quickness." The second letter takes up the situation, feelings, and pleasures of an American farmer, and the third, on "What is an American?" relates the diverting experiences of Andrew the Hebridean, in his first meeting with Indians. In the fourth we pass to the Island of Nantucket, while the fifth describes the education and employment of the islanders. In the sixth, after an account of Martha's Vineyard and the whale fishery, the author returns to a discussion of manners and customs, this topic continuing in the seventh and eighth. The ninth transfers us to Charleston and the South, where slavery brings the author to "an examination of what is called civilized society." "Would you prefer the state of men in the woods to that of men in a more improved situation? Evil preponderates in both. . . . For my part, I think the vices and miseries to be found in the latter exceed those of the former." In the tenth, a special inquiry of the correspondent abroad is met with a dissertation on snakes and on the humming-bird. The eleventh is a letter "From Mr. Iw–n Al–z, a Russian Gentleman, describing the Visit he paid at my request to Mr. John Bertram, the celebrated Pennsylvania Botanist." The twelfth and last pictures the distress of a "frontier man"—menaced by the savages, and unsettled by the revolt of the colonies,—who "would chearfully go even to the Mississippi, to find that repose to which we have been so long strangers"; with his appeal to the Father of Nature, to the Supreme Being whose creative power inhabits "the immense variety of planets," the volume closes.

Crèvecœur's pretext of an inquiring foreigner mirrored the curiosity of Europe respecting the colonies, and the way in which that curiosity was satisfied, not merely through the multiplying books of travel, but also through the exchange and publication of formal letters. Such was the origin of Jefferson's *Notes on the State of Virginia; Written in the Year 1781, Somewhat Corrected and Enlarged in the Winter of 1782, for the Use of a Foreigner of Distinction, in Answer to certain Queries Proposed by Him.* This serious piece of scientific writing, perhaps the most frequently printed treatise that has emanated from the South, was compiled by Jefferson while he was Governor of Virginia, and sent to M. Barbé de Marbois, Secretary of the French Legation. It was first issued at Paris (1784–85). The arid statistics, the details of agriculture, and the generally dry geography, important in their time, now mean less to the reader than do Jefferson's occasional flights in a loftier style, represented in the following:

The Natural Bridge, the most sublime of nature's works, though not comprehended under the present head [Cascades and Caverns], must not be pretermitted. . . . Though the sides of this bridge are provided in some parts with a parapet of fixed rocks, yet few men have resolution to walk to them and look over into the abyss. You involuntarily fall on your hands and feet, creep to the parapet, and peep over it. Looking down from this height about a minute gave me a violent headache. If the view from the top be painful and intolerable, that from below is delightful in an equal extreme. It is impossible for the emotions arising from the sublime to be felt beyond what they are here; so beautiful an arch, so elevated, so light, and springing as it were up to heaven!

The influence of the *Notes*, of their author, and of Jeffersonian ideals, is constantly met in other works of description. The
allusions to Washington himself are scarcely more frequent.
In 1794 Henry Wansey, an English manufacturer, breakfasted
with Washington, and "was struck with awe and admiration";
but about the same time, Thomas Cooper, who, in a flying
visit, found "land cheap and labour dear," remarks that "the
government is the government *of* the people and *for* the people."
And when John Davis, the pedestrian, had from 1798 to 1802
"entered, with equal interest, the mud-hut of the negro and the
log-house of the planter," he dedicated his book to Jefferson.
Isaac Weld the Irishman, author of a widely read book on the
United States and Canada, wrote one of his thirty-eight letters
from Jefferson's then unfinished establishment at Monticello.
He made mediocre pencil sketches of Niagara Falls, and the
"Rock Bridge" of Virginia, but secured a picture of Mount
Vernon from a friend. He visited the Dismal Swamp, saw
Washington in a cheerful mood at a reception in Philadelphia,
and culled observations on the Indians, helping himself at need
from Carver and Jefferson. In Weld's account, the backsliding
of the educated savage Joseph Brant became heroic.

With Weld, the strictures of the British travellers upon
American life become sharp. A mild rejoinder to foreign de-
preciation soon appeared in the fictitious *Letters of the British
Spy* by the American jurist William Wirt, which purported
to derive from the abandoned manuscript of "a meek and
harmless" young Englishman of rank who was travelling in-
cognito. Composed in a formal Addisonian manner, this
defence of American statesmen and American eloquence is
overcharged with allusions to Cicero and Demosthenes. Nevertheless, some of the descriptions cling to the mind.[1] It is easy
to perceive why the booklet went through so many editions,
when one finds in it the leading men of the nation in 1803 under
a thin disguise. Here, for example, is President Jefferson:

The . . . of the United States is in his person tall, meagre,
emaciated; his muscles relaxed, and his joints so loosely connected
as not only to disqualify him, apparently, for any vigorous exertion

[1] See also Book II, Chap. III.

of body, but to destroy everything like elegance and harmony in his air and movement.

Wirt's young nobleman denies to the President the gift of poetical fancy; yet Jefferson allowed such imaginative faculty as he possessed to dally with the theme of western exploration. As early as 1784 he was devising names for ten suggested states to the northwest—"Sylvania," "Michigania," "Metropolitamia," etc.,—after the pseudo-classical taste of the day. He was therefore ready to promote discovery in the far North-west when the moment for action arrived. Indeed, before the Lewis and Clark enterprise, he had twice made plans for the same general undertaking. More particularly, while he was Vice-President of the American Philosophical Society, in 1793, he had arranged with the French botanist Michaux, then in this country, for an expedition which was to follow the Missouri and some tributary thereof to a point where these waters might communicate with the Columbia River, opening a way to the Pacific. The scheme fell through when Michaux became involved in a French marauding project against the Spanish, and lingered among the recruits in Kentucky. It seems that Meriwether Lewis, a young neighbour of Jefferson, had desired the position of leader in the great exploration.

Lewis, who in 1801 became private secretary to Jefferson, was born in 1774 of a prominent stock in Virginia. After five years at a Latin school, he studied botany on his mother's farm, then entered the army raised to quell the Whiskey Rebellion, and, serving as an officer under Wayne, rose to be a captain. In the eyes of Jefferson, Lewis was "brave, prudent, habituated to the woods, and familiar with Indian manners and character," besides possessing "a great mass of accurate observation on all the subjects of nature." When chosen to pilot the now famous expedition which bears his name, he further prepared himself by studying with competent scientists at Philadelphia; and feeling the need of a companion for the tour, he chose a friend of his boyhood, his elder by four years, Captain William Clark, also a soldier under Wayne, experienced in Indian warfare, and practised in the construction of forts. An unpolished, but staunch and friendly man, heartily returning the warm affection of Lewis, Clark accepted the opportunity with spirit, and made ready to join him in seeking the information which Jefferson desired "for the benefit of our own country and of the world." For a time it was Jefferson's pretence that the undertaking was "a literary enterprise." But when the sale of Louisiana was ratified, there was no further need of concealing the interest of the Federal Government in the project.

Lewis left Pittsburgh on 31 August, 1803, to meet Clark in Kentucky. They wintered in Illinois, as Clark writes,

at the enterance of a Small river opposit the Mouth of Missouri Called Wood River, where they formed their party, Composed of robust helthy hardy young men.

In the spring the detachment of twenty-nine regular members and sixteen supernumeraries began the slow progress up the Missouri. They spent the next winter in a stockade in North Dakota, proceeding in the spring of 1805 to the source of the Jefferson Fork of the Missouri, and under many hardships crossing over the barrier mountains toward the end of summer. Going down the Columbia River, they reached the Pacific at the close of the autumn, to pass the winter in their Fort Clatsop—log huts enclosed by a palisade. Here they had leisure to study the natives and to compile records. In March, 1806, they began the return journey. After surmounting the difficult snow-clad barrier in June, the party divided, Lewis making his way to the Falls of the Missouri, and exploring Maria's River, Clark returning to the head of Jefferson Fork, proceeding thence to the Yellowstone River, and following this down to the Missouri. Coming together again in August, they went to St. Louis in September, having consumed about two and one-third years in the wilds.

The subsequent duties of Lewis as Governor of Louisiana Territory, and of Clark as Superintendent of Indian Affairs, delayed the preparation of the records, although Jefferson was ardent for their publication. In 1809, Lewis, while on his way to Washington and Philadelphia to take charge of the editing, met his death, probably by violence, in Tennessee; whereupon the unlettered Clark, at the urgent desire of Jefferson, undertook the task with the help of Nicholas Biddle of Philadelphia.

Biddle performed the major part of the editing, and then Paul Allen, a journalist, supervised the printing. After many vicissitudes, the work was published in February, 1814. Much of the scientific material, however, was not included; nor was a strictly accurate account of the expedition and its results ever given to the world until the recent edition (1904–1905) of the *Original Journals* by Dr. Thwaites. Of the first edition, about 1400 copies were circulated, from the sale of which Clark apparently received nothing. Though the authentic work became popular in America and Europe, being reprinted and translated, the initial delay in publication, and the presence of other diarists in the party, made room for more than one earlier account of the expedition—for example, the *Journal* of Patrick Gass, of which there were five editions before 1814, as well as a French and a German translation in that year. However made known, the achievement of Lewis and Clark has won greater fame than any other geographical exploration ever undertaken within the United States proper. The Government expedition from Pittsburgh to the Rocky Mountains in 1819, under the command of Major Long, was more fruitful in technical results; and with the vast, though unmethodical, accumulations of Schoolcraft the data on Indians in the records edited by Biddle are not to be compared in value. But the authorized account of Jefferson's great enterprise, published in the concluding year of the final war with England, marked the fulfilment of Carver's vision, and betokened the approaching establishment of the United States as the ruling power in the Western Hemisphere.

When the strife of arms was settled by the Treaty of Ghent in 1814, a literary war between Great Britain and America burst into flame. It had long been smouldering. In the *Travels* of the Rev. Andrew Burnaby, of the Church of England, there was little to offend the jealous or sensitive American. This genial clergyman went through the "Middle Settlements," beginning with Virginia, in 1759 and 1760. His slender volume, published in 1775, had reached a third edition by 1798, being revised and enlarged, and was still valued in 1812 when Pinkerton chose it for his collection of travels in all parts of the world. Burnaby's affection for the colonies is only second to his love of England. He balances the advantages and disadvantages of North and

South, and of Philadelphia, New York, and Boston. At "Prince-town" he finds "a handsome school and college for the education of dissenters, erected upon the plan of those in Scotland," with "about twenty boys in the grammar-school, and sixty in the college." There are "only two professors, besides the provost." He sees beautiful homes along the Raritan River, and handsome ladies at "Brunswick"; but the people of Rhode Island "are cunning, deceitful, and selfish"—though he adds: "After having said so much to the disadvantage of this colony, I should be guilty of injustice and ingratitude, were I not to declare that there are many worthy gentlemen in it, who see the misfortunes of their country, and lament them." The lower classes at Boston are insufferably inquisitive; yet "Arts and Sciences seem to have made a greater progress here than in any other part of America." By 1798 Burnaby might well have revised his prediction that "America is formed for happiness, but not for empire." Before this there had been critics more hostile, like J. F. D. Smyth; but in British travellers who really belong to the period about 1800, there is a new and characteristic note of displeasure. Weld remarks that the Pennsylvania farmers "live in a penurious style"; they are "greatly inferior to the English." The roads are "execrable," and the Americans in general are prying. In Ashe, who had expected too much, the reaction against both people and customs is violent; he grieves because at Carlisle, Pennsylvania, he "did not meet with a man of decent literature"; and this is the mildest of his abuse. Weld, Parkinson, Ashe, and Bradbury, in a line, raise and re-echo the note of censure. Before Bradbury's work was published, there was a dismal chorus from the great British periodicals. As early as 1814 *The Quarterly Review* was chiming in, to be duly followed by the *Edinburgh* and the *British*, and by *Blackwood's Magazine*. Both Gifford and Sydney Smith lent their voices, and Southey was supposed by the Americans to have produced one of the bitterest attacks upon them. Various causes exasperated the discussion—discontented emigrants, discontent in England at the emigration, vainglory in America, especially over the outcome of the second war, the sensitiveness of Americans to the charge of inquisitiveness and lack of reserve, and, by no means least, the pirating of English books by American publishers.

The strife was at its height from 1814 to 1825. "In the four quarters of the globe, who reads an American book? or goes to an American play? or looks at an American picture or statue?" Such were the cordial questions put by Sydney Smith in *The Edinburgh Review* for January, 1820. The sourness of the reviewers, great and small, reacted upon new books of travel, and prospective observers when they crossed the ocean came with the prepossession that democratic institutions in America had corrupted good manners. There was a recrudescence of the old theory, once formulated by Pauw, that everything deteriorated when transplanted from Europe. Fearon (1818) — "no lover of America," said Sydney Smith,—Harris (1821), Welby (1821), and Faux (1823) gave the English public the reading it enjoyed, and the publishers welcomed fresh manuscript. "Have a passage ready taken for 'Merriker," whispers Mr. Pickwick's friend Weller to Sam. "Let the gov'ner stop there till Mrs. Bardell's dead . . . and then let him come back and write a book about the 'Merrikins as 'll pay all his expenses, and more, if he blows 'em up enough." Evidently the painful animadversions had not ceased in 1837; they were perhaps generally mitigated after 1825. Captain Basil Hall in 1829, Fidler in 1833, Thomas Hamilton in 1833, Captain Marryat in 1839, and Thomas Brothers in 1840, keep up the unlucky strain, sometimes with more, and sometimes with less good humour. Brothers is of opinion that "there is in the United States more taxation, poverty, and general oppression than ever known in any other country." And in January, 1844, *The Foreign Quarterly* asserts that "As yet the American is horn-handed and pig-headed, hard, persevering, unscrupulous, carnivorous, . . . with an incredible genius for lying." Ere this, however, better sense was prevailing. Basil Hall, though preferring the manners of aristocratic England, was not unkindly, nor was Mrs. Trollope (1832) unsympathetic. Dickens himself, having followed the Ohio and the Mississippi to St. Louis, and having visited Looking-Glass Prairie, in 1842 published his *American Notes*, in which he "blows 'em up" with moderation. The courteous Sir Charles Lyell (1845) was unfortunately justified in a dislike of American boasting.

Meanwhile the Americans, sensitive as well as vainglorious

or patriotic, on their part had not been idle, whether in the magazines or in books. *Niles' Weekly Register*, and *The North American Review*, with Edward Everett as editor, hurried to the defence, and Timothy Dwight, Irving, Fenimore Cooper, and Paulding were among those who, with or without finesse, parried the foreign thrusts. Robert Walsh wrote *An Appeal from the Judgments of Great Britain respecting the United States* (1819), while John Neal of Portland carried the fight into the enemy's camp by contributing to *Blackwood's Magazine* from 1823 until 1826. After Dwight's death his *Travels* in New England and New York were published, four substantial volumes, representing vacation journeys which he had taken for reasons of health from 1796 on. They are full of exact information on every conceivable subject—on the prevailing winds, on the "excellencies of the colonists of New England," "their enterprise and industry, their love of science and learning, their love of liberty, their morality, their piety," on the superiority of soil and climate, etc. But the serious vein was not the only one for such a contest, as Paulding was aware when he wrote the anonymous *John Bull in America, or the New Munchausen* (1825), which for its time was effective as an allegorical satire upon English opinion in relation to travellers. It is now less amusing than the strictures that called it forth. But there is something trivial about the whole episode.

The best kind of reply to the taunt of Sydney Smith was the literary work of Fenimore Cooper and Washington Irving, who are more fully treated elsewhere in this history.[1] Of Cooper's novels, three more important ones had been produced before he was entangled in the controversies that occupied much of his life. *The Pioneers* reflected his early experiences on the frontier; while *The Last of the Mohicans* deserves notice because it contains, in distinct types, both the idealized and the unidealized Indian that we have seen in the travellers. Chingachgook is a true descendant of Montaigne's high-minded savage, and belongs to the family of Rousseau's "natural" man; whereas the base "Mingoes" are more like real aborigines. *The Prairie*, with its large element of description, was followed during the author's residence abroad by *Notions of the Americans Picked up by a Travelling Bachelor* (1828), a series of letters by

[1] See also Book II, Chaps. IV and VI.

an imaginary Englishman, in which there is an attempt to rectify prevailing European and British misconceptions of America, and to show the Americans how to be more refined, and how to suppress their self-satisfaction. A middle course pleased neither English nor Americans; nor did the criticism in *Homeward Bound* and *Home as Found* tend to pacify Cooper's fellow-countrymen. The turmoil of his later years did not prevent him from writing two of his most popular novels, *The Pathfinder* and *The Deerslayer*, which again disclose his conception of the forest and frontier.

Few have depicted that life with more truth and spirit than Irving. From the noisy disputes between John Bull and Jonathan we come back to him as to a contemplative traveller of some previous generation; and in truth he carries on the tradition of Carver, and of Lewis and Clark. Returning in 1832, after an absence in Europe of seventeen years, Irving found his countrymen expecting him to vindicate his patriotism, and American letters, by some work on a native theme. Instead of directly yielding to the call, he made "a wide and varied tour," joining a Government expedition to the Arkansas River, exploring the hunting-grounds of the stealthy Pawnees, witnessing the pursuit of the buffalo, and sharing the spoils of bee-hunters. The result was *A Tour on the Prairies* (1835), which represents but a part of the journey. "It is," he says, "a simple narrative of every-day occurrences"; but it describes the motley life of the border with fidelity—Osage Indians, "stern and simple in garb and aspect," with "fine Roman countenances, and broad deep chests"; gaily dressed Creeks, "quite Oriental" in appearance; and "a sprinkling of trappers, hunters, half-breeds, creoles, negroes of every hue, and all that other rabble rout of nondescript beings that keep about the frontiers, between civilized and savage life, as those equivocal birds, the bats, hover about the confines of light and darkness." Irving's next task was to write the history of John Jacob Astor's development and consolidation of the fur-trade in the North-west (after the Lewis and Clark expedition), in *Astoria, or Anecdotes of an Enterprise beyond the Rocky Mountains*, which appeared in 1836. The literary method here employed is characteristic of so many books of travel, beginning with Carver's, that Irving may be allowed to explain it in his own words:

As the journals, on which I chiefly depended, had been kept by men of business, intent upon the main object of the enterprise, and but little versed in science, or curious about matters not immediately bearing upon their interests, and as they were written often in moments of fatigue or hurry, amid the inconveniences of wild encampments, they were often meagre in their details, furnishing hints to provoke rather than narratives to satisfy inquiry. I have, therefore, availed myself occasionally of collateral lights supplied by the published journals of other travellers who have visited the scenes described, such as Messrs. Lewis and Clark, Bradbury, Brackenridge, Long, Franchère, and Ross Cox, and make a general acknowledgment of aid received from these quarters.

The work I here present to the public, is necessarily of a rambling and somewhat disjointed nature, comprising various expeditions by land and sea. The facts, however, will prove to be linked and banded together by one grand scheme, devised and conducted by a master spirit; one set of characters, also, continues throughout, appearing occasionally, though sometimes at long intervals, and the whole enterprise winds up by a regular catastrophe; so that the work, without any laboured attempt at artificial construction, actually possesses much of that unity so much sought after in works of fiction, and considered so important to the interest of every history.

While engaged upon *Astoria*, Irving had met at the house of Colonel Astor the picturesque Captain Bonneville, and learning that the Captain possessed a manuscript record of his experiences among the Rocky Mountain hunters, he secured it for a goodly sum, thereupon proceeding to rewrite and amplify it in the customary fashion. From the popular *Adventures of Captain Bonneville* (1837), one gains an indescribable sense of the buoyancy of spirit in the open prairies, and of high tension in the life of the mountaineers, sanguine and alert in the midst of dangers known or surmised.

The general influence of these travellers and observers upon commerce and immigration is rather the affair of the historian and economist. Unquestionably the effect of innumerable guides for emigrants, and statistical works on agriculture, was augmented by books of travel which in substance were not always distinct from these humbler compilations. The trenchant if malevolent Cobbett, glorying in a life of cheerful industry close to the soil, and representing America as neither a paradise nor yet a den of thieves but a good nurse for the farmer, did much in the third decade of the last century to stimulate emigration of a better sort from the mother country to the land of free endeavour. Possession of the soil, and the opportunity to gain more and more of it—as depicted by Crèvecœur—must always act as a stimulus to the human mind. Once reaching these shores, a mobile population would be allured to the West through the virile descriptions of the Mississippi Valley by a Timothy Flint, or through the animated sketches of life and manners by a James Hall. To the literature of travel may also be ascribed much of the attraction exerted by this country upon distinguished foreigners in seasons of stress or misfortune. Napoleon himself once spoke of America as a possible retreat. If Crèvecœur's portrait of the free and social colonist was "embellished with rather too flattering circumstances," it was not the less true in presenting an ideal that the Americans have striven to realize; it was real in the sense that it governed their better thoughts and actions. By disengaging and projecting the ideal form of American life, such works interpreted the new republic for England and the Continent. More than this, they interpreted one part of the new nation to another. No other class of books can have done so much to consolidate the people; their effect upon character and imagination can hardly be overestimated.

They gave wings to the imagination; and here they are especially significant for the history of literature. As the discovery of America was accompanied by an outburst of poetry in the Renaissance, other causes, naturally, contributing thereto— as the mind of a Shakespeare was caught by a chance description of the "still-vexed Bermoothes"; so the great advances in geographical discovery and natural science after the middle of the eighteenth century made themselves felt in another generation of poets, and American travels found a quick response in works of literary art. The place of the travellers in the movement known as "the return to nature" would require for adequate treatment nothing short of a dissertation; nor could one always discriminate between the literary preconceptions which the observers brought with them and the ultimate facts about man and his environment which they transmitted to the poets. Yet we recognize in the reports of American travel something ultimate, as did the poets and philosophers.

Scattered instances suffice for illustration. In the speech *On Conciliation with America*, Burke, who himself had a share in an *Account of the European Settlements* (1757), betrays an acquaintance with more recent works of a similar kind. To one of Carver's borrowed passages on Indian funeral customs Schiller owes the substance of the *Nadowessiers Todtenlied*, a poem greatly admired by Goethe. Still better known is the employment of what is striking and exotic in Carver and Bartram by Chateaubriand in the composite landscape of *René* and *Atala*, and his mingling of conventional with imaginary incidents in the *Voyage en Amérique*.

In American and English poets, also, one may see the connection between higher forms of literature and books of travel. Freneau translates the *Travels* of the Abbé Robin (Philadelphia, 1783), and writes *Stanzas on the Emigration to America and Peopling the Western Country* (*Poems*, 1786). Timothy Dwight's "Most fruitful thy soil, most inviting thy clime," in *Columbia*, echoes the sentiment of his *Travels*. Longfellow derives the myth of Hiawatha from Schoolcraft, and is said to have used Sealsfield's *Life in the New World*, and Frémont's *Expedition to the Rocky Mountains*, in *Evangeline*. In Bryant, the allusion to

the continuous woods
Where rolls the Oregon

has been traced to Carver. *Thanatopsis*, the lines *To a Waterfowl*, and *The Prairies* alike reveal the spirit of inland discovery.

The relation of English poets to American observers is most significant of all. Coleridge praises Cartwright, Hearne, and Bartram; "the impression which Bartram had left on his mind," says his grandson, "was deep and lasting." Lamb is enamoured of pious John Woolman, and eventually favours Crèvecœur, yielding to Hazlitt's recommendation. Southey commends Dwight, and employs Bartram in *Madoc*. In *Mazeppa*, Byron, an inveterate reader of travels, takes the notion of an audible aurora borealis from Hearne. But the most striking instance is Wordsworth. Commonly supposed to have refrained from describing what he had not seen with the

bodily eye, and to have read little save his own poetry, he was
in fact a systematic student in the field of travel and observation, for the ends of poetical composition. Accordingly, he
writes to Archdeacon Wrangham, perhaps in 1811: "You
inquire about old books; you might almost as well have asked
for my teeth as for any of mine. The only modern books that I
read are those of travels, or such as relate to matters of fact—
and the only modern books that I care for." What they meant
to him may be seen in *Ruth*, which is full of images from Bartram—the magnolia, the cypress, green savannas, and scarlet
flowers that set the hills on fire; in *The Complaint of a Forsaken
Indian Woman*, based on Hearne; in the address to Hartley
Coleridge, reminiscent of Carver; in Book Third of *The Prelude*, where the ideal environment for a university and its
students is clearly that of Bartram's "Alatamaha" River,
"where the generous and true sons of liberty securely dwell";
and in Book Third of *The Excursion*. Here the Solitary, a returned American traveller, first relates his dissatisfaction with
the "unknit Republic," echoing Ashe, and English opinion in
the year 1814, and then tells of his vain search for the natural
man of Rousseau. He found little more to please him than
"the Muckawiss," of Carver:

> So, westward, tow'rd the unviolated woods
> I bent my way; and, roaming far and wide,
> Failed not to greet the merry Mocking-bird;
> And, while the melancholy Muccawiss
> (The sportive bird's companion in the grove)
> Repeated o'er and o'er his plaintive cry,
> I sympathised at leisure with the sound;
> But that pure archetype of human greatness,
> I found him not. There, in his stead, appeared
> A creature, squalid, vengeful, and impure;
> Remorseless, and submissive to no law
> But superstitious fear, and abject sloth.

The Solitary is not Wordsworth, but a dramatically conceived
malcontent. The animating note that is characteristic of
American travel at its best was sounded, not by English poets
in the time of George the Third, but forty years before the

close of the French and Indian War in Berkeley's anticipatory
lines *On the Prospect of Planting Arts and Learning in America:*

> There shall be sung another golden age,
> The rise of empire and of arts . . .
> **Westward the course of empire takes its way.**

CHAPTER II

The Early Drama, 1756–1860

OUR native drama, even though it antedated the novel and the short story, has practically no history until the latter half of the eighteenth century. The first drama written in this country which is now in existence, the satirical farce, *Androborus*, was printed, it is true, in 1714. It was by Governor Richard Hunter[1] of New York, but as he was an Englishman, the interest in his work is limited to its representation of local conditions. *Androborus* was not acted, and had no influence in the development of an acting drama. The two forces which seem to have led to the production of a native play upon the stage were the indirect influence of the early performances of masques and of dramatic odes and dialogues at the colleges, and more directly, the acting of the first regular company of professional players.

The earliest college exercise, including original composition, that has survived, is Francis Hopkinson's revision of *The Masque of Alfred*, originally written by Thomson and revised by Mallet in 1751, which deals with the invasion of England by the Danes. It was performed, according to Hopkinson's statement,[2] several times during the Christmas holidays of 1756-7 in the College of Philadelphia.[3] Hopkinson's original lines number more than two hundred, besides a new prologue and epilogue, and new scenes are introduced so that the masque may be considered as in large measure original. What makes

---

[1] For a description of *Androborus*, see Ford, P. L., *The Beginnings of American Dramatic Literature* in *The New England Magazine*, Feb., 1894, New Series, vol. IX., No. 6, p. 674.

[2] See *The Pennsylvania Gazette*, 20 and 27 Jan.; 3 and 10 Feb., 1757, for a detailed account of the Masque, giving Hopkinson's lines.

[3] Now the University of Pennsylvania.

it of special interest is the fact that Thomas Godfrey, our first dramatist, who grew up under the tutelage of William Smith, Provost of the College, and who was a close friend of Hopkinson, was in all probability prompted to write by witnessing this and similar early attempts at dramatic composition.[1]

Among these college exercises others that have survived are *An Exercise Containing a Dialogue and Ode Sacred to the Memory of his late Gracious Majesty, George II*, performed at the public commencement in the College of Philadelphia, 23 May, 1761, the dialogue being by the Rev. Dr. William Smith, the first Provost, and the ode by Francis Hopkinson. A similar exercise on the accession of George III was performed at the public commencement on 18 May, 1762. The epilogue on this occasion was by the Rev. Jacob Duché, Hopkinson's classmate and afterwards chaplain of Congress. A similar entertainment, *The Military Glory of Great Britain*, was performed at the commencement in the College of New Jersey,[2] 29 September, 1762, while there is evidence of dramatic interest at Harvard College if not dramatic authorship as early as 1758.[3]

Of more direct influence, however, on early dramatic writing, were the performances of plays by the company under David Douglass. There seem to have been theatrical performances in this country since 1703,[4] but the permanent establishment of professional acting dates from the arrival of Lewis Hallam and his company from England in 1752. This company acted in Philadelphia in 1754, where Godfrey doubtless saw them, and it was to this company after its reorganization under Douglass in 1758 that he offered his play, *The Prince of Parthia*, which he had finished before the end of 1759. It was not performed at this time, but was acted on 24 April, 1767, at the Southwark Theatre, in Philadelphia, according to an advertisement in

---

[1] For Hopkinson, see also Book I, Chap. IX.

[2] Now Princeton University.

[3] Matthews, Albert, *Early Plays at Harvard*, *Nation*, vol. XCVIII, no. 2542, p. 295, 19 March, 1914.

[4] Sonneck, O. G., *Early Opera in America*, 1915, p. 7. See also, for the beginning of theatrical companies, Daly, Charles P., *When Was the Drama Introduced in America?* 1864, reprinted in *Dunlap Soc. Pub.*, Ser. 2, vol. I, 1896; Ford, P. L., *Washington and the Theatre*, Dunlap Society Pub., Ser. 2, vol. VIII, 1899. For earlier performances by amateurs, see Bruce, P. A., *An Early Virginia Play*, *Nation*, vol. LXXXVIII, no. 2276, p. 136, 11 Feb., 1909, and Neidig, W. J., *The First Play in America*, *Nation*, vol. LXXXVIII, no. 2274, p. 86, 28 Jan., 1909.

The Pennsylvania Journal and Weekly Advertiser of 23 April, which contains a list of the players who were to take part. Godfrey did not live to see his play, but died in 1763, two years before it was published. This play, the first written by an American to be produced by a professional company, is a romantic tragedy, laid in Parthia about 200 B.C., and is written in blank verse of a flexible and dignified character. It is no unworthy beginning for American dramatic poetry, but it led at the time to no school of writing. It is interesting, however, to note that at a later period the most significant literary drama in this country was produced in the field of tragedy to which *The Prince of Parthia* belongs.

The Pre-Revolutionary period was purely a tentative one. The work of Charlotte Lenox, who was born here but whose plays were written and played in England, hardly concerns us, while such plays as *Ponteach*, by Major Robert Rogers (1766), or *The Disappointment* of Col. Thomas Forrest (1767), since they were not acted, fail to be significant, however tragic the recital of Indian wrongs in the former or however comic the hoax described in the latter may be. The *Conquest of Canada*, performed at the Southwark Theatre in Philadelphia, 17 February, 1773, has been sometimes referred to as "the second American play," but its author, George Cockings, was an Englishman, who wrote the play while in Boston, and it is in any case of little value either in matter or form.

On 20 October, 1774, the Continental Congress convened and passed a recommendation in its Articles of Association— that the colonists "discountenance and discourage all horse racing and all kinds of gaming, cock fighting, exhibitions of shows, plays and other expensive diversions and entertainments." Douglass and his "American Company," which had occupied the theatres in the colonies for almost a quarter century, left for the West Indies and the first period in the history of the American drama was closed.

During the Revolution a number of political satires were written, none of them, however, in strict dramatic form. The most important are *The Adulateur* (1773) and *The Group* (1775), by Mrs. Mercy Warren, of Boston, *The Fall of British Tyranny* (1776), by John Leacock, and the anonymous farce *The Blockheads* (1776), which has been attributed to Mrs.

Warren, but which internal evidence indicates is not by her. They paint the Tory officeholders and the British soldiers in very unflattering colours, but in no worse hues than the satirists on the loyalist side portray their enemies in such products as *The Americans Roused in a Cure for the Spleen* (1775?) or *The Battle of Brooklyn* (1776). There is no conclusive evidence that any of these were acted, though on the title page of *The Group* it is represented "as lately Acted, and to be Reacted, to the Wonder of all Superior Intelligences Nigh Head Quarters at Amboyne." The literary quality is not remarkable in any event, although Mrs. Warren at times writes a blank verse of considerable distinction, but their chief interest lies in their close relation to the great conflict they represent.[1]

The authority of Congress, except when ratified by action of the several states, did not extend beyond a recommendation to discontinue plays, but with the exception of a brief season in 1778 at the Southwark Theatre in Philadelphia, the activities of the Baltimore Company which began in 1781, and the later ventures of Ryan's Company in New York, the wishes of Congress were generally respected. With the coming of peace, the feeling against plays began to lessen. Lewis Hallam, the younger, returned to Philadelphia in 1784, and when he was coldly received there took to New York the reorganized American Company that was to be so closely associated with the history of the drama in that city. From the point of view of the production of dramatic writing, however, nothing is worthy of record until 1787.

In that year, dramatic performances were given by the American Company in New York, Philadelphia, Baltimore, and Annapolis. There was a more decided interest in things theatrical, but most important was the production in New York on 16 April, 1787, of *The Contrast* by Royall Tyler, the first American comedy to be produced by a professional company. As had been the case with Godfrey, the local company served as the inspiration for Tyler. The theme of the play is the contrast between simple native dignity as typified in Colonel Manly and imported foppery and follies represented by Dimple, Charlotte, and Letitia. The most important character, however, is that of Jonathan, the servant of Manly, who is the prototype of a

[1] For Mrs. Warren see also Book I, Chap. IX.

Dunlap

long succession of stage Yankees. Tyler also wrote a comic opera in two acts, *May Day in Town or New York in an Uproar*, performed 18 May, 1787, in New York, and after his return to Boston produced a dramatic satire entitled *A Georgia Spec. or Land in the Moon*, aimed at the rage for speculating in the Georgia lands of the Yazoo Purchase. It was played in Boston and New York in 1797.[1]

Important historically as Tyler was, this period is dominated by the personality of William Dunlap, whose first acted play, *The Father*, performed in New York on 7 September, 1789, was a comedy of manners inspired by the success of *The Contrast*. The success of this play and that of his drama *Leicester*, the second American tragedy, played first under the title of *The Fatal Deception*, on 24 April, 1794, inspired him to go on. According to his own statement he wrote fifty plays[2] "and other pieces unpublished," most of which were acted successfully. These include tragedy, comedy, melodrama, farce, opera, and interlude. He is especially significant as an adaptor of German and French plays, and it was through him that Kotzebue was introduced to the American stage. His first adaptation from Kotzebue, *The Stranger*, played on 10 December, 1798, was from an English version, but the success of this led him to study German, and he adapted and produced at least thirteen plays of Kotzebue, the most significant being *False Shame*, played in 1799, and *The Virgin of the Sun* and *Fraternal Discord*, both acted in 1800. He also adapted Zschokke's *Abaellino* in 1801 with great success, while his earlier adaptation of Schiller's *Don Carlos* in 1799 had been a failure. He did not neglect American themes, however, and one of his most popular plays, *André* (1798), afterwards rewritten as *The Glory of Columbia* (1803), represents the Revolutionary period. His career as manager of the American Company from 1796 to 1805 and the influence he had upon the development of the stage at that time make it fitting to close this period with the date at which financial difficulty forced him to shut his doors. He became connected with the theatre again from 1806 to 1811 and wrote even after that, but his later contribution was comparatively

[1] For Tyler, see also Book I, Chap. IX, and Book II, Chaps. III and VI.
[2] A complete bibliography of Dunlap records sixty-five plays. See Bibliography.

unimportant. This period is noteworthy also for the beginning
of organized dramatic criticism in New York in the work of a
group headed by Peter Irving and Charles Adams, who met
after the play, wrote critiques in common, and secured their
publication.

The next period begins naturally with the work of James
N. Barker of Philadelphia and John Howard Payne of New
York. Barker's first play, *Tears and Smiles*, was produced in
1807. This comedy continued the representation of contemporary manners started in *The Contrast* and reflected also the
reproduction of recent events in the reference to the Tripoli
pirates. In his dramatization of historical American life in
The Indian Princess (1808), probably the first dramatic version
of the Pocahontas story, and *Superstition* (1824), whose motif
was the witchcraft delusion in New England, Barker represents
the American playwright working with native material. Even
in *Marmion* (1812) he put in King James's mouth a ringing
speech which, while seeming to apply to Scottish conditions,
actually reflected the feeling of America toward England in
1812. *Marmion* was played as late as 1848. Payne, unlike
Barker, represents foreign influence. From 1806 when his
Julia, or The Wanderer, was acted in New York, his dramatic
work consisted largely of adaptation from English, French, and
German sources. His complete bibliography[1] records sixty-
four plays, of which nineteen were published. His most
significant work was done in the field of tragedy, such as his
Brutus, first played in London in 1818, or in comedy like *Charles
II*, first performed in London in 1824, while the bulk of his
work is composed of melodrama or farce. It was in his opera of
Clari (1823) that the song *Home Sweet Home* was first sung.
Payne's achievement can hardly be properly rated until it is
ascertained how much of his work is original, and so far as his
treatment of native material goes, he is not so significant as
lesser dramatists such as M. M. Noah, who made a brave
attempt to dramatize American history in *She Would Be a
Soldier* (1819) and *Marion* (1821). *She Would Be a Soldier*
was based on the battle of Chippewa in 1812. It proved popular; Forrest acted the Indian Chief in 1826, and it was repeated
as late as 1848.

[1] See Bibliography.

There are several reasons why the year 1825 forms a convenient point of departure in the development of the drama. Up to about 1822, largely through the excellence of the company at the Chestnut Street Theatre where Jefferson, Warren, and Wood formed a triumvirate in comedy, Philadelphia had been the theatrical metropolis.[1] Then the growing importance of the port of New York brought an increasing number of foreign actors to that city and made it important for an actor to begin his career there. The year 1825-6, according to Ireland,[2] was remarkable in the history of the New York stage, since it witnessed the first attempt to establish Italian opera with a fully organized company, the beginning of Hackett's career as a comedian, and the combination of Placide, Hilson, Barnes, and Miss Kelly in comedy at the Park Theatre. Most important, this year marked the real beginning of Edwin Forrest's career, both in Philadelphia and in New York.

The very prominence of New York and its proximity to Europe, however much they added to its theatrical prestige, hindered the development of the drama. The succession of English actors who were brought over as "stars" resulted in little encouragement to native writers, while in Philadelphia, under the encouragement of Edwin Forrest and others, a group of dramatists arose whose work became widely known both at home and abroad. For the year 1829-30 Durang lists nine plays by American writers, among them *Pocahontas* by George Washington Custis and John Kerr's first draft of *Rip Van Winkle*.

In 1829 Forrest produced the Indian play of *Metamora* by John Augustus Stone, an actor who lived during his creative period in Philadelphia. The play was a bit bombastic and the speeches of Metamora show a curious mixture of Indian and Ossian, but they are at times very effective and some of the phrases of this play became bywords in the mouths of the people.

Forrest also inspired Robert Montgomery Bird of Philadelphia to write *The Gladiator* in 1831. It was played by Forrest in all parts of the Union and at Drury Lane in 1836. In this play Dr. Bird combined the principal sources of dramatic interest—self-preservation, love of wife, child, and brother, desire

---

[1] See Durang, C., *History of the Philadelphia Stage*, Second Series, Chap. III, and Wemyss, F. C., *Twenty-Six Years of the Life of an Actor-Manager*, vol. I, p. 74.

[2] Ireland. *Records of the New York Stage*, vol. I, p. 483.

for freedom, and personal loyalty—in one central character, expressed this combination of qualities and sentiments in
a vigorous personality, especially suited for Forrest, and
clothed the sentiments expressed in a dignified and flexible
blank verse, varied at times by prose. Bird's tragedy of Peru,
Oralloossa (1832), but more especially his *Broker of Bogota*
(1834), both produced by Forrest, are among the most significant
of American dramas. The character of Febro in *The Broker of
Bogota*, energetic, with a middle-class mind but courageous
and with a passion for his children, is admirably conceived.
Bird was also known as a novelist, and one of his romances,
Nick of the Woods, dramatized by Louisa Medina in 1838,
proved to be one of the most successful melodramas of the time.
His *Infidel* was dramatized by Benjamin H. Brewster and
played in Philadelphia in 1835, and *The Hawks of Hawk
Hollow* was put on the stage in 1841.[1]

Bird's fellow-citizen, Richard Penn Smith, while not so
great a dramatist, is significant on account of his laudable
attempts to treat native material. At least fifteen of his plays
were performed, eleven of which have been preserved in print
or in manuscript. Of his tragedy *Caius Marius*, in which
Forrest starred, we have only tradition and one scene. His
national plays, *The Eighth of January*, celebrating Jackson's
victory at New Orleans, *William Penn*, his drama of colonial
and Indian life, both played in 1829, and *The Triumph at
Plattsburg* (1830), concerned with McDonough's victory on
Lake Champlain, are vigorous plays and were well received.

Although Robert T. Conrad's historical play of *Jack Cade*,
first acted in Philadelphia in 1835, was not written originally
for Forrest, it was through his acting that it received its best
interpretation. This play was a worthy rival of Bird's dramas
for favour here and abroad. It has a deeper significance than
appears at first glance, for it was made a vehicle for the expression of democratic ideals, and this strengthened its hold on the
American people.

The most significant of this group of Philadelphia dramatists was George Henry Boker. His first play, *Calaynos*, is a
tragedy based on the hatred of the Spaniards for the Moors.
Previous to its performance in Philadelphia in 1851, it had a

[1] See also Book II, Chap. VII.

long run at the Sadlers Wells Theatre in London in 1849, where Samuel Phelps played Calaynos and G. K. Dickenson, Oliver.[1] His second tragedy, *Leonor de Guzman*, produced in 1853, was also laid in Spain and is concerned with the revenge of the injured Queen, Maria of Portugal. His comedy *The Betrothal*,[2] produced successfully in Philadelphia and New York in 1850, and played in England in 1853, is laid in Italy. With the exception of *Under a Mask*, a prose comedy, performed in Philadelphia in 1851, all of Boker's acted plays are of a distinguished quality. His masterpiece, however, was his tragedy *Francesca da Rimini*, first acted by E. L. Davenport in 1855 in New York and Philadelphia, and revived by Lawrence Barrett in 1882 and by Mr. Otis Skinner in 1901. The art with which the medieval Italian life is depicted, the music of the verse and the noble conception of Lanciotto, the wronged husband and brother, lift this tragedy to its deserved place in the first rank of verse dramas written in the English language during the nineteenth century.

It is not to be supposed that dramatic talent was limited to Philadelphia. Epes Sargent and Julia Ward Howe in Boston, Nathaniel Parker Willis of Boston and New York, Charlotte Barnes Conner and Anna Ogden Mowatt of New York, and George H. Miles of Baltimore, to mention only a few, wrote plays that were definite contributions to literature as well as practically adapted for the stage. From this point it becomes necessary, however, owing to the wealth of material and the imposed limits of the chapter, to treat the plays from the point of view of types of the drama, rather than as the work of individuals, and this is also most productive of results. Examination of printed plays before 1860, combined with search through the histories of the stage, discloses about seven hundred plays by American writers actually placed upon the boards. These figures are obviously incomplete,[3] but they show at least the

---

[1] *Calaynos*, Lond. ed., n.d., p. 8.

[2] The facts given here and in the Bibliography are based upon the manuscripts of Boker, in the possession of his family.

[3] The histories of Dunlap, Durang, Wood, Ireland, Brown, Seilhammer, Clapp, Wemyss, and the MSS. diary of Wood have been carefully examined in preparation of these figures, but inaccuracies, confusions of titles of acted and printed plays, difficulty of deciding in all cases as to the nationality of the playwright, etc., make the statements only relatively exact.

wide activity of our early playwrights notwithstanding the
difficulties under which they laboured, and to which one of
them so vigorously refers.[1]

Of greatest distinction as literature are the tragedies.
About eighty of these were performed, forty of which are
extant, and they belong usually to the type known as romantic
tragedy. In many cases there is an additional historical interest.
Among those dealing with ancient history the most significant
are Payne's *Brutus* (1818), Bird's *Gladiator* (1831), David Paul
Brown's *Sertorius, the Roman Patriot*, acted by the elder
Booth in 1830, and *Waldimar* by John J. Bailey, produced by
Charles Kean in 1831 and based on the massacre at Thessalonica
in the fourth century A.D. Dunlap's *Leicester* (1794), Barker's
Marmion (1812), and Conrad's *Jack Cade* (1835) are the best
of the dozen dealing with English history, while the historical
interest is also definite in such tragedies as John Burk's *Female
Patriotism or The Death of Joan D'Arc* (1798), Dunlap's *Virgin
of the Sun* (1800), Mrs. Ellet's *Teresa Contarini* (1835), a Venetian tragedy, Epes Sargent's *Velasco*, laid in Burgos in 1046,
and acted by E. L. Davenport in 1837, and *Bianca Visconti*, by
Nathaniel Parker Willis, based on the career of Francesco
Sforza. This play won the prize competition offered by
Josephine Clifton, who produced it in 1837 in the principal
cities of this country. It held the stage as late as 1852. George
H. Miles's prize play of *Mohammed*, performed in 1851, and
Leonor de Guzman and *Francesca da Rimini* of Boker belong also
to this group. Even in the historical tragedies, however, it is the
unhappy lot of the main character and the interest of the unfamiliar that hold the attention rather than the background,
and there is no clear line to be drawn between those which are
historical and those which are not. To the latter class belong
Bird's *Broker of Bogota*, and a tragedy of peculiar interest,
Octavia Brigaldi, by Mrs. Conner, in which she acted in the
title rôle in 1837. The play was repeated often in this country
and was successfully produced in London. It was based on the
killing, in 1828, by Colonel Beauchamp of Kentucky, of
Colonel Sharpe, who had seduced Beauchamp's wife before
their marriage.[2] Mrs. Conner transferred the scene to Milan

at the close of the fifteenth century. This preference for foreign scenes, especially in Spain or Italy, remains one of the significant features of this type of play. There has been a tendency to criticize these playwrights for failing to confine themselves to national themes, which in view of the existence of *Hamlet*, *Julius Caesar*, and *Othello* seems beside the point. But there is nothing so satisfactory in a review of our early drama as the steady progress in romantic tragedy from *The Prince of Parthia* in 1767 to *Francesca da Rimini* in 1855.

Little criticism, indeed, may be levelled at the quantity of the plays based upon native themes, historical or contemporary. Disregarding mere pantomime, theatrical history down to 1860 records performances of nearly two hundred plays with a national background, of which some forty are available for examination. First in point of time come the Indian dramas, of which the most important are Stone's *Metamora*, Bird's *Oralloossa*, and the series of plays dealing with the Pocahontas theme. The best of these are *The Indian Princess* by Barker (1808), *Pocahontas or The Settlers of Virginia* by George Washington Custis, first played in Philadelphia, 16 January, 1830, *Pocahontas*, by Robert Dale Owen, acted first 8 February, 1838, in New York, with Charlotte Cushman as Rolfe, and *The Forest Princess*, by Charlotte Barnes Conner, acted in Philadelphia, 16 February, 1848. They all emphasize the love story of Rolfe and Pocahontas and make John Smith a central character. Mrs. Conner alone takes Pocahontas to England, where she dies. Of the colonial dramas, Barker's *Superstition* (1824) and R. P. Smith's *William Penn* (1829) seem the most significant.

As was natural, the Revolution was the most appealing theme. Practically every great event from the Boston Tea Party to the Battle of Yorktown was dramatized. The treason of Arnold and André's capture was a favourite theme and it is to our credit that André usually is a heroic figure.[1] Marion and Franklin were also favourites, but everyone else runs a bad second to Washington so far as the stage is concerned. One of

---

two novels, *Beauchampe* (1842) and *Charlemont* (1856), upon this event, and C. F. Hoffman his *Greyslaer* (1840). *Beauchampe* was dramatized in 1856 by John Savage under the title of *Sybil*, which was frequently played.

[1] See Matthews, Brander, Int. to his reprint of *André* in *Dunlap Soc. Pub.*, Ser. 1, No. 4, 1887.

the most interesting scenes occurs in *Blanche of Brandywine* (1858) by J. G. Burnett, in which Howe deliberately puts himself in Washington's power in order, apparently, to offer him a dukedom. After refusing in terms which are refreshingly human, considering the usual vocabulary allotted to the Father of his Country in literature, Washington calmly lets his antagonist depart in peace. Patriotism must have covered a multitude of sins in this class of drama, for it otherwise is difficult to explain the success of John Burk's *Bunker Hill* (1797), hard to recognize as the work of the author of *Joan D'Arc*. Dunlap's *Glory of Columbia* is not bad, and such a play as *Love in '76* (1857) by Oliver Bunce must have given a good opportunity for a clever actress.

Leaving the Revolution, we find the troubles with the Barbary States celebrated in eight plays, beginning with Mrs. Rowson's *Slaves in Algiers* (1794), which is made a vehicle to express abolition sentiments in general. The War of 1812 was reflected in such popular plays as *She Would Be a Soldier* of Noah (1819), and R. P. Smith's *The Eighth of January* (1829), and *The Triumph at Plattsburg* (1830). As an illustration of the quick reflection of events upon the stage we find a statement in Durang[1] that on 8 December, 1812, there came news of the capture of the *Macedonian* by the *United States* and that on 11 December a patriotic sketch entitled *The Return from a Cruise* was performed at the Chestnut Street Theatre, in Philadelphia, including a part for Captain Decatur. Almost as prompt had been the dramatization of the victory of the *Constitution* over the *Guerrière*. The fight occurred on 31 August, 1812. On 9 September, William Dunlap's *Yankee Chronology* was played in New York, while on 28 September, the opening night, a play was on the stage in both Boston and Philadelphia. Clapp tells us[2] that "in the early days of the theatre, every public event of sufficient importance was immediately dramatized, and during the progress of the war, the spirit was kept up by the frequent production of pieces in honour of our naval victories."

The Mexican War furnished its quota of plays, none, however, of special significance. Nor was the ready appeal to the

[1] Durang, First Series, Chap. XLIX.
[2] Clapp, W. W., Jr., *Records of the Boston Stage*, 1853, p. 134.

stage limited to martial themes. We find the Anti-Masonic agitation represented in such a play as *Captain Morgan or The Conspiracy Unveiled* (1827), while toward the close of our period the adventures of Walker in Nicaragua, the Mormon emigration, and the California gold fever find dramatic expression. Most important, of course, was the great question of abolition, reflected in the run of G. L. Aiken's version of *Uncle Tom's Cabin*, which was first acted at the Museum in Troy, New York, in September, 1852, and after long runs there and elsewhere was performed almost nightly in New York City from 18 July, 1853, to 19 April, 1854. Though it was not the first[1] stage version it distanced all others as to popularity. It follows the book quite closely in its language but is melodramatic in the extreme and is really a succession of scenes rather than a play. The same criticism may be applied to Mrs. Savage's *Osawattomie Brown*, which placed on the stage of the Bowery Theatre on 16 December, 1859, a dramatic account of the raid of 1 November.

The line is not easy to draw between these patriotic spectacles, dealing with events that have now become historic, and the comedies which reflected contemporary manners and customs. Both tend to become melodrama, and it would be fruitless to classify rigidly the large number of melodramatic comedies that are recorded as having had their day on the stage. Among plays of which record of performance has been kept, about four hundred in number, the largest group would be that of comedy, and it was from this group that the most significant plays from the point of view of stage development evolved.

In our first comedy, *The Contrast*, Tyler developed the stage Yankee in Jonathan, and though J. Robinson's *Yorker's Stratagem* (1792) and Barker's *Tears and Smiles* (1807) contain Yankee characters, it was not till *The Forest Rose*, by Samuel Woodworth, was placed on the stage in 1825 that a Yankee character was developed which permanently held the boards. The part of Jonathan Plowboy was played afterward by Henry Placide, G. H. Hill, Joshua Silsbee, and others. In the preface[2] to the play it is stated that Silsbee played Jonathan for

---

[1] See Brown, T. A., *History of the New York Stage*, 1903, vol. I, pp. 312–319, for an interesting account of the different dramatizations of *Uncle Tom's Cabin*.

[2] Woodworth, S., *The Forest Rose*, Boston, 1854. For Woodworth, see also Book II, Chaps. v and vi.

over one hundred consecutive nights in London. The comedy, which was accompanied by songs, is an interesting one, the action is quick and the conversation clever. In 1829 J. H. Hackett transformed the character of Solomon Gundy in Colman's *Who Wants a Guinea?* into Solomon Swop and, re-christening the play *Jonathan in England*, made a great success in it. Other well-known Yankee parts were Lot Sap Sago in *Yankee Land* (1834) and Deuteronomy Dutiful in *The Vermont Wool Dealer* (1839), both written by C. A. Logan, Jedediah Homebred in *The Green Mountain Boy* (1833) and Solon Shingle in *The People's Lawyer* (1839), both by Joseph S. Jones, and Sy Saco in John A. Stone's prize play of *The Knight of the Golden Fleece* (1834). These plays are usually of the same type, a comedy or melodrama into which a Yankee comic character has been inserted. He bears little relation to the play, but it is this very detachment that makes him im-portant, for he is the one spot of reality among a number of stage conventions, and it is no doubt this flavour of earth that secured the warm reception which these plays received. Read now, they seem hardly to justify it, but they point forward at least to a time when in the hands of an artist like James A. Herne this same material received a more significant treatment.

Another interesting development is represented in the local drama representing actual conditions, frequently of lower life, in the larger cities. The date of the first production of such a play would be hard to determine. Dunlap[1] speaks of a *Life in New York, or The Fireman on Duty*, before 1832. As early as 1829 Hackett appeared in a play called *The Times or Life in New York*, in which he acted a Yankee character. From the cast, however, as given in Ireland[2] it seems hardly likely that there was much realism in this play, however interesting it is as a point of connection with the species just described. More promising is the description of *The New York Merchant and His Clerks*, performed in 1843, with scenery "representing the Battery, Wall St., Chatham Square and the Lunatic Asylum." These plays, however, have not survived, but there can be little doubt that when F. J. Chanfrau made his great success in *A Glance at New York* in 1848, the public had been prepared to

[1] Dunlap, *History of the American Theatre*, London, 1833, vol. II, p. 381.
[2] Ireland, vol. I, p. 624.

Comedy

enjoy the type of play he furnished. The story of the building
of this play is an interesting one. It was written by Benjamin
A. Baker, the prompter at the Olympic Theatre, who when
Mitchell, the manager, had refused to produce it, insisted on its
production at his own benefit and had the satisfaction of
witnessing the tumultuous reception that Chanfrau received
in the part of Mose, the New York fireman. Chanfrau had
made a number of imitations of firemen before on the stage, and
the play was, therefore, a growth. It is melodramatic, but
there is a reality about the scenes in the dives and streets
that points forward rather than backward. Baker continued
in *New York as It Is* (1848) to exploit Mose, and the interest
in that form of play was capitalized immediately by other
writers and actors. *Philadelphia as It Is* appeared in 1849, and
in Boston George Campbell produced in 1848 a local drama in
which a scene in a police court was introduced.[1]

The vogue of these plays continued to the end of our period
and beyond, and there is little distinction, so far as type is
concerned, to be made between them and such a later play as
Augustin Daly's *Under the Gaslight*. Such titles as *The Dry
Goods Clerk of New York* (1851), *The Seamstress of New York*
(1851), *New York by Gaslight* (1856), *The Poor of New York*
(1857), *Life in Brooklyn, its Lights and Shades, its Virtues and
Vices* (1858) illustrate the nature of the species perhaps sufficiently, while *Mose in California* (1849) and *Mose in China*
(1850) show how cosmopolitan that gentleman became.

Much more important from the artistic standpoint were the
comedies proceeding by means of social satire. Here, too, we
turn back to our first comedy, *The Contrast*, for the beginning
of the type, but while we note in 1841 the production of a
"cutting satire upon fashionable life"[2] in the comedy of
Saratoga Springs, which was very successful, it was not until
the production of *Fashion* by Anna Ogden Mowatt on 24 March,
1845, at the Park Theatre in New York that we can chronicle
a social satire of any distinction. *Fashion* is a good-humoured
satire upon the artificial qualities of society in New York, and
introduces the snob who is taken in by a French barber, the
merchant ruined by his wife's extravagance, the confidential
clerk who blackmails his employer, and as contrasts to these,

[1] Clapp, p. 457. [2] Ireland, vol. II, p. 378.

the true-hearted farmer and his granddaughter who, by her efforts to save the daughter of the self-seeking social striver, almost loses her own lover. These are all types, to be sure, but they are made alive and the dialogue is clever. The play had a great success here and abroad,[1] and may be said to have founded a school of playwriting which lasts to this day. Its immediate successors, however, hardly came up to the standard set by *Fashion*. One of the best of them, *Nature's Nobleman*, produced in New York in 1851, was written by Henry O. Pardey, an English actor, who laid his scenes in Saratoga, Cape May, and a farm in New York State, and established quite well a contrast between American and English types. Mrs. Bateman's *Self*, E. G. Wilkins's *Young New York*, Cornelius Mathews's *False Pretences; or, Both Sides of Good Society*, all played in 1856, become caricature of a descending quality. Perhaps the most clever of the later comedies of social life is *Americans in Paris* by W. H. Hurlbert, performed in 1858.

In romantic comedy, there was very little that could compare with the achievement in romantic tragedy. *The Deformed*, played in 1830, by Richard Penn Smith, has some real merit, though it owes much to Dekker. *Tortesa, the Usurer*, by N. P. Willis, was played by J. W. Wallack in 1839 in New York and later in England, where Lester Wallack played Angelo to his father's Tortesa. It is an excellent play, and the last act, in which the usurer rises to the dignity of self-sacrifice, is especially appealing. Another play in which the two Wallacks were associated, *The Veteran* (1859), written by Lester Wallack, is an entertaining comedy laid in France and Algeria. Boker's *Betrothal* has already been mentioned. Mrs. Mowatt's *Armand, or The Child of the People*, produced in 1847 in New York and in 1849 in London, is a blank verse comedy of some merit. But here again the line between comedy and melodrama is hard to draw. Especially is this true in the plays dealing with Irish life, of which there are a number. One of the most interesting records in this connection is that describing the production, in 1842, after the playwright's death, of the adaptation of the novel of *The Collegians* by Louisa Medina. This play has not survived, but the

[1] For an interesting contemporary critique of *Fashion*, see Poe's *Works*, Virginia Edition, vol. XII, pp. 112–121 and 124–129.

cast[1] of characters is significant in view of the later dramatization of the same material in Dion Boucicault's *Colleen Bawn.*

The Gothic melodrama, illustrated by Dunlap's *Fontainville Abbey*, played in 1795, or his *Abaellino*, performed in 1801, was popular and in it he had a number of followers, some of whom, like S. B. Judah, in his *Rose of Aragon*, played in 1822, preserved the original meaning of the word Gothic. More interesting, if not more artistic, was the melodrama that dealt with contemporary events, such as Woodworth's *Lafayette or The Castle of Olmutz*, played in 1824, the year of Lafayette's visit to this country. Dunlap's importation of the domestic drama of Kotzebue had also its effect. Some of the dramas of this class, notably Noah's *Wandering Boys*, played first in Charleston in 1812 under the title of *Paul and Alexis*, were vastly popular. Most important in this class was the genesis of *Rip Van Winkle.* As early as 26 May, 1828, Thomas Flynn seems to have played a version of *Rip Van Winkle* in Albany. It was written by an native of Albany.[2] In October, 1829, there was produced in Philadelphia[3] a version written in whole or part by John Kerr, in which W. Chapman and later J. H. Hackett played Rip Van Winkle and " J. Jefferson " played Knickerbocker. This version was very popular and was afterward played in New York. A later play by Charles Burke is an adaptation of this one, with certain changes, notably the preservation of Dame Van Winkle, and the final version of Boucicault and Joseph Jefferson the younger is a development in its turn from Burke's play.

The farce as a species of comedy in the broader sense has already been spoken of in connection with the treatment of certain comic themes. Payne developed a form of farce largely from foreign sources, and W. E. Burton, by the development of farcical characters like the Toodles out of material whose history goes back to sentimental domestic drama, scored one of his greatest popular successes.

The dramatization of American novels calls for a word of comment here. The work of Cooper, W. G. Simms, J. P. Kennedy, C. F. Hoffman, R. M. Bird, T. S. Fay, Mrs. Stowe,

---

[1] Ireland, vol. II, p. 393.

[2] Phelps, H. S., *Players of a Century*, Albany, 1880

[3] Durang, Second Series, Chap. L.

and others, was quickly placed on the stage. It will be noticed that it was chiefly in the sphere of the romance that this was the case, Cooper being the prime favourite. Though this work was rarely done by a dramatist of distinction, it was often popular.

What impresses one most in a survey of these types of drama is the evidence of organic growth. It is possible to trace in the development of the drama in this country before the Civil War certain fairly distinct periods. The first ends with the closing of the theatres in 1774 and has as its principal event the production of *The Prince of Parthia* in 1767. The second, from 1774 to 1787, includes the Revolutionary satirists and is a transition period. The third begins with the production of *The Contrast* in 1787 and closes with the termination of Dun-lap's first period of managership in 1805. It was a period of tentative effort, partly under the influence of German and French models. The fourth period from 1805 to 1825 is one of development, with considerable native effort, but still largely under foreign influence, both English and Continental. The fifth was a significant and creative period, from 1825 to the Civil War, with its climax in *Francesca da Rimini* in 1855.

This development was interrupted naturally by the Civil War. What would have been its course had the war not occurred it is perhaps fruitless to speculate. There were signs of a quickening of dramatic interest in the late fifties under the encouragement of such managers as Lester Wallack and Laura Keene, but the domination of the stage by Dion Boucicault and John Brougham, while it resulted in some significant plays, especially in a later period, was not an unmixed blessing from the point of view of the production of American drama. The dramatization of English and French novels with resultant long runs, indeed the very success of Boucicault's original dramas, made for conditions in which the work of new play-wrights became less in demand. The old days in which a man-ager was willing to put on a play for a few nights were going fast, and with them went our early drama. That its significance in the history of our literature has never been appreciated is due largely perhaps to the fact that some of its most important monuments are still unprinted. But of its significance both in itself and for the later drama there is no shadow of doubt.

CHAPTER III

Early Essayists

IN anticipating Dr. Johnson's advice to fashion his prose style on the model of Addison, Franklin anticipated also the practice of American essay-writers for more than a generation. Like Franklin's *Dogood Papers*, the first essays printed in colonial newspapers were written with a conscious moral purpose. With some spice of wit Timothy Dwight and John Trumbull collaborated in an imitation of *The Spectator* in 1769–70, and between 1785 and 1800 nearly a hundred series of light periodical essays were contributed to various New England journals.[1] Those of the better sort like the "Neighbour" of *The Massachusetts Spy* or the "Metabasist" in *The Farmer's Journal* of Danbury, Connecticut, when not discussing politics, filled their columns with grave moralizing or racy satire on manners. They were widely copied and recopied by other papers, and a few such as Noah Webster's *Prompter* and Mrs. Judith Murray's *Gleaner* attained the distinction of separate publication by reason either of their plain common sense or their studied correctness. In general, the imitation of English models resulted in feeble literary replicas, or in strange patchworks of Yankee homespun with Addisonian finery.

During the first decade of the nineteenth century nearly every literary device and favourite character in the long line of British essayists was reproduced in this country. Isaac Bickerstaff owned an American cousin in Launcelot Langstaff of *Salmagundi*, memories of *l'Espion turc* were evoked by Wirt's *Letters of a British Spy*, and Goldsmith's Lien Chi Altangi dropped a small corner of his mantle on Irving's Mustapha Rub-a-Dub Kheli Khan and S. L. Knapp's Shahcoolen. The shade of Johnson dictated the titles of *The Traveller*, *The Rural*

[1] Ellis, H. M., *Joseph Dennie and his Circle*, p. 51.

Wanderer, The Saunterer, and *The Loiterer,* and such editorial pseudonyms as Jonathan Oldstyle, Oliver Oldschool, and John Oldbug were significant of the attempt to catch the literary tone of the previous age. But the essay of manners, a product of leisurely urban life, was not easily adapted to the environment of a sparsely settled, bustling young republic. "Perhaps, indeed," wrote the Rev. David Graham of Pittsburg, "it is impossible to give interest and standing popularity, to a periodical essay paper, constructed upon the model of the British Essayist, in an infant country."[1] Even in the populous cities "where the inhabitants amount to several thousand" there was little interest in the art of living. Reprehensible luxury and eccentric characters were hard to discover. But by dint of persistent attempts the essay of manners was made to grow in the new soil.

Perhaps the most successful "American Addison" was Joseph Dennie (1768–1812), who was "reasonably tinged with literature" while resisting a Harvard education, and after a short trial of the law, devoted his desultory talents to periodical writing until his death. He kindled the first sparks of a reputation by the *Farrago* essays, contributed to various country newspapers, but his *Tablet,* a hopeful weekly paper devoted to *belles lettres,* failed to set Boston ablaze. Yankee readers objected to his exercises in the manner of Goldsmith and Addison as "sprightly rather than moral." While a law-student, Dennie had supplemented his income by reading sermons in unsupplied churches, and now to gain a hearing he fitted each of his lucubrations with a text and tempered his sentiments ostensibly for the pulpit. *The Lay Preacher,* commenced in 1795, won immediate applause. Seven years later John Davis, the traveller, declared it the most widely read work in America, and its popularity contributed largely to the author's success as editor, first of *The Farmer's Weekly Museum* at Walpole, New Hampshire, and finally of that notable literary gazette, the Philadelphia *Port Folio.*

Though Dennie collaborated with his friend Royall Tyler in a mélange of light prose and verse "From the Shop of Messrs. Colon & Spondee," which later developed into a series

[1] *The Pioneer, consisting of Essays, Literary, Moral and Theological,* Pittsburg, 1812. P. 31.

of "Author's Evenings" reminiscent of men and books, his scattered writings were never collected or even completely identified, and his reputation must rest almost entirely upon *The Lay Preacher*. In these papers he sometimes dallied with a trifling subject, or to the indignation of severe critics applied a sacred text to the discussion of Mrs. Radcliffe's romances, or gave free rein to his eccentric humour in denouncing French innovations. But in the main he preserved a solemn front, dimming his wit with sobriety, as in the following extract from "Watchman, what of the night?"

Duty, as well as inclination, urges the Lay Preacher to sermonize, while others slumber. To read numerous volumes in the morning, and to observe various characters at noon, will leave but little time, except the night, to digest the one or speculate upon the other. The night, therefore, is often dedicated to composition, and while the light of the paly planets discovers at his desk the Preacher, more wan than they, he may be heard repeating emphatically with Dr. Young,

"Darkness has much Divinity for me."

He is then alone, he is then at peace. No companions near, but the silent volumes on his shelf, no noise abroad, but the click of the village clock, or the bark of the village dog. The Deacon has then smoked his sixth, and *last* pipe, and asks not a question more, concerning Josephus, or the Church. Stillness aids study, and the sermon proceeds.[1]

In reality, however, Dennie was as fond of conviviality as Steele, and as elegant in dress as Goldsmith. His literary pose had little in common with his actual habits of composition, as described by a former printer's devil of *The Farmer's Museum:*

One of the best of his Lay Sermons was written at the village tavern, directly opposite to the office, in a chamber where he and his friends were amusing themselves with cards. It was delivered to me by piece-meal, at four or five different times. If he happened to be engaged in a game, when I applied for copy, he would ask some one to play his hand for him, while he could "give the devil his due." When I called for the closing paragraph of the sermon, he said, "Call again in five minutes." "No," said Tyler, "I'll write

[1] *The Lay Preacher* (1796), p. 103.

the improvement for you." He accordingly wrote the concluding
paragraph, and Dennie never saw it till it was in print.[1]

No trace of the "nights of mirth and mind" that he shared with
"Anacreon" Moore, none of the ready puns that Irving learned
to dread, can be found in the pious columns of *The Lay Preacher*.
The wonder is, not that Dennie should be forgotten, but that,
writing so evidently against the grain, he should have achieved
his extraordinary vogue.

Among many young lawyers who found time to use their
pens while waiting for briefs, Dennie is historically important
as one of the first to adopt literature as a profession. Others
who continued to write as an avocation were easily allured into
religious or political controversy, for the renown of the *Federalist*
papers was yet new. So Royall Tyler, author of several plays[2]
and a series of periodical observations entitled *Trash*, besides
a waggish account of Dennie's first appearance at the bar,
became more a chief justice and less a man of letters after the
publication of his novel, *The Algerine Captive*, in 1797.[3] David
Everett, now barely remembered as the author of

> You'd scarce expect one of my age
> To speak in public on the stage,

wrote essays called *Common Sense in Dishabille* for *The Farmer's
Museum*, but his inclination for *belles lettres* soon yielded to a
maturer passion for writing political leaders and commentaries
on the Apocalypse. Only the hardiest political writings could
survive the frost of piety in New England.

Literary essays in the South were almost neglected in the
general enthusiasm for forensic and pulpit oratory, or when
written, reflected the formal style of public speeches. The most
persistent essayist was William Wirt (1772–1834), who commenced lawyer with "a copy of Blackstone, two volumes of
Don Quixote, and a volume of Tristram Shandy," gave sufficient
attention to the first item of his library to become Attorney-
General of the United States, and left as his chief literary
monument a biography of Patrick Henry. *The Letters of a
British Spy*, first printed in the Richmond *Argus* for 1803,

[1] J. T. Buckingham, *Specimens of Newspaper Literature* (1852), vol. II, p. 197.
[2] See also Book II, Chap. II.   [3] See also Book II, Chap. VI.

justly gained him a reputation as a critic and master of eloquence.[1] A temperateness, discernment, and sincerity unusual in the journalism of the day marked his observations on
Virginia society and his strictures on the style of public men,
and his descriptive powers, best illustrated in the striking
picture of the Blind Preacher, elevated the *Spy* at once into the
class of "elegant native classical literature." Later in conjunction with friends Wirt wrote ten essays, collected as *The
Rainbow*, dealing with sundry political and social questions.
These, like *The Old Bachelor*, in which he set himself to follow
more closely the admired model of Addison, were too thickly
studded with florid passages, oratorical climaxes, and didactic
fulminations. Wirt's natural charm of manner survived only
in his playful private letters.[2] Nothing of permanent mark
came from the facile pen of William Crafts, editor of the
Charleston *Courier*, and the ornate prose of Hugh Swinton
Legaré is that of the scholar rather than of the familiar essayist.

New York and Philadelphia were comparatively free from
the blight of theology and the bane of eloquence, though the
latter city seems to have suffered from a constitutional profundity which even Dennie could not entirely overcome. It
gave to the world nothing better than the *Didactics* of Robert
Walsh. The commercial interests of Manhattan could claim
little attention from young men of wit and spirit, but leisure
and a society both cosmopolitan and congenial afforded them
ample opportunity and provocation for literary *jeux d'esprit*.
When the busy savant, Samuel Latham Mitchill, presided at
the Sour Krout crowned with cabbage leaves or burlesqued his
own erudition in jovial speeches at the Turtle Club, what
wonder if Irving and the "lads of Kilkenny" found time to
"riot at Dyde's on imperial champagne" or to sally out to
Kemble's mansion on the Passaic—the original of Cockloft
Hall—for a night of high fun and jollification. Dr. Mitchill's
Picture of New York, with a wealth of geological and antiquarian lore travestied in the first part of the "Knickerbocker"
History, records the numerous landmarks and traditions of

[1] An imitation called "The British Spy in Boston" appeared in *The Port Folio*
for 3–24, Nov., and 22 Dec., 1804. An amusing parody of these followed on 26
Jan., 1805.
[2] See also Book II, Chaps. I and XVII.

the city. Corlaer's Hook was then something more than a
memory, Hell Gate was still a menace to navigation, the Collect
was not all filled up, and the tolls levied at Kissing Bridge
formed a standing jest. In such an environment the tradition
of Steele and Goldsmith culminated not unworthily with *Salmagundi*, a buoyant series of papers ridiculing the follies of 1807.
Thereafter imitation of Addison could no further go. Moreover,
in announcing with mock gravity their intention "simply to
instruct the young, reform the old, correct the town, and casti-
gate the age" the authors of *Salmagundi* exposed the prevailing
overearnestness of the grim guardians of public virtue and
taught their readers to expect entertainment as well as instruction from writers of the essay.

James Kirke Paulding (1779–1860), Washington Irving's
chief assistant in this youthful venture, shared with his collaborator a love of English letters, a vivid recollection of the
New York of their boyhood, and a keen eye for odd whim-
whams and curiosities of character. So closely akin were they
in spirit that to identify completely the contributions of either
writer would be a hopeless task, but the papers known to have
been written wholly or in large measure by Paulding indicate
that his part in the undertaking was not inferior to Irving's.
Nor was Paulding less a master of a graceful and vivacious
style, formed by his boyish reading of *The Citizen of the World*.
It was he who first sketched the characters of the Cockloft
family, and in the case of "Mine Uncle John" he took the
likeness of a real uncle as deftly as Irving portrayed the lively
Mrs. Cooper in Sophie Sparkle or the fastidious Joseph
Dennie in Launcelot Langstaff. Aunt Charity, who "died
of a Frenchman," was apparently a joint production. The
two writers might have acquired from Steele and his successors the art of drawing crotchety characters, if not the
fondness for detecting them, but the inevitable urban setting
of the British essays afforded few models for such studies of
nature as the "Autumnal Reflections" of the seventeenth
Salmagundi paper. There Paulding—who undoubtedly had a
hand in it—discovered a happy talent for combining gentle
melancholy with landscape description which remained one of
the most attractive elements in his varied writings. Almost
the only quotable passages in his pretentious poem, *The Back-*

woodsman,[1] have to do with wild and romantic scenery, and when in 1819 he revived the name, though not the sparkle of *Salmagundi*, the serious admonitory air of his continuation was sometimes freshened by vignettes of the Hudson valley or the frontier. After the second series of "Old Sal," Paulding wrote few essays except the unremarkable *Odds and Ends* contributed in his old age to *The Literary World*, but in his *Letters from the South*, in his tales and novels,[2] and even in his prose satires he found opportunities to manifest his delight in American scenes. Unlike Irving, he never travelled, and the beauties of his native land remained in his eyes unrivalled.

While the author of *Bracebridge Hall* and the *Alhambra* was cultivating his cosmopolitan fancy in many lands, Paulding grew more and more intensely local. In accepting the cares of a family and of official position—he was eventually Secretary of the Navy under Van Buren—he lessened his opportunities to develop his literary talent, and at the same time increased his desire to exalt the glory of American letters. Unusually sensitive to the faults of his fellow-countrymen, he too often went out of his way to rail at primogeniture, lotteries, French fashions, paper money, and the charities of "those venerable married ladies, and thrice venerable spinsters, who go about our cities like roaring lions, doing good." When in such works as in *Merry Tales of the Three Wise Men of Gotham* (1826), and the *New Mirror for Travellers* (1828), he undertook to quiz political or fashionable failings, his irony was not infrequently more severe than just. The same objection may be applied with double force to the acrimonious squibs which he hurled at British critics who dared sneer at American innovations.[3] Like many of his contemporaries Paulding could not refrain from using his stylus as a dagger whenever patriotically aroused, and he lost no opportunity to flaunt the merits of republican institutions before the "crowned heads" of Europe. He may best be remembered as an author whose faults and virtues combined to make him exclusively and eminently national.

Salmagundi was but one of a number of hopeful productions issued by two or three young men in combination or even by literary clubs after the traditional fashion of periodical essays.

[1] See also Book II, Chap. v.
[2] See also Book II, Chap. VII.
[3] See also Book II, Chap. I.

In 1818–19 a Baltimore society, which claimed Wirt as a member, printed a fortnightly leaflet called *The Red Book*, containing, besides verse, occasional papers by the future novelist, John Pendleton Kennedy.[1] William Tudor, one of the Monthly Anthology Club of Boston, and first editor of *The North American Review*, collected his *Miscellanies* in 1821, and in that and the following year a more original member of the same coterie, the elder Richard Henry Dana,[2] edited and mainly wrote the six numbers of *The Idle Man*, perhaps the most notable competitor of Irving's *Sketch Book*. Much of Dana's work may be paralleled elsewhere; the half-Shandean meditation on a suitable title for his periodical, the sketches of Ned Fillagree and Bob Brazen and of the whimsical old gentleman and his club, the eulogy of Kean's acting, and the plea for a more confident and independent criticism of American books—though this last does not lack vehemence—are not essentially different from such stuff as essays were usually composed of. But the papers on " Domestic Life " and the "Musings" on the power of the imagination redeem their triteness of subject by a noble sincerity and depth of poetic insight not unworthy of a prose Wordsworth. Three numbers of *The Idle Man* are taken up by tales of gloomy intensity which fall within the compass of this chapter only as they illustrate the ease with which the periodical essay might merge with the then unrecognized short story. Not a few contributions in the *Miscellanies* of Verplanck, Bryant, and Sands (originally published as *The Talisman* for 1828, 1829, 1830) were made of a descriptive or didactic essay prefixed to a simple tale, and the gleanings from numerous annuals included by the publisher, S. G. Goodrich, in *Sketches from a Student's Window* (1841), can hardly be classed except as an indistinguishable compound of essays and stories. In none of these cases are the narratives apologues or character sketches of the sort traditionally associated with the periodical essay.

Dana, though he continued to live in Cambridge, was intimately connected with Bryant and his set. *The Idle Man* was printed in New York, and it was there, naturally enough, that the vein opened by Irving and Paulding in *Salmagundi* was most consistently followed by writers of the Knickerbocker group, many of them contributors at one time or another to

[1] See also Book II, Chap. VII.   [2] See also Book II, Chap. V.

Colonel Morris's *New York Mirror*. From that paper Theodore Sedgwick Fay, better known as the author of successful but mediocre novels, clipped enough of his occasional writings to fill two volumes entitled *Dreams and Reveries of a Quiet Man* (1832). Save for the lively satire of the *Little Genius* essays and a delicious travesty of Mrs. Trollope, there is little of other than historical interest in Fay's pictures of New York life. Distinctly in better form are the *Crayon Sketches* by William Cox, an English printer once in the employ of *The Mirror*. In his fondness for the theatre, his devotion to Scott, and his love of old English scenes and customs, Cox had much in common with Irving. Here too should be mentioned the editors, Park Benjamin of *The American Monthly Magazine* and *Brother Jonathan*, poet and miscellaneous writer; Lewis Gaylord Clark of *The Knickerbocker Magazine;* and his twin brother, Willis Gaylord Clark, a Philadelphia journalist whose "Ollapodiana" papers inherited something of Lamb and anticipated something of Holmes.[1]

Flashes of cleverness, geniality, and quiet humour, however, could not conceal the lack of originality and barrenness of invention that were becoming more and more apparent among the remoter satellites of Geoffrey Crayon. The stream of discursive literature was indeed running dry when Nathaniel Parker Willis (1806–61) burst into prominence like a spring freshet, frothy, shallow, temporary, but sweeping all before it. This prince of magazinists, precociously celebrated as a poet even before his graduation from Yale in 1823, and petted by society in this country and abroad, has suffered the fate of other ten days' wonders. Though the evanescent sparkle and glancing brilliance of his *A l'Abri*, less extravagantly known by its later title of *Letters from under a Bridge*, fully deserved Lowell's praise, though it is possible to understand the popularity of his vivid, vivacious glimpses of European society in *Pencillings by the Way* and the vogue of his clever "Slingsby" stories in *Inklings of Adventure*, yet it cannot be denied that Willis too often merited the charges of affectation and mawkishness which we still instinctively associate with the elaborately gilded backs of his many volumes. Unluckily he wrote himself out just at the time when his necessities compelled him to have

[1] See also Book II, Chap. xx.

continuous recourse to his pen for a livelihood. His later books sound like a parody of his true manner. It is unnecessary, therefore, to dwell upon the reasons for the decline of his immense reputation; they are obvious.

Nor is it needful to distinguish the paste from the genuine in the composition of the man himself; to defend him from the charge of puppyism by insisting upon his kindliness to younger authors. All that concerns us here is to indicate in what ways Willis inaugurated a temporary but essential phase in the development of the essay and indeed of American letters. The time had come to break with the smooth, dry, elegant style. Willis's romantic and sentimental ardour influenced more than his choice of subject; it dictated his whole manner. He was the most formless of writers. His eclectic, tentative genius readily expressed itself, and often with great charm, in amorphous informal blends of essay, letter, and story. Fleeting impressions, "dashes at life," ephemera, "hurry-graphs" were his forte. In an established form like the novel he was never successful. Striving to be original at all costs, he first embellished, then later mutilated the English language, sticking it full of foreign phrases, coined words, and oddities of diction culled from all times and localities. If these things seem intolerable when compared to the sure classic perfection of Irving's style, we must remember that fluidity is essential to the innovator. Willis followed no tradition, good or bad. That with no guide but his own not infallible taste he should have reached at his best an easy, supple grace of manner, never for a moment tedious, is an evidence of uncommon powers, and even his weaknesses, his not infrequent soft spots, show that at least he was independent of the methods of eighteenth-century prose.

In this respect Willis has been compared to Leigh Hunt, whom in several ways he certainly resembled, but he was not, like Hunt, an omnivorous reader. The social sense was stronger in him than literary instinct; the merits of his best work are the merits of lively chat. During his European wanderings he learned more from men than from books, and from women most of all. His Diotima was Lady Blessington, whose literary dinners and *soirées* were duly, in *The New York Mirror*, dashed at by his free pencil. At Gore House he heard gossip of Byron, saw D'Israeli in action, and met Rogers, Procter, Moore, and Bulwer, men of letters and men of the world. After such models Willis shaped his own career. He luxuriated in drawing-rooms and shone at dinners,

> The topmost bright bubble on the wave of The Town.

With his rapid glances into the kaleidoscope of society he combined—for his readers—views of famous places, anecdotes of travel, reflections by the way, descriptions of scenery, and observations on customs and characters, in all a delightfully varied mixture and exactly suited to his tastes and abilities. In America he wrote with the same minuteness and freshness of his rural life and rural neighbours at Glenmary and Idlewild, painted vivid word-pictures of such beauty spots as Nahant or Trenton Falls, or sketched fashionable life at Ballston and Saratoga in the days when those watering places were in their first glory. There where woods and streams were enlivened by flowered waistcoats, pink champagne, and the tinkle of serenades, Willis found a setting for some of his most characteristic writing. Jaunty and impermanent as the society it portrayed, his pages yet contain the most valuable deposit left by what Professor Beers has happily called the "Albuminous Age" of American literature.[1]

A more reserved, though hardly less voluminous writer than Willis, was the critic, biographer, and essayist, Henry Theodore Tuckerman, born in Boston in 1813 and from 1845 until his death in 1871 a resident of New York. As a young man he twice spent a year or two abroad, of which the fruits were an *Italian Sketch Book* in 1835 and several other volumes of travel. Meanwhile he had been reading widely, studying art, and meeting authors and painters. These things combined with a native fineness of temperament to preserve him from falling into the verbal excesses of Willis. Whatever else Tuckerman lacked, he was not wanting in good taste.

As a critic Tuckerman earned the praise of Irving for his "liberal, generous, catholic spirit." The solid merits of his *Thoughts on the Poets* were admired in Germany, where the

---

[1] Professor H. A. Beers has in every respect said the last word on Willis in his *Life* (*American Men of Letters*) and Introduction to *Selected Prose* (1885).

work was translated. But more popular in this country were *Characteristics of Literature* and *Essays, Biographical and Critical*, which illustrate various types of genius by little biographies of representative men. Addison, for instance, appeared—with no reference to Dennie—as the Lay Preacher. Many introductions, magazine articles on literature, and two books on American artists gave evidence of Tuckerman's critical versatility.

His cosmopolitan training is equally apparent in his familiar essays. *The Optimist* (1850) was nearly akin to the miscellaneous reflections sometimes imbedded in his early books of travel. It was followed by *The Criterion*, more appropriately known in England as *The Collector*, in 1866. Antiquarian in spirit, fond of mingling bits of book-lore with personal reminiscence, Tuckerman picks his meditative and discriminating way along the byways of literature and life. Authors, Pictures, Inns, Sepulchres, Holidays, Bridges, equally provoke his ready flow of illustrative anecdote and well-chosen quotation. With Longfellow and others, he did much to familiarize the American public with a wide range of literature. His cosmopolitanism, however, though of considerable service to his contemporaries, prevented him from interpreting the America that he knew to other countries or to after times. His pleasantly pedantic essays are no longer either novel or informing. Lowell and Whipple have left him scarcely a corner of his chosen field.

CHAPTER IV

Irving

WASHINGTON IRVING was born in William Street, New York City, 3 April, 1783. As this was the year in which the colonies finally achieved the independence for which they had been fighting for seven years, Irving may be regarded as the first author produced in the new republic. The writer recalls that he visited Sunnyside with his father a year or two before the death of Irving and heard him narrate, doubtless not for the first time, how, when he was a youngster a year old, his nurse had held him up in her arms while Washington was passing by on horseback, in order that the General might place his hand on the head of the child who bore his name. "My nurse told me afterwards," said Irving, "that the General lifted me in his arms up to the pommel of his saddle and bestowed upon me a formal blessing." The listening boy looked, with reverential awe, at the head that had been touched by the first president, but when later he told his father about Irving's words, the father said: "You did not see the spot that Washington touched." "And why not?" was the natural question. "You goose," came the retort, "do you not know that Mr. Irving wears a wig?"

Washington Irving was prevented by poor health from following his two elder brothers to Columbia College. His formal training was limited to a course of a few years in the public schools of the day. He had always, however, encouraged in himself a taste for reading and an interest in human affairs so that his education went on steadily from year to year. His father, a Scotchman by birth, had built up an importing business and ranked well among the leading merchants of the city. The family comprised in all five sons and two daughters. The relations to each other of these brothers and sisters were always closely sympathetic, and throughout the record of Irving's career the reader is impressed with the loyal service rendered, first, by the elder brothers to the younger, and later, when the family property had disappeared and the earnings of the youngster had become the mainstay of the family, by Washington himself to his seniors, and to his nieces.

In 1804, Irving, who had just attained his majority, made his first journey to Europe. His father had died some years earlier, and the direction of the family affairs was in the hands of the eldest brother William. The trip seems to have re-established Washington's health, which had been a cause of anxiety to his brothers. After a voyage of forty-two days he landed in Bordeaux, whence he journeyed to Paris. He then travelled by way of Marseilles to Genoa, from which point he went by stage-coach through some of the picturesque regions in Italy. It was on these trips that he secured his first impressions of the Italian hill country and of the life of the country folk, impressions that were utilized later in the *Tales of a Traveller*. From Naples, crossing to Palermo, he went by stage to Messina, and he was there in 1805 when the vessels of Nelson passed through the straits in their search for the combined French and Spanish fleet under Villeneuve, a search which culminated in the great victory at Trafalgar.

Journeying in Europe during those years of war and of national upheaval was a dangerous matter. Irving was stopped more than once, and on one occasion was arrested at some place in France on the charge of being an English spy. He seems to have borne the troublesome interruptions with a full measure of equanimity, and he used each delay to good purpose as an opportunity for a more leisurely study of the environment and of the persons with whom he came into touch. He returned to New York early in 1806, shortly after Europe had been shaken by the battle of Austerlitz.[1]

Irving was admitted to the bar in November, 1806, having previously served as attorney's clerk, first with Brockholst Livingston and later with Josiah Ogden Hoffman. The law

---

[1] During these journeys he took notes, wrote them out in a full journal, portions of which are shortly to be published, and utilized his material in elaborate letters to his relations.

failed, however, to exercise for him any fascination, and his practice did not become important. He had the opportunity of being associated as a junior with the counsel who had charge of the defence of Aaron Burr in the famous trial held in Richmond in June, 1807. The writer remembers the twinkle in the old gentleman's eye when he said in reply to some question about his legal experiences, "I was one of the counsel for Burr, and Burr was acquitted." In letters written from Richmond at the time, he was frank enough, however, to admit that he had not been called upon for any important service. During Irving's brief professional association with Hoffman, he was accepted as an intimate in the Hoffman family circle, and it was Hoffman's daughter Matilda who was the heroine in the only romance of the author's life. He became engaged to Matilda when he was barely of age, but the betrothal lasted only a few months, as she died suddenly at the age of seventeen. At the time of Irving's death it was found that he was still wearing on his breast a locket containing her miniature and a lock of hair that had been given to him half a century before.

The first literary undertaking to which Irving's pen was devoted, apart from a few ephemeral sketches for one of the daily papers, was a serial publication issued at irregular intervals during 1807–08, under the title of *Salmagundi*. In this work, Irving had the collaboration of his brother William and his friend James K. Paulding.[1] The *Salmagundi* papers, reissued later in book form, possess, in addition to their interest as humorous literature, historical value as pictures of social life in New York during the first decade of the nineteenth century.

The famous *History of New-York* was published in 1809. The mystery surrounding the disappearance of old Diedrich Knickerbocker, to whom was assigned the authorship, was preserved for a number of months. The first announcement of the book stated that the manuscript had been found by the landlord of the Columbian Hotel in New York among the effects of a departed lodger, and had been sold to the printer in order to offset the lodger's indebtedness. Before the manuscript was disposed of, Seth Handaside, the landlord, inserted in New York and Philadelphia papers an advertisement describing

[1] See also Book II, Chaps. I, III, V, VII.

Mr. Knickerbocker and asking for information about him. When acknowledgment of the authorship of the book was finally made by Irving, it was difficult for his fellow New Yorkers to believe that this unsuccessful young lawyer and attractive "man about town" could have produced a work giving evidence of such maturity and literary power. He had secured an excellent position in New York society, a society which in the earlier years of the century was still largely made up of the old Dutch families. In the "veracious chronicle" of Mr. Knickerbocker free use was made of the names of these historic families, and it is related that not a few of the young author's Dutch friends found it difficult to accord forgiveness for the liberty that had been taken with their honourable ancestors in making them the heroes of such rollicking episodes.

After a brief editorial experience in charge of a Philadelphia magazine called the *Analectic*, to which he contributed some essays later included in *The Sketch Book*, Irving enjoyed for a few months the excitement of military service. He was appointed a colonel on the staff of Governor Tompkins, and during the campaign of 1814 was charged with responsibilities in connection with the defence of the northern line of New York.

In 1810, Irving had been taken into partnership with his two brothers, Peter and Ebenezer, who were carrying on business as general merchants and importers; and on the declaration of peace in 1814 he was sent by his firm to serve as its representative in Liverpool. If the business plans of that year had proved successful, it is possible that Irving might for the rest of his life have remained absorbed in commercial undertakings, but in 1818 the firm was overtaken by disaster and the young lawyer-merchant (never much of a lawyer and by no means important as a merchant) found himself adrift in England with small funds and with no assured occupation or prospects. He had already come into friendly relations with a number of the leading authors of the day, a group which included Scott, Moore, Southey, and Jeffrey. Scott had in fact sought him out very promptly, having years earlier been fascinated by the originality and the humour shown in *The History of New-York*.

After a couple of years of desultory travelling and writing, Irving completed a series of papers which were published in

New York in 1819–20 and in London in 1820, under the title of *The Sketch Book*. It is by this volume that he is today best known among readers on both sides of the Atlantic. The book has been translated into almost every European tongue, and for many years it served, and still serves, in France, in Germany, and in Italy as a model of English style and as a text-book from which students are taught their English. In this latter rôle, it took, to a considerable extent, the place of *The Spectator*.

The publication by Murray of *The Sketch Book*, and two years later of *Bracebridge Hall*, brought Irving at once into repute in literary circles not only in Great Britain, but on the Continent. In 1826, after a year or two chiefly spent in travelling in France, Germany, and Italy, he was appointed by Alexander Everett, at that time Minister to Spain, attaché to the Legation at Madrid, and this first sojourn in Spain had an important influence in shaping the direction of Irving's future literary work. In July, 1827, he brought to completion his biography of Columbus, later followed by the account of the *Companions of Columbus* (1831). The *Columbus* was published in London and in Philadelphia in 1828 and secured at once cordial and general appreciation. Southey wrote from London: "This work places Irving in the front rank of modern biographers"; and Edward Everett said that "through the Columbus, Irving is securing the position of founder of the American school of polite learning." Irving continued absorbed and fascinated with the examination of the Spanish chronicles. He made long sojourns in Granada, living for a great part of the time within the precincts of the Alhambra, and later he spent a year or more in Seville. He occupied himself collecting material for the completion of *The Conquest of Granada*, published in 1829, and for the *Legends of the Alhambra*, published in 1832.

In 1828, Irving declined an offer of one hundred guineas to write an article for *The Quarterly Review*, of which his friend Murray was the publisher, on the ground, as he wrote, "that the Review [then under the editorship of Gifford] has been so persistently hostile to our country that I cannot draw a pen in its service." This episode may count as a fair rejoinder to certain of the home critics who were then accusing Irving (as half a century later Lowell was, in like manner, accused) of having become so much absorbed in his English sympathies as to have lost his patriotism.

In 1829, Irving was made a member of the Royal Academy of History in Madrid, and having in the same year been appointed Secretary of Legation by Louis McLane, he again took up his residence in London. Here, in 1830, the Royal Society of Literature voted to him as a recognition of his "service to history and to literature" one of its gold medals. The other medal of that year was given to Hallam for his *History of the Middle Ages*. A little later Oxford honoured Irving with the degree of Doctor of Laws. The ceremony of the installation was a serious experience for a man of his shy and retiring habits. As he sat in the Senate Hall, the students saluted him with cries of "Here comes old Knickerbocker," "How about Ichabod Crane?" "Has Rip Van Winkle waked up yet?" and "Who discovered Columbus?"

In 1832, Irving returned to New York, having been absent from his country for seventeen years. His fellow citizens welcomed him, not a little to his own discomfiture, with a banquet given in the City Hall, where the orator of the evening addressed him as the "Dutch Herodotus." Later in the year, he made a journey through the territory of the Southwest, an account of which he published under the title of *A Tour on the Prairies* (1835). His description of St. Louis as a frontier post and of the great wilderness extending to the west of the Mississippi still makes interesting reading. Returning from his journey by way of New Orleans, he visited Columbia, South Carolina, where he was the guest of Governor Hamilton. The Governor, who had just transmitted to the legislature the edict of nullification, insisted that the author must repeat his visit to the state. "Certainly," responded the guest, "I will come with the first troops."

In 1834, Irving declined a Democratic nomination for Congress, and in 1838 he put to one side the Tammany nomination for mayor of New York and also an offer from President Van Buren to make him Secretary of the Navy. In 1842, he accepted from President Tyler the appointment of Minister to Spain. The suggestion had come to the President from Daniel Webster, at that time Secretary of State. The succeeding five years were in large part devoted to the collection of material relating to the history and the legends of Spain during the Moorish occupation.

On his return to New York in 1846, he met with a serious disappointment. His books were out of print, at least in the United States, and his Philadelphia publishers assured him that, as there was no longer any public demand for his writings, it would be an unprofitable venture to put new editions upon the market. They explained that the public taste had changed, and that a new style of authorship was now in vogue. The books had in fact been out of print since 1845, but at that time Irving, still absent in Spain, had concluded that the plan for revised editions might await his return. To be told now by publishers of experience that *The Sketch Book*, *Knickerbocker*, *Columbus*, and the other books, notwithstanding their original prestige, had had their day and were not wanted by the new generation, was a serious shock to Irving not only on the ground of the blow to his confidence in himself as an author, but because his savings were inconsiderable, and he needed the continued income that he had hoped to secure from his pen.

His personal wants were few, but he had always used his resources generously among his large circle of relatives, and having neither wife nor child he had made a home at Sunnyside for an aged brother Ebenezer, and at one time for no less than five nieces. Some western land investments, which in later years became profitable, were at this time liabilities instead of resources, and his immediate financial prospects were discouraging. He had taken a desk in the office of his brother John Treat Irving, and to John he now spoke, possibly half jestingly, of the necessity of resuming the practice of the law. He was at this time sixty-five years of age, and as it was forty years since he had touched a law book, it is hardly likely that he could have made himself of much value as a counsellor.

One morning early in 1848, he came into the office in a joyful frame of mind. He tossed a letter over to his brother saying: "John, here is a fool of a publisher willing to give me $2000 a year to go on scribbling." The "fool of a publisher" was the late George P. Putnam, who had recently returned from London where he had for eight years been engaged in the attempt to induce the English public to buy American books. Mr. Putnam now proposed to issue a uniform revised edition of all of Irving's writings, with which should be associated the books that he might later bring to completion, and to pay to the author a royalty on each copy sold, guaranteeing against such royalty for a term of three years a sum increasing with each year. It may be mentioned as evidence of the accuracy of the publisher's judgment that the payments during the years in which this guaranty continued were always substantially in excess of the amounts contracted for.

In 1849, the London publisher Bohn began to print unauthorized editions of the various books of Irving. A series of litigations ensued, as a result of which the authorized publishers, Murray and Bentley, discouraged with a long fight and with the great expense incurred in securing protection under the existing copyright regulations, accepted the offer of the pirate for the use, at a purely nominal price, of their publishing rights, and Irving's works came thus to be included in Bohn's Library Series. Copyright in Great Britain, as in the United States, was in 1850 in a very unsatisfactory condition, and it was not easy to ascertain from the provisions of the British statute just what rights could be maintained by alien authors. So far as American authors were concerned, this uncertainty continued until, through the enactment of the statute of 1891, an international copyright relation was secured.

As one result of the transfer to Bohn of the control of the English editions of Irving's earlier volumes, the author found that he could not depend upon any material English receipts for his later works. For the right to publish the English edition of the *Life of Washington* (a work comprised in five volumes) Bentley paid the sum of £50, which was a sad reduction from the £3000 that Murray had given him for the *Columbus*.

In December, 1852, Irving wrote to his American publisher a letter of thanks, which is notable as an expression both of the sense of fairness and of the modest nature of the man. That this expression of friendship was not a mere empty courtesy, he had opportunity of making clear a few years later. In 1857, partly because of the mismanagement of his financial partner and partly because of the general financial disasters of the year, Mr. Putnam was compelled to make an assignment of his business. Irving received propositions from a number of other publishers for the transfer of his books, the commercial value of which was now fully appreciated. From some of these propositions he could have secured more satisfactory returns than were coming to him under the existing arrangement. He declined them all, however, writing to his publisher to the effect that as long as a Putnam remained in the publishing business, he proposed to retain for his books the Putnam imprint. He purchased from the assignee the plates and the publishing agreements; he held these plates for a year or more until Mr. Putnam was in a position to resume the control of the publication, and he then restored them to his publisher. He waived the larger proceeds to which, as the owner of the plates, he would have been entitled, and insisted that the old publishing arrangement should be resumed. Such an episode is interesting in the long and somewhat troubled history of the relations of authors with publishers, and it may be considered equally creditable to both parties.

The final, and in some respects the greatest of Irving's productions, the *Life of Washington*, was completed on his seventy-sixth birthday, 1859, and a month or two later he had the pleasure of holding in his hands the printed volume. His death came on 29 November, of the same year, and he was laid to rest in the beautiful little graveyard of the Sleepy Hollow Church. The writer has in his memory a picture of the great weather-beaten walls of the quaint little church with the background of forest trees and the surroundings of the moss-covered graves. Beyond on the roadside could be seen the grey walls of the mill, in front of which Ichabod Crane had clattered past, pursued by the headless horseman. The roadside and the neighbouring fields were crowded with vehicles, large and small, which had gathered from all parts of the countryside. It was evident from the words and from the faces of those that had come together that the man whose life was closed had not only made for himself a place in the literature of the world, but had been accepted as a personal friend by the neighbours of his home.

Washington Irving occupied an exceptional position among the literary workers of his country. It was his good fortune to begin his writing at a time when the patriotic sentiment of the nation was taking shape, and when the citizens were giving their thoughts to the constructive work that was being done by their selected leaders in framing the foundations of the new state. It was given to Irving to make clear to his countrymen that Americans were competent not merely to organize a state, but to produce literature. He was himself a clear-headed and devoted patriot, but he was able to free himself from the local feeling of antagonism toward the ancient enemy Great Britain, and from the prejudice against other nations, always based upon ignorance, that is so often confused with patriotism. Irving's early memories and his early reading had to do with the events and with the productions of colonial days. Addison and Goldsmith are the two English writers with whose works his productions, or at least those relating to English subjects, have been most frequently compared. His biography of Goldsmith shows the keenest personal sympathy with the sweetness of nature and the literary ideals of his subject. Irving's works came, therefore, to be a connecting link between the literature of England (or the English-inspired literature of the colonies) and the literary creations that were entitled to the name American, and they expressed the character, the method of thought, the ideals, and the aspiration of English folk on this side of the Atlantic.

The greatest intellectual accomplishment to be credited to New York during the first years of the republic was the production of *The Federalist*. It is fair to claim, however, that with Irving and with those writers immediately associated with his work during the first quarter of the nineteenth century, began the real literature of the country. Partly by temperament and by character, and partly, of course, as a result of the opportunities that came to him after a close personal knowledge of England, with a large understanding of things Continental, Irving, while in his convictions a sturdy American, became in his sympathies a cosmopolitan. His first noteworthy production, *The History of New-York*, is so distinctive in its imagination and humour that it is difficult to class. It is purely local in the sense that the characters and the allusions all have to do with the Dutch occupation of Manhattan Island and the Hudson River region, but, as was evidenced by the cordial appreciation given to the book on the other side of the Atlantic, the humour of Mr. Knickerbocker was accepted as a contribution to the literature of the world.

In the production of *The Sketch Book*, Irving was able not only to enhance his fame by a charming contribution to literature, but to render a special service to two countries, England and America. The book came into print at a time when the bitterness of the war which closed in 1814 was still fresh in the minds of both contestants. It was a time when it was the fashion in America to use Great Britain as a bugaboo, as a synonym for all that was to be abominated in political theories and in political action. The word "British" was associated in the minds of most Americans with an attempt at domination, while in England, on the other hand, references to the little Yankee nation were no more friendly, and things American were persistently decried and sneered at.[1]

It was of enormous value that at such a period, first in the list of patriotic Americans who through sympathetic knowledge of England have come to serve as connecting links between the two countries, Irving should have been a resident in England and should have absorbed so thoroughly the spirit of the best that there was in English life. It was in part because men honoured in Great Britain, writers like Scott, Southey, Rogers, Roscoe, Moore, men of affairs like Richard Bentley, John Murray, and many others, came not only to respect, but to have affectionate regard for, the American author, and it was in part because the books written by this man showed such sympathetic appreciation of things and of men English, that England was brought to a better understanding of the possibilities of America. If there could come from the States a man recognized as one of nature's gentlemen, and to be accepted as a companion of the best in the land, a man whose writings on things English won the highest approval of the most authoritative critics, it was evident that there were possibilities in this new English-speaking state. If one American could secure friendships in Great Britain, if one American could make a noteworthy contribution to the literature of the English tongue, the way was thrown open to other Americans to strengthen and widen the ties and the relations between the two countries. An American critic who might have been tempted to criticize some of the papers in *The Sketch Book* as unduly English in their sympathies and as indicating a surrender by the author of his American

[1] See also Book II, Chap. I.

principles, was estopped from any such folly by the fact that the same volume contained those immortal legends of the Hudson, *Rip Van Winkle* and *The Legend of Sleepy Hollow*. In these stories, poems in prose, the author utilized, as the pathway and inspiration for his imagination, the great river of which he was so fond. If Irving's descriptions of rural England were to give fresh interest to American readers in the old home of their forefathers, the skill with which he had utilized the traditional legends of the Catskill Mountains and had woven fanciful stories along the roadway of Sleepy Hollow made clear to readers on the other side of the Atlantic that imagination and literary style were not restricted to Europe.

The work begun in *The Sketch Book* was continued in *Bracebridge Hall*. Here also we have that combination (possibly paralleled in no other work of literature) of things English and things American. Squire Bracebridge is, of course, a lineal descendant of Sir Roger de Coverley. It is not necessary, however, because Irving was keenly sympathetic with Addison's mode of thought, to speak of Irving's hero as an imitation. England has produced more than one squire, and Bracebridge and the family of the Hall were the creations of the American observer. The English home of the early nineteenth century is presented in a picture that is none the less artistic because it can be accepted as trustworthy and exact. In this volume we have also a characteristic American study, *Dolph Heyliger*, a fresh romance of Irving's beloved Hudson River.

The *Tales of a Traveller*, the scenes of which were laid partly in Italy, show the versatility of the author in bringing his imagination into harmony with varied surroundings. Whether the subject be in England, in France, or in Italy, whether he is writing of the Alhambra or of the Hudson, Irving always succeeds in coming into the closest sympathy with his environment. He has the artist's touch in the ability to reproduce the atmosphere in which the scenes of his stories are placed.

The *Life of Columbus* may be considered as presenting Irving's first attempt at history, but it was an attempt that secured for him at once a place in the first rank among historians. In this biography, Irving gave ample evidence of his power of reconstituting the figures of the past. He impresses upon the reader the personality of the great discoverer, the idealist, the man who was so absorbed in his own belief that he was able to impress this upon the skeptics about him. We have before us a vivid picture of the Spanish Court from which, after patient effort, Columbus secured the grudging support for his expedition, and we come to know each member of the little crew through whose service the great task was brought to accomplishment. Irving makes clear that the opposition of the clerics and the apathy of King Ferdinand were at last overcome only through the sympathetic support given to the project by Queen Isabella.

In the *Conquest of Granada*, the narrative is given in a humorous form, but it represents the result of very thorough historic research. By the device of presenting the record through the personality of the mythical priestly chronicler, Fray Agapida, blindly devoted to the cause of the Church, Irving is able to emphasize less invidiously than if the statements were made direct, the bitterness, the barbarism, and the prejudices of the so-called Christianity of the Spaniards. Through the utterances of Agapida, we come to realize the narrowness of Ferdinand and the priestly arrogance of Ferdinand's advisers. The admiration of the reader goes out to the fierce patriotism of the great Moorish leader, El Zagal, and his sympathies are enlisted for the pathetic career of Boabdil, the last monarch of Granada. *Granada* was Irving's favourite production, and he found himself frankly disappointed that (possibly on the ground of the humorous form given to the narrative) the book failed to secure full acceptance as history and was not considered by the author's admirers to take rank with his more popular work.

The *Alhambra*, which has been called the "Spanish Sketch Book," is a beautiful expression of the thoughts and dreams of the author as he muses amid the ruins of the Palace of the Moors. The reader feels that in recording the great struggle which terminated in 1492 with the triumph of Spain, Irving's sympathies are not with the conquering Christians but with the defeated Moslems.

The *Life of Mahomet* and the supplementary volume on the successors of Mahomet followed in 1849–50. The biographies constitute good narrative and give further examples of the author's exceptional power of characterization. If they fail to reach the high standard of the *Columbus*, it is doubtless because Irving possessed no such close familiarity with the environment of his subjects. In Spain he had made long sojourns and had become imbued with the atmosphere of the Spanish legends and ideals. He knew his Italy, in like manner, from personal observation and from sympathetic relations with the peasants no less than the scholars, but Arabia was to him a distant land.

The writing of *Columbus* prepared the way for Irving's chief historical achievement. The *Life of Washington* is not only a biography presenting with wonderful precision and completeness the nature and career of a great American, but a study, and the first study of importance, of the evolution of the republic. Irving had given thought and planning to the biography for years before he was able to put a pen to the work. As early as 1832 he had confided to some of his nearer friends his ambition to associate his name with that of Washington and to devote such literary and historical ability as he possessed to the creation of a literary monument to the Father of the Republic. The work had, of necessity, been postponed during his long sojourn in England and the later residence in Spain, but he never permitted himself to put the plan to one side. As soon as the sales of the new Putnam edition of the earlier works and of the later volumes that he had been able to add to these freed him from financial care, he began the collection of material for the great history. He had already travelled over much of the country with which the career of his hero was connected. He knew by the observations of an intelligent traveller the regions of New England, New Jersey, Western Pennsylvania, and Virginia, while with the territory of New York he had from his youth been familiar. The Hudson River, which had heretofore served as the pathway for Irving's dreams of romance, was now to be studied historically as the scene of some of the most critical of the campaigns of the Revolution. Since the date of Irving's work, later historians have had the advantage of fuller material, particularly that secured from the correspondence in the homes of Revolutionary leaders, North and South, but no later historian has found occasion for any corrections of importance, either in the details of Irving's narrative, or in his analysis of the characters of the men through whom the great contest was carried on. Irving possessed one qualification which is lacking in the make-up of not a few conscientious and able historians. His strain of romance and his power of imagination enabled him to picture to himself and to make vivid the scenes described, and the nature, the purpose, and the manner of thought of each character introduced. The reader is brought into personal association with the force and dignity of the great leader; with the assumption, the vanity, the exaggerated opinion of his powers and ability of Charles Lee; with the sturdy patriotism, the simple-hearted nature, persistence, and pluck of the pioneer fighter Israel Putnam; with the skill, leadership, and unselfishness of Philip Schuyler; with the pettiness and bumptiousness of Gates; with the grace, fascination, and loyalty of Lafayette; and with the varied attainments and brilliant qualities of that wonderful youth Alexander Hamilton. We are not simply reading descriptions, we are looking at living pictures, and the historic narrative has the quality of a vitascope.

The production of this great history constituted a fitting culmination to the literary labours of its author. When Irving penned the last word of the fifth volume of the *Washington*, he was within a few months of his death. The work on this volume had in fact been a strain upon his vitality, and there were times when he needed to exert his will power to the utmost in order to complete the task allotted to himself for the day. He said pathetically from time to time to his nephew and loyal aid Pierre and to his friend Putnam, "I do not know whether I may be spared to complete this history, but I shall do my best." In this his final work, the shaping of the fifth volume, he did his best.

It may fairly be contended for this American author, whose work dates almost from the beginning of the Republic, that his writings possess vitality and continued importance for the readers of this later century. His historical works have, as indicated, a distinctive character. They are trustworthy and dignified history, while they possess the literary charm and grace of the work of a true man of letters. For the world at large, Irving will, however, doubtless best be known by his works of imagination, and the students in the gallery in Oxford who chaffed "Diedrich Knickerbocker" as he was receiving his degree were probably right in selecting as the characteristic and abiding production of the author his *Rip Van Winkle*.

CHAPTER V

Bryant and the Minor Poets

I. BRYANT

TO the old-fashioned prayers which his mother and grand-mother taught him, the little boy born in Cummington, Massachusetts, 3 November, 1794, a year before John Keats across the sea, was wont to add (so we learn from the Autobiographical Fragment),[1] his private supplication that he might "receive the gift of poetic genius, and write verses that might endure."

This inner urge and bent, witnessed so early and so long, could not be severed, early or late, from the unfathomable world. Bryant's was a boyhood and youth among the virginal woods, hills, and streams, among a farmer folk and country labours and pastimes, in a Puritan household, with a father prominent in the state as physician and legislator, whose independence and breadth are attested by a leaning toward that liberalism which was to develop into the American Unitarian movement and by his enlightened devotion, as critic and friend, to the boy's ambitions in rhyme. Private tutoring by unpretending clergymen, a year at poverty-stricken Williams College, law studies in an upland office, distasteful practice as a poor country lawyer, a happy marriage with her whose "birth was in the forest shades,"[2] death, season by season, of those nearest and dearest, travel down among the slave-holding states and out to the prairies of Illinois, where his brothers and mother were for a second time pioneers, with voyages on various

---

[1] Godwin, *Life*, vol. 1, p. 26.
[2] *Poems*, p. 82. Roslyn edition (1913), from which all poetical quotations are cited in this chapter.

occasions to the West Indies, to Europe, and to the Levant, and fifty years as a New York editor, who with the wisdom of a statesman and the courage of a reformer made *The Evening Post* America's greatest newspaper,—all this gives us a life of many visions of forest, field, and foam, of many books in diverse tongues, of many men and cities, of many problems in his own career and in the career of that nation which he made so much his own, a life not without its own adventures, struggles, joys, and griefs. So it stands recorded, a consistent and eloquent and (fortunately) a familiar chapter in American biography, even as it passed before the visionary octogenarian back in the old home, sitting "in the early twilight," whilst

> Through the gathering shade
> He looked on the fields around him
> Where yet a child he played.[1]

One might regard the events of this lifetime either as in subtle and inevitable ways harmoniously contributory to the poet-nature that was Bryant's (if not indeed often its persistent and victorious creation), or as in the main a deflection, a check. If no other American poet has written, year measured by year, so little poetry, the poetry of no other so clearly defines at once its author's character, environment, and country; if no other American poet was apparently so much occupied with other interests than poetry, not excepting the critic, diplomat, orator, and humorist Lowell, none felt his high calling, it seems, with as priestly a consecration,—no, truly, not excepting Whitman, who protested thereon sometimes a little too much.

Bryant's public career as poet fulfilled the psalmist's three-score years and ten, if we date from *The Embargo*, an anti-Jefferson satire in juvenile heroics (1808). It began with the year of Scott's *Marmion;* it was barely completed with *Sigurd the Volsung* of William Morris; it included the lives of Byron and Shelley and most that was best in those of Tennyson, Arnold, Browning. It began the year following Joel Barlow's American epic *The Columbiad*, and the publication of *The Echo* by the Hartford Wits. Longfellow and Whittier were in the cradle, Holmes and Poe unborn. Except Freneau, there were no poets

[1] *A Lifetime.*

in the country but those imitative versifiers of an already antiquated English fashion whom Bryant was himself to characterize[1] with quiet justice in the first critical appraisal of our
"literature," the first declaration of intellectual independence,
antedating Emerson's *American Scholar* by nineteen years.
He compassed the generations of all that was once or is still
most reputed in American poetry: the generations of Paulding,
Percival, Halleck, Drake, Willis, Poe, Longfellow, Whittier,
Emerson, Lowell, Whitman, Bret Harte.

Yet he was from very early, in imagination and expression,
curiously detached from what was going on in poetry around
him. *The Embargo* is a boy's echo, significant only for precocious facility and for the twofold interest in verse and politics
that was to be lifelong. Byron's voice is audible in the Spenserian stanzas and subject matter of the Phi Beta Kappa poem
of 1821, *The Ages*[2]; the New York verses, so painfully facetious
on Rhode Island coal and a mosquito, are less after Byron than
after the town wit Halleck and his coterie. Wordsworth, at the
reading of whose *Lyrical Ballads* in 1811, "a thousand springs,"
Bryant said to Dana, "seemed to gush up at once in his heart,
and the face of Nature of a sudden to change into a strange
freshness and life," was the companion into the woods and
among the flowers who more than all others helped him to find
himself; but *Thanatopsis*, so characteristic of Bryant, was
written almost certainly some weeks before he had seen the
Lyrical Ballads,[3] and, even if Bryant's eminence as poet of
nature owed much to this early reinforcement, his poetry is
not Wordsworthian either in philosophy or in mood or in
artistry. Wordsworth never left the impress on Bryant's
work that the realms of gold made upon the surprised and
spellbound boy Keats. No later prophets and craftsmen,

---

[1] *North American Review*, July, 1818.

[2] Thomson's *Liberty* may have contributed something to the choice of theme.

[3] The time relations seem to have been as follows. Bryant's father purchased
the *Lyrical Ballads* in Boston during 1810, when the son was at college (till May,
1811); Bryant "had picked it up at home" (Godwin, *Life*, vol. 1, p. 104) to take
with him to Worthington (Dec., 1811), where it was that, as a young law student,
he first read it with such surprised delight. *Thanatopsis* had been written between
May and December, apparently in the autumn (Godwin, *Life*, vol. 1, pp. 97–99),
and if (as likely) before 3 November, then written when Bryant was still a lad of
sixteen. See Van Doren, C., *The Growth of "Thanatopsis," Nation*, 7 October,
1915.

American, English, or continental, seem to have touched him at all.[1]

More obvious to the registrar of parallels are Bryant's literary relations to the poets he read, and read evidently with deeper susceptibility than has been realized, before 1811.[2] The reference is not alone to the well-known relation *Thanatopsis* bears to Blair's *Grave*, Porteus's *Death*,[3] Kirk White's *Time*, *Rosemary*, etc., and the whole Undertaker's Anthology so infinitely beneath the Lucretian grandeur of America's first great poem with its vision of

Dead men whose bones earth bosomed long ago.

The reference is equally to certain themes and moods and unclassified details in poems written long after *Thanatopsis*, all of which, though so characteristically Bryant's, make us feel him as much closer to the eighteenth century tradition than any of his contemporaries, even than Holmes with his deference to "the steel-bright epigrams of Pope"; so that we may appraise him much better by going forward from the moralizing, "nature" blank verse of Thomson, Cowper, Young, and Akenside, than backward from Wordsworth and Tennyson. In the eighteenth century tradition is the very preference for blank verse as the instrument for large and serious thought, and the lifelong preference itself for large and serious thought on Death, History, Destiny. The Biblical note too is of the former age. But the diction is, if anything, freer than the mature Wordsworth himself from eighteenth century poetic slang, and the peculiarities of this blank verse (to be mentioned later) have fewer cadences suggestive of Cowper than, perhaps, of the early poems of Southey, whose impression on those impressionable first years of Bryant's has apparently been overlooked.[4] With this early romanticism we may connect the sentimental element in the appeal of innocent and happy savages, whether

[1] Tennysonian blank-verse in *Sella* has been suggested—unconvincingly.

[2] See Autobiographical Fragment for a partial list.

[3] Winner of the Seaton Prize at Cambridge for 1759. *Death* may be found in *Musae Seatonianae*, Cambridge, 1808—a copy of which was apparently in Doctor Bryant's library.

[4] Compare Southey's *Inscriptions* (themselves imitated from Akenside), especially *In a Forest*, with *Inscription for the Entrance to a Wood*.

on Pitcairn's Island or in the pristine Indian summers; likewise the two or three tales of horror and the supernatural, in which he succeeded so poorly. But he arrived soon enough to contribute his own influence to the nineteenth-century poetry of nature.

He came to himself early, for one who had so many years in which to change, if he would change or could. The first volume, the forty-four pages of 1821, contains most, the second, 1832, certainly contains all, of the essential Bryant, the essential as to what he cared for in nature and human life, as to how he envisaged it in imagination and dwelt with it in intellect and character, and as to how he gave it expression. In the later years there is more of Bryant's playful fancy, perhaps more of ethical thinking and mood, a slight shift of emphasis, new constructions, not new materials. His world and his speech were already his: there is no new revelation and no new instrument in any one of the several succeeding issues of his verse (though there are many new, many high poems), as there are new revelations and new instruments in Byron, Tennyson, and Browning; indeed, Keats in the three years between the volumes of 1817 and 1820 lived a much longer, a more diversified life of steadily increasing vision and voice. It need hardly be remarked, then, that he experienced no intellectual and moral crisis,—neither from without, as did Wordsworth when his country took up arms against Liberty, Fraternity, and Equality and when shortly Liberty, Fraternity, and Equality danced, like the Weird Sisters, around the cauldron of horror; nor from within, like the expatriated husband and father Byron, and the political idealist Dante, and even the *flâneur* who wrote *The Ballad of Reading Gaol*.

He came, likewise, early to his fame. He was first and alone. The little world of the lovers of good things on the North Atlantic seaboard in those days, trained as it was in the English and ancient classics, quickly set the young man apart; Bryant became established, fortunately, somewhat before American literary criticism had become self-consciously patriotic, indiscriminate, vulgar. England, too, long so important an influence on American judgments of American products, early accorded him a measure of honour and thanks. It is well known that Washington Irving secured the English reprinting of the volume of 1832 in the same year, with a brief criticism by way of dedication to Samuel Rogers, whose reading of the contents was the delight of that old Maecenas and Petronius Arbiter.   It has, however, apparently not been observed that the entire contents of the volume of 1821 were reprinted, indeed in the same order, in *Specimens of the American Poets* (London, 1822) with a noteworthy comment[1] on the lines *Thanatopsis* that "there are few pieces, in the works of even the very first of our living poets, which exceed them in sublimity and compass of poetical thought."   And Bryant was spared from the beginning furor and contempt: he was never laurelled like Byron, never foolscapped like Keats by critics or public; his repute was always, like himself, dignified, quiet, secure.   And so the critical problem is initially simplified, in two ways: there is no story of struggle for recognition, and the effects of that struggle on the workman; there is no story of evolution of inner forces.   Thus the poetry of Bryant admits of treatment as one performance, one perception and one account of the world, in a more restricted sense than is generally applicable to poetic performance, where the unity is the unity of psychological succession in a changing temporal order: *Don Juan* is, perhaps, implied in the *English Bards* and *Childe Harold*, *Paradise Lost* in the *Nativity*, *Hamlet* in *Romeo and Juliet;* but, in a humbler sphere, *Among the Trees* and *The Flood of Years* are less implied than actually present in *A Forest Hymn* and *Thanatopsis*.   If Bryant's poems need sometimes the reference of date, it is for external occasion and impulse, not for artistic registration.   Three periods have been discovered for Chaucer, and four for Shakespeare; our modest American was without "periods."

The critical problem is simple, though not necessarily trivial or easy, in another way: this one performance was itself of a relatively simple character.   Bryant's poems stress perpetually a certain few ideas, grow perpetually out of a certain few emotional responses, and report in a few noble imaginative modes a certain few aspects of man and nature, with ever recurring habits of observation, architectonics, and style.   This absence of complexity is, again, emphasized by the elemental clarity and simplicity of those same few ideas, emotions, modes, methods.   Within his range he is complete, harmonious, and,

[1] P. 190.

in a deeper sense than above, impressively one. It is for this, perhaps, that of all American poets he makes the strongest impression of an organic style, as contrasted with an individual, a literary style, consciously elaborated, as in Poe and Whitman. It is partly for this, perhaps, that the most Puritan of our poets is also the most Greek. Bryant's limitations, then, are intimately engaged in the peculiar distinction of his work; and it is ungracious, as well as superficial, to quarrel with them.

Bryant's ideas, stated in bald prose, are elementary,— common property of simple minds. His metaphysics was predominantly that of the Old Testament: God is the Creator and His works and His purposes are good. Bryant communicated, however, little sense of the loving fatherhood and divine guidance in human affairs: perhaps once only, in *To a Waterfowl*, which originated in an intensely religious moment of young manhood.[1] His ethics stress the austerer loyalties of justice and truth rather than those of faith, hope, and charity. His politics in his poems, however analytic and specific he might be as publicist, reiterate only the ideals of political freedom and progress, with ever confident reference to the high destinies of America, that "Mother of a Mighty Race." His assurance of individual immortality for all men, which scarcely touches the problem of sin, rests not on revelation, not on a philosophy of the transcendental significance of intellect, struggle, and pain, but mainly on primitive man's desire to meet the loved and lost, the father, the sister, the wife. There is nothing subtle, complex, or tricky here; there are no philosophers, apparently, on his reading desk; no Spinoza, Plotinus, Berkeley, Hartley, who were behind Coleridge's discursive verse; no Thomas Aquinas who was the propedeutic for *The Divine Comedy*. And of any intricate psychology, or pseudo-psychology, such as delighted Browning, there is of course not a bit. There is in these ideas, as ideas, nothing that a noble pagan, say of republican Rome, might not have held to, even before the advent of Stoic and Academician. But there is a further paganism in the emphasis on the phenomena of life as life, on death as death. Man's life, as individual and type, is what it is—birth and toil in time; and death is what it is, save when he mentions a private grief—for men and empires it is a passing away in a

[1] Godwin, *Life*, vol. I, pp. 143–145.

universe of time and change. The original version of *Thanatopsis* is more characteristic than its inconsistent introductory and concluding lines, now the oftenest quoted of all his writings. If Bryant was the Puritan in his austerity and morale, he was quite as much the Pagan in the universality of his ideas, and in his temperamental adjustment to brute fact.

On nature and man's relation to nature, one who reads without prepossession will find the American Wordsworth equally elemental. He raises his hymn in the groves, which were God's first temples,—venerable columns, these ranks of trees, reared by Him of old. And "the great miracle still goes on"; and even the "delicate forest flower" seems

> An emanation of the indwelling Life,
> A visible token of the upholding Love,
> That are the soul of this great universe.[1]

But more frequently nature is herself enough, in the simple thought that personifies and capitalizes: it is She herself that speaks to man, in his different hours, a various language. But it is only casually, as in *Among the Trees*, that he wonders if the vegetable world may not have some

> dim and faint
> . . . sense of pleasure and of pain,
> As in our dreams;

only casually, for conscious mysticism was foreign to Bryant's intellect, and the conception had yet to be scientifically investigated in the laboratories of the Hindoo botanist Bose. Here nature, as herself the Life, is simply an hypostasis of the racial imagination in which Bryant so largely shared, just like his intimate personifications of her phenomena, her flowers, her winds, and waters; it is not a philosophic idea, but a primitive instinct. "Nature's teachings" for men are simply the ideas that suggest themselves to Bryant himself (not inevitably to everyone) when he observes what goes on, or what is before him:

> The faintest streak that on a petal lies,
> May speak instruction to initiate eyes.[2]

---

[1] *A Forest Hymn.*   [2] *The Mystery of Flowers.*

But this apparently Wordsworthian couplet can be related to no system of thought or Wordsworthian instruction. These ideas are sometimes merely analogies, where in effect the flower (be it the gentian), or the bird (be it the waterfowl), is the first term in a simile on man's moral life; in this phase Bryant's thought of nature differs from that of Homer, the Psalmist, Jesus, or any sage or seer, Pagan or Christian, only in the appositeness, more or less, of the illustrative symbol. It implies no more a philosophy of nature than similes drawn from the action of a locomotive or a motor-boat would imply a philosophy of machinery. As a fact, Bryant's one abiding idea about nature is that she is a profound influence on the human spirit, chastening, soothing, encouraging, ennobling—how, he does not say; but the fact he knows from experience, and mankind knows it with him, and has known it from long before the morning when the sorrowful, chafed soul of Achilles walked apart by the shore of the many-sounding sea.

Every poet, like every individual, has of course his favourite, his recurrent ideas: Wordsworth, again and again, adverts to the uses of old memories as a store and treasure for one's future days, again and again he sees his life as divided into three ages; Browning again and again preaches the doctrine that it is better to aim high and fail than to aim low and succeed; Emerson that the soul must live from within. But with Bryant the recurrence is peculiarly insistent and restricted in variety.

But these ideas were involved in a temperament. The chief differences among men are not in their ideas, as ideas, but in the power of the ideas over their emotions, or in the ideas considered as the overflow of their emotions. In Bryant presumably the ideas became formulas of thought, clarified and explicit, through his feelings. A man of great reserve and poise, both in life and art, his "coldness," well established in our literary tradition by some humorous lines of Lowell and a letter of Hawthorne, is a pathetic misreading. There is no sex passion; if there was in Bryant any potentiality of the young Goethe or Byron, it was early transmuted into the quiet affections for wife and home. There is no passion for friends; without being a recluse, he never craved comradeship, like Whitman, for humanity's sake, nor, like Shelley, for affinity's sake, and was, in the lifelong fellowship with such men as the elder Dana, the literary mentor who is responsible for more of Bryant's revisions in verse than any one knows,[1] spared the shocks that usually stimulate the expression of the passion of friendship. But his feelings, for woman and friend, were deep if quiet—perhaps deeper because quiet. And the other primary feelings were equally deep: awe in the presence of the cosmic process and the movements of mankind, reverence for holiness, pity for suffering, brooding resentment against injustice, rejoicing in moral victory, patriotism, susceptibility to beauty of outline and colour and sound, with peculiar susceptibility to both charm and sublimity in natural phenomena. These emotions, in Bryant, ring out through his poetry, clear, without blur or fringe, like the Italian vowels. He had no emotional crotchets, no erratic sensibilities; among other things, he was too robust and too busy. He had the "feelings of calm power and mighty sweep" of which he himself speaks, as befitting the poet.[2]

The few aspects of man and nature he reported have, in a way, been necessarily already suggested. With senses more alert to observe details in the physiognomy and voice of nature than of man, his imagination continually sees the same general vision: the Indian, shadowy type of a departed world, accoutred with feathers and tomahawk, realized, however, in almost none of his actual customs and in none of his actual feelings save that of sorrow for tribal ruin; the warriors of freedom, especially of the American Revolution; the infinite and mysterious racial past on this earth with all its crimes, triumphs, mutations, rather than with its more ethical future which he believes in more than he visualizes, an act of his thinking rather than of his imagination; the earth itself as the sepulchre of man; and, like one great primeval landscape, the mountain, the sea, the wind, the river, the seasons, the plain, the forest that undergo small change from their reality, take on few subjective peculiarities, by virtue of an imagination that seems, as it were, to absorb rather than to create its objects,—in this more like the world of phenomena in Lucretius than, say, in Tennyson, or in the partially Lucretian Meredith, certainly than in Hugo, to whom

[1] See some correspondence between Bryant and Dana apropos the 1846 edition of the *Poems*, Godwin, *Life*, vol. II, p. 14 ff.
[2] *The Poet.*

nature becomes so often monstrous and grotesque. And yet Bryant's imagination has its characteristic modes of relating its objects. Three or four huge and impressive metaphors underlie a great part of his poetry: the past as a place, an underworld,[1] dim and tremendous, most poignantly illustrated in the poem *The Past* with its personal allusions, and most sublimely in *The Death of Slavery*, a great political hymn, with Lowell's *Commemoration Ode*, and Whitman's *When Lilacs last in the Dooryard Bloomed*, the highest poetry of solemn grandeur produced by the Civil War; death as a mysterious passage-way, whether through gate[2] or cloud,[3] with the hosts ever entering and disappearing in the Beyond; mankind conceived as one vast company, a troop, a clan; and, as suggested above, nature as a multitudinous Life.

Bryant wonderfully visualized and unified the vast scope of the racial movement and the range of natural phenomena. His "broad surveys," as they have been called, are more than surveys: they are large acts of the combining imagination, presenting the significance, not merely the catalogue. These acts take us home to the most inveterate habit of his poet-mind. As method or device they seem to suggest a simple prescription for writing poetry; superficially, after one has met them again and yet again in Bryant, one might call them easy to do, because easy to understand. The task is, however, not to make a list, but to make the right list; a list not by capricious association of ideas, but by the laws of inner harmony of meaning. Again, in Bryant the list is itself often a fine, far look beyond the immediate fact—the immediate fact with which all but the poet would rest content. *The Song of the Sower* needed no suggestion from Schiller's *Song of the Bell*, which, however, Bryant doubtless knew;[4] it highly illustrates his own natural procedure:

[1] The figure is in Kirke White's *Time*:

"Where are conceal'd the days which have elapsed?
Hid in the mighty cavern of *the past*,
They rise upon us only to appal,
By indistinct and half-glimpsed images."

This is doubtless one of the many indications of how thoroughly Bryant's early reading penetrated his subconsciousness and, with boyhood's woods and mountains, contributed to his essential make-up in maturity.

[2] *Poems*, p. 260.   [3] *Ibid.*, p. 250.   [4] See *The Death of Schiller*.

> Fling wide the golden shower; we trust
> The strength of armies to the dust.

The grain shall ripen for the warrior. Then he goes on: 'O fling it wide, for all the race: for peaceful workers on sea and land, for the wedding feast, for the various unfortunate, for the communion, for Orient and Southland'—and we live, as we read, wise in the basic fact of agriculture and wise in the activities of humankind. The precise idea is handled more lightly in *The Planting of the Apple Tree*. Often the "survey"—the word is convenient—starts from some on-moving phenomenon in nature—again an immediate fact—and proceeds by compassing that phenomenon's whence or whither, what it has experienced or what it will do: let one re-read his tale of *The River*, by what haunts it flows (like, but how unlike, Tennyson's brook); *The Unknown Way*, the spots it passes (becoming a path symbolic of the mystery of life); *The Sea*, what it does under God (like and unlike Byron's apostrophe); *The Winds*, what they do on sea and land; *A Rain-Dream*, imaging the waters of the globe. Sometimes the phenomenon is static and calls his imagination to penetrate its secret history, or what changes it has seen about it, as when he looks at the fountain[1] or is among the trees.[2] Sometimes the vision rides upon or stands beside no force in Nature, but is his own direct report, as in *Fifty Years*, on the changes in individual lives, in history, in inventions, especially in these States, since his class graduated at Williams. "Broad surveys" of human affairs and of the face of earth, so dull, routine, bombastic as far as attempted in Thomson's *Liberty*, in Blair's *Grave*, in White's *Time*, become in Bryant's less pretentious poems the essential triumph of a unique imagination. The mode remained a favourite to the end: large as in *The Flood of Years*, intimate and tender in *A Lifetime*. No American poet, except Whitman, had an imagination at all like Bryant's, or, indeed, except Whitman and Emerson, as great as Bryant's.

No reminder should be needed that Bryant, like Thoreau and Burroughs, was a naturalist with wide and accurate knowledge. He knew the way of the mist on river and mountain-crest, all tints of sunset, the rising and the setting of the

---

[1] *Poems*, p. 185.   [2] *Ibid.*, p. 321.

constellations, every twig and berry and gnarled root on the forest floor, all shapes of snow on pine and shrub, the commoner insects and wild creatures, and especially the birds and the flowers; and he knew the hums and the murmurs and the boomings that rise, like a perpetual exhalation, from the breast of earth. A traveller from some other planet could take back with him no more useful account of our green home than Bryant's honest poems of nature. There is a group of his poems that details the look, habits, and habitat of single objects: *The Yellow Violet* (with an intrusive moral—but his "morals" are, contrary to traditional opinion, seldom intrusive, being part of the imaginative and emotional texture), and *Robert of Lincoln* (which is besides most fetching in its playfulness and Bryant's one success in dramatic portrayal). He was a good observer; he would never have placed, like Coleridge, a star within the nether tip of the crescent moon. There is an allied group which impart the quality of a moment in nature, as *Summer Wind:*

> It is a sultry day; the sun has drunk
> The dew that lay upon the morning grass;
> There is no rustling in the lofty elm . . .
> . . . All is silent, save the faint
> And interrupted murmur of the bee,
> Settling on the sick flowers . . . .
> . . . Why so slow?
> Gentle and voluble spirit of the air?

These, if not the most representative, are the most exquisite of all his poems.

And no reminder should be needed that he knew best the American scene, and was the first to reveal it in art. Irving, in the London edition of 1832, naturally emphasized this claim to distinction; and Emerson, many years later, at an after-dinner speech on the poet's seventieth birthday, dwelt on it with a winsome and eloquent gratitude[1] that has made all subsequent comment an impertinence.

Apart from the characteristics outlined above, Bryant had, as if a relief and release from the verities and solemnities, a love of fairyland: he had found it already, for instance, in the snow

[1] Godwin, *Life*, vol. II, p. 216 ff.

world of the *Winter Piece;* he went to it more often and eagerly from the editorial desk and the noise and heat of the Civil War: in *The Little People of the Snow*, in *Sella* (the underwater maiden), and in the fragments, *A Tale of Cloudland*, and *Castles in the Air*. Their flowing blank verse (each some hundreds of lines), unlike his early experiments in prose narrative (which in their wooden arrangement, dull plot, and stilted characterizations are of a piece with the American short story before Poe and Hawthorne), tells, in simple chronological order, of one simple type of adventure, a mortal penetrating beyond the confines of nature—again the repetition of theme and architectonics, and one more manifestation of the primitive in Bryant (for the fairy-tale is, as the anthropologists tell us, among the most primitive activities of man) as dreamer and poet.

Like Cowper and Longfellow, and so many others, Bryant turned, in later life, to a long task of translation, in his case Homer, as relief from sorrow. The literary interest was to see if he might not, by closeness to the original and simplicity of straightforward modern English, supersede the looseness and artificial Miltonic pomp of Cowper. His translation, by detailed comparison line for line with the Greek and with the English poet, will be found to be exactly what Bryant intended it. By block comparison of book for book, or version for version, it will be found to be the better translation, from the point of view of limpid and consequent story-telling—perhaps the best in English verse. Of Arnold's four Homeric characteristics, rapidity of movement, plainness of style, simplicity of ideas, nobility of manner, Bryant's translation is inadequate mainly in the first and the last, but the *Homer* is, in any case, a proof of intellectual alertness, scholarship, and technical skill. All his translations, many of them made before Longfellow's now widely-recognized activities as spokesman in America for European letters, are a witness to Bryant's knowledge of foreign tongues and literatures, to his part in the culturization of America, to the breadth of his taste and a certain dramatic adaptability (for the originals that attracted him had often not much of the specific qualities of his own verse), and to his all but impeccable artistry.

Of his artistry this study has scarcely spoken; yet it has

been throughout implied.   His qualities of thought, feeling,
imagination, were communicated, were indeed only communi-
cable, because so wrought into his diction, his rhymes, cadences,
and stanzas.   Indeed, there is no separating a poet's feeling,
say, for a beautiful flower from his manner of expressing it—
for all we know about his feeling for the flower is what he
succeeds in communicating by speech.   It is tautology to say
that a poet treats a sublime idea sublimely—for it is the sublimity in the treatment that makes us realize the sublimity of
the idea.   We can at most conceive a poet's "style" as a whole;
as, along with his individual world of meditation and vision,
another phase of his creative power—as his creation of music.
Possibly it is the deepest and most wonderful of the poet's
creations, transcending its manifestation in connection with
any single poem.   Perhaps, for instance, Milton's greatest
creative act was not *Lycidas*, or the *Sonnets*, or *Paradise Lost*,
but that music we call Miltonic.   Certainly this is the more
true the more organic the style is; and, as said before, Bryant's
style was highly organic.

An astute and sympathetic mind who might never have seen
a verse of Bryant's could deduce that style from what has been
said in this chapter—if what has been said has been correctly
said.   Such a mind would not need to be told that Bryant's
diction was severe, simple, chaste, narrower in range than that
of his political prose; that his rhymes were dignified, sonorous,
exact and emphatic rather than subtle or allusive, and narrow
in range—not from artistic poverty but because the rhyme
vocabulary of the simple and serious moods is in English itself
narrow, and much novelty and variety of rhyme is in our
speech possible only when, like Browning, one portrays the
grotesque and the eccentric, or like Shelley the fantastic, or
like Butler the comic, or like Chaucer the familiar.   Such a
mind would deduce Bryant's most fundamental rhythm, the
iambic; his most fundamental metre, the pentameter; together
with his preference for stanzaic, or periodic, treatment, whether
in blank verse or in rhyme, rather than for couplets; yes,
together with the most characteristic cadences,—like the curves
of a distant mountain range, few and clear but not monotonous;
like the waves of a broad river, slow and long but not hesitant
or ponderous, never delighting by subtle surprises, nor jarring

by abrupt stops and shifts. Indeed, and would our critic not likewise guess, especially if recently schooled at Leipzig under Sievers, the very pitch of his voice in verse—strongest in the lower octaves—as well as the intrinsic alliteration, [1]—an alliteration as natural as breathing, in its context unobtrusive as such to the conscious ear because so involved in a diction which is itself the outgrowth of very mood and meaning? In quite different ways, Bryant is, with Poe, America's finest artist in verse. Perhaps this is, with Bryant's genuineness of manhood, a reason why Bryant was the one native contemporary that Poe thoroughly respected.

What to puzzled readers seems "characteristically Bryant's blank verse" is really the total impression of both materials and manner, manner itself including diction as well as metrics. But the metrics alone do have their peculiarities, which can, however, hardly be examined here: line endings like "and the green moss," caesuras at the end of the first and of the fourth foot, the tendency to repeat the same caesura and cadence through a succession of lines, a stanza group of five or more lines with full stop followed by a single line or so, inverted accent at the beginning of a line, and a differentiated, strong cadence at the conclusion of the whole poem which gives the effect of a completion, not of a mere stopping,—these are all contributing factors.

Yet Bryant is not one of the world's master-poets. It is not so much that he contributed little or nothing to philosophic thought or spiritual revolution, not altogether that his range was narrow, not that he never created a poem of vast and multitudinous proportions, drama, epic, or tale, not that he knew nature better than human life and human life better than human nature, not that he now and then lapsed from imaginative vision into a bit of sentiment or irrelevant fancy,—not either that there is not a single dark saying, or obscure word, construction, allusion, in all his verse, for the judicious to elucidate at a club or in a monograph. He is not one of the world's master-poets, because he was not pre-eminently endowed with intellectual intensity and imaginative concentration. The character of his whole mind was discursive, enumerative,

[1] Largely on b and frequently in idiomatic pairs, as "bees and birds," "bled or broke."

tending, when measured by the masters, to the diffuse. Thus, among other results, his report of things has given man's current speech but few quotations, of either epigrammatic criticism or haunting beauty. A book could be written on this thesis, but a paragraph must suffice. It is just as well: it is better to realize what Bryant was than to exploit what he was not.

And if he was and is a true poet, he belongs to our best traditions also as critic. He was never, to be sure, the professional guide of literary taste, like Arnold and Lowell. Apart from sensible but obvious memorial addresses on Irving, Halleck, and Cooper, his best known essay is introductory to his *Library of Poetry and Song;* it enunciates fewer keen judgments on individuals, fewer profound principles, than does Emerson's introduction to his *Parnassus*, but it does enunciate the primacy of "a luminous style" and of themes central to common man, in noble paragraphs that should not be forgotten, certainly not by any one who believes that criticism gains in authority when it is the concentrated deduction of experience. Of his services as editor of a leading metropolitan paper, through nearly two generations of crisis after crisis in the nation's life, only an historian should speak. Not even Godwin, his editorial colleague, has spoken, it seems, quite the definitive word. Why should it not be spoken? The fact is, no such man ever sat, before or since, in the editorial chair; in no one other has there been such culture, scholarship, wisdom, dignity, moral idealism. Was it all in Greeley? in Dana? What those fifty years may have meant as an influence on the American press, especially as counteracting the flamboyant and vulgar, the layman may only conjecture.

There is no space to speak of his letters beyond noting that, with all their elegance, courtesy, criticism, information, they do not belong, with Cicero's, Gray's, Cowper's, Byron's, Emerson's, Meredith's, to the literature of correspondence, because they are without zest for little details of human life (whether in others or in himself), or without informal spontaneity and flashes of insight—or without whatever it be that makes a private letter ultimately a public joy.

As a whole, Bryant's prose style has quality as well as qualities, but here a word only on its relation to the style of his poetry. Bryant more than once explicitly differentiated the functions of the two harmonies[1]; but Prescott[2] was not the only one who detected in both the same qualities of mind: obviously a man is not two different beings according to whether he is playing a violin or a cello, singing or talking. Bryant, as Dowden said of Burke, saw "the life of society in a rich, concrete, imaginative way"; and not unlike Burke he had, as politician, the poet's generalizing power. But the point here of special interest is the recurrence in his prose so often, when his prose rises to things in their significance (as apart from their mere relations), of the same imaginative procedure: there is the "broad survey," as in the account of the waters of the Mississippi[3] (themselves introduced as a simile to illustrate the fame of Homer); there are his fundamental metaphors, the grammar of his dialect, as that of the past as a place, occurring in the editorial[4] on the amendment abolishing slavery, which is besides in many details of imagery almost another version of the poem on the same theme, written, says Godwin, a little later. In a public address on the electric telegraph[5] he said:

My imagination goes down to the chambers of the middle sea, to those vast depths where repose the mystic wire on beds of coral, among forests of tangle, or on the bottom of the dim blue gulfs strewn with the bones of whales and sharks, skeletons of drowned men, and ribs and masts of foundered barks, laden with wedges of gold never to be coined, and pipes of the choicest vintages of earth never to be tasted. Through these watery solitudes, among the fountains of the great deep, the abode of perpetual silence, never visited by living human presence and beyond the sight of human eye, there are gliding to and fro, by night and by day, in light and in darkness, in calm and in tempest, currents of human thought borne by the electric pulse which obeys the bidding of man.

Is not this in imagination, mood, manner, even in the recurrent blank verse cadences, veritably as if an unpublished fragment of *A Hymn of the Sea?*

So we return to the Poet. Yet when all is said, it is the whole man that is ours and that should be ours. He is the Citizen of

---

[1] Godwin, *Prose*, vol. II, p. 22.
[2] Godwin, *Life*, vol. II, p. 36.
[3] Godwin, *Prose*, vol. II, p. 269.
[4] Godwin, *Life*, vol. II, p. 235.
[5] Godwin, *Prose*, vol. II, p. 259.

our tradition; not to us today so much for his hand in the
founding of two political parties, nor for his counsels by personal letter and speech that Lincoln, the Statesman of our
tradition, heard with such grave respect, nor for his civic
activities in art, charity, and reform; but for that Mosaic
massive head, those deep, peering, brooding eyes, those white
shaggy brows, and the great beard over the old man's cloak
that, in the engraving after Sarony's photograph, has been now
for a generation familiar in so many homes of our land.

II. MINOR POETS

When Bryant, pioneer and patriarch, was laid away on that
bright June afternoon of 1878 in the cemetery at Roslyn, Long
Island, his oldest and dearest friend was still alive.   Richard
Henry Dana (1787–1879), one of the founders of *The North
American Review*[1] and of the serious tradition in our literary
criticism, is remembered, if at all, as verse-writer mainly
through Bryant's praise, as Mason is remembered through
Gray's.   How remote the short jerky stanzas of *The Buccaneer*
(1827), an ambitious tale of pirate and spectre, were from the
talents and temper of the Bostonian descendant of the Puritan
Anne Bradstreet, one may realize who reflects what Coleridge
would have done with the spell and the uncanny, and what
Byron with the crime and the movement—the two poets whom
Dana was obviously emulating.   But there are some good lines
on the sea in *The Buccaneer*, and Dana's lyric, *The Little Beach
Bird*, gets a traditional honourable mention in the manuals.

The other minor poets about Bryant lived in or near New
York.   James Kirke Paulding, humorist and proseman of no
mean reputation,[2] and collaborator with Bryant in prose
stories,[3] deserves mention here as an early representative of a
conscious movement to make poetry out of American materials,
convinced that

> Thrice happy he who first shall strike the lyre
> With homebred feeling, and with homebred fire.

[1] See Book II, Chap. xx.   [2] See also Book II, Chaps. i, iii, iv, and vii.
[3] *Tales of the Glauber Spa* (1832).

The Backwoodsman (1818), from which this conventional couplet is taken, recounts, without much plot, in sturdy heroics
more like Crabbe's realism than Goldsmith's idyllic sentiment,
the rugged life and wild surroundings of a frontiersman and
his family.   It is an honest document, if not distinguished
literature.

James Gates Percival (1795–1856) typified that crude manifestation of Romanticism, the self-constituted, the self-conscious poetic genius.   Similarly, he typified the poetic mood
that is without the poetic reason.   The stuff of him is pre-
eminently the stuff of poetry, but unclarified, uncontrolled,
unorganized.   It is often as if the personalities of Byron, Shelley,
Wordsworth, Moore, and Bryant had been merged into one
helpless hypnoidal state of metrical and emotional garrulity.
Yet every now and then an open-minded reader is surprised
by some first-hand observation, some graceful analogy, some
picturesqueness or energy, some short lyric cry; and once at
least he wrought a little gem—his simple stanzas on *Seneca
Lake*.   He typified, too, a not altogether ignoble phase of
earlier American culture in his zealous acquisitiveness, both in
science (he died as state geologist of Wisconsin), and in languages (he wrote verse in Scandinavian and German, and translated from innumerable tongues).   But he belongs chiefly to
the student of human nature; lonely, shy, unmarried, disappointed, poor, and dirty, he was in appearance and mode of
life a character for Dickens, in heart and soul a character for
Thackeray or George Eliot.   Lowell pilloried him in an essay;
Bryant was perhaps juster in his kindlier obituary criticism in
The Evening Post.   He was once a famous man.

Samuel Woodworth (1785–1842)[1] and George P. Morris
(1802–1864), Knickerbocker editors of literary journals[2] and
charitably remembered respectively for *The Old Oaken Bucket*
and *Woodman, Spare that Tree*, were popular song writers in the
sentimental fashion (perhaps more developed in America than
in England) that seems to have originated with Tom Moore.
Yet such songs had music, point, and refinement that sets them
far above their popular descendants—the raucous, vulgar
inanities born of vaudeville and cabaret.

Charles Fenno Hoffman (1806–1884), another Knicker-

[1] See Book II, Chaps. II and VI.   [2] See Book II, Chap. XX.

bocker editor[1] and a song-writer, who, says a recent critic,[2] "possessed a lyric note almost completely unknown in the America of his time,"—by which is meant a certain catchy musical lilt,—is, however, chiefly memorable for the fine ballad *Monterey:*

> We were not many, we who stood
> Before the iron sleet that day:
> Yet many a gallant spirit would
> Give half his years if but he could
> Have been with us at Monterey.

This is, or should be, a classic in a genre rare in our literature, whose poets have seldom communicated with martial fire the rapture of the strife or celebrated worthily the achievements of our arms. Bryant wrote a critical sketch for the last edition of Hoffman's poems.

Nathaniel Parker Willis, the most honoured among these literary editors of old New York,[3] began as a sentimental poetizer of Scripture for meek ladies, and then helped to establish a still existing journalistic tradition in our literature— that of the light, the pretty, the clever, the urbane negligee in prose and rhyme; while his *Lady Jane*, a story after *Don Juan* and *Fanny*, and his *Melanie*, after Byron's *Tales*, only too well illustrate the now dead but once potent influence of Byron on our minor poets, even on poets utterly unlike Byron in temperament and in mode of life.[4] Yet Willis was a true poet in a half dozen lyrics where a human form, a bit of nature, or a moral insight is registered in sincere, graceful, dignified, and, at least once (*Unseen Spirits*), noble speech. These, with his brief prose obituary notice of Poe and its tribute to Mrs. Clemm, are higher things than conventional criticism now associates with the brilliant and versatile gentleman of provincial but polished Broadway.

Joseph Rodman Drake (1795–1820) and Fitz-Greene Halleck (1790–1867) are remembered first for a romantic youthful friendship, not common in our literary history. For a time they

[1] See Book II, Chaps. VII and XX.
[2] Trent, W. P., in *American Literature*, p. 457.
[3] See also Book II, Chap. III.
[4] See Leonard, W. E., *Byron and Byronism in America* (Columbia Univ. Diss.), 1905.

amused themselves and the town by facile and often pointed
skits on contemporary politics, people, and events, under the
title Croaker and Co., after the manner of English wits of the
time, as Moore and the Smith brothers.   Halleck is said to have
written the last four lines of Drake's *American Flag*, a lyric
full of the old-fashioned expansive and defiant Americanism,
and, with its flare of imagery and blare of sound, still sure to
stir the blood of any one but a professional critic.   And it was
on Drake, dead at twenty-five, that Halleck wrote what is the
tenderest, the manliest little elegy of personal loss in American
literature, beginning with the familiar lines:

> Green be the turf above thee,
>   Friend of my better days!
> None knew thee but to love thee,
>   Nor named thee but to praise.

Yet they are remembered no less for achievements more
noteworthy than those of the other minor men in this sketch.
Drake's *Culprit Fay* is the best and in fact the one fairy story in
American verse, if we except Bryant's *Sella* and *The Little
People of the Snow*, which are indeed rather stories of mortals
in fairyland than of the tiny, tricksy creatures themselves.
Though in a sense exotic, for it roots in no folklore despite the
setting on the Hudson, *The Culprit Fay* reports quite as well as
Drayton's *Nimphidia*, its nearest analogue, the antic characteristics of the elfland of man's universal fancy.   But it is most
remarkable for its reading of nature.   The Culprit Fay's
adventures take him through woods, waters, and air, on to
the stars above, amid the iridescent, elusive, darting, rended,
prickly little objects of the real universe that heavy-lidded folk
seldom observe.   There are also—and this before Bryant's first
volume—the American plant, bird, and insect: the chickweed
and sassafras, the whippoorwill, the katydid and woodtick.
The music, though perhaps influenced by Coleridge, sang itself
under the unconscious guidance of a delicate and independent
ear—the most striking creative act in American versification
up to that time and for some time to come.   Of the obvious
faults of *The Culprit Fay* it were ungracious to speak; it was
the two days' diversion of a very young man, and published
posthumously (1835).

Halleck was the one worthy American representative of the contemporary popular English Romanticists, Scott, Campbell, and Byron—worthy, because something of their matter and manner, despite occasional crude imitation, was thoroughly natural to his vigorous feelings, to his alert though not subtle masculine intellect, and to his sounding voice. His Spenserians on *Wyoming* remind one of Campbell and Byron in stanza and phraseology. The still popular *Marco Bozzaris* reminds one of Byron in the enthusiasm for Greek freedom (also the inspiration of some of Bryant's early verse), and of Campbell in martial vigour, while its octosyllabics have the verve of Scott's. In *Alnwick Castle* and several other poems grave and gay are whimsically mixed after Byron's later manner. Indeed Byron, whose works Halleck subsequently edited, was his most kindred spirit. As early as 1819 appeared his *Fanny*, suggested by *Beppo* and in its present form sometimes reminiscent of *Don Juan*—

With the wickedness out that gave salt to the true one,

as Lowell's *Fable for Critics* observed as late as 1848—a social satire on a flashy New Yorker and his fashionable daughter, with Byronic anti-climax and Byronic digressions on Greece, European and American politics, bad literature and bad statues. But a financial failure was substituted for Byronic *crim.-cons.*, and the bluff and hearty Halleck "was never cynical in his satire, and Byron was"—to quote Bryant,[1] who speaks, however, a truer word for Halleck than for Halleck's master. *Fanny* became at once popular,[2] and remained so for a generation, stimulating to several long since forgotten imitations and doubtless serving to foster American Byronism in its pseudo-comic phases. A detailed study of Halleck would reveal, as the chief source of his genuinely individual note, his power to phrase energetically a single moment of action or of feeling with a certain fusion of imaginative vision and of intellectual

[1] Godwin, *Prose*, vol. I, p. 374.

[2] It was reprinted almost entire in *Specimens of the American Poets*, London, 1822, in which it is called a "sprightly little poem" and "one of the cleverest efforts of the American Muse." The note concludes, however, with a comment that the English edition had not apparently had "a very extensive circulation." Part of its American popularity was due to its purely local allusions.

criticism. Moreover, Halleck's *Poems*, including such unforgotten titles as *The Field of the Grounded Arms, Burns,* and *Red Jacket*, still have some literary value as a volume: the anthologies do not exhaust him.

Thus these early minor men left us some things worth keeping; but, nevertheless, taken all in all, they emphasize for us today, as they never could for their contemporaries, the relative greatness of Bryant.

CHAPTER VI

Fiction I

Brown, Cooper

THE clear victory which the first great British novelists won over popular taste did not, for some years, make them masters of the colonial public. *Pamela*, indeed, was printed as early as 1744 in Philadelphia, by Benjamin Franklin, and in the same year in New York and in Boston. But the only other novels printed in America before the Declaration of Independence seem to have been *Robinson Crusoe* (1768), *Rasselas* (1768), *The Vicar of Wakefield* (1772), *Juliet Grenville* (1774), and *The Works of Laurence Sterne M.A.* (1774). Publishers, however, were less active than importers, for diaries and library catalogues show that British editions were on many shelves. The Southern and Middle colonies may have read more novels than did New England, yet Jonathan Edwards himself, whose savage quarrel with the Northampton congregation had arisen partly over the "licentious books" [possibly *Pamela*, among others] which some of the younger members "employed to promote lascivious and obscene discourse," was later enchanted by *Sir Charles Grandison*.

Edwards did not relent in advance of the general public. After the Revolution the novel-reading habit grew, fostered by American publishers and cried out against by many moralists whose cries appeared in magazines side by side with moral tales. Nearly every grade of sophistication applied itself to the problem. It was contested that novels were lies; that they served no virtuous purpose; that they melted rigorous minds; that they crowded out better books; that they painted adventure too romantic and love too vehement, and so unfitted

Richardson in America

readers for solid reality; that, dealing with European manners, they tended to confuse and dissatisfy republican youth. In the face of such censure, native novelists appeared late and apologetically, armed for the most part with the triple plea that the tale was true, the tendency heavenward, and the scene devoutly American. Before 1800 the sweeping philippic of the older school had been forced to share the field of criticism with occasional efforts to distinguish good novels from bad. No critical game was more frequently played than that which compared Fielding and Richardson. Fielding got some robust preference, Smollett had his imitators, and Sterne fathered much "sensibility," but until Scott had definitely set a new mode for the world, the potent influence in American fiction was Richardson. The amiable ladies who produced most of these early novels commonly held, like Mrs. Rowson, that their knowledge of life had been "simply gleaned from pure nature,"[1] because they dealt with facts which had come under their own observation, but like other amateurs they saw in nature what art had assured them would be there. Nature and Richardson they found the same. Whatever bias they gave this Richardsonian universe was due to a pervading consciousness of the sex which read their novels. The result was a highly domestic world, limited in outlook, where the talk was of careless husbands, grief for dead children, the peril of many childbirths, the sentiment and the religion which enabled women to endure their sex's destiny. Over all hangs the furious menace of the seducer, who appears in such multitudes that one can defend the age only by blaming its brutality less than the pathetic example of Clarissa Harlowe.

Thus early did the American novel acquire the permanent background of neutral domestic fiction against which the notable figures stand out. A few of the early names have a shade of distinction. Mrs. Sarah Wentworth Morton (1759–1846), a "Lady of Boston," produced the first regular novel, *The Power of Sympathy* (1789). Its two volumes of stilted letters caused a scandal and were promptly suppressed, but they called forth a much better novel, *The Coquette* (1797), by Mrs. Hannah Webster Foster (1759–1840). Based upon the tragic and widely known career of Elizabeth Whitman of Hartford, it saw

[1] Preface to *Mentoria*.

thirteen editions in forty years, but it was still less popular than Mrs. Susannah Haswell Rowson's *Charlotte* (1794), one of the most popular novels ever published in America. Mrs. Rowson (1762–1824), an American only by immigration, had indeed written the novel in England (1790?), but *Charlotte Temple*, to call it by its later title, was thoroughly naturalized. It has persuaded an increasingly naïve underworld of fiction readers to buy more than a hundred editions and has built up a legend about the not too authentic tomb of Charlotte Stanley in Trinity Churchyard, New York.

A particular importance of *The Coquette* and *Charlotte Temple* was that they gave to fiction something of the saga element by stealing, in the company of facts, upon a community which winced at fiction. And this brief garment of illusion was not confined to New York and New England. In 1792–3–7 Pennsylvania saw the publication, in four volumes, of the first part of the remarkable *Modern Chivalry*. The author, Hugh Henry Brackenridge (1748–1816), son of a poor Scotch immigrant, graduate of Princeton, tutor and licensed preacher, master of an academy in Maryland, editor of *The United States Magazine* in Philadelphia (1776), chaplain in the Revolutionary army, author of patriotic tragedies and pamphlets, and lawyer and judge in Pittsburg after 1781, brought to his work a culture and experience which gave his satiric picture of American life many of the features of truth. Farrago, the hero, is a new Don Quixote, his servant Teague a witless and grotesque Sancho Panza, but the chief follies of the book are found not in them but in the public which they encounter and which would gladly make Teague hero and office-holder. No man was a more convinced democrat than Brackenridge, but he was also solid, well-read, and deeply bored by fools who canted about free men and wise majorities. Against such cant and the excesses of political ambition he directed his chief satire, but he let few current fads and affectations go unwhipped. His book had an abundant popularity, especially along the frontier which it satirized. The second part (1804–5), ostensibly the chronicle of a new Western settlement, is almost a comic history of civilization in America. It is so badly constructed, however, and so often goes over ground well trodden in the earlier part as to be generally inferior to it in interest. Here Brackenridge depos-

ited scraps of irony and censure which he had been producing since 1787, when he had set out to imitate *Hudibras*.
His prose is better than his verse, plain and simple in style, by
his own confession following that of Hume, Swift, and Fielding.
Swift was his dearest master. Very curious, if hard to follow,
are the successive revisions by which Brackenridge kept pace
with new follies.

Smollett had something to do with another novel which,
though less read than *Modern Chivalry*, deserves mention with
it, *The Algerine Captive* (1797) of Royall Tyler, poet, wit,
playwright, and jurist.[1] The first volume has some entertaining
though not subtle studies of American manners; the second, a
tale of six years' captivity in Algiers, belongs with the many
books and pamphlets called forth by the war with Tripoli.[2]
Historically important is the preface, which declared that the
American taste for novels had grown in the past seven years
from apathy to a general demand.

Apparently the time was slowly ripening to the point at
which taste begins to support those who gratify it, and it is
notable that the first American to make authorship his sole
career had already decided for fiction. Charles Brockden
Brown came of good Quaker stock long settled in Pennsylvania,
where, at Philadelphia, he was born 17 January, 1771. He was
a frail, studious child, reputed a prodigy, and encouraged by
his parents in that frantic feeding upon books which was expected, in those days, of every American boy of parts. By
the time he was sixteen he had made himself a tolerable
classical scholar, contemplated three epics—on Columbus,
Pizarro, and Cortez—and hurt his health by over-work. As
he grew older he read with a hectic, desultory sweep in every
direction open to him. With his temper and education, he
developed into a hot young philosopher in those days of revolution. He brooded over the maps of remote regions, glowed with
eager schemes for perfecting mankind, and dabbled in subterranean lore as an escape from humane Philadelphia. He
kept a journal and wrote letters heavy with self-consciousness.
Put into a law office by his family, he found that his legal studies
only confirmed him in his resolution to be a man of letters. His

[1] See also Book I, Chap. IX and Book II, Chaps. II and III.
[2] See also Book II, Chap. II.

parents and brothers, who supported him in his adventure, urged him from a path so unpromising, but Brown, though he felt the pressure of their distress, clung stoutly, if gloomily, to the pursuits of literature. He speculated, debated, and wrote for the newspapers. His first identified work, a series of papers called *The Rhapsodist*, which appeared in *The Columbian Magazine*, August–November, 1789, glorified the proud and lonely soul.

Little is known of the next few years of his life. In 1793 he seems to have gone to New York to visit his friend Dr. Elihu Hubbard Smith, formerly a medical student in Philadelphia. Removed from the scenes of his old solitude, Brown became less solitary. Smith's friends, among them S. L. Mitchill, James Kent, and William Dunlap, Brown's future biographer, who belonged to a club called the Friendly Society, forced the young misanthrope to cast part of his coat. In 1795, after another visit to New York, he began an unidentified work, apparently speculative but not a romance, to "equal in extent Caleb Williams," a book in which Brown saw "transcendant merits." In spite of the first ardour which had made him sure he could finish his task in six weeks, he lost faith in its moral utility and never got beyond fifty pages, but he had gradually given up Dr. Johnson for Godwin as his model. July, 1796, saw him cease to be even a sleeping partner in his brother's counting house. Thenceforth he was nothing but an author.

The spirit of Godwin stirred eagerly in Brown during the early days of his freedom. Toward the end of 1797 he bore witness by writing *Alcuin*, a dialogue on the rights of women which took its first principles from Mary Wollstonecraft and Godwin. On the last day of December he says he finished a romance which appears to have been *Sky-Walk*, the manuscript of which was lost before it could be published. Early in 1798 he became a contributor to the new Philadelphia *Weekly Magazine*, which contains, among the fragments which always mark Brown's trail, the first two parts of *Alcuin*, called *The Rights of Women*, and nine chapters of *Arthur Mervyn*.[1] He announced *Sky-Walk* 17 March, 1798, in a letter to the *Weekly Magazine* signed "Speratus." In this earliest public statement of his ideals of fiction Brown spoke of the need of

[1] Published in 1799, with a second part, 1800.

native romances and ascribed the "value of such works" to "their moral tendency." Only by displaying characters "of soaring passions and intellectual energy," he believed, could a novelist hope "to enchain the attention and ravish the souls of those who study and reflect." But Brown was too good a democrat to write for geniuses alone. "A contexture of facts capable of suspending the faculties of every soul in curiosity, may be joined with depth of views into human nature and all the subtleties of reasoning."

With these opinions, and his apprenticeship already served, Brown took up his residence in New York during the summer of 1798. In two ardent years, which were more social than any that had gone before, Brown did all his best work. The single month of August served to produce *Wieland*, which made a stir and is still commonly held his masterpiece. The source of its plot has been shown[1] to be, in part, the actual murder of his whole family by a religious fanatic, "Mr. J—— Y——," of Tomhannock, New York, in December, 1781. To this Brown added the mysteries of spontaneous combustion and ventriloquism to make up the "contexture of facts capable of suspending the faculties of every soul in curiosity." These were for the vulgar. The apparent scene of action is laid upon the banks of the Schuylkill; this was patriotism. But the real setting is somewhere in the feverish climate of romantic speculation, and the central interest lies in the strange, unreal creatures "of soaring passions and intellectual energy," Wieland, crushingly impelled to crime by a mysterious voice which, however, but germinates seeds of frenzy already sleeping in his nature, and Carwin, the "biloquist," a villain who sins, not as the old morality had it, because of wickedness, but because of the driving power of the spirit of evil which no man can resist and from which only the weak are immune. These were cases of speculative pathology which Brown had met in his morbid twilights, beings who had for him the reality he knew best, that of dream and passion. It is the fever in the climate which lends the book, in spite of awkward narrative, strained probabilities, and a premature solution, its shuddering power. Here at least Brown was absorbed in his subject; here at least he gave a profound unity of effect never equalled in his later works.

[1] Van Doren, C., *Early American Realism, Nation,* 12 Nov., 1914.

Close upon this August followed the plague in New York. Brown was then living with Dr. Smith in Pine Street, and Smith, firm in the opinion that yellow fever could not be contagious, insisted upon taking into the house a stricken young Italian. Of the three only Brown escaped death. He thus came hand-to-hand with a hard reality, and, like other men of many dreams and few experiences, was deeply impressed by it. The effect upon his work, however, of this month of pestilence may be easily overstated. Five years before, Brown's family had left Philadelphia for a time to escape the great plague of 1793, and Brown had put memories of that visitation into *The Man at Home*, in *The Weekly Magazine*, and the earliest chapters of *Arthur Mervyn*, both written before his removal to New York. Curiously enough, the Dr. Stevens of the novel, by his hospitality to Mervyn, behaves much as did the Dr. Smith of reality, but invention was before fact. And when, in December, 1798, Brown wrote *Ormond* (1799), he not only laid his scene in Philadelphia in 1793, but he borrowed a whole chapter from *The Man at Home*. What the plague had been to Brown in 1793 it remained: a chapter in the annals of his native city, mysterious, the stuff of passion, and therefore fully congenial to his temper and ideals of art. He used it with sombre and memorable detail, as a background for mental or social ills.

It is characteristic of Brown that, while two of his notable romances recall his most vivid personal experience, all four of them wear the colours of *Caleb Williams*. From Godwin, Brown had his favourite subject, virtue in distress, and his favourite set of characters, a patron and a client. Perhaps he comes nearest to his master in *Ormond*. Constantia Dudley won the passionate regard of Shelley, to whom she was the type of virtuous humanity oppressed by evil customs. She is Brown's picture of feminine perfection, learned, self-reliant, pure, priggish. Ormond is quite clearly the child of romance and revolution, a hero who is a villain, a creature of nature who is the master of many destinies, a free will which must act as the agent of inevitable malice. All this seems pure Godwin, but it has a certain spirit of youth and ardour which Godwin lacked. In *Arthur Mervyn* the hero has to undergo less than the cumulative agony of Caleb Williams, for the simple reason that

Brown worked too violently to be able to organize a scheme of circumstances all bearing upon a single victim. At least in the second part of the book, the plot frays helplessly into flying ends which no memory can hold together, and the characters and "moral tendency" of a story rich in incident suffer a sad confusion. Brown was no match for Godwin in the art of calm and deliberate narrative, partly because of his vehement methods of work, partly because he lacked Godwin's finished and consistent philosophy of life. The leaven of rationalism stirs in his work, but it does not, as with Godwin, pervade the mass.

Passion, not hard conviction, gives Brown his positive qualities. He had a power in keeping up suspense which no clumsiness could destroy. In presenting the physical emotions of danger and terror he had a kind of ghoulish force. Without the deftness to get full value from his material, he had still a sharp eye for what was picturesque or dramatic. In *Edgar Huntly*, for which Brown was considerably indebted to the memory of *Sky-Walk*, he made notable use of that pioneer life which was to bulk so large in American fiction for half a century. His preface repeats his earlier plea, as "Speratus," for native matter in native fiction. From that ideal he never swerved. The plague, Wieland's frenzy, Queen Mab in *Edgar Huntly*,— these he had studied from the facts as he knew them. That his books are not more realistic proves merely that he was a romancer interested primarily in ideas and abstruse mental states which he saw with his eyes closed. "Sir," he told prying John Davis, "good pens, thick paper, and ink well diluted, would facilitate my composition more than the prospect of the broadest expanse of clouds, water, or mountains rising above the clouds." But when Brown opened his eyes he always saw Pennsylvania. His strangest supernaturalisms, too, turn out in the end to have rested on acts of nature which science can explain. It was his characters he romanticized. He saw in man a dignity which only the days of hopeful revolution can bestow, and he was thus urged to study souls with a passion which took him past the outward facts of humanity to a certain essential truth which gives him, among his contemporaries, his special virtue.

In April, 1799, Brown began to edit *The Monthly Magazine*

in New York and so entered the decade of journalism which closed his life. He wrote, indeed, besides fragments of fiction, two other novels, *Clara Howard* (1801) and *Jane Talbot* (1801), but they lack his old vigour. In *Jane Talbot* he seemed to renounce Godwin; gradually he became subdued to humanity and lost his concern with romance. He returned to Philadelphia in 1801, where, two years later, he founded *The Literary Magazine*. The stolid orthodoxy of his prospectus makes it clear that he was no longer a philosopher of the old stamp, although he did write two acts of a tragedy for John Bernard, and, told the play would not act, burned the work and kept its ashes in a snuff-box. In November, 1804, he married Miss Elizabeth Linn of New York, and was thereafter an exemplary husband, father, and drudge, who produced pamphlets, large parts of his magazine, and practically the whole of the useful *American Register* (1807–11). The fame of his novels, of which he claimed to think little, became a legend, but new editions were not called for. In 1809 he was elected to honorary membership in the New York Historical Society, with such notables as Lindley Murray, Noah Webster, Benjamin Trumbull, Timothy Dwight, Josiah Quincy, and George Clinton. He died of consumption 19 February, 1810. In England he was well known for at least a generation. *Blackwood's* praised him with the fiery pen of John Neal; Scott borrowed from him the names of two characters in *Guy Mannering;* Godwin himself owed to *Wieland* a hint for *Mandeville*. In his native country Brown has stood, with occasional flickerings of interest, firmly fixed as a literary ancestor.

There is little to note in American fiction between the close of Brown's career and the beginning of Cooper's. An absurd romance, *The Asylum* (1811), probably by Isaac Mitchell, was popular. Tabitha Tenny (1762–1837) produced a funny if robustious anti-romance, *Female Quixotism* (1808?); Samuel Woodworth[1] mingled conventional history with conventional romance in *The Champions of Freedom* (1816), which celebrated the second war with England. By this time the humane and thrilling art of Scott had already begun to be effective in America, as in Europe. At the first, however, Scott's peculiar qualities seemed to defy rivalry.

[1] See also Book II, Chaps. II and V.

"Of native *novels*," said John Bristed in 1818, "we have no great stock, and none good; our democratic institutions placing all the people on a dead level of political equality; and the pretty equal diffusion of property throughout the country affords but little room for varieties, and contrasts of character; nor is there much scope for fiction, as the country is quite new, and all that has happened from the first settlement to the present hour, respecting it, is known to every one. There is, to be sure, some traditional romance about the Indians; but a novel describing these miserable barbarians, their squaws, and papooses, would not be very interesting to the present race of American readers."[1]

America, that is, without aristocracy, antiquity, and a romantic border, could not have a Scott. Seldom has time contradicted a prophet so fully and so soon as when Cooper, within three years, began to show that democracy has its contrasts, that two hundred years can be called a kind of antiquity, and that the border warfare between pioneer and Indian is one of the great chapters in the world's romance.

The task weighed less upon Cooper than it might had he been from boyhood at all bookish or, when he began his career, either scholar or conscious man of letters. But, unlike Brown, he had been trained in the world. Born at Burlington, New Jersey, 15 September, 1789, the son of Judge William Cooper and Susan Fenimore, James Cooper[2] was taken in November, 1790, to Cooperstown, the raw central village of a pioneer settlement recently established by his father on Otsego Lake, New York. Here the boy saw at first hand the varied life of the border, observed its shifts and contrivances, listened to tales of its adventures, and learned to feel the mystery of the dark forest which lay beyond the cleared circle of his own life. Judge Cooper, however, was less a typical backwoodsman than a kind of warden of the New York marches, like Judge Templeton in *The Pioneers*, and he did not keep his son in the woods but sent him, first to the rector of St. Peter's in Albany, who grounded him in Latin and hatred of Puritans, and then to Yale, where he wore his college duties so lightly as to be dis-

---

[1] *The Resources of the United States*, 1818, pp. 355–6.
[2] The family name was changed to Fenimore-Cooper by act of legislature in April, 1826. Cooper soon dropped the hyphen.

missed in his third year. Thinking the navy might furnish
better discipline than Yale, Judge Cooper shipped his son before
the mast on a merchant vessel to learn the art of seamanship
which there was then no naval academy to teach. His first
ship, the *Sterling*, sailed from New York in October, 1806, for
Falmouth and London, thence to Cartagena, back to London,
and once more to America in September of the following year.
They were chased by pirates and stopped by searching parties,
incidents Cooper never forgot. In January, 1808, he was
commissioned midshipman. He served for a time on the
Vesuvius, and later in the same year was sent with a party to
Lake Ontario to build the brig *Oneida* for service against the
British on inland waters. He visited Niagara, commanded for
a time on Lake Champlain, and in November, 1809, was ordered
to the *Wasp*. In the natural course of events he would have
fought in the War of 1812, but, having been married in January, 1811, to Miss Susan Augusta DeLancey, he resigned his
commission the following May and gave up all hope of a naval
career.

Thus at twenty-two he exchanged a stirring youth for the
quiet, if happy, life of a country proprietor. He spent the next
eleven years, except for a stay at Cooperstown (1814-17), in
his wife's native county of Westchester, New York. There,
in a manner quite casual, he began his real work. His wife
challenged him to make good his boast that he could write a
better story than an English novel he was reading to her. He
attempted it and wrote *Precaution* (1820), which, as might
have been expected from a man who, in spite of a juvenile
romance and a few doggerel verses, was little trained in authorship, is a highly conventional novel. Its scene is laid in England,
and no quality is more notable than stiff elegance and painful
piety. Cooper was dissatisfied with his book. "Ashamed to
have fallen into the track of imitation, I endeavoured to repay
the wrong done to my own views, by producing a work that
should be purely American, and of which love of country should
be the theme." [1] He chose for his hero a spy who had served
John Jay during the Revolution, according to Jay's own
account, with singular purity of motive. The work was
carelessly done and published at the author's risk, and yet

[1] *A Letter to his Countrymen*, 1834, p. 98.

with the appearance of *The Spy* (22 December, 1821), American fiction may be said to have come of age.

This stirring tale has been, for many readers, an important factor in the tradition which national piety and the old swelling rhetoric have built up around the Revolution. The share of historical fact in it, indeed, is not large, but the action takes place so near to great events that the characters are all invested with something of the dusky light of heroes, while the figure of Washington moves among them like an unsuspected god. Such a quality in the novel might have gone with impossible partiality for the Americans had not Cooper's wife belonged to a family which had been loyal during the struggle for independence. As it was, he made his loyalists not necessarily knaves and fools, and so secured a fairness of tone which, aside from all questions of justice, has a large effect upon the art of the narrative. It is clear the British are enemies worth fighting. Perhaps by chance, Cooper here hit upon a type of plot at which he excelled, a struggle between contending forces, not badly matched, arranged as a pursuit in which the pursued are, as a rule, favoured by author and reader. In the management of such a device Cooper's invention, which was great, worked easily, and the flights of Birch from friend and foe alike exhibit a power to carry on plots with sustained sweep which belongs only to the masters of narration. To rapid movement Cooper added the virtues of a very real setting. He knew Westchester and its sparse legends as Scott knew the Border; his topography was drawn with a firm hand. In his characters he was not uniformly successful. Accepting for women the romantic ideals of the day and writing of events in which, of necessity, ladies could play but a small part, Cooper tended to cast his heroines, as even that day remarked, into a conventional mould of helplessness and decorum. With the less sheltered classes of women he was much more truthful. Of his men, too, the gentlemen are likely to be mere heroes, though Lawton is an interesting dragoon, while those of a lower order have more marked characteristics. Essentially memorable and arresting is Harvey Birch, peddler and patriot, outwardly no hero at all and yet surpassingly heroic of soul. The skill with which Birch is presented, gaunt, weather-beaten, canny, mysterious—a skill which Brown lacked—should not make one overlook the half-supernatural spirit of patriotism which, like the daemonic impulses in Brown's characters, drives Birch to his destiny at once wrecking and honouring him. This romantic fate also condemns him to be sad and lonely, a dedicated soul who captures attention by his secrecy and holds it throughout his career by his adventures. No character in American historical fiction has been able to obscure this first great character, whose fame has outlasted every fashion for almost a century.

With *The Spy* Cooper proved his power to invent situations, conduct a plot, vivify history and landscape, and create a certain type of heroic character. His public success was instant. The novel reached a third edition the following March; it was approved on the stage; European readers accepted it with enthusiasm. Pleased, though perhaps surprised, at this reception of his work, Cooper threw himself into the new career thus offered him with characteristic energy. He removed to New York and hurried forward the composition of *The Pioneers*, which appeared in February, 1823, with Cooper's first bumptious preface. Technically this book made no advance upon *The Spy*. Cooper had but one method, improvisation, and the absence of any very definite pursuit deprives *The Pioneers*, though it has exciting moments, of general suspense. But it is important as his first trial at the realistic presentation of manners in America. Dealing as he did with the Otsego settlement where his boyhood had been spent, and with a time (1793) within his memory, he could write largely from the fact. Whatever romance there is in the story lies less in its plot, which is relatively simple, or in its characters, which are, for the most part, studied under a dry light with a good deal of caustic judgment, than in the essential wonder of a pioneer life. The novel is not as heroic as *The Spy* had been. Indian John, the last of his proud race, is old and broken, corrupted by the settlements; only his death dignifies him. Natty Bumppo, a composite from many Cooperstown memories, is nobler because he has not yielded but carries his virtues, which even in Cooper's boyhood were becoming archaic along the frontier, into the deeper forest. Natty stands as a protest, on behalf of simplicity and perfect freedom, against encroaching law and order. In *The Pioneers*, however, he is not yet of the proportions which he later assumed, and only at the end, when he withdraws from the field of his defeat by civilization, does he make his full appeal. Cooper may have felt that there were still possibilities in the character, but for the present he did not try to realize them. Instead, he undertook to surpass Scott's *Pirate* in seamanship and produced *The Pilot*, issued in January, 1824.[1] With this third success he practically ended his experimental stage. Like *The Spy*, his new tale made use of a Revolutionary setting; like *The Pioneers*, it was full of realistic detail based on Cooper's own experience. The result was that he not only outdid Scott in sheer narrative, but he created a new literary type, the tale of adventure on the sea, in which, though he was to have many followers in almost every modern language, he remains unsurpassed for vigour and variety. Smollett had already discovered the racy humours of seamen, but it remained for Cooper to capture for fiction the mystery and beauty, the shock and thrill of the sea. Experts say that his technical knowledge was sound; what is more important, he wrote, in *The Pilot*, a story about sailing vessels which convinces landsmen even in days of steam. The conventional element in the novel is its hero, John Paul Jones, secret, Byronic, always brooding upon a dark past and a darker fate. Thoroughly original is that worthy successor of Birch and Natty Bumppo, Long Tom Coffin, who lives and dies by the sea which has made him, as love of country made the spy and the forest made the old hunter.

Cooper had now become a national figure, although critical judgment in New England condescended to him. He founded the Bread and Cheese Club in New York, a literary society of which he was the moving spirit; he took a prominent part in the reception of Lafayette in 1824; in the same year Columbia College gave him the honorary degree of Master of Arts. He planned a series of *Legends of the Thirteen Republics*, aimed to celebrate each of the original states, which he gave up after the first, *Lionel Lincoln* (1825), for all his careful research failed to please as his earlier novels had done. During the next two years Cooper reached probably the highest point of his career in *The Last of the Mohicans* (February, 1826) and *The Prairie* (May, 1827). His own interest and the persuasion of his friends led him to continue the adventures of Natty Bumppo, and

[1] But dated 1823.

very naturally he undertook to show both the days of Natty's prime and his final fortunes. In each case Cooper projects the old hunter out of the world of remembered Otsego, into the dark forest which was giving up its secrets in 1793, or into the mighty prairies which Cooper had not seen but which stretched, in his mind's eye, for endless miles beyond the forest, another mystery and another refuge. Natty, called Hawkeye in *The Last of the Mohicans*, no longer has the hardness which marred his age in *The Pioneers*. With all his virtues of hand and head he combines a nobility of spirit which the woods have fostered in a mind never spoiled by men. He grows nobler as he grows more remote, more the poet and hero as the world in which he moves becomes more wholly his own. Chingachgook has undergone even a greater change, has got back all the cunning and pride which had been deadened in Indian John. But Hawkeye and Chingachgook are both limited by their former appearance; one must still be the canny reasoner, the other a little saddened with passing years. The purest romance of the tale lies in Uncas, the forest's youngest son, gallant, swift, courteous, a lover for whom there is no hope, the last of the Mohicans. That Uncas was idealized Cooper was ready to admit; Homer, he suggested, had his heroes. And it is clear that upon Uncas were bestowed some of the virtues which the philosophers of the age had taught the world to find in a state of nature. Still, after a century, many smile upon the state of nature who are yet able to find in Uncas the perennial appeal of youth cut off in the flower. The action and setting of the novel are on the same high plane as the characters. The forest, in which all the events take place, surrounds them with a changeless majesty that sharpens, by contrast, the restless sense of danger. Pursuit makes almost the whole plot. The pursued party moving from Fort Edward to Fort William Henry has two girls to handicap its flight and to increase the tragedy of capture. Later the girls have been captured, and sympathy passes, a thing unusual in Cooper, to the pursuing rescuers. In these tasks Hawkeye and the Mohicans are opposed by the fierce capacity of Magua, who plays villain to Uncas's hero, in moral qualities Uncas's opposite. There is never any relaxation of suspense, and the scene in which Uncas reveals himself to the Delawares is one of the most thrilling moments in fiction.

The Prairie has less swiftness than *The Last of the Mohicans*
but more poetry. In it Natty appears again, twenty years
older than in *The Pioneers*, far away on the plains beyond the
Mississippi. He owns his defeat and he still grieves over the
murdered forest, but he has given up anger for the peace of old
age. To him it seems that all his virtues are gone. Once
valiant he must now be crafty; his arms are feeble; his eyes have
so far failed him that, no longer the perfect marksman, he has
sunk to the calling of a trapper. There is a pathos in his resignation which would be too painful were it not merely a phase
of his grave and noble wisdom. He is more than ever what
Cooper called him, "a philosopher of the wilderness." The
only change is that he has left the perils and delights of the forest and has been subdued to the eloquent monotony of the
plains. Nowhere else has Cooper shown such sheer imaginative
power as in his handling of this mighty landscape. He had
never seen a prairie; indeed, it is clear that he thought of a
prairie as an ocean of land and described it partly by analogy.
But he managed to endow the huge empty distances he had not
seen with a presence as haunting as that of the populous forest
he had known in his impressionable youth. And the old
trapper, though he thinks of himself as an exile, has learned the
secrets of the new nature and belongs to it. It is his knowledge
that makes him essential to the action, which is again made up
of flight and pursuit. Once more there are girls to be rescued,
from white men as well as from Indians. There is another
Magua in Mahtoree, another Uncas in the virtuous Hard-
Heart. The Indians ride horses and are thus more difficult to
escape than the Hurons had been. The flat prairies give fewer
places of concealment. But the trapper is as ready as ever with
new arts, and the flight ends as romance prescribes. The final
scene, the death of the trapper in the arms of his young friends,
is very touching and fine, yet reticently handled. For the
most part, the minor characters, the lovers and the pedant, are
not new to Cooper and are not notable. The family of Ishmael
Bush, the squatter, however, make up a new element. They
have been forced out of civilization by its virtues, as the trapper
by its vices. They have strength without nobility and activity
without wisdom. Except when roused, they are as sluggish
as a prairie river, and like it they appear muddy and aimless.

Ishmael Bush always conveys the impression of terrific forces lying vaguely in ambush. His wife is nearly the most memorable figure among Cooper's women. She clings to her mate and cubs with a tigerish instinct that leaves her, when she has lost son and brother and retreats in a vast silent grief, still lingering in the mind, an inarticulate prairie Hecuba.

Possibly the novel owes some of its depth of atmosphere to the fact that it was finished in France and that Cooper was thus looking back upon his subject through a mist of regret. He had sailed for Europe with his family in June, 1826, to begin a foreign residence of more than seven years which had a large effect upon his later life and work. He found his books well known and society at large disposed to make much of him. In Paris he fraternized with Scott, who enjoyed and praised his American rival. Parts of his stay were in England, Holland, Germany, Switzerland, which delighted and astonished him, and Italy, which he loved. Most of his time, however, he passed at Paris, charmed with a gayer and more brilliant society than he could have known before. He did not cease to write. In January, 1828, he repeated the success of *The Pilot* with another sea tale, *The Red Rover*, which has always held a place among the most favoured of his books. The excitement is less sustained than in *The Pilot*, but portions of the narrative, notably those dealing with storms, are tremendous. The ocean here plays as great a part as Cooper had lately assigned to the prairie. One voices the calm of nature, one its tumult; both tend to the discipline of man. In 1829 he fared better than with *Lionel Lincoln* in another historical tale of New England, *The Wept of Wish-ton-Wish*, an episode of King Philip's War. It is a powerful novel, irregular and ungenial, not only because the Puritans represented were themselves unlovely, but because Cooper had an evident dislike for them which coloured all their qualities. This was followed in the next year by *The Water-Witch*, which Cooper thought his most imaginative book. It has a spirited naval battle, but it flatly failed to localize a supernatural legend in New York harbour.

Novels were not Cooper's whole concern during his years in Europe. Unabashedly, outspokenly American, he had secured from Henry Clay the post of consul at Lyons, that he might not seem, during his travels, a man without a country.

As consul, though his position was purely nominal, he felt
called upon to resent the ignorance everywhere shown by
Europeans regarding his native land, and he set out upon the
task of educating them to better views. Cooper was not Franklin. His *Notions of the Americans* (1828), while full of information and a rich mine of American opinion for that day, was too
obviously partisan to convince those at whom it was aimed.
Its proper audience was homesick Americans. He indulged,
too, in some controversy at Paris over the relative cost of
French and American government which pleased neither nation.
Finally, he applied his art to the problem and wrote three
novels "in which American opinion should be brought to bear
on European facts."[1] That is, in *The Bravo* (1831), *The Heid-
enmauer* (1832), and *The Headsman* (1833) he meant to show
by proper instances the superiority of democracy to aristocracy
as regards general happiness and justice. He claimed to be
writing for his countrymen alone, some of whom must have been
thrilled to come across a passage like "a fairer morning never
dawned upon the Alleghanies than that which illumined the
Alps," but he was not sufficiently master of his material, however stout and just his opinions, to make even *The Bravo*, the
best of the three, as good as his pioneer romances.

Before he returned to New York in November, 1833, he was
warned by his friend S. F. B. Morse that he would be disappointed. Cooper found himself, in fact, fatally cosmopolitan
in the republic he had been justifying for seven years. Always
critical, he sought to qualify too sweeping praise of America
precisely as he had qualified too sweeping censure in Europe.
But he had not learned tact while becoming a citizen of the
world, and he soon angered the public he had meant to set
right. The result was the long and dreary wrangling which
clouded the whole remainder of his life and has obscured his
fame almost to the present day. If he had attended the dinner
planned in his honour on his return, he might have found his
welcome warmer than he thought it. If he had been an observer
keen enough, he would have seen that the new phases of democracy which he disliked were in part a gift to the old seaboard of that very frontier of which he had been painter and
annalist. But he did not see these things, and so he carried on

[1] *A Letter to his Countrymen*, p. 12.

a steady fight, almost always as right in his contentions as he
was wrong-headed in his manner. From Cooperstown, gener
ally his residence, except for a few winters in New York, to the
end of his life, he lectured and scolded. His *Letter to his Countrymen* (1834), stating his position, and *The Monikins* (1835),
an unbelievably dull satire, were the first fruits of his quarrel.
He followed these with five books dealing with his European
travels and constantly irritating to the people of both continents. He indulged in a heated altercation with his fellow townsmen over some land which they thought theirs, although it was
certainly his. In 1838 he published a fictitious record, *Homeward Bound* and its sequel *Home as Found*, of the disappointment of some Americans who return from Europe and find
America what Cooper had recently found it. He proclaimed
his political principles in *The American Democrat* (1838).
Most important of all, he declared war upon the newspapers
of New York and went up and down the state suing those that
had libelled him. He won most of the suits, but though he
silenced his opponents he had put his fame into the hands of
persons who, unable to abuse, could at least neglect him.

His solid *History of the Navy of the United States of America*
(1839) turned his attention once more to naval affairs, with
which he busied himself during much of his remaining career.
He wrote *Lives of Distinguished American Naval Officers* (1842–
5), and *Ned Myers* (1843), the life of a common sailor who had
been with him on the *Sterling*. The *History* led to a furious
legal battle, but generally Cooper left his quarrels behind him
when he went upon the sea. As a cosmopolitan, he seemed to
feel freer out of sight of land, on the public highway of the
nations. His novels of this period, however, are uneven in
merit. *The Two Admirals* (1842) contains one of his best naval
battles; *Wing-and-Wing* (1842) ranks high among his sea tales,
richly romantic and glowing with the splendours of the Mediterranean. *Mercedes of Castile* (1840) has little interest beside
that essential to the first voyage of Columbus. The two parts
of *Afloat and Ashore* (1844), dealing powerfully as they do with
the evils of impressment, are notable chiefly for sea fights and
chases. *Jack Tier* (1846–8) is a lurid piratical tale of the
Mexican War: *The Crater* (1847) does poorly what *Robinson
Crusoe* does supremely; *The Sea Lions* (1849) has the distinc-

tion of marking the highest point in that religious bigotry which pervades Cooper's later novels as thoroughly as the carping spirit which kept him always alert for a chance to take some fling at his countrymen.

The real triumph of his later years was that he wrote, in the very midst of his hottest litigation, *The Pathfinder* (March, 1840) and *The Deerslayer* (August, 1841). One realizes, in reading them, that the forest more than the ocean was for Cooper a romantic sanctuary, as it was for Pathfinder the true temple, full of the "holy calm of nature," the teacher of beauty, virtue, laws. Returning to these solemn woods, Cooper was subdued once more to the spirit which had attended his first great days. The fighting years through which he had passed had left him both more mellow and more critical than at first. During the same time he had gone far enough from the original character of Leather-Stocking to become aware of traits which should be brought out or explained. It was too late to make his hero entirely consistent for the series, but Cooper apparently saw the chance to fill out the general outline, and he did it with such skill that those who read the five novels in the order of events will notice relatively few discrepancies, since *The Deerslayer* prepares for nearly all that follows. In *The Pathfinder*, undertaken to show Natty in love and to combine the forest and a ship in the same tale, Cooper was at some pains to point out how Pathfinder's candour, self-reliance, justice, and fidelity had been developed by the life he had led in the forest. Leather-Stocking, indeed, does not seem more conscious of these special gifts, but Cooper does. Still there is abundant action, another flight through the woods, a storm on Lake Ontario, a siege at a blockhouse. Chingachgook, unchanged, is with Pathfinder, who varies from his earlier character in little but his love for a young girl whom he finally surrenders to a more suitable lover. His love affair threatens for a moment to domesticate Natty, but the sacrifice restores him to his old solitude.

In the final book of the series, *The Deerslayer*, Cooper performed with full success the hard task of representing the scout in the fresh morning of his youth. Love appears too in this story, but Deerslayer, unable to love a girl who has been corrupted by the settlements, turns to the forest with his best devotion. The book is the tale of his coming of age.

Already a hunter, he kills his first man and thus enters the long career which lies before him. That career, however, had already been traced by Cooper, and the distress with which Deerslayer realizes that he has human blood on his hands becomes immeasurably eloquent. It gives the figure of the man almost a new dimension; one remembers the many deaths Natty has yet to deal. In other matters he is near his later self, for he starts life with a steady philosophy which, through all the many experiences of *The Deerslayer*, keeps him to the end as simple and honourable as at the outset.

The novel is thus an epitome of the whole career of the most memorable character American fiction has given to the world. Leather-Stocking is very fully drawn; Cooper's failure to write a sixth novel, as he at one time planned, which should show Natty in the Revolution, may be taken as a sign that he felt, however unconsciously, that the picture was finished. It is hard, indeed, to see how he could have added to the scout without taking something from the spy. More important still, the virtue of patriotism, if carried to the pitch that must have been demanded for that hero in that day, would surely have been a little alien to the cool philosopher of the woods. Justice, not partisanship, is Leather-Stocking's essential trait. In him Cooper exhibited, even better than he knew, his special idea that human character can be brought to a noble proportion and perfection in the school of pure nature. Now this idea, generally current in Cooper's youth, had an effect upon the Leather-Stocking tales of the greatest moment. Because their hero, as the natural man, had too simple a soul to call for minute analysis, it was necessary for Cooper to show him moving through a long succession of events aimed to test the firmness of his virtues. There was thus produced the panorama of the American frontier which, because of Cooper's incomparable fusion of strangeness and reality, at once became and has remained the classic record of an heroic age.

He wrote more border tales before his death. *Wyandotte* (1843) deals largely with the siege of a blockhouse near the upper Susquehanna, and *The Oak-Openings* (1848), the fruit of a journey which he made to the West in 1847, is a tale of bee hunting and Indian fighting on the shores of Lake Michigan. Full of border material, too, is the trilogy of *Littlepage Manu-*

scripts, *Satanstoe* (1845), *The Chainbearer* (1846), and *The Redskins* (1846). Having tried the autobiographical method with Miles Wallingford in *Afloat and Ashore*, Cooper now repeated it through three generations of a New York family. In the last he involved himself unduly in the question of anti-rentism and produced a book both fantastic and dull; the second is better by one of Cooper's most powerful figures, the squatter Thousandacres, another Titan of the brood of Ishmael Bush; the first, if a little beneath Cooper's best work, is so only because he was somewhat rarely at his best. No other novel, by Cooper or any other, gives so firm and convincing a picture of colonial New York. Even Cooper has no more exciting struggle than that of Corny Littlepage with the icy Hudson. But the special virtue of *Satanstoe* is a quality Cooper nowhere else displays, a positive winsomeness in the way Littlepage unfolds his memories (now sweetened by many years) and his humorous crotchets in the same words. There are pages which read almost like those of some vigorous Galt or Goldsmith. Unfortunately, Cooper did not carry this vein further. His comedy *Upside Down*, produced at Burton's Theatre, New York, 18 June, 1850, was a failure, and his last novel, *The Ways of the Hour* (1851), lacks every charm of manner. With his family and a few friends he lived his latter days in honour and affection, but he held the public at a sour distance and before his death, 14 September, 1851, set his face against a reconciliation even in the future by forbidding any biography to be authorized. The published facts of his life still leave his personality less known to the general world than that of any American writer of equal rank.

This might be somewhat strange, since Cooper was lavish of intrusions into his novels, were it not that he wrote himself down, when he spoke in his own person, not only a powerful and independent man, but a scolding, angry man, and thus made his most revealing novels his least read ones. One thinks of Scott, who, when he shows himself most, wins most love. The difference further characterizes the two men. In breadth of sympathies, humanity, geniality, humour, Cooper is less than Scott. He himself, in his review of Lockhart, said that Scott's great ability lay in taking a legend or historical episode, which Scotland furnished in splendid profusion, and repro-

ducing it with marvellous grace and tact. "This faculty of
creating a *vraisemblance*, is next to that of a high invention,
in a novelist." It is clear that Cooper felt his own inferiority
to Scott in "creating a *vraisemblance*" and that he was always
conscious of the relative barrenness of American life; it is
also tolerably clear that he himself aimed at what he thought
the higher quality of invention. Cooper's invention, indeed,
was not without a solid basis; he is not to be neglected as an
historian. No man better sums up in literature the spirit
of that idealistic, irascible, pugnacious, somewhat crude, and
half aristocratic older democracy which established the United
States. No one fixed the current heroic traditions of his day
more firmly to actual places. No one else supplied so many
facts to the great legend of the frontier. Fact no less than
fiction underlies the character which, for all time, Cooper
gave to the defeated race of red men, who, no longer a menace
as they had been to the first settlers, could now take their
place in the world of the imagination, sometimes idealized, as
in Uncas and Hard-Heart, but more often credibly imperfect
and uncivilized. It was his technical knowledge of ships and
sailors which led Cooper to write sea tales, a province of
romance in which he still takes rank, among many followers,
as teacher and master of them all. True, Cooper had not
Scott's resources of historical learning to fall back upon when
his invention flagged, any more than he had Scott's resources
of good-nature when he became involved in argument; but
when, as in the Leather-Stocking tales, his invention could
move most freely, it did unaided what Scott, with all his
subsidiary qualities, could not outdo. This is to credit Cooper
with an invention almost supreme among romancers. Certainly it is difficult to explain why, with all his faults of
clumsiness, prolixity, conventional characterization, and ill
temper, he has been the most widely read American author,
unless he is to be called one of the most impressive and
original.

CHAPTER VII

Fiction II

I T is mere coincidence that Cooper was born in the year which produced *The Power of Sympathy* and that when he died *Uncle Tom's Cabin* was passing through its serial stage, and yet the limits of his life mark almost exactly the first great period of American fiction. Paulding, Thompson, Neal, Kennedy, Simms, Melville, to mention no slighter figures, outlived him, but not, as a current fashion, the type of romance which had flourished under Cooper. Although by 1851 tales of adventure had begun to seem antiquated, they had rendered a large service to the course of literature: they had removed the stigma, for the most part, from the word novel. For the brutal scrapes of eighteenth-century fiction the new romance had substituted deeds of chivalrous daring; it had supplanted blunt fleshliness by a chaste and courtly love, and had tended to cure amorous sentimentalism by placing love below valour in the scale of virtues. Familiar life, tending to sordidness, had been succeeded by remote life, generally idealized; historical detail had been brought in to teach readers who were being entertained. Cooper, like Scott, was more elevated than Fielding and Smollett, more realistic than the Gothic romancers, more humane than Godwin or Brown. The two most common charges against the older fiction, that it pleased wickedly and that it taught nothing, had broken down before the discovery, except in illiberal sects, that the novel is fitted both for honest use and for pleasure.

In Europe, at Cooper's death, a new vogue of realism had begun, but America still had little but romance. With so vast and mysterious a hinterland free to any one who might come to take it, novelists, like farmers, were less prompt in America than in Europe to settle down to cultivate intensively known fields. There is a closer analogy, indeed, between the geographic and the imaginative frontier of the United States than has been pointed out. As the first advanced, thin, straggling, back from the Atlantic, over the Alleghanies, down the Ohio, beyond the Mississippi, across the Great Plains and the Rockies to the Pacific, the other followed, also thin and straggling but with an incessant purpose to find out new territories over which the imagination could play and to claim them for its own. "Until now," wrote Cooper in 1828, "the Americans have been tracing the outline of their great national picture. The work of filling up has just seriously commenced." He had in mind only the physical process, but his image applies as well to that other process in which he was the most effective pioneer. Two years after his death the outline of the national picture, at least of contiguous territory, was established, and the nation gave itself to the problem of occupation. In fiction, too, after the death of Cooper the main tendency for nearly a generation was away from the conquest of new borders to the closer cultivation, east of the Mississippi, of ground already marked.

As late as 1825 Jared Sparks thought ten American novels a striking output for one year, but during the second quarter of the century Cooper had many helpers in his great task. In New England Neal, Miss Sedgwick, Mrs. Child, and D. P. Thompson had already set outposts before Hawthorne came to capture that section for classic ground. Paulding and Hoffman assisted Cooper in New York, and Paulding took Swedish Delaware for himself; for Pennsylvania Bird was Brown's chief successor; Maryland had Kennedy; Virginia, without many native novels, began to undergo, in the hands of almost every romancer who dealt with the founders of the republic, that idealization which has made it, especially since the Civil War, the most romantic of American states; South Carolina passed into the pages of Simms; Georgia and the lower South brought forth a school of native humorists who abounded in the truth as well as in the fun of that border;[1] the Mississippi and the Ohio

[1] See Book II. Chap. XIX.

advanced to a place in the imagination with the Hudson, the Susquehanna, the Potomac, and the James. North of the Ohio romance achieved relatively little, but on the southern bank Kentucky, "Dark and Bloody Ground," rivalled its mother Virginia. Bird ventured into Mexico at a time when Irving and Prescott were writing romantic histories of the Spanish discovery and conquest. Melville, the most original and perennial of Cooper's contemporaries, concerned himself with the wonders of the Pacific and the deeds of Yankee whalers. Some of these novels dealt with contemporary life, but the large majority used history to lend depth to the picture which was being filled in. This was the age during which there grew up the heroic conceptions of the first settlements and of the Revolution which still prevail; the novelists stand side by side with the orators and the popular biographers in the creation of those powerful legends. Crude style and bombastic characters abound, but so do great vigour and idealism. Although such romances do not present a solid record of actual life in America at the time they were written, they offer important evidence regarding the life of the imagination, its aims, methods, and conventions, as it existed in those formative years.

The first confessed follower of Cooper, it seems, began his career on other models. John Neal (1793–1870), a native of Maine, was in Baltimore when *The Spy* appeared, engaged in the production of four long novels in six or seven months. Full of a history of the Revolution on which he had been working, he was fired by Cooper's example to write *Seventy-Six* (1823) with incredible rapidity. The work, however, is little more like Cooper than the three which had preceded it, *Logan* (1822), *Randolph* (1823), and *Errata* (1823). In all these Neal's real master was Byron, whom he followed with a fury of rant and fustian which would have made him, had he been gifted with taste and humour as well, no mean follower. Three years spent in England as a writer on American topics, where he became one of Bentham's secretaries and a utilitarian in all but atheism, modified Neal somewhat so that in his long later career he seemed almost a man of sense if never a man of humour or taste. *Brother Jonathan* (1825) and *The Down-Easters* (1833), however, which promise at first to be real pictures of New England life and character, soon run amuck into raving melodrama. For all his very unusual originality and force Neal has ceased to be read, the victim of a bad education and uncritical times. Equally unread, as novelists, are two other writers famous in their day, Catherine Maria Sedgwick (1789–1867) and Lydia Maria Child (1802–80), who, through long and busily useful years, touched fiction here and there, both beginning with historical romances in the early days of *The Spy's* fame and later drifting to more solid shores with the tide of realism. Less gifted than Neal, both had greater charm. Mrs. Child is remembered for her devoted opposition to slavery, but Miss Sedgwick was the more important novelist. *Redwood* (1824), *Hope Leslie* (1827), and *The Linwoods* (1835), her best and most popular stories, exhibit almost every convention of the fiction of her day.

One novelist of New England before Hawthorne, however, still has a wide, healthy public. Daniel Pierce Thompson (1795–1868) knew the Vermont frontier as Cooper knew that of New York. After many struggles with the bitterest poverty he got to Middlebury College, studied law, became a prominent official of his native state, and somewhat accidentally took to fiction. Of his half-dozen novels, which all possess a good share of honest realism, *Locke Amsden* (1847) gives perhaps the most truthful record of frontier life, but *The Green Mountain Boys* (1840) is the classic of Vermont. It is concerned with the struggles of the Vermonters for independence first from New York and second from Great Britain; its hero is the famous Ethan Allen. Thompson had none of Cooper's poetry and was little concerned with the magic of nature. He took over most of the tricks of the older novelists, their stock types and sentiments. But he made little effort to preach, he could tell a straight story plainly and rapidly, and he touched action with rhetoric in just the proportion needed to sell fifty editions of the book by 1860 and to make it in the twentieth century a standard book for boys which is by far the most popular romance of the immediate school of Cooper.

The Middle States had no secondary novelist who has survived so sturdily as Thompson. Charles Fenno Hoffman[1] is remembered for his lyrics, not for *Greyslaer* (1840). James Kirke Paulding,[2] though nearer Irving than Cooper, had

[1] See also Book II, Chap. v. [2] See also Book II, Chaps. i, iii, iv, and v.

considerable merit as a novelist, particularly in the matter of comedy, which most of the romancers lacked. *Koningsmarke* (1823) contains some pleasant burlesquing in its stories of adventures among the Delaware Swedes. Here, as in his later works, Paulding laughed at what he called "Blood-Pudding Literature." He was too facile in lending his pen, as parodist or follower, to whatever fashion happened to be approved to do any very individual work, but *The Dutchman's Fireside* (1831), probably his masterpiece, deserves to be mentioned with Mrs. Grant's *Memoirs of an American Lady* (1809), on which it is based, and Cooper's *Satanstoe*, much its superior, as a worthy record of colonial life along the Hudson. New Jersey and Pennsylvania appear in nothing better than the minor romances of Robert Montgomery Bird (1803–54),[1] *The Hawks of Hawk Hollow* (1835), *Sheppard Lee* (1836), and *The Adventures of Robin Day* (1839), vigorous and sometimes merry tales but not of permanent merit.

To the school of his friend Irving may be assigned the urbane John Pendleton Kennedy (1795–1870). Of excellent Virginia connections, he was born and educated in Baltimore, which, like New York, made rapid progress after the Revolution, first in commerce and then in taste. Having served bloodlessly enough in the War of 1812 and been admitted to the bar, Kennedy lived as merrily as Irving in the chosen circles of his native town. With Peter Hoffman Cruse he issued *The Red Book* (1818–19),[2] a kind of Baltimore *Salmagundi* in prose and verse, and after several years devoted to law and politics made a decided success with *Swallow Barn* (1832), obviously suggested by *Bracebridge Hall* but none the less notable as a pioneer record of the genial life of a Virginia plantation. Although the story counts for little, Kennedy's easy humour and real skill at description and the indication of character make the book distinguished. His later novels, *Horse-Shoe Robinson* (1835), in which he dealt with the Revolution in the Carolinas, and *Rob of the Bowl* (1838), which has its scene laid in colonial Maryland, are nearer Cooper, with the difference that Kennedy depended, as he had done in *Swallow Barn*, on fact not invention for almost all his action as well as for his details of topography and costume. Indeed,

[1] See also Book II, Chap. II.   [2] See also Book II, Chap. III.

he founded the career of Horse-Shoe Robinson upon that of an actual partisan with such care that the man is said later to have approved the record as authentic. Decidedly Kennedy's gift was for enriching actual events with a finer grace and culture than many of the rival romancers could command. His style is clear, his methods always simple and rational. Of his miscellaneous writings *The Annals of Quodlibet* (1840) is tolerable satire, and the *Memoirs of the Life of William Wirt* (1849), substantial biography. Kennedy's range of friendship with other authors was wide; he had a full and honourable public career in city, state, and national affairs.

South of the Potomac there were relatively few novelists during Cooper's lifetime. The great tradition of Virginia was sustained by her orators and scholars rather than by her writers of fiction, but Nathaniel Beverley Tucker (1784–1851) was both scholar and novelist. His *George Balcombe* (1836) Poe thought the best novel by an American; his *Partisan Leader* (1836), primarily famous because it prophesied disunion, is clearly a notable though little known work. No other American of the time wrote with such classical restraint and pride as Tucker. No book, of any time, surpasses *The Partisan Leader* for intense, conscious Virginianism. Mention should be made of Dr. William Alexander Caruthers (1800–46), perhaps less for his genial novels, *The Cavaliers of Virginia* (1835) and *The Knights of the Horse-Shoe* (1845), than for his widely-known sketch *Climbing the Natural Bridge.*[1] The lower states best appeared in the pages of their native humorists, who seldom wrote novels. South Carolina produced the writer who, among all the American romancers of the first half century, ranks nearest Cooper for scope and actual achievement.

William Gilmore Simms has been, to a pathetic degree, the victim of attachment to his native state. It was one of his strongest passions. He loved every foot of South Carolina, he honoured its traditions and defended its institutions even when they hurt his own fame. His best work was largely devoted to an heroic account of the Revolution in the Carolinas. But, whether his birth did not admit him to the aristocracy of Charleston, or because of a traditional disrespect for native

[1] First published in *The Knickerbocker Magazine*, July, 1838.

books, South Carolina refused Simms the honour certainly due his powers. In this the whole South was negligent; Simms had to depend too largely upon the North for publishers and a public. Unfortunately, Northern readers, though hospitable to his tales from the first, were not as familiar with Southern manners and traditions as with those nearer home, and Simms had not the mastery of illusion which might have overcome this disadvantage. The solid grounds, therefore, of his romance were partly wasted upon an audience not competent to recognize them. Time must have taught South Carolina more cordiality to her best writer had not the Civil War forced all literary matters into the background for a generation. When, later, the South became eager to establish its claims to a literature, the vogue of historical romance had passed, and Simms, not yet having found the public he deserved, never has found it.

Unlike Poe, he had not the art or patience to make himself independent of general approval. Born in Charleston, 17 April, 1806, son of a merchant of Irish birth who lost both his wife and his fortune during the winter of 1807–8, Simms got but a bare schooling and was early apprenticed to a druggist. He seems, during his youth, to have been as bookish as Brockden Brown, but it was romantic poetry and history which claimed his attention, not romantic speculation. From his grandmother, with whom he lived as a boy, he heard innumerable legends of the Revolution, South Carolina's heroic age, and cherished them with a poetic and patriotic devotion. When he was eighteen he went to visit his father, who had left Charleston for the West, become friend and follower of Andrew Jackson, and finally settled on a plantation in Mississippi. The young poet was thus shown the manners of a frontier which corresponded, in many ways, to that of Cooper, and he seems, during extended travels, to have observed its rough comedy and violent melodrama with sharp eyes. But the border was not, for Simms, his first love, and he went back, against his father's advice, to the traditions and dreams of Charleston. There he was married in 1826, was admitted to the bar the next year, published the first of his many volumes of verse, and suffered the death of his young wife. Thence, in 1832, he set out to the North on a career of authorship in which necessity confirmed his training and temper by urging him to immense industry and careless work.

It is unnecessary to say more of the miscellaneous tasks of Simms than that he wrote moderate poetry to the end of his life, including three tragedies, that he edited the apocryphal plays of Shakespeare, that he produced popular histories of South Carolina and popular biographies of Marion, Captain John Smith, the Chevalier Bayard, and General Greene, and that he kept up a ceaseless flood of contributions to periodicals. His range of interest and information was large, but he commonly dealt with American, and particularly Southern, affairs. His really significant work, as a romancer, he began in 1833 with a Godwinian tale of crime, *Martin Faber*, which was so well received that he followed it in 1834 with *Guy Rivers* and in 1835 with *The Yemassee*, two romances in which almost the full extent of his powers was instantly displayed. *Guy Rivers*, a conventional piece as regards the love affair which makes a part of the plot, is a tale of deadly strife between the laws of Georgia and a fiendish bandit. A born story-teller, like Cooper, Simms was as heedless as Cooper of structure and less careful as to style, but he was too rapid to be dull and he revealed to the reading world a new adventurous frontier. In *The Yemassee* his concern for the history of South Carolina bore fruit, a moving tale of the Yemassee War of 1715. This book is to the famous Revolutionary group what *The Spy* is to the Leather-Stocking tales, a romance standing somewhat by itself at the beginning of the author's career and yet quite the equal of any of the most representative volumes. Once again Simms took hints from current romances, but when he set himself to describing the rich landscape of South Carolina or to recounting its annals he was more fully master of his material than in *Guy Rivers* and more admirable in proportion as his subject was more congenial to him. He gave his Indians the dignity and courage which, he said, they must have had at an earlier period; he invented for them a mythology. The white and black characters have somewhat less heroic dimensions, but they are done with great vigour and some realism.

His third novel having met with popular success, Simms turned to the Revolution and published *The Partisan* (1835), designed as the first volume of a trilogy which should celebrate these valorous times. He later wavered in his scheme, and, though he finally called *Mellichampe* (1836) and *Katherine Walton* (1851) the other members of his trilogy, he grouped round them four more novels that have obvious marks of kinship. *The Partisan* traces events from the fall of Charleston to Gates's defeat at Camden; the action of *Mellichampe*, which is nearly parallel to that of *Katherine Walton*, the proper sequel of *The Partisan*, takes place in the interval between Camden and the coming of Greene; *The Scout*, originally called *The Kinsmen* (1841), illustrates the period of Greene's first triumphs; *The Sword and the Distaff* (1852), later known as *Woodcraft*, furnishes a kind of comic afterpiece for the series. Simms subsequently returned to the body of his theme and produced *The Forayers* (1853) and its sequel *Eutaw* (1856) to do honour to the American successes of the year 1781.

Of these *The Scout* is perhaps the poorest, because of the large admixture of Simms's cardinal vice, horrible melodrama; *Woodcraft* is on many grounds the best, by reason of its rather close-knit plot and the high spirits with which it tells of the exploits and courtships, after the war, of Captain Porgy, the best comic character in the whole range of the older American romance. But neither of these works is quite representative of the series; neither has quite the dignity which, lacking in his sensational tales of the border, Simms always imparted to his work when he was most under the spell of the Carolina tradition. That always warmed him; indeed at times he seems drunk with history. He had a tendency to overload his tales with solid blocks of fact derived from his wide researches, forgetting, in his passionate antiquarianism, his own belief that "the chief value of history consists in its proper employment for the purposes of art," or, rather, too much thrilled by bare events to see that they needed to be coloured into fiction if they were to fit his narrative. Simms never took his art too lightly. He held that the "modern Romance is the substitute which the people of the present day offer for the ancient epic."[1] In this sense, the seven novels are his epic of the Revolution. Marion, the Agamemnon of these wars, had already become a kind of legend, thanks to the popular memory and the fantastic ardour of Weems, but it remained for Simms to

[1] Preface to *The Yemassee* (1853).

show a whole society engaged in the task which Marion did best. Simms's defect was that he relied too much upon one plot for all his tales, a partisan and a loyalist contending for the hand of the same girl, and that he repeated certain stock scenes and personages again and again. His great virtue was that he handled the actual warfare not only with interest and power but that he managed to multiply episodes with huge fecundity. He described, in a surge of rhetoric, his favourite material:

Partisan warfare, itself, is that irregular and desultory sort of life, which is unavoidably suggestive of the deeds and feelings of chivalry—such as gave the peculiar character, and much of the charm, to the history of the middle ages. The sudden onslaught— the retreat as sudden—the midnight tramp—the moonlight *bivouack* —the swift surprise, the desperate defence—the cruel slaughter and the headlong flight—and, amid the fierce and bitter warfare, always, like a sweet star shining above the gloom, the faithful love, the constant prayer, the devoted homage and fond allegiance of the maiden heart!

The passage is almost a generalized epitome of his Revolutionary romances. It also betrays the fact that by "epic" Simms meant not Homer but Froissart. If he is more bloody, he is also more sentimental than Cooper. His women, though Nelly Floyd in *Eutaw* is strikingly pathetic and mysterious, and Matiwan in *The Yemassee* is nearly as tragic as romance can make her, are almost all fragile and colourless things, not because Southern women were, but because pseudo-chivalry prescribed. His comedy is successful only, and there not always, in the words and deeds of the gourmand Porgy. Simms is a master in the description of landscapes, from the sterile wastes of Georgia to the luxuriant swamps in which the partisans found a refuge; but he lays little emphasis on the poetry or philosophy of "nature."

In historical tales, not Cooper's forte, Simms succeeded best; he was inferior when he dealt with the border. This may have been due partly to the intrinsic superiority of the earlier frontier to that which Simms had observed. At least it shows itself chiefly in the fact that Simms grew more melodramatic, as Cooper more poetic, the farther he ventured from regions of order and law. *Richard Hurdis* (1838), *Border Beagles* (1840), *Beauchampe* (1842), and *Charlemont* (1856) are amazingly sensational. Nor was Simms happy when he abandoned native for foreign history, as in *Pelayo* (1838), *The Damsel of Darien* (1839), *Count Julian* (1845), and *Vasconselos* (1854). Even more than Cooper, he lacked judgment as to the true province of his art; like Cooper, he constantly turned aside to put his pen to service in the distracted times through which he was fated to live.

His life was singularly noble and singularly tragic. Married a second time, in 1836, to Miss Chevillette Roach, and thus master of Woodlands, a respectable plantation in his own state, he led a pleasantly feudal existence, hospitable to many guests, and helpful, as the most prosperous Southern man of letters, to nearly all the authors and journals of the South. He spent the summers in Charleston where he came to preside over a coterie of younger writers; he made not infrequent visits to New York, and was well received. Besides concerning himself unofficially with all public affairs, he served in the state legislature for the session of 1844–46. As the agitation which led to civil war grew more heated, Simms plunged into stormy apologetics for the grounds and virtues of slavery. Just on the eve of the struggle he repeated the success of *The Yemassee* with a romance of seventeenth-century Carolina, *The Cassique of Kiawah* (1859), a stirring, varied story which must be ranked with his better books. Then upon him came the disasters of war. At first he was as sure that the South would win as that the South was just. His gradual realization that it was a losing contest would have shattered him had he been of any but the strongest stuff. His house, on the line of Sherman's march, was burned in February, 1865; he witnessed the wicked burning of Columbia. When the war ended he had lost his wife, nine of his fourteen children, (two of them since 1861), many of his best friends, and the whole of his fortune, yet he managed, in a more horrid overthrow than Scott's, to drive himself to work again with courage and energy, and kept up his efforts till his death, undoubtedly hastened by his labour, on 11 June, 1870. Despite his friends and admirers, the eclipse of those last years has never been quite lifted, and the somewhat fitful republication of his romances has left him much less read than he deserves, though few competent judges will put him far below Cooper, at least as regards strength and vigour, in the type of romance in which no third American name can be associated with theirs.

West of the Alleghanies the growth of fiction during the life of Cooper was, of course, scanty. It consisted less of novels than of tales and sketches, which, produced for the most part by writers of Eastern birth dwelling for a time in the new settlements, were chiefly concerned with the representation of manners not known to the seaboard. The wittiest of these writers was Mrs. Caroline Matilda Stansbury Kirkland (1801–64), a native of New York who took advantage of a three years' stay in Michigan to produce *A New Home—Who'll Follow* (1839), a volume of keen and sprightly letters on the frontier avowedly in the manner of Miss Mitford, and a continuation, *Forest Life* (1842), which is less piquant only because it was not the first. In the later *Western Clearings* (1846) she was somewhat more regular but not so racy and natural. A more representative Western author was James Hall (1793–1868),[1] who, born in Philadelphia, went west in search of adventure, lived in Illinois and Ohio, edited an annual and a magazine, and served as interpreter between West and East much as Irving did between America and Europe. Hall's manner, indeed, is like Irving's in its leisurely, genial narrative, its abundant descriptions, and its affection for supernatural legends which could be handled smilingly. He had real powers of fidelity, the only merit he claimed, to the life he knew, but he had also a florid style and a vein of romantic sentiment which too seldom rings true. *Legends of the West* (1832), *Tales of the Border* (1834), and *The Wilderness and the War-Path* (1846) contain his best stories; he is perhaps better known, not quite justly, for such books as *Sketches of History, Life and Manners, in the West* (1835), wherein he published his wide knowledge of a section then becoming important in the national life. It is as traveller and observer, too, not as romancer, that Timothy Flint (1780–1840) has come to be remembered, though he essayed fiction as well as nearly every other type of authorship in the days when he and Hall divided the West between them as a province to be worked by their

[1] See also Book II, Chap. xx.

versatile pens. Many novels celebrated Kentucky, which, as
the first Western state of the Union, had secured a primacy
in romance, between the Alleghanies and the Mississippi,
that it has never lost. Paulding, Simms, and Bird were chief
among those who laid plots there. Bird's best novel, *Nick
of the Woods* (1837), an exciting tale of border warfare in
1782, is notable for its attempt to correct Cooper's heroic
drawing of the Indian and for its presentation of a type often
spoken of in frontier annals, the white man who, crazed by
Indian atrocities, gave his whole life to a career of ruthless
vengeance.[1] The great romance of Kentucky, however,
while perpetuated by no single novel or novelist, centres
round the life and character of Daniel Boone, who became, by
the somewhat capricious choice of tradition, a folk hero,
standing among other pioneers as Leather-Stocking stands
among native characters of fiction. A similar, though smaller,
fame belongs to David Crockett of Tennessee, who comes somewhat closer to literature by the fact of having written an
Autobiography (1834).

The region west of the Mississippi continued in the popular
mind to be a strange land for which the reports of explorers
and travellers did the work of fiction, and Cooper's *Prairie*
had few followers. In 1834, however, Albert Pike (1809–91)
published in his *Prose Sketches and Poems* some vivid tales of
life in the South-west. That same year appeared *Calavar*, in
writing which Bird had the avowed purpose of calling the
attention of his public to romantic Mexico. The next year he
repeated his success with *The Infidel*, another story of Cortez
and the Conquest. Reading these novels with their tolerable
learning in Mexican antiquities, their considerable power, and
their superior sense of the pomp of great historical events, one
is reminded how few romances of the period ventured beyond
native borders. Whatever may be said of the poets, the novelists kept themselves almost always scrupulously at home.
One set of exceptions was those who dealt with Spain and
Mexico, and even with them the motive was largely, as with
the contemporary historians, to honour the ancient bond
between America and the European nation which had discovered it. In a more distant scene Mrs. Child laid her

[1] For the play founded on this novel, see Book II, Chap. II.

Philothea (1836), a gentle, ignorant romance of the Athens of Pericles, the fruit of a real desire to escape from the clang of current life. Not much more remote from any thinkable reality was George Tucker's *Voyage to the Moon* (1827), in which a sound scholar satirized terrestrial follies in the spirit which seemed to his friends like that of Swift.[1] To a slightly later date belong the two novels of William Starbuck Mayo (1812–95), *Kaloolah* (1849) and *The Berber* (1850), stories of wild adventure in Africa. The first contains a strange mixture of satire and romance in its account of a black Utopia visited by the Yankee hero Jonathan Romer.

Contemporaries suspected, what Mayo denied, that *Kaloolah* must have taken hints from *Typee*. The suspicion was natural at a time when Melville, at the height of his first fame, had not entered the long seclusion which even yet obscures the merit of that romancer who, among all Cooper's contemporaries, has suffered least from the change of fashion in romance. Herman Melville, grandson of the conservative old gentleman upon whom Holmes wrote *The Last Leaf*, and son of a merchant of New York, was born there, 1 August, 1819. The early death of his father and the loss of the family fortune having narrowed Melville's chances for higher schooling to a few months in the Albany Classical School, he turned his hand to farming for a year, shipped before the mast to Liverpool in 1837, taught school from 1837–40, and in January, 1841, sailed from New Bedford on a whaling voyage into the Pacific. Upon the experiences of that voyage his principal work is founded. The captain of the *Acushnet*, it seems, treated the crew badly, and Melville, with the companion whom he calls Toby, escaped from the ship to the Island of Nukuheva [Nukahiva] in the Marquesas and strayed into the cannibal valley Typee [Taipi], where the savages kept Melville for four months in an "indulgent captivity." Rescued by an Australian whaler, Melville visited Tahiti and other islands of the Society group, took part in a mutiny, and once more changed ship, this time setting out for Honolulu. After some months as a clerk in Hawaii, he joined the crew of the frigate *United States* and returned by the Horn to Boston, October, 1844. "From my twenty-fifth year," he told Hawthorne, "I date my life." Why he held 1844

[1] For Tucker, see also Book II, Chap. XVII.

so important is not clear; he may then first have turned to authorship. Though he had kept no notes of his journeying, within a year he had completed his first book, *Typee*, the record of his captivity. This was followed the next year by *Omoo*,[1] which completes his island adventures. In 1849 came *Redburn*, based on his earlier voyage to Liverpool, and in 1850 *White-Jacket*, an account of life on a man-of-war.

The first two had a great vogue and aroused much wonder as to the proportion of fiction and fact which might have gone to their making. Murray published *Typee* in England in the belief that it was pure fact. There were others to rank it with Richard Henry Dana's *Two Years before the Mast* (1841) as a transcript of real events. But though little is known of Melville's actual doings in the South Seas, it is at least clear that *Typee* and *Omoo* are no more as truthful as *Two Years before the Mast* than they are as crisp and nautical as that incomparable classic of the sea. Melville must be ranked less with Dana than with George Borrow. If he knew the thin boundary between romance and reality, he was still careless of nice limits, and his work is a fusion which defies analysis. *White-Jacket*, of these four books, is probably nearest a plain record; *Redburn* has but few romantic elements. *Omoo*, as a sequel, has not the freshness of *Typee*, nor has it such unity. *Typee*, indeed, is Melville at all but his best, and must be classed with the most successful narrations of the exotic life; after seventy years, when the South Pacific seems no longer another world, the spell holds. The valley of Taipi becomes, in Melville's handling, a region of dreams and languor which stir the senses with the fragrance and colour of the landscape and the gay beauty of the brown cannibal girls. And yet Melville, thoroughly sensitive to the felicities of that life, never loses himself in it but remains the shrewd and smiling Yankee.

The charge that he had been writing romance led Melville to deserve the accusation, and he wrote *Mardi* (1849), certainly one of the strangest, maddest books ever composed by an American. As in *Typee*, two sailors escape from a tyrannical captain in the Pacific and seek their fortune on the open sea, where they finally discover the archipelago of Mardi, a para-

[1] The word is Polynesian for "rover."

dise more rich and sultry than the Marquesas, which becomes, as the story proceeds, a crazy chaos of adventure and satirical allegory. In *Mardi* for the first time appear those qualities which made a French critic call Melville "un Rabelais américain," his welter of language, his fantastic laughter, his tumultuous philosophies. He had turned, contemporaries said, from the plain though witty style of his first works to the gorgeous manner of Sir Thomas Browne; he had been infected, say later critics, with Carlylese. Whatever the process, he had surely shifted his interest from the actual to the abstruse and symbolical, and he never recovered from the dive into metaphysics which proved fatal to him as a novelist. It was, however, while on this perilous border that he produced the best of his, and one of the best of American, romances; it is the peculiar mingling of speculation and experience which lends *Moby Dick* (1851) its special power.

The time was propitious for such a book. The golden age of the whalers was drawing to a close, though no decline had yet set in, and the native imagination had been stirred by tales of deeds done on remote oceans by the most heroic Yankees of the age in the arduous calling in which New England, and especially the hard little island of Nantucket, led and taught the world. A small literature of whaling had grown up, chiefly the records of actual voyages or novels like those of Cooper in which whaling was an incident of the nautical life. But the whalers still lacked any such romantic record as the frontier had. Melville brought to the task a sound knowledge of actual whaling, much curious learning in the literature of the subject, and, above all, an imagination which worked with great power upon the facts of his own experience. Moby Dick, the strange, fierce white whale that Captain Ahab pursues with such relentless fury, was already a legend among the whalers, who knew him as "Mocha Dick."[1] It remained for Melville to lend some kind of poetic or moral significance to a struggle ordinarily conducted for no cause but profit. As he handles the story, Ahab, who has lost a leg in the jaws of the whale, is driven by a wild desire for revenge which has maddened him and which makes him identify Moby Dick with the very spirit of evil and hatred. Ahab, not Melville, is to blame if the story seems an allegory,

[1] See Reynolds, J. N., *Mocha Dick, Knickerbocker Magazine*, May, 1839.

which Melville plainly declared it was not[1]; but it contains, nevertheless, the semblance of a conflict between the ancient and scatheless forces of nature and the ineluctable enmity of man. This is the theme, but description can hardly report the extraordinary mixture in *Moby Dick* of vivid adventure, minute detail, cloudy symbolism, thrilling pictures of the sea in every mood, sly mirth and cosmic ironies, real and incredible characters, wit, speculation, humour, colour. The style is mannered but often felicitous; though the book is long, the end, after every faculty of suspense has been aroused, is swift and final. Too irregular, too bizarre, perhaps, ever to win the widest suffrage, the immense originality of *Moby Dick* must warrant the claim of its admirers that it belongs with the greatest sea romances in the whole literature of the world.

Married in 1847, Melville lived for three years in New York and then for thirteen years in a farmhouse near Pittsfield, Massachusetts. Although he did not cease to write at once, *Moby Dick* seems to have exhausted him. *Pierre* (1852) is hopelessly frantic; *Israel Potter* (1855) is not markedly original; neither are *The Piazza Tales* (1856), and *The Confidence Man* (1857). The verses which he wrote in his later years, his sole output, are in a few instances happy, but far more often jagged and harsh. Whatever the causes of his loss of power, he fretted under it and grew more metaphysical, tortured, according to Hawthorne, his good friend, by uncertainty as to a future life. That way, for Melville, was madness; his earlier works should have taught him that he was lost without a solid basis in fact. He moved restlessly about, lecturing on the South Seas during the years 1857–1860 in many cities of the United States and Canada. He visited Europe and Palestine. Finally, having returned to New York, he was appointed to a place in the Custom House in 1866, and served there for twenty years, living a private life of almost entire, though voluntary and studious, seclusion. His death, 28 September, 1891, after nearly forty silent years, removed from American literature one of its most promising and most disappointing figures. Of late his fame has shown a tendency to revive.

Another type of romance which had some vogue during the

[1] *Moby Dick*, Chap. XLV.

later years of Cooper was the religious romance, of which, though many essayed it, the chief writers were William Ware (1797–1852), and Sylvester Judd (1813–53). Ware, a clergyman and fair classical scholar, wrote three novels, *Letters from Palmyra* (1837), later called *Zenobia*, *Probus* (1838), a sequel now known as *Aurelian*, and *Julian* (1841), which, though strongly biased in favour of the creed Ware preached, and often diffuse and monotonous, had still enough force and charm to have continued to be read by those to whom all books dealing with the origins of Christianity are an equal duty and delight. Judd has not been so widely read as Ware, though generally considered a novelist of superior truth and subtlety. His first novel, *Margaret* (1845), was born of a desire to show that Unitarians could produce imaginative literature. Its special merits are its vivid fidelity to the life of rural Massachusetts just after the Revolution, its thorough, loving familiarity with the New England temper and scene, and a kind of spiritual ardour which pervades the whole book; but it is badly constructed and it runs, toward the close, into a region of misty transcendentalisms where characters and plot are lost. *Richard Edney* (1850), a companion piece with its hero a boy and its setting contemporary, suffers, either as narrative or sense, from the same theological obsession, which appears in Judd's poems as little less than pathological.

By 1851 there were, or had been, many novelists whose names could find place only in an extended account of American fiction[1]: writers of adventure stories more sensational than Simms's or of moral stories more obvious than Miss Sedgwick's and Mrs. Child's, authors for children, authors preaching causes, authors celebrating fashionable or Bohemian life in New York. Not only regular novels and romances but briefer tales multiplied. The period which could boast in Cooper but one novelist of first rank could show three such tale-tellers as Irving, Hawthorne, and Poe. The annuals and magazines met the demand for such amusement and fostered it,[2] but the novel was encouraged more than it was hurt by the new type. Prose fiction, in fact, though somewhat late in starting,

---

[1] See Northrup, C. S., *The Novelists*, in *A Manual of American Literature*, ed. Stanton, T., 1909.

[2] See Book II, Chap. xx.

had firmly established itself in the United States by the middle of the century, and Cooper, followed in Great Britain by the nautical romancers, and on the Continent by such writers about wild life as Karl Anton Postl ("Charles Sealsfield"), Friedrich Gerstäcker, and Gustave Aimard, and everywhere read, had become a world figure.

CHAPTER VIII

Transcendentalism

N EW ENGLAND transcendentalism was a late and local
manifestation of that great movement for the liberation
of humanity which, invading practically every sphere of
civilized activity, swept over Europe at the end of the eighteenth and the beginning of the nineteenth century.

With the fading of the Renaissance, Europe had passed
into an age of criticism, during which all it had inherited and
achieved in the preceding era was subjected to the test of
reason. Throughout the eighteenth century especially, the
existing structure of society was subtly undermined, and when,
at the end of that century, it finally collapsed, the revolution
which in reality had long been in preparation took on an
abrupt and miraculous appearance.

> Heaven smiles, and faiths and empires gleam
> Like wrecks of a dissolving dream,

cried Shelley, attempting to describe this remarkable period,
and his lines are scarcely an exaggeration. Smiles and wrecks,
these were the characteristic products of the time, blasted
institutions and blossoming ideals.

What those ideals were—some of them soon to be realized,
others destined to remain distant visions—is tolerably clear.
Socially this revolution meant democracy, the assertion of the
brotherhood and potential equality of men. Politically and
religiously it meant the overthrow of feudal and ecclesiastical
tyrannies and customs, and the setting up of liberal forms of
government and belief as instruments for testing the new social
doctrine. Philosophically it meant the contention, in the face
of existing rationalisms and skepticisms, that man's practical

and imaginative faculties play a part in his apprehension of the
truth. In the realm of art and literature it meant the shattering of pseudo-classic rules and forms in favour of a spirit of
freedom, the creation of works filled with the new passion for
nature and common humanity and incarnating a fresh sense of
the wonder, promise, and romance of life. In the scientific
and industrial worlds it meant those fundamental and far-
reaching changes which came with the constantly fuller recognition and adoption of the scientific method.

To the special student, each of these revolutionary movements has its separate history. But life, in spite of the student,
is not a matter of water-tight compartments, and a first fact to
be seized and held fast in any discussion of New England
transcendentalism is that the new spirit which appeared in
Europe a century and more ago was neither social, nor political,
nor industrial, nor economic, nor literary, nor scientific, nor
religious. It was all of them at once. It transcended every
phase of life—though it is true, of course, that in this particular
locality or at that particular time, in this individual or in that
social atmosphere, it did take on this or that predominant
emphasis or colour.

On this side of the Atlantic, for instance, it assumed at the
outset a pre-eminently political character, and America, in her
own Revolution and in the events which followed it, made an
early and memorable contribution to that greater revolution
of the human spirit of which the source and centre was in
Europe. But America, save in the case here and there of an
exceptional mind, remained largely unconscious, even as a
matter of political theory, of the general significance for the
world of what she had accomplished. Still less had she distilled
from her democratic practice any fresh philosophy or faith.
When, then, voices from abroad of those who were seeking a
religion for the new order of things penetrated to a community
which, religious to the core, had long been religiously starved,
those voices were bound to be heard and answered. That
is precisely what began happening near Boston shortly before
the year 1830. The result was similar to what occurs, under
like conditions, in the case of an individual.

Whoever has seen a young man of high mental and spiritual
endowment lifted out of a provincial environment and placed

suddenly in contact with the central intellectual and religious forces of his time, has a key to much of the transcendental movement in New England. The unsettling of traditional foundations, the ferment of thought and emotion, the aspirations, the excesses, the unleashing of dormant and unsuspected powers, all the effects, in fact, which attend such an experience in the case of the individual were reproduced on a wider scale when the spirit of revolutionary Europe descended upon a group of the finest minds of early nineteenth-century New England. The spirit of the eighteenth century had survived in the neighbourhood of Boston long after the eighteenth century was dead. And suddenly—so at least it seemed—this group of young men and women became intensely aware of that fact. The new ideas and ideals found their way to them through a score of channels and affected as many phases of New England life. But because of the predominant part which religion still played in that life and its traditions, it was within the religious world that the influence of the new spirit was immediate and marked. Transcendentalism was the religious conversion of early nineteenth-century New England. And because of the relative cultural eminence of New England, it became indirectly, in some measure, the religious conversion of America. Emerson's address, *The American Scholar*, is called our intellectual Declaration of Independence. With far more fundamental truth his little volume, *Nature*, might be called our religious Declaration of Independence.

New England transcendentalism, then, was the product of European forces brought to bear on New England character and conditions. To analyze the movement further it will be necessary to look somewhat more closely at the nature of those conditions and that character and to study in a little more detail the outside forces which were brought in contact with them.

The religious evolution of New England from the period of the Puritan theocracy to the beginning of the nineteenth century is on the whole, with a certain change of scale and retardation of movement, strikingly similar to the religious development during the same period abroad, a fact which, at the outset, renders futile any hope to estimate with exactness how far the two movements were parallel, how far the one was influenced by the other.

New England took no plunge, as England did, from the moral heights of Puritanism into the abyss of Restoration licentiousness. But there was a descent, which, if more gradual, was not on that account less real. Seventeenth-century Puritanism held within itself the germ of its own disintegration.[1] Already, by the second generation, under the law of psychological reaction and the exacting material demands of a pioneer community, "the decay of godliness in the land" had become conspicuous, and it seems difficult not to regard Salem witchcraft as the *reductio ad absurdum* of the extreme religious spirit. The revulsion of feeling that followed that outburst of superstition, the increasing interest in commercial and political questions, the gradual introduction of English rationalistic doctrines, the growing influence of the philosophy of Locke and of the literature of the "classical" school, all these causes, and many others, combined to accelerate the change in spiritual atmosphere, and it was not long before there was prevalent, especially in the neighbourhood of Boston, much of that temper of prose and reason which we habitually associate with the eighteenth century. With this changing mood, "heresies" began to creep into the religious world: Arminianism, Arianism, and other dissolvents of Calvinism. Interest in "morality" began to infringe on interest in theology. A line of increasingly "liberal" ministers occupied prominent Boston pulpits.[2]

The career of Jonathan Edwards serves, by contrast, to tell the story of what was happening.[3] He, if anyone, was fitted to stem the tide of encroaching secular interests. The Great Awakening, that transitory religious revival of the second generation of the eighteenth century which is in many ways the American counterpart of the Methodist movement, was designed to remedy the spiritual deadness of the time. But it merely widened the opening gulf in the religious world. The New Calvinists, as the followers of Edwards were called, went on to develop a theology of their own, while the liberals, constantly in closer touch with English thinking, grew more and more radical, until, as the two schools diverged, the term Unitarian was finally applied to them. Though 1785, the year

[1] See Book I, Chap. III.　　　　[2] See Book I, Chap. V.
[3] See Book I, Chap. IV.

in which King's Chapel in the revision of its liturgy tacitly denied the doctrine of the Trinity, is often selected as the beginning of the Unitarian movement, and though the actual schism between the Unitarian and the Trinitarian churches did not come till 1815, it is convenient, if not strictly accurate, to speak of the whole evolution of American liberalism in the eighteenth century as the Unitarian movement.

Throughout that century the position of the New England liberal had been an increasingly strong one, the typical Unitarian of the time being a man of tolerance, of intellect, of cultured tastes, of unexceptionable private morality and notable civic virtue. Emotional or spiritual in temperament, however, he was not. When, therefore, the intense fervour and the new ideals of revolutionary Europe began to make their way to New England, the Unitarian (like the orthodox Calvinist of a century before) began to find himself in an untenable position, transformed by the altered spirit of the age from a radical into a conservative. A number of Unitarian clergymen, notably the Rev. Joseph Stevens Buckminster (1784–1812), seem to have had an inkling of new things, but Buckminster died at the age of twenty-eight, and it was left to William Ellery Channing to be the first Unitarian to show something like a full appreciation of the significance for religion of the changing spirit of the time. Channing is the bridge between Unitarianism and transcendentalism.

Channing was born in Newport, Rhode Island, in 1780. His early religious environment was Calvinistic but not illiberal, his parents being orthodox in belief but tolerant in spirit. The stern Calvinism of Dr. Samuel Hopkins, Edwards's pupil, the minister to whose preaching Channing listened as a boy, shocked his delicately sensitive nature, and was doubtless one of the influences that by reaction led to his liberal religious views. During his college days at Harvard Channing's early tendency toward revolt was strengthened and his seeking for intellectual independence encouraged. Contact in his reading with radical English writers of the eighteenth century gave a direction to his thinking which, in spite of marked mental growth in later years, was never fundamentally altered.

On leaving Harvard he acted for nearly two years as tutor in a Virginia family, imbibing in the course of this experience an intense hatred of slavery. During this period, too, he became acquainted with the works of Rousseau, Godwin, and Mary Wollstonecraft, and from that time the kinship of many of his ideas with those of French Revolutionary origin can be clearly traced, though in passing through his serene and profoundly Christian mind those ideas often became scarcely recognizable.

On returning north Channing studied theology, becoming in 1803 minister of the Federal Street Society, Boston, a pulpit from which, until his death in 1842, he preached, in a spirit of singularly mingled benignity and power, sermons of constantly increasing influence that emphasized consistently the spiritual and practical as opposed to the doctrinal aspects of Christianity. Ultimately his fame even crossed the ocean, a number of his essays and reviews being translated and widely read, especially in France. The eminence he attained was due fundamentally to the gracious, almost saintly, character behind both his written and his spoken words; and it is worth remembering that all he did was accomplished in the face of a physical condition that made him essentially an invalid.

Although Channing is usually spoken of as the greatest Unitarian of his time, his sermon on *Unitarian Christianity*, preached at the ordination of Jared Sparks at Baltimore in 1819, being often called the creed of that denomination, he was, if we are to give him that name, a Unitarian of an entirely new type, and his works are full of indictments of what Emerson later called "the pale negations of Boston Unitarianism."

"Unitarianism," we find him writing, for instance, "has suffered from union with a heart-withering philosophy. . . . I fear that we must look to other schools for the thoughts which thrill us, which touch the most inward springs, and disclose to us the depths of our own souls."

Or again:

Now, religion ought to be dispensed in accommodation to this spirit and character of our age. Men desire excitement, and religion must be communicated in a more exciting form. . . . Men will not now be trifled with. . . . They want a religion which will take a strong hold upon them.

And they desire the same quality in their literature, he says elsewhere, " a poetry which pierces beneath the exterior of life to the depths of the soul."

Manifestly, as these references to changing standards in philosophy, religion, and literature make clear, a new spirit was abroad in the land, and though Channing himself had caught much of it from other and earlier sources, it is certain that German philosophy and literature, some of it directly, much more of it indirectly, was, by the third decade of the century, becoming a chief influence in its dissemination.

The impetus toward things German had come, about 1819, with the return to America from Göttingen of George Ticknor, George Bancroft, and Edward Everett, young men, all of them, of brilliant parts. The interest thus aroused was fostered by the coming to Harvard a few years later, as instructor in German, of Charles T. Follen, a political exile. From about this time, some direct knowledge of Kant, Fichte, and Schelling, of Schleiermacher, of Goethe and Schiller—of Goethe probably more than of any other German writer—gradually began to make its way into New England, while the indirect German influence was even greater, coming in part through France in the works of Madame de Staël, Cousin, and Jouffroy, but much more significantly through England, in subtle form in the poetry of Wordsworth, more openly in the writings of Coleridge,[1] and, a little later, in the essays of Carlyle.

This interest in German thought and in English romantic literature, moreover, was but the beginning of a wider literary and philosophical awakening which brought with it increasing attention to general European literature, a revitalized attitude toward the classics, and considerable exploration in the realms of Neo-Platonic philosophy and Oriental "Scriptures."

It is natural that those who began to feel the vital effect upon their own religious convictions of this new spirit in philosophy and literature should have found one another out.

---

[1] There is practically no question that of all these influences the works of Coleridge stand first in importance, and it is due to this fact that New England transcendentalism, in so far as it is a philosophy, bears a closer resemblance to the metaphysical system of Schelling (whose influence on Coleridge is well known) than to that of any other thinker.

This they had done many months before any regular gatherings were contemplated. It was not until 1836 that these were begun when on 19 September—after a still smaller preliminary conference—Ralph Waldo Emerson, Frederick Henry Hedge, Convers Francis, James Freeman Clarke, and Amos Bronson Alcott met at the house of George Ripley and formed an organization to aid an exchange of thought among those interested in the "new views" in philosophy, theology, and literature. Among those who joined the group at later meetings were Theodore Parker, Margaret Fuller, Orestes A. Brownson, Elizabeth and Sophia Peabody, Thoreau, Hawthorne, Jones Very, Christopher P. Cranch, Charles T. Follen, and William Henry Channing. For a number of years, following 1836, this group, generally referred to as the Transcendental Club, continued occasionally to come together.

Of the less familiar names among its members, several, in a fuller treatment of the subject, would deserve discussion: Hedge and Clarke, for instance, Unitarian clergymen, the former a man of wide reading and sound scholarship who did much to spread a knowledge of German philosophy, the latter a leader of his denomination and of some contemporary standing as an author; Brownson, one of the most forceful but erratic figures of the time, minister, editor, politician, and novelist—beginning life as a Presbyterian and becoming in turn Universalist, Unitarian, transcendentalist, and Roman Catholic; Very and Cranch, two of the poets of the period, the former probably the extreme mystic of the whole group, a victim for a time of religious mania, the latter a picturesque figure, painter, musician, and ventriloquist, as well as poet. Some of these men attained considerable eminence in their own time, but for the present discussion these passing comments on them must suffice.

It is characteristic of the extreme individualism of the movement that the Transcendental Club was never a really formal organization. The transcendentalists, though most of them were Unitarians, did not leave the fold and form a new church—though such an event as Emerson's withdrawal from the ministry in 1832 is symbolic of a general spiritual secession then taking place. But in spite of the absence of definite organization, there was essential unity of belief among the dissenters. This belief is as well embodied as anywhere, perhaps, in Emerson's little treatise *Nature*, a work which, appearing the same year the Club was formed, may be fittingly considered the philosophical "constitution" of transcendentalism, all the more so since the same author's better known Phi Beta Kappa Oration, *The American Scholar* (1837), and his profoundly influential *Divinity School Address* (1838) are merely applications of the doctrine of *Nature* to the realms of letters and theology.

Into any detailed discussion of what that doctrine was, into any minute exposition, in other words, of the transcendental philosophy, it is impossible here to enter. A glance, however, may be taken at a few of its central and controlling features.

The word "transcendental" in its philosophic sense goes back to Kant and the *Critique of Pure Reason*, though in New England, as elsewhere, the term lost its narrowly technical application and borrowed at the same time a new shade of meaning from the *Critique of Practical Reason*. Kant had taught that time and space are not external realities but ways in which the mind "constitutes" its world of sense. The same is true, he had contended, of cause and effect and the other categories of the mind. Furthermore, as he brought out in his second *Critique*, the ideas of God, of freedom, and of immortality are inevitable intuitions of the practical nature of man, and these intuitions, since man is essentially a practical and moral being, have therefore not a merely sentimental but a real validity. From these and other Kantian conceptions a broad generalization was made, and the word "transcendental" came to be applied, in New England, to whatever in man's mental and spiritual nature is conceived of as above experience and independent of it. Whatever transcends the experience of the senses is transcendental. Innate, original, universal, *a priori*, intuitive—these are words all of which convey a part of the thought swept under the larger meaning of the term. To the transcendentalists the name John Locke stood for the denial of innate ideas. "Sensationalism" was the prevalent description of the doctrine of his *Essay*. Transcendentalism, on the other hand, reaffirmed the soul's inherent power to grasp the truth, and upon this basis went on to erect a metaphysical structure similar in its main outlines to the leading Platonic and idealistic philosophies of the past.

According to this view of the world, the one reality is the vast spiritual background of existence, the Over-Soul, God, within which all other being is unified and from which it derives its life. Because of this indwelling of divinity, every part of the world, however small, is a microcosm, comprehending within itself, like Tennyson's flower in the crannied wall, all the laws and meaning of the whole. The soul of each individual, therefore, is identical with the soul of the world, and contains, latently, all that that larger soul contains. Thus the normal life of man is a life of continuous expansion, the making actual of the potential elements of his being. This may occur in two ways: either directly, in states which vary from the ordinary perception of truth to moments of mystical rapture in which there is a conscious influx of the divine into the human; or indirectly, through the instrumentality of nature. Nature is the embodiment of spirit in the world of sense—it is a great picture to be appreciated, a great book to be read, a great task to be performed. Through the beauty, truth, and goodness incarnate in the natural world, the individual soul comes in contact with and appropriates to itself the spirit and being of God.

From these central conceptions all the other teachings of the transcendentalists are derived: their doctrines of self-reliance and individualism, of the identity of moral and physical laws, of the essential unity of all religions, of the negative nature of evil; their spirit of complete tolerance and of absolute optimism; their defiance of tradition and disregard for all external authority.

It must not be understood, however, that metaphysics was a central interest of the transcendentalists. They were not system makers. The idealistic philosophy was to many of them more a spirit and attitude of mind than a consciously reasoned-out theory of the world, and it is as such a pervading spirit that its virtue still survives. As an explanation of the mystery of existence the transcendental philosophy makes little appeal to our own hard-headed and scientific generation; but no one, assuredly, with any measure of spiritual and poetic perception can give himself sincerely and unreservedly to one of the literary masterpieces of the transcendental school, to one of the greater essays of Emerson for example, the *Self-Reliance, Compensation, Spiritual Laws,* or *The Over-Soul,* without a consciousness, as he puts down the volume, of having passed for the time into a higher sphere of being, without a deepened conviction of the triviality, the relative unreality, of material concerns, without a sense of spaciousness, of clarity, of nobility, of power, a feeling that that much abused word "eternal" has suddenly put on a very real and concrete meaning. Against such an actual experience no mere argument can avail. Nor does the emotion thus evoked end in a vague mystical exaltation. It leaves, rather, whether the reader profit by it or not, a distinct sense of its bearing on the daily conduct of life. This spirit of uplift, together with the moral impulsion it imparts, is the heart of New England transcendentalism.

But the transcendentalists were not always at the level of their masterpieces, and from the outset two results of a movement whose essence was so intangible and ideal were practically inevitable: first, that it should be misunderstood and misinterpreted by those who viewed it from outside; and second, that it should lead to excesses among the initiated themselves which would lend colour and, in a measure, justification to its critics. So quickly, indeed, did these results appear that to the public the word "transcendental" soon came to mean, to all intents and purposes, "transcending common sense," and this use of the term gained added sanction from the difficulty of distinguishing sharply between transcendentalism and other currents of social and religious unrest then pulsing through New England. Some notion of the varieties of "dissent" and "reform" contending at that time for public attention is conveyed in Emerson's description of the Chardon Street Convention which was held in Boston in 1840:

Madmen, madwomen, men with beards, Dunkers, Muggletonians, Come-outers, Groaners, Agrarians, Seventh-day Baptists, Quakers, Abolitionists, Calvinists, Unitarians, and Philosophers.

Surely these were wild and "transcendental" times!

Of the members of the Club it was Amos Bronson Alcott,

father of Louisa May Alcott, who was particularly singled out as a target for the shafts of a jesting and unsympathetic public. The stories told of him, to be sure, were often outright inventions or gross exaggerations. But we do not need to go beyond the testimony of his daughter to discover considerable basis for the popular conception of his character. Alcott, in fact, becomes an especially significant figure as embodying in excessive degree the mystical tendency of the transcendentalists together with those extravagances and eccentricities which often accompany the mystic's habit of wrapping himself up in the clouds of his own speculation and aspiration.

Alcott was born in Connecticut in 1799. After a fragmentary education he went to Virginia planning to teach but was compelled to earn his living by peddling. For four or five years this was his chief vocation, and it is interesting to note that toward the end of this period he came in contact with North Carolina Quakers, whose religious views seem to have influenced his thinking. Following this he returned to New England and for nearly fifteen years devoted himself in the main to school-teaching, putting into practice with considerable success, especially in his last and most famous school at the Masonic Temple in Boston, radical educational theories, some of which seem to have anticipated kindergarten methods now in vogue and which earned for Alcott the title of the American Pestalozzi.

Alcott's fundamental educational conceptions were Platonic, and he exhibited an astonishing but entirely characteristic consistency in carrying out his most radical ideas. He believed in the plenary inspiration of childhood, and his method may be described as an attempt to realize in practice the thought of Wordsworth's ode on the *Intimations of Immortality*.

The publication of some of his conversations with his pupils, owing to their references to the phenomena of birth, brought adverse criticism and tended to impair the prosperity of the school. Finally, on his refusal to dismiss a coloured child whom he had received as a pupil, patronage was withdrawn and he was compelled to give up the enterprise.

After the failure of his school Alcott first tried his scheme of public "conversations," with little financial success, however. In these years, too, he showed an interest in many of the reform movements of the day, the temperance cause, woman's rights, the anti-slavery agitation. Moving with his family to Concord in 1840, he tried for a time to stick to farm work, but his taste for transcendental thought was too strong and he again began holding conversations and giving lectures. Shortly after this he removed to a farm in the town of Harvard, where, with two English friends, he instituted the community of Fruitlands.

The ideals of this miniature Utopia were extreme. The diet was strictly vegetarian, even milk and eggs being tabooed. Water was the only beverage. The "aspiring" vegetables, those which grow into the air like the fruits, were allowed, but the baser ones, like potatoes and beets, which grow downward, were forbidden. When cold weather came the experiment had proved itself, materially at least, a complete failure. This was too much for Alcott, who, losing for once his perennial serenity and turning his face to the wall, asked only to be allowed to die. He had a brave wife, however, who eventually brought him to his senses.

Following the failure of Fruitlands, the Alcotts had a long struggle against poverty first in Concord and later in Boston, Mrs. Alcott apparently being the financial mainstay of the family, her husband contributing what little he could earn from his conversations. The journal of Louisa May Alcott covering this period gives us many intimate glimpses into the life of "the pathetic family," and while the father is revealed as a man of extreme impracticality and even of unwitting selfishness, his extraordinary gentleness of temper and his unfailing optimism under adversity are not less conspicuous. When, a few years later, Miss Alcott gained literary distinction, the family was freed from financial embarrassment. The latter part of Alcott's life brought the Concord School of Philosophy and the realization of his long-cherished dream to see himself the American Plato surrounded by a group of admiring disciples.

It is singularly difficult to arrive at a just estimate of Alcott. The whole affinity of his mind was mystical, Neo-Platonic and Oriental writers being his favourite authors. The rarified nature of his subject-matter combined with a certain deficiency in power of literary expression makes his published works inadequately representative of the man, and the critic pauses between the belief that admiring contemporaries grossly over-rated the ability of an active and elevated but withal rather ordinary mind, and the opposite view that Alcott had a touch of real genius in him, a kinship in due degree with the inspired talkers of literary history. Carlyle's famous description of him gives us part of the truth:

> The good Alcott: with his long, lean face and figure, with his grey worn temples and mild radiant eyes; all bent on saving the world by a return to acorns and the golden age; he comes before one like a kind of venerable Don Quixote, whom nobody can even laugh at without loving.

But Emerson probably came nearer than anyone else to doing justice to both sides of Alcott's nature when he called his friend a "tedious archangel."

If Alcott embodied the extreme mystical and esoteric side of transcendentalism, the Brook Farm Association represents its social and experimental aspect.

George Ripley (1802–1880), the leader of this enterprise, was a graduate of Harvard and a Unitarian minister. A wide and increasing knowledge of European writers, however, gradually led his interest from theology into the sphere of social reform. He accordingly gave up his pastorate, and in 1841 he and his wife and a number of loyal friends established the Brook Farm Institute of Agriculture and Education on a farm at West Roxbury, nine miles from Boston. The association was a joint-stock company and financially it was inaugurated and conducted with considerable practical saga-city. On its theoretical side the enterprise, while the product in a general way of the speculations and example of Owen and Fourier, was not, especially at the beginning, in any precise sense an experiment in socialism. The hope of its founders was merely to make Brook Farm a self-supporting group of men and women, where all should share in the manual labour, the leisure, and the educational and cultural advantages, a place of "plain living and high thinking" where life might be lived in an atmosphere of fraternity, free from the strife and burdens of ordinary competitive society. That the attempt was far from being unsuccessful is revealed by many anecdotes which have come down showing the hearty and genuine spirit which prevailed among its members, a spirit to the happy influence of which on their later lives more than one of the survivors of the enterprise has borne witness.

The adoption in 1844, with some modifications, of the principles of Fourier seems, however, to have put an end to some of the more Arcadian features of Brook Farm; and this, together with the fact that the efforts of inexperienced farmers on a rather poor farm yielded insufficient financial return, was enough to doom the experiment to ultimate failure. The disbanding of the members was immediately occasioned by the burning in 1846 of the unfinished "phalanstery," upon which seven thousand dollars had already been expended and which was wholly uninsured.

Brook Farm, being the most tangible and visible product of this whole New England movement, has come to stand in the public mind for a perfect incarnation of the transcendental spirit. This is an error. Brook Farm was characteristic of transcendentalism in its belief that the material factors of life should be subservient to the spiritual and ideal and in its conviction that right thinking would lead toward better social conditions—in the end, indeed, to a perfect society. But it is important to notice that Ripley alone of the original members of the Transcendental Club had an active share in the enterprise and that while Emerson, Alcott, Theodore Parker, and Margaret Fuller were interested and on the whole sympathetic visitors, they were too thoroughly individualistic, too distrustful of the institutional factor in life, to be completely satisfied with the experiment. In not a few respects incidents more characteristic, in their individualism, of the transcendental spirit were Alcott's sojourn with his friends at Fruitlands and, still more so, Thoreau's experiment on the shore of Walden Pond.[1]

An achievement more intimately connected than Brook Farm with the Transcendental Club and the leading transcendentalists was *The Dial*,[2] the literary organ of the movement, the first number of which appeared in 1840 with Margaret Fuller as editor, and George Ripley as assistant editor. *The*

[1] See Book II, Chap. x.   [2] See also Book II, Chap. xx.

Dial never approached financial success, and it was only through real devotion and sacrifice on the part of its editor and of Elizabeth Peabody that it was issued as long as it was.] Miss Fuller resigned the editorship after two years and Emerson assumed it for a like period, after which it was discontinued.

Whatever defects *The Dial* may have had, a comparison of its pages with the dusty contemporaneous numbers of, let us say, *The North American Review* is not to its disadvantage and lends some weight to the assertion of its main contributors that they were dealing with subjects of deeper than passing interest. [The journal discussed questions of theology and philosophy; it contained papers on art, music, and literature, especially German literature; translations from ancient "Oriental Scriptures"; original modern "scriptures" in the form of Alcott's *Orphic Sayings;* and finally, a good deal of verse.] In this latter connection one of the most interesting features of *The Dial* to the present-day reader is the opportunity and encouragement it afforded to the literary genius of Thoreau. In addition to his and Emerson's, there were, among others, metrical contributions from Lowell, Cranch, and William Ellery Channing, the younger, the last-named one of the poets of transcendentalism, now best remembered for the single line,

> If my bark sinks, 'tis to another sea.

[*The Dial*, needless to say, did not satisfy the public.] Dozens of parodies, especially of the *Orphic Sayings*, were forthcoming, and (in the words of Colonel Higginson)

epithets, too, were showered about as freely as imitations; the Philadelphia "Gazette," for instance, calling the editors of the new journal "zanies," "Bedlamites," and "considerably madder than the Mormons."

Alcott, on the other hand, considered its policy tame and compromising. Whatever, between these extremes, our own estimate of its intrinsic merit may be, we shall not be likely to overrate its significance in the history of American literature or the importance of the part it played in our literary emancipation. Its volumes stand as a reminder that the transcendental movement was, among other things, a literary renaissance—the enthusiasm for art and literature which appeared in New

England after the long æsthetic starvation of the Puritan ascendency being comparable in kind if not in degree to the immense artistic expansion of Western Europe after a thousand years of mediæval Christianity.

No one of the leading transcendentalists illustrates this aspect of the movement more completely than does the first editor of *The Dial*, Sarah Margaret Fuller (1810–1850).

The character of Margaret Fuller's childhood and early training is the key to much in her later career. She was brought up by a father whose stern temperament and uncompromising notions on education made him peculiarly unfitted to understand and mould the delicately sensitive nature of his daughter. Under the mental tasks he imposed upon her, her health became impaired and she was overstimulated intellectually and emotionally. All the early part of her life was a struggle against the sentimentalism and self-consciousness which her early education had engendered. As a young woman she was proud and imperious, at times overbearing, in her nature. She could use her tongue sharply and sarcastically, a quality which, combined with a high temper and a tendency to tell the truth, made her many enemies; and gradually, as she became more widely known, out of these hints that she herself supplied, there emerged in the public mind a distorted conception of her personality—a view that still lingers—which made her out a woman of insufferable vanity and masculinity, a veritable intellectual virago. Along with Alcott she became a chief butt of coarse and unsympathetic critics.

As a matter of fact, however, the unloveliest features of Margaret Fuller's personality were but the reverse sides of sterling virtues, and it is to her lasting credit that she lived to master and in the main to outgrow her early defects. The family duties devolving upon her at the death of her father, the sacrifice of long-cherished plans for foreign travel, a brief period of teaching, her work as editor of *The Dial*—these experiences gave her needed self-control and contact with practical problems, and the figure that emerges from them some years later as literary critic of *The New York Tribune* and social and philanthropic worker is an exceedingly able, sensible, and admirable woman.

From her early years, Margaret Fuller read omnivorously

(at a rate like Gibbon, Emerson once said). Her linguistic equipment was good, and there is little question that she came to know Continental literature, that of Germany especially, more fully and appreciatively than any other of the transcendentalists. Her choice as editor of *The Dial* therefore was natural. She also put her literary acquirements to use— as did Alcott his educational theories and mystical lore—by holding conversations on Greek mythology and other subjects. While these at the beginning were not free from amateurishness and a narrowly self-cultural ideal, they had deeper qualities, the promise of powers more fully revealed in her *Woman in the Nineteenth Century* (1845) and her collected *Papers on Literature and Art* (1846), which, in spite of their decidedly uneven quality, reveal her on the whole as one of the best equipped, most sympathetic and genuinely philosophical critics produced in America prior to 1850.

Following Miss Fuller's removal to New York, the realistic element in her work grew stronger, her interest in social and political questions increased, and particularly during her three years in Italy from 1847 to 1850—where she was married to the Marquis Ossoli—did her intimate contact with the struggle for Italian freedom broaden and deepen her nature. In fact her career seemed just entering on its most useful phase when it was tragically cut short by her death in the wreck off Fire Island in 1850 of the ship that was bringing her back to New York, a disaster in which her husband and child also perished.

Though her later promise was thus unfulfilled, Margaret Fuller had already accomplished much.

"It has been one great object of my life," she once declared, "to introduce here the works of those great geniuses, the flower and fruit of a higher state of development, which might give the young who are soon to constitute the state, a higher standard in thought and action than would be demanded of them by their own time. . . . I feel with satisfaction that I have done a good deal to extend the influence of the great minds of Germany and Italy among my compatriots."

She had, in truth, accomplished this, and her words are suggestive of one of the greatest achievements of the transcendental movement on its literary side.

If Margaret Fuller is the literary critic of transcendentalism, Theodore Parker (1810–1860) is its theologian and reformer. Parker was a graduate of Harvard and of the Harvard Divinity School, and held pastorates near or in Boston during the whole of his ministerial career. He carried to its extreme form the theological reaction from eighteenth-century Unitarianism begun by Channing, his South Boston sermon in 1841 on *The Transient and Permanent in Christianity* being generally considered a milestone not only in the history of transcendentalism but in the development of American theology.

Parker, though his nature was not lacking in qualities of engaging simplicity and kindliness, was a man of warlike and aggressive temperament, of indomitable energy whether in thought or action, "our Savonarola," as Emerson called him. During the earlier part of his life, much of his tremendous power of activity was expended upon books, and he became a man of immense erudition, the most widely read member of the transcendental group. His learning, however, savoured a little too much, as Lowell suggested, of an attempt to tear up the whole tree of knowledge by the roots, and he surely misconstrued his own nature when he declared "I was meant for a philosopher, and the times call for a *stump orator*." His mind was in reality more practical than metaphysical in its cast, and it was with the turning of his interest to the slavery question and especially with the arousing of all the fires of his nature at the passage of the Fugitive Slave Law that the tremendous will power and earnestness of the man came out to the full. During the years of this controversy, he interspersed an endless mass of correspondence, lectures, sermons, and addresses with deeds of conspicuous moral and physical courage. He was chairman of the executive committee of the Vigilance Committee, sheltered fugitive slaves in his own house and aided their escape in all ways possible, was indicted but never brought to trial in connection with the famous Burns Affair, and came into intimate relations with John Brown. It was the strain of labours of this sort that led to his premature death in 1860.

These anti-slavery activities of Parker came, of course, after the crest of the transcendental movement, but they are mentioned here as an illustration of that tendency in transcendentalism, already noted in connection with Brook Farm and the life of Margaret Fuller, to pass from its early sentimental and romantic stage into a phase of social or political activity. Parker's life reveals with special clearness the link between transcendentalism and the abolition movement. There is probably little likelihood of exaggerating the relation between a philosophy which taught the divinity of every human soul and the agitation for the freedom of the Southern slaves.

Although the transcendental philosophy was of course only one of many forces that led to abolitionism in New England, the connection between the two is a powerful reminder that, in spite of its underlying unity of spirit, transcendentalism was an exceedingly varied and complex movement. Even the present rapid survey of a few of its characteristic incidents and leading figures has served perhaps to emphasize that fact.

In Channing, for instance, to glance back for a moment, we perceive it as a force mellowing and humanizing the stern Calvinistic tradition and touching with emotion the prosaic rationalism of the Unitarians. In Emerson it shines forth as an unfailing sense of the unity of the soul with God and nature, a religious aspiration constantly translated into incentives toward the noble conduct of life. In Alcott we behold it at first touching education and the child, then volatilizing into clouds of Oriental mysticism. In Margaret Fuller we catch its significance as a literary renaissance, an effort for culture, for criticism, passing over at last into an effort for social betterment—which latter note is struck earlier and more resoundingly in the social Utopianism of Ripley and the other Brook Farmers. In Parker it takes on particularly the form of extreme theological radicalism, a radicalism successfully undergoing the test of practical application in the abolition movement. In Thoreau it is present—in none of the group more ethereally—as a spiritualized feeling for nature, a fine dissolvent of convention, a pervasive and contagious influence toward natural and simple living.

These considerations, together with the implication of such names as Hawthorne, Dana, Curtis, and a dozen others, show how impossible it is not only to define the nature but to fix the limits of transcendentalism. Transcendentalism was, in fact, simply the focus and energizing centre of that larger area of illumination and activity which is coextensive with the whole movement of literary and spiritual expansion that transformed New England during the second and third quarters of the nineteenth century. For purposes of historical and critical discrimination, to be sure, it is convenient, as we have done, to treat transcendentalism as a distinct and separate movement. But in reality it was not. In reality it was so blended with wider currents of spiritual change that the relation between the two can never be precisely determined. All that can be asserted with any certainty is that the fundamentally religious complexion of New England life makes it a fair presumption that the religious phase of the whole development was as nearly central and determinative as any.

It is equally difficult, as may now be seen more clearly than at the outset of our discussion, to separate the European and the American contributions to transcendentalism. That spirit of freedom, of individualism, of revolution, of romance, which was abroad throughout the Western world during this period, took on a peculiar local colour in New England. Distilled in the New England alembic, French Revolutionary dogmas, German philosophy, Oriental mysticism, assume a semblance that often makes them scarcely recognizable. Yet, however fresh the utterance, an alert sense can usually detect, if not its particular source, at least its general European kinship.

When Emerson in the opening pages of *Nature* exhorts his countrymen to come forth and live their own lives, reminding them that "the sun shines to-day also," we catch echoes of Rousseau's "Man is born free; and is everywhere in chains." When Thoreau proclaims an intention "to brag as lustily as chanticleer in the morning, standing on his roost, if only to wake my neighbours up," we feel that here is the homely New England version of Shelley's cry to the West Wind:

> Be through my lips to unawakened earth
> The trumpet of a prophecy!

When Thoreau, on another occasion, writes that he was not aware "that the capacity to hear the woodpecker had slumbered within me so long," the words have all the spontaneity of underived utterance, and yet who can deny that the peculiar turn of that expression goes back through German or we know not what other channels to Plato and still remoter Eastern sources?

This mention of the East is suggestive of all the weaknesses of transcendentalism: its tendency to neglect proximate and to refer everything to primal causes; its attempt to attain the spiritual not by subduing but by turning its back on the material; its proneness to substitute passivity and receptiveness for alertness and creative force; its traces of a paralysing pantheism and fatalism; its ineffectualness; its atrophy of will. More than a touch of each of these qualities transcendentalism indisputably has; but if this were all there were to it, we should brand it as one more vain revival of a philosophy of life long since proved futile.

But who can doubt that there is in it also something the precise opposite of all this, the strange union of which with its Oriental elements makes it precisely the unique thing it is? Who can doubt that in speaking the last word of transcendentalism we should come back from India, even from Europe, to Concord and Boston? For, at bottom, it is the strong local flavour of it all, a smell of the soil through the universal generalizations, a dash of Yankee practicality in the midst of the Oriental mysticism, a sturdy Puritan pugnacity and grasp of fact underneath its serenest and most Olympian detachments, that gives this movement its reality and grip, and rescues it in large part not only from the ineffectiveness of the East but from the sentimental, the romantic, and the anarchic excesses of many of its related European movements.

These men were no mere dreamers. Emerson resigning his pulpit rather than administer the Lord's Supper or pray when he did not feel like praying, Thoreau going to jail for a refusal to pay his taxes, Alcott closing his school sooner than dismiss a coloured pupil (yes! even Alcott planting "aspiring" vegetables), Parker risking reputation and life in the anti-slavery crusade—these are typical examples of the fact that when these men were put to the test of acting up to their principles they were not found wanting. The Puritan character was the rock on which transcendentalism was built.

How inherent in the religious development of New England that character has been may be seen by glancing at three of her foremost spiritual figures: Jonathan Edwards, Ralph Waldo Emerson, and William James (James, curiously enough, though a New Englander only by adoption, being scarcely less representative of the most recent phase of New England religious evolution than Emerson and Edwards were of two of its earlier stages). Edwards, the last great apostle of theocratic dogmatism; Emerson, the prophet of a generation of romantic aspiration; James, the pragmatic philosopher of a scientific and democratic age—how far apart, at first thought, they seem! And not merely far apart, but often hostile. Emerson gave much of his best effort to demolishing the remnants of the Calvinistic structure Edwards had done so much to fortify. James's career was one long assault on that philosophy of the Absolute which is the intellectualized counterpart of the religion of the Over-Soul. The respective attitudes of the three men toward nature well illustrate their differences. To Edwards, in spite of his feeling for natural beauty, nature is essentially evil and is consistently set over against grace, which is of God. To Emerson, God and Nature are merely two aspects of a single spirit. To James, endlessly interesting as the natural world is in its instrumental capacity, in any ultimate sense nature is merely "so much weather." And yet, under analysis, such distinctions turn out to be partly nominal and relatively superficial, for, deeper than all their differences of doctrine, there is a community of spirit among these men, a something central and controlling in them all, something which in its day was the driving force of transcendentalism, the innate idealism and individualism of the New England mind.

CHAPTER IX

Emerson

I T becomes more and more apparent that Emerson, judged by
an international or even by a broad national standard,
is the outstanding figure of American letters. Others
may have surpassed him in artistic sensitiveness, or, to a
criticism averse to the stricter canons of form and taste, may
seem to be more original or more broadly national than he,
but as a steady force in the transmutation of life into
ideas and as an authority in the direction of life itself he has
obtained a recognition such as no other of his countrymen can
claim. And he owes this pre-eminence not only to his personal
endowment of genius, but to the fact also that, as the most
perfect exponent of a transient experiment in civilization, he
stands for something that the world is not likely to let die.

Ralph Waldo Emerson, born in Boston, 25 May, 1803,
gathered into himself the very quintessence of what has been
called the Brahminism of New England, as transmitted through
the Bulkeleys, the Blisses, the Moodys, and the direct paternal
line. Peter Bulkeley, preferring the wilderness of Satan to
Laudian conformity, founded Concord in 1636; William
Emerson, his descendant in the fifth generation, was builder of
the Old Manse in the same town and a sturdy preacher to the
minute-men at the beginning of the Revolution; and of many
other ministerial ancestors stories abound which show how
deeply implanted in this stock was the pride of rebellion against
traditional forms and institutions, united with a determination
to force all mankind to worship God in the spirit. With
William, son of him of Concord and father of our poet, the
fires of zeal began to wane. Though the faithful pastor of the
First Church (Unitarian) of Boston, it is recorded of him that he

entered the ministry against his will. Yet he too had his un-fulfilled dream of "coming out" by establishing a church in Washington which should require no sort of profession of faith. He died when the future philosopher was a boy of ten, leaving the family to shift for itself as best it could. Mrs. Emerson cared for the material welfare of the household by taking in boarders. The chief intellectual guidance fell to the Aunt Mary Moody Emerson, of whom her nephew drew a portrait in his *Lectures and Biographies*. "She gave high counsels," he says. Indubitably she did; but a perusal of her letters and of the extracts from her journals leaves the impression that the pure but dislocated enthusiasms of her mind served rather to push Emerson in the direction of his weaker inclination than to fortify him against himself. When a balloon is tugging at its moorings there may be need of low counsels.

In 1817, Emerson entered Harvard College, and in due course of time graduated. Then, after teaching for a while in his brother's school in Boston, he returned to Cambridge to study for the ministry, and was in the autumn of 1826 licensed to preach. Three years later he was called, first as assistant to Henry Ware, to the Second Church of Boston. His ministra-tion there was quietly successful, but brief. In 1832, he gave up his charge on the ground that he could not conscientiously celebrate the Communion, even in the symbolic form customary among the Unitarians. He was for the moment much adrift, his occupation gone, his health broken, his wife lost after a short period of happiness. In this state he went abroad to travel in Italy, France, and England. One memorable incident of the journey must be recorded, his visit to Carlyle at Craigenput-tock, with all that it entailed of friendship and influence; but beyond that he returned with little more baggage than he took with him. He now made his residence in Concord, living first with his mother and then with his second wife. Thence-forth there was to be no radical change in his life, but only the gradual widening of the circle. The house that he now bought he continued to inhabit until it was burned down in 1872; and then his friends, in a manner showing exemplary tact, sub-scribed money for rebuilding it on the same lines. For a number of years he preached in various pulpits, and once even considered the call to a settled charge in New Bedford, but he could not overcome his aversion to the ritual of the Lord's Supper and to regular prayers.

Meanwhile, by the medium of lectures delivered here and there and by printed essays, he was making of himself a kind of lay preacher to the world. His method of working out the more characteristic of these discourses has long been known: he would commonly select a theme, and then ransack his note-books for pertinent passages which could be strung together with the addition of such developing and connecting material as was necessary. But since the publication of his *Journals* it has been possible to follow him more precisely in this pro-cedure and to see more clearly how it conforms with the inmost structure of his mind. These remarkable records were begun in early youth and continued, though at the close in the form of brief memoranda, to the end of his life. The first entry pre-served (not the first written, for it is from *Blotting Book No. XVII*) dates from his junior year at college and contains notes for a prize dissertation on the Character of Socrates. Among the sentences is this:

What is God? said the disciples, and Plato replied, It is hard to learn and impossible to divulge.

And the last page of the record, in the twelfth volume, repeats what is really the same thought:

The best part of truth is certainly that which hovers in gleams and suggestions unpossessed before man. His recorded knowledge is dead and cold. But this chorus of thoughts and hopes, these dawning truths, like great stars just lifting themselves into his horizon, they are his future, and console him for the ridiculous brevity and meanness of his civic life.

There is of course much variety of matter in the *Journals*— shrewd observations on men and books, chronicles of the day's events, etc.—but through it all runs this thread of self-com-munion, the poetry, it might be called, of the New England conscience deprived of its concrete deity and buoying itself on gleams and suggestions of eternal beauty and holiness. Of the same stuff, not seldom indeed of the same words, are those essays of his that have deeply counted; they are but a repetition to the world of fragments of this long inner conversation.

Where they fail to reach the reader's heart, it is not because they are fundamentally disjointed, as if made up of sentences jostled together like so many mutually repellent particles; but because from the manner of his composition Emerson often missed what he might have learned from Plato's *Phaedrus* was the essence of good rhetoric, that is to say, the consciousness of his hearer's mind as well as of his own. We hear him, as it were, talking to himself, with no attempt to convince by argument or enlighten by analysis. If our dormant intuition answers to his, we are profoundly kindled and confirmed; otherwise his sentences may rattle ineffectually about our ears.

Emerson's first published work was *Nature* (1836), which contains the gist of his transcendental attitude towards the phenomenal world, as a kind of beautiful symbol of the inner spiritual life, floating dreamlike before the eye, yet, it is to be noted, having discipline as one of its lessons for the attentive soul. The most characteristic and influential of his books are the two volumes of *Essays*, issued respectively in 1841 and 1844. In the former of these are those great discourses on *Self-Reliance*, *Compensation*, and *The Over-Soul*, into which was distilled the very quintessence of the volatile and heady liquid known as Emersonianism. Other volumes followed in due course. The latter publications, however, beginning with *Letters and Social Aims* (1875), are made up mainly of gleanings from the field already harvested, and were even gathered by hands not his own.

Two of his addresses (now both included in the volume with *Nature*) deserve special notice for the attention they attracted at the time. The first of these is the oration before the Phi Beta Kappa Society of Harvard, in 1837, a high but scarcely practical appeal to the American scholar to raise himself above the dust of pedantries, even out of the routine of what is "decent, indolent, complaisant," and to reach after the inspiration of "the Divine Soul which also inspires all men." The other lecture was delivered the next year before the senior class in Divinity College, Cambridge, and held up to the prospective preacher about the same ideal as was presented to the scholar. Historical Christianity is condemned because "it is not the doctrine of the soul, but an exaggeration of the personal, the positive, the ritual. It has dwelt, it dwells, with noxious exaggeration about the *person* of Jesus." The founder of Christianity saw, indeed, "with open eye the mystery of the soul," but what as a man he saw and knew of man's divinity cannot be given to man to-day by instruction, but only on the terms of a like intuition. The Unitarians of Massachusetts had travelled far from the Calvinistic creed of the Pilgrim Fathers, but Emerson's suave displacement of the person of Jesus for the "chorus of thoughts and hopes" in any human soul, perhaps even more his implicit rejection of all rites and institutions, raised loud protest among the worshippers of the day. For the most part he answered the criticism by silence, but in a letter replying to one of the more courteous of his opponents he used these significant words:

I could not give an account of myself, if challenged. I could not possibly give you one of the "arguments" you cruelly hint at, on which any doctrine of mine stands; for I do not know what arguments are in reference to any expression of a thought.

There may be some guile in this pretence to complete intellectual innocence, but it is nevertheless a fair statement of a literary method which seeks, and obtains, its effect by throwing a direct light into the soul of the hearer and bidding him look there and acknowledge what he sees.

Of the events of these years there is not much to relate. A journey to Europe, in 1847, resulted in the only two of his books which may be said to have been composed as units: *Representative Men* (published in 1850, from a series of lectures delivered in London), which displays Emerson's great powers as an ethical critic, in the larger use of that phrase, and *English Traits* (1856), which proves that his eyes were observing the world about him with Yankee shrewdness all the while that he seemed to be gazing into transcendental clouds. Into the question of slavery and disunion which was now agitating the country, he entered slowly. It was natural that one to whom the power and meaning of institutions had little appeal and to whom liberty was the all-including virtue, should have been drawn to the side of the Abolitionists, but at first there was a philosophical aloofness in his attitude. Only after the passing of the Fugitive Slave Law and Webster's defection were his passions deeply engaged. Then he spoke ringing words:

There is infamy in the air. I have a new experience. I awake in the morning with a painful sensation, which I carry about all day, and which, when traced home, is the odious remembrance of that ignominy which has fallen on Massachusetts, which robs the landscape of beauty, and takes the sunshine out of every hour.

And the war came to him as a welcome relief from a situation which had grown intolerable.

A third trip to Europe was made in 1872, when his central will was already loosening and his faculties were losing their edge. It was at this time that Charles Eliot Norton talked with Carlyle, and heard the old man, eight years older than Emerson, expatiate on the fundamental difference in their tempers. And on the voyage home in the same boat, Norton, who so fully represents the judgment of New England, had much conversation with Emerson, and recorded his opinion in words that, whether welcome or not, should not be forgotten:

Emerson was the greatest talker in the ship's company. He talked with all men, and yet was fresh and zealous for talk at night. His serene sweetness, the pure whiteness of his soul, the reflection of his soul in his face, were never more apparent to me; but never before in intercourse with him had I been so impressed with the limits of his mind. His optimistic philosophy has hardened into a creed, with the usual effects of a creed in closing the avenues of truth. He can accept nothing as fact that tells against his dogma. His optimism becomes a bigotry, and, though of a nobler type than the common American conceit of the preeminent excellence of American things as they are, has hardly less of the quality of fatalism. To him this is the best of all possible worlds, and the best of all possible times. He refuses to believe in disorder or evil. . . . But such inveterate and persistent optimism, though it may show only its pleasant side in such a character as Emerson's, is dangerous doctrine for a people. It degenerates into fatalistic indifference to moral considerations, and to personal responsibilities; it is at the root of much of the irrational sentimentalism in our American politics, of much of our national disregard of honour in our public men, of much of our unwillingness to accept hard truths, and of much of the common tendency to disregard the distinctions

between right and wrong, and to excuse guilt on the plea of good
intentions or good nature.[1]

For some time there had been a gradual relaxation of
Emerson's hold on life. Though always an approachable
man and fond of conversation, there was in him a certain lack
of human warmth, of "bottom," to use his own word, which
he recognized and deplored. Commenting in his *Journal* (24
May, 1864) on the burial of Hawthorne, he notes the statement of James Freeman Clarke that the novelist had "shown
a sympathy with the crime in our nature," and adds: "I
thought there was a tragic element in the event, that might
be more fully rendered,—in the painful solitude of the man,
which, I suppose, could not longer be endured, and he died of
it." A touch of this romantic isolation, though never morose
or "painful," there was in himself, a failure to knit himself
strongly into the bonds of society. "I have felt sure of him,"
he says of Hawthorne in the same passage, "in his neighbourhood, and in his necessities of sympathy and intelligence,—
that I could well wait his time,—his unwillingness and caprice,
—and might one day conquer a friendship. . . . Now it appears that I waited too long." Eighteen years later, standing
by the body of Longfellow, he was heard to say: "That gentleman was a sweet, beautiful soul, but I have entirely forgotten
his name." Such forgetfulness, like a serene and hazy cloud,
hovered over Emerson's brain in his closing years. A month
afterwards, on 27 April, 1882, he himself faded away peacefully.

To one who examines the events of Emerson's quiet life
with a view to their spiritual bearing it will appear that his
most decisive act was the surrender of his pulpit in 1832.
Nearly a century earlier, in 1750, the greatest of American
theologians had suffered what now befell the purest of American
seers; and though the manner of their parting was different
(Jonathan Edwards had been unwillingly ejected, whereas
Emerson left with good will on both sides), yet there is significance in the fact that the cause of separation in both cases was
the administration of the Lord's Supper. Nor is there less
significance in the altered attitude of the later man towards
this vital question. Both in a way turned from the ritualistic

[1] *Letters of Charles Eliot Norton*, vol. I, pp. 503 and 506.

and traditional use of the Communion, and in this showed themselves leaders of the spirit which had carried the New England Fathers across the ocean as rebels against the Laudian tyranny of institutions. Edwards had revolted against the practice of Communion as a mere act of acquiescence in the authority of religion; he was determined that only those should approach the Table who could give evidence of a true conversion, by conversion meaning a complete emotional realization of the dogma of divine Grace and election. The eucharist was not a rite by conforming with which in humility men were to be made participators in the larger religious experience of the race, but a jealously guarded privilege of the few who already knew themselves set apart from the world. He was attempting to push to its logical issue the Puritan notion of religion as a matter of individual and inward experience, and if he failed it was because life can never be rigidly logical and because the worshippers of his day were already beginning to lose their intellectual grasp on the Calvinistic creed.[1] By Emerson's time, among the Unitarians of Boston, there could be no question of ritualistic grace or absolute conversion, but his act, nevertheless, like that of Edwards, was the intrusion of unyielding consistency among those who were content to rest in habit and compromise. In his old age Emerson gave this account of his conduct to Charles Eliot Norton:

He had come to the conviction that he could not administer the Lord's Supper as a divinely appointed, sacred ordinance of religion. And, after much debate with himself, he told his people that he could henceforth conduct the service only as a memorial service, without attributing to it any deeper significance. A parish meeting was held; the parish, though most kindly affected to him, could not bring themselves to accept his view,—it would be tantamount to admitting that they were no longer Christians. He resigned his charge, but an effort was made to induce him to remain, he administering the Lord's Supper in his sense, the people receiving it in theirs. But he saw that such an arrangement was impossible, and held to his resignation.[2]

Emerson had come to the inevitable conclusion of New England individualism; he had, in a word, "come out." Ed-

[1] See also Book I, Chaps. IV and V.
[2] *Letters of Charles Eliot Norton*, vol. I, p. 509.

wards had denied the communal efficacy, so to speak, of rites, but had insisted on inner conformity with an established creed. Emerson disavowed even a conformity in faith, demanding in its stead the entire liberty of each soul to rise on its own spiritual impulse. He was perspicacious and honest enough to acknowledge to himself the danger of such a stand. "I know very well," he wrote in his journal at the time of his decision, "that it is a bad sign in a man to be too conscientious, and stick at gnats. The most desperate scoundrels have been the over-refiners. Without accommodation society is impracticable." But, he adds, he could "not go habitually to an institution which they esteem holiest with indifference and dislike"; and again, looking deeper into his heart, "This is the end of my opposition, that I am not interested in it."

Emerson's act of renunciation was not only important as determining the nature of his career, but significant also of the transition of New England from theological dogmatism to romantic liberty. Much has been written about the influences that shaped his thoughts and about the relation of his transcendentalism to German metaphysics. In his later years it is clear that the speculations of Kant and Schelling and Fichte were known to him and occasionally coloured his language, but his *Journals* prove conclusively enough that the whole stamp of his mind was taken before these sources were open to him. Indirectly, no doubt, something of the German spirit came to him pretty early through Carlyle, and a passage in his *Journal* for 13 December, 1829, shows that he was at that time already deeply engaged in the Teutonized rhapsodies of Coleridge. But it would be easy to lay too much stress even on this indirect affiliation. Long before that date, as early as his senior year in college, he is yearning "to separate the soul for sublime contemplation till it has lost the sense of circumstances," and otherwise giving implicit expression to the full circle of transcendental faith. He was in fact a product of the great romantic movement that was sweeping over the world as it listed; his ideas, so far as they came to him from books, go back mainly to the Greek philosophers and the poets and preachers of seventeenth-century England, as these were interpreted under the light of the new movement. When he

Emerson

declared, in *Nature*, that "the vision of genius comes by renouncing the too officious activity of the understanding, and giving leave and amplest privilege to the spontaneous sentiment," he was stating in precise terms an idea familiar to Blake and to the romanticists of every land—the elevation of enthusiasm above judgment, of emotion above reason, of spontaneity above discipline, and of unlimited expansion above centripetal control. But there was another element as strongly formative of Emerson's disposition as was the current of romanticism, and that was his ancestral inheritance. Romantic spontaneity moved in various directions in accordance with the field in which it worked; in an Emerson, with all the divinity of Massachusetts in his veins, it might move to repudiate theological dogma and deny Jehovah, but it could not get out of hearing of the question "What is God?" It could not fall into the too common confusion of spiritual aspiration with the sicklier lusts of the flesh; it could never, for all its centrifugal wandering, overstep the bounds of character. Emersonianism may be defined as romanticism rooted in Puritan divinity.

In literary form and style the privilege of spontaneous sentiment showed itself with Emerson not in that fluency which in many of his contemporaries meant mere longwindedness, but in the habit of waiting for the momentary inspiration to the neglect of meditated construction and regularity. He has indeed succeeded in sustaining himself to the end in three or four poems of some compass, but his noblest work in verse must be sought in those quatrains which need no context for their comprehension and might be called spiritual ejaculations. Matthew Arnold has quoted for approval the two familiar stanzas,

> So nigh is grandeur to our dust,
> So near is God to man,
> When Duty whispers low, *Thou must*,
> The youth replies, *I can.*

and,

> Though love repine and reason chafe,
> There came a voice without reply:
> "'Tis man's perdition to be safe,
> When for the truth he ought to die."

These quatrains are, he says, "exceptional" in Emerson. They are that, and something more: they are exceptional in literature. One would have to search far to find anything in English equal to them in their own kind. They have the cleanness and radiance of the couplets of Simonides. They may look easy, but as a matter of fact the ethical epigram is an extremely difficult *genre*, and to attain this union of gravity and simplicity requires the nicest art. Less epigrammatic in tone but even more exquisitely finished are the lines entitled *Days*, pre-eminent in his works for what may truly be called a haunting beauty:

> Daughters of Time, the hypocritic Days,
> Muffled and dumb like barefoot dervishes,
> And marching single in an endless file,
> Bring diadems and faggots in their hands.
> To each they offer gifts after his will,
> Bread, kingdoms, stars, and sky that holds them all.
> I, in my pleachèd garden, watched the pomp,
> Forgot my morning wishes, hastily
> Took a few herbs and apples, and the Day
> Turned and departed silent. I, too late,
> Under her solemn fillet saw the scorn.

And as his verse, so is his prose. Though in one sense, so far as he writes always with two or three dominant ideas in his mind, he is one of the most consistent and persistent of expositors, yet he is really himself only in those moments of inspiration when his words strike with almost irresistible force on the heart, and awake an echoing response: "This is true; this I have myself dimly felt." Sometimes the memorable paragraph or sentence is purely didactic; sometimes it is highly metaphorical, as is the case with the closing paragraph of the *Conduct of Life:*

> There is no chance, and no anarchy, in the universe. All is system and gradation. Every god is there sitting in his sphere. The young mortal enters the hall of the firmament; there is he alone with them alone, they pouring on him benedictions and gifts, and beckoning him up to their thrones. On the instant, and incessantly, fall snowstorms of illusions. He fancies himself in a vast crowd which sways this way and that, and whose movement and doings

he must obey: he fancies himself poor, orphaned, insignificant. The mad crowd drives hither and thither, now furiously command- ing this thing to be done, now that. What is he that he should resist their will, and think or act for himself? Every moment, new changes, and new showers of deceptions, to baffle and distract him. And when, by and by, for an instant, the air clears, and the cloud lifts a little, there are the gods still sitting around him on their thrones,—they alone with him alone.

There is, it need scarcely be said, a good deal in the works of Emerson—literary criticism, characterization of men and movements, reflection on the state of society—which lies out- side of this ethical category; but even in such essays his guiding ideas are felt in the background. Nor are these ideas hard to discover. The whole circle of them, ever revolving upon itself, is likely to be present, explicit or implicit, in any one of his great passages, as it is in the paragraph just cited—the clear call to self-reliance, announcing that "a man should learn to detect and watch that gleam of light which flashes across his mind from within"; the firm assurance that, through all the balanced play of circumstance, "there is a deeper fact in the soul than compensation, to wit, its own nature"; the intuition, despite all the mists of illusion, of the Over-Soul which is above us and still ourselves: "We live in succession, in division, in parts, in particles; meanwhile within man is the soul of the whole; the wise silence; the universal beauty . . .; the eternal *One*."

Emerson's philosophy is thus a kind of reconciled dualism, and a man's attitude towards it in the end will be determined by his sense of its sufficiency or insufficiency to meet the facts of experience. One of Emerson's biographers has attempted to set forth this philosophy as "a synthesis and an anticipation." It is a synthesis because in it we find, as Emerson had already found in Plato and Plotinus, a reconciliation of "the many and the one," the everlasting flux and the motionless calm at the heart of things:

An ample and generous recognition of this transiency and slipperiness both in the nature of things and in man's soul seems more and more a necessary ingredient in any estimate of the uni- verse which shall satisfy the intellect of the coming man. But it seems equally true that the coming man who shall resolve our problems will never content himself with a universe a-tilt, a universe in cascade, so to speak; the craving for permanence in some form cannot be jauntly evaded. Is there any known mind which fore-shadows the desired combination so clearly as Emerson's? Who has felt more profoundly the evanescence and evasiveness of things? . . . Yet Emerson was quite as firm in his insistence on a single unalterable reality as in his refusal to believe that any aspect or estimate of that reality could be final.[1]

The necessity of the dualism that underlies Emerson's philosophy could scarcely be put more neatly, and the kind of synthesis, or reconciliation, in which Emerson floated is admirably expressed. But it is not so plain that this synthesis antici-pates the solution of the troublesome problems of life. There will be those who will ask whether the power of religion for mature minds does not depend finally on its feeling for evil. How otherwise, in fact, shall religion meet those harder questions of experience when its aid is most needed? And in like manner they will say that the power of philosophy as the *dux vitae* depends on its acquaintance with the scope and difficulties of scepticism. Both religion and philosophy would seem, in such a view, to rest not only on a statement of the dualism of good and evil, knowledge and ignorance, but on a realization of the full meaning and gravity, practical and intellectual, of this dualism. Now Emerson certainly recognizes the dualism of experience, but it is a fair question whether he realizes its full meaning and seriousness. He accepts it a trifle too jauntly, is reconciled to its existence with no apparent pang, is sometimes too ready to wave aside its consequences, as if a statement of the fact were an escape from its terrible perplexities. Carlyle meant something of the sort when he worried over Emerson's inability to see the hand of the devil in human life. Hence it is that Emerson often loses value for his admirers in proportion to their maturity and experience. He is above all the poet of religion and philosophy for the young; whereas men, as they grow older, are inclined to turn from him, in their more serious moods, to those sages who have supple-mented insight with a firm grasp of the darker facts of human nature. That is undoubtedly true; nevertheless, as time passes, the deficiencies of this brief period of New England, of which

[1] O. W. Firkins. *Ralph Waldo Emerson*, p. 364.

Emerson was the perfect spokesman, may well be more and more condoned for its rarity and beauty. One of the wings of the spirit is hope, and nowhere is there to be found a purer hope than in the books of our New England sage; rather, it might be said that he went beyond hope to the assurance of present happiness. The world had never before seen anything quite of this kind, and may not see its like again.

INDEX

376 Index

Index 377

THE CAMBRIDGE HISTORY

OF

AMERICAN LITERATURE

Volume II

Early National Literature: Part II
Later National Literature: Part I

The Cambridge History

of

American Literature

Edited by

William Peterfield Trent

John Erskine

Stuart P. Sherman

Carl Van Doren

In Three Volumes

Early National Literature: Part II
Later National Literature: Part I

MACMILLAN PUBLISHING CO., INC.

New York

PREFACE

*T*HE *Cambridge History of American Literature* was originally planned to appear in two volumes, but the abundance of the material submitted and the importance of
having the biography comprehensive and practically complete,
made it necessary for the publishers to extend the work to four.

In the later volumes, the editors have found increasing
difficulty in connection with the problem of how far to include
living writers, some of whom could not be omitted without
making the record obviously inaccurate. We have felt justified
in dealing with certain contemporaries who before 1900 had
written notable books and who have exerted important influence in our literary history, even when, as for example in the
case of Professor Brander Matthews, these writers have, as
contributors, been associated with the present work to the
advantage of the readers and to our own satisfaction.

THE EDITORS.

May 1, 1918.

CONTENTS

Contents

Contents

CHAPTER XXII
DIVINES AND MORALISTS, 1783–1860

By Samuel Lee Wolff, Ph.D., Instructor in English, Extension Teaching, Columbia University.

CHAPTER XXIII
WRITERS OF FAMILIAR VERSE

By Brander Matthews, D.C.L., Litt.D., LL.D., Professor of Dramatic Literature in Columbia University.

CHAPTER XXIV
LOWELL

By Ashley H. Thorndike, Ph.D., L.H.D., Professor of English in Columbia University.

BOOK III
LATER NATIONAL LITERATURE: PART I

CHAPTER I
WHITMAN

By Emory Holloway, A.M., Assistant Professor of English in Adelphi College.

Contents

CHAPTER II

POETS OF THE CIVIL WAR I: THE NORTH

By WILL D. HOWE.

CHAPTER III

POETS OF THE CIVIL WAR II: THE SOUTH

By EDWIN MIMS, Ph.D., Professor of English in Vanderbilt University.

CHAPTER IV

THE NEW SOUTH: LANIER

By DUDLEY MILES, Ph.D., Chairman of the Department of English in the Evander Childs High School, New York City.

Contents

Book II (*Continued*)

CHAPTER X

Thoreau

THE life of a village community is not seldom enriched by the inclusion of a rebel, an original who refuses obstinately to conform to type, and succeeds in following out his idea, in contrast to the humdrum routine of his fellows. When the community happens to be Concord, the picturesque and historic village where the Revolution began, the Weimar of American literature, and when the rebel happens to be an American faun, the conjunction must result in no ordinary enrichment. There on 12 July, 1817, just after the second war with Britain, David Henry Thoreau was born to a small farmer and artisan who kept a shop and painted signs. The French-looking surname came by way of the Channel Islands, for the author's grandfather was born in Jersey, and, in spite of his British origin, had served as a sailor in a Continental privateer. Thoreau passed his life in the village of his birth, and now his name is indissolubly associated with it.

For a generation which plumes itself upon its "breadth," no slight effort is needed to picture the life of a typical New England village before the Transcendental movement had broken up the hard old Puritanic crust. It was a rigid and limited life made up of work, thrift, duty, and meetings. Caricatured and ridiculed though it be, that old stern life moulded men and women of the toughest moral and intellectual fibre. Puritanism was an intellectual creed, and led directly to the cultivation of the intellect. The minister and the schoolmaster were twin ruling powers. None questioned the value of education; it was almost a fetish. So as a child in a Puritan community, Henry Thoreau followed the regular routine of the common school until he was ripe for the university.

Thoreau became a man of letters, but he was also a wild man, a faun; he became Emerson's man, and—although it is rather difficult to fit into the picture—he was a Harvard man. He went up at sixteen and took his degree at twenty. His portrait at this time shows a smooth, grave face dominated by a Roman nose and overhung by a bush of fine brown hair. What benefit he derived from his college years is a matter both of record and of inference. "What I was learning in college was chiefly, I think, to express myself," he writes five years after leaving Harvard. Perhaps the most significant memorial of his college career is the Latin letter he wrote to his sister Helen, in 1840. It gave him pleasure to use the language of Virgil and Cicero, for one of the many paradoxes in Thoreau's life was the union of true American contempt for tradition with an unaffected love of the classics. After a diatribe against the narrow religiosity of New England, he draws breath to praise "the Ionian father of the rest," with the enthusiasm of Keats.

There are few books which deserve to be remembered in our wisest hours, but the Iliad is brightest in the serenest days, and embodies still all the sunlight that fell in Asia Minor. No modern joy or ecstasy of ours can lower its height, or dim its lustre, but there it lies in the east of literature, as it were the earliest and latest production of the mind.

From the wildwood simplicity of Walden, he startles the reader with deliverances which might have come from the Bodleian.

Those who have not learned to read the ancient classics in the language in which they were written must have a very imperfect knowledge of the history of the human race. . . . Homer has never been printed in English, nor Æschylus, nor Virgil even,—works as refined, as solidly done, as beautiful almost as the morning itself; for later writers, say what we will of their genius, have rarely if ever equalled the elaborate beauty and finish and the lifelong and heroic literary labours of the ancients.

Thoreau translated the *Prometheus Vinctus* and tried his hand at Pindar. His pages are sown with classical allusions and quotations. The sunset at Cape Cod brings a line of Homer into his memory "with a rush," as the shining torch of the sun falls into the ocean. He has words of just appreciation for Anacreon. His odes

charm us by their serenity and freedom from exaggeration and passion, and by a certain flower-like beauty, which does not propose itself, but must be approached and studied like a natural object.

Such genuine admiration for Greek genius is rare at any time, and certainly not many American hands could have been busy translating Æschylus, Pindar, and Anacreon in the hurried forties and fifties of the nineteenth century. This large and solid academic basis for Thoreau's culture is not generally observed. His devotion to the Greeks rings truer than his various utterances on Indian literature and philosophy. Besides, he was well seen in the English classics from Chaucer downwards. A few pages of *A Week* yield quotations from Emerson, Ovid, Quarles, Channing, *Relations des Jesuits*, Gower, Lydgate, Virgil, Tennyson, Percy's *Reliques*, Byron, Milton, Shakespeare, Spenser, Simonides. As Lowell remarks, "His literature was extensive and recondite." The truth is, Thoreau was a man of letters, whose great ambition was to study and to write books.

During and after his college career, Thoreau taught school, like the hero of *Elsie Venner*. He is quite frank about this episode. "As I did not teach for the good of my fellow-men, but simply for a livelihood, this was a failure." Brief as was his apprenticeship to the schoolmaster trade, one might possibly conjecture that it left some mark upon him. The many citations of recondite literature do not escape the suspicion of parade and pedantry. There is a certain gusto with which he inserts the botanical name of a plant after the picturesque vernacular, and distinguishes between *Rana palustris* and *Rana pipiens*. In general, the tone he adopts towards the world is that of the pedagogue dealing habitually with inferior minds.

After his college days comes an episode which his biographers seem inclined to slur over, perhaps from a false sense of the dignity of biography, and that is the two years, from 25 April.

1841, to May, 1843, which Thoreau spent under Emerson's roof. By the time Thoreau left Harvard, Emerson had become a power in the spiritual life of America. His brief career as a Unitarian minister was already far behind him; he had made his pilgrimage to Europe; he had penetrated the wilds of Scotland to Craigenputtock because one Thomas Carlyle, another unrecognized genius, lived there. He had given in Boston those lectures on *Great Men* and *The Philosophy of History* which foreshadow the great address commonly called the declaration of independence for American literature.[1] He had brought out his Scottish friend's odd book, *Sartor Resartus*, a publication which accelerated the Transcendental movement. Emerson discovered the youth Thoreau as a true poet, and communicated the discovery in a letter to Carlyle. Thoreau became a member of Emerson's household, apparently as general "help," a relationship which all Americans will understand but which will be the despair of Europeans.

> The most practical and handy person in all matters of every day life, a good mechanic and gardener, methodical in his habits, observant and kindly in the domestic world,

is the character Emerson gives him. There must have been a cash nexus, but the essence of the relationship was the tie uniting master and pupil, sage and disciple. This long and close association with the great literary force of that time had no slight effect in moulding Thoreau's character and determining his bent.

His biographer, who knew him personally, says that he imitated Emerson's tones and manners so that it was annoying to listen to him.

The imitation of Emerson in Thoreau's writing is equally apparent. Lowell saw and condemned it in his criticism of *A Week*. In prose there is the sentence which reads like an oracle. It may be the profoundest wisdom, or it may be the merest matter of moonshine. When Thoreau writes "Ancient history has an air of antiquity," or, "Give me a sentence which no intelligence can understand," the critic can only fall

[1] See Book II, Chap. IX.

back on the Gilbertian comment upon the young man who "expresses himself in terms too deep for me." The imitation of Emerson's poetry is even more marked and results in what Lowell calls Thoreau's "worsification." He had no candid friend to tell him what Dryden told "Cousin Swift." There was, on the other hand, no little benefit in mere contact with such a personality as Emerson, much more in continual and close intercourse with him. The stimulus to thought must have been most potent, and Emerson's influence could not but stiffen Thoreau in his natural independence and confirm him in his design of living his own life.

The village rebel who will not conform rebels first against the local religion. It is the obvious thing to rebel against. What Thoreau dissented from was New England Puritanism, as is plainly shown in "Sunday" of *A Week*. The atmosphere of that lost religion hangs about the letter of his roommate at Harvard, who became a minister in due course. One thinks of the letters young Mr. Tennyson of Trinity was exchanging with other Cambridge "Apostles" about the same time. The salutation is "Friend Thoreau," which seems to have been the accepted convention at the time. Perhaps the most significant sentence in it runs:

I hear that you are comfortably located in your native town, as the guardian of its children, in the immediate vicinity, I suppose, of one of our most distinguished apostles of the future, R. W. Emerson, and situated under the ministry of our old friend Reverend Barzillai Frost, to whom please make my remembrances.

It does not appear that Thoreau after reaching manhood was ever "situated under the ministry" of the Reverend Barzillai Frost. In "Civil Disobedience," he writes:

Some years ago, the State met me on behalf of the Church and commanded me to pay a certain sum toward the support of a clergyman, whose preaching my father attended, but never I myself. "Pay" it said, "or be locked up in jail." I declined to pay. But unfortunately, another man saw fit to pay it.

The recusant even rendered the authorities a reason in writing for his recusancy.

Know all men by these presents that I Henry Thoreau do not wish to be regarded as a member of any incorporated society which I have not joined.

Opposition to the State followed naturally on opposition to the Church. To his honour, Thoreau took a stand against slavery when it was anything but popular to do so, even in the State of Massachusetts. In all his words on this theme there is a fire not to be found elsewhere. What roused him was the spectacle of fugitive slaves escaping to the free North, and, through the action of Northern courts, dragged back into slavery. The State was clearly in the wrong; Thoreau, in his own phrase, "declared war on the State," by refusing to pay his poll-tax. He believed that such passive resistance by a number of taxpayers would bring about the abolition of slavery. He was therefore quite consistent with himself when he stood forth from the crowd as the champion of John Brown in his history-making raid on Harper's Ferry. Public opinion, North and South, condemned the raid as the outrage of a fanatic attempting to kindle a servile war. Thoreau was of the remnant who saw its true bearing.

It was in the first year of his Walden hermitage that Thoreau was arrested and lodged in jail for refusing to pay his poll-tax. He tells how he was going to the cobbler's, with a shoe to be mended, when the Law laid hold of him, how he spent the evening very pleasantly with the other inmates of the lock-up, how he was released next morning, and immediately started off with a berry-picking party. This "grand refusal" struck the imagination of Stevenson, who considers it the most significant act of Thoreau, and more important than his retreat in Walden. A parallel might be found in Stevenson's account of his brief incarceration in a French prison in the epilogue to *An Inland Voyage*. Again, some friend paid Thoreau's poll-tax for him, but he never wavered in his reasoned policy of passive resistance to an unjust, slavery-supporting State. At the same time, he never refused to pay the highway tax, because, "I am as desirous of being a good neighbour as I am of being a bad subject." "I simply wish," he continues, "to refuse allegiance to the State, to withdraw and stand aloof from it effectually."

His next step was a more remote withdrawal, an attempt to stand aloof from his kind. It was an attempt to live by himself and to himself, in fact, to turn modern hermit. Apparently the idea had long been germinating in his mind. On that far-off Harvard commencement of 1837, he took part in a "conference," an obsolete academic exercise resembling a medieval "disputation." He took one side of an argument and a fellow-student, afterwards a judge, maintained the opposite. The subject debated was "The Commercial Spirit." In his set speech, the grave, shock-headed graduate from Concord suggested that

the order of things should be somewhat reversed; the seventh should be man's day of toil, wherein to earn his living by the sweat of his brow; and the other six his Sabbath of the affections and the soul— in which to range this widespread garden, and drink in the soft influences and sublime revelations of Nature.

The young collegian's division of time may have provoked a smile, but the day was to come when he was to make the actual experiment. Thoreau had turned against the Church, he had turned against the State, and now he turned against organized society. He perceived that man was bound to the wheel of circumstance, he was the passive, unquestioning slave of a vain and sordid routine. One man at least would wrench himself free from the mill at which he saw his fellows ceaselessly toiling. He would carry out his boyhood's dream, and, by reorganization of his life, obtain freedom for the things that matter. By making life more simple, he would cheat circumstance and really begin to live.

I dream of looking abroad summer and winter, with free gaze from some mountainside, while my eyes revolve in an Egyptian slime of health—I to be nature looking into nature with such easy sympathy as the blue-eyed grass in the meadow looks in the face of the sky. From such recess, I would put forth sublime thoughts daily, as the plant puts forth leaves.

It only remained to choose his "recess."

Apparently the suggestion as to the particular recess came from his friend, Channing, who writes,

I see nothing for you in this earth but that field which I once christened "Briars"; go out upon that, build yourself a hut, and there begin the grand process of devouring yourself alive.

Thoreau was a natural ascetic. He ate little flesh meat, but subsisted almost entirely on vegetable food; he drank nothing but water; he never married. He refers in a letter to a nameless lady who wished to marry *him*, and he calls the inverted courtship "tragic." In the Age of Faith he would have fled to the wilderness for the same reason that he built his hut by Walden pond, in order to save his soul. Salvation for him meant escape from endless labour for the acquisition of useless things. By another paradox of his career, he freed himself from New England thrift by being still more thrifty. By denying himself and faring more scantily than his neighbours, he secured leisure for pursuits they could not comprehend. Thoreau is a prophet of the simple life, perhaps the first in America. He uses the very term.

I do believe in simplicity. When the mathematician would solve a difficult problem, he first frees the equation from all encumbrances, and reduces it to its simplest terms. So simplify the problem of life, distinguish the necessary and the real.

He was preaching to his friend Blake what he had already practised. He had felled the pines with his borrowed axe, and dug his cellar, and built his

tight shingled and plastered house, ten feet wide by fifteen long, and eight feet posts, with a garret and a closet, a large window on each side, two trap-doors, one door at the end, and a brick fireplace opposite.

It was a little smaller than the room he occupied at Harvard. The materials cost less than twenty-nine dollars; and by cultivating beans and other vegetables he was able to support himself at an annual expense of a little more than eight dollars. This was removing the encumbrances from the equation, with a vengeance, but Thoreau could make a "dinner" of berries. The experiment lasted from March, 1845, until September, 1847, and then having satisfied himself that the thing could be done, he gave it up.

Two years later, Thoreau published his first book, *A Week on the Concord and Merrimack Rivers*. The actual voyage was performed by the two brothers Henry and John in the late summer of 1839 in a boat of their own making, "painted green below with a border of blue, with reference to the two elements in which it was to spend its existence." During his Walden retirement, Thoreau worked over the original record of his pleasant outing, expanding it greatly by the inclusion of very various material, and had it published at his own risk by Monroe in 1849. It was the year of the Argonauts, of the gold-rush to California, and such literary treasure as the odd book contained was not much regarded. Though favourably reviewed by Ripley and by Lowell, it did not please the public, and over seven hundred copies out of an impression of one thousand were thrown back on the author's hands. It is another of the paradoxes of Thoreau's career that since his death, this failure has been edited with almost benedictine care.

Lowell's praise of *A Week* can hardly be termed excessive. After dwelling on its weak points, its lack of unity, its imitation of Emerson, its dolorous verse, he continues,

the prose work is done conscientiously and neatly. The style is compact and the language has an antique purity like wine grown colourless with age.

The truth is that Thoreau with all his genuine appreciation of the classics never learned their lessons of proportion, restraint, "nothing too much." Nor was the example of his master Emerson likely to correct his own tendency to formlessness. The principle of selection is absent. The week's excursion is only an excuse for including Emersonian essays on friendship and chastity, or dissertations on the Laws of Menu, or translations of Anacreon, till the reader asks resentfully what they are doing in this dory-modelled *galère*, painted green below with a border of blue, on the Merrimack and Concord, lucid streams. If he had possessed the artistic instinct of Stevenson, or had undergone Stevenson's rigid self-imposed discipline in the writer's craft, he might have made *A Week* as complete a little masterpiece as *An Inland Voyage*. *A Week* fails on account of its scattering aim. It is neither a record of a week's excursion, nor a book of essays, but a jumble of the two. Thoreau's American contempt for tradition accounts for the artistic failure.

Where Thoreau is not the transcendental essayist, but the first-hand observer of nature, he is delightful. When discoursing on such a theme as the common sunfish, the reader wishes he would never end.

The breams are so careful of their charge that you may stand close by in the water and examine them at your leisure. I have stood over them half an hour at a time, and stroked them familiarly without frightening them, suffering them to nibble my fingers harmlessly, and seen them erect their dorsal fins in anger when my hand approached their ova, and have even gently taken them out of the water with my hand. . . . As you stand thus stooping over the bream in its nest, the edges of the dorsal and caudal fins have a singular dusty golden reflection, and its eyes, which stand out from its head, are transparent and colourless. Seen in its native element, it is a very beautiful and compact fish, perfect in all its parts, and looks like a brilliant coin fresh from the mint.

If the whole book had been of this texture, it would be a classic. Another element in the book which Thoreau valued slightly—those incidental glimpses of a vanished America—will be prized by later generations. His accounts of the mountain people he discovered, of the girl combing her black hair, of his surly host, Rice, and his strange inn, of the old farmer praying in the dim morning pasture, of the canal boatmen, of the lockmen's house, and the small-voiced but sincere hospitality of the Yankee housewife offering the obsolete refreshment of "molasses and ginger," read like pages Irving forgot to put into *The Sketch Book*. These things are seen with the naturalist's clear grave eyes and recorded in plain words with no attempt at oracular profundity. For the sake of more such true pictures of reality, how gladly would the modern reader forego the disquisitions on Persius and Ossian.

The next year, 1850, Thoreau and his friend Channing made a brief raid across the border into Quebec, though the record of his experience was not published until 1866, with the title *A Yankee in Canada*. Stevenson found the book dull.

Still, it has an interest of its own for the light it sheds on Thoreau's peculiar temperament, and particularly on his robust Americanism, a sentiment based on traditional dislike of Britain and on contempt for monarchy as an effete institution. Patriotism is a curious passion. It does not seem possible to love one's own country except by hating some other country. Emerson defines Thoreau almost in these terms:

> No truer American existed than Thoreau. His preference of his country and condition was genuine, and his aversion from English and European manners and tastes almost reached contempt.

With no great love for the institutions of his own land, he showed his instinctive preference for them during his one brief sojourn under an alien flag. His attitude throughout is one of consistent patronage to all he sees and hears. The red-coats in the citadel at Quebec have the manhood drilled out of them. Britain, he believes, is "red in the knuckles" with holding on to the Canadas, and must soon relax her grasp. Towards the great mystery of historical Christianity, he is equally contemptuous. The devout worshippers in the Cathedral at Montreal, absorbed in prayer and regardless of gazing strangers, suggest the parallel of his fellow Yankees going to meeting on a week-day, after the cattle-fair. The Sisters of Charity whom he saw in the street looked as if they had cried their eyes out, "insulting the daylight with their presence." That the soldier and the religious had something valuable to which he was a stranger, never occurred to him. In other words, he was blind to the romance of war and the poetry of faith. Even the natural courtesy of the *habitants* seems to him mere servility. For the American of Thoreau's generation, history began with the musketry of the embattled farmers at Concord bridge. Before that day, there was only a dark welter of wicked kings and mad tories. These limitations prevented him from realizing, as Parkman did, the epic struggle which ended on the Plains of Abraham. He indeed transcribes the inscription on the monument to Wolfe and Montcalm, but the splendour and pathos of their fate leave him unmoved. Still, this rigid and narrow provincialism gives salt to his books and explains his revolt against convention.

It was his Americanism which drove Thoreau to realize himself in his own way.

In 1854, Thoreau published the book by which he will always be best known, *Walden, or Life in the Woods*. It is by far the deepest, richest, and most closely jointed of his books. It shows Thoreau at his best, and contains all that he had to say to the world. In fact, he is a man of one book, and that book is *Walden*. In plan, it is open to the same objection as *A Week*, and might almost plead guilty to the charge of obtaining a hearing under false pretences. "Life in the woods" suggests the atmosphere of *As You Like It* and the Robin Hood ballads, but not moralizings on economy and the duty of being yourself. The reader who takes up the book with the idea that he is going to enjoy another *Robinson Crusoe* will not be pleased to find that every now and then he will have to listen to a lay sermon, or a lyceum lecture.

Still it is the adventurous, *Robinson Crusoe* part that is imperishable. How a man resolved to live in a new way, how he borrowed an axe and began felling pines on the ground that sloped southward to a wonderful pond, how he trimmed his rafters, dug his cellar, bought an Irish labourer's shanty, transported the materials to a new site and raised the frame, appeal to the open-air instinct of every man. Even how he maintained the fire on the hearth, and grubbed out the fat pine roots to feed it, are matters of absorbing interest. His struggle with the weeds and poor soil of the two-acre patch on which he raised his beans and potatoes, every item of his various accounts, his food, his daily routine, his house-cleaning, have the fascination of a narrative by Defoe. The reader follows the solitary in his swim across the lake, or through the wood to the village, or about the hut, or along the rows of beans, with a zest he can hardly explain to himself. The reason is that Henry Thoreau in Walden wood is the same as the mariner of York on the Island of Desolation; he represents once more the struggle of primitive man to obtain food and shelter, in fact the epic of civilization. The interest of the theme is perennial.

Walden is also the memorial of an American faun, of a wild man who lived in the woods, who carried an umbrella like Robinson Crusoe, to weatherfend his head, and used a microscope to study insects with. About the same time, just after leaving Harvard, Thoreau found his first arrowhead and began his first journal, and the two streams of tendency ran side by side in his nature till the end. Intercourse with nature was even more necessary to Thoreau than intercourse with books. Intercourse with human beings he thought he did not need, but he was always tramping off to the village for a chat. He was not a real solitary, for visitors were always coming to view the progress of the odd experiment in living. Still Thoreau differed widely from the ordinary gregarious man in that he could manage to be alone for long periods with the woods and the sky. A friend called him a poet-naturalist; but the description is not exact. He hardly views nature as a poet, and he is surpassed by not a few observers of nature, who have had the stimulus of Darwin. The merely pictorial in nature does not much interest him, probably because he had seen no pictures. To Thoreau nature is no divinity as she is to Wordsworth; she is simply the pleasantest of companions, or rather the pleasantest environment for a natural man. In a house, in a town, he is like a creature caged. It is characteristic that after swimming across the lake, he would sit in his doorway all morning, "in a wise passiveness," as Wordsworth would term it. So wild creatures live in the wild, when not hunger-driven. The wild things found him to be of their own kind; a mouse made friends with him, a hen partridge led her brood about his hut, he could take a fish out of the water in his hand. Thoreau is perhaps the first to suggest the pleasure of hunting animals without a gun, of learning about them without any desire to kill. He was not influenced by Darwin, or such a conception as the struggle for existence. Nature to him was not red in tooth and claw with ravin; it was a gentle, friendly, peaceful alternative to the mean greed and futile toil of man. The atmosphere of Walden is always serene and free from cloud or storm. Rain and winter come in their season; but they never seem to touch him; the rain does not wet, and the winter does not chill. There may be a thousand nooks in New England more beautiful than Walden, but they remain unknown, while the pine-clad slope which this strange being discovered and haunted for two years is charted as a permanent addition to the world-wide map of Romance.

Thoreau has two styles, the oracular and the simple; and

in *Walden* the simple prevails. Like the water of the pond, it is clear, colourless and wholesome. Thoreau is a careful writer, with an instinct for the right word which was developed and strengthened by a lifelong devotion to the best books. His love of the classics must have tended to purify his style and increase its natural dignity. *Walden* is generally free from oracular phrases and grotesque locutions like "eyes revolve in an Egyptian slime of health." It must always retain the deep unfailing value of all autobiography, personal memoirs, "confessions." The record of a life will never fail of an audience. When a man declares, "Thus I did, thus I thought, thus I felt," other men are always eager to attend his tale.

The Walden experiment was not unlike the other Transcendental experiment of Brook Farm. Both were declarations of independence; both were attempts to place life on a new basis; both broke down. The Greek dog-sage in his tub, the English Quaker in his suit of leather, the Yankee land-surveyor in his wooden hut are three object lessons to the world of the ancient truth that "a man's life consisteth not in the abundance of the things that he possesseth." The Walden experiment is open to all the criticism of Lowell: "it presupposed all the complicated civilization which it theoretically abjured." Even for Thoreau it was not a success. In the first year, his Homer lay open on the table, but he was so busy that he could only read it by snatches; in the second year, he was forced to set up a prosaic stove in the place of the romantic fire-place. Thoreau's ideal of a world of book men, or contemplatives, is a dream. Still, the experience of the ascetic always shames the grossness of the worldly wiseman. If a man can live for a year for eight dollars, we certainly spend too much on things we could do without. Thoreau's experiment will always have its appeal to hot, ambitious spirits on their first awakening to the intricacy of life. The hero of *Locksley Hall* longs to escape from civilization to summer isles of Eden. At least one American man of letters has followed Thoreau's example by going into retreat.

After living in his hut for two years, Thoreau supported himself for three more by cultivating his garden, like Candide. Thus he obtained the freedoms he desired, the leisure to think, and to read, and to write, and to be himself. Then he went back to his land-surveying, his communing with the spirits of the wild, and the compilation of his voluminous journals. From the latter, several volumes have been quarried for the definitive edition of his works. They must always be of more interest to the admirer of Thoreau and the student of literature than to the general reader.

Then came the break-down of his health. It was the irony of fate that the man who lived according to nature, who obeyed the dictates of spare temperance, who never seemed to tire, should die of tuberculosis, the scourge of civilized life. His latest portrait, a daguerreotype taken in New Bedford, seven months before his death, shows a hairy, innocent, pathetic face; the eyes have the mute appeal of the consumptive. In 1861, the stricken man made a trip to the West, in the vain hope of restoration to health by change of air. He died in his birth-place, Concord, on 2 May, 1862, in the second year of the Civil War. He has been blamed for expressing his sense of detachment from that terrible conflict, but if, like Mercutio, he cries, "A plague on both your houses!" it must be remembered that, like Mercutio, he was a dying man. His last letter, dictated to his sister, concludes, "I am enjoying existence as much as ever, and regret nothing."

Emerson has written an appreciation of Thoreau with intimate knowledge and tender humanity. To that estimate, little can be added, or taken away. Lowell and Stevenson have appraised his character and his work, none too gently. Of himself he said, "I am a mystic, a Transcendentalist, and a natural philosopher."

CHAPTER XI

Hawthorne

THE romances of Hawthorne can hardly be understood apart from the current of Transcendentalism in which his genius was formed. Most foreigners and many of his countrymen have thought of him as an affectionate student of the New England past, in a small way comparable to Scott with his love of Border history, and especially they have thought of him as a kind of portrait painter, who magically resharpened for us the already fading lineaments of Puritanism. Reflection might suggest, however, that the portrait he restored bears an unlucky resemblance in its sombreness and its unloveliness to the portrait of Edward Randolph in the *Twice Told Tales*, and a little further thought would perhaps convince us that Hawthorne usually treats Puritanism, not as the central theme in his canvas, but as a dark background for the ideas and for the experiences which more deeply concern him. Those ideas and experiences have little to do with Puritanism except by contrast; they were partly furnished to his imagination by the enthusiastic but uncritical thinkers among his acquaintance who kindled rapturously at Alcott's conversations or basked in the indefiniteness of Emerson's lectures, and partly they were furnished by his own contact with Alcott and Emerson and with their writings. Like them, he was less a Puritan than a lover of the present, and if he seemed often to deal with things long past, it was only because he had the faculty, more than other men, of recognizing in the present whatever had served its purpose or was worn out or dead.

But if as a Transcendentalist he stood aloof from Puritanism, his temperament forced him to stand aloof also from the other

Transcendentalists. Although their philosophy, as they liked to say, was a "questioning" of life, he differed from them all in being a true skeptic. To be quite precise, let us say that he drew the inspiration of his romances not so much from their ideas as from the neglected but inevitable conclusions of their ideas. Alcott and Emerson uttered between them a set of doctrines so full of apparent contradictions as to seem almost double-faced. They preached the sacredness of fact as against the authority of tradition; they made much of physical heredity, of evolution, of fate; they pointed out the inadequacy of any moral scheme to comprehend all the surprises of nature; yet being inveterate optimists, both of them, and both at certain moments curiously mystical, and both enjoying an outward orthodoxy of manners and culture, they soothed their hearers and seemed less dangerous than they were. Their sincerity, of course, was unquestionable, but they obscured even to themselves the startling conclusions of their own surmises, and having shaken their moral world to its foundation, they allowed the structure to settle again, and all this in such a glamour of temperamental cheerfulness that those who felt only the eloquence of their mood could depart conscious of spiritual uplift, and none but the few who attended to the implications of their specific ideas went away troubled. How few these critics were is attested by the lonely position in which their spokesman, Hawthorne, seems to stand. He was no mystic; what attracted him in Transcendentalism was its free inquiry, its radicalism, its contact with actual life. In his stories, therefore, he was a philosophical experimenter, in whose method was no room for optimism nor for prepossessions of any kind; he had recourse to life in order to try out the efficacy or the consequences of Transcendental ideas, and if the result was hardly what he expected, he still pursued the hypothesis to the bitter end. He was really the questioner, the detached observer, that other Transcendentalists thought they were. The soul, Emerson had said, "accepts whatever befalls, as part of its lesson. It is a watcher more than a doer, and it is a doer only that it may the better watch." The description is truer of Hawthorne's soul than of Emerson's. In accepting whatever befalls, Emerson was convinced, as he says in the essay on *Circles*, that there is a saccharine principle

in all things; small wonder that Hawthorne seems an alien
among such cheerful sages. When Emerson says that either
love or crime leads all souls to the good, that there is no straight
line in nature, that evil in the end will bless, Hawthorne examines the doctrine somewhat dubiously in Hepzibah and
Clifford Pyncheon and in Donatello; and when the cheerful
philosopher tells us to trust ourselves, to follow our own nature,
to live from the Devil if we are the Devil's children, Hawthorne
projects the advice experimentally in *The Scarlet Letter* and in
The Blithedale Romance.

Those who classify Hawthorne in a loose way as the
romancer of Puritanism sometimes speak of him also as a psychologist. The term needs defining. To him, as to other Transcendentalists, the fortune of a human soul was the most critical
of experiences, comparatively negligible were the doings of
society as a whole or the outward panorama of events and
scenes. If to be thus interested in the soul is to be a psychologist, then Hawthorne was one, as to some extent are all
who write of human nature. But if the term denotes attention
to motives and to fine mental processes, to the anatomy, as
it were, of character, then Hawthorne was no such psychologist
as, let us say, Henry James or George Meredith. It is important to realize how broad and general his ideas and his art were,
how completely he avoided the special and the minute. He
studied no subtle character, nor any character subtly. He was
a moralist rather than a psychologist. Were it not sufficiently
evident in the stories themselves, the notes preserved in his
journals would show that his imagination was engaged first
by a moral idea, which he afterwards incorporated in plot and
in persons. When he is most successful the plot seems actually
to occur, and the persons really live; when his imagination
fails him, the incidents seem allegorical and the figures become
shadowy; but in either case the abstract idea from which he
started is likely to be clear enough, and his own personality
will probably be felt as standing outside the story, looking on.
Since he is neither novelist nor preacher, but only an investigator of moral ideas, it is equally beside the mark to expect of
him Balzac's sense of the social panorama, or Bunyan's certi-
tude of faith.

A writer who pictures life chiefly in order to project abstract ideas is not likely to reveal in his art more of himself than his general disposition. Hawthorne's biography makes rich and human reading, for he was an admirable man in all ways and his private life was in the best sense fortunate; if at first he endured poverty, he earned success later, and even in the obscure years he had the admiration of loyal friends. But only in a few instances does his biography aid directly in the understanding of his works, and then for the most part by explaining his contact with Transcendental ideas. Of the non-literary events in his life it is enough to say that he was born in Salem, Massachusetts, 4 July, 1804, of an old New England family; that after his father's death he was educated by his mother's brothers, and in 1825 he was graduated from Bowdoin College; that among his classmates he made three lifelong friends—Longfellow, the poet, Franklin Pierce, later President of the United States, and Horatio Bridge, who first appreciated his genius; that chiefly through Bridge's thoughtfulness he was made weigher and gauger at the Boston Custom House, 1839–1841, and surveyor at the Salem Custom House, 1846–1850; that President Pierce appointed him to the consulship of Liverpool, 1853–1857; that he lived in Italy for two years, 1857–1859, and that while travelling for his health, attended by Pierce, he died at Plymouth, New Hampshire, 18 May, 1864.

The facts of his literary record are hardly more numerous, but they invite more comment. His college letters to his mother and his sisters show how early he mastered his superb style. Indeed, they are much better written than his first published story, *Fanshawe* (1828), which was probably composed, in part at least, during his college days. From 1825 to 1837 he lived at home in Salem, laboriously perfecting his short stories and sketches, and publishing them anonymously or under assumed names, chiefly in Goodrich's annual, *The Token*, and in *The New England Magazine*. He gives an idealized account of this period in his sketches *The Devil in Manuscript* and *The Journal of a Solitary Man*. In 1837, again through Bridge's good offices, a publisher was found for the *Twice Told Tales* (enlarged edition in two volumes, 1842). With this practical beginning of his reputation coincided his first acquaintance with the Peabody family. In all the biographies his love for Sophia Peabody has naturally filled a large place, but no sufficient estimate has perhaps been made of the intellectual enrichment his love brought him. It was through the Peabodys that he became really alive to the philosophical currents of his time. Transcendentalism had, of course, enfolded him, as it had the average New Englander, in its general atmosphere, and its temper is felt in some of his earliest writings, but it can hardly be said to have possessed his thought as it did later, and he had been in personal contact with none of the leaders. The Peabodys, however, were on intimate terms with Emerson, the young rhapsodist of *Nature*, whose recent triumph in *The American Scholar* had more recently been rendered equivocal by his *Divinity School Address;* and Alcott, Emerson's inspirer, they knew still better, for Elizabeth and to some extent Sophia had assisted at his Temple school in Boston, and Elizabeth had published in her *Records of a School* (1835) verbatim reports of Alcott's conversations with his pupils. When *The Dial* was founded in 1840, Elizabeth Peabody, who by that time had organized a remarkable book store, became its publisher. It was not extraordinary, therefore, that Hawthorne was drawn, though with some mental qualms, into the full tide of Transcendentalism, nor that upon the termination of his service in the Boston Custom House, in 1841, he joined the Brook Farm venture,[1] in the hope of establishing a home there. His note-books tell us the most interesting aspects of this passage in his life. At the end of a year and a half, completely disillusioned with the community experiment, he married and settled at Concord, in the Old Manse, where for neighbours he had Emerson, Alcott, and Thoreau, all busy with *The Dial*, and where Thoreau was shortly to undertake his Walden solitude. In Concord most of the stories were written which Hawthorne published in 1846 as *Mosses from an Old Manse*. A still later collection, *The Snow Image* (1852), gathered up practically all of the remaining sketches which he cared to preserve. His longer romances show a tendency to rework or develop this earlier material, or to draw upon actual scenes and events for their narrative fabric; the controlling problems, however, which the romances deal with are more obviously than in the shorter stories suggested

[1] See Book II, Chap. viii.

by Transcendental ideas. *The Scarlet Letter* (1850) is developed from a brief description in *Endicott and the Red Cross*, one of the *Twice Told Tales*. In *The House of the Seven Gables* (1851), Hawthorne makes use of such a curse as was pronounced on his own ancestor, John Hawthorne, or Hathorne, a severe magistrate in witchcraft times. In *The Blithedale Romance* (1852) it is hard not to identify Hawthorne's Brook Farm experience, though he warned us against the temptation. The outward details of *The Marble Faun* (1860) are clearly the observations of his two years in Italy.

Besides the short stories and the romances, Hawthorne wrote several important books for children—the series called *Grandfather's Chair* (1841–1842) and the two *Wonderbooks* (1852–1853). He also edited his friend Bridge's *Journal of an African Cruiser* (1845), wrote a campaign life of his friend Pierce (1852), and published some of his notes on England under the title of *Our Old Home* (1863).

If it is just to see in the early writings a picture of his native temper before he was consciously engaged with Transcendental doctrines, it is also true that from the first his mind was of another order than Alcott's or Emerson's, and that though he might be interested in the same ideas, he would treat them very differently. Most philosophers can be classed roughly among those who conceive of the ideal ends of life as already existing in heaven, in some order or pattern which may be imitated on earth, or among those who think of the ideal as of something which does not yet exist, but which is implicit in the universe, and toward which the universe evolves. A philosopher of the first or Platonic type, if he notices facts at all, is likely to be disconcerted by them, since they rarely conform to his ideal or serve to authorize it; his comfort is in rising superior to actual life—that is, in ignoring it. Alcott was an almost pure example of this type. The other kind of philosopher is likely to entertain a respect amounting almost to reverence for any concrete existing condition, because as two points determine a straight line, so a recent moment observed against the past gives indication of the order to come. Emerson was partly, like Alcott, a Platonist, but he had also a profound and inconsistent disposition toward this other way of thought; having two points of view at once, therefore, he is not only perplexing at times, but really contradictory, and it is not strange that he should have proved in one aspect of his genius inspiring to Maeterlinck and in the other aspect acceptable to Nietzsche. Hawthorne belonged altogether to the second type of thinker. Concerned primarily with the actual world before him, he found a natural use for the past in the explanation it might give of the present, but the present was to him just as naturally the more important moment, and most interesting of all was the occasional hint or prophecy of that to which time through its past and present changes might be tending. He was a radical, therefore, but he saw clearly that this particular present will soon be no more sacred than any other moment of the past, and that to devote oneself to any cause as though it were a final remedy of circumstances, promising rest thereafter, is merely to postpone stagnation for a while. With this insight he could not readily give his faith to any reform or reformer; even the crusade for abolition and the war for the Union left him cold, for he wisely doubted whether measures conceived in the root-and-branch spirit might not raise more evils in the state than they were intended to cure. True reform, the only kind that could enlist his sympathy, must work hand in hand with nature's slowly evolving but inevitable order, and so long as that order can be but partially or infrequently discerned, it is best to do nothing violent, nothing headlong. Even when we discern the order, from time to time, we should become humble, observing how little it resembles our own morality, our own dreams of perfection.

It needs no fine perception to discover these principles or attitudes in Hawthorne, for they are displayed quite simply on the surface of his early stories. The significance he attached to the present world, whatever it might be, can be seen in the important group of essay sketches such as *A Rill from the Town Pump*, *David Swan*, *Sights from a Steeple*, and *Main Street*. Some resemblance has been found between this department of his work and the essays of Addison and of Irving, and certainly Addison's cheerfulness is here, and often something more than Irving's fancy. But neither *The Spectator* nor *The Sketch Book* would suggest that Addison or Irving was in the habit of keeping a diary; whereas Hawthorne's simple studies, of the group just referred to, are in form nothing more than episodes in a journal. The fact is of some consequence in understanding his genius. When the American and European notebooks were finally included in the complete editions of his writings, they took their place, not as an appendix or illustration of more perfect things, but on equal terms with his other works; for the journal manner was suited to his realistic, unprejudiced search into the world about him, and his lifelong preoccupation with his diary was not, as with most novelists, for the sake of books to be written later, but was itself the satisfaction of a primary literary interest. Like the journals, the essay sketches take the scene as they find it, extract from it all that observation can, and then discard it, having proved no point and exhibited no characters in continuous interplay, but having uncovered possibilities, hints, causes, coincidences. In the simpler essays Hawthorne observed these possibilities and coincidences in a kind of stationary cross-section, and left them undeveloped; but in more elaborate stories he played with the ironic contrasts between the order which we foresee in life and the order which time brings to pass. Emerson often came out of his mysticism and contemplated the "beautiful necessity," the inevitable consequence of things, to which man must submit himself before he has either happiness or power. Hawthorne was inclined to stress rather man's inability to submit himself to this necessity, since he seldom guesses correctly what it would be. *Mr. Higginbotham's Catastrophe* is a lighter treatment of this theme of consequences; *Edward Fane's Rosebud* and *The Wives of the Dead* are in a darker tone. Or sometimes Hawthorne would turn the irony in another direction, by emphasizing the incredible swiftness with which the present becomes the past, and the insidiousness with which antiquity begins to show its symptoms even in what seems youthful and emancipated. *The May-pole of Merry Mount* brings this idea home, less in the overthrow of the maskers at Merry Mount than in the expressed faith of the stern Puritan leader that the troubles of life come soon and unexpectedly—a confession which somehow brings a chill over his own righteous success. A still better illustration is *Endicott and the Red Cross*, which shows the Puritans, who crossed the ocean for freedom of conscience and who in the moment of the story proclaim themselves champions of religious liberty, as having nevertheless instituted already the pillory and the stocks for those who disagree with them.

The Transcendental ideas which chiefly occupied Hawthorne's thought in the long romances were the doctrines of self-reliance, of compensation, and of what Emerson expressed in his essay on *Circles*. The ideal of self-reliance was that a man should live according to his own nature, by listening to the dictates of the over-soul as revealed in his impulses; to this end he should keep himself free of the imprisoning past, and of conventional society, which embodies the past. To Alcott or to Emerson this doctrine was so obviously sound that they stated it with every emphasis of rhetoric and with no qualifications. "Whoso would be a man must be a non-conformist." Hawthorne doubtless felt the truth of the doctrine as keenly as any one, but he was alive also to the unsocial results which might follow a narrow practice of it. A man consciously and entirely free of the past and on his guard against it might indeed possess his soul, but he might also miss the essence of culture, and having renounced the finer instruments of the art of life, he might so isolate himself from his fellows as to become ineffective in his noblest virtues. Since nature is unfolding a necessary order in and around us, an order which we apprehend with difficulty, the great danger of asserting ourselves is that we may thereby place ourselves outside of our true development, and never return to it. This danger of stepping out of the order, of doing violence to our proper destiny, gave Hawthorne the theme of such stories as *Wakefield*, *The Prophetic Pictures*, and *Rappaccini's Daughter*. The doctrine of compensation, in one form or another, was peculiarly dear to Transcendental optimism. Every action carries its reward or punishment with it. The thief is punished, though the police never find him, for the price of theft is loss of innocence, fear of arrest, suspicion of other men. What compensation is destined for the victim of the thief, optimistic Transcendentalism preferred not to investigate, but it was into just such a neglected area of morals that Hawthorne liked to push his inquiry. His observations brought him into a certain agreement with the doctrine; because a natural order constantly unfolds in the world, he believed in the efficacy of mere time to break down conventions and to reveal a nobler law, and in his historical scenes—*Howe's Masquerade*, for example, or *The Gray Champion*—he liked to show a fossilized past at the moment when it is shattered. He could believe that life does so far make restitution, but in daily life he could find no compensation for the injuries suffered by the innocent, nor could he persuade himself that a noble bearing of wrongs will necessarily lead to spiritual profit. Indeed, though Emerson's sunny temperament had spread its glamour over his discussion of this theory, to Hawthorne the theory seemed, so far as it was true, one of the darkest and most perplexing. Still less could he agree with Emerson's exaggeration of the same doctrine in *Circles*. Optimism here, taking the bit in its teeth, contended that as there is in experience no such thing as a straight line, so there is practically no such thing as evil—a prophetic application, it would seem, of Riemannian geometry to morals; that what seems hopelessly bad will in the end be found to contain the good principle; and, quite illogically, that what seems to be good will actually prove to be so.

> In vain produced, all rays return;
> Evil will bless and ice will burn.

In a famous passage in *Circles*, Emerson acknowledges the awkwardness of this position, and explains that his temperament dictates it. Hawthorne could not undertake any such cheerfulness, but he was profoundly concerned with the moral phenomena by which Emerson may have justified his faith. Here springs that paradox of experience, that mystery of sin, the question as to what sin is, which threw its shadow over three at least of the four romances. Since we rarely discern our true destiny, the human being who steps out of what seems the moral order may really have chanced upon a sounder morality; through what appears to be sin, therefore, may sometimes come the regeneration of a soul—not through repentance, be it observed, but through sincere adherence to the sin. Conversely, though a man should devote himself to the highest ideal he is aware of, if that ideal does not lie in the true order of nature, his devotion may bring him to an evil end. These possibilities, together with the implications of self-reliance and compensation, furnish the moral problems of Hawthorne's romances.

Hester Prynne, for example, in *The Scarlet Letter*, illustrates self-reliance in a way that some Emersonians may have found not altogether comfortable. Since her love for Dimmesdale was the one sincere passion of her life, she obeyed it utterly, though a conventional judgment would have said that she was stepping out of the moral order. There is nothing in the story to suggest condemnation of her or of the minister in their sin; the only blame attaches to Dimmesdale's cowardice, his lack of self-reliance, his unreadiness to make public acknowledgment of his love. The passion itself, as the two lovers still agree at the close of their hard experience, was sacred, and never caused them repentance. The doctrine of compensation is illustrated in Chillingworth, who, having determined on a fiendish revenge, becomes himself a fiend. There is a kind of comment on Emerson's cheerful doctrine in the fact that this gloomy soul, marked for perdition, is a firm believer in compensation; he wronged Hester's youth by marrying her, and therefore he bears her no ill will for wronging him, but he argues that since the minister had never received a justifying harm at his hands, the secret lover should therefore be punished by the injured husband. As Chillingworth discusses the matter with Hester, compensation seems to be at one moment sheer fatalism, at another moment a primitive exacting of an eye for an eye, but never does it come to a happy issue. The optimistic turn in the doctrine is illustrated by Hester—or perhaps it is better to say that she illustrates the optimism of *Circles*. She has sinned, but the sin leads her straightway to a larger life. Like Adam and Eve driven out of Paradise, she finds she has a career at last. Social ostracism first gives her leisure for meditation and a just angle from which to attack social problems, and then it permits her to enter upon a life of mercy and good works which would have been closed to a conventional woman. Hawthorne had described the original wearer of the scarlet letter in *Endicott and the Red Cross* as a woman who braved her shame by embroidering the guilty "A" into an elaborate and beautiful emblem; so in the romance he lets the sin elaborate itself, so far as Hester's nature is concerned, into nothing but beauty. She becomes more loving, more sympathetic, more tender; and intellectually she becomes emancipated from the narrowness of her age, so that even now she seems prophetic of what the noblest women may be. Thoughts were her companions which, says Hawthorne, would have been held more dangerous than the sin of the scarlet letter, had they been seen knocking at her door. She saw how completely the social scheme must be altered before woman can enjoy a true equality with man, and she suspected the losses in the best of manhood and womanhood which might be the incidental or temporary price of the belated justice.

The greatness of *The Scarlet Letter*, on repeated readings, seems to lie in this social interest, this inexorable study of the world as it is, which distinguishes Hawthorne from other Transcendentalists. The Puritan environment is represented as already dying, young as it was in the new world; at the outset of the story Hawthorne shows us that these courageous founders of religious liberty in the wilderness felt the necessity at once of building a prison and of setting up a pillory. The ideals which a little while before were an inner light for the community, carrying inevitable conviction, were now stiffened into convention and leaned upon force. In making the point that Hawthorne was no special admirer of Puritanism, we must add that neither was he a special critic of it; he used the Puritan moment in our history merely to illustrate the truth of all moments, that society conventionalizes its ideals and becomes cruel, and that time, which annihilates one set of conventions, substitutes another. But some specific criticism of Puritan New England, of New England in his own day, may be discerned in the fortunes of Hester, and may be still more clearly felt in Zenobia and in Miriam, the later heroines; these are all represented as physically beautiful, and as in some way estranged from life, and we wonder whether it was not their beauty rather than their conduct that alienated them from their environment. What career has a beautiful woman in New England?—Hawthorne seems to ask, and he seems to imply that if she is conventional she may live down the handicap of beauty, but meantime she is dangerous to others and

to herself. The danger to herself is indicated by the fact that
Hester, Zenobia, and probably Miriam, were all married for
their beauty, when they were very young, to men who could
not appreciate their greatness of soul, and whom therefore
they were forced to divorce or to desert.

The House of the Seven Gables is so quiet a story that Hawthorne's characteristic criticism of self-reliance or of compensation is not at first disturbing, but in none of his books does he
take more essential issue with Alcott and Emerson.   On the
surface of the romance lies the theme of long-delayed retribution—the curse of old Maule falling on each generation of the
usurping Pyncheons. But what punishment does after all
overtake the thoroughly bad man who allows his innocent
cousin to rest in jail for years? He dies of apoplexy, as he
would have died had he been the innocent cousin. And
what happens to his victims? It is easy to guess how Emerson
might have treated Clifford and Hepzibah; the innocence of
the imprisoned brother would somehow have been its own
reward, and the loyalty of the devoted sister, waiting for his
release, would have ennobled her character. But confinement
in prison is not likely to sweeten even innocence; Hawthorne
shows Clifford on his return to the old house a broken man,
irritable and unappreciative. Hepzibah's long waiting proved
for her a solitude almost as complete as prison confinement;
Hawthorne shows her as a shrivelled old maid, angular and
grim, with hardly a grace remaining. He had no more wish
than Emerson would have had to decry the ethical beauty of
her patient loyalty, but he could not help seeing that she, like
Clifford, was the victim of gross wrong, and that it is disastrous
to be even an innocent victim. Similarly he insists on a precise account of self-reliance in Holgrave, the descendant of
old Maule. Emerson himself could not have portrayed a
more thorough-going critic of the past.

"Shall we never, never get rid of this Past?" asks Holgrave. "It
lies upon the Present like a giant's dead body. In fact, the case is
just as if a young giant were compelled to waste all his strength in
carrying about the corpse of the old giant, his grandfather, who died
a long while ago, and only needs to be decently buried. . . . A
dead man, if he happen to have made a will, disposes of wealth no

onger his own; or, if he die intestate, it is distributed in accordance with the notions of men much longer dead than he. A dead man sits on all our judgment-seats; and living judges do but search out and repeat his decisions. We read in dead men's books! We laugh at dead men's jokes, and cry at dead men's pathos! We are sick of dead men's diseases, physical and moral, and die of the same remedies with which dead doctors killed their patients! We worship the living Deity according to dead men's forms and creeds. Whatever we seek to do, of our own free motion, a dead man's icy hand obstructs us! Turn our eyes to what point we may, a dead man's white, immitigable face encounters them, and freezes our very heart! And we must be dead ourselves before we can begin to have our proper influence on our own world, which will then be no longer our world, but the world of another generation, with which we shall have no shadow of a right to interfere."

How far Hawthorne agrees with Holgrave we cannot tell, but there is no doubt what sort of character he thought would result from a sincere practice of such philosophy. Holgrave is free of the past, and thereby he is practically free of the present too; his honesty and his emancipation attract the reader, yet he has little or no influence. Few men really wish to detach themselves so far. Even Phœbe, the young girl whom he marries, who has the natural freshness of innocence, seems curiously social in comparison with this conscientious rover whose one dread is that he may take root somewhere.

Hawthorne showed an increasing disposition to discuss these philosophical questions in frank comment outside the plot of his romances. Hollingsworth, in *The Blithedale Romance*, illustrates his fear of tampering with the natural order of things, especially by organized reform; and Zenobia illustrates his reflections on self-reliance, especially where woman is concerned. Hollingsworth was a determined social reformer; he wished to reform criminals through an appeal to their higher instincts. Hawthorne observed that such philanthropy, admirable in its intention, often proceeded on slight knowledge of the facts. "He ought to have commenced his investigation of the subject by perpetrating some huge sin in his proper person, and examining the condition of his higher instincts afterwards." As a matter of fact, Hollingsworth does ruin two lives, Zenobia's and Priscilla's, in the selfish pursuit of his philanthropic ideal, and, if he had chosen, might well have furnished the state of his own heart for examination. Hawthorne comments again, making his familiar point that a good ideal brings a man to a good end only if it does not lead him out of the natural sympathies of life:

> The moral which presents itself to my reflections, as drawn from Hollingsworth's character and errors, is simply this—that admitting what is called philanthropy, when adopted as a profession, to be often useful by its energetic impulse to society at large it is perilous to the individual whose ruling passion, in one exclusive channel, it thus becomes. It ruins, or is fearfully apt to ruin, the heart, the rich juices of which God never meant should be pressed violently out and distilled into alcoholic liquor by an unnatural process, but should render life sweet, bland, and gently beneficent and insensibly influence other hearts and other lives to the same blessed end.

Zenobia is a modern and conscious Hester—or rather, her experience is the reverse of Hester's, for she is a woman naturally emancipated who is ruined by disappointed love. It is this difference in their problems that makes her seem less noble than Hester, less tragic than pitiful. But in portraying her, Hawthorne raises more especially the question he had suggested in *The Scarlet Letter:* is not such a woman, so beautiful and so intellectual, an exotic creature in our society? Here is the modern woman whom Hester dreamed of, but the old misfortune still overtakes her; like Hester, she has married one who could not appreciate her, but she has never found the lover who should have been her mate, and she has no true companionship with other women. She seems to be a foreigner, and in the New England thought of Hawthorne's time foreigners had the right to be, like Zenobia, physically beautiful.

The Marble Faun repeats in Miriam the problem of Hester and of Zenobia, and in Hilda, the simple Puritan girl who finds peace in the Roman Catholic confessional, the story illustrates beautifully Hawthorne's faith that some of our most unconventional impulses lead us to a practical morality. But the philosophy of the book centres in Donatello, that wonderful creature who begins life with the animal-like innocence which radical thought seems often to desire for man, and who develops an immortal soul by committing an impulsive murder. The doctrine of *Circles* has its most elaborate illustration here; here is the evolution of good out of sin—not out of repentance for sin. But if the doctrine is sound, our theology needs thorough revision, and Hawthorne suggests the logical change in our conception of sin:

Is sin then—which we deem such a dreadful blackness in the universe—is it, like sorrow, merely an element of human education, through which we struggle to a higher and purer state than we could otherwise have attained? Did Adam fall that we might ultimately rise to a far higher Paradise than his?

These problems, suggested by the Transcendental philosophy, occupied Hawthorne to the last. It was not in his disposition to suggest answers to them. His distinction in American literature is the extent to which he projected them experimentally into life, and the sincerity with which he modified them to conform to stubborn and perplexing facts.

CHAPTER XII

Longfellow

HENRY WADSWORTH LONGFELLOW was born in Portland, Maine, 27 February, 1807. In view of what America as a whole then was and of what he was destined to accomplish for the literature of the country, it is difficult to see how he could have been more fortunately circumstanced with respect to stock and environment. Both the Longfellows and his mother's people, the Wadsworths, were well-to-do, and they represented the best New England, particularly Massachusetts, traditions, which, with the spread of Unitarianism, were losing some of their rigidity. Thus the child experienced little that was specially straitening, and he received a training well adapted to bring out the talents that soon manifested themselves. His native town furnished the influence of the sea and sea-faring men; the virgin District soon to be the State of Maine, afforded other impressive features of nature; and the frontier situation, even if it could not make strenuous a constitutionally gentle and refined disposition, at least inculcated feelings of sympathy with a pioneer, rugged, prevailingly practical population, which were to be of great use to a poet who in after years could point to his successful fulfilment of the threefold function of transmitter of Old World culture to the New, shaper into verse of aboriginal, colonial, and Revolutionary material, both legendary and historical, and lyric interpreter of the simple thoughts and feelings of an unsophisticated people. His career was well foreshadowed when he published anonymously at the age of thirteen, in a local newspaper, a Revolutionary battle-lyric.

After a good schooling and an introduction to the best reading old and new, including Irving's *Sketch Book*, Longfellow, in the autumn of 1822, entered Bowdoin College as a

ophomore, having Nathaniel Hawthorne as a classmate.
Here, as at home, he continued to come under unpretentious,
wholesome influences, to which were added those of rural
seclusion. Before he graduated in 1825, he was writing verse
rather copiously, and some of it was published in a literary
journal just founded in Boston. As is not surprising, it was
overpraised by a provincial public, but for a wonder, in view
of the vogue of Byron, it was not stormily romantic. His
success gave point to his plans for leading a literary life, but
his more experienced father held out for the law, although he
was willing to give his son a year of grace to be spent in less
uncongenial studies at Harvard. This plan was abandoned
because it was found feasible for Longfellow to fit himself to
become the first incumbent of a chair of modern languages to
be established at Bowdoin.

Travel and study in Europe were essential to such a design,
and the middle of June, 1826, saw the youth of nineteen beginning at Havre a European sojourn of a little more than three
years. Temperament and immaturity, combined doubtless
with a shrewd perception of the fact that great erudition was
not a prerequisite to successful language-teaching in Maine,
made it natural that Longfellow should become rather a sentimental pilgrim than a delving student or a philosophical
observer, and that he should make but slight use of Ticknor's
recommendation of Göttingen as a centre and source of the
exact scholarship so much needed in America. German sentiment and romance were later to mean much to the poet; but
Latin colour and picturesqueness meant more to the young
traveller. France, Spain, where he met Irving, and Italy,
from whose greatest writer his mature and declining years
derived their chief solace, were in turn visited, their manners
noted, their literatures studied, their languages in more than
polite measure mastered. Then several months were given
to Germany, including a little studying at Göttingen, and in
August, 1829, the neophyte professor was back in America
ready to take up the duties of his chair.

Those duties occupied him until his second visit to Europe,
which took place nearly six years later. He was a conscientious and successful teacher and compiler of text-books, he
lectured on literary history, he wrote for *The North American*

Review essays flavoured with scholarship, he gave a pledge to society by taking to himself, in 1831, a wife, Mary Storer Potter, of Portland. Except for some verse translations from the Spanish and certain traces of the poet to be discovered in a series of travel-sketches, which appeared in a volume entitled *Outre-Mer: a Pilgrimage beyond the Sea* (1835), one might have been justified in supposing that without doubt the undergraduate whose heart was set on "future eminence in literature" would end his life as a distinguished academic personage, not as the most popular poet of his generation. His fate seemed sealed with his acceptance of the Smith Chair of Modern Languages at Harvard, in succession to Ticknor, and with his departure for Europe in April, 1835, in order that by study of the northern literatures he might the better qualify himself for his important post.

His second period of training in Europe, although shorter, rendered Longfellow a greater service than his first. As he was more mature, his genius was better prepared to receive a definitive bent, and his experiences determined that that bent should take an emotional rather than an emphatically intellectual direction. After a short visit to England he spent some months in Sweden and Denmark studying their literatures with results obvious to the reader of his later poetry. Then he went to Holland, where his wife fell ill and died in the autumn. This meant that the ensuing winter at Heidelberg saw no notable progress made by the young professor in his German studies, but did see a deep absorption of the spirit of German romanticism by the young widower and the future poet. The sentimental prose romance *Hyperion* and the collection of poems entitled *Voices of the Night*, both published in 1839, show what bereavement and the new environment, physical as well as mental and spiritual, had brought to the man entering his fourth decade. We track the footsteps of the naïve hero of *Hyperion* with less confiding delight than our grandfathers and grandmothers probably experienced, but then we are less sentimental and more widely travelled than they were, facts which of course do not warrant us in arrogating to ourselves a taste necessarily superior to theirs. *Hyperion* doubtless meant more to the author and his countrymen than a scholarly monograph would have meant, for what

America needed just then, apparently, was some one who, like Longfellow, could carry on the work begun by Irving of interpreting the Old World to the New. The younger man was not only better endowed with the faculty of specific poetic utterance, but he was naturally more fully qualified than his predecessor to gratify the taste of a generation that was beginning to be affected by the work of the newer English romantic poets. Thus we are not surprised to find the Smith Professor writing poems on European subjects instead of grammars and histories of literature, and editing in place of textbooks a small collection of poems entitled *The Waif* (1843), a similar volume, *The Estray* (1847), and the comprehensive and useful *Poets and Poetry of Europe* (1845). Even the thirty-one volumes of the much later *Poems of Places* (1876–1879) with which Longfellow's name is more or less associated, bear witness to the influence of the teacher-poet's second sojourn in Europe both upon him and upon American culture.

But the greatest influence of that sojourn, exhibited after he took up his duties at Harvard in December, 1836, is to be seen in the simple, wholesomely emotional, and unblushingly didactic poems with which Longfellow now began to win the hearts of his provincial readers. *The Psalm of Life* is perhaps the best known and the best chosen example of these "household poems," shall we call them? With its companion pieces *The Reaper and the Flowers*, *The Light of Stars*, and *Footsteps of Angels*, it is undoubtedly amenable to some of the harsh criticism it has received from those persons who seem to imagine that taste thrives only on its own exigency. But it is hard to see how verses of subtler quality would have so sung themselves through the length and breadth of young America, or could have laid so broad and deep a foundation for the fame of the most heartily loved poet of his generation.

Long before that poet had reached the zenith of his reputation the professor had grown weary of his chair. At first he worked hard enough to justify weariness, particularly at the uncongenial task of supervising the instruction in the elementary language courses given by his assistants; but gradually, whatever enthusiasm he may have had for a scholarly, academic career wore itself out, and toward the end of his eighteen years of service—he resigned in 1854—he was almost querulous in his attitude toward a calling without the aid of which he would probably have remained a somewhat local and minor writer, his disposition scarcely prompting him to draw inspiration from Transcendentalism or the anti-slavery movement, and his genius not qualifying him to probe the heart or to wander in shadowland.

Whatever its irksomeness, however, his position at Harvard brought with it compensations. He soon secured a congenial habitat—the now famous Craigie House—he gathered about him a group of sympathetic friends, he became a distinguished figure in the most cultured community in America, the Cambridge of Lowell's essay and of Colonel Higginson's books, he added to his happiness and his income by a second marriage—to Miss Frances Elizabeth Appleton in 1843—and he found time and incentive to write whatever he had in his mind and heart to say. Reading his letters and his diaries, putting together the biographical details furnished by others, and constructing as best one can the man's life and spirit from his writings, one is forced to the conclusion that except for a single great tragedy—the accidental burning to death of his wife in 1861—Longfellow's is one of the most serenely fortunate careers ever led by a man of letters. Some of his critics have wished that it might have been otherwise, apparently supposing that, if he had been more unfortunate, his poetry would have been more to their liking. It is not, however, on record that any critic has deliberately wooed infelicity in order to qualify himself for a fuller enjoyment of Longfellow's placid verses.

In 1842 a third visit was made to Europe, this time a short one for the sake of health. It was preceded by the *Ballads and Other Poems* (1841), and followed by the *Poems on Slavery* (1842). These justly enhanced his reputation, but the meritorious anti-slavery verses proved no prelude to active participation in the great conflict that was leading up to the Civil War. The prior volume with such pieces as *The Village Blacksmith, God's Acre, Maidenhood*, and the egregiously anabatic *Excelsior*, strengthened his hold upon the popular heart, and in the successful ballads proper, such as *The Wreck of the Hesperus* and *The Skeleton in Armor*, it gave him, in addition, some incentive to address his readers in narrative verse, the form of poetry in which, during his middle period, he made himself easily the chief American master. Neither in these earlier volumes, to which may be added *The Belfry of Bruges and Other Poems* (1846), nor in *Evangeline* (1847) and succeeding tales in verse, did Longfellow show himself to be a consummate metrical and verbal artist of the highest order or a poet of sustained imaginative flight; nor was he, in compensation, one of those writers who produce a strong effect through their subtle knowledge of human character or their exceptional ability to describe and interpret nature or their profound understanding of a country or a period. Yet even in these particulars he was capable of exhibiting distinguished merit—witness his command of the simpler rhythms, his wide-reaching metrical experimentation, his feeling for the sea, his sympathetic attitude toward the Middle Ages displayed in *The Golden Legend* (1851), his presentation of the larger natural features of America in *Evangeline*—and in his lyrical appeal, especially through his semi-didactic poems of reflection and sentiment, as well as in his general narrative power, he was during his life, and he still remains, unapproached by any other American poet.

The years immediately preceding his second marriage in 1843 were partly devoted to the composition of a poetical drama in three acts, *The Spanish Student*, which was published serially in 1842, and the next year was issued in book form. It is generally and justly regarded as a failure, since Longfellow exhibited neither in it nor in later poems cast in similar form —*The New England Tragedies* (1868), *Judas Maccabaeus* (1872), and *Michael Angelo* (1883),—the slightest trace of dramatic genius. A poet of literary derivation, so to phrase it, inspired by his own wide reading, and a useful transmitter of culture he could not help being from first to last, and his growing reputation naturally prompted him to undertake elaborate works in a form of art practised by preceding poets in every age. His countrymen were not exigent critics, and were inclined to resent it when he was accused, as by Poe and by Margaret Fuller, of unoriginality; latter-day readers are likely to skim, or else altogether to neglect the dramas that are protected from complete oblivion by the venerated and still venerable name. If they desire any justification for their conduct, such prudent readers may ejaculate "*habent sua fata libelli*," or may recall the facts that Dr. Samuel Johnson wrote *Irene* and William Wordsworth, *The Borderers*.

In all probability, neither of these ominous dramatic productions was in Longfellow's mind when he was writing *The Spanish Student*, or planning his presumptive masterpiece, *Christus: A Mystery*, which finally saw the light in 1872, more than twenty years after the first appearance of its second part, *The Golden Legend*, one of the most attractive and yet one of the least widely read of its author's books. Poems Swedish and German, ominous in no bad sense, were in his mind when he wrote his sentimental idyllic narrative in hexameters, *Evangeline*, not perhaps the best of his longer poems, but certainly the most popular both at home and abroad. Hawthorne, from whom Longfellow secured the theme of the Acadian maiden's vain search for her lover, might have made more of the pathetic story, but he would have done it for fewer readers. Other writers might have improved the local colour of the poem, still others might have laboured more heroically to keep the hexameters from making forays across the borders of prose, but it may be doubted whether any contemporary could have written, on the whole, a better *Evangeline*, at least one more suited to the taste of the period. Few of his contemporaries, however, have left behind a more negligible prose romance than the story of an impossible New England village which Longfellow published in 1849 under the title *Kavanagh; A Tale*.

The end of the fifties saw the culmination of his genius in the appearance of *The Courtship of Miles Standish and Other Poems* (1858). This narrative poem, another experiment in hexameters, seems to surpass Longfellow's other successful achievements in the same category because it is more racy of New England, fuller of humour, superior in movement and in characterization. It is less popular than *Evangeline*, partly no doubt because it is less sweet, and it seems to have made less impression than its predecessor the Indian epic *Hiawatha* (1855)—another metrical experiment, this time in rhymeless trochaic tetrameters—partly because it is less ambitious and exotic. The popularity of *Hiawatha* is not undeserved, however, since novelty and quaintness may well be set over against facility and factitiousness, and since, being in a certain sense

American, the poem may justly make more of a local appeal
than such a work as *The Golden Legend* based on *Der Arme
Heinrich*. Yet it may be doubted whether either *Hiawatha*
or *Miles Standish* did as much to establish Longfellow as the
most admired poet of his time as some of the unpretentious
poems contained in the collection entitled *The Seaside and the
Fireside* (1850), such poems, for example, as the tender *Resignation*, to say nothing of the patriotic close of *The Building
of the Ship*.

From the date of the tragic accident to his wife—July,
1861—to his death 24 March, 1882, at his home in Cambridge,
Longfellow's life takes on dignity without losing its quiet
charm, and his genius—shall we say, mellows, or slowly
abates in energy? There was no marked falling off in
the number of published volumes, in the range of his interests, in his hold upon his intimate friends, such as Charles
Eliot Norton and James Russell Lowell, in his endeavours,
conscious and unconscious, to deserve the affectionate
gratitude of his countrymen. Even in the South, for a
time rent away from the rest of the country politically, and
for a longer period estranged in sentiment, his was a Northern
name not anathema to the rising generation, and in Great
Britain he rivalled in popularity Tennyson himself. But, as
might have been expected, these years saw the production of
little, except for some excellent sonnets, that adds permanently
to his fame as a poet.

True, he added considerably to the mass of his narrative
poetry by the three series of *Tales of a Wayside Inn*, the first of
which appeared under its own name in 1863, the second and
third of which were included respectively in *Three Books of
Song* (1872—along with *Judas Maccabaeus*), and in *Aftermath*
(1874), but save for the spirited *Paul Revere's Ride* and the
Saga of King Olaf, of the first series, these tales in verse have
made only a mild impression. This is about all that may
justly be said with regard to the twelve poems collected in
Flower-de-luce (1867); it is more than should be said of *The
New England Tragedies*, the third part of *Christus*, consisting
of *John Endicott* and *Giles Cory of the Salem Farms*. These,
with the first part of the ambitious trilogy, *The Divine Tragedy*
(1871), constitute what may best be ambiguously denominated

"efforts." Longfellow was more fortunately employed when he put himself in the company of Cowper and Bryant, and sought solace for his private woes in an extensive piece of poetical translation. Perhaps his true genius as a translator, seen early in the *Coplas de Manrique* (1833), is better exemplified in his numerous renderings of lyrics, particularly, as in Uhland's *The Castle by the Sea*, from the German, than in the faithful, meritorious version of *The Divine Comedy*, which appeared in three volumes between 1867 and 1870; but, despite a certain lack of metrical charm resulting from the facile character of the rhymeless lines printed in threes, the version of the masterpiece to which Longfellow gave so many years of love and study seems worthy of his pains and of the praise it has received from other admirers of Dante.

After the appearance of the translation of Dante and of the *Christus*, two works *de longue haleine* which show that the retired professor of nearly twenty years' standing was not open to the charge of idleness, Longfellow had still about a decade to live and to continue his writing. Some of the titles of his collections of verse have been already given; others are *The Masque of Pandora, and Other Poems* (1875), *Kéramos; and Other Poems* (1878), *Ultima Thule* (1880), and *In the Harbor* (1882—posthumous). The first of these volumes contained one of the most dignified and impressive of all his poems, one of the best occasional poems in American literature, the *Morituri Salutamus*, written for the semi-centennial of the poet's class at Bowdoin. It also contained *A Book of Sonnets*, fourteen in all, considerably extended in number in later editions of the poetical works. Some notable sonnets had been published with the translation of Dante, and to these Longfellow's later achievements in the same form are worthy pendants. High praise has been given to them by many critically minded readers of a later generation, who have wished, in default of admiration for Longfellow's earlier work, to combine patriotism with acumen in their praise of a poet whose reputation seemed to require rather delicate handling. Both the sonnets and their American encomiasts are fortunately unamenable to comments lacking in amiability, although it is open to doubt whether even such a pathetic sonnet as *The Cross of Snow*, written at the close of the poet's life in memory of his unfortunate second wife, will ever mean to the great public what *The Bridge* and *The Day is Done* have meant. It is perhaps more to the purpose to express satisfaction that the poet was capable of making the double appeal—to the reader who thinks he knows what to think and to the reader who knows he knows how to feel.

It may be gathered from this brief survey of a long life and a productive career that Longfellow's reputation, in the opinion of the present writer, was amply deserved in the poet's day, and rested in the main on his gifts as a story-teller in verse, on his power to transplant to American literature some of the colour and melody and romantic charm of the complex European literatures he had studied, and, more especially, on his skill in expressing in comparatively artless lyrics of senti- ment and reflection homely and wholesome thoughts and feelings which he shared with his countrymen of all classes throughout a broad land the occupation of which proceeded apace during his own span of years. Whatever he accom- plished beyond this as teacher and editor and writer of prose, and as self-conscious poet seeking success in the more elabo- rate traditional forms of his art, is worthy, to say the least, of as much praise as the similar work of his predecessors, contem- poraries, and successors among American poets, and is not clearly doomed to a speedier death than the elaborate produc- tions of his contemporaries and successors among the British poets. His place is not with the few eminent poets of the world, or even of his century, as the admiration of the mass of his countrymen and the critical lucubrations of some of them might be held to imply; but it is, legitimately and permanently, in the forefront of the small band of important writers in verse and in prose who during the first century of the republic's existence laid firmly and upon more or less democratic lines the foundations of a native literature.

CHAPTER XIII

Whittier

IT was in 1638, when the great Puritan emigration to Massachusetts was beginning to slacken, that Thomas Whittier, a youth of eighteen, possibly of Huguenot extraction, landed in New England and made a home for himself on the shores of the Merrimac River. The substantial oak farmhouse which, late in life, he erected for his large family near Haverhill, is still standing. Descended from him in the fourth generation, John Greenleaf Whittier, the poet, was born in this house, 17 December, 1807. This is the homestead described with minute and loving fidelity in *Snow-Bound*, and it is typical of the many thousands of its sort that dotted the New England country-side, rearing in the old Puritan tradition a sturdy pioneer stock that was to blossom later in the fine flower of political and ethical passion, of statesmanship and oratory and letters. Though Whittier's family tree was originally Puritan, a Quaker scion was grafted upon it in the second American generation, when Joseph Whittier, the youngest son of the pioneer, married Mary Peaslee, whose father had been an associate and disciple of George Fox. The descendants in this line remained faithful to the doctrines of the Society of Friends, and the poet, although he persisted in the characteristic and quaint (although ungrammatical) use of the second person singular pronoun in address, found the principle of non-resistance something of a strain in the days when his fondest hopes were bound up in the holy cause for which his friends were bearing arms and laying down their lives upon the battle-field.

> The levelled gun, the battle brand
>   We may not take,
> But, calmly loyal, we can stand
> And suffer for our suffering land
>   For conscience' sake.

The temperament of the New England Quaker was not unlike that of the New England Puritan. The one could be as cantankerous as the other, on occasion, but when the early Puritan intolerance of the sect had been smoothed away, the Quaker was found to be a man whose ideals were essentially those of the founders of Massachusetts, contributing to those ideals his own element of kindly sympathy, his own insistence upon the dignity of the individual, and his own uncompromising spirit of democracy. These traits were permanently stamped upon Whittier's character, and all rested upon a foundation of unshakable faith in the spiritual order of the world. Christianity has perhaps never assumed a purer or lovelier guise than it took in the lives of those New England Quakers of whom Whittier was the type.

The life of the household in which the poet grew to manhood is reproduced in *Snow-Bound* with a fidelity which makes of that poem, for its truthfulness and sincerity, one of the imperishable things in American literature—a document whose significance is becoming fully apparent only now that the phase of life it describes has all but vanished from American life, whether in New England or elsewhere. The home which *Snow-Bound* describes was a comfortable one, as New England farmsteads went, and, in poetical retrospect, its gracious human aspects are raised to a prominence which somewhat obscures the hard facts of the daily life of the household. It was a life of toil, with meagre opportunities for recreation, and the young Whittier did not have the constitution needed for its requirements. The physical disabilities under which he laboured all his life were doubtless traceable to the hardships of these early years on the farm.

Whittier had but little education of the formal sort. There were sessions of the district school for a few weeks every year, and these he attended off and on. In his twentieth year, an academy was opened in Haverhill, and in this institution he was enrolled as a student for two terms, earning the money to pay for his tuition. Meanwhile, he had been acquiring the best kind of education by devouring every book that he could lay his hands on, including the few on the family shelf—mostly the writings of pious Quakers—and

> The Bible towering o'er the rest,
> Of all other books the best.

One evening the district school teacher, Joshua Coffin, brought to the house a volume of Burns, and read from it to the family. This reading was a revelation to the boy of fourteen, who eagerly sought permission to keep the book for a while. The Scotch poet aroused in him the poetical stirrings which were to occupy his mind from that time on, and marked an epoch in the intellectual development of his boyhood. It was Burns, as he confessed many years later, who made him see

> through all familiar things
> The romance underlying;
> The joys and griefs that plume the wings
> Of Fancy skyward flying,

and so shaped his imaginings that he became, in a more exact sense than is usually connoted by such literary analogies, the Burns of his own New England country.

From this time on, Whittier was an industrious scribbler of rhymes. Most of them have been lost, but enough remain to reveal a promise which may perhaps be characterized as similar to that of the *Poems by Two Brothers*, or the *Poems by Victor and Cazire*. The first of his verses to appear in print were sent, unknown to the author, by his sister Mary to *The Free Press*, a weekly paper just established by William Lloyd Garrison in Newburyport. The boy's surprise was great when he read his own composition in an issue of the paper that was delivered at the Whittier farm in the summer of 1826. Other pieces followed, and one day shortly afterward, Garrison made a journey to the farm for the purpose of hunting up his promising contributor. He found Whittier at work in the field, urged the poet's father to send him to the academy, and thus began what was to be the life-long friendship of these two remarkable personalities. During the next two years Whittier published in the Haverhill *Gazette* nearly one hundred poems, besides prose articles on *Burns, War,* and *Temperance.* In 1828, a volume to be entitled *The Poems of Adrian* was projected, but this venture was abandoned. In the summer of that year his schooldays came to an end, and he began to look about for a means of earning his living. An offer was made him of the editorship of *The Philanthropist,* a paper devoted to the cause of what is called "temperance" in the current perverted sense of that term, but this offer he declined in a letter containing this significant confession: "I would rather have the memory of a Howard, a Wilberforce, and a Clarkson than the undying fame of Byron." By this time, he had acquired a considerable local reputation as a young writer of promise, and various modest openings already lay in his path.

During the next four years of his life (1828–32), Whittier was the editor of papers in Boston and Haverhill, and of *The New England Review,* in Hartford, Connecticut, besides contributing to many others. He became a partisan of Clay and the protective system, and looked askance at Jackson, "the blood-thirsty old man at the head of our government." The death of the elder Whittier in 1830 kept him for some time in Haverhill for the settlement of the family affairs. His interest in politics became more and more pronounced, and he thought seriously of standing for an election to Congress in 1832 but gave up the idea because he would, at the time of the election, be a few weeks short of the legal age requirement. When he identified himself, the next year, with the unpopular cause of the abolitionists, he gave up all hopes of political advancement.

Whittier's first published book was entitled *Legends of New England, in Prose and Verse.* It appeared in 1831, and was followed in 1832 by a pamphlet containing *Moll Pitcher.* Both these publications he afterwards did his best to suppress. Reform still appealed to him even more than poetry, and he wrote upon one occasion: "I set a higher value on my name as appended to the Antislavery Declaration of 1833 than on the title-page of any book." This Declaration was issued by the Convention held in Philadelphia, in 1833, to which Whittier was a delegate.   In taking this momentous decision, he builded better than he knew, for the poet in him was aroused, and the *Voices of Freedom* which from that time flowed from his pen were the utterances of a deeply-stirred soul, as different as possible from the imitative exercises which had hitherto engaged him.

The incidents of Whittier's life during the following few years may be briefly summarized.   In 1835 he served a term in the Massachusetts Legislature.   In 1836, the Haverhill homestead was sold, and he bought in Amesbury, a few miles down the Merrimac, the cottage which was to be his home for the rest of his life.   He occupied various editorial positions, which, together with activities in connection with the abolitionist agitation, kept him moving about until 1840, when he found his health badly broken and returned to Amesbury, there to remain for the greater part of the half-century that was still vouchsafed to him.   In his abolitionist activities he proved his mettle, often suffering indignities at the hands of mobs and being on several occasions in no small physical peril.   His shrewd and persuasive political activities made him a force to be reckoned with, and he kept in close touch with the leaders and movements of the time, allying himself with the Liberty Party of 1840, which, like the scriptural mustard seed, was destined to wax into so great a tree.

In 1836, Whittier published *Mogg Megone*, and, in the following year, a collection of his miscellaneous poems.   In 1849, a comprehensive collection of his poems appeared, followed a year later by *Songs of Labor and Other Poems*.   The first English edition of his collected poems also appeared in 1850.   These volumes included all that he thought worth preserving of the work of twenty years.   In 1857, the "blue and gold" collected edition of the poems was published in Boston. From this time onward small volumes of new poems appeared at intervals of about two years down to the year of the author's death, *At Sundown*, the last of the series, bearing the date of that very year (1892).   Of special significance are the idyl entitled *Snow-Bound* (1866) and the cycle called *The Tent on the Beach* (1867).   These two volumes marked a broadening of Whittier's fame, a higher recognition of his standing as an artist, and a noticeable measure of release from the financial difficulties under which he long had struggled. For the rest, the ballads, lyrics, and occasional pieces which made him most famous are scattered somewhat indiscriminately through the score or more of his volumes. For upwards of half a century verse flowed profusely from his pen, and his career did not fall into the distinctive periods that it is the task and the delight of the critic to define and to characterize in the work of many other poets.

From 1840 onward Whittier made Amesbury his home, although he allowed himself many protracted visits to friends and relatives, to Danvers and Newburyport, to the waters and mountains of New Hampshire, to Maine and the Isles of Shoals. From 1847 to 1860 he was associated, at long distance, with *The National Era*, a weekly paper published at Washington, and best remembered as the periodical in which *Uncle Tom's Cabin* was first given to the world. This paper was the chief medium for his expression until the establishment of *The Atlantic Monthly* in 1857, in whose pages a large part of his later work appeared. His seventieth birthday, in 1877, was made the occasion of a celebration more elaborate than had before been the reward of any American poet. He attended the Boston dinner then given in his honour, feeling

> Like him who in the old Arabian joke
> A beggar slept and crownéd Caliph woke.

His eightieth birthday was also celebrated, bringing to him a striking memorial signed by all the members of the Supreme Court bench, nearly all the members of both houses of Congress, and many private citizens of the highest distinction, making it clear that the nation held him in love and veneration as one of its greatest spiritual assets. He was visiting at the house of a friend, a few miles from Amesbury just over the New Hampshire border, when a cerebral hemorrhage brought him to a peaceful death, 7 September, 1892. "Love to all the world," were the words that played upon his lips just before the end.

In the classification of Whittier's work, the narrative poems are the first to call for consideration. "Of all our poets he is the most natural balladist," says E. C. Stedman, and throughout his entire life he was always ready to turn from the strenuous exactions of the causes which claimed his most ardent sympathies to the delightful relaxation of story-telling. From childhood he was steeped in the legendry of New England, its tales of Indian raids, of Quaker persecutions, of picturesque pioneers, and of romantic adventure; while the wide reading which made Whittier in later life a cultivated man fed his narrative faculty with old-world themes, ranging all the way from the Norse to the Oriental. The grim tragic economy of the folk-ballad, as it sprang from the heart of the people in England, Denmark, or Germany, never imparted its secret to him, although in *The Sisters* he came near to plucking the heart out of that mystery; but the ballad was to him the occasion for a rambling narration, diffuse in its unfolding and unrestrained in its form, often with decorative illustrations drawn from quite unexpected sources, and usually shaped to the point of a rather obtrusive moral. Such pieces as *Maud Muller* and *Barclay of Ury* would doubtless have been better poems without the moralizing tags which conclude them, but probably they would also have been less popular. Whittier's public expected a certain element of sermonizing in his verse and the America of his time paid scant heed to the cry that "art for art's sake" should be the guiding principle of poetic practice. The best of Whittier's ballads, nevertheless, are comparatively unburdened with didacticism. Among these may be mentioned *Pentucket*, with its memories of old-time Indian raids along the Merrimac; *Cassandra Southwick*, a tale of the Quaker persecutions; *The Angels of Buena Vista*, an echo from the battle-fields of the Mexican War; *The Garrison of Cape Ann*, which tells how the New Englander of old vanquished the powers of darkness; *Skipper Ireson's Ride*, a spirited song of the vengeance wrought by the women of Marblehead upon a sea-captain thought to have abandoned the crew of a sinking ship; *Mabel Martin*, an idyl of the days of witchcraft, and *Amy Wentworth*, a dainty romance of the old colonial time. Upon these ballads, and many others, New England childhood has been nurtured for a century, gaining from them its special sense of a heritage of no mean spiritual content, rich also in picturesque associations and romantic memories.

The high-water mark of Whittier's artistic achievement was undoubtedly reached in the years that gave birth to *Snow-*

Bound and *The Tent on the Beach*. The latter and less important of these two works is a cycle of narratives in verse, linked together in the fashion of Longfellow's *Tales of a Wayside Inn*. The company are three in number, "Fields the lettered magnate and Taylor the free cosmopolite" being foregathered on Salisbury Beach with Whittier, who thus describes himself:

> And one there was, a dreamer born,
>   Who, with a mission to fulfil,
> Had left the Muses' haunts to turn
>   The crank of an opinion-mill,
> Making his rustic reed of song
> A weapon in the war with wrong.

The poems which make up the cycle fall into the general class of Whittier's narrative verse; the thousand lines of octosyllabic rhyme which are entitled *Snow-Bound* are almost in a class by themselves. This idyllic description of the Whittier household shut in for a week by

> The chill embargo of the snow,

which bids us

> pause to view
> These Flemish pictures of old days,

is not only a poem but a social document of the highest value. In the words of T. W. Higginson,

Here we have absolutely photographed the Puritan Colonial interior, as it existed till within the memory of old men still living. No other book, no other picture preserves it to us; all other books, all other pictures combined, leave us still ignorant of the atmosphere which this one page re-creates for us; it is more imperishable than any interior painted by Gerard Douw.

It has been said of Whittier that he could never be concise— and a diffuse style is undoubtedly one of the greatest artistic defects of the body of his verse—but the criticism falls flat in the presence of the lines which describe the fireplace on that winter evening.

This poem has often been compared with *The Cotter's Saturday Night* and it means to the American all and more than Burns's famous poem means to the Scotsman. There is also much aptitude in a comparison with Crabbe, but it has qualities of wistful sentiment and tender reminiscence that are not to be found in the poet of *The Village* and *The Borough*. Akin to *Snow-Bound*, and to be mentioned as offering a foretaste of its subtle charm, is the short poem *The Barefoot Boy*, dated some ten years earlier, and cast in the same mould of retrospective yearning for the happy and wholesome days of childhood.

The most considerable section of Whittier's verse in point of volume is that in which the poet voices the burning indignation fanned in his breast by the curse of negro slavery in America. His fellow-poets—Holmes, Longfellow, Lowell, and Emerson—were all enlisted in the warfare against this monstrous evil, and did yeoman service in the cause of freedom, but Whittier alone gave himself heart and soul to the crusade, from early manhood until the cause was won, from the time of his first association with Garrison to the time when his jubilant *Laus Deo* acclaimed the writing into the fundamental law of the republic of the ban upon slavery throughout the extent of its domain. Every step in the history of the conflict, which is the history of the United States for the period of a full generation, was seized upon by Whittier as a pretext for poetical expression—the terrorizing of the pioneer abolitionists, the war which the annexation of Texas made inevitable, the efforts of Clay and Webster to heal the wounds of dissension by compromise, the outrage of the Fugitive Slave Law, the struggle for freedom in the Territory of Kansas, the growth of the modern Republican party, and the holocaust of the Civil War. The majority of the poems occasioned by these themes are too entirely of and for the moment to have any lasting value, but their immediate effect was potent in strengthening the mighty moral resolve of the nation, and they made Whittier perhaps the best beloved of contemporary American poets. When this mass of work is sifted by criticism, only a few pieces seem to preserve much of the fire which made them so effective at the time of their publication. We may still be stirred by the stanzas of *Le Marais du Cygne* and the marching-song of *The Kansas Emigrants:*

> We cross the prairies as of old
>   The pilgrims crossed the sea,
> To make the West, as they the East,
>   The homestead of the free!

The ballad of *Barbara Frietchie* still has power to thrill its readers, and the terrible *Ichabod*, occasioned by Webster's willingness to make terms with the abhorred evil of slavery, has lost little or none of its original force. "It is a fearful thing," says Swinburne, paraphrasing the Scriptures in praise of Victor Hugo, "for a malefactor to fall into the hands of an ever-living poet." And nowhere in the *Châtiments* of the French poet is there to be found a greater finality of condemnation than that with which Whittier stamped the subject of this truly great poem.

It will have been observed that many of the pieces already mentioned belong to the class of occasional or personal compositions. This class constitutes a large fraction of the total of Whittier's work. The long list of his friendly tributes and poems written for occasions includes many that are merely trivial or without any special appeal to readers for whom the incidents or personalities commemorated have no longer any meaning. Whittier had neither the wit nor the erudition that have preserved many of the occasional pieces of Holmes and Lowell from decay. The tributes to Garrison, Sumner, and a few others still stand out as significant from this mass of metrical exercises, and when a great occasion inspired Whittier to song, the result was likely to be memorable, as in the verses which celebrate the Emancipation Proclamation, the Thirteenth Amendment to the Federal Constitution, the Chicago Fire of 1871, and the Centennial Exhibition of 1876.

The deep and sincere religious feeling of the *Centennial Hymn* is characteristic of the entire body of Whittier's verse, and not merely of the poems specifically religious in their subject-matter. His consciousness was shot through with a sense of the divine. and the essential spirituality of his thought suffuses his expression like the sunlight in cloud-banked western skies. But his religious faith was far from being of the dogmatic type. "I regard Christianity as a life rather than as a creed," he once said, and the whole of his writing exemplifies the statement. He found in the doctrines of the Society of Friends exactly the framework which his nature needed, saying that "after a candid and kindly survey" of all the other creeds, "I turn to my own Society, thankful to the Divine Providence which placed me where I am; and with an unshaken faith in the one distinctive doctrine of Quakerism —the Light Within—the immanence of the Divine Spirit in Christianity." In this doctrine, he says elsewhere, "will yet be found the stronghold of Christendom, the sure, safe place from superstition on the one hand and scientific doubt on the other." The perfect expression of this simple and serene faith is found in *The Eternal Goodness*, and still again in the very last of all his poems. The sunset song of Tennyson's soul, just before "crossing the bar" that divides the harbour of Time from the ocean of Eternity, illustrates no better than do these final lines of Whittier the matchless beauty that may crown the simplest modes of expression, if only they are based upon perfect faith and perfect sincerity.

While Whittier was primarily a poet, his activities as a reformer and philanthropist, and his editorial work in connection with the many papers that claimed his services, made him an important writer of prose. The amount of his prose writing is very great, and, although the larger part of it is too ephemeral to have any place in the history of American literature, the part which has been thought worthy of inclusion in the standard edition of his collected works fills three of the seven volumes. Much of this writing is controversial in character, like the early tract on *Justice and Expediency*, but the greater part of it belongs to the permanent literature of New England history and thought. The most important titles are *The Stranger in Lowell*, *The Supernaturalism of New England*, *Leaves from Margaret Smith's Journal in the Province of Massachusetts Bay*, and *Literary Recreations and Miscellanies*. The story of Margaret Smith is almost a work of fiction. It recounts the imagined observations of a young woman who comes from England on a visit to the Bay Colony in its early days. She meets the chief worthies of the time, describes the landscape and the crude pioneer life, and writes of witch-hunting, Quaker-baiting, and Indian warfare. G. R. Carpenter says of this work that "no single modern volume could be found which has so penetrated the secret of colonial times in Massachusetts, for it is almost line by line a transcript and imaginative interpretation of old letters, journals, and memoirs." Its Quaker authorship, moreover, gives it just the detachment needed to save it from the danger of accepting too unreservedly the view of New England colonial life that the leaders of the Puritan theocracy so zealously sought to perpetuate.

In the history of English literature in the larger sense, Whittier is probably no more than a poet of the third rank. His native endowment was rich, but it was supplemented by neither the technical training nor the discipline required for the development of the artist. He was extremely careless about his rhymes—"good Yankee rhymes, but out of New England they would be cashiered," he once said of them. The construction of his stanzas was diffuse and often slovenly. The organ voice and the lyric cry were not, except at rare moments, his to command. But no American who lived in the shadow of slavery and internecine strife, none who grew to manhood in the generation succeeding those epic days, would dream of measuring his love and veneration for Whittier by the scale of absolute art. Whittier's verse is so inwrought with the nation's passion during that period of heightened consciousness that preserved the Union and redeemed it from the curse of slavery that it cannot be coldly and critically considered by any one who has had a vital sense of the agonies and exaltations of that critical time. To such, the invocation of Stedman's *Ad Vatem* will always be a truer expression of their feeling than any critical judgment, for they can never forget their debt to him for

> righteous anger, burning scorn
> Of the oppressor, love to humankind,
> Sweet fealty to country and to home,
> Peace, stainless purity, high thoughts of heaven,
> And the clear, natural music of [his] song.

Fifty years ago, the verdict of thoughtful Americans acclaimed Whittier as the foremost American poet, with the possible exception of Longfellow, and while now there would be more dissentients from that judgment than there were then, his fame still rests upon a very solid basis of acceptance and esteem. And especially to those who have sprung from the soil of New England, he will always be the incomparable poet of their childhood home, of its landscape, its legendry, and the spiritual essence of its history.

CHAPTER XIV

Poe

THE saddest and the strangest figure in American literary history is that of Edgar Allan Poe. Few writers have lived a life so full of struggle and disappointment, and none have lived and died more completely out of sympathy with their times. His life has been made the subject of minute and prolonged investigation, yet there are still periods in his history that have not been satisfactorily cleared up. And the widest differences of opinion have existed as to his place and his achievements. But there are few today who will not readily concede to him a place among the foremost writers of America, whether in prose or in verse, and there are not wanting those who account him one of the two or three writers of indisputable genius that America has produced.

Poe was born at Boston, 19 January, 1809, the son of actor parents of small means and of romantic proclivities. Before the end of his third year he was left an orphan, his mother dying in wretched poverty at Richmond, Virginia, 8 December, 1811, and his father a few weeks later, if we may believe the poet's own statement. He was promptly taken under the protection of a prosperous tobacco exporter of Richmond, John Allan, in whose family he lived, ostensibly as an adopted child, until 1827. In his sixth year he attended for a short time the school of William Ewing in Richmond. In the summer of 1815 he went with his foster-father to England, and for the next five years, with the exception of a few months spent in Scotland shortly after reaching England, he lived in London, attending first a boarding school kept by the Misses Dubourg in Sloane Street, and later the academy of the Rev. John Bransby in Stoke Newington. He impressed Bransby as a "quick and clever boy," though embarrassed by "an extravagant amount of pocket-money"; and John Allan wrote of him in 1818 that he was "a fine boy" and read "Latin pretty sharply." In 1816 Allan described him as "thin as a razor," but in 1819 he wrote that he was "growing wonderfully."

On his return to Richmond in the summer of 1820, Poe entered an academy kept, first, by Joseph H. Clarke and, later, by William Burke, under whom he continued his work in the languages, earning the admiration of his fellows by his readiness at "capping verses" from the Latin and by his skill in declamation. He also wrote verses of his own, and it is said that a sheaf of his juvenilia was collected in 1822 or 1823 in the hope that they might be published in volume form. But before the end of 1824 he had somehow broken with his foster-father, and the breach between the two was never to be entirely healed. "The boy possesses not a spark of affection for us," wrote John Allan in November, 1824, "not a particle of gratitude for all my care and kindness towards him. . . . I fear his associates have led him to adopt a line of thinking and acting very contrary to what he possessed when in England." The immediate cause of the breach we do not know; but a parting of the ways between the two, who were radically dissimilar in tastes and ideals, was inevitable sooner or later.

The year 1826 Poe spent as a student at the University of Virginia. Here he made a creditable record in his classes, winning honourable mention in Latin and French; and he at no time fell under the censure of his instructors. At the end of the year, however, because of his having accumulated gambling debts of some twenty-five hundred dollars, he was withdrawn from college; and with the beginning of the next year he was placed by his adoptive father in his counting-house in Richmond, in the hope that he might develop a taste for a business career. But he had small leaning that way; besides, he had been disappointed in a love-affair, having become engaged before going to college to Miss Sarah Elmira Royster, of Richmond, who, in consequence of a misunderstanding, had jilted him in his absence and had betrothed herself to another. Smarting under this disappointment and completely out of sympathy with the life marked out for him by his foster-father, Poe now determined to run away: and at some time in March, 1827, he left Richmond for parts unknown. In May he appeared at Boston, and there, 26 May, he was mustered into the army of the United States. The next two years he served as a soldier in barracks, being stationed first at Boston, then at Charleston, South Carolina, and finally at Fortress Monroe. In the spring or summer of 1827 he brought out at Boston his first volume of poems, *Tamerlane and Other Poems*, a collection of ten fugitive pieces, all brief save one, and all plainly imitative either of Byron or of Moore.

In February, 1829, Mrs. Allan died, and in April Poe was discharged from the army, a substitute having been provided, and efforts were made to obtain for him an appointment to West Point. Some time intervened, however, before an appointment could be procured, and it was not until July, 1830, that he was admitted to the Academy. In the preceding December he had published at Baltimore a second volume of poems, made up largely of his earlier pieces revised, but containing his long poem *Al Aaraaf*, the most ambitious and the most promising of his earlier productions. At West Point he took high rank in his classes; but in October, 1830, John Allan had married a second time, and Poe, concluding that there was no longer any prospect of succeeding to a fortune, determined with the beginning of the new year to bring about his dismissal from the Academy. He adopted the very effective means of absenting himself from roll calls and from classes, was court-martialled in consequence, and 6 March, 1831, was formally expelled. In April a third volume of his poems appeared, containing some of the best work that he ever did, but in a state much inferior to that in which he ultimately left it.

During the ensuing four years Poe seems to have made his home in Baltimore, though it is impossible to trace his history with complete certainty throughout this period. Much of his time, no doubt, was given to his prose tales, five of which appeared in the Philadelphia *Saturday Courier*, in 1832,[1] and a sixth—for which he won a prize of a hundred dollars—in the Baltimore *Saturday Visiter* in October, 1833; and he also worked at intervals during these years on a play, *Politian*, which, though published in part, was never completed. That

[1] These stories were originally submitted in competition for a prize—won, as it happens, by Delia Bacon.

he lived in poverty and in much obscurity is evident from the reminiscences of John Pendleton Kennedy, the novelist,[1] who had been one of the judges in the *Visiter's* contest in 1833 and who now proved his most helpful friend.

In the summer of 1835, Poe went to Richmond to assist in the editing of *The Southern Literary Messenger*, and before the end of the year he had been promoted to be editor-in-chief of that magazine. He was now fairly launched on his career as man of letters. In the columns of the *Messenger* he republished, with slight revisions, the tales that had already appeared, and in addition a number of new tales and poems, together with a long line of book reviews, which promptly won for the *Messenger* a popularity such as no other Southern magazine has ever enjoyed. In May, 1836, relying on his suddenly acquired prosperity, he married. His wife was Virginia Clemm,[2] a child of thirteen and the daughter of a paternal aunt, in whose home he had lived for a time in Baltimore. In the fall he was absent from his post for several weeks in consequence of illness brought on by excessive indulgence in drink; and though on his recovery he returned to his duties with his accustomed vigour, he was unable to satisfy his employer as to his stability of habit; and with the initial number of the *Messenger* for 1837 his resignation as editor was formally announced.

From Richmond he went to New York, where he hoped to find employment with *The New York Review*. In October, 1837, he was in Richmond again, posing as editor still of the *Messenger*, though we cannot be certain that he contributed anything to its columns at this time. At the end of the year he was again in New York; and in the following summer he moved to Philadelphia. In July he published at New York, in book form, the longest of his tales, *The Narrative of Arthur Gordon Pym*.

The next six years (1838–1844) he spent in Philadelphia. During the first year he was engaged largely in hack-writing, busying himself with a work on conchology (published in

---

[1] Tuckerman, *Life of Kennedy*, pp. 373 f.

[2] A license for marriage to Virginia Clemm was procured at Baltimore in September, 1835, but it has not been established that there was a wedding at that time.

1839) among other things, though he also composed at this time some of the best of his tales. In May, 1839, he became associate editor of *Burton's Gentleman's Magazine*, but a year later he quarrelled with Burton and lost his place. From April, 1841, to May, 1842, he edited *Graham's Magazine*. And in 1843 he had for a while some tacit connection with a Philadelphia weekly, *The Saturday Museum*. In *Burton's* and in *Graham's* he published a number of the ablest of his book-reviews and some of the most striking of his tales. At the end of 1839 he brought out at Philadelphia a collection of his tales, in two volumes; and in 1843 a further edition of his tales was projected, of which, however, only one fascicle, containing but two of his stories, was published. In the same year he won a prize of a hundred dollars for his story *The Gold Bug*. But at no time during these years was his income from his writings or from his editorial labours sufficient to enable him to live in comfort. During his later years in Philadelphia, moreover, his weakness for drink had grown on him, and he had as a result lost many of his friends; his wife, too, frail from childhood, had become an invalid in 1841 or in 1842; and so, early in 1844, the poet concluded to seek a new field.

In April, 1844, he moved with his family to New York; and there, either in the city or at Fordham, a few miles out, he lived during the remaining five years allotted to him. The year 1844 was uneventful, but the year 1845 proved to be the pivotal year of his history. At the end of January appeared in the New York *Evening Mirror*, on which he had held a minor editorial position for several months, *The Raven;* and he became at once the most talked of man of letters in America. In the summer he published a new volume of his tales, and in the fall, a collected edition of his poems, *The Raven and Other Poems.* Early in the year he became assistant editor of *The Broadway Journal;* in July he became sole editor, and in October editor and proprietor of this paper; and thus was enabled to realize an ambition that he had cherished for more than a decade, to edit a paper of his own. But owing to financial embarrassments arising from various causes, he was compelled to give up this paper at the end of the year. During the first half of 1846 he was ill, so he himself claimed, for several months. In the middle of the year (May to October) he published, in Godey's *Lady's Book*, his *Literati*, a series of bio-graphical-critical papers dealing with the chief living writers of Gotham; and the year was further made memorable by the controversy with Thomas Dunn English engendered by the publication of the *Literati*, and by a scandal growing out of his friendship with the poetess, Mrs. F. S. Osgood. Early in 1847 the poet's wife died, and throughout the year, as indeed during the preceding year, the family suffered keenly from the pinch of poverty. The year 1848 saw the culmination of two unhappy love-affairs—first, with Mrs. Shew, who had nursed the poet through a spell of illness following the death of his wife, and then with Mrs. Whitman, the Rhode Island poetess; and this year also witnessed the publication of his *Eureka*, a philosophical disquisition on the origin and composition of the universe.

The year 1849 opened auspiciously for the poet; during the first half he wrote at least one new tale, and several new poems, including the lines *For Annie*, *Eldorado*, a revised and much enlarged version of *The Bells*, and the last of his poems, *Annabel Lee*. In the summer of 1849 he went to Richmond, where he renewed his addresses to the sweetheart of his boy-hood, Miss Royster, now the widow Mrs. Shelton and wealthy, and they became engaged for a second time. Late in Septem-ber Poe left Richmond for the North, intending to bring his mother-in-law, who remained loyal to him throughout the years, to the South for the marriage; but at Baltimore he was induced to break a temperance pledge that he had made in the summer, and as a result he fell into excesses from the effects of which he died 7 October, 1849. He lies buried in the churchyard of Westminster Presbyterian Church, Baltimore.

Such are the leading facts that have been established con-cerning Poe's life. But despite the labours of his biographers —and no American writer has had more and abler biographers —there are still certain periods of his life for which our know-ledge is exceedingly meagre and unsatisfactory. We have, for instance, no specific knowledge as to how or where he spent the two months intervening between his departure from Rich-mond in March, 1827, and his mustering into the army at the end of May. We are likewise ignorant both as to his where-abouts and as to his activities during the year immediately pre-ceding his winning of the *Visiter's* prize in October, 1833; and the entire period from 1831 to 1835 is obscure. He sinks out of sight again for six months in the middle of 1837. And a hiatus of several months also occurs in his history during the first half of the year 1846. For this obscurity Poe is himself mainly responsible. He took pleasure in mystifying his public about himself; and in a few instances he deliberately misstated the facts. [1]

As to Poe's character and personality the most divergent views have been expressed. According to Griswold, whom he chose as his literary executor, Poe was a "naturally unamiable character," arrogant, "irascible, envious," without "moral susceptibility" or sense of gratitude, and exhibiting "scarcely any virtue in either his life or his writings." According to the Richmond editor, John M. Daniel, who saw him frequently during the summer of 1849, he was sour of nature, capricious, selfish, a misanthrope, possessing "little moral sense." In the view of Lowell's friend, C. F. Briggs, with whom he was associated for several months in 1845 as co-editor of the *Broadway Journal*, he was "badly made up," a "characterless character," and "utterly deficient of high motive." And Horace Greeley was disturbed lest Mrs. Whitman should marry him, giving it as his opinion that such a union would be a "terrible conjunction." To N. P. Willis, on the other hand, who perhaps knew him better than any other outside of his immediate family during his last half-dozen years, there appeared, during several months of close association with him in 1844–1845, "but one presentment of the man,—a quiet, patient, industrious, and most gentlemanly person, commanding the utmost respect and good feeling by his unvarying deportment and ability"; and in subsequent years he saw, so he declares, nothing of the arrogance, vanity, and depravity of heart "that were commonly attributed to him." And George R. Graham, editor of the magazine that bore his name, testifies that, when he knew him best (in the first half of the forties), "he had the docility and kind-heartedness of a child," and that "no man was more quickly touched by a kindness, none more prompt to make return for an injury," and, further, that he was "the soul

[1] See, in particular, in this connection, an autobiographical memorandum sent to Griswold in 1841 (*Works of Poe*, ed. Harrison, Vol. I, pp. 344–346), in which most of the dates are inaccurately given, and in which we have one of several apocryphal accounts of a voyage to Europe in 1827.

of honour in all his transactions." Kennedy notes that he was
"irregular, eccentric, and querulous," but adds—as if in set rejoinder to Griswold's charge that he was incapable of gratitude
for service done—that "he always remembered my kindness
with gratitude." As time has passed and we have come to know
more about Poe's life, it has become more and more evident
that the view of his character held by Griswold and those who
sided with him was unduly harsh,[1] though it remains clear,
nevertheless, that Poe was not without regrettable traits and
serious weaknesses. It is plain, first of all, that he was abnormally proud and sensitive and impulsive; it is equally plain
that he was thoroughly undignified and ungenerous in his
attacks on certain of his contemporaries who had aroused his
envy or incurred his dislike. We have already noted that he
was not invariably accurate of statement, especially in matters
pertaining peculiarly to himself; we know, too, that he was an
incessant borrower, and that he neglected in some instances
to make good his borrowings at the appointed time,—though
there is no conclusive evidence of dishonesty of intent on his
part. And all the world knows that he sometimes drank to
excess. But it is also clear—contrary to the popular assumption—that Poe was not a confirmed inebriate: the volume and
the quality of his writings sufficiently demonstrate this; and it
is not to be denied that he made repeated and manful efforts
to shake off the tyranny of drink. Nor can we read his letters
—in which we see the true Poe more plainly than elsewhere—
without being convinced that he also possessed amiable traits
and noble impulses. In any estimate of his character, moreover, it is but just to take into account—as, indeed, most of his
recent biographers have done—the influences exerted on his
character by heredity and by his early environment[2]; and it
should also be borne in mind that he suffered during most of
his later career from serious physical infirmities.[3]

[1] It is due to Griswold, however, to say that his account of Poe's life, though
inaccurate at many points and jaundiced throughout, is more to be relied on
than is now commonly assumed. For exposing most of Griswold's inaccuracies
we are indebted to Poe's English biographer, the late John H. Ingram.

[2] His father before him was highly impulsive and was over-fond of drink,
and his foster-father was not only given to wine-bibbing but was an arch-hypocrite
besides.

[3] The clash of opinion with respect to Poe's character appears to be due

It was as critic that Poe first attracted widespread attention. As editor of the *Messenger* and *Burton's* and *Graham's* his chief function was that of book-reviewer; and much of the work that he did for other periodicals was of the nature of book-reviews and gossip about books and authors. The bulk of his work in this field is journalistic in style and of ephemeral interest, much of it being the merest hack-writing; but there remains a small body of critical matter that possesses genuine worth and distinction, and that entitles Poe to an honourable place among the literary critics of America.[1] Assuredly no other American critic of his day, save Lowell, may take rank above him. This residue of good work comprises a score of masterly book-reviews, including the memorable notices of Longfellow's *Ballads*, Hawthorne's *Twice-Told Tales*, and Dickens's *Barnaby Rudge;* some half-dozen essays in the theory of criticism, of which the earliest is his *Letter to B——*, and the most significant is his *Poetic Principle;* and a series of *obiter dicta*, collected under the title *Marginalia*, which have justly[2] been held to contain much of his best work as critic.[2]

His most distinctive gifts as critic were clearness of intellect and a faculty for analysis. Few Americans of his time had finer intellectual endowments. He also had the poet's "faculty of ideality," on which he laid great stress in his judgments of others. And he was the most independent and fearless of critics, disdaining not to attack either high or low. He had not read very widely; but he knew his Milton well, and probably his Shakespeare and his Pope, and he was familiar

---

mainly, as Willis suggested, to the fact that most of the contemporary judgments adverse to him were based on his conduct during his spells of inebriation, at which times (as he pathetically admitted more than once) he was largely irresponsible. Most of these estimates, too, are based, naturally, on the poet's later years, after both body and mind had become enfeebled. Poe himself urged, in partial explanation of his irregularities in his later years, the plea of insanity; and there is reason to believe that he was at one time addicted to the use of opium.

[1] "Poe's critical writing was so much superior to the best of what had preceded it," remarks William Morton Payne (*American Literary Criticism*, 1904, p. 14), "that one might almost be pardoned for saying that this department of our literature began when, in 1835, The Southern Literary Messenger engaged his services."

[2] F. C. Prescott, *Selections from the Critical Writings of Edgar Allan Poe*, p. xix; J. M. Robertson, *New Essays towards a Critical Method*, p. 117.

with the chief Romantic poets of the age immediately preceding his own; while as editor and magazinist he kept in close touch with contemporary literature. On the other hand, he was prone to exaggerate technical blemishes and to under-estimate ethical and philosophical significance. And his taste was not always impeccable. By his contemporaries he was thought of as inexcusably harsh in his criticisms: by one of them he is dubbed the "tomahawk man," by another the "broad-axe man"; and Lowell remarks, in his sketch of him, that he seemed "sometimes to mistake his phial of prussic-acid for his inkstand." What is more to his discredit, he stooped now and then to log-rolling both on his own account and on behalf of his friends, and his unfavourable judgments appear to have been actuated in some instances by animus and jealousy. But most of his critical judgments have been sustained by time. And despite the arrogance charged against him by Griswold and others, it is to be set down to his credit that he ungrudgingly conceded to Longfellow and Lowell the primacy among the American poets of his time and that he generously proclaimed Hawthorne to be without a peer in his peculiar field. His chief hobbies as critic were originality—and, *per contra*, imitation and plagiarism—"unity or totality of effect," consistency and "keeping," verisimilitude, "the heresy of the didactic," provinciality, metrical imperfections of whatever sort, and verbal inaccuracies and infelicities; some of which hobbies—as plagiarism—he rode over-hard. But his influence in an age when wholesale adulation was the rule, and when art counted for but little, was naturally wholesome.

Among the best known of his critical *dicta* is his characterization of the short story in his notice of Hawthorne's *Twice-Told Tales* (1842). Probably no other passage in American literary criticism has been quoted so often as the following extract from this review:

A skilful literary artist has constructed a tale. If wise, he has not fashioned his thoughts to accommodate his incidents; but having conceived, with deliberate care, a certain unique or single *effect* to be wrought out, he then invents such incidents—he then combines such events as may best aid him in establishing this preconceived effect. If his very initial sentence tend not to the outbring-ing of this effect, then he has failed in his first step. In the whole composition there should be no word written, of which the tend-ency, direct or indirect, is not to the one pre-established design. And by such means, with such care and skill, a picture is at length painted which leaves in the mind of him who contemplates it with a kindred art, a sense of the fullest satisfaction. The idea of the tale has been presented unblemished, because undisturbed; and this is an end unattainable by the novel.[1]

Scarcely less famous are some of his deliverances on the mean-ing and the province and aims of poetry. Poetry he defined as the "rhythmical creation of beauty," holding with Cole-ridge, his chief master as critic, that its "immediate object" is "pleasure, not truth"; and that "with the intellect or with the conscience it has only collateral relations." "Poetry and passion" he held to be "discordant." And humour, also, he believed to be "antagonistical to that which is the soul of the muse proper." Sadness he declared to be the most poetic of moods; and "indefinitiveness" one of the chief essentials of lyric excellence. A long poem he held, with Bryant, to be a "contradiction in terms."

Poe's critical doctrines find their best exemplification in his own poems. He is, first of all, a poet of beauty, paying little heed to morality or to the life of his fellow-men. He is, in the second place, a master-craftsman, who has produced a dozen poems of a melody incomparable so far as the western world is concerned; and he has achieved an all but flawless construc-tion of the whole in such poems as *The Raven, The Haunted Palace*, and *The Conqueror Worm;* while in *The Bells* he has performed a feat in onomatopœia quite unapproached before or since in the English language. He is, moreover, one of the most original of poets. And the best of his verse exhibits a spontaneity and finish and perfection of phrase, as well as, at times, a vividness of imagery, that it is difficult to match elsewhere in American poetry.

But his poems of extraordinary worth are exceedingly few —scarcely above a score at most—in which must be included the earlier lines *To Helen, Israfel, The City in the Sea, The Sleeper,*

[1] *Works of Poe*, ed. Harrison, Vol. XI, p. 108.

The Haunted Palace, Dream-Land, The Raven, Ulalume, For Annie, and *Annabel Lee.* And most of his earlier verses are manifestly imitative, Byron and Moore and Coleridge and Shelley being his chief models; while much of his earlier work, including all of the volume of 1827, and some of his latest—notably the verses addressed to Mrs. Osgood and Mrs. Shew and Mrs. Lewis—are either fragmentary and "incondite" or mere "verses," or both. It has been justly said that "there is almost no poet between whose best and worst verse there is a wider disparity."[1] His range, too, is narrower than that of any other American poet of front rank. Consistently with one of his theories already adverted to, he wrote no long poem, save the juvenile *Tamerlane* and *Al Aaraaf*, both of them extremely crude performances (though *Al Aaraaf* contains excellent passages and played a large part in his development as poet), and an abortive play, *Politian*, which he never saw fit to publish in its entirety; so that he lives as poet solely by reason of his lyrics. And within the realm of the lyric he confined himself to the narrowest range of ideas. Nature he employed merely as ornament or as symbol or to fill in the background; and nowhere in his poems does he deal with the life about him, except in so far as he writes of friends and kindred. His most constant theme—if we exclude the poet himself, for few writers have so constantly reflected themselves in their work—is either the death of a beautiful woman and the grief occasioned thereby, or the realm of shades—the spirit-world—a subject to which he was strongly attracted, especially in his middle years. Hence, although most European critics have accorded him first place among American poets, most American critics have hesitated to accept their verdict.

Much of the excellence of his best poems arises from the never-ending revisions to which he subjected them. *The Raven*, for example, exists in upwards of a dozen variant forms, and some of his earlier verses were so radically altered as to be scarcely recognizable in their final recast. His melody, especially in his later poems, grows in large measure out of his all but unexampled use of parallelism and of the refrain.[2] Not a little of his charm, moreover, both in his earlier and in

[1] J. M. Robertson, *New Essays*, p. 76.
[2] C. A. Smith, *Repetition and Parallelism in English Verse*, pp. 44 f.

his later work, results from his use of symbolism. It is idle to complain that his best verses—as *Israfel* or *The Haunted Palace* —are superficial; and it is futile to contend that such poems as *Annabel Lee* or the sonnet *To My Mother* are not sincere, or that his poems, one and all, lack spontaneity. But it is not to be denied that some of his best-known poems—as *Lenore* and *The Raven*—exhibit too much of artifice; that *The Conqueror Worm* and passages in still other poems approach too near to the melodramatic; and that, with many readers, his verses must suffer by reason of their sombreness of tone.

Poe's tales, which exceed in number his fully authenticated poems, have been held by some of the most judicious of his critics to constitute his chief claim to our attention.[1] There are those who will not subscribe to this view, but it is plain that he was the most important figure in the history of the short story during his half-century. Hawthorne alone may be thought of as vying with him for this distinction; but although the New Englander is infinitely Poe's superior in some respects—as in the creation of character and in wholesomeness and sanity—he must yield place to him in the creation of incident, in the construction of plot, and in the depicting of an intensely vivid situation. Whether or not we allow Poe the distinction of having invented the short story will depend on our interpretation of terms; but at least he invented the detective story, and more than any other he gave to the short story its vogue in America.

Like his poems, his tales are notably unequal. Some of his earlier efforts—especially his satirical and humorous extravaganzas, as *Lionizing* and *Bon-Bon*—are properly to be characterized as rubbish; and he was capable in his later years of descending to such inferior work as *The Sphinx*, *Mellonta Tauta*, and *X-ing a Paragrab*. One feels, indeed, that Lowell's famous characterization of him:

Three fifths of him genius and two fifths sheer fudge,

applies with entire justice to him as a maker of short stories. The best of his narrative work is to be found in his analytical

[1] E. C. Stedman in the Stedman-Woodberry edition of Poe, Vol. x, p. xiii; and Robertson, *l. c.*, p. 75.

tales, as *The Gold Bug* or *The Descent into the Maelstrom,* in certain stories in which he combines his analytical gift with the imaginative and inventive gift, as *The Cask of Amontillado* and *William Wilson,* or in certain studies of the pure imagination, as *The Fall of the House of Usher* and *The Masque of the Red Death.* In all of these he displays a skill of construction and of condensation surpassed by few if any other workers in his field. In some—as in *The Masque of the Red Death,* or in *Eleonora,* or in his landscape studies—he shows himself a master of English style; and in two of his briefer studies—*Shadow* and *Silence*—he approaches the eloquence and splendour of De Quincey.

His main limitations as a writer of the short story are to be found in the feebleness and flimsiness of his poorer work; in his all but complete lack of healthy humour; in his incapacity to create or to depict character; in his morbidness of mood and grotesqueness of situation.[1] He suffers also in comparison with other leading short-story writers of America and England in consequence of his disdain of the ethical in art (though neither his tales nor his poems are entirely lacking in ethical value); he suffers, again, in comparison with certain present-day masters of the short story in consequence of his lack of variety in theme and form; and he was never expert in the management of dialogue.

By reason of his fondness for the terrible and for the *outré,* he is to be classed with the Gothic romancers: he makes constant use of Gothic machinery, of apparitions, cataleptic attacks, premature burial, and life after death. In several of his stories—as also in his long poems, *Tamerlane* and *Al Aaraaf* —he follows in the steps of the Orientalists. On the other hand, in some of his tales of incident he achieves a realism and a minuteness of detail that betray unmistakably the influence of Defoe. And it is easy to demonstrate an indebtedness to divers

[1] His friend, P. P. Cooke, wrote of him in 1847: "For my individual part, having the seventy or more tales, analytic, mystic, grotesque, arabesque, always wonderful, often great, which his industry and fertility have already given us, I would like to read one cheerful book made by his *invention,* with little or no aid from its twin brother *imagination,* . . . a book full of homely doings, of successful toils, of ingenious shifts and contrivances, of ruddy firesides—a book healthy and happy throughout" (*Southern Literary Messenger,* January, 1848, p. 37).

of his contemporaries, as James and Bulwer and Disraeli and Macaulay. It has been proved also that he knew the German romancer, E. T. A. Hoffmann, if not in the original, at least in translation, and that he caught his manner and appropriated his themes.[1] For the rest, he drew for his materials largely on the magazines and newspapers of his day, finding in a famous newspaper sensation of the forties the suggestion of his *Mystery of Marie Rogêt* (as he had found in another sensation, of the twenties, the plot of his *Politian*), and taking advantage of certain contemporary fads in his myth-making about mesmerism, ballooning, premature burial, and the like; and he boldly pilfered from government reports, scientific treatises, and works of reference such material as he found serviceable in some of his tales of adventure. Hence his originality may be said to consist rather in combination and adaptation than in more obviously inventive exercises of the fancy.

Poe's influence has been far-reaching. As poet, he has had many imitators both in his own country and abroad, but especially in France and England.[2] As romancer he has probably wielded a larger influence than any English writer since Scott. And as critic it is doubtful whether any other of his countrymen has contributed so much toward keeping the balance right between art-for-art's-sake and didacticism. His fame abroad is admittedly larger than that of any other American writer, and his vogue has been steadily growing among his own people.

[1] Palmer Cobb, *The Influence of E. T. A. Hoffmann on the Tales of Edgar Allan Poe*. Woodberry, *Life of Poe*, vol. I, pp. 379–381, and *passim*.

[2] In the view of Edmund Gosse, "there is hardly one [of the later English poets] whose verse-music does not show traces of Poe's influence" (*Questions at Issue*, p. 90). On Poe's influence and vogue in France, see L. P. Betz, *Edgar Poe in der franzoesischen Litteratur: Studien zur vergleichenden Litteraturgeschichte der neueren Zeit* (1902), pp. 16–82; C. H. Page in *The* [New York] *Nation* for 14 January, 1909; and G. D. Morris, *Fenimore Cooper et Edgar Poe*, pp. 67 f. (Paris, 1912).

CHAPTER XV

Publicists and Orators, 1800–1850

IN America, political theory and political philosophy have always been closely associated with practical politics and with the problems of very immediate interest. The cogent and effective theory of the American Revolution was distinctly part of a determined effort to reach results in civil organization. And so too in the first half of the nineteenth century, a period by no means without its contribution to the philosophy of the state, most of the political theory appeared in speeches and pamphlets directed to the accomplishment of a present and very concrete purpose. The Americans have been charged with incapacity for sustained theorizing, or for prolonged logical discussion; and yet one may safely say that no other people of modern times have so widely used political theory or so generally discussed practical affairs on a theoretical basis. The whole nature of our institutions has prompted men to indulge in argument which was legalistic and was often tinctured with philosophy. Even the unlearned could not speak and think of democracy and its hopes without indulging in visions; they could not discuss the presence of slavery without touching the border of the deepest problems of social order; they could not speak of union or states' rights without entering at least the outer portal of philosophic argument. But we need not look for detached theoretical treatises; the statesman, the politician, and the jurist were busily using such learning as they had and such aptitude for theory as they possessed in the concrete and difficult problems which were begotten by democracy in a country which, to use Calhoun's words, was "rapidly—I was about to say fearfully —growing." Calhoun himself, a philosopher of real distinction, probably never claimed a higher rôle than that of statesman; and though he published two treatises which belong in the field of political theory, they were produced because of an immediate tangible condition and they were partly vitiated for permanent service because of their defence of a decaying institution which dimmed his own outlook on the world.

The first few decades of the century, if they produced no notable pieces of abstract political theory, gave alluring opportunity for oratory and offered also an unusual field for the jurist. The orator had big themes—democracy, slavery, free labour, expansion, states' rights, nationalism, as well as the well-worn subjects of banks and tariffs and lands and commerce. The jurist was called to the novel task of construing constitutions, of passing on the fundamental law of a federal republic, and more—the task of developing and adjusting a system of private law suited to the needs of a new people and a new country. In both of these fields of action and of thought the Americans did much; in oratory appeared Webster, Clay, Calhoun, Randolph, Choate, Benton, and John Quincy Adams, and others only less worthy of note; in jurisprudence, Marshall and Kent and Story and Wheaton, by judicial opinion or by written text, laid the foundations of American public and private law and ably performed a creative task such as rarely, if ever, before fell to the lot of the jurist.

Much of the oratory of the time was of a kind which appeals but little to the reader of the present day. The speeches that have come down to us are often diffuse and occasionally florid. Nothing else could be expected from the leaders of a nation which was full of eager life and was assured of its own high destiny, a nation in which a man to be a popular leader must have power in appealing to the multitude, uncritical in its attitude toward literary form, provided the speaker himself have vitality, assurance, and a plentiful store of winged words. This, it is true, is not altogether just, for Webster's diction was on the whole restrained and strong; Calhoun rarely declaimed; Clay and Benton and Adams were always earnest and did not merely toy with words; Everett's orations, polished and academic, never descended into the lower realms of commonplace word-juggling for applause. And yet it is probably right to say that most of the speaking of the time was affected by the fact that orators were appealing to a wide constituency, to a people engaged in very practical tasks, but self-confident, buoyant, and withal emotional or at least idealistic.

The jurists of the time may here be considered first, although, as already said, it is not possible to disassociate the greatest among them from the problems which enlisted the enthusiasm and interest of the orator and political leader. If one turns, for example, to the decisions which John Marshall (1755–1835) gave as chief justice, one at once thinks of the work of Calhoun and other great particularists, who in the field of active politics put forth theories totally at variance with those coming from the Court. It is, therefore, quite impossible to detach Marshall from the most important movements of his time; for his words lose significance unless we see that they marked out lines of social and political progress and profoundly affected the character and career of the nation. And thus too, if the establishment of a widely accepted system of jurisprudence is necessary for the building up of a common industrial and social life for the nation at large, the work of Joseph Story, James Kent, and others, cannot be assigned to any narrow field of technical jurisprudence of interest to the professional lawyer alone.

The appointment of Marshall to the chief justiceship (January, 1801) was of great significance, for in the course of a few years he showed the importance of the Federal judiciary and the great authority of his office. For thirty-four years he presided over the Court and gave out a series of decisions which fixed permanently the principles of constitutional construction. His task was in some respects more that of the statesman than the lawyer; he was called upon to consider public questions of far-reaching importance and to lay down principles which he must gather from the nature of the United States, which was itself, in its composite organization, an experiment, a new form of political order. He was the first judge in history on whom fell the duty of interpreting and expounding the fundamental basis of the state; for, though the Supreme Court had been in existence twelve years before Marshall took his seat on the bench, not much had been done to prepare the way or to throw light on the solution of perplexing problems which Marshall had to solve. Ordinary legal learning and, above all, learning in the domain of ordinary private law could not avail him much; indeed one may question whether, had his mind been stored with vast legal lore, he could have entered on his work without falling into traps of pedantry or finding himself clogged by precedent and technicality. He brought to his great undertaking considerable experience in public affairs, an interest and a viewpoint arising from practical participation in government, and no small amount of learning in international and municipal law and in what we should now call political science.

The layman reading Marshall's decisions will be struck by the fact that he did not balance an opinion on a long line of precedents or seek refuge behind the thoughts and words of others. Few references to authority are to be found, and in some of his greatest cases there is not a single citation of precedent. He begins with simple statements, founded, one is led to think, in common sense, and then, with a careful but not overwrought analysis, he leads one forward to his conclusions, always with a directness and a simplicity which are characteristic of strong mental grasp but conceal the cleverness with which the road has been chosen or the arguments exposed. By his very statement of the issues involved in a case he could quietly disclose to the litigants against whom he was ruling the far-reaching and perhaps destructive consequences of their own contentions. And, as we have said, he did this, as he must needs do it in constitutional decisions, not by an elaborate dissecting of precedent and legal authority, but by a calm outlook upon the field and a searching analysis of the elements involved in the discussion. In his most important cases he appears to rise far above the details of the immediate controversy, one might almost say above the merits of the particular case, and to have his eye on the big principles affecting the future growth of the nation. And thus he created American constitutional law; at least, not to exaggerate, he marked out the broad lines of constitutional construction and fashioned the fundamental principles on which union and government might rest.

To select his opinions for separate comment, or to choose those most noteworthy, is not an easy task. Probably *Marbury vs. Madison* is the most famous, because in that decision the Supreme Court exercised, for the first time, the power to declare an act of Congress unconstitutional. The principle on which Marshall gave the decision had been stated several times before, for the state courts had announced it when declaring statutes void and, among others, Hamilton had clearly set forth the doctrine in *The Federalist*. Moreover, modern scholars are not altogether content with the method of approach which Marshall followed in reaching his conclusion that a court had the right to declare a law void. Withal, however, the case is of signal importance and there would be considerable difficulty in presenting the power of the court with more simplicity and cogency.

In the decade after the War of 1812, Marshall rendered a series of opinions of the first importance. Thoroughly permeated with the conviction that the states of the Union must be kept within their proper bounds, he gave to the task of interpreting the Constitution and maintaining the authority of the national government his greatest power. Possibly his ablest decision, certainly the one most elaborately wrought out, is *Cohens vs. Virginia*, in which the question arose as to the right of the Supreme Court to exercise its appellate jurisdiction over the judgment of a state court involving the validity of state legislation. The contention of the counsel for the state struck at the very root of the judicial system of the Union, with its authority to review state decisions which involved the binding effect of the Federal Constitution and laws: and so to the discussion of this fundamental question Marshall brought his heaviest artillery. In a series of powerful paragraphs he proclaimed the principle of nationalism and the existence of a real union resting on the will and determination of the people:

"That the United States," he said, "form, for many, and for most important purposes, a single nation, has not yet been denied. In war, we are one people. In making peace, we are one people. In all commercial regulations, we are one and the same people. In many other respects, the American people are one; and the government which is alone capable of controlling and managing their interests in all these respects, is the government of the Union. It is their government. and in that character they have no other. America has chosen to be, in many respects, and to many purposes, a nation; and for all these purposes, her government is complete; to all these objects, it is competent."

These words give us some idea of the simplicity of the style, the evidence of power and confidence, the eloquence which can raise a judicial opinion into the realm of literature. This decision, emphatically maintaining the appellate authority of the Court and the supremacy of the national law when the law is consonant with the Constitution, left no further ground for legal discussion, though the men of Virginia, fretting under the authority of the Court, poured out their wrath in many words.[1]

In other decisions of vast influence on developing America, Marshall announced his doctrine of nationalism and marked out the limits of state competence. One of these, the case of *McCulloch vs. Maryland*, gave with renewed elaboration the doctrine of implied powers in the hands of the national government and laid down principles limiting the rights of the states. Here too Marshall examined the character of the Union and the scope of governmental authority under the Constitution, and did so with remarkable clearness. In the well-known case of *Dartmouth College vs. Woodward*, Marshall declared that a charter of a private corporation was a contract, inviolable by state authority. This decision is probably more sharply criticized by the modern lawyer than any other, and yet it is still standing and has stood for a century, the bulwark of the corporations, saving them at least from unreasonable and purely gratuitous attacks upon their privileges and property. A third case, *Gibbons vs. Ogden*, proclaiming in broad terms the extent of Federal power over interstate commerce, served as the foundation on which later decisions rested and at least suggested the legal foundation for the great development of nation-wide commerce. Thus, it will be seen, his work was of significance not alone because it furnished theories and principles of national organization and helped in determining the character of the Union, but also because, in passing on questions of state competence, his vision was sufficiently wide and

[1] See William E. Dodd, *Chief Justice Marshall and Virginia*, in *American Historical Review*, XII (1907), 776–787.

far-reaching to comprehend the need for secure industrial growth.

Though Marshall's best-known decisions were in the field of constitutional law, where he was easily master, his work was by no means confined to that subject, for many problems besides those involving constitutional construction came before the court.   During his term as chief justice he rendered over five hundred opinions, dealing with almost every one of the main divisions of modern jurisprudence.   But he did even more; he placed the Court itself in a position of authority and influence, dignified and made potent the whole Federal judicial system, and thus helped to build up that respect for the Federal courts which has been of such tremendous importance in the development of American life.   This in fact was no easy task; the Supreme Court itself was often fiercely attacked; it often went counter to the intense prejudice of parties, states, and sections.   But by virtue of his own integrity and inherent power he compelled respect and overcame prejudice.

In the general field of constitutional law, Joseph Story (1779–1845) must be placed next to Marshall, though he did much less than the great chief justice of a purely constructive or creative character.   His work as associate justice on the Supreme Bench was important, but his most substantial contribution was his *Commentaries on the Constitution*, which appeared in 1833 and long remained the only extensive and authoritative treatise on the subject.   It passed through various editions, the best known, the fourth, containing copious annotations by Thomas M. Cooley, a distinguished publicist of a later generation. Thus for fifty years after its first appearance it furnished students of the law with the principles which Marshall and Story himself had done so much to establish by their decisions, and it doubtless had great influence on the thinking of bench and bar for two generations at least.   It would be difficult to overestimate the importance of such volumes in the days when the critical case system was not used by beginners, when texts were comparatively few, and when practising attorneys and judges were not provided with long series of reports, in days also when the layman was interested in problems concerning the nature of the Union and the powers of government.

If Story's name is associated in our minds with that of

Marshall, because Story's *Commentaries* carried forward the Marshall tradition, we may also justly associate him with James Kent (1763–1847). Both were judges, both also teachers and writers, and by their published works on various fields of American law they gave it coherence, stability, and strength. Though Marshall has undimmed honour as the founder of constitutional law, we look to these two men as the chief influences in building up other branches of American jurisprudence.

They began their work when there was practically nothing written on American law, and when there was a feeling of opposition to the English common law, even as it was presented in Coke and Blackstone. The times were critical, and the work of these two men in laying the foundations of American law, in seizing upon the principles of the common law and adapting them to American conditions, and in building up, in general, a coherent and usable system was of great importance. A competent author, attributing much to the influence of these men, asserts that the achievements of the seventy-five years before the Civil War compare favourably with those of any period of growth and adjustment in legal history, and declares that the "closest analogy, both in the time taken and the amount and character of the work accomplished, is the classical period in England—the age of Coke."[1] Kent's *Commentaries on American Law* (1826–1830) was of very great effect; it was long read by students of the law and occupied a place of distinction by the side of Blackstone's famous work. Story, in addition to his work as a teacher of law in Harvard and to his duties on the bench of the Federal Supreme Court, wrote a number of volumes which did perhaps even more than those of Kent to standardize and shape the law. His *Conflict of Laws* and *Equity Jurisprudence* were of transcendent value, restating and formulating in convenient form the judge-made law of the past and making it adaptable to American conditions. Of the former treatise it has even been said that "It forthwith systematized, one might almost say, created, a whole branch of the law of England." Kent's decisions, when he was chancellor of New York, fashioned and made applicable in America the principles of equity, and

---

[1] Roscoe Pound, *The Place of Judge Story in the Making of American Law.* *Proceedings of the Cambridge Historical Society,* vol. VII (1914), p. 39.

Story's treatise on the same subject had as much or even greater influence in establishing and maintaining the system of equity jurisprudence.

What two men could do in expounding the law, making it intelligible and effective, and showing the strength and reasonableness of fundamental principles, in short, what could be done in fashioning the main lines of a growing jurisprudence for a rapidly growing country, these two men accomplished. The layman commonly thinks of the law as fixed, or as developing only by the addition of statutes passed by some legislative body, but the truth is that law grows, and the common law above all, as questions and problems arise; judges on the bench and writers of text-books who do more than merely chronicle decisions, have great opportunity to direct the law into new channels and to determine the course of its development. Such power and influence naturally belonged in unusual measure to Kent and Story, because of their learning, because they taught and wrote as well as gave opinions from the bench, and above all because the period in which they worked was a formative period in the early life of a nation, during which law, like everything else, had to find expression and formulation.

To the list of jurists deserving special mention must be added Henry Wheaton (1785–1848). His early important work was that of reporter of the Supreme Court; but in 1827 he was appointed *chargé d'affaires* to Denmark, and a few years later minister to the court of Prussia. His diplomatic experience was doubtless of much service to him in his career as a publicist. In 1836 appeared the work by which he is chiefly known, the *Elements of International Law*. It passed through various editions, was translated into foreign languages, and is justly considered one of the most valuable contributions to the science of international law made during the nineteenth century.

With the possible exception of Marshall and Webster,[1] John C. Calhoun (1782–1850) was the most important statesman and writer on public affairs in the forty years preceding 1850. A South Carolinian, he belonged by birth, not to the lowland planter class, but to the men of the up-country. At an early day his father purchased a slave, not a usual possession for an up-country man, and when John Calhoun grew to manhood

[1] For whom see Book II, Chap. xvi.

he married a distant cousin of social standing and with some means, and thus the young man was connected with the social aristocracy and the slave-owning interests of the state. These simple facts stand out prominently in any effort to understand him in his development, because he became the learned and devoted advocate of the slave interests and defended, with his logic and his power in debate, the economical and social régime of the South. In 1811 he entered Congress, and was at once one of the leaders among the new young men, who were out of patience with the dallying methods of the older Jeffersonian politicians. For some years he was an ardent nationalist; possibly it is too much to say that he committed himself by votes or speeches to an interpretation of the Constitution radically opposed to state sovereignty; but in these earlier days we find in his spirit no traces of sectionalism or of any narrow particularism. In the latter part of the decade between 1820 and 1830, overcome by the unrest in his state and moved, it would seem, by its economic difficulties, he succumbed to the pressure of his surroundings and became the leader in formulating doctrines which South Carolina put forth to the world to defend itself against the tariff—shrewdly reasoned and highly elaborated doctrines of state sovereignty, the basis of nullification and secession.

Though other Southern states were at first by no means in agreement with South Carolina, when she presented to the world the theories which Calhoun so neatly phrased and so ably defended, he came to be, as the days went by, the leader of his section as well as the idol of his state. Sometimes he was a leader so far in advance that Southern people scarcely knew that they were slowly following his footsteps. More and more the South was identified with slavery; and more and more the people took their cue from Calhoun. He did not pose as a friend of disruption, and probably was a sincere friend of the Union; but the Union, he insisted with increasing fervour, must be a Union respecting the rights of the states, a Union which would hold together only if its government respected the varying conditions and the different interests of states and, indeed, of sections. He thus became the chief defender of two things or two ideas, slavery and particularism, to which the developing character of the nineteenth century was utterly opposed; slavery here and everywhere was doomed to be beaten down by the tide of humanitarianism, while localism, and sectionalism, and all other tendencies to exclusiveness and segregation, were at variance with those great forces of aggregation and of nation-building which were manifest in the whole civilized world. Calhoun's great talents were actually devoted to elaboration and vehement promulgation of theories to the effect that the American Union was a clever political system devised for the express purpose of protecting peculiar local interests against external attack; and the chief local interest was the "peculiar institution" of the South!

Calhoun's important contributions to the theory of American government began in 1828 in connection with the agitation in South Carolina about the tariff question. From that time on, his attention was largely devoted to inculcating the doctrine that the state had the right under the Constitution to protect its local interest against national aggression. His task was, and needed to be, in the presence of the growing power of the North, to develop principles for the protection of the minority, and in his quest for these doctrines he worked out a notable series of constitutional principles and philosophical theories.

Between 1828 and 1833 he developed his theories in defence of nullification by a single state. The basis of the right is of course the sovereignty of the state, and Calhoun insisted on indivisibility of sovereignty. "I maintain," he said, "that sovereignty is in its nature indivisible. It is the supreme power in a state, and we might just as well speak of half a square, or half of a triangle, as half a sovereignty." Probably it is not quite evident that one cannot justly speak of half a square; but without cavilling at his illustration we may see that in these words he swept aside statements which had been common before this time, to the effect that states, coming into the Union, surrendered a portion of their sovereignty and retained the remainder. Beneath his whole reasoning, therefore, lay the principles of what we may call organic philosophy, the recognition of the vital character of the body politic, though, of course, in this case, the body politic was the commonwealth, not the nation. He also believed that mere agreement could not establish law or political unity. This notion, at variance with the older one that men by consent could form themselves, artificially as it were, into a new entity, was beginning to take its hold on the philosophic world, and it was Calhoun's appreciation of this notion and his use of it in concrete political controversy which constitutes one of his signal contributions to the history of political theory.

He did not, in these early days, dwell on the right of secession. In fact he did not wish, especially then, to emphasize that right; he relied, rather, on the right of nullification, that is, on the power of any state to declare, not through its legislature but through a convention representing the sovereignty of the state, that a federal law is void and must not be enforced within the state. Nullification, in fact, was put forth as a device whereby the state might be preserved, with its authority untouched, without having to resort to secession from the Union. It was, therefore, as he conceived it, conservative in a twofold sense: it conserved the right of the individual state, and it saved the Union; for, without nullification, secession was the only remedy for wrong. To preserve the appearance of constitutional method, he insisted that when a law was nullified the judgment of all the states should be sought, and they, by a three-fourths vote, might declare that the disputed power belonged to the national government. It is quite unnecessary to assert that Calhoun was insincere in announcing this method of passing on controverted points; the protection of the minority and the real desirability of maintaining the Union were cogent in his mind; the Union was too much of a reality for him to think easily of its being altogether at the beck and nod of a single state. It is plain, however, that one more than one-fourth of the states could, by his plan, pronounce a measure void; and, moreover, if three-fourths declared it constitutional, such declaration could not deter a state, all-powerful in its sovereignty, from seceding. A resort to nullification was, in Calhoun's mind, a means of determining whether the states supported the government, which was only their agent, and, if they did support it, then and only then might secession be resorted to. Secession, in other words, though theoretically within the competence of any state, would not as a rule be justified simply because of the action of the central government, for the government was the agent of the states; until the principals acted, the individual state should content itself with nullification.

At the very outset, as we have seen, Calhoun announced principles calculated to defend the minority. His later and more elaborate treatises, notably his *Disquisition on Government* and his *Discourse on the Constitution and Government of the United States*, pushed to the end his theories as to the constitutional guarantees of minority. Here we find a very able discussion of constitutional principles so cogently expressed that they challenge one's admiration if they do not carry conviction. Intent upon disproving the notion that a mere majority of individuals, mere numbers, can decide upon rights or impose decisions on others, he insists that each interest or portion of the community must have a negative, and thus only when there is concurrence of the elements can there be the right to exercise power; where this principle of negation and concurrence does not exist, government rests on force; where they do exist, there is constitutionalism; a majority may be tyrannical, and therefore an unrestrained majority is inconsistent with constitutional liberty. It would be hard to deny that our constitutional system rests in part on the belief that majorities have not all power over the individual; but Calhoun's theory was different from this: interests, individual communities, must have, through the negative, the power of self-defence—and this meant, in reality, the South as a section and slavery as an interest. Through his whole career from 1828 till his death in 1850 there appears consistently this right of a minority to protect itself.

One other word must be said of Calhoun's work; for he did much more than outline the principles of state sovereignty. In the thirties, when the South began to defend slavery as never before, Calhoun stepped forward as a leader; and henceforward he was prepared to defend slavery as an institution and to use his theories concerning the Union to safeguard the institution at every turn. Here was the unnatural union: constitutional theory skilfully adapted to warding off intrusion was wedded to an economic, social, and moral condition of society. This union was all the more significant because slavery, though defended by theories of localism, was in need of recognition and of protection by national law; it needed in

fact to expand, if it were to hold its own; and thus Calhoun's
doctrine of the individual rights of the individual states must
so be turned, by infinitely cautious curves of logic, as to justify
the protection of slaves on the high seas, the existence of
slavery in the District of Columbia, national guardianship
of slavery in the national domain, the denunciation of free
speech on the subject at the North.   No one save a giant
among clever logicians and a devotee among enthusiasts
could have played the rôle with success.   His arguments and
assertions are cogent and philosophical, keen, yet exhibiting
a certain breadth and firmness of grasp.   He early recognized
the danger of a moral agitation against slavery; he did not
say that the Union could not exist half slave and half free;
but he did announce (1837) that "Abolition and the Union
cannot co-exist"; the fell spirit of abolitionism, based as it
was, or pretended to be, on moral grounds, was irreconcilable
with the safety of slaves.   To meet the attack of moral crusad-
ers, he laid down the philosophy of slaveholding and above
all its value in America:

I hold that in the present state of civilization, where two races of
different origin, and distinguished by colour, and other physical
differences, as well as intellectual, are brought together, the relation now existing in the slaveholding states between the two, is,
instead of an evil, a good—a positive good.

He also declared—what may perhaps appear today to be a
gruesome fact, or at least something near the fact—that, as
social and political equality between the races was impossible,
"to change the present condition of the African race . . .
would be but to change the form of slavery."   If the black
race must exist among us deprived of social equality, political
rights, and, largely, of industrial opportunity, have the former
slaves become freemen or have they passed into a new form of
servitude?
    Calhoun's written treatises on government and the rights
of the South do not differ essentially from his spoken words
on the same subjects.   They are often metaphysical and
subtle; but his doctrines rested on certain philosophical conceptions; and in presenting his theories he used language that

was calm and clear, as clear at least as the nature of his delicately wrought system might well allow.   In his speeches, he rarely, if ever, sought to stir his audience by mere flights of eloquence; he spoke, rather, as a man with his back to the wall, striking hard blows, seeking to defend himself and his section, unconsciously appealing to the emotions, if appealing at all, because his own position was not free from pathos; for here was a great man defending a losing cause and heroically beating back the forces that were hourly gaining in numbers and strength.   Even when discussing subjects which now appear of bygone interest, he commonly struck at fundamentals and at principles with such force and precision that many of his words still have vitality; and much that he said will long retain interest for the academic student of politics.   With the possible exception of Hamilton there is no other politician in our history whose writings today—decades after the disappearance of the subjects discussed—contain so much deserving attention and challenging respect even from the unbeliever. History offers few examples of such leadership, such success in mapping out for some millions of people a course of conduct and the ideas and beliefs on which conduct rests.

We have spoken of Calhoun as the great Southerner who presented with logical power the doctrines on which the South came to rest its case in defence of slavery.   There were, however, others almost as able and gifted who wrote and spoke on similar lines.   In the early years of the century, the Southerners were on the whole nationalistic in sentiment; opposition to national authority came from the North-east; but after the War of 1812 the conditions changed; the South, partly doubtless because it felt economic distress, began to complain.   The first formidable protest came from Virginia and was directed against the Federal Court and its great chief justice, himself a Virginian, who was declared to be interpreting the Constitution in violation of states' rights and to be intent on building up a consolidated government, or as we should now say a unitary state.   Jefferson, thoroughly disliking Marshall and all his works, was in or behind these attacks, but the great protagonists were Judge Spencer Roane (1762–1822) and John Taylor (1750–1824) of Caroline.   Roane's argument was chiefly directed against the assumed right of final review of constitutional questions by the Federal Court in cases involving the validity of state legislation.   Taylor in a number of very able books and pamphlets discussed the same subject; but he treated also the nature of the Union in a manner so critical and acute that, more nearly than any one else, he foreshadowed Calhoun and suggested the clear undimmed features of state sovereignty. Naturally we cannot omit from this list of Southern advocates Robert Y. Hayne (1791–1839), who was Webster's opponent in the "great debate" of 1830; for he made a deep impression and presented Calhoun's theories with eloquence and vigour.

Among the men of Congress who indulged in far-flung speech and whom we shall have to class as orators, John Randolph (1773–1833) of Roanoke claims our first attention. Totally without the qualities for party leadership, unable to retain the devotion or following of friends, unable to handle a big constitutional question with confident learning and logic, unable to develop theories and to win people by the force of his argument or the steady adherence to a cause and a principle, he nevertheless played a conspicuous rôle during the first quarter of the nineteenth century, and, if we judge now only by the records of his speeches, he was gifted with a power of expression, a cutting brilliant invective and devilish cleverness in criticism and attack, such as few speakers have ever possessed.   He was essentially a busy fault-finder, an active, alert, denunciatory enemy, at his best—or perhaps we should say, his worst—when dealing out taunts and pouring out the vial of his wrath on the less gifted but more wise.   It should also be said of him that by his vehement defence of the slavery interest, though he professed opposition to slavery in itself, and by his attack on the growing power of the Federal government, he prepared the way for the later arguments and positions of Calhoun, the real leader of the South.   One passage will illustrate almost as well as many the character of his declamation:

"We are the eel," he said of the South, "that is being flayed, while the cookmaid pats us on the head and cries, with the clown in King Lear, 'Down, wantons, down! . . .'   If, under a power to regulate trade, you prevent exportation; if, with the most approved spring lancets, you draw the last drop of blood from our veins; if, *secundum artem*, you draw the last shilling from our pockets, what are the checks of the Constitution to us? A fig for the Constitution! When the scorpion's sting is probing us to the quick, shall we stop to chop logic? Shall we get some learned and cunning clerk to say whether the power to do this is to be found in the Constitution, and then, if he, from whatever motive, shall maintain the affirmative, shall we, like the animal whose fleece forms so material a portion of this bill [tariff, 1824], quietly lie down and be shorn?"

Randolph's idiosyncrasies have been variously accounted for. He said himself that his unprosperous life was the fruit of an ungovernable temper; but his temper and his violent vagaries were such evidences of a morbid mind that there is temptation simply to consider him mentally unbalanced if not insane. His very maddening skill with words recalls the adage about children and edged tools, for it seems a pity that one so unsedate should have had such weapons of offence in his arsenal.

From scarcely any point of view can the orations of Henry Clay (1777–1852) be classed as literature of the same grade and importance as those of Webster and Calhoun. And yet just why one should say this is not quite clear even to oneself. The conclusion, if it be just, rests on the fact that today his speeches seem unprofitable and to be wanting in carrying power and effect. If in order to be classed as literature orations must either be marked by beauty of language and peculiar felicity of word and phrase, or contain, though without distinction of language, a profound and philosophic discussion of matters of lasting human interest, then Clay's speeches can scarcely deserve a high place in literature. But if Clay's words do not now move us deeply, they did move and captivate the men to whom he spoke, and that is the aim of oratory. He was more nearly the great popular orator of his time than was any other; in power over a general audience and in ability to touch the chord of human sympathy, no one was quite his equal, at least in the field of politics. This is much to say of an orator in a generation of free oratory, when men were not hesitant in the use of burning words or hindered by sophisticated self-restraint. No one else had the gracious manner, the voice and the presence, or those nameless qualities of personal charm, which are powerful and dominant in all the relations of life. If he could not win men by his logic or his facts, he could win and hold them simply because of himself. Randolph could arouse the interest of the crowd and amaze his audience by the brilliance of his epigrams; Rufus Choate could pour out strains of sonorous sentences which might for the time dazzle his admirers and confound his adversaries; Everett was able, with admirable grace and with decorous regard for niceties of expression, to utter polished periods which were almost too elegant to be convincing. But Clay conquered because he made friends and held them to himself; he enlisted their sympathies; with gracious persuasiveness he appealed to the hearts and the simple emotions of the crowd before him.

From the time when he became Speaker in 1811 and helped to bring on the war with England, to and through the compromise of 1850, Clay was intimately connected with all the great political movements of his day. The recognition of the South American republics, the tariff, the bank, the public lands, the distribution of the surplus revenue, the slavery question in all its phases, expansion, and the Mexican War can scarce be studied better than in the story of his life. Despite this fact or because of it, despite the fact that his life was in unusual degree the public life of a generation or more, it is perhaps not unjust to think of his speeches as occasional and of his work as that of an opportunist—a fairly consistent opportunist, it must be said, for he did not always trim his sails for popular favour, but represented instinctively and honestly, on the whole, certain human impulses of the people, and above all those elements of nationalism, conservatism, and democracy which were inherent in the strangely mingled Whig party of which he was the founder and guide. Though Jackson was for a time more popular and more successful, and though Webster's eloquence appealed more to the New Englander and to the book-read classes, Clay held for decades the devotion of large portions of the people and peculiarly embodied the sense and sensibility of the nation at large. It is only when one understands the intricacies of political controversy, the sentiments of Jacksonian democracy in the West, all the entanglements of banks, and tariffs, and roads, and slavery, that we can account for Clay's failure to attain the presidency, which he so ardently desired.

The thing which lifts him into a place of undoubted significance in the course of American history is this: he embodied the spirit of developing nationalism and gave it constant expression. As Jackson, though a nationalist, represented the attitude of domineering individualism so characteristic of the untutored frontier, Clay in a wider and a deeper way appealed to the lofty sentiments of the whole people. It is not a question now of broad interpretation of the Constitution, or of any theory of governmental authority, or of any opposition to states' rights, or of anything that was legalistic or even argumentative in character; it is a question of the spirit which made America a nation, the sense of national existence, of power, of bigness, of duty, in a word, of reality. Without this sense, without this feeling in the hearts of Americans, the Union could not have resisted the corroding influence of slavery and could not have made itself, by a mighty effort, the huge, self-conscious, personal being that it is today. Of course, this was the work of others also; it was the natural product of modern life and culture; it rested on the elaborate argumentation of Webster and Marshall; but Clay by the spell of an attractive presence, by personal charm, and by the lure of a fervid eloquence awakened and developed this sentiment and made it irresistibly strong.

Perhaps the student of American literature might justly pass by the work of John Quincy Adams (1767–1848), on the ground that it possesses nothing of real literary merit and deserves no special distinction; he was not a great orator, if one judge by grace of expression and by power of public appeal, and he was not a writer gifted with special originality or charm of style. He was, however, for fifty years and more a prominent figure in public life—foreign minister, senator, secretary of state, president, representative in Congress; he prepared able state papers; for nearly twenty years and at an age when most men enjoy retirement from active service, he played a conspicuous rôle in Congress, speaking in behalf of free speech and the right of petition and defending the cause of free labour against the demands of slavery; he left for the use of succeeding generations a diary of his life, a source of comfort to the historical investigator and a pleasure to the lay reader of history, a diary astonishingly full and minute, filled with reflections and with stern and caustic comments on men and events. The years after his presidency, when he was a representative in Congress, have given his name a peculiar lustre, for he laboured there boldly and almost alone.

He was too intense in his devotion to what he thought right, too unbending, too severe, too outspoken, too blunt perhaps, to be a political leader or a popular idol, but that he had power is plain, for by dint of fearless speech he won the well-earned title of "old man eloquent,"—and eloquent he undoubtedly was, when he rose to his height in defence of principles he believed just and sacred. Without descending into vulgar abuse, he could indulge in scathing attack, while his wide learning and experience in public affairs gave him advantage over most of his adversaries.

From even a hurried sketch of this period we cannot omit to mention the names of a few other men who were well known in this time and deserve to be known now. Albert Gallatin (1761–1849), one of the ablest and most learned of American statesmen, served his country in Congress, as foreign minister, and as secretary of the treasury; he was an administrator rather than a publicist or orator, but some of his pamphlets and reports were of marked ability. Roger Brooke Taney (1777–1864), secretary of the treasury under Jackson, and chief justice of the United States from 1836 to 1864, was a learned jurist, whose fame was clouded for the later part of his life by his opinion in the Dred Scott case. Josiah Quincy (1772–1864), an orator of no mean power, represented during the earlier part of his life the narrow New England Federalism which was so bitterly opposed to the politics of Jefferson and Madison. Edward Everett (1794–1865) occupied various public positions—member of Congress, governor of Massachusetts, minister to England, president of Harvard College. Although long active in political affairs he won chief destinction by lectures on literary subjects and by orations of an occasional character. In no other speeches of his generation, probably in no others in our whole history, do we find the same precision and elegance or equal refinement, ease, and grace; in no others are there such marks of real distinction in expression.

More than a word should be given to Thomas H. Benton (1782–1858), if the real importance of his work be given proper recognition; but we must content ourselves with a brief statement. For over thirty years, from the time of the Missouri Compromise until almost the outbreak of the Civil War, he was prominent in public life, an active, untiring representative of the active, untiring West. No man, not even Clay or Jackson or Lincoln, better typified the young, self-confident Western democracy; he represented the West of his day not only in the measures he advocated and the principles he followed, but in his very manner of speech—earnest, assured, buoyant, boastful, idealistic. If one would know America and its differences, how training and environment have affected oratory as well as views of public policy, one could get no better lesson than by comparing the full-blooded oratory of Benton with the acrid speech of Josiah Quincy or the polite eloquence of Everett. After Benton's retirement from Congress, he prepared and published his *Thirty Years' View*, a political history of the decades between 1820 and 1850 written from the viewpoint of an actor in the scenes described, with copious extracts from his own speeches and without special care to diminish the importance of his own influence. After this, though he was now past threescore and ten, he prepared his *Abridgment of the Debates of Congress from 1787 to 1856*, the last sentences of which he is said to have dictated in whispers from his deathbed.

Though only the most noteworthy persons have been spoken of in this chapter, enough has been said to indicate that in the first fifty years of the nineteenth century there was much good oratory and a large amount of able writing on subjects of political interest. As we look back on those decades, the years seem to be hurrying past with great rapidity, changing the primitive United States in the span of a single lifetime from a row of scattered republics scarcely realizing national existence into a great empire stretching across the continent. And in those hurrying years, all sorts of questions arose to be vehemently and earnestly discussed before an increasing number of eager hearers who felt that their destiny was in their own hands. These crowding problems full of intense human meaning; this developing democracy with all its trials, hopes, and determinations; this people, beset with slavery and boasting its freedom, bent upon the big job of taking possession of a continent and turning wilderness into farms and villages—these form the background of the oratory and the public tasks of the day. If no single piece of the very highest value in literature came out of the mêlée, we cannot wonder. And yet in the restless years there were men to be classed well up among the world's orators—for their themes were inspiring and a multitude was ready to hang upon their words. And in addition to all this product of earnest political strife and fervid declamation, is the fact, surprising, almost disconcerting, that the years produced jurists and publicists of erudition who quietly and methodically, amid all the hurry and change, framed the basic laws for a new nation, or, grasping essentials of older systems, gave them new life and form.

CHAPTER XVI

Webster

WE may take it for granted that Webster knew well how large a place he would fill in the history of his time. He was singularly free from small vanities and petty conceit but he was too great a man not to be conscious of his own intellectual power or of the part which he had played in his day and generation. His feeling about himself comes out in the famous passage of the Seventh of March speech when he asked: "What States are to secede? What is to remain American? What am I to be?" A remarkable question that last one! With the exception of Washington and Lincoln, who in our history could have solemnly put it forth in a public speech without being laughed at and ridiculed? Yet Webster uttered the words in a speech in the Senate, and a political opponent said that the tone of that question made him shudder as if some dire calamity were at hand. Laughter and ridicule fled before this naked assertion of a personality, and men not only shrank from the visions which it conjured up but accepted it as very solemn and entirely natural. The power of the orator was one reason, no doubt, for the impression, but the greatness of the man himself was the controlling cause.

Yet despite this just sense of his place in the history of his time and of his own greatness, Webster would have been profoundly surprised to find himself included as a marked figure in the history of our literature.[1] Except for a fragment of an autobiography and some private letters he never wrote anything in the literary sense. In his day public men did not turn to the newspaper or the magazine for an opportunity to express their views upon public questions. The age of pamphlets, so

---

[1] There are used here, with modifications, two or three passages from an address delivered by the writer at the unveiling of the Webster monument in Washington, 14 January, 1900.

much used by the framers of the Constitution and the founders of our government, had passed away. That of the magazine and the review had not arrived. Men in public life trusted to their speeches in Parliament or Congress or before the people, almost as in the days of Fox and Pitt, to make their arguments and opinions known, and they would have thought any other course hardly consistent with their dignity. Moreover, Webster did not give his leisure, as many statesmen have done, to writing memoirs or history or to the discussion in book form of some question which interested him. The reason was simple. When Webster was not in office or when he had an interval between the sessions of Congress, he gave his time to the practice of his profession, and great cases before the courts absorbed all his energy.[1]

---

[1] Daniel Webster was born in Salisbury [now Franklin], New Hampshire, 18 January, 1782, of pioneer stock. A frail child, and therefore spared the hard work of his father's farm, he was sent to Phillips Exeter Academy and to Dartmouth College, from which he graduated in 1801. He taught school as a make-shift, studied law, and was admitted to the bar in 1805. He practised first at Boscawen and then at Portsmouth, where he rapidly rose to prominence both as lawyer and public speaker. In 1813 he was sent to the House of Representatives as a Federalist member from Massachusetts, and thus came in close contact with Clay, then speaker, and Calhoun. Within a year Webster was a marked man in Congress. After four years, during which he struck many heavy blows at the administration, he resumed the practice of law. The great cases which he argued—the Dartmouth College Case, *M'Culloch v. Maryland*, *Gibbons v. Ogden*, *Ogden v. Saunders*—brought him into the first rank of American lawyers by the time he was forty. Meanwhile his reputation as the greatest American orator was built up by his oration at Plymouth in 1820, the Bunker Hill oration of 1825, and the speech in which he commemorated Adams and Jefferson in 1826. He returned to the House of Representatives in 1823 and in 1827 entered the Senate, in which he served till 1841.

Ever since 1800 Webster had been the exponent of a doctrine of nationalism which now made him the chief defender of the idea of union. His debate with Hayne of South Carolina in 1830, commonly called "The Great Debate," is a classic statement of the doctrine and the idea. For twenty years Webster was the voice of New England. He failed of election as President, but he had a notable, if brief, career as secretary of state under Harrison and Tyler, 1841–43, during which he concluded with Great Britain the important Webster-Ashburton Treaty. Once more in the Senate after 1845, Webster opposed the annexation of Texas and the Mexican War. As the struggle over slavery grew more violent he turned to the side of Clay and in the famous "Seventh of March Speech" defended Clay's Compromise Bill, with the result that he was bitterly denounced in the North as a renegade. The same year he became secretary of state again. He died under a kind of cloud, 24 October, 1852, but there can be little doubt that he, more than any other one man, contributed to the growth of that sentiment of union which sustained the national idea during the Civil War.—THE EDITORS.

He loved literature undoubtedly. He had been educated, both at school and at college, upon the old classical system, and it is obvious that he always retained his knowledge of Latin: in fact, he was a good Latin scholar. There is no evidence that he was a good Greek scholar or even kept up the Greek of his youth. He knew the history of Greece and Rome and much of modern history, but he was not a student of history, and this he realized. It is also apparent that he was fond of pure literature, and he never forgot at least the eighteenth century poets who were the standard poets of his youth. The story of his dispute with Rufus Choate over a quotation illustrates not his knowledge of Pope, which is unimportant, but his love of literature, which is significant. At a most exciting moment in the trial of a case very famous in its day, Webster was observed to write a few words upon a slip of paper and pass it to Choate. The spectators thought something very vital to the case was going on, but what Webster wrote was this:

> Lo! where Mæotis sleeps and softly flows
> The freezing Tanais through a waste of snows.

Choate wrote "wrong" on the slip and then:

> Lo! where Mæotis sleeps and *hardly* flows
> The freezing Tanais through a waste of snows.

Webster wrote "right" against his version and offered a bet. The volume of Pope containing *The Dunciad* was sent for, and it appeared that Choate was right. Webster wrote the words "Spurious Edition" on the book, and the consultation between the two great lawyers ended.

The fact, however, that in Johnson's phrase he had literature and loved it, although it tells us of the man, would not give him a place in literary history. Yet he has that place and his right to it rests and must rest upon his speeches, for speeches and addresses are all that Webster has left to us to prove his literary quality, and it very rarely happens that a literary reputation can be based upon speeches actually spoken and delivered. The reason for this rarity of speeches which give a title to a place in literature lies, if we pause to reflect upon it, in the very nature of the speech itself.

Charles Fox was the author of the famous aphorism that "no good speech ever read well." This is a declaration in epigrammatic form that the speech which is prepared like an essay and then read or recited, which, in other words, is primarily literature and not oratory, is not a thoroughly good speech, and of the soundness of the doctrine there can hardly be a doubt. But the theory, however valid, is not without its dangers. Charles Fox lived up to his own principle. He was, it may well be thought, the greatest of English orators at the moment of speech, but he is little read and seldom quoted now. What he actually said has faded from the minds of men despite its enchanting, its enormous effect at the moment. On the other hand, the speech which is literature before it is spoken is ineffective or only partially effective at the moment, and if it is read afterwards, however much we may enjoy the essay, we never mistake it for the genuine eloquence of the spoken word.

Macaulay is an example of this latter class, as Fox is of the former. Macaulay's speeches are essays, eloquent and rhetorical, but still essays—literature, and not speeches. He was listened to with interest and delight, but he was not a parliamentary debater or speaker of the first order. The highest oratory, therefore, must combine in exact balance the living force and freshness of the spoken word with the literary qualities which alone ensure endurance. The best examples of this perfection are to be found in the world of imagination, in the two speeches of Brutus and Mark Antony following the death of Cæsar. They are speeches and nothing else— one cool, stately, reasonable; the other a passionate, revolutionary appeal, hot from the heart and pouring from the lips with unpremeditated art, and yet they both have the literary quality, absolutely supreme in this instance, because Shakespeare wrote them.

It is not the preparation or even the writing out beforehand which makes a speech into an essay, for these things can both be done without detracting from the spontaneity, without dulling the sound of the voice which the wholly great speech must have, even on the printed page. The speech loses when the literary quality becomes predominant, and absolute success as high as it is rare comes only from the nice balance of the two essential ingredients. This balance and combination are found in Demosthenes and Isocrates, although one may venture to think that those two great masters, as they have come down to us, lean, if at all, too much to the literary side. In Cicero, although in matter and manner the best judges would rank him below the Greek masters, the combination is quite perfect. One of his most famous speeches, it is said, was never delivered at all, and none the less it is a speech and nothing else, instinct with life and yet with the impalpable literary feeling all through it, the perfect production of a very beautiful and subtle art. Among English orators Burke undoubtedly comes nearest to a complete union of the two qualities, and while the words of Fox and Pitt are unread and unquoted, except by historians, Burke's gorgeous sentences are recited and repeated and his philosophic discussion of great general principles are studied and admired by successive generations. Yet there is no doubt that Burke erred somewhat on the literary side, and we find the proof of this in the fact that he often spoke to empty benches, and that Goldsmith could say of him:

> Too deep for his hearers still went on refining,
> And thought of convincing while they thought of dining.

Burke was a literary man as well as an orator and a statesman; Webster, as has just been said, was not a literary man at all. He was an orator pure and simple; his speeches, good, bad, or indifferent, are speeches—never essays or anything but speeches—and yet upon all alike is the literary touch. In all, certainly in all the great speeches, is the fine literary quality, always felt, never seen, ever present, never obtrusive. He had the combination of Shakespeare's Brutus or Antony, of Demosthenes or Cicero, and when he rose to his greatest heights he reached a place beyond the fear of rivalry. The practical proof and exhibition of this fact is apparent if we turn to any serious and large debate in Congress, for there we shall find Webster quoted, as he is in every session, twenty times as often as any other public man in our history. He said many profound, many luminous, many suggestive things;

he was an authority on many policies and on the interpretation of the Constitution. But there have been others of whom all this might be said—there were kings before Agamemnon—but they are rarely quoted, while Webster is quoted constantly. He had strong competitors in his own day and in his own field, able, acute, and brilliant men. He rose superior to them, it appears, in his lifetime; and now that they are all dead Webster's words are familiar to hundreds while his rivals are little more than names. So far as familiarity in the mouths of men goes, it is Eclipse first and the rest nowhere. That which has made this possible is his rare combination of speech and literature; it is the literary quality, the literary savour which keeps what Webster said fresh, strong, and living. When we open the volumes of his speeches it is not like unrolling the wrappings of an Egyptian mummy, to find within a dry and shrivelled form, a faint perfume alone surviving faintly to recall the vanished days, as when

> Some queen, long dead, was young.

Rather it is like the opening of Charlemagne's tomb, when his imperial successor started back before the enthroned figure of the great emperor looking out upon him, instinct with life under the red glare of the torches.

Let us apply another and surer test. How many speeches to a jury in a criminal trial possessing neither political nor public interest survive in fresh remembrance seventy years after their delivery? One can hardly think of jury speeches of any kind which stand this ordeal except, in a limited way, some few of Erskine's, and those all have the advantages of historical significance, dealing as they do with constitutional and political questions of great moment. But there is one of Webster's speeches to a jury which lives to-day, and no more crucial test could be applied than the accomplishment of such a feat. The White murder case was simply a criminal trial, without a vestige of historical, political, or general public interest. Yet Webster's speech for the prosecution has been read and recited until well-nigh hackneyed. It is in readers and manuals, and is still declaimed by schoolboys. Some of its phrases are familiar quotations and have passed into general speech. Let us recall a single passage:

He has done the murder. No eye has seen him; no ear has heard him. The secret is his own, and it is safe.

Ah, gentlemen, that was a dreadful mistake. Such a secret can be safe nowhere. The whole creation of God has neither nook nor corner where the guilty can bestow it and say it is safe. . . . A thousand eyes turn at once to explore every man, everything, every circumstance connected with the time and place; a thousand ears catch every whisper; a thousand excited minds intensely dwell on the scene, shedding all their light, and ready to kindle the slightest circumstance into a blaze of discovery. Meantime the guilty soul can not keep its own secret. It is false to itself; or, rather, it feels an irresistible impulse of conscience to be true to itself. It labours under its guilty possession, and knows not what to do with it. The human heart was not made for the residence of such an inhabitant. It finds itself preyed on by a torment which it dares not acknowledge to God or man. A vulture is devouring it, and it can ask no sympathy or assistance either from heaven or earth. The secret which the murderer possesses soon comes to possess him, and, like the evil spirits of which we read, it overcomes him and leads him whithersoever it will. He feels it beating at his heart, rising to his throat, and demanding disclosure. He thinks the whole world sees it in his face, reads it in his eyes, and almost hears its workings in the very silence of his thoughts. It has become his master. It betrays his discretion, it breaks down his courage, it conquers his prudence. When suspicions from without begin to embarrass him and the net of circumstance to entangle him, the fatal secret struggles with still greater violence to burst forth. It must be confessed; it will be confessed. There is no refuge from confession but suicide, and suicide is confession.

Those are words spoken to men, not written for them. It is a speech and nothing else, and yet we feel all through it the literary value and quality which make it imperishable. If now we go back to Webster's earlier days we can trace throughout his speeches, once he had escaped from the flowers of eloquence which burdened his youth, the literary touch appearing with increasing frequency until it came continually, quite naturally and without effort. As the sureness of the literary touch increased, so did the taste become refined until it was finally almost unerring.

The *Discourse*, as he called it, delivered at Plymouth in 1820 upon the two hundredth anniversary of the landing of the Pilgrims, was the first of the great occasional addresses which gave so much fame to Webster as an orator, wholly apart from that which he achieved in Congress or in the courts. It was evidently prepared with extreme care and has less of the effect of words actually spoken than his later work of the same character. The perfect combination of the literary quality with the spoken word, to which he afterwards attained, has not yet been reached. The Plymouth *Discourse* shows his wide knowledge of history, and the historical illustrations are given with an easy mastery of his subject and with a conciseness that saves him from the rambling digression which is at once the temptation and the danger of the historical parallel. There are also many passages which contain, in the manner of Burke, philosophical considerations of the science of government and which deal with the general principles affecting social and political problems. The history and philosophy are all eminently appropriate to his subject and to an address of that character. They give it weight, seriousness, and the permanence which lasts far beyond the moment of speech. The manner in which they are used and introduced is distinctly literary. But we also find in this address something more, the purely literary quality in the style and in the thought.

It is this literary quality which concerns us here, and to appreciate it we must mark the distinction, often a very narrow one, between the rhetorical and the literary. Rhetoric is of course in its place a branch of literature, but it may be of the utmost excellence and yet lack the highest literary quality. Rhetoric is out of place in purely literary work which is not dramatic in character. Yet curiously enough it is not misplaced in poetry. Rhetorical verse, although not the highest kind of poetry, may yet be in its own sphere very admirable indeed.

> You have the Pyrrhic dance as yet,
>   Where is the Pyrrhic phalanx gone?
> Of two such lessons, why forget
>   The nobler and the manlier one?
> You have the letters Cadmus gave—
> Think ye he meant them for a slave?

That is rhetorical poetry and it is very fine of its kind, very splendid even. Byron was a great master of rhetorical verse,

often too much so for his own good, but none the less the rhetoric is not out of place. On the other hand, to put rhetoric,
except in dramatic passages, into literary prose is almost as
bad as to write metred prose, of which Dickens was guilty in
the description of the death of Little Nell. But when we come
to giving the literary touch to rhetoric the exact reverse is the
case. The rhetoric is at once lifted up and illuminated. The
only objection is that the art is as rare as it is difficult, to be
found in only a few great masters of speech in human history.
It was precisely in this rare and difficult art that Webster
excelled. His rhetoric was always unimpeachable, but his
peculiar power lay in the fact that he was able to give to it
with ever-increasing ease the imperishable literary quality.

We detect the first gleams of this beautiful art in the
Plymouth oration. It is not necessary to take as an example
the celebrated passage about the slave trade, where the rhetoric
predominates; less familiar sentences prove the point. He is
speaking of Rome:

Although the time might come, when darkness should settle
on all her hills; when foreign or domestic violence should overturn
her altars and her temples; when ignorance and despotism should
fill the places where Laws, and Arts and Liberty had flourished;
when the feet of barbarism should trample on the tombs of her
consuls and the walls of her Senate-house and forum echo only
to the voice of savage triumph.

A little farther on, speaking of the human love of home and
birth-place, a well-worn theme, he says:

When the heart has laid down what it loved most, then it is
desirous of laying itself down. No sculptured marble, no enduring
monument, no honourable inscription, no ever burning taper that
would drive away the darkness of the tomb, can soften our sense
of the reality of death, and hallow to our feelings the ground which
is to cover us, like the consciousness that we shall sleep, dust to
dust, with the objects of our affections.

The thought in these passages is simple, oft-recurrent,
entirely familiar, expressed by many other orators with great
effect and received by genuinely moved audiences with much
applause. The first time one looks upon them, if one could

extricate them from the limbo of forgotten speeches, they might sound as well as Webster's words. But listen to them again, read them, and it will be found that Webster's sentences have a quality which all the others lack. Literature is interwoven with Webster's rhetoric, and it is this that preserves what he said from the forgetfulness which has overwhelmed others who in public speech have said the same things but just a little differently and without the magic literary touch.

Let us take one more example from his early days. In 1826, speaking in the House upon the Monroe Doctrine, Webster said:

I look on the message of December, 1823, as forming a bright page in our history. I will neither help to erase it or tear it out; nor shall it be by any act of mine blurred or blotted. It did honor to the sagacity of the government and I will not diminish that honor. It elevated the hopes and gratified the patriotism of the people. Over those hopes I will not bring a mildew; nor will I put that gratified patriotism to shame.

Rhetorically this passage is all that could be desired. The sentences are short, effective, possessing both balance and precision. But when we come to the last we find the literary touch. It is only one word, "mildew," but that single word is imaginative and strikes us at once. Leave it out and change the sentence slightly; the rhetoric remains excellent as before, but the whole effect is altered.

Let us take one or two other familiar passages from the later speeches when the style was perfected and when the literary quality had become a second nature. As Webster stood one summer morning on the ramparts of Quebec, and heard the sound of drums and saw the English troops on parade, the thought of England's vast world empire came strongly to his mind. The thought was very natural under the circumstances, not at all remarkable nor in the least original. Some years later, in a speech in the Senate, he put his thought into words, and this, as everyone knows, is the way he did it:

A power which has dotted over the surface of the whole globe with her possessions and military posts, whose morning drumbeat, following the sun and keeping company with the hours, circles the earth with one continuous and unbroken strain of the martial airs of England.

The sentence has followed the drumbeat round the world and has been repeated in England and in the antipodes by men who never heard of Webster and probably did not know that this splendid description of the British Empire was due to an American. It is not the thought which has carried these words so far through time and space. It is the beauty of the imagery and the magic of the style. Let me take one more very simple example of the quality which distinguishes Webster's speeches above those of others, which makes his words and serious thoughts live on when others, equally weighty and serious, perhaps, sleep or die. In his first Bunker Hill oration he apostrophized the monument, just as anyone else might have tried to do, and this is what he said:

Let it rise, let it rise till it meet the sun in his coming; let the earliest light of morning gild it, and parting day linger and play on its summit.

Here the thought is nothing, the style everything. No one can repeat those words and be deaf to their music or insensible to the rhythm and beauty of the prose with the Saxon words relieved just sufficiently by the Latin derivatives. The ease with which it is done may be due to training, but the ability to do it comes from natural gifts which, as Goethe says, "we value more as we get older because they can not be stuck on." Possibly to some people it may seem very simple to utter such a sentence. One can only repeat what Scott says somewhere about Swift's style, perhaps the purest and strongest we have in the language. "Swift's style," said Scott, "seems so simple that one would think any child might write as he does, and yet if we try we find to our despair that it is impossible."

It is not easy to say how much Webster's literary art was due to intentional cultivation and how far it was purely instinctive. Undoubtedly he had a natural gift as certainly as he had an ear for the arrangement and cadence of words; but we know that he cared for style and had strong preferences in the choice of the words he used to express his thought. We have the right to infer, therefore, that he was quite aware of the art which he practised so admirably. The highly conscious art which we see in Sterne, or in Walter Pater in our own time, to take two examples at random, and which is so effective in its results, is not apparent in Webster. He would probably not have been one of the greatest of orators if it had been, for then the writer would have absorbed the speaker. We are conscious of his art, although he does not seem to be conscious of it himself. Yet, however much we may speculate as to the proportions of intentional art and of unaided natural gifts in the style of all he said, there can be no question that he possessed and had mastered the rare combination which confers the lasting quality of literature upon the speech without losing the living force of the written word. It is this most rare achievement which gives to Webster, who never wrote book or essay or verse, his uncontested place in the history of American literature.

CHAPTER XVII

Writers on American History, 1783--1850[1]

THE Revolutionary War gave our historians new motives for writing. A glorious struggle was to be described; the states, just raised out of the rank of colonies, began to demand the preservation of their earliest history; and the nation, inspired by great hopes for the future, felt that it must have loyal men to prepare the record of common growth and common achievement. The men who responded to these impulses were, perhaps, less cultured than the best of the old historians. It was long before there appeared among them one who could be ranked with Hutchinson, though some of them wrote well and displayed great industry. The stream was wider than formerly, but it was not so deep.

Of those who wrote about the Revolution, in one phase or another, the best were the Rev. William Gordon, Dr. David Ramsay, William Henry Drayton, General William Moultrie, John Marshall, and William Wirt. Less scholarly but more widely influential were Mrs. Mercy Warren and "Parson" Weems.

Gordon, who was born in England, preached at Roxbury, Massachusetts, from 1770 to 1786. He was an active Whig, and after his return to England he wrote in four volumes a history of the Revolution (1788), which was widely read by the English, and in America was honoured with a pirated edition and long extracts in the newspapers. We now know that Gordon copied freely from *The Annual Register*, of which the parts dealing with America were at that time written by Edmund Burke. It is even charged that Gordon tempered his

[1] For a more extended treatment of the historians of the period, see the author's *Middle Group of American Historians* (1917).

narrative to please the feelings of his friends in England. His book is but slightly esteemed. Dr. Ramsay (1749–1815), of South Carolina, though educated to be a physician, was more a politician and *littérateur* than a scientist. His *History of the Revolution of South Carolina* (1785) and *History of the American Revolution* (1789) were well received by an uncritical generation. It remained for a later age to discover that the second of these books, long accepted as an original work, was largely drawn from *The Annual Register*. Drayton and Moultrie were prominent South Carolinians, one a political and the other a military defender of the Whig cause. Each wrote an excellent account of what he had seen in his own state. Marshall[1] and Wirt[2] were Virginia lawyers who thought it their duty to portray the lives of two great men of the Revolution. From the first we have the *Life of Washington* (1804–07) in five volumes, a heavy book without literary style and smacking of Federalist opinions. It displeased the followers of Jefferson but had a wide circulation among those who did not agree with the great Republican leader. For posterity it has value chiefly as a solid source of information. Wirt's *Life of Patrick Henry* (1817) is much unlike Marshall's book. It was well written—Wirt had a polished style—but it was a hasty and inadequate picture of a most important life. A better but less readable biography was William Tudor's *Life of James Otis* (1823).

Mrs. Mercy Otis Warren (1728–1814),[3] a sister of James Otis, was the wife of James Warren of Boston. Her three-volume *History of the American Revolution* (1805), a loosely written book which contained many biographical sketches, was popular and for a long time furnished the average New Englander his knowledge of the Revolution. Five years earlier had appeared the most successful historical book of the day, Weems's *Life of Washington*. The author was a versatile man, who could be buffoon, fiddler, parson, or hawker of his book as occasion demanded. He had not known Washington, but he created the impression that he wrote from personal knowledge by announcing himself as "formerly Rector of Mt. Vernon Parish." The book was a romance, interlarded with pious

---

[1] See also Book II, Chap. xv.   [2] See also Book II, Chaps. I and III.
[3] See also Book I, Chap. IX, and Book II, Chap. II.

stories. It was slightly esteemed by educated men of the day but was acceptable to the unsophisticated. Except as a curiosity, it is beneath contempt or criticism.

Of the state histories that appeared in this period a few are worthy of mention. Jeremy Belknap (1744–98) wrote a *History of New Hampshire* (three volumes, 1784–92), which is of the first rank in our historical compositions. Had its theme been more extended, it would have become a household memory in the country. Benjamin Trumbull's (1735–1820) *History of Connecticut* (2 vols., 1818) and Robert Proud's (1728–1813) *History of Pennsylvania* (2 vols., 1797–98) were of scholarly standards but heavy in style. George Richards Minot (1758–1802), a brilliant Massachusetts lawyer, wrote a *History of the Insurrection in Massachusetts* (1788), dealing with Shays' Rebellion, and followed it by a continuation of Hutchinson's *History of Massachusetts* (2 vols., 1798–1803). The books were well written and have maintained their credit. Here should be mentioned Henry M. Brackenridge's (1786–1871) *History of the Western Insurrection* (1817), a fair-minded narrative of the Whisky Insurrection, which was very popular and ran through several editions. Three Southern books which may here be spoken of are hardly up to the standard of the state histories. Dr. Ramsay's *History of South Carolina* (2 vols., 1809) was not equal to his work on the Revolution. John D. Burk (d. 1808) wrote a less valuable work in his *History of Virginia* (3 vols., 1804–05).[1] He was an ardent Republican who rhapsodized on liberty. Dr. Hugh Williamson (1735–1819), who wrote a *History of North Carolina* (2 vols., 1812), was a Pennsylvanian by birth, clergyman and physician by education, merchant and politician by necessity. He lived a while in Edenton, North Carolina, was elected a member of the Continental Congress, and served in the Constitutional Convention. In 1793 he removed to New York, where he acquired a high reputation for learning. His history, however, was thin and disappointing.

These men worked under the disadvantage that they were writing at a time when the minds of the people were absorbed with the struggle for national existence. Ebenezer Hazard, in 1779, described the situation as follows:

---

[1] After his death the book was continued in a fourth volume.

The war and the numerous avocations consequent upon it, have thrown every man's mind into such an unsettled and confused state that but few can think steadily upon any subject. They hear of useful designs, they give you all the encouragement which can be derived from the warmest approbation of your plan, they will even promise you assistance. Politics intrude,—kick you and your designs out of their heads; and when you appear again, why they really forgot that the matter had been mentioned to them. I have been repeatedly served so with reference to my collection.[1]

After the war came the years of constitution-making, and then a long period during which foreign affairs occupied most minds exclusively. It was a time, also, when unusual business opportunities enthralled the best intellects in the country. Thus there were few competent persons to whom the quiet task of writing history made appeal. It is not strange that Hazard had few people to encourage him.

Our post-Revolutionary period has been compared with the years following the French Revolution, in which there was a notable outburst of literary activity. The contrast is unfair. The French Revolution came upon an old and well-developed society, kept down by outworn social ideals, and when it had passed the shackles were broken. In the United States an immature society was relieved of the power that had hitherto done no more than impose irritating checks on its development. This wilful young people were given an opportunity to do as they pleased. They had no rich culture waiting to fill a new era with its splendour. They were fighting their way up from the bottom, and the process was necessarily slow.

A third group of historians was those who undertook to write general histories of the United States. They were inspired with the spirit of nationality, whatever their views of the new Union. They wished to depict the relations of the colonies to one another and their struggle against Britain's policy of strict control. The first histories presenting a general account of the colonies came from England, where as early as 1708 John Oldmixon, in his *British Empire in America*, made a sorry attempt to treat English America as a whole. In 1780 George Chalmers published his *Political Annals of the*

[1] "The Belknap Papers," *Mass. Hist. Soc. Col.*, 5th Ser., vol. II, p. 12.

Present United Colonies, followed in 1782 by another work called *Introduction to the History of the Revolt of the American Colonies*. Chalmers was an able writer and gave at least continuity to his subject. He was, however, strongly British in sympathy, and his work was not esteemed in the United States. It stimulated more than one American to write what he considered a true history of the rise and progress of the Revolutionary struggle.

Of the Americans who undertook to do the same thing, and to do it in a spirit more friendly to the cause of America, the first man worthy of notice here was the Rev. Abiel Holmes (1763–1837), whose *American Annals* (2 vols., 1805) represented much accurate and careful work. It marked the author as a man of scientific mind, worthy of equal respect with his son, the delightful Autocrat. The next to take up the task was Benjamin Trumbull, whose history of Connecticut has already been mentioned. He planned to write a history of the United States in three volumes and prepared for it by collecting many documents. The first and only volume, published in 1810, carried the narrative to the year 1765. Accuracy of statement and a spiritless style are the chief characteristics of the work.

Somewhat later came Timothy Pitkin's (1766–1847) *Political and Civil History of the United States* (2 vols., 1828). The author was a man of great industry and painstaking care. He had a fancy for statistical knowledge, and wrote also a valuable *Statistical View of the Commerce of the United States* (1817). His political history has the merits and the demerits to be expected in a statistician. Although it is marked by accuracy and a just sense of industrial development, its style is disjointed and difficult. Pitkin strove for fairness, but he saw the history of the country as a man of New England would see it. His own section bulked large in his treatment, and he did not get the point of view of the rest of the Union.

Twenty-one years after Pitkin's book was published, New England found a still abler and more satisfying historian in Richard Hildreth (1807–65), who in 1849 gave to the world the first three volumes of his *History of the United States;* three more appeared in 1852. The six volumes cover the years 1492 to 1821. For the lover of entertaining literature the book is a failure, but for one who enjoys a solid presentation of facts it has merit. Few other men have written down so many statements of fact in so small a compass with such great reliability. In the preface Hildreth said that he wished to describe the fathers of the nation as they were,

unbedaubed with patriotic rouge, wrapped up in no fine-spun cloaks of excuses and apologies, without stilts, buskins, tinsel, or bedizzenment, in their own proper persons, often rude, hard, narrow, superstitious and mistaken, but always earnest, downright, manly, and sincere. The result of their labours is eulogy enough; their best apology is to tell the story as it was.

There can be no doubt that the author tried in all honesty to carry out his purpose. "We encounter [in Hildreth]," said *The Edinburgh Review*, "the muse of American history descended from her stump, and recounting her narrative in a key adapted to our own ears."

An historian who did not liberate himself entirely from patriotic bias was John Gorham Palfrey (1798–1881). Although he falls slightly without the limits of time assigned to this chapter, he was by nature and purpose a member of what has been called the "filio-pietistic" group. Bred a Unitarian minister, and pastor for a time of Brattle Square Church, Boston, he served as Dexter Professor of Sacred Literature in Harvard University (1830–39). From 1836 to 1843 he was editor of *The North American Review*. He held several political offices in his State, and was a member of Congress in 1847–49. From 1861 to 1867 he was postmaster of Boston. He wrote many tracts, religious, political, and historical. Nevertheless, he kept true to his love for the history of New England. In 1858–64 he brought out in three volumes a *History of New England during the Stuart Dynasty*. It won instant recognition and the author followed up his success with two more volumes, *History of New England from the Revolution of the 17th Century to the Revolution of the 18th* (1875–90). The two parts were later shorn of their most irrelevant passages and issued as a *Compendious History of New England* in four handy volumes. So far as the mere statement of facts goes, it is safe to say that Palfrey has given us a complete and sufficient history of colonial New England. He has not been careless or slothful. But to Palfrey all that New Englanders did and thought was good. He did not question the spirit of Puritanism, and he did not find its narrowness unpleasant; he accepted it as a thing of course. He was the last of the complacent defenders of the old régime in the land of Bradford and Winthrop. Before he had retired from the scene Charles Francis Adams's severe blows were beginning to tell.

Over against these books from the North we must place a Southern history, the existence of which was due to the belief that the South had not received fair consideration at the hands of men who knew little about its life and natural environment. Such a book was George Tucker's (1775–1861) *History of the United States* (4 vols., 1856–58), which carried the story of the national development to the year 1841. The author was a lawyer in Virginia, a well-known and voluminous writer on political subjects. His *History* was not an extreme Republican book, as some have thought. It represented the ideas which one would expect from a conservative Virginian of the old school; it was well written, but not brilliant. Had it been offered to a section more accustomed to reading history, it would have been recognized as a standard book of its kind; as it is, it is known chiefly for the impression it made on those who held views it was intended to counteract. Tucker[1] wrote also a *Life of Thomas Jefferson* (2 vols., 1837), probably the best of the early lives of this statesman.

The last of the general historians who fall within this chapter's limits is George Bancroft, who, during his lifetime, held a larger place in the minds of his countrymen than any other historian who has lived in the United States. This he did partly because of his literary worth, partly because of his political activity, and partly because of his social prominence. President Arthur once said that the President is "permitted to accept the invitations of members of the cabinet, supreme court judges, and—Mr. George Bancroft."

Bancroft was born in Massachusetts in 1800 and died in Washington in 1891. Having graduated from Harvard in 1817, he went to Göttingen on funds subscribed by Harvard and its friends. Back in America in 1822 with a doctor's degree, he settled for a year at Harvard as tutor in Greek. He brought

---

[1] See also Book II, Chap. VII.

home from Europe many affectations of manner and such marked eccentricities that his influence at Harvard was under-mined; at the end of a year he left, to become, with Joseph G. Cogswell, proprietor of a boys' school at Northampton, Massachusetts. As a schoolmaster Bancroft was a failure, and he retired from the school in 1831. Meanwhile, he had begun to write. School-books, translations, and articles for *The North American Review* came out in rapid succession. By 1831 he had established the literary habit and had the reputation of being a ready and effective writer.

At this time Bancroft had begun to support the Democratic party. He was accused of doing it to obtain Federal office, but the charge was not substantiated. He was ever a defender of the doctrine of equality held by Jefferson, Jackson, and Lincoln. In America he saw organized democracy which was to make humanity happy: to write its history became his hope. In 1834 appeared the first volume of his *History of the United States from the Discovery of the American Continent*. At the time neither Hildreth nor Tucker had written, and only Pitkin, Holmes, and Trumbull had undertaken a task like his. They were all didactic. Bancroft produced a work of a different character. There was a lofty and sonorous sense of detachment in his sentences. To the present age they seem sheer affectation; but to the men who had been reading the bald statements of fact hitherto offered as history, they seemed admirable. Edward Everett read the first volume through in twenty-four hours and wrote:

I think you have written a Work which will last while the memory of America lasts; and which will instantly take its place among the classics of our language. It is full of learning, information, common sense, and philosophy; full of taste and eloquence; full of life and power. You give us not wretched paste-board men; not a sort of chronological table, with the dates written out at length, after the manner of most historians;—but you give us real, individual, living, men and women, with their passions, interests, and peculiarities.

Theodore Parker wrote: "I think you are likely to make, what I long since told you I looked for from *you*, the most noble and splendid piece of historical composition, not only in English, but in any tongue." Emerson said of the *History:* "It is noble matter, and I am heartily glad to have it nobly treated." Bancroft is less than a quarter of a century dead, and these beautiful laurels are already withered. A new age has accepted other standards than his.

Bancroft, our first historian who had studied in Germany, was well known at home and abroad as a hard student and a man of great learning. The abundant foot-notes in the first volumes of his history show how freely he used the sources in foreign languages. His experience in Germany led him to admire German scholarship in all its phases. At Göttingen he studied under Heeren, who was stressing the unity of history. In the preface of his first volume, Bancroft wrote: "The United States of America constitute an essential portion of a great political system, embracing all the political nations of the earth." He did not, however, try to work out this theory in his volume, but told, like others, the story of voyages, settlements, colonies, and the common struggle for freedom.

His progress was leisurely. The second volume appeared three years after the first, the third in 1840. The fourth and fifth were published in 1852. The sixth came in 1854, the seventh in 1858, the eighth in 1860, the ninth in 1866, and the tenth in 1874. During these years his literary work was interrupted by political service. He was secretary of the navy from 1845 to 1846, minister to Great Britain from 1846 to 1849, and minister to Germany from 1867 to 1874. The tenth volume carried the work to the end of the Revolution; but in 1882 came two additional volumes with the title *History of the Formation of the Constitution of the United States.* Hildreth wrote more rapidly, and his *History,* nearly as long as Bancroft's, seems to have been written in six years.

Another group of men, by collecting materials, compiling, and editing, rendered marked service to history in the first half of the nineteenth century. Beginning to collect for their own comfort they laid the foundations of great collections which have endured and grown and are now indispensable. The men who did this work are not to be forgotten; they were as truly servants of the historic muse as those who held her stylus.

Of the efforts of Prince and Hutchinson as early collectors of documents mention has already been made.[1] After the Revolution the first activity of that kind was due to the interest of Ebenezer Hazard (1744–1817) and Jeremy Belknap. Born the same year, they both graduated from college in 1762. Becoming fast friends, they left to posterity a correspondence which gives us our best glimpse of the conditions under which historical writing went forward in the two decades after the war.

Hazard first of the two began to collect documents. In 1777 he was appointed surveyor of post-roads and in 1782 postmaster-general. As surveyor he travelled over many parts of the country. He thus had opportunity to copy historical documents, and formed the design of publishing a documentary history of the Revolution. He rightly thought it a proper time to make collections of papers which otherwise would be lost. Congress gave him permission to take copies of such papers as were in its hands, free of expense of copying, and voted one thousand pounds for his expenses in securing copies elsewhere. This particular scheme was not realized, and there is no evidence that Hazard used the money voted. Dismissed from the office of postmaster-general in 1789 to make room for a politician, he soon afterwards announced a work with the title *Historical Collections, State Papers, and Other Authentic Documents;* and in 1792 the first volume was published. It contained papers, many of them very rare, relating to the American colonies before 1660. In 1794 came Volume II, most of it given up to the records of the New England Confederation. The two volumes did not pay expenses, and the editor, absorbed in business, lost interest in their continuation. Judged by what he published merely, Hazard had only a moderate influence on history in the United States. It is as the first collector and editor of documents after the Revolution that we must estimate him. He had the notion, shared by Sparks and Force in a later period, that it is possible to present the history of a people in a collection of documents. It was his failure to satisfy the general reader with such a collection that caused Hazard's publication to remain unsold, and to be a source of discouragement to its compiler.

[1] See Book I, Chap. II.

Hazard influenced the work of Belknap, who, as a minister
in Dover, New Hampshire, from 1767 to 1778, early became
interested in the history of the colony and began to collect
documents relating to it.   In this task he was aided by Governor Benning Wentworth.   Though Belknap had doubts about
the propriety of a minister's dabbling in history, the inclination was too strong to be resisted; and receiving encouragement
from his friends, he proceeded as he had begun.   In 1784
he published the first volume of his *History of New Hampshire*.   Financially it was as great a failure as Hazard's *Collections*.   It was many years before he sold enough copies to pay
the printer, but, unlike Hazard, Belknap was not discouraged.
Having resigned his parish at Dover, after a disagreeable wrangle
over his salary, in the following year he accepted a call to the
church in Federal Street, Boston.   From this time history
became a chief phase of his activity.   He was in the midst of
a congenial group of educated men, and one literary demand
after another was made on him.   The editors of magazines
appealed to him for articles; whatever co-operative work of
history was projected—and there were several—he was sought
for the enterprise.   In 1792 he published Volumes II and III
of his *History of New Hampshire*.   The sales were large enough
to wipe out the debts incurred by the first volume.

To *The Columbian Magazine* of Philadelphia he contributed
from time to time a number of very well prepared biographical
sketches of persons associated with the early history of America; and in 1794 they appeared in Volume I of an *American
Biography*.   Other sketches came out in a second volume (1798).
A third was planned, but the author died before it could be
written.   These sketches were based on the best sources then
available and were written in the author's best style.   For the
same magazine Belknap also wrote a series of satirical letters
dealing with the early history of New England.   They were
published in a separate volume called *The Foresters* (1792),
enlarged in an edition of 1796.   Belknap died suddenly, in
the midst of literary schemes, in 1798.   He was the best
American historian of his day, and the most zealous in preserving historical memorials.

Probably Belknap's greatest service was his efforts in
founding the Massachusetts Historical Society.   While he

had valuable aid from other men, he was the force that brought these others together; and until the time of his death he was the leader in the actual work of the society. Belknap himself said that he got the idea from John Pintard of New York. The project was launched in 1791, in accordance with plans prepared by Belknap. The membership was limited to thirty corresponding and thirty resident members, only ten of the latter being elected at first. The object was to collect, preserve, and publish historical materials. As long as he lived Belknap was a most active member, visiting nearby towns for document, supervising the publications, and finally leaving the Society his own manuscripts.

One of the friends of Belknap and Hazard—and a connection of Hazard's by marriage—was Jedidiah Morse (1761–1826), minister at Charlestown, Massachusetts. He was the author of the first American geography (1789), a book containing much more than mere geographical description. To gather the accounts of natural resources, means of communication, and statistics the author made many journeys. He also collected facts for his *Annals of the American Revolution* (1824), a compilation which posterity does not esteem highly. But it served its day, and was for a time widely read. Morse was probably indebted to Hazard and Belknap for the impetus that set him to writing. The latter complained that it was only Morse who could make money out of what he wrote.

When Morse published his thin work, two other men, Jared Sparks and Peter Force, were planning much greater enterprises. One was a New England man, a Harvard graduate, a minister of accepted standing, and a member of the most select literary circle of Boston. The other was a self-taught printer's boy who became publisher and editor, with a passion for collecting. Each served well the cause of historical research.

Jared Sparks was born at Willington, Connecticut, in 1789. His youth was clouded by misfortune, but his intellectual ability brought him into notice, and friends sent him to college. He took a high rank at Harvard, where he was looked upon as a man of great promise. A residence of four years in the South as a Unitarian minister in Baltimore gave Sparks a national feeling and probably stimulated his interest in national history.

In 1823 he returned to Boston to be the editor of *The North American Review*. This journal was then languishing under the editorship of Edward Everett, but Sparks secured control and placed it on a sound basis. In 1830, when he sold his last remaining share in the enterprise, he had received $19,000 besides an annual salary of $2200.

Sparks gave up the *Review* to devote himself to history. As early as 1824 he formed a plan to produce a complete edition of Washington's writings. He intended to write history that paid and did not think it discreditable to have an eye on the popular demand. In 1826 and 1827 he made journeys through the original thirteen states collecting materials from unpublished documents. In 1828 and 1829 he visited Europe and was given access to the British and French archives. By this time he was full of enthusiasm. "I have got a passion for Revolutionary history," he said, "and the more I look into it the more I am convinced that no complete history of the American Revolution has been written." At this time he was full of schemes, each connected with the Revolution, and several works came out of them. But always in the back of his mind lay the plan of a great documentary history of the Revolution. While preparing the edition of Washington he learned from President John Quincy Adams that in 1818 Congress had appropriated money to publish the foreign correspondence of the Continental Congress during the Revolution. Adams was then too busy to give the matter his attention, and nothing was done about it. Sparks caught at the suggestion that he should take it up, and he made an agreement with Secretary Clay by which he was to print and sell to Congress one thousand copies of this correspondence at $2.12½ a copy and to have $400 a volume for copying and editing. The work was done in eighteen months and for the entire set of twelve volumes the editor received $30,300. As his chief expense was for printing and translations, his net earnings must have been considerable. In the following year (1830), he proposed to Secretary Van Buren that the work be continued through the period of the Continental Congress. Van Buren agreed, and Congress passed the necessary act, but at the last moment the new secretary of state, Edward Livingston, made the contract with Frank P. Blair. Livingston blandly admitted that Sparks should have had the appointment but said that Blair's selection was demanded by the politicians.

The writings of Washington now occupied Sparks's time, but before they began to appear he brought out *The Life of Gouverneur Morris* (1832), in three volumes. In 1834 appeared Volume II of *The Life and Writings of George Washington*, and the rest of the twelve volumes followed regularly until the series was complete in 1837. The last to appear was the biography, the first volume in the set. The general verdict of the day was that it was a work worthy of the exalted subject. From 1836 to 1840 was published *The Works of Benjamin Franklin*, in ten volumes, and between 1834 and 1838 came the first series, and between 1844 and 1847 the second series, of *The Library of American Biography*, in all twenty-five volumes. In 1853 he issued *The Correspondence of the American Revolution*, a series of letters to Washington in four volumes.

Sparks's letters are full of his greater plan, and he recurred to the idea again and again until he was an old man, but he did not carry out his purpose. In fact, Sparks suffered an eclipse about 1840. After that date he did little besides editing the second series of the *American Biography* and writing several pamphlets and addresses. From 1838 to 1849 he was professor of history at Harvard, but the conditions were such that he had more than half his time for writing. From 1849 to 1853 he was Harvard's president, retiring to do literary work. It is hard to explain the paucity of results during these last years without assuming that he had lost his zeal after the achievement of his first great work, the Washington cycle. He died in 1866.

As a historian Sparks is to be measured by the *American Biography*, the best work of the kind then prepared. Even here his chief service was as an editor; for he wrote comparatively few of the individual sketches. Those he did write, however, were well done. His greatest editorial achievement was the *Washington*, an epoch-making work. It set a new standard of scholarship, founded upon accurate and broad knowledge, for American students of history. Edward Everett spoke truly when he said of it in *The North American Review:* "The American press has produced no work of higher value."

But Sparks had serious faults. In 1833 he sent Judge Story a specimen volume of his work accompanied by manuscript copies of the letters in it. Story could thus see in what respects liberties had been taken with the texts. He said in reply:

There is not an instance in which you have failed to give the identical sense with more accuracy and clearness [than in the original]. You have done exactly what I think Washington would have desired you to do, if he were living. I cannot, therefore, in any manner object to it on my own account.

But he added that he feared the critics would take objections to the changes of literary form. Had the hint been taken, Sparks's reputation as an editor would be higher.

The editor's Nemesis at length overtook him. In 1847 appeared the *Life and Correspondence of Joseph Reed*, containing many letters from Washington to Reed, his secretary. The editor had printed them as they were sent by the author. The public now had two copies of certain letters, one published by Sparks and one by Reed. Sharp eyes soon discovered discrepancies, and Sparks was charged in the press with correcting, embellishing, and altering to suit his own purposes letters which should have been reproduced literally. In 1851 Lord Mahon's *History of England* reached its sixth volume, in which an appendix repeated the charges. Then followed a long controversy in which Sparks was put to his mettle to defend himself. It is known that Washington in his old age corrected many of his letters which he had kept in letter books. Sparks sought excuse in saying that this indicated that Washington wished all his letters revised, and that he had merely done what Washington himself would have done. Needless to say, this excuse did not satisfy the critics. The controversy probably served a good turn to scholarship. Coming in connection with the first great work of editing in the field of American history, it attracted wide attention, and fixed in the minds of scholars the necessity of accurate reproduction of documents. It should be said for Sparks that many others of his time thought that an editor ought to correct the letters he reproduced. Exact reproduction, however, had become the rule with the best editors.

Peter Force was born in New Jersey in 1790. When very small he accompanied his father to New York, where, after a short term at school, he became a printer's boy. He proved intelligent and reliable and rose to the first place in the business. In 1816 he became managing partner in a shop which his former master established in Washington to execute a government contract. In 1823 he became editor and proprietor of *The National Journal*, then in the interest of Monroe's administration and later an Adams organ. In 1830 his party had disintegrated, and, being of all men least able to find another, he saw his paper run into a decline that left him without employment.

Earlier than this he had made plans for publishing a great collection of documents on the American Revolution. Sparks was just bringing his *Diplomatic Correspondence* to a successful close, and the profits of the enterprise had attracted the attention of more than one Washington editor. It seemed a favourable time to attempt the execution of Force's scheme. He found a partner in Matthew St. Clair Clarke, clerk of the House of Representatives, who had money enough to launch the enterprise and political influence enough to get it authorized by Congress. Accordingly, after some negotiations Congress on 2 March, 1833, at the very time the compromise tariff bill and the "Force Bill" disposed of the South Carolina crisis, passed a brief law authorizing the secretary of state to contract with Force and Clarke for the publication of a documentary history of the American Revolution, provided it did not cost more proportionally than Sparks's work.

Edward Livingston was then secretary of state. His contemporaries considered him an impractical man, and the contract he now made goes far to support their view. It was agreed that the work should be published in folio form, the government to take fifteen hundred copies at $1\frac{7}{8}$ cents a page a copy. Thus $22,500 would be paid for each volume of eight hundred pages. No limit was set to the number of volumes, and as the mass of materials was large the work might be made to extend to many volumes. Among Force's manuscripts, in the Library of Congress, is a memorandum in which he and Clarke estimated their profits, not including the expenses of collecting materials, at $11,000 on a volume of eight hundred and fifty pages. Force had begun to collect, according to his own statement, as early as 1822; but his efforts had evidently been desultory. He now gave all his time to the work, his partner advancing the necessary funds.

By 1834 a storm of denunciation broke over them. Clarke had lost his office through the triumph of the Jackson men in the House. He was believed, before going, to have filched this fat job, by which he could publish an indefinite number of volumes at a great profit. The secretary of state was called on for an investigation, and there was an angry debate in the House; but nobody could discover means to annul a contract about which the only complaint was that it was unwisely made. Moreover, the plan announced provided for six series each containing several volumes, covering the whole existence of the country from the days of settlement until the adoption of the constitution. The title was *The American Archives.*

In 1837 the initial volume, the first of the fourth series, was before the public. It was made on such a comprehensive scale that the completed series would necessarily be gigantic. Moreover, the character of the contents was alarming. By "documents" most people understood manuscript materials, or rare fugitive papers; but here were included whole sections of the debates in Parliament, the journals of the Continental Congress, and many state laws, all previously accessible in print. It was Force's idea to make a complete collection of Revolutionary material. In 1839 the second volume of the fourth series appeared, and in 1840 the third volume. Such was the feeling that in 1843 the publishers had not been paid for the third volume and could not get $6000 of the amount due on the second. Under these circumstances a compromise was made. The publishers agreed that the series should not exceed twenty volumes at a maximum average cost of $20,400 each, and that the secretary of state should approve the materials offered for publication. About this time Clarke sold his interest in the series to Rives, the partner of F. P. Blair.

For several years matters now proceeded satisfactorily. The fourth volume appeared in 1843, the fifth in 1844, and the sixth, completing the fourth series, in 1846. The first volume of the fifth series came in 1848, the second in 1851, and the third in 1853. Marcy was secretary of state in 1855, and when the material for the fourth volume was submitted, he refused to approve it in any part. To Force he said: "I do not believe in your work, sir! It is of no use to anybody. I never read a page of it and never expect to." Neither he nor his successor, Lewis Cass, could be induced to change this decision, and *The American Archives* came to an end with Volume III of the fifth series, nine volumes in all having been issued.

In 1832 Force thought the series would contain not more than five volumes, eleven years later it was limited to twenty, but when nine had been published the story of the Revolution had been carried only to the end of 1776. At this rate it would have taken over thirty volumes to bring the story to the treaty of peace; and if it had been limited to twenty it must have been left incomplete. One other fact may have aroused Marcy's disapprobation. By 1855 each Congress had formed the habit of ordering copies of the work for its own members not previously in the House, a species of graft unlikely to be terminated by Congress itself. On the other hand, it is undeniable that Marcy did not appreciate Force's work and that he was illiberal, if not narrow-minded.

Early in the series Force adopted the following division of the matter bearing on the period any given volume was to cover: (1) The proceedings, papers, and correspondence of the Continental Congress; (2) The proceedings, papers, and correspondence of the assemblies, conventions, and councils of safety of the several states; (3) The proceedings, papers, and correspondence of the British Government and of the officers acting under it in our Revolution; (4) Miscellaneous letters and papers relating to the Revolution. This material was presented with accuracy and completeness, but poorly arranged, and with very few editorial notes. The indexes in the fourth series were inadequate, but the deficiency was remedied in the fifth.

After the rejection of his work Force continued in Washington, completing his collections and putting them into shape for publication, if fortune should bring the opportunity. The outbreak of the war removed the last hope of this kind. In 1867 he was too old to complete his task, and sold his library to the Government for $100,000. It contained 22,529 printed volumes, about 40,000 pamphlets, some valuable newspaper files, and enough transcripts to make 129 bound volumes. The collection was placed in the Library of Congress, where Force's manuscripts remain unpublished. In 1879 Congress called for a report on the value of the collection, and received a lucid statement from the Librarian of Congress. No practical results followed.[1]

Aside from the *Archives* Force is best remembered for four volumes of *Tracts* published from 1836 to 1846. They were mostly reprints of rare pamphlets relating to the earliest period of American history, and their publication was accomplished with financial sacrifices. "Whenever I found a little more money in my purse than I absolutely needed," he said, "I printed a volume of *Tracts*." Several pamphlets of his own composition were also published, none of them of much importance. They serve to show us how little of an author he was.

Bancroft and Sparks collected documents, and Sparks published documents, but each was an historian first of all. Force collected documents and published them, without a thought of editing or interpreting them. If his great work had been more discreetly conducted, it might have weathered the storm of popular criticism. But Force was not discreet. In all the confusion around him he never relaxed an inch in his plan of making a complete and all-inclusive collection.

Force has had no successor, probably because his example raised up such a large school of local collectors and compilers that there has been no room for one vast treasure. The work he did not do has been carried on by many workers and has resulted in many restricted collections. Force played a large part in awakening the interest of this group; and in doing so he contributed much to the progress of American historical scholarship in the last fifty years, its latest and most fruitful period.

[1] For a discussion of the value of Force's collection see Bassett, *Middle Group of American Historians*, p. 298.

CHAPTER XVIII

Prescott and Motley

I. PRESCOTT

TO write, his first resolve; to select a topic, his second—herein lies a cardinal difference between William Hickling Prescott (1796–1859) and the typical research student who only at last commits the results of his labours to paper. Not that Prescott plunged into his task without preparation. His self-training was long and minute, but the methods were so exceptional as to be well worth noting in some detail.

Prescott's choice of a career was hampered at the outset by defective eyesight and fragile health. A seemingly trivial incident had left a permanent mark upon his life. When he was a junior at Harvard, a crust of bread thrown by one of a careless group of skylarking students hit Prescott in the very disk of the left eye, the blow being so sudden that the lid did not have time to protect its charge. The victim's whole system received a nervous shock. Later it was discovered that the one eye was destroyed and that the sight of the other could be preserved only by assiduous watchfulness. Prescott was able, however, to complete his college course, and maintained his standing so well that he received the appointment as Latin poet at Commencement and amidst applause delivered his hexameters *Ad Spem*. That was in August, 1814. He had all that a young Bostonian of a century ago could wish for, except health. He was handsome, with good and sound inheritance, cultivated surroundings, sympathetic and congenial parents and well-to-do family circumstances, and he was as well equipped for intellectual life as Harvard could make him. But ill-health barred the way to active life. All the capacity for work, for the steady occupation that enriched forty years of quiet student pursuits, had to be resolutely wooed. What was won needed careful husbanding to ensure the maximum return for the minimum nerve expenditure. But, shackled by physical limitations as he was, Prescott was fortunate in not being a prisoner of poverty. His was a case where an assured income made the labour he delighted in physic pain and then grow profitable in its turn. Far from the harvest he wanted, he was able to gather expensive source material without financial limitations.

Seven years after graduation, Prescott was still on the eve of setting himself to serious work within his capacity. By that date he had been married a year to Susan Amory, found in the circle of cultivated, prosperous Bostonians in which the Prescotts moved, and he was wonderfully fortunate in his wife. She was a splendid comrade for her husband in the sheltered life that had to be his lot. Prescott's early ventures at travelling, while they gave him a little experience of life in the Azores and slight glimpses of England and Paris, proved conclusively that changes exposed him to the risk of incapacitating suffering, though with favourable conditions he might exert himself to good effect. Thus it was, in 1821, that he decided to take up his pen as an occupation. Very deliberately he proceeded to examine the tools of expression that were ready to his hand. He found them very defective. He had no well-based accurate knowledge of English, let alone modern languages. Accordingly, on 30 October, 1821, he planned a preliminary course to lay accurate foundations for a literary career. Blair's *Rhetoric*, Lindley Murray, the introductory chapter of Johnson's *Dictionary* were studied as though the student were a small schoolboy instead of a Harvard graduate of seven years standing. At the same time he ploughed through a long course of English literature. Ascham, Bacon, Browne, Raleigh, and Milton, besides the sermons of eminent divines, were read to him in chronological series, while he used his own sight for an hour of Latin daily. At the end of the year he felt he had broken ground only. A temporary improvement in his eye enabled him to plunge into French authors from Froissart to Chateaubriand, still devoting a part of each day to hearing English drama from Heywood to Dryden. With his friend Ticknor, Prescott kept up a third line of English reading, connected with Scandinavian and Teutonic themes and compositions. In 1823, Sismondi's *Littérature du Midi* prepared him for Italian letters, which he proceeded to explore systematically and intelligently. Two articles in *The North American Review* contained his impressions on this field; they were written *con amore*, as the change from French to Italian had been to him especially stimulating and refreshing. The latter language was far more to his taste than the former. German was his next desire, but it had to be abandoned as too difficult for his partial eyesight. Then, through Ticknor's interest in things Spanish, Prescott turned to that language as his next venture. Once embarked, he sailed on in Spanish interests until his death, although he was not attracted immediately. "I am battling with the Spanish," he wrote to Bancroft in 1824, "but I have not the heart for it that I had for the Italian. I doubt whether there are many valuable things that the key of knowledge will unlock in that language." Still he continued to play with the key for a long time until, out of a list of subjects for a book, he made his choice. "What new and interesting topics may be admitted—not forced into— the reign of Ferdinand and Isabella?" he noted in 1825. In 1847 he endorsed the entry, "A fortunate choice."

The whole sweep of events taking place on the Peninsula seems to have flashed before his vision: the constitutions of Castile and of Aragon, of the Moorish dynasties, the causes of their decay and dissolution, the Inquisition, the conquest of Granada, the discoveries in the unknown West, monarchical power *versus* aristocracy; and he saw their relation to the whole world. Prescott had assimilated literary expression in its best forms in order to fit himself to express something in his turn; when that something had crystallized into definite form, it was as a narrator that he entered on his task of giving it a proper treatment. He began to see his story in episodes for the framing of which he had already provided the material.

A tentative bibliography was despatched to Edward Everett, United States Minister at Madrid, on 29 January, 1826. To Everett's natural suggestion that Prescott would be wise to come to Spain and look over the ground for himself, the latter answered in some detail that his one chance of success was to work even with limited resources at home rather than to jeopardize his future by groping with half sight in archives abroad. The explanation, written by his own hand, brought on an access of misery to his eye, and he recovered lost ground very slowly.

Under fresh limitations, but now with his scene firmly set, he began a systematic course of international and legal history, in addition to a general survey of Spain, geographically, economically, ecclesiastically, and civilly, especially with reference to fifteenth-century conditions. This necessitated the consultation of several hundred volumes in working days of about four hours each, with actual reading power of an hour a day at best, a few minutes or nothing, at worst. The imported sources arrived, but the author lingered on at the threshold before plunging into Spanish details. He recurred to Montesquieu's *Ésprit des lois*, to Voltaire, and to other philosophical considerations of history and human conditions; he heard governmental, theological, and chivalric works, many biographies and the classics, the last now in translation that they might be read aloud. Much of this was, of course, mere intellectual pabulum, never to be concretely adapted to his expressed results. By this time he had acquired a capacity of holding firmly in his mind the portions he saw he could use, while putting aside the non-essential. Such methods have rarely been applied so deliberately and consciously by an historical writer.

Having decided that he would use secondary material when a phase of his subject had been adequately treated by French or Spanish writers, Prescott began original work by mastering the chronicles of Andres Bernaldez as a first-hand source. Luckily the secretary devoted to his service was an able young Harvard graduate, a Mr. English, capable of supplementing the author's eyes, and sympathetic with his methods. The copy of Bernaldez obtained was in manuscript of no easy style.

The actual composition of *Ferdinand and Isabella* began in 1829, after eight years of preliminary reading, both general and special, at large and with the goal in mind. When it came to the literary form of the narrative, Prescott followed

Mably as a guide, having read his *Étude de l'histoire* ten times. He would think out a chapter on the same structural plan as for a romance or a drama, letting the events develop towards some obvious point or conclusion. Count d'Haussonville thinks this tendency to group transactions artistically a defect in historical narration, but other critics are more lenient, finding the result very readable. For six years the author worked on. Everything pertinent to his subject, and accessible at that time, that could be taken out of Spain, was imported in original or in transcript and digested very slowly. Prescott worked his direct quotations into his text, as a rule, instead of giving excerpts thrown or jerked into the narrative. At the same time, his references are precise and accurate. When the three volumes were concluded, the author again reaped an advantage from his full purse. No typewriting was available to break the fall from handwriting to the pitiless printed page, and to read handwriting was forbidden to Prescott. Feeling the need of meeting his copy face to face, he had four copies printed in large type on one side of the page. Then he was able to go over the whole, little by little, with his own sight. Submitted to the criticism of various friends, the book excited only delighted approval and stimulating comment, encouraging the author to have 1250 copies printed at his own expense by the American Stationers' Company (1836–37). Such a success America had never before seen or heard of. The edition was exhausted in five weeks. It was not surprising that the American reviews were favourable. There was no one capable of passing upon the sources. That the style was easy and the story illuminating was sufficient to make people gratefully acknowledge the introduction to Spanish history at a moment when Spanish eyes were turned anxiously towards the west. But in England there were at least two scholars who knew the subject and could pass a competent opinion on the American's work: Don Pascual de Gayangos, Spaniard and archivist in London, and Richard Ford, author of a handbook on Spain. Both accepted the new book with some puzzled queries as to how it could emanate from America. Basil Hall and Mrs. Trollope had given forth their impressions of the United States, and their readers were not prepared for scholarly yet graceful and novel historical work.

Yet such was the rating of *Ferdinand and Isabella* pronounced by these competent specialists in Spanish lore. One sympathetic and appreciative review came from the hand of Count de Circourt, a man described by Lamartine as "a living chest of human knowledge," which gave the unknown and modest American immense satisfaction. He was actually received at once into the international circle of authoritative scholarship. Hallam, Guizot, Milman, Sismondi, Thierry, were among those to give Prescott not condescending but cordial welcome as one of their own rank. Such an authority as C. P. Gooch states in 1913 that the work published in 1837 has not been superseded to this day. Research has brought, indeed, masses of documents to light that Prescott never heard of. Critics differ from him in conclusions—strange if they did not. Yet there is more serious difference of opinion between Vignaud and Harrisse, both writing on Columbus in the twentieth century, than between Prescott and Justin Winsor, in the first and second halves of the nineteenth.

Stimulated by the prompt recognition accorded to him, Prescott turned to his next venture, *The Conquest of Mexico*. It is characteristic of his methods that his first step towards beginning the narration in which one figure, Hernando Cortes, was to hold the centre of the stage, was the examination of certain celebrated biographical records of exploits—Voltaire's *Charles XII*, Livy's *Hannibal*, Irving's *Columbus*. His criticism of the last is that the interest flags at the end. That is just what can be said of his own *Mexico*, finished in 1844. Where the glow of achievement is ahead of his hero, the narrative marches and carries the reader on. Or is it that Bernal Diaz carries the story triumphantly up to the Aztec city? Prescott's method of assimilating his authority, instead of giving excerpts, was used to good purpose here, and his paraphrases are very vivid. For instance, in describing the Spanish army as it came in sight of the lake-city: "A scene so new and wonderful filled their rude hearts with amazement. It seemed like enchantment and they could find nothing to compare it with but the magic pictures in Amadis de Gaula." This is a clever turn to the simple statement by the chronicler of the Spaniards' first impressions of the Aztec city. Bernal Diaz, the veteran soldier, unskilled in letters, moved to set down his recollections of the great events in which he had participated half a century back, because Gomara's official history gave Cortes undue, and his comrades insufficient, credit for the Conquest, was a delightful guide to follow. His untaught phrases are alive and Prescott makes them more so. While later judgment discounts some of the conquistadore's statements, it cannot deny the fact that it was these glowing descriptions that affected the European imagination of the sixteenth century. For the ultimate rating of the veracity of the complaisant adventurer archæology has brought its later contribution, and of that science Prescott was ignorant, as was the rest of the world when he wrote. He almost relinquished the idea of his *Mexico* on hearing that Washington Irving had a similar scheme in mind. This would have been a real loss, as Irving's gentle raking over of unknown ground could not have produced as good fruit as Prescott's digging certainly did. Both *The Conquest of Mexico* and *The Conquest of Peru* were important works in the development of American literature and the American attitude towards knowledge. Neither the reputation nor the libraries of New England could have spared them.

The courtesy that Irving showed to a younger aspirant in his field was repeated by Prescott himself towards Motley, the latter ready to abandon his *Rise of the Dutch Republic* for fear lest Prescott's *Philip II* would fill the whole field adequately. There was a division of labour, again lucky, as Prescott's biography would have been a meagre substitute for the glowing partisan book. Count d'Haussonville ranks the incomplete *Philip II* as Prescott's best work. That is a dictum hard to accept. The author's attitude towards his central figure is less slashing than Motley's, less appreciative than Martin Hume's. In so much it may be called just, but there is a certain meagreness in the treatment. Robertson seems to have affected his style, although his work on that author's *Charles V* was not done until two volumes of *Philip II* had seen the light in 1855.

Between *Peru* and *Philip II* Prescott made a journey to England, where he was wonderfully received and fêted during his four months' visit. Oxford gave him a doctorate. In 1845 the French Institute and the Royal Society of Berlin, and in 1847 two learned societies of England, had made him a member, so that his status as a scholar was perfectly assured, and his own charm gained him permanent friendship after formal courtesy had made connecting links. During the remainder of his life, noted English scholars and statesmen kept up a correspondence with him. Perhaps the friendship accorded to him by Alexander von Humboldt on account of *Mexico* and *Peru* was one of the most grateful of the many won by the real merit of his literary labours. Fortunately he never lost the powers of enjoyment or of active occupation as death came very suddenly in 1859.

Prescott has been called a great amateur in the historical field, and in one sense, the term applies. Born only a year after Leopold Ranke, Prescott missed the influence spread abroad, eventually far beyond German university circles, by the great German scholar. The very vocabulary now used had not come into being. Prescott made his own standards. Nor did he have the incidental training that has been the strength of many an historian. Not trained in the methods of the École des Chartes, nor in the precise legal knowledge of jurisprudence, like Maitland, nor in active political service for his own state, nor in a school of philosophy, still less in the academic methods of research, Prescott simply assimilated language first and then events, and painted pictures of the past by a skilful union of the two. His style is a fine instrument of expression. His language plays him no tricks. He holds it in his own control, firmly, like a well-wrought, highly-tempered tool. His own temperament manifests itself very little in his writing. Nor is there any echo of contemporary politics in his treatment of the past. He is as aloof from the events passing in the United States as from those that he depicts. Possibly this is due to the peculiar state of affairs in those ante-bellum decades of the nineteenth century. He was a Bostonian who hated strife and felt that agitation was disagreeable. Thus nothing of his personal opinions and experience peeps out from between his lines as do those of Bancroft, Motley, and a score of French and Netherland writers whose pages are coloured by their attitude towards their immediate present. Perhaps had Prescott survived the outbreak of the Civil War his sentiments would have changed.

Those of many compromisers did. But he passed from the scene before the outbreak, and thus is crystallized as a figure detached from strife, a non-partisan, hard-working yet leisurely historian, sheltered from the hard things of life, almost untouched by his generation, endowed with the best New England could give to a few of her sons, and with the type of New England conscience that led him to use the talents he had but which also permitted him to hold aloof from his country's troubles as from something almost unclean.

Yet how many of his fellow-countrymen found his work grateful can be seen from the number of his books that were scattered over the land. Since 1837, editions of his books have appeared at frequent intervals. Exact figures seem difficult to obtain, but many thousand copies have been sold, while several editions of translations have appeared in Spain, in France, in Italy, in Germany, and in Holland.

II. MOTLEY

John Lothrop Motley (1814–77) was like Prescott in being a son of Massachusetts and born with a silver spoon of pure Boston metal in his mouth. In each case New England gave to her child a heritage of sturdy character, of convinced opinions of the Channing school, of the finest lineage she had woven from British material; to birth-right she added the best quality of education that had thus far been evolved on her soil. Of this late post-colonial education it can be said that, full of short-comings as it was, it usually had this characteristic— its disciples were inspired with a desire for more. To each of these Bostonians fate granted the boon of remarkable personal beauty. These endowments fell, however, upon characters of somewhat different tendencies, while their lives took them over different courses. Prescott was a prisoner within the bounds of congenial private life, his professional activity limited to the area of his own book-room filled with the imported source-material which he could not go to seek; while Motley made his own researches, touched the past with his own fingers, so close did he come to the documents, and had, in addition, the stimulus of world contact, of hearing statesmen's voices, of activities of which Prescott was wholly ignorant. Moreover, Prescott died in 1859, just too soon to fling off the shackles of repression which choked the free speech of Americans of his temperament before the Civil War.   On the other hand, Motley, in every line of his later work on the sixteenth and seventeenth centuries, shows the exhilarating effect produced by the casting of the die and the ending of the compromise restraint.   Born the very year Prescott finished his Harvard course, Motley was two-thirds of a generation behind the elder historian.   Thus, though the immediate environment of the two Bostonians was the same, the storm brewing beyond the confines of Massachusetts had burst and had forced her conservative citizens out of their aloofness, and the Commonwealth was involved in a close bond with the other units of the Union, while Motley and his labours were still in a stage to be affected, as Prescott and his work never were, by contemporaneous politics.

From his early childhood, Motley was overflowing with expression. He was possessed to act out what he read; he made miniature theatres; he declaimed in season and out. His zeal for dramatic effect was in his blood—even though he did not evince the slightest histrionic ability or tendency. That is, he could not possibly have been an actor. It was literary expression that attracted him. He was so precocious that it would not have been surprising had his promise died out. Luckily, the colonial energy of the race was also in his blood and a New England strain well woven into the woof of his conscience so that his abilities found enduring record when, at last, he developed the powers of industry. His Harvard career was begun at the age of thirteen and completed at seventeen—an age young even for the time—and it is not surprising that his election to Phi Beta Kappa was gained only by stretching a point in his favour and including one more than the sixteen men legitimately chosen as the maximum number to be taken from each class. His class work did not give him high rank—indeed, he was rusticated for negligence—but his personality was so charming and his kind of cultivated human interest so convincing, that he could not be passed over. His facility in grasping the gist of a book was marvellous, but as it did not presage minute and accurate research, there was natural astonishment among his contemporaries over the industry evinced by his later work.

Harvard was followed by two years of study at Göttingen and Berlin and of foreign travel. George Bancroft, then fresh from his own German experience, had been a teacher in Motley's school at Northampton. Probably it was due to his influence that German was taught, as it was not a usual subject in the school curricula of the twenties. The young student was thus partially prepared for his plunge into Hanoverian university life and did not lose his first months in struggling over linguistic elements. Perhaps the most interesting contribution to his training given by the Göttingen episode was his acquaintance and intimate association with Count Bismarck, the foundations of a life-long friendship. The American had an exceptional opportunity to know a contemporary from an environment totally different from his own by heritage and tendency. Later, he had the still rarer chance of glimpses at the inside happenings or intentions of Prussian politics. He saw a master mind in the making and in the doing, as few of his generation could. The friendship has, moreover, permitted posterity some peeps at the Iron Chancellor in his moments of relaxation, a few of his intimate letters to the American having been published among those of Motley. Most delightful are the young student's own letters home during his *Wanderjahre*. He worked hard, indeed, at law in both universities, but it was the glimpses of Europe and the human side of its life, both past and present, that were the really vital part of the educational results for the young American. Intellectual Germany was still palpitating with the influence of Goethe, whom he was just too late to see, and he was deeply impressed by the atmosphere. He met scholars, such as Tieck, then at work on his translation of Shakespeare, and he learned what minute research could be. At the same time Motley retained an impressionistic attitude towards history which was wholly un-German. He always saw the past instinct with life. He is constantly reconstructing. "If you will allow me to mount my hobby, as Tristram Shandy would say," he writes from Rome in 1834, "and call fancy to the aid of history, the scene will be different, at least more lively." Thus he and his imagination travelled together, congenial companions.

When the wanderer returned to Boston he continued his
preparation for law, but it never became his serious profession.
He had to write, and his first venture was a novel called *Morton's Hope*. Published anonymously, it fell flat. Nor did it
deserve success, although, at first view, the writer seems to
have had both the training and the qualifications for a romancer. Foreign travel and study had widened his vision; he
had really studied languages on the basis of a good preliminary education; and he had a fertile and graphic imagination.
Moreover, at the time of writing, he was fairly bubbling over
with personal happiness. The novel appeared in 1839, two
years after his marriage to the sister of Park Benjamin, an
intimate friend of Motley, while another intimate friend,
Joseph Lewis Stackpole, married Mrs. Motley's sister. A
close circle of friends was thus formed—affectionate yet all
critical of each other. Mary Benjamin Motley seems, from
all testimony, to have been a very rare person, whose comradeship with her husband was singularly perfect throughout her life.
But despite such good auspices, *Morton's Hope* failed. The critics
scarcely noticed the book, although one did admit that it must
have been "written by a person of uncommon resources of mind
and scholarship." As a work of art the story deserved oblivion.
It is full of chronological anachronisms, the diction is bombastic and strained, the composition is faulty. The one interest in
the book is that there are certain autobiographical suggestions
in the reflections and self-contemplations of the hero. There is
an underlying thread of aspirations, "disguised," says Dr.
Holmes, "under a series of incidents, which are flung together
with no more regard to the unities than a pack of cards."

The failure of his first venture did not deter Motley from
making another trial in the same direction. His second novel
Merry Mount, not published until 1849, was semi-historic in
character. The scene is laid in Massachusetts in 1628—"in
that crepuscular period which immediately preceded the rise
of the Massachusetts Colony and possesses more of the elements
of romance than any subsequent epoch," writes the author in
his preface. The book plays with theological revolt and separatist movements, and introduces adventurers of somewhat
dime-novel calibre to shock Puritan sentiments and to impress
Indians by aristocratic hauteur.

But with all his knowledge of fundamental facts and of local colour, the author failed to command attention. *Merry Mount* is not bad, but it is dull. The characters do not carry the slightest conviction. They are simple bundles of attributes, and some of the bundles have a sensational taint. Contemporary reviews did not slight the book. *The North American Review* actually devoted seventeen pages to an abstract of the tale, in order to prove that the early settlement of New England was not a good field for fiction: "Later events only make the period interesting," "The conditions are too hard," "Romantic elements are lacking." The reviewer concludes with saying that he has been agreeably disappointed, on the whole, but he does not consider the romance a fair specimen of what the writer can achieve.[1]

Between the production of the two novels, Motley had had fresh experiences. In 1841 he was appointed secretary to the legation at St. Petersburg and spent some months in the Russian capital, long enough to be convinced that he did not wish to have his wife and children join him. So he resigned his post before his year was out. Once again in America, he began to give utterance to his opinions on political events, the failure of Henry Clay to secure the presidential nomination having roused him to mournful expressions of his conviction that all that was fine in American public life had been overpowered by mediocrity if not by evil. He had a little taste of public life himself; he served in the Massachusetts legislature for one term (1849). The one measure he seems to have worked for was an endowment of higher education at the expense of the common schools. "Failure was inevitable," says George S. Boutwell, a fellow legislator. "Neither Webster nor Choate could have carried the bill." Motley had written a report as Chairman of the Committee on Education, thinking that he had achieved a fine document, and was much surprised at the unanimity of its condemnation. He had no more desire for Massachusetts political life. By this date, Motley was thirty-five, no longer a youth, yet all his failures seem those of immaturity. It sometimes happens when a boy is precocious that the reputation of being in advance of his years lingers about him after the time when a man of

[1] *North American Review*, January, 1849.

more normal powers makes his public appearance. But
Motley began to show himself in another light than that of
romancer or legislator; his essays were proving that he could
conquer some of the glaring faults of his style and write on
sober themes. His articles on Peter the Great, on Balzac,
and on Talvi's *Geschichte der Colonisation von New England*
were scholarly and original. He had no desire, however, to
dissipate his store of energy in ephemeral reviews. Before the
publication of his half-historical *Merry Mount* he had selected
the theme of the contest between the Netherlands and Spain
for an extensive work, had been checked momentarily by the
news of Prescott's projected *Philip II*, had been spurred on by
the kindly words of the elder American, and had then devoted
himself to going to the foundations of the story of the events.
He says in reference to hearing of Prescott's work:

It seemed to me that I had nothing to do but to renounce authorship. For I had not at first made up my mind to write a history
and then cast about to take up a subject. My subject had taken
me up, drawn me on, and absorbed me into itself. It was necessary for me, it seemed, to write the book I had been thinking much
of, even if it were destined to fall dead from the press, and I had
no inclination or interest to write any other.

Thus Prescott's courtesy did as much service to Motley as
Washington Irving's did to the author of *The Conquest of
Mexico*. To the world, too, it would have been a loss had *The
Rise of the Dutch Republic* never come to light. It was indeed
a work of love. Motley gave up every other thought and
worked to one end only. He made no such preliminary preparation as did Prescott. Yet in a way, his whole career had
been leading up to it. He had burned to express himself.
He planted source-material in his mind, and the story flowered from it, naturally. For nearly ten years he plodded on,
at first in Boston and then in archives abroad, in Berlin, Dresden, The Hague, and Brussels. He bathed in local colour.
In 1855 he had his three volumes ready for the printer. Then
came a difficulty. No publisher would look at the formidable
mass of manuscript with the slightest interest. No one would
believe in the chances of returns from such an expensive undertaking as its publication. Like his compatriot, Motley was

obliged to take his own risks, and *The Rise of the Dutch Republic* was published at the author's expense by John Chapman in London, and by Harpers in New York. The sale of fifteen thousand copies in two years proved the fallibility of human judgment. The reviews were not, however, as uniformly favourable as in Prescott's case. *The Saturday Review*[1] brought heavy artillery to bear on the ambitious American in the same number with a censorious attack upon Browning's *Men and Women* and three columns upon the lack of interest in Miss Yonge's unpretentious domestic tale, *The Daisy Chain*. The *Review's* slashing denunciation of his flashy chapter headings was peculiarly annoying to Motley, because he had disapproved of their adoption. He comments upon this in a letter to his father, in connection with the remark that every book notice had condemned them unequivocally. *The Literary Gazette*[2] found virtues in the volumes, but added: "The book is far too ponderous both in matter and style to be popular," and commiserated Motley because his literary skill fell so far short of his diligence and learning that other writers would enter into the fruits of his labours and write more popular histories out of his store. The sequence of the prophecy proved singularly true. Motley's *Rise of the Dutch Republic* has been quarried and retold in every conceivable form. One has only to glance along the shelves in the Library of Congress to see how many books are based on Motley, with due credit to him, while many more volumes, serious and romantic, less frankly owe their being to his pages. At the same time, this use of fragments has not been due to the unpopular character of the full work, as is proved by the continued sales of the three volumes.

As a compensation for the *Saturday's* strictures on his work, *The Westminster Review* for the month following (April, 1856), had as its leading article a comprehensive paper by J. A. Froude which did full justice to the unknown American writer.

A history as complete as industry and genius can make it now lies before us of the first twenty years of the Revolt of the United Provinces. . . . It has been the result of many years of silent

---

[1] 23 March, 1856.   [2] 19 April, 1856.

thoughtful, unobtrusive labour, and unless we are strangely mistaken, unless we are ourselves altogether unfit for this office of criticis-
ing which we have undertaken, the book is one which will take its
place among the finest histories in this or in any language. . . .
All the essentials of a great writer Mr. Motley eminently possesses.
His mind is broad, his industry unwearied.

Froude did not like Motley's estimate of Queen Elizabeth,
adding: "It is ungracious, however, even to find so slight a
fault with these admirable volumes." This gentle animad-
version is amusing, because all the eminent authorities on the
period treated do just what Froude does. They like the way
Motley has navigated the whole sea of difficulties but think
he has lost his way on their private pools. In Holland and
Belgium at the time of the appearance of *The Rise of the Dutch
Republic* there were, among other scholars, three eminent
archivists and one rising historian: Groen van Prinsterer,
Bakhuysen van der Brink, and Professor Fruin in Holland, and
Gachard in Brussels. They all received the book with pleasure
as well as with profound surprise that any foreigner had cast
his plummet down their deeps with so much assiduity. Mingled
with their real and cordial approval there was a reserve on
the part of each regarding the treatment of his own particular
thesis. Groen thought that Motley did not really feel the
Protestant impulse in all that happened; Bakhuysen considered that he did not understand phases of the relations with
Germany; Gachard, himself less fervent in his opinions than
the Hollanders, criticized Motley's partisanship; while Fruin,
the first man to hold a chair at Leyden University exclusively devoted to "Vaderlandsche Geschiedenis," criticized the whole work on a larger and more ample scale. He
thought that the author did not grasp fully the actual development of the congeries of provinces, found many weak spots
in the generalizations, and held that, closely as Motley had
followed original authorities, he had erred seriously in not
testing the exact weight and authenticity of the witnesses
whom he had summoned to help him tell his tale.

The English original excited immediate interest in Holland,
but the most exhaustive reviews were reserved until the Dutch
version appeared in 1859, made by no less an authority than

Bakhuysen himself, who said: "Motley's work seems to me to make such an excellent foundation for the history of the growth of the Commonwealth of the United Netherlands that it seems almost a duty to bring forth one's own possessions in order to rear up a structure on this foundation." Fruin repeated the words at the beginning of his review. He added a cordial appreciation of the industry and conscientiousness of the American.

> We have discovered no unused source. . . . I take it for granted that everyone has read the work of the American. . . . It would be a scandal if our countrymen neglected to read what the foreigner counted of sufficient importance to discuss. . . . Motley shines in narrative [*Hij is een bekwam stylist*] but he is less fortunate in his explanations of cause and effect. What the witnesses whom he summons testify, he narrates better than they can tell, but he fails to weigh their personality and trustworthiness with sufficient accuracy. The "how" is good, the "why" defective. He is far behind Ranke in his comprehension of the beginnings of the revolt.

Then the Dutch historian proceeded to write one of the most valuable articles that ever came from his pen, *Het voorspel van den tachtigjarigen oorlog*. Herein he carefully reviewed the ground with exact references to his authorities and gave a less passionate and less biassed picture than Motley of Philip's relations to the Netherlands and to the thread of events that preceded the final outbreak. Motley could not complain of lack of appreciation in the Netherlands, and had reason to flatter himself that his work was a spur to the Netherlanders to look to their own dykes and consider carefully what was true among their writers of the sixteenth century and what needed to be winnowed. Besides, there was an interest aroused in the texts, and several valuable works, used by Motley in manuscript, were printed within a few years after the publication of his work. Now nearly everything important is in print, and the stimulus to the incessant output during the last half century was certainly largely due to the American.

Scarcely taking breath after the publication of this first great effort, the author plunged into the sequel and brought out two volumes of *The United Netherlands* in 1860. This time neither publisher nor public was shy. The English reviews were very favourable, on the whole; even *The Saturday Review*[1] was almost commendatory though it did not find the style satisfactory. Perhaps the most severe stricture was that the figurative language was uncultivated in tone, but the general attitude of the censor is quite different from that taken four years previous. *The Westminster Review* was more lavish in its praise. *The Edinburgh Review* was a trifle patronizing, but still Motley was given credit.

The American reviews had no reservations in their praise of both works. It is a trifle amusing to note the conclusion of the comments—a long and serious article—on *The Rise of the Dutch Republic* in the *North American:* "upon the whole it seems to us that the first William was a greater man than his great-grandson and namesake." This sounds as though, indeed, the elder Prince of Orange had needed an introduction to the American public in 1856.

In Holland the second book received the same greeting as did the first, a greeting marked by pride and pleasure that a stranger had devoted so much of his life to their affairs, tempered by some careful and discriminating criticism. Professor Fruin wrote: "We have delayed too long in noticing this important work. No one can put down the book until it is finished. Through the beautiful style, the vivid narrative, the artistic descriptions, this work shines out above the works on history in our own language." Fruin took Motley's notes and verified every reference: "Even where we differ from his opinion, we must do honour to his good faith, to his keen perception, to his industrious and accurate investigation." The review was another of Fruin's fine essays on Dutch history. Fruin once more criticized Motley's failure to differentiate the values of his authorities and considered him often tempted to expand a phase simply because he had a rich store of material bearing upon it, but without due regard to the need of that phase in the narrative. Letters between Leicester and his officers led him on to tell a detailed story of petty English quarrels which would have been more suitable for a separate publication. That Motley's vivid imagination inspired him with interlinear visions, hardly substantiated by a strict construction of the text, was gently intimated by Fruin with one

[1] January, 1861.

or two striking examples. Undoubtedly this is the same imagination that led the tourist to people the Rome before his eye with actors once within her walls. Life was, indeed, breathed into skeleton facts—some new joints being supplied —and life, too, into years of discussion as to the eternal verity of Motley's conception. One item in *The Rise of the Dutch Republic* gave Fruin especial concern. That was the use of the term "William the Silent." He wished that the American had lent his weight towards eliminating the unsuitable adjective from the historical vocabulary. Criticism such as this of Fruin's was the highest compliment that could have been paid to Motley.

The spring of 1861, momentous in the history of the United States, found Motley still in London. He had been abroad at work in the archives ever since the winter of 1856–57, which he had spent in Boston. The first public news of the imminent Civil War must have come to him on Monday, 29 April. That was the day when the Earl of Malmesbury opened the session in the House of Lords with the assumption that "Almost all your Lordships must have read the account that arrived this morning from America, and must have learned with pain as well as astonishment that civil war has broken out." Humanely rejoicing that no blood had been shed, the Earl proceeded to ask what the noble Lords were going to do towards settling this most unnatural quarrel. Lord Woodhouse replied that, after mature deliberation, the Government had decided that advice on internal matters would be intrusive unless solicited. From that Monday on, the London *Times* gave much space to comments on the terrible anachronism of war in general, on the horror of seeing thirty million Anglo-Saxons slaying each other like the Indians whom they had displaced, etc., etc. All civil wars known to history were reviewed. In each of these, asserted the *Times*, a vital principle had been at stake. Each had been justified by the crying needs of religion or civil liberty. But in the United States, no principle was involved. Day after day this statement was reiterated in varying forms. Admitting that, on the whole, they inclined rather to the Northern cause, they still declared that, nevertheless, the actual issue between the two sections was a mere shadow.

It is curious how long the idea of the causelessness of the strife prevailed in Europe. As late as April, 1863, Bismarck wrote to Motley in a familiar letter: "Do you all know exactly why you are waging furious war with each other? Certainly all do not know, but they kill each other *con amore*, that is the way the business comes to them. Your battles are bloody; ours are wordy." This query was, perhaps, half humorous, but the *Times* was in dead earnest in its opinion that the war was unjustifiable. It went further, after a little, and declared that the spirit of George III had passed into Seward and that his reluctance to let the South go its own way was couched in language quite as tyrannical as that of the British monarch to his colonies when they desired "secession."

Under the stimulus of these daily reiterations, Motley wrote two long letters, to which the *Times* gave prominent space, on *The Causes of the Civil War*. They appeared on Thursday, 23 May, and Friday, 24 May, and were reprinted in New York within a few weeks. The line of argument followed was that the United States was no confederacy from which a part could be lopped and both parts continue to live. A confederation of sovereign bodies had been tested and found wanting; then a more perfect government had been formed by the people themselves, at large, not in states as units. The government to which the Constitution of the United States gave birth was different in kind from its predecessor. It could not be divided any more than Scotland could be severed from the British Empire. It was a plea for the sacredness of the Union as an organic, vitalized whole. The tariff, as an irritating cause of division, was discussed, while slavery was touched on very lightly.

The Queen's Proclamation of Neutrality had already checked the press in its references to President Davis as precisely on a par with President Lincoln, and Motley's words were allowed to be worth noting, as coming from one already recognized as an historian of European reputation. For a time, at least, the English newspapers changed their tone, while in America there was warm appreciation of Motley's statement of the case.

Shortly after this incident, Motley returned home and was in Boston when the first Massachusetts regiments left their

camp at Brook Farm (singularly peaceful spot for a training
ground!) and marched off to war. He regretted that his forty-
seven years disqualified him from enlisting without previous
training, but he was stirred to the depths of his being by the
emotion of the summer months of 1861. That emotion, carried
abroad, kept him a fervent American during his years of foreign
residence. John Bigelow considers that he was denationalized,
but he was not. He only tried to hold fast to ideals crystallized at a moment of high pressure. He did not feel the meaner
elements that obtruded themselves during the long-drawn-
out contest.

Although he did not enlist, he was summoned to do other
work for the republic, and accepted the mission to Austria,
where, it was felt, the sentiment he had shown in his London
letters would be serviceable. His own historical work was
put aside for the six years in which he lived at Vienna, upholding the dignity of the United States. A cultivated, polished, high-minded American official was a great asset to the
United States at that juncture, when there was a disposition
abroad to count the Northerners as commercial sordid folk.
Here was a Yankee of the Yankees as a living witness that
the name was not counted as a term of reproach by those who
bore it.

His office was no sinecure. In addition to the complica-
tions arising from the war, there were others connected with
Maximilian's expedition to Mexico, in which he showed good
judgment. The unexpected elevation of Andrew Johnson to
the presidency in 1865 brought a new element to be reckoned
with. It chanced that, just at a moment when Johnson was
feeling very sore about the defection of Republicans from his
support, a letter came to him from Paris accusing various official Americans abroad of malignant criticism towards the
administration. A passage about Motley was as follows: "Mr.
Motley does not pretend to conceal his 'disgust' as he terms
it elegantly, at your whole conduct. He tells every traveller
that Sumner is wholly justified and that you have deserted
your principles in common with Mr. Seward, who, he says, is
hopelessly degraded." Under the influence of his general
feeling of distrust and suspicion, the president told Seward to
send a formal query to each person mentioned, asking the

truth of the accusation against them. Later Seward told John Bigelow that no one resented the query, drawn up by a clerk and signed by himself as secretary of state, except Motley. In all other cases, it was taken as it was meant, a simple matter of office routine. Probably, had the President not been over-sensitive about the attitude of his subordinates, the accusing document would have been put in the waste-paper basket. No one knew the "George McCrackin" from whom it purported to come. Motley, however, did not take it as a formula. Such a question addressed to him seemed an insult, and he lost no time in replying, perhaps only less hotly than he felt, offering his resignation at the end of his denial of the charge that he had maligned the new administration. The secretary of state would have taken no notice of a resignation offered under a momentary smart, but when Johnson said "Let him go," Seward did not try to stay his hand. According to the story Seward told John Bigelow in 1869, it would seem a fair conclusion that the minister was too hot and the secretary too cold and too indifferent, when an effort on his part to interpose would have been natural under the circumstances. The result was that Motley left Vienna with a very sharp wound to his self-respect.

Luckily for the ex-diplomat, the seventeenth century was waiting till he should be released from the claims of the nineteenth, and he plunged at once into the next period of his Netherland story. *The History of the United Netherlands* was concluded by two more volumes issued in 1868. A continuation centred about John of Barneveld was finally published in 1874. Motley returned from Vienna to Boston and was settled there at the time of Grant's first campaign, into which he entered with much interest. At the suggestion of Sumner, he was honoured by Grant with the appointment to the Court of St. James, the highest diplomatic post in his gift. That was pleasant after the Vienna incident. Unfortunately, Grant identified him with Sumner, and when a breach came between the president and the senator from Massachusetts, the former found a pretext to recall Motley, and again a secretary of state failed to protect the minister. Moreover, the explanatory letter written by Hamilton Fish was not phrased in a manner to soothe the diplomat's feelings, so that the incident ended with added discomfiture for Motley. Again work was the refuge from the annoyances to which he had been subjected, but they were not forgotten. It is rather curious to note how the author's unpleasant experience colours the story of the relations between Maurice of Nassau and John of Barneveld. The inability of the soldier, acting as statesman, to understand the diplomat is dwelt on in a fashion to show that General Grant was in the historian's thoughts when he wrote of Count Maurice. Indeed, *John of Barneveld* is a reflection of autobiography almost as much as *Morton's Hope*. Every point having to do with the ambitions of the individual province and the needs of the United Netherlands is coloured by the crisis through which the United States had just passed. Sometimes the implied parallel is apt, sometimes both strained and forced. It was Motley's tendency, in general, to indulge in comparisons and metaphor that once more troubled *The Saturday Review.*[1] The carping critic evidently thought that all the expressions to which he objected were American. He did not realize that any worker in sixteenth century historical sources is living in the midst of just such language as was found objectionable. Sober documents are permeated with idioms not to be counted Americanisms; the letters of Elizabethan statesmen overflow with quaint twists and turns. Thus Motley's natural tendency in this direction was constantly fed during his researches into contemporary material. It was natural for him, writing from Vienna during a terrible drought, to declare that there was nothing green in Austria but the Archduke Maximilian, dreaming of an American empire (1863). It was phrases like that in history which shocked the reviewer. Other reviews in Great Britain and America were almost unanimous in their high praise for *John of Barneveld*. *The Edinburgh Review* said: "We can hardly give too much praise to the subtle alchemy of the brain which has enabled him [Motley] to produce out of dull, crabbed, and often illegible State-papers, the vivid, graphic, and sparkling narrative which he has given to the world."

In the Netherlands, the book was viewed from a different standpoint. The period treated was one marked by the bitterest kind of theological disputes. Motley thought he could discuss these impartially, but his attempt only brought down upon his head a flood of pained criticism from the heirs to both sides of the controversy,—no dead question in Holland. The old archivist, Groen van Prinsterer, fervent Calvinist as he was, declared that only an Arminian, such as an American Unitarian was, could be so antagonistic to the principles of the Reformation espoused by Maurice. (Perhaps Groen did not believe that Maurice had once declared that he did not know whether Predestination was green or blue!) Motley had become the ardent apologist of Barneveld and latitudinarian doctrine, the orthodox Hollanders felt, and a battle was started that raged for years. Groen devoted a whole book to the topic. At the same time, Dutch scholars paid warm tributes to the American's conscientious use of sources, though they might not accept his interpretation. No one accused him of neglecting what was obtainable. They only thought "He cannot understand." By that time the handsome American with his air of distinction was a well-known figure in The Hague. In 1871, the Queen of the Netherlands offered him a house in the Dutch capital, where he spent part of the years when he was working at *John of Barneveld*.

The death of Mrs. Motley in 1874 was a blow from which her husband never recovered, although he tried to resume his work and complete the story of the Eighty Years' War. The sub-title of the Barneveld volumes had been *A View of the Primary Causes and Movements of the Thirty Years' War*. But Motley was never to take the public with him beyond that view. His own death came in 1877, and he was buried in England.

What is the judgment of posterity upon the work into which Motley poured so much vigorous painstaking effort? This much can be said: he was first a brilliant searchlight, sweeping over an unknown field, and then an able draughtsman in describing the scene. Every new generation claims to have a light in its own hand which enables it to judge the past with greater accuracy than its predecessors. Scholars of today in Holland, Blok, Japikse, Colenbrander, all consider that the American failed to treat Netherland history on scientific lines. He did not understand Europe at large, he did not understand the Church. In his hands Philip II was treated too severely, as was Maurice in his conflict with Barneveld. There was a lack of perspective in his every estimate. Not only that, but in making one period so dominant, he dislocated the perspective of the whole history of the Netherlands. For the last thirty years scholars in Belgium as well as Holland have been working over the ground, bringing small dark places into sober light, shading down other points too highly illuminated. A fair result will be reached at last. But the great light was a pleasant thing.

CHAPTER XIX

Early Humorists

A LTHOUGH American literature was, even at the beginning, not without its humour, much of the early writing which seems to us whimsical and amusing may have had no humorous appeal for contemporary readers. From an early period, however, we can discern symptoms of the two kinds of humour which were to be represented by American writers: the one following closely English models, especially Addison, Steele, Defoe, and Goldsmith in the eighteenth century, and Lamb, Hood, Jerrold, and Dickens in the nineteenth century; the other springing from American soil and the new conditions of American life, and assuming a character as new to the world as the country that produced it. Franklin,[1] Irving,[2] Holmes[3] belong to what we may call the classical tradition; the present chapter is concerned with those aspects of American humour which are more essentially native, at least in form and tone.

The great period of American humorous writing has been the last three quarters of the nineteenth century. For all the preceding periods a very brief sketch must here suffice. In the seventeenth century the conditions of colonial life were not propitious to any sort of writing, humorous or other. To secure the means of a livelihood was a practical problem which left little time for the cultivation of the more genial side of life. In bleak surroundings where there was little physical comfort, and under the gloom of Puritanism, most writers were practical and serious. But there are a few exceptions. *New England's Annoyances* (1630),[4] a piece of anonymous

---

[1] See Book I, Chap. VI.   [2] See Book II, Chap. IV.
[3] See Book II, Chap. XXIII.   [4] See Bibliography to Book I, Chap. IX.

doggerel, shows that even the Puritans could smile as they regarded some of their discomforts. Nathaniel Ward[1] wrote *The Simple Cobler of Aggawam in America* (1647), which Moses Coit Tyler called "the most eccentric and amusing book that was produced in America during the colonial period," although Ward insisted that it should be accepted as a trustworthy account of the spiritual state of New England. John Josselyn, who wrote *New England's Rareties* (1672), declared that most of what he wrote was true; he admits that some things which he recorded he had heard but not seen: for example, that "Indians commonly carry on their discussions in perfect hexameter verse, extempore," and that "in New England there is a species of frog which chirps in the spring like swallows and croaks like toads in autumn, some of which when they sit upon their breech are a foot high, while up in the country they are as big as a child of a year old."

In the eighteenth century humour assumed a more important place in American literature, being represented less by naïve recitals of incongruous situations and incidents and more by a conscious recognition of the incongruity. The narratives of William Byrd (1674–1744),[2] perhaps the wittiest and most accomplished Virginian of the colonial time, are remarkable for their civil geniality amid rude circumstances, and for their touches of cultivated irony. Madam Sarah Kemble Knight (1666–1727),[3] in her diary written in the pauses of her horseback journeys between Boston and New York in 1704 and 1705, recorded in a most amusing manner the humours of the rough roads, the perilous crossing of rivers, the intolerable inns, and the coarse speech of the inland rustics. John Seccomb (1708–93) wrote a piece of verse called *Father Abbey's Will* (1732) facetiously describing the estate of Matthew Abdy, sweeper, bed-maker, and bottle-washer to Harvard College. These lines found their way into *The Gentleman's Magazine.* Joseph Green,[4] who became well known for his puns, has left us some mischievous lines on *Doctor Byles's Cat* (1733). The popular impression of Green is embodied in an epitaph which was written for him by one of his friends:

---

[1] See also Book I, Chap. III.
[3] *Ibid.*
[2] See also Book I, Chap. I.
[4] See also Book I, Chap. IX.

Siste, Viator, Here lies one
Whose life was whim, whose soul was pun,
And if you go too near his hearse,
He'll joke you both in prose and verse.

These few specimens show, if they show nothing more, that other spirits than Cotton Mather and Jonathan Edwards were alive in America in the eighteenth century.

The Revolution produced its humour chiefly in the form of political satire; the principal names are Francis Hopkinson, John Trumbull, Joel Barlow, Philip Freneau.[1] The first two were perhaps most important in this connection. Hopkinson's *Battle of the Kegs* was as good for the American cause as the winning of a real battle. In the grim year of 1778, this poem went into every American camp, cheered the patriots, and provoked hearty laughter at the awkwardness and stupidity of the enemy. And Trumbull in *McFingal* produced a Hudibrastic epic whose anger and irresistible logic reflected ingeniously the temper of a colony of sturdy militiamen that had taken upon themselves the task of offering opposition to the mother country—a task in itself not without its incongruous aspect.

During the period that followed the Revolution the colonists doubtless told their stories of war and sea, "swapped yarns," and recounted deeds of adventure along the frontier, but little has remained to show the character of the writing and to enable us to know what impression it made upon the time. There was not a little humorous political and satirical verse. Certain writers, like William Austin, Irving, Paulding, Drake, Halleck, Sands, Verplanck, brought into American literature an estimable sort of humour, but little was produced by any of them that had an emphatically native quality.

About the time of Andrew Jackson, along with the birth of popular national self-consciousness, the emergence of the frontier as a social entity in the nation's imagination, and the rise to power of the newspaper (for almost without exception the professional American humorists have been newspapermen), the kind of humour that we think of as American took

[1] For these four poets see Book I, Chap. IX.

on new life. It first found voice in New England, the section
which was eventually to shudder at the tide of boisterous,
outlandish mirth that set in from the new South and the
newer West, along and beyond that "highway of humour,"
the Mississippi.

First in point of time among the new humorists came
Seba Smith (1792–1868), whose *Letters of Major Jack Downing*
appeared in 1830. Almost immediately after his graduation
from Bowdoin College in 1818, Smith began to contribute a
series of political articles in the New England dialect to the
papers of Portland, Maine. These illustrated fairly well the
peculiarities of New England speech and manners, and doubtless had a great influence in encouraging similar sketches in
other parts of the country. Smith was in several ways a
pioneer. He led the way for *The Biglow Papers* and all those
writings which have exploited back-country New England
speech and character. He anticipated, in the person of Jack
Downing, confidant of Jackson, David Ross Locke's Petroleum V. Nasby, confidant of Andrew Johnson. He was the
first in America, as Finley Peter Dunne, with his Mr. Dooley,
is the latest, to create a homely character and through him
to make shrewd comments on politics and life. Charles
Augustus Davis (1795–1867) of New York created a pseudo
Jack Downing (often confused with Smith's) who was intimate
with Van Buren and the National Bank in the thirties and with
Lincoln in the sixties. In 1835, only two years after Smith's
first collected volume appeared, Judge Thomas Chandler
Haliburton, a prolific Nova Scotian, began the series of short
sketches from which emerged one of the most famous of the
early Yankee characters, Sam Slick the Clockmaker.

It must suffice barely to mention a number of the earlier
volumes of American humour which attained popularity but
which today are known only to the student. David Crockett's
Autobiography (1834) may not belong here, though it is certainly one of the raciest of all the books in its kind.

Crayon Sketches (1833), by William Cox (d. 1851), an
English journalist working in New York, consists of a series
of amusing essays contributed to *The New York Mirror*, satir-
izing the literary infirmities of the times and hitting off
well-known actors. Especially popular were the sketches of

himself and the burlesque biography of the old city constable, Jacob Hays. *The Life and Adventures of Dr. Didimus Duckworth, A. N. Q. to which is added the History of a Steam Doctor* (1833), is a mock-heroic biography of a spoiled child, in the style of broadest farce; *The Perils of Pearl Street* (1834) tells of the fortunes and misfortunes of a country lad who comes to New York in search of wealth. Both were written by Asa Green (d. 1837), a New England physician, who moved to New York and established himself as bookseller. A clever book, hustling with action, is *Novellettes of a Traveller, or, Odds and Ends from the Knapsack of Thomas Singularity, Journeyman Printer* (1834), which was written by Henry Junius Nott (1797–1837), of South Carolina, distinguished at the bar for his learning and afterwards as professor of *belles-lettres*. The *Ollapodiana Papers*, in the style of a more boisterous Lamb, were contributed to *The Knickerbocker Magazine*[1] by Willis Gaylord Clark (1810–41), whose twin brother, Lewis Gaylord Clark (d. 1873), for a long time editor of the *Knickerbocker*, was an accomplished journalist and humorist of the chatting sort. *The Motley Book* (1838) was a collection of original sketches and tales by Cornelius Mathews (1817–89), a versatile poet, dramatist, and journalist who was very prolific during the forties and whose *Career of Puffer Hopkins* (1841) is one of the most interesting of minor American political satires. The sprightly and observant *Sketches of Paris* (1838), by John Sanderson (1783–1844), were made a good deal of in London and Paris for a decade or so after their first appearance. George P. Morris (1802–64),[2] one of the founders of *The New York Mirror*, collected in 1838 a volume of his sketches of New York life; the leading one, called *The Little Frenchman and his Water Lots*, is a pathetic but graphic account of a little French merchant duped by a Manhattan real estate dealer. The *Annals of Quodlibet, a Political Satire by Solomon Secondthought, Schoolmaster* (1840), by John Pendleton Kennedy, has been treated elsewhere in this history.[3] The influence of Dickens is potent in *Charcoal Sketches or Scenes in a Metropolis* (1840), by Joseph Clay Neal (1807–47), whose

---

[1] See also Book II. Chaps. III and XX.
[2] See also Book II, Chap. V.
[3] See Book II, Chap. VII.

work was seen through the press in England by Dickens himself.

Of more importance in these times was *Georgia Scenes* (1835), a series of inimitable and clear-cut pictures of the rude life of the South-east, by Augustus Baldwin Longstreet (1790–1870). Longstreet, who was the son of a prominent inventor, graduated at Yale, and won distinction as lawyer, judge, newspaper editor, Methodist minister, and president of Emory College. His realistic descriptions of country parties, debating societies, horse-trades, fox-hunts, shooting-matches, brutal fights, and the adventures of his hero, the practical joker Ned Brace, insured a fruitful career to humour in the South, which before the Civil War enlisted at least a dozen considerable names in its ranks. From Georgia also came *Major Jones's Courtship* (1840), intimate and comic letters by William Tappan Thompson (1812–82), who had an interesting career as editor and soldier in Ohio, Pennsylvania, Florida, Maryland, and Georgia. One of the best of early Southern humorists was an Alabama editor, Johnson J. Hooper (1815–62), whose *Adventures of Captain Simon Suggs* (1846) was admired by Thackeray. Captain Suggs is an amusing rascal, who lives by his wits and who is presented with rare irony by an author who had perhaps the most delicate touch of his time and section. Charles Henry Smith, "Bill Arp so-called" (1826–1903), wrote from Georgia a series of letters, beginning with the mildly defiant "Bill Arp to Abe Linkhorn," which marked him as a brave and sensitive voice for the Confederacy. After the war Bill Arp was the first to smile and relieve the gloom. A trifle later, and farther north, appeared the letters of Moses Adams, in real life George W. Bagby (1828–83), of Virginia, editor of *The Southern Literary Messenger* and other periodicals and among the earliest to master negro psychology and dialect in literature. Tennessee is represented in this period by George Washington Harris, "Sut Lovengood" (1814–69); and Kentucky by George Denison Prentice (1802–70), who came from Connecticut in 1830 and made *The Louisville Journal* a powerful Whig organ as well as a repository for the widely quoted epigrammatic paragraphs which he collected in 1859 as *Prenticeana*.

Perhaps the most significant volume of humour by a Southerner before the Civil War was *The Flush Times of Alabama and Mississippi* (1853), by Joseph Glover Baldwin (1815–64), who was born in Virginia, practised law in Alabama, and spent the late years of his life in California. Like Lincoln. as a lawyer he had learned much from riding the circuit, and traced in his book the evolution of a country barrister with considerable skill and imagination. Although chiefly concerned with the Flush-time bar, Baldwin described as well most of the sharpers, boasters, liars, spread-eagle orators, the types of honesty and dishonesty, efficiency and inefficiency, in the newly rich and rapidly filling South. Unlike some of the books of his time, this one does not degenerate into mere horse-play or farce. We may still find interest in the characters of Simon Suggs, Jr., Esquire, and Ovid Bolus, the former a good trader and the mean boy of the school, the latter a great spend-thrift and liar although handsome and possessed of a generous and winning manner.

In the North and West meanwhile, humorous books were growing steadily in number and importance. During the late forties Mrs. Frances Miriam Whitcher (1811–52) wrote for several journals a series of articles purporting to come from the pen of the Widow Bedott, "an egregiously wise and re-spectable and broadly humorous matron." Such was the demand for her writings that after her death two collections were published, *The Widow Bedott Papers* (1855) and *Widow Sprigg, Mary Elmer, and Other Sketches* (1867). Her humour is spirited but often obvious. Frederick Swartout Cozzens (1818–69), a New York wine merchant with literature as a hobby, cultivated a pleasant vein of mild, dry humour which produced *The Sparrowgrass Papers* (1856), describing the expe-riences of a New York cockney who retires to Yonkers to live *The Travels, Voyages, and Adventures of Gilbert Go-Ahead* (1856), recording the deeds of a shrewd clock-selling Yankee in differ-ent parts of the world, was probably by the most prodigious literary hack of his day, Samuel Griswold Goodrich (1793–1860), "Peter Parley." A widely travelled New York naval officer, Henry Augustus Wise (1819–69), wrote several extravagant volumes of sea exploits, of which *Tales for the Marines* (1855) was probably best known. Thomas Bangs Thorpe (1815–78), a Massachusetts man who went as a journalist to Louisiana and became known as the author of highly coloured tales of the South-west, adopted the name of "Tom Owen, the Bee-Hunter," an eccentric person who had picturesque adventures on the frontier. Two other men, Samuel A. Hammett (1816–65) of Connecticut and John Ludlum McConnel (1826–62) of Illinois, travelled in the West and South-west and described their experiences in racy volumes.

Mrs. Partington, the American Mrs. Malaprop, was created by Benjamin Penhallow Shillaber (1814–90) of *The Boston Post* and forms the central figure in at least three books, *Life and Sayings of Mrs. Partington* (1854), *Partingtonian Patchwork* (1873), and *Ike and his Friends* (1879). Her character and manner of expression may be seen in her chance remarks:

> I am not so young as I was once, and I don't believe I shall ever be, if I live to the age of Samson, which, heaven knows as well as I do, I don't want to, for I wouldn't be a centurion or an octagon and survive my factories and become idiomatic by any means. But then there is no knowing how a thing will turn out until it takes place, and we shall come to an end some day, though we may never live to see it.

Her benevolent face, her use of catnip tea, her faith in the almanac, her domestic virtue, and her knowledge of the most significant facts in the life of every person in the village immediately made a large circle of readers recognize the lifelike portrayal of a person known in every American community. It is interesting to observe that her nephew Ike and his experience with the dog and cat and with "spirits" is a striking prototype of Tom Sawyer in his relationship to his Aunt Polly.

Three New York writers of broad burlesque in both prose and verse may be mentioned together. There appeared in *The New York Herald* a series of satirical lyrics in the assumed character of an Irish private in the Union Army who rapidly became famous. These were written by Charles Graham Halpine (1829 –68), a versatile Irish journalist and poet who had been with General Hunter in South Carolina, and were published subsequently in two volumes as *Life and Adventures, Songs, Services and Speeches of Private Miles O'Reilly* (1864). The best of this collection is the amusing account of the visit of the hero to the President, the members of the Cabinet, and foreign ministers

at the White House.   Mortimer Thompson (1832–75), actor,
salesman, journalist, rhymester, was one of the most spirited
of mid-century humorists, though his work is little more
than (to use his own phrase) "a series of unpremeditated extravagances."   He indulged in impudent prefaces, incredible
titles, fantastic illustrations, and breathless satire upon every
current popular enthusiasm.   He went to Niagara and wrote
back contemptuous letters to *The New York Tribune*.   His
Plu-Ri-Bus-Tah (1856) burlesqued *Hiawatha* in meter and
the American eagle in attitude.   His pseudonym was characteristically "Q. C. Philander Doesticks, P.B."   In their day
The Orpheus C. Kerr[1] *Papers* (1862–68) had a great vogue.
They furnished sharp satire upon civil and military affairs in the
darker days of the war.   Lincoln read with great satisfaction
their burlesque of the unescapable office-seeker of the time.
The lampooning seems rather reckless today and the characterization overbroad.   Newell was also a writer of serious and
burlesque poems; he was well read, a clever wag, and an effective parodist.

George Horatio Derby (1823–61) has been called the real
father of the new school of humour which began to flourish
toward the middle of the nineteenth century.   His sketches,
with the signature "John Phœnix," began to appear about
1850, and were afterwards collected in two volumes, *Phœnixiana*
(1855) and *Squibob Papers* (1859).   Derby had graduated
from West Point, had served in the Mexican War, and, as
an engineer, had been engaged in surveying in the West and
South.   As a means of relaxation from his strenuous and
exacting work, he set about writing down in humorous fashion
his observations upon the life about him.   In his books are
to be found most of the elements used by humorists of more
recent times.   He delighted in the use of big words, high-
sounding phrases and figures of speech, and euphemistic
statements.   We quote a short example:

This resplendent luminary, like a youth on the Fourth of July,
has its first quarter; like a ruined spendthrift, its last quarter;
and like an omnibus, is occasionally full and new.   The evenings
in which it appears between these last stages are beautifully illumined by its clear, mellow light.

[1] Orpheus C. Kerr = Office Seeker.

As a Western humorist, the first to introduce the spirit of the Pacific Coast into humorous literature, he influenced his admirer, Mark Twain, and as a writer of easy, fertile monologue he anticipated "Josh Billings," and "Artemus Ward," two of his most famous successors.

For the present discussion there remain three men who, in the history of American humour, stand out more prominently than all others from colonial days to Mark Twain: Henry Wheeler Shaw, "Josh Billings" (1818–85); David Ross Locke, "Petroleum V. Nasby" (1833–88); and Charles Farrar Browne, "Artemus Ward" (1834–67).

The first of these, a child of Massachusetts, wandered out to Ohio and finally settled as an auctioneer in New York State, where he began to contribute to various newspapers and magazines. His early writings attracted no attention until, in 1860, he changed his spelling in the *Essa on the Muel*, and then he achieved a popularity which never failed him. As a lecturer and as a witty philosopher he was not surpassed in his day. He is the comic essayist of America rather than her comic story-teller. His humour and his only strength lie in his use of the aphorism which is old but which he brings forth with as much sententiousness as if it were new. "With me everything must be put in two or three lines," he once said. He was not one to write humorously merely to amuse. He took delight in ridiculing humbug, quackery, and falsity of all kinds. His burlesque *Farmers' Allminax* (1870–80) were exceedingly popular.

Locke was born in New York State and became in turn journeyman printer, reporter, and editor in an Ohio town only a few miles west of Cleveland and Artemus Ward, whom indeed Locke began by imitating. In 1861 he began a series of letters in his paper over the signature "Petroleum V. Nasby." These letters were supposed to come from a pastor of the New Dispensation with "Copperhead" sympathies. Shortly afterwards "Nasby" settled in "Confedrit X Roads," Kentucky, where he drank whiskey, and preached to negro-hating Democrats of the type of "Deekin Pogram." After the war he received a commission as postmaster from Andrew Johnson. "Nasby" is a type of the backwoods preacher, reformer, workingman, postmaster, and chronic office-seeker, remarkable for his unswerving fidelity to the simple principles of personal and political selfishness. To him the luxuries of life are a place under the government, a glass of whiskey, a clean shirt, and a dollar bill. No writer ever achieved popularity more quickly. The letters were published in all the Northern papers, were as eagerly expected as news of the battles, and universally read by the Federal soldiers. "Nasby" was not only a humorist but he was a great force in carrying on the reconstructive measures of the Republican party after the war by his laughable but coarse and merciless pictures of the lowest elements in the Western States that had been opposed to the policy of equal justice.

Of all the humorists mentioned in this chapter "Artemus Ward" alone was known beyond the seas. He was born in Maine, travelled as a wandering printer in the South and West, and really began his career in 1857 when he was called to the local editorship of *The Cleveland Plain Dealer*. To this paper he began to contribute articles purporting to describe the experiences of Artemus Ward, an itinerant showman. He began to lecture in 1861 and had an unprecedented success on the platform in this country and in England, where he was a noted contributor to *Punch* and where he died. He had many and varied experiences and in them all saw nothing but humanity. He wrote of people and of their doings, not unkindly or profanely, but always as a moralist, waging warfare with abounding good humour upon all things that were merely sentimental and insincere and doing good service by exposing them in vivid caricatures. Although it was his genius for misspelling that first attracted attention — he was the first of the misspellers — his plaintive personality proved more attractive still, and may prove permanently so.

Derby, Shaw, Locke, and Browne carried to an extreme numerous tricks already invented by earlier American humorists, particularly the tricks of gigantic exaggeration and calm-faced mendacity, but they are plainly in the main channel of American humour, which had its origin in the first comments of settlers upon the conditions of the frontier, long drew its principal inspiration from the differences between that frontier and the more settled and compact regions of the country, and reached its highest development in Mark Twain, in his youth a child of the American frontier, admirer and imitator of Derby and Browne, and eventually a man of the world and one of its greatest humorists.

CHAPTER XX

Magazines, Annuals, and Gift-books, 1783–1850

I. MAGAZINES

O F the short-lived literary journals that were founded before and during the American Revolution, none appears to have survived the closing years of that struggle. Hardly had peace been declared, however, before new magazines were undertaken, and throughout the years covered by this chapter much of the literary history of America is bound up with a history of its periodicals. A complete account of American magazines during the early part of this period would be to a great extent a story of literary Chauvinism, of absurd literary ambition on the part of individuals and of communities, of misplaced faith in the literary tastes and interests of the people. The many failures are reminders of the unattained intellectual ambitions of the nation; a few commercially prosperous magazines furnish an index to the taste of the average reader; and a few show the best that was being thought and written. In a brief presentation only the most general tendencies can be considered and a few magazines cited as examples of important types. For convenience the period may be divided roughly into two sub-periods, one extending from the close of the Revolution to the close of the War of 1812, the other from 1815 to 1850.[1]

---

[1] In this treatment it will be unnecessary to draw any sharp line between "literary" magazines and those that were largely religious or scientific. The distinction between magazines and newspapers is more troublesome. By agreement with the author of the following chapter literary weeklies, except in one or two cases to be noted, will be considered as newspapers rather than as magazines.

During the period between the first and the second wars with Great Britain Americans were unduly sensitive over the lack of a national literature, and absurdly determined that such a literature should at once be produced. A considerable number of magazines were projected with the deliberate purpose of improving literary conditions, and of avoiding the taunts that crystallized in Sydney Smith's notorious question. The feeling of patriotism is reflected in such titles as *The Columbian Magazine, The American Magazine, The American Museum, The American Apollo, The Monthly Magazine and American Review, The United States Magazine, The American Universal Magazine, The American Moral and Sentimental Magazine, The National Magazine*—all of which were used before 1800. The rapid growth of periodicals was encouraged by the liberality of the post office. While under the Act of 1793 the postage on a single-sheet letter varied from eight to twenty-five cents according to distance, the postage on magazines was one and one-half cents a sheet for distances up to one hundred miles, and two and one-half cents per sheet for all greater distances— a rate but slightly higher than that charged for newspapers.

The chief centres of publication during the early period were Philadelphia, Boston, and New York, but almost every city which boasted a group of men with literary interests undertook at some time or other its literary magazine. Even Lexington, Kentucky, in what was then the extreme West, maintained as early as 1803 *The Medley*, by no means the least creditable of these ventures.

In this early time the different types of periodical were not sharply differentiated, yet it is possible to distinguish a few heavy and ambitious reviews, modelled on the British quarterlies, several literary miscellanies, which followed as nearly as might be the traditions of *The London Magazine* and *The Gentleman's Magazine*, and the more popular "Museums" and "Instructors" which contained interesting anecdotes and information gathered from all sources. Most of the more serious magazines gave summaries of current events. Few, if any, confined themselves to original articles, and some reprinted serially English works of a much earlier day. Such titles as *The American Museum, or Repository of Ancient and Modern Fugitive Pieces, Prose and Poetical* (Philadelphia,

1787), *The Universal Asylum and Columbian Magazine* (Philadelphia, 1790), *The Omnium Gatherum* (Boston, 1809) are significant. *Salmagundi* (New York, 1807) written by Washington Irving, William Irving, and James K. Paulding, was the only notable periodical essay which was published independently. As a rule the many imitators of *The Spectator* contributed their effusions to some newspaper or magazine.

No literary periodical established before 1800 deserves individual consideration. *The Literary Magazine and American Register* (Philadelphia, 1803–1807) was a serious and creditable work, containing reviews and miscellaneous contributions in prose and verse, but it is better remembered because of its editor, Charles Brockden Brown,[1] than because of its intrinsic merits. A more important Philadelphia periodical was *The Port Folio*, during the editorship of Joseph Dennie.[2] Dennie, who signed himself "Oliver Oldschool," and accepted complacently the nickname of the "American Addison," was a conservative in letters, though he welcomed some of the earlier work of the romantic school in England. During his editorship *The Port Folio* was devoted to what at the time was called "elegant literature"; and though to a taste less influenced by eighteenth-century standards it seems formal and sentimental, it exerted a strong influence for good during a critical period of American literature. Among the contributors were Charles Brockden Brown and John Quincy Adams.

The most important of the Boston magazines before 1815 was *The Monthly Anthology*.[3] This was established in 1803 by one Phineas Adams, but after six months it passed into the control of The Anthology Club, founded by the Rev. William Emerson, which conducted it until it was abandoned in 1811. The Anthology Club included at various times from seven to sixteen Boston gentlemen of literary interests, and a few honorary non-resident members. Each member

---

[1] See also Book II, Chap. vi.

[2] *The Port Folio* was founded in 1801 as a weekly newspaper. In 1806 it changed its form and took on most of the characteristics of a magazine, though it was still published weekly; in 1809 it became a monthly. Dennie died in 1812. *The Port Folio* continued until 1827. For Dennie, see also Book II, Chap. iii.

[3] The original title was *The Monthly Anthology and Magazine of Polite Literature*. With the change of proprietorship the sub-title became *The Massachusetts Magazine*, and a little later *The Boston Review*.

was expected to contribute to the magazine. Books were assigned for review, manuscripts were accepted or rejected, and the policy of the magazine was determined by vote at the weekly meetings of the Club. *The Monthly Anthology* is notable for the high quality of some of its articles, and as the best example of a magazine which was actually edited "by a society of gentlemen" purely for the love of literature. It should also be remembered as, in a way, the forerunner of *The North American Review*.

In the years immediately following the close of the War of 1812 national life received a new impulse. The desire for a national literature was undiminished, though it was perhaps becoming more intelligent. Within a few years Americans were gratified by finding that in Irving and Cooper they had at least two authors who were highly appreciated abroad, and before 1850 many of the more distinguished writers of the century had established their reputations. With a real gain in literary prestige came an improvement in the tone and sanity of periodical literature, though to the close of the period far too many magazines were absurd in their pretensions and given to an excess of literary patriotism.

The return of peace soon brought another large crop of new periodicals. Boston, New York, and Philadelphia still led, of course, in the number of these ventures, but every town of literary pretensions tried to maintain a magazine. The South had its fair share; and in the region west of the Alleghanies there was a surprisingly large number. Cincinnati and Lexington were the most important publishing centres in this region, but several less famous towns in the Ohio Valley had their literary periodicals at an early date. By 1831 James Hall[1] was publishing *The Illinois Monthly Magazine* at Vandalia, and before 1850 Chicago and other cities in the central West had followed the prevailing fashion.

The different types of periodicals were a little more sharply distinguished than in the preceding period. There were several serious reviews, of which *The North American Review* was the most important, and *The American Quarterly Review* (Philadelphia, 1827-37) was perhaps the heaviest. There was a multitude of general literary magazines, con-

[1] See also Book II, Chap. VII.

taining fiction, essays, poetry, scientific and historical articles, and reviews. Magazines especially for ladies made their appearance, and one, *Godey's Lady's Book*, attained great vogue. It should also be remembered that this was a prosperous time for the popular literary weeklies, such as Willis's *Mirror* and *Home Journal*, which published the same class of contributions as the lighter literary and the ladies' magazines, but which are excluded from the scope of this chapter. In Philadelphia and Boston were published a number of periodicals that aimed at instruction, some of them reprinting classical works of English literature in large instalments, others giving in popular form miscellaneous information derived from encyclopædias and similar sources. Theological controversies, especially those over the Unitarian schism in New England, called forth a number of religious periodicals that are of importance to the student of American literature. There are also journals devoted to temperance and kindred reforms, and others too nondescript to classify.

The most important of the more serious periodicals was *The North American Review*, founded at Boston in 1815. The first editor, William Tudor, and several of the early contributors had been members of the Anthology Club. Tudor in later reminiscences gave as the reasons for establishing the magazine a desire to emancipate America from undue subservience to England in literary matters, and to neutralize the effects of the French Revolution on American political thought. But the *Review* was less flamboyant and absurd in its patriotism than many of its contemporaries, and to this fact may have been due its success. As first established it was a bi-monthly and published poetry, fiction, and other miscellaneous contributions, but in 1818 it became a quarterly and restricted the nature of its contents. The list of early contributors includes the names of Edward T. Channing, Richard Henry Dana, Jared Sparks, Edward Everett, Alexander H. Everett, John Adams, William Cullen Bryant, Gulian C. Verplanck, George Ticknor, Daniel Webster, Nathaniel Bowditch, George Bancroft, Caleb Cushing, Lewis Cass, and many more of the Americans best known in literary and political life. Like most such enterprises it was financially unprofitable at first, and it was never highly remunerative; but its literary importance was soon recognized abroad as well as at home. Until the founding of *The Atlantic Monthly* in 1857 it was the most valuable organ of the best conservative thought in New England; and it continued its traditions until 1878, when it suffered a change of management and of habitat, and to some extent of ideals.

Although the greater New England writers of the nineteenth century were well started on their careers by 1850, Boston succeeded in maintaining no general literary magazines of the first rank before *The Atlantic Monthly*. Several were begun with brilliant prospects and distinguished lists of contributors, but, sometimes for unexplained reasons, each in turn failed. Among those best remembered are *The United States Literary Gazette* (1825–27), to which Longfellow was a frequent contributor, *The New England Magazine* (Boston 1831–35), in which Holmes published two papers to which he gave the name "The Autocrat of the Breakfast Table," and Lowell's *Pioneer*. This last ran for but three issues in 1843, and left the promoters heavily in debt, though its list of contributors contained such names as those of Poe and Hawthorne. *The North American Review* furnished an opportunity for the publication of serious essays, but much of the lighter work of Longfellow, Hawthorne, Whittier, Lowell, and their contemporaries was contributed to the magazines of New York and Philadelphia. In what might be called informational periodicals Boston continued strong. Interest in one of the least of these, *The Magazine of Useful and Entertaining Knowledge*, has been preserved by the fact that Hawthorne was for a time the editor. *Littell's Living Age*, the best of the reprints from foreign journals, was begun in 1844.

The most picturesque of the Boston periodicals of the time was *The Dial*, published quarterly by a group of New England Transcendentalists from 1840 to 1844. Such an organ of the new thought had long been talked of, and as early as 1835 Emerson had proposed to Carlyle that the latter come to America and act as editor. It was not until July, 1840, however, that the first number of *The Dial* appeared, with Margaret Fuller as editor, and Emerson, Alcott, and Thoreau among the contributors. The magazine was never financially successful, the smallness of its subscription list being indicated by the rarity of complete sets today. Margaret Fuller, after serving gratuitously for two years, reluctantly resigned the editorship, and Emerson as reluctantly took it up, noting in his diary: "I wish it to live, but I do not wish to be its life. Neither do I like to put it into the hands of the Humanity and Reform Men, because they trample on letters and poetry; nor in the hands of the scholars, for they are dead and dry." After spending much time and some money Emerson too felt forced to abandon the undertaking, and *The Dial* came to an end with the close of the fourth volume. Among contributors other than those already noted were C. P. Cranch, George Ripley, William H. Channing, William Ellery Channing, Theodore Parker, James Freeman Clarke, James Russell Lowell, Charles A. Dana, and Jones Very. In its own day *The Dial* was regarded reverently by a few, but by the great mass of readers it was ignored or taken as a joke. A later generation still finds many things in its pages amusing but has come to recognize it as the best single exponent of New England Transcendentalism, and of the peculiar aspects of culture that accompanied that movement.[1]

Although *The Dial* was unique, several earlier and later Boston magazines appealed to much the same constituency. In 1838 the Reverend Orestes A. Brownson began to issue *The Boston Quarterly Review*, and the next year he urged the Transcendentalists to contribute to his journal rather than to found *The Dial*. After five years *The Boston Quarterly Review* was merged with *The Democratic Review* of New York. A more important periodical was *Brownson's Quarterly Review*, founded in 1844 after the editor had been converted to the Roman Catholic faith. An immediate successor of *The Dial* was *The Harbinger*, established in 1845 by the members of the Brook Farm community as an organ of Fourierism. From 1847 to 1850 the Reverend Theodore Parker, one of the most virile of the Transcendental group, conducted *The Massachusetts Quarterly Review*, which he humorously characterized as "*The Dial* with a beard."

One of the earliest of the popular New York magazines to attain permanency was *The Knickerbocker*.[2] This first

---

[1] See also Book II, Chap. VIII.

[2] Owing to some whim of Hoffman, the first editor, the spelling adopted for the earlier issues was Knickerbacker.

appeared 1 January, 1833, with Charles Fenno Hoffman[1] as editor. Bryant, Paulding, and Sands contributed to the first number. Hoffman was soon succeeded in the editorship by Timothy Flint[2] and Samuel Daly Langtree, and in April, 1834, the magazine passed into the control of Lewis Gaylord Clark,[3] who continued in the editorship until *The Knickerbocker* was abandoned in 1859. Clark's own writings in the "Editor's Table" department show little of the literary skill, taste, and knowledge which have characterized similar work by other editors of American magazines, but in spite of his apparent deficiencies he secured for many years the co-operation of the best writers of the country, and conducted what was in many ways the best general literary magazine. *The Knickerbocker Gallery*, an elaborate gift book published for the benefit of the editor in 1855, and made up of brief poems and essays donated by contributors to the magazine, contained pieces by Washington Irving, William Cullen Bryant, Henry Wadsworth Longfellow, Oliver Wendell Holmes, James Russell Lowell, N. P. Willis, Fitz-Greene Halleck, Donald Grant Mitchell, George H. Boker, Bayard Taylor, T. W. Parsons, Epes Sargent, J. G. Saxe, James T. Fields, Charles Godfrey Leland, George William Curtis, Park Benjamin, Rufus W. Griswold, Richard Henry Stoddard, C. F. Briggs, and many more; and among other contributors of the early time were Miss Sedgwick, James Gates Percival, Richard Henry Wilde, Mrs. Sigourney, William Gilmore Simms, J. G. Whittier, Horace Greeley, and James Fenimore Cooper. The importance of *The Knickerbocker Magazine* may be judged by this list of names; yet in dignity of tone and especially in the quality of its humour it was somewhat below the standard of several of its successors.

New York, like Boston, saw many ambitious attempts at literary periodicals. Only the special student of bibliography and literary biography will follow in detail the amalgamations and kaleidoscopic changes of such ventures as *The Atlantic Magazine*, *The New York Review and Athenæum Magazine*, and *The New York Literary Gazette*, even though the names of Bryant and Sands appear among the editors, and Halleck,

Dana, Willis, Longfellow, and Bancroft among the contributors. Of somewhat longer continuance and greater importance was *The Democratic Review*, already mentioned as having absorbed *The Boston Quarterly Review.* In 1850, at the very close of the period, *Harper's Magazine* was established in New York, and at once took high rank.

Godey's Lady's Book, long the most popular of a class of magazines that has flourished in Philadelphia, was founded by Louis A. Godey in 1830, though not until after Mrs. Sarah J. Hale assumed the editorship in 1837 did it attain its greatest vogue. The success of the *Lady's Book* was largely due to its coloured fashion plates and a quantity of light and sentimental poetry and fiction, but its financial success enabled it to make seductive offers to distinguished writers, and it secured occasional contributions from Poe, Longfellow, Holmes, and others.

A later Philadelphia magazine was *Graham's*, established in 1841 by the union of *The Casket*, which had formerly been owned by George R. Graham and Charles J. Peterson, and *Burton's Gentleman's Magazine*, a monthly now remembered chiefly because Poe was for a time associate editor. Poe retained for something over a year a similar position on the new *Graham's Magazine*, and among his successors was the Rev. Rufus W. Griswold. The magazine achieved great popularity, and is said for a time to have brought its owner large financial returns. According to a somewhat dubious tradition its decline began when Graham published a harshly unfavourable review of *Uncle Tom's Cabin.* Among the contributors to *Graham's* in its best days were Cooper, Longfellow, Lowell, Hawthorne, and Simms.

Most of the Southern magazines were still conducted in a spirit of patriotism and local literary pride, rather than as paying business ventures. The most famous of these, *The Southern Literary Messenger*, was founded at Richmond in 1834. It was at first a semi-monthly, but soon changed to a monthly, though its appearance seems to have been at times somewhat irregular. Poe began to contribute to the *Messenger* in 1835, and later in the same year became editor. His tales and poems, and particularly his reviews, which were more independent in tone than had been common in America, added greatly to the fame of the magazine, but his editorship ceased with the beginning of the year 1837. Among later editors were Benjamin Blake Minor, who was both editor and proprietor from 1843 to 1847, and who later wrote a reminiscent history of the magazine; and John R. Thompson, who was Minor's immediate successor. Though it was distinctly Southern in tone the *Messenger* numbered among its contributors many distinguished Northerners—more, probably, than any other Southern magazine.

The rapid development of a distinctive Western literature and of Western periodicals is partly explained by the comparative isolation of the country west of the Alleghanies. In the early years of the century settlers in the Ohio and Mississippi valleys found difficulty in obtaining Eastern magazines regularly and promptly, and set about supplying their own needs. In this they were, of course, greatly encouraged by their local patriotism. *The Western Review and Miscellaneous Magazine* (Lexington, 1819–21), *The Western Monthly Review* (Cincinnati, 1827–30), *The Western Monthly Magazine* (Cincinnati, 1833–37), and other contemporary and later magazines were serious, well-considered, and, for the time and place, highly creditable; but as difficulties of communication were overcome they lost much of their significance, and Western authors exerted their greatest influence on American letters not through their local journals but by their contributions to the more cosmopolitan magazines of the seaboard cities.

To the very end of the period the publication of magazines continued to be a precarious and usually an unsuccessful undertaking. Few of the journals mentioned in the preceding pages were alive in 1850, and of these a much smaller number survived the Civil War. Indeed, of the more important literary periodicals founded before 1850, but one, *The North American Review*, was so firmly established that it lasted through the century. *Harper's*, the earliest of the literary magazines of high grade familiar today, was founded in 1850; and Boston waited seven years longer for the *Atlantic*. The short life and the financial difficulties of the earlier ventures must not always, however, be interpreted as signs of literary mediocrity, or of deficient appreciation on the part of American readers. At times such journals as the *Knicker-*

bocker and *Graham's*, and even others less successful, boasted lists of contributors quite as distinguished as those which most later magazines have been able to show. It is true that in the last sixty years there has been great development in the arts of magazine editorship and of magazine authorship—the writing of articles especially adapted for publication in a periodical. But in the same time have come improvement and cheapening of the processes of printing and of illustration, and the development of advertising. Indeed, it is probable that it is chiefly in the mechanical and business rather than in the editorial departments that the better early magazines are at a disadvantage as compared with those of a later time.

Futile as the early experiments seemed, and slight as was the reward that they brought their editors and publishers, they did good service in their day. By offering a ready means for the publication of literary attempts and for the exchange of ideas on literary matters they did much to clear the literary atmosphere and to make American men of letters sane and self-respecting. Today the student of the taste and the ideals of that time finds in their files his most valuable sources of material.

II. ANNUALS AND GIFT-BOOKS

The publications described as literary annuals and gift-books varied in many respects but they agreed in being intended not primarily to be read but to be given away. They were "Keepsakes," and "Souvenirs," and "Forget-me-nots," and "Tokens." Many of them bore as sub-titles such phrases as "A gift for the holidays," or "A Christmas, New Year's and birthday present." Almost or quite all of those published in America were literary miscellanies, the contents being original, or, in case of some of the cheaper volumes, "selected." A few, such as *The Odd-Fellows' Offering* and *The Masonic Token* were intended primarily for the members of certain organizations—there were religious annuals and temperance annuals, an anti-slavery annual, and even a "Knownothing Token"; but most such books made a general appeal to those who wished to bestow an "elegant" offering indicative of "refined" sentiment. They varied in size and elaborateness from large paper volumes selling for twelve dollars each to diminutive and inexpensive souvenirs which a Sunday-school teacher might present to members of her class. The bindings of the best were in leather, elaborately tooled and sometimes inlaid with mother-of-pearl, or in richly watered silk. The "embellishments," as the pictures were commonly called, were most frequently engravings on steel, though there were many coloured plates, some coloured by hand.

The annual proper was supposed to be published from year to year, though many never made a second appearance. The year was frequently made a part of the title, as *The Gift of Friendship, a Token of Remembrance for 1848*, though sometimes the date appeared only at the foot of the title-page, or on the binding. The entire absence of a date was indicative of a desire to make unsold remainders available for the next year's market, or of still more questionable practices on the part of the publishers. Among these practices was that of reprinting an old annual with a new name, sometimes with change of plates and of leading article; or that of bestowing on an inferior work a name that had been made popular by another publisher. These devious procedures bring despair to bibliographers today, and they may originally have been one reason why the whole tribe of annuals fell into something of disrepute. A few of the annuals were in reality bound volumes of popular magazines with date-lines and other indications of periodical publication removed. The gift-books which are here considered resembled the annuals in form and purpose, but were avowedly not members of a series.

The annuals came as a late accompaniment of the wave of sentimentality in literature and art that swept over England and America during the early years of the nineteenth century. The fashion of issuing them is said to have started in Germany, whence it spread to England and a little later to America. *The Atlantic Souvenir* of 1826 was the first of the American annuals proper, though before that time there had been a few illustrated miscellanies which might be classed as gift-books. The number increased rapidly until, according to Mr. Faxon's excellent bibliography, "from 1846 to 1852 an average of sixty appeared each year." By the beginning of the Civil War the day of the annuals was over, though the list of holiday books has each year contained a few miscellanies intended chiefly as gifts.

A student's first impressions of the annuals are usually gained from the "embellishments." In respect of illustrations the American annuals rarely equalled the best of their English prototypes, yet the publishers enlisted the services of the foremost American engravers. John Cheney seems to have developed his talent in connection with his work for *The Token*, and he also executed plates for many other annuals. John Sartain and Alexander H. Ritchie were among the most prolific and successful of the workers in mezzotint. Publishers of the cheaper annuals employed cruder engravers, or used old plates, often so worn as to be almost worthless. It is in the subjects of the pictures rather than in the workmanship of the engravers that the sentimental character of the annuals reveals itself. Many of these were taken from British paintings, others were by American artists; they were likely to be female figures and faces, romantic landscapes, or pictures hinting at pathetic or chastely amorous tales. In an annual taken at random, *Leaflets of Memory* for 1845, the illustrations are entitled "Julia," "Was it for this?" "We part no more," "The heart's best dream," "The Christian slave," "The past and present," "The rose of the ruin," "The Grecian maid," "Myrrha." Pictures designed for fine editions of standard authors were often introduced with change of name, and not infrequently the process of illustration was reversed, and poems or tales were written to fit the renamed plate.

It is not strange that volumes which are so palpably indicative of the commercial side of publishing, and that appealed to a constituency often more "elegant" and "refined" than intellectual, should be treated in later years with scant respect. Charles Lamb, Thackeray, and George Eliot all indulged in humour at the expense of the annuals and their admirers, and in America Miss Agnes Repplier and others who have given them passing notice adopt the same tone. They were not, however, without literary importance. Their exuberances and peculiarities register for the literary historian some of the less admirable qualities of popular taste; and they really contain much work of value. At a time when most of the literary magazines were living but a precarious existence many of the annuals were well established and financially successful. It was the annuals and not the magazines that were able to pay what was considered a lavish price for a few verses or a short tale by a popular author. It is too true that they often depended on the names of one or two distinguished contributors to sell a volume composed largely of cheaper material; but men like Poe, Irving, Bryant, Whittier, Emerson, Longfellow, Lowell, and Holmes were not ashamed to contribute to annuals, and often furnished some of their best work. The better editors were also alert for modest and unknown merit. It was in annuals that most of Hawthorne's *Twice Told Tales* first saw the light, and these were all printed without the author's name. Change of taste has left the twentieth century reader sadly out of sympathy with the annuals, but they invite from the student more attention than they have yet received.

Few of the annuals deserve individual consideration. *The Atlantic Souvenir*, already mentioned as the earliest of its kind in America, was published by H. C. Carey and I. Lea of Philadelphia from 1826 to 1832. It was a small and not a very elaborate volume, but it contained poems, essays, and tales by some of the most popular writers of the day. After the issue for 1832 it was merged with *The Token*, published by Gray & Bowen, of Boston, and later volumes of the latter bore the title *The Token and Atlantic Souvenir*. *The Token* was first issued in 1828 with Samuel G. Goodrich as both editor and publisher, and Goodrich continued to edit it until its demise in 1842, except the second volume, which bore the name of N. P. Willis on the title-page. *The Token* was one of the best of the earlier annuals as regards literary content, and though less showy than many of its later rivals it contained illustrations of high merit. A large number of Hawthorne's tales and sketches were first published in *The Token*, and among the contributors were N. P. Willis, Miss Sedgwick, Longfellow, Mrs. Child, and other writers whose names are less impressive now than they were in their own day. John Cheney was for a time employed exclusively on work for *The Token*, and throughout the quality of the engraving was good. The popularity and the intrinsic merit of *The Token* offered temptations to piratical publishers. After the abandonment of the legitimate series, *The Token* for 1838, one of the best volumes, ap-

peared in at least ten re-issues by different publishers, with
changes of title and of plates, and in some instances with
abridgment of contents.   The volume for 1840 was similarly
treated at least five times.   The name was also adopted by a
New York publisher for the reprint of a cheap annual which
appeared without date in the later fifties.

The Rose of Sharon, a Religious Souvenir (Boston, 1840 to
1858) boasted a longer continuous existence than any of the
other American annuals.   The first ten volumes were edited by
Miss Sarah C. Edgarton, the last eight by Mrs. Caroline M.
Sawyer.   The volume for 1857 was reissued, merely with
change of date, "for 1858"; and a publisher at Auburn, New
York, borrowed the title for a wholly different work in 1849.
The Rose of Sharon was somewhat showy in binding, but was
good in typography and illustrations, and in literary contents
was an average example of the better grade of annuals.   *The
Opal, A Pure Gift for the Holy Days*, published by John C.
Riker, New York, survived only from 1844 to 1849 inclusive,
but it was made attractive by contributions from Poe, Willis,
Longfellow, and Whittier, and by plates by Cheney and Sartain.

Among annuals that differ a little from the ordinary was
The Talisman, which was published at New York for 1828,
1829, and 1830.   The literary contents were prepared in collaboration by William Cullen Bryant, Robert C. Sands, and
Gulian C. Verplanck, and the illustrations were by artist
friends of the authors, among them Henry Inman and S. F.
B. Morse.   The volumes were unpretending in appearance,
but the literary quality was high.   *The Boston Book* (Boston,
1836, 1837, 1841, 1850) is, in the words of the editor, "a compilation of specimens,—or, essentially, a specimen, in the
aggregate—of the modern literature of the metropolis of the
North."   *The Liberty Bell, by Friends of Freedom*, published
nearly every year from 1839 to 1858 for the benefit of the
annual anti-slavery fair or anti-slavery bazaar in Boston,
contained contributions from all the leading anti-slavery
writers of New England.

Others of the better known annuals were *The Amaranth,
The Christmas Blossoms and New Year's Wreath, The Diadem,
The Forget-Me-Not, Friendship's Offering, The Garland, The Gem
of the Season, The Gift, The Gift of Friendship, The Hyacinth*

The Keepsake, The Keepsake of Friendship, Leaflets of Memory, The Lily, The Lily of the Valley, The Magnolia, The Mayflower, The Odd-Fellows' Offering, The Religious Souvenir, The Remember Me. These and others had each its especial admirers, and the critic of today hardly need attempt the task of deciding on their respective merits.

CHAPTER XXI

Newspapers, 1775–1860

THE turbulent years between 1775 and 1783 were a time of great trial and disturbance among newspapers. Interruption, suppression, and lack of support so checked their growth that at the close of the war they were in most respects less thriving than at the beginning of it. Although there were forty-three newspapers in the United States when the treaty of peace was signed, as compared with thirty-seven on the date of the battle of Lexington, only a dozen had had continuous existence between the two events, and most of those had experienced delays and difficulties through lack of paper, type, and patronage. Not one newspaper in the principal cities, Boston, New York, and Philadelphia, continued publication throughout the war. When the colonial forces were in possession, royalist papers were suppressed, and at times of British occupation Revolutionary papers moved away, or were discontinued, or they became royalist, only to suffer at the next turn of military fortunes. Thus there was an exodus of papers from the cities along the coast to smaller inland places, where alone it was possible for them to continue without interruption. Scarcity of paper was acute; type worn out could not be replaced. The appearance of the newspapers deteriorated, and issues sometimes failed to appear at all. Mail service, never good, was poorer than ever; foreign newspapers, an important source of information, could be obtained but rarely; many of the ablest writers who had filled the columns with dissertations upon colonial rights and government were now otherwise occupied.

News from a distance was less full and regular than before; yet when great events happened reports spread over the country with great rapidity, through messengers in the service of patriotic organizations. The newspapers made use of such assistance, and did service in further spreading the tidings, though they seldom overtook the flying word of mouth. Naturally, reporting was still imperfect. The Salem *Gazette* printed a full but coloured account of the battle of Lexington, giving details of the burning, pillage, and barbarities charged to the British, and praising the militia who were filled with "higher sentiments of humanity." The Declaration of Independence was published by Congress, 6 July, 1776, in the Philadelphia *Evening Post*, from which it was copied by most of the papers; but some of them did not mention it until two weeks later, and even then found room for only a synopsis. When they were permitted to do so they printed fairly full accounts of the proceedings of provincial assemblies and of Congress, which were copied widely, as were all official reports and proclamations. On the whole, however, a relatively small proportion of such material and an inadequate account of the progress of the war is found in the contemporaneous newspapers.

The general spirit of the time found fuller utterance in mottoes, editorials, letters, and poems. In the beginning both editorials and communications urged united resistance to oppression, praised patriotism, and denounced tyranny; as events and public sentiment developed these grew more vigorous, often a little more radical than the populace. Later, the idea of independence took form, and theories of government were discussed. More interesting and valuable as specimens of literature than these discussions were the poems inspired by the stirring events of the time. Long narratives of battles and of heroic deaths were mingled with eulogies of departed heroes. Songs meant to inspire and thrill were not lacking. Humour, pathos, and satire sought to stir the feelings of the public. Much of the poetry of the Revolution is to be found in the columns of dingy newspapers, from the vivid and popular satires and narratives of Freneau[1] to the saddest effusions of the most commonplace schoolmaster.

The newspapers of the Revolution were an effective force working towards the unification of sentiment, the awakening of a consciousness of a common purpose, interest, and destiny

[1] See Book I, Chap. IX.

among the separate colonies, and of a determination to see the war through to a successful issue. They were more single-minded than the people themselves, and they bore no small share of the burden of arousing and supporting the often discouraged and indifferent public spirit. Many of the papers, however, which were kept alive or brought to life during the war could not adapt themselves to the new conditions of peace.

Perhaps a dozen of the survivors held their own in the new time, notably the Boston *Gazette*, which declined rapidly in the following decade, *The Connecticut Courant* of Hartford, *The Providence Gazette*, and *The Pennsylvania Packet* of Philadelphia, to which may be added such representative papers as *The Massachusetts Spy*, the Boston *Independent Chronicle*, the New York *Journal* and *Packet*, the Newport *Mercury*, *The Maryland Gazette* of Annapolis, *The Pennsylvania Gazette* and *The Pennsylvania Journal*, both of Philadelphia. Practically all were of four small pages, each of three or four columns, issued weekly. *The Pennsylvania Packet*, which appeared three times a week, became in 1784 the first daily paper. In the same year the New York *Journal* was published twice a week, as were several of the papers begun in that year. There was a notable extension to new fields. In Vermont, where the first paper, established in 1781, had soon died, another arose in 1783; in Maine two were started in 1785. In 1786 the first one west of the Alleghanies appeared at Pittsburg, and following the westward tide of immigration *The Kentucky Gazette* was begun at Lexington in 1787.

Conditions were hardly more favourable to newspapers than during the recent conflict. The sources of news were much the same; the means of communication and the postal system were little improved. Newspapers were not carried in the mails but by favour of the postmen, and the money of one state was of dubious value in another. Consequently circulations were small, rarely reaching a thousand; subscribers were slow in paying; and advertisements were not plentiful. Newspapers remained subject to provincial laws of libel, in accordance with the old common law, and were, as in Massachusetts for a short time in 1785, subject to special state taxes on paper or on advertisements. But public sentiment was growing strongly against all legal restrictions, and in general the papers practised freedom, not to say license, of utterance.

With independence had come the consciousness of a great destiny. The collective spirit aroused by the war, though clouded by conflicting local difficulties, was intense, and the principal interest of the newspapers was to create a nation out of the loose confederation. Business and commerce were their next care; but in an effort to be all things to all men, the small page included a little of whatever might "interest, instruct, or amuse." Political intelligence occupied first place; news, in the modern sense, was subordinated. A new idea, quite as much as a fire, a murder, or a prodigy, was a matter of news moment. There were always a few items of local interest, usually placed with paragraphs of editorial miscellany. Correspondents, in return for the paper, sent items; private letters, often no doubt written with a view to such use, were a fruitful source of news; but the chief resource was the newspapers which every office received as exchanges, carried in the post free of charge, and the newspapers from abroad.

The newspaper continued to compete with the magazine by supplying moral, descriptive, and sentimental essays, poetry, anecdotes, reflections, and articles on trade, education, and conduct. Imitators of the English writers of periodical essays, the beginning of whose activities almost coincided with that of American newspapers,[1] multiplied in numbers, until towards the close of the century it was a poor paper that did not maintain at least one series. The "Lay Preacher" essays of Joseph Dennie[2] gave *The Farmers' Museum* of Walpole, New Hampshire, as wide a reputation as that of any paper in its day.

The editor, usually reflecting the sentiment of a group or a faction, began to emerge as a distinct power. He closely followed the drift of events and expressed vigorous opinions. But as yet the principal discussions were contributed not by the editors but by "the master minds of the country." The growing importance of the newspaper was shown in the discussions preceding the Federal Convention, and notably in the country-wide debate on the adoption of the Constitution, in which the

[1] See Book I, Chap. VII, and Book II, Chap. III.
[2] See Book II, Chap. III.

newspaper largely displaced the pamphlet. When Hamilton, Madison, and Jay united to produce the *Federalist* essays,[1] they chose to publish them in *The Independent Journal* and *The Daily Advertiser*, from which they were copied by practically every paper in America long before they were made into a book. When the first Congress assembled 4 March, 1789, the administration felt the need of a paper, and, under the influence of Hamilton, John Fenno issued at New York, 15 April, the first number of *The Gazette of the United States*, the earliest of a series of administration organs. The seat of government became the journalistic centre of the country, and as long as party politics remained the staple news interest the administration organs and their opponents were the chief sources of news for the papers of the country.

One question of great importance to the press was early raised and settled. Reports of state legislative proceedings had always been permitted in the colonies, though in Massachusetts the reporters had been denied the use of the chaplain's pulpit as a desk. As soon as the first Congress assembled, the newspapers began to print the proceedings and debates, whereupon, in September, a Mr. Burke moved that representatives of the press should be excluded from the sessions. After a warm debate the resolution was withdrawn, never again to be revived, at a time when the taking of notes in the British Parliament was still forbidden.

Partisan bitterness increased during the last decade of the century. New England papers were generally Federalist; in Pennsylvania there was a balance; in the West and South the anti-Federalist press predominated. Though the Federalists were vigorously supported by such able papers as Russell's *Columbian Centinel* in Boston, Thomas's *Massachusetts Spy*, *The Connecticut Courant*, and, after 1793, Noah Webster's daily *Minerva* (soon renamed *Commercial Advertiser*) in New York, *The Gazette of the United States*, which in 1790 followed Congress and the capital to Philadelphia, was at the centre of conflict, "a paper of pure Toryism," as Thomas Jefferson said, "disseminating the doctrines of monarchy, aristocracy, and the exclusion of the people." To offset the influence of this, Jefferson and Madison induced Philip Freneau, who had been

[1] See Book I, Chap. VIII.

editing *The Daily Advertiser* in New York, to set up a "half weekly," to "go through the states and furnish a Whig vehicle of intelligence." Freneau's *National Gazette*, which first appeared 31 October, 1791, soon became the most outspoken critic of the administration of Adams, Hamilton, and Washington, and an ardent advocate of the French Revolution. Fenno and Freneau, in *The Gazette of the United States* and *The National Gazette*, at once came to grips, and the campaign of personal and party abuse in partisan news reports, in virulent editorials, in poems and skits of every kind, was echoed from one end of the country to the other.

This decade of violence was nevertheless one of development in both the quality and the power of newspapers. News reporting was extended to new fields of local affairs, and the intense rivalry of all too numerous competitors awoke the beginnings of that rush for the earliest reports which was to become the dominant trait in American journalism. The editor evolved into a new type. As a man of literary skill, or a politician, or a lawyer with a gift for polemical writing, he began to supersede the contributors of essays as the strongest writer on the paper. Much of the best writing, and of the rankest scurrility, be it said, was produced by editors born and trained abroad, like Bache of the *Aurora*, Cobbett, Cooper, Gales, Cheetham, Callender, Lyon, and Holt. Of the whole number of papers in the country towards the end of the decade, more than one hundred and fifty, at least twenty opposed to the administration were conducted by aliens. The power wielded by these anti-administration editors impressed John Adams, who in 1801 wrote: "If we had been blessed with common sense, we should not have been overthrown by Philip Freneau, Duane, Callender, Cooper, and Lyon, or their great patron and protector. A group of foreign liars encouraged by a few ambitious native gentlemen have discomfited the education, the talents, the virtues, and the prosperity of the country."

The most obvious example of that Federalist lack of common sense was the passage of the Alien and Sedition laws in 1797 to protect the government and its chief officers from the libels of politicians and editors. The result was a dozen convictions and a storm of outraged public opinion that threw

the party from power and gave the radical Republican press
renewed confidence and the material benefit of patronage
when the anti-Federalists took control of the government.
The passing of the Federalist party made a radical change in
journalistic supremacy, but for a third of a century the newspapers were to continue primarily party organs; the tone
remained strongly partisan, though it gradually gained poise
and attained a degree of literary excellence and professional
dignity.

The number and geographical distribution of newspapers
grew apace. Whereas in 1800 there were between 150 and 200
all told, by 1810 there were 366, and during the next two
decades the increase was at least equally rapid. With astonishing promptness the press followed the sparse population as it
trickled westward and down the Ohio or penetrated the more
northerly forests. By 1835 papers had spread to the Mississippi
River and beyond, from Texas to St. Louis, throughout Ohio,
Indiana, Illinois, Michigan, and into Wisconsin. These pioneer
papers, poorly written, poorly printed, and partisan often
beyond all reason, served a greater than a merely local purpose
in sending weekly to the seat of government their hundreds of
messages of good and evil report, of politics and trade, of
weather and crops, that helped immeasurably to bind the far-
flung population into a nation. Every congressman wrote
regularly to his own local paper; other correspondents were
called upon for like service, and in some instances the country
editors established extensive and reliable lines of intelligence;
but most of them depended on the bundle of exchanges from
Washington, Philadelphia, and New York, and reciprocally the
city papers made good use of their country exchanges.

Meanwhile the daily newspapers were increasing in number.
The first had appeared in Philadelphia and New York in 1784
and 1785; in 1796 one appeared in Boston. By 1810 there were
twenty-seven in the country—one in the city of Washington,
five in Maryland, seven in New York, nine in Pennsylvania,
three in South Carolina, and two in Louisiana. As early as
1835 the Detroit *Free Press* began its long career.

The political and journalistic situation made the administration organ one of the characteristic features of the period.
Fenno's *Gazette* had served the purpose for Washington and

Adams; but the first great example of the type was *The National Intelligencer* established in October, 1800, by Samuel Harrison Smith, to support the administration of Jefferson and of successive presidents until after Jackson it was thrown into the opposition, and *The United States Telegraph*, edited by Duff Green, became the official paper. It was replaced at the close of 1830 by a new paper, *The Globe*, under the editorship of Francis P. Blair, one of the ablest of all ante-bellum political editors, who, with John P. Rives, conducted it until the changing standards and conditions in journalism rendered the administration organ obsolescent. *The Globe* was displaced in 1841 by another paper called *The National Intelligencer*, which in turn gave way to *The Madisonian*. Thomas Ritchie was in 1845 called from his long service on *The Richmond Enquirer* to found, on the remains of *The Globe*, the Washington *Union*, to speak for the Polk administration and to reconcile the factions of democracy. Neither the *Union* nor its successors, which maintained the semblance of official support until 1860, ever occupied the commanding position held by the *Telegraph* and *The Globe*, but for forty years the administration organs had been the leaders when political journalism was dominant. Their influence was shared and increased by such political editors as M. M. Noah[1] and James Watson Webb of the New York *Courier and Enquirer*, Solomon Southwick of the Albany *Register*, Edwin Croswell, who edited *The Argus* and who, supported by Van Buren and others, formed what was known as the "Albany Regency." The "Regency," the Richmond "Junta," which centred in the *Enquirer*, and the "Kitchen Cabinet" headed by the editor of *The Globe*, formed one of the most powerful political and journalistic cabals that the country has ever known. Their decline, in the late thirties, was coincident with great changes, both political and journalistic, and though successors arose, their kind was not again so prominent or influential. The newspaper of national scope was passing away, yielding to the influence of the telegraph and the railroad, which robbed the Washington press of its claim to prestige as the chief source of political news. At the same time politics was losing its predominating importance. The public

[1] See also Book II, Chap. II.

had many other interests, and by a new spirit and type of journalism was being trained to make greater and more various demands upon the journalistic resources of its papers.

The administration organ presents but one aspect of a tendency in which political newspapers generally gained in editorial individuality, and both the papers and their editors acquired greater personal and editorial influence. The beginnings of the era of personal journalism, the chief figures in which will be discussed in later paragraphs, were to be found early in the century. Even before Nathan Hale had shown the way to editorial responsibility, Thomas Ritchie, in the Richmond *Enquirer* in the second decade of the century, had combined with an effective development of the established use of anonymous letters on current questions a system of editorial discussion that soon extended his reputation and the influence of his newspaper far beyond the boundaries of Virginia. Washington Barrow and the Nashville *Banner*, Amos Kendall and *The Argus of Western America*, G. W. Kendall and the New Orleans *Picayune*, John M. Francis and the Troy *Times*, and Charles Hammond and the Cincinnati *Gazette*, to mention but a few among many, illustrate the rise of editors to individual power and prominence in the third and later decades. Notable among these political editors was John M. Daniel, who just before 1850 became editor of the Richmond *Examiner* and soon made it the leading newspaper of the South. Perhaps no better example need be sought of brilliant invective and literary pungency in American journalism just prior to and during the Civil War than in Daniel's contributions to the *Examiner*.

Though it could still be said that "too many of our gazettes are in the hands of persons destitute at once of the urbanity of gentlemen, the information of scholars, and the principles of virtue," a fact due largely to the intensity of party spirit, the profession was by no means without editors who exhibited all these qualities, and put them into American journalism. William Coleman, for instance, who, encouraged by Hamilton, founded the New York *Evening Post*[1] in 1801, was a man of high purposes, good training, and noble ideals. The *Evening Post*, reflecting variously the fine qualities of the editor,

[1] See also Book II, Chap. v.

exemplified the improvement in tone and illustrated the growing importance of editorial writing, as did a dozen or more papers in the early decades of the century. Indeed the problem most seriously discussed at the earliest state meetings of editors and publishers, held in the thirties, was that of improving the tone of the press. They tried to attain by joint resolution a degree of editorial self-restraint which few individual editors had as yet acquired. Under the influence of Thomas Ritchie, vigorous and unsparing political editor but always a gentleman, who presided at the first meeting of Virginia journalists, the newspaper men in one state after another resolved to "abandon the infamous practice of pampering the vilest of appetites by violating the sanctity of private life, and indulging in gross personalities and indecorous language," and to "conduct all controversies between themselves with decency, decorum, and moderation." Ritchie found in the low tone of the newspapers a reason why journalism in America did not occupy as high a place in public regard as it did in England and France. The editorial page was assuming something of its modern form. The editorial signed with a pseudonym gradually passed away, but unsigned editorial comment and leading articles did not become an established feature until after 1814, when Nathan Hale made them a characteristic of the newly established Boston *Daily Advertiser*. From that time on they grew in importance until in the succeeding period of personal journalism they were the most vital part of the greater papers.

As the magazines were still few and offered poor pay, if any at all, the newspaper became the means of support of innumerable authors, and even in this age of the political press there were as many literary as political editors. In contrast with the situation today, when the magazines are generally conducted by men whose tastes and ideals have been formed in journalism rather than in literature, and assume more and more the characteristics of timeliness, until the middle of the century the newspapers owed their character to men of literary tastes and pursuits. When Bennett the elder referred slurringly to the "poets of the *Post*" and the *Post* declared that Bennett was not a journalist, a momentous divergence and change of ideals was indicated.

Changes which came about in the thirties well-nigh re-
volutionized the newspapers. Within a decade the cheap
newspaper was begun; steam presses were introduced; a radical
alteration took place in the idea of news values, reporting, and
correspondence; freedom from party control was found possible;
and important modifications took place in the party press.

Several of these changes are exemplified in the work of
James Gordon Bennett (1794–1872), though he originated few
of them. In more than ten years of unsuccessful effort as a
political journalist he had become familiar with· the increasing
enterprise in news-gathering that had already distinguished
American methods. He despised the journalism of the day—
the seriousness of tone, the phlegmatic dignity, the party
affiliations, the sense of responsibility. He believed journalists
were fools to think that they could best serve their own purposes by serving the politicians. As Washington correspondent
for the New York *Enquirer*, he wrote vivacious, gossipy
prattle, full of insignificant and entertaining detail, to which he
added keen characterization and deft allusions. Bennett saw a
public who would not buy a serious paper at any price, who
had a vast and indiscriminate curiosity better satisfied with
gossip than discussion, with sensation rather than fact, who
could be reached through their appetites and passions.

The idea which he did much to develop rested on the
success of the one-cent press created by the establishment of
the New York *Sun* in 1833. To pay at such a price these
papers must have large circulations, sought among the public
that had not been accustomed to buy papers, and gained by
printing news of the street, shop, and factory. To reach this
public Bennett began the New York *Herald*, a small paper,
fresh, sprightly, terse, and "newsy."

"In journalistic débuts of this kind," he wrote, "many talk of
principle—political principle, party principle—as a sort of steel
trap to catch the public. We . . . disdain . . . all principle, as
it is called, all party, all politics. Our only guide shall be good.
sound, practical common sense, applicable to the business and
bosoms of men engaged in every-day life."

News was but a commodity, the furnishing of which was a business transaction only, which ignored the social responsibility

of the press, "the grave importance of our vocation," prized of the elder journalists and of the still powerful six-cent papers. The *Herald*, like the *Sun*, was at once successful, and was remarkably influential in altering journalistic practices.

This idea of news and the newspaper for its own sake, the unprecedented aggressiveness in news-gathering, and the blatant methods by which the cheap papers were popularized aroused the antagonism of the older papers, but created a competition which could not be ignored. Systems of more rapid news-gathering and distribution quickly appeared. Sporadic attempts at co-operation in obtaining news had already been made; in 1848 the *Journal of Commerce, Courier and Enquirer, Tribune, Herald, Sun,* and *Express* formed the New York Associated Press to obtain news for the members jointly. Out of this idea grew other local, then state, and finally national associations. European news, which, thanks to steamship service, could now be obtained when but half as old as before, became an important feature. In the forties several papers sent correspondents abroad, and in the next decade this field was highly developed.

The literary departments of newspapers were being stimulated by the rise of literary or semi-literary weeklies. Some of these, such as *The Notion* in Boston, and *The New World* and *Brother Jonathan* in New York, were devoted mainly to the reprinting of English novels and other literary successes. Others, like *The New York Mirror*, contained sketches of life and manners, society verse, stories, and essays, as well as some news. The *Mirror* and its kind were a source of much material for newspapers. N. P. Willis's[1] *Pencillings by the Way*, for instance, were copied by five hundred newspapers. Another class of weeklies of general circulation contained much literary material combined with a larger proportion of politics and affairs. Such a paper was Greeley's *New Yorker*, "devoted mainly to current literature, but giving regularly a digest of all important news," and maintaining a good editorial page. Neither magazine nor newspaper, these weeklies were something of each. From the former they doubtless took away a good many readers; to the latter they were an incentive to the

[1] See also Book II. Chap. II.

maintaining of literary departments which in a few papers, like the *Tribune*, became important.

Newspapers in foreign languages, especially the German, multiplied rapidly about the middle of the century. Some of the ablest journalists of the middle of the century, not only of papers in the German language but also of papers in English, were liberal-minded Germans who sought in America the freedom of speech which was denied them in their native country.

The telegraph, in 1844 shown to be practical, and put to successful use during the Mexican War, led to numerous far-reaching results in journalism. Telegraphic columns became a leading feature; news associations grew as the wires lengthened; but the greatest effect on the journalism of the country at large was to decentralize the press by rendering the inland papers, in such cities as Chicago, Louisville, Cincinnati, St. Louis, and New Orleans independent of those in Washington and New York. A change made in the postal laws in 1845 favoured the local circulation of newspapers. The country circulation of most of the large Eastern papers was so curtailed that only one or two, like the New York *Tribune*, were able to maintain through their weekly editions something of their national character; the organs in Washington, even Niles's *Weekly Register*, which had been a most useful vehicle for the disseminating of political information, were still further shorn of their usefulness and soon eliminated; and the already vigorous provincial press became numerous and powerful.

In a period of wide-spread unrest and change many specialized forms of journalism sprang up—religious, educational, agricultural, and commercial, which there is no space here to discuss. Workingmen were questioning the justice of existing economic systems and raising a new labour problem; the socialistic ideas of Cabet and Fourier were spreading; Unitarianism and Transcendentalism were creating and expressing new spiritual values; temperance, prohibition, and the political status of women were being discussed; abolition was a general irritant and a nightmare to politicians. The subject of controversy most critically related to journalism was abolition. The abolitionist press which began with *The Emancipator* of 1820, and had its chief representative in William Lloyd Garrison's *Liberator*, first issued 1 January, 1831, forced the slavery question upon the newspapers, and there ensued a struggle for the freedom of the press more acute than any since that caused by the Alien and Sedition laws. Many abolitionist papers were excluded from the mails; their circulation was forcibly prevented in the South; in Boston, New York, Baltimore, Cincinnati, Alton, and elsewhere, editors were assaulted, offices were attacked and destroyed; rewards were offered in the South for the capture of Greeley and Garrison; in a few instances editors, like Lovejoy at Alton, lost their lives at the hands of mobs.

Out of the period of restless change in the thirties there emerged a few great editors whose force and ability gave them and their newspapers an influence hitherto unequalled, and made the period between 1840 and 1860 that of personal journalism. These few men not only interpreted and reflected the spirit of the time, but were of great influence in shaping and directing public opinion. Consequently the scope, character, and influence of newspapers was in the period immensely widened and enriched, and rendered relatively free from the worst subjection to political control.

Naturally, the outstanding feature of this personal journalism was the editorial. Rescued from the slough of ponderousness into which it had fallen in its abject and uninspired party service, the editorial was revived, invigorated, and endowed with a vitality that made it the centre about which all other features of the newspaper were grouped. It was individual; however large the staff of writers, the editorials were regarded as the utterance of the editor. "Greeley says" was the customary preface to quotations from the *Tribune*, and indeed many editorials were signed. James Gordon Bennett, Samuel Bowles (1826–78), Horace Greeley (1811–72), and Henry J. Raymond (1820–69) are the outstanding figures of the period. Of Bennett's influence something has already been said; especially, he freed his paper from party control. His power was great, but it came from his genius in gathering and presenting news rather than from editorial discussion, for he had no great moral, social or political ideals, and his influence, always lawless and uncertain, can hardly be regarded as characteristic of the period. Of the others named, and many besides, it could be said with approximate truth that their ideal was "a full presentation and a liberal discussion of all questions of public concernment, from an entirely independent position, and a faithful and impartial exhibition of all movements of interest at home and abroad." As all three were not only upright and independent, but in various measure gifted with the quality of statesmanship at once philosophical and practical, their newspapers were powerful moulders of opinion at a critical period in the history of the nation.

The news field was immeasurably broadened; news style was improved; interviews, newly introduced, lent the ease and freshness of dialogue and direct quotation. There was a notable improvement in the reporting of business, markets, and finance. In a few papers the literary department was conducted by staffs as able as any today. A foreign news service was developed which in intelligence, fidelity, and general excellence reached the highest standard yet attained in American journalism. A favourite feature was the series of letters from the editor or other member of the staff who travelled and wrote of what he heard or saw. Bowles, Olmsted, Greeley, Bayard Taylor, Bennett, and many others thus observed life and conditions at home or abroad; and they wrote so entertainingly and to such purpose that the letters—those of Olmsted and Taylor, for instance—are still sources of entertainment or information.

The growth of these papers meant the development of great staffs of workers that exceeded in numbers anything dreamed of in the preceding period. Although later journalism has far exceeded in this respect the time we are now considering, still the scope, complexity, and excellence of our modern metropolitan journalism in all its aspects were clearly begun between 1840 and 1860.

The highest development in provincial journalism during this period is typified in the Springfield *Republican*. Established by Samuel Bowles in 1824 as a country weekly, it was converted into a daily in 1844 by his energetic and ambitious son, who bore the same name. From the beginning it was a clean, well written, honest, independent, and conservative paper that reported all of the happenings of its own vicinity, with brief mention of the gist of important events generally.

As rapidly as possible its news-gathering was extended until within a few years its columns contained departments of items from every town and hamlet along the Connecticut valley, as well as from Springfield. Bowles believed that the newspaper should be a power in the moral, religious, and literary, as well as the political life of the community, and he tried to make his paper fulfill those functions, not for the world at large but for the people of western Massachusetts. With the aid of J. G. Holland and others who joined the staff the paper attained excellent literary quality and a high moral tone. Probably its success rested most of all upon its political discussions. The excellence of its short, crisp, pithy editorial paragraphs and longer discussions, free from pedantry and heaviness, based always on fundamental ideas and principles, made the *Republican* widely known and respected. Its opinions soon reached all New England, and after the formation of the Republican party they extended far beyond the limits of any section. But in spite of the extent of its influence, the *Republican* held steadily to its purpose as a provincial newspaper; it told all the news, gave all sides a fair hearing, preserved its self-respect and independence, frowned on all "isms," and presented invariably the personal opinions of its editor, whom all its readers knew.

The New York *Tribune* under Horace Greeley exhibited the best features of the new and semi-independent personal journalism based upon political beginnings and inspired with an enthusiasm for service that is one of the fine characteristics of the period. In editing the *New Yorker* Greeley had acquired experience in literary journalism and in political news; his *Jeffersonian* and *Log Cabin*, popular campaign papers, had brought him into contact with politicians and extended his acquaintance with the masses. Being with all his independence a staunch party man, he was chosen to manage a party organ when one was needed to support the Whig administration of Harrison, and the prospectus of the New York *Tribune* appeared 3 April, 1841. Greeley's ambition was to make the *Tribune* not only a good party paper, but also the first paper in America, and he succeeded by imparting to it a certain idealistic character with a practical appeal which no other journal possessed. His sound judgment appeared in the unusually able staff which he gathered about him. Almost from the first, the staff which made the *Tribune* represented a broad catholicity of interests and tastes, in the world of thought as well as in the world of action, and a solid excellence in ability and in organization which were largely the result of the genius of Greeley and over which he was the master spirit. It included Henry J. Raymond, who later became Greeley's rival on the *Times*, George M. Snow, George William Curtis, Charles A. Dana, Bayard Taylor, George Ripley, William H. Fry, Margaret Fuller, Edmund Quincy, and Charles T. Congdon. It is easy to understand how with such a group of writers the idea of the literary newspaper, which had been alive from the beginning of the century, should have advanced well-nigh to its greatest perfection.

The great popular strength of the *Tribune* doubtless lay in its disinterested sympathy with all the ideals and sentiments which stirred the popular mind in the forties and fifties. "We cannot afford," Greeley wrote, "to reject unexamined any idea which proposes to improve the moral, intellectual, or social condition of mankind." He pointed out that the proper course of an editor, in contrast to that of the time-server, was to have "an ear open to the plaints of the wronged and suffering, though they can never repay advocacy, and those who mainly support newspapers will be annoyed and often exposed by it; a heart as sensitive to oppression and degradation in the next street as if they were practiced in Brazil or Japan; a pen as ready to expose and reprove the crimes whereby wealth is amassed and luxury enjoyed in our own country as if they had only been committed by Turks or Pagans in Asia some centuries ago." In conformity with these principles Greeley lent his support to all proposals for ameliorating the condition of the labouring men by industrial education, by improved methods of farming, or even by such radical means as the socialistic Fourier Association. He strongly advocated the protective tariff because he believed that it was for the advantage of the workingman; and the same sympathy led him to give serious attention to the discussion of women's rights with special reference to the equal economic status of women. There were besides many lesser causes in which the *Tribune* displayed its spirit of liberalism, such as temperance reform, capital punishment, the Irish repeals, and the liberation of Hungary. On the most important question of the time, the abolition of slavery, Greeley's views were intimately connected with party policy. His antipathy to slavery, based on moral and economic grounds, placed him from the first among the mildly radical reformers. But his views underwent gradual intensification. Acknowledged the most influential Whig editor in 1844, he had by 1850 become the most influential anti-slavery editor—the spokesman not of Whigs merely but of a great class of Northerners who were thoroughly antagonistic to slavery but who had not been satisfied with either the non-political war of Garrison or the one-plank political efforts of the Free Soil party. This influence was greatly increased between 1850 and 1854 by some of the most vigorous and trenchant editorial writing America has ever known. The circulation of the *Tribune* in 1850 was, all told, a little less than sixty thousand, two-thirds of which was the *Weekly*. In 1854 the *Weekly* alone had a circulation of 112,000 copies. But Rhodes has pointed out that even this figure is not the measure of the *Tribune's* peculiar influence, "for it was pre-eminently the journal of the rural districts, and one copy did service for many readers. To the people in the Adirondack wilderness it was a political bible, and the well-known scarcity of Democrats there was attributed to it. Yet it was as freely read by the intelligent people living on the Western Reserve of Ohio," and in Wisconsin and Illinois. The work of Greeley and his associates in these years gave a new strength and a new scope and outlook to American journalism.

Henry Jarvis Raymond, who began his journalistic career on the *Tribune* and gained further experience in editing the respectable, old-fashioned, political *Courier and Enquirer*, perceived that there was an opening for a type of newspaper which should stand midway between Greeley, the moralist and reformer, and Bennett, the cynical, non-moral newsmonger. He was able to interest friends in raising the hundred thousand dollars which he thought essential to the success of his enterprise. This sum is significant of the development of American daily journalism, for Greeley had started the *Tribune* only ten years earlier with a capital of one thousand dollars, and Bennett had founded the *Herald* with nothing at all. On this sound financial basis, Raymond began the career of the New York *Times*, 18 September, 1851, and made it a success from the outset. He perfected his news-gathering forces and

brought into play his intimate acquaintance with men of af
fairs to open up the sources of information. Above all he set
a new standard for foreign service. The American public never
had a more general and intelligent interest in European affairs
than in the middle years of the nineteenth century. The leading papers directed their best efforts toward sustaining and
improving their foreign service, and Raymond used a brief
vacation in Europe to establish for his paper a system of correspondence as trustworthy, if not as inclusive, as that of the
Herald or *Tribune*. If our newspapers today are immeasurably in advance of those of sixty years ago in almost every
field of journalism, there is only here and there anything to
compare in worth with the foreign correspondence of that
time. The men who wrote from the news centres of Europe
were persons of wide political knowledge and experience, and
social consequence. They had time and ability to do their
work thoroughly, carefully, and intelligently, innocent of superficial effort toward sensation, of the practices of inaccurate
brevity and irresponsible haste which began with the laying
of the Atlantic cable.

The theory of journalism announced by Raymond in the
Times marks another advance over the party principles of his
predecessors. He thought that a newspaper might assume the
rôle now of a party paper, now of an organ of non-partisan,
independent thought, and still be regarded by the great body
of its readers as steadily guided by principles of sincere public
policy. An active ambition for political preferment prevented
him from achieving this ideal. Although he professed conservatism only in those cases where conservatism was essential to the
public good and radicalism in everything which might require
radical treatment and radical reform, the spirit of opposition
to the *Tribune*, as well as his temperamental leanings, carried
him definitely to the conservative side. He was by nature
inclined to accept the established order and make the best of
it. Change, if it came, should come not through radical agitation and revolution, but by cautious and gradual evolution.
The world needed brushing, not harrowing. Such ideas, as he
applied them to journalism, appealed to moderate men, reflected the opinions of a large and influential class somewhere
between the advanced thinkers and theorists and the mass of

men more likely to be swayed by passions of approbation or protest than by reason.

It was the tone of the *Times* that especially distinguished it from its contemporaries. In his first issue Raymond announced his purpose to write in temperate and measured language and to get into a passion as rarely as possible. "There are few things in this world which it is worth while to get angry about; and they are just the things anger will not improve." In controversy he meant to avoid abusive language. His style was gentle, candid, and decisive, and achieved its purpose by facility, clearness, and moderation rather than by powerful fervor and invective. His editorials were generally cautious, impersonal, and finished in form. With abundant self-respect and courtesy, he avoided, as one of his coadjutors said, vulgar abuse of individuals, unjust criticism, or narrow and personal ideas. He had that degree and kind of intelligence which enabled him to appreciate two principles of modern journalism —the application of social ethics to editorial conduct and the maintenance of a comprehensive spirit. As he used them, these were positive, not negative virtues.

Raymond's contribution to journalism, then, was not the introduction of revolutionizing innovations in any department of the profession but a general improving and refining of its tone, a balancing of its parts, sensitizing it to discreet and cultivated popular taste. Taking the London *Times* as his model, he tried to combine in his paper the English standard of trustworthiness, stability, inclusiveness, and exclusiveness, with the energy and news initiative of the best American journalism; to preserve in it an integrity of motive and a decorum of conduct such as he possessed as a gentleman. To his success American journalism is deeply indebted.

CHAPTER XXII

Divines and Moralists, 1783–1860

THE writings of the American clergy between the Revolution and the Civil War have Jonathan Edwards[1] for their point of departure, and carry onward the tendencies he brought to a focus. Let us rather say two focuses: for Edwards is great precisely in the intensity with which he manifests a tough-mindedness and a tender-mindedness that are universal. He is at once dogmatist and mystic; he works out his theology into dualistic metaphysics, yet he knows himself to be one with God; though he philosophizes away the Freedom of the Will, and preaches Hell for sinners, yet he meditates also the Benevolence of the Deity, and is translated into mystical rhapsodies upon the divine love and upon Nature as its symbol and emanation. The primacy he gives to motivation places him with those who insist that reward and punishment must be held up before depraved mankind to keep it even outwardly decent; his insistence upon an inner light and a love for universal being faces him toward the believers in man's essential goodness and perfectibility. He never reconciled these tendencies in his own thinking; nor have they been reconciled since in that American literature which in various phases, mixtures, and proportions they have continued to colour.

Historically, at the close of the American Revolution the tender-minded derive from the Cambridge Platonists and their successors the English deists. Their thought is developed by Shaftesbury and the "benevolists"; favoured by Berkeley; much re-enforced by the works of Paley, and by Butler's

[1] See Book I, Chap. IV for Edwards. For divines other than Congregational and Unitarian see Book III, Chap. XVII.

Analogy; and developed again in various directions by Rousseau, William Godwin, and, later, Kant and Coleridge. They are the liberals, transcendentalists, and romantics, and Plato is their ultimate master, though he contributes his realism to their opponents. The tough-minded derive from Aristotle, St. Augustine, and, of course, Calvin; find themselves close kin to Hobbes and Locke, to the "motivists," and, later, to Reid and Dugald Stewart; and are the classics—the orthodox. In the large, the thought of American divines and moralists from Edwards to Beecher moves from tough to tender, parallel with the romantic movement in secular literature; while Beecher's contemporary, Mark Hopkins, toughly reacting against romanticism, anticipates the present secular return toward greater sharpness in realizing evil and the fundamental cleavages in things.

Our secular and our theological literature, thus closely akin in ideas, have also a strong personal connection, almost a family connection. With us, divinity has seldom been more, and has usually been less, than a generation removed from literary scholarship or the literary imagination. Andrews Norton is father to Charles Eliot Norton, William Henry Furness to Horace Howard Furness, Abiel Holmes to Oliver Wendell Holmes, Charles Lowell to James Russell Lowell. James Russell Lowell and Robert Traill Spence Lowell are brothers; so are Henry Wadsworth Longfellow and Samuel Longfellow. There is something filial in the scholar Ticknor's pious task of editing the sermons of the Rev. Joseph Stevens Buckminster, one generation before him. Emerson's forefathers had been clergymen for seven generations; and within his single life the early days as preacher and the later days as *sacer vates* were "bound each to each by natural piety." So were those of John Gorham Palfrey, George Ripley, and Octavius Brooks Frothingham, and of such clerical families as the Channings, the Abbotts, the Wares, the Beechers, the Muhlenbergs, and the Dwights, whose *pietas*, priestly, educational, juristic, and literary, has extended unto the third generation and beyond. It would be easy, but needless, to multiply examples in proof of the close and various personal connections between our divinity and our scholarship and literature.

The family tradition is evident at once in Edwards's disciples.

The sons of Jonathan, whether after the flesh or after the spirit, included Jonathan Edwards the younger (1745–1801), a systematic theologian, President of Union College, Schenectady, from 1799 to his death; David Brainerd (1718–47), author of a diary of his mystical experiences; Joseph Bellamy (1719–90); Samuel Hopkins (1721–1803); and Edwards's grandson Timothy Dwight (1752–1817). Of these, Hopkins and Dwight are for many reasons the most important. The younger Edwards, after graduating at Princeton in 1765, was Hopkins's disciple; Bellamy's chief works were all published before the Revolution; and Brainerd, a young consumptive, who was to have been Edwards's son-in-law, died before him. Hopkins, moreover, exercised an influence which went beyond theology into literature; and Dwight produced something uncommonly like literature itself.

Hopkins was born of Puritan stock at Waterbury, Connecticut. Roused to religious conviction at Yale by his college mate, David Brainerd, and by the revivalist Tennent, he heard Edwards before graduating in 1741, and, still not sure that he was a Christian, "concluded to go and live with Mr. Edwards" at Northampton as a student of divinity—which he did off and on till 1743. Then he was settled and ordained at Housatonic (later Great Barrington), where he had to contend with Indian attacks, malaria, and the Dutch settlers in his congregation; taking comfort, however, in a second intimate contact with Edwards while the latter was conducting the mission to the Stockbridge Indians. In 1769 the poverty of Hopkins's congregation, together with their opposition to his stiff doctrine, led to his dismissal.

In the next year he accepted a call to the First Congregational Church at Newport. The Rev. Ezra Stiles, then minister of the Second Congregational Church and later (1777–95) President of Yale, opposed the call, but preached a learned sermon at Hopkins's installation, and remained on friendly terms with him despite radical differences in doctrine and temper. In Newport, too, Hopkins became acquainted with the Channing family: William Ellery Channing, then a boy, heard him preach and was repelled by his harsh doctrine. Though the Revolutionary War wrecked his church, he remained with it, and in the lean years following wrote his

System of Doctrines Contained in Divine Revelation Explained and Defended (1793). After 1770 he also produced his sermons and pamphlets against slavery, probably the most readable of his works, being somewhat less impeded than the others by the pitiless iteration and verbose pedantry of his style. He seems to have aided in procuring the passage of the Rhode Island laws of 1774 and 1784, respectively forbidding the importation of negroes and declaring free all children born of slaves after the next 1 March. In failing health and with a dwindling congregation, he ministered faithfully until his death in 1803.

The formula associated with Hopkins's name, and most definitely set forth in his posthumous *Dialogue between a Semi-Calvinist and a Calvinist*, is "Willingness to be damned for the glory of God." It is the upshot of all his strict Calvinist theory of decrees, election, and evidences. Rejecting the benevolists' belief in a mild Deity, he transfers "universal benevolence" from God to man—of whom he then requires it. The germs of the doctrine are to be found in Edwards's theory of virtue as consisting in love for universal being; and some of Mrs. Edwards's own religious experiences while Hopkins resided at her house might well have suggested to him his extension of the doctrine. For with him the willingness to be damned is not merely the acme of mystical devotion, but an indispensable evidence of grace—a necessary, though not a sufficient, condition of salvation. If you are not willing to be damned, then you are sure to be.

Hopkins thus carried onward and reduced to a system the materials which Edwards left unco-ordinated. So tough-minded was he that in his hands what might otherwise have been an efflorescence of tender mysticism became a dogma of terror. Naturally it roused intense opposition, but this, together with the logical completeness of the system, focussed attention upon it; so that it remained a powerful influence until the time of general emancipation from theological terrors.

Hopkins personally met his own requirements of benevolence. His combination of terrific doctrine with a kindly and self denying personal life among his Newport parishioners is the underlying theme of Harriet Beecher Stowe's novel,

The Minister's Wooing.[1] His philanthropic opposition to the slave trade, said to be the first open opposition by an American clergyman, rendered him so unpopular among the prosperous traders of Newport that he was left to die in poverty with the feeling that his work was unaccomplished. Futile, he must have felt, was his letter of remonstrance and admonition (1802) to his revered master's grandson, Aaron Burr, upon the latter's dangerous courses; and his *Farewell to the World* is a pathetic review of the state of man as he then beheld it in all portions of the globe, particularly in Newport among his congregation. It is not a hopeful view. Hopkins could not foresee the success of his opposition to slavery; and he could scarcely have believed, even if told, that his doctrine of disinterested benevolence had so impressed young Channing with the boundlessness of human generosity and the infinite worth of man that it became with him one of the points of departure for a new hopefulness.

Timothy Dwight (1752–1817) could have had no such doubts of his present success. After a varied experience as student (graduated 1769) and tutor at Yale, as an army chaplain during the Revolution, as a farmer, as a member of the Connecticut legislature, and as preacher, schoolmaster, and writer of verse[2] at Greenfield, Connecticut, he became, at the age of forty-three, Dr. Stiles's successor in the presidency of Yale. He seems to have been the prototype of the modern college president,—appreciative of scholarship, but primarily a practical administrator. He raised the college to financial prosperity; he broadened the curriculum, especially by introducing courses in science; and to the infidels then numerous among the student body he brought religious conviction.

His divinity (*Theology Explained and Defended*, 1818–19), though schematic, is also controversial, aiming perhaps less to systematize than to convince, and establishing orthodoxy by refuting heresy. It consists of the sermons—essentially Hopkinsian—which he delivered from the college pulpit week after week and year after year, repeating the full set every four years so that each student generation might have the benefit of the whole course.

---

[1] The romance indicated by the title was suggested in part by an incident of Hopkins's ministry at Great Barrington.

[2] For his verse see Book I, Chap. IX.

As a contribution to American prose it is much less important than his four posthumously published volumes of *Travels in New England and New York* (1821–22). These record a series of journeys, on horseback or in a gig or "sulky," which Dwight undertook for his health, usually during college vacations, beginning in September, 1796, and continuing at intervals until 1815. The book is the upshot of his experience of life; he was engaged upon the manuscript within nine months of his death, and probably within a few days of it.

He professes as his motive for writing, the humanistic desire to vivify the past; he had wished to know "the manner in which New England appeared or to mine own eye would have appeared eighty or one hundred years before"; and, finding this impossible for himself, he resolved to make it possible for posterity. A second professed motive was the desire to refute foreign misrepresentations of America; and with this in view he cast his material into the form of letters and topical essays addressed to an imaginary Englishman.[1]

These definite purposes do not prevent the book from being an *omnium gatherum*. For Dwight does not use them as a basis of selection or exclusion of material, but admits anything that happens to interest him; and as he is interested in anything he sees and thinks of, the unity of his book is far to seek. Now, in emulation of the early New England annalists, he chronicles a great storm or an egregious murder; now, in a vein reminiscent of White's *Selborne*, he tells of the habits of birds, of the fitness of trees for particular soils, or of the right weather for maple sap; now, for chapter after stodgy chapter, he repeats and summarizes the Connecticut constitution and laws, the system of land tenure, the powers and duties of officers of government, and the penal system, even down to the fines imposed for

[1] Thomas Jefferson's *Notes on Virginia* (1786) has these points in common with Dwight's *Travels:* it purports to answer questions asked by a foreigner; it gives information about the constitution and laws, religion and manners, public revenue and expense, manufactures, commerce, money, histories, and memorials; it refutes the views of Buffon and of the Abbé Raynal upon the bad climate and soil of America, and upon the degeneracy of its animals and men. (See also Book II, Chap. I.) An immediate predecessor of Dwight in this *genre* was Ezra Stiles, who bequeathed to Dwight his *Literary Diary*, and whose *Itineraries* Dwight may well have seen in MS. Investigation would probably show that Dwight owed much to Jefferson and to Stiles.

various offences. Yet his commentary upon this tedious material—shrewd and lucid, well-balanced both in judgment and in style, and above all practical—places it in a kind of Blackstonian tradition.   For the rest, he mingles topographical accounts of the regions he passes through with sketches of the characters and lives of distinguished residents, descriptions of scenery, estimates of inns and innkeepers, bits of historical narrative, and statistics of industry, wealth, religion, and climate.

Dwight's descriptive powers are high but unsustained. At Canajoharie, he tells us, the Mohawk runs below, in a gorge, while above is a

long narrow stripe of azure seen overhead. On both sides rise stupendous walls of a deep black, awful with their hanging precipices, which are hollowed with a thousand fantastical forms. . . . As you advance up the stream . . . you suddenly arrive at a cascade sixty feet in height, where the water descends with a sufficient approximation to perpendicularity to convert the current from a sheet into a mass of foam perfectly white and elegant.

The passages that he does not thus spoil, as, for example, his description of the Notch of the White Mountains, of a view in the Catskills, or of the "oak openings" of the Genesee River, are very few. His narratives, too, while interesting as raw material of literature, are seldom more. The woman one hundred and two years old who, when "the bell was heard to toll for a funeral, . . . burst into tears and said, 'When will the bell toll for me? It seems that the bell will never toll for me,'" might have appealed poignantly to Hawthorne. Dwight's traveller, who rode across a bridge in the dark, and only in the morning discovered that the bridge had not a plank on it and that his horse had found his way across the naked frame, was in fact used by Henry Ward Beecher as an illustration rather less effective than the original. Dwight's tale of how the regicide Goff, then a venerable man in concealment in the house of the minister at Hadley, had suddenly appeared during an Indian raid upon the congregation, rallied them, and disappeared, may well have actually suggested Hawthorne's story of *The Gray Champion*. But Dwight has no *flair* for imaginative material; nor is he content to leave even his expository effects unspoiled. His narrative of the Saratoga campaign is solid historical writing; but alas, hard at its heels follows the judgment that Saratoga was more important than Marathon.

In description, in narrative, in its dry controversial humour, Dwight's style is a sound eighteenth-century style, very serviceable in conveying his keen judgments upon statecraft and college management; an administrator's style, clean in structure, sharp and low-toned in diction, modelled upon Johnson and Burke, but with an occasional richer rhythm. "The bloom of immortality, already deeply faded, now withered away." The apostle Eliot, when he died, "undoubtedly went to receive the benedictions of multitudes, who, but for him, had finally perished." Sometimes there are short passages of a sober eloquence not unlike Edwards's own. Of the congregation to whom Dr. Swift had been a faithful pastor Dwight observes: "Many of them will probably remember him with gratitude throughout eternity." But such pieces of Attic diction or noble rhythm may be followed in the very next sentence by a banality. As in his descriptions and narratives, so in the general body of his prose, the passages of power or beauty are not sustained. He has merely stumbled upon them.

From first to last Dwight has either no æsthetic standards or only the standards of cocksure provincialism. "Longitude from Yale College," the legend upon the map prefixed to each of his volumes, might be their motto. His opinions upon Elizabethan writers, upon architecture, upon the drama, upon Greek and Roman literature, would be incredible if they did not stare us in the face from cold type. His genuine powers are rendered nugatory by his incompetence in the realms of taste and imagination. He is the complete Puritan, inhospitable to art but thoroughly efficient in dealing with things; and—to modify Arnold's formula concerning the Philistine—a maker of farms that produce, of sermons that edify, of a college that educates, and of characters that wear. His want of adequate standards leaves his book a miscellany, not so much because there are all sorts of things in it as because of their huge artistic incongruities; not so much because of the variety of its contents as because of the unplumbed gaps between their literary levels.

Yet this is not to say that after some acquaintance with the *Travels* the reader does not perceive a dominant interest

204 Divines and Moralists, 1783–1860

emerge. This is Dwight's interest in watching the world confirm his creed. Streams erode their banks, waterfalls recede, puddingstone is compounded, in order to support the Mosaic chronology, which infidel geologists had been heard to assail. Insects found alive in wood known to be eighty years old, seeds that germinate after centuries, frogs found alive by diggers far under ground, are not mere curiosities: they prove that a species supposed to be new may well have been the offspring of such durable creatures, and hence that there is no new species and no spontaneous generation. Dwight chronicles them to support the Biblical account of the origin of all species by creation at the beginning, an account which even in his time was being questioned by precursors of the evolutionary philosophy. His interest in other marvels, again, such as floating islands and mysterious bright spots in the clouds, is much the same as Cotton Mather's interest in *magnalia*— What hath God wrought! Every detail of the creation is full of manifest providences. The rich vegetable mould on the surface of new lands, for example, which yields an abundant crop to the pioneer almost without effort on his part, has been placed there for that very purpose, to support him during the first years of his settlement, when his energies, being required to build his house and clear more land, are diverted from the soil. Then, when the beneficent mould has disappeared, the poor soil has its providential purpose too, for by now the settler has time to cultivate it, indeed, must cultivate it if he is to live; so that he has a motive for industry and the other virtues which make him respectable. Thus both the presence and the absence of vegetable mould are effects of the final causes which make the world for man.

Carrying his theology into his judgments upon life, Dwight is interested above all, then, in seeing how a depraved humanity actually gets along in the world. His picture of the trim green New England landscape, with its white spires and prosperous villages, and his picture of the unkempt and sprawling German settlements along the Mohawk, though they may at first seem intended to produce an imaginative contrast, at length reveal his purpose of showing what it is that makes people become respectable. In fact the whole book is a collection of materials toward a genetic psychology of respectability.

Dwight's observations of certain portions of Long Island and Westchester County, of the whole of Rhode Island (which he considers "missionary ground"), of the Indian settlements in parts of Connecticut, of the Irish settlements in central New York, and, generally speaking, of the world outside New England Congregationalism, all strengthen his conviction of the general depravity of man, and help him to confute the doctrines of Rousseau and William Godwin that men are good by nature but have been corrupted by civilization. His theology here coincides with his politics—his inveterate abhorrence of French "atheistic" democracy and Jeffersonianism in general. The *Travels* is a Federalist document, exhibiting in its most sensible consequences the view that men are presumably bad until something makes them good. Bent therefore upon discovering and applying the incentives that will make them good—for Dwight is a convinced motivist—he exemplifies everywhere the sanctions furnished by thrift, by education, by strong government, and by strong religion. Probably there exists no completer application of Calvinistic principles to secular life. Dwight is the last of the Puritans.

The term "Unitarian" was accepted by the leaders of the movement only after much reluctance and delay. The doctrine designated by it is not perhaps the characteristic note of the movement at all, for it suggests mere static belief or disbelief in a proposition; whereas Unitarianism was a dynamic tendency, and to be designated rather by some such term as "Liberal Christianity." Liberty, tolerance, the free play of the intellect, the enfranchisement of the soul from its terrors, faith in the possibilities and the worth of man,—these are more characteristic of it than the denial of the divinity of Jesus, though its high concept of humanity, indeed, renders its humanization of Christ no derogation.

Thus interpreted, Unitarianism has points of contact with whatever is liberal and hopeful in any religion. Its affiliation with Deism, Natural Religion, Benevolism, and other liberal tendencies of eighteenth-century Europe, need not be traced here. It is sufficient to observe that in America the Unitarians drew strength from the liberal wing of any or all of the Protestant churches. The less strict Calvinists, like Ezra Stiles,

Jonathan Mayhew, and Charles Chauncy, are thus accounted to have been upon the verge of Unitarianism. Mayhew (died 1766)[1] had been a champion not more of civil than of religious liberty. Stiles exhibited the Unitarian tolerance: he was the friend not only of Hopkins but of the Boston progressives and of the Newport rabbis. His administration at Yale is said to have broadened and secularized the college. In his pursuit of the intellectual life he touched another side of Unitarianism: he and Cotton Mather were the two American scholars whom Timothy Dwight considered able to stand comparison with British scholars. Chauncy[2] had condemned the more violent manifestations of the Great Awakening of 1740. In the pre-Revolutionary controversy concerning the establishment of Episcopacy in America, he had opposed the Anglican views of William White of Philadelphia (afterward the first Bishop of Pennsylvania), asserted that the English Church had best leave the American to develop independently, and contended for the right of the congregation to ordain its own minister. He leaned also toward the Arminian emphasis upon human choice as a genuine factor in salvation, thus falling in with the Unitarian tendency to magnify man. At the same time he is credited with "high" Arianism, and with a touch of Universalism. He had written, too, upon the benevolence of the Deity. He is thus found upon several characteristic Unitarian pathways.

It was the Boston Episcopalians, however, rather than the Congregationalists, who took the first decisive step. In 1785, the congregation of King's Chapel, having adopted a modification of the Anglican liturgy, from which all Trinitarian doctrine had been omitted, ordained and installed as its rector James Freeman, who, together with William Hazlitt (father of the essayist), had performed the revision. This ordination is usually held to mark the formal beginning of Unitarianism in New England.

The Rev. Joseph Buckminster (1751–1812) of Portsmouth, New Hampshire, a strict Calvinist, from first to last was doomed to lift up his voice against the liberal movement in vain. He protested against the Rev. Mr. Foster's Sermon at New Braintree (1788), which, he thought, offered salvation upon too easy

---

[1] See also Book I, Chap. v.   [2] See *ibid.*

terms; in a series of letters (1811) to the Rev. Hosea Ballou (1771–1852)[1] he protested against that pioneer Universalist's preaching the final salvation of all mankind; and above all he protested against the defection of his own son, the Rev. Joseph Stevens Buckminster (1784–1812), whose ordination sermon (1805) he nevertheless preached, not without a note of fatherly foreboding.

The Buckminsters were of the Edwards stock. The staunch and earnest father was a contemporary of Dwight, Barlow, and Trumbull at Yale; the scholarly, eloquent, and saintly son was an immediate predecessor of Andrews Norton, and a contemporary of W. E. Channing, Charles Lowell, and Washington Allston at Harvard. But for his father's opposition, he might have become assistant to James Freeman, whom he heard with admiration at King's Chapel. He taught Daniel Webster Latin at Phillips Exeter, and tried to persuade his pupil to take part in the school exercises in public speaking. His work, in fact, is full of seeds which the future brought to fruition. Its new note of secular culture, against which his father had warned him—its allusions to art, to foreign books and travel (he was abroad in 1806–07), and to classical philosophy and literature — becomes increasingly characteristic of nineteenth-century clerical writing. In quietly removing emphasis from the staggering conditions of salvation to the process of religious training, Buckminster anticipates Jacob Abbott and Horace Bushnell. He anticipates Andrews Norton both in attaching prime importance to philology and history, as evidences of Christianity, and in a large conception of theology as including the widest range of scholarship,—as bounded, in fact, only by the limits of human knowledge. Buckminster realized Norton's idea of a "learned and able theologian—disciplined in habits of correct reasoning—[and] informed by extensive learning." Norton seems to have laid upon himself the task of continuing the work that his admired friend had "died too young to do." "Hearing Buckminster," said Norton, "one seemed to be walking in the triumphal procession of Truth."

Despite warning and opposition, then, "liberal Christian-

---

[1] Great-uncle of Hosea Ballou 2d, who was a founder and the first President of Tufts College.

ity" continued to flourish, until in 1805 the Rev. Henry Ware, an outspoken Unitarian, was appointed to the Hollis Professorship of Divinity in Harvard College. This invasion of the school whose initial purpose had been the production of Congregational ministers roused the Congregationalists of every shade of opinion to the defence of their discipline; and from extreme Hopkinsians to moderate Calvinists, they combined to establish at Andover a new theological seminary, which was opened in 1808.

During the era of orthodoxy Andover Seminary published *The Andover Review*, and had its famous teachers, such as Leonard Woods, Moses Stuart, Austen Phelps, and Edwards A. Park; yet in the course of time even this stronghold yielded to the irresistible trend toward liberalism. In 1886, five of its professors who had published a volume of advanced theological thought were tried for heresy, and acquitted. The legal proceedings for their removal also failed. By a bit of historical irony, the counsel for the defence was Theodore William Dwight, a grandson of Timothy. In 1908, the wheel having come full circle, Andover Seminary removed to Cambridge and became affiliated with Harvard University.

The Princeton Theological Seminary, founded by the Presbyterian branch of the Calvinists, was opened in 1812, and had its strong men also: Archibald Alexander (1772-1851) and his sons James W. (1804-59) and Joseph A. Alexander (1809-60); Charles Hodge (1797-1878), who in 1825 established the organ of the Seminary, afterwards named *The Princeton Review*; and James McCosh (1811-94), President of Princeton College 1868-88. Princeton has always remained Presbyterian.

These conservative reactions in the early nineteenth century widened the cleavage between the Calvinists and the Unitarians, which by 1819 had become so marked that William Ellery Channing, who in that year preached the ordination sermon of Jared Sparks at Baltimore, adopted for it the title *Unitarian Christianity*. Thenceforth the separate establishment of the Unitarians was unquestioned.

As Channing[1] was their great mild preacher, so Andrews Norton was their hard-headed champion. Descended from

[1] See Book II, Chap. VIII.

the Rev. John Norton, the notable minister of Ipswich and of
Boston, Andrews Norton was born in 1786 at Hingham. In
1804 he graduated at Harvard, and spent the next fifteen years
as graduate student, tutor, and lecturer, there and at Bowdoin.
In 1819 he was appointed Dexter Professor of Sacred Literature
in Harvard College, acting also from 1813 to 1821 as the
College Librarian. His *Statement of Reasons for Not Believing
the Doctrine of Trinitarians*, first published in 1819 in a controversy with Professor Stuart of Andover, soon became a
Unitarian classic. In 1833 and 1834 he was engaged with
Charles Folsom in editing *The Select Journal of Foreign Periodical Literature*, one of the numerous magazines of that period
of growing international culture. The first number contains
Macaulay's *Essay on Hampden*, reprinted from *The Edinburgh Review;* Paulin Paris's *Letter upon the Romances
upon the Twelve Peers of France*, from Férussac's *Bulletin
Universel* ("translated from the French with notes by Professor
Longfellow"); and reviews from *The Foreign Quarterly Review*
and elsewhere. For a number of years Norton contributed
also to *The North American Review*, and was influential in its
management.

Emerson's celebrated *Divinity School Address*[1] in 1838
brought to a head Norton's distaste for the Transcendental
movement. A year later he addressed to the alumni of the
Harvard Theological School at their Commencement reunion
his *Discourse on the Latest Form of Infidelity*, which, by opposing Spinoza, Schleiermacher, Strauss, and Hegel, whom
apparently Norton considered responsible for much Transcendental error, refutes Emerson by indirection, without
mentioning him or taking explicit issue with his views. Yet
the clash of their opinions is uncompromising. Where Emerson insisted upon intuition, Norton requires an outer revelation
evidenced by historical documents. Where Emerson insisted
that genuine religion cannot be received at second-hand, but is
intuitive and immediate, Norton emphasizes the dependence
of laymen upon expert authority and mediation in difficult
matters of research and exegesis. Where Emerson rejected any
conception of a miracle that would oppose it to the ordinary
course of nature, implying that nature is miraculous enough,

[1] See also Book II, Chap. IX.

and that miracles are happening all the time, Norton reiterates that miracles are suspensions of the course of nature, are historical, and are evidence of the divine mission of Christ. George Ripley's answer to Norton's *Discourse* led to a controversy which belongs to the history of the Transcendental movement.[1]

Norton's opposition to intuitionalism appears throughout his works. His *Views of Calvinism* scores the proposition (which had found support even at Andover Seminary) that "The truths of Christianity have always been addressed to the intuitive perceptions of the common mind." Norton points out the inconsistency between the Calvinist doctrine that the common mind is naturally so depraved as to be unable to perceive religious truth, and the new Andover doctrine, adopted from Transcendentalism, that the common mind has absolute intuitions of religious truth. He thus hits out in opposite directions, against both the orthodox and the Transcendentalists, but on the same ground, namely, his rejection of intuitions. The violence of this rejection, indeed, carried him too far; so that when in the warmth of controversy he rejected all but the historical or external evidences of Christianity, he laid himself open to George Ripley's charge of narrowness.

From the very first, however, for example in his *Defence of Liberal Christianity* (1812), Norton had been consistent in pleading for the historical and linguistic interpretation of the Bible, and the consideration of dogma less as prescribed by authority than as developed by history. His final contributions to scholarship, the *Evidences of the Genuineness of the Gospels* (1837–44), and the *Translation of the Gospels* and *Internal Evidences of the Genuineness of the Gospels* (both published posthumously in 1855), take the same line. Even by "internal evidences" Norton does not mean evidences of spiritual truth. He is concerned not with establishing Christianity but with the genuineness of certain documents; thus his remarks are limited generally to matters of historical and linguistic exegesis and logical probability. Least of all does he consider what might by some be defined as internal evidence, the adaptability of Christianity to the character of man, or the intuition that Christianity is true.

[1] See Book II, Chap. VIII.

Norton is the representative Unitarian in taking the position, typical of that body, precisely half-way between Calvinism and Transcendentalism, engaging impartially in controversy on the one hand with Moses Stuart and on the other with George Ripley. The common basis of his opposition to both is his opposition to Plato. Platonism, his researches led him to believe, had in its Neo-Platonic avatar at Alexandria produced, among other doctrines of emanation, the doctrine of the Trinity. Platonism also, believing the soul to have been in contact with ideal archetypes whose memory it retained in this life, was the very fountain of the doctrine of intuitions. Norton's opposition to Emerson and Ripley was thus of a piece with his opposition to Philo Judæus and Moses Stuart, the opposition of an exact scholar to what he considered loose, effusive, and sentimental thinking. Indeed, though Norton never says so in so many words, he seems to have recognized the Platonism of the Transcendental movement, and to have condemned it upon the same grounds as those upon which he condemned Plato himself. Anti-Platonism is the key to Norton's position.

Norton's teaching is praised by his disciple William Henry Furness (1802–96), who carried it to the First Unitarian Church in Philadelphia; and it must, in fact, have been a powerful stimulus to anyone who could taste his austerity and his intellectual keenness. He is not wholly free from banalities, those devils that stand ever ready at the clerical elbow; he prefers Mrs. Stowe to Goethe; but the great body of his work is ascetically pure in taste as in style. It can still be read with pleasure, indeed with a certain intellectual thrill.

The work of enfranchisement was carried on in their several modes by three notable contemporaries: Horace Bushnell (1802–76), Henry Ward Beecher (1813–87), and Mark Hopkins (1802–87), each in his way a liberator.

Superficially, Bushnell may seem to have been a reactionary. Born in Litchfield Township, Connecticut, he graduated at Yale in 1827, whither, after a short experience in journalism, he returned as tutor, student of law, and finally student of theology. In 1833 he was ordained pastor of the North Congregational Church in Hartford, where he remained until 1859. In 1856, while in California for his health, he was active in organizing at Oakland the "College of California," which in 1869 was merged in the University of California, and the presidency of which he declined. He thus belongs by birth, by training, and by professional activity to that hinterland— consisting of the valleys of the Connecticut and the Housatonic, and of the Litchfield and Berkshire Hills—whose orthodoxy has stood out against the liberal movements of the coast line from Boston to Newport.

Bushnell disliked what to his richly mystical temperament seemed the baldness of Unitarianism, and he re-established on a new basis many of the institutes of orthodoxy, notably the Trinity and the Atonement. Yet he consistently opposed all dogma, not because it was bigoted on the one hand or lax on the other, but because of the inadequacy of language as such to convey the religious mysteries which his piety bade him hold fast despite their logical contradictions. Mere logic he distrusted so deeply that its contradictions, dilemmas, antinomies were to him no arguments against a belief. According to a well-known anecdote, Bushnell, finding a college-mate stropping his razor all in one direction, bade him oppose his strokes to each other, a procedure which has been accepted as typical of Bushnell's dialectic, and which is not unlike Hegel's. Contradictories merely led him to a higher resultant—a mystical synthesis and a sort of *credo quia impossibile*. He saved impossible dogmas by turning them into sacraments.

At the same time, the rationalist in him offered to weaker faiths a *modus vivendi*. The Trinity, whose essence was a mystery inexpressible in language, was reconcilable with the divine unity in that it was a mode and an instrument by which the Absolute revealed itself to and worked upon finite souls. This epistemological view, which is said to go back to Sabellius, was perhaps a novelty in American theology; its pragmatism and distrust of logic seem even to be anticipations. In much the same way Bushnell retained the doctrine of the Atonement by attributing to it a moral effect upon the human soul, instead of the old-fashioned governmental or legalistic function of paying a debt, expiating a crime, or mending a broken law. These positions he promulgated in his *God in Christ* (1849), with its introductory *Dissertation on the Nature of Language as Related to Thought and Spirit*, in *Christ in*

Theology (1851), and in *The Vicarious Sacrifice* (1856). For
the old revivals, with their sudden superemotional conversions,
he also substituted the concept of a gradual education in
Christianity; *Christian Nurture* (1847), like Jacob Abbott's
The Young Christian (1832), directs the attention of those who
would be of the faith toward the possibility of growing in it by
a process open to all mankind, the process of training. In his
attitude toward the abolition of slavery, Bushnell was likewise
detached from the extremists. Here, too, he believed less in
drastic measures than in education and in the gradual workings
of nature under Providence. In the same way he assumed
toward the scientific movement of the mid-nineteenth century
an attitude at once decisive and concessive. Whatever science
might have to say about the rigour of causation and necessity
within the physical world, man was always to be recognized as
an essentially free supernatural being, placed literally above
nature by his alliance with the divine. Yet the two realms,
of necessity and of freedom, were held together by a Deity
immanent in both (*Nature and the Supernatural*, 1858).

Without being a compromiser, Bushnell thus works *rap-
prochements* everywhere. His thought holds all subjects
suspended in a sort of Platonic solvent, conciliating opposites—
not without sometimes confusing them. Yet he continues with
vigour the tradition of Plato, Hegel, and Coleridge, and is a
genuine religious thinker, whose importance in the history of
American thought has perhaps not been generally recognized.
In many ways he suggests William James. Moreover, he has
a style, nervous, clean, and racy. Kept fresh by its " anti-
septic " virtue, his *Literary Varieties*—the volumes of essays
entitled *Work and Play* (1864), and *Moral Uses of Dark Things*
(1868) and *Building Eras in Religion* (1881)—will still richly
reward a reader. Indeed, all of Bushnell's prose, though
manifestly influenced by Emerson, by Carlyle, and by Ruskin,
yet possesses its own peculiar vitality, a pulsation that at its
best may be likened, to use a metaphor of his own, to the beat
of wings.

Henry Ward Beecher, too, was born in the orthodox up-
lands of Litchfield, and of a strictly Calvinistic sire. Lyman
Beecher (1775–1863) had studied theology under Timothy
Dwight at Yale; had occupied, after 1798, first the Presby-

terian pulpit at Easthampton, Long Island, next the Congregational pulpit at Litchfield, and lastly that of the Park
Street Church in Boston; until in 1832 he became President
of the newly established Lane Theological Seminary in Cincinnati. He is best known, perhaps, for his *Six Sermons on
Intemperance*, but he was a dogmatist as well as a moralist,
staunchly supporting the Calvinism of his native tradition.

His son Henry, graduating at Amherst in 1834 in no
doubt as to his vocation, at once entered the Lane Theological
Seminary, and studied under his father and under Calvin
Stowe (1802–86), an Oriental scholar of real attainment,
who in 1836 married Beecher's sister Harriet. Beecher served
his apprenticeship in the pulpit at Lawrenceburg and Indianapolis, whence in 1847 he was called to the new Brooklyn
congregation of Plymouth Church. The liberal movement
of his thought paralleled his geographical wanderings from
the region of orthodoxy, through the region of culture,
to the practical West, and back to the metropolitan East.
He had had his fill of dogmatic theology in youth, and never
took much further interest in it. He became more and more
a minister, looking rather to the needs of humanity than
to the theory of divinity. In the West, under the stress of
primitive conditions, he soon threw overboard a system of
doctrines in which, he found, plain people were not interested;
so that by the time he took the Brooklyn pulpit, which soon
became a national platform, he was preaching straight at
human nature, and touching it with a more and more liberating
hand as he advanced in years.

From his *Seven Lectures to Young Men* (1844) to his *Evolution and Religion* (1885) he came a long way. The *Lectures* are
addressed apparently not to young men in general, but to young
employees—clerks, mechanics, salesmen, and apprentices.
Hence their flavour of *Poor Richard* and the *Industrious
Apprentice*. Guided to his audience by Franklin and Hogarth,
Beecher combines allegory with vivid eighteenth-century
realism; bigoted invective against the theatre and novels, with
"characters," the Sluggard, the Busybody, the Dandy, the
Pleasure-Loving Business Man, the Cynic, the Libertine.
This antique literary material explains the excessively old-
fashioned flavour of the book. Though Beecher grew im-

measurably away from it, he seems never to have disavowed or changed it, and for fifty years it remained perhaps his most popular work.

To Beecher's Western period also belong short pieces which first appeared in an Indiana agricultural paper and were later (1859) reprinted as *Plain and Pleasant Talk about Fruit, Flowers and Farming*. Of no intrinsic literary importance, they are of interest as showing the sources of much of Beecher's imagery. He was always close to the soil, and he drew from natural phenomena some of his most effective "illustrations." The *Star Papers* (1855 and 1859) and the *Eyes and Ears* (1862), collections of short essays, are good reading even now. With naïveté and self-depreciation, Beecher records his impressions of his first tour in Europe, tells of holiday outings among the Connecticut hills and trout streams, and gives plainly and modestly his very sensible opinions upon such subjects as sudden conversion, mischievous self-examination, and total depravity. The latter doctrine he rejects, accepting the doctrine of men's sinfulness and the necessity of their atonement not because Adam fell but because sin is actual and present. With regard to conversion, he takes the empiricist view that only in rare cases does the inner clock strike twelve when men have found grace; they may have it, yet not have infallible evidence. Hence he deprecates excessive introspection and hesitation, and says "Go ahead." His reminiscences, too, of old Litchfield at a time when that lucky town held Miss Pierce's Female Seminary and the celebrated Law School of Judge Gould and Judge Tapping Reeve, are discursive essays of permanent interest. His story of how, having as a boy of thirteen visited the Charlestown Navy Yard, he stole a cannon ball and went away with it in his hat, is as enjoyable as Franklin's apologues of *The Axe to Grind* and of *Paying too Dear for One's Whistle*. The *Essay on Apple Pie* is not *toto cælo* removed from the *Essay on Roast Pig*. *Home Revisited*, the record of a few days in Indianapolis, recalls the first of his sermons which he considered a success because it was aimed at his hearers; and tells by the way of his awe of Jonathan Edwards. "I never could read . . . *Sinners in the Hands of an Angry God* . . . at one sitting. I think a person of moral sensibilities, alone at midnight, reading that awful discourse, would well nigh go crazy." Through many of these pieces there breathes a frank sensuous enjoyment of physical beauty, which passes easily into religious exaltation. Beecher revels in the form and colour of great painting, and in the sounds, sights, and colours of landscape; the pictures in the Louvre and the glories of a sunset are to him literally revelations. These volumes testify once more to the richness of his mental imagery, and to its decided growth in range and in culture after his removal to the East.

Meanwhile, during all the years from his first pulpit to the beginning of the Civil War, his opposition to slavery had been deepening. He never joined the Abolitionists, but untiringly opposed the extension of slavery, and during the decade from 1850 to 1860, in lectures and in contributions to periodicals, denounced the various compromises and outrages that led up to the conflict. *Freedom and War* (1863), a volume of spirited sermons and addresses from the Brooklyn pulpit, exhibits the growth of his opinions up to the moment when he began to advocate immediate abolition—a moment just before the Emancipation Proclamation itself.

In educating public opinion upon slavery, Beecher had been unconsciously preparing his own armament for uses which he could not have guessed. While upon a vacation in England in the autumn of 1863 he was asked to speak on the war, and in the course of eleven days delivered almost impromptu, at Manchester, Glasgow, Edinburgh, Liverpool, and London, the series of addresses which gave him perhaps his greatest celebrity. Some of his audiences, notably those at Liverpool and Glasgow, were most tumultuous, and had actually to be conquered by the speaker. He conquered them, and won over the English middle class to sympathy with the Union cause. The determination of the British government to maintain strict neutrality is said to have been largely due to Beecher's effect upon public opinion. As literature, the addresses in England, though of course they bear the marks of their hasty composition and contested delivery, yet reveal the easy mastery of his material which Beecher had been storing up in his years of preparatory writing and speaking. Their lucidity and humour are still delightful; they still throw off visibly the live sparks that were struck out in the original clash between the speaker and his hearers; they reproduce the time in its very form and pressure; and in their way, too, they are classics of argumentation, for Beecher realizes the essential Aristotelian form of rhetoric—the orator's persuasion of an audience confronting him. The history of slavery and of secession could hardly be read in a more interesting form.

In *Norwood, or Village Life in New England* (1868), advertised as "Mr. Beecher's only novel," Beecher attempted an excursion into imaginative literature, but failed for want of breath. He had no power of construction and very little power of characterization. The personages are lay figures moving through an action prescribed for them by the author, and speaking his language, not their own. The general woodenness of the book, and several delightful absurdities, lay it open to easy parody. So much allowed, *Norwood*, if taken not as a novel but as a series of sketches of New England types, descriptions of New England scenery, and discussions not too profound of topics in religion, politics, and æsthetics, has distinct merit. This is much the same merit that is exhibited, under much the same limitations, by Beecher's short essays: though he had imagination, he had no architectonic.

Beneath the routine activities of the next twenty years— his regular sermons, the public addresses for which he was more and more in request, and his sentimental *Life of Jesus the Christ* (1871), Beecher was quietly conducting an earnest study of the evolutionary philosophy. From the very beginning of his acquaintance with the new way of thinking, he seems to have felt that it would be his latest and his last instrument for enfranchising the soul; and when he had accomplished his task of educating public opinion at home and abroad toward the abolition of slavery, he turned to this other task of spiritual emancipation. "If I had preached thirty years ago," he says in one of the sermons of his *Evolution and Religion* (1885), "what I preach now, it would have been a great mischief to you; but for thirty years I have been cautious, and have fed you as you could bear it."

Beecher did not, it would seem, understand the full power of the instrument he was employing, and as he was a man of images and not of ideas he never brought his own self-contradictions to a clear issue. In his prevailing mood he makes the assumption, which comes down to him from Platonism, natural religion, and Transcendentalism, that nature is a symbol of God and the moral order, is a continuing revelation of God, is sympathetic with humanity, and is parallel, analogous, and favourable to religion and morals. Often, however, he realizes to some extent, and frankly declares, as far as he realizes it, the inevitable implication of the theory of natural selection, that nature is alien to the moral strivings of man, and is thoroughly unmoral if not immoral. When he is conscious of his self-contradiction at all, Beecher seems merely puzzled by it as by one mystery among many. It would of course be fatal to his work if that work were a philosophical system—which it is not.

Despite his indecision upon this central problem, really the problem of evil itself, Beecher succeeds in giving sight and freedom to souls weighed down and blinded by the old unhappy dogma of depravity. Without denying man's sinfulness, he reverses the whole prospect of humanity by simply declaring that it is not true that men were created innocent but fell and incurred a debt which they could never hope to pay; but rather that the human race began low down, has not come up very far, and has the opportunity for limitless development upward.

Beecher's close contact with his audience and the abundance of his imagery are the sources of his peculiar power. They keep his style homely and racy (Robert South he declared to have been his chief model), and hold his thought and feeling near to human needs. He deliberately cultivated both. He carried pocketfuls of gems, which he loved to turn over and examine; he haunted picture-galleries and jewellers' shops. Like Whitman, whom he is said to have influenced, he walked the streets, spent whole days among the docks and ferry boats, made himself familiar with all sorts of trades, and talked with all sorts of people. These sources of power were also at times sources of weakness. Beecher came to depend upon hearers rather than readers; his hand faltered when he felt himself out of contact with an audience; and as he could not bring himself to revise with any degree of care the reports of his oral discourse, the form in which much of it has come to us is distinctly sub-literary. His exuberance of imagery also upon occasion betrayed him into incongruity and bathos. Yet his

Mark Hopkins

writings as a whole produce a deepening impression of merit.
Here was a large personality, all of a piece, singularly free
from repressions, and with no closet for a skeleton to lurk in.
Beecher's openness of soul—exhibiting frankly his delight in
beautiful things and in human contacts—is perhaps his characteristic note, and together with the great historical interest
of his work will probably go far to render it permanent.

Mark Hopkins was one of a group of clerical college presidents and teachers in whom the old interest in systems was
transferred from theology to "anthropology." The group
includes men like Francis Wayland (1796–1865), President of
Brown University (1827–55); Archibald Alexander (1772–
1851), professor at Princeton; James McCosh (1811–94),
President of Princeton (1868–88); and Noah Porter (1811–
94), President of Yale (1871–86). All of these turn from
dogmatic theology to psychology, ethics, and the relations of
the human mind to Christianity. They produce textbooks on
"Christian Evidences," "Moral Science" or "Moral Philosophy," and "Mental Philosophy," for the most part in a
vein of Scottish dualistic realism modified by Sir William
Hamilton's Kantian importations.

Mark Hopkins, like Beecher, came of tough-minded stock
in a tough-minded region. He was the grandson of Mark, one
of three younger brothers who were reared by the benevolent
Samuel Hopkins. He was born at Stockbridge, graduated in
1824 at Williams College, and spent the next two years there
as tutor. In 1829 he took a degree in medicine at the Berkshire Medical College in Pittsfield, but in 1830 returned to
Williamstown as Professor of Moral Philosophy and Rhetoric.
Though licensed in 1833, he did not accept a pulpit, but in
1836 became President of Williams College, where he did main
service until his resignation in 1872. He remained at Williamstown as President Emeritus, and as a general counsellor to the
college and to the very wide community of his pupils.

The influence to which they testify is accounted for not
only by his strong, gentle, and sympathetic personality, but
also by his mastery of those pregnant generalizations which
interest growing minds. He was from first to last a man of
ideas. It would be too much to expect that among so many
ideas even the majority should be original, and in point of fact

Hopkins derived nearly all from his Calvinistic tradition and from his reading. His works refer explicitly to an exceedingly large number of authors. But the success with which, as a teacher, he caused his pupils to wheel his ideas into action, is surely originality enough. Those ideas, if not themselves a liberal education, gave to the education of hundreds its coherence, articulation, and aim. The winged word of his pupil James A. Garfield, variously reported, asserts that the essence of a college is a student at one end of a log and Mark Hopkins at the other.

Literary quality was only a by-product of a mind thus primarily engaged in forming character. Hopkins's prose is exceedingly uneven. Probably nothing in it was obscure when he spoke it aloud with his own significant intonations; but as a text for the eye it abounds in pitfalls. Yet he so reiterated, developed, illustrated, and enforced his ideas as to produce a total effect of lucidity. He has moments, too, of eloquence and charm.

From the Edwardean tradition Hopkins received the concept of universal benevolence, the dogmatic side of which interested him, however, much less than its usefulness as a basis of ethics. From his very early essay on *The Connection between Taste and Morals* down to his latest volume on *The Scriptural Idea of Man*, he so used it. In his mind it coincided fruitfully with the Aristotelian notion of a scale of things in which each lower member is the condition of a higher; the State, for instance, in which the best life for the citizen is conditioned upon the existence of slaves. Hopkins combined these or kindred ideas into a scale of forces and beings each member of which had a worth higher than that of the one upon which it was conditioned. Thus he established at once a series of ethical values and a series of physical phenomena, each built upon all the preceding and all leading up to the highest, which took up all the lower, and benevolence toward which was the basis of morals. As early as 1857 Hopkins's baccalaureate sermon, *The Higher and the Lower Good*, explained gravity as conditioning cohesion, cohesion as conditioning chemical affinity, and so on up through regularity of form, organic life, sensitive life, rational life, and moral life. Thenceforward this conception reappeared in all his more important works.

Essential to its working also was the assumption that each stage was lifted into the next higher stage by the addition of some external force. It will be observed that this gave Hopkins a full-fledged evolutionary process, worked, however, not from within but from without, by means of accessions of matter and force effected by an external artificer. It was this last phase of his theory that gradually drew to itself the chief emphasis and the most important functions of the whole, and became in Hopkins's hands his great instrument of liberation.

To Hopkins's thinking, the evolutionary philosophy threatened the destruction of personality, the personality of God and of man, both of whom seemed about to be swallowed up in a mechanistic nature. Hopkins has no illusions on the subject. Charm she never so wisely, Nature cannot persuade him of her virtue. She is not, except in some very early Platonistic effusions of his, the symbol of a divine moral order, but is rather a machine grinding out uniform cycles under mechanical necessity, and making no answer to the human demand for purpose and freedom. These elements must be supplied from without; and it is a detached Deity who supplies them.

The germ of this portion of Hopkins's system appears in one of his earliest published works, that entitled *On the Argument from Nature for the Divine Existence* (1833), a review of Whewell's Bridgewater Treatise on *Astronomy and General Physics Considered with Reference to Natural Theology*. Here Hopkins already discredits the "argument from design" and finds evidence of the existence of God much less in nature than in man. Nature, though full of "contrivance," is often irrational and neither wise nor good; only in man is there found a glimmering of wisdom and goodness, only there a moral valuation,— which must be the effect of a cause not different in kind, and hence of the Deity. This argument, too, runs throughout Hopkins's system, parallel with his use of the scale of conditioning and conditioned; so that when he beholds the menace of the evolutionary philosophy, he has his weapons ready.

Tyndall's *Belfast Address* (1874), with its assertion of the complete immanence of all the developing forces within matter itself, realized Hopkins's worst fears; and thenceforth he held evolutionism to this its extreme logic. With a flexibility that was little short of marvellous in one well past his threescore years and ten and confronted by a new and complex hypothesis, he seized at once the fundamental issue between evolutionism and Christianity. This, he saw, was essentially the old issue of immanence against transcendence. Many a younger mind even now fails to grasp this ultimate implication as Hopkins grasped it the moment Tyndall pointed it out; many a Christian even now thinks himself a thorough-going evolutionist when he believes that a detached God created the universe and left it thenceforth to evolve. Hopkins perceived and turned to account with much acumen these same intellectual compromises, futilities, and divisions within the camp of the evolutionists themselves. Spencer, with his utterly detached transcendent Absolute; Fiske, with his old argument from nature to his new unknowable power distinct from matter; and, Hopkins might have added, Wallace, with his several special creations of "higher faculties," one every little while;—these, clearly enough, not only were divided among themselves, but were not carrying the evolutionary argument "whithersoever it led." They were only clouding the issue. All such compromises he refused, and with an intellectual honesty and courage even more admirable than his flexibility, pushed the question to its ultimate form and squarely faced it there. About each professor of evolution he asks, in effect: "Does he, or does he not, say that this power is inherent in matter? If he does, he is properly an evolutionist. If he does not, . . . but says that the results are due to the action of a being . . . that is separable from matter and uses it, then he is not properly an evolutionist." So facing the question, Hopkins had no need of the Bishop of Oxford's weapons. For at least a generation his own mind, as if anticipating the struggle to come, had been forging its sword.

Hopkins, then, uncompromisingly groups together evolutionism, with its mechanistic nature, its continuity, uniformity, necessity, law, monism, immanence, and tendency to pantheism, over against a scale of being that rises into personality, with its freedom, its choice of ends, its discontinuity, its movement *per saltum*, its realism as to species, its supernatural man, and its transcendent Deity. The sum of God's attributes, indeed, is that he is a person; and for Hopkins religion is faith in a person. This order of ideas, suggested as early as the Williams College Semicentennial Address of 1843, grows stronger and stronger in the series of his works; with deepening earnestness he declares that, deprived of personality and of the scale of moral values conditioned by it, the world will go forever circling through mechanical revolutions, but that progress is impossible.

It is a matter for serious inquiry whether the future is not with him. The world has of course moved beyond a denial of the facts of evolution; but it may have to admit that from the accepted and undeniable facts it has been drawing the falsest inferences. The romantic "return to Nature" has led man into the suicidal fallacy that he ought to imitate her in the conduct of his own affairs, and that because he has been evolved by natural selection he must continue its wild work. A reaction against these romantic horrors is now in sight. Many are feeling that romanticism, having given us its best, has had its day; and that "as the Nineteenth Century put man into nature, so it will be the business of the Twentieth to take him out." If man shall indeed acknowledge that he has been following the law for thing rather than the law for man, if he shall understand how it was by following nature's senseless competitive ways, instead of subjecting his self-assertiveness to man's ethical scale, that he betrayed his race to mutual slaughter, and how it was a pseudo-scientific philosophy that brought him to this *doloroso passo*, he will turn from his ghastly naturalism to a controlling humanism such as has never yet been realized.

CHAPTER XXIII

Writers of Familiar Verse

I. Holmes

ONE of the best known passages in *Elsie Venner* is that in which Holmes asserted the existence of an aristocracy in New England, or at least a caste, which "by the repetition of the same influences, generation after generation," has "acquired a distinct organization and physiognomy." This caste is composed of those whose ancestors have had the advantage of college training and have practised one or another of the three learned professions. The young man born in this selected group is commonly slender, with a smooth face and with features regular and of a certain delicacy. "His eye is bright and quick,—his lips play over the thought much as a pianist's fingers dance over their music,—and his whole air, though it may be timid, and even awkward, has nothing clownish." Teachers discover that he "will take to his books as a pointer or setter to his field work." He may be intended for the bar while his father was a minister and his grandfather a physician; and by the very fact of this heredity he "belongs to the Brahmin caste of New England."

The man who thus described this caste was himself a Brahmin of the strictest sect, endowed with its best qualities, and devoid of its less estimable characteristics,—the tendency to anæmia and to the semi-hysterical outlook of the dyspeptic reformer. He was energetic, wholesome to the core, sound and sane, unfailingly alert, fundamentally open-minded, never tempted to crankiness or freakishness. He was born in an illustrious year, 1809, which saw the birth of Darwin and Lincoln, of Tennyson and Gladstone, of Chopin, Mendelssohn, and Edgar Allan Poe. It was toward the end of August that the Rev. Abiel Holmes, author of the *Annals of America*,[1] made a brief entry at the foot of a page in his almanac, "—29. son b." The son was named Oliver Wendell Holmes, the Wendell being the maiden name of his mother, descended from an Evert Jansen Wendell who had been one of the early settlers of Albany; and thus her son could claim a remote relationship with the Dutch poet Vondel:

And Vondel was a Wendell who spelt it with a V.

Through his father, the Calvinist minister, and his grandfather, a physician who had served in the Revolution with the Continental troops, Holmes was descended from Anne, daughter of Thomas Dudley, governor of Massachusetts Bay, and wife of Simon Bradstreet, twice governor of the province.[2] The author of the *Autocrat* shared with R. H. Dana, author of *Two Years before the Mast*, the honour of descent from this literary ancestress. Holmes was born in Cambridge, in an old gambrel-roofed house that had served as General Ward's headquarters at the outbreak of the Revolution: "The plan for fortifying Bunker's Hill was laid, as commonly believed, in the southeast room, the floor of which was covered with dents, made, it is alleged, by the butts of the soldiers' muskets." Holmes's mother, it may be recorded here, to account in a measure for the veracity and the vigour of his *Grandmother's Story of Bunker-Hill Battle*, was only a little girl of six when she was hurried off from Boston, then taken by the British, who were preceded by rumours that "the redcoats were coming, killing and murdering everybody as they went along."

It was in Cambridge that Holmes grew to boyhood, playing under the Washington Elm. He was sent to what was then known as a "dame's school." He had an early inclination to verse, and composed rhyming lines in imitation of Pope and Goldsmith before he knew how to write; and Pope and Goldsmith remained his masters in metrical composition to the end of his long life. His father had a library of between one and two thousand volumes, and in this the son browsed at

[1] See Book II, Chap. XVII.
[2] For Anne Bradstreet, see Book I, Chap. IX.

will, reading in books rather than through them. "I like books," he told us later; "I was born and bred among them and have the easy feeling when I get into their presence, that a stable boy has among horses." When he was fifteen he was sent to Phillips Academy at Andover; and at sixteen he entered Harvard, graduating in 1829, eight years after Emerson and nine before Lowell. Among his classmates were James Freeman Clarke[1] and S. F. Smith, the author of *America* (1832). He wrote freely for the college papers, both in prose and verse, preserving in his collected works only a very few of his earlier humorous lyrics.

Upon his graduation he hesitated as to his profession, spending a year at the Dana Law School without awakening any liking for the law, and confessing later that "the seduction of verse-writing" had made this period "less profitable than it should have been." Yet it was while he was supposed to be studying law, and when he was just twenty-one, that he wrote the first of his poems to achieve an immediate and lasting popularity. This was the fiery lyric on *Old Ironsides*, protesting against the breaking up of the frigate *Constitution*, victor in the naval duel with the *Guerrière*. The glowing stanzas were written in a white heat of indignation against the proposed degradation of a national glory; they were published in 1830 in the Boston *Advertiser;* they were copied in newspapers all over the country; they were reprinted on broadsides; and they accomplished their purpose of saving the ship, which did not go out of commission for more than half a century after Holmes had rhymed his fervent appeal for its preservation.

At last he turned from the law to medicine, the profession of his grandfather. He studied for a while at the private school of Dr. James Jackson; and then he crossed the Atlantic to profit by the superior instruction to be had in Paris. Half a century later he recorded:

I was in Europe about two years and a half, from April, 1833, to October, 1835. I sailed in the packet ship " Philadelphia " from New York to Portsmouth, where we arrived after a passage of twenty-four days. . . . I then crossed the channel to Havre, from

[1] See Book II, Chap. VIII.

which I went to Paris. In the spring and summer of 1834 I made my principal visit to England and Scotland. . . . I returned in the packet ship "Utica," sailing from Havre, and reaching New York after a passage of forty-two days.

On his return to America he settled in Boston as a practising physician, taking as his motto "the smallest fevers thankfully received." He was twenty-seven when he obtained the degree of doctor of medicine and when he issued his earliest volume of poems. Nothing that he had written before or that he was to write later was more characteristic than one of the lyrics in this book,—*The Last Leaf.* He won several prizes for dissertations upon medical themes, published together in 1838; and the next year he was appointed professor of anatomy and physiology in the medical school of Dartmouth College, a position which he held for only a brief period. In 1840 he married Amelia Lee Jackson. He had resumed his practice in Boston, and he continued to contribute freely to the literature of his profession. He was always justly proud of his share in diminishing the danger from puerperal fever and of his trenchant attack upon *Homeopathy and its Kindred Delusions* (1842). Then in 1847 he was called to Harvard as professor of anatomy and physiology; and this position he was to fill with distinction for thirty-five years.

The career of Holmes was placid and uneventful even beyond the average of literary careers. Nothing happened to him other than the commonplaces of life; he took part in nothing unusual; he practised medicine for a few years and he taught medical students for many years; he wrote prose and verse in abundance; and in the fulness of years he died. The only dates that call for record here are those of the publication of his successive books. Until he was almost at the summit of his half-century he was known to the general public only as a writer of verse. He used prose for his discussions of medical questions; and whenever he was moved to express his opinions on other themes he chose the medium of metre. Those were the fertile years of the Lyceum System, and Holmes went the rounds of the lecture-halls like many others of the New England authors who were his contemporaries; but even as a lecturer he preferred rhyming verse to the customary colloquial prose.

Then quite unexpectedly, when he was forty-eight, an age when most men shrink from any new departure disconcerting to their indurated habits, he revealed himself in an entirely new aspect. *The Atlantic Monthly* was started in 1857 with Lowell as its editor; and to its early numbers Holmes contributed *The Autocrat of the Breakfast-Table*. Lowell had insisted as a condition precedent to his acceptance of the editorship that Holmes should be a constant contributor, awakening him "from a kind of lethargy in which" he was "half-slumbering."

Much of the vogue of the new magazine was due to the novel flavour of Holmes's series of papers; and he was persuaded to follow up his first success with kindred volumes entitled *The Professor at the Breakfast-Table* (1860), *The Poet at the Breakfast-Table* (1872), and *Over the Teacups* (1890). For the same monthly he wrote many disconnected essays, some of which he sent forth in 1863 under the appropriate name *Soundings from the Atlantic*. In the several volumes of the Breakfast Table series there is a thin thread of story and the obligatory wedding winds them up at the end; and in his three attempts at fiction, *Elsie Venner* (1861), *The Guardian Angel* (1867), and *A Mortal Antipathy* (1885), the thread is only a little strengthened and there is no overt abandonment of the leisurely method of the essayist. From the telling of fictitious biographies to the writing of the lives of two of his friends was only a step; and he published a memoir of John Lothrop Motley in 1878 and a study of Emerson in 1884.

It was in 1883, when he was seventy-four, that he resigned his professorship; and it was in 1886, when he was seventy-seven, that he paid his second visit to Europe. He spent the summer mainly in England, and in London he was "the lion of the season." It was almost exactly half a century since his first voyage across the ocean; and on his return from this second voyage he wrote out a pleasantly personal narrative of *Our Hundred Days in Europe*. At intervals, for nearly sixty years, he had sent forth volumes of verse; the latest to appear (in 1888) was aptly entitled *Before the Curfew*,—as Longfellow had called his final volume *In the Harbor* and Whittier had felicitously styled his last book *At Sundown*. On 7 October, 1894, Holmes died at the ripe age of eighty-five, unusual even among the long-lived American poets of his generation, of whom he was the last to survive.

During his second visit to London, Holmes was the guest of honour at a dinner of the Rabelais Club, founded to cherish the memory of an earlier humorist who was also a practitioner of medicine; and in his letter accepting the invitation he took occasion to confess his regard for another physician-author, Ambroise Paré, whom he termed "good, wise, quaint, shrewd, chatty." And all five of these characteristics he possessed himself. He was a gentleman and a scholar—to revive the fine old phrase—who was also a physician learned in the lore of the healing art and keenly interested in its history. He was a gentleman and a scholar, who was also a man of the world, in the best sense of that abused term,— a man of the world holding a modest place as a man of science. And at bottom he was a Yankee, with a true Yankee inventiveness,—the hand-stereoscope he devised being the outward and visible sign of this native gift, which was exhibited incessantly in his writings, notably in *The Physiology of Verse* and in *The Human Wheel, its Spokes and Felloes.* In prose and in verse he disclosed an unfailing Yankee cleverness, whittling his rhymes and sharpening his phrases with an innate dexterity.

"The secret of a man who is universally interesting is that he is universally interested," William Dean Howells has told us; "and this was above all the secret of the charm Doctor Holmes had for every one." There is zest and gusto in all that he wrote, and the reader can share the writer's own enjoyment. Especially was the writer interested in himself, as the true essayist must be. His delight in talking about himself was complacent, contagious, and innocent. "I have always been good company for myself," Holmes once confessed; and this is one reason why he has been pleasantly companionable to countless readers who found in him a friendly quality which took them captive. His egotism was as patent as Montaigne's, even if it was not so frank in its expression nor so searching in its analysis. The more of himself he revealed, the more he won the hearts of his fellow men, who relished the gentleness and the firmness of the character so openly disclosed, its kindliness, its urbanity and amenity, its lack of all acerbity or acridity, its total freedom from the rennet of meanness which curdles the milk of human kindness.

In a letter which Whittier wrote for a celebration of Holmes's seventy-fifth birthday, the Quaker poet singled out for praise the Boston bard's "genial nature, entire freedom from jealousy and envy, quick tenderness, large charity, hatred of sham, pretence and unreality, and his reverent sense of the eternal and permanent." This is keen criticism. Holmes was a wit, but there was no bitterness in his laughter, because it lacked scorn; and there was in it no echo of the cruel sterility of Voltaire's irony. We can say of Holmes what Moore said of Sheridan, that his wit

> ne'er carried a heart-stain away on its blade.

We can say this with the weightier emphasis when we recall the cheerful courtesy with which he met the vindictive and virulent retorts evoked by his dissolvent analysis of the abhorrent and horrible aspects of Calvinism, a disestablished code inherited from a less civilized past. Holmes's influence was civilizing and humanizing; and it was more important than we are likely now to recognize. He had in a high degree the social instinct which has given grace to French life and which was perhaps accentuated in him during his two years' stay in Paris in his malleable youth. He was the constant exponent of good manners and of right feeling, at a period in the evolution of American society when the need for this was even more evident than it is now.

It was in a score of his poems and in the successive volumes of the *Breakfast-Table* series that Holmes most completely disclosed himself. His two biographies and his three novels are far less important,—in fact, these other prose writings are important chiefly because they are the work of the "Autocrat"; and it may be well to deal with them briefly before considering his major work, in which he is expressing the essence of his cheerful optimism. The less significant of his two memoirs is that of Motley, a labour of love undertaken in the months that followed hard upon the death of the historian. "To love a character," said Stevenson, "is the only heroic way of understanding it." Possibly an author could write a vigorous life of a man he hated, since hatred is the other side of love. But no author could paint a vital portrait of a personality which left him indifferent; to his biographer at least a man must be a hero; and no valet has yet written an acceptable account of his master's life. But love needs to be controlled by judgment; and Holmes, at the time he composed his memoir, felt too keenly the injustice from which Motley had suffered to be able to survey the career and to estimate the character of the eminent historian with the detachment necessary to the painting of a portrait for posterity. What he did was to put forward an apology for Motley, with undue insistence upon the temporary griefs of the man and with less adequate consideration of the histories by which his fame is supported.

The biography of Emerson is far better, even if it also is not wholly satisfactory. It is in no sense an apology, for there was nothing in Emerson to extenuate. It is less personal, more detached, more disinterested, more comprehensive. It is admirably planned, with the adroitly articulated skeleton which we have a right to expect from a professor of anatomy. It is rich in appreciation and abundant in phrases of unforgettable felicity, for Holmes was ever the neatest of craftsmen. But when all is said, we cannot repress the conviction that he was out of his natural element when he undertook to deal with a figure so elusive as Emerson's. Holmes's very qualities, his concreteness, his sense of reality, his social instinct, tended to unfit him for interpreting an intangible personality like Emerson. He was characteristically witty when he compared Emerson to those "living organisms so transparent that we can see their hearts beating and their blood flowing through their transparent tissues"; but he did not altogether succeed in making us feel the ultimate purpose for which Emerson's heart beat and his blood flowed. The interest of the biography—and it has its full share of the interest which animated all that Holmes wrote—is kept alive rather by the adroitness of its author than by the revelation of its subject.

Such also is the interest of his three novels; they appeal to those who relish the flavour of Holmes's personality rather than to those who expect a work of fiction to be first of all a story, and secondly a story peopled with accusable characters.

In one of the prefaces to *Elsie Venner* Holmes cited the remark
of a dear old lady who spoke of the tale as "a medicated novel";
and he declared that he was "always pleased with her discriminating criticism." It is not unfair to say that all three
novels were conceived by a physician and composed by an
essayist. Holmes, so Leslie Stephen asserted, lacked the
"essential quality of an inspired novelist," which is "to get
absorbed in his story and to feel as though he were watching
instead of contriving the development of a situation."

Of *Elsie Venner* Holmes himself said that the "only use of
the story is to bring the dogma of inherited guilt and its consequences into a clearer point of view"; and he declared that his
"heroine found her origin not in fable or romance, but in a
physiological conception, fertilized by a theological dogma."
In other words, *Elsie Venner* is a novel-with-a-purpose; it is a
fiction devised by a nineteenth-century physician to attack
eighteenth-century Calvinism. Perhaps a born story-teller
could have so constructed his narrative as to fascinate the
reader in spite of the argument it was intended to carry, but
Holmes was not a born story-teller. He described characters
and places, not for their bearing on the story itself, and not
even for suggesting the appropriate atmosphere of the action,
but mainly if not solely for their own sake, and quite in the
manner of the character-writers who had blazed the trail for
the early essayists. By the side of figures thoroughly known
and delicately delineated, there are others, not a few, outlined
in the primary colours and trembling on the very verge of
caricature. In this we can discover the unfortunate influence
of Dickens, as we can perceive the fortunate influence of Hawthorne in the treatment of the abnormal heroine. And equally
obvious is the influence of Thackeray, who also began and
ended his career as an essayist. Thackeray, even if he had a
bias toward moralizing, confessed to the Brookfields that he
found his ethical lectures very convenient when he had to pad
out his copy to fill the allotted number of pages in the monthly
parts in which his larger novels originally appeared. But
Thackeray, after all, was a born story-teller, an inspired
novelist, who got absorbed in his story and felt as though he
were watching and not inventing his situations. Holmes
lingered by the way and chatted with the reader, not from any

external necessity, but because digression and even disquisition is to the essayist the breath of life.

In *The Guardian Angel*, the heroine is a composite photograph of half a dozen warring ancestors of whom now one and now another emerges into view to insist upon the reappearance of his or her identity in Myrtle Hazard. Yet, when all deductions are made, both *Elsie Venner* and *The Guardian Angel* have many a chapter that only Holmes could have written, rich in wisdom, in wit, in whimsy, and in knowledge of the world. But this can scarcely be said of *A Mortal Antipathy*, the latest of the medicated fictions and the feeblest, written when its author had long passed threescore years and ten. The physiological theme is too far-fetched, too unusual, too abnormal, to win acceptance even if it had been handled by a master of fiction; and we may doubt whether even Balzac could have dealt with it triumphantly. As Holmes dealt with it, it did not justify itself; the narrative was too fragmentary for fiction and too forced, while the intercalary papers lacked the freshness of view and the unpremeditated ease of Holmes's earlier manner as an essayist.

"The prologue of life is finished at twenty; then come five acts of a decade each, and the play is over, with now and then a pleasant or a tedious afterpiece, when half the lights are put out, and half the orchestra is gone." When Holmes wrote this, he could not foresee that he would be able to keep in their seats more than half of the spectators, if not the most of them, to the very end of his pleasant afterpiece. He was not forty when he first discoursed as the "Autocrat" and he was twice forty when he gossiped "Over the Teacups." In the octogenarian book he may be a little less spontaneous and a little more self-centred than in its predecessor of twoscore years earlier; and the shadowy figures who take part in its conversations may seem to talk a little because they are aware that they were created on purpose to converse, instead of talking freely for the fun of it as the solider persons who met around the breakfast table were wont to do. Yet the latest of the group, even if its wit be less pungent, has almost as many samples of shrewd sagacity as adorned the two books that came after the *Autocrat*. "Habits are the crutches of old age," Holmes tells us; and he never lost the habit of cheerfulness. There is no hypocritic praising of past times; on the contrary there is a blithe and buoyant recognition of the gains garnered in eighty years.

Over the Teacups may be a little inferior to *The Poet at the Breakfast-Table* but only as the *Poet* is a little inferior to the *Professor* and the *Professor* to the *Autocrat*, because the freshness had faded and because we were no longer taken by surprise. The *Autocrat* struck the centre of the target and the hit was acclaimed with delight; the later books went to the same mark, even if they were not winged by an aim as unerring. No doubt, a part of the immediate success of the *Autocrat* was due to its novelty,—novelty of form and novelty of content. Holmes was characteristically shrewd when he declared that "the first of my series came from my mind almost with an explosion, like the champagne cork; it startled me a little to see what I had written and to hear what people said about it. After that first explosion the flow was more sober, and I looked upon the product of my wine-press more coolly"; and he added, "continuations almost always sag a little." Perhaps the novelty of form was more apparent than real, since Steele and Addison had given us a group of characters talking at large as they clustered about Sir Roger de Coverley. But there is this salient difference, that in *The Spectator* the talk is mainly for the purpose of creating character, whereas in the *Autocrat* the characters have been created that they might listen.

Yet in so far as the *Autocrat* has a model, this is plainly enough the eighteenth-century essay, invented by Steele, improved by Addison, clumsily attempted by Johnson, and lightly varied by Goldsmith. Steele is the originator of the form, since the earlier essay of Montaigne and of Bacon makes no use of dialogue; it has only one interlocutor, the essayist himself, recording only his own feelings, his own opinions, and his own judgments. Steele was probably influenced by the English character-writers, perhaps also by the lighter satires of Horace, and quite possibly by the comedies of Molière,— notably by the *Précieuses Ridicules* and the *Femmes Savantes*. The outline Steele sketched the less original Addison filled with a richer colour. As Holmes had begun when a child by imitating the verse of Pope and Goldsmith, so as a man when he wrote prose he followed the pattern set by Steele and Addison. Although he was not born until the ninth year of the nineteenth century, he was really a survivor from the eighteenth century; and his prose like his verse has the eighteenth-century characteristics, despite the fact that he himself was ever alert to apprehend the new scientific spirit of the century in which he lived.

The real novelty of the *Autocrat* was in its content, that is to say, in Holmes himself, the master talker of the Breakfast-Table, in the skill with which the accent of conversation is caught. The other characters are responsible for an occasional remark not without individuality and point; but the Autocrat himself tends to be a monopolist and to intermit his discourse only that his adversary in the verbal combat may lay himself open to a series of sharp thrusts in retort. This is as it should be, since the others who gather about the breakfast table were but ordinary mortals, after all, whereas the Autocrat was an extraordinary mortal, an artist in conversation, gifted by nature and trained by long experience, a man who had thought widely if not deeply about life, who had read the records of the past and who could revive them to shed light on the present, a physician abreast of modern science and swift to bring its new discoveries to bear on the old problems of life. In reading the *Breakfast-Table* series in swift succession the reader cannot help remarking the frequency with which Holmes draws on his professional experience; he sees men and women through the clear spectacles of the family physician;—and perhaps one reason why he arrogates to himself the major part of the conversation is in revenge for the silence imposed on the practitioner by the tedious and interminable talk of his patients about themselves to which the family physician has perforce to submit. Holmes used medical analogies and dropped into the terminology of the anatomist and physiologist with the same frequency that Shakespeare employed the vocabulary of the theatre, even in incongruous situations finding material for figures of speech in his own experience on the stage.

Holmes is not only a man of science and a man of the world, he is also a humorist and a wit,—a wit who has no antipathy even to the humble but useful pun,—a humorist abounding in whimsy. And as a result of this fourfold equipment his talk is excellent merely as talk. It has the flavour of the spoken word; it is absolutely unacademic and totally devoid of pedantry. Therefore it is not only delightful but stimulating; it continually makes the reader think for himself and turn back upon himself. Despite its acuteness, its liveliness, its briskness, its vivacity, it never lacks seriousness, without ever becoming ponderous.

It may be that Holmes does not attain to the high seriousness, the deep seriousness, of enduring philosophy; and it cannot be denied that there are pages here and there which are not as valid today as when they were written. It would be doing the Autocrat an ill-service to compare him with his remote and mighty predecessors Montaigne and Bacon. And it may be admitted that there is more or less warrant for the remark of John Burroughs, to the effect that Holmes always reminded him "of certain of our bird songsters, such as the brown thrasher or the cat-bird, whose performances always seem to imply a spectator and to challenge his admiration." Holmes seems "to write with his eye upon his reader, and to calculate the advance upon his reader's surprise and pleasure." To admit this would be only to acknowledge the truth of the French saying that every man has the defects of his qualities. But it cannot be admitted if it implies that Holmes was unduly self-conscious or affected or pretentious. In fact, much of the charm of the Autocrat is due to the entire absence of affectation and to the apparent spontaneity of the talk which pours so easily from his lips and which discloses so abundantly the winning personality of Holmes himself. "Every book is, in an intimate sense, a circular letter to the friends of him who writes it," so Stevenson has told us; and Holmes was fortunate in that his circular letter made a friend of every one who received it.

The qualities which give charm to Holmes's prose are those which please us also in his verse. He has left a dozen or a score of lyrics secure in the anthologies of the future. But he wrote too easily and he wrote too much to maintain a high average in the three hundred double-columned pages in which his complete poems are collected. No poet or prose man can take down to posterity a baggage wagon of his works, and he is lucky if he can save enough to fill a saddle-bag. Holmes's reputation as a poet will rise when his verses are winnowed and garnered into a thin volume of a scant hundred pages wherein *Old Ironsides* and *The Last Leaf, The Chambered Nautilus* and *Homesick in Heaven, The Wonderful "One-Hoss Shay"* and *The Broomstick Train, Grandmother's Story of Bunker-Hill Battle,* and a handful more are unincumbered by the hundreds of occasional verses which were each of them good enough for its special occasion and yet not good enough to demand remembrance after the event.

There are a few of Holmes's loftier poems in which we feel that the inspiration is equal to the aspiration; but there are only a few of them, with *The Chambered Nautilus* at the head, accompanied by *Homesick in Heaven,*—not overpraised by Howells when he called it one of the "most profoundly pathetic of the language." And Stedman was right also when he suggested that Holmes's serious poetry had scarcely been the serious work of his life. Even at its best this serious poetry is the result of his intelligence rather than of his imagination. It lacks depth of feeling and largeness of vision. It has a French felicity of fancy, a French dexterity of craftsmanship, a French point and polish; and also a French inadequacy of emotion. "Assuredly we love poetry in France," said Anatole France when he was discussing the verse of Sainte-Beuve; "but we love it in our own fashion; we insist that it shall be eloquent, and we willingly excuse it from being poetic." *Old Ironsides,* fiery as its lines ring out, is eloquent rather than truly poetic.

Here again Holmes declares himself as a survival from the eighteenth century, when English literature conformed to French principles. His favourite reading as a child was Pope's *Homer,* the couplets of which "stimulated his imagination in spite of their formal symmetry." And even their formal symmetry was not displeasing to his natural taste:

> And so the hand that takes the lyre for you
> Plays the old tune on strings that once were new.
> Nor let the rhymester of the hour deride
> The straight-backed measure with its stately stride;
> It gave the mighty voice of Dryden scope;
> It sheathed the steel-bright epigrams of Pope;
> In Goldsmith's verse it learned a sweeter strain,
> Byron and Campbell wore its clanking chain;
> I smile to listen while the critic's scorn
> Flouts the proud purple kings have nobly worn.

The even merit of its occasional verse is one of the obvious qualities of the eighteenth century which we find also in Holmes. Late in life he admitted that he had become rather too well known in connection with "occasions." He was intensely loyal to Boston; and he felt that he had no right to refuse the summons to stand and deliver whenever the city received an honoured guest or when an honoured citizen died or went away or came back. As he explained in one of these occasional pieces,

> I'm a florist in verse, and what *would* people say
> If I came to a banquet without my bouquet?

Late in life Holmes admitted that "many a trifling performance has had more good honest work put into it than the minister's sermon of that week had cost him"; he confessed to strenuous effort over his copy of verses, insisting that "if a vessel glides off the ways smoothly and easily at her launching, it does not mean that no great pains have been taken to secure the result"; and he proudly reminded his readers that "Pindar's great odes were occasional poems . . . and yet they have come down among the most precious bequests of antiquity to modern times." The noblest example of English prose in the nineteenth century, Lincoln's Gettysburg address, was also evoked by an occasion. Even if Holmes's occasional verse has not the lofty elevation of Pindar's odes or the pathetic simplicity of Lincoln's little speech, it has almost always an exquisite propriety to the event itself, an unfailing happiness of epithet, a perfect adequacy to the moment of local importance. Its chief fault, if not its only defect, is that there is too much of it, even if its average is higher than might reasonably be expected.

In a letter to Lowell, Holmes declared, speaking of Bostonians in particular and yet perhaps also of Americans in general, that "we Boston people are so bright and wide-awake . . . that we have been in danger of thinking our local scale was the absolute one of excellence—forgetting that 212 Fahrenheit is but 100 centigrade." There is one department of poetry in which Holmes can withstand without any danger of shrinking the application of the centigrade scale; this is the department of *vers de société*, so called, although it is never merely society verse. Perhaps Cowper's term best describes it, "familiar verse," the lyric commingled of humour and pathos, brief and brilliant and buoyant, seemingly unaffected and unpremeditated, and yet—if we may judge by the infrequency of supreme success—undeniably difficult, despite its apparent ease. Dr. Johnson, who was himself quite incapable of it, too heavy-footed to achieve its lightness, too polysyllabic to attain its vernacular terseness, was yet shrewd enough to see that it is

less difficult to write a volume of lines, swelled with epithets, brightened with figures, and stiffened by transpositions, than to produce a few couplets, grand only by naked elegance and simple purity, which require so much care and skill that I doubt whether any of our authors have yet been able for twenty lines together nicely to observe the true definition of easy poetry.

In this "easy poetry," which is the metrical equivalent of the essay in its charm, in its grace and in its colloquial liberty, Holmes has few rivals in our language. It was with strict justice that Locker-Lampson, in the preface to the first edition of *Lyra Elegantiarum* (1867)—to this day the most satisfactory anthology of *vers de société*,—declared that Holmes was "perhaps the best living writer of this species of verse." It may be recorded also that Locker-Lampson paid Holmes the even sincerer compliment of imitation, borrowing for two of his delightful lyrics not only the spirit but also the stanza Holmes had invented for *The Last Leaf*. With characteristic frankness the London lyrist once told an American admirer that this stanza might seem easy but it was difficult, so difficult that no one had handled it with complete success—except Holmes and himself.

Locker-Lampson derived directly from Praed, whose verses have an electric and dazzling brilliance, whereas in Holmes the radiance is more subdued and less blinding. Of all the writers of familiar verse no one has ever surpassed Holmes in the delicate blending of pathos with humour, as exemplified most strikingly in *The Last Leaf*, in which fantasy plays hide and seek with sentiment. Scarcely less delightful in its eighteenth-century quaintness is the family portrait, *Dorothy Q;* and close to those two masterpieces are lesser lyrics like *Contentment, Bill and Joe,* and the lines *On Lending a Punch Bowl* and *To an Insect:*

> I love to hear thine earnest voice,
>   Wherever thou art hid,
> Thou testy little dogmatist,
>   Thou pretty Katydid!
> Thou mindest me of gentlefolks,—
>   Old gentlefolks are they,—
> Thou say'st an undisputed thing
>   In such a solemn way.

These are only a few of the best of his lighter lyrics, now sprightly and sparkling, and now softer and more appealing, often evoking the swift smile, although never demanding the loud laugh, and sometimes starting the tear on its way to the eyelid; and in them Holmes proved that Stedman was only just when he declared that familiar verse may be "picturesque, even dramatic," and that it may "rise to a high degree of humor and of sage and tender thought."

II. Minor Writers

It is in a half dozen of the ineffably graceful lyrics of the Greek anthology and in a like number of the more personal songs of Horace that we may find the earliest analogue of English familiar verse, better and more abundant than the French *vers de société*, even though the native English form has been compelled to borrow a French name for itself.   The Greek anthology has the freedom of the fields and of the solitary hillside, and therefore it lacks a little of the social tone which is the dominating quality of familiar verse.   Yet Horace is never rustic—he belongs to the town; and Stevenson is right in saying that Horace is urban, even when read outdoors; he has the abundant urbanity and the total absence of rusticity which familiar verse must ever reveal.   Familiar verse is a species of poetry which can flourish only where men and women meet frequently, without undue parade, not wearing their hearts on their sleeves, and hiding their deeper feelings behind the semi-transparent mask of conventional detachment from the serious duties of life.

Familiar verse can develop only when men congregate in cities; it is a town-product; and Boston can claim a share in Holmes's success in this difficult department of song.   Other

Americans in other cities have been inspired to risk the dangers of familiar verse and to rhyme the sayings and doings of their fellow citizens. Sometimes they give to their airy nothings a local habitation and a name as easily recognizable as the background of *Dorothy Q.* Could *Nothing to Wear*, detailing the sad plight of Miss Flora McFlimsy of Madison Square, and the *Visit from Saint Nicholas* on

> the night before Christmas, when all through the house,
> Not a creature was stirring, not even a mouse

—could either of these have been composed elsewhere than in New York? And could *The Truth about Horace* have been told with such stern veracity anywhere else than in Chicago?

In the first century of the American republic there were only a few large cities, and yet urban amenity was to be discovered here and there in towns where the social organization had advanced beyond its elementary stages. Benjamin Franklin, a pioneer in so many different departments of human endeavour, seems to have been the earliest American to adventure himself among the difficulties of this lighter poetry, so closely akin to prose in its directness and in its seeming lack of effort; and perhaps his lines on *Paper* could open an American selection of familiar verse only by favouritism. Philip Freneau[1] essayed it more than once; so did Royall Tyler,[2] our first writer of comedy; so did John Quincy Adams[3] and James Kirke Paulding[4] and Washington Irving,[5]—prose men all of them, dropping into rhyme only occasionally, and only when the spirit moved them. And it is a significant fact, supported by a host of examples in both branches of English literature, British and American, that it is in familiar verse that the expert essayist is most likely to be successful when he risks himself in the realm of rhyme.

Yet it is possible also to select specimens of this special type from the major poets, the sport of their frolicsome moods, and no adequate anthology would fail to include Bryant's *Robert of Lincoln*, Emerson's *Humble-Bee*, Whittier's *In School Days* and Longfellow's *Catawba Wine*. From Lowell the

[1] See Book I, Chap. IX.
[2] *Ibid.*
[3] See Book II, Chap. XV.
[4] See Book II, Chap. V.
[5] See Book II, Chap. IV.

examples would be half a dozen at least, with *Auf Wiedersehen* and *Without and Within* as the first flowers to be picked. Indeed, Lowell is Holmes's only chief rival among American poets in the limited field of familiar verse, but he is less meticulous in finish and polish and more likely to charge his lines with a meaning too large for the lyric which aims above all else at lightness and brightness.

Three other American poets of high ambition, Stedman,[1] Aldrich,[2] and Bret Harte,[3] gave a more abundant share of their attention to the poetry which is blithe and buoyant; and in any selection of the best in this kind, it would be inexcusable to omit Stedman's *Pan in Wall Street*, Aldrich's *In an Atelier*, or Bret Harte's *Her Letter*. Nor would any competent editor exclude from such a collection Weir Mitchell's *Decanter of Madeira*, George Arnold's *Jolly Old Pedagogue*, or Charles Henry Webb's *Dum Vivimus Vivamus*. Nor would it be difficult largely to increase this list of examples chosen from the verse of men whose reputation has been won mainly in other fields.

Three of our lighter lyrists demand a little more detailed consideration,—John Godfrey Saxe (1816–87), Eugene Field[4] (1850–95), and Henry Cuyler Bunner[5] (1855–96), though the last two belong to a period somewhat later than that chiefly considered in this chapter. Of these Saxe is the earliest and the least important. He is not only the earliest, he is also the most old-fashioned in his method and the least individual in his outlook. His verse is modelled upon Praed's, to whose dazzling brilliance he could not attain; and he borrowed also the pattern of Hood in his more broadly comic lyrics. He was clever and facile; but he was a little too easy-going to achieve the delicate fineness which we have a right to demand in familiar verse. He does not understand that the thinner the theme the more care must be exercised to redeem its exeguity by certainty of touch and by infinite solicitude in execution. The immanent difficulty of familiar verse is due to the fact that poetry of this type at its best ought to be humorous without broadening into mere fun, while it ought also to be pathetic without slopping over into sentimentality. Saxe is quite free from senti-

[1] See Book III, Chap. x.   [2] *Ibid.*
[3] See Book III, Chaps. v. and vi.   [4] See also Book III, Chap. ix.
[5] See also Book III, Chap. vi.

mentality, in fact he does not often succeed in suggesting sentiment. His defect is that his verse tends to be frankly laughter-provoking. It is in *Little Jerry* that he has hinted the sentiment which sustains humour, as it is in *The Mourner à la Mode* that he has echoed the more worldly manner of mere society verse.

Eugene Field is like Saxe in one respect at least,—that his verse is frankly comic more often than not. His humour is bold, exuberant, energetic, spontaneous, and easy; and there is cause for wonder, therefore, that he was able to restrain himself on occasion and to curb his comic verse within the strictest bounds of familiar verse, endowing it with genuine sentiment without foregoing either blitheness or brilliancy. He had far more freshness than Saxe, a more fertile originality, and knowledge of men and of books both wider and deeper. He is superior also in technical dexterity, in variety of rhythm, and in fertility of rhyme. His feeling is more spontaneous, his sentiment more abundant and finer in feeling. He can when he chooses hint at the tear which trembles above the lips that seem to smile. There is warrant for the wide popularity of his *Little Boy Blue*, in which the pathos is pure and tender, without any taint of mawkish sentimentality. Only a little narrower in its appeal is *Old Times, Old Friends, Old Loves*. Field's command of sentiment is so certain that he can impart true feeling even to stanzas as frolicsome and as rollicking as those which delight us in *Apple Pie and Cheese*.

The youngest of these three younger practitioners of familiar verse, Henry Cuyler Bunner, could also be broadly comic; he had an ample outlook on literature and on life; and he was truly a poet, who won a memorable position among our lyrists by lyrics of a loftier flight than mere comic verse. His lyre was a winged instrument on which he could strike at will the resonant note of patriotism or the gentler strain of peaceful sentiment. *The Way to Arcady* is almost too poetical, its spirit is almost too ethereal, to let it fall within the narrow circle of social verse; it has a simple grace and a light freedom not often discoverable since the songs of the Elizabethan dramatists. In certain of his brisker and brighter poems Bunner reveals himself as a disciple of Austin Dobson; in others he is treading the trail of Herrick or following in the footsteps of Heine. He sat at the feet of many

masters and learned what they had to teach him, standing
forth in time upon his own feet and giving voice to a note of his
own.   No one of his predecessors in social verse could be credited with the suggesting of *Forfeits* or *Candor*, the *Chaperon*
or *One, Two, Three*, exquisite in its certainty of execution, in the
skill with which the sadness of the theme is relieved by the
joyousness of the treatment.   It is the abiding quality of
Bunner's familiar verse that it discloses the spirit of the true
poet, even while it confines itself within the bounds of the
brevity, the brilliancy, and the buoyancy which are the ham-
pering limitations of familiar verse.

CHAPTER XXIV

Lowell

NEITHER Lowell's poetry nor prose has that obvious unity of effect which characterizes the work of so many nineteenth century writers. His work does not recall, even in the minds of its admirers, a group of impressions so distinct and fixed as those summoned by the poetry of Whittier, Poe, or Whitman, or by that of Swinburne, Morris, or Browning, or by the prose of Thoreau or Emerson, of Ruskin or Arnold. His work, indeed, does not have the marks of a dominant or of a peculiar personality; nor does it add to literature a new group of ideas or a new departure in workmanship. Though its volume is large, and though a number both of his poems and his essays have won a wide familiarity, there is difficulty in summarizing their qualities of form or matter in a way that will indicate with justice his importance in American literature.

This somewhat miscellaneous appeal made by his writing may be ascribed in part, no doubt, to a lack of literary power that prevented him from winning the triumphs that belong to the great conquests of the imagination, but it is also due in large measure to the variety of responses which his rich personality made to the changing movements of American life. Other writers were surer of their message or of their art, but perhaps the career of no other affords a more varied and interesting commentary on the course of American letters, or responds as constantly to the occasions and needs of the nation's experience. It is impossible to consider him apart from his time and environment, or to judge his writing apart from its value for the United States. It has left something for posterity, but its best energy was expended in the manifold tasks which letters must perform as a builder of national civilization. It is this service which makes him an eminent and in some ways our most representative man of letters.

The briefest summary of the events of his life will indicate the variety of his interests and occupations. Born in 1819 in Cambridge, Massachusetts, in the colonial house where he was to spend most of his life, he went to Harvard College, studied law—and abandoned it for a career of letters. He contributed verses and sketches to the magazines, edited a few numbers of an unsuccessful literary journal, *The Pioneer*, brought out his first volume of poems, *A Year's Life*, in 1841, a second volume in 1843, and a collection of essays, *Conversations on Some of the Old Poets*, in 1844.

In December of this year he was married to the poetess Maria White. The nine years of their married life until her death in 1853 mark a distinct period in Lowell's literary work. He contributed constantly both prose and verse to various journals, at first largely for those of the anti-slavery propaganda; and the Mexican War gave the opportunity for *The Biglow Papers*, the first of which appeared in *The Boston Courier* of 17 June, 1846. In 1848 appeared a second collection of poems, the completed *Biglow Papers*, and *The Fable for Critics*. Lowell had won, in both popular and critical regard, an assured place in what was already an important national literature. The fifteen months which the family spent in Europe in 1851–52 seem to have increased his desire to widen the range of his poetry, but the ambitions that thronged with the return to America were interrupted by the death of his wife. A period of uncertainty followed his bereavement, and circumstances gave him a new occupation.

In 1855 he delivered in Boston a course of twelve lectures (unpublished) on English poetry, and as a result of their success was appointed to succeed Longfellow as Smith Professor of the French and Spanish Languages and Literatures and Professor of Belles Lettres in Harvard College. A few months were spent in Dresden in preparation for a course on German literature, and in the fall of 1856 he began twenty years work as a teacher. In the following year he was married to Frances Dunlap and resumed life in Elmwood. His professorship turned his mind to criticism and scholarship, but did not hasten that stronger poetic flight for which he had felt himself preparing. A brief-lived literary magazine, *Putnam's Monthly*, in 1853–54 had given place to one or two of his best known essays, and a new literary enterprise, *The Atlantic Monthly*, in 1857 gave further opportunity for his prose. Lowell was editor of the new magazine for two years and a regular contributor of reviews and articles until 1863, when he joined with Charles Eliot Norton in editing *The North American Review*. For the next dozen years his essays both political and literary appeared mainly in this review.

During the Civil War, Lowell's chief contributions to poetry were the new series of *Biglow Papers* which began in the *Atlantic* in 1861. It was not until the war was over that the great themes of national triumph through sacrifice called forth the four memorial odes. Miscellaneous verse of the preceding twenty years was collected in *Under the Willows* (1868); but the odes and longer poems, as *The Cathedral* (1870), *Agassiz* (1874), best represent both the emotional impulses that followed the war and the maturity of Lowell's art.

The political interests which had engaged much of his prose writing before and during the war had not interrupted his increasing devotion to the study and criticism of literature. He had been directing his attention less to contemporary letters and more to the masters of English and to a few of the masters of foreign literature, notably Dante. The result of these studies was a long succession of essays which make up the volumes *Among My Books* (1870), *My Study Windows* (1871), and *Among My Books, Second Series* (1876). It is these books which are his main contributions to literary criticism.

Lowell and his wife spent two years (1872–74) in Europe, and after a brief resumption of his professorship he was appointed minister to Spain in 1877, and in 1880 was transferred to England. After his retirement in 1885 he spent a considerable part of his time in England until his death in 1891. The mission was a recognition of his distinction not merely as a man of letters but as a representative of the best American culture, and this distinction Lowell maintained in a number of addresses on both literary and political themes, represented by the volume *Democracy and Other Addresses* (1886). Although his poetry became infrequent there was enough for a nnal volume, *Heartsease and Rue*, in 1880.

To all these varied activities as poet, essayist, humorist, editor, teacher, scholar, and diplomat, must be added that of letter writer. For Lowell's letters, in addition to their annals of his personal experiences and friendships, contribute something to literature and history which perhaps has ceased with the day of the typewriter—a record of the intimate association of the high-minded. His work as a man of letters may be considered most readily by the main divisions of verse and prose; but the separation is not always significant. The poetry is mostly bounded by the years 1840 and 1870, and the best of the essays by 1860 and 1890; but there is hardly a year of his half century which did not see both prose and verse. Nor can the subject matter be divided by the two forms, for both require attention from the historian of either the literary or the political progress of the half-century. Both respond to the changing events of his own life, and to the greater changes that transformed the nation of 1840 into that of 1890.

Lowell's youth was spent among books. Before he left college he had become a wide if desultory reader, and the study of law failed to detach him from what was to become a life-long devotion to the easy chair and the library. To the inheritance of English blood, law, language, and religion that bound New England to the mother country, he added an enthusiastic appreciation for English literature. Naturally this appreciation was directed by the Romanticism which had reached its full flower in English letters, by its leaders, Wordsworth, Keats, Lamb, or by the gods of its idolatry, Shakespeare, Spenser, and Dante. His feeling was like that which Keats had experienced twenty years before, when English poetry had opened out a new world inviting to fresh beauty and new enterprise. And this world of British letters had added since then the clarion voice of Carlyle and the exquisite art of Keats himself and of Tennyson. It is easy to trace in Lowell's early verse imitation and reminiscence of the English poets of the preceding half-century; but even more important was his acceptance of their faith in poetry. With Wordsworth he believed that it was to be the moral guide and spiritual inspirer, with Keats he saw it opening new doors to the abode of beauty. He shared the assurance of *Sartor Resartus* that literature was to supply the new priesthood that was to direct the new age.

There were also new ideas and impulses astir in the New England of Lowell's youth. The narrow Puritanism had given way to Unitarianism and Transcendentalism[1] and literature. During the first twenty years of Lowell's life, American literature had taken a bulk and character which might risk comparison with the literature of any European nation during that period. In his teens he was reading Emerson, Longfellow, Holmes, Whittier, Hawthorne, and Prescott, and most of these men were his neighbours and ready to welcome and direct his first attempts at letters. There is a sense of an intellectual and imaginative dawn to be found in Lowell's essays and verse, a dawn that is to gladden the granite and pines of his native land. With a loving admiration for the old literature, there is a loyal national pride in the new; or, rather, there is a sectional pride; for the patriotism is mainly a sectional patriotism, a fervour for the New England hills and men. Boston was then a long way from New York and Philadelphia—although Lowell's literary adventures carried him to both cities—and the rest of the nation was separated by barriers of manners and habit. He was patriotically American because his beloved and awakened New England was expected to lead the nation.

Lowell's early poems do not show much novelty of theme or manner. They are on about the same subjects that all men were writing verse upon in the forties, and written with the same vocabulary, images, and rhythms. Love, nature, liberty, idealism, classic story, personal moods are the themes, but there is some novelty in the ingenuity of the phrases and in the new fauna and flora. If he was following the English romanticists he was transferring their worship of beauty to a New England landscape and their religious musings to the turmoil of idealism that stirred the youth of Massachusetts. He writes of the dandelion and the pine-tree, and his seasons are the riotous June or the Indian summer of Cambridge, his landscape that of Beaver Brook. All is descriptive or reflective; there is no narrative except when it is the mere text for sentiment and moral.

Some union of art and morality, of Keats and Carlyle, Poe and Emerson—that was the poet's endeavour. He wrote to Briggs in 1846:

[1] See also Book II, Chaps. VIII and XXII.

Then I feel how great is the office of Poet, could I but even dare to hope to fill it. Then it seems as if my heart would break in pouring out one glorious song that should be the gospel of Reform, full of consolation and strength to the oppressed, yet falling gently and restoringly as dew on the withered youth-flowers of the oppressor. That way my madness lies.[1]

It is easy to smile at this youthful fervency, as Lowell himself smiled a year or two later in *The Fable for Critics*.

> There is Lowell, who's striving Parnassus to climb
> With a whole bale of isms tied together with rhyme.
> The top of the hill he will ne'er come nigh reaching
> Till he learns the distinction 'twixt singing and preaching.

But, with most nineteenth-century poets, Lowell was a preacher as well as a singer. Poverty, tyranny, doubt, industrialism, are the themes that for England distracted the attention of the Muse; in the United States, the mid-century vision of beauty was clouded by the presence of slavery. And if Lowell was conscious that the isms, even that of the anti-slavery cause, burdened his climb up Parnassus, there was never any doubt of the imperative nature of the summons of moral reform.

The American reader should indeed have a special sympathy for this avowal of high purpose; for is not this gospel of reform the better genius of our nation? The material advance which has conquered a continent has made us self-confident, disregardful of the past, and careless of reflection, but it has inspired us with a faith in our power to rebuild and move on. The evils which beset us do not daunt us, and the virtues we possess we would fain impose upon others. We believe in propaganda, we are uneasy without some cause to further, some improvement to promote. If we ever determine what the American idea is, we shall evangelize the world.

It was perhaps this spirit of reform which Lowell had sought to express in his *Prometheus* and which he had in mind when in another letter to Briggs he declares "I am the first who has endeavoured to express the American Idea, and I shall be popular by and by."[2] Popularity came first, however, when

---

[1] Scudder, *Life*, Vol. I, p. 267.   [2] *Ibid.*

fervour was linked with wit and humour in *The Biglow Papers* with their racy Yankee dialect and their burning zeal against the aggressiveness of the slave-holding South.

The art of these verses has no resemblance to the art of Keats, and their gospel of reform is not a glorious song of consolation; but their rapid fire of wit and common sense was perhaps a better expression of Lowell's temperament than any of his more studied measures. Certainly no poems have ever more distinctly revealed the New England temper. When collected they were imbedded in a paraphernalia of apparatus in which the wit is often laboured, and some of them are no more than clever journalism; but the best have become a lasting part of our popular literature. If this is due in part to their vernacular homeliness, and in part to their wit, it is also due to the moral fire of their democracy. As Horace Scudder insisted, there is a connection between them and another popular success of a different kind, *The Vision of Sir Launfal*. There "it is the holy zeal which attacks slavery issuing in this fable of a beautiful charity."[1]

In 1850 Lowell wrote to Briggs:

I begin to feel that I must enter a new year of apprenticeship. My poems have thus far had a regular and natural sequence. First, Love and the mere happiness of existence beginning to be conscious of itself, then Freedom—both being the sides which Beauty presented to me—and now I am going to try more after Beauty herself. Next, if I live, I shall present Life as I have seen it.

But, as often, Life proved a jealous mistress who would not yield the field to Beauty. Change and bereavement followed, and his professorship and editorship gave little incentive for verse. The moral exaltation which had seemed the promise of America found itself involved with all the turmoil of emotions that accompany terrific war. For these, Hosea's dialect was scarcely an adequate vehicle of expression, and the second series of *Biglow Papers*, if not inferior in skill, somehow lacks the entire sufficiency of the first; even when, as in the tenth paper, both the pathos and valour of the great conflict sound through the verse. The passions that the war aroused were

[1] Scudder. *Life*. Vol. L p. 268.

too overpowering for poetry except the brief expression of dominant feeling, as in the fine stanza written in October, 1861.

> God, give us peace! not such as lulls to sleep,
> But sword on thigh, and brow with purpose knit!
> And let our Ship of State to harbor sweep,
> Her ports all up, her battle-lanterns lit,
> And her leashed thunders gathering for their leap!

In the poems written in the decade after the war there is a greater depth of thought and a maturity of feeling. The cause which he served broadened into the issue of the life of a national democracy; and he was called upon to sing its victories and the sacrifice by which they were won. The odes are so noble in sentiment and so splendid in parts that one cannot forbear to regret that they do not bring an even more perfect beauty to their great theme. The far-fetched figure, the halting measure, the forced rhythm occasionally intrude on verse where the feeling demands all the majesty of poetic mastery. And yet, national anniversaries have rarely if ever aroused such pæans as these in which New England mourns her slain but passes on her heritage to the larger nation. Eloquence rises again and again to passionate melody, yet the feeling never loses the restraining guide of thought. Lowell never attains greater mastery than in the thoughtful analysis and noble beauty of the stanzas on Lincoln in the *Commemoration Ode*.

The war and its aftermath left Lowell's poetic faculty somewhat spent. Now and then a theme would arouse his imagination to its earlier spontaneity. Chartres revisited summoned back the recollections of its first impressions and stirred him to search again the mysteries and confusions of faith. The death of Agassiz recalled the Cambridge of old and its brave spirits. But the visits of the Muse grew rarer, and Lowell came to find his most characteristic expression in the prose essay. As the close of the war relieved him from the pressing necessity of political writing, he naturally returned to literature.

Mrs. Browning, in one of her letters to her husband, complains of the *Conversations on Some of the Old Poets*, which she has just been reading, that Lowell is saying over again the same things that every one knows. There is, no doubt, a certain truth in the charge, even when applied to his maturer essays. Lowell introduces no new principle or methods into literary criticism and he makes no search after novelties. In these respects and in the part that his essays have played in changing the direction of literary criticism, they may be regarded as less important than those which Matthew Arnold was writing during the same decade. But this is mainly due to the fact that Arnold's literary criticism was a part of a definite propaganda. When he gave up poetry and turned to prose, it was with the pronounced intention of getting at the British public, of entering on controversy, of preaching a new gospel, that of Culture, which was to have its main ally in criticism. Lowell's increasing use of prose was made from no such incentive. The great cause to which he had been devoted had been won. It was in part as a relief from controversy and propaganda that he turned from political subjects to the leisurely appreciation of his favourite authors. The essays have no reforms to propose. They are the summing up of many hours spent in his library and his class-room.

The influence of the college makes itself felt in various ways. Agassiz in science and Child in letters were among Lowell's colleagues, and his years as a professor had given him both an opportunity for wide reading and an acquaintance with the sterner exactions of scholarship. In some cases, as in the careful review of Richard Grant White's edition of Shakespeare, the criticism is precise and textual. In all cases the reflections about the great masters formed through years of intimacy have undergone the seasoning discipline of a broad and adequate scholarship. Lowell did not write on a subject unless he knew a good deal about it, nor did he fail to avail himself of the best that scholarship had accumulated; and such habits have not been matters of course among literary critics. Not only Lowell's thoroughness and accuracy, but his very freedom from the bias of propaganda and from the desire for novelty give his criticism an enduring sanity, a sanity which is happily united with a rich and discriminating sympathy.

Lowell's essays indeed may be warmly defended from any charge of ineffectuality. If he did not proclaim a definite evangel, yet scarcely less potently than Arnold he preached the gospel of culture. To a nation torn by war and largely engaged in the indispensable work of economic reconstruction, he taught by both precept and example the value of criticism. In the renewed task of making a nation, he turned confidently to literature as the record of human activity that contains most that is vital for the spirit. The cause of culture, indeed, called for a different service in the two countries. For Arnold in England, literature was to be given a renewed allegiance in the face of industrialism and science, and literature itself was to be directed away from the dangers of romanticism into a wiser and better poised criticism of conduct. For Lowell in the United States, the nation was to be reminded of the value for it of the great traditions of the old world and the need of linking both conduct and letters to the best that the past could offer.

One example may further suggest the different tasks of literary criticism in the two countries. It was unnecessary for Arnold to preach the value of medieval art. The Middle Ages were still very much present in England, and they had been summoned for various purposes by Scott, Carlyle, Tennyson, Ruskin, and Morris. In the United States, the Middle Ages are as remote as Persia or Egypt, and their significance for us discernible mainly through literature. Lowell took occasion later to defend his land against the implication in Ruskin's remark that he could not live in a country that had neither castles nor cathedrals. But for "our past well-nigh desolate of æsthetic stimulus" his essays were supplying the past of Milton and Spenser, of Chaucer and Dante. The essays on the two medieval poets are among his best and have done their part in stimulating among thoughtful Americans a study and appreciation of the great centuries of human progress that preceded Columbus's discovery.

The personal essay as a literary form seems to require maturity of mind, breadth of experience and reading, a responsive humour, and intensity and discrimination in taste. These qualities Lowell brought to his essay writing, whether the subject be drawn from nature or society or the world of books. Nowhere else, unless in his letters, is his personality more fully and charmingly revealed. The essays are full of good things. Allusion and quotation, epigram and description, whimsical epithet and graphic phrase crowd one another along the page, but all move in the train of Wit and Wisdom, our constant companions along the way.

The glimpses of New England village life that one receives in the essays will appeal to some readers with a charm like that of personality. The village has often been celebrated in literature from Sweet Auburn to Spoon River, but full justice has scarcely been done to the individuality and distinction of the New England village of the mid-nineteenth century. Cambridge was one of the best representatives of the type, but there were many of them. Each was likely to have a college, or at least an academy, one orthodox and one Unitarian church, a few pleasant colonial houses, and many elms. Everyone who lived in the village had been born there, was proud of that accident, loved whatever natural beauty its trees and meadows afforded, and enjoyed a conscious satisfaction that it was not like other places. Among the residents there might be a great personage, or even a poet, and there were certain to be enough teachers, ministers, doctors, judges, and writers to make up a coterie where ideas circulated. During the long winters, in fact, every one did considerable reading and thinking.

It was for the cultivated men and women of these villages that Lowell wrote. They of all persons delighted in his essay *On a Certain Condescension in Foreigners*, with its urbane reproof of criticism of our lack of urbanity; for the village cherished some dignity of manners and would accept a pre-destined hell easier than condescension from anybody. The old villages have faded, but their June gardens and winter nights, their serious talk and eager reading, their self-reliance, mitigated by a sense of humour, live again in Lowell's prose.

Wit becomes less exuberant and sagacity is the leading spirit in Lowell's later writing. Village society is disappearing, Cambridge is becoming a large city and Harvard a university, and Lowell is in Europe. Both as a poet and an essayist, he had appeared in part as a mediator or ambassador between the culture of the old world and the new, between the ideals of England and of the United States. In continuing this function as a foreign minister, he did not escape some censure that he v losing his faith in American democracy. To the reader of his later addresses, that criticism must seem groundless. To be sure, his long residence abroad increased his liking for England and Englishmen; and the course of American politics was a rather dismal sequel to the *Gettysburg Address* and the *Commemoration Ode.* After vanquishing slavery, the nation found itself facing still more dangerous evils, and was somewhat loth to gird its loins for the struggle. Lowell had greeted the dawn that was brightening the New England of his youth, and had seen the noonday of heroic effort in the Civil War. Now, as his own days were lengthening, he could be excused if he saw only a dubious twilight in the America of the eighties.

As a matter of fact there is little doubt and no indifference in these later writings. The maturing years had widened Lowell's perspective without vanquishing the idealism of his youth. He could look back on the course of the industrial revolution which had transformed his New England as well as older lands; and he could foresee the impending revolution that science had already begun in men's standards and processes. The effect of these movements on his own thought are manifest in his poetry and essays mainly by implication and suggestion; but in the utterances of the last decade of his life he often looks upon both his own career and the American purpose directly from this more modern point of view.

In his address at Manchester, in 1884, on Democracy, he declared:

> By temperament and education of a conservative turn, I saw the last years of that quaint Arcadia which French travellers saw with delighted amazement a century ago, and have watched the change (to me a sad one) from an agricultural to a proletary population.

Nevertheless, though opposing the single tax and State Socialism, he could see with hopefulness the portents in the air and even believe that democracy was to be the fulcrum for a Socialism possessing "the secret of an orderly and benign construction. He is willing to rebuild his house and believes that uilded better. The forward call is to be found in es as well as in the ardent verse of youth, the call of image of something better and nobler and more we are."

earnestness, this desire for perfection, this zeal

to reform a changing but evil world, characterizes English literature of the years 1830–1880, and American literature of the same epoch. Literature in those years has preached many creeds and many reforms, and it has lost something in simplicity and certainty because it has been so much in earnest. So Lowell's writing loses in certainty of art and unity of effect from its very responsiveness to the shifting opportunities for usefulness. But its contribution to civilization is not lessened, for it has done its best to teach a new people to guide their steps by the great men and great ideas of the past.

In the address on Democracy, Lowell held forth as arguments in favour of our national institutions two of their products, Lincoln and Emerson. We surely need not despair of our democracy so long as it can produce men of letters like Lowell and utilize them in the service of the common weal.

Book III

CHAPTER I

Whitman

WALT WHITMAN once declared his *Leaves of Grass* to be "the most personal of all books ever published."

> This is no book;
> Who touches this, touches a man.

Thus he fits Hazlitt's description of Montaigne as one who dared to set down as a writer what he thought as a man. This being the claim of the volume, it becomes highly important to determine the character of the author. Evidently Whitman was not, in any conventional sense of the term, that "average man" whose praises he sang, else even his novel form of expression would hardly have sufficed to keep his poetry so long a time from the masses. He was a man and a writer who could be hated as an impostor or adored as a Messiah but who was in any case a challenge to discussion. Much light is thrown on his character, of course, by the autobiographical parts of his writings; but here it is frequently difficult to determine which incidents belong to his outward and which to his inner, or imaginative, life, so deftly do his vicarious mystical experiences blend with the sublimations of his own deeds, and so carefully have many of those deeds been mystified or concealed. [1]

[1] For instance, a poem, *Once I Pass'd Through a Populous City*, taken by many biographers to support the theory that Whitman had a romance with a lady of high social standing during his 1848 visit to New Orleans, proves to have been addressed, in the original draft of the poem, not to a lady but to a "rude and ignorant man":

Much remains for painstaking research to accomplish. This chapter attempts to set forth only the facts of his biography which are well established or establishable.

Born in the same year as Lowell, Whitman may be said to represent the roots and trunk of democracy, while Lowell may be likened to its flowers or fruits. Whitman, for his part, could hardly have been, or wished to be, a flower; it was not in his ancestry, his education, or his environment. Blending in his own nature the courage, the determination, and the uncompromising Puritan idealism of good, if somewhat decadent, English ancestry with the placid slowness,[1] self-esteem, stubbornness, and mysticism of better Dutch (and Quaker) ancestry, Walt[2] Whitman was born 31 May, 1819, at the hamlet of West Hills, a few miles south of Huntington, Long Island. His father, Walter Whitman, was a farmer and later a somewhat nomadic carpenter and moderately successful housebuilder, who, although, like the poet's excellent mother, he had even less education than their nine children were destined to have, was something of a free thinker. The Whitmans moved to Brooklyn about 1823–25,[3] but Walt, until he went to live in Washington during the Civil War, continued to be more or less under the wholesome influence of the country. Throughout childhood, youth, and earlier manhood he returned to spend summers, falls, or even whole years at various parts of the Island, either as a healthy roamer enjoying all he saw, or as a school-teacher, or as the editor of a country paper, or as a poet reading Dante in an old wood and Shakespeare, Æschylus, and Homer within sound of the lonely sea, and mewing his strength for the bold flights of his

---

on the other hand, the poem *Out of the Rolling Ocean, the Crowd*, to which no biographer has attached particular personal significance, can be shown to have been addressed, about 1864, to a married woman with whom Whitman was in love and with whom he maintained for a time a correspondence notwithstanding the jealous objections of her husband.

[1] This description does not allow for a high temper, displayed on occasion, which Whitman seems to have inherited from his father.

[2] Shortened from Walter to distinguish the son from his father, but not used in connection with his published writings until 1855.

[3] The exact date is uncertain. Whitman gives 1822–3 once, 1823 twice, 1824 twice, and 1825 once; the earliest record in the directory of the city (Spooner) is 1825. At any rate Whitman was probably accurate in his statement that he was "still in frocks."

fancy. Perhaps it was a certain disadvantage that while he was thus "absorbing" and learning to champion the common people, the "powerful uneducated persons," among whom he moved on equal terms though not as an equal, he was little thrown, in any influential way, among people of refinement or taste. In his old age nobility and common humanity jostled each other in his hospitable little parlour—or kitchen; but during his youth the breadth of his view and the democracy of his sympathy were somewhat limited, not so much in theory as in fact, by the conditions that surrounded him. At the same time his native "egotism," as he frankly calls what Emerson would probably have softened to "self-reliance" had it been a trifle less arrogant, was being abnormally developed, even for a genius, by conditions little fitted to correct it. Nevertheless, he thus early learned lessons from nature and from human nature which were as indispensable to the inspiring and shaping of his liberating art and his democratic philosophy as was his outdoor life in developing his remarkably sensitive and healthy physical constitution.

Whitman's youth in Brooklyn, though full of interest, was uneventful. As a child of six he was flattered by Lafayette's chancing to lay his hands on him during a visit to the city in 1825. He attended the public school for a few years, impressing his teacher, Benjamin Buel Halleck, only with his good nature, his clumsiness, and his poverty of special promise. He ran with the boys of the street and was familiar with the city and its environs, especially with Fulton Ferry, whose slip was not far from his home. Not Irving, not Charles Lamb was more intimately or passionately fond of city life, with its opportunities for human contact and for varied sights, than was Whitman, both as boy and man. When about eleven years old he left school to become an office-boy, first to a lawyer and then to a doctor, the former of whom kindly afforded him opportunities for reading such books as the *Arabian Nights* and the poetry and romances of Scott. At twelve he was learning to set type, in a building once used as Washington's headquarters, under the instruction of a veteran printer who had many tales to tell of Revolutionary heroism. Next he went to set type for a few dollars a week on Aldin Spooner's *Star*. He had already felt the satisfaction of authorship when "sentimental bits" had appeared from his pen in the newspapers. Later he became a compositor on unknown journals in New York.

In May, 1836, Whitman went down to his father's farm at Hempstead, and then began a wandering career as a well-liked but not altogether successful country school-teacher. He taught somewhat after the fashion of the transcendentalists, substituting moral suasion for the ferule, and "boarding round" in at least seven different districts in Queens and Suffolk counties, but seldom remaining more than a few months at any one school. His mind was but half on his work, and after two years of teaching he sought (June, 1838), a more congenial occupation in starting a village newspaper, *The Long Islander*, at Huntington. On this he did all the work, even to delivering the papers on horseback; but he did it so irregularly that in less than a year his financial backers entrusted the little sheet to more punctual hands. Again teaching had to be resorted to. When living at Jamaica (1839–41) Whitman spent some of his time, apparently after school hours, in learning the printing business in the office of James J. Brenton's *Long Island Democrat*, to the pages of which he contributed a considerable number of sketches and essays replete with juvenile philosophy, as well as a number of patriotic and sentimental poems in conventional measures. The poet's tendency to dream—to loaf and invite his soul—to the neglect of more earthly duties, a tendency that was to become a tradition wherever he thereafter worked, had already marked him as an unusual person. He was even then dreaming of composing a ponderous and prophetic book to teach men, among other things, the danger of riches. The Quaker's attitude toward truth and the mystic's attitude toward nature were already discernible in his writings. But his life was unhappy, full of irresolution and unrest, and frequently given to a morbid brooding on death, while his enormous capacity for sentimental friendship, equalled only by his capacity for taking delight in external nature, had already taught him to sing of unreturned affection, and drove him, no doubt, to take refuge, like Narcissus, in self-admiration. Yet he took part in the sports and merry-makings of the village and was interested in the political campaigns of the day, himself attaining some prominence as a stump speaker in Queens County and even in New York City.

Then, in the summer of 1841, he definitely and finally threw in his lot with the city, and the second important period of his development began. Heretofore the highly sensitive youth had been almost ladylike in his sentiments, often morbid in his contrary moods, but puritanically strict in word and deed. At twenty-two his passionate nature demanded a sort of reaction. He "sounded all experiences of life, with all their passions, pleasures, and abandonments,"[1] and became, in another sphere of indulgence, something of a dandy. He was developing his personality meanwhile, and he was learning to write.

Whitman's early pieces written in New York reflect the wave of sentimentality which was, in the forties, sweeping over the country, and display, along with their humanitarian feeling, a fondness for melodramatic extravagance which caused him later to wish them all "quietly dropp'd in oblivion." He was a reformer pleading for the abolition of intemperance (including the use of tobacco, tea, and coffee), of capital punishment, and of slavery; and urging, as the constructive side of his reform, the need of a native American drama, opera, and literature. His interest in the theatre and the opera was a vital one, the constant satisfaction of which was made possible by his having a pressman's pass. Here he received many hints for his declamatory and rhythmical style of verse. Altogether more than a score of tales, sketches, essays, and poems have been found which belong to this period. To these must be added a crude and hasty dime novelette, *Franklin Evans*,[2] addressed, in the cause of temperance, not to the "critics" but to "THE PEOPLE," and evidently written to order. In this period Whitman was connected with some of the best city magazines and newspapers as contributor, compositor, or editor. The most important position that he held was that of editor of *The Daily*

---

[1] John Burroughs, in *Notes on Walt Whitman as Poet and Person*, 1867, p. 81. The substance, if not the phrasing, of this indefinite though suggestive passage was supplied by Whitman himself.

[2] This was republished, in compressed form, under the caption *Fortunes of a Country Boy*, by J. R. S. in *The Brooklyn Eagle* (November, 1846) as an "original novel." *Death in the School Room, The Child's Champion, Little Jane, The Death of Wind-Foot*, and a few poems were similarly twice published by Whitman, in the lax fashion of the day. See Bibliography.

[and *Weekly*] *Brooklyn Eagle*, a connection which extended from February, 1846, to January, 1848, when a "row with the boss," on account of Whitman's unreliability, and with "the party," on account of his progressive Barnburner politics, made it necessary for him to shift for a new position. This was readily found on *The Daily Crescent*, a paper about to be launched in New Orleans.

The trip which, with his favourite brother Jeff, Whitman made in the spring of 1848 by rail, stage, and Mississippi steamboat to New Orleans, his residence in that city for three months, and his return by way of the Mississippi and the Great Lakes[1] were rather less important than has commonly been supposed. It is doubtful whether the experience brought into his life a great but secret romance,[2] and it appears certain that he was not by it first made conscious of his mission as a poetic prophet. But the journey did give him a new and permanent respect for the undeveloped possibilities of his country, especially in the South and West, and it gave him opportunities for the study of the French and Spanish elements in New Orleans; while his observation of the South's "peculiar institution" caused him to remain, though a radical Free-Soiler, one careful not to be classed with the Abolitionists. But if this journey was of only measurable importance, perhaps others were of greater; for, though details are almost entirely unknown, it is practically certain that he made still other visits to the South.[3]

Notwithstanding the attractiveness that the new atmosphere had for all that was Southern in Whitman's temperament, he soon haughtily resigned his position, because of a

---

[1] Whitman's fullest and best account of the trip south was printed in the early numbers of the *Crescent*. This was not preserved in his collected prose editions, but a considerable portion of it was reprinted in *The Yale Review*, September, 1915.

[2] Whitman never married. In old age he confided to John Addington Symonds the information that, though unmarried, he had had six children, from intimate relations with whom he had been prevented by circumstances "connected with their fortune and benefit." For a fuller discussion of this confession and the questions arising out of it than is here possible the reader is referred to the biographies by Binns, Perry, Edward Carpenter, Bazalgette, De Sélincourt, and Traubel.

[3] Several lines of evidence point to this conclusion. Here it will be sufficient to refer to Whitman's autobiographical note published in *The Critic*, 28 February, 1885, over the pseudonym "George Selwyn." See Bibliography.

difference with his employers, and left for home 27 May. Almost immediately after his arrival he was engaged by Judge Samuel E. Johnson to edit (and nominally to own) a new Free-Soil paper, the weekly[1] *Brooklyn Freeman*, as the organ of those Democrats with whom Whitman, but not the party leaders behind the *Eagle*, had sympathized the year before. The new paper appeared 9 September, but it had the hard fortune to be burnt out, with no insurance, in a great conflagration that swept the city that very night. But the *Freeman* was revived in November, and, though a small and apparently a very outspoken sheet, it attained a large circulation. The nature of the political warfare in those days of personal invective may be suggested by Whitman's valedictory, published when, without explanation, he resigned the paper, 11 September, 1849, into the hands of those who would compromise, as he would not, with his political opponents:

To those who have been my friends, I take occasion to proffer the warmest thanks of a grateful heart. My enemies—and old hunkers generally—I disdain and defy the same as ever.

Of the next six years of Whitman's life comparatively little is known. He is said to have been connected with certain newspapers,[2] to have run a book-store and printing establishment, and to have assisted his aging father, now suffering from paralysis, in building small houses for sale. He had here an opportunity for money-making which, to the disappointment of the family, he allowed to pass unimproved. What is more important, he was growing rapidly in his inner life, as he attended lectures, read miscellaneous magazine articles, Shakespeare, Epictetus, the Hebrew and the Hindoo bibles, and Emerson, and loafed on the shores of Coney Island, timing the new poetry he was composing to the rhythmic beat of the sea. Somewhere in this period probably belongs the mystical experience, described in the poem *Song of Myself*, Section 5,

[1] Changed to a daily in April, 1849.

[2] An article in the Springfield *Republican*, 28 March, 1892, states that Whitman helped to edit Levi D. Slamm's *Plebeian;* and a letter from Whitman's friend, T. H. Rome, the first printer of the *Leaves of Grass*, to Wm. E. Benjamin (September, 1898) mentions the fact that after his return from New Orleans Whitman conducted for a short time an advertising sheet called *The Salesman*. See also Hearne's city directory for 1851 and 1852.

which clarified his vision "of the world as love" and fused his
purposes in life, and which some biographers, attaching to it
more significance than did Whitman himself and forgetting
that he had other such experiences, are inclined to consider the
most important fact in his biography.   At any rate, the book of
which he had dreamed since adolescence and of which he had
as early as 1847[1] written many passages was now, in 1854–5,
written and rewritten, and printed in Brooklyn, without a
publisher, in July, 1855.

The purpose of the author in writing this unique volume
may be stated in his own comprehensive words, written in 1876:

I dwelt on Birth and Life, clothing my ideas in pictures, days,
transactions of my time, to give them positive place, identity—
saturating them with the vehemence of pride and audacity of freedom necessary to loosen the mind of still-to-be-form'd America from
the folds, the superstitions, and all the long, tenacious and stifling
anti-democratic authorities of Asiatic and European past—my enclosing purport being to express, above all artificial regulation and
aid, the eternal Bodily Character of One's-Self.

The plan for his poetic life-work was to have been completed,
he tells us in the Preface to the 1876 edition, by composing

a further, equally needed volume, based on those convictions of
perpetuity and conservation which, enveloping all precedents,
make the unseen soul govern absolutely at last.

The perfecting of this latter work, dealing with the soul and
immortality, had proved beyond his powers and failing health,
but a fair idea of what it meant to set forth is to be found, no
doubt, in *The Two Rivulets* (1876).

If Emerson's *American Scholar* address was the intellectual declaration of American independence, this first
edition of *Leaves of Grass*, though only a thin imperial
octavo of ninety-five pages with a hastily written but
vigorous and far-sighted explanatory preface, was the first
gun in a major campaign of the war that was to win that

---

[1] A Whitman manuscript notebook in the possession of Thomas B.
Harned, one of the poet's friends and literary executors, preserves these earliest
known specimens of modern free verse.   They are shortly to be published by the
present writer.

independence. Of the form taken by so audacious a message space is wanting for accurate description. It may be said, however, that, denying to itself rhyme, regular metre, stanza forms, literary allusions, and "stock 'poetical' touches" in general, it frequently achieved, nevertheless, a deep and satisfying rhythm of its own—sometimes pregnant gnomic utterances, sometimes a chant or recitative, occasionally a burst of pure lyricism. Just where, if anywhere, Whitman found the hint for this flexible prose-poetic form critics have not agreed. Perhaps Biblical prosody, *Ossian*, the blank verse of Shakespeare and Bryant, the writings of Blake, the prose of Carlyle and Emerson, and his own impassioned declamation all assisted; but full allowance must be made for the unquestioned originality of his own genius, working slowly but courageously for the fuller liberation of song.[1]

The book, expecting opposition, was met by almost complete disregard. Except for a few copies which found their way to England and were later to secure for Whitman ardent disciples and his first English editor, William Michael Rossetti, there was practically no sale. Most of the reviews in the periodicals that noticed the book at all were as scandalized as had been anticipated; but a highly congratulatory letter from Emerson, who evidently recognized in Whitman the disciple he then professed to be, compensated for all neglect or abuse from other quarters, and a sentence from it was put to good, if indelicate, use as advertising on the back of the second edition (1856), a volume much larger than the first and more open to criticism because of its attempt to combat prudery in America by a naturalistic but fragmentary treatment of the facts of sex. Of this patent and confessed indebtedness to

[1] In one of the anonymous reviews which Whitman saw fit to write, in 1855, of his own first edition, he disclaims any model: "The style of these poems, therefore, is simply their own style, just born and red. Nature may have given the hint to the author of 'Leaves of Grass,' but there exists no book or fragment of a book which can have given the hint to them." *In Re Walt Whitman*, p. 16.

The first poem known to have been published in this measure was *Blood-Money*, which appeared in Horace Greeley's *Tribune* (Supplement), 22 March, 1850. But *Isle of La Belle Rivière*, published in the Cincinnati *Post*, 30 April, 1892, was written, in what is now called imagist verse, at the age of thirty (1849–50), while *New Year's Day, 1848*, written in an album just before Whitman's departure for New Orleans, shows a tendency to break away from conventional forms. By far more important are the Harned manuscript notebook specimens already mentioned.

Emerson, who had brought the simmering pot of Whitman's literary and patriotic ambition to a boil, Whitman had no cause to feel ashamed; for though lacking Emerson's sanity and mature idealism, he had a greater sympathetic, active, and emotional equipment than had the Concord sage. If Whitman was, as he said, "a child, very old," Emerson was a man, very young. It was almost as if the older champion of individuality had meditated the philosophy by which the younger was to live; but whereas the Emersonian gospel, addressing itself to the idealism of its readers, "breeds the giant which destroys itself," Whitmanism, appealing strongly to the religious sentiment, has already had the ironical fate of developing something not unlike a cult, both at home and in other countries.

Of course such a book failed to bring in royalties, and Whitman again fell back on the drudgery of editing a newspaper, in this instance the bantling *Daily Times* (Brooklyn). Just when this editorship began (1856 or 1857) is not easily determined, but it ended probably in the early part of 1859, after the editor had repeatedly rebuked certain church officials for the, as he thought, unfair treatment they had accorded to one Judge Culver, then the defendant in an ecclesiastical trial. At odd times Whitman wrote the new poems, including that incomparable lyric, *Out of the Cradle Endlessly Rocking*, which appeared now and then in the pages of the Bohemian *Saturday Press*, and the many others which were to be included in the 1860 edition of the *Leaves*. The country was full of lecturers in 1858, and Whitman planned to become one, both to support himself and to supplement the *Leaves*, which could hardly as yet have been called a success. But though he disciplined himself in a style of oratory only less novel than that of his poetry, writing "barrels of lectures" on religion, democracy, language, æsthetics, and politics, and though the desire thus to present his message in a more personal fashion than any sort of authorship, even his own, could afford, persisted throughout life, only a few memorial addresses—such as the tribute to Lincoln—and a few public readings of his own poems written for college commencements or other special occasions ever came of it.

Meanwhile Whitman was widening the circle of his acquaintance. Emerson not only called on him frequently when in the city but sent Alcott, Moncure Conway, and Thoreau to do likewise. Lord Houghton also came, and Bryant crossed the river to share with him long walks into the country. These were the days of Whitman's Bohemianism. A negligent, open-throated attire and great soft hat that one might associate with a carpenter or a sailor he insisted on wearing, Richter-like, wherever he went. In the earlier years of his journalism he had worn a high hat, cane, and boutonnière; now the dandy had given place to a man dressed in a habit more in keeping with his new rôle as the national bard of democracy *en masse*. The affectations in his dress were, however, of less importance than the inner character of the man. And that character was one of great human sympathy and magnetism, possessing a charm which those who felt it most were least able to explain. He spent, as from childhood he had done, much time among the people—boatmen, pilots, omnibus drivers, mechanics, fishermen —going anywhere to "feed his hunger for faces." He visited prisons, attended the sick in hospitals, drove all one winter the stage of a disabled driver, and mingled as a meditative observer among the liberal-minded and light-hearted Bohemians at Pfaff's restaurant. In 1860 he went to Boston and published, through Thayer and Eldridge, his third edition, full of the echoes of this life, in which he had not always been a mere observer. Until the war drove its publishers to the wall, the book had a fair sale. The poems of two new groups— *Enfans d'Adam*, celebrating the love, usually physiological, between the sexes, and *Calamus*, celebrating that "adhesiveness" or "manly attachment" which Whitman then considered the true cement of a democracy—have in the past provoked much severe criticism and indignant defence, and the former were the occasion, at various times, of a threatened official prosecution, of a temporary exclusion of the book from the mails, and of the author's being dismissed from a government clerkship. Emerson had urged Whitman to be more tactful and worldly-wise, but the latter's inner conviction that he was right and his stubborn determination to go ahead in the chosen course blinded him to the value of tact and condemned him to suffer from a reputation that he did not really deserve. Whatever may be the true interpretation of these poems, one finds it difficult to understand either the character or the writings of Whitman unless one's eye is kept on the chronology of his publications, a feat which his method of grouping has rendered rather difficult; for he was a growth, as his poems were, in which a heroic and loving soul gradually freed itself from the passions of a very human and earthly body. His reaction from the asceticism of his adolescence was strong, tumultuous, almost tragic, but it was only a reaction; and when the war had passed over him with its purification and its pain, and when he had suffered severely in his personal affections, he sang more and more of the soul.

Whitman's optimistic faith in democracy was put to the severest possible test by the outbreak of the Civil War. But he did not come into personal touch with its heroic and pathetic sides until, in December, 1862, he went down to the front at Fredericksburg to look after his younger brother, an officer in a volunteer regiment, who had received a slight wound in battle. Shortly after the outbreak of hostilities Whitman had begun writing (June, 1861) for the weekly *Brooklyn Standard* a serial history of the city, entitled *Brooklyniana*, based on his own reminiscences, his conversations with older citizens, and his rather desultory historical reading. He had likewise been composing a few of the vivid war poems in *Drum-Taps*. But as the war became more serious he suspended this writing and took a loitering trip through many of his old haunts on Long Island, fishing, sailing, meeting people in the unceremonious manner of the country, and doubtless pondering the gloomy problems of the war. The early Whitman, so inadequately reported in the biographies, was preparing to give place to the well-known serious and noble Whitman of the Washington hospitals; and this leisurely visit was, one chooses to think, a farewell to the light-hearted irresponsibility of his protracted youth. Returning to Brooklyn in the fall, he took up the *Brooklyniana* again and occupied himself with it almost until the accident to George Whitman called him to the Virginia battle-field.

Thence he casually drifted into the finest employment of his life, that of caring for sick and wounded soldiers on the field and, especially, in the many military hospitals in and about Washington. He lived frugally, supporting himself for a time by doing copying [1] and by contributing wonderfully vivid sketches of his

---

[1] It is probable that Whitman had been reduced to the necessity of doing copying before, for the Brooklyn city directory (Lain) for 1860 gives "Walt Whitman, copyist."

experiences to the Brooklyn *Eagle* and *Union* and the New York *Times*.[1] To supply the little comforts and necessities of the hundred thousand soldiers, Northern and Southern, to whom, as he estimated, he ministered courage and cheer, he privately raised several thousand dollars from friends and correspondents in the North. When he obtained a salaried position in 1865, a generous portion of his earnings went into the same fund. But chiefly he gave himself, in undisguised affection. The full tenderness, almost motherliness, of this large-hearted, self-sacrificing man can be fully understood only in the modest but realistic account of his daily activities preserved in the letters written to his mother at the time and in the hospital-notebook jottings printed in *Specimen Days*. It would be a questionable service to Whitman to affirm that these three years of slow martyrdom sanctified the whole of his life; but it is literally true that the deepest and best instincts in him never before had found such full and beautiful expression. Partly, at least, as a result of his hospital service his magnificent health was lost, and the last twenty years of his life were those of a paralytic cripple.

Whitman's poetic power was still at its height. *Drum-Taps*, —the poetic complement to *Specimen Days* and *The Wound-Dresser*,—a booklet charged with the pathos and the spirituality of the war, was published in 1865, with the profoundly moving dirge for the martyred Lincoln. In *Democratic Vistas* (1871) he made use of prose, though with unequal success.

This period was also important because of the friendships that it made or fostered. Perhaps the most important was that with William Douglas O'Connor. When, in 1865, Whitman had been employed for several months in the Interior Department under Secretary Harlan, the latter, on learning that he was the author of *Leaves of Grass*, had him summarily dismissed; then O'Connor came to his friend's defence in a brilliant and passionate, though ill-advised, polemic, *The Good Gray Poet*, the title of which gave the bard a fit and enduring sobriquet. The advertising value of such a polemic, or of such an incident, though it was rated highly by Whitman and by some of his friends, may now be questioned. Thanks to such

---

[1] Most of these letters were reprinted in *Specimen Days* or in *The Wound-Dresser*. See Bibliography.

staunch friends, however, Whitman was soon settled, for the eight following years, in a comfortable clerkship in the Attorney-General's Department. Another close friend and enthusiastic disciple then and later was John Burroughs, who published in 1867 the first biographical and critical study of the poet. An attachment more similar to those of the New York days was Whitman's singular friendship for Pete Doyle, an unschooled young Confederate soldier, now a street-car conductor, with whom, notwithstanding the disparity in their ages and interests, the poet spent much of his leisure time. To him Whitman wrote the letters which were, after his death, published by one of his literary executors under the appropriate title *Calamus*. But this comfortable and congenial life was destined to a sudden end. Just when Whitman was beginning to make literary friends abroad—Rudolf Schmidt in Denmark, Freiligrath in Germany, Madame Blanc in France, Edward Dowden in Ireland, and in England William Rossetti, Swinburne,[1] Robert Buchanan, Roden Noel, John Addington Symonds, Tennyson, and Anne Gilchrist—and when he was beginning to become somewhat favourably known abroad through Rossetti's expurgated selection, *Poems by Walt Whitman* (1868), and through fragmentary translations in Continental countries, an attack of paralysis (January, 1873) compelled him first to suspend and finally to give up his clerical work. Taking his savings, enough to tide him over the first few years of invalidism, he went to live with his brother, Colonel George Whitman, in Camden, New Jersey. A leisurely trip to Colorado in 1879, a longer one to Canada in the following year, and various briefer visits and lecture journeys—now to New York, now to visit his friend Burroughs at his home on the Hudson, now to his own Long Island birthplace, but oftenest to recuperate and to write charming nature descriptions at his retreat on Timber Creek—except for these furloughs Whitman was to spend the remainder of his days, and to be buried, in Camden. In March, 1884, he bought a little house (328 Mickle Street, now 330) with the proceeds from the very successful Philadelphia edition of the *Leaves* in 1882.

This period, the final act of Whitman's unique life, was natur-

[1] Swinburne, who had in *Songs before Sunrise* hailed Whitman as a new force in literature, considerably retracted his praise in later publications.

ally not a climax of achievement, though it was a severe test of his patience and optimism, a test which, on the whole, he stood with unassuming courage. He sent forth occasional contributions to various American and British magazines and newspapers, besides new editions of his works. The most notable of these latter was the autographed Centennial or Author's Edition in two volumes of prose and verse (1876), designed to be sold in England, his best market, in order to relieve the straitened circumstances of the author, who was then "paralyzed . . . poor . . . expecting death," and who had been fleeced by his New York publishers; *Specimen Days and Collect* (1882-3), a "diary of an invalid," which contains some of Whitman's most characteristic prose and is a storehouse of autobiographical data; and *November Boughs* (1888), containing reprints of short poems that Whitman had been writing regularly for the New York *Herald* and of miscellaneous prose essays that had appeared elsewhere, the most significant of these being *A Backward Glance O'er Travel'd Roads*.

New friends were made, as faithful as the old. One was Dr. Richard Maurice Bucke, of Canada, who, like Burroughs, hailed the *Leaves of Grass* as "the bible of democracy" and wrote (1883) the first comprehensive biography of its author, to set him forth as a mystical saviour of the modern world. Another was Thomas B. Harned, in whose hospitable home the poet met, during these later years, not a few American and foreign notables. A third was Horace Traubel, who until Whitman's death was his daily visitor, who, without pay, assisted him in his dealings with printers and publishers, and who has for some years been publishing a minute diary of his talks with the poet during 1888-92. These three friends became, by Whitman's will, his literary executors. Space is wanting to mention even the most prominent of that host of other visitors, American and foreign, who made Camden the object of their pilgrimages, some with a selfish desire to secure the poet's bold autograph, others with a reverent wish to pay homage to a liberator of the soul. One of the most sincere and unreserved of these tributes was that proffered by Mrs. Anne Gilchrist, the English author (then a widow), who through his poetry came to love the man [1] and who

---

[1] The love-letters of Anne Gilchrist and Walt Whitman are now being edited by Thomas B. Harned and will soon be published.

later with her children spent two years (1876–1878) in Philadelphia in order to be near him. Assistance of a substantial nature from abroad, due in part to the efforts of Mrs. Gilchrist, who had been the first woman to defend the *Children of Adam* poems in print, together with similar if somewhat later help from a growing number of friends and readers in America, lightened the burdens of Whitman's last years, affording him comforts that would otherwise have been denied him and giving him hope that the tide of disapproval and misunderstanding which he had been breasting for half a lifetime was beginning at last to turn. When a complication of maladies finally resulted in his death, 26 March, 1892, he had "positively appeared," a prophet and a poet not without honour even in his own country. He was buried, with unique but impressive ceremony, beside a number of near relatives, in a massive and costly tomb which he had built for the purpose the preceding year. Most of his property, valued at a few thousand dollars, was left for the support of an imbecile brother, to care for whom Whitman had for many years saved money from his own small income.

The influence of Whitman has in the past taken three directions. Those of his readers who, like himself, attach most significance to the revolutionary and the religious elements in his writings have naturally been somewhat indifferent as to whether a place could be found for Whitman among the recognized literary coteries. To them he has been a seer profound enough and a lover sincere enough to render ordinary literary criticism an impertinence—unless such criticism would content itself with mere exegesis. On the other hand a growing number of readers have seen in Whitman—quite aside from a personality which, for all its philosophical breadth and its friendly sweetness, was hampered by an occasionally repellent sentimental egotism and a marked deficiency in taste—a genuine artist and a true poet. All manner of liberal political, sociological, and religious movements have been fathered on Whitman the seer and prophet; while Whitman the poet has become the legitimate founder of the various forms of modern free verse. Criticism that confounds this twofold claim and this twofold appeal of Whitman's writings is destined to make little progress, as is also that criticism which considers the two methods of approach to be necessarily exclusive. Still a third class of readers, uninterested in poets or prophets, as such, have gone to Whitman for the refreshing presence of a man and a writer who was entirely himself and who loved nature and his fellow men.

CHAPTER II

Poets of the Civil War I

THE NORTH

WITH the opening of the Civil War the people of the loyal states were stirred to a more intense realization of the high responsibilities of citizenship in a republic. At once the country was confronted by the gigantic task of feeding and clothing the men in the field, of caring for the sick and wounded, of raising the crops, and keeping the shops and factories going. Such a radical readjustment of forces called out powers hitherto unsuspected either in the nation or in its individual citizens. The great present seemed to engulf the petty troubles and ill feelings, social and political, of the past, and the people of the North found themselves moved by a national spirit which knew few of the bounds of the old provincialism. Like the shot at Lexington almost a hundred years before, the guns at Sumter struck the note of a new era. The country marched to war with the gay step of youth; it came back solemnly, as if tried by fire. As it went, the bands played *Annie Laurie,* and the men sang the sentimental songs of adolescent America; they returned chanting

Mine eyes have seen the glory of the coming of the Lord.

Readers of poetry in the fifties had enjoyed the verse of Bryant[1] and Longfellow[2] and of others who modestly portrayed aspects of quiet nature, mildly moralized upon conduct, or willingly submitted to the spell of beauty. For not a few of the poets, poetry was something apart from the actuality of

[1] See also Book II, Chap. v.   [2] See also Book II, Chap. xii.

life, too often little more than commonplace sentiment inspired by earlier poets. It is interesting to find Longfellow writing in his diary in 1856:

> Dined with Agassiz to meet Emerson and others. I was amused and annoyed to see how soon the conversation drifted off into politics. It was not until after in the library that we got upon anything really interesting.

Longfellow, Taylor, Story, and Stoddard (in his early days) were practitioners of the poetic art rather than workers in the real material of human experience. There were other singers, however, who, though surrounded by much that was crude and raw, petty and vulgar, still had visions and felt pulses throbbing beneath the rude exterior of American life. Of such were Lowell, Whittier, Whitman, and various more ephemeral writers who felt the stirring times. To them it was not satisfying merely to dream of the past or yearn for the land of the Lotos Eaters. As if called to a great service, they saw a work to be done and prepared for its doing. Stedman at twenty-eight could write:

> I have cared nothing for politics—have been disgusted with American life and doings. Now for the first time I am proud of my country and my grand heroic brethren. The greatness of the crisis, the Homeric grandeur of the contest, surrounds and elevates us all. . . . Henceforth the sentimental and poetic will fuse with the intellectual to dignify and elevate the race.

Stedman[1] himself, brought up in an older school of lovers of beauty, turned to a more resonant lyre, and wrote such pieces as *How Old Brown Took Harper's Ferry*, *Kearny at Seven Pines*, *Wanted—A Man*, *Gettysburg*, and the stirring romance *Alice of Monmouth*—pieces full of metrical energy, strong, high spirit, and convinced devotion to the union. Stoddard,[2] writer of delicate "Melodies and Catches," rose to the grave, noble tones of his Horatian ode *Abraham Lincoln*, among the finest of all the poems commemorative of the chief personage of the War. Lowell[3] wrote a second series of *The Biglow Papers*,

---

[1] See also Book III, Chap. x.   [2] See *ibid.*
[3] See Book II, Chap. xxiv.

confirming his right to be called the great American satirist in verse; and Whittier,[1] already, like Lowell, no uncertain voice speaking against slavery, almost forgot his Quaker traditions in the eager strophes with which he encouraged the fighters for freedom and exulted over the victory of their aims. Whitman,[2] already the prophet, though as yet hardly heard, of a mystical union of his people, composed, during the struggle to destroy the Union of the states, battle-pieces that are without rancour, and, after that Union had been assured, splendid hymns of triumph that contain no insults to the conquered, vying with Lowell for the honour of producing the loftiest and best Northern poetry of the War.

The purpose of this chapter is to tell not of the major poets of the mid-century period, most of whom, in the intervals of full poetic careers traced elsewhere in this history, lent powerful voices to the cause of anti-slavery and union, but of some of the lesser figures whose best or most significant work deals almost wholly with the conflict. At least one of them has not received his due share of praise—Henry Howard Brownell (1820–1872), called by Holmes "Our Battle Laureate." Born at Providence, he went with his family to Hartford, where he graduated from Trinity College in 1841. After a short season of teaching in Mobile, he returned to Hartford, was admitted to the bar, and began the practice of his profession, while also joining his brother in literary work. His early devotion to the sea, stimulated by frequent voyages, inspired him to sing of its awe and its beauty. Like his brother, who lost his life in 1859 exploring South America, he had the spirit of an adventurer, but, though his little volume of *Poems* (1847) had contained some lines of verse ringing with denunciation of ease and lazy comfort at a time when such a question as slavery was pressing for answer, he had dealt, for the most part not originally or strikingly, only with the eternal themes of minor poets—love, disappointments, passing beauty, the hard fate of the poetical tribe—and did not really find expression for himself until the Civil War. For a Hartford paper he composed a rhymed version of Farragut's orders to his fleet before the attack upon New Orleans. The verses so pleased the Commodore that he wrote to Brownell in terms of hearty appreciation and afterwards made the poet

[1] See also Book II, Chap. XIII. [2] See also Book III, Chap. I.

his secretary. Brownell thus had an opportunity, in actual service, to become acquainted with the details of warfare. The best of his pieces, all included in *Lyrics of a Day* (1864) and *War-Lyrics* (1866), still deserve praise as strong as that pronounced by Lowell and Aldrich in Brownell's own generation. His power lay in combining vivid detail with lyric exultation, accurate pictures of still life with fiery episodes of heroic action. No other Northern poet reported real warfare so accurately. Some of Brownell's lines read like rhymed journalism, but he had everywhere such intensity of visualization, such fiery passion, and such natural, racy language dignified by sincerity that he rarely suffered any descent into prose, though he tended to *longeurs*. Energy and swift movement are not his only qualities. In the midst of *The Bay Fight* he does not forget the actual men engaged. He can pass from scenes of fighting to the calm, sad picture of Lincoln watching from on high the troops that have not returned for the Grand Review in Washington. Perhaps nothing in his verse seems more striking, in the twentieth century, than his terrific confidence in the cause of the Union and equally terrific condemnation of all Southern "traitors." His moral energy is as much the secret of his power as are his poetical vigour and veracity.

Less important than Brownell as a war poet was George Henry Boker,[1] a native of Pennsylvania, who, though primarily a dramatist, was from 1861 to 1871 the efficient secretary of the Union League of Philadelphia, and prominent in patriotic activities throughout the struggle. His *Poems of the War* appeared in 1864. It contained a few pieces, some of them still remembered, which adequately represent the faith and deep feeling of that time. Most interesting are the *Dirge for a Soldier, On Board the Cumberland, The Ballad of New Orleans, Upon the Hill before Centreville, The Black Regiment, The Battle of Lookout Mountain*. Boker's lyrics, however, lack the passionate truthfulness of Brownell's, and play too much with allegory and ancient mythology for the best effect. The *Dirge*, called forth by the death of General Kearny, is spontaneous and haunting. Bayard Taylor,[2] a friend of Boker, while ardently sympathetic toward the Union cause, and a speaker in its behalf in America and England, shows a slighter imprint of the conflict

[1] See also Book II, Chap. II.   [2] See also Book III, Chap. X.

in his verse. Even his *National Ode*, delivered on a great occasion in 1876, failed to rise to the dignity and power expected of it. It seems, for all its large weight of thought and knowledge, unimportant when compared with Lowell's *Commemoration Ode*. Still a third Pennsylvanian, Thomas Buchanan Read,[1] wrote, in *Sheridan's Ride*, one of the most rousing of all the martial ballads called forth by the war.

Herman Melville,[2] who said in the preface to his *Battle-Pieces and Aspects of the War* (1866) "I seem, in most of these verses, to have but placed a harp in a window, and noted the contrasted airs which wayward winds have played upon the strings," suffered in his verse as in his minor romances from a fatal formlessness, but he had moments of contagious enthusiasm. He celebrated some of the most striking incidents of the war in *The Victor of Antietam*, *The Cumberland*, *Running the Batteries*, *Sheridan at Cedar Creek*, *The Fall of Richmond*, and *The Surrender at Appomattox*. Most intimately associated with hostilities of all was Charles Graham Halpine,[3] better known as Miles O'Reilly, who entered the Union army and became a brigadier-general. Although his verse lacks metrical skill, it is vigorous and full of feeling, generally free of animosities, and in the tone of the soldier rather than of the bitter poet who stays at home.

To get a really vivid idea of the lyric expression of the time one should look less to individual writers or groups of writers than to the subjects which were most commonly their themes. The John Brown affair found many poets: Stedman in *How Old Brown Took Harper's Ferry*, Brownell in *The Battle of Charlestown*, fiercely ironic, Whittier in *Brown of Ossawatomie*, and, above all, the anonymous author (he may have been Charles Sprague Hall) of *John Brown's Body*, which, set to the air of an old Methodist hymn, became the most popular marching song of the Union armies, and survived innumerable parodies and rival versions—to be sung not only by American but by British troops in the present war. The secession of South Carolina called forth the earnest, affectionate *Brother Jonathan's Lament for Sister Caroline* by Oliver Wendell Holmes. Stedman and Brownell were but two of the many stirred to

---

[1] See also Book III, Chap. x.   [2] See also Book II, Chap. vii.
[3] See also Book II, Chap. xix.

verse by the attack on Sumter. The spirit of the volunteers
was celebrated in *A Call to True Men* by Robert Traill Spence
Lowell, *Who's Ready?* by Elizabeth Stuart Phelps, *The Heart
of the War* by J. G. Holland; Theodore Tilton published in
The Independent for 18 April, 1861, his clanging and exciting
tocsin *The Great Bell Roland;* even Bryant had a strange fire in
Our Country's Call:

> Lay down the axe; fling by the spade;
>   Leave in its track the toiling plough;
> The rifle and the bayonet-blade
>   For arms like yours were fitter now;
> And let the hands that ply the pen
>   Quit the light task, and learn to wield
> The horseman's crooked brand, and rein
>   The charger on the battle-field.

Thereafter the passion of events is recorded in the poems of
the war, North and South. Bayard Taylor's *Through Baltimore* cried out against the opposition offered by Southern
sympathizers to the passage through Baltimore streets of the
Sixth Massachusetts. A. J. H. Duganne, in his impetuous
Bethel, sang of the heroism but not the blunders of that battle,
the chief victim of which, Theodore Winthrop,[1] was the subject
of Thomas William Parsons's lofty *Dirge for One Who Fell in
Battle*. Bull Run, theme of many exultant Southern ballads and
satires,[2] brought from Boker the impassioned *Upon the Hill before Centreville*. In the controversy with England which followed
the seizure of Mason and Slidell, Lowell wrote his spirited and
determined *Jonathan to John*, second in the new series of *Biglow Papers*. During September, 1861, Mrs. Ethelinda (Ethel
Lynn) Beers wrote *The Picket-Guard* (attributed in the South
to Lamar Fontaine or Thaddeus Oliver), a widely popular piece
expressing sympathy with the minor and unnoted victims of
the conflict. Also popular was the anonymous *Tardy George*,
that is, General McClellan, of whom the North demanded more
activity than he ever attained. In the same cause, though without the mention of names, was *Wanted—A Man*, by Stedman,
who shortly after had to write another elegy, *Kearny at Seven
Pines*, upon the gallant officer commemorated by Boker in the

[1] See also Book III, Chap. XI.   [2] See also Book III, Chap. III.

Dirge for a Soldier. Thomas Dunn English's *The Charge by the Ford* and Melville's *Malvern Hill* deal with the later events of McClellan's first campaign. Lincoln's call for new troops gave rise to the sentimental but immensely effective *Three Hundred Thousand More* by James Sloan Gibbons and to Bret Harte's *The Reveille* (sometimes called *The Drum*), which is said to have played a large part in holding California loyal. The advance of Lee to Antietam, his repulse there, and his retreat found a record in Whittier's *Barbara Frietchie*, Melville's *The Victor of Antietam*, Boker's *The Crossing at Fredericksburg*, John Boyle O'Reilly's *At Fredericksburg*, and Aldrich's exquisite sonnets *Fredericksburg* and *By the Potomac*.

Meanwhile the war in the West was not without its poet-annalists, of whom the most notable perhaps was Forceythe Willson (1837–67), a native of New York who lived in Indiana from 1852 to 1864 and wrote Union editorials for the Louisville *Journal.* During the first year of the war he began his sombre, disheartened *In State*, a poem which spoke of the Union as dead and lying on its bier:

> The Sisterhood that was so sweet,
> The Starry System sphered complete,
> Which the mazed Orient used to greet,
> The Four and Thirty fallen Stars glimmer and glitter at her feet.

The next year he wrote *Boy Brittan* to commemorate a seventeen-year-old lieutenant killed in the attack on Fort Henry, and the year after published his masterpiece, *The Old Sergeant*, which Holmes thought "the finest thing since the war began,"—the death-scene of a nameless soldier wounded at Shiloh. Richer in melody than Brownell, Willson was like him in directness and realism; his output, however, was very slight. The struggle for the possession of Missouri was recorded in Stoddard's *The Little Drummer*, Henry Peterson's *The Death of Lyon*, and Boker's *Zagonyi*. During the Confederate attempt to recapture Corinth in October, 1862, the Eighth Wisconsin imaginatively carried, instead of a flag, a live eagle which circled over the battlefield and which gave Brownell his occasion for *The Eagle of Corinth*.

This same year on the sea the duel between the *Merrimac* and the *Cumberland* stirred the poets as did almost no other

episode of the entire war.   Thomas Buchanan Read wrote
The Attack; Longfellow, *The Cumberland;* Boker, *On Board
the Cumberland;* Melville, *The Cumberland;* Weir Mitchell,
How the Cumberland Went Down,—all of them poems which,
with a larger eloquence than then appeared, sounded the knell
of the wooden battleship.   As might have been expected, de-
feat had more poets than victory; Boker, however, wrote *The
Cruise of the Monitor*, and Lucy Larcom *The Sinking of the
Merrimac.*   For the capture of New Orleans there were Boker's
The Ballad of New Orleans and *The Varuna* (the name of a
Federal ship sunk during the action), while Brownell's *The River
Fight* was as triumphant as the attack.

> Do you know of the dreary land,
> If land such region may seem,
> Where 'tis neither sea nor strand,
> Ocean nor good dry land,
>   But the nightmare marsh of a dream—
> Where the Mighty River his death-road takes,
> 'Mid pools, and windings that coil like snakes,
> (A hundred leagues of bayous and lakes,)
>   To die in the great Gulf Stream?
>
>   .   .   .   .   .   .
>
> Would you hear of the River-Fight?
> It was two, of a soft spring night—
>   God's stars looked down on all,
> And all was clear and bright
> But the low fog's clinging breath—
> Up the River of Death
>   Sailed the Great Admiral.
>
> On our high poop-deck he stood,
>   And round him ranged the men
> Who have made their birthright good
>   Of manhood, once and agen—
> Lords of helm and of sail,
> Tried in tempest and gale,
>   Bronzed in battle and wreck—
> Bell and Bailey grandly led
> Each his Line of the Blue and Red—
> Wainwright stood by our starboard rail:
>   Thornton fought the deck.

And I mind me of more than they,
  Of the youthful, steadfast ones,
  That have shown them worthy sons
Of the Seamen passed away—
(Tyson conned our helm, that day,
  Watson stood by his guns.)

.   .   .   .   .   o

Lord of mercy and frown,
Ruling o'er sea and shore,
Send us such scene once more!
All in Line of Battle
Where the black ships bear down
On tyrant fort and town,
'Mid cannon cloud and rattle—
And the great guns once more
Thunder back the roar
Of the traitor walls ashore,
And the traitor flags come down!

It was in New England that Emancipation was most eagerly acclaimed. Emerson's *Boston Hymn*, written in honour of Lincoln's Proclamation, can hardly be matched for pungency and pregnancy of matter by any other American poem for an occasion. Whittier, who had already hailed Frémont's action in freeing the slaves or secessionists in Missouri in the poem *To John C. Frémont*, and the abolition of slavery in the District of Columbia in his hopeful *Astræa at the Capital*, hailed the actual Proclamation with passion, and, later, the passage of the constitutional amendment abolishing slavery with the rapt exultation of *Laus Deo*. Stedman's *Treason's Last Device* glowed with anger at a proposal made, as late as 1863, to bar New England from the Union because of an opposition to slavery that made that section very obnoxious to the South.

Boker in the spring of 1863 greeted the news of the Federal advance with his *Hooker's Across;* and Chancellorsville, which called forth so many Confederate poems [1] on the death of Stonewall Jackson, led George Parsons Lathrop to write his dashing ballad, *Keenan's Charge*. Perhaps it was again because poets

[1] See also Book III, Chap. III.

sing best in defeat that no Union poem on Gettysburg quite equals Will Henry Thompson's later *High Tide* (1888). Stedman, however, made a ringing ballad, *Gettysburg*, and Bret Harte preserved a real episode of the day in his *John Burns of Gettysburg*. Best of all, of course, was Lincoln's famous address at the battle-field on 19 November, 1863, which lacks nothing of poetry but its outer forms.

As Grant rose to fame the poets kept pace with his deeds: Melville with *Running the Batteries* and Boker with *Before Vicksburg* dealt with the struggle to open the Mississippi. Lookout Mountain was commemorated by Boker—*The Battle of Lookout Mountain*—and William Dean Howells—*The Battle in the Clouds*. Two poems this year honoured the negro soldiers that the Union army had begun to use. Boker's *The Black Regiment* concerns itself with the assault on Fort Hudson; Brownell's *Bury Them* is a stern and terrible poem on the slaughter of the Fifty-Fourth Massachusetts, with their Colonel, Robert Gould Shaw, at Fort Wagner, South Carolina. The Confederates buried Shaw in a pit under a heap of his men, and Brownell thought of them as dragon's teeth buried in "the sacred, strong Slave-Sod" only to rise—Southerners are supposed to be speaking—as sabres and bayonets:

> And our hearts wax strange and chill,
> With an ominous shudder and thrill,
>   Even here, on the strong Slave-Sod,
> Lest, haply, we be found
> (Ah, dread no brave hath drowned!)
>   Fighting against Great God.

In the fourth year of the war the note of triumph passed from the Southern to the Northern poets. S. H. M. Byers's *Sherman's March to the Sea* and Halpine's *The Song of Sherman's Army* are almost gay, and Henry Clay Work's *Marching Through Georgia* if not gay is nothing else. Holmes's *Sherman's in Savannah* rhymed the name of the fallen city with "banner." Strangely haunting is Whitman's *Ethiopia Saluting the Colors*. Also haunting, but sad, is Melville's *A Dirge for McPherson*——

> *True fame is his, for life is o'er*
> *Sarpedon of the mighty war*——

while his *Sheridan at Cedar Creek*, *The Fall of Richmond*, and *The Surrender at Appomattox*, though never widely known, are full of that distinction which Melville, with all his irregularities, was never long without, in prose or verse. Thomas Buchanan Read's famous *Sheridan's Ride* is a better ballad than Melville's piece on the same theme, but purely as poetry it is inferior. Henry Clay Work's *The Year of Jubilee*, supposed to be written by a slave full of delight in the coming freedom, is too amusing and racy to need to have its poetical merits estimated. Read's *The Eagle and the Vulture* and Weir Mitchell's *Kearsarge* echoed the doom of the *Alabama*. Farragut was so fortunate as to have two poets among his officers at Mobile Bay: William Tuckey Meredith, who wrote *Farragut*——

> Farragut, Farragut,
> Old Heart of Oak,
> Daring Dave Farragut,
> Thunderbolt stroke——

and Brownell, whose *The Bay Fight*, though perhaps too long, can hardly be matched for martial energy.

In the armies themselves the most popular verses were naturally less fine than those which have chiefly been remembered as the poetic fruits of the war. It was to furnish more worthy words to the tune of *John Brown's Body* that Julia Ward Howe wrote her noble poem *The Battle Hymn of the Republic*, but the words proved too fine to suit the soldiers, who would not sing of "grapes of wrath" or "the beauty of the lilies." They preferred instead such pieces as *Three Hundred Thousand More*, *Marching Through Georgia*, and *The Year of Jubilee*, which have been already mentioned, the equally favoured *The Battle Cry of Freedom*, *Tramp, Tramp, Tramp*, and *Just Before the Battle*, *Mother*, of George Frederick Root, and Walter Kittredge's *Tenting on the Old Camp Ground*. Now forgotten, but famous in its day, was William B. Bradbury's *Marching Along*, most frequently sung by soldiers of the Army of the Potomac. The song perhaps most frequently heard from soldiers of both sides in the conflict was *When This Cruel War Is Over* by C. C. Sawyer. In the Northern version "blue" rhymes with "true"; with cheerful unconcern for the rhyme, the Southerners substituted "gray." This song was sentimental, without poetic merit or rhythm, without even a trick of melody to recommend it, but it voiced the eager longing for peace and was heard in every camp many times every day. Other popular songs were the *Song of the Soldiers* by Halpine and

> I'd rather be a soldier,
> A tramping, camping soldier

by John Savage.

All these are primarily concerned with the military side of the conflict. Civil matters, too, found poetic voices: Bret Harte's *The Copperhead* and *The Copperhead Convention*, and Thomas Clarke's *Sir Copp*, stinging denunciations; F. W. Lander's *Rhode Island to the South*, full of prophetic challenge; Richard Realf's *Io Triumphe*, hopeful and resolute; W. A. Devon's *Give Me Your Hand, Johnny Bull*, a friendly, earnest bid for British sympathy. Still more interesting are the numerous pieces that reveal the feelings of sorrowing men and women at home, and of soldiers sick for home. Specially memorable are Lucy Larcom's *Waiting for News*, Kate Putnam Osgood's extraordinarily pathetic *Driving Home the Cows*, C. D. Shanly's *The Brier Wood Pipe*, Augusta Cooper Bristol's *Term of Service Ended*, Read's *The Brave at Home*, *The Drummer Boy's Burial* (anonymous), and William Winter's *After All*. From civil life came the tender and moving note of reconciliation in Francis Miles Finch's *The Blue and the Gray*, written in 1867 when the news came that the women of Columbus, Mississippi, had decorated the graves both of Northern and Southern soldiers.

To civil life, too, belongs the supreme poetry that the war called forth, associated, for the most part, with the name of Lincoln. Stoddard's *Abraham Lincoln*, Whitman's *When Lilacs Last in the Door-yard Bloomed* (not to be mentioned with the popular but less valuable *O Captain! My Captain!*), and Lowell's *Ode Recited at the Harvard Commemoration*. Whitman had written not a few vivid descriptions of war scenes, and he stands alone among all the poets of his time in his noble freedom from partisanship, but his chanting was never elsewhere so rapt or melodious. Lowell, a fiery partisan, had in his second series of *Biglow Papers* applied his satirical powers to every step of the conflict, and had at times risen to thrilling elevation, as in *Mr. Hosea Biglow to the Editor of The Atlantic Monthly*, but in his *Ode* he outstripped himself and brought American civic poetry to its highest point. An intensely pacific people had the happiness to have poets who sang peace better than they had sung war, when they had won, even at the price of war, a peace which left them purged of slavery and still a nation.

Much of this verse has naturally lost its appeal, but its national and historical significance cannot be overlooked. As Stedman afterwards wrote:

One who underrates the significance of our literature, prose or verse, as both the expression and the stimulant of national feeling, as of import in the past and to the future of America, and therefore of the world, is deficient in that critical insight which can judge even of its own day unwarped by personal taste or deference to public impression. He shuts his eyes to the fact that at times, notably throughout the years resulting in the Civil War, this literature has been a "force."

CHAPTER III

Poets of the Civil War II

THE SOUTH

AMONG the many reasons that have been suggested for the lack of literature in the ante-bellum South—the absorption in politics, the pre-eminence of the spoken word as compared with the written, the absence of centres of thought and life—must be considered the failure of the people as a whole to appreciate the literary efforts of their writers, and, what is more important, the failure of writers of talent to devote themselves to literature as a profession. The popular orator, William L. Yancey, expressed the views of many when he said in a grandiose way: "Our poetry is our lives; our fiction will come when truth has ceased to satisfy us; as for our history, we have made about all that has glorified the United States." A. B. Meek, author of *The Land of the South*, in the preface to a volume of his poems (1857) said: "The author is not a poet by profession or ambition; he has written only at long intervals or at the instigation of trivial or transient causes. The present volume is composed of occasional effusions through many years of my life." Some years later Margaret J. Preston wrote to Hayne:

Poetry has been only my pastime, not the occupation or mission of my life, which has been too busy a one with the duties of wifehood, motherhood, mistress, hostess, neighbor, and friend. . . . I think I can truly say that I have never neglected the concoction of a pudding for the sake of a poem, or a sauce for a sonnet. Art is a jealous mistress and I have served her with my left hand only.

Of a great many Southern poets, then, it may be said that they were "amateurs quick to feel the poetic instinct and the influence of other poets, content with an occasional poem or a single volume, and thenceforth prone to lead a life of culture rather than of creative activity."

The result was that the South, in 1860, had found no adequate expression of her life, no interpretation of her ideals, not even a description of her natural scenery. What writing there was, with few exceptions, was not of the soil nor of the people. Poe,[1] Edward Coate Pinkney (1802–28), author of the exquisite love-compliment *A Health*, and Richard Henry Wilde (1789–1847), who wrote the fragrant *Stanzas* beginning "My life is like the summer rose," might have written anywhere. One poem of the War of 1812, one or two of the Mexican War, and some half dozen other lyrics constituted, despite the appearance of not a few volumes of well-meant verse,[2] the poetic output of the South before the Civil War.

The Civil War aroused intense emotions that found expression in a large body of lyric poetry, written by some men who were professedly poets and by more who were but occasionally such. It is difficult for one of the present generation to realize the unity and the fervour of the Southern people at the beginning of the war. Most intelligent Southerners would now agree with President Wilson that the principles for which the South fought "meant stand-still in the midst of change; it was conservative, not creative; it was against drift and destiny; it protected an impossible institution and a belated order of society; it withstood a creative and an imperial idea, the idea of a united people and a single law of freedom." But it was given to few men, if any, on either side to understand the issues thus clearly defined. In fact, as soon as Fort Sumter was attacked and Maryland was invaded there was no longer a question of political issues—it was rather, to Southerners, a struggle of human passions, of liberty against despotism, and of the invasion of the sacred rights of home and common wealth. As Sidney Lanier,[3] himself then a young man just graduating at a Georgia college, said:

An afflatus of war was breathed upon us. Like a great wind it drew on, and blew upon men, women, and children. Its sound mingled with the serenity of the church organ, and arose with the earnest words of preachers praying for guidance in the matter. It

[1] See Book II, Chap. xiv.
[2] See Bibliography
[3] See also Book III, Chap. iv.

thundered splendidly in the impassioned appeals of orators to the people, it whistled through the streets, it stole into the firesides, it clinked glasses in bar-rooms, it lifted the gray hairs of our wise men in conventions, it thrilled through the lectures in college halls, it rustled the thumbed book leaves of the schoolrooms, it arrayed the sanctity of a righteous cause in the brilliant trappings of military display, it offered tests to all allegiances and loyalties,—of church, of state; of private loves, public devotions; of personal consanguinities, of social ties.

Of this solidarity of Southern opinion and feeling no better evidence could be given than the fact that practically all those who wrote poetry during the Civil War were either participants in the actual struggle or were intimately connected with those who were. Theodore O'Hara, who had been in active service during the Mexican War and had written *The Bivouac of the Dead* in honour of those who died in that war, was colonel of an Alabama regiment and later a staff officer in the Confederate Army. Henry Rootes Jackson, who had also fought in the Mexican War and had written *My Wife and Child* and *The Red Old Hills of Georgia*, served under Hood in the battles around Atlanta, commanded a brigade in the Army of Tennessee, and was captured in the battle of Nashville. Their poems of the Mexican War were frequently quoted, and in fact were printed in nearly all the Southern anthologies of the Civil War. James Barron Hope, who had been Virginia's official poet at the Jamestown celebration and the unveiling of the Washington monument in Richmond (1858), was quartermaster and captain in the Army of Virginia, and came out of the struggle broken in fortune and in health. Albert Pike,[1] born in Massachusetts and author of *Hymns to the Gods* (1839), was Confederate Commissioner to the Indians and afterwards a brigadier-general. Margaret Junkin Preston, born in Philadelphia, revealed in *Beechenbrook*—a poetical transcript of her experiences and impressions of the war—what the war meant to a woman who was the wife of one of the most distinguished colonels of Lee's army, the sister-in-law of Stonewall Jackson, and the friend of Lee. John R. Thompson, successor to Poe as the editor of *The Southern Literary Messenger*, became assistant secretary to the Commonwealth of Virginia and was

[1] See also Book II, Chap. VII.

later sent to England in the hope that his poems and articles might help to win English sympathy for the Confederacy. Of the younger poets Paul Hamilton Hayne, Henry Timrod, and James Ryder Randall volunteered for service but were prevented by delicate constitutions from remaining in the army, though as staff officers, correspondents, or poets they followed the events of the war with the keenest interest. Henry Lynden Flash was on the staff of General Joseph Wheeler and was thus prepared by his experience to write his tributes to Zollicoffer, Polk, and Jackson. Dr. Francis O. Ticknor was in charge of the hospital work at Columbus, Georgia, and ministered to the needs of soldiers, among them the brave Tennessean whom he made immortal in *Little Giffen*. Abram J. (Father) Ryan could never have written *The Conquered Banner* and *The Sword of Robert Lee* if he had not visualized as a chaplain the heroism and tragedy of the long struggle. William Gordon McCabe, who went from the University of Virginia as one of the Southern Guards, was a poet of the trenches, giving expression in his *Dreaming in the Trenches* and *Christmas Night of '62* to the quieter and gentler aspects of a soldier's life. Sidney Lanier and John B. Tabb,[1] after living the romantic life of soldiers, sealed a memorable friendship by a common suffering in the prison at Point Lookout.

The feeling of the South as represented by all these poets first expressed itself in music. Southern soldiers were quick to seize upon *Dixie*, the words of which had been written by Dan D. Emmett for Bryant's minstrels in 1859. Except for the refrain and a few haunting phrases, the words were totally inadequate, but the music proved to be the chief inspiration of Southern armies throughout the long conflict. Sung for the first time by Mrs. John Wood in New Orleans late in 1860, it was taken up by the Louisiana regiments and was soon heard by the camp-fires and hearthstones of the South. From New Orleans, too, came *The Bonnie Blue Flag*, an old Hibernian melody, with words written by an Irish comedian, Harry McCarthy, a volunteer soldier in the Confederate Army from Arkansas. The enthusiasm aroused by its first rendition at the Varieties Theatre in 1861 is well described by a later writer. The

[1] See Book III, Chap. IV.

theatre was filled with soldiers from Texas, Arkansas, and Louisiana on their way to the front. McCarthy appeared on the stage accompanied by his sister waving a Confederate flag. "Before the first verse was ended the audience was quivering with excitement. After he sang the second stanza the audience joined in the chorus and sang it over and over again amid the most intensive excitement. It was wafted to the streets and in twenty-four hours it was all over the Southern Army." For the crude words of both these melodies were soon substituted various versions more dignified and intellectually more worthy of the Southern cause. Of all these, the most striking version of *Dixie* was written by Albert Pike, and the most stirring words for *The Bonnie Blue Flag* by Mrs. Annie Chambers Ketchum. But not even these versions took the place in the army, or have since taken the place in the affections of the Southern people, held by the first forms.

If New Orleans may lay claim to the first popular melodies, it was natural that from Charleston should come the first notable expression in verse of the South's feeling with regard to the war. Aside from the fact that this city was the meeting place of the convention which proclaimed the secession of South Carolina, aside from the fact, too, that the first incident of the war was connected with Fort Sumter, Charleston, at the outbreak of the war, was the one Southern city that might have been considered a literary centre. Here for many years Simms,[1] as the editor of many magazines and as a prolific romancer, had made his brave fight for literary independence, and here he had gathered about him in his later years a group of young men, two of whom especially were to respond as poets to the call of the new nation. He himself was now an old man, moving among his friends "like a Titan maimed." As the struggle tightened about Charleston in the later years of the war, he wrote some fiery appeals against the besieging foe, but there is in his verse excitement rather than inspiration, heat rather than light.

Of the group of friends and younger men who gathered about Simms, the most promising was Paul Hamilton Hayne (1830–86). The descendant of several generations of Caro-iina gentlemen and gentlewomen, he had deliberately turned

[1] See also Book II, Chap. VII.

away from the attractive profession of law and politics and had definitely chosen literature as his profession. In his first published poem he had announced his dedication to the poet's life in words that are in striking contrast to the views of the Southern people in general, and even of Southern poets, who had looked on the writing of poetry as a pastime and not a passion. Before the war he had edited *Russell's Magazine* (1857–60) and had published three volumes of poetry—poems characterized by a certain imitativeness and yet a genuine love of nature and a feeling for idyllic life. When the war came he volunteered, only to find that his delicate health would not allow him to share the hardships of a campaign. From the first, however, he hailed his native state as his mother, who, like a priestess "blessed with wondrous vision of the things to come," would not wait till the sister nations would join her in the conflict. While he wrote constantly of many incidents of the war in other places, Charleston was the centre of his tenderest affections; perhaps his greatest poem of those years was *The Battle of Charleston Harbor*. In certain reminiscences that he wrote after the war, as well as in the poems written during the war, one realizes what a charm this city, with its distinct flavour and atmosphere, had for him. If to Henry James and Owen Wister Charleston is today "the most appealing, the most lovely, the most wistful town in America," how much more so was it to a sensitive soul who from infancy had known its legends and its history, and whose most tragic thought in his later life was that he was an exile from the City by the Sea.

Henry Timrod (1829–67), the friend of Simms and Hayne, had also definitely dedicated himself to the work of a poet, having already published a volume of poems in Boston (1860) and many individual poems in *Russell's Magazine* and *The Southern Literary Messenger*. A poet by natural temperament, he was a critical student of the classics and of the best English poetry. A poet hitherto of nature and of love, he was now to show himself the greatest Southern poet of the Civil War. Even before the Southern Confederacy was formed he wrote *The Cotton Boll*, which struck a new note in that it was almost the first Southern poem of local colour. The single boll of cotton which he holds in his hand as he reclines beneath an immemorial pine suggests the great plantation near Charleston

from which it came, and then all the cotton fields of the South,
from gray Atlantic dawns to the evening star; and not only
cotton fields, but the rivers and mountains and forests of this
land, which blesses the world with its mighty commerce,
joining "with a delicate web remotest strands." In offices of
peace and love his country's mission lies; but now the enemy is
coming—war is inevitable. In words of passionate indignation and patriotism he exclaims:

> Oh, help us, Lord! to roll the crimson flood
> Back on its course, and, while our banners wing
> Northward, strike with us! till the Goth shall cling
> To his own blasted altar-stones, and crave
> Mercy; and we shall grant it, and dictate
> The lenient future of his fate
> There, where some rotting ships and crumbling quays
> Shall one day mark the Port which ruled the Western seas.

The closing lines—partly ridiculous and partly pathetic in the
light of today—are typical of the absolute confidence of the
South.

When the Confederate Congress met in Montgomery in
February, 1861, Timrod hailed the birth of the new nation
in his stateliest ode, *Ethnogenesis*. All nature's blessings are
with the South and take part with her against the North, mad
and blinded in its rage. The strength of pine and palm,
the firmness and calm of the hills, the snow of Southern summers (cotton), the abundance of the harvests, the heart of
woman, the chivalry of men are arrayed against materialism
and fanaticism. To doubt the end were want of trust in God.
The poem closes with a passage that still remains the most
felicitous expression of the Southern temperament. Although
the poet's vision of a separate nation was an illusion, there will
never be a time when these words should not be quoted in any
characterization of the natural warmth and cordiality of the
Southern people:

> The hour perchance is not yet wholly ripe
> When all shall own it, but the type
> Whereby we shall be known in every land
> Is that vast gulf which lips our Southern strand,

And through the cold, untempered ocean pours
Its genial streams, that far off Arctic shores
May sometimes catch upon the softened breeze
Strange tropic warmth and hints of summer seas.

With the outbreak of hostilities in April, Timrod wrote his passionate lyric *A Cry to Arms*, and later, *Carolina*. But none of Timrod's poems had the lyric quality that fits them for popular music. The union of music and poetry in a splendid impassioned utterance came from James Ryder Randall (1839–1909). Seldom in history have the man, the moment, and the word met in such happy conjunction as in the composition of *My Maryland*. Randall, a native of Baltimore—just from college in Maryland, and, as he said, full of poetry and romance —was teaching English literature in Poydras College at Pointe Coupee, Louisiana, when he read in the New Orleans *Delta* an account of the attack on the Massachusetts troops as they passed through Baltimore:

This account [he said in later years] excited me greatly; I had long been absent from my native city, and the startling event there inflamed my mind. That night I could not sleep, for my nerves were all unstrung, and I could not dismiss what I had read in the paper from my mind. About midnight I arose, lit a candle, and went to my desk. Some powerful spirit appeared to possess me, and almost involuntarily I proceeded to write the song of *My Maryland*. I remember that the idea appeared to first take shape as music in the brain—some wild air that I cannot now recall. The whole poem was dashed off rapidly when once begun. It was not composed in cold blood, but under what may be called a conflagration of the senses, if not an inspiration of the intellect.

He read the poem the next morning to his students, and at their suggestion sent it to the New Orleans *Delta*, from which it was copied in nearly every Southern journal. The finding of an appropriate melody for the words was the achievement of the Cary sisters of Baltimore. A glee club, which was in the habit of singing at their home, sang the words to the tune *Lauriger Horatius*, well known as a college tune that had come from a modification of the German *Tannenbaum, O Tannenbaum*. A few weeks later, shortly after the battle of Manassas.

the two sisters and their brother went through the Southern lines. One night while visiting the headquarters of General Beauregard they were serenaded by a regiment of soldiers from New Orleans, who in turn asked for a song. One of the sisters sang *My Maryland;* the refrain was speedily caught up and tossed back from hundreds of rebel throats, who shouted, "We will break her chains; she shall be free!" Soon the words which had been read far and wide were being sung in every part of the South—had become indeed a great national song, the Marseillaise of the Confederacy.

The words—too familiar to be quoted—suggest every aspect of the great struggle from the Southern standpoint. They summarize in passionate, concentrated lines the points of view that are scattered here and there throughout all the anthologies of Southern poetry. The feeling of an exiled son at the invasion of his home, the crushing of liberty under the despot's heel, the peerless chivalry of Maryland's former heroes of history and tradition, his love for the state as a mother, the appeal for a sister state's aid to Virginia, and, on the other hand, the fierce indignation at the "vandal," the "despot," the "Northern scum"—all these are suggestive of the passion of a people giving themselves entirely to the great struggle.

The popular melodies, the odes of Timrod, and the lyric cry of Randall—all of them the best illustrations of their various types—were prophetic of an outburst of poetry in all parts of the South. Such papers as the Charleston *Mercury*, the Richmond *Examiner*, the Louisville *Courier*, the New Orleans *Delta*, and such magazines as *The Southern Literary Messenger*, *The Southern Field and Fireside*, and *The Southern Illustrated News* published constantly poems written by men and women in all sections. As there were no general means of communication, many poems were attributed to various authors and many were published anonymously. On account of the lack of publishing houses practically no volumes of poetry were published during the war. The problem, therefore, of making anthologies of these poems was a difficult one—much more difficult than was the case in the North, where so many poets already famous were writing constantly during the war, and where there were so many means of communication and of publication. Southern readers had to be satisfied with scrap-

books in which were treasured many of the poems that in this
way became the common property of a good many people.

Of distinctly different quality from the poems already
referred to, and all other "literary" poems, are certain crude
vernacular verses. With some of the characteristics of popular
ballads, they had much currency in the camps. A writer in the
Southern Bivouac (July, 1885) recalls and characterizes some of
these as follows:

As the long contest dragged on, and war, losing much of its
earlier illusions, became a stern, bitter, and exceedingly monotonous reality, these "high-toned" lyrics were tacitly voted rather too
romantic and poetical for the actual field, and were remitted to the
parlor and the piano stool. The soldiers chanted in quite other
fashion on the march or seated at the campfire. In these crude
rhymes, some of them improvised for the moment, there was less of
flourish but more of meaning, not so much bravado but a good deal
more point. They were sappy with the homely satire of the camps,
which stings friend and foe alike. Innumerable verses were composed and sung to popular refrains. The Army of Virginia and the
Army of Tennessee had each its history rudely chronicled as fast
as made in this rough minstrelsy. Every corps and command contributed some commemorative stanza. The current events of
campaigns were told in improvised verse as rapidly as they occurred
and were thereafter skillfully recited by the rhapsodist who professed to know the whole fragmentary epic.

Forms of such rhymed narratives may be seen in typical
stanzas:

> Marse Robert said, "My soldiers,
>   You've nothing now to fear,
> For Longstreet's on the right of them,
>   And Jackson's in the rear."

> The Fourteenth Louisiana,
>   They charged 'em with a yell;
> They bagged them buck-tailed rangers
>   And sent 'em off to hell.

> O Morgan crossed the river,
>   And I went across with him;
> I was captured in Ohio
>   Because I could not swim.

No matter where this song was sung, or by whom, or which of its multitude of stanzas happened to be selected by the minstrel, the following verse always closed it:

> But now my song is ended,
>   And I haven't got much time,
> I'm going to run the blockade
>   To see that girl of mine.

Some of these poems are found in *Rebel Rhymes and Rhapsodies* (1864) edited by Frank Moore as a companion volume to two other volumes of war poetry of the North. In his preface to this first anthology of Southern war poetry Moore says:

It has been the purpose of the editor to present as full a selection of the songs and ballads of the Southern people as will illustrate the spirit which actuates them in their rebellion against the government and laws of the United States. Most of these pieces have been published in the magazines and periodicals of the South, while many are copies of ballad-sheets and songs circulated in the Rebel armies, and which have come into the possession of the forces of the Union in their various moves and advances during the present conflict.

We find in the volume many humorous poems of the kind just described. The more serious include two poems each by Randall and Ticknor, one each by Hayne, Hope, Flash, Meek, Pike, Simms, and J. R. Thompson, Timrod's *A Cry to Arms* and Palmer's *Stonewall Jackson's Way*, the last two published, however, anonymously. There are also many parodies of famous songs such as *Annie Laurie, Gideon's Band, Bannockburn, Columbia, Wait for the Wagon, The Star Spangled Banner,* etc.

It was probably this collection that formed the basis of the selections from Southern poetry published as an appendix to

Richard Grant White's *Poetry, Lyrical, Narrative, and Satirical of the Civil War* (1866). In his preface White says:

> I have read all that I could discover of the war poetry, written by the confederated enemies of my government, and have preserved here all that, in a most catholic spirit, I deemed of any intrinsic merit or incidental interest. It was my original purpose to embody them with the substance of the volume, giving each piece its place in the order of time; but finding so little of this poetry which possesses any kind of interest, instead of scattering it sparsely through the collection, I put it in an appendix. The secessionists fought much better than they wrote; and it is worthy of remark that the best poem on that side, "The Conquered Banner" was published in a New York newspaper, *The Freeman's Journal.*

Omitting the humorous poems published by Moore, White has only the ten or twelve of a more serious and important nature, and these, in the main, not the ones that might be considered the most important by the leading Southern poets. The selections are a good illustration either of the difficulty of getting hold of Southern poems or of a provincial point of view that happily no longer exists.

Inadequate as these anthologies were, they were much better than the volume entitled *War Lyrics and Songs of the South*, published in London in 1866, and edited by "a faithful few Southern women" who had thrown "hastily together this book of poems," in the hope that

> its sale to the charitable might secure a fund for the relief of the crippled and invalid men who fought as soldiers in the war in the South; the impoverished women and children, widows and orphans, as well as those who from sorrow, need, sickness, and other adversity have lost their health and their *minds.*

In this volume *The Virginians of the Valley*, by Ticknor, and *Stonewall Jackson's Way* and *The Conquered Banner*, both published anonymously, are the only poems of any value. An illustration of the carelessness of the editors is that Henry R. Jackson's *My Wife and Child* is attributed to General J. T. [T. J., or Stonewall] Jackson. More than half of the volume is given up to *Songs of the Southland and Other Poems* by "Kentucky."

In the following year Miss Emily V. Mason of Virginia edited *The Southern Poems of the Civil War*. She had from the beginning of the war conceived the design of "collecting and preserving the various war poems which (born of the excited state of the public mind) then inundated our public newspapers." With her collection, supplemented by those of her friends, she made an edition of 247 poems, not only as a memorial to the lost cause, but "to aid the education of the daughters of our desolate land" and especially to fit a certain number to be teachers. The volume proved popular, for by 1869 a third and enlarged edition was published, consisting of 288 poems. The first edition is notable for the large number of women writers selected from, 71 in all, the only noteworthy one being Mrs. Preston. There are thirteen poems on Stonewall Jackson, only two poems by Timrod, an indiscriminate list by Randall, and many anonymous poems. In the third edition we have eight by Timrod, four by Father Ryan, and good, though not the best, selections by Lucas, McCabe, Flash, and others.

The improvement in this edition may doubtless be attributed to William Gilmore Simms's *War Poetry of the South* (1866). It was a noble task undertaken by this "weary old Titan" of Southern letters to preserve the writings of the younger poets, many of whom had been inspired by his friendship or by his lifelong devotion to Southern letters. The spirit in which he made the book is indicated in the following words from the preface:

Though sectional in its character, and indicative of a temper and a feeling which were in conflict with nationality, yet, now that the States of the Union have been resolved into one nation, this collection is essentially as much the property of the whole as are the captured cannon which were employed against it during the progress of the late war. It belongs to the national literature, and will hereafter be regarded as constituting a proper part of it, just as legitimately to be recognized by the nation as are the rival ballads of the cavaliers and roundheads by the English in the great civil conflict of their country.

Not much can be said for the critical standards which allowed Simms to publish so much unworthy poetry, none more so than the seven poems from his own pen. His desire to give a place to representative poets of all states, and especially to his personal friends, is in part responsible. Furthermore, the book was thrown hastily together without any arrangement of the material with regard to authorship or chronology. When all has been said, however, we find in this volume the first anthology of practically all the important poems produced by the South during the war—seven each by Randall, J. R. Thompson, and Simms himself, six by Hayne, three by Ticknor, three by Flash, and, above all, eleven by Timrod. It is this recognition of Timrod's greatness as a poet, this first setting him forth as the poet of the South who expressed in adequate verse every aspect of the struggle, that increases the value of the book and our appreciation of Simms's critical judgment.

In 1869 appeared *The Southern Amaranth*, characterized by its editor, Miss Sallie A. Brock, as "a carefully selected collection of poems growing out of and in reference to the late war." In the preface of March, 1868, she expresses a wish to render to her Southern sisters "some assistance in gathering up the remains of the Confederate dead." Her regret is that "a vast number of beautiful and worthy productions are compelled for want of space to be crowded out of this volume." In florid style she exclaims:

The Muse of the Southland is one of tireless wing, and though her theme is lofty and glorious as the golden sunset splendor upon the purple sky of evening, her song is often as sad as the weary echoes of the winter wind through her matchless forests—the mournful wailings of broken hearts.

The most striking new features of the volume are Timrod's *Ode on the Confederate Dead* (written in 1867) and Dr. Ticknor's *Little Giffen of Tennessee*, which, though probably written in 1863, was not published until October, 1867, in *The Land We Love*. The latter poem is not given, however, as it appears in the revised form of later years, the last stanza being especially faulty.

All these anthologies had appeared with but little introductory material or notes regarding the lives of the writers or the circumstances under which the poems were written. They were all practically a conglomeration of poems with little to aid the student of literary history. In 1869 James Wood Davidson's *Living Writers of the South* was published in New York, with salient facts as to the biographies and bibliographies of some 241 writers—166 men and 75 women. Of these he puts down 112 as having written "verse" and eight as having written "poetry." He adds:

> Some of these specimens are poor enough, in all conscience,—some inartistic of course; and some, it may be, frivolous,—but each in its way and all together have their use in the general design. Some of the writers have talents and character, with corresponding results, which enable them to stand in the front rank of American authorship. Some have limited ability. And some have none.

These words are typical of the judgment and sense that run through the volume. There are, for instance, critical estimates, biographical sketches, and bibliographies of Simms, Hayne, Mrs. Preston, Flash, and Randall, and surprisingly short ones of Ticknor and Lucas. It required courage on the author's part to characterize the poems of the veteran Simms as "prosaic, commonplace, and Tupperesque." After citing some sixty-five titles of his books of all kinds he remarks: "He has not written an epic; why, I have no idea, but we may be infinitely grateful that he has not."

In his criticism of Flash, for whom he shows much enthusiasm, Davidson puts his finger upon the cardinal defects of many of the Southern poets. Flash, he says, "has never written anything which was not finished at a single sitting, and has never been more than two hours writing anything he has ever published." He wrote his poem on Polk when his foreman told him that he lacked six or seven inches for the makeup of *The Daily Confederate*. "You have written about Zollicoffer and Jackson, you might as well write about Polk, who was killed the other day." Flash quickly responded to the suggestion, and in five minutes the poem was in the hands of the composer, and in twenty minutes was being printed. Paying full tribute to Flash's good qualities, the author warns him that without work there is not the remotest chance for an enduring reputation, and at the same time makes the same suggestion to others who may have acquired "a reverence for inspiration so called, and a contempt for the art of versification."

Apart from his critical judgment Davidson shows the ability of a careful editor in weighing evidence as to the authorship of *All Quiet Along the Potomac*—a poem that all Southerners had claimed as the work of Lamar Fontaine.[1] Davidson publishes Fontaine's letter claiming positively the authorship, but side by side with it is one from Joel Chandler Harris, who was at that time, according to the editor, planning an edition of Southern poems, and who after much deliberation expresses the opinion that Mrs. Beers is the author of the poem. He quotes also a letter to the same effect from the editor of *Harper's Magazine.* While he himself does not express an opinion, it is not difficult for the reader to be convinced by the reasoning submitted by Joel Chandler Harris. The mention of Harris suggests that in this volume he himself appears as the author of several poems which are as unlike his later writings as anything could well be. Davidson has the credit too of publishing for the first time in this volume McCabe's *Dreaming in the Trenches* and *Christmas Night of '62*, and certain recent poems of Maurice Thompson and Sidney Lanier. He also has much to say of poems that do not relate to the war.

In 1882 Francis F. Browne of Chicago carried out the purpose that Richard Grant White had expressed by publishing *Bugle Echoes*—a collection of poems of the Civil War, Northern and Southern. Drawing upon the anthologies that have been discussed and upon separate editions of Southern poets, such as Hayne's edition of Timrod (1873), of Ticknor (1879), of Hayne (1882), he finds a much larger number of Southern poems that fit into his plan of suggesting the story of the Civil War by poems written at the time. Thus for the first time a systematic arrangement was made of this material. The result is altogether striking. The Southern poems, while slightly fewer in number (the proportion is 60 to 85), measure up well with those of the North. Side by side in this volume appear Bryant's *Our Country's Call* and Timrod's *A Cry to Arms,* Whitman's *Beat, Beat Drums* and Randall's *My Maryland,* Pike's *Dixie* and *The Battle Hymn of the Republic,* Holmes's *Voyage of the Good Ship Union* and Ticknor's *Virginians of the Valley,* Lowell's *Commemoration Ode* and Timrod's *Ode to the Confederate Dead,* and at the very end Finch's *The Blue*

[1] Now by some ascribed to Thaddeus Oliver (1826-64).

and the Gray and Lanier's *The Tournament*—both of them prophetic of a new national era. Not only was Browne's idea happy and well executed; his introduction and notes are invaluable. He established the fact that the author of *Stonewall Jackson's Way* was Dr. J. W. Palmer. He printed in connection with the poems valuable letters as to the circumstances under which were written *My Maryland* and *The Conquered Banner*. The volume as a whole was so marked by a careful critical judgment and good taste as to distinguish it from the hastily prepared anthologies by Southerners.

Two books of similar nature are Eggleston's *American War Ballads* and Burton E. Stevenson's *Poems of American History*, in both of which the poems are published in chronological order, and in Stevenson's book with the historical setting which interprets many of the individual poems. In later years selections from Southern writers by Miss Manly and Miss Clarke and Professors Trent, Kent, and Fulton, and biographical sketches by Baskervill and Link, have brought the best poems and poets within the reach of a larger circle of students and readers. *The Library of Southern Literature* is a valuable mine of selections and biographical material.

When one tries to make a general estimate of this war poetry as a whole, there are three standpoints from which it may be considered. Judged from the standpoint of absolute criticism, it affords another illustration of the contention that war produces a quantity of mediocre poetry but little of enduring worth. Four or five poems at best have stood the winnowing process of time and judicial criticism. Randall's *My Maryland*, Ticknor's *Little Giffen of Tennessee*, and Timrod's *Ode* on the Confederate dead in Magnolia Cemetery might well be included in any anthology of lyric poetry, ancient or modern. If we consider the poems from the standpoint of either literary or social history, a larger number must be considered significant. They rightly find their place in such a collection as Stedman's *American Anthology* as affording material for the comprehensive survey of American poetry, or in the books of Stevenson and Browne, where the various stages of the Civil War are suggested in poems rather than in army orders, political tracts, or newspaper comment. When President Lincoln said at the end of the war that the Northern army had captured *Dixie* he might have extended his remarks to other poems that have become a part of our national heritage.

Still another interest attaches to it. Much of it is an adequate, if not felicitous and final, expression of the ideas and emotions of Southerners at a time when they felt as one people. The emotional fervour that swept over the South was somehow the inspiration of a literature different from that of any other era in its history. Southern literature before the war had been marked by its absorption in politics, or its divorce from real life, or its amateurishness and sentimentalism. A people that had been all too inclined to underrate poetry and to discourage literary production found their deepest emotions expressed in martial strains, or in meditative lyrics. Written for local newspapers, preserved in scrap-books, collected in volumes like those of Simms and Miss Mason, sifted by the later editors and collectors, they preserve heroes and incidents, landscapes and sentiments that will always endear them to the Southern people.

If we consider the poems from this last point of view, they serve to suggest the principal events of the war in rapid review. The gauntlet was thrown down in the poems hitherto cited and also in Tucker's *The Southern Cross*, Miles's *God Save the South*, Randall's *Battle Cry of the South*, Mrs. Warfield's *Chant of Defiance*, Thompson's *Coercion*, and Hope's *Oath of Freedom*. Among the group of Virginia poets who wrote of the early battles on Virginia soil, John R. Thompson (1822–73) and Mrs. Preston (1820–97) stand out as the most conspicuous. Of distinctly higher quality than the crude rhymes already referred to were Thompson's humorous poems on some of the early Southern victories. His *On to Richmond*, modelled on Southey's *March to Moscow*, is an exceedingly clever poem. His mastery of double and triple rhymes, his unfailing sense of the value of words, and his happy use of the refrain ("the pleasant excursion to Richmond") make this poem one of the marked achievements of the period. Scarcely less successful in their brilliant satire are his *Farewell to Pope*, *England's Neutrality*, and *The Devil's Delight*.

The humour of these poems soon gave way, however, to the more heroic and tragic aspects of the war. Thompson himself wrote dirges for Ashby and Latané, both of them the finest types of Virginia gentlemen. Mrs. Preston wrote a still more beautiful tribute to Ashby, in which she expresses one of the favourite ideas of the South—that the struggle was between the cavaliers and men of low breeding. The tragic aspects of Virginia and the heroism of her people were visualized also by a Georgia poet, Francis O. Ticknor (1822–74), whose wife was one of the distinguished Nelsons of the Old Dominion. His *Our Left* is the most vivid account of the second battle of Manassas. *Virginia* is the best tribute we have to the commonwealth that bore the brunt of the struggle. The more popular *Virginians of the Valley* suggests the most romantic story of early years and adds that the same spirit pervades their descendants:

> We thought they slept! the men who kept
>   The names of noble sires,
> And slumbered, while the darkness crept
>   Around their vigil fires!
> But aye! the golden horse-shoe Knights
>   Their Old Dominion keep,
> Whose foes have found enchanted ground,
>   But not a Knight asleep.

One phase of the struggle ends with Lee's whole army crossing the Potomac into Maryland—an event celebrated by Hayne in his *Beyond the Potomac*. Then the fighting changed to the West, and we have Thompson's poem on Joseph E. Johnston in which he exhorts the West to emulate Virginia in its struggle for freedom. Requier's *Clouds in the West* is followed by Flash's tribute to Zollicoffer, Ticknor's poem on Albert Sidney Johnston, Hayne's *The Swamp Fox*—a spirited characterization of Morgan, who seems to the poet a re-incarnation of the South Carolina Revolutionary patriot Marion. Connected also with the battles of the West were Ticknor's *Loyal* and *Little Giffen of Tennessee*—the latter based on a story of real life and a striking illustration of the heroism with which the sons of the masses threw themselves into the Southern struggle. This poem, so dramatic in its quality, so concise in its expression, so vital in its phrasing, is destined to outlive all the tributes to the great leaders of the Confederacy. Mrs. Preston's *Only a Private* and Mrs. Townsend's *The Georgia*

Volunteer and the anonymous *Barefooted Boys* are poems of the same general tenor, but they lack the freshness and the vigour of Ticknor's poem.

With the publication of Hayne's poems on Vicksburg and the battle of New Orleans, the scene shifts again to Virginia, and especially to the dramatic death of Stonewall Jackson after some of the fiercest battles of the war. This event more than any other pierced the heart of the South and called forth scores of poems from all sections. One of the early collectors claimed to have found forty-eight of these; at least four or five rise to a high level of expression. No other poem gives anything like so adequate an expression of Jackson—his personal appearance, his religious faith, his impressive commands, his almost magical control of his men—as *Stonewall Jackson's Way* by John Williamson Palmer (1825–1906). Excellent also are Margaret J. Preston's *Stonewall Jackson's Grave* and *Under the Shade of the Trees*, Flash's *Death of Stonewall Jackson*, Randall's *The Lone Sentry*, and the anonymous *The Brigade Must Not Know, Sir*.

In 1863 Charleston was attacked by the Northern fleet and her group of devoted poets gathered about her in suspense. Timrod described the dawn of the eventful day as the city in the broad sunlight of heroic deeds waited for the foe. The hostile smoke of the enemy's fleet "creeps like a harmless mist above the brine." He knows not what will happen—the triumph or the tomb. With his *Carmen Triumphale* he sings the rapturous joy of the victory. Paul Hamilton Hayne sang a nobler song of victory, giving the details of the battle, ending in the triumphant victory of Sumter's volleyed lightning, and closing with an apostrophe to his native city:

O glorious Empress of the main, from out thy storied spires
Thou well mayst peal thy bells of joy and light thy festal fires,—
Since Heaven this day hath striven for thee, hath nerved thy
    dauntless sons,
And thou in clear-eyed faith hast seen God's angels near the guns.

This victory was short-lived, however, for on 27 August, by a land attack, Fort Sumter was reduced to a shapeless mass of ruin, though the city itself stood unshaken. As the fate of the city became more and more uncertain, William Gilmore

Simms, now in his old age, did all in his power to rouse the Spirit of the inhabitants.   In a series of poems, *Do Ye Quail? The Angel of the Church*, and *Our City by the Sea*, he presents in passionate words the claims of the historic city upon its inhabitants.   Especially vivid is his plea for St. Michael's church, whose spire for full a hundred years had been a people's point of light, and the sweet, clear music of whose bells, made liquid-soft in Southern air, had been a benediction in the life of the city.

But the words of her poets could not avail the doomed city when, in 1865, Sherman's army marched north from Savannah. Timrod, now a citizen of Columbia, wrote his greatest lyric, *Carolina*, which comes nearest to *My Maryland* of all the poems of the war in its indignation and power.   He reproaches the idle hands and craven calm of the inhabitants, but calls upon the descendants of Rutledge, Laurens, and Marion to rouse themselves against the despot who treads their sacred sands. The answer to this appeal was the burning of Columbia. Hayne and John Dickson Bruns still had hope that Charleston might escape the doom.   As Timrod from Charleston had given to the world the first expression of the new nation's hope, so his friend and fellow townsman, Dr. Bruns, was to utter the last appeal for Charleston in his *The Foe at the Gates*.   There is nothing more tragic in the Civil War than the fall of Charleston—the proud, passionate, and romantic city that had issued her challenge to the South to join her in the conflict with the North.   In her last despairing cry the poet calls upon her children to ring round her and catch one last glance from her imploring eye:

> From all her fanes let solemn bells be tolled;
> Heap with kind hands her costly funeral pyre,
> And thus, with pæan sung and anthem rolled,
> Give her unspotted to the God of Fire.

The fall of Charleston was the beginning of the end.   Various poems on Lee, notably Ticknor's *Lee*, Thompson's *Lee to the Rear*, and the anonymous *Silent March*, suggest the last battles in Virginia.   The dominant note of the later poetry is that of melancholy, now and then tempered by a sort of pathetic longing for peace.   Eggleston tells us that the most popular poem on both sides came to be C. C. Sawyer's *When This Cruel War Is Over*.[1] The sentiment of the poem is echoed in poems on peace by George Herbert Sass, Ticknor, Bruns, and Timrod. Very different from the concluding lines of the *Cotton Boll* is Timrod's pathetic yearning for peace, in the poem entitled *Christmas:*

> Peace in the quiet dales,
> Made rankly fertile by the blood of men,
> Peace in the woodland, and the lonely glen,
> Peace, in the peopled vales!
>
> .   .   .   .
>
> Peace on the whirring marts,
> Peace where the scholar thinks, the hunter roams,
> Peace, God of Peace! peace, peace, in all our homes,
> And peace in all our hearts!

When peace came, the defeat of the South, its unconquerable loyalty to the lost cause, and its sad resignation at the inevitable found expression in Mrs. Preston's *Acceptation*, Requier's *Ashes of Glory*, Flash's *The Confederate Flag*, and, above all, Father Ryan's *The Sword of Robert Lee* and *The Conquered Banner*. Not until the end of the war did the last-named poet suddenly flash forth as the most popular of all Southern poets. *The Conquered Banner* was written under somewhat the same circumstance as *My Maryland*—written in less than an hour as he brooded over the thought of the dead soldiers and the lost cause. He wrote other poems, chiefly religious, but none that has ever stirred the hearts of the people like these two written in the shadow of defeat.

Somewhat different in tone and spirit is *The Land Where We Were Dreaming*, by Daniel B. Lucas. Written and first printed in Montreal, whither the author had fled at the end of the war, it is a striking expression of a Southerner's awakening from the illusions which had so long dominated the thought of the people. There is the same loyalty to the leaders and the principles of the South, but a glimpse of reality that augured a readjustment for the future.

Two years after the war, Timrod, suffering from tuberculosis and the direst poverty, wrote his greatest poem, the *Ode*

Sung on the Occasion of Decorating the Graves of the Confederate Dead at Magnolia Cemetery, Charleston, S. C., 1867. The poem is a fit ending to any consideration of Southern War Poetry, for it is the last word to be said of those who died and of those who would honour their memory.

I

Sleep sweetly in your humble graves,
   Sleep, martyrs of a fallen cause;
Though yet no marble column craves
   The pilgrim here to pause.

II

In seeds of laurel in the earth
   The blossom of your fame is blown,
And somewhere, waiting for its birth,
   The shaft is in the stone!

III

Meanwhile, behalf the tardy years
   Which keep in trust your storied tombs,
Behold! your sisters bring their tears
   And these memorial blooms.

IV

Small tributes! but your shades will smile
   More proudly on these wreaths to-day,
Than when some cannon-moulded pile
   Shall overlook this bay.

V

Stoop, angels, hither from the skies!
   There is no holier spot of ground
Than where defeated valor lies,
   By mourning beauty crowned!

The question inevitably arises as to how these poets developed after the Civil War. One would naturally suppose that many of the younger ones especially would grow in power and influence. But all the causes generally assigned for the lack of poetry in the ante-bellum South prevailed in the new era; and thereto were added poverty, widespread disaster, and an overwhelming confusion in the public mind. Lanier tersely expressed the chief limitation under which the writer laboured when he wrote to Bayard Taylor: "Perhaps you know that with us of the younger generation of the South since the war, pretty much the whole of life has been merely not dying." Simms wrote to Hayne just before his death in 1870: "I am rapidly passing from a stage where you young men are to succeed me," and inscribed for his tombstone the poignant words: "Here lies one who, after a reasonably long life, distinguished chiefly by unceasing labours, has left all his better works undone." Meek, O'Hara, John R. Thompson, and Henry Timrod were all dead by 1875. Randall spent many years in the drudgery of a newspaper office, never recapturing the first fine careless rapture of his great song. Ticknor and Bruns followed with devotion the life of a doctor, while McCabe became one of the best-known schoolmasters of Virginia—a position which seemed to deaden his poetic inspiration, though he remained an inimitable raconteur, and the friend of some of the most gifted poets of England and America. Mrs. Preston continued to write as late as 1887, when she published *Colonial Ballads*, but she added nothing to her fame. Flash became a merchant and lived for many years in the Far West.

Paul Hamilton Hayne alone made progress after the war. With magnificent courage and faith, after the destruction of his city and his home, he moved to a small cabin of his own building in the pine barrens near Augusta, Georgia. Here on a writing desk made out of a carpenter's work-bench he wrote poems for the remainder of his life. To Mrs. Preston he wrote: "No, no! By my brain—my literary craft—I will win my bread and water; by my poems I will live or I will starve." In 1872 he brought out a volume of *Legends and Lyrics;* in 1875 *The Mountain of the Lovers and Other Poems;* and in 1882, a complete edition of his poems. Two or three of his best poems were written in his last years, notably *A Little While I Fain Would Linger Yet*, and *In Harbor*. While Hayne did not strike a deeply original note, he cultivated faithfully the talents with which he was endowed. His best poems are characterized by delicacy of feeling, conscientious workmanship, and a certain assimilation of the best qualities of other poets. His magnanimous spirit after the war, as revealed in his tributes to Whittier and Longfellow, his revelation of the picturesqueness of the Southern landscapes and especially of the pine forests of Georgia, are the substantial features of his poetry. As a connecting link between Simms and Lanier he has a permanent place in the literary history of the South.

CHAPTER IV

The New South: Lanier

THE conditions of Reconstruction were inimical to the production of literature. The life of the South, always sluggish, now became stagnant. A country of farms and plantations, there were in it few large cities to foster an intellectual life. The large planters whose travel and whose experience in government and statesmanship rendered them the natural leaders were downcast by the sudden destruction of their wealth in slaves and soil. The poor whites lived too close to mother earth and were too densely ignorant to furnish a public for literary activity. The isolation of the whole South was heart-sickening. The roads were unfit for teams. The railroads had been destroyed Cities like Columbia, South Carolina, reputed to be the most beautiful on the continent, stood a wilderness of ruins, "like Tadmor alone in the desert." Not one of the railways that formerly entered it had so much left as the iron on its track.

The newspapers were few and ill-informed. For many years they devoted their meagre talents to vituperation of Republican acts and policies. There was, to be sure, a short-lived effort at literary activity, as if the section might make good with the pen what had been lost by the sword. But even so catholic a venture as *The Land We Love*, edited by General D. H. Hill, which was devoted to literature, military history, and agriculture, had soon to die of inanition. Journals of opinion, like *De Bow's Review*, in New Orleans, maintaining a precarious existence in scattered centres of the region, had at length to give up the struggle. Schools and colleges were few and far between. Even the will to attend them had to be fostered with perseverance and great care. In fine, the intellectual stagnation of the South made literature impossible except for those with an unquenchable longing for expression.

Worse even than stagnation was the hopelessness of the outlook. The leaders, the owners of plantations, were reduced from affluence to poverty. Many a family that had been comfortable or even rich was now thankful for a supper of cornmeal. Plantations were for sale at a song. The "richest estates" of North Carolina were at first to be bought for from one to ten dollars an acre. A hundred acres four miles from Macon, Georgia the birthplace of Lanier, was offered for fifty cents an acre. The Southerner was convinced that the negro would not work in freedom. Two books give unforgettable pictures of the efforts of the planters to meet the new industrial situation. *Ten Years on a Georgia Plantation* by the daughter of Fanny Kemble, Frances Butler Leigh, details the childishness of the negro under the novel conditions of freedom. Mrs. Leigh can hardly be claimed as a Southern author, but Susan Dabney Smedes (1840—) must take high rank as one. Her *Memorials of a Southern Planter* is an artless but absorbing picture of a class made extinct by the war. Without any of the theatrical effectiveness common in the older Southern prose, she relates in simple, dignified words the history of her father, Thomas Dabney, a planter of Mississippi. The war brought out in him such lofty nobility as is seldom seen in actual life. On laying down the volume Gladstone exclaimed "Let no man say, with this book before him, that the age of chivalry is gone, or that Thomas Dabney was not worthy to sit beside Sir Perceval at the 'table round' of King Arthur." His struggle to keep the plantation ended in its sale. A like fate awaited others. It was only slowly through the years that the large holdings were broken up into small farms and reduced to a more intense cultivation by intelligent diversification of crops.

Hopelessness of the economic outlook was deepened to despair by political and social conditions. By 1870 the seceded states were nominally reconstructed. But the Republican measures were such as poured salt and iron filings into the open wounds of civil war. Negro soldiers were set over their former masters. The intelligent voters were disqualified. The state governments were handed over to Northern carpet-baggers and

Southern scalawags, and the ignorant freedmen were given the right to vote. These former slaves marched through legislative halls on plush carpets, sat with their feet on mahogany desks, and spat into imported cuspidors. In one capital they resorted to a free and continuous lunch, with ample food and drink. All these luxuries were paid for out of the pockets of their former masters. This proud race, accustomed to generations of autocratic government, ground its teeth in silent rage. But by 1876 it had by fraud or violence overturned the inverted pyramid, and once more placed the state governments in the hands of responsible men, and returned many of its former leaders to the national Congress. The reins of government had been restored to the white man.

This atmosphere of turmoil was not conducive to a fine or vigorous literary product. Even so late as 1880 in Alabama "the assessed value of guns, dirks, and pistols was nearly twice that of the libraries and five times that of the farm implements of the state." For there continued the race problem to set the Southerners apart as a peculiar people. In many neighbourhoods the blacks outnumbered the whites two to one, three to one, four to one, and in the Yazoo bottom lands of Mississippi as many as fifteen to one. Their presence was viewed as a peril. It continued to be viewed as a peril during the twenty years following 1880, though the South became more and more a modern industrial community.

During that period Northern capital flowed in to draw iron and coal from the South's mines, to build factories along its streams, to spin a web of railways over its territory, to gather more and more its population into the humming hives of cities. The stagnation of the years immediately following the war gave way to an alerter life. Hopelessness and despondency waned gradually. With leisure and an interest in literature came visions of new beauty, a new-found joy in life, an impulse to share with others the creations of one's mind and spirit. Yet it was even more due to the Northern periodical and the Northern publisher that in the seventies and still more in the eighties the South found a voice in literature. That voice, in prose, spoke at first in the sonorous accents of the antebellum orator. Only as means of publication were multiplied and made more available did it take on the natural tones of everyday use. Poetry in the seventies tended to give way to prose fiction.[1]

Of course, those who had written before the war still tried to gain a livelihood from the pen, but they continued the manner and traditions of the Old South. John Esten Cooke,[2] for example, carried on in Virginia the tradition of the school of Scott and Cooper, then elsewhere becoming archaic. George William Bagby (1828–83),[3] also of Virginia, renewed his newspaper productions and added the lyceum to his resources. But so intense a lover of the Old Dominion and its civilization could suffer no sea-change even in the fiery baptism of war. He tried to deliver his lecture *The Virginia Negro* in New York, but the reception was unmistakably cool. Life "befo' de war" had not yet become for the North a charming memory from a land of romance.

Richard Malcolm Johnston (1822–98)[4] in his various writings evinces an equal devotion to the earlier times before the railroad came to central Georgia. They form a sympathetic record of the ways and characters of that humble but picturesque era. Johnston, though a slave-holder, was unwaveringly opposed to secession and the war. Nevertheless, reduced by the surrender at Appomattox from an estate of fifty thousand dollars to poverty, to him the situation seemed so hopeless that he removed, with the school he kept, to Baltimore. The autobiography, the eighty stories, and the three novels which he there produced, it is interesting to note, were written largely to assuage a sad longing for his boyhood home. These writings show him to have been, in spite of his political opinions, of the old school of Southern gentlemen.

More typical both in opinions and in fervour was Charles Colcock Jones, Jr. (1831–93). Born in Savannah, he graduated from Princeton in 1852 and the Harvard Law School in 1855. His Southern convictions, however, still intact, were intensified by his service in the artillery of the Confederate States. When the guns were stilled by the surrender of Lee, he, like Johnston, joined that numerous caravan which, seeing no hope in its own section, sought fortune in other regions. New York and the practice of law were his goals.

---

[1] See Book III, Chaps. VI and XI.   [2] See also Book III, Chap. XI.
[3] See also Book II, Chap. XIX.   [4] See also Book III, Chap. VI.

Although he remained North twelve years, he moved no jot nor tittle from his early point of view. On his return south in 1877 to a suburb of Augusta, Georgia, he became at once conspicuous for his devotion to the Lost Cause, and when he died in 1893, his body, wrapped in the flag of the Confederacy, was given a soldier's burial.

The style and the spirit of his numerous public addresses may be seen in a single sentence taken from *Sons of Confederate Veterans*, delivered so late as 1891:

Under the absurd guise of a New South, flaunting the banners of utilitarianism,—lifting the standards of speculation and expediency, —elevating the colors whereon are emblazoned consolidation of wealth and centralization of government,—lowering the flag of intellectual, moral, and refined supremacy in the presence of the petty guidons of ignorance, personal ambition and diabolism,— supplanting the iron cross with the golden calf,—and crooking

"the pregnant hinges of the knee
Where thrift may follow fawning"

not a few there are who, ignoring the elevating influence of heroic impulses, manly endeavor, and virtuous sentiments, would fain convert this region into a money-worshiping domain; and, careless of the landmarks of the fathers, impatient of the restraints of a calm, enlightened, conservative civilization, viewing with indifferent eye the tokens of Confederate valor, and slighting the graves of Confederate dead, would counsel no oblation save at the shrine of Mammon.

This turgid style was much admired for the magniloquent swing of the phrases and the unending procession of lofty and sectional notions. It so well comported with his tall, stately figure and Chesterfieldian manners that he employed it even in his history of the aboriginal, colonial, and Revolutionary epochs of Georgia. The book was the product of careful research in the records then available, so that Bancroft hailed the author as "the Macaulay of the South." But he is a Macaulay muffled in a pompous dress. His *Antiquities of the Southern Indians, Particularly of the Georgia Tribes*, which appeared so early as 1873, along with many other monographs established his reputation as an archæologist. He was, indeed, the most fertile Southern author of the period. His publications number eighty, including fourteen books, ten pamphlets, twenty-two magazine articles, and twenty-nine addresses. His indefatigable industry demonstrated the energy and the diligence of the old order, yet his writings are characteristically aristocratic and grandiose when compared with the more scientific researches of later scholars like John Bell Henneman (1864–1908), whose voluminous editorial labours represent very well the activity of the new generation.

Strange to say, the breath of the new era first faintly stirred those who had been in the thick of the fight. It was, perhaps, not so strange that men like Zebulon Baird Vance (1830–94) and Benjamin Harvey Hill (1823–82) should be reconciled to the outcome. Vance was not only a strong Union man but he opposed secession with all the fire of his oratory until the moment that he heard of the attack on Sumter. It seems natural, then, that after the war he should sing again the glories of the Union, one and indivisible. His *Sketches of North Carolina*, however, which had appeared serially in *The Norfolk Landmark*, show much the same fond longing for the past which charms in Johnston and Bagby. Hill in Georgia fought for the preservation of national unity even in the secession convention, yet, once in the war, he was as fervent in the support of the Confederacy. This fervour was intensified by the Reconstruction policy of the National Government. His *Notes on the Situation* in 1869 were vitriolic in their denunciation. Much of this belligerent attitude appears in his speeches in Congress. They have a narrative quality which, though less lofty, is more telling than the ringing rhetoric of some of his peers.

The case of General John Brown Gordon (1832–1904) is even more memorable. His brilliant record in the Confederate armies was closed by his generous address to his soldiers after the surrender at Appomattox, in which he exhorted them to bear their trials bravely, to go home in peace, to obey the laws, to rebuild the country, and to work for the weal and harmony of the Republic. In spite of the iniquities of Reconstruction, his political career was instinct with the same chivalrous spirit, which found its most widely echoing expression in that speech in the Senate in 1893 when he pledged the South to maintain law and order. His *Reminiscences of the Civil War*, with its oratorical swing and fluency, diffused throughout the North that generous recognition of the foe and that proud acceptance of the result which have overcome the passions of sectionalism on both sides of Mason and Dixon's line.

The noblest example of this reconciling spirit among antebellum leaders is Lucius Quintus Cincinnatus Lamar (1825–93). Born and reared in Georgia, and a strict disciple of Calhoun, he removed at the age of twenty-four to Mississippi, which eventually became his home. So thoroughly imbued was he with the justice of the extreme Southern attitude that, as chairman of the Committee of Fifteen, he brought in the ordinance of secession for Mississippi. He came out of the ordeal of war with the vision of a new heaven and a new earth, for the first heaven and the first earth had passed away. But the dark years of Reconstruction fell over his soul like a pall. Pondering on the supreme necessity of getting his people into harmonious relations with the Federal Government, he saw no hope except in their going to work to restore their material prosperity and to establish their institutions of education. In 1872 he was elected a representative of Mississippi, the first Democrat of the Old South to enter the halls of Congress. To one object he was consecrated: the perfect reconciliation of the North and the South. The opportunity to remove from the North a wellnigh universal suspicion of the South and to rescue the nation from the perils of an increasing sectional hate came to him sooner than he anticipated. The death of Charles Sumner was the occasion of resolutions in both houses of Congress. On 28 April, 1874, Lamar delivered that Eulogy of Sumner which melted the distinguished audience to tears, which rang through the nation in a day, and which echoes still. Filled with the patriot's pride and faith, it revealed the Southern people to their better selves and began in the North to mitigate the estrangements of a generation. Yet the loftiness of its sentiment is not the passport to posterity which it should be. The long Southern roll of the eloquence needs the revealing tones of a voice to bring out its majesty. Frequently the sentences become for the average modern reader too far prolonged or too intricately involved to surrender their meaning at once. The same drawback may be found in Lamar's other deliverances, even the carefully prepared oration at the unveiling of the Calhoun monument at Charleston. But with those who read speeches the Eulogy of Sumner will live as the noble expression of a patriot and a seer, whose gentleness and devotion will win him a bright and quiet niche in the dark and troublous vestibule of Reconstruction.

Another disciple of Calhoun, Jabez Lamar Monroe Curry (1825–1903), born in Georgia but reared in Alabama, learned at the University of Georgia to regard the Arch-Secessionist as second only to Aristotle. Going to Harvard in 1843 to study law, he was soon fired by Horace Mann with a passion for universal education. It was therefore natural, although he became a United States Congressman and a member of the Confederate Congress, that after the war he should enter educational work, in order that the youth of his section might be fitted to build worthily and helpfully in the tumble-down world that surrounded them. As agent of the Peabody and Slater Funds, he aided more than any other one man to develop an irresistible public opinion for the education of the whole people, both white and black, in the Southern States. Today the most valuable of his educational writings is the *History of the Peabody Education Fund*, which records the progress of one of the most beneficent philanthropies since the war. He is thus on the side of the constructionists as opposed to those forensic champions who revelled in the abstract notions of States' rights and liberty, but where he develops the theory of secession, as in *Civil History of the Government of the Confederate States* or *The Southern States of the American Union*, there is a pugnacious reiteration of outworn arguments which will appeal chiefly to the historical student or the partisan. His numerous other writings dealing with the South, even when they utter a national spirit or retail personal experiences, lack the colour and the vigour which render Gordon's reminiscences still interesting. His life of Gladstone lacks power to portray and to analyze.

But the figures we have passed in review, revered and stately though they be, and eloquently as they avowed the new spirit of allegiance to a common country, in reality belonged to an earlier generation than that of the Reconstruction period. Those who did not, like Bagby and Johnston, sing the glories of an aristocratic civilization resting on slavery, were at least imbued, like Vance and Hill and Gordon, with the elder spirit, which regarded politics as the only arena toward which ambition beckoned. Their writings are consequently concerned with lofty ideals of human rights and the limits of governmental action. They are rhythmic with the cadences of an oratory which too frequently forsook cold argument for fervid appeals to tradition and class interests. Rare was the apostle like Curry who preached the democratic necessity of developing both the black and the white races. Rarer still was the seer like Lamar who divined that the hope of the future lay in going to work to develop the material resources of the section.

Not till we reach the fascinating figure of Henry Woodfin Grady (1851–89) do we find a true representative of the new generation. He is recognized by common consent as the chief latter-day orator of his section. Born in Athens, Georgia, he grew up in the turmoil of the Civil War, often visited the camp of his father's soldiers, and could never forget the scene when Major Grady's remains were brought back from one of the last battles around Petersburg. His sunny disposition and his inexhaustible flow of animal spirits made him a general favourite with the professors at the University of Georgia, where he developed that style which was later to win him fame both South and North. After graduation he became a journalist. The journalism of Georgia, like that of the whole South, was then in a deplorable state. The State governments were still in the hands of the carpet-baggers. The editors drew what comfort they could from denouncing the Republicans as the authors of all evil. Into this sullen circle came Grady with the bright, racy humour which had captivated his classmates, with a freshness and an individuality which caused many a Georgia editor to open his eyes. His own editorial ventures were brilliant in their audacity but dismal in their financial returns. By 1875 he had dissipated his fortune. Borrowing fifty dollars, he gave twenty to his wife, and with the remainder, with characteristic impetuosity, bought a ticket to New York. There, by a single article, he won the position of Southern correspondent of the New York *Herald*. His reports of the South Carolina riots of 1876 and of the Florida election frauds of the same year were so graphic and complete that they established his future. In 1879 he was enabled to purchase a quarter interest in *The*

Atlanta Constitution, a medium through which he impressed himself upon his state and his section.

In 1886, by reason of a speech on *The New South* delivered 22 December before the New England Society of New York City, he became the spokesman of the new era, and the title of that speech became the watchword of a vast movement. Though it aroused the ire of the old school, as seen above in the denunciation of "the banners of utilitarianism" by Charles Colcock Jones, Jr., it expressed a new sense of the economic basis of society and of the social conditions which must obtain more and more in the regenerated South. Some of his later speeches are notable. *The South and her Problem*, delivered in Dallas, 26 October, 1887, and *The Farmer and the Cities*, at Elberton, Georgia, in June, 1889, show him as the evangel of the new gospel to his own section. His treatment of the negro problem before the Boston Merchants' Association in December, 1889, was more cogent in argument than his other addresses, but less ardent in appeal. Yet one of the auditors characterized it as "a cannon-ball in full flight, fringed with flowers." Weakened by his exertions on this trip in the unexpected cold of the Northern winter, he returned to Atlanta to die 23 December, 1889.

One singular feature of Grady's career, and one significant of the new era, was that he never held public office. His ambition shows the change which had come over the spirit of the South:

My ambition is a simple one. I shall be satisfied with the labors of my life if, when those labors are over, my son, looking abroad upon a better and grander Georgia—a Georgia that has filled the destiny God intended her for—when her towns and cities are hives of industry, and her country-side the exhaustless fields from which their stores are drawn—when every stream dances on its way to the music of spindles, and every forest echoes back the roar of the passing train—when her valleys smile with abundant harvests, and from her hillsides come the tinkling of bells as her herds and flocks go forth from their folds—when more than two million people proclaim her perfect independence and bless her with their love—I shall be more than content, I say, if my son, looking upon such scenes as these, can stand up and say: "My father bore a part in this work, and his name lives in the memory of this people."

This ambition dictated the character of his journalism and the substance of his speeches. In his newspaper he endeavoured without shadow of turning to draw attention to the material resources of the South and to develop her industries. In his speeches he displayed even greater brilliancy, fervour, and versatility in presenting the various phases of the topic. Incapable of rancour himself, he with magnanimous sincerity and a whole heart endeavoured to remove the barriers to harmony and co-operation between the sections. In short, he became the orator of the peacemakers.

This purpose in part explains the form of those addresses. He was delivering an appeal to his public, not conducting a legal argument. He was moving his auditors to a new point of view, not convincing them of a scientific truth. He threw into the effort all the ardour of a generous and enthusiastic nature. The pictures of his fancy, the constant balancing of phrases and ideas, the play of wit and humour and pathos were employed with the instinctive effectiveness of one who has learned to sway audiences. They reflect, too, in many ways the sonorous models of Southern oratory that formed the pattern and ideal for his youthful attempts. Yet there is a greater definiteness of thought, a closer linking of word and idea, on the whole a simpler and more vivid style than obtained in the old school. To the ears of the sophisticated, of course, his periods are cloying in their fluency. To thousands of untutored youths all over the South, on the other hand, his words have seemed the echoes of a silver tongue flowing like the honey of Hybla. His picture of "a country home, a quiet, modest house, sheltered by great trees," his vision of the returning Confederate soldier, "this hero in gray with the heart of gold," have been declaimed from hundreds of school and college platforms all over the South. His continued popularity proves that his sentiment was not merely a device for moving an audience but was the outpouring of Grady's real nature, full of quick sympathy and unfathomed tenderness. In character and disposition Grady belonged with the Old South; in vision and purpose he was the herald of the New.

No account of the New South in literature would be complete without notice of the life and writings of Booker T. Washington[1]

1 See also Book III. Chap

(1859–1915). He was not only a product of Reconstruction but he contributed much to the progress and prosperity of his section in the new era. Born two or three years before the war on a Virginia plantation, his mother a slave, his father he knew not who, he a few years after the war joined in that rush for an education which seized great numbers of the freedmen. The acuteness of that struggle, the inspiring tenacity with which it was maintained, form one of the bright pages in that dark period. When he had completed his studies in Hampton, he turned aside from the opportunities for political preferment which lured many of his race to destruction, and devoted his days and his nights to the upbuilding of his fellow freedmen. In 1881 he was called to the obscure village of Tuskegee in Alabama to take charge of what was to be a normal school for coloured people. Thereafter his name and Tuskegee became synonymous for negro progress. For he there worked out with dauntless persistence a scheme for education which would fit the negro to his actual surroundings. Consecrating all of his vast energy to that cause, he became long before his death the foremost representative of his race in the world, a writer known in every section of his own country, and one of the most eloquent speakers of his generation.

Of his addresses, typical is the five-minute speech delivered at the Atlanta exposition 17 September, 1895, which made him the recognized leader of his race. Aside from the fact that it presented a platform so simple, yet so fundamental in its assumptions, that both black and white could stand thereon, it illustrates well the guiding principles of his rhetoric, that every word shall mean something. There is in it little of that fatally easy use of superlatives, that sonorous succession of periods, which so tickled the ears of old-time audiences. There is little of the habitual resort to cunning balance and alliteration which even Grady constantly introduced to secure his effects. It is simple, direct, vivid, yet sustained by a high devotion to the future of his race. Not only in its message but in its style it speaks of the New South.

His writings display the same characteristics. Of these, his autobiography, consisting of *Up from Slavery* and *Working with Hands*, forms one of the noblest records America has to show. *Up from Slavery* in particular, the annals of his childhood and rise to fame, with its mingled pathos and humour, its etching of the past, its modest story of a quiet but heart-stirring achievement, has already become one of the classics of its type. Of his other voluminous writings, dealing almost exclusively with the colored race, weighty is *The Future of the American Negro*, which contains his views on the enigma which ever confronts the South. Not founding his argument on those lofty conceptions of right and justice which aroused such fanatical zeal before the war, but with a sanity of outlook upon the industrial situation in the South and an unclouded vision of the progress of his race in the past and of the necessary steps in future advance, he discusses the various aspects of the problem with a dispassionate but illuminating calm. Though his contact with the more steadfast and aspiring kind of negro may have filled him with undue hope, yet no reader can fail to admire his self-forgetful devotion to his race, or refuse to accord him a high place among the prose writers of the New South.

The poets, also, represent the effects of Reconstruction on literature in the South. They belonged to a younger generation. They felt in their own persons the wreck of their section. Their outlook upon life and their practice of their art were formed or deeply changed by the hopeless struggles of reconstruction and restoration. Their more sensitive souls felt and recorded the underlying attitudes of their generation. Both their lives and their writings merit close attention.

The first voices were proud and defiant. They echoed in more poignant phrases the Berserker rage of the Southern editorial columns. Most notable of these myriad voices of the press was Carlyle McKinley (1847–1904), of the Charleston *News and Courier*. At fifteen he forsook the quiet campus of the University of Georgia and distinguished himself by bravery in the trenches before Sherman at Atlanta. Like most Southern youths after the war, he drifted about for a time between two worlds, one dead, the other powerless to be born. In 1875 he joined the staff of the *News and Courier*, and after a brief excursion into commercial life in New York he returned in 1881 as associate editor, where in failing health he remained the rest of his days.

His prose was greatly admired, especially his *An Appeal to Pharaoh* (1889), an argument for deportation, a solution of the negro problem to which thousands of Southerners in the early de-spair of Reconstruction turned with hope, until the enthusiasm of Grady and the doctrine of Booker T. Washington brought to light a more adequate economic and sociological basis.

Nevertheless, it is in poetry that the man and the period are revealed. Not only did McKinley love the South with his whole heart, but the Lost Cause was dear to him in a pas-sionate degree. Early in Reconstruction his *At Timrod's Grave* voiced the complaint of Southern poets:

> For singing, Fate hath given sighs,
> For music, we make moan.

His undaunted demeanour under the manifold injustices of Reconstruction speaks for his state and his section. Typical is his *South Carolina—1876:*

> They've wasted all her royal dower;
> They've wrought her wrong with evil power;
> And is she faint, or doth she cower?
> —She scorns them in her weakest hour!
>
> She bides her time—a patient Fate!
> Her sons are gathering in the gate!
> She knows to counsel and to wait,
> And vengeance knoweth no "too late."

In later years he came to take refuge in poetry from the dis-tresses of life, to find in it an anodyne. Probably the best ex-ample of this mood, *Sapelo*, illustrates not only the finish of his verse, which lifts him above the rhymesters of his section, but at the same time the lack of that inspiration or individ-ual power which would give him a secure place in the poetical annals of our country.

It is individuality of style that strikingly distinguishes another Reconstruction poet who could never forget the Lost Cause and who sought solace in the realms of poesy. John Banister Tabb (1845–1909) was born and reared at The Forest, a plantation near Richmond. The only blemish on the bright untroubled period of his boyhood with a loved mother and kind tutors was weakness of the eyes, which at the age of twelve an occulist pronounced incurable. His youthful passions were poetry and music, yet when the conflict came he soon forsook these nymphs to fly to arms and war. In 1862 he entered the navy as a captain's clerk and after two years of service was captured on a blockade runner and confined to Point Lookout Prison. There Sidney Lanier's flute-playing made the two men firm friends for life. Unlike Lanier, however, Tabb could not forget the prison and the victorious Northern armies which dispersed his wealth. In the blank years following the war he first studied music and then resigned himself to teaching. He was ordained a Catholic priest in 1884, but remained in St. Charles College at Ellicott City, Maryland, till his death, for as teacher of literature, especially of his favourite poets, Poe, Keats, and Shelley, he was eminently successful. His total blindness in 1906 he bore with equanimity until his death in 1909.

His career reveals the character of his mind. He was detached from life and sought to pierce below its aspects to the soul beneath. Nature, to be sure, he loved. His memory dwelt fondly on the Virginia scenery of his boyhood, the rolling slopes and "smooth-sliding" streams, the kildee and the wood-robin of that Utopian period. In Maryland he liked to take walks and come back with flowers and leaves. More than thirty birds are celebrated in his poems. Yet even when they stir the deepest emotion these voices of nature speak to him of some facet of human life. The call of the robin in the waning daylight reminds him of the shadowy but inevitable approach of Death:

> Come, ere oblivion speed to me, flying
> Swifter than thou.

It is his underlying philosophy that God speaks to man through the multiform aspects of nature; that

> Love, of sweet Nature the Lord,
> Hath fashioned each manifold chord
> To utter His visible Word;

that the poet acts merely as interpreter. Indeed, so intent is Tabb on the thought symbolized that he comes to find loveliness in nature only as its aspects may be interpreted. More

than that, everywhere in his unformulated but profoundly-
felt philosophy,—and not in mere figure of speech,—all the
outwardly beautiful objects in nature live and breathe and
have their being in God as much as we.   Almost might St.
Francis of Assisi have written *Brotherhood:*

> Knew not the Sun, sweet Violet,
>   The while he gleaned the snow,
> That thou in darkness sepulchred,
>   Wast slumbering below?
> Or spun a splendor of surprise
> Around him to behold thee rise?
>
> Saw not the Star, sweet Violet,
> What time a drop of dew
> Let fall his image from the sky
>   Into thy deeper blue?
> Nor waxed he tremulous and dim
> When rival Dawn supplanted him?
>
> And dreamest thou, sweet Violet,
>   That I, the vanished Star,
> The Dewdrop, and the morning Sun,
>   Thy closest kinsmen are—
> So near that, waking or asleep,
> We each and all thine image keep?

Quite in keeping with this detachment from mundane
affairs, this preoccupation with the abstract relationships of
life, is Tabb's absorption in the dogmas of the Church.   That
they should have engaged his imagination so deeply reveals the
strength of his other-worldliness, the extent to which he fled
from the ordinary interests of men.   One human feeling, however, he displayed in a beautiful degree—friendship.   His
affection for Sidney Lanier in particular was one of the bright
strands in his life.   Their few months together in prison reveal
an affinity between them that was not dimmed by the lapse of
years.

Yet, as we shall see, their poetic styles were in sharp contrast.   An English critic has compared "the long, voluminous,
rushing flow of Lanier with the minute, delicately carved work"
of Tabb rather to the credit of Tabb, who, he says, "piping on

his flute can do things which Lanier's great four-manual organ could never accomplish." It surely will be conceded that Tabb's poetic manner is as individual as Lanier's. Yet his first poems in 1883, some nineteen lyrics and a few sonnets, reveal little of this originality or indeed of poetical promise. The shortest poems were in ten lines, whereas his later style tends to quatrains. Working in such small compass, he has polished his technique to a point near perfection. The diction is of extreme simplicity. The measures flow on without a ripple. The figures are suggested in the most concise phrasing. In short, his poems are a series of the most delicate cameos. Contrast and endless comparison are the basis of his style, which is largely coloured by the frequency of scriptural allusions, the constant introduction and personification of abstract ideas, and the subtle intermixture of symbolism. He was so wrapped up in his poetic fancies that his figures often pass over into conceits. Who else could give to the spiritual inquiry "Is thy servant a dog?" such a turn as this:

> So *must* he be who, in the crowded street,
> Where shameless Sin and flaunting Pleasure meet,
> Amid the noisome footprints finds the sweet
> Faint vestiges of Thy feet.

In his *Child's Verse* the effect is natural enough, for his puns, no matter how far fetched they appear to the sober eye, there strike one as flashes of wit. But in serious poetry the effect is different. The mind hardly has time to link the symbol and the interpretation. The compression does not permit full grasp of the significance.

In spite of these shortcomings, however, we must concede that Father Tabb, though he lived constantly in a rarefied religious atmosphere, far removed from the daily interests of man, yet was endowed with an ear sensitive to those overtones which escape most men and that he was often visited with those intuitions which reveal nooks of beauty, aspects of cheer. Though his lute was of few strings, he played it with exquisite tone.

Another class of Reconstruction poets felt less keenly the sting of defeat. Some in fact came to catch the new national spirit and have even expressed in poetry their devotion to the common flag. Verse was for them not so much an avenue of escape from the cares and tribulation of this life as a means of self-expression. A humble and rather negative representative is John Henry Boner (1845–1903), whom North Carolina now claims as her chief poet of the period, although in Reconstruction times she drove him from her borders. Coming from a quite different class of society from that of Tabb or McKinley, he found it easy to become a Republican after the war. Not till his demise did his fellow citizens forgive him. In 1870, when, after a campaign that approached civil war, a Democratic governor was elected, the Republicans took care of Boner by placing him in the Government Printing Office in Washington, for which he was fitted by his earlier trade as printer; but when the Democrats again gained control of the national government, Boner was dismissed on the ground of offensive partisanship. Fortunately his poetry had won him the ear of Edmund Clarence Stedman, who obtained for him in New York various tasks of compilation. He eventually became editor of *The Literary Digest*, which he conducted with ability until his resignation in 1897.

All this time, however, he cherished memories of the South and the scenes of his boyhood. In particular, the theme that pleased Stedman, the music of the pines as the wind sighed through them or the moon rose beyond them, haunted him with a gentle yearning. *The Light'ood Fire* lightens his memory with fond pictures. *Crismus Times is Come* is an unusually faithful representation of the negro character and religion. These effusions are carefully finished. The versification is smooth, often liquid. The descriptive passages are clear and sometimes vivid. The tone of melancholy that pervades his best efforts casts the charm of subdued light over both the measures and the man. Nevertheless, Boner is deficient in imagination, and adds no new note, no original element, to American verse. He will consequently live as a poet of one poem—*Poe's Cottage at Fordham*. The subject enlisted a deeper interest than even the events of Boner's own life and much deeper than the swirling progress of his adopted section. The lines well up from a sympathy that interprets and enshrines. They flow with a haunting melody worthy of the magician in metre whom they celebrate.

Less sectional, more completely national in spirit, was Robert Burns Wilson (1850–1916). He was endowed with a double gift—the gifts of painting and poetry, each of them genuine. It must be conceded that he did not have to break the shackles of sectionalism. Born in Pennsylvania and moving early to Virginia, he looked back, not on memories of conflict, but on scenes of quiet peace. He early studied art. At barely twenty he received further impetus while on a canoe trip with John W. Alexander. Much of his later success may be attributed to Alexander's influence and assistance. In painting he sought "to catch the passing and elusive things in nature, which do not sit for their pictures." It is just the mood and feeling of these evanescent aspects of nature which form the substance of his poetry. Visions of Kentucky woods and fields float by on the wings of music, but there is usually some melancholy cadence or echo in the strain. The most famous, and probably the best of his poems, *When Evening Cometh On*, is characteristic of his method of presenting pictures suffused with emotion in order to create a dominant mood. In spite of the variety of measures which he employs, there is a weakness in his repetition of similar themes in successive volumes.

During the Spanish-American War Wilson made clear how truly the South had become national. His *Remember the Maine* not only occupied the front page of the New York *Herald* but was reprinted all over the country. His *Such is the Death the Soldier Dies*, which appeared originally in *The Atlantic Monthly*, was at once welcomed for the gentle pathos of its picture and its sentiment. Many stirring and martial poems by other Southerners attest the genuineness of the national spirit which had followed the dark and bitter days of Reconstruction. Not by any surcease of sorrow but by the genuine fire of a new vision did Southern poetry bud forth into a patriotic cry. The days of McKinley and his *South Carolina—1876* had given way to the new conception of a united country and eager, confident prospects for the future.

The most salient figure in this change, in fact the most distinguished man of letters of the New South, is Sidney Lanier, who, like Wilson, was endowed with a double gift—music and poetry. He was born in Macon, Georgia, 3 February, 1846.

His father was a lawyer of undistinguished abilities but of cultured and literary tastes. His mother was devotedly religious, and reared her family in the strict Presbyterian faith. His grandfather's hotel, the Lanier House, was the centre of a cordial, hospitable social life. The city of Macon, a prosperous commercial centre, counted among its citizens many wealthy plantation owners but few who aspired to higher education or intellectual achievement. Even his father's literary interests seem to have been confined to Shakespeare and Addison and Sir Walter Scott—to the items of that self-sufficient culture which reigned everywhere in the South before the Civil War.

Although Scott and Froissart fired Lanier's young mind with ideals of chivalry, the thing which set him apart from the Macon school boys was his remarkable musical ability. At seven he had made himself a reed flageolet, and on receiving a flute at Christmas he soon organized quartets and bands among his playfellows. Indeed, it was because of his leadership in serenading parties at Oglethorpe, which he had entered shortly before his fifteenth birthday, that his father brought him home to spend a year in the Macon post office. When he returned to Oglethorpe as a junior he began to play the violin with such effect that he would at times lose consciousness for hours. His father, fearing this stimulation, induced him to return to the flute and discouraged him as much as possible from devotion to music. The result is seen in the boy's journal:

The prime inclination—that is, natural bent (which I have checked, though) of my nature is to music, and for that I have the greatest talent; indeed, not boasting, for God gave it me, I have an extraordinary musical talent, and feel it within me plainly that I could rise as high as any composer. But I cannot bring myself to believe that I was intended for a musician, because it seems so small a business in comparison with other things which, it seems to me, I might do.

His later life seems to bear out the assumption that America, by his father's solicitude and the social pressure of Southern opinion at the time, was deprived of another distinguished name in music.

The life at Oglethorpe was a period of intellectual advance for Lanier. The major influence was exerted by James Woodrow of the department of science, who took the boy on long rambles, or on long drives, when the two of them would talk about everything either of them was interested in. Woodrow thought so much of Lanier that he secured for him an appointment as tutor. Better still, he gave the future poet a zest for science that remained with him to the end, and a vision of the intellectual life which shaped his aspirations and his future conduct. Giving up music as a possible career, Lanier resolved to spend two years in Heidelberg and to return to a professorship in some American college.

Then came the cataclysm of Civil War, and with it for Lanier a period of storm and stress that tossed him this way and that for a dozen years. At the outbreak he was enthusiastic at the prospect of a South more wealthy than history had yet seen. Macon, he thought, was to become a great art centre whose streets were to be lined with marble statues like unto Athens of old. At the close of the college year he, like nearly all the other teachers and the students of Oglethorpe, enlisted for service. The war itself was not an unmixed evil to Lanier. Although he saw some exciting service as a signal-man along the James River, he was for three years allowed ample time for study and for cherishing that passion for the very highest which grew with his years. He now began to contemplate a literary life as his vocation. To his father he wrote in 1864, "Gradually I find that my whole soul is merging itself into this business of writing, and especially of writing poetry." He began his novel, *Tiger Lilies*, and sent several poems to his father for criticism. In 1864, however, he was transferred to Wilmington, North Carolina, where he served as signal officer on the blockade runners. In November he was captured in the Gulf Stream and sent to Point Lookout Prison in Maryland. There he continued to play the flute, which won him the friendship of Tabb. He busied himself with German poetry, but the prison conditions were so loathsome as to induce a breakdown in health. He came out emaciated to a skeleton, and when he finally reached Macon in March he fell ill and lingered near death for two months. Thereafter his life was an unavailing search for health.

The fact that members of his family "who used to roll in wealth are, everyday, with their own hands ploughing the little patch of ground which the war has left them, while their wives do the cooking and washing," did not disturb him. What he felt most keenly was the intellectual stagnation of the South. Already in 1866 he was, with characteristic breadth and lack of prejudice, writing thus to a Northern friend:

You are all so alive up there, and we are all so dead down here! I begin to have serious thoughts of emigrating to your country, so that I may live a little. There is not enough attrition of mind on mind here to bring out any sparks from a man.

Even among these untoward surroundings he continued to foster his literary ambitions. In another letter he continues:

We have no newspapers here with circulation enough to excite our ambition, and, of course, the Northern papers are beyond our reach. Our literary life, too, is a lonely and somewhat cheerless one; for beyond our father, a man of considerable literary acquirements and exquisite taste, we have not been able to find a single individual who sympathized in such pursuits enough to warrant showing him our little productions—so scarce is "general cultivation" here.

I am thirsty to know what is going on in the great art world up there; you have no idea how benighted we all are. I have only recently begun to get into the doings of literary men through "The Round Table" which I have just commenced taking.

That journal not only satisfied his thirst for the doings of the great world but helped to foster the national spirit which he was to voice more clearly than other poets of his section, and to fire his own ambition for a literary career. Several of his earlier poems appeared in its pages.

To the same inspiration may be traced his visit to New York in 1867 to find a publisher for *Tiger Lilies*. Possibly it was the reputation he gained from its publication which caused him to marry in the face of the precarious future. The setting up of the state governments under the Reconstruction Act of 1867 made the prospect for him, as for hundreds of others, even darker and more discouraging. Despairing of earning a living by his pen, and seeing that Southern colleges were so poor as "to hold out absolutely no inducement in the way of support to a professor," he yielded in January, 1869, to his father's solicitation and betook himself to the study of law.

The work in the law office kept him very busy. He did indeed write a few humorous dialect poems, published in various local papers, but in general his resignation was that expressed in a letter to Paul Hamilton Hayne in 1870:

> I've not put pen to paper, in the literary way, for a long time. How I thirst to do so, how I long to sing a thousand various songs that oppress me, unsung,—is inexpressible. Yet, the mere work that brings bread gives me no time. I know not, after all, if this is a sorrowful thing. Nobody likes my poems, except two or three friends,—who are themselves poets, and can supply themselves!

But music regained its ascendancy over him. Letters to his wife written in 1869, 1870, and 1871, on visits to New York, reveal the intensity of his pleasure in a violin solo, or the singing of Nilsson, or Theodore Thomas's orchestra, where he plunged into an amber sea of music and came away from what he felt might have been heaven.

The turning point of his life came in San Antonio, Texas, whither he went in the winter of 1872–3 for his health. He filled in part of his time there with literary projects, but the inspiration of his stay was found in a group of German musicians, who received "amid a storm of applause" his flute-playing before the *Maennerchor*. In February, 1873, he played before "a very elegant-looking company of ladies and gentlemen." He reported:

> I had not played three seconds before a profound silence reigned among the people. . . . When I allowed the last note to die, a simultaneous cry of pleasure broke forth from men and women that almost amounted to a shout, and I stood and received the congratulations that thereupon came in, so wrought up by my own playing with (hidden) thoughts, that I could but smile mechanically, and make stereotyped returns to the pleasant sayings, what time my heart worked falteringly, like a mouth that is about to cry.

Two weeks later he wrote:

I have writ the most beautiful piece "Field-larks and Black-birds," wherein I have mirrored Mr. Field-lark's pretty eloquence so that I doubt he would know the difference betwixt the flute and his own voice.

In the summer he confessed to Hayne:

Are you, by the way, a musician? Strange, that I have never before asked this question,—when so much of my own life consists of music. I don't know that I've ever told you, that whatever turn I have for art is purely musical; poetry being, with me, a mere tangent into which I shoot sometimes. I could play passably on several instruments before I could write legibly; and since then, the very deepest of my life has been filled with music, which I have studied and cultivated far more than poetry.

Inspired with this new faith, he again repaired to New York, this time determined to settle his future. He revelled in the musical associations which he quickly formed. By November he had been engaged by Asger Hamerik for the position of first flute in the new Peabody Orchestra forming in Baltimore. On 29 November he wrote his declaration of independence to his father:

Why should I, nay, how *can* I, settle myself down to be a third-rate struggling lawyer for the balance of my little life as long as there is a certainty almost absolute that I can do some other thing so much better. Several persons, from whose judgment there can be no appeal, have told me, for instance, that I am the greatest flute-player in the world; and several others, of equally authoritative judgment, have given me an almost equal encouragement to work with my pen. . . . My dear father, think how for twenty years, through poverty, through pain, through weariness, through sickness, through the uncongenial atmosphere of a farcical college and of a bare army and then of an exacting business life, through all the discouragements of being wholly unacquainted with literary people and literary ways—I say, think how, in spite of all these depressing circumstances, and of a thousand more which I could enumerate, those two figures of music and poetry have steadily kept in my heart so that I could not banish them. Does it not seem to you as to me, that I begin to have a right to enroll myself among the devotees of those two sublime arts, after having followed them so long and so humbly, and through so much bitterness.

Thus he entered upon the third and final period of his life, one of feverish activity. During the winter succeeding his great resolution he grew rapidly in the intellectual grasp of music. He had the soul of an artist, and gradually acquired the technical skill to bring the most out of his instrument. Still the strength of his renderings always resided in the emotion he imparted. His conductor testifies:

His conception of music was not reached by any analytical study of note by note, was intuitive, spontaneous; like a woman's reason: he felt it so, because he felt it so, and his delicate perception required no more logical form of reasoning. His playing appealed to the musically learned and unlearned—for he would mesmerize the listener; but the artist felt in his performance the superiority of the momentary living inspiration to all the rules and shifts of mere technical scholarship.

The next year he still yearned for a musical career. He told Dr. Leopold Damrosch, then conductor of the Philharmonic Society of New York, that music "is not a matter of mere preference, it is a spiritual necessity. I must be a musician, I cannot help it." But the conference with Damrosch impressed Lanier with the great handicap he suffered in lack of thorough technical training. Though he continued to gain intense joy from music, literature more and more occupied his thoughts and monopolized his time.

In February, 1875, *Corn*, which he had conceived the preceding summer and had rewritten during the winter, appeared in *Lippincott's Magazine.* It was one of the earliest Southern poems to receive publication in a Northern periodical. Notable, too, is the fact that the verses are not an effort to escape into some dreamland but the presentation of a widespread problem of Georgia agriculture.

Corn attracted favourable attention, notably from Gibson Peacock, editor of the Philadelphia *Evening Bulletin.* Within a month Lanier was at work on a second ambitious poem, *The Symphony*, which appeared in June, and which brought him the friendship of Bayard Taylor. The firm of Lippincott was able to fill Lanier's time with hackwork. The whole summer was spent in preparing "a sort of spiritualized guidebook" to Florida. Yet he was happy. He wrote of himself as one

who, after many days and nights of tribulation and bloody sweat, has finally emerged from all doubt into the quiet and yet joyful activity of one who knows exactly what his *Great Passion* is and what his God desires him to do. As for me, life has resolved simply into a time during which I must get upon paper as many as possible of the poems with which my heart is stuffed like a schoolboy's pocket.

When at the instance of Bayard Taylor he was appointed to write the cantata for the Centennial Exposition to be held in Philadelphia, he was jubilant. His patriotic fervour produced also *The Psalm of the West.* A place among American poets he challenged by bringing out a slender volume of poems late in the same year.

Because of a severe illness he was ordered South for the winter of 1876–7, but there he continued to throw off "a sort of spray of little songs" and to hope for "that repose which ought to fill the artist's firmament while he is creating."

The four remaining years of his life were spent in an unavailing search for that repose. He endeavoured to make sure where next week's dinners were coming from before carrying out his ambitions for creative work. He continued his connection with the Peabody Orchestra, but his chief endeavour turned him aside, this time into the field of scholarship. He wandered about in Old and Middle English, and ranged far in the Elizabethan period. These enthusiastic studies resulted in lectures at the Peabody Institute, and in 1879 in his appointment as lecturer in Johns Hopkins University. *The Science of English Verse* and *The English Novel* are the products of those two years, besides some books for boys and many poems. But consumption had made such advances that it was feared that he would not live to complete his last series of lectures. Indeed, those who listened to him momentarily feared that he would not survive to the end of the hour. In May, 1881, he was taken to the mountains of North Carolina, where he died 7 September.

What shall be said of the product of this eager and varied effort? Shall we lament the incompleteness and immaturity of a life fourteen years longer than Keats's and ten years longer than Shelley's? Shall we bemoan the constant battle with disease, which yet left to Stevenson the energy for an exquisitely wrought style? Shall we bewail the hard necessity of winning his daily bread in a land devastated by civil war and depressed by corrupt government, and the consequent removal to a more congenial and invigorating clime far from friends and family? Or shall we endeavour merely to disengage the essential characteristics and achievements of this troublous activity, so that his contribution to our American heritage may stand out clear?

He did, of course, engage in too much hackwork for his own good or his reputation. Yet so exuberant was his activity that he dispatched all of these tasks with zest. His "sort of spiritualized guide-book" to Florida contains many descriptions over which he must have lingered and which bear witness to a quick eye and a rich humour. He puts into the whole book, too, much of himself, his love of music, his over-refining intellect, his relish of local tradition. His boys' books, the Froissart and King Arthur and the rest, reveal even more of the man. He had from early youth cherished a recurring interest in the deeds and heroes of chivalry. They answered to an innate knightliness of spirit which was fostered by his Southern up-bringing. He would pick up the volume as it came fresh from the printers, familiar though it was by reason of the preparation and the proof-reading, and con page after page with pure delight. In his introductions he never learned to address his young readers, but through the mature style gleams his absorption in this fresh new world of romance.

The same personal reaction appears in his critical writings. The zeal with which he pursued these researches during the last years of his life astonishes one who remembers the meagre initiation he had received at college into the methods of scholarship. The attainments, too, of those few years are considerable. He read with an assiduity that helped to shorten his days and with a whole-souled enthusiasm and moral earnestness that lent to his utterances much of the fluency and high seriousness of Ruskin. But even greater than Ruskin's is his tendency to wander. He did not keep the goal in view.

He did not sift and arrange and clarify with a dominant impression in mind. He sauntered along the broad highway, frequently wandering off into the leafy woods and lingering there intent on the strange foliage. Consequently his critical writings are an amazing collection of individual vagaries and intuitive insights. *Shakespeare and his Forerunners* contains such surprising pronouncements as that Drummond of Hawthornden is "one of the chief glories of the English tongue." Yet he could often divine an essential quality, as in his remark on Chaucer's works as "full of cunning hints and twinkle-eyed suggestions which peep between the lines like the comely faces of country children between the fence-bars as one rides by."

The same want of the perspective and balance that come from broad and profound knowledge characterizes his lectures on *The English Novel.* His effort to trace the conception of personality from the time of the Greeks was a perilous undertaking for one who knew so little of Greek life and was so little acquainted with the sociological implications of any such investigation. The limitations of his upbringing also militated against success. The strict Presbyterian training of his childhood as well as an inherent moral bias conspired to give him a strongly ethical view of literature:

Indeed, we may say that he who has not yet perceived how artistic beauty and moral beauty are convergent lines which run back into a common ideal origin, and who is therefore not afire with moral beauty just as with artistic beauty; that he, in short, who has not come to that state of quiet and eternal frenzy in which the beauty of holiness and the holiness of beauty mean one thing, burn as one fire, shine as one light within him, he is not the great artist.

Consequently he fervently wished that the novels of Fielding and Richardson might be "blotted from the face of the earth." Consequently, too, "in some particulars *Silas Marner* is the most remarkable novel in our language," and its author the greatest of English novelists. The preachments in which he again reminds one of Ruskin are the most interesting portions, because in them the man Lanier shines out and his cherished and innate convictions lie bare.

The most valuable critical work of Lanier is undoubtedly

his *Science of English Verse.* For the consideration of the structure of English verse he was peculiarly well prepared. His own unusually sensitive organism enabled him to respond very delicately to musical effects in verse. Besides, the early impulse to science given by Professor Woodrow in that "farcical college" of his boyhood stimulated him to an investigation of the physics of sound and to a desire for reducing to law the apparent chaos of English versification. The result was pioneer work which appealed to many as the most sensible treatment of the subject which had then appeared. What differentiates this treatment from preceding ones is the insistence that the laws of music and verse are identical, that every foot represents a mathematically equal time interval. Length of interval, and not accent, is therefore the determining element in prosody. The valuable feature of this theory is that it emphasizes the relation of music and poetry and the fundamental importance of rhythm in poetry. Its unfortunate feature is that it insists too strongly on law. No such mathematical relation exists. Accent normally appears at equal time intervals and an accented syllable tends to acquire length. But Lanier wrote long before the psychological investigation of rhythm had begun. He therefore could not see the impossibility of trying to reduce to one rule all the innumerable individual senses of rhythm. Not only no two poets but no two readers would exactly coincide in their sense of rhythm. Lanier was on the right road. He merely made the mistake of taking his own sense of rhythm for a universal law.

Of his other prose writings the letters are the most important. They reveal the man with unusual fullness—the pulsating sea of emotion in which he lived, his exuberance, his passionate love of music, his wavering literary ambition, his buoyancy and humour and occasional despondency, together with his intellectual interests and preferences. Few letters written in America are more interesting. Yet on first dipping into them one is repelled by the same qualities which frequently give one pause in his other writings. The style seems highly artificial, fanciful in its imagery, strained and rhetorical in its phrasing, bookish and precious in its diction. Even in his last years he was rarely simple and direct, for he had from boyhood so steeped himself in the older writers of our tongue, Shakespeare in particular, that a plain and natural way of putting things would have seemed to him insipid, inane, and inartistic. The literary glamour which he casts over his writings, which draws attention from the thought itself to some supposed felicity of expression, never entirely left him. Yet some of his later books, particularly where he is pouring forth his convictions on music, literature, and life, possess all the fluency of the Old South, without ceasing to be strong, luminous, and eloquent.

These shortcomings have been explained away on the ground that his prose is the prose of a poet. Certainly it is as a poet that he jumps to the front rank among Southern writers. The single volume of his verse, gathered with loving care by his wife three years after his death, is paramount among his writings. Upon that corner-stone must be reared whatever reputation he may attain in American letters. Yet his poetry too suffers from defects similar to those in his prose. His verse in general betrays a lack of spontaneity without obtaining that finish, that technical polish, that wedding of word and thought which Tabb achieved. There are, to be sure, moments of fine phrasing, intermittent flashes from the heaven of song:

> Music is love in search of a word

or

> For when God frowns, 'tis then ye shine.

But the general impression is of an elaborated verse, not a gush of words from the heart. Indeed, it seems to have been Lanier's practice to write out the ideas of his poems in prose before turning them into verse. Not many of his poems sang themselves over in his soul before he committed them to paper. He was, on the other hand, forever haunted by ideas for poems. As an obscure lawyer in Georgia he complained to Paul Hamilton Hayne of the "thousand various songs that oppress me, unsung." Even after he had won the ear of the nation, he wrote to Gibson Peacock:

I'm taken with a poem pretty nearly every day, and have to content myself with making a note of its train of thought on the back of whatever letter is in my pocket. I don't write it out because I find my poetry now wholly unsatisfactory.

Sometimes a poem, like *The Symphony*, would shake him like a James River ague until he had finished it. Sometimes he would revise patiently, as in *Corn*. In general it is true that he did not work in that calm serenity which might have brought him closer to perfection of form. There is one blemish, however, that no amount of revision would have eliminated. His exuberant fancy betrayed him into conceits as far fetched as ever disfigured Donne or Crashaw or Tabb. An ox in a clover field becomes "the Course-of-Things," and the rising sun is "the Build-fire Bee." He did not see the grotesqueness of such comparisons, but cultivated them as original adornments to his verse.

Some of the dissatisfaction with the form of his verse is due to his theory that the principles of music and of metrics are identical. His sense of rhythm did not allow sufficient emphasis for accent as marking the equal intervals of time. But he was, naturally, enamoured of his own theory and felt happier when he put it into practice. Of *Special Pleading*, composed in 1875, he wrote: "I have allowed myself to treat words, similes, and metres with such freedom as I desired. The result convinces me I can do so safely." Thereafter he developed his own peculiar style more courageously, sometimes with beautiful effect, but often with the resulting impression of a straining for form. In *Sunrise*, for example, there is a passage descriptive of approaching dawn, beginning,

> Oh, what if a sound should be made!

which is unsurpassed in American poetry for its rendering of the ecstasy in the poet's heart. Yet only a few lines above this marvellous description is a section beginning,

> Ye lispers, whisperers, singers in storms

which illustrates how far his attention wandered from the thought in his elaboration of form, how he forgot that words are primarily symbolic, and that beauty of verse depends on poetic and beautiful thoughts.

Indeed, it must be confessed that Lanier's thought is liable on analysis to be found commonplace and prosaic. This quality is partly due to a didacticism that issued from an unswerving devotion to the ideal. From his youth he cherished a longing for the very highest. How amid the uninspiring surroundings of his boyhood he should have developed this allegiance to the "sweet, living lands of Art" is another of those mysteries with which the history of literature abounds. Yet there is no mystery about the moral purpose which led him to employ poetry to combat intolerance, brutality, and commercialism. It was bred into him at his mother's knee. There is no cynicism in his verse. There is a very strong religious strain. Not only does he curiously eschew all mythological allusions as being pagan in spirit, but he expresses a deeply religious view of life in many poems, as in *The Crystal* and that quaint but unsurpassed *Ballad of Trees and the Master*.

His idealism is also revealed in his eager intellectual interests. Here too he triumphed over his untoward surroundings, as the brief sketch of his life has indicated. Pathetic witness to this inherent bent is found in a letter to Bayard Taylor:

I could never describe to you what a mere drought and famine my life has been, as regards that multitude of matters which I fancy one absorbs when one is in an atmosphere of art, or when one is in conversational relationship with men of letters, with travellers, with persons who have either seen, or written, or done large things. Perhaps you know that, with us of the younger generation in the South since the war, pretty much the whole of life has been merely not dying.

Such complaints did not remain topics of conversation or correspondence. He sought in poetry no refuge from the hard conditions of life. Rather is he one of the leaders of the New South because he grasped at the intellectual and social problems of the time. He dealt with the necessity of planting corn for cotton, with the nascent oppression of labour by capital, with the mission of music and art. His reading of Emerson in the winter of 1876–7 revived an earlier penchant for metaphysics and led to such poems as *A Florida Sunday* and *Individuality*. If these abstruse problems are not handled with power, they at least do honour to the author's lofty purpose and sincerity of execution.

It must be conceded, too, that the profound and abiding interests of his life—love and nature—are peculiarly Southern

in their colouring and substance. It is characteristic that love
is for him not that fleshly passion which has thrilled and burned
in verse since Sappho. It is a kneeling adoration, an ideal
emotion, the only love which one of his purity of life would
avow. He has been well called the Sir Galahad of American
literature. *My Springs* shows how deep and sincere was the
inspiration he received from his dearest partner in misfortune
and ill-health. But there was mingled with the personal devotion to one woman a chivalric devotion to women which came
partly from the Southern ideals of his day. There is in his
poetry no better expression of this than in *The Symphony*.

Nature was to him almost equally dear, and even more
Southern in its appeal. He found nothing within to answer
to the wild and rugged majesty of the mountains. He felt no
expansion of the soul in viewing the limitless plains of Texas.
The broad sand-flats of Florida roused only a longing for the
Georgia hills. Indeed, the only scene which called forth a love
of broad, free places was the long and often viewed marshes at
Brunswick, Georgia, which will go down in American literature
in the eloquent and musical *Marshes of Glynn*. It remains
true, however, that his love for nature was a delicate and
passionate love, the love of an attentive and scrupulous observer of leaves and plants and the thousand minute details of
the summer woods. So personal was the solace and uplifting
of nature that he addressed her various forms with terms of
endearment, more warm than Tabb, yet precisely like St.
Francis of Assisi. He sings of the "fair cousin Cloud," the
"friendly, sisterly, sweetheart leaves." Of himself it was
true that,

> With hands agrope he felt smooth nature's grace,
> Drew her to breast and kissed her sweetheart face.

The Southern aspect of nature lives again in his verse.

Though his abiding interests were Southern, he was not
narrowly Southern in his outlook. On the contrary, it has
already been indicated that much of Lanier's distinction
among Reconstruction poets lies not only in his interest in the
problems of his own time but likewise his sympathy and
comprehension in voicing the new idea of nationality. The

freedom from prejudice which led him to resume relations with a Northern friend at the close of the war, fitted him to sing the meditations of Columbia at the Philadelphia Centennial in 1876. There was nothing mean or narrow in his make-up. The breadth of his own soul and the exalted purpose of his life responded quickly to the new outlook before the nation. He leaped far ahead of his section in grasping and appropriating what he might of the new quickening spirit, but he was largely influential, with Lamar and Grady, in bringing the South to share in that quickening influence. He likewise revealed to the North, even before Grady, the possibilities of the recently vanquished section, and thereby hastened that spiritual *rapprochement* which went on steadily increasing to the end of the century, as we have seen in the patriotic glow of Wilson's poems. If Lanier had only had for poetic expression that genius which he apparently possessed for music, what position might he not have attained? With what full-throated ease then would the South at the Reconstruction period have sung out its inmost heart!

CHAPTER V

Dialect Writers

I. Negro Dialect: Joel Chandler Harris

APART from its purely literary significance, *Uncle Remus: his Songs and his Sayings* makes a threefold claim upon our interest. (1) In the character of Uncle Remus the author has done more than add a new figure to literature; he has typified a race and thus perpetuated a vanishing civilization. (2) In the stories told by Uncle Remus the author has brought the folk-tales of the negro into literature and thus laid the foundation for the scientific study of negro folk-lore. His work has, therefore, a purely historical and ethnological value not possessed in equal degree by any other volume of American short stories. (3) In the language spoken by Uncle Remus the author has reproduced a dialect so accurately and so adequately that each story is worth studying as marking a stage in the development of primitive English.

The life of Joel Chandler Harris was comparatively uneventful though it was an ideal preparation for the work that he was to do. He was born in Eatonton, Putnam County, Georgia, 9 December, 1848,—a date now celebrated annually in all Georgia schools. It is a remarkable fact that the middle counties of Georgia have produced the most representative humorists of the South. Among those who were born or who at some time lived in this part of Georgia may be mentioned A. B. Longstreet,[1] the author of *Georgia Scenes;* Richard Malcolm Johnston,[2] the author of *The Dukesborough Tales;* William

[1] See also Book II. Chap. XIX.　　[2] See also Book III. Chaps. IV and VI.

Tappan Thompson,[1] the author of *Major Jones's Courtship;* and Harry Stillwell Edwards, the author of *Two Runaways and Other Stories.* In the same section were born the two poets Francis O. Ticknor,[2] author of *Little Giffen of Tennessee,* and Sidney Lanier.[3] Middle Georgia was also before the war the most democratic part of the slaveholding states, a circumstance not without its influence upon the development of Harris's genius.

"The sons of the richest men," he tells us,[4] "were put in the fields to work side by side with the negroes, and were thus taught to understand the importance of individual effort that leads to personal independence. It thus happened that there was a cordial, and even an affectionate, understanding between the slaves and their owners, that perhaps had no parallel elsewhere. The poorer whites had no reason to hold their heads down because they had to work for their living. The richest slave owners did not feel themselves above those who had few negroes or none. When a man called his neighbor "Colonel," or "Judge," it was to show his respect, nothing more. For the rest, the humblest held their heads as high as the richest, and were as quick, perhaps quicker, in a quarrel."

Young Harris owed little to the schools but much to a country printing office and to a large library in which it was his privilege to browse at will. At the age of twelve he read one morning the announcement that a new newspaper, *The Countryman*, was to be started a few miles from Eatonton. The editor, Joseph Addison Turner, the owner of a large plantation and many slaves, was a man of sound but old-fashioned literary taste and wished his paper to be modelled after *The Spectator* of Addison and Steele. This announcement kindled the ambition of young Harris, who was already familiar with the best literature of Queen Anne's time and to whom the very name *Spectator* recalled days and nights of indescribable delight. He applied at once for the vacant position of office boy, received a favourable answer, and devoted the rest of his life to journalism in his native State. The duties of his new position were not onerous, and he found time, or took time, to hunt foxes, coons, opossums, and rabbits

---

[1] See also Book II, Chap. XIX.   [2] See also Book III, Chap. III.
[3] See also Book III, Chap. IV.   [4] *Stories of Georgia* (1896), p. 24.

whenever he wished, and to make himself familiar with every nook and corner of the surrounding country.

It was in these early years that Harris laid the foundation for his future work. There was not a negro myth or legend in which he was not interested; there was not a negro custom or peculiarity that he did not know; and there was not a sound or idiom of the negro language that he could not reproduce.

"No man who has ever written," says Thomas Nelson Page, "has known one-tenth part about the negro that Mr. Harris knows, and for those who hereafter shall wish to find not merely the words but the real language of the negro of that section and the habits of mind of all American negroes of the old time, his works will prove the best thesaurus."

In addition to his interest in the life about him Harris soon came to have an equal interest in Turner's large library. Among his favourite books were the writings of Sir Thomas Browne, the essays of Addison and Steele, and later the Bible and Shakespeare. His best loved writer, however, from first to last, and the one whose genius was most like his own, was Goldsmith.

"The only way to describe my experience with *The Vicar of Wakefield*," he said in his later years, "is to acknowledge that I am a crank. It touches me more deeply, it gives me the 'all-overs' more severely than all others. Its simplicity, its air of extreme wonderment, have touched and continue to touch me deeply."

Among the writers of New England Harris seems to have cared least for Emerson and most for Lowell.

"Culture," he once wrote, "is a very fine thing, indeed, but it is never of much account either in life or in literature, unless it is used as a cat uses a mouse, as a source of mirth and luxury. It is at its finest in this country when it is grafted on the sturdiness that has made the nation what it is, and when it is fortified by the strong common sense that has developed and preserved the republic. This is culture with a definite aim and purpose . . . and we feel the ardent spirit of it in pretty much everything Mr. Lowell has written."

In the march through Georgia, General Sherman's army devastated the Turner plantation, and *The Countryman* was of course discontinued. After various experiences with different newspapers Harris joined the staff of *The Atlanta Constitution* in 1876. At this time he was known chiefly as an essayist and poet, but he began almost immediately to publish some of the plantation legends that he had heard from the lips of the negroes before and during the war. The first volume of these stories, *Uncle Remus: his Songs and his Sayings, the Folk-Lore of the Old Plantation*, was published in 1880. It contained thirty-four plantation legends or negro folk-tales, a few plantation proverbs, nine negro songs, a story of the war, and twenty-one sayings or opinions of Uncle Remus, all supposed to be sung or narrated by Uncle Remus himself. In 1883 appeared *Nights with Uncle Remus: Myths and Legends of the Old Plantation*. This contained sixty-nine new legends and was prefaced by an interesting Introduction. Among the new legends were a few told by Daddy Jack, a representative of the dialect spoken on the coastal rice plantations of South Carolina and Georgia. These two volumes represent the author's best work in the domain of negro dialect and folk-lore, and were accorded instant recognition as opening a new and deeply interesting field both to literature and ethnology. Among the later works that continue the Uncle Remus tradition may be mentioned *Uncle Remus and his Friends* (1892), *Mr. Rabbit at Home* (1895), *The Tar-Baby Story and Other Rhymes of Uncle Remus* (1904), *Told by Uncle Remus* (1905), *Uncle Remus and Brer Rabbit* (1907), and *Uncle Remus and the Little Boy* (1910). There were also numerous stories of the War and of the Reconstruction period.

A year before his death Harris founded *Uncle Remus's Magazine*, which survived him only a few years. Immediately after his death in 1908 the Uncle Remus Memorial Association was formed, the purpose of which was to purchase the home of the writer of the Uncle Remus stories, near Atlanta, and to convert it into a suitable memorial. This has now been done.

The significance of Uncle Remus as a study in negro character can best be understood by a comparison of Harris's work with that of others, especially his predecessors, in the same field. The negroes themselves, by the way, can show an orator, two prose-writers, and one poet of merited eminence. These are Frederick Douglass (1817–95); Booker T. Washington (c. 1859–1915); W. E. Burghardt DuBois, and Paul Lawrence Dunbar (1872–1906). *Up from Slavery* (1901) by Washington and *The Souls of Black Folk* (1903) by DuBois are works of almost diametrically opposite styles. The former makes its appeal by its simplicity and restraint; the latter by its emotionalism, its note of lyric intensity. Neither author, however, is of unmixed negro blood, and neither has come as close to the heart of his race as did Dunbar, a pure negro, in his *Lyrics of Lowly Life* (1896). He was the first American negro of pure African descent "to feel the negro life æsthetically and to express it lyrically."[1] His dialect poems, it may be added, are better than the poems that he wrote in standard English. Indeed, Dunbar's command of correct English was always somewhat meagre and uncertain.

Negro writers, however, were not the first to put their own race into literature or to realize the value of their own folk-lore.

"The possibilities of negro folk-lore," says a recent negro writer,[2] "have carried it across the line, so that it has had strong influence on the work of such Southern writers as Thomas Nelson Page and Frank L. Stanton, and on that of George W. Cable. Its chief monument so far has been in the Uncle Remus tales of Brer Rabbit and Brer Fox told by Joel Chandler Harris."

The chief writers who preceded Harris in the attempt to portray negro character were William Gilmore Simms,[3] Edgar Allan Poe,[4] Harriet Beecher Stowe,[5] Stephen Collins Foster, and Irwin Russell. Hector, the negro slave in Simms's *Yemassee* (1835), and Jupiter in Poe's *Gold-Bug* (1843) are alike in many respects. Both belong to the type of faithful body servant,[6] both are natives of the coastal region of South Carolina, both illustrate a primitive sort of humour, and both

---

[1] See Introduction by William Dean Howells to *Lyrics of Lowly Life*.
[2] See Benjamin Griffith Brawley's *The Negro in Literature and Art* (Atlanta, 1910), p. 5.
[3] See also Book II, Chap. VII.   [4] See also Book II, Chap. XIV.
[5] See also Book III, Chap. XI.
[6] For the body servant in later literature see *The Negro in Southern Literature since the War*, by B. M. Drake (Dissertation, Vanderbilt University, Nashville, 1898), pp. 21–22

speak an anglicized form of Gullah (Gulla) dialect. Of the
two, Hector is the better portrayed. His refusal (in Chapter
51) to accept freedom when it is offered to him by his owner
is by no means surprising; it is an evidence rather of Simms's
familiarity with negro character and a reminder of the
anomalous position in which a freedman in those days found
himself.[1] Neither Hector nor Jupiter, however, can be said
to have any individuality of his own. They are mere types,
not individuals. Apart from their masters they have no
separate existence at all.

The best-known negro character in fiction is, of course,
Uncle Tom, the hero of *Uncle Tom's Cabin* (1852). The dramatic power shown in this book is undeniable. More than any
other one book it hastened the Civil War and made necessary
the emancipation of all slaves. But Uncle Tom is portrayed so
plainly for a purpose, the scenes in the book are so skilfully
arranged to excite public indignation, that one can hardly call
it a great work of art or even a work of art at all. Mrs. Stowe
knew the negro chiefly as she had seen him on the right bank of
the Ohio River. Ohio was a free state and the negroes that Mrs.
Stowe talked with in Cincinnati were those that had fled from
Kentucky. Uncle Tom is the type of a good man, a man of
sterling piety, subjected to bitter servitude and maltreatment;
but there is little about him that is distinctively negro. There
is no African background. The language that he speaks is a
low grade of highly evangelized English but no more distinctive
of the negro than of illiterate whites. Let one compare his
language on any page with that of Uncle Remus and the difference will be at once felt. For instance, Uncle Remus is telling
what he is going to do to the negro that steals his hogs:

"An' I boun'," continued Uncle Remus, driving the corncob
stopper a little tighter in his deceitful jug and gathering up his bag,
"an' I boun' dat my ole muskit'll go off 'tween me an' dat same
nigger yit, an' he'll be at de bad een', an' dis seetful jug'll 'fuse
ter go ter de funer'l."

The quaint indirectness of that is more distinctive of the old-
time negro speech than anything ever said by Uncle Tom.

[1] See in this connection the powerful story by Joel Chandler Harris, *Free Joe
and the Rest of the World* (in *Free Joe and Other Georgian Sketches*).

If the novel with a purpose is not a suitable theatre for the display of negro character, neither is the comic minstrel show. The songs written by Stephen Collins Foster (1826–64) retain still their deserved popularity but they do not portray the negro from within. *Old Black Joe*, *Old Uncle Ned*, *My Old Kentucky Home*, *Old Folks at Home*, or *Way Down upon the Suwanee River* are the best-known songs ever written by an American. Words, music, and sentiment are welded into perfect unity and harmony. *"Old Folks at Home,"* says Louis C. Elson,[1] "is the chief American folk-song, and Stephen Collins Foster is as truly the folk-song genius of America as Weber or Silcher have been of Germany." On the contrary, Foster can hardly be called a writer of folk-songs at all. His songs are pure sentimentality. The old-time negro, however, was religious, musical, humorous, loyal, emotional, improvident, diplomatic, philosophical, almost everything in fact except sentimental. These songs are not folk-songs, therefore, because the dialect is purely artificial, because neither words nor music originated with the negroes, and because the sentiment they express is alien to the race by whom these songs are supposed to be sung. They are sung, in fact, so far as the writer's observation goes, only by white people, never by negroes, except in a minstrel show.

The man who really discovered the literary material latent in negro character and in negro dialect was Irwin Russell (1853–79), of Mississippi. The two men best qualified to pass judgment, Joel Chandler Harris and Thomas Nelson Page, have both borne grateful testimony to Russell's genius and to their indebtedness to him. It is noteworthy also that the first marble bust that the State of Mississippi has placed in her Hall of Fame is that of Irwin Russell.

Russell's greatest poem is *Christmas Night in the Quarters* (1878). In its fidelity to the humble life that it seeks to portray, in the simplicity of its style, the genuineness of its feeling, the distinctness of its pictures, and the sympathy that inspires it, *Christmas Night* belongs in the class with Burns's *Cotter's Saturday Night* and Whittier's *Snow-Bound*. "Burns," said Russell, "is my idol. He seems to me the greatest man that God ever created, beside whom all other poets are utterly

[1] *History of American Music* (1904).

insignificant." This poem differs from the works hitherto considered in three important respects: the negro is the central character, the poem being written not to exploit him but to portray him; the dialect, both in its grammar and its rhetoric, is an improvement on everything that had preceded it; and the mingling of humour and religion, though admirably true to life, had been hitherto unachieved.

It is evident, therefore, that Joel Chandler Harris came at a time when the interest in the negro was at its height. His value as literary material had been realized in part, but no satisfactory portrait of him had been drawn. The war, too, with its attendant saturnalia of Reconstruction, was over, and the negro was trying to fit himself into a new political and industrial régime. It will be seen also that Uncle Remus is a very different character from those by which the negro had hitherto found representation in literature. The character of Uncle Remus is noteworthy not only because it represents both a type and an individual, but because the type is now nearly extinct. Before the war every large plantation or group of plantations had its Uncle Remus; today he lingers here and there in a few villages of the South, but is regarded more as a curiosity, a specimen, a relic of the past than as a part of the present.

As portrayed by Harris, Uncle Remus sums up the past and dimly hints the future. The character was modelled in part after that of an old negro, Uncle George Terrell, whom Harris had learned to know intimately on the Turner plantation. The Uncle Remus of the stories is eighty years old, but still moves and speaks with the vigour of youth.

He had always exercised authority over his fellow-servants. He had been the captain of the corn-pile, the stoutest at the log-rolling, the swiftest with the hoe, the neatest with the plough, and the plantation hands still looked upon him as their leader.[1]

His life spanned three distinct and widely divergent periods; he had looked out upon three worlds—the South before the war, the South during the war, and the South after the war. He is tenderly cared for by his former owners, "Mars John"

---

[1] *Nights with Uncle Remus.* p. 400.

and "Miss Sally"; he has his own little patch of ground around his cabin; and he is devotedly attached to Miss Sally's "little boy." In spite of their difference in years, the child and the old man have one point in common: they both look out upon the world with eager, wide-eyed interest. Uncle Remus expresses their common point of view in a conversation with Brer Ab. Brer Ab had been telling Uncle Remus of some of the miraculous things seen by a coloured woman in a trance:

"She say she meet er angel in de road, and he pinted straight ter de mornin' star, and tell her fer ter prepar'. Hit look mighty cu'us, Brer Remus." "Cum down ter dat, Brer Ab," said Uncle Remus, wiping his spectacles carefully, and readjusting them—"cum down ter dat, an' dey ain't nuffin' dat ain't cu'us."[1]

Acting on this Aristotelian maxim, Uncle Remus explains to the little boy the mysteries of animal life, especially as they embody themselves in the character of the rabbit and the fox. The humour is entirely unconscious. It is not that of the Uebermensch, for the humour of the Uebermensch springs from the consciousness of intellectual power, and is, moreover direct, cynical, self-assertive, masterful. The humour of Uncle Remus represents the world of the Underman; it has no reasoned philosophy but springs from the universal desire to correlate the unknown with the known and to explain the most mysterious things by reference to the most obvious. If the rabbit lost his long tail on a certain historic occasion, then all the rabbits since born will have short tails. In fact, Uncle Remus's philosophy is perfectly consistent in one thing: all physical characteristics, whether native or acquired, find their explanation not in past conditions but in past events. The slow influence of environment yields place to a prompt and obliging heredity.

After all, however, the language of Uncle Remus is more interesting than his philosophy. In the picturesqueness of his phrases, in the unexpectedness of his comparisons, in the variety of his figures of speech, in the perfect harmony between the thing said and the way of saying it, the reader finds not only a keen æsthetic delight but even an intellectual satisfac-

---

[1] *Uncle Remus: his Songs and his Sayings*, p. 212.

tion. It is probable that Uncle Remus's vocabulary would be found, on investigation, to be narrowly limited. If so, he is a striking evidence of the varied effects that can be produced with but few words provided these words have been thoroughly assimilated. He leaves the impression not of weakness but of strength, not of contractedness but of freedom. What he says has not only been thought through but seen through and felt through.

It is only after repeated readings that one realizes how completely the character of Uncle Remus is revealed, or rather how completely he is made to reveal himself. There are not many subjects within his range, or beyond it, on which he has not somewhere registered an interesting opinion. If animals are his specialty, he is none the less willing to comment on negroes before and after the war, his favourite dishes, revivals, courtship, Christmas, witches, and religion. These are some of the elemental things about which his thoughts play and through which we come at last to know him and to revere him. Nowhere in American literature has an author succeeded better in harmonizing a typical character with an individual character than has been done in the character of Uncle Remus. What James Fenimore Cooper did for the Indian, Harris has in fact done for the negro. Just as Chingachgook is the last of the Mohicans, so Uncle Remus is the last of the old-time negroes. In literature he is also the first.

But Uncle Remus is interesting not merely in himself but also for the folk-tales of which he is the mouthpiece. These tales mark indeed the beginning of the scientific study of negro folk-lore in America. The author had, however, no ethnological purpose in publishing the Uncle Remus stories, and was greatly surprised to learn afterwards that variants of some of his tales had been found among the Indians of North and South America, and in the native literature of India and Siam. Variants of the Tar-Baby story, for example, have been found among the Natchez, Creek, and Yuchi Indians[1]; among the West Indian islanders[2]; in Brazil[3]; in Cape Colony[4]; among the

---

[1] *Journal of American Folk-Lore*, July–Sept., 1913, p. 194.
[2] Andrew Lang's *At the Sign of the Ship* (*Longman's Magazine*, Feb., 1889).
[3] Romero's *Contos do Brazil*.
[4] *South African Folk-Lore Journal*, vol. I.

Bushmen of South Africa[1]; along the lower Congo[2]; in West Central Africa[3]; among the Hottentots[4]; and among the Jatakas or "Birth-Stories" of Buddha.[5]

As to the accuracy with which the Uncle Remus stories are reproduced, the author speaks as follows:[6]

> With respect to the folk-lore series, my purpose has been to preserve the legends themselves in their original simplicity, and to wed them permanently to the quaint dialect—if, indeed it can be called a dialect—through the medium of which they have become a part of the domestic history of every Southern family; and I have endeavored to give the whole a genuine flavor of the old plantation. Each legend has its variants, but in every instance I have retained that particular version which seemed to me to be the most characteristic, and have given it without embellishment and without exaggeration.

The animals that figure in these stories are, in addition to the fox and the rabbit, the opossum, the cow, the bull, the terrapin, the turtle, the wolf, the frog, the bear, the lion, the tiger, the pig, the billy goat, the deer, the alligator, the snake, the wildcat, the ram, the mink, the weasel, and the dog; among their feathered friends are the buzzard, the partridge, the guinea-fowl, the hawk, the sparrow, the chicken, and the goose. Why the rabbit should be the hero rather than the fox has been differently explained. Harris's own view seems, however, most in accord with the facts:

> The story of the rabbit and the fox, as told by the Southern negroes . . . seems to me to be to a certain extent allegorical, albeit such an interpretation may be unreasonable. At least it is a fable thoroughly characteristic of the negro; and it needs no scientific investigation to show why he selects as his hero the weakest and most harmless of all animals, and brings him out victorious in contests with the bear, the wolf, and the fox. It is not virtue that triumphs, but helplessness; it is not malice but mischievousness.

---

[1] James A Honeÿ's *South African Folk-Tales* (1910), p. 79.
[2] *The Sun*, New York, 17 March, 1912.
[3] *The Times*, New York, 24 Aug., 1913.
[4] Toni von Held's *Märchen und Sagen der afrikanischen Neger* (Jena, 1904). p. 72.
[5] *Indian Fairy Tales*, selected and edited by Joseph Jacobs (1910), p. 251.
[6] *Uncle Remus: his Songs and his Sayings*, Introduction, p. 3.

The origin of these tales is still in a measure unsettled, and there is urgent need of more scientific investigation of them. For a while it was thought that the negroes learned these stories from the Indians. It is at least certain that many of the Uncle Remus stories are current among the Indians of North and South America. It is equally certain that more is known of Indian folk-lore than of negro folk-lore. The present status of the question is overwhelmingly in favour of an African origin. The negro slaves, in other words, brought these stories with them from Africa to Brazil and the United States. The Indians in both countries learned them from the negroes.

Of the negro dialect in general as spoken in the United States today, there are four varieties:

(1) The dialect of Virginia, especially of Eastern or Tidewater Virginia. It is best represented in the works of Thomas Nelson Page. Broad *a* is retained in this dialect and there is a vanishing *y* sound (as in *few*) heard after *c* and *g* when broad *a* follows: *larst* (*last*), *farst* (*fast*), *grahss* (*grass*), *pahsture* (*pasture*), *chahmber* (*chamber*), *pahf* (*path*), *cyarn'* (*can't*), *kyars* (*cars*), *gyardin* (*garden*). Broad *a* is also heard in *cyar* (*carry*) and *dyah* (*there*). Such forms as *gyardin*, *seegyar*, *kyards*, *kyarvin' knife* are also used by Uncle Remus, but they are evidences of Virginia influence. Uncle Remus himself says, though he had dropped the broad *a*, that he "come from Ferginny."

(2) The dialect of the Sea Islands of the South Atlantic States, known as the Gullah (or Gulla) dialect. The name is probably derived from Angola, as many of the rice-field negroes of South Carolina and Georgia are known to have come from the west coast of Africa. This diminishing dialect is spoken on the rice plantations of coastal South Carolina and Georgia as the Uncle Remus dialect is spoken on the cotton and tobacco plantations further inland. Gullah diverges widely from English and in its most primitive state is, as Harris says, "merely a confused and untranslatable mixture of English and African words." Though it was used in a diluted form here and there by Poe and Simms and though Harris employs it for some of the stories in his *Nights with Uncle Remus*, it can hardly be said to have found a place in literature. It has given us, however, the only pure African word still current in

negro speech, the word *buckra*, meaning *boss* or *overseer*. *Tote*, meaning *to carry*, which long claimed a place beside *buckra*, has been found in American writings of so early a date as to preclude the theory of African origin.

(3) The dialect spoken by the Creole negroes of Louisiana. This dialect is of course not English but French, and is best represented, though sparingly, in the works of George W. Cable. Its musical quality and the extent to which elision and contraction have been carried may be seen in the following love song of the Creole negro Bras-Coupé, one of the characters in Cable's *Grandissimes*. An interlinear translation is added:

> En haut la montagne, zami,
> *On the mountain chain, my friends,*
> Mo pé coupé canne, zami,
> *I've been cutting cane, my friends,*
> Pou' fé i'a' zen', zami,
> *Money for to gain, my friends,*
> Pou' mo baille Palmyre.
> *For my fair Palmyre.*
> Ah! Palmyre, Palmyre, mo c'ere,
> *Ah! Palmyre, Palmyre, my dear,*
> Mo l'aimé 'ou —mo l'aimé 'ou.
> *I love you—I love you.*

(4) The Uncle Remus dialect, or the dialect spoken by the negroes in the great inland sections of the South and South-west. Though there have been changes in vocabulary and a decline in vigour and picturesqueness of expression, due to the influence of negro schools and to the passing of the old plantation life, this is the dialect still spoken by the majority of the older negroes in the country districts of the South, especially of the far South. The characteristics of this dialect consist wholly in adaptation of existing English words and endings, not in the introduction of new words or new endings. The plurals of all nouns tend to become regular. Thus Uncle Remus says *foots* (*feet*), *toofies* (*teeth*), and *gooses* (*geese*), though the old plural *year* is retained. The relative pronoun *who* is not used, its place being taken by *which* (or *w'ich*), *what* (or *w'at*), *dat*, and the more interesting *which he* and *which dey*, corresponding to Chaucer's *that he* and *that they*. Thus: "She holler so loud dat

Brer Rabbit, *which he* wuz gwine by, got de idee dat she wuz callin' him."

Another interesting characteristic of the Uncle Remus speech is found in the present tense of verbs. Uncle Remus does not say, for example, *I make, you make, he makes, we make, you make, they make,* but *I makes, you makes, he makes, we makes, you makes, dey makes.* Negro dialect, like the dialect of all illiterate peoples, is an ear dialect. The eye has nothing to do with it. The law of analogy, therefore, which is nothing more than the rule of the majority, has unfettered operation. The illiterate man, whether black or white, hearing the third person singular with its invariable *s*-ending far more frequently than he hears any other form of the present tense, makes it his norm and uses it for all forms of both numbers. The same is true of the verb *to be,* though *is* has not in the language of Uncle Remus entirely succeeded in dispossessing *am* and *are.*

II. Dialects of the Whites

Why dialect should have been so sparingly used by American writers before the Civil War and why it should have become so constituent a part of American fiction immediately after the Civil War are questions not easily answered. A partial explanation would seem to lie in the increasing sectionalism from 1830 to 1860 which, culminating in 1865, gave place not only to an increasing sense of national solidarity but to a keener interest in how the other half lived. Sectionalism meant indifference and ignorance; union means reciprocal interest and understanding. There can at least be no doubt that the American short story[1] has been the chief vehicle of dialect since the Civil War, and the American short story, by its fidelity to local usages, has done more during these years to acquaint or re-acquaint the North with the South and the East with the West than any other type of literature. Bret Harte, writing in 1899, mentioned as the leading short-story writers then living Joel Chandler Harris, George W. Cable, Mark Twain, Charles Egbert Craddock (Miss Murfree), and Mary E. Wilkins (now Mrs. Freeman). These names, together with that of Bret Harte himself, indicate that ex-

[1] See Book III. Chap. vi

cellence in dialect and excellence in the short story have been almost synonymous in American literature since the Civil War. They indicate also that dialect has been both an expression and a cause of the interstate knowledge and interstate sympathy that have linked the far separated sections of the United States into closer bonds of union and fellowship.

The resemblances, however, existing among the dialects of the different sections of the United States are so great, and the differences so slight, that one hesitates to call these speech peculiarities dialects at all. The reign of the newspaper, diffused educational facilities, increasing means of travel and transportation, together with the American passion for a standardized average of correctness, have checked the tendency to dialect that the colonists brought with them. The effort now making in England, through the Society for Pure English, to restore the old words and racy idioms that survive in the Cornish, Sussex, and Northumbrian dialects and thus to enrich and revitalize standard English, could hardly find imitation in this country, because there are no American dialects that offer corresponding rewards. The differences between the New England dialect, the Southern dialect, and the Western dialect, for example, are differences in pronunciation, in intonation, in stress, and slurring, not primarily in the loss or preservation of old words or old idioms. The speech of the mountain districts, especially that of the Southern Appalachian region, retains, it is true, a few words and locutions of old and honourable origin; but these are by no means numerous enough to be used for regenerative purposes on a large scale. *Hit* (*it*), *holp* (*helped*), *ax* (*ask*), *afeard* (*afraid*), *fray* (*combat*), *fraction* (as in *Troilus and Cressida* II, III, 107), *antic* (*clown*), *humans* (*human beings*), *mought* (*might*), *Old Christmas* (*6 January*), *hone* (*yearn*), *tilth* (*agriculture*), *back a letter* (*address an envelope*), and a few others may be heard in the mountains of Virginia, North Carolina, Tennessee, and Kentucky. But to affirm that in this dialect or in the dialect of any other part of the United States is to be found our best reservoir of fresh and vigorous English or our surest safeguard against slovenly pronunciation would be manifestly absurd.

While much remains to be done in accurately classifying American speech peculiarities, it needs no proof that the strongest impetus to a fresh study and appraisal of American dialect was given by James Russell Lowell[1] in his *Biglow Papers* (1848, 1866) and in the Introductions with which he prefaced them. The early masters of the short story, Irving, Poe, and Hawthorne, looked askance at dialect, as did Longfellow and Whittier in their abolition poems. But Bret Harte[2] gave new force to Lowell's views by his effective use of dialect in the stories of the forty-niners, and from 1870 to the present time dialect has played a leading part in the attempt to portray and interpret American character against the background of social environment. Edward Eggleston,[3] who brought a new dialect into literature in *The Hoosier Schoolmaster* (1871), spoke for all his colleagues when he said:

If I were a dispassionate critic, and were set to judge my own novels as the writings of another, I should say that what distinguishes them from other works of fiction is the prominence which they give to social conditions; that the individual characters are here treated to a greater degree than elsewhere as parts of a study of a society—as in some sense the logical results of the environment. Whatever may be the rank assigned to these stories as works of literary art, they will always have a certain value as materials for the student of social history.

With the exception of the negro dialects and those that are more French or German than English, American dialects fall into three groups, those of New England, the South, and the West. The dialect employed by Bret Harte has often been criticized as belonging to no one of these groups. The charge is made that it is merely an importation of cockney English. The critics, however, when pressed for proof, have been able to cite only the use of *which* in such initial sentences as

Which I wish to remark,
And my language is plain.

This is undoubtedly cockney English, but it is American as well, though it has always been and still is rarely heard.[4]

[1] See Book II, Chap. xxiv.   [2] See Book III, Chap. vi.
[3] See Book III, Chap. xi.
[4] See Henry Childs Merwin's *Life of Bret Harte* (1911), pp. 325–327. Some of Mr. Merwin's citations, however, are not pertinent but belong to the *which he* construction noted in Uncle Remus.

Bret Harte's dialect has also been subjected to criticism on the charge of being too clever. It seems at times to be the author's own creation rather than a transcript of speech actually current in California at the time. Much of this criticism turns on the failure to distinguish between dialect and slang, slang having a right to be original. The society, moreover, that Bret Harte portrays was unique in its compositeness. There were preachers, teachers, lawyers, and doctors among those who flocked to California as well as toughs, tramps, dead-beats, and illiterates. "The faith, courage, vigor, youth, and capacity for adventure necessary to this emigration," says Bret Harte, "produced a body of men as strongly distinctive as were the companions of Jason." William Grey[1] describes the pioneers with whom he went to California as "a fine-looking and well educated body of men,—all young." That the language of these men should be picturesque and representative in its idiom and as intellectual as the occasion might demand, is not surprising. Investigation has shown that of Bret Harte's three hundred dialect words and phrases a mere handful remain unidentified as American.

The term Western, however, usually has reference not to the Pacific slope but to the Middle West and South-west. The Western dialect is currently understood to be the dialect found in the writings of Mark Twain,[2] Edward Eggleston, Hamlin Garland,[3] Owen Wister, and James Whitcomb Riley.[4] But this dialect is also composite. The original sources are chiefly New England and the South, with a mingling here and there of German and Scandinavian elements. Thus the pioneer dialect of Southern Ohio, Indiana, and Illinois was mainly Southern, while the northern portions of these States reflect the New England influence. The speech of Nebraska shows the influence of Swedish and Pennsylvania German settlers. Western and Central New York was settled chiefly by New Englanders, but in the last few decades there are evidences of Irish, German, and Scandinavian influences. Eastern New York and Pennsylvania were intermediate in their speech habits between New England and the South, their dialect showing traces of both.

[1] *Pioneer Times in California.*
[2] See Book III, Chap. VIII.
[3] See Book III, Chap. VI.
[4] See Book III, Chap. X.

Even cultivated Indianians, particularly those of Southern antecedents, have the habit of clinging to their words; they do not bite them off sharply. . . . In New England and in Virginia the Italian *a* finds recognition, whereas in the intermediate region the narrower sound of the vowel prevails; and likewise the softening of *r* is noted in New England and among the Virginians and other Southerners, while in the intermediate territory and at the West *r* receives its full sound. The shrill nasal tone is still marked in the back country folk of New England, while the Southern and South-western farmer's speech is fuller and more open-mouthed. . . . At the South and in New England, where there is less mingling of elements, the old usages will probably endure much longer; and it is a fair assumption that in the Mississippi Valley and in the Trans-Missouri country, a normal American speech free of local idiosyncrasies will appear first.[1]

This New England dialect which has spread so widely through the West and North-west was summarized by Lowell in the following seven general rules[2]:

1. The genuine Yankee never gives the rough sound to the *r* when he can help it, and often displays considerable ingenuity in avoiding it even before a vowel.

2. He seldom sounds the final *g*, a piece of self-denial, if we consider his partiality for nasals. The same of the final *d*, as *han'* and *stan'* for *hand* and *stand*.

3. The *h* in such words as *while*, *when*, *where*, he omits altogether.

4. In regard to *a*, he shows some inconsistency, sometimes giving a close and obscure sound, as *hev* for *have*, *hendy* for *handy*, *ez* for *as*, *thet* for *that*, and again giving it the broad sound it has in *father*, as *hânsome* for *handsome*.

5. To the sound *ou* he prefixes an *e* (hard to exemplify otherwise than orally). . . .

6. *Au* in such words as *daughter* and *slaughter*, he pronounces *ah*.

7. To the dish thus seasoned add a drawl *ad libitum*.

The New England dialect may perhaps best be studied in such later writers as Rose Terry Cooke,[3] Sarah Orne Jewett,[4] and Mary E. Wilkins Freeman.[5]

---

[1] Meredith Nicholson, *The Hoosiers* (1900), pp. 58–60.
[2] *The Biglow Papers*, first series, Introduction.
[3] See Book III, Chap. vi.   [4] *Ibid.*   [5] *Ibid.*

What is known as the Southern dialect may be formulated also in seven general rules:

1. *Like* does duty for *as if* in such sentences as "He looks like he was sick." This construction, says Lowell, is "never found in New England."

2. *'Low* (*allow*), meaning *think* and *say*, though "never heard in New England" (Lowell), is very common among white and black illiterates, as it is in the pages of Bret Harte. *Guess* in the New England sense is also used, but New England *cal'late* (*calculate*) is unknown.

3. Such words as *tune, news, duty* (but not *true, rule, sue, dude*) have the vanishing *y*-sound heard in *few*.[1] This pronunciation, like the retention of broad *a*, can hardly be called dialectal; but it is almost a shibboleth of the Southerner to the manner born, and helps to differentiate him from the Westerner and Northerner.

4. The vanishing *y*-sound heard in *gyarden, cyards, Cyarter, Gyarfield*, is common in Virginia but less so in other parts of the South.

5. The same may be said of broad *a.* intermediate *a* (halfway between *father* and *fat*) being distinctively academic and acquired.

6. *More, store, floor, four, door*, and similar words are usually pronounced *mo, sto, flo, fo, do* by negroes. Among the white population the *r* is not pronounced but these words have two distinct syllables, the last syllable having the obscure *uh* sound heard in *mower* or *stower*. The tendency in the North and West to pronounce long *o* as *au* (in *autumnal* rather than in *autumn*) is not observable in the South.

7. The most distinctive idiom in the South is the use of *you all*, meaning not *all of you* but *you folks, you people, you boys, you girls*. It may be addressed to one person but always implies more than one. If a Southerner says to a clerk in a store, "Do you all keep shoes here?" he means by *you all* not the single clerk but the entire firm or force that owns or operates the store.[2]

Notable writers of the Southern dialect besides Harris, Page, and Cable, are Richard Malcolm Johnston,[3] Charles Egbert Craddock,[4] and O. Henry.[5]

[1] See *Some Variant Pronunciations in the New South*, by William A. Read, *Dialect Notes*, Vol. III, Part vii, 1911.

[2] There is an interesting paragraph on this idiom in Jespersen's *Modern English Grammar*, Part II, Syntax, First Volume (Heidelberg, 1914), pages 47–48. He compares it with East Anglian *you together*, "used as a kind of plural of *you*."

[3] See also Book III, Chaps. IV and VI.   [4] *Ibid.*, Chap. VI.   [5] *Ibid*

An analogy may be noted, by way of retrospect, between the three dialects of Chaucer's time and the three that, with many modifications, have survived in the United States. The Northern or Northumbrian dialect was spoken north of the Humber, the Midland between the Humber and Thames, and the Southern south of the Thames. The Midland gained the supremacy largely because it was a compromise between the other two. The situation a century ago in the United States was not dissimilar. New England, with Massachusetts as the speech centre, may be likened to Northumbria not only in relative position but in a corresponding preference for certain austerities of pronunciation. The South, with Virginia as the speech centre, differed from New England in pronunciation not as widely but in much the same way as Southern England differed from Northern England. The Middle States, with New York as the speech centre, was, like Midland England, intermediate in speech habits as well as in geographical position. Even today if a Bostonian and a Tidewater Virginian were to visit New York City for the first time they would observe less that would be arrestive in speech, barring foreign elements, than the Bostonian would find in Richmond or the Virginian in Boston. That New York, therefore, in spite of its unparalleled growth in population, has not influenced the dialect of the West as have New England and the South, is due partly to the lack of dialectal distinction in the speech of New York and partly to the more migratory habits of New Englanders and Southerners. If "in the Mississippi Valley and in the Trans-Missouri country a normal American speech free of local idiosyncrasies will first appear," as seems not unlikely, a compromise English dialect will have won its second and greatest victory.

CHAPTER VI

The Short Story

THE period between the Civil War in America and the outbreak of the Great War in Europe in 1914 may be termed in the history of prose fiction the Era of the Short Story. Everywhere, in France, in Russia, in England, in America, more and more the impressionistic prose tale, the *conte*—short, effective, a single blow, a moment of atmosphere, a glimpse at a climactic instant—came, especially in the magazines, to dominate fictional literature. Formless at first, often overloaded with mawkishness, with essay effects, with moralizing purpose, and dominating background, it grew constantly in proportion and restraint and artistic finish until it was hailed as a new *genre*, a peculiar product of nineteenth century conditions, one especially adapted to the American temperament and the American *kultur*.

That the prose story was no innovation peculiar to later literature, is an axiom that must precede every discussion of it. It is as old as the race; it has cropped out abundantly in every literature and every period. That it has taken widely differing forms during its long history is also axiomatic. Every generation and every race has had its own ideals in the matter, has set its own fashions. One needs remember only *The Book of Ruth*, *The Thousand and one Nights*, the Elizabethan novella, the Sir Roger de Coverley papers, Johnson's *Rambler*, Hannah More's moral tales, and the morbid romance of the early nineteenth-century annuals. The modern short story is only the latest fashion in story telling—short fiction *à la mode*.

In America the evolution of the form may be traced through at least four stages. It began with the eighteenth-century tale of the Hannah More type, colourless, formless, undramatic, "subservient," to use a contemporary phrase, "only to the interest of virtue"—a form peculiarly adapted to flourish in the Puritanic atmosphere of the new nation. Such stories as *Chariessa, or a Pattern for the Sex* and *The Danger of Sporting with Innocent Credulity*, both from Carey's *Columbian Magazine* established in 1786, satisfied the American reading public for half a century.

Then came the work of Washington Irving[1]—the blending of the moral tale with the Addisonian essay, especially in its Sir Roger de Coverley phase. The evolution was a peculiar one, a natural result of that isolation of early America which belated all its art forms and kept it always a full generation behind the literary fashions of London. Irving's early enthusiasms came from the shelves of the paternal library rather than from the book stalls of the vital centres where flowed the current literature of the day. To the impressionable youth Addison and Steele and Goldsmith were as fresh and new as they had been to their first readers. The result appears in his first publication, *Salmagundi*, a youthful *Spectator*, and later in his first serious work, *The Sketch Book*, another essay periodical since it was issued in monthly numbers—a latter-day *Bee*. Never did he outgrow this formative influence: always he was of the eighteenth century, an essayist, a moralist, a sketcher of manners, an antiquarian with a reverence for the past, a sentimentalist. His sketchy moral essays and his studies of manners and character grew naturally into expository stories, illustrations, narratives of a traveller set in an atmosphere attractive to the untravelled American of the time, all imagination and longing. He added to the moral tale of his day characterization, humour, atmosphere, literary charm, but he added no element of constructive art. He lacked the dramatic; he overloaded his tales with descriptions and essay material; and he ended them feebly. His stories, even the classic *Rip Van Winkle*, are elaborations with pictorial intent rather than dramas with culminative movement and sharp outlines. They are essays rather than short stories.

Irving advanced the short story more by his influence than by his art. The popularity of *The Sketch Book* and the others that followed it, the tremendous fact of their author's European

[1] See also Book II, Chap. IV.

fame, the alluring pictures of lands across the sea, the romantic atmosphere, the vagueness and the wonder of it, laid hold mightily upon the imagination of America. They came just in time to capture the young group of writers that was to rule the mid-century. The twenties and the thirties in America were dominated by *The Sketch Book*. All at once came an outburst of Irvingesque sketches and tales. That the unit of measure in American fiction is a short one is to be accounted for in a very great degree by the tremendous influence of Irving in its early formative period.

For the new form there sprang up in the twenties a new vehicle, the annual. For two decades the book-stands were loaded with flamboyantly bound gift books—*The Token*, *The Talisman*, *The Pearl*, *The Amaranth*, and the others, elaborate *Sketch Books* varied soon by echoes from the new romanticism of Europe. Never before such a gushing of sentiment, of mawkish pathos, of crude terror effects, and vague Germanic mysticism. From out of it all but a single figure has survived, the sombre Hawthorne[1] who was genius enough to turn even the stuff of the annuals into a form that was to persist and dominate. Hawthorne added soul to the short story and made it a form that could be taken seriously even by those who had contended that it was inferior to the longer forms of fiction. He centred his effort about a single situation and gave to the whole tale unity of impression. Instead of elaboration of detail, suggestion; instead of picturings of external effects, subjective analysis and psychologic delineation of character. Hawthorne was the first to lift the short story into the higher realms of art.

The forties belong to Poe.[2] With him came for the first time the science of the short story, the treatment of it as a distinct art form with its own rules and its own fields. Laws the form was bound to have if it was to persist. As the century progressed and as modern science swept from men's minds the vague and the generalizing and the disorderly, there came

[1] See also Book II, Chap. XI. Here may be mentioned, however, one short story before Hawthorne which seems rather to anticipate him than to follow Irving, William Austin's tantalizing *Peter Rugg, the Missing Man*, of which the first part appeared in 1824. [For Austin, see also the Bibliography for Book II, Chap. XIX.]

[2] See also Book II, Chap. XIV.

necessarily the demand for more reality, for sharper outlines, for greater attention to logical order. The modern short story is but the fiction natural, and indeed inevitable, in a scientific age, and Poe was the first to perceive the new tendency and to formulate its laws.

In Poe's opinion the short story owed its vogue in America to the great number of literary magazines that sprang up during the mid years of the century. "The whole tendency of the age is magazineward," he wrote in the early forties. The quarterlies are

quite out of keeping with the rush of the age. We now demand the legal artillery of the intellect; we need the curt, the condensed, the pointed, the readily diffused—in place of the voluminous, the verbose, the detailed, the inaccessible. . . . It is a sign of the times—an indication of an era in which men are forced upon the curt, the condensed, the well digested, in place of the voluminous—in a word, upon journalism in lieu of dissertation.

Fiction, he contended, to be scientific must be brief, must yield a totality of impression at a single sitting. The writer must concentrate upon a single effect.

If his very initial sentence tend not to the outbringing of this effect, he has failed in his first step. In the whole composition there should be no word written of which the tendency, direct or indirect, is not to the one pre-established design.

As he wrote this, Poe was thinking of his own art more than of Hawthorne's. He had been a magazinist all his life, and he had learned to view the tale from the standpoint of the editor. He who has but a brief space at his command in which to make his impression, must condense, must plan, must study his every word and phrase. All of his stories are single strokes, swift moments of emotion, Defoe-like massings of details with exactness of diction, skilful openings, harrowing closes.

More than this we may not say. He did not work in the deeps of the human heart like Hawthorne; he was an artist and only an artist, and even in his art he did not advance further than to formulate the best short story technique of his day. His tales are not to be classified at all with the products of later art. They lack sharpness of outline, *finesse*, and that sense of reality which makes of a tale an actual piece of human life. His creations are *tours de force;* they reflect no earthly soil, they are weak in characterization, and their dialogue—as witness the conversation of the negroes in *The Gold Bug*—is wooden and lifeless. Poe was a critic, keenly observant of the tendencies of his day, sensitive to literary values, scientific, with powers of analysis that amounted to genius. He was not the creator of the short story; he was the first to feel the new demand of his age and to forecast the new art and formulate its laws.

In the realm of the short story Poe was a prophet, peering into the next age, rather than a leader of his own time. Until later years his influence was small. He had applied his new art to the old sensational material of the thirties—old wine in new bottles. The annuals and all they stood for were passing rapidly. *Putnam's Magazine* noted in February, 1853, the great change that had come over the literature for the holiday period.

It used to be the custom to issue when Christmas approached an almost endless variety of "Gifts," "Remembrances," "Gems," "Tokens," "Wreathes," "Irises," "Albums," &c, with very bad mezzotint engravings and worse letter-press,—ephemeral works, destined to perish in a few weeks; but that custom appears to be rapidly passing away.

The decline of the old type of story explains why Hawthorne turned to the production of long romances. The age of the Hawthornesque short story had passed. With the fifties had come a new atmosphere. To realize it one has but to read for a time in *Godey's Lady's Book* and *Graham's Magazine* and the annuals and then to turn to *Harper's Magazine*, established in 1850, *Putnam's Magazine*, in 1853, and *The Atlantic Monthly*, in 1857.

In England it was the period of Dickens and Thackeray and Reade and George Eliot, the golden age of the later novel. American magazines like *Harper's* were publishing serial after serial by British pens, yet the demand for short fiction increased rather than declined. During its first year *The Atlantic Monthly* published upward of thirty-three short stories by twenty-three different authors, or an average of almost three in every number. It was no longer fiction of the earlier type. A new demand had come to the short story writer; in the "Introductory" to the first volume of *Putnam's Magazine* the editor announced that American writers and American themes were to predominate, adding that "local reality is a point of utmost importance." In the first volume of the *Atlantic*, Emerson struck the new note: "How far off from life and manners and motives the novel still is. Life lies about us dumb"; and in the same volume a reviewer of George Eliot notes "the decline of the ideal hero and heroine." "The public is learning that men and women are better than heroes and heroines." By 1861 a writer like Rebecca Harding Davis could open her grim short story, *Life in the Iron Mills*, with a note like this;

I want you to hide your disgust, take no heed to your clean clothes, and come right down with me,—here into the thickest of the fog and mud and effluvia. I want you to hear this story. There is a secret down here, in this nightmare fog, that has lain dumb for centuries: I want to make it a real thing for you.

The fifties and sixties in America stand for the dawning of definiteness, of localized reality, of a feeling left on the reader of actuality and truth to human life.

The first significant figure of the transition was Rose Terry (1827–92), later better known as Rose Terry Cooke, who has the distinction of having contributed seven short stories to the first eight numbers of the *Atlantic*. Born in Connecticut—the heart of New England, a school teacher with experience in country districts, she wrote with knowledge and conviction of the area of life that she knew. In her long series of stories beginning in the forties with unlocalized romantic tales in *Graham's* and extending throughout the transition period into the seventies and eighties, and ending with a final collection as late as 1891, one may trace every phase of the American short story in half a century. Her early *Atlantic* narratives lean decidedly in the direction of the *Young Ladies' Repository* type of fiction, sentimental, leisurely, moralizing, and yet even in the poorest of them there is a sense of actuality that was new in American short fiction. They were not romances; they were homely fragments of New England rural

life. The heroine may be introduced in this unromantic fashion:
"Mrs. Griswold was paring apples and Lizzie straining squash."
Here for the first time we may find dialect that rings true, and,
moreover, here for the first time are sprightliness and rollicking
humour, varied at times with tragedy and true pathos. As
one traces her work from *Atlantic* to *Atlantic*, a gradual increase
in power impresses one until after her declaration of independence at the opening of *Miss Lucinda* (August, 1861)—"I
offer you no tragedy in high life, no sentimental history of
fashion and wealth, but only a little story about a woman who
could not be a heroine"—it is felt that she has found herself
and that with her later work like *Odd Miss Todd, Freedom
Wheeler's Controversy with Providence, The Deacon's Week*,
and last of all and in many ways her best, *The Town and Country
Mouse*, the final story in her collection *Huckleberries*, she has
passed into the new period and taken a secure place with the
small group of masters of the short story. Unlike Harriet
Prescott Spofford, whose gorgeous *In a Cellar* and *The Amber
Gods* fluttered for a time the readers of the early sixties, she
was able to heed the voice of the new period and to grow and
outgrow, and it was this power that made her the pioneer
and the leader not only of the group of depicters of New England life, but of the whole later school of makers of localized
short fiction realistically rendered.

Rose Terry came gradually, an evolution, without noise or
sensation; not so Fitz-James O'Brien (1828–62), who, after his
The Diamond Lens (January, 1858), was hailed loudly as a new
Poe. O'Brien's career in America was meteoric. He appeared
unheralded, in 1852, an adventurer who had been educated in
Dublin University, and who had squandered a rich patrimony
in London. For ten years he lived in the Bohemian circles of
New York, writing impetuously, when the mood was upon
him, temperamental, Celtic-souled material which he published
here and there in the magazines—*Harper's, Putnam's*, the
Atlantic, until, enlisting in one of the first regiments of volunteers, he fell in one of the earliest skirmishes of the Civil War.
His short stories *What Was It?* and *The Wondersmith* have
undoubted power, but they are not to be compared with the
best work of Hawthorne and Poe. What O'Brien might have
done had he lived into the next period of the short story it is

idle to conjecture. As it is, he must be regarded only as an episode, a passing sensation, and he might be dismissed unmentioned but for the fact that he was an undoubted influence in the period of transition. To the art and the impressionism of Poe he added the new element of actuality. His shuddery tale *What Was It?* is laid in a New York boarding-house with convincingness. Even his Hawthorne-like fantasia *The Wondersmith* has as a background a New York slum street drawn with all the pitiless realism of a Zola. O'Brien added the sense of actuality to Poe's unlocalized romance, but his influence was not large.

Another figure in the transition was Edward Everett Hale[1] (1822–1909), whose *The Man without a Country*, first published in 1863, has been accepted generally as an American classic. Little else that he has written, and he wrote much in many fields, gives promise of surviving, and the reasons why this should survive are not immediately evident. As a short story it would seem to have almost fatal defects. It may be used as an example of mid-century diffuseness, its moralizing intent is only thinly veiled, it is episodic, and it does not culminate. Undoubtedly its timeliness—it is a document in the history of the war—and its genuine atmosphere of patriotism account partly for its success, but there are more vital reasons. It is really a work of art. With all its episodes it presents but a single situation, and that situation at the close has been so worked upon that it becomes to the reader a haunting presence, never to be forgotten. Moreover, there is reality to the story. Everything is in the concrete. The author adds specific detail to detail with the skill of a Defoe until, in spite of its manifest impossibility, the tale becomes alive, a piece of actual history, a human document. Few modern writers have surpassed Hale in what may be called the art of verisimilitude. He was the precursor of Stockton. A story like *My Double and how he Undid me* is manifestly a *tour de force*, yet one is in danger of gravely accepting it as a fact. Hale added to the short story not alone the sense of reality; he added plausibility as well.

With Henry James[2] the period of transition came to an end. From 1865, when he published his first story, until 1875,

[1] See also Book III, Chap. XIII.   [2] See also Book III, Chap. XII.

the date of *Roderick Hudson*, he devoted himself to short fiction, contributing fourteen stories to the *Atlantic* alone, and he brought to his work not only the best art America had evolved, but the best of England and France as well.   He was a scientist, an observer, a tabulator, as cool and accurate as even his brother William James, the psychologist.   Unlike O'Brien and the others, he threw away completely the machinery of the mid-century tale—not without regret it would appear from his *Romance of Certain Old Clothes* and other early tales—and sought only the uncoloured truth.   The art of Poe, especially the French adaptations of that art, he retained, but he rejected all the rest of Poe's outfit.   That he understood the full possibilities of the supernatural as short story material we know from his grim tale *The Turn of the Screw*, but the field was little to his taste.   He was a naturalist rather than a supernaturalist, and his sensitive and fastidious soul could not endure the harsh and the horrible.   In his second story, *My Friend Bingham* (1866), he wrote: "I am of a deep aversion to stories of a painful nature . . . the literature of horrors needs no extension."   He rejected allegory and mystery and vague impressionism as unscientific.   He condemned the tradition that "a serious story of manners shall close with the factitious happiness of a fairy tale."   He was a scientist; his second paper in the *Atlantic* is a defence of George Eliot, scientist. To both of them the first requisite of fiction was the truth, the truth told directly, simply, concretely.

An age of science could no longer tolerate the unrelieved black and white of the earlier periods, but demanded shades, traces of white found even in the black.   According to James, a short story was the analysis of a situation, the psychological phenomena of a group of men and women at an interesting moment.   Given two, three, four different temperaments, bring them into a certain situation, and what would be the action and reaction?   The story was a problem to be solved. Little was to be said *about* the characters: they were to reveal themselves, gradually, slowly as they do in actual life, by long continued dialogue, by little unconscious actions and reactions, by personal peculiarities in dress, manners, movement, revealed by a thousand subtle hints, descriptive touches, insinuations. Under such conditions the movement of the story must be slow: in some of his work there seems to be no story at all, only the analysis of a situation. The method requires space: James has stretched the length of the short story to its extreme. *The Aspern Papers*, the bare story of which could have been told in three pages, dragged through three magazine instalments. Twenty-eight of the one hundred and three stories in Henry James's final list are long enough to appear as volumes. Yet one may not doubt they are short stories: they are each of them the presentation of a single situation and they leave each of them a unity of impression.

James was the most consummate artist American literature has produced. He was fastidious by nature and by early training. He had studied his art in France as men study sculpture in Italy, and he had learned the French mastery of form. Nowhere in his writings may we find slovenly work. His opening and closing paragraphs are always models, his dialogue moves naturally and inevitably,—in all the story despite its length nothing too much,—and everywhere a brilliancy new in American fiction. He is seldom spontaneous; always is he the conscious artist; always is he intellectual; always is he working in the clay of actual life, a realist who never forgets his problem to soar into the uncharted and the unscientific realms of the metaphysical and the romantic.

The chief criticism of the short stories of James must concern their spirit rather than their form. The tendency of science has been to repudiate the spiritual. Romance with intuition in place of sense perception found at least the heart. With James the short story became an art form simply, cold and brilliant, a study of the surface of society, manners, endless phenomena jotted down in a note-book, human life from the standpoint of the laboratory and the test tube. Beyond the brilliant art of Henry James, the impressionistic study of situations from the standpoint of scientific truth, the American short story has never advanced. He gave distinctness to the form. Nevertheless, he is not a supreme master: that dominating factor in life that eludes scapel and test-tube he never found, and, neglecting it, he falls inevitably into second place as an interpreter of human life.

That James and others of his school, like T. B. Aldrich, for instance, and H. C. Bunner, could have directed the short story permanently into the channels that it has followed in France, is doubtful. The great success in the middle seventies of the anonymous *Saxe Holm's Stories*, with their mid-century sentiment and romantic atmosphere, would imply that America at heart was still what it was in the days of Hawthorne and the annuals. What might have happened had James and Howells and Aldrich had full control it is idle to speculate; what did happen was the sudden appearance of a short story that stampeded America and for two decades set the style in short fiction. Bret Harte's *The Luck of Roaring Camp*, whatever one may think of its merits, must be admitted to be the most influential short story ever written in America.

Francis Bret Harte[1] was born in 1839 at Albany, where his father, a scholar and an itinerant teacher of languages, happened at the time to be stationed. A youth of frail physique, he became a precocious reader, preferring a Hawthorne-like seclusion among books to playground activities among boys of his own age. From his childhood he was predisposed to literature; he dreamed over it, and he began to make poems even in his early school days. His removal to California at the age of fifteen, five years after the first gold rush, came from no initiative of his. To the delicate youth dreaming over his books it was an exile at the barbarous ends of the world. For a time he lived at his mother's home at Oakland—after a nine years' widowhood she had married again—and then half heartedly he began to support himself as a school teacher, as a private tutor, as a druggist's clerk, and later as a type-setter on a rural newspaper. There is little doubt that for a time he saw something of mining life during a visit to Humboldt County, but the experience was brief. He had no taste for the rough life of the border. The greater part of his seventeen years in California he spent in San Francisco, first as type-setter, then as editor in various newspaper and magazine establishments. He was a man of the city, a professional literary worker, a poet, and a dreamer over the work of the older poets and romancers.

Harte came to the short story by way of Irving. His first dream was to do for the lands of the Spanish missions what Irving had done for the highlands of the Hudson. As early as

[1] See also Book III. Chap. v.

1863 he had contributed to *The Atlantic Monthly* his *Legend of Monte del Diablo*, which, with half a dozen other pieces written during the same period, breathed the soul of *The Sketch Book*. Poe had affected him not at all, but he had read much in the French, and he had been from his boyhood a devotee of Dickens. When in 1868, therefore, he found himself editor of the new *Overland Monthly*, which was to be the *Atlantic Monthly* of the Pacific coast, it was not strange that he should have evolved for its second number a short story like *The Luck of Roaring Camp*. The time was ready for such a production, and the place was ready: it could have come only during the decade following the war, and, moreover, it could have come only from California.

The story was woven of four strands: first, there was the Dickens sentiment, melodrama, theatric presentation of lowly material; second, there was the French art that had been adapted from Poe—form, *finesse*, nothing too much; third, there was the unusualness of background, new skies, strange types, presented by one who seemingly had been a part of what he told, a voice of the new spirit of the age in America; and, finally, over it all there was a reminiscence of Irving, that impalpable atmosphere of romance which covers it with the soft haze of remembered things, of the far-off and the idealized. Only the third was new, the "local colour" we have come to call it, that touch of strangeness added to the picture by means of strongly picturesque characters and scenes hitherto unknown to the reader. A mere spice of novelty it was, a detail of stage setting wholly subsidiary to the vital elements of the tale, and yet it was largely this single element that gave *The Luck of Roaring Camp* its enormous vogue and that made its author —at least in America—the most influential writer of short stories in a generation.

And yet Harte was an effect rather than a cause. America was ready for local colour. He was the voice that started the avalanche that was bound to come sooner or later. The Civil War had liberated America from provincialism. It had done away with the boundaries of New England, of the South, of New York, of the West. The new emphasis was now upon the nation rather than upon the state or section. The first railroad across the continent was completed in 1868. Now everywhere were problems national in scope. The tremendous activities of the war were now transferred to the breaking of the great West, to the building of new cities and industries, and to the extending into every part of the continent of a network of communication. Books of travel like Bowles's *Across the Continent* and King's *The Great South* began to appear, and all at once the nation awoke to a realization of its own riches, of its own picturesque diversity. The long period of the settlement had bred individualism; it had covered America with little isolated areas as provincial as if they were the only settlements on the continent. The era following the war was an era of self-discovery. America was as full of new and interesting life and environment as even Europe, and for two decades and more American writers exploited the strange new riches of the land as the first wave of placer miners excitedly rifle the nugget pockets of a new-found bonanza. Eagerly the public read of the picturesque conditions that had evolved from the California rush of '49; it wondered at the new world that Mark Twain revealed in his *Jumping Frog of Calaveras County*, and that Cable opened in old Creole New Orleans, and at the grotesque Hoosier types revealed by Eggleston; it thrilled with astonishment at Charles Egbert Craddock's pictures of the dwellers in the Tennessee Mountains, and at Octave Thanet's revelations of life in the canebrakes of Arkansas; and it lingered over the Old South before the war as revealed by Johnston, and Harris, and Page.

Never was movement launched with more impetus. No sooner had *The Luck of Roaring Camp* reached the East than the foremost publishing house of Boston hailed it as a new classic. Its author immediately was offered ten thousand dollars a year to write for *The Atlantic Monthly*, and the progress of his train east as he came to accept his unprecedented commission was indicated by daily bulletins in the newspapers as if he were a royal personage on a tour of the land. When was short story ever so advertised before? No wonder that everybody at the earliest opportunity read it, and later, in 1870, bought the book of short stories to which it gave the title.

Harte's arrival in Boston marks the climax of his career. We need not follow him to Europe whither he afterwards went to spend the rest of his life, or read widely in his voluminous

later product.   The work in that first collection containing
The Luck of Roaring Camp he never surpassed, though over
and over for years he repeated its characters and backgrounds
in stories of California life.   If he is to endure it will be on
account of the title story, or *Tennessee's Partner*, or *The Out-
casts of Poker Flat*.

Like James, Harte was a conscious artist, a workman who
had served a careful apprenticeship.   His stories are models
of condensation, his characters are as distinct and as striking
as are those of Dickens, his climaxes are dramatic, and his
closing effect is always impressively theatric.   Sentiment he
used with a free hand, but he kept it more within control than
did the creator of Little Nell.   Fiction with him, as with Poe,
was a deliberate thing, to be written with the reader always
in mind.   His unit necessarily was short.   He had no power
to trace the growth of a soul or to record the steps of an evolution.   His one attempt at a novel, *Gabriel Conroy*, was a
failure.   He could make a situation dramatic, he could make
alive a climactic moment in a reckless career, but he was
powerless to deal with the resultant effects from a complexity
of motives and situations.   What he added to the short story
of his time, aside from the obvious local colour, was the dramatic element.   His stories move, they culminate, they may be
translated with little change into acting plays.   Moreover,
Harte was the first prominently to bring into the short story
the element of paradox.   It is the object of the theatrical
always to move strongly the emotions, to keep interest taut
by swift change and by unexpected turns.   With Harte paradox became almost a mannerism.   Everywhere anticlimax:
in a desperado suddenly an outburst of Christlike self-sacrifice;
from a mild youth with seraphic countenance a fiendish outburst; from a seeming clergyman, all in a moment, profanity.

The weakness of Harte was his lack of sincerity and of
moral background.   Unlike Cable and Page, he stood apart
from his material, cold and unmoved, and sought not the
truth but effect upon the reader.   Every one of his extreme
characters may have had somewhere a counterpart, and every
separate incident, no matter how startling, may actually have
happened at some time during the mining era, but the assembling of all this mass of exceptions and of isolated extremes into

pictures that give the impression that they represent the ordinary course of life everywhere in California during a period is in reality a violation of the truth. The stories are unnatural: they have about them the atmosphere of the theatre. They are melodrama: they are compounded of the stage properties of the showman. Great as has been his influence, Harte cannot rank with the supreme masters of the short story. Lacking sincerity and sympathy and moral background, he becomes a picturesque incident rather than a permanent force.

After the enormous publicity given to Harte and the universal praise accorded his work both in America and in Europe, one might expect to find that a sudden change came over the spirit of American fiction. A change there was, indeed, but it was not sudden. One may leaf through whole volumes of such periodicals as *Harper's Magazine* and find no hint of the new vogue. Artists like James and Aldrich went on with their work as if *The Luck of Roaring Camp* had never been written. The writers who were to be influenced—that group which later was to be known as the "local colour school" —in 1870 were just beginning to find themselves, and they fell under the spell of Harte just as Longfellow and his circle in earlier days had fallen under the spell of Irving. It was not until the eighties and the early nineties that the tide which had begun in *The Overland Monthly* in 1868 came to its full.

Perhaps the most interesting transition during the period is that which may be traced in the work of Constance Fenimore Woolson (1838–94), a grandniece of Cooper, a native of New Hampshire, and a dweller successively by the Great Lakes, in the South, and in Italy, where she died. At the beginning of the seventies Miss Woolson was writing unlocalized poetic stories for *Harper's*, *A Merry Christmas*, *An October Idyl*, and the like, tales that might have come from the early period of Rose Terry Cooke. But soon one notes a change, a new sense of the value of background and of strongly individualized types for characters. By 1874 she was choosing the West for her materials. Her *Solomon* is a study of a unique character in an isolated German settlement on One-leg Creek which flows into the Tuscarawas River in Ohio, and her *Jeanette* and most of the other stories in *Castle Nowhere* (1875) deal with the primitive French habitants on Mackinac and

the islands of Lake Superior. She had been reading Harte.
Later, in the South, she was stirred by the desolation and the
poverty wrought by the war, and now with her heart in her
work she wrote the first post-bellum Southern short stories
founded upon the contrast between what was and what had
been. And still later in Italy she caught again the soul of a
people and wrought it into the tales to be collected under
the title *The Front Yard*. With each volume there had been
an increase in definiteness, in picturesque characterization, in
dramatic effect. She worked without dialect and she threw
over her work the soft evening light, yet was she a realist, as
Harte never was, and unlike him too she worked always with
insight and sympathy. Stories like her *The Front Yard* are
constructed of the materials of life itself. One cannot forget
them.

A transition from another source is to be found in the stories
of Sarah Orne Jewett (1849–1909), who also stands on the
border line between the real and the romantic. She was
affected not at all by Harte, but by Mrs. Stowe and Rose Terry
Cooke. In her *Deephaven* (1877) she struck the new note of
the decade, concreteness, geographical locality made so definite
and so minutely real that it may be reckoned with as one of
the characters in the story. Rose Terry Cooke had written
of New England; Miss Jewett wrote of Deephaven, which was
Berwick, Maine, her native town. Mrs. Stowe and Mrs.
Cooke wrote of the New England flood tide; Miss Jewett wrote
of the ebb, not despairingly like Miss Wilkins and the depressed
realists, but reverently and gently. Over all her work is the
hint of a glory departed, that Irving-like atmosphere which is
the soul of romance. She delighted in decaying old seaports
with their legends of other and better days, of old sea captains
mellow and reminiscent, and of dear old ladies serene in spite
of the buffets of time.

Her knowledge of her materials was intimate and thorough.
All through her girlhood she had ridden much with her father, a
country doctor, as he went his daily round among his patients.
From him she learned the soul of the region, and she sympathized with it, and later she interpreted it in story after story
based accurately upon what she knew. Unlike Mrs. Cooke
she came late enough to avoid the mid-century gush of senti-

ment. With her it became pathos, the pathos of sympathy and understanding; there is a grip of it in each one of her tales. One does not cry over a story like *A White Heron*, but one feels at the end of it like finding the sturdy little heroine and calling her a good girl. No art can go farther. Her delight was in the simple and the idyllic rather than in the dramatic. A story like *A Native of Winby* has very little of plot; but no tale was ever more worth the telling. It is a quivering bit of human life, a section of New England, a tale as true as a soul's record of yesterday.

There remains the element of style. She was one of the few creators of the short story after the seventies who put into her work anything like distinction. She was of the old school in this, of the school of Irving and Hawthorne and Poe. Indeed her style has often been likened to Hawthorne's, effortless, limpid, sun-clear in its flowing sentences, and softened and mellowed into a Sleepy-Hollow atmosphere—the perfect style, it would seem, for recording the fading glories of an old régime.

Her best stories are perhaps *Miss Tempy's Watchers*, *The Dulham Ladies*, *The Queen's Twin*, *A White Heron*, and *A Native of Winby*. Lightness of touch, humour, pathos, perfect naturalness—these are the points of her strength. She was a romanticist, equipped with a camera and a fountain pen.

To touch the seventies anywhere is to touch romance. Even Howells was not fully a realist until into the eighties. The new local colour work was not primarily realism. The new writers who now sprang up to portray local peculiarities in all parts of the land sought, even as Harte had done, to throw an idealized atmosphere over their pictures. One thinks of Mrs. Jackson and *Ramona*[1] and of Eggleston and *The Hoosier Schoolmaster*,[2] and, in the realm of the short story, of George W. Cable and Charles Egbert Craddock.

Cable was one of the discoveries of Edward King during his tour of the South for *Scribner's Monthly* in 1872. It was in New Orleans that he found him working as a humble clerk by day, and by night dreaming over a collection of reading matter as foreign to his work-day world as that which once had engaged another dreaming clerk, Charles Lamb. Among his enthusiasms were the old Spanish and French archives of

See also Book III, Chap. XI.   [2] *Ibid.*

the city; old relations of the priest-explorers; French novels—Hugo, Mérimée, About; English literature and American—Thackeray, Dickens, Poe, Irving. The composite of all this, plus a unique and evanescent quality which we call personality, was already finding form in sketches and stories which Cable was writing for himself and for the New Orleans papers. Some of his stories he showed to King, who advised him to send them to *Scribner's*. One of these, *'Sieur George*, was published the following year; others came at intervals. The young artist was not to be hurried; it was not for half a dozen years that enough had accumulated to make a volume. He had grown slowly upon the American consciousness, but the growth had been steady and sound. *Old Creole Days* (1879) was accepted at once as a masterpiece, and there has been no revulsion of feeling.

This collection, together with *Madame Delphine* the sum-total of his really distinctive short stories, owes its charm not alone to quaintness and strangeness of materials. It is as redolent of Cable as *The Luck of Roaring Camp* is of Harte. Cable's technique and his atmospheres may have been influenced by the French, but his style,—epigrammatic, Gallic in its swift shiftings and witty insinuations, daintily light, exquisitely pathetic at times, exotic always in its flavour of the old Creole city so strange to Northern readers,—all this is his own. No one has excelled him as a painter of dainty femininity, as a master of innuendo and suggestion, as a creator of exotic atmospheres. Whether his backgrounds are realistically true we do not ask, and whether his characters are actual types we do not care. They are true to the fundamentals of human life, they are alive, they satisfy, and they are presented ever with exquisite art. *Old Creole Days* stands unique, one of the undisputed masterpieces in the realm of the short story.

Two distinct schools ruled the short fiction of the seventies, that vital seed-time of a period: the school of unlocalized art, timeless and placeless, as Poe and Hawthorne had written it, and the new "local colour" school of Harte, which was going more and more to extremes. A few there were like Henry James who went on with their work utterly oblivious of the new demand for the violently localized. T. B. Aldrich[1]

---

[1] See also Book III, Chap. x.

was one. His little story *Marjorie Daw* was published in the *Atlantic* five years after Harte's sensational début. A trivial thing it was compared with such tragedies as *Tennessee's Partner* or *Madame Delphine*, an American humorous anecdote elaborately expanded, with a "point" at the end to be followed by laughter, yet its appearance marked a new stage in the history of the American short story. Tales already there had been that had held a sensation in the last sentence. *The Amber Gods* had ended with the startling words: "I must have died at ten minutes past one." But in *Marjorie Daw* the device was handled with a skill that made the story a model for later writers. After Aldrich, Stockton and Bunner and O. Henry.

Aldrich brought a style to the short story as distinctive as Cable's, a certain patrician elegance, yet a naturalness and a simplicity that concealed everywhere its art, for art is the soul of it; every sentence, every word a studied contribution toward the final effect. There is no moral, no hidden meaning, no exotic background to be displayed, no chastening tragedy; it is a mere whimsicality light as air, a bit of American comedy. The laugh comes not from what is told but from the picture supplied by the reader's imagination. All of Aldrich's thin repertoire of short stories is of the same texture. He may be compared with no American writer. To find a counterpart of *Marjorie Daw* one must go to the French—to Daudet for its whimsical lightness of touch, and to Maupassant for its exquisite technique.

But the interest created by the appearance of *Marjorie Daw* was mild compared with that accorded to Frank R. Stockton's *The Lady or the Tiger?* (1884). Stockton (1834–1902)[1] had not the technique of Aldrich nor his naturalness and ease. Certainly he had not his atmosphere of the *beau monde* and his grace of style, but in whimsicality and unexpectedness and in that subtle art that makes the obviously impossible seem perfectly plausible and commonplace, he surpassed not only him but Edward Everett Hale and all others. After Stockton and *The Lady or the Tiger?* it was realized even by the uncritical that short story writing had become a subtle art and that the master of its subtleties had his reader at his mercy.

[1] See also Book III, **Chap. XI.**

The best of Stockton's short work is to be found in his *Negative Gravity*, *The Transferred Ghost*, *The Remarkable Wreck of the "Thomas Hyke,"* and *The Late Mrs. Null*. It is like nothing else in American literature: everywhere paradox presented with the utmost gravity, everywhere topsy-turviness and anticlimax and the grotesquely unexpected. There is little of substance in it all; it is *opéra bouffe*, amusing, delightful, ephemeral. Even now Stockton is remembered only for *The Lady or the Tiger?* and the present generation considers even that story clumsy work when compared with the creations of his successor, O. Henry.

Another who did much to advance the short story toward the mechanical perfection it had attained to at the close of the century was Henry Cuyler Bunner[1] (1855–96), editor of *Puck* and creator of some of the most exquisite *vers de société* of the period. The title of one of his collections, *Made in France: French Tales with a U. S. Twist*, forms an introduction to his fiction. Not that he was an imitator; few have been more original or have put more of their own personality into their work. His genius was Gallic. Like Aldrich, he approached the short story from the fastidious standpoint of the lyric poet. With him, as with Aldrich, art was a matter of exquisite touches, of infinite compression, of almost imperceptible shadings. The lurid splashes and the heavy emphasis of the local colourists offended his sensitive taste: he would work with suggestion, with microscopic focussings, and always with dignity and elegance. He was more American than Henry James, more even than Aldrich. He chose always distinctively native subjects,—New York City was his favourite theme,—and his work had more depth of soul than Stockton's or Aldrich's. The story may be trivial, a mere expanded anecdote, yet it is sure to be so vitally treated that, like Maupassant's work, it grips and remains, and, what is more, it lifts and chastens or explains. It may be said with assurance that *Short Sixes* marks one of the high places which have been attained by the American short story.

In the same group belongs Ambrose Bierce (1838–1914?), though in mere point of time he is to be counted with the California group of the early *Overland Monthly* days. A

[1] See also Book II, Chap. XXIII, and Book III, Chap. IX.

soldier of the Civil War, editor of the San Francisco *News Letter* in 1866, associate editor, with the younger Tom Hood, of *London Fun* in 1872, author in London of the brilliant satirical fables *Cobwebs from an Empty Skull* in 1874, then in California again as editor of *The Argonaut* and *The Wasp*, and finally a resident of Washington, D. C., he was one of the most cosmopolitan of American writers. It was not until 1891 that his *Tales of Soldiers and Civilians*, later changed to *In the Midst of Life*, gave him a place with the short story writers, a very prominent place some critics would insist. Power undoubtedly he had, a certain scintillating brilliance, and a technique almost uncanny. His world was the world of Poe, timeless and placeless, ghastly often, chilling always and unnerving. At his best he was Poe returned after a half century equipped with the short story art of the new generation. Few have surpassed him in precision of diction, in reserve, in the use of subtle insinuation and of haunting climax. Some of his tales cling in one's soul like a memory of the morgue. His failure was his artificiality and his lack of sincerity and of truth to the facts of human life. Like Poe, he was a man of the intellect only, a craftsman of exquisite subtlety, an artist merely for the sake of his art.

With the eighties the short story came in America fully to its own. Up to 1884 it had generally been regarded as a magazine form, a rather trivial thing as compared with the stately novel. Hawthorne had abandoned the form early with the implication that he had used it as a prentice exercise. Harte no sooner had gained recognition than he began on *Gabriel Conroy*. Henry James, though it must be noted that it was after his long English residence, while revising his work declared that he had felt a sense of relief when he abandoned the frail craft of the short story where he ever had felt in danger of running ashore. Scarcely one of the later group of short story writers but sooner or later sought permanence in what, though they might not have confessed it, seemed to them the more permanent and dignified form of fiction.

Beginning in 1884, however, collections more and more began to dominate the output of fiction. Henry James in 1885 gathered up his scattered work of a decade and put it forth as *Stories Revived*. Others followed him, until seven years later the critic Copeland could devote an entire *Atlantic* article to the short-story collections of the year. The full triumph came in 1891, which produced this significant list of collections: *Elsket, and Other Stories*, Thomas Nelson Page; *Balaam and his Master*, Joel Chandler Harris; *Flute and Violin*, James Lane Allen; *Otto the Knight*, Octave Thanet (Alice French); *Main-Travelled Roads*, Hamlin Garland; *Gallegher, and Other Stories*, Richard Harding Davis; *Fourteen to One*, Elizabeth Stuart Phelps; *Huckleberries Gathered from New England Hills*, Rose Terry Cooke; *Iduna, and Other Stories*, George A. Hibbard; *Three Tales*, William Douglas O'Connor; *Uncle of an Angel*, Thomas A. Janvier; *Zadoc Pine, and Other Stories*, Bunner; *With My Friends*, Brander Matthews; *Rudder Grangers Abroad*, Stockton; *The Adventures of Three Worthies*, Clinton Ross.

1884 was the climactic year in the history of the short story inasmuch as it produced *The Lady or the Tiger?* and *In the Tennessee Mountains*, each one of them a literary sensation that advertised the form tremendously. No book since Harte's *The Luck of Roaring Camp* had been launched with such impetus as the latter of these. For six years the name of Charles Egbert Craddock had been appealing more and more to the national imagination because of a series in the *Atlantic* of strongly impressionistic studies of life in the Tennessee mountains. Now suddenly it came to light that the author was a woman, Miss Mary N. Murfree. The sensation in the *Atlantic* office spread everywhere and gave tremendous vogue not only to the book but to the type of short story that it represented. No one had gone quite so far before: the dialect was pressed to an extreme that made it almost unintelligible; grotesque localisms in manners and point of view were made central; and all was displayed before a curtain of mountains splashed with broad colours. The year was notable too because it produced Brander Matthews's *The Philosophy of the Short-story*, a magazine article later expanded into a volume, the first scientific handling of the art of the form since Poe's review of Hawthorne.

Realism, or more exactly, perhaps, naturalism, ruled the decade. From all sections of the country came now a tide of short fiction the chief characteristic of which was its fidelity to local conditions. The *Century* published Page's *Marse Chan*, a story entirely in negro dialect. Joel Chandler Harris[1] contributed his inimitable Uncle Remus studies of negro folk-lore and added to them short stories of the mountain "crackers." *Mingo and Other Sketches*, which appeared the same year as *In the Tennessee Mountains*, deals with the Craddock region and people but with surer hand. Harris was himself a native of Georgia hills, though he was by no means a "cracker," and he spoke with the sympathy and the knowledge of a native, not as an outside spectator and an exhibitor like Miss Murfree. The same may be said of Richard Malcolm Johnston (1822–98), whose *Dukesborough Tales*, dealing with rural life in the Georgia of his youth, first were given to Northern readers in 1883.

The evolution of Johnston's art is an interesting study. He was inspired not by Irving or by any of the Northerners, but by Longstreet,[2] whose brutally realistic *Georgia Scenes* had appeared as early as 1835. In 1857 Johnston had written *The Goose Pond School* and had followed it with other realistic studies for *The Southern Magazine*. Later they were gathered for a Southern edition entitled *Georgia Sketches*, and still later, in 1871, he had reissued them in Baltimore as *Dukesborough Tales*. He, therefore, must be reckoned with Harte as a pioneer, though his work had few readers and no influence until it was again reissued by the Harpers in 1883. Even then, and afterwards when he had added new and more artistically handled material, he was not a highly significant figure. Studies of provincial Georgia life he could make, some of them bitingly true, but his range was small and his soundings, even within his narrow area, were not deep. He must be classified with the makers of sketches like Longstreet rather than with the short story writers of the period in which he first became known.

So completely was local colour the vogue of the eighties that the novelist was regarded as a kind of specialist who moved in a narrow field of his own and who was to be reprimanded if he stepped beyond its limits. The movement had three phases: first, the Irvingesque school that romanticized its material and threw over it a softened light,—Harte, Miss

[1] See also Book III, Chap. v.   [2] See also Book II, Chap. xix.

Jewett, Cable, Page; second, the exhibitors of strange material objectively presented,—Charles Egbert Craddock, Octave
Thanet, and the dialect recorders of the eighties; and third,
the veritists of the nineties who told what they considered to
be the unidealized truth concerning the life they knew,—
Garland, Miss Wilkins, Frank Norris,[1] and the rest. This third
group approached its task scientifically, stated its doctrines
with clearness,—as for example in Hamlin Garland's *Crumbling
Idols*,—and then proceeded to work out its careful pictures
with deliberate art. Garland's *Main-Travelled Roads*, stories
of the settlement period of the Middle Border, have no
golden light upon them. They tell the truth with brutal
directness and they tell it with an art that convinces. They
are not mere stories; they are living documents in the history
of the West. So with the Maupassant-like pictures of later
New England conditions by Mary E. Wilkins Freeman, in *A
Humble Romance* (1887) and *A New England Nun* (1891).
If the florid, sentimental school of the mid-century went to
one extreme, she went to the other. Nowhere in English
may one find more of repression, more pitiless studies of repressed lives, more bare searchings into the soul of a decadent
social system. She wrote with conviction and a full heart of
the life from which she herself had sprung, yet she held herself
so firmly in control that her pictures are as sharp and cold as
engravings on steel.

With the nineties came the full perfection of short story
art. Within their limited field *A New England Nun* and *Main-
Travelled Roads* may not be surpassed. In another area of the
short story James Lane Allen's *Flute and Violin* stands by
itself, and in still another such work as Margaretta Wade
Deland's *Old Chester Tales*, Grace King's *Monsieur Motte*,
and Alice Brown's *Meadow Grass*. No more exquisite work,
however, may be found in the whole range of the local colour
school than that in Kate Chopin's (1851–1904) *Bayou Folks*
(1894). She was of Celtic blood and spontaneously a story-
teller. She wrote with abandon, yet always it was with the
restrained art that we have got into the habit of calling French.
Such stories as *Désirée's Baby*, the final sentence of which
grips one by the throat like a sudden hand out of the dark, and

[1] See also Book III, Chap. XI.

Madame Célestin's Divorce, with its delicious humour and its glimpse into the feminine heart, are among the few unquestioned masterpieces of American short story art.

The local colour vogue during the period undoubtedly was an element toward the making of the American fictional unit short. He who would deal with the social régime of a provincial neighbourhood must of necessity be brief. There was no background of established manners in the corners of America, or in the centres, for that matter, sufficient to afford material for a Richardson or a Thackeray. Harte and Charles Egbert Craddock and most of the others attempted novels and failed. One may make a moving drama of the culminating moment in Mother Shipton's or Tennessee's life, but a complete novel written about either of them would be only a succession of picaresque adventures. The short story was peculiarly the vehicle for recording American life, so squalid, yet so glorious and moving, during the era when the country had no manners but only the rudiments of what were to become manners.

Beginning about 1898 with the early work of O. Henry and Jack London, there has come what may be called the last period in the history of the short story—the work of the present day. It is the period of magazines devoted wholly to short stories, of syndicates which handle little else, of text books and college courses on the art of the short story, and even of correspondence courses in which the art of making marketable stories may be learned through the mails. In America the short story seems to have become an obsession.

The demand of the decade has been for "stories with a punch." The material must be out of the ordinary; it must not only breathe the breath of unfamiliar regions but it must give the impression that it is a bit of autobiography, or at least a section of life that has passed under the author's own eyes. The short story work of F. Hopkinson Smith (1838–1915)[1] may be taken as an illustration. There is in it the breath of foreign parts, the sense of cosmopolitanism, breezy knowledge of the world. Everywhere alertness, wide-awakeness, efficiency, in an easy colloquial style of narrative that has about it a businesslike ring. His brilliant narratives in such

[1] See also Book III, Chap. XI.

a collection as *At Close Range* are the work of one who would have made a most efficient special reporter for a city daily. Here are modern instances in all parts of the world, engagingly told. He has been everywhere, he has seen everything, he has learned all the world's rituals and all its secrets. There is no leisurely approach, no sentimental colourings, no literary effects; they are life seen in flashes, a vivid fragment snipped from the moving film of human life.

It may be illustrated also by Jack London's (1876–1916)[1] headlong art: strangeness always,—Alaska of the gold rush, the ultimate South Seas, the unknown recesses of the prize ring, the no-man's land of the hobo,—impressionistic studies in sensation. He was writing for money and for little else, and he studied his market like a broker. Earlier literature was aristocratic,—it was written for the refined few; the latest literature is democratic,—it is written for the mass, and the mass is uncritical and unrefined. Its demands are gross: sensation, movement, physical thrill. London gave the mass what it demanded, every sensation which the brutal underworld he knew afforded him, and he sold his work well. Of the graces demanded in the earlier periods, finish, elegance of style, melody, elevation in tone, he knew nothing. He had immediacy—he told vivid stories of physical prowess in the world of the present moment; he had the note of authority—he wrote only of wild epic things of which he had himself been a large part; he had sensation—the appeal of crude physical horror, the strange and the unheard-of in hitherto unknown regions; and he had a barbaric style—a lurid wealth of adjectives, a melodramatic intensity, and a headlong rush of incident that sweeps the reader along as in a stampede. Force undoubtedly he had and freshness of material, but, lacking poise and moral background and beauty of style, he must be passed as an ephemeral sensation.

From the multitude of the later short story writers Richard Harding Davis[1] (1864–1916), whose literary life, from the appearance of *Gallegher* in 1891 to his death, coincided almost exactly with the modern period in American literature, may be chosen as the typical figure. Reared in a literary home,— his mother was the author of *Life in the Iron Mills*,—educated

---

[1] See also Book III, Chap. XI. [2] *Ibid.*

at Lehigh University, trained in a city newspaper office until he became one of the most successful special correspondents of his generation, he was admirably fitted to give to the reading public—enormous now because of the universality of the public school and the newspaper and the popular magazine—what it most wanted.   He had what Jack London lacked utterly, literary traditions, poise, a certain patrician touch, and an innate love of the romantic.   What he might have become in an earlier and more literary era it is not hard to conjecture; what he did become was the result of the spirit of the age, for he became a journalist, a recorder of the ephemeral moment for the ephemeral moment, a reporter with pen marvellously facile and ready, a literary craftsman who mastered every detail of his craft.

That Davis satisfied his generation goes without saying. A good newspaper man, he gave it what it desired, up-to-dateness, swift action, strangeness of setting presented with the authority of an eye-witness, and, moreover, a sprinkling of sentiment and mystery and romance. All of his work is brilliant, and there are parts that have the touch of distinction, but nowhere does it satisfy the supreme tests.   He attempted too much, he skimmed over too much ground, he observed too much of the superficial and not enough of the real underlying heart of life.   He was a facile sketcher of surfaces, a versatile entertainer, a craftsman rather than a critic of human life, an artist enamoured with his art rather than a creator who worked with the deeper materials of the human tragedy and comedy.

The period closes with the work of William Sydney Porter, better known as O. Henry (1862–1910), whose sudden rise and enormous popularity are one of the romances of the history of the short story.   Only the bare facts of his biography need detain us: his Southern origin, his limited education, his sixteen years in Texas, his unfortunate experience as a bank clerk, his flight to South America, his return after a few months to serve a sentence in the Ohio State prison, and finally his last years in New York City—as picturesque a life as may be found in the annals of literature.

His short story career began almost by accident, the result of his enforced leisure in prison. His first story, *Whistling*

Dick's Christmas Stocking, redolent of Bret Harte, was pub·
lished in *McClure's Magazine* in 1899. Following it irregularly,
came a series of Western and South American tales, and then
finally a most remarkable output of stories dealing with the
human comedy and tragedy of New York City.

Nowhere is there anything just like them. In his best
work—and his tales of the great metropolis are his best—he is
unique. The soul of his art is unexpectedness. Humour at
every turn there is, and sentiment and philosophy and surprise.
One never may be sure of himself. The end is always a sensation. No foresight may predict it, and the sensation always
is genuine. Whatever else O. Henry was, he was an artist, a
master of plot and diction, a genuine humorist, and a philosopher. His weakness lay in the very nature of his art. He was
an entertainer bent only on amusing and surprising his reader.
Everywhere brilliancy, but too often is it joined to cheapness;
art, yet art merging swiftly into caricature. Like Harte, he
cannot be trusted. Both writers on the whole may be said to
have lowered the standards of American literature, since both
worked in the surface of life with theatric intent and always
without moral background. O. Henry moves, but he never
lifts. All is fortissimo; he slaps the reader on the back and
laughs loudly as if he were in a bar-room. His characters,
with few exceptions, are extremes, caricatures. Even his
shop girls, in the limning of whom he did his best work, are
not really individuals; rather are they types, symbols. His
work was literary vaudeville, brilliant, highly amusing, and
yet vaudeville.

On the whole the short story episode in American literary
history has been a symptom not of strength but of weakness.
"Short story writing is a young man's game," says H. G. Wells,
and it may be added that it is also the natural device of the
young nation just emerging from its adolescent period. To
see life in true perspective, to know the truth in its breadth
and depth, demands that we fix our attention not on fragments of life, on snatches of experience, on glimpses, swift
impressions, but on wholes. America has not had the time to
look steadily and long at any phase of the human play. All
it has wanted has been momentary impressions artistically
given, surface and sensations. It has been satisfied with clever-

ness rather than mastery, entertainment rather than instruction, with journalism rather than literature. What the coming
period is to be it is not within the province of the historian
to seek

CHAPTER VII

Books for Children

THE titles of the earliest American books for children sufficiently indicate their sole intention. John Cotton's *Milk for Babes, drawn out of the Breast of both Testaments,* published in London in 1646, was reprinted in Massachusetts ten years later as *Spiritual Milk for Boston Babes in either England.* Cotton Mather in 1700 revised an English book and issued it with the title *A Token for the Children of New-England. Or Some Examples of Children to whom the Fear of God was Remarkably Budding, before they Dyed.* In these books and the few others of early times the child was not recognized to have any individual needs or even an undeveloped mentality. The famous and very widely read *New England Primer* (c. 1690) was the first book to add elementary teaching, but its character still remained entirely religious. It sought, however, to be more attractive than earlier school books and employed illustrations; and it no doubt succeeded in exhilarating children whose sole portion had been drowsy sermons.

About midway in the eighteenth century, the desire to furnish amusement together with instruction, religious or mundane, ventured to show its head in reckless juveniles which came chiefly from the London shop of John Newbery. But it required half a century to convince parents that the combination was not pernicious—even parents who were allowing their children to read abridged editions of *Clarissa* and *Tom Jones* as well as *Moll Flanders.* As for the meagre American product, even *The Children's Magazine* (Hartford, 1789) made almost no attempt to approach the child's level. In Noah Webster's *Spelling Book* (1783), eight short illustrated fables formed the only concession to childish interest. The solitary instance of the amusement book proper was *Songs for the Nursery*, an edition of Mother Goose published in Boston some seventy years before; and it remained solitary for almost as many to come. By 1800, however, the somewhat more humanized instruction of Mrs. Barbauld and Mrs. Trimmer and Miss Edgeworth and Miss More had crossed the water.

Home production arose through the desire for suitable Sunday reading. Our first juvenile books were by preachers or their maiden relatives. The Rev. Henry Ware asked Miss Sedgwick in 1834, at the height of her popularity, for narratives "between a tale and a tract, which should provide illustrations of Christianity." The demands of her audience may be guessed from a letter entreating her to change a game of marbles to kite-flying, "because marbles are immoral as by betting they involve an appeal to God." This is perhaps an extreme application of the prescription of the Sunday School Union that their tales must avoid "even the most indirect insinuation of anything which can militate against the strictest ideas of propriety." But the services of an educated and practiced writer like Miss Sedgwick were unusual. Most of the earlier books were controversial; ignorant authoresses prattled of theology as glibly as their heroines declaimed their religious experiences. At first in great demand, the strongly sectarian books began to give way; the Sunday School Union itself was tending to break down sect distinctions, and the publishers complained that dogmatic preachings limited their sales. At a much later period those books grew in favour which had the least direct religious teaching, until finally the Sunday School library, designed to instruct, remained only to allure; and at the end of the nineteenth century the old-fashioned Sunday School book had happily vanished.

Down to the decade 1880–90, however, it still sold in enormous quantities; and its influence for three generations had been as morbid as it was weighty. These books presented parodies of child-life in Edgeworthian contrast. There was a spiritually faultless but organically feeble child who died after converting someone during a gasping illness, and there was a more healthy but worldly companion who refused to attend Sunday School and lived to a miserable end. In the long line of authors of these books, the two prime offenders demand mention not so much for the greater bulk of their sins as for their greater popularity. Susan Warner (1319–85)[1] under the pen name of Elizabeth Wetherell published her two chief stories *The Wide Wide World* in 1850 and *Queechy* in 1852. Both were phenomenally successful and widely translated. Their heroines when not undergoing brutal treatment for their aggressive rectitude are confidently flirtatious. But Miss Warner, as she showed elsewhere than in these tear-drenched pages, had simple tenderness and charm. Her successor had little of either, and even more of religious self-consciousness and effusive sentimentality. Yet in the *Elsie* books Martha Finley (1828–1909) attained an even longer popularity. With her the "ministering child" reached a burlesque of itself; Elsie Dinsmore, who begins the long series as an infant and ends it as a grandmother, made all previous prigs appear reticent and recreant. With Mrs. A. D. T. Whitney (1824–1906) the latest phase of the impulse, though not escaping sentimentality and self-righteousness, steered a middle course. Her many popular books, notably *Faith Gartney's Girlhood* (1863), continue to be widely read and possess an endearing quality which her predecessors forfeited by their obviousness. Hardly Sunday School books and yet chiefly the product of the same strong religious purpose are Mrs. Elizabeth Stuart Phelps Ward's even more naturalistic infantiles and juveniles. They show the girl prig on the decided decline.

The early writers of Sunday School literature, who alone were doing native work, are nameless now; but the decade 1830–40 brought forward our first group of juvenile authors, who, though they all assisted in supplying the Sunday School trade, wrote also for children much that was not intended to meet it specifically. Five were women, who wrote for girls; and two were men, who wrote for both sexes but rather for boys. Unlike the men, the women had already attained much contemporary fame. Mrs. Sarah J. Hale and Miss Eliza Leslie were popular magazinists and editors; Mrs. Sigourney was called the American Mrs. Hemans and read in every home; critics disputed whether our most important woman writer was Mrs. Child[2] or Miss Sedgwick.[3] The children's stories

---

[1] See also Book III, Chap. XI.   [2] See also Book II, Chap. VII.
[3] *Ibid.*

and verse of Mrs. Sigourney have disappeared, as have Mrs. Hale's with the exception of one nursery rhyme. The merit in the others' popular work failed to compensate for their old-fashioned style in a later day. Miss Leslie brightly narrated simple incidents unusually free from sanctimoniousness. Miss Sedgwick was less direct and simple, but her books are still extant. Their ample preaching never loses sight of the story; and as this is a good one, she headed the list of favourites in the annual report of the New York City library in 1847, with Dana's *Two Years Before the Mast* second. But as Miss Sedgwick herself preferred Hume and Shakespeare at the age of eight, it is not surprising that her children's stories have a somewhat adult tone. So do those of Mrs. Child, who was devouring Milton and Homer at fifteen. Her magazine, *Juvenile Miscellany*, established in 1827, continued for eight years, and was snuffed out at the height of its popularity by Boston's disapproval of her conversion to Anti-Slavery. It is a landmark in the history of juvenile writing. Even more important is *The Youth's Companion*, established the same year by Nathaniel Willis, father of N. P. Willis. The *Companion* may perhaps serve to illustrate the changing view. Taking a hint from the perseverance with which death had been dangled before the eyes of Puritan children, it exiled the word from its pages, which distribute lively and wholesome entertainment to the present day. However stilted the work of these decades may now appear, it had unprecedented humanity and naturalness; and the children of Miss Leslie, Miss Sedgwick, and Mrs. Child at their worst were never the puppets of the sensible Miss Edgeworth, and at their best had charm. Lucy Larcom's tribute to Mrs. Child in her *New England Girlhood* may be bestowed upon all these writers: "I have always been glad that I could tell her how happy she had helped to make my girlhood."

A far more powerful influence, however, came from the two men. These were Samuel Griswold Goodrich (1793–1860) and Jacob Abbott (1803–79). The son of a clergyman, Goodrich set out with a theory and an admiration for the method of Miss Hannah More. "Could not history, natural history, geography, biography, become the elements of juvenile works in place of fairies and giants and mere monsters of the imagination?" The hero of his first book accompanies an informed adult through America, meets with adventures, sees historical places. His books soon succumbed to their purpose and lost fictional interest, but seven millions of them were sold before detailed description palled. He wrote or edited one hundred and twenty books; and his pseudonym Peter Parley was stolen by many imitators, especially in England. He did a very important work in simplifying information books for children; and *Parley's Magazine*, which he conducted for nine years, and also the chief juvenile annual, which he edited, contributed to create opportunity for and to popularize children's writing. Jacob Abbott kept his heroes in their New England home, busying them only with rambles and picnics in woods and fields. A professor of mathematics, he had an appreciation of fact even more imperious than his rival's, and almost equalled him in fecundity. From 1832 until his death in 1879 he was exhaustless in quantity if not in invention. The *Rollo*, *Lucy*, *Jonas*, and *Franconia* books provide simple pictures of cheerful children, but place main emphasis upon dispensing information on all subjects about which curious youngsters may pester their parents. Beech-nut, the village encyclopedia in the *Franconia* books, is an original creation, life-like if omniscient; but although Abbott in his other series has similar vehicular youthful prodigies, they are wooden. The voluminous information of the *Rollo* books and the rest made convenient burlesque in later genera-tions, but Abbott's work had conspicuous common sense; and in pre-homeopathic days his sugar-coated pills were extraordinarily popular. Both of these men naïvely indicated that their purpose was not primarily fictional. About their work, Gulian Verplanck, editing *The Fairy Book*, was as testy as Charles Lamb with Mrs. Barbauld and Mrs. Trimmer. "Dismal trash all of them!" he cried. "Something half-way between stupid story-books and bad school-books; being so ingeniously written as to be unfit for any useful purpose in the school and too dull for any entertainment out of it." But Peter Parley had much naturalness of style in contrast with earlier stiffness, and Abbott showed genuine lightness of touch. Their enormous sales prove their attractiveness; and Noah Brooks, himself an important juvenile writer, has recorded that, however tame they seemed later, they were thrilling in interest compared with all previous juveniles.

Although before the end of the nineteenth century America was to lead the world in its special literature for children, the chief authors of the first half of the century did not intentionally contribute to it. Cooper's stories[1] bequeathed to a later generation the Indian, the Yankee Trader, and the Scout; but neither he nor Irving[2] in *Sleepy Hollow* and *Rip Van Winkle*, nor Dana in the book that still remains one of the most popular with boys,[3] wrote directly for them. Nor (except occasionally) did Mrs. Stowe,[4] whose *Uncle Tom's Cabin* is now almost exclusively a juvenile. The one author of general fame who did so was Hawthorne.[5] His *Grandfather's Chair*, *Wonder Book*, and *Tanglewood Tales* have among children's books as high rank as his other work has in the adult field, and are certainly more widely read. He tells the Greek myths in a happy and paternal spirit, as he does numerous legends of New England; and his style has its usual distinction. With the advent of several excellent magazines for children, sheltered by established publishers and commanding their writers, the literary attitude began to change. "Some of my friends," Isaac Watts had written, "imagine that my time is employed in too mean a service while I write for babes"; and down to the middle of the nineteenth century critics still mistook juvenile books for puerile books. The time was approaching when two editors of the austere *Atlantic Monthly*, Aldrich and Horace Scudder, would think writing for children not unworthy of their accomplished pens, and the editor of the massive *North American Review*, Charles Eliot Norton, would edit also a boy's library. It was perceived that simplicity need not be inane, and that to entertain children without enfeebling their intellect or stultifying their sentiment afforded scope for mature skill and judgment. *Our Young Folks*, published by Ticknor and Fields (about 1865), enlisted Mrs. Stowe, Whittier, Higginson, Aldrich, Elizabeth Stuart Phelps, E. E. Hale, Rose Terry Cook,

---

[1] See also Book II, Chap. VI.   [2] See also Book II, Chap. IV.

[3] Interesting evidence of the simplicity and straightforwardness of the style of *Two Years Before the Mast*, which like that of *Robinson Crusoe* so commended it to boys, is found in the fact that quotations from it long formed the material upon oculists' cards for testing the eyesight.

[4] See also Book III, Chap. XI.   [5] See also Book II, Chap. XI.

Bayard Taylor. It was edited by J. T. Trowbridge, Gail Hamilton, and Lucy Larcom; and later was merged into *St. Nicholas*, edited by Mrs. Mary Mapes Dodge (1838–96). With these magazines a new era begins.

The notable success of the period was made, however, by one whose work for adults was only mediocre. Louisa M. Alcott (1832–88) was asked by a publisher in 1867 for a girl's book, and began her task reluctantly. But wisely deciding not to write down, she merely spoke out, with no more than the pleasant moralizing of the Alcott household, her youthful memories. Out of the incidents of her own girlhood she constructed *Little Women* (1868), and its abiding charm lies in its atmosphere of real life and its real portraits. It at once gained the heights of popularity and was translated into many languages. The public kept demanding other stories; and *An Old-Fashioned Girl* (1869), *Little Men* (1871), *Eight Cousins* (1874), *Rose in Bloom* (1876), and *Under the Lilacs* (1878) were almost as popular and as meritorious. Some of these were written for *St. Nicholas*, in which Mrs. Mary Mapes Dodge was nearly equalling her achievement. The two books which next to Miss Alcott's have the most assured position are Mrs. Dodge's *Hans Brinker* (1865) and *Donald and Dorothy* (1883). The former still remains the best story about Holland, and was awarded a prize by the French Academy; the latter runs it close for naturalness and interest. A little later these artistic successes were matched by *Betty Leicester* of Sarah Orne Jewett,[1] whose work for young people has the charm and distinction of her short stories for adults. *St. Nicholas* became in itself a library of choice literature for children, and many of the books which this chapter mentions appeared there. It encouraged writers for younger children also, and there were now some magazines devoted to them alone. For them Rebecca Clarke (1833–1906) had already written much, under the name of Sophie May. The *Little Prudy* and *Dotty Dimple* books have quaintness and tenderness, but, as with most of the writers of her time, grow thinner as their series lengthen. These and Margaret Sidney's *Little Pepper* stories are standard achievements in infantile writing. The *Katy* books of Sarah Woolsey, under the name

[1] See also Book III, Chap. vi

of Susan Coolidge, have a similar excellence for children somewhat older, but also outlast their material.

When the object of juvenile writing became, in the sixties,
wholesome amusement rather than instruction, a result at once
evident was that far more books were written for boys than for
girls. "Simple, lively books for girls are much needed," wrote
Miss Alcott in her journal; and seemed to fear that her liveliness was more suitable for the youthful male. Women
apparently combated more than men the idea that mere entertainment was harmless. But the respectable of the sterner
sex so shared it at first that it was seized upon only by the con-
coctors of lurid melodrama, shameless persons who hid under
such pseudonyms as "Nick Carter." A rage for these dime
dreadfuls swept the country, and perhaps it was the tardy
desire not "to leave all the good tunes to the devil" which
energized the next group of writers for boys. Some of them at
any rate were ministers, and the books of others were still too
much under the compulsion of preaching, even if by story
rather than by precept. Chief among these writers (who wrote
solely for children) were Elijah Kellogg[1] (1813–1901), William
Taylor Adams (1822–97), and Horatio Alger, Jr. (1832–99).
Their careers began about 1860. Kellogg's several series of
stories of Maine deal with the adventures of fishermen and
farmers. Though more carefully written than were the other
two, they have no merit of literary form beyond the great one
of telling a straightforward story unimpeded by inessentials,
but their pictures of a sturdy and rugged people are vivid and
unaffected. Pictures of equal local value and interest F. R.
Goulding was giving at the same time in stories of boy-life on
the Southern seaboard. *The Young Marooners* (1852) has decided merit. Adams's pseudonym, "Oliver Optic," speedily became as profitable as Goodrich's, and it also was placed at the
head of a magazine. He wrote over one hundred volumes besides
innumerable short stories, and their popularity has never since
been equalled. Principal of a public school and Sunday School
superintendent, he lived to hear his books called trashy by a
more exacting age. Their style is, it is true, slovenly, and their
smart heroes are given to cheap declamation; but their material

---

[1] His sounding declamatory piece *Spartacus to the Gladiators* was long familiar
to every school boy.

is all clean, effective, and interesting. *The Starry Flag, Soldier Boy*, and *Young America* series merited the delight of two generations of boys. Horatio Alger, Jr., once a Unitarian minister, wrote seventy volumes, most of their titles summoning apt alliteration's artful aid. They told of bootblacks and newsboys, from systematic personal observation in the streets of New York City. His simple and invariable formula scored— by pluck and perseverance his hero rose single-handed to fame and fortune. The books of all three writers aroused admiration for sterling qualities; but the more sophisticated boys of a later generation began to complain that the Optic and Alger books were all alike, and conscientious librarians began to see that in them the element of luck was overemphasized. Two other writers grew very popular before the trend at the close of the century toward the study of adolescent psychology and adolescent citizenship discovered something pernicious in action unaccompanied by reflection and analysis. These were Harry Castlemon and Edward S. Ellis. The former revelled in exciting and incredible adventures upon unrecognizable frontiers, and the latter yarned blithely of hunting and Indians without a thought of preparing boys for social service.

Meanwhile, writers more serious in purpose had been following the historical and biographical trail of Goodrich and Abbott, bringing to it more literary nicety and greater research. An early contemporary of the two had been John Frost (1800– 59), a forgotten schoolmaster whose one hundred juveniles sold by the ton in his day and were republished as late as 1890. John Abbott (Jacob's brother), followed by James Parton, Elbridge Brooks, E. E. Hale, and Hezekiah Butterworth, made important contributions to the new department of biography for children. These and other writers, among them Edward Eggleston[1] and George Cary Eggleston, began also to combine history and fiction so well that the reader did not know where one left off and the other began. This species they developed more successfully than did their extremely popular English rivals, Henty and his school. Their fiction was more credible and their background more accurate. Charles Carleton Coffin's historical series from colonial times to the close of the

[1] See also Book III, Chap. XI.

Civil War present in story form perhaps the best short histories of the campaigns they cover; Noah Brooks's *Boy Emigrants* exhibits frontier life accurately; John Bennett's *Master Skylark* belongs to the highest type of historical juvenile.

The informational path trod first by Goodrich and Abbott grew to be the main road for future juveniles. Today the *How To Make* books are perhaps the most distinctive, as they are among the best-selling. What probably remains the most distinguished treatment for young children of foreign life and scenes and of nature was given by Jane Andrews (1833–87) in her *Seven Little Sisters* (1861) and *Stories Mother Nature Told*. She was the pioneer of the great crowd of present-day nature writers for children and still compares in dignity and interest of treatment with all her successors. Of these, those who steer warily between the scientific and lifeless and the sentimental and the superficial are still living. In less philosophical or imaginative setting, the books of actual adventure by Paul du Chaillu deserve mention.

The revolt from Goodrich and Abbott took not only the form of stories of unmixed action but also of the novel assertion that innocent pranks are a legitimate subject for children's books. These J. T. Trowbridge (1827–1916) and James Otis Kaler (1846–), authors respectively of the delightful *Cudjo's Cave* (1864) and *Toby Tyler* (1867), ventured to exploit with no uneasy eye on the moral effect. Thomas Bailey Aldrich[1] made a notable success artistic as well as popular with his *Story of a Bad Boy*. A semi-idealized record of his own New England childhood, its only intention was to record zestfully what had really been the life of a boy engaged in no adventurous actions other than ordinary escapades. It was a departure when published in 1869. A half-dozen years later appeared another masterpiece of pranks regarded at the time as by no means innocent. *Tom Sawyer* (1876) and its sequel *Huckleberry Finn* (1884), by Samuel L. Clemens,[2] raised a tempest in the cambric-teapot world and are even yet looked at askance in some children's libraries. But in spite of moralists they immediately took the foremost place as stories of the American boy, and in a surprisingly short while became world classics. They are not explicitly treated as boy's stories

[1] See also Book III, Chaps. VI and X.   [2] See also Book III, Chap. VIII.

throughout, and in each are description and social observation beyond the appreciation of young readers; yet they have doubtless never failed with boy as with man to reap the highest triumph possible to fiction, the reader's recognition of his own psychology and temperament. The general unimprovingness of both of these books was balanced, for moralists, by the excess of serious purpose in the author's third book for young people, *The Prince and the Pauper* (1882). It is an impressive panorama of splendid scenes of ancient legal and royal cruelty.

The distinct Americanism, so noteworthy in Mark Twain, was an important characteristic of American juveniles from the beginning. In the school-readers after the Revolution were most naïve attempts to enshrine patriotism with the other virtues. Indeed, it was the impatience that children began to manifest at forever reading books with unfamiliar local colour which turned the attention of writers to this hitherto neglected branch of literature. "Our Sabbath School library books were nearly all English reprints and most of our every-day reading came to us from over the sea," wrote Lucy Larcom. Goodrich and Abbott and the women of the thirties no longer talk of English flowers and birds. When Goodrich took his boy heroes abroad, their comments were often aggressively American; and it is amusing to see that though he censured the horrors of giants for sensitive children he revelled in Indian atrocities. Miss Sedgwick was particularly praised by the *North American* for her native atmosphere and incidents, when children's books were all following the English moralists. Since the Civil War historical juveniles have covered every phase of national development. It has, indeed, several times been observed that one can get more of American life from the juvenile than from the adult fiction of the period. To a large extent, this is implicit in the problem of interesting children. Hawthorne's *Grandfather's Chair*, points out Horace Scudder, discussing the art of writing for them to which he so greatly contributed, is more actual than even *The Blithedale Romance*.

Just as markedly American have been the spiritual characteristics of American juveniles. "Those English children had to be so prim and methodical," wrote Lucy Larcom, "they were never allowed to romp and run wild." The growing independence of American children appeared in the successive books written to appeal to them. Parents and guardians, so important in English books, figure very little. In the most popular books, boys and girls are thrown on the world or leave home to seek their fortunes or have adult responsibilities. The reforming child was an American creation and persevered in America some time after she had been happily throttled in England; and her strenuosity was even more offensive because of the lack of grown-up authority. American book-children are always the king-pins of their households as well as of their stories, and often their sagacious ability is thrown into relief by weak-minded parents. Miss Alcott recorded that innumerable letters from her child admirers forced her to provide a wedding for her first heroine. It cannot be denied that all this reflects the attitude of American life. Also, one may gather from children's stories—with less misgiving—that the United States evinced in the first half of the century more interest in education than did any other country and in the second half more interest in the analytic study of child-life by reason of an earlier appropriation of the kindergarten theory. On account of this interest, the moral and the educational as leading features were suppressed sooner. As the growing psychological study of the child demanded that his initiative be unhampered by patterns, so his pranks began to be recorded, as more personal (as well as more interesting) than his good behaviour. Finally, it may be said that because of this kindergarten impulse more conscientious, intelligent work has been done in American writing for children than has been the case elsewhere.

But in one way, equally characteristic of the American temperament and American adult literature, children's writers have lagged behind the European world. In the domain of pure fancy very little has been accomplished. As the century entered its closing decades protests were heard against the prevailing realism, and appeals for the restoration of those idealistic qualities which enkindle the child's imagination elsewhere. In fairy tales, Frank R. Stockton[1] stands almost alone in having done any considerable quantity of work possessing literary value. The wise humorous style of his fanciful tales and their grotesque droll material make them exceptional.

[1] See also Book III, Chaps. VI and XI.

Howard Pyle also did work of distinction in this field, much assisted by his eccentric illustrations; and his *Robin Hood* (1883)
is capital romance.   In nonsense books, the imitators of Lewis
Carroll and Edward Lear were many in the last years of the
century; but the best of them, Charles Carryl in *Davy and The
Goblin* (1885), only invite comparison.   Somewhat earlier,
Lucretia P. Hale in *Peterkin Papers* (1882) created a new form
of nonsense of a more literal sort; and this for spontaneous
fun and clever foolishness is remarkable.   Fairy tales seem
to have no foothold in America—the stories in verse of Palmer
Cox, the *Brownie* books, being perhaps the sole instance the
century afforded of nation-wide popularity (and these owing
more to the author's illustrations than to the text).   For this
condition publishers may be somewhat responsible, as they can
sufficiently supply the market with uncopyrighted European
material for which no royalties need be paid.   Less likely to
have been discouraged by unfair foreign competition, and certainly in themselves more indigenous, are stories which endow
animals with human motives and speech.   A local counterpart of European folk-lore is the lore of Uncle Remus, created
by Joel Chandler Harris.[1]   He was far more successful than
Hawthorne in the setting he gave these tales, which, like the
Greek myths, are the common property of a race; Uncle
Remus himself is a fine characterization, well-observed, humorous, and full of reverent kindliness.

The class of juvenile poetry furnished no writer distinguished
by any body of work, but an anthology of high order could be
compiled.   First in time and perhaps in merit would come a
one-poem writer, Clement C. Moore (1779–1863).   In December, 1823, he published *A Visit from St. Nicholas*, which is unique
for its period in being entirely free from didacticism and from
laboured inanity masquerading as simplicity; it still remains
unexcelled in America as a joyous narrative of childhood.
Mrs. Hale's *Mary Had a Little Lamb* yet gambols in children's
hearts—for as inexplicable a reason as much of the mechanical
nonsense of Mother Goose.   The longevity of jingles has never
been an indication of their merit, as witness the permanence of
such ditties as *Upidee* and *Good-bye, my Lover, Good-bye*.   Lucy
Larcom and Alice and Phœbe Cary published books of child-

[1] See also Book III, Chap. v.

hood songs; and other women followed with no particular success. Eugene Field[1] and James Whitcomb Riley[2] wrote many tender and charming poems about children, but with some notable exceptions they are as much from the adult point of view as were Longfellow's. The point of view of youthful patriots was skilfully considered in *Poems and Ballads upon Important Episodes in American History* (1887) by Hezekiah Butterworth, long connected with *The Youth's Companion*. The best verse is scattered in magazines and newspapers, particularly as publishers have learned from librarians that American children as a rule do not care for poetry. Mrs. Dodge wrote for her magazine many neat and attractive rhymes. In this field there are, however, several living writers of conspicuous artistic success.

Nor is it surprising that some of the best work in fiction also must, similarly, go unmentioned here. The juvenile has only lately received artistic cultivation, and its flowering is very recent. More striking than in any other department of literature, where contrasts are all striking enough, is the comparison of the earlier with the latter part of the century. Where then existed not a single book of value, there could now be mentioned half a thousand of real merit. American literature for children has reached a comparative eminence which it shows in no other department.

[1] See also Book II, Chap. XXIII, and Book III, Chap. IX.
[2] See also Book III, Chap. X.

INDEX

THE CAMBRIDGE HISTORY

OF

AMERICAN LITERATURE

Volume III

Later National Literature: Parts II and III

The Cambridge History

of

American Literature

Edited by

William Peterfield Trent

John Erskine

Stuart P. Sherman

Carl Van Doren

In Three Volumes

Later National Literature: Parts II and III

MACMILLAN PUBLISHING CO., INC.

New York

PRINTED IN THE UNITED STATES OF AMERICA

PREFACE

IN the final volumes of *The Cambridge History of American Literature* will be found several chapters which cover periods beginning much earlier than the Later National Period to which the volumes are specifically devoted. They are placed here partly because it has been found convenient to hold them till the last, inasmuch as they deal with large groups of writers not readily classified elsewhere, and also because in almost every case the bulk of the material discussed in them was produced after 1850.

The delay in the publication of these volumes has been due, not only to the unsettled conditions of the time, but equally to the realization, as the work has advanced, that the number of pioneer tasks still to be undertaken in the study of American literature was larger than could be entirely foreseen. We cannot claim to have accomplished all or nearly all of them. But it would be equivalent to a failure to acknowledge our appreciation of the aid rendered by our sixty-four contributors, who have faithfully laboured to bring this history to a completion, if we did not express a belief that the work as a whole furnishes a new and important basis for the understanding of American life and culture.

THE EDITORS.

10 September, 1920.

CONTENTS

CHAPTER XI

THE LATER NOVEL: HOWELLS

By CARL VAN DOREN, Ph.D., Literary Editor of *The Nation*, Associate in English in Columbia University.

CHAPTER XII

HENRY JAMES

By JOSEPH WARREN BEACH, Ph.D., Associate Professor of English in the University of Minnesota.

CHAPTER XIII

LATER ESSAYISTS

By GEORGE S. HELLMAN, A.M.

CHAPTER XIV

TRAVELLERS AND EXPLORERS, 1846–1900

By FREDERICK S. DELLENBAUGH.

Contents

CHAPTER XV

LATER HISTORIANS

By JOHN SPENCER BASSETT, Ph.D., LL.D., Professor of American History in Smith College.

CHAPTER XVI

LATER THEOLOGY

By AMBROSE WHITE VERNON, A.M., D.D., Professor of Biography in Carleton College.

CHAPTER XVII

LATER PHILOSOPHY

By MORRIS R. COHEN, Ph.D., Professor of Philosophy in the College of the City of New York.

Contents

CHAPTER XVIII

THE DRAMA, 1860–1918

By MONTROSE J. MOSES.

CHAPTER XIX

LATER MAGAZINES

By WILLIAM B. CAIRNS, Ph.D., Associate Professor of American Literature in the University of Wisconsin.

CHAPTER XX

NEWSPAPERS SINCE 1860

By FRANK W. SCOTT, Ph.D., Assistant Professor of English in the University of Illinois.

Contents

CHAPTER XXI

POLITICAL WRITING SINCE 1850

By WILLIAM KENNETH BOYD, Ph.D., Professor of History in Trinity College, Durham, North Carolina.

CHAPTER XXII

LINCOLN

By NATHANIEL WRIGHT STEPHENSON, Professor of History in the College of Charleston.

CHAPTER XXIII

EDUCATION

By PAUL MONROE, PhD., LL.D., Professor of the History of Education in Teachers College, Columbia University.

BOOK III: PART III
CHAPTER XXIV

ECONOMISTS

By EDWIN R. A. SELIGMAN, Ph.D., LL.D., McVickar Professor of Political Economy in Columbia University.

CHAPTER XXV

SCHOLARS

By SAMUEL LEE WOLFF, Ph.D., Lecturer in English in Columbia University.

Contents

CHAPTER XXVI

PATRIOTIC SONGS AND HYMNS

By PERCY H. BOYNTON, A.M., Associate Professor of English in the University of Chicago.

CHAPTER XXVII

ORAL LITERATURE

By LOUISE POUND, Ph.D., Professor of English in the University of Nebraska.

CHAPTER XXVIII

TWO NEW RELIGIONS

By LYMAN P. POWELL, D.D., LL.D.

CHAPTER XXIX

BOOK PUBLISHERS AND PUBLISHING

By EARL L. BRADSHER, Ph.D., Adjunct Professor of English in the University of Texas.

CHAPTER XXX

THE ENGLISH LANGUAGE IN AMERICA

By HARRY MORGAN AYRES, Ph.D., Associate Professor of
English in Columbia University, Associate Editor of
The Weekly Review.

CHAPTER XXXI

NON-ENGLISH WRITINGS I

GERMAN, FRENCH, YIDDISH

1. German

By ALBERT BERNHARDT FAUST, Ph.D., Professor of
German in Cornell University.

2. French

By the late EDWARD J. FORTIER, Assistant Professor of
French in Columbia University.

3. Yiddish

By NATHANIEL BUCHWALD.

Contents

CHAPTER XXXII

NON-ENGLISH WRITINGS II

Aboriginal

By MARY AUSTIN.

___

Book III (*Continued*)

CHAPTER VIII

Mark Twain

SAMUEL LANGHORNE CLEMENS, more widely known as Mark Twain, was of the "bully breed" which Whitman had prophesied. Writing outside "the genteel tradition," he avowedly sought to please the masses, and he was elected to his high place in American literature by a tremendous popular vote, which was justified even in the opinion of severe critics by his exhibition of a masterpiece or so not unworthy of Le Sage or Cervantes. Time will diminish his bulk as it must that of every author of twenty-five volumes; but the great public which discovered him still cherishes most of his books; and his works, his character, and his career have now, and will continue to have, in addition to their strictly literary significance, a large illustrative value, which has been happily emphasized by Albert Bigelow Paine's admirable biography and collection of letters. Mark Twain is one of our great representative men. He is a fulfilled promise of American life. He proves the virtues of the land and the society in which he was born and fostered. He incarnates the spirit of an epoch of American history when the nation, territorially and spiritually enlarged, entered lustily upon new adventures. In the retrospect he looms for us with Whitman and Lincoln, recognizably his countrymen, out of the shadows of the Civil War, an unmistakable native son of an eager, westward-moving people—unconventional, self-reliant, mirthful, profane.

I

realistic, cynical, boisterous, popular, tender-hearted, touched
with chivalry, and permeated to the marrow of his bones with
the sentiment of democratic society and with loyalty to American institutions.

By his birth at Florida, Missouri, 30 November, 1835, he
was a Middle-Westerner; but by his inheritance from the restless, sanguine, unprosperous Virginian, his father, who had
drifted with his family and slaves through Kentucky and
Tennessee, he was a bit of a Southerner and still more of a mi-
grant and a seeker of fortune.   His boyhood he spent in the
indolent semi-Southern town of Hannibal, Missouri, which, as
he fondly represents it, slept for the most part like a cat in the
sun, but stretched and rubbed its eyes when the Mississippi
steamboats called, teasing his imagination with hints of the
unexplored reaches of the river.   When in 1847 his father died
in poverty brightened by visions of wealth from the sale of
his land in Tennessee, the son was glad to drop his lessons and
go to work in the office of the Hannibal *Journal*.   There,
mainly under his visionary brother Orion, he served as printer
and assistant editor for the next six years, and in verse and
satirical skits made the first trials of his humour.   In 1853,
having promised his mother with hand on the Testament "not
to throw a card or drink a drop of liquor," he set out on an excursion into the world, and worked his way for three or four
years as printer in St. Louis, New York, Philadelphia, Keokuk,
and Cincinnati.

Through the winter of 1856–7 he pleased himself with a
project for making his fortune by collecting cocoa at the headwaters of the Amazon; and in the spring of 1857 he actually
took passage on the *Paul Jones* for New Orleans.   But falling
into conversation with the pilot, Horace Bixby, he engaged himself with characteristic impulsiveness as an apprentice to that
exacting, admired, and, as it then seemed to him, magnificently
salaried king of the river.   In return for five hundred dollars
payable out of his first wages Bixby undertook to teach him the
Mississippi from New Orleans to St. Louis so that he should
have it "by heart."   He mastered his twelve hundred miles of
shifting current, and became a licensed pilot.   In the process
he acquired without the slightest consciousness of its uses
his richest store of literary material.

"In that brief, sharp schooling," he wrote many years later, "I got personally and familiarly acquainted with all the different types of human nature that are to be found in fiction, biography, or history. When I find a well-drawn character in fiction or biography, I generally take a warm personal interest in him, for the reason that I have known him before—met him on the river."

This chapter of his experience was ended abruptly by the outbreak of the Civil War and the closing of the river. His brief and inglorious part in the ensuing conflict he has described, with decorations, in his *Private History of a Campaign that Failed*, a little work which indicates that he rushed to the aid of the Confederacy without much conviction, and that two weeks later he rushed away with still less regret. Eventually, it should be remarked, General Grant became his greatest living hero, and his attitude towards slavery became as passionately Northern as that of Mrs. Stowe.

Meanwhile he went West. On 26 July, 1861, he was sitting on the mail-bags behind the six galloping horses of the overland stage headed for Carson City, Nevada, as assistant to his brother Orion, who through the good offices of a friend in Lincoln's cabinet had been appointed Territorial secretary. On his arrival, finding himself without salary or duties, he explored the mining camps and caught the prevailing passion for huge quick wealth. First he bought "wild-cat" stock; then he located a vast timber claim on Lake Tahoe; then he tried quartz mining in the silver regions; prospected for gold in the placer country; and, in daily expectation of striking it fabulously rich, sank his brother's salary in the most promising "leads."

That his claims did not "pan out" well is clear from his accepting in 1862 a position as local reporter for the Virginia City *Enterprise* at twenty-five dollars a week, having commended himself to the editor by a series of letters signed "Josh." Thus began his literary career. In reporting for this paper the sessions of the Legislature at Carson City he first employed the signature "Mark Twain," a name previously used by a pilot-correspondent of the New Orleans *Picayune* but ultimately commemorating the leadsman's cry on the Mississippi. His effervescent spirits, excited by the stirring and heroically convivial life of a community of pioneers, found easy outlet in the robust humour and slashing satire of frontier journalism. In 1863 Artemus Ward[1] spent three glorious weeks revelling with the newspaper men in Virginia City, recognized the talent of Mark Twain, and encouraged him to send his name eastward with a contribution to the New York Sunday *Mercury*. A duel occasioned by some journalistic vivacities resulted in his migration in 1864 to San Francisco, where in 1864 and 1865 he wrote for *The Morning Call*, *The Golden Era*, and *The Californian;* and fraternized with the brilliant young coterie of which Bret Harte[2] was recognized as the most conspicuous light. In a pocket-hunting excursion in January, 1865, he picked up a very few nuggets and the nucleus for the story of *Jim Smiley and his Jumping Frog*, which appeared in the New York *Saturday Press* in November and swiftly attained wide celebrity. In the following spring he visited the Sandwich Islands on a commission from the Sacramento *Union*, called upon his first king, explored the crater of Kilauea, struck up a friendship with the American ministers to China and Japan, and made a great "scoop" by interviewing a group of shipwrecked sailors in the hospital at Honolulu. Later he wrote up the story for *Harper's Magazine;* his appearance there in 1866 he calls his *début* as a literary person.

Returning to San Francisco, he made his first appearance as a humorous lecturer in a discourse on the Sandwich Islands, delivered with his sober, inimitable, irresistible drawl to a crowded and applausive house on the evening of 2 October, 1866. From this point his main course was determined. Realizing that he had a substantial literary capital, he set out to invest it so that it would in every sense of the word yield the largest returns obtainable. To the enterprise of purveying literary entertainment he, first in America, applied the wide-ranging vision and versatile talents of our modern men of action and captains of industry: collecting his "raw material," distributing it around the world from the lecture platform, sending it to the daily press, reworking it into book form, inventing his own type-setting machinery, and controlling his own printing, publishing, and selling agencies. He did not foresee this all in 1866; but it must have begun to dawn.

[1] See Book II, Chap. XIX. [2] See Book III, Chap. VI.

By repeating his Sandwich Islands lecture widely in California and Nevada he provided himself with means to travel, and revisited his home, returning by way of Panama and New York. In May, 1867, he published his first book, *The Celebrated Jumping Frog of Calaveras County, and Other Sketches*, and lectured in Cooper Institute. Then on 8 June he sailed on the *Quaker City* for a five months' excursion through the Mediterranean to the Holy Land, first reported in letters to *The Alta-California* and the New York *Tribune*, and immortalized by his book *Innocents Abroad*. On 2 February, 1870, he married his most sympathetic reader and severest censor, Olivia Langdon of Elmira, New York, a sister of one of the *Quaker City* pilgrims who had shown him her photograph in the Bay of Smyrna. After a brief unprofitable attempt to edit a newspaper in Buffalo, he moved in 1871 to Hartford, Connecticut, and in 1874 built there the home in which he lived for the next seventeen years.

He formed a close association with his neighbour Charles Dudley Warner[1]; was taken under the editorial wing of William Dean Howells[2] and into his intimate friendship; contributed to *The Atlantic Monthly, Harper's Magazine*, and *The North American Review;* and ultimately made some progress with such festive New Englanders as O. W. Holmes,[3] F. J. Child,[4] and T. B. Aldrich[5]; but his head was white before he became as much of a lion in Boston and New York as he had been in Carson City and San Francisco. At various times he made extended sojourns in England, Italy, France, Germany, and Austria, particularly in his later years in seasons of pecuniary retrenchment. He reaped a fortune by contracting for the publication of Grant's *Memoirs* and his royalties were steadily large; but bad ventures in his publishing business, his somewhat lavish style of living, and his unperfected type-setting machine, in which he sank $200,000, pushed him finally into bankruptcy. He had extended his reputation in 1873 by lecturing for two months in London; he made a big reading tour with G. W. Cable[6] in 1884–5; and in 1895, at the age of sixty,

---

[1] See Book III, Chap. XIII.
[3] See Book II, Chap. XXIII.
[5] See Book III. Chaps. VI, VII, and X.
[2] See Book III, Chap. XI.
[4] See Book III, Chap. XXIII.
[6] See Book III, Chap. VI.

disdaining the advantages of bankruptcy, he set out on a lecturing tour of the world which took on something of the aspect of a royal progress and ended in the triumphant discharge of all his obligations. Then he collected another fortune and built himself his mansion Stormfield in Redding, Connecticut.

In his last years he spent a good deal of time in New York and Washington, and a variety of causes kept him pretty steadily in the public eye as a figure of national interest: his valiant assumption of his debts, his great tour, his growing habit of commenting on public affairs, the publication of sections of his autobiography, his domestic bereavements, and the foreign tributes and honours which gradually assured his somewhat incredulous countrymen that he was a great man of letters. His first academic recognition had come from Yale University, which created him Master of Arts in 1888; in 1901 Yale and in 1902 the University of Missouri conferred upon him the degree of Doctor of Letters; but the crowning academic glory fell in 1907 when the University of Oxford called him across the sea and robed him in scarlet and made him Doctor of Literature, amid, as he noted, "a very satisfactory hurrah" from the audience. On his return from a trip to the Bermudas he died 21 April, 1910.

Mark Twain's literary independence is generally conceded. Except for a certain flavour of Dickens in *The Gilded Age* there is hardly an indication of any important relationship between him and modern writers. He was a lover of the elemental in the midst of the refinements of an English and an American Victorian Age. "I can't stand George Eliot and Hawthorne and those people," he said. "And as for 'The Bostonians,' I would rather be damned to John Bunyan's heaven than read that." Modern fiction generally impressed him as namby-pamby and artificial. Jane Austen was his pet abhorrence, but he also detested Scott, primarily for his Toryism, and he poked fun at Cooper for his inaccuracies. His taste for books was eminently masculine. The literary nourishment of his style he appears to have found chiefly in history, travel, biography, and such works of imagination as one puts on a "five-foot shelf" —Shakespeare and the Bible, Suetonius's *Lives of The Cæsars*, Malory, Cellini, *Don Quixote, Gil Blas*, the *Memoirs of Casanova*, Lecky's *History of Civilization*, and Carlyle's *French Revolution.*

In his prose as in the verse of Whitman there is an appearance of free improvisation concealing a more or less novel and deliberate art. "So far as I know," wrote W. D. Howells in 1901, "Mr. Clemens is the first writer to use in extended writing the fashion we all use in thinking, and to set down the thing that comes into his mind without fear or favour of the thing that went before, or the thing that may be about to follow." Beside this assertion of a spontaneity approaching artlessness let us put Professor Matthews's caution: "His colloquial ease should not hide from us his mastery of all the devices of rhetoric." In a letter to Aldrich he acknowledges great indebtedness to Bret Harte, "who trimmed and trained and schooled me patiently until he changed me from an awkward utterer of coarse grotesquenesses to a writer of paragraphs and chapters that have found a certain favour in the eyes of even some of the very decentest people in the land." Finally, let the reader who doubts whether he was conscious of his own art read carefully his little article, *How to Tell a Story*, beginning: "I do not claim that I can tell a story as it ought to be told. I only claim to know how a story ought to be told, for I have been almost daily in the company of the most expert story-tellers for many years." The art which he had learned of such American masters of oral rhetoric as Artemus Ward, John Phoenix,[1] and J. H. Riley he tested and developed in print and by word of mouth with constant reference to its immediate effect upon a large audience. Those principles the observance of which he found essential to holding and entertaining his public he adopted and followed; but literary "laws" which proved irrelevant to his business as entertainer of the masses he disregarded at pleasure as negligible or out of place in a democratic Æsthetic. Howells calls him "the Lincoln of our literature"; and with that hint we may add that his power and limitations are alike related to his magnanimous ambition to beguile all the people all the time.

Let us begin our illustration of his literary character with a review of his five great books of travel. Against every one of them the charge might be brought that it is ill-composed: the chapters follow a certain chronological and geographical order; but the paragraphs frequently seem to owe their juxtaposition to the most casual association of ideas. This license.

[1] See Book II, Chap. XIX.

however, is the law and studied practice of his humour. "To bring incongruities and absurdities together in a wandering and sometimes purposeless way, and seem innocently unaware that they are absurdities, is the basis," he declares, "of the American art." He is speaking here specifically of the humorous story; but obviously he applies the same principle to the book of travel, which, as he conceives it, is a joyous miscellany. It is a miscellany but with ingredients preconsidered and formulable. He is as inflexible as Aristotle on the importance of choosing a great subject. He holds with the classicists that the proper study of mankind is man. He traverses in each book territory of world-wide interest. He describes what meets his eye with rapid, vivid, unconventional eloquence. He sketches the historical background in a highly personal fashion and gives to his interlarded legends an individual twist. While he imparts a good quantity of information, useful and diverting, he keeps the thread of his personal adventures spinning, rhapsodizes for a page, then clowns it for another, or introduces an elaborate burlesque on the enthusiasm of previous travellers. It is a prepared concoction.

The Innocents Abroad justified the formula on which it was constructed by selling nearly a hundred thousand copies at three dollars and a half apiece within the first three years. Its initial success was due partly to its novelty and partly to the wide interest which the excursion itself had excited. Both these advantages it has now relinquished, yet, as his biographer tells us, it remains the most popular of all Mark Twain's travel books, and still "outsells every other book in its particular field." Time has not reduced the rich variety of its famous topics, though time has somewhat altered the nature of curiosity with regard to the conduct of the pilgrims; but even though their type of tourist were now quite extinct one might still gratify the historical sense by acquaintance with a representative group of Americans on a tremendous picnic with spirits high in rebound from the long depression of the Civil War. One hears in the book the rollicking voice of the ex-pilot, ex-miner, the joyously insolent Western American, emancipated from all terror of the minor or Sunday-school vices, fortified by certain tolerant democratic standards of his own, well acquainted with the great American cities, equipped with ideas of natural beauty and sublimity acquired on the Missis-sippi, the Great Plains, the Rockies, the Pacific, the Sandwich Islands, setting out to see with his own unawed eyes how much truth there is in the reported wonders of the "little old world." Mark Twain describes Europe and the East for men, roughly speaking, like himself. He does not undertake to tell them how they ought to look at objects of interest, but quite resolutely how these objects of interest strike a thoroughly honest Western-American eye. He is obliged to report that the barbers, billiard tables, and hotel accommodations of Paris are inferior; that the paintings of the Old Masters are often in a bad state of repair and, at best, betray to a democrat a nauseous adulation of princely patrons; that the French grisettes wear mustaches; that Vesuvius and Lake Como are nothing to Kilauea and Lake Tahoe; that priest-ridden Italy is a "museum of magnificence and misery"; and that under close inspection the glamour of the Holy Land gives way to vivid impressions of fleas, beggars, hungry dogs, sandy wastes, and the odours of camels. But this young traveller with so much of the iconoclastic Don Juan in him has also a strain of Childe Harold. For him as for Byron the deepest charm of the old world is the charm of desolation and decay, felt when the dingy palaces of Venetian doges or the ruined marbles of Athens are bathed in the moon-light. And he like Byron gains many an effect of his violent humour by the abruptness of his transitions from the sublime to the ridiculous or *vice versa*. He interprets, for example, with noble gravity the face of the Sphinx:

After years of waiting, it was before me at last. The great face was so sad, so earnest, so longing, so patient. There was a dignity not of earth in its mien, and in its countenance a benignity such as never anything human wore. It was stone, but it seemed sentient. If ever image of stone thought, it was thinking. . . . All who know what pathos there is in memories of days that are accomplished and faces that have vanished—albeit only a trifling score of years gone by—will have some appreciation of the pathos that dwells in those grave eyes that look so steadfastly back upon the things they knew before History was born—before Tradition had being—things that were, and forms that moved, in a vague era which even Poetry and Romance scarce know of—and passed one by one away and

left the stony dreamer solitary in the midst of a strange new age
and uncomprehended scenes.

But one turns the page and comes upon the engineer who feeds
his locomotive with mummies, occasionally calling out pet-
tishly, "D—n these plebeians, they don't burn worth a cent—
pass out a king."

In *Roughing It* (1872) he chose a subject doubtless less
interesting to some good people of the Atlantic seaboard than a
European tour—the narrative of his journey across the plains
to Carson City, and his life and adventures in Nevada, California, and the Sandwich Islands. Various critics, however,
have preferred it to *Innocents Abroad* as a truer book; and in a
sense the preference is justifiable. As literal history, to be sure,
or as autobiography, it is untrustworthy. Mark Twain follows
his own advice to Rudyard Kipling: "Young man, first get
your facts; then distort them as you please." He distorts the
facts in *Roughing It*, and vitalizes them by a poetical enlargement and interpretation thoroughly characteristic of native
Western humour. In painting frontier manners, no longer an
outsider, as he was in Europe, he abandons the attitude of one
exposing illusions, and seeks to exhibit the West under the
glamour of imagination. His coyote, turning with a smile
upon the pursuing hound and vanishing with a "rushing sound,
and the sudden splitting of a long crack in the atmosphere"—
his coyote is a beast of fable; so is his jackrabbit; so is his bron-
cho; so is his Brigham Young. On all his pioneers, his stage-
drivers, his miners, his desperadoes, his boon-companions he
has breathed with a heroizing emotion recollected in literary
tranquillity. In the clear light of the vanished El Dorado of
his youth they and their mountains and forests loom for him
larger than common nature, more passionate, more picturesque.

A Tramp Abroad (1880) sprang from no such fund of delightful experience and mellow recollection but from an expedition to Europe deliberately undertaken in order to escape
from the growing harassment of business responsibilities and to
collect material for a book. Before he could work himself into
a satisfactory writing mood he found it necessary to invent a
new humorous attitude and literary character. His new invention has three parts. In the first place, he announces him

self an enthusiastic and intrepid pedestrian but actually presents himself as a languid and timorous person travelling luxuriously with agent and courier by railway, steamboat, carriage, raft, or by any means to avoid the use of his legs. Secondly, he professes himself a devoted student of art and decorates his pages with infantile sketches. Finally, he assumes the air of a philologist seriously studying the German language. The first of these devices he handles in many places ingeniously and pleasantly, presenting an amusing satire on the indolent middle-aged tourist who climbs his Alps by telescope and gets his thrills on his hotel veranda out of the books of Edward Whymper; but in the elaborate burlesque ascent of the Riffleberg the humour becomes crudely farcical and tiresome. His drawings are not very expressive; and from their fewness it may be inferred that he discovered the fact. Some fellow philologists have found inexhaustible satisfaction in the German legends in German-English and in the appendices treating of "the awful German language" and the German newspaper—possibly also in the violent attack on Wagnerian opera. Other favourite passages of various qualities are those dealing with the grand affair between M. Gambetta and M. Fourtou, the sunrise on Mt. Riga, and the 47-mile hunt for a sock in Chapter XIII; but the humorous jewel of the collection is "Baker's Bluejay Yarn" in Chapter III—a trivial incident touched with imagination and related in a supremely delicious manner. The serious writing, as in the description of the Jungfrau and Heidelberg and the student duels, is so good that one wishes there were more of it.

For *Life on the Mississippi* (1883) Mark Twain drew again from the treasure of Western material which he had amassed before he became a professional humorist; and that distinguished connoisseur, the ex-Emperor William II of Germany, therein agreeing with the *portier* of the author's lodging in Berlin, informed the author that it was his favourite American book. More strictly speaking, it is the first twenty of the fifty-five chapters that do for the Mississippi Valley what *Roughing It* does for the Far West, namely, invest it with the charm of recollected experience and imaginative apprehension. The latter part of the book, which might have been called "The Mississippi Revisited," is the journalistic record of an excursion

made with a stenographer in 1882; it contains interesting autobiographical notes, admirable descriptive passages, a remarkable
diatribe on Sir Walter Scott for perpetuating outworn chivalry
in the South, an account of a meeting with G. W. Cable and
Joel Chandler Harris in New Orleans, and miscellaneous yarns
and information; but it is of distinctly secondary value. Steadily throughout the first twenty chapters the writer is elate with
his youthful memories of the drowsy towns by the river, the
old barbaric raftsmen, the pride and power of the ancient race
of pilots, and the high art and mystery of piloting those infinitely various waters in the days before the war. The moon-
light, one of his characters fancies, was brighter before the war;
and he himself, travelled now and acquainted with glory, has
experienced, he believes, nothing so satisfying to his inmost
sense as his life in that epical calling with its manly rigours, its
robust hilarity, its deep, wholesome, unreflective happiness.
The spirit that, years before, inspired Emerson's blandly expressed desire to make Concord and Boston Bay as memorable
as the storied places of Europe becomes in these pages clear,
strong, resounding: it is the new national pride declaring the
spiritual independence of America. Not in peevish envy, with
no anxiety about the ultimate answer, out of his knowledge and
the depths of his conviction Mark Twain cries: "What are all
the rivers of Damascus to the Father of Waters?"

The material for *Following the Equator* (1897) he collected
under the strain of debt, ill health, and the fatigues of the immense lecture-tour undertaken in 1895. In Australasia, to
which the first half of the book is given, the people impress him
as Englishmen democratized, that is to say, as Americans, and
the cities and towns offer little noteworthy. In order to exhibit
novelties he is obliged to present the history of the early settlers, the aborigines, and the fauna; and as he gets up his facts
by visits to museums and hasty digestion of Australasian literature, his treatment strikes one as, for him, noticeably second-
hand and uninspired. He also introduces later a good deal of
"lifted" material of a vivid sort in his account of the Sepoy
Mutiny, Suttee, and the Thugs—and here we may note his
taste for the collection of atrocious incident. India, however,
for which Kipling had sharpened his appetite, inspired him to
the task of imparting his oppressed sense of her historic and

scenic immensities, stricken with plagues, famines, ferocious beasts, superstitions, over-population, and swooning heat:

a haunting sense of the myriads of human lives that have blossomed and withered, and perished here, repeating and repeating and repeating, century after century, and age after age, the barren and meaningless process; it is this sense that gives to this forlorn, uncomely land power to speak to the spirit and make friends with it; to speak to it with a voice bitter with satire, but eloquent with melancholy.

There are satirical and witty disquisitions on imperialistic morality apropos of Madagascar, the Jameson Raid, Cecil Rhodes, and the British dealings with the Boers. The barbarity of the civilized in contact with the so-called backward peoples excites his indignation, but history and travel show him its universality and quiet his sensibilities to a state of tolerant contempt for all unregenerate mankind: "Christian governments are as frank to-day, as open and above-board, in discussing projects for raiding each other's clothes-lines as ever they were before the Golden Rule came smiling into this inhospitable world and couldn't get a night's lodging anywhere."

Mark Twain's fiction, a large and highly diversified section of his total output, should be regarded as, hardly less than the travel books, the work of a humorist whose most characteristic form was a medley in divers keys. His critical champions used to allege that recognition of his sterling literary talent was delayed by his reputation as a creator of laughter. At the present time the danger is perhaps rather that some of his novels and tales will be unduly disparaged precisely because criticism has been persuaded to take them too seriously. With an instinct for an ingenious plot and unquestionable power of characterization within certain limits, Mark Twain sometimes lacked the ability and the patience and even the desire to carry a long piece of fiction through in the key on which he began. He would begin a story, for example, on the key of impressive realism, shift to commonplace melodrama, and end with roaring farce; and this amounts to saying that he did not himself steadily take his fiction writing seriously. He sometimes took it very lightly, like an improvising humorist; and the discords which affect the severely critical ear as blemishes probably struck his own ear as a joke. There is amusement in the most uneven of his novels if one relaxes to the point of reading it in the mixed moods in which it was written.

The most uneven of his novels is *The Gilded Age*, begun in collaboration with Charles Dudley Warner in February, 1873, on the spur of a dinner-table challenge, and finished in the following April. The authors were proud of their performance; and it has admirable points. The title is a masterly epigraph on the flushed, corrupt period of the Reconstruction. The stage is set as for the representation of "the great American novel," with scenes in New York, Philadelphia, Washington, St. Louis, and villages of New England and Tennessee. The plot is designed to bring typical Easterners and Westerners into diverting sentimental, financial, and political relations. There is a lively satirical play upon a wide range of clearly conceived characters and caricatures, exhibiting most of the elementary passions from love-making and fortune-hunting to bribing Congressmen and murder; and the sanguine, speculative Colonel Sellers, said to have been modelled on a relative of Mark Twain's but certainly also modelled on Orion Clemens and on Mark Twain himself, is an American rival to Micawber. The book bristles with interesting intentions and accomplishments; yet its total effect is a bewildering dissonance of moods and styles, which fills one with regret that Mark Twain did not cut loose from his literary partner and work out by himself the story of Obedstown, Tennessee, opened by him with a rich realistic flow in the first eleven chapters. With all its demerits on its head, the novel sold forty thousand copies within a couple of months after publication, and a play built around the character of Sellers was immensely successful on the stage. Later, in collaboration with Howells, Mark Twain made a second Sellers play showing the hero aspiring to an English earldom; and this he worked over into *The American Claimant* (1891), a generally farcical romance streaked with admirable realistic passages. One may mention here also, as springing perhaps from experience not utterly remote from that of Sellers, Clemens's exhibition of the effect upon character produced by expectation of unearned wealth in two capital short stories: *The Man that Corrupted Hadleyburg* (1899) and *The $30,000 Bequest* (1904).

Tom Sawyer, his second extended effort in fiction and his first masterpiece, he began as a play in 1872 and published in its present form in 1876. The long incubation contributed to its unsurpassed unity of tone. But the decisive fact is that his irresponsible and frequently extravagant fancy is here held in check by a serious artistic purpose, namely, to make an essentially faithful representation of the life of a real boy intimately known to him by memory and by introspection and by those deductions of the imaginative faculty which start from a solid basis of actuality. His own boyhood, we may believe, and that of his companions in Hannibal, lives in this intensely vital narrative. It is significant of his unwonted austerity in the composition that he wrote to Howells on its completion: "It is not a boy's book at all. It will only be read by adults. It is only written for adults." He had some justification for feeling that his newly finished manuscript broke a long taboo. He had taken a hero who was neither a model of youthful virtues nor a horrible example but was distinguished chiefly by pluck, imagination, and vanity, and had made him leader of a group of average little Missouri rascals running loose in an ordinary small river town and displaying, among other spontaneous impulses, all the "natural cussedness" of boyhood. Furthermore he had made a central incident of a rather horrid murder. Remembering the juvenile fiction of the Sunday-school library,[1] he suspected that the story of these fighting, fibbing, pilfering, smoking, swearing scapegraces was not for young people. But Howells, after reading about Aunt Polly, the whitewashing of the fenee, Tom's schoolboy love, Huck and the wart-cure, and the pirates' island, ordered the profanity deleted, and declared it the best boy story ever written; and that was near the truth. In the two sequels *Tom Sawyer Abroad* (1894) and *Tom Sawyer, Detective* (1896), the plots are rather flimsy contrivances of the humorous fancy, but the stories are partly redeemed by the established reality of the actors and the raciness of the narrative which comes from the mouth of Huck Finn.

The Prince and the Pauper (1881), a first venture in historical romance, was deliberately written for children and tested in the process of composition on the author's daughters. The

[1] See Book III, Chap. VII.

plot, suggested by Charlotte M. Yonge's *The Prince and the Page*, is fascinating to the youthful imagination; and the notion underlying it is to the older reader the most characteristic element in the book. The exchange of clothes and stations effected by Tom Canty and Prince Edward, later Edward VI, provided for the prince opportunities for feeling the common lot which the democratic author would gladly have given to all the monarchs of Europe. Occasionally writing over the heads of his audience, he utilizes the situation to express his inveterate sense of the evil of monarchical institutions and in particular his peculiarly flaming indignation at obsolete English penal laws. Humorous situations, sometimes tragically humorous, are abundant; but neither in the simple and vigorous prose of the narrative nor in the archaic style of the dialogue does one find at full strength the idiom and the first-hand observation for which one values *Tom Sawyer*. *The Prince and the Pauper* is a distinguished book in the class to which *Little Lord Fauntleroy* was added in 1886; but it is overshadowed by Mark Twain's own work.

The Adventures of Huckleberry Finn (1884) overshadows it; but that is nothing. *Huckleberry Finn* exceeds even *Tom Sawyer* almost as clearly as *Tom Sawyer* exceeds *The Prince and the Pauper*. Mark Twain had conceived the tale in 1876 as a sequel to the story of Tom. In the course of its long gestation he had revisited the Mississippi Valley and had published his superb commemoration of his own early life on the river. He wrote his second masterpiece of Mississippi fiction with a desire to express what in *Tom Sawyer* he had hardly attempted, what, indeed, came slowly into his possession, his sense of the half-barbaric charm and the romantic possibilities in that grey wilderness of moving water and the rough men who trafficked on it. He had given power to the earlier story by the representation of characters and incidents which are typical of the whole of American boyhood in rural communities in many parts of the country. He gave power to *Huckleberry Finn* by a selection of unusual characters and extraordinary incidents which are inseparably related to and illustrative of their special environment. He shifted heroes, displacing quick-witted, imaginative Tom by the village drunkard's son, because Huck in his hard, nonchalant, adventurous adolescence is a more distinctive product of the frontier. He changed the narrator, letting Huck tell his own story, in order to invest the entire narrative in its native garb and colour. Huck perhaps exhibits now and then a little more humour and feeling for nature than a picaro is entitled to possess; but in the main his point of view is well maintained. His strange captivity in his father's cabin, the great flight down the river, the mysteries of fog and night and current, the colloquy on King Sollermun, the superbly incidental narrative of the Grangerford-Shepherdson feud, the appealing devotion and affectionateness of Nigger Jim, Huck's case of conscience,—all are stamped with the peculiar comment of Huck's earthy, callous, but not insensitive soul. The stuff and manner of the tale are unique, and it is as imperishably substantial as *Robinson Crusoe*, whether one admire it with Andrew Lang as "a nearly flawless gem of romance and humour" or with Professor Matthews as "a marvellously accurate portrayal of a whole civilization."

A Connecticut Yankee in King Arthur's Court (1889) is a work of humorous invention set in motion by G. W. Cable, who first brought Malory's *Morte d'Arthur* to Mark Twain's attention. For assignable reasons it has not had the universal admiration enjoyed by *Huckleberry Finn;* Andrew Lang, for example, could not bring himself to read it; yet one might plausibly argue that it represents Mark Twain more completely than any other single book on his list, and so may serve as a touchstone to distinguish those who care for the man from those who only care for some of his stories. It displays every variety of his style from the mock-heroic and shirt-sleeve journalese of the Yankee's familiar vein to the careful euphonies of his descriptions of English landscape and the Dantean mordancy of the chapter "In the Queen's Dungeons." It exhibits his humour in moods from the grimmest to the gayest, mingling scenes of pathos, terror, and excruciating cruelty with hilarious comic inventions and adventures, which prove their validity for the imagination by abiding in the memory: the sewing-machine worked by the bowing hermit, the mules blushing at the jokes of the pilgrims, the expedition with Alisande, the contests with Merlin, the expedition with King Arthur, Launcelot and the bicycle squad, and the annihilation of the chivalry of England. The hero is, despite the title, no mere Yankee but Mark Twain's "personal representative"—acquainted with the machine shops of New Haven but acquainted also with navigation on the Mississippi and with Western journalism and with the use of the lariat. The moment that he enters "the holy gloom" of history he becomes, as Mark Twain became when he went to Europe, the representative of democratic America, preaching the gospel of commonsense and practical improvement and liberty and equality and free thought inherited from Franklin, Paine, Jefferson, and Ingersoll. Those to whom Malory's romance is a sacred book may fairly complain that the exhibition of the Arthurian realm is a brutal and libellous travesty, attributing to the legendary period of Arthur horrors which belong to medieval Spain and Italy. Mark Twain admits the charge. He takes his horrors where he finds them. His wide-sweeping satirical purpose requires a comprehensive display of human ignorance, folly, and iniquity. He must vent the flame of indignation which swept through him whenever he fixed his attention on human history—indignation against removable dirt, ignorance, injustice, and cruelty. As a radical American, he ascribed a great share of these evils to monarchy, aristocracy, and an established church, and he made his contemporary references pointed and painful to English sensibilities. *A Connecticut Yankee* is his *Don Quixote*, a sincere book, full of lifelong convictions earnestly held, a book charged with a rude iconoclastic humour, intended like the work of Cervantes to hasten the end of an obsolescent civilization. Whether it will finally be judged a great book will depend in considerable measure on factors outside itself, particularly on the prosperity of western democratic sentiment in the world at large. Since the War of the German Invasions there has been an increase of Quixotism in his sense, and what used to be considered his unnecessary rage at windmills now looks like prophetic tilting at giants.

The volume containing *Pudd'nhead Wilson* and *Those Extraordinary Twins*, published in 1894, one is predisposed to value because it is another specimen from the Mississippi "lead." It adds, however, relatively so little that is distinctive to the record that one is tempted to use it as an unsurpassable illustration of haphazard method in composition. The picture of a two-headed freak had given him the cue for a "howling farce." When he began to write, the contemplated short story swiftly expanded, and there developed unexpectedly under his hand serious characters and a tragic situation unrelated to the initiating impulse. After long study he extracted the "farce" by "Cæsarean operation," and appended it with amusing explanations to the "tragedy" which it had set in motion. *Pudd'nhead Wilson*, disfigured by vestiges of the farce in the incredible Italian twins, is, like *The Gilded Age*, a discordant medley with powerful character-drawing in Roxana and her half-breed son, and with a somewhat feebly indicated novelty in the philosophical detective Pudd'nhead.

The last certified claimant for a position in the front rank of the novels is *Joan of Arc* (1896), a romance containing as its core the ascertained facts concerning one of the most problematic figures in secular history, and as its important imaginative expansion Mark Twain's conception of her familiar charm and his pictures of the battles and scenes of state and trials through which she passed. As in the somewhat similar case of the supernatural powers of Jesus, of which he was certainly sceptical, he says nothing to raise a doubt of the Maid's divine assistance; he neither explained nor attempted to explain away Joan's mystery. Her character, her Voices, and her mission he presents throughout with an air of absolute reverence and indeed at times with almost breathless adoration. For the reader in whom illusion is not destroyed by constant involuntary attention to the line where fact meets fiction the total impression is doubtless both beautiful and deeply moving. In the last section, at least, which deals with the trial and martyrdom, the most impatient reader of historical romance can hardly escape the pang of actuality; he is too near the facts. Recognizing that the book was quite out of his customary vein, Mark Twain published it first anonymously; yet in 1908 he wrote: "I like the *Joan of Arc* best of all my books and it is the best; I know it perfectly well. And besides, it furnished me seven times the pleasure afforded me by any of the others; 12 years of preparation & 2 years of writing. The others needed no preparation, & got none." This much we must admit: we are glad to have *Joan of Arc* on the shelf beside *A Connecticut Yankee* to complete our conception of that versatile and representative American whom we call Mark Twain.

Without it, and its little companion-piece, *In Defence of Harriet Shelley* (1894), we should have a harder task to prove, against those that take him for a hard unsanctified philistine, his invincible chivalry and fineness in relation to womankind, feelings precious in a free society, and fostered, as we like to think, by a thoroughly established American tradition.

But if we value a book in proportion to its saturation with its author's most distinctive qualities and in proportion to its power, exerted or latent, to affect the general literary current, we shall hardly rate *Joan of Arc* among Mark Twain's most interesting or significant books. In its utterly reverent treatment of the traditional and the supernatural it impresses one as a counterpoise obviously unequal to the task of making a balance with the great burden of naturalistic and radically iconoclastic writing in the other scale.

Mark Twain counts as an influence because he is an innovator. The great notes of his innovation from *Innocents Abroad* to *A Connecticut Yankee* are: first, the disillusioned treatment of history; second, the fearless exploitation of "the natural man," or, the next thing to it, "the free-born American"; and, lastly, a certain strain of naturalistic pessimism. In the first class go the foreign-travel books, *The Prince and the Pauper*, and *A Connecticut Yankee;* and the impulse properly proceeding from them is imaginative satire. In the second class go *Roughing It*, *Tom Sawyer*, *Life on the Mississippi*, *Huckleberry Finn*, *Adam's Diary*, and *Eve's Diary;* and from such work has proceeded an observable impulse to the cultivation of the indigenous, the elemental, the primitive, and, perhaps, the brutal and the sensual. For the third class one can glean representative paragraphs only here and there among the writings published in Mark Twain's lifetime; but the posthumously published philosophical dialogue *What is Man?* (1905) and *The Mysterious Stranger* (1916), a romance, and some of the letters are steeped in a naturalistic melancholy and tinged with a philosophical bitterness of which American literature before Mark Twain showed hardly a trace. That strain seems likely to be influential too, and, unfortunately, not always in connection with the fine bravado of his American faith, which occasionally required an antidote to its natural insolence.

CHAPTER IX

Minor Humorists

THE eccentric and racy touch of the Civil War humorists vanished early in the seventies, and humour underwent a period of organization, levelling, and standardization. Its cruder manifestations disappeared; editors no longer burst upon their readers with the discovery of unsuspected females —Ann Tiquity, Ann Gelic, and Ann O'Dyne—in Webster's Unabridged; parodying became less inevitable; and "reverses" such as P. T. Barnum's

Lewd did I live & evil I did dwel

lost their fascination for keen minds. The dialect of the immigrant replaced the twang of the crossroads. And at the same time the native flavour and homely philosophy of the older humour ceased to illuminate the work of the fun-makers.

The channels of humorous journalism were meanwhile clearly marked out. Casual newspaper paragraphers like J. M. Bailey of *The Danbury* [Connecticut] *News*, C. B. Lewis of *The Detroit Free Press*, and R. J. Burdette of *The Burlington* [Iowa] *Hawkeye* gave their otherwise obscure journals a nation-wide prominence, and demonstrated the commercial value of daily humour. Their books, compiled from newspaper clippings, have, however, long been covered by *les neiges d'antan*. Eugene Field set the measure of the humorist's output at one column a day "leaded agate, first line brevier." He aspired also to produce work of permanent literary quality. His standards in both respects are kept up at the present time by such experienced "colyumists" as Bert Leston Taylor ("B. L. T.") of

[1] See Book II, Chap. XIX.

The Chicago Tribune and in New York by Franklin P. Adams ("F. P. A.") of *The Tribune* and Don Marquis of *The Evening Sun*. The column that soothes tired business men on train, subway, or trolley has long been supplemented for family, club, and barber-shop consumption by the humorous weeklies: *Puck*, founded in 1877; *Judge*, 1881; and most notably *Life*, 1883. Taking their cue rather from the best of the college funny papers, such as *The Harvard Lampoon*, founded 1876, than from *Punch*, these weekly magazines have supplied the public with its best periodical humour. H. C. Bunner,[1] one time editor of *Puck*, and John Ames Mitchell and Edward S. Martin, founders of *Life*, should be mentioned among the writers who have given a high tone to comic journalism.

Besides its submission to the great American genius for commercialization, whatever national quality may be found in the humour of the last half century consists mainly in a tendency to regard fun-making as an end in itself rather than as an agent to criticism. Though no longer relying on the mechanical misspellings of Artemus Ward or Josh Billings, the next crop of humorists wrought effects in dialect rather than in character and preferred absurdities of their own invention to incongruities observed in the social scheme. Irony was alien to their minds, and satire, when they used it, took for its victims Mormons, mothers-in-law, undertakers, and other beings whose removal would in no way imperil the pillars of society. Jesters made it their function to tickle the sides of a nation content and prosperous, conscious of having made in the Civil War the great sacrifice of a generation, and confident after Grant's election that the fruits of victory would be apportioned among the truly deserving. There may be significance in the fact that the two comic writers who deserted journalism for other professions became one a popular preacher the other a successful manufacturer and conspicuous advocate of high tariff. At any rate, the words prefixed to one of the most widely circulated humorous books of the time might well have served as a motto for them all: "Fun is the most conservative element of society, and it ought to be cherished and encouraged by all lawful means."[2]

[1] See also Book II, Chap. XXIII, and Book III, Chap. VI.
[2] "Max Adeler," *Out of the Hurly-Burly*, 1874, p. 6.

Such being the case, the typical work of such humorists cannot stand high in comparison with the subtler manifestations of the Comic Spirit. That, at least, would be the conclusion if American humour were regarded as a mere stage in an inevitable progress from pioneer jocularity to urbane irony. But it is possible that the national preference for unreflective merriment is not thoughtless and immature, but deliberate, permanent, and full grown. While Americans can picture Lincoln deferring discussion of the Emancipation Proclamation to read aloud a chapter from Artemus Ward, the laughter of sheer full-throated relief may well seem to them more manly than the comedy that wakens thoughtful laughter. American humour, then, may claim to be of a different school from the comedy of the Old World, operating on human nature by the lenitives and tonics of mirth instead of by the scalpel of criticism.

One of the most decided believers in recreative humour was a man of many interests whose humorous writing was originally done merely for his own amusement. Charles Godfrey Leland (1824–1903), a native of Philadelphia and a graduate of Princeton, after three years of student life at Heidelberg and Munich and three days as captain of a barricade in the Paris revolution of 1848, found the practice of law in the city of his birth a listless occupation. Turning journalist, he worked successively as managing editor under P. T. Barnum and R. W. Griswold. He gave early and able support to Lincoln's administration, besides seeing service in an emergency regiment during the Gettysburg campaign. The later years of his long life were spent in cultivating a wide circle of friends in America and Europe, in a disinterested and successful effort to establish industrial art as a branch of public education, and in the study of gipsy lore, tinkers' language, Indian legends, Italian witches, and all things exotic, mysterious, and occult. During this time he wrote with extreme fluency more than fifty books on the most varied subjects, not to mention uncounted contributions to periodicals. He would doubtless have wished to be remembered chiefly for his services to education.

His generation, however, persisted in thinking of him exclusively as the author of *Hans Breitmann's Ballads*, often to his annoyance identifying him with the hero of his lays. Indistinguishable Leland and Breitmann are only in certain ballads describing European cities with quiet sentimental charm. But the huge, bearded Hans Breitmann who gorges, guzzles, and scuffles at the famous "barty," drinks lager from his boots among the rebel dead, and cynically takes advantage of the "circumswindles" of American politics, is of course not a projection of the author's personality but "a German gentleman who drinks, fights, and plunders." In this conception Leland discovered a vein of genuine humour, the converse of that in *Innocents Abroad.*[1] Mark Twain's double-edged satire disclosed the imperviousness of the native American to the finer subtleties and superfluities of European culture. Leland revealed the demoralization of an over-complex European in the rarefied social atmosphere of the New World. Released from accustomed exterior control and given nothing for his native idealisms to work on, "der Breitmann solfe de infinide ash von eternal shpree."[2]

As a cavalry commander and "bummer" in the Civil War this compound of *geist* and thirst finds his real vocation. *Breitmann in Maryland*, describing, with a ringing "gling, glang, gloria!" refrain, the wild ride of German troopers to capture a rebel tavern, catches the fire and swiftness of an *echtdeutsch* ballad. A more unusual blend of moods—satire, sentiment, excitement, pathos—may be found in *Breitmann's Going to Church*. In later ballads Breitmann enters the Franco-Prussian War, but in proportion as he becomes an Uhlan "mad with durst for bier and blut" he loses significance as an American figure. The fun tends to be kept up by mechanical expedients, as in the ballad of *Breitmann in a Balloon*.

Decidedly more amusing are the burlesques of Teutonic legends, such as the celebrated *De Maiden mid Nodings on*. These have nothing of the real Breitmann about them but the German-American dialect. Some clever macaronics in many tongues further indicate that German-English was not the only jargon at Leland's command. Part of his reputation as being "at the very head of Pidgin English learning and literature" was earned by his publication of songs and stories in the China-English dialect, by his discovery of the last refinement

[1] See Book III, Chap. VIII.
[2] *I. e.* "Breitmann solves the Infinite as one eternal spree."

in vagabond lore, a tinkers' language called Shelta, and by his vast collection of curious mixtures of speech from all parts of the world. Much of his folklore study brought into play his keen sense of drollery. But in spite of his *Egyptian Sketch-Book*, his *Brand-New Ballads*, and the sly meditations of his *Flaxius*, Leland may fairly be considered a humorist of only one character. Hans Breitmann, created by accident to fill a space in *Graham's Magazine* in 1856 and revived for the last time in a prose and verse sketch-book of the Tyrol in 1895, remains the outstanding representative of his genius.

Opportunities for humorous studies of more varied kinds existed in plenty in Leland's career, had he cared to make use of them. One can hardly open his entertaining *Memoirs* without stumbling upon hints that would have provided twenty lesser men with sufficient stock in trade. A single incident from the Gettysburg campaign must suffice for illustration:

There came shambling to me an odd figure. There had been some slight attempt by him to look like a soldier—he had a *feather* in his hat—but he carried his rifle as if after deer or racoons, and as if he were used to it. "Say, Cap!" he exclaimed, "kin you tell me where a chap could get some ammynition?" "Go to your quartermaster," I replied. "Ain't got no quartermaster." "Well then to your commanding officer—to your regiment." "Ain't got no commanding officer nowher this side o' God, nor no regiment. . . . I'll jest tell you, Cap, how it is. I live in the south line of New York State, and when I heard that the rebs had got inter Pennsylvany, forty of us held a meetin' and 'pinted me Cap'n. So we came down here cross country, and 'rived this a'ternoon, and findin' fightin' goin' on, went straight for the bush. And gettin' cover, we shot the darndest sight of rebels you ever *did* see. And now all our ammynition is expended, I've come to town for more, for there's some of 'em still left—who want killin' badly." [1]

Had this unique bushwhacker but grown in Leland's imagination as did Jost of the Pennsylvania cavalry, the original of Hans Breitmann in his military phase, we might have possessed a character more truly American and not less rich in humorous significance. But Leland was not merely a humorist, and to deplore the loss of what he left undone is at once

[1] C. G. Leland, *Memoirs*, vol. I., pp. 51–52.

to be ungrateful for his many services in other fields and to express the highest appreciation of what he contributed to international comedy.

Of the deluge of humorists who followed, Charles Heber Clark ("Max Adeler"), like Leland, became better known in England than in the United States. *Out of the Hurly-Burly* (1874), his first and best book, links together facetious extravagances in prose and verse on a thread of narrative describing the perplexities of the suburbanite. Its delightful illustrations by A. B. Frost contributed almost as much as the text to the popularity of the book. Clark's travesties of the obituary lyric have been long remembered. At times rivalling the mock horrors of the *Bab Ballads*, his mortuary burlesques go far to justify Augustine Birrell's dictum that the essence of American humour consists in speaking lightly of dreadful subjects.

In spite of his pseudonym Clark was not one of the many dialect writers. The verbal humours of German-American speech were further exhibited, however, in the *Yawcob Strauss* rhymes of Charles Follen Adams. Negro dialect and certain broad aspects of darky pretentiousness were turned to laughable effect by Charles Bertrand Lewis ("M. Quad") in *The Lime-Kiln Club* (1887) and other sketches. At the close of the century Bowery slang gained a temporary currency through the Chimmie Fadden stories of Edward Waterman Townsend, but Faddenism never seriously disturbed the cult of Mr. Dooley, whose Irish-American witticisms deserve more extended mention. A remarkable type of later slang, that invented by an author and yet perfectly intelligible to all alert Americans, reached its apogee in the work of George Ade, whose *Fables in Slang* (1900) have been followed by several volumes of a similar method.

Humorists who did not rely upon dialect for their main effect usually began on the humour of a particular locality and gradually extended their range. Miss Marietta Holley as "Josiah Allen's Wife" from up-state New York has for more than forty years applied shrewd observation and the homeliest common sense to the popular amusements and fashionable problems of the day. *My Opinions and Betsy Bobbett's* (1873) and *Samantha at Saratoga* (1887) established her reputation as a keen deviser of ludicrous incidents and impossible social blunders. James Montgomery Bailey ("The *Danbury News* Man") and Robert Jones Burdette ("The *Hawkeye* Man") attained a more than local vogue as newspaper comedians, Bailey excelling in quaintly exaggerated pictures of familiar domestic occurrences, Burdette in the unexpected collocation of dissimilar ideas. Edgar Wilson Nye ("Bill Nye"), once of *The Laramie* [Wyoming] *Boomerang*, was also fond of surprising turns of phrase, but his most characteristic vein lay in a sort of affected, zealous idiocy. No better example of his manner is available than one already selected by a skilled hand:

The condition of our navy need not give rise to any serious apprehension. The yard in which it is placed at Brooklyn is enclosed by a high brick wall affording it ample protection. A man on board the *Atlanta* at anchor at Brooklyn is quite as safe as he would be at home. The guns on board the *Atlanta* are breechloaders; this is a great improvement on the old-style gun, because in former times in case of a naval combat the man who went outside the ship to load the gun while it was raining frequently contracted pneumonia.[1]

The lecture platform gave both Nye and Burdette an opportunity to display at best advantage their comical solemnity, and much of their notoriety rose from their public appearances. Nye especially was fortunate in his collaborators, touring at one time with Mark Twain and again with James Whitcomb Riley[2] and Eugene Field.

The last named, greatest of newspaper paragraphers and in his own right something more, qualified as a Middle Westerner by his birth in St. Louis (1850) and by his New England ancestry and bringing up. After three years in three colleges, a trip to Europe, and an early marriage, he served his apprenticeship to journalism on several Missouri papers. From *The Denver* [Colorado] *Tribune* his first humorous skit, *The Tribune Primer* (1882), was reprinted. The best years of his life were spent in Chicago as contributing editor to *The Chicago Record*. In his daily column of "Sharps and Flats" appeared his most characteristic verse,[3] tales, and miscellaneous paragraphs, later

---

[1] Quoted by S. Leacock, *American Humour, Nineteenth Century*, vol. lxxvi, p. 453.

[2] See Book III, Chap. x.   [3] See Book II, Chap. XXIII.

collected to form *A Little Book of Western Verse* (1889), *A Little Book of Profitable Tales* (1889), and other volumes. He was still in the prime of life and at the height of his celebrity as a household poet, humorist, and lecturer, when he wrote in the assumed character of a veteran bibliomaniac: "I am aweary and will rest a little while; lie thou there, my pen, for a dream—a pleasant dream—calleth me away." A few weeks later (4 November, 1895) death visited the writer as he slept.

Field's best known pieces of verse and prose exploiting sentimental and pathetic themes, especially Christmas festivities and the deaths of little children, emerge from a background of humorous writing illustrated by the rank and file of his contributions to "Sharps and Flats." The waggery of his natural bent finds unmixed expression in the early and unsuccessful book, *Culture's Garland; Being Memoranda of the Gradual Rise of Literature, Art, Music and Society in Chicago and other Western Ganglia* (1887), which engagingly blends the atmosphere of cultivation, so long anticipated by Chicagoans, with whiffs from the very real and ever-present stockyards. Only a few gleams of wit, however, relieve the profitable sentimentality of the later *Tales*.

A better balanced expression of his undeniable personal charm is to be found in *A Little Book of Western Verse*, virile and funny in the ballads of the miners' camp on Red Hoss Mountain; otherwise "Western" only as it exemplifies a readiness to try anything once.[1] Among many lullabies, Christmas hymns, and lyrics of infant mortality, the playful side of Field's genius is sufficiently represented by imitations of Old English ballads, echoes of Horatian themes, a few rollicking nursery songs, and much personal, political, and literary gossip cleverly versified. A bit of flippancy like *The Little Peach of Emerald Hue* goes to show that Field's humour could on occasion conquer the sentimental strain in him. But only too often his children die from the fatal effects of contact with the angels.

In his more ambitious pieces Field not infrequently falls into an over-refinement and false simplicity of style. When not too consciously doing his best, however, nothing could seem

---

[1] "I want to dip around in all sorts of versification, simply to show people that determination and perseverance can accomplish much in this direction." S. Thompson, *Eugene Field*, vol. ii., p. 120.

more effortless than the easy play of his wit. One thrust at a gang of politicians junketing at their constituents' expense deserves to be recalled as a fair example of his skill:

BLUE CUT, TENN., May 2, 1885.—The second section of the train bearing the Illinois Legislature to New Orleans was stopped near this station by bandits last night. After relieving the bandits of their watches and money, the excursionists proceeded on their journey with increased enthusiasm.[1]

Political sarcasms like the foregoing, though frequently employed, have ordinarily been powerless to influence either the character of American politics or the fortunes of any particular politician. On the contrary, they have had, like Ford jokes, a certain advertising value, being considered less marks of discontent than the banter of satisfaction with which healthy Americans accompany their doings. Most unusual, therefore, is the spectacle of the national frame of mind changed in consequence of the work of a humorist. Yet that result may fairly be claimed for the "Dooleys" written by Finley Peter Dunne during the Spanish-American War. The American public, conscious of a chivalrous mission in the war, uncertain of the strength of the adversary, and angry at the bustling incompetence and greedy profiteering at home, lost its sense of humour. Its regeneration from the slough of perfervid earnestness was accelerated by the cool remarks of the Irish saloonkeeper of Archey Road, Chicago. As Mr. Dooley commented on the great charge of the army mules at Tampa with reflections on other jackasses, pictured the Cuban towns captured by war-correspondents and the Spanish fleet sunk by dispatch boats, celebrated General Miles's uniform and the pugnacity of "Cousin George Dooley" (Admiral Dewey), the national fever cooled, and the nation, realizing its superfluous power, burst into saving laughter.

"We're a gr-reat people," said Mr. Hennessy, earnestly.
"We ar-re," said Mr. Dooley. "We ar-re that. An' th' best iv it is, we know we ar-re."

Mr. Dooley for some years continued to give his opinions on the men and affairs of peace with a shrewdness that recalls

[1] S. Thompson, *Eugene Field*, vol. ii., p. 204.

the pungent insight of Josh Billings and makes him one of the most quotable writers. Americans of the present generation are not likely to forget some of his sayings, least of all the remark of Father Kelly:

"Hogan," he says, "I'll go into th' battle with a prayer book in wan hand an' a soord in th' other," he says; "an' if th' wurruk calls f'r two hands, 'tis not th' soord I'll dhrop," he says.

When not busied with comments on current events, Mr. Dooley sometimes had leisure to relate incidents of the life about him in the gas-house district. As an interpreter of the city, however, he yields to Sydney Porter ("O. Henry").[1] The O. Henry story is the last word in deft manipulation, but as a humorist Porter is not deeply philosophical. His neat situations, surprising turns, and verbal cleverness show a refinement upon the methods of predecessors, indeed, but not a new comic attitude. Unsurpassed in daring extravaganza when he can give himself completely to gaiety, he becomes immediately sober in the presence of thought or sentiment. In these respects he represents the norm of recent American humour at a high pitch of technical perfection, and his death in 1910 may fittingly be taken as the close of the period. Just at present, judicious Americans are importing their best current humour from Canada.

[1] See Book III, Chap. **VI.**

CHAPTER X

Later Poets

IN the expanding, heterogeneous America of the second half of the nineteenth century, poetry lost its clearly defined tendencies and became various and experimental. It did not cease to be provincial; for although no one region dominated as New England had dominated in the first half of the century, the provincial accent was as unmistakable, and the purely national accent as rare, as before. The East, rapidly becoming the so-called "effete East," produced a poetry to which the West was indifferent; the West, still the West of "carnivorous animals of a superior rank," produced a poetry that the cultivated classes of the East regarded as vulgar. In a broad way it may perhaps be said that the poetry of this period was dedicated either to beauty or to "life"; to a revered past, or to the present and the future; to the civilization of Asia and Europe, or to the ideals and manners of America, at least the West of America. The virtue of the poetry of beauty was its fidelity to a noble tradition, its repetition, with a difference, of familiar and justly approved types of beauty; its defect was mechanical repetition, petty embellishment. The virtue of the poetry of "life" was fidelity to experience, vitality of utterance; its defect, crudity, meanness, insensitiveness to fineness of feeling and beauty of expression. Where the poets are many and all are minor it is difficult to make a choice, but on the whole it seems that the outstanding poets of the East were Emily Dickinson, Aldrich, Bayard Taylor, R. H. Stoddard, Stedman, Gilder, and Hovey; and of the West, Bret Harte, Joaquin Miller, Sill, Riley, and Moody.[1]

None of these has gained more with time than has Emily

[1] For the South, see Book III, Chap. IV.

Dickinson. Despite her defective sense of form, which makes her a better New Englander than Easterner, she has acquired a permanent following of discriminating readers through her extraordinary insight into the life of the mind and the soul. This insight is that of a latter-day Puritan, completely divorced from the outward stir of life, retiring, by preference, deeper and deeper within. Born in 1830 at Amherst, Massachusetts, she lived there all her life, and in 1886 died there. The inwardness and moral ruggedness of Puritanism she inherited mainly through her father, Edward Dickinson, lawyer and treasurer of Amherst College, a Puritan of the old type, whose heart, according to his daughter, was "pure and terrible." Her affection for him was so largely compounded with awe that in a sense they were strangers. "I have a brother and sister," she wrote to her poetical preceptor, Thomas Wentworth Higginson[1]; "my mother does not care for thought, and father, too busy with his briefs to notice what we do. He buys me many books, but begs me not to read them, because he fears they jiggle the mind. They are religious, except me." Of course, she too was religious, and intensely so, breathing as she did the intoxicating air of Transcendentalism. In person she described herself as "small, like the wren; and my hair is bold like the chestnut burr; and my eyes, like the sherry in the glass that the guest leaves." "You ask of my companions. Hills, sir, and the sundown, and a dog large as myself." These, and not her family, were actually her companions, together with a few books and her own soul. She had an alert introspection that brought her more than the wealth of the Indies. There is no better example of the New England tendency to moral revery than this last pale Indian-summer flower of Puritanism. She is said literally to have spent years without passing the doorstep, and many more years without leaving her father's grounds. After the death of her parents, not to mention her dog Carlo, she retired still further within herself, till the sounds of the everyday world must have come to her as from a previous state of existence.

"I find ecstacy in living," she said to Higginson, and spoke truly, as her poems show. In an unexpected light on orchards, in a wistful mood of meadow or wood-border held secure for a

[1] See Book III. Chap. XIII.

moment before it vanished; in the few books that she read—her Keats, her Shakespeare, her *Revelation;* in the echoes, obscure in origin, that stirred within her own mind and soul, now a tenuous melody, now a deep harmony, a haunting question, or a memorable affirmation;—everywhere she displayed something of the mystic's insight and joy. And she expressed her experience in her poems, forgetting the world altogether, intent only on the satisfaction of giving her fluid life lasting form, her verse being her journal. Yet the impulse to expression was probably not strong, because she wrote no poems, save one or two, as she herself asserts, until the winter 1861–62, when she was over thirty years old. In the spring of 1862 she wrote a letter to Higginson beginning, "Are you too deeply occupied to say if my verse is alive? The mind is so near itself it cannot see distinctly, and I have none to ask." Discerning the divine spark in her shapeless verse, he welcomed her advances, and became her "preceptor," loyally listened to but, as was inevitable, mainly unheeded. Soon perceiving this, Higginson continued to encourage her, for many years, without trying to divert her lightning-flashes. In "H. H."—Helen Hunt Jackson,[1] herself a poetess of some distinction, and her early schoolmate at Amherst she had another sympathetic friend, who, suspecting the extent of her production, asked for the post of literary executor. At length, in 1890, a volume edited by Higginson and Mabel Loomis Todd was published, *Poems by Emily Dickinson*, arranged under various heads according to subject. The book succeeded at once, six editions being sold in the first six months; so that a second series, and later a third, seemed to be justified. From the first selection to the third, however, there is a perceptible declension.

The subject division adopted by her editors serves well enough: Life, Love, Nature, Time and Eternity. A mystical poetess sequestered in a Berkshire village, she naturally concerned herself with neither past nor present, but with the things that are timeless. Apparently deriving no inspiration from the war to which Massachusetts, including her preceptorial colonel, gave itself so freely, she spent her days in brooding over the mystery of pain, the true nature of success, the refuge of the tomb, the witchcraft of the bee's murmur, the election of love,

[1] See also Book III, Chaps. VI and XI.

the relation of deed to thought and will. On such subjects she jotted down hundreds of little poems.

Though she had an Emersonian faith that fame, if it belonged to her, could not escape her, she cared nothing at all about having it; like not a few Transcendentalists, she might have written on the lintels of her door-post, *Whim*. That was her guiding divinity, Whim in a high sense: not unruliness, for all her impishness, but complete subjection to the inner dictate. She obeyed it in her mode of life, in her friendships, in her letters, in her poems. It makes her poetry eminently spontaneous—as fresh and artless as experience itself—in spite of the fact that she was not a spontaneous singer. The ringing bursts of melody that are characteristic of the born lyrical poet, such as Burns, she was incapable of; but she had insight, and intense, or rather tense, emotion, and expressed herself with an eye single to the truth. Something she derived from her reading, no doubt, from Emerson, the Brownings, Sir Thomas Browne; but rarely was poet less indebted. From her silent thought she derived what is essential in her work, and her whole effort was to state her findings precisely. She could not deliberately arrange her thoughts; "when I try to organize," she said, "my little force explodes and leaves me bare and charred." If she revised her work, as she did industriously, it was to render it not more attractive but truer.

Her poems are remarkable for their condensation, their vividness of image, their delicate or pungent satire and irony, their childlike responsiveness to experience, their subtle feeling for nature, their startling abruptness in dealing with themes commonly regarded as trite, their excellence in imaginative insight and still greater excellence in fancy. Typical is such a poem as that in which she celebrates the happiness of a little stone on the road, or that in which she remarks with gleeful irony upon the dignity that burial has in store for each of us— coach and footmen, bells in the village, "as we ride grand along." Emily Dickinson takes us to strange places; one never knows what is in store. But always she is penetrating and dainty, both intimate and aloof, challenging lively thought on our part while remaining, herself, a charmingly elfish mystery. Her place in American letters will be inconspicuous but secure.

Also born a New Englander, Thomas Bailey Aldrich remained essentially a New Englander all his days. It is true that he never sympathized with the occupations of the New England mind in his time, and that his dedication of his art to beauty is not in the tradition of that "reformatory and didactic" section, and that, on the other hand, New York left its metropolitan imprint on nearly all his work. Yet most of his career belongs to New England, and he himself liked to say that if he was not genuine Boston he was at least Boston-plated; nor is it quite fanciful to assert that his somewhat painful artistic integrity is largely a re-orientation of New England principle and thoroughness. In him, Puritan morality, after passing through Hawthorne, half artist and half moralist, becomes wholly artistic.

Aldrich's Salem was Portsmouth, New Hampshire, the "Rivermouth" of *The Story of a Bad Boy*, sleepy, elm-shaded, full of traditions, bordered by the ocean, where he spent many an hour, as he wrote reminiscently, " a little shade wandering along shore, picking up shells, and dreaming of a big ship to come and carry him across the blue water." Three years of his boyhood he lived in New Orleans, imbibing sights and moods quite other than those of the North Shore boy, travelling, too, up and down the Mississippi and receiving impressions never to be forgotten. A professed and hot-headed Southerner, he returned to Portsmouth to prepare for college. but, on the death of his father, gave up Harvard and went to New York at the age of seventeen, where he entered upon a career as counting-room clerk, contributor to periodicals, and assistant editor of the *Home Journal* under N. P. Willis.[1] During these early years he published several volumes of poems. The first, *The Bells* (1855), does little more than indicate his juvenile masters—Chatterton, Keats, Tennyson, Longfellow, Poe, Willis, among whom Tennyson is perhaps the most important in the light of his later work. The fourth, *The Ballad of Babie Bell, and Other Poems* (1859), marks his first success—*Babie Bell* itself he wrote when but nineteen. Then came the war, and adventurous war correspondence, but Aldrich was by nature nearly as timeless as Hawthorne, and in 1862 returned to his versecraft by no means transformed. Two or three of his poems, including *The Shaw Memorial Ode*, show the influence of war idealism, but most of

[1] See Book II, Chap. III.

his best work apparently owes nothing to the incitements of those stirring days. To him, indeed, the victory of 1865 meant not Appomatox but marriage, an excellent editorial position in Boston, and the publication of his collected poems in the renowned Blue and Gold series of Ticknor and Fields—an event in Boston, as Bliss Perry remarks, equivalent to election to the French Academy.

In New York he had been associated with the foremost writers of the "school" there—most intimately with Bayard Taylor, the Stoddards, Stedman, William Winter, and Fitz-James O'Brien. These and other members of the group agreed in condemning Boston and respectability in general, and espousing beauty and an enfranchised moral life. Yet their freedom was one of manners rather than of morals; even the Bohemians—headed by the satiric Henry Clapp—who fore-gathered at Pfaff's below the pavement at 647 Broadway and gave free rein to their impulses, seem to have had the usual impulses of the Hebraizing Anglo-Saxon if not of the Puritan. Aldrich was not a Bohemian of any type; nor was he by temperament a Manhattan journalist, but rather a gently mirthful New Englander, who felt eminently at home in the company of Longfellow, Lowell, Holmes, and others whom he met through Fields, and who preferred the "respectable" social standing of a knight of the pen in Boston to the incomplete Bohemianism of New York. For nine years he edited Ticknor and Fields's *Every Saturday*, while in the next room Fields and William Dean Howells edited *The Atlantic Monthly;* then, upon Howells's resignation in 1881, he entered upon a nine-years' editorship of the *Atlantic*. Travel was an item of importance in these later years. He wandered through Spain, one of his old castles in the air, and through the rich Orient, where his poetic fancy was always at ease, and he travelled round the world twice. Travel, and reading in foreign literature, added to an attractive cosmopolitanism in his spirit that marks him off from some of his Boston friends. He retained to the end a boyishness of disposition that made him personally winning, together with an intellectual liveliness that earned him a national reputation as a wit and the friendly admiration of no less a man than Mark Twain. He died in Boston in 1907.

Aldrich's unfailing good fortune was only a fitting reward

for a single-hearted devotion to art that is too rare in the history
of American literature. His faith as an artist was that, while
many fine thoughts have perished through inadequate expression, even a light fancy may be immortal by reason of its "perfect wording." There is here a suggestion of embellishment
that marks the limit of Aldrich's reach. It was well enough for
him to object to "Kiplingese" and to the negligée dialect of
James Whitcomb Riley, but he himself went to the other extreme in his solicitude for beautiful form. Even more than his
master Tennyson, he loved fine form so ardently that he cared
too little whether the embodied thought was equally distinguished. That he realized his danger is indicated by his verses
At the Funeral of a Minor Poet. Some thought the poet's
workmanship, he says,

> more costly than the thing
> Moulded or carved, as in those ornaments
> Found at Mycenæ;

and yet in defence it may be said that Nature herself works
thus, lavishing endless patience "upon a single leaf of grass or
a thrush's song"; or, as he puts it in one of his prose papers,
"A little thing may be perfect, but perfection is not a little
thing."

Many of Aldrich's poems, however, have substance enough
to deserve the embalming power of fine form. Their extraordinary neatness, precision, and delicacy, their fascinating
melody, are again and again conjoined with a mood or conception so subtly true or so vividly felt that we discern in them the
classic imprint. *Latakia, On Lynn Terrace, Resurgam, Sleep,
Frost-Work, Invita Minerva, The Flight of the Goddess, Books and
Seasons, Memory, Enamoured Architect of Airy Rhyme, Palabras
Cariñosas,* are poems that we may re-read repeatedly with an
ever renewed sense of their beauty. They offer no profound
criticism of life; but much great literature does not. Aldrich's
other work—his long narrative poems, of which he regarded
Wyndham Towers and *Friar Jerome* as the best; his *Judith of
Bethulía,* a dramatic poem; and his occasional poems, such as
the *Ode on the Unveiling of the Shaw Memorial on Boston Common*—is work in kinds in which other American poets have
done better. But none of them has done better than he in

vers de societé, in sonnets, and very short poems generally; indeed, the quality of Aldrich is the more apparent the shorter the poem, many of his best poems being quatrains. In *Songs and Sonnets*, a selection from his work published in 1906, the shorter poems have been brought together in a captivating little volume. Aldrich called Herrick "a great little poet"; he merits the title himself.[1]

In the Transcendental period, it was said that one could not throw a stone in Boston without hitting a poet; in the latter half of the century one's chances would have been little better. Representative, perhaps, of the countless lesser poets of New England in this period are Thomas William Parsons (1819–92), a Boston dentist who translated the *Inferno* admirably in *terza rima* and wrote poems of small merit save *On a Bust of Dante*, which, through its Dantesque elevation and purity of form, deserves to rank with the best American lyrics; William Wetmore Story (1819–95), of Salem, lawyer, later sculptor in Italy, his adopted home, a poet influenced by Tennyson and Browning, whose passionate *Cleopatra* and lofty *Praxiteles and Phryne* are among his most successful work; Lucy Larcom (1826–93), who spent her girlhood in the Lowell cotton mills, and whose lyrics, too often sentimental, show the influence of Whittier; Celia Thaxter (1836–94), whose father was lighthouse keeper on the Isles of Shoals, where the blended beauties and austerities of sea and rocks evoked many poems of nature in her sympathetic temperament; and J. G. Holland (1819–81),[2] who lived in Massachusetts till 1870, when he founded *Scribner's Monthly* (now *The Century Magazine*) in New York, a versatile author whose poems, such as the long *Bitter Sweet* and *Kathrina*, little read now, were widely popular in their day.

Of the New York authors, the most prominent in the first part of the half century was Bayard Taylor. As Aldrich belongs not only to New York but also to New England, so Taylor belongs not only to New York but also to Pennsylvania, where he was born in Kennett Square in 1825. By that time the State had lost what literary glories it had ever had, and although a new brood of native writers had just been born—T. Buchanan Read in 1822, Boker[3] in 1823, Leland[4] in 1824—New York was

---

[1] For Aldrich's prose see Book III, Chap. VI.   [2] See Book III, Chap. XI.
[3] See Book II, Chap. II.   [4] See Book III, Chap. IX.

already obviously destined to be the literary centre of the future.

Bayard Taylor is fairly representative of his State by virtue of his Quaker descent and his mixed English and German blood. Aside from the abounding life of nature in which he immersed himself as a boy, he found inhibitions on all sides: in his moral and religious life, in his practical life as a farmer's son, and in his intellectual life as a boy for whose education means were wanting. Gifted with the impetus of genius, he broke away from these hindrances, and embarked upon that varied and adventurous career of expansion that marks both his greatness and his littleness. He read all the books, especially poetry and travel, he could lay his hands on; he wrote verse from his seventh year onward; he drew and painted; he dreamed of foreign lands; he aspired to the heights—envying the bird, the weathercock, the balloonist. He had the expansiveness that often accompanies vigorous health of mind and body—at seventeen was six feet tall and enjoyed a magnetic power that foreshadowed his friendships and his personal impressiveness. Two years later, in 1844, having won the interest of Rufus W. Griswold, he was enabled to publish his first book, *Ximena*, in Philadelphia; though in later years, recognizing the emptiness of the fifteen poems that made up the book, he repented of it.

Already, in a sense, his poetry was subordinate to his travels; *Ximena* was intended to supply the means necessary for the voyage abroad that he had long cherished for its own sake and for its educational value. At a time when American pilgrims were a curiosity, he wandered through Europe for two years, virtually without funds, enduring and enjoying every manner of hardship and adventure. Particularly in Germany, where he was subsequently to marry and to find the material for his most ardent literary studies, he felt more at home than in repressive Kennett. *Views Afoot* (1846) told the story of these years, and launched Taylor upon a career of travel and journalistic distinction that made his fame international. Of all the lands that he lived in or roamed through, the countries of the Orient captivated this eager romanticist most completely.

It needed not [says Stedman] Hicks's picture of the bronzed traveller, in his turban and Asiatic costume, smoking, cross-legged, upon a roof-top of Damascus, to show us how much of a Syrian he was. We saw it in the down-drooping eyelids which made his profile like Tennyson's; in his acquiline nose, with the expressive tremor of the nostrils as he spoke; in his thinly tufted chin, his close-curling hair, his love of spices, music, coffee, colours, and perfumes.

The author of *Poems of the Orient* (1854) was indeed a fitting leader and high priest of the cult of the East that was one characteristic of the New York school.

After his first voyage to Europe, Taylor determined, in 1847, to try to make a living as a writer in New York; "this mighty New York," as he calls it with his appetite for large experience, "*here* is the metropolis of a continent!" It was the New York of Bryant, Halleck, and Willis to which he had come; it was under Willis's wing that he came to know the literary life of the city. When Greeley, the next year, invited him to a post on the *Tribune*, Taylor formed a connection that was to give him a sense of security for many years. In the newspaper rooms he now wrote for fifteen hours a day. He also contrived to see a good deal of R. H. Stoddard, Boker, Read, William Winter, and later Aldrich, who were to be his closest friends. He knew the Bohemians well enough not to be one of them; though he could scarcely avoid having some traits in common with them, since Bohemianism in one form or another has been a characteristic of New York literary life from the days of the Knickerbocker school. When the war came he sold a share of his *Tribune* stock so that his brother might enlist in the army; this he regarded as his "bit." The next year he was in Washington as war correspondent for the *Tribune*, but his activity in that capacity was cut short by a chance, too good to be sacrificed, to see Russia and Central Asia as Secretary of the Legation in Russia. His *Gettysburg Ode*, despite the fact that his brother died on that field, is distinguished neither in its poetry nor in its grasp of the significance of the war.[1] Meanwhile he had built, in his old Pennsylvania haunts, a manorial house named Cedarcroft, at a cost of $17,000, then a good deal of money,—a roomy dwelling with, typically, a tower that commanded an extended view of the gentle Pennsylvania countryside. Cedarcroft became a haven of refuge from his

[1] See also Book III, Chap. II.

arduous travels, where he might write undisturbed, and con verse at ease with Boker and Stedman and the rest, and smoke his narghile, and shock the good people of Kennett through his Continental *Gemüthlichkeit* in the use of liquor; it became also, unfortunately, as Stoddard says, "a Napoleonic business for a poet," who, in committing himself to earning a large income, sometimes $18,000 a year, by writing prose, appreciably injured his poetry.

And poetry was his passion, his religion, as he says with proud humility in *Porphyrogenitus*. In 1874 he told Howells that he was trying desperately to bury his old reputation as a traveller and writer of travel books "several thousand fathoms deep" and to create a new one. His prose he wrote with fatal facility, performing prodigies of speed, but his poetry he composed with the most painstaking care, spending hours over a couplet, if necessary, till it satisfied him. Like Aldrich, he despised American dialect verse. He venerated the great traditions of poesy, and never threw off the influence of his best-loved masters, Tennyson and Shelley. The "Immortal Brother" of his *Ode to Shelley* has left traces in most of his poetical work.

But, after all, it is Goethe, rather than Shelley, who is the index to Taylor's mind. He was so devoted to Goethe, and to German literature generally, that Whitelaw Reid found it necessary to say that "those who did not know him, have sometimes described him as more German than American." Some acquaintance with the German language he picked up at home; far more he gathered in his hibernation in Germany in the first year of his wanderings abroad; in time he spoke it like a native and composed poems in it, including a *Jubel-lied* (Berlin, 1870) celebrating German unity. He enjoyed life in Germany much as an earlier and greater Pennsylvanian cosmopolite, Franklin, enjoyed life in London and Paris, but his loyalty to America was never in question. He came to know the great men of Germany, including Bismarck, who, commenting on a novel by Taylor, remarked that the villain was allowed to escape too easily. In 1869 he was made non-resident professor of German literature at Cornell, where he gave courses of lectures. In 1870 he completed his admirable translation of *Faust* in the original metres, which he had projected twenty years before, and over which he had laboured with something of the devotion of Carlyle. This translation will doubtless come to be regarded as Bayard Taylor's foremost achievement. It was largely instrumental in obtaining for him the appointment, in 1878, as Minister to Germany, whither he sailed thoroughly worn out with congratulations and flowers and champagne. Excessively hard work had taken its revenges, and he was never to enjoy the great future that the new life in Germany held out to him—he was never, for one thing, to carry out his fond plan of writing the biography of Goethe, a task for which he was well fitted. He died soon after reaching Germany.

His death is the symbol of his life. His whole career, his poetical achievement most of all, was an approximation to high distinction that was frustrated through both outer and inner forces. He was cast in a large, a Goethean mould; he aspired highly and in many directions, seeking self-realization, but he lacked—outwardly—freedom from worldly troubles and—inwardly—Goethe's ideal of *Entsagung*. His buoyant enthusiasm, his capacity for hard work, tended to deploy in the void because of his lack of concentration and true harmony. He sought what he liked to call "cosmical experience," but in his eagerness he lost himself.

The consequences are plainly visible in his poetry. It is the poetry of a man who has "aspired" rather than "attained." It is, to begin with, dangerously versatile. Aside from his varied experiments in prose, Taylor wrote lyrics, pastorals, idylls, odes, dramatic lyrics, lyrical dramas, translations, poems in German, poems in every mood and every metre, poems consciously or unconsciously imitative of a host of poets (he had a remarkable but ill-controlled verbal memory), poems on themes Oriental, Greek, Norse, American from coast to coast, poems classical, sentimental, romantic, realistic, poems of love, of nature, of art. In most of this work he was acceptable to his age; in very little is he acceptable to a later time. His poetry, again, is diffuse, as the poetry of a fifteen-hour-a-day journalist is likely to be. Despite a certain buoyant resonance, a resonance, however, rarely full enough; despite a frequent delicacy of perception and expression; despite a sense of melody that seldom fails; despite a simplicity of method and phrasing that betokens sincerity;—despite all these merits and others, his poetry attracts mildly because it is diffuse, and it is diffuse, fundamentally, because it is shallow.   In his ode on Goethe, written three years before Taylor died, conscious of his "lighter muscle" he asks with an undercurrent of sadness:

> How charge with music powers so vast and free,
> Save one be great as he?

Taylor, with all his aspiration and energy, was ill-educated, ill-disciplined, emotionally and intellectually unsymmetrical. He was too fond of his narghile and of melon-seeds brought all the way from Nijni-Novgorod.   He learned modern Greek before he learned ancient Greek.   His few good poems, such as the popular *Bedouin Song, John Reed, The Quaker Widow, Euphorion*, are far too few.   He had latent powers, if not supreme power, but it was misdirected.   To his contemporaries, he was a distinguished poet as well as traveller; to us he is an interesting personality. [1]

While Shelley was Taylor's poet, Richard Henry Stoddard found in Keats, as he says in a verse tribute, the Master of his soul.   As a boy, he "lived for Song," and throughout his life, in surroundings essentially alien and "an age too late," he dedicated himself to poetry with a happiness and dignity, and with a degree of success in his own day, quite out of proportion to the merit of his achievement.

A New Englander like Aldrich and Stedman, he was born in the same year with Taylor (1825), in Hingham, Massachusetts, where his ancestors were hardy sailors.   In his *Recollections* he tells of his grandfather's house by the sea, where his mother sang melancholy hymns at nightfall, and of the ancient church and cemetery that gave tone to the family life—"dying seemed to be the most laudable industry of the time."   His father being lost at sea, the pale widow and her delicate boy removed to Boston, and later to New York, where she married again. After a few years of schooling, Richard was set to work, first as errand-boy, as shop-boy, and as legal copyist,—spending part of his petty earnings in the purchase of the English poets, —later as blacksmith and as moulder in an iron foundry.   On the threshold of manhood, he worked in the foundry for three hard years, with ever one consolation: "the day would end, night would come, and then I could write poetry."   In 1849 he

---

[1] For Taylor's travels see Book III, Chap. xv

published his first volume, *Footprints*, of which he tells us one copy was sold before the edition was given to the flames. Leaving the foundry, he supported himself, like Aldrich and Taylor, as a journalist, becoming in time literary editor of the *World* and *Mail and Express*. Meanwhile he had married Elizabeth Barstow, of Mattapoisett, Massachusetts, "one of those irrepressible girls," says her husband, "who are sometimes born in staid Puritan families," who later attained some distinction as novelist and poetess ("for she became," says Stoddard, "the best writer of blank verse of any woman in America"), and had secured a clerkship in the New York Custom House which he held till 1870. He lived in New York through many of its varied decades till 1903, a prominent figure in the literary life, a close friend of Taylor, Stedman, and the others. In his somewhat austere devotion to beauty he was far removed from the Bohemians; he states specifically with regard to Pfaff's " I never went inside the place." His life lacked the advantages—and disadvantages—of much travel, though, like his friends, he poetized the magical Orient (in *The Book of the East*). His personality was that of a somewhat angular individualist, outspoken, vigorous, inflexible in his support of the right. He was a product of Puritan New England as well as a disciple of Keats.

New England didacticism, however, is all but absent from his poetry. Here and there is a trace, now and then a whole poem, such as *On the Town*, a harlot's plea for justice, which has also, it is true, a modernly realistic aspect; but otherwise the world of sin that Hawthorne loved to brood over and the New England poets sought to improve, is far away. He began his career as a palpable imitator of Keats's sensuousness, magical epithet, and praise of beauty. His *Autumn* is little more than a frank copy of the ode by Keats. Other early poems are full of echoes of Milton and Wordsworth. Though he soon passed into his own manner, which was never highly individualized, one can discern his masters everywhere. Some of his best narrative poetry, such as *Leonatus* and *Imogen*, is agreeably reminiscent of Keats. His blank verse, as in the tribute to Bryant, *The Dead Master*, often has power and accomplished variety, but it is not individual. Indeed, it may not be unfair to say that Stoddard was mainly a passionate lover of poetry, more passionate than the others of the New York group, and not so much a natural creator of it. Creation was, to him, an inevitable accident; enjoyment of others' poetry was a leading function of life. Most of his work is the expression of commonplace sentiment and tame emotion. Its merit is melody and deftness, in phrasing, in rhyming, in imagery. Consequently his best work is doubtless that which the public of his day knew him by, his lyrics, as in the pleasant volume *Songs of Summer*, diverse snatches of song without attachment to time or place, also without much meaning or purpose, but so well fashioned that one can understand why Stoddard was once a prominent poet. His *Lincoln, an Horation Ode*, however, still has power.[1]

If Bayard Taylor's handicap was travel, and Stoddard's uncongenial labour, Stedman's was business. Though born of an old New England family in Hartford, Connecticut, and educated at Yale, he immersed himself so thoroughly in Wall Street that he belongs to New York. Probably he owed less to his father, lumber merchant and devout Christian, than to his mother, Elizabeth Dodge Stedman, a poetess notable chiefly for her ardent emotional life. Of her son she wrote: "As soon as he could speak he lisped in rhyme, and as soon as he could write, which was at the age of six years, he gave shape and measure to his dreams. He was a sedate and solemn baby." In college, as the youngest in a class of more than one hundred, he developed his infantile devotion to poetry, winning prizes, but losing his sedateness and solemnity. According to the Faculty Records, "Stedman, Soph. was dismissed for having been present at a 'dance house' near the head of the wharf," this being apparently his culminating indiscretion. As soon as he realized his error, he said in applying for his degree years later, he "resolved to obtain a higher culture"; and, taking himself in hand, he transformed his raw, strong-willed, high-spirited youth to an attractive type of energetic, idealistic manhood. In 1855 he became a broker in New York. Associating himself with Greeley's *Tribune*, he presently found himself the popular author of three lively, rather journalistic poems—*The Diamond Wedding, The Ballad of Lager Bier*, and *How Old Brown Took Harper's Ferry*. In 1860, the year of his first volume, *Poems, Lyric and Idyllic*, he joined the staff of the

[1] See also Book III, Chap. II.

World. For this newspaper he went to the front, in 1861, as war correspondent. A man of thirty years when the war was over, he turned to the life of Wall Street, becoming, six years later, an active member of the Stock Exchange. He held his seat till 1900. "There was no such market for literary wares at that day as has since arisen, and I needed to be independent in order to write and study." Perhaps so; it was a bitter problem to solve; yet there is little question that Stedman's choice limited his literary achievement in quality as well as quantity. To be sure, he could not have foreseen the financial misfortunes that beset his way to independence. At the same time, he had a talent for business that might better not have been developed, since it flourished at the expense of a rarer talent that he possessed for literary criticism and for poetry. With more knowledge and the discipline of hard thinking, his literary criticism, at its best in *Poets of America* (1885), might have contributed much to a department of our literature that is all too weak. He had high, if not the highest, seriousness, without the admixture of sentimentalism that often accompanies ideality and range.

His distinction as a literary critic and as an editor of anthologies and other works seems to have given rise to an unwarranted presumption in his favour as a poet. If he had a voice of his own, he spoke in uncertain tones; in the main his poetry is an echo of the romantic poets and Tennyson. He seems to have written frequently in cold blood; at least he told Winter that "it was his custom to select with care the particular form of verse that he designed to use, and sometimes to invent the rhymes and write them at the ends of the lines which they were to terminate,—thus making a skeleton of a poem, as a ground-work on which to build." Aside from his war verse[1] he wrote poems on New York themes, the best of which is *Pan in Wall Street;* on New England life and ideals, including the charming lines entitled *The Doorstep;* on *The Carib Sea;* on special occasions, including poems on Greeley and several of the New England poets; and on various other themes, notably in *The Hand of Lincoln* and *Stanzas for Music*. In most of this work—limited in quantity to a single volume—Stedman's muse is decorously uplifted rather than elevated of its own

[1] See Book III, Chap. II.

nature; it rarely sings freely, and, if it never offends, also never stirs deeply. At a public meeting in his memory, his friend William Winter expressed Stedman's literary faith in a compact phrase when he said: "He steadfastly adhered to the stately, lovely, ancient traditions of English poetry." Undidactic, devoted to the dignity and beauty of letters, he expressed himself in the idiom of the tradition of beauty in literature, both classical and modern. His protracted studies in Theocritus and the other early idyllists were typical of his scholarly love of literature. He himself is the *Pan in Wall Street* of one of his few fascinating poems: among the bulls and bears he too held

> a Pan's-pipe (fashioned
> Like those of old),

and upon it he could sing arrestingly if not greatly.[1]

Though subordinate in genius to the greater New Englanders,—Emerson, Lowell, Whittier, and the rest,—the poets of the New York school made a positive contribution to our literature. Aside from the intrinsic merit of their work, they are important on account of their influence. Holding that poetry is amply justified through its beauty and the happiness produced in us by its beauty, and that the moral element is ancillary, if not accidental or irrelevant, they prepared the way for the highly accomplished versecraft that is characteristic of the declining years of the century. Whether this highly accomplished, often precious, poetry is itself admirable is scarcely open to question: it is not great, but it provided a discipline that American poets had never had and that they needed.

Of the lesser luminaries in New York little need be said. They include William Winter (1836–1917), who early came from Massachusetts, primarily a dramatic critic[2] but also the author of verses resembling those of his poet friends: Emma Lazarus (1849–87), born in New York of Portuguese Jewish ancestry, some of whose work is remarkable for its Hebraic intensity[3]; and the Cary sisters, Alice (1820–71) and Phoebe (1824–71), who came from Ohio, importing the sentimental and moralizing tendency of the age along with a sweetness and beauty by virtue of which they still have some charm. Two

---

[1] For his prose see Book III, Chap. XIII. [3] See Book III, Chap. XIII.
[2] See Book III, Chap. XIII.

Philadelphians already mentioned, George H. Boker (1823–90)[1] and Thomas B. Read (1822–72),[2] may be named here again on account of their association with writers of the New York group. Boker, distinguished as a dramatist, began authorship with *The Lesson of Life, and Other Poems* in 1847 and continued to write verse. Read's first volume appeared in Philadelphia in the same year. Among his poems are *The New Pastoral* (1855), a long poem dealing with American pioneer life, *The Wagoner of the Alleghanies* (1862), a tale of the Revolutionary War, and many short lyrics, of which the best known is *Sheridan's Ride*.

Although Richard Watson Gilder (1844–1909) belongs to the same general group with Taylor, Stoddard, and the other "squires of poesy," as they called themselves a trifle ostentatiously, he is associated with a later and more public-spirited period of New York culture.

Born at Bordentown, New Jersey, he was educated at his father's schools, first at Bordentown, then at Flushing. The latter school failing, his father re-entered the active ministry shortly before the Civil War. In the war, the father served as chaplain till his death in 1864; a son served in a Zouave regiment; and Richard, a boy of nineteen, enlisted in Landis's Philadelphia Battery when the Confederate invasion threatened eastern Pennsylvania. The war over, Richard Watson Gilder became a journalist in Newark, soon after in New York, where, in 1870, he became the assistant editor of the new periodical known as *Scribner's Monthly*. When his chief, Dr. J. G. Holland, died in 1881, Gilder assumed control of the *Century*, as it was now called, giving it unsparingly his best energy for more than a quarter of a century. Partly through his own interests, partly through his wife's (Helena de Kay's) association with fellow painters, he found himself surrounded by friends of a type very different from those of the Bohemians and squires of poesy—La Farge, Saint-Gaudens, Stanford White, Joseph Jefferson, Madame Modjeska, and, in the summers on Cape Cod, President Cleveland. Again, unlike the earlier members of the New York group, he became an ardent and enlightened humanitarian and publicist, serving the cause of good government in city and nation. "That I am

[1] See Book II, Chap. II. [2] See Book III, Chap. II.

drawn into too many things," he wrote in a letter, "is perhaps true." He was right; both his health and his work, in various fields, were impaired. In another letter he refers to his "insufficient but irrepressible verse," which describes it well enough.

He began verse writing under happy auspices. Milton was his master at the age of ten or twelve, and his father encouraged him to write. Years later, he chanced to meet Helena de Kay at the very time that he came upon Rossetti's translation of the *Vita Nuova;* the result of the conjunction was the love sonnets of *The New Day*, his first volume, which was published in 1875. With its slow, heavily-freighted lines, its solemn music and carefully composed imagery, its intense feeling not fully articulate, its occasional vagueness of meaning, it contrasts with the obvious and more lively American poetry of that day and the day before. The vagueness of meaning Gilder happily escaped in his later work; the other qualities he retained and improved.

Of virtually all of his poetry, the dominant trait is a brooding intensity,—suggested by the dark, peering eyes of the man himself,—expressed in language distilled and richly associative, "the low, melodious pour of musicked words." He was passionately responsive to music, to

> The deep-souled viola, the 'cello grave,
> The many-mooded, singing violin,
> The infinite, triumphing, ivoried clavier

—his own poetry has the quality of orchestral instruments, oftenest the grave 'cello. Many of his poems are concerned with other arts, especially painting and acting, for art was to this "stickler for form," as he called himself, a large part of life. He naturally wrote on *Modjeska, Eleonora Duse, A Monument of Saint-Gaudens, An Hour in a Studio*, and *In Praise of Portraiture* as well as on *MacDowell, The Pathetic Symphony, A Fantasy of Chopin, Paderewski*, and *Beethoven*. He had, too, a love of the Orient,—an artist's love as well as a reflective poet's, —that led him to add *In Palestine, and Other Poems* (1898) to New York's considerable body of literature on the East.

Yet art was by no means a tower of ivory to this public man.

The youth of the Gettysburg campaign became the laureate of the Civil War heroes, and the volume of his poems entitled *For the Country* (1897) is as typical as any. It includes *Sheridan* and *Sherman* and the excellent sonnet on *The Life-Mask of Abraham Lincoln*. Gilder took his place eagerly in the "wild, new, teeming world of men" that America meant to him, and desired a part, as he stated in a poem written abroad, in making it not only free and strong but also noble and pure—a land of justice lifting a light for all the world and leading into the Age of Peace.

New York fostered if not produced one other important poet, Richard Hovey, who was born in 1864, when Gilder was a young man. Follower of Whitman and the Elizabethans, and poet in his own right, Hovey won the enthusiasm of both the conventional school—especially Stedman—and the eager modernists who began to attract attention near the close of the century. The odd mixture of loyalties in his verse is paralleled by the curious variety in his life. Born in Illinois, he lived in Washington, D. C., graduated from Dartmouth College, New Hampshire, studied at the General Theological Seminary, New York, became lay assistant at the Church of St. Mary the Virgin, accepted literature as his profession, and ended his brief career as professor of English literature in Barnard College and lecturer in Columbia University. Several years, also, he lived abroad—familiarizing himself, for one thing, with Verlaine, Mallarmé, and the later symbolists, and becoming one of the first American disciples and translators of Maeterlinck.

Hovey's early death deprived us of a poet who had not yet reached the height of his powers. Finer work than he actually produced lay ahead unrealized, but it was probably not the unfinished dramatic work which he had come to regard as his *magnum opus,—Launcelot and Guenevere: A Poem in Dramas*, which he began to publish in 1891. This was not to be merely a rehandling of ancient poetic material by an idle singer of an empty day but a profound treatment of a modern problem in terms of the past—the conflict of the individual and society, and the establishment of a right relation between them. Hovey planned nine plays, though he completed only four. He expected to arrange them in three trilogies: in the first, Launcelot and Guenevere were to disregard society; in the second they were to disregard themselves; and in the third their problem was to be resolved. It was a tremendous theme, worthy of a poet of an ampler intellectual endowment than Hovey's. How high a flight he attempted may be seen in *Taliesin: A Masque* (1900), the last play that he completed, a poet's poem which to some readers has been Hovey at his most exalted, while others have roundly condemned its exuberant fancy, imagination, and metaphysics. It is, at all events, a remarkable feat in rhythm-building, astonishing in the easy mastery with which the poet passes from one movement to another and in the variety of musical effects. The other plays are clearer and more substantial; in *The Marriage of Guenevere* (1895), for example, the Queen is revealed with a definiteness unequalled in the Arthurian tradition, though it is by no means certain that the modern touch is in this respect an unmixed advantage. All the plays are deftly and fluently written, but they fail in sustained power. The note of the *improvvisatore* is never away.

This note is not so fatal in the lyric. Hovey's lyrics time will doubtless adjudge his best work. He has little weight, little insight of the profounder sort, but he has, on the other hand, unusual fervor and *élan*, and much insight of the merely subtle sort. Sensitive, tingling with life, he responds to the world with a gaiety not so much thoughtless as thought-banishing, a gaiety alien to the dominant moods of modern life and hence always open to the suspicion of affectation. His quality is very evident in the three series of *Songs from Vagabondia* (1893, 1896, 1900) written collaboratively with Bliss Carman. They express impetuously, a little artificially at times, the vagabondage of the soul that runs like a gypsy thread through the romantic literature of the century. *The Wander-Lovers*, which sets its pace in the first line, "Down the world with Marna!" is in its way a nearly perfect thing. In a distinct part of Hovey's work, his poems of masculine comradeship and college fraternity, this Bohemian mood is expressed in a really notable way. *Spring*, for instance, read at a fraternity convention in 1896, contains, in a charming natural setting, the lines beginning "Give a rouse, then, in the May-time" which, set to music by Frederic Field Bullard, are familiar to college youth from coast to coast. This kind of thing Hovey could do better than any other of our poets.

His poems on serious themes lack the delightful assurance of *The Wander-Lovers* and *Spring*. *The Call of the Bugles*, one of his several Spanish War poems, is only intermittently buoyant and martial, is too long, and is scarcely American in its sentiment "Great is war—great and fair!" In a rarer mood of Hovey's is *Unmanifest Destiny*, in which, as in *Seaward*, his elegy on the death of Thomas William Parsons, his tone is impressively reverent and his music richly solemn.

Another Columbia University poet of latter-day New York was the accomplished Frank Dempster Sherman (1860–1916), professor of graphics, an ardent philatelist and collector of book-plates, author of *Madrigals and Catches* (1887), *Lyrics for a Lute* (1890), *Little Folk Lyrics* (1892), and *Lyrics of Joy* (1904). The titles indicate of themselves the poetic *genres* to which he devoted himself. Whether he dealt with love, or nature, or books, his lines were short and jocund. His range was narrow, and quite out of the modern current; but his love of music and image were so genuine that his poems reached a cordial if small audience.

This brings us to the poetry of the West. The poets of the East are, in one sense, a survival from the past; in another sense, a bridge leading from the past into the future. The West, on the other hand, having the initiative, the irreverence, and the breezy optimism of a new country, set about creating a literature fashioned in its own image. If that image was unbeautiful, it was at least sturdy and forward-looking. At times the West did not hesitate to use the past, but its own force nearly always gave the past a new direction. It was this element of novelty that delighted ordinary readers even in the conservative East and caused England to find in Western poetry, as it found in Whitman, the authentic voice of the New World at last beginning to express itself:

> Nothing of Europe here—
> Or, then, of Europe fronting mornward still.

For this hasty generalization there is some semblance of justification, since, after all, as Professor Turner has shown impressively, all of the United States save the Atlantic seaboard has at some time been a democratic West in opposition to an aristocratic East. And yet, if the West was not a fixed region,

it was merely a phase in national development, and the voice
of that phase is not the voice of the nation itself.

The immigrant character of the Far West is illustrated by
its chief writers, Harte, Miller, and Sill. Bret Harte, born in
Albany, never became quite saturated with the spirit of the
West, and spent a little more than half of his total years in the
State of New York and in Great Britain. His poetry is that of
a gifted man of letters who perceived the literary possibilities
of the material lying about him in his impressionable young
manhood in California. The picturesque California of the
early fifties he presented adroitly not only in his short stories
but also in such poems as *Plain Language from Truthful James*
(generally known as *The Heathen Chinee*), *The Society upon the
Stanislaus*, *Dickens in Camp*, and *Jim*. Some of these poems
were dramatic monologues, commonly in dialect; Harte's
poems in conventional English were less successful, though
some of his *Spanish Idyls and Legends* depict attractively the
fading glory of Spanish rule in the West. Most of his poems
contain humour and pathos, often blended, as in the short
stories; in most of them the deft technique, especially the surprising turn at the end, adds much to the reader's pleasure.
His range was considerable but his excellence nowhere great
enough to lift him above the minor poets.[1]

Harte's *East and West Poems*, which came out in 1871,
exploited "the Pike," a recurrent figure in our literature since
the work of George W. Harris[2] and other Southerners. The
Pike County Ballads of John Hay (1838–1905), published in
the same year, reached an extensive audience, English as well as
American; to the English reviews, indeed, Hay was likely to be
the poet of *Jim Bludso* and *Little Breeches* rather than one of
the authors of a monumental life of Lincoln.[3] Since 1871 dialect
poems portraying humble life in a definite region have contributed a striking localism to our minor poetry.

Possibly the truest representative of the Far West in the
poetry of the nineteenth century is Joaquin Miller (1841–1913).
Like Whitman, whom he resembles in more ways than one,
Miller won a following first of all in England, ever watchful for

[1] For Harte's stories see Book III, Chap. vi.
[2] See Book II, Chap. xix.
[3] See Book III, Chap. xv.

signs of the indigenous in American literature and finding them
in Miller's poetry as in his leonine mane, flannel shirt, and high
boots. In 1870–71 the "Oregon Byron," then in London,
achieved a popularity as sudden as that of his master. *Songs of
the Sierras*, first published many thousand miles from the Sierras
themselves, was widely applauded, and Tennyson, Browning,
Swinburne, and Rossetti received this "typical American"
author as a brother bard. Then America, too, discovered him,
and he was soon known from London to San Francisco. Although his debt to Byron, Coleridge, and other romanticists is
obvious to any reader, his verse is by no means purely imitative.
If his subject matter had been less novel, it is hard to say what
his poetry would have been; certainly we may say that it owes
at least as much to its novelty of theme as to its essential qualities. The element of imitation, plain as it is, is superficial; his
poetry may best be regarded, as Miller regarded it himself,
as indirect autobiography, as the extraordinary product of an
extraordinary life.

"My cradle," he wrote in a lively prose account of his life,
"was a covered wagon, pointed West." In this wagon he was
born, he tells us, as it was crossing the border line of Indiana
and Ohio, in the year 1841, and he was named Cincinnatus
Hiner Miller. His family settled on the Middle Western frontier, where they suffered many hardships without becoming
dispirited. Fascinated, however, by accounts of the Far West,
the family began, in March, 1852, a three-thousand-mile journey to Oregon, lasting more than seven months, beset by
cholera, tornadoes, and hostile Indians. Thus as a boy of eleven
Joaquin Miller came to know that terrible and alluring westward
journey to the ultimate frontier. After only two years on the
Oregon farm, he began a roving life of adventure that led him
into half a dozen Indian campaigns, and into repeated struggles
with mountain flood and prairie fire, desert thirst and buffalo
stampede, until he understood the life of that region outwardly,
perhaps inwardly too, as nobody else in American literature.
In the course of this life bristling with action he found time to
write verse constantly, publishing, first, *Specimens* in 1868; a
year later *Joaquin et al*, whence his rechristening derisively as
"Joaquin Miller"; and another year later, at his own expense,
in London, *Pacific Poems*, which had an astonishing reception

before being promptly republished as *Songs of the Sierras.* Of the many volumes that followed, none fulfilled the promise that readers not unnaturally found in the *Songs.* He wrote dramas, too, and novels, uniformly without success.

Little as Joaquin Miller had in common with the Pre-Raphaelites, his view of poetry—"To me a poem is a picture," he stated at a Rossetti dinner—was not uncongenial to them. One would expect his work to be concerned with action first of all, but it is not: nearly always the action, even in the ostensibly narrative poems, is subordinate to the description. He loved the West as he loved nothing else, and his best work is a pictorial treatment of it: the West from Central America to Alaska, from the Great Plains to the coast, its grand Sierras,—"white stairs of heaven,"—its canyons, its great rivers, its ocean,—"the great white, braided, bounding sea,"—its chaparral and manzanita, its buffaloes and noble horses, its stars overhead "large as lilies." Then the figures that peopled this vast setting—gold-miners, Indians, Mexicans, and the romantic adventurers who are commonly his heroes, restless, rebellious, and misunderstood. All these Miller had lived among till he knew them as well as he, at least, could know anything, and in his best work they stand forth vividly. His poems of the personal life are forgotten, but the power of *Yosemite* lives. One reads again and again, with renewed pleasure, such poems as *Exodus for Oregon* and *Westward Ho!*, which picture the heroic wanderings of the pioneers across the continent, "A mighty nation moving west," in long wagon trains, with their yoked steers, shouting drivers, crashing whips, "blunt, untutor'd men," and "brave and silent women." This westward movement is the theme of Miller's most impressive poems, from *Columbus* who sailed "on and on" (a phrase that recurs repeatedly in these poems) to *The Last Taschastas*, an old chief who is driven, in an open boat, from the Pacific shore, as the Indians of the Atlantic coast had been driven westward centuries earlier. More than anyone else, Joaquin Miller is the poet of our receding frontier.

In narrative poetry he could use to the full his immense energy, which is his chief excellence. He was not a man of ideas; he reflected objectively less perhaps than Byron, and certainly was less fond of introspection, despite his later years as a sort of hermit on the heights above Oakland, where he built the cairn upon which his ashes rest. Primarily he was a man of action in an active society. If there was something of the theatrical about him, it became so habitual, as C. W. Stoddard testifies, as to be natural. Compared with Harte at least, who exploited the West, he is the unfeigned expression of the West. If he had not much culture, he fortunately did not pretend to have, but relied upon the force within him. His "rough, broken gallop," as a London reviewer described his style, has a charm that draws the reader "on and on," disregarding the defects of his quality—his lack of proportion, his crudity in music and in taste. In the end, his defects may be fatal, so far as purely literary values are concerned, but he had the good fortune to record the Western scene in poetry as no one else has done, an achievement that will not soon be forgotten. He was so Western as almost to be a caricature of his section, as Emily Dickinson is of New England.

Edward Rowland Sill (1841–87), another of the more prominent Far Western poets, born in the same year with Joaquin Miller, wrote quite apart from the literary movements of both West and East, though his artistic ideals had some resemblance to those of the New York school and his temperament was that of a New Englander. Twenty-two years of his life belong to California, but he was born in Connecticut and died in Ohio. He was descended from old New England families, whose heads were mainly ministers on his mother's side and physicians on his father's side. At Yale College he was a "dreamy, impetuous, sensitive, thoughtful youth" who read widely aside from the curriculum, who impressed his comrades with his attractive personality, pure character, and literary talent, and who confronted the world in a spirit of independent inquiry. "He must translate human experience into his own thought and language." He published *Dream-Doomed*, *Music*, and other poems in the college literary magazine, and was the class poet of 1861; his *Commencement Poem*, included in his collected verse, was long regarded at Yale as the best class poem that had been delivered there. Graduating at twenty, in poor health, he made the trip to California by way of Cape Horn. For half a dozen years he engaged in miscellaneous occupations, on a ranch, in a post-office, eventually becoming much attached to this alien land.

In order to study theology he attended the Divinity School at Harvard; but he quickly gave over this ambition and entered upon a still briefer career as journalist in New York. Then followed his school-teaching years, first in Ohio and afterwards in California, where he eventually became professor of English in the State University. This post he held, with distinction as a teacher, for eight years, resigning in 1882 mainly on account of the failing health that dogged his steps most of his life. In Cuyahoga Falls, Ohio, he continued his literary pursuits to his death at the age of forty-six, in 1887.

The struggle between faith and doubt, forced upon him by the spirit of the age even before he was a man, survived all the changing scenes of his life. In another age his Puritan inwardness might have made of him a poet of faith, if not a minister of the Gospel. But he never attained conviction, was always gently questioning, finding, it seems, a certain twilight gratification in his inconclusive brooding. This habit of brooding was alleviated by a delicate sense of humour, which removed all suspicion of morbidity, and was intensified by his modesty. "You should see," he wrote to a friend, "the equanimity with which I write thing after thing—both prose and verse—and stow them away, never sending them anywhere, or thinking of printing any book of them, at present, if ever." Most of his published work, indeed, is posthumous—to use his word, post-humorous—and there is very little of it, only a volume of collected prose and a volume of collected poetry. To the *Atlantic* he sent a number of poems, some of which were printed under a pen-name, and in the "Contributors' Club" his prose enjoyed complete anonymity.

Among his prose studies is an essay on *Principles of Criticism*, which contains a statement of the ideal that his own poetry followed:

In the poem, the requirement is that it shall be full of lovely images, that it shall be in every way musical, that it shall bring about us troops of high and pure associations,—the very words so chosen that they come "trailing clouds of glory" in their suggestiveness; and in its matter, that it shall bring us both thought and feeling, for whose intermingling the musical form of speech alone is fitted; and that, coming from a pure and rich nature, it shall leave us purer and richer than it found us.

It is not too much to say that these are the characteristics of Sill's poetry at its best. We are the purer and richer for reading him; he rouses life in the dark, disused corners of our being as many greater poets do not. In *The Fool's Prayer* and *Opportunity*, his two best known poems, he attacks us rather too directly, in the New England didactic strain. Yet even here the "moral," though obvious, exists in solution rather than in a crystallized statement. Nearly always his instinct was to be suggestive, to reach the reader's emotion by indirection, by surprise. Always clear, he is also quietly subtle; his meaning steals upon us like the mood of a peaceful evening. His diction is so simple that an unpracticed reader does not suspect how delicately the poet has felt the "troops of high and pure associations" that accompany his plain words. So, too, his poems are musical, frequently, with a melody that is unheard. He was devoted to music all his life, playing a number of instruments with skill if not virtuosity. He wrote about music in prose and verse. In nature, sound seemed to attract him especially, most of all the fitful surf-music of the wind, which he used in his poems repeatedly. He had, too, a pictorial sense, which gave him a command of the "lovely images" that he regarded as essential in verse. Indeed, he had all the qualities needed for the highest excellence in poetry except a vigorous creative imagination. His imagination was perhaps mainly inarticulate, for though he wrote all his life he seems to have lacked the intense eagerness or the steady, resolute progress in creation that we associate with the great artist. His overmodest mind, moreover, together with his unresolved struggle of faith and doubt, encouraged his tendency to rest in the unrecorded thought—to read widely, to feel and reflect abundantly, rather than to shape his conception in the concrete poem.

Among his many poems that peer within to the shadowy mood and the curious speculation, there are also poems, and a larger number than one would expect, presenting the scene of that "purer world" of the Far West to which this typical New England spirit attached itself with few moments of regret,— the soaring pines filled with the sound of chanting winds, the surf with its "curdling rivulets of green," the city of San Francisco across the bay like a sea-dragon crawled upon the shore, the flowery fields now white, now orange or sea-blue, the great redwood forest dreaming in silence disturbed only by the sob of a distant dove, and overhead, by night, the clear stars that he loved because they made him, as he said, victor over time and space. In these poems we come to know the Western scene, not as it appeals to a man of action and large, blunt emotion, but as it rouses the feeling of a temperament subtly æsthetic and spiritual.

Harte, Miller, and Sill were born far from the Pacific coast region with which they are associated; the case is otherwise with the leading poets of the Middle West,—the Piatts, Carleton, Riley, and Moody. "The wedded poets," John James Piatt (1835–1917), born in Indiana, and Sarah Morgan Piatt (1836–1912), born in Kentucky, together produced a large number of volumes of verse, little of which has survived its age. They used conventional forms, and wrote with care and skill; today, however, what interest they still have depends on the themes of their Western poems, such as *The Mower in Ohio* and *Fires in Illinois*. With the Piatts may be named Madison Cawein (1865–1915), of Kentucky, notable for his delicately fanciful sense of the camaraderie of nature. Will Carleton (1845–1912), born in Michigan and brought up on a farm, became a journalist, first in the West and later in the East, and a popular reader of his own work. In 1873 he published *Farm Ballads*, a group of crudely sentimental pieces directed at the common heart of humanity; forty thousand copies were sold within a year and a half. Poems like *Out of the Old House*, *Nancy*, and *Gone with a Handsomer Man* were not too good for anybody.

Carleton's success foreshadows the still greater success of another journalist and public reader of his own verse, the "People's Laureate," James Whitcomb Riley. Of Pennsylvania Dutch and Irish stock, the latter predominating, he was born in 1849 in the country town of Greenfield, Indiana, where his father had attained a considerable local reputation as a lawyer and orator. In his boyhood Riley was, as he says, "always ready to declaim and took natively to anything dramatic or theatrical." He was fond of poetry before he could read it, carrying a copy of Quarles's *Divine Emblems* about with him for the sake of its "feel." In later years his favourite authors were Burns in poetry and Dickens in prose. With his father he often went to the courthouse, where, being allowed to mingle freely with the country people, he came to know the dialect and the hearts and minds of the people who were in after years to be the subject of his poems. For a time he devoted himself to music—the banjo, the guitar, the violin, the drum.

In a few weeks I had beat myself into the more enviable position of snare drummer. Then I wanted to travel with a circus, and dangle my legs before admiring thousands over the back seat of a Golden Chariot. In a dearth of comic songs for the banjo and guitar, I had written two or three myself, and the idea took possession of me that I might be a clown, introduced as a character-song-man and the composer of my own ballads.

For a time, too, he was a "house, sign, and ornamental painter," covering, he tells us, "all the barns and fences in the State with advertisements." Persuaded by his father, he read law, only to find himself running away with a travelling medicine man, whose company was composed, he says, of "good straight boys, jolly chirping vagabonds like myself. Sometimes I assisted the musical olio with dialect recitations and character sketches from the back step of the wagon." This life suited him; "I laughed all the time."

Returning to Greenfield, he entered journalism, and began to publish in various papers elsewhere. Lean and uncertain years followed, till, in 1877, he was invited to take a place on *The Indianapolis Journal.* In this newspaper he printed his dialect poems by "Benjamin F. Johnson of Boone," which were welcomed so warmly that a pamphlet edition was sold locally, with the title *The Old Swimmin' Hole and 'Leven More Poems* (1883). This marks the beginning of his widespread success as a poet of the people, which led to his success as a public reader of his own work. Early in his career he had been given valuable encouragement by the Eastern people's laureate, Longfellow, and in 1887, when he appeared before a New York audience, he was introduced as a "true poet" by the author of *The Biglow Papers.* By 1912 schools in many parts of the country celebrated "Riley Day"; by 1915 he was honoured by official recognition, the Secretary of the Interior suggesting that one of his poems be read in each school-house in the land.

When he died in the year following, some thirty-five thousand people are said to have passed his body as it lay in state under the dome of the Indiana capitol. The impression that Riley made—and still makes—on the American public was indeed extraordinary.

It is to be accounted for, in part, by his personality. His sunny, gentle nature won the affection of those who met him, and he had a group of loyal friends who presented him to the public in his true character. But in the main his popularity depends on the excellence and the limits of his achievement. Essentially sincere, he nevertheless aimed at the public a little too deliberately. "In my readings," he informs us, "I had an opportunity to study and find out for myself what the public wants, and afterwards I would endeavour to use the knowledge gained in my writing." The public wants, he concluded, "simple sentiments that come from the heart" and not intellectual excellence; he must therefore compose poems, he says expressively, "simply heart high."

This he did. Even his poems in conventional English, of which he wrote not a few, fail to rise above simple sentiments; there is scarcely a trace of thought or passion in even so pleasantly sentimental a poem as *An Old Sweetheart of Mine*. Nor, in all his dialect verse, is there more than a suggestion here and there of the profundity of emotion—not to mention profundity of thought—of the great poets. He wrote of the everyday life of rustic America, of "home" and "old times,"—magic words with him,—of childhood, of simple well-tried pleasures and sensibly received pains. He had genuine sympathy for ordinary folk, for animals, for nature. In his presentation of character,—Old John Clevenger, Bee Fessler, Myle Jones's wife, and the rest of his large gallery,—he showed an understanding born of sympathy and humour; in his pictures of nature, as in *When the Frost is on the Punkin*, responsiveness and distinct vision, though to be sure he fails to go much below the physical, even the air being "so appetizin" merely. His "philosophy" is that of the prudent farmer; it is made up of the most patent truisms, though some of them are freshly worded. If there is nowhere the quality of *The Biglow Papers*, still less of Burns, there is at least a wholesomeness of mood and mind, uncommon in the restlessly brooding nineteenth century, that offers some justi-

fication for Riley's enormous vogue. Though there are capacities in the American mind and character that he does not appeal
to, it is undeniable that he appeals urgently to the normal
thoughts and feelings of the divine average.

This is not true of the last of the greater Western poets who
are no longer living—William Vaughn Moody. His small, discriminating audience regarded him as a poet of the highest
promise, whose early death was a public loss. Wholly without
the sectional point of view, he was also free from the restrictions in vision characteristic of certain decades in American life.
He was neither Middle Western nor late Victorian, but American and modern.

Born, like Riley, in Indiana, in 1869,—at the beginning of
an era of industrial development and clearer national consciousness,—the son of a steamboat captain, with English,
French, and German strains in his blood, and educated in a
New England college, Moody naturally attained a larger outlook on life than most of the poets of the half century. After
graduating from Harvard, he stayed in Cambridge for two
years, and then, in 1895, returned to the Middle West as instructor in English in the University of Chicago. Although
conscientious as a teacher, he chafed at the routine,—measuring
time in terms of committee meetings and quantities of "themes,"
—and at his environment, finding himself, he soon reported,
"fanatically homesick for civilization," though it is doubtful
whether he could have found a congenial post as a teacher
anywhere in the "booming" America of his day. Fond of outdoor activity, he found relief in swimming, bicycling, and
walking in this country and abroad, from Arizona to Greece.
He was a vigorously sensuous, full-blooded, ruddy-faced,
youthful poet, intensely curious of experience, ardently devoted to "It," his term for "the sum total of all that is beautiful and worthy of loyalty in the world"—chief of all, poetry
as an expression of life. The decisions of his life prove the
sincerity of this devotion. Achieving a sudden success through
his drama *The Great Divide*,[1] he was besieged by publishers who
offered him as much as fifty thousand dollars for the play in the
form of a novel; but he did not believe in "novelization" and
preferred to follow his own artistic bent. So, too, after vir-

[1] See Book III, Chap. XVIII.

tually severing his connection with the University of Chicago in 1902, when offered a professorship at full salary if he would lecture for a single quarter annually, he declined, valuing his independence so highly that he accepted hardship with it, rather than a prosperous subjection.

Before his early death in 1910 he had made his way to a mode of expression quite his own. His imitative and experimental period extended into his manhood years; it took this florid Westerner, for example, a curiously long time to pass from the shadow of Rossetti, and his debt to Browning is visible in some of his best work. Answering a friend's criticism of *Wilding Flower* (later named *Heart's Wild Flower*), he said: "'Paltry roof' is paltry I freely admit; 'wind-control' and 'moonward melodist' are rococo as hell." The remark has the downrightness, with a trace of humour, which is common in his letters, and which helped him to become more than a moonward melodist. The same letter contains another sentence that suggests at once the strength and the weakness of his work. "I think you are not tolerant enough for the instinct for conquest in language, the attempt to push out its boundaries, to win for it continually some new swiftness, some rare compression, to distill from it a more opaline drop." This eagerness of expression gives vitality to all of Moody's work; but it also gives it a sense of effort, of straining to obtain an intensity that must, after all, come inevitably and easily.

In his dramas in blank verse, this characteristic eagerness dominates not only style but theme. His trilogy of poetic dramas aims to do no less than to reveal the need of God to man and of man to God. *The Fire-Bringer* (1904) is concerned with the Prometheus legend; *The Masque of Judgment* (1900) with the eventual meaning to God of his decree of man's destruction; and *The Death of Eve* (1901), unhappily never completed, was to show the impossibility of separation. The plan is stupendous; there is perhaps none greater in literature; but certainly it may be questioned whether the problem is soluble at all, and if it is, whether Moody was the poet needed for so lofty an enterprise. It is true that the fragmentary member of the trilogy is finely done, in a manner grandly simple despite the complex and murky emotional states evolved, and that the conception of Eve as the instrument of reconciliation between man and God is carried out with impressive power. Still, it cannot be denied that the other dramas are vague and inchoate, lacking the lucidity and impact of the true classic, and that, therefore, even if Moody might have improved the trilogy later, his actual accomplishment is, at best, splendidly tentative and grandiose.

Possibly the lyrics contained in these dramas are the best part of them; and it is in the lyric, unquestionably, that Moody did his most important work. Dainty lyricism was beyond his sober touch; and the commonplace theme never appealed to him, any more than the commonplace mode of expression. Given a substantial conception, however, he could use his intellectual power and his large emotional reservoirs in such a manner as to repel the plain man and delight the lover, say, of Shelley and Browning. Such poems as *Gloucester Moors*, with its vivid sense of the earth sailing through space like a gallant ship with a dubious crew (a conception previously used more than once by Sill), and *The Menagerie*, with its grimly humorous description of the evolutionary ancestors of "A little man in trousers, slightly jagged," are of a kind unmatched in American poetry. They have the sophisticated, questioning spirit of the new century. Closer to tradition are his patriotic poems, the *Ode in Time of Hesitation*, written in 1900 when the relation of the United States to the former Spanish colonies was in question, and the lines *On a Soldier Fallen in the Philippines*, with its desolating sense of a dishonourable cause. These poems appeared when the public was warmly debating the questions they deal with. To that fact, and to their beauty and assured tone, is owing the thrill that welcomed them, as if a new Lowell had come to voice our conscience in memorable verse. But they form a tiny group; and indeed the total bulk of Moody's lyrics is inconsiderable. What he might have done had he not been cut off at the height of his powers it is vain to wonder.

Moody brings us to the new century, in years and in spirit. In his work is a turbulence unknown in the facile and edifying poetry of our "albuminous" Victorian era, a passionate discontent with old forms, old themes, old thoughts. In the twentieth century our poets have more and more believed that, if their work was to be vital, they must return to the laboratory of poetry to study afresh the raw materials and to seek a new formula in accord with the time spirit. In this effort they have naturally derived more help from Whitman, a poet *in posse*, than from anyone else. To him, and of course to others, they owe their usual form, free verse, and their point of view, that of an exaggerated individualism, often combined with humanitarian emotion and an intimate feeling for nature. But though their intellectual outlook is still in the main that of Whitman's century, their poetic energy is so fresh and vital that it may reasonably be expected to prelude a new vision of life adequate to the new era. From the point of view of a conventional public, the new poetry has been bizarre and not always sincere; but the new poets themselves—to mention only Edwin Arlington Robinson, Robert Frost, Vachel Lindsay, Edgar Lee Masters, Carl Sandburg, and Amy Lowell, of the many poets who may be studied in W. S. Braithwaite's annual anthologies—have for the most part honestly sought to see life more truly than it has been envisaged by the poets of the past, and to reveal their findings to other men by means of a form entirely dictated by the substance—the very substance externalized. Recent years have brought forth an extraordinary number of poets, a great mass of verse, not a few remarkable poems, and the promise of still higher achievement when the new poetry has found its intellectual and artistic standards through some kind of genuine discipline.

Vol.

CHAPTER XI

The Later Novel: Howells

THE romance of the school of Cooper was not only falling into disuse among most writers of capacity at the time of his death but was rapidly descending into the hands of fertile hacks who for fifty years were to hold an immense audience without more than barely deserving a history. It was in that very year (1851) that Robert Bonner bought the New York *Ledger* and began to make it the congenial home of a sensationalism which, hitherto most nearly anticipated by such a romancer as Joseph Holt Ingraham, reached unsurpassable dimensions with the prolific Sylvanus Cobb, Jr. From the *Ledger* no step in advance had to be taken by the inventors of the "dime novel," which was started upon its long career by the publishing firm of Beadle and Adams of New York in 1860.[1] Edward S. Ellis's *Seth Jones or The Captive of the Frontier* (1860), one of the earliest of the sort, its hero formerly a scout under Ethan Allen but now adventuring in Western New York, sold over 600,000 copies in half a dozen languages. Though no other single dime novel was perhaps ever so popular, the type prospered, depending almost exclusively upon native authors and native material: first the old frontier of Cooper and then the trans-Mississippi region, with its Indians, its Mexicans, its bandits, its troopers, and above all, its cowboys, among whom "Buffalo Bill" (Col. William F. Cody) achieved a primacy much like that of Daniel Boone among the older order of scouts. Cheap, conventional, hasty,—Albert W. Aiken long averaged one such novel a week, and Col. Ingram Prentiss produced in all over

[1] Charles M. Harvey, *The Dime Novel in American Life*, *Atlantic*, July, 1907.

66

six hundred,—they were exciting, innocent enough, and scrupulously devoted to the doctrines of poetic justice, but they lacked all distinction, and Frank Norris could justly grieve that the epic days of Western settlement found only such tawdry Homers. In the fourth quarter of the century the detective story rivalled the frontier tale; after 1900, both, though reduced to the price of five cents apiece, gave way before the still more exciting and easily comprehended moving picture.

One successor of Cooper, however, upheld for a time the dignity of old-fashioned romance. John Esten Cooke (1830–8ʊ,, born in the Valley of Virginia and brought up in Richmond, cherished a passion as intense as Simms's for his native state and deliberately set out to celebrate its past and its beauty. *Leather Stocking and Silk* (1854) and *The Last of the Foresters* (1856), both narratives of life in the Valley, recall Cooper by more than their titles; but in *The Youth of Jefferson* (1854), still more in *The Virginia Comedians* (1854) and its sequel *Henry St. John, Gentleman* (1859), Cooke seems as completely Virginian as Beverley Tucker[1] before him, though less stately in his tread. All three of these novels have their scenes laid in Williamsburg, the old capital of the Dominion; they reproduce a society strangely made up of luxury, daintiness, elegance, penury, ugliness, brutality. At times the dialogue of Cooke's impetuous cavaliers and merry girls nearly catches the flavour of the Forest of Arden, but there is generally something stilted in their speech or behaviour that spoils the gay illusion. Nevertheless, *The Virginia Comedians* may justly be called the best Virginia novel of the old régime, unless possibly *Swallow Barn*[2] should be excepted, for reality as well as for colour and spirit. During the Civil War Cooke fought, as captain of cavalry, under Stuart, and had experiences which he afterwards turned to use in a series of Confederate romances, most notable of which is *Surry of Eagle's Nest* (1866). But in this and in the related tales *Hilt to Hilt* (1869) and *Mohun* (1869), as well as in numerous later novels, he continued to practice an old manner which grew steadily more archaic as the realists gained ground. Towards the end of his life he participated, without changing his habits, in the revival of the historical romance which began

[1] See Book II, Chap. VII.　　　　　　　　　　　*Ibid.*

in the eighties; but his pleasant, plaintive *My Lady Poka-hontas* (1885) cannot really compare for charm with his *Virginia A History of the People* (1883), a high-minded and fascinating work. Cooke was the last of Cooper's school; but he was also the first of those who contributed to the poetic idealization of the antebellum South which has been one of the most prominent aspects of American fiction since 1865.

Less close to Cooper was another novelist who fought in the Civil War, and gave his life in one of the earliest battles, Theodore Winthrop (1828–61). Of a stock as eminent in New England and New York as Cooke's in Virginia, Winthrop had a more cosmopolitan upbringing than Cooke: after Yale he travelled in Europe, in the American tropics, in California while the gold fever was still new, and in the North-west. His work at first found so delayed a favour with publishers that his books were all posthumous—*Cecil Dreeme* (1861), *John Brent* (1862), *Edwin Brothertoft* (1862), *The Canoe and the Saddle* (1863), and *Life in the Open Air and Other Papers* (1863).[1] Time might, it is urged, have made Winthrop the legitimate successor of Hawthorne, but in fact he progressed little beyond the qualities of Brockden Brown, whom he considerably resembles in his strenuous nativism, his melodramatic plots, his abnormal characters, his command over the mysterious, and his breathless style. Of the three novels *John Brent* is easily the most interesting by reason of its vigorous narrative of adventures in the Far West, at that time a region still barely touched by fiction, and its magnificent hero, the black horse Don Fulano. That Winthrop's real talent looked forward in this direction rather than backward to Hawthorne appears still more clearly from *The Canoe and the Saddle*, a fresh, vivid, amusing, and truthful record of his own journey across the Cascade Mountains, and an established classic of the North-west. His death, however, prevented further achievement, and the Pacific Coast had to wait for Mark Twain[2] and Bret Harte.[3]

What chiefly characterized American fiction of the decade 1850–60, leaving out of account romancers like Hawthorne,

---

[1] *Mr. Waddy's Return*, written earliest of all, was first published in 1904, edited and condensed by Burton Egbert Stevenson.

[2] See Book III, Chap. VIII.

[3] See Book III, Chap. VI.

Cooke, and Winthrop, was domestic sentimentalism, which for a time attained a hearing rare in literary history, and produced one novel of enormous influence and reputation. In that decade flowered Mrs. E. D. E. N. Southworth, Mary Jane Holmes, and Augusta Jane Evans (Wilson), all more or less in the *Charlotte Temple* tradition; Anne and Susan Warner[1] and Maria S. Cummins, pious historians of precocious young girls; and—not so far above them—the almost equally tender and tearful Donald Grant Mitchell ("Ik Marvel")[2] and George William Curtis,[3] young men who, however, afterwards took themselves to sterner tasks. Professor Ingraham gave up his blood-and-thunder, became a clergyman, and wrote the long-popular biblical romance *The Prince of the House of David* (1855). Indeed, the decade was eminently clerical, and though Mitchell and Curtis might recall Irving and Thackeray respectively, they were less representative than the most effective writer of the whole movement, who was daughter, sister, wife, and mother of clergymen.

Harriet Beecher, born in Litchfield, Connecticut, 14 June, 1811, passed her childhood and girlhood, indeed practically her entire life, in an atmosphere of piety which, much as she eventually lost of its original Calvinistic rigour, not only indoctrinated her with orthodox opinions but furnished her with an intensely evangelical point of view and a sort of Scriptural eloquence. Her youth was spent in a more diversified world than might be thought: from her mother's people, who were emphatically High Church and, in spite of the Revolution, some of them still Tory at heart, she learned a faith and ritual less austere than that of her father, Lyman Beecher[4]; she had good teaching at the Litchfield Academy, especially in composition; like all her family, she was highly susceptible to external nature and passionately acquainted with the lovely Litchfield hills; she read very widely, and not only theology, of which she read too much for her happiness, but the accepted secular authors of the eighteenth century, as well as Burns and Byron and Scott. At the same time, she justified her Beecher lineage by her ready adaptation to the actual conditions under which she lived during Lyman Beecher's pastorates

---

[1] See Book III, Chap. VII.   [2] See Book III, Chap. XIII.   [3] *Ibid.*
[4] See Book II, Chap. XXII.

in Litchfield and Boston, and during her own career as pupil and then teacher in the school conducted at Hartford by her strong but morbid sister Catherine. Although Harriet Beecher was still a thorough child of New England when she went, in 1832, to live in Cincinnati, to which her father had been called as president of the Lane Theological Seminary, and although her earliest sketches and tales, collected in a volume called *The Mayflower* (1843), deal largely with memories of her old home set down with an exile's affection, she grew rapidly in knowledge and experience. Married in 1836 to Professor Calvin E. Stowe of the Seminary, mother by 1850 of seven children, she returned in that year to Brunswick, Maine, where Professor Stowe had accepted a position in Bowdoin College. There, deeply stirred by the passing of the Fugitive Slave Law, she began *Uncle Tom's Cabin; or, Life among the Lowly*, which ran as a serial in *The National Era* of Washington from June, 1851, to April, 1852, and then, on its appearance in two volumes in March, 1852, met with a popular reception never before or since accorded to a novel. Its sales went to the millions. Over five hundred thousand Englishwomen signed an address of thanks to the author; Scotland raised a thousand pounds by a penny offering among its poorest people to help free the slaves; in France and Germany the book was everywhere read and discussed; while there were Russians who emancipated their serfs out of the pity which the tale aroused. In the United States, thanks in part to the stage,[1] which produced a version as early as September, 1852, the piece belongs not only to literature but to folklore.

That *Uncle Tom's Cabin* stands higher in the history of reform than in the history of the art of fiction no one needs to say again. Dickens, Kingsley, and Mrs. Gaskell had already set the novel to humanitarian tunes, and Mrs. Stowe did not have to invent a type. She had, however, no particular foreign master, not even Scott, all of whose historical romances she had been reading just before she began *Uncle Tom*. Instead she adhered to the native tradition, which went back to the eighteenth century, of sentimental, pious, instructive narratives written by women chiefly for women. Leave out the merely domestic elements of the book—slave families

---

[1] See above, Vol. I, p. 227.

broken up by sale, ailing and dying children, negro women at the mercy of their masters, white households which at the best are slovenly and extravagant by reason of irresponsible servants—and little remains. To understand why the story touched the world so deeply it is necessary to understand how tense the struggle over slavery had grown, how thickly charged was the moral atmosphere awaiting a fatal spark. But the mere fact of an audience already prepared will not explain the mystery of a work which shook a powerful institution and which, for all its defects of taste and style and construction, still has amazing power. Richard Hildreth's[1] *The Slave; or Memoirs of Archy Moore* (1836) and Mrs. M. V. Victor's once popular "dime novel" *Maum Guinea; or, Christmas among the Slaves* (1861) no longer move. They both lack the ringing voice, the swiftness, the fullness, the humour, the authentic passion of the greater book.

It has often been pointed out that Mrs. Stowe did not mean to be sectional, that she deliberately made her chief villain a New Englander, and that she expected to be blamed less by the South than by the North, which she thought peculiarly guilty because it tolerated slavery without the excuse either of habit or of interest. Bitterly attacked by Southerners of all sorts, however, she defended herself with *A Key to Uncle Tom's Cabin; Presenting the Original Facts and Documents upon which the Story is Founded* (1853), and then, after a triumphant visit to Europe and a removal to Andover, essayed another novel to illustrate the evil effects of slavery especially upon the whites. *Dred; A Tale of the Great Dismal Swamp* (1856)[2] has had its critical partisans, but posterity has not sustained them. Grave faults of construction, slight knowledge of the scene (North Carolina), a less simple and compact story than in *Uncle Tom's Cabin*, and a larger share of disquisition,—these weigh the book down, and most readers carry away only fragmentary memories, of Dred's thunderous eloquence, of Tom Gordon's shameless abuse of his power as master, and of Old Tiff's grotesque and beautiful fidelity.

After *Dred* Mrs. Stowe wrote no more anti-slavery novels, although during the Civil War she sent to the women of Eng-

[1] See Book II, Chap. xvii.
[2] Also known as *Nina Gordon* from the English title.

land an open letter reminding them that they, so many of whom now sympathized with the defenders of slavery, had less than ten years ago hailed *Uncle Tom's Cabin* as a mighty stroke for justice and freedom. A considerable part of her later life (she died 1 July, 1896) was spent in Florida, where she had taken a plantation on the St. John's River for the double purpose of establishing there as a planter one of her sons who had been wounded at Gettysburg and of assisting the freedmen, about whom and their relation to the former masters she had more enlightened views than were then generally current in the North. Now an international figure, she let her pen respond too facilely to the many demands made upon it: she wrote numerous didactic and religious essays and tales, particularly attentive to the follies of fashionable New York society, in which she had had little experience; she was chosen by Lady Byron to publish the most serious charges ever brought against the poet. In another department of her work, however, Mrs. Stowe stood on surer ground, and her novels of New England life—particularly *The Minister's Wooing* (1859), *The Pearl of Orr's Island* (1862), *Oldtown Folks* (1869), *Poganuc People* (1878)—cannot go unmentioned.

Weak in structure and sentimental she remained. Her heroines wrestle with problems of conscience happily alien to all but a few New England and Noncomformist British bosoms; her bold seducers, like Ellery Davenport in *Oldtown Folks* and Aaron Burr in *The Minister's Wooing*, are villains to frighten schoolgirls; she writes always as from the pulpit, or at least the parsonage. But where no abstract idea governs her she can be direct, accurate, and convincing. The earlier chapters of *The Pearl of Orr's Island* must be counted, as Whittier thought, among the purest, truest idyls of New England. It is harder now to agree with Lowell in placing *The Minister's Wooing* first among her novels, and yet no other imaginative treatment so well sets forth the strange, dusky old Puritan world of the later eighteenth century, when Newport was the centre at once of Hopkinsian divinity[1] and the African slave trade. Mrs. Stowe wisely did not put on the airs of an historical romancer but wrote like a contemporary of the earlier Newport with an added flavour from her own youthful recollections.

[1] See Book II, Chap. xxii.

This flavour was indispensable to her. When her memory of the New England she had known in her girlhood and had loved so truly that Cotton Mather's *Magnolia* had seemed "wonderful stories . . . that made me feel the very ground I trod on to be consecrated by some special dealing of God's providence,"—when this memory worked freely and humorously upon materials which it was enough merely to remember and set down, she was at her later best. These conditions she most fully realized in *Poganuc People*, crisp, sweet, spare (for her), never quite sufficiently praised, and in *Oldtown Folks*, like the other a series of sketches rather than a novel, but—perhaps all the more because of that—still outstanding, for fidelity and point, among the innumerable stories dealing with New England.

Adaptable to literary as to other circumstances, Mrs. Stowe had actually in *Oldtown Folks* fallen in with the imperious current proceeding from the example of Bret Harte, whose *Luck of Roaring Camp* stands at the very headwaters of American "local colour" fiction and largely gave it its direction. Elsewhere in this history that movement, so far as it concerns the short story, its chief form, has been traced[1]; in the novel a similar fondness for local manners and types appeared, but not so prompt a revolution in method, for the good reason that most writers who followed Bret Harte followed him in the dimensions of their work as well as in its subjects, and left the novel standing for a few years a little out of the central channel of imaginative production. Domestic sentimentalism, of course, did not noticeably abate, carried on with large popular success by Josiah Gilbert Holland (1819–81) of Massachusetts and Edward Payson Roe (1838–88) of New York until nearly the end of the century, when others took up the useful burden. Both Holland and Roe were clergymen, a sign that the old suspicion of the novel was nearly dead, even among those petty sects and sectarians that so long feared the effects of it. Holland, whose first novel had appeared in 1857, was popular moralist and poet[2] as well as novelist and first editor of *Scribner's Magazine* (founded 1870); but Roe contented himself with fiction. Chaplain of cavalry and of one of the Federal hospitals during the Civil War, he

---

[1] See Book III, Chap. VI.   [2] See Book III, Chap. X.

later gave up the ministry in the firm conviction that he could reach thousands with novels and only hundreds with his voice. His simple formula included: first, some topical material, historical event, or current issue; second, characters and incidents selected directly from his personal observation or from newspapers; third, an abundance of "nature" descriptions with much praise of the rural virtues; and fourth, plots concerned almost invariably, and not very deviously, with the simultaneous pursuit of wives, fortunes, and salvation. *Barriers Burned Away* (1872), *The Opening of a Chestnut Burr* (1874), and *Without a Home* (1881) are said to have been his most widely read books.

The greatest, however, and practically the ultimate victory over village opposition to the novel was won by *Ben-Hur A Tale of the Christ* (1880), a book of larger pretension and broader scope than any of Roe's or Holland's modest narratives, the only American novel, indeed, which can be compared with *Uncle Tom's Cabin* as a true folk possession.[1] Its author, Gen. Lew Wallace (1827–1905), an Indiana lawyer, a soldier in both the Mexican and the Civil War, had already published *The Fair God* (1873), an elaborate romance of the conquest of Mexico. A chance conversation with the notorious popular skeptic Col. Robert G. Ingersoll led Wallace to researches into the character and doctrines of Jesus which not only convinced him but bore further fruit in a tale which thousands have read who have read no other novel except perhaps *Uncle Tom's Cabin* and have hardly thought of either as a novel at all, and through which still more thousands know the geography, ethnology, and customs of first-century Judaea and Antioch as through no other source. Without doubt the outstanding element in the story is the revenge of Ben-Hur upon his false friend Messala, a revenge which takes the Prince of Jerusalem through the galleys and the palaestra and which leaves Messala, after the thrilling episode of the chariot race, crippled and stripped of his fortune. And yet, following even such pagan deeds, Ben-Hur's discovery that he cannot serve the Messiah with the sword does not quite seem an anticlimax, though the conclusion, dealing with the Passion, like the introductory

---

[1] An edition numbering a million copies was ordered by a Chicago mail order house in 1913 and promptly distributed.

chapters on the meeting of the Magi, falls somewhat below the level of the revenge theme in energy and simplicity. Compared with other romances of this sort, however, with William Ware's[1] or Ingraham's, for instance, *Ben-Hur* easily passes them all, by a vitality which has a touch of genius. It passes, too, Wallace's third romance, written while he was ambassador to Turkey, *The Prince of India or Why Constantinople Fell* (1893), a long, dull romance with the Wandering Jew as principal figure.

Edward Eggleston (1837–1902), a clergyman like Holland and Roe, and like General Wallace a native of Indiana, though nourished in the school which made the domestic-sentimental-pious romance the dominant type of fiction between 1850 and 1870, must yet be considered the pioneer figure in the new realism which succeeded it in the eighties. As a Methodist on the frontier he had been brought up, though of cultivated Virginia stock, to think novels and all such works of the imagination evil things, but his diversified experience as an itinerant preacher, or "circuit rider," and as editor and journalist, his wholesome religion, and the studious habit which eventually made him a sound historical scholar, took him out of these narrow channels of opinion. It is highly significant that whereas Mrs. Stowe or her followers would have thought of themselves as writing fiction considerably for the sake of its moral consequences, Eggleston, having read Taine's *Art in the Netherlands,*[2] undertook to portray the life of southern Indiana in the faithful, undoctrinaire spirit of a Dutch painter. His first novel, *The Hoosier Schoolmaster* (1871), remains his most famous. Indiana's singularities had already been exposed by Bayard Rush Hall ("Robert Carlton") in *The New Purchase* (1855), and there was growing up a considerable literature[3] reporting

that curious poor-whitey race which is called "tar-heel" in the northern Carolina, "sand-hiller" in the southern, "corn-cracker" in Kentucky, "yahoo" in Mississippi, and in California "Pike" . . . the Hoosiers of the dark regions of Indiana and the Egyptians of southern Illinois.[4]

---

[1] See Book II, Chap. VII.   [2] Published in English at New York in 1871.
[3] See *The Discovery of Pike County* in F. L. Pattee's *American Literature since 1870* (1915).
[4] *Roxy*, Chap. XXVI.

All Eggleston's essential novels are concerned with this phase of American life, whatever the scene: Indiana in *The Hoosier Schoolmaster*, *The End of the World* (1872), and *Roxy* (1878); Ohio in *The Circuit Rider* (1874); Illinois in *The Graysons* (1887); Minnesota in *The Mystery of Metropolisville* (1873). Light is thrown upon his aims in fiction by the fact that he subsequently aspired to write "A History of Life in the United States," which he carried through two erudite, humane, and graceful volumes.[1] His Hoosier novels, simple in plot, clear-cut in characterization, concise and lucid in language, unwaveringly accurate in their setting, manners, and dialect, are indispensable documents, even finished chapters, for his uncompleted masterpiece. The *Schoolmaster*, as first in the field and fresh and pointed, still remains most famous; but *Roxy* is perhaps most interesting of them all, and *The Circuit Rider* the most informing. *The Graysons* deserves credit for the reserve with which it admits the youthful Lincoln into its narrative, uses him at a crucial moment, and then lets him withdraw without one hint of his future greatness. If the morals of these tales seem a little easy to read, they nevertheless lack all that is sentimental, strained, or perfervid. Without Mrs. Stowe's rush of narrative, neither has Eggleston her verbosity. Even where, in his fidelity to violent frontier conditions, his incidents seem melodramatic, the handling is sure and direct, for the reason, as he says of *The Circuit Rider*, that whatever is incredible in the story is true. No novelist is more candid, few more convincing. With greater range and fire he might have been an international figure as well as the earliest American realist whose work is still remembered.[2]

It was perhaps a certain bareness in Middle Western life, lacking both the longer memories of the Atlantic States and the splendid golden expectations of California, that thus early established in the upper Mississippi valley the realistic tradition which descends unbroken through the work of Eggleston, E. W. Howe, Hamlin Garland, and Edgar Lee Masters.

[1] See Book II, Chap. xv.
[2] Mention should be made here of Col. John W. De Forest (1826–1906), who has not deserved that his novels should be forgotten as they have been, even *Miss Ravenel's Conversion from Secession to Loyalty* (1867), which survives only in the thoroughly merited praise of W. D. Howells (*My Literary Passions*, 1895, p. 233), but which still seems strong and natural.

From the Middle West, too, came the principal exponent of native realism, in himself almost an entire literary movement, almost an academy. William Dean Howells was born at Martin's Ferry, Ohio, 1 March, 1837, the grandson of a Welsh Quaker and the son of a country printer and editor. Like his friend Mark Twain he saw little of schools and nothing of colleges, and like him he got his systematic literary training from enforced duties as a printer and journalist. But, unlike Mark Twain, he fell as naturally into the best classical traditions as Goldsmith or Irving, who, with Cervantes, earliest delighted him. In *My Literary Passions* Howells has delicately recorded the development of his taste. At first he desired to write verse, and devoted months to imitating Pope in a youthful fanaticism for regularity and exactness. From this worship he turned, at about sixteen, to Shakespeare, particularly to the histories; then to Chaucer, admired for his sense of earth in human life; and to Dickens, whose magic, Howells saw, was rough. Macaulay taught him to like criticism and furnished him an early model of prose style. Thackeray, Longfellow, Tennyson followed in due course. Having taught himself some Latin and Greek and more French and Spanish, Howells took up German and came under the spell of Heine, who dominated him longer than any other author and who showed him once for all that the dialect and subjects of literature should be the dialect and facts of life.

Poems in the manner of Heine won Howells a place in the *Atlantic*, then the very zenith of his aspiration, and in 1860 he undertook the reverent pilgrimage to New England which he recounts with such winning grace in *Literary Friends and Acquaintance*. Already a journalist of promise, and something of a poet, he made friends wherever he went and was reconfirmed in his literary ambitions. At the outbreak of the Civil War appointed United States consul at Venice, married at Paris in 1862 to Miss Elinor G. Mead of Vermont, he spent four years of almost undisturbed leisure in studying Italian literature, notably Dante, as the great authoritative voice of an age, and Goldoni, whom Howells called "the first of the realists." In Italy, though he wrote poetry for the most part, he formed the habit of close, sympathetic, humorous observation and discovered the ripe, easy style which made him, beginning with

Venetian Life (1866) and *Italian Journeys* (1867), one of the happiest of our literary travellers. From such work he moved, by the avenue of journalism, only gradually to fiction. On his return to the United States in 1865 he became, first, editorial contributor to *The Nation* for a few months, and then assistant editor and editor of the *Atlantic* until 1881.

The literary notices which he wrote for the *Atlantic* during these years of preparation would show, had he written nothing else, how strong and steady was his drift toward his mature creed. Not alone by deliberate thought nor even by the stimulus of polemic was he carried forward, but rather by a natural process of growth which, more than an artistic matter, included his entire philosophy. From his childhood he had been intensely humane—sensitive and charitable. This humaneness now revealed itself as a passionate love for the truth of human life and a suspicion, a quiet scorn, of those romantic dreams and superstitious exaggerations by which less contented lovers of life try to enrich it or to escape it. "Ah! poor Real Life," he wrote in his first novel, "can I make others share the delight I find in thy foolish and insipid face?" Perhaps *Their Wedding Journey* (1871) ought hardly to be called a novel, but it is a valuable Howells document in its zeal for common actuality and in its method, so nearly that of his travel books. *A Chance Acquaintance* (1873), more strictly a novel, for the first time showed that Howells could not only report customs and sketch characters felicitously but could also organize a plot with delicate skill. A young Bostonian, passionately in love with an intelligent but unsophisticated inland girl, who returns his love, is so little able to overcome his ingrained provincial snobbishness that he steadily condescends to her until in the end he suddenly sees, as she sees, that he has played an ignoble and vulgar part which convincingly separates them. Nothing could be more subtle than the turn by which their relative positions are reversed. The style of *A Chance Acquaintance*, while not more graceful than that of Howells's earlier books, is more assured and crisp. The central idea is clearly conceived and the outlines sharp without being in any way cruel or cynical. The descriptions are exquisite, the dialogue both natural and revealing, and over and through all is a lambent mirth, an undeceived kindliness of wisdom, which was to remain his essential quality.

In 1869 he had published a metrical novel, *No Love Lost*, and in 1871 a volume of *Suburban Sketches;* he continued to write criticism and later began to write farces; but an increasing share of his energy now went to novels. The study of the conflict between different manners or grades of sophistication, taken up at about the same time by Henry James,[1] concerned Howells largely, and appears in *A Foregone Conclusion* (1875), *The Lady of the Aroostook* (1879), and *A Fearful Responsibility* (1881). Writing of spiritualism and Shakerism in *An Undiscovered Country* (1880), he made clear his suspicion of those types of otherworldliness. And in 1882, with the publication of *A Modern Instance*, Howells assumed his proper rank as the chief native American realist.

The superiority of this book to all that had gone before can less justly be said to lie in its firmer grasp of its materials, for Howells from the first was extraordinarily sure of grasp, than in its larger control of larger materials. It has a richer timbre, a graver, deeper tone. Marcia Gaylord, the most passionate of all his heroines, is of all of them the most clearly yet lovingly conceived and elaborated. In the career of her husband, Bartley J. Hubbard, Howells accomplishes the difficult feat of tracing a metamorphosis, the increase of selfishness and vanity, fed in this case by Marcia's very devotion, into monstrous growths of evil without a redeeming tincture even of boldness—mere contemptibility. The process seems as simple as arithmetic, but, like all genuine growth, it actually resists analysis. The winter scenes of the earlier chapters, faithful and vivid beyond any prose which had yet been written about New England, drawn with an eye intensely on the fact, have still the larger bearings of a criticism of American village life in general. The subsequent adventures of the Hubbards in Boston, though so intensely local in setting and incident, are applicable everywhere. Squire Gaylord's arraignment of his son-in-law in the Indiana courtroom vibrates with a passion seldom met in Howells; and Bartley's virtual offer of his former wife to his former friend belongs with the unforgettable, unforgivable basenesses in fiction. After these episodes, however, it

[1] See Book III. Chap. XII.

must be owned that an anticlimax follows in Halleck's discovery that his New England conscience will now forever hold him from Marcia because he had loved her before she was free.

Between 1881, when Howells resigned from the *Atlantic*, and 1886, when he began to write for *Harper's*, he had some years of leisure, particularly signalized by the publication in 1884 of the novel which brought him to the height of his reputation as well as of his art. The theme of *The Rise of Silas Lapham* is the universal one, very dear in a republic, of the rising fortunes of a man who has no aid but virtue and capacity. Lapham, a country-bred, "self-made" Vermonter, appears when he has already achieved wealth, and finds himself drawn, involuntarily enough, into the more difficult task of adjusting himself and his family to the manners of fastidious Boston. A writer primarily satirical might have been contented to make game of the situation. Howells, keenly as he sets forth the conflict of standards, goes beyond satire to a depth of meaning which comes only from a profound understanding of the part which artificial distinctions play in human life and a mellow pity that such little things can have such large consequences of pain and error. The conflict, however, while constantly pervasive in the book, does not usurp the action; the Lapham family has serious concerns that might arise in any social stratum. Most intense and dramatic of these is the fact that the suitor of one daughter is believed by the whole family to be in love with the other until the very moment of his declaration. The distress into which they are thrown is presented with a degree of comprehension rare in any novel, and here matched with a common sense which rises to something half-inspired in Lapham's perception—reduced to words, however, by a friendly clergyman—that in such a case superfluous self-sacrifice would be morbid and that, since none is guilty, one had better suffer than three. A certain rightness and soundness of feeling, indeed, govern the entire narrative. As it proceeds, as Lapham falls into heavy business vicissitudes and finally to comparative poverty again, and yet all the time rises in spiritual worth, the record steadily grows in that dignity and significance which, according to Howells's creed, is founded only on absolute truth.

Silas Lapham marked the culmination of Howells's art,

approached the next year in the exquisite interlude *Indian Summer*, gayly, lightly, sweetly, pungently narrating the loves of a man of forty, and not quite approached in *The Minister's Charge* (1887), which shows a homespun poet moving in the direction of comfortable prose. But Howells had not yet shaped his final philosophy, which grew up within him after he had left Boston for New York in 1886 and had established his connection with *Harper's Magazine*. Again, as from the *Atlantic* literary notices, light falls upon his growth from the monthly articles which he wrote for "The Editor's Study" between 1886 and 1891. Chiefly discussions of current books, concerned with poetry, history, biography nearly as much as with fiction, these essays remarkably encouraged the growth of realism in America, and most eloquently commended to native readers such Latin realists as Valera, Valdés, Galdós, and Verga, and the great Russians Turgenev, Dostoevsky, and Tolstoy. It will not do to say that these foreign realists moulded Howells, for his development, whatever his readiness to assimilate, was always from within outward, but it helps to distinguish between the Howells who lived before 1886 and the one who lived after that date, to say that the earlier man had one of his supreme literary passions for the art of Turgenev, and that the later Howells, knowing Tolstoy, had become impatient of even the most secret artifice. For Tolstoy was Howells's great passion. "As much as one merely human being can help another I believe," said Howells, "that he has helped me; he has not influenced me in æsthetics only, but in ethics, too, so that I can never again see life in the way I saw it before I knew him." Tolstoy's novels seemed to Howells as perfect as his doctrine. "To my thinking they transcend in truth, which is the highest beauty, all other works of fiction that have been written. . . . [He] has a method which not only seems without artifice, but is so."

This was some ten years after Howells had first read Tolstoy, ten years during which, in spite of Tolstoy's example, he had not at all reverted to the preacher but had published many merry farces and had begun to be sunnily reminiscent in *A Boy's Town* (1890). But though too much himself to be converted from his artistic practice, Howells had broadened his field and deepened his inquiries. *A Hazard of New Fortunes*

(1889), in which Basil and Isabel March, the bridal couple of *Their Wedding Journey*, now grown middle aged, give up Boston, as Howells had himself recently done, for a future in New York, is not content to point out merely the unfamiliar fashions of life which they meet but is full of conscience regarding certain evils of the modern social order. Or rather, Howells had turned from the clash of those lighter manners which belong to Comedy and had set himself to discuss the deeper manners of the race which belong to morals and religion. He wrote at a moment of hope:

We had passed through a period of strong emotioning in the direction of the humaner economics, if I may phrase it so; the rich seemed not so much to despise the poor, the poor did not so hopelessly repine. The solution of the riddle of the painful earth through the dreams of Henry George, through the dreams of Edward Bellamy, through the dreams of all the generous visionaries of the past, seemed not impossibly far off.[1]

In this mood Howells's theme compelled him so much that the story moved forward almost without his conscious agency, "though," he carefully insists, "I should not like to intimate anything mystical in the fact." *A Hazard of New Fortunes* outdoes all Howells's novels in the conduct of different groups of characters, in the superb naturalness with which now one and now another rises to the surface of the narrative and then retreats without a trace of management. New Englanders, New Yorkers, Southerners, Westerners, all appear in their true native colours, as do the most diverse ranks of society, and many professions, in their proper dress and gesture. The episode of the street-car strike, brought in near the end, dramatizes the struggle which has been heretofore in the novel rather a shadow than a fact, but Howells, artist first then partisan, employs it almost wholly as a sort of focal point to which the attention of all his characters is drawn, with the result that, having already revealed themselves generally, they are more particularly revealed in their varying degrees of sympathy for the great injustice out of which class war arises. In this manner, without extravagant emphasis,

[1] Preface dated July, 1909.

Howells judges a generation at the same time that he portrays it in the best of all novels of New York.

Howells's Tolstoyanism appears still more frankly in his two Utopian tales, *A Traveller from Altruria* (1894) and *Through the Eye of the Needle* (1907), in which he compares America with the lovely land of Altruria, where all work is honourable and servants are unknown, where capital and interest are only memories, where equality is complete, and men and women, in the midst of beauty, lead lives that are just, temperate, and kind. The stern tones of Tolstoy Howells never learned, or at least never used, for he could not lose his habitual kindness, even when he spoke most firmly. It was kindness, not timidity, however, for though he held steadily to his art he did not keep silence before even the most popular injustices. He plead for the Chicago "anarchists" and he condemned the annexation of the Philippines in clear, strong tones; no good cause lacked the support of his voice. He was extraordinarily fecund. After 1892 he succeeded George William Curtis in "The Easy Chair" of *Harper's* and wrote monthly articles which, less exclusively literary than the "Editor's Study" pieces, carried on the same tradition. His most significant critical writings, chiefly concerned with the art he himself practiced, are found in *Criticism and Fiction* (1891), *Heroines of Fiction* (1901), and *Literature and Life* (1902). Reminiscences and travels assume a still larger place in his later work. After *A Boy's Town* came *My Literary Passions* (1895), and then *Literary Friends and Acquaintance* (1900), of accounts of the classic age of Boston and Cambridge easily the best. He revisited Europe and left records in *London Films* (1905), *Certain Delightful English Towns* (1906), *Roman Holidays* (1908), *Seven English Cities* (1909), *Familiar Spanish Travels* (1913), in which he occasionally drew his matter out thin but in which he was never for a page dull, or untruthful, or sour, after the ancient habit of travellers. *My Mark Twain* (1910) is incomparably the finest of all the interpretations of Howells's great friend, while *Years of My Youth* (1916), written when the author was nearly eighty, is the work of a master whom age had made wise and left strong. In 1909 he was chosen president of the American Academy, and six years later he received

the National Institute's gold medal "for distinguished work
in fiction." He died 11 May, 1920.

The Institute rightly judged that, important as Howells is
as critic and memoir-writer, he must be considered first of all a
novelist. His later books of fiction make up a long list. That
he could produce such an array of fiction is sign enough that he
had not been overpowered by humanitarianism; a better sign
is the fact that these later novels are even kinder, gayer,
mellower than the early ones. In them his investigation moves
over a wide area, which includes the solid realism of *The Landlord at Lion's Head* (1897) and *The Kentons* (1902); the sombre
study of a crime in *The Quality of Mercy* (1892); the keen
statement of problems in *An Imperative Duty* (1892) and *The
Son of Royal Langbrith* (1904); happier topics as in *Miss
Bellard's Inspiration* (1905); and, very notably, subtle explorations of what is or what seems to be the supersensual world in
The Shadow of a Dream (1890), *Questionable Shapes* (1903)—
short stories, *Between the Dark and the Daylight* (1907)—short
stories, and *The Leatherwood God* (1916), which last, the study
of a frontier impostor who proclaims himself a god, best hints
at Howells's views of the relation between the real world which
he had so long explored and so lovingly portrayed and those
vast spaces which appear to be beyond it for the futile tempting
of religionists and romanticists.

Holding so firmly to his religion of reality, and with his
varied powers, it is not perhaps to be wondered at that Howells
produced in his fourscore books the most considerable transcript of American life yet made by one man. Nor, of course,
should it be wondered at, that in spite of his doctrine of imper-
sonality the world of America as he has set it down is full of
his benignance and noble health, never illicit or savage and
but rarely sordid. His natural gentleness and reserve, even
more than the decorous traditions of the seventies and
eighties, kept him from the violent frankness of, say, Zola,
whose books Howells thought "indecent through the facts
that they nakedly represent." What Howells invariably
practiced was a kind of selective realism, choosing his material as a sage chooses his words, decently. Most of his
stories end "happily," that is, in congenial marriages with good
expectations. He did not mind employing one favoured situ-

ation—in which a humorous husband and a serious wife find themselves responsible for a young girl during her courtship—so often as to suggest a personal experience. Not without some complaint, he nevertheless not too rebelliously accepted the modern novelist's fate of writing largely for women, a sex which in Howells's world appears as often shallow and changeful and almost always quite unreasonable. Thus limited as to subjects by his temper and his times, he was likewise limited as to treatment. On every ground he preferred to make relatively little of impassioned or tragic moments, believing that the true bulk of life is to be represented by its commonplaces. "It will not do," he wrote, speaking of the ducal palace at Weimar, "to lift either houses or men far out of the average; they become spectacles, ceremonies; they cease to have charm, to have character, which belong to the levels of life, where alone there are ease and comfort, and human nature may be itself, with all the little delightful differences repressed in those who represent and typify."[1] (The pendulum had swung far since the days when Cooper and Hawthorne repined over the democratic barrenness of American manners!) No one has written more engaging commonplaces than Howells, though perhaps something like the century which has elapsed since the death of Jane Austen—Howells's ideal among English novelists—will have to pass before the historian can be sure that work artistically flawless may be kept alive, lacking malice or intensity, by ease and grace and charm, by kind wisdom and thoughtful mirth.

Hawthorne and Mrs. Stowe, romance and sentiment, had divided first honours in American fiction during the twenty years 1850–1870; the seventies belonged primarily to the short story of the school of Bret Harte. The novel of that decade, thus a little neglected, profited in at least one respect: it ceased to be the form of fiction on which all beginners tried their pens and passed rather into the hands of men whose eyes looked a little beyond easy conquests and an immediate market. This fact, with the rapid growth of the artistic conscience in the cosmopolitanizing years which followed the Civil War, serves to explain in part the remarkable florescence, the little renaissance of fiction in the eighties.[2] The short story may specially

[1] *Their Silver Wedding Journey* (1899), chap. lx.
[2] *A Renaissance in the Eighties*, *Nation*, 12 October, 1918.

claim Bret Harte, Aldrich, Stockton, Bunner, Rose Terry Cooke, Sarah Orne Jewett, Mary E. Wilkins Freeman, Cable, Constance Fenimore Woolson, Charles Egbert Craddock, Johnston, Page, [1] and Joel Chandler Harris, [2]—though they all wrote novels of merit,—because their talents were for pungency, fancy, brevity. But to the novel of the decade three of the five major American novelists, Mark Twain, Howells, Henry James, contributed their greatest triumphs; then appeared *Ben-Hur*, for a good while rivalled in popularity by Judge Albion Winegar Tourgee's *A Fool's Errand* (1879), a fiery document upon Reconstruction in the South; and there were such diverse pieces as Edward Bellamy's much-read Utopian romance *Looking Backward* (1888), dainty exotics like Blanche Willis Howard's *Guenn A Wave on the Breton Coast* (1884) and Arthur Sherburne Hardy's *Passe Rose* (1889), E. W. Howe's grim *The Story of a Country Town* (1883), Helen Hunt Jackson's *Ramona* (1884), passionately pleading the cause of the Indians of California, Miss Woolson's *East Angels* (1886), just less than a classic, Henry Adams's[3] *Democracy* (1880) and John Hay's[4] *The Bread-Winners* (1884), excursions into fiction of two men whose largest gifts lay elsewhere, the earlier army novels of General Charles King, and the earlier detective stories of Anna Katharine Green (Rohlfs). As a rule these novels seem more deftly built than the novels of the sixties or seventies, more sophisticated. People talked somewhat less than formerly about "The Great American Novel," that strange eidolon so clearly descended from the large aspirations of men like Timothy Dwight and Joel Barlow[5] but by 1850 thought of less as an epic which should enshrine the national past than as a great prose performance reflecting the national present

In the eighties began the career of that later American writer who gave to the novel his most complete allegiance, undeterred by the vogue of briefer narratives or other forms of literature. Francis Marion Crawford, son of the sculptor Thomas Crawford and nephew of Julia Ward Howe, was born at Bagni di Lucca, Tuscany, in 1854. He prepared for college at St. Paul's School, New Hampshire, and entered Harvard,

---

[1] For these writers see Book III, Chap. VI. [2] See Book III, Chap. V.
[3] See Book III, Chap. XV. [4] See Book III, Chaps. X and XV.
[5] See Book I, Chap. IX.

but soon left it to study in Europe, successively at Cambridge, Heidelberg, and Rome. Having become interested in Sanscrit, and having lost his expectations of a fortune, he went to India and there edited *The Indian Herald* at Allahabad. In 1881 he returned to America, spent another year upon Sanscrit with Professor Lanman of Harvard, and wrote his first novel, *Mr. Isaacs* (1882), on the advice of an uncle who had been struck by Crawford's oral account of the central personage. The success of the experiment was so prompt and complete that its author recognized his vocation once for all, much as does George Wood in *The Three Fates* (1892), a novel admitted to be partly autobiographical. Crawford went to Italy in 1883, and thereafter spent most of his life at Sorrento. He still travelled, grew wealthy from the sale of his novels, became a Roman Catholic, and died in 1909.

Except that toward the end of his life he partly turned from fiction to sober—and not remarkably spirited—history, Crawford can hardly be said to have changed his methods from his earliest novel to his latest. Improvisation was his knack and forte; he wrote much and speedily. His settings he took down, for the most part, from personal observation in the many localities he knew at first hand; his characters, too, are frequently studies from actual persons. In his plots, commonly held his peculiar merit, Crawford cannot be called distinctly original: he employs much of the paraphernalia of melodrama—lost or hidden wills, forgeries, great persons in disguise, sudden legacies, physical violence; moreover, it is almost a formula with him to carry a story by natural motives until about the last third, when melodrama enters to perplex the narrative and to arouse due suspense until the triumphant and satisfying dénouement. And yet so fresh, strong, and veracious is the movement that it nearly obscures these conventional elements. Movement, indeed, not plot in the stricter sense, is Crawford's chief excellence. He could not tell a story badly, but flowed on without breaking or faltering, managing his material and disposing his characters and scenes without apparent effort, in a style always clear and bright. This lightness of movement is accompanied, perhaps accounted for, by an absence of profound ideas or of any of that rich colour of life which comes only—as in Scott, Balzac, Tolstoy—when fiction is deeply based in a native soil. As to his ideas, Crawford appears to have had few that were unusual, and at least he suspected such ideas as the substance of fiction, about the aims and uses of which he is very explicit in *The Novel: What It Is* (1893). Novelists he called "public amusers," who must always write largely about love and in Anglo-Saxon countries must write under the eyes of the ubiquitous young girl. They might therefore as well be reconciled to the exigencies of their business. For his own part he thought problem novels odious, cared nothing for dialect or local colour, believed it a mistake to make a novel too minute a picture of one generation lest another should think it "old-fashioned," and preferred to regard the novel as a sort of "pocket theatre"—with ideals, it should be added, much like those of the British and American stage from 1870 to 1890.

Thus far Crawford was carried by his cosmopolitan training and ideals: he believed that human beings are much the same everywhere and can be made intelligible everywhere if reported lucidly and discreetly. Reading his books is like conversing with a remarkably humane, sharp-eyed traveller who appears —at least at first—to have seen every nook and corner of the world. *Zoroaster* (1885), *Khaled* (1891), and *Via Crucis* (1898) have their scenes laid in Asia; *Paul Patoff* (1887), in Constantinople; *The Witch of Prague* (1891), in Bohemia; *Dr. Claudius* (1883), *Greifenstein* (1889), and *A Cigarette-Maker's Romance* (1890), in Germany; *In the Palace of the King* (1900), in Spain; *A Tale of a Lonely Parish* (1886) and *Fair Margaret* (1905), in England; *An American Politician* (1885), *The Three Fates* (1892), *Marion Darche* (1893), *Katharine Lauderdale* (1894), and *The Ralstons* (1895), in America; and, most important group of all, the Italian tales of which *A Roman Singer* (1884), *Marzio's Crucifix* (1887), *The Children of the King* (1892), and *Pietro Gh sleri* (1893) are but little less interesting than the famous Roman series,—*Saracinesca* (1887), *Sant' Ilario* (1889), *Don Orsino* (1892), and *Corleone* (1896). The Saracinesca cycle most of all promises to survive, partly because as a cycle it is imposing but even more particularly because here Crawford's merits appear to best advantage. After all, though he considered himself an American, and though he knew many parts of the globe, he knew the inner circles of

Rome better than any other section of society, and really minute knowledge came, as it did not always in his stories of America, for instance, and almost never did in his historical tales, to the aid of his invariable qualities of movement and lucidity and large general knowledge of life. If in this admirable cycle, which is to Crawford's total work much what the Leather-Stocking cycle is to Cooper's, Crawford actually achieved less than Cooper, it is to some extent for the reason that some cosmopolitanism finds it even harder than does some provincialism to impart to fiction true depth and body; that reality, like charity, often begins at home.

In the eighties realism was the dominant creed in fiction, which in practice followed its creed somewhat closely, with exceptions, of course, among the purely popular novelists like Roe and General Wallace. The same decade, however, saw the beginnings of two movements which became marked in the nineties, both of them natural outcomes of the official realism of Howells and James. One led, by reaction, to the rococo type of historical romance which flourished enormously at the end of the century; and the other to the harsher naturalism which shook off the decorums of the first realists, contended with the historical romancers, first succumbed to them, and then succeeded them in power and favour. The historical tendency, less than the naturalistic a matter of doctrine, came at first from the South and West: from writers who painted the amiable colours of antebellum plantation life—Cable, Page, Joel Chandler Harris; or from California, from writers who tried to catch the charm of old Spanish days—Bret Harte and Helen Hunt Jackson; or from the Mississippi Valley, from writers who, thanks to Parkman, had discovered the richness and variety of the French régime there—Constance Fenimore Woolson and Mary Hartwell Catherwood. Of all these Mrs. Jackson wrote perhaps the best single romance in *Ramona* (1884), a story aimed to carry forward an indictment, already begun in the same author's *A Century of Dishonor* (1881), against the treatment of the Indians by their white conquerors. Ramona, however, and her Temecula husband Alessandro have so little Indian blood that their wrongs seem less those of Indians than the wrongs which all the older Californians, Indian or Spanish, suffered from the predacious vanguard of the Anglo-Saxon conquest. **And the romance** dominates the problem. For Mrs. Jackson, Spanish California had been a paradise of patriarchal estates set in fertile valleys, steeped in drowsy antiquity, and cherished by fine unworldly priests. Her tragic story derives much of its impressiveness from the pomp of its setting, the strength of its contrasts, its passionate colour and poetry. Mrs. Catherwood wrote graceful and engaging but not quite permanent tales, from *The Romance of Dollard* (1889) to *Lazarre* (1901), which added a definite little province to our historical fiction—the French in the interior of the continent.

But the later historical romance is best studied in the work of Dr. Silas Weir Mitchell (1829–1913) of Pennsylvania, who, on the advice of Oliver Wendell Holmes, early set aside his literary ambitions until he should have established himself in a profession, became one of the most eminent of medical specialists, particularly in nervous diseases, and only after he was fifty gave much time to verse or fiction, which, indeed, he continued to produce with no diminution of power until the very year of his death. His special knowledge enabled him to write authoritatively of difficult and wayward states of body and mind; as in *The Case of George Dedlow* (1880), so circumstantial in its impossibilities, *Roland Blake* (1886), which George Meredith greatly admired, *The Autobiography of a Quack* (1900), concerning the dishonourable fringes of the medical profession, and *Constance Trescott* (1905), considered by Dr. Mitchell his best-constructed novel and certainly his most thorough-going study of a pathological mood. His psychological stories, however, had on the whole neither the appeal nor the merit of his historical romances, which began with *Hephzibah Guinness* (1880) and extended to *Westways* (1913). *Westways* is a large and truthful chronicle of the effects of the Civil War in Pennsylvania, but Mitchell's best work belongs to the Revolutionary and Washington cycle: *Hugh Wynne Free Quaker Sometimes Brevet Lieutenant-Colonel on the Staff of his Excellency General Washington* (1896), *The Youth of Washington Told in the Form of an Autobiography* (1904), and *The Red City A Novel of the Second Administration of President Washington* (1908). Dr. Mitchell's own favourite among his books, *The Adventures of François, Foundling, Thief,*

Juggler, and Fencing-Master during the French Revolution (1898),
stands as close to the American stories as did Paris to the city
of Franklin in the later eighteenth century. Revolutionary
these narratives are only by virtue of the time in which they
take place, for their sympathies are almost wholly with the
aristocrats in France, with the respectable and Federalist
classes in America. Philadelphia, generally the centre of the
action, appears under a softer, mellower light than has been
thrown by our romaneers upon any other Revolutionary city,
and Washington, though drawn, like Philadelphia, as much to
the life as Dr. Mitchell could draw him, is a demigod still.

By the time *The Red City* appeared its type was losing
vogue, but *Hugh Wynne* and *The Adventures of François* came
on the high tide of the remarkable outburst of historical romance just preceding the Spanish War. The best books of the
sort need but to be named: Mark Twain's *Personal Recollections
of Joan of Arc* (1896), Frederic Jesup Stimson's *King Noanett*
(1896), James Lane Allen's *The Choir Invisible* (1897), Charles
Major's *When Knighthood Was in Flower* (1898), Mary Johnston's *Prisoners of Hope* (1898) and *To Have and To Hold*
(1899), Paul Leicester Ford's *Janice Meredith* (1899), Winston Churchill's *Richard Carvel* (1899) and *The Crisis* (1901),
Booth Tarkington's *Monsieur Beaucaire* (1900), Maurice
Thompson's *Alice of Old Vincennes* (1900), Henry Har-
land's *The Cardinal's Snuff-Box* (1901). In part they were
an American version of the movement led in England by
Robert Louis Stevenson, Rider Haggard, Conan Doyle, and
Anthony Hope; the "Ruritanian" romance, for instance, of
Anthony Hope was so popular as to be delightfully parodied in
George Ade's *The Slim Princess* (1907); all these tales were
courtly, high-sounding, decorative, and poetical. But their
enormous popularity—some of them sold half a million copies
in the two or three years of their brief heyday—points to some
native condition. In the history of the American imagination
they must be thought of as marking that moment at which, in
the excitement which accompanied the Spanish War, the nation
suddenly rediscovered a longer and more picturesque past than
it had been popularly aware of since the Civil War. The
episode was brief, and most of the books now seem gilt where
some of them once looked like gold, but it was a vivid moment

in the national consciousness, and if it founded no new legends it deepened o d ones.

Romance did not have the field entirely during these years, for there was also a strong naturalistic trend, which dated from the eighties, when Henry James had seemed too foreign and Howells too hopeful. In 1883 Edgar Watson Howe, of Kansas, had published *The Story of a Country Town*, a book almost painfully overlooked and yet worthy to be mentioned with *Wuthering Heights* or *Moby Dick* for power and terror. Unlike those two it lacks locality, as if the bare, sunburned Kansas plain had no real depth, no mystery in itself, and could find no native motif but the smoldering discontent of that inarticulate frontier. Sternest, grimmest of American novels, it moves with the cold tread and the hard diction of a saga. No shallow mind could have conceived the blind, black, impossible passion of Joe Erring or have conducted it to the purgation and tranquillity which succeeds the catastrophe. Plainly, the author had deliberately hardened his heart against the too facile views of contemporary novelists. It is this stiffening of the conscience which goes with all the later naturalistic writers in America; they are polemic haters of the national optimism. Howe's early experiment was fol- lowed, not imitated, by a brilliant group of writers undoubt- edly nearer to Zola than to Howells: Hamlin Garland,[1] best in short stories, who stressed the sordid facts of Middle Western farm life and who spoke for the group in his volume of essays *Crumbling Idols* (1894); Henry Blake Fuller, who wrote *The Chevalier of Pensieri-Vani* (1890) under the ægis of Charles Eliot Norton and then the realistic novel of Chicago, *The Cliff- Dwellers* (1893); Harold Frederic, who after his lucid and accurate romance of the Mohawk, *In the Valley* (1890), followed Ambrose Bierce[2] with energetic Civil War stories and later made a sensation with *The Damnation of Theron Ware* (1896) and *The Market-Place* (1899); and the notable pair who promised much but died young, Stephen Crane (1871–1900) and Frank Norris (1870–1902).

Crane was a genius who intensely admired Tolstoy and somewhat febrilely aimed at ¬bsolute truthfulness in his fiction. *Maggie A Girl of the Streets* (1896), written when he

[1] See Book III, Chap. vi.   [2] *Ibid.*

was but twenty-one, gave a horrible picture of a degenerate Irish family in New York and the tragedy of its eldest daughter; its violent plain speaking seemed very new when it appeared. Crane's great success, however, attended *The Red Badge of Courage An Episode of the American Civil War* (1895), a reconstruction, by a man who at the time of writing knew war only from books, of the mental states of a recruit when first under fire. A greater war has made the theme widely familiar, but Crane's performance still seems more than an amazingly clever *tour de force;* it is a real feat of the imagination. Norris had larger aims than Crane and on the whole achieved more, though no one of his books excels the *Red Badge*. He was one of the least sectional of American novelists, with a vision of his native land which attached him to the movement, then under discussion, to "continentalize" American literature by breaking up the parochial habits of the local colour school. He had a certain epic disposition, tended to vast plans, and conceived trilogies. His "Epic of the Wheat"—*The Octopus* (1901), *The Pit* (1903), and *The Wolf* (never written)—he thought of as the history of the cosmic spirit of wheat moving from the place of its production in California to the place of its consumption in Europe. Another trilogy to which he meant to give years of work would have centred about the battle of Gettysburg, one part for each day, and would have sought to present what Norris considered the American spirit as his Epic of the Wheat presented an impersonal force of nature. Such conceptions explain his grandiose manner and the passion of his naturalism, which he was even willing to call romanticism provided he could mean by it the search for truths deeper than the surface truths of orthodox realism. He had a strong vein of mysticism; he habitually occupied himself with "elemental" emotions. His heroes are nearly all violent men, wilful, passionate, combative; his heroines—thick-haired, large-armed women—are endowed with a rich and deep, if slow, vitality. Love in Norris's world is the mating of vikings and valkyries. Love, however, is not his sole concern. The Pacific and California novels, *Moran of the Lady Letty* (1898), *Blix* (1899), *McTeague* (1899), *A Man's Woman* (1900), as well as *The Octopus*, are full of ardently detailed actualities; *The Pit* is a valuable representation of a "corner" on the Chicago Board of Trade. In all these his eagerness to be truthful gave Norris a large energy, particularly in scenes of action, but his speed and vividness are not matched by his body and meaning.

Much the same thing may be said of Jack London (1876–1916), one or two of whose novels will likely outlast his short stories,[1] important as they were in his best days, and close kin as his stories and novels are in subjects, style, and temper. Norris's "elemental" in London became "abysmal" passions. He carried the cult of "red-blood" to its logical, if not ridiculous, extreme. And yet he has a sort of Wild-Irish power that will not go unnoted. *John Barleycorn* (1913) is an amazingly candid confession of London's own struggles with alcohol. *Martin Eden* (1909), also autobiographical, though assumed names appear in it, recounts the terrific labours by which in three years London made himself from a common sailor into a popular author. *The Sea-Wolf* (1904) reveals at its fullest his appetite for cold ferocity in its record of the words and deeds of Wolf Larsen, a Nietzschean, Herculean, Satanic ship captain, whose incredible strength terminates credibly in sudden paralysis and impotence. Most popular of all, and best equipped for survival, is *The Call of the Wild* (1903), the story of a dog stolen from civilization to draw a sledge in Alaska, eventually to escape from human control and go back to the wild as leader of a pack of wolves. As in most animal tales, the narrative is sentimentalized, but there runs through it, along with its deadly perils and adventures, an effective sensitiveness to the Alaskan wastes, a robust, moving, genuine current of poetry.

A real, however narrow, gulf separates London from such colleagued naturalists as Richard Harding Davis, better in short stories[2] than in novels, and often romantic, or even from David Graham Phillips (1867–1911), whose bitter war upon society and "Society" culminated in the two volumes of *Susan Lenox* (1917), the only extended portrait of an American courtesan No one of them all had quite London's boyish energy, quite his romantic audacity in naturalism. And the tendency of fiction is just at present away from the world of "elemental" excitement to more civil phases of life, a newer form of realism having succeeded alike the episode of naturalism and the

[1] See Book III, Chap. VI.   [2] *Ibid*

antithetical episode of historical romance. At the same time there are still novels of many types: domestic and sentimental romances; tales of wild adventure; stories written to exploit a single character in the tradition of F. Hopkinson Smith's[1] *Colonel Carter of Cartersville* (1891), Edward Noyes Westcott's *David Harum* (1898), and Owen Wister's *The Virginian* (1905); a few records of exotic life at the ends of the earth; narratives, nicely skirting salaciousness, of "fast" New York; affectionate, idealized portrayals, as in the work of James Lane Allen for Kentucky, of particular states or neighbourhoods. But no tendency quite so clearly prevails as romance in the thirties, sentimentalism in the fifties, realism in the eighties, or naturalism at the turn of the century.

[1] See Book III, Chap. VI.

CHAPTER XII

Henry James

HENRY JAMES was born an American and died an Englishman. He might never have formally transferred his allegiance had it not been for the War and our long delay in espousing the Allied cause. He became a British subject in July, 1915. The transfer had, however, been virtually made many decades earlier. Of the two ruling passions of James, one was surely his passion for "Europe." Of this infatuation the reader will find the most explicit record in his fragmentary book of reminiscences, *The Middle Years* (1917), record and whimsical apology which may well serve the needs of other Americans pleading indulgence for the same offence. James loved Europe, as do all "passionate pilgrims," for the thick-crowding literary and historical associations which made it seem more alive than the more bustling scene this side the water. Going to breakfast in London was an adventure,—being not, as at Harvard, merely one of the incidents of boarding, but a social function, calling up "the ghosts of Byron and Sheridan and Scott and Moore and Lockhart and Rogers and *tutti quanti.*" In America, James had never so taken breakfast except once with a Boston lady frankly reminiscent of London, and once with Howells fresh from his Venetian post, and so "all in the Venetian manner." Everybody in Victorian London had, as he calls it, references—that is, associations, appeal to the historic imagination; and, as he humorously confesses, "a reference was then, to my mind, whether in a person or an object, the most becoming ornament possible." It was "with bated breath" that he approached the paintings of Titian in the old National Gallery; and when, in the presence of the Bacchus and Ariadne, he became aware, at the same moment, of the auburn head and eager talk of Swinburne, his cup for that day ran over. With the best of introductions to the Rome of Story, the London of Lord Houghton, the highest ambition of James was to establish "connections" of his own with a world in which everything so bristled with connections; and it is he who lets us know with what joy he found himself, on the occasion of his first visit to George Eliot, running for the doctor in her service, since thereby "a relation had been dramatically determined."

But it is only in the light of his other ruling passion that we can rightly understand the force of his passion for Europe. Even more rooted was his love for art, the art of representation. All his pilgriming n London and elsewhere was by way of collecting a fund of material to draw upon "as soon as ever one should seriously get to work." And is it surprising that he should have been impressed with the greater eligibility of the foreign material; that his impressions of New York and Boston seemed to him "negative" or "thin" or "flat" beside the corresponding impressions of London? The old world was one which had been lived in and had taken on the expressive character of places long associated with human use. It was not simply the individual object of observation, but the "cross-references"; or, again, the association of one object with another and with the past, making up altogether a "composition." Whatever person or setting caught his attention, it was always because it "would fall into a picture or a scene." Of the heroine of *The American*, a young French woman of rank, the hero observed that she was "a kind of historical formation." And along with his material, James found abroad a favourable air in which to do his work. There he found those stimulating contacts, there he could observe from within those movements in the world of art, which were of such prime importance for his own development. Lambert Strether, in *The Ambassadors*, represents the deprivations of a man of letters, strikingly suggestive in many ways of James himself, condemned to labour in the provincial darkness of "Woollett, Massachusetts."

In all this our American author seems identified with anything but the American scene; and the case is not altered when we consider his stories on the side of form. His form is not American, nor his preoccupation with form. It is as strictly international as that of Poe. James was a profound admirer of Hawthorne; but so was he an admirer of Balzac and of George Sand, and it is probably to later models than any of these that he owes whatever is most characteristic in his technique. There is at any rate nothing here drawn from American sources rather than from European; nothing which we can claim as our production.

Yet we have reasons for our claim upon him. This very passion for Europe, as he has exhibited it in himself and in so many of his creatures, this European "adventure" of Lambert Strether and Isabel Archer (of *The Portrait of a Lady*)—what more purely American product can be conceived? Even to the conscientiousness with which young James did his London sightseeing, mindful of his own feeble health, which threatened to cut it short, and above all mindful "that what he was doing, could he but put it through, would be intimately good for him!"

Altogether his theme turned out to be quite as much American character as European setting. We must not forget how predominantly his novels, and how frequently his short stories, have for their subject Americans,—Americans abroad, or even Americans at home seen in the light of foreign observation. In this connection the novels in particular may be divided into three groups, falling chronologically into three periods. In the first period, extending from *Roderick Hudson* to *The Bostonians*, 1875 to 1885, the leading characters are invariably Americans, though the scene is half the time abroad. In the second period, from *The Princess Casamassima* to *The Sacred Fount*, 1885 to 1901, the novels confine themselves rather strictly to English society. In the third period, from *The Wings of the Dove* to the novels left unfinished at the author's death, 1902 to 1917, James returned to his engrossing, and by far his most interesting, theme of Americans in Paris or Venice or London. Not a very original contribution to literature is the American scene itself—the New York of *Washington Square* (1881), the Boston of *The Europeans* (1878) and *The Bostonians;* and none of these novels was included by James in the New York Edition. His American settings are but palely conceived; and his figures do not find here the proper background to bring them out and set off their special character. But the crusading Americans—variegated types, comic and romantic—with the foreign settings in which they so perfectly find themselves, these make up a local province as distinct in colour and feature as those of Cable[1] and Bret Harte,[2] —a province quite as American, in its way, and for the artist quite as much of a *trouvaille*, or lucky strike.

These Americans abroad fall naturally into two classes. The first are treated in the mildly comic vein, as examples of American crudeness or simplicity. Such are the unhappy Ruck family of *The Pension Beaurepas*,—poor Mr. Ruck who had come abroad in hopes of regaining health and escaping financial worries, and his ladies whose interest in the old world is confined to the shops where money can be spent. Perhaps we might refer to this class Christopher Newman, the self-possessed and efficient American business man, hero of *The American* (1877); though in his case the comedy of character is by no means broad, and is strictly subordinate to the larger comedy of social contrast. In general, these people are treated not unkindly; and there is the one famous instance of *Daisy Miller*, in which the fresh little American girl is so tenderly handled as to set tears flowing—a most unusual proceeding with James. Generally the Americans emerge from the international comedy with the reader's esteem for sterling virtues not always exhibited by the more sophisticated Europeans. In the later group of stories in particular, the American character, presented with no hint of comic bias, actually shines with the lustre of a superior spiritual fineness. This is what Rebecca West has in mind in her somewhat impatient reference to James's characters as American old maids, or words to that effect.

And here we have the very heart of his Americanism, if we may make bold to call it that. There is something in James's estimate of spiritual values so fine, so immaterial, so indifferent to success or happiness or whatever merely practical issues, as to suggest nothing so much as the transcendentalism of Emerson, the otherworldliness of Hawthorne. There is here a psychology not of Scott or Thackeray, not even of George Eliot, still less of any conceivable Continental novelist; and one can hardly refer it to any but a New England origin.

[1] See Book III, Chap. VI.　　　　[2] *Ibid.*

William James, the novelist's grandfather, was an Irishman settled in Albany. He was described in a New York newspaper of 1832 as "the Albany business man"; and he laboured so well at business that he left several millions to be divided among twelve heirs. Otherwise the relatives of the novelist were quite innocent of practical affairs. His father, Henry James,[1] was a philosopher-clergyman, a friend of Emerson's, who carried with him everywhere the entire works of Swedenborg. Henry James, Jr., was born 15 April, 1843, in New York; but he went to Europe as a babe in arms. Two years later, still in long clothes and waggling his feet, he noted from the carriage window "a stately square surrounded with high-roofed houses and having in the centre a tall and glorious column"—the reader will recognize the Place Vendôme. From the earliest times, in New York and Albany, all his conceptions of culture had a transatlantic origin. The caricatures of Gavarni, Nash's lithographs of *The Mansions of England*, the novels of Dickens read aloud in the family circle, —these fed his imagination. He and his brothers went regularly to a New York bookseller for a boys' magazine published in London. Even their sense of a "political order" was derived from Leech's drawings in *Punch*. Their education was amazingly various and spasmodic,—better adapted, one might suppose, to the formation of novelists than of philosophers. Dozens of private schools and tutors succeeded one another in bewildering rapidity in New York, not to speak of later instruction in Bonn and Geneva, in Paris and London.

All this while the main occupation of the future novelist was the contemplative observation of character. The world of Albany and New York was a world not of vulgar persons but of artistic "values." Everyone was interesting as a "type": type of "personal France" or of French "adventuress" (referring to early governesses), type of orphan cousins, type of wild young man. Cousin Henry was a kind of Mr. Dick, cousin Helen a kind of Miss Trotwood. James's account in *A Small Boy and Others* shows him in those early days a mere vessel of impressions suitable to the uses of art. All this was fostered by the kind of discipline, or no discipline, maintained by their metaphysical father. For religion, the boys went to all the

[1] See also Book III, Chap. XVII.

churches, and, we gather, in much the spirit in which they approached any other æsthetic experience. As for livelihood, or occupation, the father was always inclined to discourage any immediate decision upon that point, lest a young man might prematurely limit the development of his inner life. We are reminded how small a place is taken in the stories of James by what men do to earn a living. In America, it seemed, there were—apart from the unique case of Daniel Webster—but two possible destinies for a young man. Either he went into business or he went to the dogs. But the immediate family and connections of James were always aspiring to that more liberal foreign order in which was offered the third alternative of a person neither busy nor tipsy,—a cultivated person of leisure.

In 1860 the family went to live in Newport, so that the older brother might work in the studio of William Morris Hunt; and Henry, who had earlier haunted the galleries of Paris with his brother, welcomed this occasion to frequent a place devoted to the making of pictures. In 1862, William being at Lawrence Scientific School, Henry entered the Harvard Law School; still noting, in boarding-house or lecture-room, personalities, chiaroscuro, *mise en scène*, more than the precedents of law. The Civil War was the one distinctly American fact which seems to have penetrated the consciousness of Henry James. While he was prevented by lameness from going to war himself, it was brought home to him, for one thing, by the participation of two of his brothers. But the war, like everything else, was followed by him, however breathlessly, as a spectacle rich in artistic values. In 1864 the family were living in Boston, and from 1866 they were definitely settled in Cambridge, William entering the Harvard Medical School in that year; and in these days the young author was forming excitingly important literary connections. One friendship dating from this time was that with E. L. Godkin, editor of the newly founded *Nation*.[1] But most important no doubt was that with the Nortons of Shady Hill, who later introduced him to London society.

In 1870 died the person to whom James refers with the greatest personal affection, his cousin Mary Temple, the model for Milly Theale in *The Wings of the Dove*, as he tells us, and

[1] See Book III, Chap. xx.

also—as we guess—for Isabel Archer of *The Portrait of a Lady*
and more than one other of his loveliest American women.
Of her death he says "we felt it together as the end of our
youth." So far he brings the family record in his *Notes of a
Son and Brother* (1914). Meanwhile in 1869 occurred the
visit to London recorded in *The Middle Years*. To 1872
belongs a perhaps equally memorable visit to Italy. And
from that time forward until his death, 28 February, 1916,
he lived abroad; during the first years largely in Italy and
France ("inimitable France" and "incomparable Italy"), and
then, from about the year 1880, in the England of his adoption,—making his bachelor home in London or in the old
Cinque Port of Rye. But he continued almost to the end to
publish his novels and tales in the great American magazines,
so that his first appeal was generally to the public here.

Evidences of the honour in which he was held in England
were the Order of Merit conferred upon him at New Year's,
1916; and his portrait by Sargent, undertaken on the occasion
of his seventieth birthday, at the invitation of some two hundred and fifty English friends. At the outbreak of the War,
none was more enthusiastic for the cause of the Allies, which
was associated with everything he held most precious. His
feeling for England at this time, on looking out across the
channel from his Sussex home, is described in what is perhaps
his latest piece of writing, *Within the Rim*, published in the
Fortnightly Review in August, 1917. It has been said that his
mortal illness was provoked by the vigour with which he took
up the work of relief for suffering Belgium and France.

James began his literary career as an anonymous contributor of reviews to *The North American Review* and *The Nation;*
and such reviews and literary news-letters he continued to
write for many years. Only a small part of his critical writing
has appeared in book form; and it still remains for the curious
to trace the development of his literary theory from the
beginning. His books of fiction were frequently supplemented,
too, with books of impressions, in which he might commune
at length with the spirit of places,—English, French, American,
Italian. He also wrote many plays, a few of which made
brief appearances on the London stage. But they were

"talky" and untheatrical; and he succeeded neither in purging the theatre of the commercialism he deprecated nor even in taking the public fancy himself. His first attempts at fiction were printed in *The Atlantic Monthly* and *The Galaxy;* but he hardly emerges as an author of account before the appearance of *The Passionate Pilgrim* in 1871. His first important novel was *Roderick Hudson*, published in *The Atlantic* in 1875. His first and only approach to popularity, whether in long or short story, was made by *Daisy Miller* in 1878. The New York Edition of his novels and tales, published during the years 1907 to 1909, is of the greatest interest because of the extended discussion of his own work and the account of his imaginative processes found in the Prefaces. It is, however, very far from being a complete collection even of his works of fiction. It is simply the choice made by James at that late date, and according to his taste as it had then developed, of such of his stories as he wished to be known by. It remains to be seen how far posterity will submit to his judgment in the matter.

The threefold grouping of his novels already suggested was in connection with the treatment of American themes. In reference to form and method a more illuminating division would be one of two periods: first, *Roderick Hudson* to *The Tragic Muse*, 1875–1890; and second, *The Spoils of Poynton* to *The Sense of the Past*, 1896–1917.

In the novels of the first group, he includes, in general, more material than in the later ones, more incident, a greater number of characters, a more extended period of time; and he treats his material in the larger, more open, more lively manner of the main English tradition. He also chooses, in the earlier period, what may be considered more ambitious themes in the matter of psychology. In *Roderick Hudson*, for example, he undertakes to trace the degeneration of a man of genius, a young American sculptor, when given the freedom of the artistic life in Rome. This evolutionary—or revolutionary— process of character, suggestive of George Eliot, is a "larger order ' than he would ever have taken on in the later period. In *The Tragic Muse* he reverts to the theme of the artistic tempera- ment—this time in disagreement with the world of affairs; and he develops it by means of two great interrelated stories, one dealing with an actress, one with a painter. In the later years he would not have undertaken thus to tell two stories at the same time; and perhaps the artistic temperament itself would have seemed to him too ambitious a theme. In the earlier period, again, we find him sometimes treating subjects touching on political or the more practical social problems, though indeed his interest was never primarily in the problems. *The Bostonians* is a somewhat satirical study, at one and the same time, of the Boston character and of feminism; while in *The Princess Casamassima* the leading persons are revolutionary socialists, and political murder lurks in the background. Probably the best, as well as the best liked, of the earlier novels is *The Portrait of a Lady* (1881), which records at length the European initiation of a generous-souled American girl.

In the course of six years between the first and second periods no novel of James was published; but during that interim came the culmination of his long activity as a short-story writer. It was his tendency always to subordinate incident to character, to subordinate character as such to situation—or the relations among the characters; and in situation or character, to prefer something rather out of the ordinary, some aspect or type not too obviously interesting but calling for insight and subtlety in the interpretation. Good examples, in the short story, of this predilection are *The Pupil*, *The Real Thing*, and *The Altar of the Dead*, all appearing in the early nineties; and a little later, *The Beldonald Holbein* and *The Turn of the Screw*. most haunting of ghost stories. In *The Beldonald Holbein* the beautiful great lady has chosen for her companion a supposedly unattractive middle-aged American woman, who will admirably serve as a foil to her beauty. But certain painters of her acquaintance having discovered that the foil is herself remarkably "beautiful"—that is, distinguished, significant of feature, a subject worthy of Holbein—it becomes necessary to send her back home and get another companion with less character engraved upon her countenance. How one of the artists gets his revenge by painting Lady Beldonald in all the splendour of her mediocrity is not the point of interest; the point of interest is the fine discrimination shown by artist —and author, and reader—in evidence of their superior good taste.

Each tale of James is thus an "initiation" into some social or artistic or spiritual value not obvious to the vulgar. And each tale is a quiet picture, a social study, rather than the smart anecdote prescribed by our doctors of the "short-story." James is not rigorous in his limitation of the short story to the magazine length; so that his tales are as likely to take the form of the more leisurely *nouvelle* as of the brief and sketchy *conte*. And so it was not surprising to find a tale intended originally for a magazine short story enlarging itself by insensible degrees into what is practically a novel. Such was the case with *The Spoils of Poynton*, one of his finest stories, which has the length of a novel, together with the restricted subject-matter, the continuity, and economy of the short story.

But these traits, it is clear, had already grown to be James's ideals for a narrative of whatever length. They were the ideals of many of the foreign novelists whose personal influence had swayed him in Paris; and to a considerable extent those of George Eliot, whose influence upon him must have been mediate, working through her French imitators, as well as emanating directly from her own work. More and more, serious novelists were denying themselves the breezy and picturesque variety of materials. the broad free stroke, of the old masters, in favour of a dramatic limitation, a dramatic closeness of weave, a scientific minuteness of detail, an intimate psychological notation, and a pictorial (as distinguished from picturesque) consistency of tone,—all of which we find in their extremest development in the later novels of James. This is what makes the international character of his art. Note should be taken, of course, of a certain fussiness and long-windedness, as well as a certain tendency to the abstract, which are partly to be set down to the score of personal idiosyncrasy. But in general he is clearly following the ideals of George Eliot, of Flaubert, of Turgenev. Perhaps too we should admit the suggestion of F. M. Hueffer, who would trace back the lineage of James, through Stendhal and other French writers, ultimately to Richardson, the early master of the technique of manifold fine strokes, of the close and sentimental study of souls.

Along with *The Spoils of Poynton* may be mentioned,

among the later novels, *The Sacred Fount* (1901) and *What Maisie Knew* (1897) as partaking somewhat of the nature of long short stories. *What Maisie Knew* is, by the way, in a class by itself, not merely for reasons of technique too special to be considered here, but also by reason of the great charm of the little girl,—so naïve, so earnest, so much a lady and so much a girl, whose experience of evil is the subject of the story.

For the full-fledged novels of the later period, it will suffice to state briefly the themes of *The Awkward Age* (1899) and *The Golden Bowl* (1904)—without prejudice, however, to the special claims of *The Ambassadors*, the novel considered by James himself to be his most perfect work of art. *The Awkward Age* is concerned with the adjustment called for in a certain London circle by the emergence of the *jeune fille* and the consideration due her innocence of the world. The adjustments prove to be very extensive, but almost wholly subjective, and leaving things very much where they were before so far as any outward signs go. The book is almost literally all talk,—the talk of people the most "civilized" and "modern," people the most shy of "vulgarity," who have ever been put in a book. It is a fascinating performance—for those who have the patience to read it. *The Golden Bowl* is a study of a theme not unlike that of *The Portrait of a Lady*. It is the story of an American girl who marries an Italian prince, and the strategy by which she wins his loyal affection. The time covered is much shorter than that in the *Portrait*, the important characters only about half as many, the amount of action much smaller: and there is little change of scene as compared with the earlier novel. The length of the book is about the same; and the space saved by these various economies is devoted to the leisurely development of a single situation as it shaped itself gradually in the minds of those participating, the steady deepening of a sense of mystery and misgiving, the tightening of emotional tension, to a degree that means great drama for all readers for whom it does not mean a very dull book.

For many readers it certainly means a very dull book. In this recipe for a story almost everything has been discarded which was the staple of the earlier English novel, even of George Eliot,—exciting incident, dramatic situation, highly-coloured character and dialogue, humour, philosophy, social comment. Indeed, we may almost say the story itself has been thrown out with the rest. For in the later novels and tales of James there is not so much a story told as a *situation revealed;* revealed to the characters and so to us; and the process of gradual revelation, the calculated "release" of one item after another—that is the plot. It is as if we were present at the painting of a picture by a distinguished artist, as if we were invited to follow the successive strokes by which this or that detail of his conception was made to bloom upon the canvas; and when the last bit of oil had been applied, he should turn to us and say "Now you have heard Sordello's story told." Some of us would be satisfied with the excitement of having assisted at such a function, considering also the picture which had thus come into being. Others,—and it is human nature, no doubt,—would exclaim in vexed bewilderment "But *I* have heard no *story* told!"

The stories of James tend to be records of seeing rather than of doing. The characters are more like patients than agents; their business seems to be to register impressions; to receive illumination rather than to make up their minds and set about deeds. But this is a way of conceiving our human business by no means confined to these novels; is it not more or less characteristic of the whole period in which James wrote? One passes by insensible degrees from the world of Renan to that of Pater and Swinburne, and thence to that of Oscar Wilde and of writers yet living, in whom the cult of impressions has been carried to lengths yet more extreme.

Among all these names the most significant here seems to be that of Walter Pater, whose style and tone of writing— corresponding to his intellectual quality and bias—more nearly anticipate the style of James than do those of any other writer, English or French. It does not matter that Pater's subject is the art of the past and James's the life of the present. No two writers were ever more concerned with mere "impressions," and impressions mean for them discriminations, intimate impressions, subtle and finely sympathetic interpretations. None ever found it necessary, in order to render the special quality of their impressions, to try them in so many different lights, to accompany their statements with so many qualifications and reservations: impulses giving rise to sentences more curiously complex and of longer breath than were ever penned by writers of like pith and moment. They were both of them averse to that raising of the voice, that vehement or emphatic manner, characteristic of the earlier Victorians and supposed to be associated with strong feelings and firm principles. These reasonable and well-bred writers, if they ever had strong feelings or firm principles, could be trusted to dissimulate them under a tone of quiet urbanity. They abhorred abrupt transitions and violent attitudes. They proceed ever in their discourse smoothly and without marked inflection, softly, as among tea-tables, or like persons with weak hearts who must guard themselves against excitement. There is a kind of hieratic gentleness and fastidiousness,—and yet withal a hint of breathless awe, of restrained enthusiasm,—in the manner in which they celebrate the mysteries of their religion of culture, their religion of art.

This, we say of James, is anything but American, indigenous; this is the *Zeitgeist;* this is the spirit of England in the "æsthetic nineties" reacting against the spirit of England in the time of Carlyle. But then we think of the "passionate pilgrimage" of Isabel Archer and the others; we think of James's *Middle Years;* we think, it may be, of ourselves and eastward prostrations of our own. And we realize that what the romancer has conjured up is a world not strange to our experience. His genius is not the less American for presenting us, before all things, this vision of a bride rushing into the arms of her bridegroom: vision of the mystic marriage (shall we say?) of new-world faith and old-world culture.

CHAPTER XIII

Later Essayists

WHEN, speaking to his classmates on their graduation from college, William Ellery Channing[1] made the address entitled *The Present Age* (1798), the note that he uttered was one that thenceforth reverberated throughout our national life and literature. It showed affiliation with the French Revolution, and with the England of Burns, Shelley, and Wordsworth; and notable is the emphasis on the possibility of all human progress, not alone American progress, and on the importance of that culture which shall be shared by all classes of mankind. To material objects Channing gave their due, but regarded them merely as the manifestations of character and of power that have in higher fields their most inspiring representation; and beauty was for him a vast treasury of benediction wherefrom he wished his fellow men to draw the priceless blessings available to the poorest purse. Thus the essay on *Self-Culture*, written as an address in 1838, is a composition to which the writings of Emerson, Curtis, Higginson, Mabie, and later authors owe a decided, even if in some cases unconscious, debt—the practical and poetical blending of humanity with the humanities.

As Channing was the earliest in that firmament of lecturer-essayists where Emerson shone as the most benignant star, so Nathaniel Parker Willis[2] is the prototype of later semi-literary American journalists. Now, the mark of the journalist, the trait which surely establishes both his immediate success and his final oblivion, is the intentness of seizure on what the present can give, in swift, exciting, easily apprehensible interest. It was always the present that fascinated Willis; and, save in fleeting mo-

[1] See Book II, Chap. VIII.   [2] *Ibid.*, Chap. III.

109

ments of early days, his vision did not seek the future with any sincere scrutiny. Revelling in personalities, he is expository only secondarily, if at all; and inspiring never. The writer of our own time who works up an interview with some man of mark is following Willis not alone in his interest in the superficialities of personality, but often in the very tricks of style, varying from gaudy metaphor to the epithet that has the tang of the unexpected. Our journalists, by and large, remain lesser members of the Willis tribe.

Still a third writer, Washington Irving,[1] exerted a notable influence as the originator of a literary form which, for want of a better phrase, might be called the story-essay, wherein the narrative element runs its gentle course over a bed of personal reflections and descriptive comment of individual flavour. He had a whole school of followers,[2] and even Hawthorne[3] for a time moved among them; while two more natural inheritors of his moods of tender sentiment and gentle satire are Donald Grant Mitchell (1822-1908) and George William Curtis, with whom the history of our later essayists may well begin.

The two volumes, *Reveries of a Bachelor* (1850) and *Dream Life* (1851), which Mitchell, as a young writer, issued under the pseudonym of Ik Marvel, are volumes that strike the same chords whose artistically modulated music resounds in so much of Irving, to whom the latter volume was dedicated; while in *The Lorgnette, or Studies of the Town* (1850) we have a series of papers directly modelled on *Salmagundi*. These sketches, despite the facile manner of their kindly satire, belong in the topical realm of ephemera, and are of interest mainly to the historical critic, who, harking back to the days of *The Spectator* and *The Tatler*, finds in them another nexus between English and American literature. Not so, however, can we dismiss *Reveries of a Bachelor* and *Dream Life*. Their hold on the affections of later generations is secure despite that naïve sentimentality frequently displayed by American literature in the period just preceding the Civil War. Both these books present a series of pictures in the imaginary life of their author, and there is a general adherence to the concept of life as a succession of the seasons. This parallel does not, however,

[1] See Book II, Chap. IV.   [2] *Ibid.*, Chap. VII.   [3] *Ibid.*, Chap. XI.

lead into paths of wintry regret. We find even December logic taking on a golden hue in such a sentence as this from the *Reveries:* "Affliction has tempered joy, and joy adorned affliction. Life and all its troubles have become distilled into a holy incense rising ever from your fireside—an offering to your household Gods." "And what if age comes"—Mitchell writes further on, in the vein of Browning's *Rabbi Ben Ezra*—"what else proves the wine? It is but retreating towards the pure sky depths." The note of joy in the springtime of life, the accent of sympathy for young griefs as well as young loves, echo from these charming pages; while the ingenuousness of Ik Marvel's sentiments is embedded in an old-fashioned form of sentimental phraseology which brings a smile to the lips of the sophisticated critic. But after all it is the smile in the reader's heart that attests the lasting human appeal of both the *Reveries* and *Dream Life*. These books were written while their author was still in his twenties, and they have the immaturity, both of technique and philosophy, which precedes the labour of the craftsman and the experiences of the man; yet they have also, with the aroma of youth, that even subtler fragrance—the gift of the gods to all who comprehend the value of the dreaming hour.

There are two elements in these works secondary in interest only to the major themes of love, sorrow, and ambition. One is the immediate affection for nature, nowhere more beautifully expressed than in this springtime picture: "The dandelions lay along the hillocks like stars in a sky of green." The other note is of love for old books. These themes are repeatedly found in Mitchell's later writings; and *My Farm of Edgewood* (1863)—Edgewood was his country home near New Haven —began a series of volumes among the earliest of a steadily increasing department of American literature revolving around agricultural and rural themes.

Mitchell's own experiences with the soil of his native Connecticut are, in *My Farm of Edgewood*, recounted with the seriousness of the scientific farmer and the grace of the man of letters. In *Wet Days at Edgewood* (1865) his pleasant discourse ranges from ancient country poets to the latest practical studies of soil cultivation; while in the yet later volume *Rural Studies, with Hints for Country Places* (1867) he continues in confidential

mood to the widening circles of those readers whose love for
country life his own writings had in no small measure developed.
Thus Mitchell figures in a very personal way in the large group
of American writers on nature, and deserves recognition as an
influential pioneer in directing, with the urbanity of the scholar,
the attention of his countrymen to non-urban delights. This
point is emphasized because, all told, American essayists have,
in their treatment of nature, covered an exceptionally wide
range, and approached this theme, both as to style and interpretation, in ways that repay the most interested study:
Audubon,[1] the important naturalist, indulging in exaggerated
poetical rhetoric in acquainting us with the habits of birds;
Emerson[2] and Thoreau,[3] not impervious to the interest of
nature's details, yet winning from them the highest spiritual
sustenance for the world of men; Agassiz[4] and Warner and
Mabie and Burroughs and John Muir, approaching each according to his temperament and qualifications this ever bountiful theme. From some of these authors we derive knowledge
concerning animal life and plant life; from others, messages of
the intimate relationship between human life and the great
world of nature. But Mitchell, in his Edgewood writings,
stands as one whose main interest sprang from the soil itself.

Towards the end of his long life, Mitchell wrote four volumes
on *English Lands, Letters, and Kings* (1890), and two on *American Lands and Letters* (1897–99). Here are many shrewd observations concerning his contemporaries, as well as pungent
estimates, often mingled with humour, of the writings and
character of earlier authors; but these books, with their wealth
of pictures, were intended for the public at large, and cannot
be considered as original contributions to critical literature.
In them we have the somewhat obvious fruit of his travels,
experiences, and readings, but in a manner that has less flavour
than the gleanings of travel, published in far younger days,
such as *A New Sheaf from the Old Fields of Continental Europe*
(1847). Those earlier descriptive papers and legends, so
immediately related to Irving's *Tales of a Traveller*, are more in
accord with Mitchell's fame as the author of the *Reveries* and
Dream Life, and through them Mitchell is most pleasantly

---

[1] See Book III, Chap. xxvi.   [2] See Book II, Chap. ix.
[3] *Ibid.*, Chap. x.   [4] See Book III, Chap. xxvi.

affiliated with many other American essayists—Emerson, Bryant,[1] Bayard Taylor,[2] Curtis—who made their travels the basis of a great body of work that varies from the decorous pace of well-phrased description to graceful flights of fancy and even to soarings of the creative imagination.

Before we leave Mitchell there is, however, to be noted one point which differentiates him from the majority of American essayists. Again like Irving, whose life Mitchell's parallels in details of ill health, early travels abroad, the study and abandonment of law, and the tenure of official position in Europe, the author of *Dream Life* held to the belief that a writer is not called upon to take an active part in the great political and social questions of his day, if he feels that he can best express himself and, in the long run, most effectively serve mankind through adherence to his literary art along the lines of his own predilections. Irving, of course, was at one time most adversely criticized by his countrymen for just such an attitude, and his protracted stay abroad was misconstrued as a form of national renegadism. Mitchell escaped hostile comment for his general abstention from participation in those public topics, ranging from the abolition of slavery and the preservation of the Union to Civil Service reform, woman suffrage, national copyright, and other themes of social betterment that led Whittier,[3] Lowell,[4] Curtis, and Higginson, and indeed almost all the leading American poets and essayists for the last fifty years, to become, at times, propagandists. This absence of the outright didactic note is a decided characteristic of Ik Marvel, leaving him none the less creditably in the brotherhood of those authors whose message remains abidingly sweet and wholesome.

The most remarkable blending of the man of letters and the devoted public servant among American authors is manifested in the life and writings of George William Curtis (1824–92). In all the literary essays and addresses of Curtis, and in even the briefest of his papers for "The Easy Chair," is apparent his incomparably suave diction; but here, too, is that firmness of thought clothing his civic aspirations in the impregnable armour of dauntless and logical convictions. And

---

[1] See Book II, Chap. v. [2] See Book III, Chaps. x and xiv.
[3] See Book II, Chap. xiii. [4] *Ibid.*, Chap. xxiv.

how graciously the two great streams in our essay literature—the Puritan stream softened by the elemental thought of the brotherhood of man, with Channing as its fountainhead, and the genial flow of benign art, with Irving as its fountainhead—have their confluence in Curtis! "Honor," he writes, "is conscious and willing loyalty to the highest inward leading. It is the quality which cannot be insulted"; thus expressing the thought which underlay the memorable phrase of a later essayist, Woodrow Wilson, President of the United States. One recalls in this connection another of Curtis's sentences: "Reputation is favorable notoriety as distinguished from fame, which is permanent approval of great deeds and noble thoughts by the best intelligence of mankind."

The literary career of Curtis falls into two parts. Born in Providence, he went, as a boy, to New York, where, for a short while, he held a clerkship. His first direct connection with other men of letters came with his sojourn in 1842 at Brook Farm; and this was followed by travels in Europe and in Egypt and Syria. The result was a series of delightful books, based on letters that he had sent to the New York *Tribune;* and in them we find Curtis giving full and original vent to his nimble fancy and his graceful descriptive powers. *The Nile Notes of a Howadji* (1856), *The Howadji in Syria* (1852), and *Lotus Eaters* (1852) are thus delectable resting places for the literary student who seeks to cover the territory of our travel literature. In *Potiphar Papers* (1853), Curtis resorted to our chief city, continuing the *Salmagundi* tradition of local satire, not without immediate evidence of the influence of Thackeray; chastizing with somewhat gentle blows of the moralist's whip the more obvious faults of a community too much given to ostentation; and pointing with no very stern finger at the social excrescences of his (and other) times. But a more individual flavour comes to the front in *Prue and I* (1856), one of the most charming of American books, wherein the poor man endowed with the gift of imagination is shown to be a far richer and infinitely more sympathetic figure than the millionaire whose festivities he contemplates with the eye of a philosopher whom love has blessed. About this same period, Curtis began those papers which made the "Editor's Easy Chair" in *Harper's Monthly* a national, as well as a literary, institution; and he began, also.

his public lectures, which, till the time of his death some forty years later, were so beneficially to affect the national life. Prior to 1860 Curtis was almost exclusively a man of letters; and had not civic duties spoken to him with peremptory voice, his early work bids us believe that he would have rounded out his career with many volumes of the most graciously conceived and gracefully expressed essays and fiction. But with his entrance, during Lincoln's first candidacy, into the field of politics, his literary activities were made largely subservient to his civic endeavours and aspirations. First one of the pillars of the Republican party, and later chairman of the Independent Republicans who rebelled against the nomination of Blaine; the chief exponent and the most influential advocate of Civil Service reform; the kindly but firm leader in every forward moving social cause, Curtis, during the latter half of his life, gave up the chance that was his to achieve preponderant literary fame, winning, instead, his high title in the citizenship of his country. What he said of Lowell may even more cordially be said of him—that he had the "grace, charm, and courtesy of established social order, blending with the masculine force and the creative energy of the Puritan spirit." The intimacy between Curtis, Lowell, and Norton, so fully revealed in the letters of the three, embodies one of the rarest and most fragrant episodes of friendship among American men of letters. Each influenced the others, strengthening that faith in one's self which, among civilized men, is the elementary religion. Each of these three was true to the conviction that acts which primarily serve ambition are seldom in accordance with the ambition to serve. Yet Curtis, for all his unfearing rectitude, felt most keenly that only those who are virtuous have the right to judge severely; but a part of their virtue consists in the frequent kindly abnegation of this right.

In his essays and addresses on Burns, on Bryant, on Sumner, on Wendell Phillips, Curtis combines the qualities of the scholar, the lover of romance, and the radical reformer; while in his attitude towards nature, as apart from his interpretation and exposition of the deeds of individuals, he shows a kinship with Thoreau in his rarest moods. Lowell would have spurned the thought that Thoreau was our most nobly imaginative nature writer (to whom Emerson owed a debt that has not yet

been fully appreciated); and indeed, one recalls how Lowell, as
editor of *The Atlantic Monthly*, objected to a paragraph of
Thoreau's wherein the pines were made to tower into a higher
heaven than might be reached by the souls of lesser men.
Curtis we cannot imagine thus adopting the theologian's views.

What man of you all [writes Curtis in his paper on *Autumn Days*]
what man of you all is as true and noble for a man as the oak upon
yon hill-top for an oak? The oak obeys every law, regularly
increases and develops, stretches its shady arms of blessing, proudly
wears its leafy coronel, and drops abundant acorns for future oaks
as faithful; but who of you all does not violate the law of your life?

And a little further on: "A stately elm is the archbishop of my
green diocese. In full canonicals he stands sublime. His
flowing robes fill the blithe air with sacred grace." It is in
sentences like these that Curtis takes firm place beside Thoreau,
both of them ambassadors bringing messages from the world of
nature to the world of men—and beside John Muir (1838–
1914), who, though born in Scotland, was thoroughly naturalized in America, as inventive as any Yankee, and a passionate
foster-son of the western mountains.

To sit in judgment on the authors whose lives outran that
of Curtis—men whose hospitality was extended to so many
younger writers, and whose personal inspiration has quickened
unforgettable hours—is no easy task; and far more grateful it
would be to saunter in informal essay fashion along the paths of
past days, placing wreaths of affectionate reverence in homes
where Norton, Higginson, Stedman dwell no more. But we
are here concerned less with the charm of men in their social
intercourse than with the printed pages which are to succeeding generations their sole direct heritage—direct heritage
because who shall gauge those influences which, emanating
from personalities like Norton's and Stedman's, come to flower
long after the hand that cast the initial seed has withered in
the grave? The bibliographer of Charles Eliot Norton (1827–
1908) finds comparatively little to record that is of importance
to the American essay. A study of Dante; notes of travel and
study in Italy; some papers published in *The Atlantic Monthly;*
and, later in life, historical studies concerning church building in
the Middle Ages,—these indicate to some extent the trend of

Norton's interests, and form a distinguished contribution in those particular fields of literature and art.[1] It is, however, to his letters, published after his death, that we must have recourse for fuller appreciation of his place in the annals of our literary culture. The revelation is a fine one. We behold a being of simple and unswerving rectitude, with a capacity for noble friendships, and with a rare power for instilling enthusiasm. Not only to the large group of students who came, at an impressionable age, under the influence of the Professor of the Fine Arts at Harvard University, but also to men like Ruskin, Lowell, Howells, and other intellectual leaders on both sides of the Atlantic, the clear-visioned Norton spoke heartening words. In a letter, in 1874, to Carlyle, Norton wrote of his aim

to give the students some definite notions of the Fine Arts as a mode in which men in past times have expressed their thoughts, faiths, sentiments, and desires; to show the political, moral, and social conditions which have determined the forms of the Arts, and to quicken so far as may be, in the youth of a land barren of visible memorials of former times, the sense of connection with the past and gratitude for the effort and labours of other nations and former generations.

This was Norton's gift to America: an accentuation of the continuity and permanence of the ideal aspects of the race life. Culture, with both its æsthetic and moral implications, was the inheritance of this New Englander, in whose idealism was inwoven that Brahminical strain which, while it strengthens, at times compresses; and so we find him, in his letters as in his life, a standard-bearer of cultivation who yet lacked the buoyant enthusiasm of American democracy. His early letters never overflow with the spirits of youth; the missives of middle life contain frequent sentences reflecting upon the unsatisfactoriness of American society; and this morally Hebraic descendant of ultra-religious Puritan forbears, sounds, in his later letters, a note of impatient agnosticism. But withal, how fine a quality flavours his correspondence, his comments on Whitman, Sumner, Lincoln, Wendell Phillips, and other subjects of his pen! Norton stands among American essayists and lecturers as the most unyielding critic of vulgarity in the

[1] See also Book III, Chap. xxv.

social life of his day and of futile sentimentalizing in the
political life. We miss in his letters that sense of humour which
is the touchstone of the philosopher, and which Norton's
friend Curtis used as a literary force in his public career.
We miss also the light touch of fancy and the quick thrust
of wit; while, at times, fastidiousness of language and thought
accentuates Norton's aloofness from the ways of other
men. When George E. Woodberry sent Norton, in 1881, his
verses on America, Norton commented on their surplusage of
patriotism in this manner: "We love our country, but with
keen-eyed and disciplined passion, not blindly exalting her.
. . . To do justice to the America that may be, we must not
exalt the America that is, beyond her worth." This kind of
integrity of judgment, this almost bleak disregard of the
popular aspect of things, this stoical insistence on the discipline
of passion, made Norton a force to be reckoned with, even
when, almost alone among our American men of letters, he took
fearless issue with the national administration at the time of
the war with Spain. Yet his power with the written word was
not sufficiently forceful to assure any very vital hold on men of
a later day. He was a phenomenon of æsthetic intuition and of
intellectual purity to whom we willingly offer tribute of admiration; yet we are aware of that pessimistic drop of acid which
made his blood run a little more coldly than that of his fellow
authors, precipitating the residue of an ultimately weary expression of New England culture.

One of our earlier essayists, Henry T. Tuckerman,[1] in his
Defense of Enthusiasm attacked the New England philosophy
of life because of its too preponderant insistence on mental
capacity and moral tendencies, and wrote: "It seems as if the
great art of human culture consists chiefly in preserving the
glow and freshness of the heart." Had Tuckerman lived in
the later decades of the last century, he might, indeed, have
felt out of sympathy with Norton, but not with many of our
other essayists. The Civil War brought New England emotionally into the full flow of that larger national life for which
Emerson and his school had prepared it, and while the later
American essayists have abstained from chauvinism, and have
written with the scholar's appreciation of what foreign culture

[1] See Book II, Chap. III.

has to offer, theirs is a consistent and hopeful interpretation of American ideals. Consider, for instance, Thomas Wentworth Higginson (1823–1911). At the age of twenty-seven he gave up his pastorate at Newburyport because he ran counter to the sentiments of his congregation, believing that his foremost duty was to preach a word for mankind in attacking the institution of slavery. With Theodore Parker and Wendell Phillips he became one of the leaders of the Abolition movement, daring, in aiding the fugitive slaves, to obey a law higher for him than that of Congress. In the dangers of the battlefield he shared, when, as colonel of the first regiment of free coloured soldiers, he served in the inevitable conflict. His writings, beginning in 1853 and continuing almost incessantly for well over threescore years, carried him into fields of history, literature, education, and politics, and reveal him as sympathetically familiar with the culture of the ancients as with the creative thought of modern democracy. In his translation of Epictetus, in his delightful essay on Sappho, he was the scholar of catholic tastes, whose shelves in his simple Cambridge home gave equally gracious welcome to the message of the Stoics and the appealing human lyricism of Heine; yet who wrote in the fly-leaf of a copy of his own volume of essays entitled *Old Cambridge*, wherein he discusses the literary epochs of his native town and writes at length on Holmes, Longfellow, and Lowell: "This book is one of my favourites among my too numerous productions because it reproduces so fully the men and traditions which surrounded my early youth." These traditions, whose finest essence his own life emphasizes, connoted for him those duties of citizenship that made him a militant intellectual leader to the end of his long life; perhaps not the least of his services being his espousal of the cause of woman suffrage, whereto his admiration for Margaret Fuller, whose life he wrote, contributed a quota of immediately personal enthusiasm. Yet so varied was Higginson's culture, so easy flowing his style, so wide the fund of quotations on which he loved to draw, and so pleasant his wit, that his essays, even when propagandist, are literature. And through them all runs a stream of optimism which, let it be admitted, is to a great degree a matter of temperament yet no less constructive an element on that account. But for this optimism, this

American faith in moulding the living material of his own day into the finer forms inherent in his country's institutions. Emerson, the most influential of our essayists, would have had a lesser hold on the minds of his fellow citizens; and the value of Higginson comes largely from a similar happy endowment.

The ministry, whose record in our annals is so frequently interwoven with that of American literature, had its greatest literary figures in New England. A distinguished exception was Moncure D. Conway (1832–1907), who, like Higginson, gave up his pulpit because of his anti-slavery pronouncements. A Virginian by birth, he did his most important work as an editor in Boston, where he conducted *The Dial* and *The Commonwealth;* and as a lecturer in England, especially in his illuminating discourses during the Civil War. In later life, again in America, he wrote many papers of sterling worth, essays notable because of their high ethical plane; yet, lacking the authentic fire of genius, the light of his writings has now merely become mingled in the wide effulgence emanating from that group of great citizen-writers in whose ranks he marched with so firm a tread.

Probably the most immediately successful exponent of practical optimism in the Cambridge group was Edward Everett Hale (1822–1909), Higginson's senior by but a year, and like Higginson a clergyman and one of the Overseers of Harvard University. There is a pleasant logic in the fact that this grand-nephew of the Revolutionary patriot whose only regret, as he mounted the scaffold, was that he had but one life to lose for his country, should have written a tale that, despite the startling improbability of its plot, is, in its stirring presentation of the value of patriotism, a masterpiece of our literature. But while the fame of Edward Everett Hale would be assured if he had done nothing further than to write, during the Civil War times, *The Man Without a Country*, [1] let it not be forgotten that his volume published in 1870, entitled *Ten Times One is Ten*, led to the establishment of philanthropic societies the world over, the nature of whose charitable activities is suggested in their motto: "Look up and not down; look forward and not back; look out and not in; lend a hand." Hale's magazine with the final phrase of the preceding motto

[1] See Book III, Chap. VI.

as its title was a journal of progress and a record of charity, wherein were continued those ideas of liberal Christianity that underlie an earlier publication, *Old and New*, which he had founded in 1869. To both he contributed many papers, while articles on historical and literary themes came frequently from his pen, in addition to many stories of discovery and adventure, of invention, of war, and of the sea. In his recently published letters there is further disclosure of his mental fertility and of his kind and practical Christianity; although his style is simple to the point of bareness, and the ordinary literary graces are absent.

Hale is not the only American author whose fame is intimately inwoven with a single piece of work. The same period in our history that brought forth his masterpiece is responsible for the immortal poem to which the marching feet and the dedicated hearts of myriad soldiers kept time as they swept on to bloody struggles with *The Battle Hymn of the Republic* on their lips. But Julia Ward Howe (1819–1910) was not alone the creator of the most potent of our battle poems.[1] Her place is secure in the record of many liberalizing movements, especially those which had to do with the social and political elevation of her own sex; and, beyond this, she was the author of delightful papers ranging in subject matter from a paper on Aristophanes, prepared as a lecture at the Concord School of Philosophy, to illuminating studies of social manners—such as *The Salon in America* and *Is Polite Society Polite?*—full of intelligent criticism and that discriminating humour which is yet too serious to indulge in any easy satire. Her achievement, as a whole, entitles her to rank as the most notable woman of letters born and bred in the metropolis of America; although another woman belonging, like Julia Ward Howe, to an old New York family displayed at least equal intellectual rarity. Nor was the regard wherein Emma Lazarus (1849–87) was held by such men as Emerson, Gilder, Stedman, Channing, Eggleston, Dana, and Godkin due alone to those poems and essays which did more than the writings of any other American author to instil among Christians a sympathy for that people of whom Emma Lazarus was so brave an exponent. Quite apart from her poems and articles on Jewish themes, there can be no

[1] See Book III, Chap. II.

question that, if one excepts Margaret Fuller, there was no woman among our authors more ardent than Emma Lazarus in her interminable search for æsthetic culture, no woman whose conversation, to quote the words of the great editor Charles A. Dana, was more "deeply interesting and intensely instructive." Stedman once said that she was the "natural companion of scholars and thinkers," a comment borne out by Emerson's abiding affection and admiration for her. In the field of prose, some of her most memorable achievements were her essays on *Russian Christianity versus American Judaism*, and her paper on Disraeli. The first of these, written some twoscore years ago at the time of Russian massacres, presents, without undue apology, or undue praise of her race, the basic attitude that should be taken in regard to the persecution of the Jews, and as the problem is still one that civilization has not solved with fearless honour, let us listen again to Emma Lazarus, as, reverting to the thought expressed by one of our most high-minded statesmen, she concludes that essay:

Mr. Evarts has put the question upon the only ground which Americans need consider or act upon. It is not that it is the oppression of Jews by Russians—it is the oppression of men and women by men and women; and we are men and women!

To this trio of noble women—Margaret Fuller, Julia Ward Howe, Emma Lazarus—there should be added the name of Harriet Beecher Stowe (1812–96),[1] who, like Hale with his one great story, and Julia Ward Howe with her one great poem, is remembered on account of her one great novel. *Uncle Tom's Cabin* has thrown her essays into the shade, where their existence remains unknown to the large majority of present-day readers. Yet those who love to have recourse to old pages of *The Atlantic Monthly* find her an essayist of charm and range. Her *House and Home Papers*, published under the pseudonym of Christopher Crowfield, wherein the father of the family discusses all manner of domestic topics, have their keynote in the thought that whereas to keep a house is a practical affair "in the region of weights, measure, colour . . . to keep a home lies not merely in the sphere of all these, but it takes in

[1] See Book III, Chap. XL.

the intellectual, the social, the spiritual, the immortal." The relationship of parents to children, and the nature of childhood itself; the servant question; matters of house decoration; the inherited predilections of Aunt Mehitable, with her "scrupulous lustrations of every pane of glass"; discussions concerning education, hospitality, pastimes; helpful considerations regarding the temptations that assail human nature, are all mingled in a sane atmosphere of simplicity and true worth which embraces, but in no Puritan spirit, the quietly heroical approach to life, the desire not only to enjoy but the willingness also "to encounter labour and sacrifice."

It was Mrs. Stowe's famous brother, Henry Ward Beecher,[1] who introduced to the world of letters the most likable of all the later American essayists, Charles Dudley Warner (1829–1900), when, in 1870, Beecher wrote the preface to Warner's first book, *My Summer in a Garden*. In these papers, as in his *Saunterings* (1872), based on European travels, and his *Backlog Studies* (1873), there are a genial humour and a grace of style decidedly reminiscent of Washington Irving, whose life Warner was later to write in a most sympathetic way. In the long course of his lectures and essays we find many stimulating appeals for greater personal and national culture, and helpful discussions in the field of social topics, especially in connection with prison reform. His travel essays, recording adventures and observations in Europe and America, Africa and Asia, are enjoyable additions to this branch of our literature; while Warner's activities as an abolitionist bring him further into touch with his fellow writers of the second half of the nineteenth century. He, more than any other of the later essayists, affected his lesser contemporaries of the pen. His papers, with their fireside warmth, their sketchy touch, their humorous and intimate personal note, were studied by many writers for magazines and newspapers, a host of commonplace scribes who found it easier to imitate the Warner flavour than to create any original atmosphere in their own writings.

For a delicious example of Warner's style one might turn to that part of *My Summer in a Garden* where the adult agriculturist has an entirely ordinary experience in which his labours are set at naught by the universal characteristics of

[1] See Book II, Chap. XXII.

boyhood. Here Warner rounds out a paragraph which begins with an expression of semi-comic awe, with a reference to the Greek conception of fate as that element in human affairs against which are hopeless the prescience of the wisest minds, the provisions of the most arduous hands. The most baffling and sombre of themes is lightly and delightfully touched, while the author instils in our attitude towards a pear tree that sense of human companionship which, elsewhere in his pages, makes peas and beans and the upspringing asparagus warm and living things.

There are two other papers of Warner's from which a few lines may indicate how he influenced the thought of his times, and how he is directly related to other American essayists. One is *The Relation of Literature to Life*, an address introductory to a course of five lectures delivered at various universities. Warner differed from others of our critics in his belief that the development of American letters would be along lines diverging from, rather than continuing in, the channels of English literature, and his first precept, as a student and expositor of American literature, was "to study the people for whom it was produced." In the light of our national character would thus be revealed the light of our works of authorship; and Warner clearly understood that in the first century of the United States the national character expressed itself most widely in those activities of invention, material production and construction, path-finding, and path-clearing, which have led to concrete prosperity—all of which Warner summarizes in the phrase "the ideal of Crœsus." But side by side with the more material tendencies, he perceived those finer currents which bear the rarer cargo of American idealism. Thus while Warner with frankness pointed out that the majority of people look upon literature as a decoration rather than as an essential element in their lives, and while he saw that culture had its own unfortunate arrogances, yet he showed how poetry (and all that poetry connotes) supplies the highest wants of a people: that literature is power as well as pleasure. In his *Thoughts Suggested by Mr. Froude's Progress*, Warner wrote:

When we speak of progress we may mean men or things. We may mean the lifting of the race as a whole by reason of more power over the material world, by reason of what we call the conquest of nature; or we may mean a higher development of the individual man, so that he shall be better and happier.

In progress of both these kinds Warner had faith. He never forsook the American birthright of optimism, while the ethical note in his writings, continuing the New England tradition, was uttered with so much grace and fine whimsicality of style that it lost didactic harshness.

There can be no doubt that American literature has considerably suffered from the platitudinous didactic note. It is for this reason that, with sentiments of utmost civic respect, with full appreciation for the fluent diction of the most prolific of our later essay writers, we must regard Hamilton Wright Mabie (1845–1916) as a teacher of sweetness and sanity, as a fair-minded expositor of literature, as a friendly observer of nature, but not as an important man of letters. Lacking colour, sharpness of outline, light and shade,—all those qualities which the great stylists have as effectually at their command as have the greatest painters,—he represents perhaps more convincingly than any other of our essayists both the possibilities and limitations inherent in writers seeking to bring "sweetness and light" to a generation of readers whose early education comes from the public schools, and who, for later enlightenment, turn to innumerable magazines. As the editor of *The Independent*, as a lecturer, as an indefatigable author of volumes of essays, Mabie was a useful teacher in his own day, but there is little in his writings that those who are conversant with his European and American contemporaries cannot find expressed elsewhere with more force and originality.

Mabie was a voluminous writer on literary topics, but two keener students of literature, among the American writers in the second half of the nineteenth century, were Edwin Percy Whipple (1819–86) and Edmund Clarence Stedman (1833–1908). Whipple is a critic whose attainments have been neglected by later readers, yet whose works have force and clarity of expression, sharp insight, frequent wit. He was born in Gloucester, Massachusetts, the very year that Washington Irving's *Sketch Book* marked the commencement of American *belles-lettres;* but his first book, *Essays and Reviews*

(1848), allies him rather with the Macaulay school of essayists than with the more personal and leisurely Irving tradition. Indeed, it was Whipple's brilliant article on Macaulay, written in 1843, that made its author known to the literary world of Boston, where Whipple, a young man of twenty-four, was then employed in the brokerage business; and Macaulay's style is reflected in much of the earlier work of his American admirer. In the lectures and essays contained in the volumes entitled *Literature and Life* (1871) and *Character and Characteristic Men* (1877) Whipple continued to reveal that really keen penetration into the strata of values and that ready entrance into the temperament of his subject which had been shown in his earlier appraisals of men and books. There are few better essays on British critics than Whipple's paper wherein, in discussing Jeffrey, to whose charm of wit he is "by no means insensible," Whipple not only refers with succinct phraseology to the "cool and provoking dogmatism" and "the insulting tone of fairness" of the British critic; but goes deeper into the nature of æsthetics, as where he writes: "By making beauty dependent on the association of external things with the ordinary emotions and affections of our nature, by denying its existence both as an inward sense and as outward reality, he substantially annihilates it." Then again, of Hazlitt: "He was naturally shy and despairing of his own powers, but his dogmatism was of that turbulent kind which comes from passion and self-distrust." Sheridan, Fielding, Carlyle, and the earlier English dramatists, beginning with Marlowe and Ben Jonson, are all treated with the sympathy of the man of letters who is, at the same time, the student of national and epochal tendencies; and so, too, in his estimates of Rufus Choate, Emerson, Motley, Sumner, and others of our own writers.

In the centennial year of American independence, Whipple contributed to *Harper's Magazine* a paper entitled *The First Century of the Republic*, in which he reviewed the development of American literature and showed how its course had been "subsidiary to the general movement of the American mind." In agreeing with this point of view, Stedman, in his *Poets of America* (1885), expands the thesis: "Our imagination has found exercise in the subjugation of a continent, in war, politics, and government, in inventive and constructive energy, in developing and controlling our material heritage." It was because Stedman was so enthusiastic a follower of all the efforts and advances of the human mind, an alert man of affairs, experienced in business and finance, as well as a poet,[1] that he possessed in such generous measure the ability to judge both scientifically and poetically. His volumes *Victorian Poets* (1876) and *Poets of America*—those standard works of fine sanity and even finer vision—reveal the great eclectic who with warm heart and open mind had a thousand approaches to life. His understanding of philosophy and his vibrating sense of melody are evident, but perhaps nowhere more significantly than in his appraisal of the poetry of Emerson, where he uses a metaphor suggested by science and the practical affairs of everyday life. Emerson, writes Stedman, "had seasons when feeling and expression were in circuit, and others when the wires were down." Only Stedman could thus have evalued the electric spark, the brilliant mysterious vitality of Emerson's poetry, negated at times by the insufficiency of his art.

Stedman's essays were almost exclusively in the field of literary criticism, but there have been published since his death two copious volumes of letters revealing in delightful fashion the range of his interest and the charm of his temperament. Beauty was his guide, and friendship was his passion. He had that spirituality which led him to write to John Hay —the most enjoyable of letter writers among our literary statesmen—that the earth "is smaller than either your soul or mine"; and though Stedman's manliness remained undaunted before cruel onsets of fate—frequent illness, the loss of fortune, the death of near and dear—he could be moved almost to woman's tears when the love of friends brought to him unexpected tribute. "For of Heavenly Love we may dream, but know nothing, while from the currents that flow between earthly hearts—young and old—we do gain our most real and exquisite compensation." In the hurried life of New York this poet who was a broker on the Stock Exchange made time to correspond not alone with his many confrères in fame but with a host of younger writers; and it was his chivalric boast that no letter from a woman ever remained unanswered. The

[1] See also Book III, Chap. X.

broadness of his sympathies in art, in drama, in music, as well as in letters, coupled with his generous interest in the effort of all those who even at the furthest radius came within his circle, made of Stedman one of the finest influences in the development of New York's cultural life. "New York," Stedman wrote in his essay on Bayard Taylor, "is still too practical to do much more than affect an æsthetic sentiment." This judgment was pronounced more than a score of years ago, and if it is now increasingly open to qualification, Stedman is one of those whom we have therefor most to thank.

Another, and to a marked degree, is William Winter (1836–1917).[1] For many years the dean of American dramatic critics, he ever rode full tilt and fearless against the commercialism rampant on our stage. He was the most winning of our essayists on Shakespeare, having in his own nature more than a touch of Hamlet. Erudite in the technique of the playwright, Winter was still more versed in the lyric knowledge of the poet and in that high wisdom which realizes both the potentialities and the obligations of dramatic art; and thus his critiques in the daily press were concerned with the eternal, as opposed to the diurnal, aspect of things. But while his standards were uncompromising, his style was gracious, courteous, tender even—as we should expect of a poet; and in such a series of papers as are included in his *Gray Days and Gold* (1894) we see how great a part sentiment played in the life and writings of that brave antagonist of all the blatant and all the insidious influences which drag down the art of a nation. The past lured him with every manner of associations, and his writings on Shakespeare's England have the charm of old days—one of the characteristics most appealing in the work of Washington Irving. Indeed, with a greater strain of melancholy, and a lesser strain of humour, William Winter was, in the closing years of the nineteenth century, the last and most winsome descendant of our first great essayist; and especially by the English public should he continue to be read as one who held that land in the tenderest regard.

The marked enjoyment in things of old—old books, old places, the myriad associations binding together the blossoms of the years—which casts glamour on many of the pages

[1] See also Book III, Chap. XVIII.

of Winter, underlies the literary work of Laurence Hutton (1843–1904),[1] his companion in the field of dramatic criticism and along the byways of foreign travel. Among collectors Hutton is remembered for the treasures he amassed, especially books relating to the theatre and play-bills. The corollary of this enthusiasm is found in his papers and addresses on the drama, wherefrom arises winningly the human note. He wrote, also, a series of volumes describing literary pilgrimages in England, Italy, and many another land,—volumes that place him graciously in the large company of American essayists whose theme has been that of travel; and with him our own journey fittingly ends.

The scope of present-day essayists is far wider than that of the men of the preceding century. The tendency is away from the traditional essay of morals or of literary culture, partially because the classics are no longer part and parcel of our education, and largely because science and social economics are more and more requisitioning the pens of many of our most brilliant contemporary essayists. We have, however, many writers, of course, whose work continues the literary tradition; and to name Howells, Woodberry, Santayana, Woodrow Wilson, Henry Van Dyke, Brander Matthews, Paul Elmer More, Agnes Repplier, and John Burroughs—foremost among nature writers—were yet to omit others well deserving of inclusion lest too long a catalogue of ships should still overlook some bark of letters already worthily launched. Our grateful task has been to write of the men who have gone by, a group of noble gentlemen, whose attitude towards life was that of the idealist, and whose courtesy of spirit and courtesy of phrase are permeating traits of their work. Not even in the harshest days of the Civil War is there a brow-beating epithet or sneering causticity. If the American essayists and critics owe a debt to the English writers of the eighteenth and nineteenth centuries—as indeed they do—they have removed from their inheritance all taint of bitterness and cruel satire, and our critical literature has (with the exception of Poe in his uninspired moments) no mean, no biassed, no tyrannical—and no fulsome—appraiser of literary values or of the motives of men's actions. If, however, we turn to our group of later essayists

---

[1] See also Book III, Chap. XVIII.

as a whole, we are soon aware that they leave something to be desired, and that we must have recourse to European essays for the supplying of this want. As our fiction has refused to portray life with full verity, to dissect with searching candour the hidden motives in individual life, so, too, have our essay writers abstained from the subtle workings of the mind in the field of personal emotions and desires. There is, however, a distinction to be made when we seek to explain these limitations in American fiction and American essays. In the first case is preponderantly involved the purpose of popular appeal along the lines of least resistance, with financial success as the writer's reward. In the second case, the purpose of educating the mind of a nation not yet ready to appreciate art in all its ramifications, has, whether directly or unconsciously, led our essayists to refrain from themes which Continental writers have made luminous to peoples inheriting the Renaissance rather than the Puritan traditions. The group of essayists that we are leaving may indeed have theoretically subscribed to the French dictum that style is the man, yet they wrote, rather, under the propulsion of the idea that mankind is more than style.

CHAPTER XIV

Travellers and Explorers, 1846–1900

THE central world-belt of human progress up to the present era lies along the fortieth parallel of north latitude with general limits ten degrees on each side. That the region now the United States falls almost entirely within this belt explains the instinctive drift of Europeans westward to, and across, this particular untrodden field. The Anglo-Saxon branch, attaining a dominance of power therein, halted briefly at the obstacle of the Appalachian mountain system, passed that barrier, and marched on its predestined course to the western ocean with a development of accompanying literature described up to 1846 in a former chapter [1]—and continued in this to the year 1900, with a slight extension at each end.

A new order of events developed speedily with the triumph of the Texans over Santa Anna and the creation of the Lone Star Republic in 1841 with its premeditated intention of annexation to the United States. This intention the Mexican Republic declared would be, if consummated, a cause of war, but the movement was not halted. The constant influx of pioneers from the "States" made annexation a foregone conclusion, while books that now appeared like Colonel Edward Stiff's *The Texan Emigrant* (1840) aided and abetted the prospective addition to the American republic. He offers for a frontispiece a map of Texas which has small consideration for the expansive Texan idea that the new republic's western limits were where the Texan pleased to place them, quite regardless of Mexican contention, for the Colonel draws the

[1] Book II, Chap. I.

western boundary at the Nueces River exactly where the
Mexicans declared it must be.

The ambitious Texans, however, were not of his mind.
They wanted territory and they understood that far beyond
the world of intervening desert unknown to them flowed the
Rio Grande del Norte, whose valley was productive and for
some two centuries had been cultivated by a Spanish population with the attractive city of Santa Fé a trade centre worth
owning. The story of *The Spanish Conquest of New Mexico*
(1869) by W. W. H. Davis and *El Gringo, or New Mexico and
her People* (1857) by the same author, who spent some years in
the region, show that the Spaniards in entering and building
up New Mexico had no thought of the Texans that were to be.
Samuel Cozzens in *The Marvellous Country or Three Years in
Arizona and New Mexico* (1873) gives more of the story, with
modern additions, and *Historical Sketches of New Mexico* (1883)
by ex-Governor L. Bradford Prince, who still lives in Santa Fé,
is another important volume on this subject.

Although the Rio Grande settlements and the capital city
of Santa Fé were so far from the outermost fringe of Texan life
that the Texans actually knew little about them, these had
fixed their minds on extending Texas to the Rio Grande, and to
the Rio Grande it must go. Therefore they decided to march
across the unknown and formally annex the old-time towns
and villages, whose inhabitants were supposed to be eager to
become Texans. A grand caravan accordingly was organized,
partly military, partly mercantile, to proceed to the conquest.
The expedition moved off into the wilderness with far rosier
expectations than facts warranted. Disaster was not long in
falling upon the party, and worse disaster awaited their straggling remnant at the hands of the tyrannical, cruel, and unruly
governor of New Mexico, Armijo.

Probably the most interesting and valuable book on this
phase of Texan enterprise, and withal one having considerable
literary charm, is *The Narrative of the Texan Santa Fé Expedition* (1844) by George Wilkins Kendall. Kendall was one of
the survivors. He was finally released from the wretched
prison in Mexico into which he was cast with others who had not
succumbed to the desert, or to the brutality of Armijo, at
the request of the United States Minister, Waddy Thompson,

whose *Recollections of Mexico* (1846) mentions this release of Kendall and his companions in misery, as well as the release of the prisoners taken by the Mexicans at Mier in 1842. The capture, sufferings, and release of these latter unfortunates are told by William Preston Stapp in his book *The Prisoners of Perote* (1845). It is interesting to note that Waddy Thompson was no longer a United States official when he requested the freedom of the captives; General Santa Anna granted the request as a personal favour. Thompson gives an estimate of Santa Anna's character which is not so black as the usual descriptions.

Kendall printed a map, which he compiled, to give such information as was possible of the wilderness the caravan had struggled through, and in this he was aided by notes from Josiah Gregg, then living and doing business as a merchant at Santa Fé. In the year of the appearance of Kendall's book, Gregg alone published the now famous volumes *Commerce of the Prairies* (1844). This is the classic of the Plains, in which he describes the Santa Fé Trail and its history. The Atchison, Topeka, and Santa Fé Railway approximately follows the route of the Santa Fé Trail, and the latter almost paralleled the great Kaw Indian trail which ran about four or five miles farther south. Everywhere the possible highways had long ago been traced out by the Indians, and the main routes of the white men usually followed, with more or less exactness, according to method of transportation, these roads of the natives.

Colonel Henry Inman, who had early experience on the Plains, wrote *The Old Santa Fé Trail* (1897). Some of his historical data are not quite correct, but there is much of value derived from his own knowledge, and he gives accounts of the frontiersmen he had met. With W. F. Cody, the last of the "Buffalo Bills," he wrote *The Great Salt Lake Trail* (1898), the trail being the one from Omaha up the Platte and to Salt Lake by way of Echo Canyon. The Santa Fé Trail has also been perpetuated in poetry, by Sharlot M. Hall with a vivid poem of that title in *Out West* (1903), and the modern route for automobiles by Vachel Lindsay, with a more original poem, also of that title, in *The Congo and Other Poems* (1914).

Many of the early travellers and explorers kept no records,

and some who did refrained from publishing until long after
their experiences, as in the case of Osborne Russell, who had a
Rocky Mountain career between 1834 and 1843. *The Journal
of a Trapper* from his pen did not appear till 1914, when it was
privately printed at Boise, Idaho. These delays were sometimes due to the reluctance of publishers to print the writings
of unknown and "unliterary" men.

While the Santa Fé Trail linked the Missouri with the Rio
Grande as early as 1822, there was for a long time no overland
highway to the Oregon country, the usual route being up the
Missouri first by keelboat and then by steamboat. Audubon
travelled that course in 1843 in the steamer *Omega* as far as
Fort Union, and he kept a full journal. This was mislaid and
fifty years elapsed before it was given to the world in *Audubon
and his Journals* by his granddaughter, Maria R. Audubon.
His son, John Woodhouse Audubon, in 1849–50 made a journey from New York to Texas and thence overland through
Mexico and Arizona to the gold fields of California, which is
recorded in *John W. Audubon's Western Journal* (1906), edited
by Frank H. Hodder.

The literature connected with the route up the Missouri
River is voluminous and it is vital to the historical annals of the
West. A great deal of it falls before 1846. H. M. Chittenden
gives a *History of Early Steamboat Navigation of the Missouri
River. Life and Adventures of Joseph La Barge, Pioneer Navigator and Indian Trader* (1903); and with this title may be
coupled an important paper on the subject read by Phil. E.
Chappel before the Kansas State Historical Society (1904) and
printed in the Society's Publications (vol. ix), with the title
"A History of the Missouri River." He writes from personal
knowledge and adds a list of the steamboats.

A change was coming in this direction. Notwithstanding
the phenomenal scepticism as to the value of Oregon displayed
in Congress, the "common people" were learning by word of
mouth from trappers and explorers that good homes were to be
had there for the taking. They saw a vision of being land-
owners—a vision that became a life-preserver amid the dis-
comfort, danger, and disaster which befell a large proportion of
them in the journey to the land of promise. Presently, from the
same Independence that saw the wagon track vanish south-

westward with its caravans for Santa Fé, another track faded into the plains to the north-west and hammered its devious sagebrush course over mountains, over valleys, through difficult canyons, across dangerous rivers or deserts of death to the Columbia River, to Oregon, to California. This was the path that Francis Parkman,[1] just out of college, followed in 1846 as far as Fort Laramie; an experience which gave us *The California and Oregon Trail* (1849). Ezra Meeker travelled it in 1852 and back again in 1906, and in *The Ox-Team, or the Old Oregon Trail* (1906) he relates what befell him in this long, wild journey with an ox-team—a real "bull-whacker's" tale.

Mrs. Ann Boyd had experiences on this difficult highway in the late forties, and she presents the record in *The Oregon Trail* (1862). A rare volume on the same road is Joel Palmer's *Journal of Travels Over the Rocky Mountains to the Mouth of the Columbia River* (1847). For those desiring to identify in detail the route and distances of the Oregon Trail of early days there is a complete exposition in the masterly work by H. M. Chittenden, *History of the American Fur Trade in the Far West* (1902).

The chain binding Europe by the west to Cathay, of which the Santa Fé and the Oregon trails were preliminary links, was being forged to completion by this steady march of pioneers across the salubrious uplands of the Far West. At the same time the surrounding seas were breaking under the prows of American ships. T. J. Jacobs writes of the cruise of the clipper ship *Margaret Oakley* in *Scenes, Incidents, and Adventures in the Pacific Ocean* (1844); and the United States government took a hand in maritime exploration by sending Captain Charles Wilkes with six ships and a large company of scientific men on an important cruise to explore and survey the South Seas. From Australia, Wilkes steered for the South Pole and on 19 January, 1840, he was the first to see the Antarctic Continent, albeit only a very short time before the French navigator D'Urville also sighted it. For 1500 miles Wilkes skirted the icy coast, and the region he reported was accordingly named Wilkes Land. He also visited Hawaii, California, and Oregon, carrying on some survey work in the latter region. Five volumes were published: *The Narrative of the United States Exploring Expedition During the Years 1838, 1839, 1840, 1841,*

[1] See also Book III, Chap. xv.

1842 (1845), but the scientific data have not been issued, although many of the projected volumes are printed.[1] There is extant the manuscript journal of Captain Hudson, who commanded one of the ships; and Lieutenant (later Admiral) Colvocoresses attached to this command published *Four Years in the Government Exploring Expedition commanded by Captain Charles Wilkes*, etc. (1852). They saw Antarctic land frequently, and he says that on one day they saw "distinctly from sixty to seventy miles of coast, and a mountain in the interior which we estimated to be 2500 feet high." There are in this volume certain ethnological notes on the South Sea Islanders that are important.

Wilkes also published separately a volume, *Western America Including California and Oregon* (1849). Data on the same region are contained in the fourth and fifth of the five narrative volumes.

A prominent American sailor on the seas in the early fifties and onward was Captain S. Samuels. He began his career as cabin-boy at the age of eleven in 1836, and in ten years was a captain. He commanded the famous *Dreadnaught*, the swiftest ship of her time. He tells a thrilling story, for which Bishop Potter wrote the introduction, in *From the Forecastle to the Cabin* (1887).

South America was not forgotten by our American travellers and explorers, and a naval expedition in 1851–53 carried on an *Exploration of the Valley of the Amazon* (1854) under William L. Herndon and Lardner Gibbon, while, earlier than this, John Lloyd Stephens was investigating the intermediate part of the Western Hemisphere, publishing his admirable results in *Incidents of Travel in Central America, Chiapas, and Yucatan* (1841) and *Incidents of Travel in Yucatan* (1843). E. G. Squier's operations came out in *Nicaragua* (1856) and *The States of Central America* (1858). Far away in Turkey the Rev. Doctor William Goodell was having the experiences which he recounts in *Forty Years in the Turkish Empire* (1876), edited by his son-in-law, E. D. G. Prime. Dr. Goodell belonged to a class of workers, the religious missionaries, who travelled far and wide seeking out all manner of places. They also became active in the Far West at an early date. Samuel Parker for

[1] For contents of these volumes see MS. catalogue in the Library of Congress.

the Presbyterian Church went to Oregon in 1836, taking with him a physician, Marcus Whitman. Parker wrote *A Journal of an Exploring Tour Beyond the Rocky Mountains* (1838), one of the valuable books of the period. Whitman became so deeply interested in the religious welfare of the Indians that he turned missionary and established a working centre at Waiilatpu. Later, in the winter of 1842–43, he made the now much discussed overland journey by the southern route to Washington. This adventure is recorded in *How Marcus Whitman Saved Oregon* (1895) by O. W. Nixon. Whitman is said to have exposed nefarious British designs to the American government, but this service has been disputed on good authority. W. I. Marshall is one of those who oppose the "saviour" idea, and he presents his views in the *Report of the American Historical Association* (1900) and also in *Acquisition of Oregon, and the Long Suppressed Evidence about Marcus Whitman* (1911). At any rate, Whitman was a splendid character and devoted his life to work among the Indians, who, imagining some superstitious grievance against the whites, murdered many of them, including their own benefactor and his wife, and held the others prisoners. M. Cannon in his account of pioneer days tells the story of this massacre in *Waiilatpu, Its Rise and Fall* (1915).

The captives were rescued by the skill and determined bearing of one of the greatest frontiersmen of the West, Peter Skene Ogden. Ogden, while not an American, was next thing to it, as his father was born in Newark, New Jersey, but the family, being royalists, travelled to more genial climes at the outbreak of the trouble with George III. T. C. Elliott, in a very entertaining and instructive pamphlet, *Peter Skene Ogden, Fur Trader* (1910), relates the remarkable career of Ogden, chiefly in the region south of the forty-ninth parallel. Ogden wrote *Traits of American Indian Life and Character by a Fur Trader* (1853), revised in manuscript by Jesse Applegate. Ogden is said to have taken it to Washington Irving, who was prevented by circumstances from editing it.

Most of the travellers who penetrated the Western wilderness in those early days were close and quite accurate observers, and many of their books, like Gregg's and Kendall's and Edwin Bryant's, have become of immeasurable historical value. Another whose works take a similar high place is Thomas

Jefferson Farnham.   No library of Americana can be considered complete which lacks his *Travels in the Great Western Prairies, the Anahuac and Rocky Mountains and in the Oregon Territory* (1843), and his *Life, Adventures and Travels in California* (1849). Farnham followed some seldom travelled trails, and he tells not only what he saw but what he heard—giving in the latter field one of the early descriptions of the Grand Canyon of the Colorado, not accurate but interesting. A missionary who roamed widely over Oregon was Father P. J. De Smet, and his writings are among the most vital, especially *Oregon Missions and Travels over the Rocky Mountains in 1845-46* (1847) and *Letters and Sketches* (1843).

The Santa Fé Trail coupled the Rio Grande and the mighty Missouri, as has been mentioned, by a well-beaten and more or less easy and comfortable way which halted at the city of Santa Fé.   Thence on to Los Angeles there were two or three routes open to the traveller, taking any one of which was sure to make him wish he had chosen another.   One led down the Rio Grande into Mexico, thence westward and up to the Gila through Tucson, following the Gila on west to the Colorado, the Mohave desert, and to Cajon Pass; the other turned north from Santa Fé and straggled over the mountains, to cross the Grand River and the Green at the first opportunity the canyons permitted (that on the Green being at what was afterwards known as Gunnison Crossing), thence through the Wasatch, down to the Virgin, and by that stream to the Mohave desert, and across that stretch of Hades by the grace of God.   This trail was laid out in 1830 by William Wolfskill, an American, but as it was travelled mostly by Spaniards it was called the Spanish Trail.   Between this and the extreme southern route was a possible way down the Gila, and another between that and the majestic Grand Canyon, followed in 1776 eastward as far as the Hopi (Moqui) villages by Garces the Spanish missionary; but to take either intermediate route at that time was almost like signing one's death warrant.   They were not often taken before 1846.   Much about the early trails and trappers and missionaries is told in *Breaking the Wilderness* (1905) by Frederick S. Dellenbaugh.

The Oregon Trail, bearing far to the north, through South Pass and down Snake River, was extended to the Columbia and thence around south to California, but, before the "Days of '49," although Ogden, Jedediah Smith, and Frémont had dared the mid-passage across the Great Basin, there was no real route directly to the rich, inviting mission settlements of the Franciscan friars: settlements that were a world unto themselves delightfully described by Alfred Robinson in *Life in California During a Residence of Several Years in that Territory, Etc. By an American* (1846). And in *Two Years Before the Mast* (1840) R. H. Dana has some interesting chapters on this primitive California paradise. The historical side is presented by Fr. Zephyrin Englehardt in an extensive work, *The Missions and Missionaries of California* (1911).

In the early forties California was nothing more than a detached colony nominally belonging to Mexico but ruled over, so far as it was ruled at all, by the Mission friars and the military governor in an arbitrary and personal fashion. Its rich soil and attractive coast were coveted by France, by Great Britain, and by the United States. This great prize slipping from Mexico's fist had its northern limit at the forty-second parallel and its eastern along the upper Arkansas and down that river to the 100th meridian, down that to Red River, along that stream to a point north of the Sabine, and by the Sabine to the Gulf of Mexico. Texas took away the portion from the Sabine to the Nueces and claimed to the Rio Grande. Thus matters stood at the time of the annexation of Texas, with its claim of a western boundary at the Rio Grande which the United States had undertaken to maintain with the sword.

There was one statesman in Congress who had a clear perception of conditions and possibilities. This was Thomas Hart Benton, whose home was in St. Louis and was the rendezvous for leading trappers and explorers. His famous phrase as he pointed to the sunset and said "There lies the road to India" recognized the approach to each other of Europe and Cathay westward across the Rocky Mountains and has appropriately been carved on his monument. In his *Thirty Years' View . . . 1820 to 1850* (1861) there is continual evidence of his firm belief in the phenomenal value of the Far West region and in a development which has since taken place. Benton was one of the chief political figures of the time. Biographies of him have been written by Theodore Roosevelt (1887) and by William M. Meigs (1904).

As the fourth decade of the nineteenth century opened, California was receiving many emigrants from the Eastern States, chiefly by the Oregon Trail. About this time appears on the scene a striking personality, John A. Sutter, independent, indefatigable, who immediately created a unique fortified settlement which, having been born in Switzerland, he called New Helvetia, but which was known generally as Sutter's Fort. It was begun in 1841 and completed in 1845, on the site of the present city of Sacramento. Although Sutter was Swiss he may be classed as an American in view of all the circumstances connected with his life. His fort mounted carronades and cannon and was garrisoned by about forty well armed, drilled, uniformed Indians. There were extra arms for more if needed. In his "Diary"[1] printed in *the Argonaut* (San Francisco, 26 Jan., 2, 9, 16 Feb., 1878) Sutter tells of his own doings, and in the *Life and Times of John A. Sutter* (1907) T. J. Schoonover relates the entire story of this remarkable pioneer, the good friend of everybody but "bankrupted by thieves."

By 1846 the dispute with Great Britain over Oregon was settled and the Americans there knew where they belonged. They had been warmly defended and assisted by the then head of Hudson Bay Company affairs in that region, John McLoughlin, who himself finally became an American. The story of his life is given by Frederick V. Holman, *John McLoughlin, The Father of Oregon* (1900), and in *McLoughlin and Old Oregon* (1900) by Mrs. Emery Dye.

Benton's son-in-law, John C. Frémont, had conducted an expedition in 1842 along the Oregon Trail to the Wind River Mountains, and he was selected to carry on a new reconnaissance, ostensibly to connect the survey of the Oregon Trail with survey work done on the Pacific Coast by Wilkes. But this 1843-44 expedition did not halt in Oregon. It headed southward into Mexican territory along the eastern edge of the Sierras, hunting for a mythical Buenaventura River that would have made a fine military base had it existed. Not discovering that entrancing Elysian valley, Frémont crossed the high Sierras in dead winter to Sutter's Fort, returning by the

[1] See also *Reminiscences* in MS., Bancroft Collection.

Spanish Trail to Utah and breaking through the Wasatch east of Utah Lake. His *Report of the Exploring Expedition to the Rocky Mountains in the Year 1842 and to Oregon and Northern California in the Years 1843–44* (1845) was a revelation to most of the world. Ten thousand copies were printed by the government, and it was reprinted by professional publishers, minus the scientific matter, in their regular lists.

The very day Frémont handed in this report, 1 March, 1845, the United States flung the gauntlet in the face of Mexico by admitting Texas and assuming the Texan boundary affair. War was inevitable and everybody knew it. Therefore when Frémont headed a new "topographical surveying" expedition to the Far West he had a force of sixty well-armed marksmen. When he reached California and found an incipient rebellion already organized by Americans, he placed himself with this powerful party and the American flag at its head, supplanting the Bear Flag of the revolutionists and giving immediate notice thereby to the other covetous nations that California was only for the United States.

The Bear Flag revolt from its beginning may be studied in *Scraps of California History Never Before Published. A Biographical Sketch of William B. Ide*, etc. (1880), privately printed by Simeon Ide. In H. H. Bancroft's *History of California*, vol. v, is another account; and the revolt and Frémont are sharply criticized by Josiah Royce in *California from the Conquest in 1846 to the Second Vigilance Committee in San Francisco* (1888). Royce also gave his analysis of Frémont's character in the *Atlantic Monthly* in 1890.

Frémont tells his own story in *Memoirs of My Life* (1887; only vol. 1 of the projected two volumes was published). This contains a sketch of "The Life of Senator Benton in Connection with Western Explorations" from the pen of his daughter, Jessie Benton Frémont. Frémont's career up to the time he ran for President was written by John Bigelow as a campaign document in 1856: *Memoir of the Life of John C. Frémont*. Another *Life of Frémont* (1856) is by Charles W. Upham, but there was no single volume containing all the story of this active explorer and politician till *Frémont and '49*, by Frederick S. Dellenbaugh, appeared in 1914.

California now attracted world attention, and there are a

great number of interesting and valuable books relating to it. *Los Gringos* (1849), by Lieutenant Wise, U. S. N., describes the cruise of an American man-of-war which took active part in the conquest along the coast. One of the most trustworthy of all the volumes of this period is by Edwin Bryant, "late Alcalde of San Francisco," *What I saw in California in 1846–1847* (1848). This will always stand in the first rank of Western Americana, with Farnham, Gregg, etc. Bryant was in Frémont's California Battalion during the conquest. The book has been cheaply reprinted, with a "blood and thunder" title-page supplanting the original, as *Rocky Mountain Adventures* (1889).

While the conquest of California was proceeding to its logical end an agricultural conquest of the valley of the Great Salt Lake was begun by the Mormons, or Latter Day Saints as they called themselves. Their late neighbours in Illinois had inaugurated such great opposition to Mormon methods that it culminated in the murder, by a mob, in Carthage jail, of Joseph Smith, the prophet and originator of the sect, and a migration was imperative. The Mormons now possessed a martyr, the essential basis of religious success, and they needed an independent field for expansion. Their new leader, Brigham Young, discovered it in the Salt Lake Valley described glowingly in Frémont's report. Brigham thought of founding a separate state in this Mexican territory, but the events of the Mexican war moved so rapidly that, even while he planned, the valley fell under American rule. The Mormons went forward nevertheless and arrived on the shore of the American Dead Sea in August, 1847. Brigham complained that the valley was not as represented by Frémont—that it was really a desert. Frémont had seen on the Rio Grande what irrigation can do, and the Mormons resorted to it with an agricultural success now well known.

The transit to the new home across the wide and unsettled plains and mountains was a huge undertaking and entailed much hardship. T. L. Kane, a non-Mormon, accompanied the famous "hand cart expedition" and tells about it in *The Mormons* (1850). The literature connected with the Mormons is voluminous. One of the latest, most comprehensive, and most exact general books is W. J. Linn's *Story of the Mormons* (1902).

It has been charged that the Mormon leaders employed a gang of cut-throats to discourage Gentiles from settling among them, and Bill Hickman, when he became an apostate, claimed to have been the leader of it. He issued a book, *Brigham's Destroying Angel Being the Life Confession and Startling Disclosures of the Notorious Bill Hickman Written by Himself with Explanatory Notes by J. H. Beadle* (1872). Beadle also published *Western Wilds* (1877), *Life in Utah* (1870), *The Undeveloped West* (1873), and "The Story of Marcus Whitman Refuted" in *American Catholic Historical Researches* (1879). Mrs. Stenhouse, who apostatized, wrote *Tell it All* (1874), a faithful account of her sad life as a Mormon.

While Frémont was aiding Commodore Stockton to clinch the claim of the United States to California, the history of which is told in *Despatches Relating to Military and Naval Operations in California* (1849) and in *A Sketch of the Life of R. F. Stockton with his Correspondence with the Navy Department Respecting his Conquest of California and the Defense of J. C. Fremont* (1856), the war in Mexico was in full swing. General Stephen Kearny, with an army, was marching overland for the Pacific Coast by way of Santa Fé, where he halted long enough to raise the flag and destroy opposition.

Kearny was a noble officer whose early death in the Mexican campaign prevented his writing about the California campaign. Valentine Mott Porter wrote a sketch of him in *Publications of the Historical Society of Southern California*, vol. VIII (1911); and *A Diary of the March with Kearny, Fort Leavenworth to Santa Fé* (1846) by G. R. Gibson gives details concerning that part of the journey. Gibson also wrote two other diaries on a trip to Chihuahua and return in 1847. The journals of Captain Johnson and of Colonel P. St. George Cooke on the march from Santa Fé to California appeared in *House Executive Document 41, 1st Sess. 30th Congress*, and Colonel Cooke's "The Journal of a March from Santa Fé to San Diego 1846-47" was printed in *Sen. Ex. Doc. 2 Special Sess. 31st Cong.* Other literary productions of Colonel Cooke were *The Conquest of New Mexico and California* (1878) and *Scenes and Adventures in Army Life* (1857).

Kearny, before proceeding to California, planned for the holding of New Mexico, and one of the memorable expeditions of the war resulted, that of Colonel A. W. Doniphan. It was accurately recorded by John T. Hughes in *Doniphan's Expedition; Containing an Account of the Conquest of New Mexico, General Kearny's Overland Expedition to California, Doniphan's Campaign Against the Navajos, his Unparalleled March upon Chihuahua and Durango and the Operations of General Price at Santa Fé, with a Sketch of the Life of Colonel Doniphan* (1847). Hughes wrote another book now very hard to obtain, *California, Its History, Population, Climate, Soil, Productions, and Harbours, and an Account of the Revolution in California and the Conquest of the Country by the United States, 1846–47* (1848).

William E. Connelley has reprinted the Hughes *Doniphan* with Hughes's diary and other related matter in *Doniphan's Expedition* (1907). With the advance guard of the Army of the West went Major William H. Emory, and his *Notes of a Military Reconnaissance from Fort Leavenworth to San Diego, California, 1846–47* (1848) is an important contribution to the documents on this famous march.

The Rev. Walter Colton was in California before the conquest and he wrote an exceedingly valuable book, *Three Years in California, 1846–49* (1850), as well as another, *Deck and Port, or Incidents of a Cruise in the United States Frigate Congress*, etc. (1850). Still another volume of this period is *Notes on a Voyage to California Together with Scenes in Eldorado in 1849* (1878) by S. C. Upham. The name Eldorado enters so commonly into the literature of the Far West that we may at this point note the volume *The Gilded Man* (1893), by A. F. Bandelier, which describes and explains the term and its origin. In a certain ceremonial in Peru a man was covered from head to foot with gold dust and this gave rise to the expression as meaning fabulous wealth.

With the prospect of closer contact with the Orient by way of the Occident, relations with some of the far off Eastern countries began to be more intimately considered. Caleb Cushing as Commissioner of the United States went to China in 1843 and in 1845 negotiated the first treaty between the United States and China. Missionaries, too, were at their task. Volumes of the *Chinese Repository* edited by Dr. Bridgman were publishing at Canton, and from these volumes, and his own personal observation and study of native authorities for twelve years,

S. Wells Williams, who went to China as a printer for the Board of Foreign Missions, who mastered the Chinese language, and who lectured in the United States to obtain money to pay for a font of Chinese type, produced *The Middle Kingdom. A Survey of the Geography, Government, Education, Social Life, Arts, Religion, etc., of the Chinese Empire and its Inhabitants* (1848), a book that remains today one of the supreme authorities on the subject.

Another traveller in that region was the afterwards eccentric George Francis Train. Only twenty-four years of age, he met with much success in commercial ventures in China, and a book was the outcome: *An American Merchant in Europe, Asia, and Australia* (1857). The last years of Train's life were mainly spent on a bench in Madison Square Park, New York, refusing conversation with all adults.

The year following the conclusion of the Mexican War, which completed the sway of the United States over the entire West between the Gila River and the forty-ninth parallel, one of the large events of the world happened. A certain Marshall was employed by Sutter in the construction of a saw-mill up in the mountains, and one morning in January, 1848, when he picked from the sluiceway a particle of metal half the size of a pea, shining in the sun, it made his heart thump, for he believed it to be gold. Gold it proved to be. The great news was quick in reaching the outermost ends of the earth, calling men of all kinds, of all nationalities, pell-mell to Eldorado to pick up a fortune. Men of Cathay, men of Europe, men of the Red Indian race, all mingled on common terms in the scramble. Centuries of creeping along the fortieth parallel had at last tied together the far ends of the earth. "Marshall's Own Account of the Gold Discovery" appeared in *The Century Magazine*, vol. XIX. Gold had been discovered some years before, but the psychological moment had not arrived for its exploitation. A vast literature developed on the subject, one of the earliest books being *The Emigrant's Guide to the Gold Mines, and Adventures with the Gold Diggers of California in August 1848* (1848), by Henry I. Simpson, of the New York Volunteers. This book has become rare. Another early but not scarce "gold" item is Theodore T. Johnson's *Sights and Scenes in the Gold Regions, and Scenes by the Way* (1849).

The gold seekers got as far as Salt Lake over the Oregon Trail by Bear River; or from Ft. Bridger by the new way Hastings had found a little farther south, and more direct, through Echo Canyon. From Salt Lake the chief trail west led down the Humboldt River to the Sierra and over that mighty barrier by what became known as Donner Pass to commemorate the Donner party and the shocking result of their miscalculation, the details of which are given in *The Expedition of the Donner Party and its Tragic Fate* (1911) by Mrs. Eliza P. Donner Houghton. "The Diary of one of the Donner Party" by Patrick Breen, edited by F. J. Taggart, is given in *Publications of Pacific Coast History*, vol. v. (1910); and C. F. McGlashan published a *History of the Donner Party* (1880). This ill-fated caravan originated in Illinois. John Carroll Power in a *History of the Early Settlers of Sangamon County, Ill.* (1876) gives the daily journal of the "Reed and Donner Emigrating Party."

The difficulties of travel by ox and mule team, the necessity of obtaining communication better from a military point of view, and other considerations led to talk of a railway to California. George Wilkes published in 1845 a volume now rare, *Project of a National Railroad from the Atlantic to the Pacific Ocean, for the Purpose of Obtaining a Short Route to Oregon.* In 1848, Asa Whitney made addresses, memorials, and petitions for a transcontinental railway, and he gave his plan in a Congressional document, *Miscellaneous 28, Senate, 30th Congress 1:* "Memorial of Asa Whitney for grants of land to enable him to build a railway from Lake Michigan to the Pacific." Whitney issued a volume in the same line, from personal exploration: *Project for a Railroad to the Pacific with Reports and Other Facts Relating Thereto* (1849).

No one was more enthusiastic or confident of the feasibility of a railway than Frémont, unless it was his father-in-law, Benton. They were both positive that neither rivers, nor hot deserts, nor the deep mountain snows of winter would interfere seriously with the operation of trains. Frémont projected his fourth expedition especially to prove that winter would be no obstacle, and he attempted crossing the highest mountains in the winter of 1848–49. He met with sad disaster in Colorado, for which he blamed the guide for misleading him. This dreadful experience he describes in his *Memoirs,* and it is related in other books on Frémont's expeditions; and Micajah McGehee, who was of the party, gives all the terror of theu struggle in "Rough Times in Rough Places" in *The Century Magazine*, vol. XIX. After this catastrophe Frémont proceeded to California by the far southern route of upper Mexico and the Gila, arriving just as the great gold excitement was in its first heat.

Thousands were now preparing to follow thousands to the fortune-field that lay against what Frémont previously had named the Golden Gate. It mattered not that the way was beset with impossibilities for the greenhorn (or in later nomenclature, the tenderfoot); to California he was bound through fair and foul. Not the least of the troubles arose from Indians, those people who already possessed the country and were satisfied with it. They disliked to see their game destroyed by these new hordes, their springs polluted by cattle, their families treated with brutality or contempt according to the physical strength of the pioneer party. The latter on their part regarded the Indians as merely a dangerous nuisance, to be got rid of by any possible means. Sometimes when the trapper's or pioneer's confidence ran high with power, the Indian, armed only with a bow and arrows, was pursued and shot as sport from horseback, just as the sportsman chases antelope or buffalo.

The misconception of Indian life and character so common among the white people [remarks Francis LaFlesche, himself an Indian, in his preface to his charming little story of his boy life, *The Middle Five: Indian Boys at School* (1900)] has been largely due to ignorance of the Indian's language, of his mode of thought, his beliefs, his ideals, and his native institutions.

We have heretofore viewed the Indians chiefly through the eyes of those who were interested in exploiting them; or of exterminating them. Perhaps it is time to listen to their own words.

Another educated Indian, Dr. Charles A. Eastman (Ohiyesa), a full-blood Sioux, writing on this subject in *The Soul of the Indian* (1900), declares:

The native American has been generally despised by his white conquerors for his poverty and simplicity. They forget, perhaps, that his religion forbade the accumulation of wealth and the enjoyment of luxury.   To him as to other single minded men in every age and race, from Diogenes to the brothers of Saint Francis, from the Montanists to the Shakers, the love of possessions has appeared a snare, and the burdens of a complex society a source of needless peril and temptation.   It is my personal belief after thirty-five years experience of it, that there is no such thing as Christian Civilization.   I believe that Christianity and modern civilization are opposed and irreconcilable and that the spirit of Christianity and of our ancient religion is essentially the same. . . .   Since there is nothing left us but remembrance, at least let that remembrance be just.

With reference to the treachery of the whites, at times, in the treatment of Indians it is permissible to refer the reader to the *Massacre of Cheyenne Indians, 38th Congress, 2nd Sess., House Doc., Jan. 10th, 1865*, wherein the Committee on the Conduct of the War, Benjamin F. Wade, Chairman, reports on an unprovoked attack by Colorado militia on a Cheyenne village in which sixty-nine, two thirds women and children, were killed and the bodies left on the field.

The Indian side of much of the trouble of the years following 1861 may be read in "Forty Years with the Cheyennes," written by George Bent for *The Frontier*, a Colorado Springs monthly. Bent's mother was Owl Woman of the Southern Cheyennes, and his father, Col. William Bent, the widely known proprietor of Bent's Fort on the Arkansas, also called Fort William. Young Bent left school to join the Confederate army, was captured, paroled, and sent to his father.   He then went to his mother's people and remained with them.

There was at least one American of early Western days who looked on the Indian with more sympathy.   This was George Catlin, now famous for his paintings and books.   Thanks to a kind Providence, not to our foresight, his invaluable painted records of a life that is past are now the property of the United States.   Thomas Donaldson gives an exhaustive review of Catlin, his paintings in the National Museum, and his books in *Part V, Report of the U. S. National Museum* (1885).

We are not here concerned with Catlin's paintings and only note his literary output.   His *Letters and Notes on the Manners and Customs of the North American Indians, Written During*

Eight Years Travel Among the Wildest Tribes of Indians in North America in 1832, 33, 34, 35, 36, 37, 38, and 39, with Four Hundred Illustrations Carefully Engraved from his Original Paintings was published first in London, at his own expense, in 1841. The same year it was brought out in New York. Another of his volumes was *Catlin's Notes of Eight Years Travels and Residence in Europe with his North American Indian Collection, with Anecdotes and Adventures of Three Different Parties of American Indians whom he Introduced to the Courts of England, France and Belgium* (1848). A book of his that raised strong doubts as to his veracity was *Okeepa, A Religious Ceremony, and other Customs of the Mandans*, which was published in Philadelphia in 1867, and gave one of the earliest accounts of the extraordinary Okeepa ceremonial: a self-sacrificial affair akin to the Sun Dance of the Dakotas. The book today is recognized as veracious and valuable. He wrote *Life among the Indians* (1861) for young folk, and in 1837 he brought out a *Catalogue of Catlin's Indian Gallery of Portraits, Landscapes, Manners, Customs, and Costumes, etc.* His well-known, and now rare, *North American Indian Portfolio, Twenty-five large Tinted Drawings on Stone, some Coloured by Hand in Imitation of the Author's Sketches*, appeared in London in 1844; his *Steam Raft* in 1850; *Shut your Mouth* in 1865; and *Last Rambles amongst the Indians of the Rocky Mountains and the Andes* in London in 1868.

His viewpoint was totally different from that of the trapper or pioneer, explorer or traveller. Catlin was interested in the Indian as a man. "The Indians have always loved me," he declares, "and why should I not love the Indians?" He wrote a "Creed," part of which was: "I love the people who have always made me welcome to the best they had. I love the people who have never raised a hand against me, or stolen my property, where there was no law to punish for either."

The Mormons soon adopted a conciliatory policy towards the Indians, feeling it was more profitable to deal justly with them, to pay them, than to fight them. It was obligatory to have a cool clear-headed man to carry out such a policy, and Brigham Young selected Jacob Hamblin for the service. No better choice could have been made. Slow of speech, quick of thought and action, this Leatherstocking of Utah was usually called "Old Jacob." He tells an interesting story through James A. Little in *Jacob Hamblin, a Narrative of his Personal Experiences* (1881). A devoted Mormon, he was never unfriendly to other sects and often assisted persons of opposite faith, at least on two occasions saving lives.

The list of books on Indians is enormous, the Bureau of Ethnology alone having produced a great many, including the series of thirty-two invaluable *Annual Reports* inaugurated by J. W. Powell, as well as more than fifty-eight equally important *Bulletins*. George Bird Grinnell's *Indians of Today* (1900) and *The North Americans of Yesterday* (1901) by Frederick S. Dellenbaugh are two volumes which present a wide general survey.

A famous man associated with Indians throughout his life was Kit Carson, one of the most remarkable and upright characters of the Far West. Dewitt C. Peters persuaded Carson to dictate to him the story of his life. The last and complete edition is *Kit Carson's Life and Adventures* (1873). George D. Brewerton in *Harper's Magazine* (1853) wrote an account of "A Ride with Kit Carson through the Great American Desert and the Rocky Mountains." This ride was made in 1848 and was over the Spanish Trail eastward from Los Angeles. The springs are few and far between in Southern Nevada and South-Eastern California, and in studying this route and the literature pertaining to the region Walter C. Mendenhall's *Some Desert Watering Places* (U. S. Water Supply Paper 224, 1909) is most useful.

Some experiences were published long afterward, as in the case of William Lewis Manly's *Death Valley in '49*, which was never printed till 1894. It is deeply interesting. The author, arrived at Green River, decided with several others to shorten the journey by taking to the river, and was hurled through the torrential waters of Red Canyon and Lodore Later he joined a California caravan to suffer terribly in Death Valley.

John Bidwell, an "earliest" pioneer, has contributed to *The Century Magazine*, vol. XIX, and to *Out West Magazine*, vol. XX, some invaluable reminiscences. He was with the first emigrant train to California. It crossed in 1841. In 1853 Captain Howard Stansbury made a report on his *Explo-*

ration and Survey of the Valley of Great Salt Lake, the valley where the Mormons already were proving by irrigation the accuracy of Frémont's statement as to its fertility.

Congress took up with energy the matter of a railway to the Pacific, and several exploration routes were planned. Frémont was to survey one, but the leadership was given instead to Captain Gunnison, who proceeded by the "Central Route" over the Sangre de Cristo Pass. Gunnison was killed by Indians at Sevier Lake. He had been stationed at Salt Lake when assisting Stansbury, and while there made a study of Mormonism, *The Mormons, or the Latter Day Saints in the Valley of the Great Salt Lake* (1852). Mrs. Gunnison believed that the Mormons had instigated the murder of her husband, and Judge Drummond, who tried the case, was of this opinion also, and so stated in a letter to Mrs. Gunnison printed in the edition of 1890. He believed that the murder was carried out by Bill Hickman and eight others. One Mormon was among those slain.

A series of large quarto volumes (thirteen in number, as the last or twelfth volume was issued in two parts) was published on railway surveys by the government: *Reports of Explorations and Surveys to Ascertain the most Practicable and Economical Route for a Railroad from the Mississippi River to the Pacific Ocean* (1855 to 1859). The explorers wrote with grace and facility, as a rule, and these reports form an indispensable library of information on the Far West of the fifties.

While these surveys were going on, an epoch-making link in the chain that was forging between Europe and Cathay was placed by Americans cruising in Asiatic waters: Commodore Perry visited Japan and negotiated the first treaty between a Western people and the Japanese. The record of this achievement is given in a *Narrative of the Expedition of an American Squadron to the China Seas and Japan Performed in the Years 1852, 1853, and 1854. Compiled from the Original Notes and Journals of Commodore Perry and his Officers at his Request and under his Supervision by Francis L. Hawkes* (1856).

A transcontinental railway became more and more a necessity from numerous points of view, not the least of which was the interchange of products across the Pacific. Preliminary wagon roads were surveyed, and for this purpose Lieutenant

E. F. Beale in returning to California struck across a little ahead of Gunnison on the same route. With him was Gwin Harris Heap, who wrote the narrative of the journey: *Central Route to the Pacific from the Valley of the Mississippi to California* (1854), an attractive and interesting story.

Following almost the same route, as far as Gunnison's crossing of Green River, came later in the same year the indefatigable Frémont on his fifth expedition. At Gunnison Crossing he swung to the south through the "High Plateau" country, a southern extension of the Wasatch uplift, and after much suffering in the midwinter of 1853–54 the starving party dragged into the Mormon settlement of Parowan with the loss of one man. Every family in the town immediately took in some of the men and gave them the kindest care. When able, Frémont proceeded westward till he met the high Sierras icy wall, where he deflected south to the first available pass. To the end of his life he never forgot the generous behavior of the Mormons.

At this time Mrs. Frémont reports in her *Far West Sketches* (1890) a most remarkable vision she had of her husband's plight, which came to her in the night at Washington. Mrs. Frémont wrote other interesting books, *The Story of the Guard* (1863), *A Year of American Travel* (1878), *Souvenirs of my Time* (1887), and the "Origin of the Frémont Explorations" in *The Century Magazine* (1890). The *Recollections* (1912) of her daughter, Elizabeth Benton Frémont, belong to the story of Frémont's career.

Frémont published no account, and no data, of the fifth and last expedition excepting a letter to *The National Intelligencer* (1854), reprinted in Bigelow's *Life*. The narrative was to appear in the second volume of his *Memoirs*, but this was not published. His exact route therefore cannot be located. The main reliance for the narrative is *Incidents of Travel and Adventure in the Far West with Frémont's Last Expedition* (1857), by S. N. Carvalho, artist to the expedition.

One of the phenomenally reckless, daredevil frontiersmen was James P. Beckwourth, a man of mixed blood, who dictated a marvellous story of his escapades to T. D. Bonner. This was published in 1856 as *The Life and Adventures of James P. Beckwourth*. Somewhat highly coloured, no doubt, by Beckwourth's fancy, it still remains a valuable record of the time. Another book in this class is *The Adventures of James Capen Adams of California*, edited by Theodore H. Hittell (1860 and 1911); and still another is William F. Drannan's *Thirty-One Years on the Plains and Mountains, or The Last Voice from the Plains* (1900), wherein he describes his intimacy with Kit Carson and other frontiersmen, all apparently from memory, as was the case with the life records of most of the rougher class of hunters. Drannan published another book, *Captain W. F. Drannan, Chief of Scouts, etc.* Joe Meek was a brilliant example of the early trapper and had a varied experience which Mrs. Frances Fuller Victor records in her fine work *The River of the West* (1870).

An extremely scarce volume is *Reid's Tramp: or a Journal of the Incidents of Ten Months' Travel Through Texas, New Mexico, Arizona, etc.* This volume by John C. Reid was published in 1858 at Selma, Alabama. The United States, after the Mexican War, had bought from Mexico a strip south of the Gila River known as the "Gadsden Purchase," and to this many pioneers flocked expecting a new Eden, Eldorado, Elysian Fields, or what not. Reid remarks: "We may review the history of the fall, death, and interment of these hopes in a far-off country of irremediable disappointment." We know of the existence of but four copies of Reid's book.

After the Gadsden Purchase the matter of the Mexican boundary was ready for determination. The work was under the direction of Major W. H. Emory, who made an excellent *Report on the United States and Mexican Boundary Survey* (1857) in two fine volumes, the first two chapters of volume I containing a very interesting personal account. One of the boundary commissioners, John Russell Bartlett, published his own account in two volumes of *Personal Narrative of Explorations and Incidents in Texas, New Mexico, California, Sonora, and Chihuahua During the Years 1850, '51, '52, and 1853* (1854), a valuable addition to the literature of the South-west.

On the north the boundary was also surveyed, and Archibald Campbell and W. J. Twining wrote *Reports upon the Survey of the Boundary between the Territory of the United States and the Possessions of Great Britain from the Lake of the Woods to the Summit of the Rocky Mountains* (1878). Previously the boundary along the 49th parallel had been surveyed to the Gulf of Georgia in settling the Oregon question.

A volume published for the author, Philip Tome, in Buffalo in 1854, now very rare, is *Pioneer Life, or Thirty Years a Hunter. Being Scenes and Adventures in the Life of Philip Tome, Fifteen Years Interpreter for Cornplanter and George Blacksnake, Chiefs on the Alleghany River.* Cornplanter, a half-breed Seneca, was one of the most distinguished of the Iroquois leaders.

In the early fifties Joaquin Miller[1] was taken to California overland by his parents, and the impressions he received coloured his entire life. His poem, *The Ship in the Desert* (1875), is a string of "these scenes and descriptions of a mighty land of mystery, and wild and savage grandeur."

> What scenes they passed, what camps at morn,
> What weary columns kept the road:
> What herds of troubled cattle low'd,
> And trumpeted like lifted horn;
> And everywhere, or road or rest,
> All things were pointing to the West;
> A weary, long and lonesome track,
> And all led on, but one looked back.

Joaquin Miller also wrote the prose volume *Life Among the Modocs* (1874).

A period was now beginning when the literature of the Far West was not to be confined to the tales of trappers and explorers. About 1860 a young printer obtained employment in the composing-room of *The Golden Era* in San Francisco, and he was a contributor to that paper as well. He was invited to the home of the Frémonts (who were then living on their Black Point estate near the Golden Gate) because of the talent, the genius, they discovered in his manuscripts. From that moment the career of Bret Harte[2] flowed on successfully to the end. About the same time there appeared on this remote and primitive literary stage another genius who was dubbed the "Wild Humorist of the Pacific Slope." He tried mining with no success and then turned to his pen. *The Jumping Frog* (1867) carried the name of the former Mississippi pilot to the outer world, and "Mark Twain" became a star among the

---

[1] See Book III, Chap. x.   [2] *Ibid.*, Chap. vi.

literary lights of the United States.[1]   Further mention here of either of these brilliant members of the American literary fraternity is unnecessary except perhaps to note Mark Twain's *Life on the Mississippi* (1883) and his *Letter to the California Pioneers* (1911), in the second of which he describes his life as a miner. An early literary explorer to the Pacific Coast was Theodore Winthrop,[2] who wrote *The Canoe and Saddle, Adventures Among the Northwestern Rivers and Forests; and Isthmiana* (1862).

One of our inveterate travellers of the purely literary type was Bayard Taylor.[3]   Among the first he went to California and published *Eldorado, or Adventures in the Path of Empire* (1850).   Taylor was a voluminous writer and his works describe many parts of the globe.   China was one country that found him an early visitor, from which journey came *A Visit to India, China, and Japan in 1853* (1855).

The interesting experiences and reminiscences of one of the most prominent Americans in China during many decades, Dr. William A. P. Martin, first president of the Imperial University, are told in Dr. Martin's book, *A Cycle of Cathay* (1897), an indispensable work in this field.   William Elliot Griffis visited the Orient too, and gave us *The Mikado's Empire* (1876) and *Corea, The Hermit Nation* (1882).   The road to the East from the West, which Benton so dramatically pointed out, was being followed with enthusiasm.   Lafcadio Hearn made Japan his own.   His *Glimpses of Unfamiliar Japan* (1894), *Leaves from the Diary of an Impressionist* (1911), *Out of the East* (1895), *In Ghostly Japan* (1899), and others are too well known to require comment.   A contribution of much interest to this literature is Eliza Ruhamah Scidmore's *Jinrikisha Days in Japan* (1891).   She declares that "Japan six times revisited is as full of charm and novelty as when I first went ashore from the wreck of the *Tokio*."

A missionary who wrote *Adventures in Patagonia* (1880) wrote also *Life in Hawaii* (1882), both of them "foundation" books.   He became identified with everything Hawaiian, and wrote many letters from there to *The American Journal of Science* and to *The Missionary Herald*.   This indefatigable worker in the missionary realm was the Rev. Titus Coan, whose

---

[1] See Book III, Chap. VIII.   [2] *Ibid.*, Chap. XI.
[3] *Ibid.*, Chap. X.

son, Dr. Titus Munson Coan, has written a brochure on *The Climate of Hawaii* (1901) and on *The Natives of Hawaii: A Study in Polynesian Charm* (1901).

The South Seas enthrall the visitor with this "Polynesian charm"; a drifting away from material things on "tropic spray 'which knows not if it be sea or sun'"; a plunge into a conservatory of blossoms producing a sort of narcosis—at least such was the effect in former days, and Charles Warren Stoddard caught and presented this earlier *delicioso* in his classic *South Sea Idyls* (1873), "the lightest, sweetest, wildest things that ever were written about the life of the summer ocean," declares W. D. Howells in the introduction which he wrote. "No one need ever write of the South Seas again." Full of whales were these South Seas, too, as well as of the fragrance of tropic fruits, and the life of the whaler in pursuit of them there, as well as in the northern waters, has found numerous recorders. But who has painted it as delightfully, as masterfully, as Herman Melville[1] in *Moby Dick?* And who can forget, once lost in its wonderful glow, that other story of Melville's, the story of life among cannibals, told in *Typee?* And there is *Omoo*, hardly less absorbing, telling of life in Tahiti. These books of his belong to our American classics. He wrote also *White Jacket*, of life on a man-of-war, *Redburn*, and *Mardi and a Voyage Thither*.

"Wherever ship has sailed, there have I been," said Columbus, and the men—and women—of America were scarcely behind him in travel and exploration. They tested out the far far seas, the solitudes of continents, the innermost secrets of the rivers. But there was one river, wild, rock-bound, and recalcitrant, the Colorado, which, like a raging dragon, refused to come to terms and was so fierce withal that trapper and pioneer shunned its canyon tentacles and passed by. Finally the government sent Lieutenant J. C. Ives to attack it at its mouth, which is defended by a monstrous tidal wave, and to ascend in his little iron steamer, *The Explorer*. Ives reached the foot of Black Canyon, while Captain Johnson with another steamer succeeded in reaching a somewhat higher point. Johnson's journal has not been published, but Ives wrote an interesting *Report upon the Colorado River of the West Explored*

[1] See Book II, Chap. VII.

in 1857 and 1858, published in 1861, the year the memorable shot was fired at Fort Sumter. The Colorado was forgotten.

So far the explorer had merely examined the dragon's teeth, but in 1867 Major J. W. Powell, a veteran of the Federal army, investigating the geology of the Territory of Colorado, conceived the idea of exploring the mysterious and fateful canyons by descending through their entire length of a thousand miles in small boats.

The same year an uneducated man, James White, was rescued near Callville from a raft on which he had come down the river some distance. His condition was pitiful. He was interviewed by Dr. Parry, who happened to be there with a railway survey party, and Parry told White that he must have come through the "Big" canyon. White therefore said he had, when assured that he had, although he did not know the topography of the canyons—neither did Dr. Parry, nor any one else. The White story was first told in General Palmer's *Report of Surveys Across the Continent in 1867–68 on the 35th and 32nd Parallels, etc.* (1869). It was repeated in William A. Bell's *New Tracks in North America* (1869) and quite recently has been republished with notes and comments by Thomas F. Dawson in *The Grand Canyon, Doc. 42, Senate, 65th Cong., 1st Sess.* (1917).

Mr. Dawson, like others who have not run the huge and numerous rapids of the Grand Canyon, believes that White went through on his frail little raft, but all who know the Canyon well are certain that White did not make the passage and that the story that he did rests entirely on what Dr. Parry thought. It is only necessary to add that White found but one big rapid in his course, whereas there are dozens in the distance it is claimed that he travelled. The river falls 1850 feet in the Grand Canyon, 480 in Marble Canyon, and 690 between this and the junction of the Green and Grand, or a total of 3020 feet in the distance White is said to have gone.

In the spring of 1869 Major Powell started from the Union Pacific Railway in Wyoming and descended, in partly decked rowboats, through the thousand miles of canyons so closely connected that they are well-nigh one, with a total descent of 5375 feet to the mouth of the Virgin. In 1871–72 he made a second descent to complete the exploration and to obtain the

required topographical and geological data, prevented by disaster and lack of trained men on the first voyage.   The account of the first voyage is given in Powell's *Exploration of the
Colorado River of the West* (1875), a report to the government.
He did not include a narrative of the second descent, which is
related in *A Canyon Voyage* (1908) by Frederick S. Dellenbaugh,
a member of the party.   The same author's *The Romance of the
Colorado River* (1902) tells the history of this unique river from
the Spanish discovery in 1540, and gives a table of altitudes
along the river.   A recent experience (1911) in navigating the
river which has been chronicled by Ellsworth Kolb in *Through
the Grand Canyon from Wyoming to Mexico* (1914) furnishes
valuable data.

In 1889 Frank M. Brown attempted a railway survey
through the canyons from Gunnison Crossing down.   He was
drowned in Marble Canyon, as were two of his men.   His engineer, Robert B. Stanton, returned to the task the same year
with better boats and successfully completed the descent.   He
relates what befell him and his men in an article in *Scribner's
Magazine* for November, 1890, "Through the Grand Canyon
of the Colorado," and there are other magazine articles on the
subject.

It is interesting to note that the first proper maps of the
United States were made of Far Western territory, and this was
due to the initiative of several energetic explorers.   Clarence
King inaugurated a geological survey with map work in conjunction with it, the results appearing in seven volumes, *Report
of the Geological Exploration of the Fortieth Parallel 1870–80*.
King wrote a charming volume, too, *Mountaineering in the Sierra
Nevada* (1871), and later that literary gem in *The Century
Magazine* (1886), "The Helmet of Mambrino," the "helmet"
and the original manuscript being preserved in the library of
the Century Association.

Powell's *Colorado River Exploring Expedition* developed
into the *Rocky Mountain Survey*, and Dr. F. V. Hayden
conducted a series of surveys in Colorado, etc., called the
Geographical and Geological Survey of the Territories.   At the
same time the army put into the Western field Lieut. George
M. Wheeler, who conducted *Geographical Surveys West of the
100th Meridian*.   Wheeler, in 1871, ascended the Colorado

River as far as Diamond Creek. Seven volumes were produced by the Wheeler Survey, eleven by the Hayden, and a considerable number by the Powell Survey. At the same time they turned out topographic maps of excellent character, all things considered—in most cases better than any then existing of the Eastern part of the country.

In connection with the Powell Survey Captain C. E. Dutton studied the geology of certain districts and wrote several books that are almost unique in their combination of literary charm with scientific accuracy: *Physical Geology of the Grand Canyon District* (1880–81), *Tertiary History of the Grand Canyon* (1882), and *The High Plateaus of Utah* (1880).

Powell established the Bureau of Ethnology and from this issued the large number of volumes before referred to, a mine of information on the North American Indian. Many workers were in the field. One of the most picturesque of these labours was Frank H. Cushing's initiation into the Zuñi tribe described in his *Adventures in Zuñi* (1883). He wrote, too, *Zuñi Folk Tales* (1901); and, in the Bureau reports, other articles on the Zuñi.[1] A remarkable ceremonial of another Puebloan group was written down by Captain John G. Bourke in *The Snake Dance of the Moquis* [*Hopi*] *of Arizona* (1884). The Puebloans for many centuries have built villages of adobe and stone in the Southwest in canyons, in valleys, and on mesas. One of these cliff-bound plateaus, the Mesa Encantada, was the source of some controversy as to whether or not its summit was once occupied. Its walls were scaled and some evidences of the former presence of natives were found. Professor William Libbey and F. W. Hodge both have written on the subject.

While the pioneers were pouring into the West, exterminating the buffalo for hide-and-tallow profits, described by W. T. Hornaday in *The Extermination of the American Bison* (1889), and dispossessing the Plains Indians generally, the latter became restless and unruly. Under the spell of their crafty "medicine" priest, Sitting Bull, the Sioux were greatly disturbed. The army was ordered to compel their obedience and in 1876 made a determined move expected to crush the Indians. General Crook was defeated in one of the first encounters; and a few days later General Custer was annihilated with his immediate

[1] See also Book III, Chap. XXXIII.

command. The Sioux were superior in numbers and in arms. The courage of Custer was of no avail.

Custer wrote *My Life on the Plains* (1874) and a number of articles for *The Galaxy*. General W. B. Hazen, who had a quarrel with Custer, privately published *Some Corrections of "My Life on the Plains"* (1875). Frederick Whittaker wrote a *Complete Life of General George A. Custer* (1876), full of details, and the whole written in a painstaking way. A large amount of information given in an exceedingly pleasant manner is found in the books of the General's widow, Elizabeth Bacon Custer: *Boots and Saddles, or Life in Dakota with General Custer* (1885); *Tenting on the Plains, or General Custer in Kansas and Texas* (1887); *Following the Guidon* (1890). Mrs. Custer also wrote the introduction for *George Armstrong Custer* (1916) by Frederick S. Dellenbaugh. There was comparatively little trouble with the Sioux Indians after the massacre of Custer, for even they seemed to be impressed by its horror; just as the Modocs were when they destroyed the attacking troops— afterwards Scar-faced Charley said his "heart was sick of seeing so many men killed."

One of the primary causes of Indian difficulties was the rapid growth of the cattle and sheep industry on the Plains. The remarkably nutritive grasses which had fattened buffalo by the tens of thousands now fattened cattle and sheep in like numbers. As cattle and sheep will not feed on the same range, or rather cattle will not on a sheep range, there were clashes that were well-nigh battles between the sheep and the cattle men. Large tracts were bought or claimed, and fenced in— another cause of trouble. And still another was the character of the cattle herders. There were suddenly many of them in the later seventies. They lived in camps and for some reason they dropped to a lower state of degradation than any class of men, red or white, that the Far West had seen. Beside a full-fledged "cowboy" of the earlier period of their brief reign the Indian pales to a mere recalcitrant Quaker. With the further development of the country the cowboy became more civilized and later on he redeemed himself by writing poetry and books. The reason for this desirable transformation from debauchery to inspiration may be read in the lines:

When the last free trail is a prim fenced land,
And our graves grow weeds through forgetful Mays.

The country was becoming agricultural; the trails were being
fenced in; the herds growing smaller for lack of vast, unpaid-
for, free range; they were of necessity differently handled; and
the cowboy's pistol was confronted by the sheriff's. In short,
the wild cowboy was a wild cowboy no more. The quotation
is from the admirable volume of poems of the West by Charles
Badger Clark, Jr., *Sun and Saddle Leather* (1915), which contains "The Glory Trail" (known among the camps as "High
Chin Bob") and another equally rhythmical, "The Christmas
Trail," one stanza of which is:

> The coyote's Winter howl cuts the dusk behind the hill,
> But the ranch's shinin' window I kin see:
> And though I don't deserve it, and I reckon never will,
> There'll be room beside the fire kep' for me.
> Skimp my plate 'cause I'm late. Let me hit the old kid gait,
> For to-night I'm stumblin' tired of the new,
> And I'm ridin' up the Christmas trail to you,
>   Old Folks,
> I'm a-ridin' up the Christmas trail to you.

The man who wrote this, we may be sure, never "shot up" a
Western saloon. Another volume of this delightful verse reflecting the freedom of the Western skies is *Out Where the West
Begins*, by Arthur Chapman, and two more are, *Riders of the
Stars* and *Songs of the Outlands*, both in ink of mountain hue,
from the pen of Herbert Knibbs. These are the things we
expect from men who have ridden the sagebrush plain, scamp-
ered up the painted cliffs with a horizon waving in the blue, or
slept in the winter white under the whispering pines.

Besides this native poetry we have some excellent prose
work in this field; *Ten Years a Cowboy* (1908) by C. C. Post;
The Log of a Cowboy (1903) by Andy Adams, as well as *The
Outlet* by the same author, the latter relating to the great cattle
drives formerly undertaken from Texas to the North-west.
Charles M. Russell, the "Cowboy Artist," who has preserved
with his brush some of the thrilling pictures of this ephemeral
and showy savagery, has expressed himself in a literary manner

in *Studies of Western Life* (1890). And it is necessary to mention in this connection the drawings of Frederick Remington, as
well as Owen Wister's later classic of cowboy life, *The Virginian*
(1905).

In the golden days of '49 there was a road to the Californian
Eldorado by way of the Isthmus of Panama. There were no
Indians that way but there was the Chagres River, until a
railway was built. There is a particular literature of the Isthmus. *A Story of Life on the Isthmus* (1853) was written by
Joseph Warren Fabens; and an even earlier one *The Isthmus
of Panama and What I Saw There* (1839) is by Chauncey D.
Griswold. Then there is *Five Years at Panama* (1889) by
Wolfred Nelson, and numerous others between these dates,
including an exceedingly scarce volume, *The Panama Massacre* (1857), which presents the evidence in the case of the
massacre of Americans in 1856. A few years after this event
Tracy Robinson appeared on the Isthmus and for forty-six
years he made it his home. This veteran published his *Panama,
a Personal Record of Forty-six Years, 1861–1907* only a short time
before his death.

Frederick Law Olmsted was specially interested in the South
and in 1856 he wrote *A Journey in the Seaboard Slave States
with Remarks on Their Economy;* in 1857, *A Journey through
Texas;* in 1861, *The Cotton Kingdom* (made up from the two
preceding books); and in 1863, *A Journey in the Back Country*.
A very scarce item is a Southerner's impressions of the North
in *Sketches on a Tour Through the Northern and Eastern States,
the Canadas, and Nova Scotia* (1840) by J. C. Meyers, one
traveller who was not impelled towards the Golden Gate.
Burroughs in the Catskills and Thoreau[1] in his favourite
haunts and on his *Yankee Trip in Canada* (1866) hardly need
mention, but there were some other outdoor men along the
eastern part of the continent. Lucius L. Hubbard in 1884
wrote *Woods and Lakes of Maine, a Trip from Moosehead Lake
to New Brunswick in a Birch Canoe;* Charles A. J. Farrar in
1886, *Down in the West Branch, or Camps and Tramps around
Katahdin;* and another, *From Lake to Lake, or A Trip across the
Country, A Narrative of the Wilds of Maine*.

Although J. T. Headley wrote *Letters from the Backwoods*

[1] See Book II, Chap. x.

and the Adirondacks in 1850, and others gave accounts of the splendid "wilderness" of Northern New York, it remained for W. H. H. Murray, a clergyman, to stir up sportsmen and travellers on this topic with his enthusiastic book on the region, *Adventures in the Wilderness, or Camp Life in the Adirondacks* (1869), which earned for him the title of "Adirondack" Murray.

American travellers and explorers extended their researches to the veritable ends of the earth, and their literary product was enormous. Africa came in for examination, too. Paul B. DuChaillu explored in West Africa in 1855–59 and reported the surprising gorilla; and in 1863–65 he reported pygmies, both bringing the reproach of prevarication against him. He was not long in being vindicated. He published *Explorations and Adventures in Equatorial Africa* (1861), *A Journey to Ashango Land* (1867), *The Country of the Dwarfs* (1872), and *Stories of the Gorilla Country* (1868). Then he turned his attention to the north and gave us *The Land of the Midnight Sun* (1881), *The Viking Age* (1889), *The Land of the Long Night* (1899).

An American newspaper correspondent was sent to seek the lost Livingstone, and Henry M. Stanley tells his remarkable story in *How I Found Livingstone* (1872). He became the foremost African explorer, and wrote *Coomassie and Magdala* (1874), *Through the Dark Continent* (1878), *In Darkest Africa* (1890), *The Congo and the Founding of its Free State* (1885). This "free" state turned out to be anything but free and became the centre of a storm of controversy. *The Story of the Congo Free State* (1905) by H. W. Wack controverts the charges, but those who know refuse to accept it.

Another part of Africa long had received attention: Egypt. The list of American travellers and explorers in that ancient land is almost beyond recording. Here again Bayard Taylor is found with his *A Journey to Central Africa* (1854), and George W. Curtis[1] wrote *Nile Notes of a Howadji* (1851); W. C. Prime gives us *Boat Life in Egypt and Nubia* (1868); Bishop Potter, *The Gates of the East, or a Winter in Egypt* (1876).

But the most prominent American in the Egyptian region was Charles Chaillé-Long, who carried on some extensive explorations along the upper Nile. His chief literary works are: *Central Africa . . . an Account of Expeditions to Lake Victoria*

[1] See Book III. Chap. XIII.

Nyanza, etc. (1877), *The Three Prophets: Chinese Gordon, Mohammed Ahmed (el Maahdi), Arabi-Pasha* (1884), and *My Life in Four Continents* (1912).

Italy is not behind Egypt as regards American travel-literature. There is W. D. Howells[1] with *Italian Journeys* in 1867 and *Venetian Life* of the year before; James Jarvis Jackson with *Italian Sights and Papal Principalities Seen through American Spectacles* (1856), and Helen Hunt Jackson's *Bits of Travel* (1873).

Then there are another score or two on Spain; John Hay's *Castilian Days* (1871); Washington Irving's many contributions; Edward Everett Hale's *Seven Spanish Cities* (1899); William H. Bishop's *A House Hunter in Europe* [France, Italy, Spain] (1893); and Bayard Taylor's *The Land of the Saracens* (1855). Raphael Pumpelly went *Across America and Asia* and tells about it in the book of that title published in 1870; W. W. Rockhill made many journeys in Oriental lands. He published *Diary of a Journey through Mongolia and Tibet in 1891-1892* (1894). "Sunset" [S. S.] Cox tells of the *Diversions of a Diplomat in Turkey* (1887); Charles Dudley Warner[2] of *In the Levant* (1895); W. T. Hornaday of *Two Years in the Jungle* [India, Ceylon, etc.] (1886); and Samuel M. Zwemer of *Arabia the Cradle of Islam* (1900). The last named has also written on Arabia, which he has studied long at first hand, other important volumes, beyond the horizon of this chapter.

Many Americans travelled in Russia, too, and wrote volumes about that enigmatical country: Nathan Appleton, *Russian Life and Society as Seen in 1866–67* and *A Journey to Russia with General Banks 1869* (1904); Edna Dean Proctor, *A Russian Journey* (1873); Miss Isabel Hapgood, *Russian Rambles* (1895); C. A. Dana, *Eastern Journeys* (1898); Eugene Schuyler, *Notes of a Journey in Russian Turkestan, Etc.* (1876); and Poultney Bigelow, *Paddles and Politics down the Danube; A Canoe Voyage from the Black Forest to the Black Sea* (1892).

Charles Augustus Stoddard was another ubiquitous traveller whose works are difficult to classify in one group. His *Across Russia from the Baltic to the Danube* (1891) takes us into rather out-of-the-way paths, and then he strikes for *Spanish Cities with Glimpses of Gibraltar and Tangier* (1892), only to jump to *Beyond the Rockies* (1894), with *A Spring Journey in California* (1895) and some *Cruising in the Caribbees* the same year.

Albert Payson Terhune shows us *Syria from the Saddle* (1896) with his customary virility; John Bell Bouton takes us *Round-about to Moscow* (1887), where we instinctively think of George Kennan and his *The Siberian Exile System* (1891) and follow him into *Tent Life in Siberia* through two editions, 1871 and 1910. From there we run back *On Canada's Frontier* (1892) with Julian Ralph, and then *Down Historic Waterways* (1888) with Reuben Gold Thwaites, who also leads us *On the Storied Ohio* (1897), after which he holds up the mirror to previous travellers in thirty-two volumes of *Early Western Travels* (1904–06). If we are interested in botany, there is Bradford Torrey, who contributed to *Reports* on Western exploration, and wrote independently *A Florida Sketch Book* (1894), *Spring Notes from Tennessee* (1895), and *Footing it in Franconia* (1901).

The war with Spain landed the United States in the Philippines, clear across the wide western ocean, thus at last forging the final link in the chain stretching westward from Europe to Cathay, and proving ultimately Senator Benton's prophecy as he pointed towards the sunset and said: "There lies the road to India."

The various islands of the Philippine group were occupied by different tribes in varying stages of progress, and it became the problem of the new governing power to give each protection from the other and an opportunity to develop. In carrying out this broad policy not only were schools established and towns remodelled, but battles were fought with such tribes as were recalcitrant and unruly like the wild Moros.

The literature which has grown out of all this effort is large and of vast importance civically, ethnologically, and politically, for it is the history of harmonizing antagonistic primitive groups, guiding them into proper channels of progress, and fitting them for eventual self government, a task never before set for itself by any conqueror; and a task which has led to impatience and misunderstanding not only among the warring tribes but among people at home who were ignorant of the situation. Arthur Judson Brown describes *The New Era in the Philippines* (1903); James H. Blount asks (in *The North American Review*, 1907)

"Philippine Independence, When?"; William H. Taft in *The Outlook* (1902) gives a statement on "Civil Government in the Philippines"; William B. Freer writes *The Philippine Experiences of an American Teacher, A Narrative of Work and Travel in the Philippine Islands* (1906); and Dean C. Worcester, to whom more than to any other individual belongs the credit for a remarkable achievement by the United States in this far-off region, wrote *The Philippine Islands and their People, A Record of Personal Observation and Experience* (1898). A most interesting and instructive "inside" account is Albert Sonnichsen's *Ten Months a Captive among Filipinos* (1901). Sonnichsen was not treated badly by Filipinos, and he was fortunate in not falling into the clutches of some of the less developed tribes.

An ethnological survey was begun and has been carried forward by the bureau having this science in charge. An example of results is the admirable study by Albert Ernest Jenks of *The Bontoc Igorot* (1905), a volume of 266 pages printed at Manila. These Bontoc Igorots occupy a district near the centre of the northern part of the island of Luzon, and are typical primitive Malayan stock, intelligent and amenable. "I recall," says Mr. Jenks, "with great pleasure the months spent in Bontoc pueblo, and I have a most sincere interest in and respect for the Bontoc Igorot."

Besides the outlying possession of the Philippines, the United States became owner by purchase in 1867 of Russian America, afterwards named Alaska. Seward was ridiculed for making such a purchase in the "frozen" north, and it was long derided as Seward's "Ice-box." The vast number of publications favourably describing this region belie this term, and it is now well understood that Seward secured a treasure house for a pittance.

Seward's "Address on Alaska at Sitka, August 12, 1869," in *Old South Leaflets*, Vol. 6, No. 133 (1904) is interesting in this connection. There are a great number of reports, and narratives like those of the veteran William H. Dall; Captain W. R. Abercrombie's *Alaska, 1899, Copper River Exploring Expedition* (1900); Henry T. Allen's *Report of an Expedition to the Copper, Tanana, and Koyukuk Rivers in the Territory of Alaska in the Year 1885* (1887); M. M. Ballou's *The New Eldorado, a Summer*

Tour in Alaska (1889); Reports by A. H. Brooks; Miss Scidmore's *Alaska* (1885), etc.

In 1899 a private expedition was organized which cruised in a chartered ship along the Alaskan coast and across Bering Sea to Siberia. A large party of scientific men were guests of the projector, Edward Henry Harriman, and there were also several artists. The results were published in a series of volumes now issued by the Smithsonian Institution. The first two are narrative, with chapters by John Burroughs, John Muir, G. K. Gilbert, and others, and reproductions of paintings by R. Swain Gifford, Louis A. Fuertes, and Frederick S. Dellenbaugh. Burroughs in addition wrote a volume entitled *Far and Near* (1904), and there were magazine articles and other books. The same year as the Harriman Expedition, Angelo Heilprin published *Alaska and the Klondike, A Journey to the New Eldorado*. Gold had been found not only in the Klondike but at Nome, in the sands of the beach, where a few square feet yielded a fortune, and in other parts.

On the bleaker eastern arctic shores of North America no gold had been found to lead armies of fortune-seekers through incredible hardships, but men will suffer as much, or more, for an idea, and there was the idea of Polar exploration with the *ignis fatuus* of the Pole ever beckoning. A library of many shelves would not hold all the books relating to this fateful quest. Americans joined the English early in this field, inspired by a desire to discover the actual fate of Franklin. In 1850 Elisha Kent Kane accompanied a party equipped by Grinnell with two ships under Lieutenant De Haven. They reached Smith Sound as described in *The United States Grinnell Expedition in Search of Sir John Franklin* (1854). Kane went north again in 1853 and reached 78° 41'. This expedition is recorded in his *Arctic Explorations: The Second Grinnell Expedition* (1856).

Dr. I. I. Hayes followed this up by taking advantage of experience acquired with Kane and in going to the ice regions in 1860. He wrote *The Open Polar Sea* (1867), *An Arctic Boat Journey* (1860), *The Land of Desolation* (1881); and the Smithsonian printed his "Physical Observations in the Arctic Seas" (Volume 15).

One of the most devoted and interesting of all Arctic explor-

ers was Charles Francis Hall.   His heart was so thoroughly in
the work, at first a search for Franklin, that he made three
fruitful expeditions and would have continued had he not
mysteriously died in full health on the last journey.   The first
expedition was on an ordinary whaling ship to the Eskimos,
with whom he lived for two years in 1860–62.   On the second
trip he again lived with Eskimos in 1864–69, and on the third
voyage in 1871 in the *Polaris* he got to 82° 11', at the Polar ocean
via Smith Sound.   His *Narrative of the [Third or Polaris] North
Polar Expedition* (1876) was edited by C. H. Davis: the *Narrative of the Second Arctic Expedition to Repulse Bay* (1879) was
edited by Prof. J. E. Nourse.   That of Hall's first journey was
published in 1864, the year in which he started on his second,
with the title *Arctic Researches and Life among the Eskimaux*. He
was the first, or one of the first, to note that the Eskimos knew
the geography of their environment and could make maps
of it.   Some reproductions of such maps occur in Hall's volumes.
E. V. Blake's *Arctic Experiences* (1874) contains an account of
Captain George E. Tyson's drift on the ice-floe, a history of the
Polaris expedition, and the rescue of the *Polaris* survivors.

The next American to push north with the great idea was
Lieutenant De Long under the auspices of the New York
Herald.   A vessel named the *Jeanette*, supplied with provisions for
three years, sailed in July, 1879, from San Francisco, entering
the Polar Sea through Bering Strait.   The *Jeanette* was sunk
by ice in June, 1881.   The crew got to Herald Island and thence
steered for the mouth of the Lena River in three boats, of
which one was lost; and the crew of another, including De Long,
starved and froze to death on land, while George W. Melville
and nine more reached a small native village.   After a fruitless
search for the others he came home, to return again to the
search.   He wrote *In the Lena Delta, A Narrative of the Search
for Lieutenant Commander De Long, and his Companions* (1885).
Another volume is, *The Narrative of the Jeanette Arctic Expedition as Related by the Survivors, etc. Revised by Raymond Lee
Newcomb* (1882).   The naval officer in command of the search
party (1882–84), Giles Bates Harber, found De Long's body
and nine other remains, and brought them home for burial.
He wrote a *Report of Lieut. G. B. Harber of his Search for
Missing People of the Jeanette Expedition* (1884).   William

H. Gilder wrote *Ice Pack and Tundra* (1883) on the same subject.

A Polar expedition which accomplished its important work and yet met with disaster was that of Greely, which co-operated with eight other international stations meteorologically. His disaster was due to inefficiency in the efforts of those at home to get the annual supplies through. One of Greely's assistants, Lieutenant Lockwood, reached the highest latitude up to that time: 83° 24′. Lockwood's journal of his trip farthest north is given in vol. I of the *Report* mentioned below and also is described in *The White World* (1902) by David L. Brainard, now General Brainard, who accompanied Lockwood, under the title "Farthest North with Greely," an excellent account of this memorable effort. Charles Lanman in *Farthest North* (1885) tells the life story of Lieutenant Lockwood, who died later at winter quarters of starvation. This was the Lady Franklin Bay Expedition, but it is seldom referred to except as the Greely Expedition. A full account is given in *Report on the Proceedings of the United States Expedition to Lady Franklin Bay, Grinnell Land*, by A. W. Greely (1888); and Greely also wrote *Three Years of Arctic Service* (1886). Winfield S. Schley, afterwards Admiral Schley, commanded the second relief expedition, and it was his energy and determination which put his ships at Cape Sabine just in time to save the survivors, who had to be carried on board. Schley made a report published in House Documents of the 49th Congress and wrote, with J. R. Soley, *The Rescue of Greely* (1885).

Evelyn B. Baldwin led the first Ziegler expedition and tells the story in *The Search for the North Pole* (1896), and Anthony Fiala headed the second Ziegler expedition, recorded in his *Fighting the Polar Ice* (1906).

Not only was the outer approach towards the Pole hazardous and difficult, but the mathematical point lay in the midst of a wide frozen ocean with hundreds of miles of barrier ice constantly on the move and frequently splitting into broad "leads" of open water, interposing forbidding obstacles to progress or to return. One American had set his heart on reaching this "inaccessible spot," and after twenty-three years of amazing perseverance, Robert Edwin Peary succeeded, 6 April, 1909, in placing the flag of the United States at the point where all meridians meet under the North Star. Peary deserved every honour his countrymen could give him, but, alas, at the moment of triumph the voice of an impostor dimmed the glory.

The North Pole was won by the adoption of Eskimo clothing, snow houses, and a relay dog-sledge system. Peary's account of his long continued efforts to attain this object of centuries is found in numerous reports, lectures, and articles, but his chief literary production is the several volumes: *Northward over the Great Ice* (1898), *Snowland Folk* (1904), *Nearest the Pole* (1907), and *The North Pole* (1910), the last the story of the final success. Besides the conquest of the Pole, Peary determined the insularity of Greenland and added much other information to the Polar records. *My Arctic Journal* (1893) by Mrs. Josephine Debitsch Peary is interesting and valuable in North Pole literature.

In travel and exploration in the period which we have thus briefly reviewed, there are many notable and thrilling events, but there is nothing that exhibits the striving after an ideal regardless of pecuniary profit or physical comfort better than the determination of Peary to reach the frozen centre of the Northern Hemisphere. He has a competent successor in Vilhjálmur Stefánsson, another American whose whole heart is in Arctic exploration, and whose bold and original method of relying on his rifle for food, even on the wide ice of the Polar ocean, has been rewarded by an astonishing success, a success which has revealed, or at least emphasized, the facts that everywhere in the farthest North there exists a large amount of game.

Stefánsson and his literary output do not properly belong to this chapter, but in closing it may be permissible to refer to him and his volume, *My Life with the Eskimo* (1913), since he has accomplished much that must be considered in connection with all earlier Arctic exploration.

CHAPTER XV

Later Historians

" IT it evident," said an intelligent librarian in 1876, "that diligent workers in preserving the history of the nation have been numerous and that whatever neglect there has been in the pursuit of science or literature, we cannot be said to have equally neglected our own history."[1] This opinion, when uttered, was supported by facts. It could not be held today, partly because science and literature have made great progress in recent years, and partly because the writing of history has recently undergone a singular development. Although the United States contains at present several times as many educated people as in 1876, there exists among them no historian who has the recognition enjoyed fifty years ago by Bancroft, Parkman, and some others. To explain this change is not the purpose here. It is sufficient to observe the progress of the change, leaving the reader to make his own deductions in regard to its causes.

When the period began, history writing was proceeding on the old lines. Books were written about men and events with an idea of pleasing the reader, stimulating his admiration for his country or for exceptional men, or satisfying a commendable desire for information. Such histories had to be well written and had an advantage if they contained what our grandfathers called "elevated sentiment." They always had a point of view, and generally made the reader like or dislike one side or the other of some controversy. These books were naturally in constant demand among a people who were still in the habit of viewing everything in a matter-of-fact way, and to whom but

---

[1] Henry A. Homes, *Public Libraries in the United States*, U. S. Bureau of Education, 1876, pp. 312-325.

one political party was right and but one kind of man was great.

The change that came into these ideas amounts to a revolution. The scientific trend of the mid-century period reached history and transformed it. Detachment of the author from his feelings, accuracy of statement, dependence on original sources, study of institutions, and increasing attention to social and economic phenomena became the chief characteristics of a new school of historians. Under such conditions history became didactic, informational, and philosophical; and at the same time it became less unified and vivid. This change came at a time when the general tendency in literature was toward the clever and amusing. In the view of the serious-minded man, history today is better written than ever before, but it does not maintain the place it held in 1876 in the esteem of the average reader of intelligence. This chapter deals with the transition from the old to the new school.

Three Underlying Movements. Accompanying the development of the new school are three movements which are not to be ignored by one who wishes to understand the subject as a whole: the wide growth of historical societies, the creation and publication of historical "collections" and other documents, and the transformation of historical instruction in the colleges and universities.

The beginning of the first goes back to 1791, when the Massachusetts Historical Society was founded through the efforts of Jeremy Belknap.[1] Other societies followed, among them the New York Historical Society in 1804, the American Antiquarian Society in 1812, the Pennsylvania, Rhode Island, and Maine Historical Societies in 1822, the New Hampshire Historical Society in 1823, the Georgia Historical Society in 1839, the Maryland Historical Society in 1844, the New Jersey Historical Society in 1845, the Virginia Historical Society in 1851, and the Delaware Historical Society in 1864. Through Belknap's efforts the Massachusetts society had a vigorous life from the beginning, collecting and publishing valuable material steadily. None of the other societies mentioned did so well. Most of them were the offsprings of local pride and lived thin and shallow lives until we come to the period treated in this

[1] See Book II, Chap. XVII.

chapter. For example, the New York society, in the richest city in the Union, kept up a battle for existence for forty years and was saved from bankruptcy only by aid from the State treasury. In sixty-four years it published eight small volumes of Collections, besides a number of "discourses" in pamphlet form. In the late forties it took on new life, obtained money for a building of its own, and in 1857 began to raise the publication fund which resulted in a series of annual Collections from 1868 to the present.

It is difficult to determine the origin of this renewed activity which appeared in other societies than the New York Historical Society. It was largely affected by Sparks's, Bancroft's, and Force's activities in the fourth decade of the century,[1] efforts so widely discussed that they must have stimulated new efforts everywhere. The return of John Romeyn Brodhead from Europe in 1844 with his excellent collection of transcripts on New York history and their publication by the State were another strong impulse to progress, and others can probably be discovered in the general development of the intellectual conditions of the day. It is clear that with the end of the Civil War the historical societies of the Atlantic States had passed out of their dubious phase of existence and had begun to exercise the important influence they have lately had in support of history.

Beyond the Alleghanies we find trace of the same awakening. State historical societies were established in Ohio in 1831, in Wisconsin and Minnesota in 1849, in Iowa in 1857, in Kansas in 1875, in Nebraska in 1878, and in Illinois and Missouri in 1899. Besides these state societies were several important privately projected societies: as the Chicago Historical Society, founded in 1855, and the Missouri Historical Society established in 1886. Within the latter part of the period under discussion the creation of societies has proceeded rapidly throughout the country.

Among the men who made this growth possible no one stands higher than Lyman Copeland Draper (1815-91), whose persistent efforts made the Wisconsin society pre-eminent among State historical societies. Fired by the example of Force and Sparks in Revolutionary history, he made his field

[1] See Book II, Chap. XVII.

the Revolutionary struggle on the Western border, extending it later to the entire Western region. He travelled widely in the West, visiting the explorers who still lived, ransacking old garrets, winning the confidence of important men, and collecting finally a vast treasure of material out of which he hoped to write a detailed history of the frontier. In 1853 he became corresponding secretary and chief executive officer of the State Historical Society of Wisconsin. His efforts were constantly and wisely directed towards increasing its collections, enlarging the scope of its publications, and inducing the State to appropriate the funds necessary for development. He is rightly called the father of the Society. To it he bequeathed his large collection of historical material, itself a worthy nucleus of any society's possessions. His work was continued after his death by Reuben Gold Thwaites (1853–1913), who was an active writer of history as well as an eminent librarian. His service to Western history has not been surpassed.

To crown the series of events attending the creation of historical societies came the organization of the American Historical Association in 1884. Herbert Baxter Adams, of the Johns Hopkins University, was the most active person in bringing together the distinguished group of scholars who launched the enterprise and got it incorporated by the national government in 1889. In 1895 *The American Historical Review* was established in connection with the work of the Association. Taken together these two expressions of historical effort have bound up the interests of scattered American scholars, intensified their purpose, clarified their understanding, and enabled them to lay better foundations for a national school of history than we could have expected to evolve under the old individualistic method of procedure. They have had, also, an important influence on the writing of history, although it is probable that their best work is in the nature of a foundation for a greater structure to be erected in the future.

The origin of the great collections of historical documents in the United States goes back to similar enterprises in Europe. In France the series known as the *Acta Sanctorum* had been projected in the seventeenth century, but the movement had its fruition after the end of the Napoleonic wars, when several national series were authorized at public expense.

Among them the most conspicuous were the *Rolls Series* in Great Britain, projected in 1823, the *Monumenta Germanica* in Germany, launched in 1823, and the *Documents Inèdits* in France, begun in 1835. The desire to do something similar for the United States led Peter Force to attempt his *American Archives*, which was authorized by an act of Congress passed 2 March, 1833. It was published at a large profit to the compilers and smacked so much of jobbery that great dissatisfaction was created in Congress and among the executive officers. The result was that it was discontinued by Secretary of State Marcy in 1855 when only nine volumes had been published. Force's materials were badly arranged and his editorial notes were nearly nil, but his ideal was good. Had it been carried out with a fairer regard for economy it might have escaped the rock on which it foundered. As it was, it served to call attention to a field in which much needed to be done, and it is probable that the collections of documents undertaken about that time in the states owed their inception in a considerable measure to his widely heralded scheme.

Of these efforts the most noticeable was Brodhead's transcripts, already mentioned in this chapter. In 1849 the legislature of New York ordered that they should be published at the expense of the state. They appeared in due time in ten quarto volumes, with an index in an eleventh volume, and with the title *New York Colonial Documents*. With some supplementary volumes they form a clear and sufficient and permanent foundation for New York colonial history.

In Pennsylvania a similar movement occurred at nearly the same time. It began in 1837 when the legislature, acting on the suggestion of the Historical Society of Pennsylvania, authorized the publication of the series eventually known as *The Colonial Records of Pennsylvania*. Failure of funds in the panic days that followed caused the suspension of the series when only three volumes had been published, but it was resumed in 1851 on an enlarged basis. The *Colonial Records* were continued through sixteen volumes, and another series, *The Pennsylvania Archives*, was authorized. The former contains the minutes of the provincial council, and the latter is devoted to other documents of historical importance on the colonial period. These works were edited with much care by Samuel Hazard, son of that Ebenezer Hazard[1] who as a friend and mentor of Jeremy Belknap had made himself one of the first collectors and publishers of historical documents in this country. Many other states have followed the examples of New York and Pennsylvania. North Carolina, however, deserves special mention. Through the efforts of her Secretary of State, William L. Saunders, ten large volumes of her *Colonial Records*, followed by sixteen volumes of *State Records*, were published by the State between the years 1886 and 1905. They deal with great completeness with the history of North Carolina from the earliest days to the adoption of the Constitution of the United States, and they place the state in the lead among Southern states in this essential phase of historical development.

The part taken by colleges and universities in promoting historical literature is equally important with the services of the historical societies and the projectors of great collections of documents. The process by which instruction shifted from the old haphazard method into the modern mode of instruction which regards history as an exhibition of the life process of organized society, falls almost entirely within our present period of discussion. The transition was made gradually. It means that the older subjects, with the strictly text-book methods, have for the most part been relegated to the preparatory schools and the lower college classes, while lectures by specialists have become the means of instructing and inspiring the upper classmen among the undergraduates, and special research in seminaries has been employed to make historical scholars out of graduate students.

The origin of the movement was in Germany, from whose universities many enthusiastic American students returned to infuse new life into institutions in their native land or to give direction to the instruction in newly established seats of learning. In the former the change came gradually, as in Harvard, which established the first distinct chair of history when Jared Sparks was made McLean Professor in 1839. It is not believed that the "occasional examinations and lectures" he was required to give greatly advanced historical instruction in the college. Distinct progress, however, was made under his suc-

[1] See Book II. Chap. XVII.

:essors, and the new life that came to the institution in the time of President Eliot completed the transformation in history as in other branches of instruction. Similar courses of development occurred in other universities.

Before this process was completed at Harvard or at any other Eastern university it was well established under the influence of Andrew D. White (1832-1918) at the University of Michigan and Cornell University. Returning from Europe he became professor of history in the former institution in 1857 and captivated the students by his brilliant lectures. In his classes was Charles Kendall Adams (1835-1902), who so impressed the master that he was made professor of history in Michigan when White became president of Cornell in 1867. Adams became president of the University of Wisconsin in 1891. Thus it happened that the influence of Andrew D. White in promoting modern historical instruction was brought to bear on three of the leading universities of the country, and that three strong departments of history sprang into existence.

At Columbia University the zeal and wisdom of Professor John W. Burgess brought into existence a department of political science in which history had an important place, with results that have been far reaching. He gathered around him an able group of assistants and set standards which have had much influence in a university which, as the event showed, was about to take a large place in our educational life. At Johns Hopkins the same kind of work was done by Herbert B. Adams (1850-1901), whose name will ever have place in the story of historical development in this country. He was born at Shutesbury, Massachusetts, graduated at Amherst in 1872, was awarded the doctorate at Heidelberg in 1876, and was appointed a fellow at the Johns Hopkins University in the same year. The illustrious position of that university offered a stage for the development of his talents. Among the mature and capable students who gathered around him he became an enthusiastic leader. No man knew better how to stimulate a young man to attempt authorship. In establishing *The Johns Hopkins University Studies in Historical and Political Science* he opened a new door of publication to American students. He took personal interest in his students after they left the university and sought to save them from the dry rot that menaces the young doctor when he

first realizes academic success. It was in this work for historical study and in the organization of the American Historical Association that Adams's best service was done. He wrote
many monographs on subjects of occasional importance. His
one large book, *The Life and Writings of Jared Sparks* (2 vols.,
1893) was received with disfavour by a public whom Adams and
men like him had already taught to condemn Sparks's uncritical
methods. Other directors of historical research have been
keener critics of their students and have given them a larger
portion of the divine doubts that makes the historian proof
against credulity; but no other has sent them forth with a
stronger desire to become historians.

One of the effects of the development of graduate instruction is that teachers of history write most of the history now
being written in the United States. The historian who is
merely a historian is rarely encountered. Whether the result
be good or bad is not a part of this discussion; but the process
promotes the separation of the writer from his readers, which
may or may not be fortunate. The professor-historian, having
his subsistence in his college salary, may defy the bad taste of
his public and write history in accordance with the best canons
of the schools: he may come to despise the just demand that
history be so written that it may maintain its place in the literature that appeals to serious and intelligent people who are not
specialists.

Minor Historians of the Old School. When the writing of
history began to undergo the change that has been described,
a number of men were doing creditable work in the old way.
Although they worked in limited fields, they produced books
which are still respected by persons interested in those fields,
and their names are essentially connected with the history of
our historians. A "minor" historian is not necessarily an unimportant historian.

One of the striking things in this connection is the rise of
New York as a centre for such historians. While Boston gloried
in the possession of Sparks, Palfrey, Hildreth, Prescott, Motley,
and Parkman, New York produced a group of smaller men who
made the vocation of historian both pleasant and respectable
in the metropolis of wealth. Among them was Dr. John Wake-

field Francis (1789–1861), genial friend of letters and literary men and last of a series of literary doctors which included Cadwallader Colden,[1] David Hosack, Hugh Williamson, and Samuel L. Mitchill,[2] not to mention Benjamin Rush and David Ramsay[3], who lived elsewhere. Francis's *Old New York* (1858) is a charming description of the city under a generation then vanishing. Others of the group were: Henry Onderdonck, Jr. (1804–86), who wrote *Annals of Hempstead* (1878), *Queens County in Olden Times* (1865), and other books on Long Island history; Gabriel Furman (1800–53), who left a most accurate book in his *Notes . . . Relating to the Town of Brooklyn* (1824); Rev. Francis Lister Hawks (1789–1866), best remembered for his *History of North Carolina* (1857–58) and his documents relating to the Anglican Church in the colonies; and Henry Barton Dawson (1821–1889), a turbulent spirit who served history best as editor of *The Historical Magazine*. John Romeyn Brodhead (1814-73), whose transcripts have been mentioned, wrote an excellent *History of New York, 1609–1691* (1853–71). He was one of the best esteemed members of the New York group.

Two Catholic historians added much to its efficiency: Edward Bailey O'Callaghan (1797–1873) and John Dawson Gilmary Shea (1824–92). The first was an educated Irishman, an agitator in the Canadian rebellion of 1837 who fled for safety to Albany when the uprising collapsed, and a historian of good ability. His *History of New Netherland* (1846–48) and the *Documentary History of New York* (1849–51) introduced him to the reading public. He became connected with the office of Secretary of State in Albany, edited the ten volumes of Brodhead's transcripts, and brought out many other documents and reprints, always working hard and conscientiously. Shea, who was educated to be a Jesuit priest but withdrew from his novitiate before taking final vows, was most interested in church history. His largest work was a *History of the Catholic Church in the United States* (1886-92), in four volumes; but he is best known in secular history for his studies in the French history of North America. His Cramoisy edition of the *Jesuit Relations* (1857–66) and his editions of Charlevoix's *History of New France* (1866–72),

[1] See Book I, Chap. II. [2] See Book II, Chap. II.
[3] See Book II, Chap. XVII.

Hennepin's *Description of Louisiana* (1880), and other similar original works were valuable additions to the assets of historians in this particular field. By calling attention to the French origins of our trans-Alleghany region O'Callaghan and Shea gave balance to a period of our history which had previously been too much accented on the English side, and opened the way for the fuller and more appreciated volumes of Francis Parkman.

Two college professors belong in this group of historians, one a teacher of chemistry the other a teacher of Greek but both best remembered as historians. Henry Martyn Baird (1832–1906) took for his theme the history of the Huguenots, which he presented in the following instalments: *History of the Rise of the Huguenots* (2 vols., 1879), *The Huguenots and Henry of Navarre* (2 vols., 1886), and *The Huguenots and the Revocation of the Edict of Nantes* (2 vols., 1895). Besides these books he wrote a short life of *Theodore Beza* (1899). His work was done carefully and in great detail. It was well written, but it always took the side of the Huguenots, and it is to be classed with the history of the old school, of which it was a notable and successful specimen.

John William Draper (1811–82) had won an assured position as a scientist before he turned to history. Like Professor Baird he was a member of the faculty of New York University. At the middle of the century the idea that history is an exact science, an idea that grew out of the teachings of Auguste Comte, had been widely advocated by scientific men. Two men, Buckle in London and Draper in New York, working independently of each other, undertook to give the idea its application. Buckle published the first volume of his *History of Civilization in England* in 1857, and the second in 1861; further efforts ceased with his death in 1862. Draper published his book, *The History of the Intellectual Development of Europe*, in 1862. We are assured that it was practically complete before the first volume of Buckle appeared and that it remained in the author's hands in manuscript during the interval.

In our day the world has not a great interest in history as an exact science; but in 1862 the work of Comte, Buckle, Darwin, and Spencer had prepared it for another attitude. Draper reaped the harvest thus made ready, and his book quickly passed through several editions, in the United States and Europe. Its thesis was that history results from the action on human activity of climate, soil, natural resources, and other physical surroundings. Having stated it in principle, he took up the history of nation after nation, showing to his own satisfaction that his theory operated successfully in each. He had little history to begin with and his statements, taken from uncritical secondary works, were full of errors. The same failing appears even more plainly in his *History of the American Civil War* (3 vols., 1867). His popularity was largely promoted by his clear and vivid style and by the frankness with which he repudiated what Comte called theological and metaphysical states of knowledge, demanding that all truth should be studied scientifically. Since most of his criticisms were aimed at the Roman church he did not arouse the ire of the Protestants. His *History of the Conflict between Religion and Science* (1874), his last work, found place in the same series in which appeared Bagehot's *Physics and Politics*, Spencer's *Sociology*, and Tyndall's *Forms of Water*. It was one of the most widely demanded of the group.

Draper's history of the Civil War brings him into relation with a group of patriotic writers who attempted to record the history of that struggle. The books that first appeared, as William Swinton's *Campaigns of the Army of the Potomac* (1866) and Horace Greeley's *American Conflict* (2 vols., 1864–66), were tinged with prejudice, however much the authors strove to keep it down. After ten years or more had passed a calmer attitude existed, and we encounter a number of books in which is discerned a serious striving to attain impartiality. In this stage the first notable effort was the series published by the Scribners known as *Campaigns of the Civil War* (13 vols., 1881–90), in which prominent military men co-operated. It was followed by a similar series called *The Navy in the Civil War* (3 vols., 1885). Another co-operative work, much read at the time and still valuable, was *Battles and Leaders of the Civil War* (4 vols., 1887–89), a collection of short papers written by participants in the war, and presenting the views on both sides of the struggle. Robert Underwood Johnson and Clarence Clough Buel were the editors whose good judgment and industry made the series a striking success. The same spirit of impartiality was observed in *The Story of the Civil War* by John Codman Ropes (1836–99), which came to an end after two volumes had been published (1894 and 1898). To many people Ropes's volumes seemed to promise the best military history of the war we were likely to have.

A large number of books of personal experience appeared from the hands of men who had taken a prominent part in the war, and some of them have merit as literature. The most notable in content and style was Ulysses Simpson Grant's *Personal Memoirs* (2 vols., 1885, 1886). It was written in simple and direct language and dealt with things in which the humblest citizens could feel interest. Other important books of similar nature were: William Tecumseh Sherman's *Memoirs* (2 vols., 1875); Philip Henry Sheridan's *Personal Memoirs* (2 vols., 1888); George Brinton McClellan's *My Own Story* (1887); and Charles Anderson Dana's *Recollections of the Civil War* (1898).

Apart from all other works on the Civil War is that which appeared with the title *Abraham Lincoln, a History* (10 vols., 1890), by John George Nicolay and John Hay, both of whom had been private secretaries of the war president. In completeness of treatment, clearness of statement, and fair discussion of the men and problems that Lincoln encountered, it is one of the best historical works of the generation in which it was written. Of the joint authors Nicolay (1832–1901) was an historian of unusual breadth of view and industry while Hay[1] (1838–1905) was noted for his clear and natural style.

The Southern histories of the war pass through the two stages just described in the Northern histories. Immediately after the conflict ended there were published such books as Edward Albert Pollard's *The Lost Cause* (1866) and Alexander Hamilton Stephens's *Constitutional View of the Late War between the States* (2 vols., 1868–70), both warmly Southern. So much belated that it might have been less apologetic was Jefferson Davis's *Rise and Fall of the Confederate Government* (2 vols., 1881). It was, however, what might have been expected under the circumstances, an official statement of the Southern side of the question. No fair and ample Southern history of the war has been published.

[1] See also Book III, Chaps. x and xi.

"*The Great Subject.*" Reverence for worthy deeds or men characterized the histories written by the men mentioned in the preceding section. To them succeeded a group who were carried away by what John Carter Brown called "the great subject," that is, the age of discovery and exploration. Columbus and the men and things of his age were their chief interest. Some of them were collectors of rare books in this field, others were historians merely, and still others were both collectors and writers. The efforts of all were closely interrelated. The significance of the group is that here was the first theme on which the American historians made an exhaustive search into the original sources of information and wrote out their conclusions with acute reasoning regardless of preconceived opinions. It was a transition phase from the old to the new school.

Book collectors who were historians existed in England and the United States long before the period now under discussion. Among them were Peter Force, George Bancroft, Jared Sparks, William H. Prescott, and most other writers of history. Public libraries were undeveloped, and it was difficult for a man to write history who was not able to buy a large portion of the books he used in collecting information. By 1840 the library of Harvard University was recognized as one of the important buyers when a rich collection came into the markets, but it was only with the advent of the Astor Library in 1854 and the donation of James Lenox's rich collection to the public in 1870 that New York had public libraries in which a student of history could find what he needed. The Boston Public Library, incorporated in 1848, the Athenæum, a private foundation, and the Harvard College library gave the same kind of support to the historians of Boston.

Meanwhile a group of wealthy men had taken up the occupation of collector, most of them dealing in early Americana. John Carter Brown, of Providence, led off in the movement, and found worthy seconds in James Lenox and Samuel L. M. Barlow of New York, George Brinsley of Hartford, and Colonel Thomas Aspinwall, who was long the American consul in London. The collections of the first two became permanent and were converted into libraries open to the public. The collections of the others were placed on the market and passed for the most part, after various vicissitudes, into the public libraries.

It was the persistent idea of most of these collectors to gather every item possible on Columbus and his associates. The process naturally stimulated interest in history writing.

The best outgrowth of this movement was Henry Harrisse (1823–1910). He was born in Paris, removed to the United States when still a boy, graduated from the University of South Carolina, taught in the University of North Carolina, and at length became a lawyer with a small practice in New York City. Here he came into contact with Samuel L. M. Barlow, who proved his fast friend and mentor. Thus inspired he decided to write a history of the rise, decline, and fall of the Spanish empire in America. His first step was to undertake to make a bibliography of the Columbian period, using Barlow's library as a basis and examining further the other collections in the city. The results he embodied in his *Notes on Columbus* (1866), in which not only titles were given but much additional information in regard to editions and contents. Favourable criticisms came from collectors and he decided to make a bibliography of Americana for the years 1492 to 1551. Thus was prepared his *Bibliotheca Americana Vetustissima*, which appeared in 1866. The few interested in the subject were loud in their praise, but the general public were so indifferent that the publisher threw a large part of the edition on the market at a sacrifice. Harrisse was so indignant that he set out for France, unwilling to reside in a country in which his researches were so slightly esteemed.

In Paris he received a warm welcome. Ernest Desjardins brought him to the notice of the Société de Géographie in flattering terms, declaring him the author of "the first work of solid erudition which American science has produced." He assumed a prominent place at once among French savants. Continuing his profession of lawyer he was retained to give advice to the American government in regard to legal matters connected with the construction of the Panama Canal. The remuneration was so satisfactory that he was able, by good management, to lay the foundation of a fortune amounting at his death to a million francs. Freed from financial anxieties he could give himself to a career of scholarly labour.

Thirty volumes and a large number of pamphlets remain to attest the persistence of his efforts. He entered the hitherto uncharted region of the discoverers, explored it with the greatest attention to details, debated every disputed point with great ability, and revealed to the world not only its metes and bounds but its most salient interior features. Not all of his conclusions have been accepted by his successors, but no man has opposed him without acknowledging that Harrisse made possible the investigations of his critics. Of his *Discovery of North America* (1892), a comprehensive view of the whole field of his labour made when he had advanced far in his own development, Professor Edward Gaylord Bourne said that it was "the greatest contribution to the history of American geography since Humboldt's *Examen.*"

Harrisse gave a large portion of his thought to three great figures in the period of discovery, Columbus, Cabot, and Vespuccius, planning an exhaustive book on each. On the first he produced his *Jean et Sebastien Cabot* (1882), besides several smaller pieces; and on the second he wrote his *Christophe Colombe* (2 vols., 1884–85). On the third he collected a great mass of material, discussing some of the points in monographs, but death intervened before a final and exhaustive work was actually written. Like a true explorer he was ever seeking new knowledge, correcting in one voyage errors made in another. He did not hesitate to alter his views when newly discovered facts demanded it. He was strong in defending his opinions and did not escape controversies with those who opposed them. But he was a true scholar and no love of ease or honour tempted him away from the joyful toil of his studies. Although he spent the best part of his life in Paris, he considered himself an American to the end. He bequeathed his annotated set of his own writings together with the most valuable of his manuscripts and maps to the Library of Congress.

Harrisse's achievements tend to dwarf the work of two New York historians who took a high stand in the circle out of which he got his first impulses to historical scholarship. James Carson Brevoort (1818–87) was a business man who gave his leisure to history. His *Verrazano, the Navigator* (1874) was an important book on that phase of our early history. Henry Cruse Murphy (1810–82), a lawyer and Democratic leader of high character, found himself stranded when the Civil War swept his party into a hopeless minority. Unwilling to twist himself into a Republican he retired from politics and devoted himself to history and the care of the large library he had collected. One of his books, *The Voyage of Verrazano* (1875), taking the opposite side from Brevoort's, was received as the best on its side of the controversy.

These men represent the early manifestations of "the great subject." Two others, Justin Winsor (1831–97) and Edward Gaylord Bourne (1860–1908), stand at the point of its fruition. Alike in scholarship and deep interest in the earliest phase of our history, they were widely apart in their use of language to express their ideas. Winsor wrote a tedious page, filled with details; Bourne wrote in a simple and well digested style which did not lack in clearness and charm of expression.

Winsor was of a prosperous Boston mercantile family and began life with every opportunity that a Boston boy could desire. He withdrew from Harvard because he disliked the routine of the college classes but read widely in the best literature. Determined to become a literary man he gave himself to poetry and the drama until he realized that he was not likely to succeed in creative literature. During this period of his life he wrote much for the Boston periodicals and projected a definitive life of David Garrick which was never completed. In 1868 he became librarian of the Boston Public Library and served with such success that he was called to the same position at Harvard in 1877, where he remained the rest of his life.

It was about this time that he assumed editorial direction of a co-operative history of Boston, for which the leading men of the city had been selected to write special chapters. The work was published in four volumes as *The Memorial History of Boston* (1880–82). Winsor's part was so well done that he was asked by the publishers to undertake a similar work on American history. Thus was written and published his *Narrative and Critical History of America* (8 vols., 1886–89), probably the most stimulating book in American history that has been produced in this country. The editor's part was the best and consisted chiefly in an abundance of bibliographical and cartological notes. Before the appearance of the book the student had been left to stumble as he could toward his bibliography. Now he had in one work such a wealth of this information that he could always have a point of departure for his studies and need not hesitate in the early stages of any investigation. The book, however, was richer in its suggestions on colonial and Revolutionary history than on the later period; and this was because the editor's interest was strongest in our early history.

Winsor came under the influence of "the great subject," and probably his most intense study was given to the achievement of the explorers. He was a high authority on early American cartography. His interest in the period of discovery led him to write his *Christopher Columbus and How he Received and Imparted the Spirit of Discovery* (1891). It was a minute and conscientious discussion of the career of the discoverer and of the progress of geographical knowledge in the Columbian period. He carried on the history of discoveries and explorations in three other books: *From Cartier to Frontenac* (1894), *The Mississippi Basin* (1895), and *The Westward Movement* (1897). These books proved disappointing to persons who sought readable narratives. They were filled with details and poorly constructed; but the maps and cartological information in them were very valuable.

In fact, in Winsor's philosophy the historian's function was to burrow into the past for the facts that had been overlooked by other writers, and when the facts were found he took little pains how he arranged them before the eyes of the reader.

I may confess [he said], that I have made history a thing of shreds and patches. I have only to say that the life of the world is a thing of shreds and patches, and it is only when we consider the well rounded life of the individual that we find permeating the record a reasonable constancy of purpose. This is the province of biography, and we must not confound biography with history.

Of "shreds-and-patches" history Justin Winsor was a master. He was loved of the student and nearly unknown to the reader.

Professor Bourne was the son of a village minister in New England. Unlike Winsor, his life was always overcast with the problem of earning a living. Lameness from childhood handicapped his efforts and eventually resulted in his death when he had just demonstrated his capacity for historical work of the first class. Wide information, good judgment, and a keen eye for inaccuracies characterized his work. A sense of proportion is ever found in the structure of his books, and his language is clear and sometimes graceful. In the latter part of his life he came under the sway of "the great subject," and when he died he was the leading Americanist in the United States. One small book, *Spain in America* (1905), remains as an expression of this phase of his activity; but it is so well done that it is not likely to be superseded as long as we hold our present views on the period of the explorers. In his *Essays in Historical Criticism* he gave the student and general reader a model of sound historical analysis and showed how to test historical statement in a practical way. Most of the *Essays* had previously been published in various places. The most notable was the paper called *The Legend of Marcus Whitman*, which was received with angry protest from those to whom the legend had become dear.

Four Literary Historians. The members of this group had something to do with Motley and Prescott on the one hand and something with the new school on the other; but they were first of all artists in expression, working in the field of history with such success as they were able to attain. They were John Foster Kirk (1824–1904), Francis Parkman (1823–93), Edward Eggleston (1837–1902), and John Fiske (1842–1901).

Kirk was the efficient literary secretary of William H. Prescott[1] during the latter part of the career of this nearly blind historian, travelling with him on both sides of the Atlantic and meeting many of the leading men of the day. During this period he began to write for *The North American Review* and other magazines. Prescott and his friends encouraged his efforts, and after the death of his employer in 1859 he embarked definitely on the sea of authorship. It was natural for him to select a subject in Prescott's field. He chose the career of Charles the Bold, founder of the Burgundian power and great-grandfather of Charles V. It was a subject worthy of a brilliant pen, and his book *The Life of Charles the Bold* (3 vols., 1863) met all expectations. While it rested on secondary authorities and has been rendered obsolete by later investigations, it was worthy to rank with the books by Robertson, Prescott, and Motley which had already made the Burgundian-Austrian cycle a famous period in historiography. Vividness and colour were its notable qualities. The great expectations it

---

[1] See Book II, Chap. xviii.

raised were doomed to disappointment; for although the author lived forty-one years after its publication, his *Charles the Bold* remains his one important book. From 1870 to 1886 he edited *Lippincott's Magazine*, and for five years later was engaged in preparing a supplement to *Allibone's Dictionary*. The remainder of his life was given to a new dictionary which the Lippincott's proposed to publish. This submergence of literary talents by hack work brought regret to many who knew Kirk's talents. When Edward A. Freemen was introduced to him he exclaimed: "Why did you stop? I looked for more books on European history from you and have been much disappointed."

Francis Parkman had the best of Boston's inheritance except health, and against the effects of that handicap he interposed a resolute spirit which enabled him to devote to his books the few hours he could snatch from a constant state of pain. From early life he had the desire to write the history of the New England border wars. During his college vacations he visited the scenes of these conflicts, and he read always widely in the books on that subject. When he graduated at Harvard in 1844 he knew the New England Indians thoroughly. Much of the next two years was spent in visiting the historic spots on the Pennsylvania border and in the region beyond. In 1846 he made a journey to the land of the Sioux, where he spent some weeks in the camps of a native tribe, studying the Indian in the savage state. His experiences were described in a series of letters in *The Knickerbocker Magazine* and republished in his first book, *The California and Oregon Trail* (1849), still considered one of our best descriptions of Indian life.

Now prepared for his main task, Parkman took a striking incident of Indian history and wrote on it his *Conspiracy of Pontiac* (1851). In this book he placed much introductory matter on the Indians, together with a comprehensive review of the history of the French settlements before 1761, when the conspiracy of Pontiac began. From this large use of preliminary materials it would seem that he had not yet determined to undertake the series of volumes in which he later treated the same period. The *Pontiac* was well received and it was a good book from a young author. But it lacked conciseness and was overdrawn.

For several years after its publication Parkman suffered great physical pain, and he seemed about to lose the use of his eyes and limbs. But he never gave up his ambition or ceased to collect information about the Indians. In this interval he wrote *Vassall Morton* (1856), a novel which did not succeed. Turning back to history he revised his entire plan and outlined his *France and England in North America*. The series was limited to the period before the Pontiac war. It embraced the whole story of French colonization in North America from the Huguenot colonies of the sixteenth century to the fall of Quebec. The various parts appeared as follows: *The Pioneers of France in the New World* (1865); *The Jesuits in North America* (1867); *La Salle and the Discovery of the Great West* (1869); *The Old Régime in Canada* (1874); *Count Frontenac and New France under Louis XIV* (1877); *Montcalm and Wolfe* (2 vols., 1884); and *A Half Century of Conflict* (2 vols., 1892). He described the series as including "the whole course of the American conflict between France and England, or in other words, the history of the American forest; for this was the light in which I regarded it. My theme fascinated me, and I was haunted with wilderness images day and night." Parkman's purposes were wholly American. He loved the vast recesses of murmuring pines, with their tragedies, adventures, and earnest striving. Prescott and Motley might paint the gorgeous scenes of royal courts and Bancroft might interrupt his labours in writing the panegyric of democracy to play a complacent rôle as minister at Berlin, but Parkman never ceased to find his chief interest in the American forest and its denizens.

His avowed method of writing was "while scrupulously and rigorously adhering to the truth of facts, to animate them with the life of the past, and, so far as might be, clothe the skeleton with flesh. Faithfulness to the truth of history involves far more than research, however patient and scrupulous, into special facts. The narrator must seek to imbue himself with the life and spirit of the time." Few writers have achieved their ideal of expression as well as he. What Cooper[1] did in the realm of fiction Parkman did with even better fidelity to nature in the realm of history. He never studied in the seminar school, but he understood its lessons instinctively and made them his

[1] See Book II, Chap. VI.

own without loss of the best things in the old school—vigour, harmony, and colour.

Edward Eggleston entered history through the door of fiction.[1] He was born in Indiana of the Western branch of a leading Virginia family, had scant educational opportunities, spent several years as an itinerant Methodist minister, became an editor in Chicago and New York, and in 1871 published the widely read story of frontier life, *The Hoosier Schoolmaster.* Two years later he retired from the profession of editor, and became pastor of a Brooklyn Congregational church, with the expressed understanding that he was not to conform to specific dogmas.   Increasing skepticism made him give up this position in 1879.   The step was taken after internal struggles which left him in a state of nervous prostration.   Rest brought restoration and he turned to history as a serious study.   Fiction he still followed as a breadwinning art, but from 1880 to his death in 1902 he considered himself primarily a historian.

Social history was his field.   What his Hoosier stories did for the Indiana backwoods, he wished his histories to do in simple narrative for the life of all the people.   To his brother he described his plan in the following words:

I am going to write a series of volumes which together shall constitute a History of Life in the United States—not a history of the United States, bear in mind, but a history of the life there, the life of the people, the sources of their ideas and habits, the course of their development from beginnings.   These beginnings will be carefully studied in the first volume.   Beyond that my plans for the ordering of the material are not fully formed.   It will be a work designed to answer the questions " How ?" and " Whence ?" and "Why?"   All this will require a great deal of research, but I stand ready to give ten years of my life to the task, if necessary.

Ten years allow brief space to write such a history for a man of less desultory habits of work than Eggleston had.   At the end of twenty-two years he had finished only two of the proposed volumes, *The Beginners of a Nation* (1897) and *The Transit of Civilization* (1901).   They carried the story of colonial life to the year 1640.   Had the work proceeded on the same scale to the end of the nineteenth century it would have

[1] See also Book III, Chap. XI.

gone to forty volumes. Eggleston had undertaken it without realizing its greatness. The plan, however, was worthily made; and the two volumes completed deserve more esteem than they will get as fragments of a too ambitious dream by a man already old when he dreamed. They are characterized by accuracy, breadth of view, and great charm of narration. Eggleston combined research and good literary style as truly as Parkman, but he worked less persistently and gauged the situation less wisely.

There was a time when John Fiske seemed likely to pass into our literary history as the man who best combined the virtues of the new and old schools. Time has defeated the hope by discovering that he lacked accuracy. Nature gave him two excellent gifts, the art of writing and the art of lecturing as few others could write or lecture. Each was performed with great facility and in the use of each he surpassed most of his contemporaries. In early life he became an evolutionist and was much disliked by the orthodox until he finally appeared in the rôle of reconciler of evolution and religion. As the leading defender of the philosophy of Darwin and Spencer in the United States he gained a wide influence and wrote constantly.[1] By 1885 the battle of evolution had been won in high places and Fiske seems to have had no desire to pursue it in the lower circles. At the same time he was gradually drifting away from Spencer, through attempting to bring religion into the scope of his philosophy. After 1885 he wrote nothing philosophical.

In the same year he published *American Political Ideals*, a short sketch of our political history, and it opened a new field of activity. In 1879 he had given six lectures on "America's Place in History" in the Old South Church, Boston. With a fine sense of the picturesque, he selected such subjects as the old sea kings, the Spanish and French explorers, and the causes of the Revolution. It was his first handling of historical events and the result was a revelation to himself. His own words were: "This thing takes the people, you see: they understand and feel it all, as they can't when I lecture on abstract things." Other lectures followed and met with such great success that he fully committed himself to history.

One of these courses was on the period following the Revolution and was published as *The Critical Period of American His-*

[1] See Book III, Chap. XVII.

tory (1888); another saw the light as *The Beginnings of New England* (1889); while still another after being presented many times on the platform was published as *The American Revolution* (2 vols., 1891). Before these volumes appeared he had made plans for a series to cover the whole period of American history, and he proposed to make these re-baked lectures fit into the scheme. It was necessary to go back to the beginnings and he accordingly set to work on *The Discovery of America* (2 vols., 1892). This was followed by *Old Virginia and her Neighbors* (2 vols., 1897) and *The Dutch and Quaker Colonies* (2 vols., 1899). Another instalment, *New France and New England*, carrying the story down to the Revolution, was not published until 1902, the year after Fiske died. A group of lectures was published in 1900 in a fascinating volume called *The Mississippi Valley in the Civil War.* He wrote two text-books which had remarkable success: *Civil Government in the United States* (1890) and *A History of the United States for Schools* (1892). A biography of his friend Edward L. Youmans (1892), a volume called *A Century of Science and Other Essays* (1899), and two posthumous works, *Essays, Historical and Literary* (1902) and *How the United States Became a Nation* (1904), completed his historical works.

It has been said that Fiske applied the principles of evolution to history, and he asserted that such was his purpose. But a brief examination of his books is enough to show that he was the historian of episodes and human action. It is the dramatic rather than the philosophical that occupies his attention. In preparing to write he read many books and out of his capacious memory he wrote with feverish haste. Too ready dependence on memory, an unwillingness to look deeply into minute sources, and an extreme tendency to the picturesque undermined his sense of accuracy. None of the other men in the group under treatment equalled him in mere power of narration.

Historians of the Latest Period.[1] Of the men in this group not one rejected the dogma of the supremacy of accuracy, but in

---

[1] This chapter does not deal with living historians, even though it is necessary, in carrying out such a policy, to omit any discussion of so excellent an historian as James Ford Rhodes.

varying degrees they cherished the notion that history should have literary merits. In all of them the new school triumphed but the old yielded slowly. It was only with Mahan and Henry Adams that style became an unconscious expression of clearly formed ideas. That it was always good is too much to assert; but at its best it was a subordinate part of the historian's purpose. The men of this group, the most conspicuous of our recently deceased historians, all worked in constant fear of inaccuracies.

Henry Charles Lea (1825–1909) may be placed at the head of the group. He was a prosperous Philadelphia publisher, the grandson of Mathew Carey,[1] the publisher, nephew of Henry C. Carey,[2] the economist, and son of Isaac Lea, a naturalist notable in his day. To this family inheritance add a general Quaker background and we may understand the origin of his desire to describe some of the most striking phases of the history of religious zeal. In two book-reviews published in 1859 he managed to introduce a great deal about compurgation, the wager of battle, and ordeals. His interest in the subject was so much aroused that he subsequently revised the essays in a volume called *Superstition and Force* (1866). It was followed by *The History of Sacerdotal Celibacy* (1867) and *Studies in Church History* (1869). These books were written in such hours as he could snatch from business. Convinced that the two kinds of labour could not be carried on jointly with perfect success, he gave up authorship for a time. In 1880 he was able to retire from active business and devote himself to literature. The books written in this second period are richer in the evidences of research and broader in plan and judgment. They are *The History of the Inquisition in the Middle Ages* (3 vols., 1888), *Chapters from the Religious History of Spain Connected with the Inquisition* (1890), *History of Auricular Confession* (3 vols., 1896), *The Moriscoes in Spain* (1901), *History of the Inquisition in Spain* (4 vols., 1906–1908), and *History of the Inquisition in the Spanish Dependencies* (1908). When Lea died he was preparing a history of witchcraft.

These works are monuments of industry and learning, and they deal with a most difficult class of phenomena in a scientific spirit. They have encountered the opposition of most Catholic

---

[1] See Book III, Chap. **xxix.**　　　　　[2] *Ibid.*, Chap. XXIV.

writers, but some, notably Lord Acton, have given them their approval.   Lea did not hesitate to lay evils at the doors to which he thought they belonged.   "I have always sought," he said "even though infinitesimally, to contribute to the betterment of the world, by indicating the consequences of evil and of inconsiderate and misdirected zeal."   He was accused of interpreting his documents improperly and of showing only the dark side of the mediæval church.   As to the first point it is difficult to find a man who can pass upon its truth.   Lea himself was, perhaps, the fairest critic in the field.   That he was not narrowly prejudiced is shown by his treatment of the motives of Philip II in his inaugural address as president of the American Historical Association.   As to the second charge, we should remember that Lea did not propose to write about the light sides of the church.   He was dealing with a dark phase of history, and he did not try to make it lighter than he thought it should be made.

Another publisher who became a historian was Hubert Howe Bancroft (1832–1918), of San Francisco, who gave us our most conspicuous group of local histories.   Having formed a large collection of materials on the history of the Pacific coast, he decided to embody the contents in a comprehensive work.   He adopted the method of the business man who has a task too large for his own efforts.   He employed assistants to prepare statements of the facts for large sections of the proposed history. Originally he seems to have intended to use these statements as the basis of a narrative from his own hand; but as the work progressed he came to use them with slight changes.   We have his own word that the assistants were capable investigators and there is independent evidence to show that some of them deserved his confidence.   But his failure to give credit leaves us in a state of doubt concerning the value of any particular part.   Bancroft considered himself the author of the work. We must look upon him as the director of a useful enterprise, but it is not possible to consider him its author.

His *Works* contain thirty-nine large volumes with the following titles: *Native Races of the Pacific States* (vols. 1–5, 1874), *History of Central America* (vols. 6–8, 1883–87), *History of Mexico* (vols. 9–14, 1883–87), *History of the Northern Mexican States and Texas* (vols. 15–16, 1884–89), *History of Arizona*

and New Mexico (vol. 17, 1889), *History of California* (vols.
18–24, 1884–90), *History of Nevada, Colorado, and Wyoming*
(vol. 25, 1890), *History of Utah* (vol. 26, 1889), *History of the
North-West Coast* (vols. 27–28, 1884), *History of Oregon* (vols.
29–30, 1886–88), *History of Washington, Idaho, and Montana*
(vol. 31, 1890), *History of British Columbia* (vol. 32, 1887),
History of Alaska (vol. 33, 1886), *California Pastorals* (vol. 34,
1888), *California inter Pocula* (vol. 35, 1888), *Popular Tribunals*
(vols. 36–37, 1887), *Essays and Miscellany* (vol. 38, 1890),
and *Literary Industries* (vol. 39, 1890).

Neither Bancroft nor his assistants had the preliminary
training to save them from the ordinary pitfalls along the path
of the scholar. They carried to their tasks uncritical enthusiasms and made good books which, nevertheless, had some
serious defects. In a period when the reviewer generally appraised a book for its style Bancroft's early volumes generally
received approbation. Francis Parkman himself gave *The
Native Races* high credit in *The North American Review*. But
the work did not escape the eyes of Lewis H. Morgan, whose
revolutionary theory of Indian culture was then new to the
world. In an article called "Montezuma's Dinner" Morgan
completely reversed Parkman's verdict and implanted a doubt
in the minds of the intelligent public which extended to other
volumes of the series. Bancroft's comments on Morgan's
criticism suggest that he did not understand Morgan's theory,
now generally accepted by scholars.

Alfred Thayer Mahan (1840–1914) graduated at the Naval
Academy at Annapolis in 1859, served the usual course at sea,
and was ordered to duty at the Naval War College shortly
after it was established in 1885. A course of lectures prepared
for that service was the basis of a book, *The Influence of Sea
Power in History, 1660–1783* (1890), which established his
reputation as an historian. Following the same idea he pub
lished *Influence of Sea Power on the French Revolution* (1892),
Life of Farragut (1892), *The Life of Nelson, the Embodiment of the
Sea Power of Great Britain* (2 vols., 1897), *Sea Power in its Relation to the War of 1812* (1905), and *From Sail to Steam* (1907),
the last a book relating to his own career. In his later years
he wrote, also, many articles for the magazines, and out of them
were formed several volumes of essays.

Rear-Admiral Mahan is the best example we have had in the United States of a man who wrote history successfully for propaganda. He wished to show that a nation that would play a large rôle in the world must have a great navy. He won immediate fame in Great Britain, where his books served to strengthen the naval policy of the government. They were also greatly appreciated in Germany, and it is said that they opened the eyes of the German government to the need of a great navy. In his own country he was highly esteemed as an historian, but he never had the satisfaction of seeing the government adopt a great naval policy.

While Mahan was a scholarly historian, he cannot be pronounced a man of research. With a thesis to prove it was not necessary to go to the sources to prove it. His early books were written entirely from secondary materials; but he used sources in his later work, particularly in the book on the War of 1812, of which he said: "It is by far the most thorough work I have done." Something of his mental character may be seen in the following statement in reference to a book which most students find uninteresting: "Though not a lawyer, nor a student of constitutions, I found Stubbs's *Constitutional History of England* fascinating. I have not analyzed my pleasure, but I believe it to have been due to arrangement of data by a man exceptionally gifted for vivid presentation, who had so lived with his subject that it had realized itself to him as a living whole, which he successfully conveyed to his readers."

Three sons of Charles Francis Adams, grandsons of John Quincy Adams, became historians, and two of them, Charles Francis Adams, Jr. (1835–1915) and Henry Adams (1838–1918), fall within the limits assigned to this chapter. Both of them had the Puritan mind, so strong in their ancestry, as well as that independent Adams spirit which put the family, from John Adams to Henry, out of touch with the dominant thought of Boston. Turning to history, both of them became able critics of conventional views and won high respect from an age turning towards cosmopolitan ideals. The elder of the two, however, did not go all the way in revolt. New Englander he remained to the last. He loved Boston, although he rapped its knuckles at times, and he sought to reform its intellectual life. The younger clung to Boston for many years,

giving himself to a phase of our history in which the town had a
deep interest; but finally, having reached a stage of disillusionment, as he considered it, he broke local ties, turned toward
the unanchored spaces of the remote past, and became a master
in the realm of detached thinking.

After serving in the army until 1865 Charles Francis Adams,
Jr., gave himself to the study of the railroad situation, writing
and publishing articles that led to his appointment on the
Massachusetts railroad commission in 1869.   In the same year
he published a remarkable essay, *A Chapter in Erie*, exposing
the methods by which some of the leading railroad directors
manipulated the stocks of their roads for their own benefit.   He
became a government director of the Union Pacific Railroad in
1882 and served as its president from 1884 to 1890.   Retiring
from this position he gave the remainder of his life to history.
The results of his labours appeared in many books and pamphlets, the most important of which were *Chapters of Erie and
Other Essays*—in collaboration with Henry Adams—(1871),
Railroads, their Origin and Problems (1878), *Notes on Railroad
Accidents* (1879), *The New English Canaan of Thomas Morton*
(new edition with introduction, 1883), *Richard Henry Dana, a
Biography* (2 vols., 1890), *History of Quincy* (1891), *History of
Braintree* (1891), *Three Episodes of Massachusetts History* (2
vols., 1892), *Massachusetts, its Historians and History* (1893),
Charles Francis Adams, the First (1900), *Three Phi Beta Kappa
Addresses* (1907), *Studies, Military and Diplomatic* (1911),
Trans-Atlantic Historical Solidarity (1913), and *Charles Francis
Adams, an Autobiography* (1916).

He was not content to be merely an historian but did many
things to promote historical interests.   He was in constant
demand for historical addresses.   Several of his discourses were
made in the South, where his appreciation of Southern character
was warmly received, and his words did much to promote good
feeling between the two sections.   As vice-president and president of the Massachusetts Historical Society he was the leader
of an important group of historians.   It was in these extra-
literary activities that he served history best.

The historical career of Henry Adams falls into two periods.
One of them began with his return from London in 1868, where
he had been private secretary to his father, then minister to

Great Britain, and continued until 1892, when he turned his back on all he had been doing and began again what he termed his "education." The second extended from that change of purpose to his death. The editorship of *The North American Review* (1869–76) and an assistant-professorship in history at Harvard (1870–77) ushered in the first period. Teaching did not suit him and he resigned because he felt that his efforts were failures. His mind was too original to go through life in the routine of college instruction. He now turned to American history, producing by much industry in fourteen years the following books: *Documents Relating to New England Federalism* (1877) *Life of Albert Gallatin* (1879), *Writings of Albert Gallatin* (1879), *John Randolph* (1882), *History of the United States during the Administrations of Jefferson and Madison* (9 vols., 1889–91), and *Historical Essays* (1891). The best scholarship and excellent literary form characterize all these books. No better historical work has been done in this country. Yet the books were little read and the author became discouraged. He concluded that what he had been doing was without value to the world, since it was not noticed by the world.

Then began the second period of his literary life. Settling down to a quiet life of study, and following his taste, he delved long and patiently in the Middle Ages. The result appeared in *Mont Saint Michel and Chartres* (1904, 1913), probably the best expression of the spirit of the Middle Ages yet published in the English language. It was followed by *Essays in Anglo-Saxon Law* (1905), *The Education of Henry Adams* (1906, 1918), *A Letter to American Teachers of History* (1910), and *Life of George Cabot* (1911). Two of these books, the *Mont Saint Michel* and the *Education*, deserve to rank among the best American books that have yet been written. The first is a model of literary construction and a fine illustration of how a skilled writer may use the history of a small piece of activity as a means of interpreting a great phase of human life. Through the *Education* runs a note of futility, not entirely counterbalanced by the brilliant character-sketching and wise observations upon the times. But the *Mont Saint Michel* redeems this fault. It shows us Henry Adams at his best, and under its charm we are prepared to overlook the aloofness which limited his interests while it depressed his spirits.

In the *Education* Henry Adams defined history in these words: "To historians the single interest is the law of reaction between force and force—between mind and nature—the law of progress." He thus announced in his maturity his allegiance to the most modern concept of history. In his early historical writings he dealt with the relations of men with men, as Parkman, Lea, Mahan, and many others dealt. In his revised opinions he conceived that the story of man's progress as affected by natural forces was the true task of the historian. It is a concept to which the best modern thinkers have been slowly moving. Adams grasped it with the greatest boldness and in the *Mont Saint Michel* gave future historians an example of how to realize it in actual literature.

CHAPTER XVI

Later Theology

A MERICAN theology since the Civil War represents an age of transition, of much fortunate silence, of expectant waiting, as on a threshold. But there are one or two sturdy souls, like William G. T. Shedd (1820–94) and Charles Hodge (1797–1878), who gathered up the olden time with a disdain of the new. Yet perhaps disdain is scarcely the word to associate with Charles Hodge. His three huge volumes on *Systematic Theology* (1873) are found now mostly in public libraries and in the attic chambers of aging parsons. Theology is out of vogue, and his volumes represent a system which is less and less widely held as the years go by. But Charles Hodge had a genuine religious experience. Disdain certainly fades from the lips of any tolerant modern man as he browses in these books. The table of contents is schematical, wooden. The first volume, after an introduction, deals with "Theology Proper," the second volume is devoted to "Anthropology," and the third is divided between "Soteriology" and "Eschatology." But though "Evolution" is in the air—and indeed in the first volume—there is no apologetic explanation of the division. Hodge is not ashamed of the tenets of past ages. He does not write for the public but to the public. But he writes with transparent sincerity. There is no evasion. There is neither condescension nor cringing. There is nothing left at loose ends. There is no sparing of thought. His weighty opponents are fairly treated and his words are devoid of sarcasm—the weapon of conscious and obtrusive superiority. He does not pretend to understand God nor those who seem to him to claim that they do. He only claims to apprehend the Word of God. In his introduction he reaches, on what he regards as rational grounds, the conclusion that the Scriptures are the Word of God and therefore that their teachings are infallible. Thereon he stands unmoved. Approaching the profound subject of the decrees of God, for every Calvinist thrilling in its audacity, he says simply:

It must be remembered that theology is not philosophy. It does not assume to discover truth, or to reconcile what it teaches as true with all other truths. Its province is simply to state what God has revealed in His Word and to vindicate those statements, as far as possible, from misconceptions and objections. This limited and humble office of theology it is especially necessary to bear in mind, when we come to speak of the acts and purposes of God. All that is proposed is simply to state what the Spirit has seen fit to reveal on that subject.

So he looks without flinching over the vast unsunned spaces to the place of eternal punishment. On the "Duration of Future Punishment" he writes:

It is obvious that this is a question which can be decided only by divine revelation. No one can reasonably presume to decide how long the wicked are to suffer for their sins upon any general principles of right and wrong. The conditions of the problem are not within our grasp. What the infinitely wise and good God may see fit to do with His creatures, or what the exigencies of a government, embracing the whole universe and continuing throughout eternal ages, may demand, it is not for such worms of the dust, as we are, to determine. If we believe the Bible to be the Word of God, all we have to do is to ascertain what it teaches on this subject, and humbly submit. . . . It should constrain us to humility and to silence on this subject that the most solemn and explicit declarations of the everlasting misery of the wicked recorded in the Scriptures, fell from the lips of Him, who, though equal with God, was found in fashion as a man, and humbled Himself unto death, even the death of the cross, for us men and our salvation.

There is a strange sublimity and extraordinary perspicuity about the style of Charles Hodge. It is not style at all. He is writing a treatise for students. His sentences are constantly interrupted by 1) 2) 3), A) B) C), and the like. Yet, notwithstanding the nature of the doctrine and the ponderous character of the subject, there are few books which open the mind on the fields of grandeur more frequently than this systematic theology. Its prose is not unworthy of being associated in one's mind with that of Milton. Out of the depths this man has cried unto God and found Him.

But, undeniably, theology has gone out of fashion. Huge treatises like those of Hodge or Shedd or Augustus Strong never found many readers, but they found their way to many bookshelves. They were treated with reverence. Now they are utterly ignored. The chief reason for this contempt of theology is that men impugn its ancient authority. Hodge rightly declared that theology was to be differentiated from philosophy by its source of authority. It dealt with revelation while philosophy dealt with speculation. Its function was the interpretation of absolute truth, committed to men by the Holy Ghost through the pages of the Scripture. In our period this supposedly infallible book was subjected to the most searching examination. The ordinary canons of historical and literary criticism were applied to it and as a result the awesome phrase "Thus saith the Lord" came to bear diverse connotations. It was in the eighties and nineties that the authority of the Scripture, already long questioned in Europe, became a vital question in American thought. Then a series of heresy trials—five within the Presbyterian Church—concentrated the attention of religious people upon the subject. The most prominent figure in the great controversy in America was Charles Augustus Briggs (1841–1913), professor in Union Theological Seminary in New York from 1874 to 1913. This controversy was preceded by a bitter controversy in the ancient Congregational Seminary at Andover, Massachusetts, on questions of the future state, into which Briggs also entered. But the main question was the nature of Biblical inspiration. After a defence conducted by himself with great skill and acumen, he was acquitted of the charges of heresy by his Presbytery in January, 1893, but upon appeal to the General Assembly was convicted and suspended from the ministry of the Presbyterian Church in March of the same year.

Apart from some minor peculiarities of personal temper, no one could well have been found better able than Briggs to commend the newer views on the Scriptures to the conservative circles of America and particularly to the members of the Presbyterian Church who occupied so large a place in the educational life of the country. He was the leading authority on the history of the Westminster Assembly which framed the Presbyterian standards. In his treatise *Whither* (1889) he is at great pains to show that the doctrine of inerrancy of Scripture is a modern development of orthodox opinion, and that it was with careful forethought that the Assembly refrained from committing itself and the Church to any specific doctrine of inspiration or to the statement that the Bible is the Word of God. It had proclaimed indeed that the Bible was the only infallible rule of faith and practice but refused to extend its authority beyond the moral and religious sphere. "The Church ought to be in advance of the Confession. But the Confession is in advance of the Church so that the children of the Puritans must first advance to the high mark of their own standards before they can go beyond them into the higher reaches of Christian theology."[1] His own temper was conservative in a very high degree. He rejoiced that he was essentially at one with historic Christendom. At the end of his life he occupied the chair of Irenics at the Seminary which proved so loyal to him, and as a priest in the Protestant Episcopal Church gave much of his energy to the reunion of Christendom. Moreover, the field upon which he chiefly laboured in his six student years in Germany and in the Seminary was the Old Testament. And although he frankly admitted that "in every department of Biblical study we come upon errors," it was with questions of Old Testament literature that he was primarily concerned. The application of the canons of criticism to the New Testament was fortunately deferred. The figure of Jesus, indeed, was first brought into the realm of criticism in America by his utterances in regard to the Old Testament books which were under discussion. The Bible was discovered by the American public to be literature by way of the Old Testament. It was, however, no literary interest which impelled the discovery, but rather the deepest loyalty to religious truth. With the same fearless loyalty to fact with which Hodge faced hell, did Briggs and his fellows descry errors in a book which they held to be the repository of eternal truth.

[1] *Whither*, p. 296.

To claim beforehand that inspiration or any such divine process must be this or that, that it must have certain characteristics, is to venture beyond our limits. In all humility, instead of dictating what God should do, let us inquire reverently what God has done,— in what form concretely the revelation of His will has come to men. All *a priori* definition of inspiration is not only unscientific but irreverent, presumptuous, lacking in the humility with which we should approach a divine, supernatural fact.

So speaks another who later was the object of heresy proceedings in the Presbyterian Church, Professor Llewelyn J. Evans of Lane Theological Seminary in Cincinnati.[1]

Now although the discovery of errors in Scripture, of pseudepigraphs in the Old Testament, of unfulfillable prophecies,—the asseveration of which occupied so prominent a place in the trial of Briggs,—of authors separated by centuries within the confines of the Pentateuch alone, of false ascriptions of late laws to the holy but dimming figure of Moses, have undoubtedly helped us to regard the Bible as primarily a product of human literary and religious genius, they have also gradually changed both the conception of the place of the Bible in our religion and of our religion itself. We find these changes emerging even in the pages of Briggs.

If a man use it [the Bible] as a means of grace, it is of small importance what he may think of its inspiration. If it bring him to the presence of the living God and give him a personal acquaintance with Jesus Christ, that is its main purpose. . . . They [the Scriptural errors] intimate that the authority of God and His gracious discipline transcend the highest possibilities of human speech or human writing, and that the religion of Jesus Christ is not only the religion of the Bible, but the religion of personal communion with the living God.[2]

The beginning at least of the profound change in a man's religion which comes about through the change in his religious authority is delicately portrayed by Professor William N. Clarke (1841-1912) of Colgate College. Professor Clarke's theological books have been the most popular attempt of our period to pre-

[1] See his *Biblical Scholarship and Inspiration*, 1891, pp. 12, 13, 20.
[2] *The Bible, Church and Reason*, 1892, pp. 82, 117.

serve in systematic form the essentials of historic Christianity without inhospitality to modern science and criticism. In his *Sixty Years with the Bible* (1909) he writes:

I have described the change by saying that I passed on from using the Bible in the light of its statements to using it in the light of its principles. At first I said, The Scriptures limit me to this; later I said, The Scriptures open my way to this. As for the Bible, I am not bound to work all its statements into my system; nay, I am bound not to work them all in; for some of them are not congenial to the spirit of Jesus and some express truths in forms which cannot be of permanent validity.

Popular interest in the authority of the Bible was prepared for by the appearance of the Revised Version of the Bible just a decade before the dramatic trial of Charles A. Briggs. Thirty-four of the leading Hebrew and Greek scholars of America united with sixty-seven Englishmen in this great undertaking, which Philip Schaff, the chairman of the American revisers, declared to be "the noblest monument of Christian union and co-operation in this nineteenth century." After a laborious toil of eight years, during which "no sectarian question was ever raised," the New Testament was given to the public. "The rapidity and extent of its sale surpassed all expectations and are without a parallel in the history of the book-trade." The New Testament appeared in 1881 and the Old Testament in 1885. Although one of the Old Testament revisers took pains to say in his *Companion to the Revised Old Testament* that "they have no fellowship with that disposition which of late years has appeared among some who profess and call themselves Christians to speak lightly of the Scriptures as a partial and imperfect record of revelation," and although the Old Testament Committee was presided over by Professor Wm. H. Green of Princeton Seminary and the New Testament Committee by ex-President Theodore D. Woolsey of Yale College, both eminently conservative scholars, the mere publication of a new translation of the Scriptures, founded upon a revised Hebrew and Greek text, prepared the public mind for some modification of the concept of infallibility which had possessed it hitherto. The printing of the Bible in paragraphs like other books—instead of in the oracular verses—and the appearance of portions of the Old Testament in poetic form helped greatly in convincing the plain people of the country that the Bible was to be subsumed under the genus literature rather than kept as a sacred oracle in mysterious isolation.

Nor did the fact that the most brilliant attacks upon the infallibility of the Bible and many of its ablest defences originated in Germany militate against the progress of the newer thought in America as much as might have been expected. Our scholars felt themselves dependent upon European thought. Providentially, too, German theological scholarship had been introduced to American minds by the presence and fecundity of Philip Schaff (1819–93), a man of most conservative temper, who, in an amazing number of volumes, chiefly in the domain of Church History, had commended the thoroughness and sanity of German research to the American public from his chair in Wittenberg, Pennsylvania, and later in Union Theological Seminary, New York.

It cannot be said that during the period under consideration American scholarship contributed anything of material value to the higher criticism of the Bible. It has to its credit the great New Testament Lexicon (1893) of Professor J. Henry Thayer of Andover Seminary and the equally pre-eminent Hebrew Lexicon (1891) edited by President Francis Brown of Union Seminary, assisted by Professor Briggs of Union and Professor Driver of Oxford. But in the higher discipline its work was of a more mediating and imitative character. Few of our leading scholars took an unyielding attitude to the spirit of the times. Manfully and with unassuming temper, Green of Princeton defended the ancient opinions in a debate with President Harper of the University of Chicago and later in his books, *The Higher Criticism of the Pentateuch* (1895), *The Unity of the Book of Genesis* (1895), and *General Introduction to the Old Testament* (1898). With the exception of more searching work by still living scholars, still fewer of our writers took radical ground. Here we may mention only the lucid books of Orello Cone of St. Lawrence University, Levi L. Paine's suggestive *Evolution of Trinitarianism* (1900) with its appendix challenging the apostolic authorship of the fourth Gospel, and particularly Edward H. Hall's *Papias and his Contemporaries* (1899), which connects the Gospel of John with the Gnostic

movement of the second century. The majority of our scholars took a moderately progressive stand. As the pregnant
debate approached the New Testament, American scholarship
maintained largely a dignified silence but refused to move the
previous question. The most substantial contribution of our
scholars in the whole field of Biblical literature is probably Ezra
Abbot's *Authorship of the Fourth Gospel* (1880), which, while
it defends the widely disputed apostolic authorship of the book,
admits the cogency of opposing opinion and the discrepancies
between the fourth Gospel and the other three. George P.
Fisher, Professor of Church History in the Yale Divinity School
and author of a very usable *History of the Christian Church*,
sensed the vital import of the criticism of the gospels and
devoted the greater part of his careful and well-poised works
on *The Supernatural Origin of Christianity* (1870) and *Grounds
of Theistic and Christian Belief* (1883) to a vigorous and able
defence of the historicity of the gospels. But while doing so
with full conviction, he is clear-sighted enough to declare:

> The Bible is one thing and Christianity is another. The religion
> of Christ, in the right signification of these terms, is not to be con-
> founded with the Scriptures, even of the New Testament. The
> point of view from which the Bible, in its relation to Christianity,
> is looked on as the Koran appears to devout Mohammedans, is a
> mistaken one. The entire conception, according to which the
> energies of the Divine Being, as exerted in the Christian revelation,
> are thought to have been concentrated on the production of a book,
> is a misconception and one that is prolific of error.

Or as T. T. Munger, Professor Fisher's neighbour in New
Haven, has it in his notable essay on the New Theology: "It
[the Bible] is not a revelation but is a history of a revelation; it
is a chosen and indispensable means of the redemption of the
world, but it is not the absolute means,—that is in the Spirit."
While Marvin R. Vincent is right in saying that "Germany
furnishes the most and the best," our theologians have maintained an open mind in the study of the book upon which their
whole discipline rests.

One reason, then, for the waning prestige of theology is
the fact that its source of authority can no longer be regarded
as lying in a class apart from all other works of the human

spirit. Its aloofness and uniqueness are even more threatened, however, by the doctrine of evolution, which subsumes not only the Christian religion but the entire nature of man under universal rubrics. At first this doctrine shocked not only the theological but also the scientific thinkers of America. Louis Agassiz and Asa Gray opposed it almost as vigorously as did Charles Hodge, who declared "that a more absolutely incredible theory was never propounded for acceptance among men." The burden of his logical and able *What is Darwinism?* (1874) is expressed in these sentences:

> The conclusion of the whole matter is that the denial of design in nature is virtually the denial of God. Mr. Darwin's theory does deny all design in nature, therefore, his theory is virtually atheistical; his theory, not he himself. He believes in a Creator. But—He is virtually consigned, so far as we are concerned, to non-existence.

That this attitude toward evolution was speedily changed among theologians was due partly to President James McCosh (1811–94) of Princeton. He had but recently come from Great Britain to America. Many of his long list of books, expounding the Scottish "Common Sense" philosophy, had been written. There was no question of his complete orthodoxy, of his intense religious zeal, or of his international standing as thinker and educator. He, however, gave liberal recognition to "powers modifying evolution." These agents are light, life, sensation, instinct and intelligence, morality. "As evolution by physical causes cannot [produce them], we infer that God does it by an immediate fiat, even as He created matter. . . . It makes God continue the work of creation, and if God's creation be a good work, why should He not continue it?"[1]

In wide circles this acceptance of evolution of species went hand in hand with the denial of the unlimited sway of evolution. Chasms which "no evolution can leap" were insisted upon, "between the inorganic and the organic, between the irrational and the rational, between the non-moral and the moral." It was widely felt that "Natural Selection" is inadequate to account for the entire process of evolution, and Darwin's variability of species was emphasized. Thus for example

[1] *Religious Aspect of Evolution*, p. 54.

Lewis Diman, who left the pastorate for a professorship of history in Brown University, asserts in his Lowell lectures on *The Theistic Argument* (1882):

Some internal principle of transformation must be admitted. . . . If we allow that the modifications of an organ are the result of some more or less conscious tendency which serves as a directing principle, then we are brought to recognize finality as the very foundation of nature. . . . To affirm that life is the continuous adjustment of inner relations to outer relations is to affirm nothing to the point, since the adjustment is the very fact for which we are seeking to account.

Or as the scintillating Joseph Cook from his lecture-throne in Tremont Temple, Boston, put it: "The law of development explains much but not itself." Gradually, however the imagination of theologians, like that of other men, refused to accentuate the small gaps of the stupendous process and evolution, not very clearly defined or delimited, became accepted as God's method of creation.

Belief in the unique sonship of Christ is a difficulty in the complete acceptance of evolution. George Harris of Andover Seminary and later President of Amherst College writes: "There is no reason to suppose that any other man will be thus God-filled. . . . We may well believe that he was one who transcended the human."[1] Because Christ produced "a new moral type," Harris feels that we need not deny either his nature miracles or his resurrection. Among the most thoroughgoing Christian evolutionists of our period may be mentioned President Hyde (1858-1917) of Bowdoin College and President John Bascom (1827-1911) of the University of Wisconsin. The latter, in his *Evolution and Religion or Faith as a Part of a Complete Cosmic System* (1915), rejoices in the breadth of view and the boundless hope with which the doctrine of evolution invests its believers. In youth Bascom studied both law and theology; in mature years he taught sociology and philosophy; he occupied influential positions in the educational institutions of the East and the West. His lapidary style and his avoidance of the concrete have kept his numerous works confined to a small circle of readers, but they are thankful for them.

[1] *Moral Evolution*, chapter XVI.

Evolution [he writes] implies a movement perfectly coherent in every portion of it. It is one therefore which can be traced in all its parts by the mind—one in which we, as intelligent agents, are partakers, first, as diligently inquiring into it; second, as concurrently active under it, and third, as in no inconsiderable degree modifying its results. . . . The secret of evolution lies here—We always lie under the creative hand at the centre of creative forces. . . . We are constantly speaking of the eternal and immutable character of truth. . . . These adjectives are hardly applicable. The universe does not tarry in its nest. It is ever becoming another and superior product. . . . We must accept the truth as giving us directions of thought, axes of growth, and no final product whatever.

A third great factor in destroying the isolation of Christianity from human life, worthy to be mentioned with Biblical criticism and the theory of evolution, was the wide-spreading interest in the foreign missionary enterprise. The various monographs in the excellent *American Church History* series indicate that missions share with education and the federation of the sects the chief interest of the denominational life of this period. An increasingly large number of intelligent men and women went into the lands "occupied" by other religions for the sake of Christianizing them. They returned frequently with the reports of their activity, their successes, and their difficulties. The chief difficulty which confronted them in the civilized lands of the East was the firmly rooted conceptions and emotions at the base of Hinduism, Buddhism, Confucianism, and Mohammedanism. It became borne in upon the Christian consciousness that Christianity and religion were not synonymous. Before they realized it, the churches were face to face with the discipline of "Comparative Religion"—what Nash called "the most significant debate the world has ever known."[1] James Freeman Clarke, one of the tenderest and truest ministers of Jesus in New England, composed a series of Lowell lectures on *Ten Great Religions* (1871) which went through at least twenty-two editions, and brought a knowledge of the high aspirations of other religious leaders to Christian people. Toward the end of our period, the World's Parliament of Religions, held in conjunction with the Columbian Exposition in Chicago, composed of representatives of ten religions,

[1] *Ethics and Revelation*, p. 92.

visited by more than one hundred and fifty thousand people, gave dramatic underscoring to the "Brotherhood of Religions" —the phrase in which they were welcomed by one of the authorities—and adopted as its motto the words from Malachi: "Have we not all one Father? hath not one God created us?"

It was possible, of course, to take the ground—and it was at first widely taken—that these religions were so many evidences of the sinfulness of mankind.   James S. Dennis, author of the three-volume work on *Christian Missions and Social Progress* (1898)—a mine of rare and accurate sociological material—holds: "They are the corruptions and perversion of a primitive, monotheistic faith, which was directly taught by God to the early progenitors of the race. . . . They are gross caricatures and fragmentary semblances of the true religion." W. C. Wilkinson of the University of Chicago, speaking at the Parliament of Religions, declared: "The attitude of Christianity towards religions other than itself is an attitude of universal, absolute, eternal, unappeasable hostility, while toward all men its attitude is an attitude of grace, mercy, peace for whosoever will."   And the noble and eloquent Bishop J. M. Thoburn of India castigates the preposterous view that the great religions were all originated and developed by God Himself and that they all have been and still are serving their purpose in the education of the human race, and declares that he has "no more respect for Mohammedanism as a system than for Mormonism."

As time went on, however, a wise agnosticism regarding the origin of the religions of the Eastern world came to be combined with an ever more intelligently founded conviction of the moral supremacy of Christianity.   Arthur H. Smith, brilliant speaker and keen observer, has given a record of his twenty-two years of life in China in the popular books *Chinese Characteristics* (1894) and *Village Life in China* (1899).   He finds the Confucian classics to be "the best chart ever constructed by man" and feels that "perhaps it is not too much to say that its authors may have had in some sense a divine guidance."   He still insists, however, that the Chinese lack "character and conscience" and that they must have "a knowledge of God and a new conception of man" to attain them. William N. Clarke, after a tour of the missions abroad, sums up thus:

in Confucianism, where the religious movement is ethical, the ethics become human and religion is lost. In Buddhism, where it is philosophical, the philosophy becomes pessimistic and religion dies out. In Hinduism, where it is emotional, the emotion becomes degrading and religion is defiled. In Mohammedanism, where it is doctrinal, the doctrine becomes cold and lifeless and religion is atrophied. . . . A personal God, possessing a moral character and offering himself in personal relations to man, is known in Christianity alone.

But a still more outspoken sympathy and reverence for the religions which Christianity is to "complete" are to be found among missionaries and their devoutest supporters. George William Knox, for fifteen years a missionary in Japan and afterward Professor of the Philosophy and History of Religion in Union Theological Seminary, who died in Corea while Union Seminary Lecturer in the East, thus expresses himself in *The Spirit of the Orient* (1906):

If God rules, we cannot join in the wholesale condemnation of the East as if it were a blot on His creation. . . . As one thinks of Confucianism, its vast antiquity, its immense influence over such multitudes, its practical common sense, its freedom from all that is superstitious or licentious or cruel or priestly, of the intelligent men it has led to high views of righteousness, one cannot but regard it as a revelation from the God of truth and righteousness.

As we should expect, this viewpoint was strongly urged at the Parliament of Religions in Chicago. Dr. Barrows, its organizer, asked the frank question: "Why should not Christians be glad to learn what God has wrought through Buddha and Zoroaster?" And Robert Hume, a missionary from India who had been prominently identified with the liberal wing in the Andover controversy, and author of *Missions from the Modern View* (1905), declared:

By the contact of Christian and Hindu thought, each will help the other. . . . The Hindu's recognition of the immanence of God in every part of his universe will quicken the present movement of western thought to recognize everywhere a present and a living God. The Hindu's longing for unity will help the western mind . . . to appreciate . . . that there has been and will be one plan and one purpose from the least atom to the highest intelligence. From the testimony of Hindu thought, Christians will more appreciate the superiority of the spiritual and invisible over the material and the seen, of the eternal over the evanescent.

At the close of the Parliament, two lectureships were established to conserve the temper and purpose of that remarkable assemblage. One of these is named the Barrows lectureship, and upon its incumbent is laid the duty of delivering a series of lectures, interpretative of the Christian spirit, in the intellectual centres of the East. Charles Cuthbert Hall, the President of Union Theological Seminary, was twice the Barrows lecturer. As the result of this last strenuous and congenial service he laid down his devoted life. Between those two periods of Oriental travel he delivered the Cole lectures before Vanderbilt University, on the *The Universal Elements of the Christian Religion* (1905). Their chief impression concerns the folly of further sectarianism in the Protestant communion, but upon the matter immediately occupying us the lecturer declares in words thoroughly and inclusively typical of our period:

When one stands in the heart of the venerable East; feels the atmosphere charged with religious impulse; reads on the faces of the people marks of the unsatisfied soul; considers the monumental expression of the religious idea in grand and enduring architectural forms, then the suggestion that all this means nothing—that it is to be stamped out and exterminated before Christianity can rise upon its ruins,—becomes an unthinkable suggestion. I look with reverence upon the hopes and yearnings of non-Christian faiths, believing them to contain flickering and broken lights of God, which shall be purged and purified and consummated through the absolute self-revelation of the Father in Christ Incarnate."

As a result then of these three great world-movements of thought—the science of Biblical criticism, the theory of evolution, and the emergence of comparative religion—Christian theology has renounced its lofty isolation and become a department of human knowledge. But though finding religion at the heart of common human life, instead of in a holy sphere apart from it, modern theologians have not found it empty of significance. They have discovered the world to be not, as Plato feared, a creature marked by changing cycles but the theatre and stuff of a steady upward movement, culminating in man. They have found the Christian Bible to contain the most significant segment of man's history, to be the transcript of that strenuous and sublime process by which the foundations of reverence and justice and truth were laid for Love to build upon. They have discovered Jesus of Nazareth to be Love's supreme creation and channel. They believe the Christian function to be the transformation of human life by the energy of that Love. They find that mankind is to be led, as George W. Knox said, "not along the road of dialectics to our God but by the great highway of service to our fellowmen." Consequently, with a growing scorn for sectarian problems and debates, they are applying themselves to the outstanding tasks of human society. Here many scholars and pastors have wrought nobly. In the earlier stages of this modern thought the books of Josiah Strong and C. Loring Brace and Edward Everett Hale[1] were of much avail. William J. Tucker made the chair of Practical Theology at Andover seem one of Sociology and directed the founding of the first settlement house in Boston. Joseph Tuckerman founded a pastorship-at-large in the same city and helped to crystallize Unitarian social sympathy in paths of definite service to the poor. These men and many others have contributed to what E. Winchester Donald of Trinity Church, Boston, so happily called in his Lowell lectures "The Expansion of Religion." From this social viewpoint, two eminent educators, in particular, have wrought at a revolution in theology, William DeWitt Hyde, already mentioned, and Walter Rauschenbusch (1861-1918) of Rochester Theological Seminary—the latter perhaps the most creative spirit in the American theological world. The heart of their gospel may be presented, though inadequately, in a few sentences:

This glorious work of helping to complete God's fair creation; this high task of making human life and human society the realization of the Father's loving will for all his children; this is the real substance of the spiritual life, of which the services and devotions of the church are but the outward forms. They ought not to be separated. Yet if we can have but one, social service is of infinitely more worth than pious profession. . . . The world has been re-

[1] See Book III, Chaps. VI and XIII.

deemed from the moment when Christ came into it; from the moment when Love was consciously accepted as the true law of human life. This Christian principle of loving service and willing self-sacrifice for the glory of God and the good of man . . . is the spiritual principle of the modern world. . . . It is not always explicitly conscious of the historic source of its inspiration; it is not always in intellectual sympathy with the formulas in which the Christian tradition is expressed. But . . . the presence of this Spirit of Love as the accepted and accredited ideal of conduct and character is itself the proof that the world has been redeemed. It is the promise and potency of its complete redemption.[1]

The religion that lived in the heart of Jesus and spoke in his words not only had a social faith; it was a social faith. . . . The Kingdom of God calls for no ceremonial, for no specific doings. . . . Like Jesus, it makes love to God and love to man the sole outlet for the energy of religion and thereby harnesses that energy to the ethical purification of the natural social relations of men. . . . We are a wasteful nation. But the most terrible waste of all has been the waste of the power of religion on dress performances. . . . The Kingdom of God deals not only with the immortal souls of men, but with their bodies, their nourishment, their homes, their cleanliness, and it makes those who serve these fundamental needs of life, veritable ministers of God. . . . If the Kingdom of God on earth once more became the central object of religion, Christianity would necessarily resume the attitude of attack with which it set out. It had the temper of the pioneer. But where it has taken the existing order for granted and has devoted itself to saving souls, it has become a conservative force, bent on maintaining the great institution of the church and preserving the treasure of doctrine and supernatural grace committed to it. When we accept the faith of the Kingdom of God, we take the same attitude toward our own social order which missionaries take toward the social life of heathenism. . . . The Church would have to "about face." The centre of gravity in the whole Christian structure of history would be shifted from the past to the future.[2]

Many Christian pastors have attempted to live in the spirit of this gospel, but it is scarcely invidious to single out Washington Gladden (1836-1918) as the best-known and most effective worker for the regeneration of the social organism in the pulpit of our period. He was pastor in North Adams and Springfield,

[1] Hyde, *Social Theology*, pp. 215-16, 229-30.
[2] Rauschenbusch, *Christianizing the Social Order*, pp. 96-102.

Massachusetts, and, for over thirty years, in Columbus, Ohio. He was the author of many books on the social and religious readjustment, of which perhaps *On Being a Christian* (1876), *Applied Christianity* (1886), *Who Wrote the Bible?* (1891), *Tools and the Man* (1893), *The Christian Pastor* (1898), and *The Labor Question* (1911) have had the largest sale. No one of these volumes, however, was written merely in order to be published; they grew out of the pressing problems of his ministry. His fine-spirited *Recollections* (1909) indicates the stormy theological and sociological times through which he lived. He refused to be silent and he was fortunately mediatory by nature. His fairness won him a hearing and his good-will gave him effectiveness. He challenged the official conservatism of the Congregational churches, he threw his influence into the struggle for untrammelled investigation of the Bible, he insisted upon a larger share of the profits of industry for the labourers, he initiated the movement for the change of the time of election in Ohio from October to November, he had himself elected to the city council in Columbus when important franchises were to be decided, and became firmly convinced of the necessity of municipal ownership of public works. He writes: "Dishonest men can be bought and ignorant men can be manipulated. This is the kind of government which private capital, invested in public-service industries, naturally feels that it must have. . . . I do not think that the people of any city can afford to have ten or twenty or two hundred millions of dollars directly and consciously interested in promoting bad government." During a fierce street-car strike in Cleveland in 1886 he journeyed thither and spoke to a great meeting of employers and employees on "Is it Peace or War?" openly favouring the right of the workingmen to combine for the defence of their interests. In a later street-car strike in his own city he intervened, insisting upon the arbitration which the labourers desired and the employers refused. He was an enemy of war. As late as 1909 he declared that he wished secession had been tried: "I cannot help wishing that the ethical passion of the North for liberty had been matched with a faith equally compelling in the cogency of good-will." An enemy of socialism, he became at length convinced that the functions of government should be extended. His opinions moved slowly but somewhat in advance of the opinion of the churches. When he died in 1918 the New York *Evening Post* remarked: "Washington Gladden seemed to have an extra sense. . . . In matters affecting religion and church organization, in matters political, in matters social, in matters international, he had an almost uncanny way of anticipating what was to come." The truth of this comment may be tested by a paragraph from his essay on *The Strength and Weakness of Socialism*, written as far back as 1886.

Out of unrestricted competition arise many wrongs that the State must redress and many abuses which it must check. It may become the duty of the State to reform its taxation, so that its burdens shall rest less heavily upon the lower classes; to repress monopolies of all sorts; to prevent and punish gambling; to regulate or control the railroads and telegraphs; to limit the ownership of land; to modify the laws of inheritance; and possibly to levy a progressive income-tax, so that the enormous fortunes should bear more rather than less than their share of the public burdens.

He was a strong believer in profit-sharing; he was president of an association for Christian education of the negroes and Indians and backward peoples; he was the moderator of the Congregational National Council; he was the champion of international peace. He was withal a Christian pastor and conscientious preacher. He said, indeed:

I maintain that good sermons may be and ought to be good literature; that the free, direct, conversational handling of a theme in the presence of an audience makes good reading in a book. If I am permitted to judge my own work, I should say that the best of my books as literature is the book of sermons, *Where Does the Sky Begin?*

The one man who, in our period, best demonstrated this thesis of Washington Gladden is Phillips Brooks (1835–93).[1] He was most fortunately constituted and placed to be a great preacher. Just about the time of his birth in Boston, his family gave up its pew in the Unitarian meeting-house and, as a

---

[1] The volume the writer of this chapter would recommend as an introduction to Brooks's writings is the fourth series of his sermons, entitled *Twenty Sermons*, published in 1886. The new edition (1910) is entitled *Visions and Tasks*.

compromise between its Unitarian and Congregational strands, took one in St. Paul's Episcopal Church, its freedom and strength becoming tinged with mystery and wrapped about in dignified historicity. And when Phillips Brooks, after an unsuccessful experiment in teaching in the Boston Latin School, hesitatingly determined to be a minister, his mind seemed to rest in the solidarity of humanity, in the perpetual and abiding emotions, conceptions, and satisfactions which underlie all change. The strong conservatism, so often noted in college students, seemed to remain with him long after the undergraduate years and to be a constitutive element of his character.

With the great controversies of his times he was not unacquainted. He took the gradually prevailing view with regard to them all. He believed the great books of other religions to be "younger brothers" of the Bible. He travelled with sympathetic interest in India and Japan. "No mischief," he thought, "can begin to equal the mischief which must come from the obstinate dishonesty of men who refuse to recognize any of the new light which has been thrown upon the Bible." When Heber Newton was threatened with a trial for heresy because of his belief in the methods and some of the more radical conclusions of the higher criticism, Brooks invited him to preach in his pulpit. He says remarkably little regarding the Darwinian controversy. He had but a superficial acquaintance with science. He finds his comfort in believing that "the orderliness of nature must make more certain the existence of an orderer," and suggests that "Christ's truth of the Father Life of God has the most intimate connection with Darwin's doctrine of development, which is simply the continual indwelling and action of creative power." He added, however, but little to the controversies. Save where, as in the problem of comparative religion, they came into close contact with his own gospel of the universal sonship of man to God, he was not fundamentally interested in them. His sympathetic sermon on Gamaliel, who left the upshot of controversies to God, is characteristic. In the Theological Seminary at Alexandria he wrote in his student's notebook:

Truth has laid her strong piers in the past Eternity and the Eternity to come and now she is bridging the interval with this life of ours. . . . Controversies grow tame and tiresome to the mind which has looked on Truth. . . . We walk the bridge of life. Can we not trust its safety on the two great resting-places of God's wisdom?

Phillips Brooks was habitually more aware of the background than of the foreground. Occasionally, indeed, it was otherwise. In his Philadelphia ministry he spoke out boldly, at the conclusion of the War, for negro suffrage. In his later life the radical in him showed itself more conspicuously. He rose in his place in the Church Congress to plead for the use of the Revised Version of the Bible in public worship, and in the Convention of 1886 he protested vigorously against the proposal to strike the words "Protestant Episcopal" from the title of his Church. On his return from the Convention to Boston, he even went so far as to declare from the pulpit that if the name were changed, he did not see how any one could remain in the Church who, like himself, disbelieved in the doctrine of Apostolic Succession. But in the main he lived above controversy. He believed neither in "insisting on full requirements of doctrine nor on paring them down. . . . The duty of such times as these is to go deeper into the spirituality of our truths. . . . Jesus let the shell stand as he found it, until the new life within could burst it for itself." His rare biographer, A. V. G. Allen, makes this significant comment upon a Thanksgiving sermon of his:

He offers no solution of the conflict between religion and science. But it means something that in the disorder of thought and feeling, so many men are fleeing to the study of orderly nature. He urges his hearers to make much of the experiences of life which are perpetual, joy, sorrow, friendship, work, charity, relation with one's brethren, for these are eternal.

For Brooks this was no evasion. It was digging below the questions of the day to the eternal, unquestioned, proven truths of human experience. It was losing one's self in humanity. He occasionally looked forward, and increasingly, but he loved best to look from the present backward and upward. Just after his graduation from Harvard, we find this in his notebook:

A spark of original thought . . . strengthens a man's feeling of individuality, but weakens his sense of race. It is an inspiring, ennobling, elevating, but not a social thing. But what a kindly power, what a warm human family feeling clusters around the thought which we find common to our mind and to some old mind which was thinking away back in the twilight of time. . . . So when we recognize a common impulse or rule of life . . . we must feel humanity in its spirit, bearing witness with our spirits, that it is the offspring of a common divinity.

His native conservatism lived through the awakening years of the Seminary. We find these musings in his notebook:

Originality is a fine thing, but first have you the head to bear it? . . . Our best and strongest thoughts, like men's earliest and ruder homes, are found or hollowed in the old primæval rock. . . . Not till our pride rebels against the architecture of these first homes and we go out and build more stately houses of theory and speculation and discovery and science, do we begin to feel the feebleness that is in us.

As his biographer keenly says: "Nowhere in these notebooks does Brooks regard himself as a pioneer in search of new thought. . . . He does not test truth by individual experiences but by the larger experiences of humanity." He told the Yale theological students in his middle life that a part of the Christian assurance lies in the fact that the Christian message is "the identical message which has come down from the beginning." Part of his satisfaction in preaching lay in his confidence that he was in his proper communion. He rejoiced "in her strong historic spirit, her sense of union with the ages which have passed out of sight." The insignia of spiritual truth to him were largely antiquity and catholicity. He had profound faith in the people. He believed in prophets when they had been accepted by the people; that is, usually some ages after they have lived and died. Few prominent men have let their friends and the public decide in their crises more than Brooks—and in nearly every case against his own original instinct. He relied on the heart of humanity as the supreme judge. Out of this primitive conviction of his grew his one essential message, that every man who has ever lived is a son of God. Consequently when a great doctrine came before him which had the ages of experience behind it or upon it, the question he asked was not " Is it true? " but "Why is it true?" or "Wherein resides its truth?" So it was with the great pivotal doctrine of the divinity of Christ, or, as he preferred to call it, the Incarnation. He found its truth to reside in the fact that Christ had lived out the secret yearnings and possibilities of humanity; Christ was the prophecy of the Christ that was everywhere to be. On the great question of the miracles he was orthodox. He lived in a time when Biblical criticism in this country was in its earlier stages. He could honestly write to a German inquirer: "There is nothing in the results of modern scholarship which conflicts with the statements in the Apostles' and Nicene Creeds concerning the birth of Jesus." As Allen remarks, Brooks was in the habit of "sheathing his critical facuities where the people's faith was concerned." He used the Bible, therefore, pretty much as he found it, or rather he used what he found beneath it.

It was toward middle life, about the time that a fresh study of the Gospels found expression in the *Influence of Jesus* (1880), that his emphasis seemed to shift from historic Christianity to the personal Christ. Over and over he insisted on the centrality of Christ. "Not Christianity but Christ! Not a doctrine but a person! Christianity only for Christ! . . . Our religion is—Christ. To believe in Him is what? To say a Creed? To join a church? No, but to have a great, strong, divine Master, whom we perfectly love." And how perfectly he loved him and how Christ responded to the embraces of this man's love, a letter on the eve of his consecration to the bishopric shows:

These last years have a peace and fulness which there did not use to be. I do not think it is the mere quietness of advancing age. I am sure it is not indifference to anything which I used to care for. I am sure that it is a deeper knowledge and truer love of Christ. . . . I cannot tell you how personal this grows to me. He is here. He knows me and I know Him. It is no figure of speech. It is the reallest thing in the world. And every day makes it realler. And one wonders with delight what it will grow to as the years go on.

And yet, notwithstanding his anchorage in the past, he believed in a port ahead, for each individual primarily, but also for the race. Even his ecstatic and unreserved loyalty to the incarnate Christ did not serve as an iron door let down athwart the highway of progress. He intimated that his teaching regarding divorce was determined by temporary circumstances and that his scheme of punishments is not an essential factor of his religion. It is true, naturally, with his strong belief in immortality and in the individual's sonship to God, that he held that society is here for the sake of the individual and not the individual for the sake of society. But in the later years we find almost a new note in his writings. "Life may become too strong for literature," he says. "It may be the former methods and standards are not sufficient for the expression of the growing life, its new activities, its unexpected energies, its feverish problems. . . . A man must believe in the future more than he reverences the past." In a speech before the Boston Chamber of Commerce he is reported as having said that "the world was bound to press onward and find an escape from the things that terrified it, not by retreat but by a perpetual progress into the large calm that lay beyond." In the sermon which gives the title to his volume *The Light of the World* (1890),—wherein is succinctly set forth his gospel, "the essential possibility and richness of humanity and its essential belonging to divinity,"— we have these majestic words:

It is so hard for us to believe in the mystery of man. "Behold man is this," we say, shutting down some near gate which falls only just beyond, quite in sight of, what human nature already has attained. If man would go beyond that, he must be something else than man. And just then something breaks the gate away, and, lo far out beyond where we can see, stretches the mystery of man, the beautiful, the awful mystery of man. To him, to man, all lower lives have climbed, and, having come to him, have found a field where evolution may go on for ever.

Such passages are rare in his writings, for usually his gaze takes in the past with Christ resplendent in it and does not lose itself in the future; then gratitude gets the upper hand of struggle. He rarely preaches an entirely "social" sermon. In *The Christian City*, wherein he departs from his custom, he beseeches Londoners to take heart because the modern city is so Christian, though unconsciously. *The Giant with the Wounded Heel* is one of the finest and most characteristic of his sermons. He believes the giant, man, is constantly crushing the serpent, and he is content to see a pretty large wound in his heel.

This largeness and poise of view is the most distinctive characteristic of Phillips Brooks. It stamps him with the mark of intellect. Occasionally he seems to value the mind for itself and to ascribe to it standards of its own. "The ink of the learned is as precious as the blood of the martyrs." Once he admits, without catching himself, that the mind is "the noblest part of us." In the sermon where this admission is made, *The Mind's Love for God*, he declares: "You cannot know that one idea is necessarily true because it seems to help you, nor that another idea is false because it wounds and seems to hinder you. Your mind is your faculty for judging what is true." But these are isolated sayings. Ordinarily he refuses to think of the intellect as a thing apart from the entire man, and he finds truth, as did his Master, inherent in life, a personal quality, discovered, determined, and determinable by personal ends. When he first began to think, Socrates was almost the ideal figure. But later, Socrates seemed thin in comparison with Christ. "Socrates brings an argument to meet an objection. Jesus always brings a nature to meet a nature; a whole being which the truth has filled with strength to meet another whole being, which error has filled with feebleness." In his sermon on the death of Lincoln he discloses his inner thought:

A great many people have discussed very crudely whether Abraham Lincoln was an intellectual man or not, as if intellect were a thing, always of the same sort, which you could precipitate from the other constituents of a man's nature and weigh by itself. . . . The fact is that in all the simplest characters, the line between the mental and moral nature is always vague and indistinct. They run together, and in their best combination you are unable to discriminate, in the wisdom which is their result, how much is moral and how much is intellectual.

In his student days he confides to his notebook: "A fresh thought may be spoiled by sheer admiration. It was given us to work in and to live by. . . . It will give its blessing to us only on its knees. From this point of view, thought is as holy a thing as prayer, for both are worship." The best description, perhaps, of his own mind is to be found in his enumeration of the "intellectual characteristics which Christ's disciples gathered from their Master," namely: "A poetic conception of the world we live in, a willing acceptance of mystery, an expectation of progress by development, an absence of fastidiousness that comes from a sense of the possibilities of all humanity, and a perpetual enlargement of thought from the arbitrary into the essential."

These peculiar intellectual characteristics, rooted in their passionate reverence for humanity, for its ideals and its achievements, determine the place of Brooks among the great preachers of the world. He is at his best when he preaches by indirection. Enlargement is his effect. A man sees his own time in relation to all time, discovers his greatness by the greatness of which he is a part. Brooks's mission was not to advance the frontiers of knowledge, not even of spiritual knowledge, but rather to annex the cleared areas to the old domains. His abiding preoccupation—fatal to the scientist, detrimental to the sociologist, fortunate for the fame and immediate influence of the preacher—was to hold the present, changing into the future, loyal to the past. He was not the stuff of which martyrs are made, but his soul was of that vastness which kept the public from making martyrs of the truthful. He seems to watch and bless rather than to urge forward. His great service to his age was that of a mediator. Standing himself as a trinitarian and a supernaturalist, rejoicing in the greenness of the historic pastures, he discovered at the base of his doctrines the same essential spiritual food which others sought on freer uplands and less confined stretches. He ministered to orthodox and unorthodox alike beneath their differences. He did much to keep spiritual evolution free from the bitterness and contempt of revolution.

CHAPTER XVII

Later Philosophy

THE prevailing other-worldliness of American philosophers seems to be the only explanation for our failure to develop an original and vigorous political philosophy to meet our unique political experience. On a priori grounds it seems indisputable that philosophy must share the characteristics of the life of which it is a part and on which it is its business to reflect. But we actually do not know with certainty what kind of philosophy any given set of historic conditions will always produce. Thus no one has convincingly pointed out any direct and really significant influence on American philosophy exercised by our colonial organization, by the Revolutionary War, by the slavery struggle, by the Civil War, by our unprecedented immigration, or by the open frontier life which our historians now generally regard as the key to American history. The fact that, excepting some passages in Calhoun,[1] none of our important philosophic writings mentions the existence of slavery or of the negro race, that liberal democratic philosophers like Jefferson[2] could continue to own and even sell slaves and still fervently believe that all men are created free and equal, ought to serve as a reminder of the air-tight compartments into which the human mind is frequently divided, and of the extent to which one's professed philosophy can be entirely disconnected from the routine of one's daily occupation. Indeed, it would seem that most of our philosophy is not a reflection on life but, like music or Utopian

[1] See Book II, Chap. xv. The keen pamphlet on *Slavery and Freedom* by A. T. Bledsoe, the most versatile of our Southern philosophers, and the references to the ethics of slavery in Wayland's *Moral Philosophy*, can hardly be considered as derogating from the statement in the text. [2] See Book I, Chap. viii.

and romantic literature, an escape from it, a turning one's back upon its prosaic monotony. But though genuine philosophy never restricts itself to purely local and temporal affairs, the history of philosophy, as part of the history of the intellectual life of any country, is largely concerned with the life of various national or local traditions, with their growth and struggles, and the interaction between them and the general currents of life into which they must fit, with the general conditions, that is, under which intellectual life is carried on.

The main traditions of American philosophy have been British, that is, English and Scotch; and the Declaration of Independence has had no more influence in the realm of metaphysical speculation than it has had in the realm of our common law. French and German influences have, indeed, not been absent. The community of Western civilization which found in Latin its common language has never been completely broken up. But French and German influences have not been any greater in the United States than in Great Britain. Up to very recently our philosophers have mostly been theologians, and the latter, like the lawyers, cultivate intense loyalty to ancient traditions. In our early national period French free-thought exercised considerable influence, especially in the South; but the free thought of Voltaire, Condillac, and Volney was, after all, an adaptation of Locke and English deism; and its American apostles like Thomas Paine,[1] Priestley, and Thomas Cooper were, like Franklin[2] and Jefferson, characteristically British—as were Hume and Gibbon in their day. This movement of intellectual liberalism was almost completely annihilated in the greater portion of the country by the evangelical or revivalist movement. The triumph of revivalism was rendered easier by the weakly organized intellectual life and the economic bankruptcy of the older Southern aristocracy, as reflected in the financial difficulties which embarrassed Jefferson, Madison, and Monroe in their old age. The second French wave, the eclectic philosophy of Cousin and Jouffroy, was at bottom simply the Scotch realism of Reid and Stewart over again, with only slight traces of Schelling.

With the organization of our graduate schools on German models, and with a large number of our teachers taking their

[1] See Book I, Chap. VIII.   [2] See Book I, Chap. VI.

doctors' degrees in Germany, Germanic terms and mannerisms gained an apparent ascendancy in our philosophic teachings and writings; but in its substance, philosophy in America has followed the modes prevailing in Great Britain. The first serious attempt to introduce German philosophy into this country came with Coleridge's *Aids to Reflection* (1829), and the apologetic tone of President Marsh's introductory essay showed how powerfully the philosophy of Locke and Reid had become entrenched as a part of the Christian thought of America. Some acquaintance with German philosophy was shown by New England radicals like Theodore Parker,[1] but in the main their interest in things Germanic was restricted to the realm of belles-lettres, biblical criticism, and philology. Though some stray bits of Schelling's romantic nature-philosophy became merged in American transcendentalism, the latter was really a form of Neoplatonism directly descended from the Cambridge platonism of More and Cudworth. Hickok's *Rational Psychology* (1848) is our only philosophic work of the first two-thirds of the nineteenth century to show any direct and serious assimilation of Kant's thought. Hickok, however, professes to reject the whole transcendental philosophy, and, in the main, the Kantian elements in his system are no larger than in the writings of British thinkers like Hamilton and Whewell. The Hegelian influence, which made itself strongly felt in the work of William T. Harris, was even more potent in Great Britain.

In 1835 De Tocqueville reported that in no part of the civilized world was less attention paid to philosophy than in the United States.[2] Whether because of absorption in the material conquest of a vast continent, or because of a narrow orthodoxy which was then hindering free intellectual life in England as well as in the United States, the fact remains that nowhere else were free theoretic inquiries held in such little honour. As our colleges were originally all sectarian or denominational, clergymen occupied all the chairs of philosophy. Despite the multitude of sects, the Scottish common-sense philosophy introduced at the end of the eighteenth century at Princeton by Presi-

---

[1] See Book II. Chap. VIII.

[2] One gets the same impression from Harriet Martineau's *Society in America* and from the account of Philarète Chasles.

dent Witherspoon, spread until it formed almost the sole basis of philosophic instruction. Here and there some notice was taken of Mill and Positivism, and Edward's *Freedom of the Will*[1] continued to agitate thoughtful minds inside and outside of the colleges, but in the main both idealism and empiricism were suspected as leading to pantheism or to downright atheism. The creation of the earth before man was a potent argument against Berkeleian idealism or denial of matter. The Scottish common-sense realism was a democratic philosophy in the sense that it did not depart widely from the popular views as to the nature of the material world, the soul, and God.[2] It did not rely on subtle arguments, but appealed to established beliefs. It could easily be reconciled with the most literal interpretation of the Bible and could thus be used as a club against freethinkers. Above all, it was eminently teachable. It eliminated all disturbing doubts by direct appeal to the testimony of consciousness, and readily settled all questions by elevating disputed opinions into indubitable principles. It could thus be authoritatively taught to adolescent minds, and students could readily recite on it. Unfortunately, however, philosophy does not thrive under the rod of authority; and in spite of many acute minds like Bowen, Mahan, Bledsoe, or Tappan, or powerful minds like Shedd and Hickok,[3] American philosophy before the Civil War produced not a single original philosophic work of commanding importance. To the modern reader it is all an arid desert of commonplace opinion covered with the dust of pedantic language.

The storm which broke the stagnant air and aroused many American minds from this dogmatic torpor came with the controversy over evolution which followed the publication of Lyell's *Geology*, Darwin's *Origin of Species*, and Spencer's *First Principles*. The evolutionary philosophy was flanked on the

---

[1] See Book I, Chap. IV.

[2] It is interesting to note that Jefferson was converted to it by Stewart.

[3] Soldier, lawyer, minister, publicist, and editor, as well as professor of mathematics, Albert T. Bledsoe deserves to be better known. His *Philosophy of Mathematics* is still worth reading. So also is Shedd's *Philosophy of History*, which illustrates the independence of the evolutionary conception of history from the thought of Spencer or Darwin. For sheer intellectual power, however, and for comprehensive grasp of technical philosophy Hickok is easily the foremost figure in American philosophy between the time of Jonathan Edwards and the period of the Civil War. He left, however, no influential disciples except Presidents Seeley and Bascom.

left by the empirical or positivistic philosophy of Comte, Mill, Lewes, Buckle, and Bain, and on the right by the dialectic evolutionism of Hegel. The work of John Fiske, the leader of the evolutionary host, of Chauncey Wright, who nobly represented scientific empiricism, and of William T. Harris, the saintly and practical minded Hegelian, united to give American philosophy a wider basis. With these the history of the modern period of American philosophy begins.

To understand the profound revolution in religious and philosophic thought caused by the advent of the hypothesis of organic evolution, we must remember that natural history was, after Paley, an integral part of American theology. The current religious philosophy rested very largely on what were then called the evidences of design in the organic world; and the theory of natural selection rendered all these arguments futile. The mass of geologic and biologic evidence marshalled with such skill and transparent honesty by Darwin proved an overwhelming blow against those who accepted the biblical account of the creation of man and of animals as literal history. Modern physical science had dispossessed theology from its proud position as the authoritative source of truth on astronomic questions. If, then, the biblical account of creation and its specific declaration, "According to their kind created He them," were to be disregarded, could Protestant Christianity, relying on the authority of the Bible, survive? These fears for the safety of religion proved groundless, but there is no doubt that the evolutionary movement profoundly shook the position of theology and theologians. Not only was the intellectual eminence of our theologians seriously damaged in the eyes of the community as a result of the controversy, but theology was profoundly altered by the evolutionary philosophy. As a religious doctrine the latter was in effect a revival of an older deism, according to which the world was the manifestation of an immanent Power expressing itself in general laws revealed by natural reason and experience, instead of being specially created and governed by divine interventions or occasional miracles revealed to us by supernatural authority.

In the realm of pure philosophy Spencer and his disciple Fiske brought no new ideas of any importance. Their doctrine of the relativity of human knowledge was a common possession of both English and Scottish writers, and their agnosticism, based on our supposed inability to know the infinite, had been common coin since the days of Kant. But the idea of universal evolution or development, though as old as Greek philosophy and fully exploited in all departments of human thought by Hegel, received a most impressive popular impetus from the work of Darwin and Spencer, and stirred the popular imagination as few intellectual achievements had done since the rise of the Copernican astronomy. Just as the displacement of man's abode as the centre of the universe led by way of compensation to a modern idealism which said "The whole cosmos is in our mind," so the discovery of man's essential kinship with brute creation led to the renewal of an idealistic philosophy which made human development and perfection the end of the cosmic process travailing through the æons. Thus, instead of doing away with all teleology, the evolutionary philosophy itself became a teleology, replacing bleak Calvinism with the warm, rosy outlook of a perpetual and universal upward progress.

This absorption of the evolutionary philosophy by theology is clearly brought out in the works of John Fiske (1842–1901). In his main philosophic work, the *Outlines of Cosmic Philosophy*, which he delivered as lectures in Harvard in 1869–71, he followed Spencer so closely in his agnosticism and opposition to anthropomorphic theism that he brought down the wrath of the orthodox and made a permanent position for himself in the department of philosophy at Harvard impossible. Yet his own cosmic theism and his attempt to reconcile the existence of evil with that of a benevolent, omnipotent, quasi-psychical Power should have shown discerning theologians that here was a precious ally. In his later writings Fiske, though never expressly withdrawing his earlier argument that the ideas of personality and infinity are incompatible, did emphasize more and more the personality of God; and his original contrast between cosmic and anthropomorphic theism reduced itself to a contrast between the immanent theology of Athanasius and the transcendent theology of St. Augustine. By making man's spiritual development the goal of the whole evolutionary process, Fiske replaced man in his old position as head of the universe even as in the days of Dante and Aquinas.

What primarily attracted Fiske to the evolutionary philo-

sophy was precisely that which made that philosophy so popular, the easy way in which it could serve as a universal key to
open up a comprehensive view on every subject of human interest. Despite his services to popular science, Fiske was not
himself a scientific investigator. His knowledge of biology was
second-hand, neither extensive nor very accurate, and even less
can be said about his knowledge of physics. But he was widely
read in history, in which he was always primarily interested.
The evolutionary philosophy appealed to him above all as a
clue to the tangled, complicated mass of facts that constitutes
human history. Like Buckle, Fiske wanted to eliminate the marvellous or catastrophic view of history and reduce it to simple
laws. In his historic writings, however, he does not seem to have
used the evolutionary philosophy to throw new light on past
events, and in his actual historic representation his dramatic
instinct gave full scope to the part of great men, to issues of
battles, and to like incidents. [1]

The extent to which Fiske as a philosopher was dominated
by traditional views is best seen when we ask for the ethical
and political teaching of his evolutionary philosophy. Only a
few pages of the *Cosmic Philosophy* are devoted to this topic,
and the results do not in any respect rise above the commonplace. He naïvely accepts the crude popular analysis which
makes morality synonymous with yielding to the "dictates of
sympathy" instead of to the "dictates of selfishness." The
conception of evolution as consisting of slow, imperceptible
changes—thus ignoring all saltations or mutations—is made to
support the ordinary conservative aversion for radical change.
The philosophy of Voltaire and the encyclopædists is sweepingly
condemned as socially subversive; and against Comte it is
maintained that society cannot be organized on the basis of
scientific philosophy, not even the evolutionary philosophy.
Statesmen should study history, but men cannot be taught the
higher state of civilization; they can only be bred in it. Just
how the latter process is to take place we are not told. Fiske
left nothing of a theory of education. [2] He belittles the importance of social institutions and concludes by making social

[1] For his historical writings see Book III, Chap. xv.
[2] His important *aperçu* as to the significance of prolonged infancy as the basis
of civilization relates to his theory of social and moral evolution.

salvation depend upon a change of heart in individual men—quite in the tradition of the Protestant theology which he had inherited.

Fiske was not an original or a logically rigorous thinker, and his knowledge of the history of science and philosophy was by no means adequate; but he was a remarkably lucid, vigorous, and engaging writer who had no fear of repeating the same point. His *Cosmic Philosophy* went through sixteen editions, and this, as well as his other books, which sold by the thousands, undoubtedly exerted wide influence. Thus he greatly aided the spread of the Berkeleian argument that all we know of matter is states of consciousness, and at the same time of the argument (really inconsistent with this) for a psychical parallelism according to which matter and mind form parallel streams of causality without one causing the other. But above all, he made fashionable the evolutionary myth according to which everything has a function, evolves, and necessarily passes through certain stages. Thus he also introduced a new intellectual orthodoxy according to which the elect pride themselves on following the "dynamic" rather than the "static" point of view.

The pietistic philosophy which gained complete control of the American college and of dominant public opinion did not completely break all communication between America and foreign liberal thought as represented by Comte, Fourier, and even Proudhon, or by Bentham, Grote, and Mill. Even the arch-skeptic Hume continued to be reprinted in this country; and the vitality of the sensualistic or quasi-materialistic tradition in the medical profession is evidenced by James Rush's *Analysis of the Human Intellect* (1865). Despite, however, the presence with us of men of such first-rate scientific eminence as Joseph Henry, Benjamin Peirce, or Nathaniel Bowditch, scientific thought was not sufficiently organized to demand a philosophy more in consonance with its own procedure. Even in Great Britain, where science was earlier and better organized by means of the Association for the Advancement of Science (1832), Mill's effort to revive and continue Hume's attempt to introduce the experimental method of natural sciences into mental and moral questions found acceptance very slowly. Toward the end of his life Mill testified that for one British

philosopher who believed in the experimental method twenty
were followers of the a priori method. Empiricism was certainly not the dominant characteristic of Anglo-Saxon thought
in the period when Coleridge, Hamilton, and Whewell were in
the foreground. Slowly the scientific mode of thought spread,
however, and found in Mill's *Logic* its most convenient formulation. Chauncey Wright (1830–75), a computer for the
Nautical Almanac who had made important contributions to
mathematics and physics, had, like most of the thinking men of
his day, been brought up on Hamilton. But his reading of Mill
converted Wright completely; and while never a disciple of Mill
to the extent that Fiske was of Spencer, he was in a fair way to
re-enforce and develop Mill's logic in a most original manner
when an untimely death cut him off. All his papers, published
mostly in *The North American Review* (1864–73), fill only one
volume. But if the test of a philosopher be intellectual keenness and persistent devotion to the truth rather than skill in
making sweeping generalizations plausible, Chauncey Wright
deserves a foremost place in American philosophy. Unlike
Fiske, Wright knew at first hand the technique of biologic as
well as mathematical and physical research, and his contribution to the discussion of natural selection was highly valued by
Darwin. But he rejects the evolutionary philosophy of Spencer, not only because of its inadequate grasp of modern physics,
nor merely because, like all cosmogonic philosophies, it goes
beyond the bounds of known fact, but primarily because it is
metaphysical, that is, it deals with the general laws of physics
as abstract elements out of which a picture of the universe is
to be drawn. To draw such a picture of the universe is a part
of religion and of poetic or myth-making art. It does not belong to science. For whenever we go beyond the limited body
of observed fact we order things according to our imagination
and inevitably develop a cosmos as if it were an epic poem, with a
beginning, middle, and end. The scientist, according to Wright,
is interested in a general law like gravitation not as a description of the cosmos, but rather as a means for extending his
knowledge of a field of concrete fact. Metaphysics speculated
about universal gravitation before Newton. What Newton
found was a law which enabled him to deduce the facts of the
solar system and led to the discovery of many more facts which

would not otherwise have come to light,—the existence of the planet Neptune, for instance. If the philosopher wishes to be scientific, let him discipline himself by carrying on an original investigation in some department of empirical science so as to gain a clear idea how knowledge is actually used as a basis for discovering new truths. Anticipating the instrumentalism of Dewey, as well as the pragmatism of James, Wright points out that the principles of modern mathematical and physical philosophy are rather the eyes with which nature is seen than the elements and constitution of the object discovered, that general laws are finders, not merely summaries of truth.

Wright does not underestimate the value of religious or metaphysical philosophies, though they may be full of vague ideas, crude fancies, and unverified convictions; for they "constitute more of human happiness and human wealth than the narrow material standards of science have been able to measure." But scientific philosophy must be clearly distinguished from these. The motives of science arise in rational curiosity or wonder, while religious and metaphysical philosophies arise from the desire—not to discover new truths but—to defend our emotional and vital preferences by exhibiting them as entirely free from inconsistency. Logical refutation of every opposing philosophy affords us satisfaction but does not convince our opponents; because the choice of ultimate metaphysical dogmas is a matter of character (or temperament, as James later said) and not of logic.

Wright's own choice, which he does not pretend to demonstrate, is for the view attributed to Aristotle, that creation is not a progression toward a single end, but rather an endless succession of changes, simple and constant in their elements, though infinite in their combinations, which constitute an order without beginning and without termination. This distinction between elements and their combination enabled him to unite the belief in the universality of physical causation which is the scientist's protection against the refined superstitions of teleology with the Aristotelian belief in accidents which keeps the scientist from erecting his discoveries into metaphysical dogmas. Scientific research must postulate the universality of the causal relation between elementary facts and cannot make use of any teleology, since there is no scientific test for distinguishing which facts are ends and which are only means. But there is no evidence that any law like that of gravity is absolutely exact or more than approximately true or that it holds beyond the observable stars. The inductive or empirical character of the actual laws of science explains the reality of accidents or phenomena which could not have been predicted from any finite human knowledge of their antecedents. The rise of self-consciousness, the use of the voice as a means of communication, or the properties of new chemical combinations, all illustrate phenomena which are subject to law yet unpredictable. Though life is subject to the law of conservation of energy, nothing characteristic of life can be deduced from such a law.

Wright's penetrating and well-founded reflections on the nature of scientific method did not attract widespread attention. The vast majority come to philosophy to find or to confirm some simple "scheme of things entire." And though all scientists are empirical in their own field, most of them demand some absolute finality when they come to philosophy. Wright's profound modesty and austere self-control in the presence of glittering and tempting generalizations and his willingness to live in a world subject to the uncertainties of "cosmic weather" will never attract more than a few. But the character of his thought, though rare, is nevertheless indicative of a tendency toward the scientific philosophy, the negative side of which was more crudely and more popularly represented by Draper's *History of the Intellectual Development of Europe* (1862)[1] and in many articles in *The Popular Science Monthly*. But at least two great American philosophers were directly and profoundly influenced by Chauncey Wright, and those were Charles Peirce and William James.

To the modern reader the writings of William T. Harris—even his last and most finished book, *Psychologic Foundations of Education* (1898)—sound rather obsolete and somewhat mechanical. But the position of the author, who from 1867 to 1910 was regarded as the intellectual leader of the educational profession in the United States, who for over twenty-five years edited *The Journal of Speculative Philosophy*, and who was the chief organizer of the Concord School of Philosophy,[2]

[1] See Book III, Chap. xv.
[2] The Concord School, of which Alcott was the nominal head and Harris the

gave his writings an amount of influence far beyond what
the reader might expect. Sweetly generous, devout, and enterprising, Harris was an ideal apostle of philosophy to the
American people, calling upon them to enter the world's great
intellectual heritage and assuring them that the truths of religion
—God, freedom, and immortality—have always been best protected by true philosophy and are in no need of the ill-advised
guardians who, by discouraging free inquiry, transform religion
into fetishism.

Just as the work of Chauncey Wright may be summarized
in its attack on the pretentiousness and inadequate scientific
basis of the Spencerian evolutionary philosophy, so the work
of William T. Harris may be summed up as an attack against
agnosticism. On its psychologic side Harris's argument is
directed against Spencer's assumption (directly derived from
Sir William Hamilton) that we cannot conceive the infinite.
Against this Harris clearly points out that Hamilton and Spencer are confusing the process of conception and the process of
imagination. It is true that we cannot form a picture or an
image of the infinite, but neither can we form an image of any
motion or process as such. This, however, need not prevent us
from grasping or conceiving any universal process of which the
imagination fixes the dead static result at any moment. On
the objective side Harris reaches the same result by the dialectic
argument that the finite particular cannot be the ultimate
reality. Particular things are given in sense perception, but
the scientific understanding shows us that every object depends
on other things to make it what it is; everything depends upon
an environment. Science in its development must thus emphasize dynamic processes, and its highest point is reached in
the discovery of the correlation of all forces. But the moment
we begin to reason as to the nature of these processes or activities, we are inevitably led to the idea of self-activity; for since
every finite object gets its activity from some other object, the
ultimate source of all activity must be that which is not limited
by something else, and that is an infinite or self-limited Activity. Thus the stages of sense-perception, understanding,

directing genius, thus represented the union of New England transcendentalism
with Germanic scholarship and idealism. As such its history is a significant
incident in the intellectual life of America.

and reason lead to atomism or materialism, pantheism, and theism respectively.

With the simplicity that comes from undiluted sincerity, Harris repeats this argument over and over again, finding in it the clue to fruitful insight in all fields of human interest. It is the weapon with which he refutes all empiricism, which bases truth on the knowledge of particulars. All such philosophy, he says, stops at the stage of understanding and fails to note that a particular fact possesses whatever unity or character it has only in virtue of some universal. Time, space, and causality cannot, therefore, be derived from particular experiences, but are, as Kant maintained, the a priori conditions of all experience.

In social philosophy Harris follows Hegel rather closely with a characteristic New England emphasis on the freedom of the will. Thus the state is "a social unit in which the individual exists not for himself, but for the use of that unit"; but social order is not to be secured by external authority, but by free choice. Like his master, Hegel, Harris intellectualizes religion and art, the function of both being to reveal ultimate or philosophic truth, religion in the form of dogmatic faith, art by sensuous representation which "piques the soul to ascend out of the stage of sense perception into reflection and free thought."

Like all Hegelians and most believers in the adequacy of one system, Harris frequently thinks he has gained insight when he has translated a fact into his own terminology[1]; and the allegoric method of interpreting works of art and great literary masterpieces, notably Dante's *Divine Comedy* and Goethe's *Faust*, easily lent itself to that result. Still the general result of Harris's theoretic as well as his practical activity was undoubtedly to broaden the basis and subject matter of American philosophy. His *Journal of Speculative Philosophy* (1867–93) the first journal in the English language devoted exclusively to philosophy, made the thought of Plato and Aristotle as well as that of the German philosophers accessible to American readers. When it was objected that America needed something more original, he justly replied that an originality which cherished its own idiosyncrasies was despicable. His convic-

---

[1] Harris, for instance, believed that he found a new insight into the nature of light when he characterized it as "a point making itself valid outside of itself." See a similar account of gravity, in *Psychologic Foundations of Education*, p. 22.

tion that a worthy originality can come only through deep acquaintance with the best of ancient and modern thought stands justified by at least one fact. The most original American thinkers, Peirce, Royce, James, and Dewey, were also the most learned, and their first philosophic papers appeared in *The Journal of Speculative Philosophy.*

The general spread of the evolutionary theory, popular science, and more accurate historical acquaintance with European thought affected the American colleges only very slowly. An examination of the catalogues of American colleges will bear out the picture of dismal unenlightenment which Stanley Hall drew in 1879 of the state of philosophic teaching.[1] The beginning of a better order of things may be dated from the election of a layman, Charles W. Eliot, as President of Harvard College in 1869 or from the introduction of post-graduate instruction at Johns Hopkins in 1876. As the American colleges began to expand and as training for the educational profession became an important consideration, teachers of philosophy and psychology began to be selected with some regard for professional training and competency rather than exclusively for piety or pastoral experience. Such professional training an increasing number obtained in Germany, where, if they did not always get much fresh wisdom, they did generally learn the meaning of scientific accuracy in experimental psychology and philologic accuracy in the history of philosophy. It was through men of this class that the idealistic philosophy of Kant and Hegel was introduced into the American colleges.[2] In this they were aided by the spread of German idealism in the English and Scottish universities, which found expression in the works of J. F. Ferrier, Hutchison Stirling, F. H. Bradley, T. H. Green, Bosanquet, John and Edward Caird, Mahaffy, and William Wallace.

The definitive triumph of the idealistic movement may be dated from the founding in 1892 of *The Philosophical Review* under the editorship of Jacob Gould Schurman and James Edwin

[1] *Mind*, vol. iv, 1879. Professor Gildersleeve of Johns Hopkins has testified that in his youth positions as college teachers were generally given to those who had failed in missionary work abroad.

[2] Typical of this class was G. S. Morris, Professor of Philosophy at Johns Hopkins, translator of Überweg's *History of Philosophy*, and editor of a series of expositions of German philosophic classics by Dewey, Watson, Harris, and Everett.

Creighton. As this review has always been open to scholarly contributions in all the various fields of philosophy, the character of its contributions during its first decade bears ample evidence to the complete dominance of the Kantian and Hegelian idealism. The old Scottish philosophy could not hold its own before the superior finesse and technical equipment of the new school.[1] At bottom, too, it realized the necessity of an alliance with the new rationalistic philosophy in the fight for a theistic and spiritual view of the world against scientific positivism and popular materialism. At Harvard Francis Bowen continued for many years to oppose dialectic Hegelianism as well as the "mind philosophy" of the British empiricists; but his assistant and successor, the gentle and classical minded G. H. Palmer, turned in the main to the Hegelian idealism introduced at Harvard in 1869 by C. C. Everett. At Princeton James McCosh, the leader of the Scottish school, poured forth an interminable list of books defending common-sense realism and attacking without excessive refinements all its opponents, including the Hegelians with their "thinking in trinities." But most of his attention had to be devoted to rendering the new evolutionary philosophy harmless to the cause of orthodoxy. His successor, Ormond, so expanded the realism of his master with Berkeleian and Kantian elements as to make it lose its historic identity. A similar development took place at Yale. Noah Porter had studied in Germany under Trendelenburg, and his great textbook on *The Human Mind* (1868) showed a painstaking, if not a penetrating, knowledge of Herbart, Lotze, and Wundt as well as of the British empiricists. But he remained substantially an adherent of a Scottish intuitive philosophy. Like McCosh, but with greater urbanity, he directed his energy mainly against popular agnosticism and materialism. His pupil and successor, George Trumbull Ladd, while professing to be eclectic and independent, follows in the main the method of Lotze,[2] and in the

---

[1] This increased technical interest necessarily led philosophy to become less popular and somewhat more narrow in its aims. Hence popular thought came to draw its inspiration either from the vague but sweeping generalizations of Spencer or other popularizers of science, or from mystic culture—theosophy, spiritualism, or "new thought"—which except in the writings of Horatio Dresser have nothing to do with the philosophy treated in this chapter.

[2] A more direct follower of Lotze was Borden P. Bowne, one of the keenest of American metaphysicians.

end bases his spiritualistic metaphysics on epistemology quite in the Kantian fashion. A leader in the introduction of modern physiologic psychology into this country, Ladd stands for a philosophy that criticizes the procedures and fundamental ideas of the special sciences. But his primary interest in philosophy is to make better Christian citizens. His idealism is a branch of modern Christian apologetics, justifying the ways of God and defending the church and the established moral and social order.

Its most distinguished and also its most influential leader the idealistic school found in Josiah Royce at Harvard. To understand his development, however, we must first take some note of Charles S. Peirce.

If philosophic eminence were measured not by the number of finished treatises of dignified length but by the extent to which a man brought forth new and fruitful ideas of radical importance, then Charles S. Peirce (1840–1914) would easily be the greatest figure in American philosophy. Unrivalled in his wide and thorough knowledge of the methods and history of the exact sciences (logic, mathematics, and physics), he was also endowed with the bountiful but capricious originality of genius. Few are the genuine contributions of America to philosophy of which the germinal idea is not to be found in some of his stray papers.

Peirce was too restless a pioneer or explorer to be able to settle down and imitate the great masters who build complete systems like stately palaces towering to the moon. He was rather of those who are always trying to penetrate the jungle that surrounds our patch of cultivated science; and his writings are all rough, cryptic sketches of new fields, without much regard to the limitations of the human understanding, so that James found his lectures on pragmatism "flashes of brilliant light against Cimmerian darkness." Overt departure from the conventional moral code and inability to work in harness made it impossible for Peirce to keep any permanent academic position, and thus he was deprived of a needed incentive to intelligibility and to ordinary consistency. Intellectual pioneers are rarely gregarious creatures. In their isolation they lose touch with those who follow the beaten paths, and when they return to the community they speak strangely of strange sights, so that few have the faith to follow them and change their trails into high roads. Peirce was fortunate in that two powerful minds, Josiah Royce and William James, were able to follow some of the directions from his Pisgah heights and thus take possession of rich philosophic domains. What further gains philosophy might make by developing other of his numerous suggestive ideas, is not an affair of history. We may note, however, that in our own day the field of mathematical logic which he developed has become the ground which supports our latest philosophic movement, neo-realism.

Peirce was by antecedents, training, and occupation a scientist. A son of Benjamin Peirce, the great mathematician, he had a thorough knowledge of pure mathematics and of modern laboratory methods. He made important contributions not only to mathematical or symbolic logic but also to photometric astronomy, geodesy, and psycho-physics, as well as to philology. For many years he was engaged in the United States Coast and Geodetic Survey, and one of his researches on the pendulum received unusual attention from the International Geodetic Congress to which he was the first American delegate. He was, therefore, predominantly concerned with a philosophy of science.

Science, according to Peirce, is a method of banishing doubt and arriving at stable ideas. Commonly we fix beliefs by reiterating them, by surrounding them with emotional safeguards, and by avoiding anything which casts doubt upon them—by "the will to believe." This method breaks down when the community ceases to be homogeneous. Social effort, by the method of authority, to eliminate diversity of beliefs also fails in the end to prevent reflective doubts from cropping up. Hence we must finally resort to the method of free inquiry and let science stabilize our ideas by clarifying them. How can this be done? Early in his life in Cambridge Peirce came under the personal influence of Chauncey Wright, and in a little club of which Wright was the strongest spirit he first developed the doctrine of pragmatism. The Newtonian experimental philosopher, as Wright had pointed out, always translates general propositions into prescriptions for attaining new experimental facts, and this led Peirce to formulate the general maxim of pragmatism that the meaning of any concept is to be found in "all the conceivable experimental phenomena which the affirmation or denial of a concept could imply."[1]

In his earlier statements of the pragmatic maxim Peirce[2] emphasized the consequences for conduct that follow from the acceptance or rejection of an idea; but the stoical maxim that the end of man is action did not appeal to him as much at sixty as it did at thirty. Indeed, if we want to clarify the meaning of the idea of pragmatism, let us apply the pragmatic maxim to it. What will be the effect of accepting it? Obviously it will be to develop certain general ideas or habits of looking at things. As Peirce accepts the view that the good must be in the evolutionary process, he concludes that it cannot be in individual reactions in their segregation, but rather in something general or continuous, namely, in the growth of concrete reasonableness, "becoming governed by law, becoming instinct with general ideas."[3] In this emphasis on general ideas Peirce's pragmatism differs sharply from that of his follower, James, who, like most modern psychologists, was a thorough nominalist and always emphasized particular sensible experience. Peirce's belief in the reality and potency of general ideas was connected in his mind with a vast philosophic system of which he left only some fragmentary outlines.[4] He called it synechistic tychistic agapism (from the Greek words for continuity, chance, and love). It assumed the primacy of mind and chance and regarded matter and law as the result of habit. The principal law of mind is that ideas literally spread themselves and become more general or inclusive, so that people who form communities or churches develop distinct general ideas. The nourishing love which parents have for their children or thinkers for their own ideas is the creative cause of evolution. Stated thus baldly these views sound fantastic. But Peirce re-enforces them with such a wealth of illustration from modern mathematics and physics as to make them extraordinarily suggestive to all whose minds are not closed against new ideas.

Peirce was one of the very few modern scientific thinkers to lay hands on that sacred cow of philosophy, the belief that

[1] *Monist*, vol. xv, p. 162. [2] *Popular Science Monthly*, 1878-9.
[3] These phrases (from the article on *Pragmatism* in Baldwin's *Dictionary of Philosophy*) strongly suggest the central idea of Santayana's philosophy, but the present writer does not know whether Santayana was ever acquainted with Peirce's writings. [4] See his articles in the *Monist*, vols. i, ii, and iii.

everything happens absolutely in accordance with certain simple eternal laws. He was too well acquainted with laboratory methods and the theory of probability to share the common belief that the existence of such universal laws is demonstrated by science. "Try to verify any law of nature and you will find that the more precise your observations, the more certain they will be to show irregular departures from law." The Platonic faith that nature is created on simple geometric lines has undoubtedly been a powerful weapon against those who would have supernatural interferences interrupt the work of science. But there is no empirical evidence to prevent us from saying that all the so-called constants of nature are merely instances of variation between limits so near each other that their difference can be neglected for practical purposes. Impressed by the modern theory of gases and the statistical view of nature as developed by Willard Gibbs and Maxwell, and perhaps also influenced by Wright's doctrine as to "cosmic weather," Peirce came to believe in the primacy of chance. What we call law is habit, and what we call matter is inert mind. The universe develops from a chaos of feeling, and the tendency to law is itself the result of an accidental variation which has grown habitual with things. The limiting ratios which we call laws of nature are thus themselves slowly changing in time. This conception of the universe growing in its very constitution may sound mythologic. But it has at least the merit of an empirically supported rational alternative to the mechanical mythology. In many respects it anticipated the philosophy of Bergson. In the hands of James this tychism becomes a gospel of wonderful power in releasing men from the oppression of a fixed or "block" universe, but in the hands of Peirce it was a philosophic support for the application of the fruitful theorems of scientific probability to all walks of life.

Unlike most of America's distinguished philosophers, Josiah Royce (1855–1916) was not brought up in New England. He was born in a mining town in California and received his philosophic education in the university of his own state, at Johns Hopkins, and at Göttingen, where he studied under Lotze. Many diverse elements stimulated his subtle and acquisitive mind to philosophic reflection; the theistic evolutionism of the geologist Le Conte, the fine literary spirit of E. R.

Sill.[1] and his own reading of Mill and Spencer as well as of the great German philosophers, Kant, Schelling, Hegel, and Schopenhauer.

In 1882 he went to Harvard, where his prodigious learning, his keen and catholic appreciation of poetry, and the biblical eloquence with which he expressed a rich inner experience, at once made a profound impression. His singularly pure and loyal, though shy, spirit attracted a few strong friendships; but his life at Cambridge was in the main one of philosophic detachment. As a citizen of the great intellectual world, however, he closely followed its multitudinous events; and his successive books only partly reflected his unusually active and varied intellectual interests. In his earliest published papers he is inclined to follow Kant in denying the possibility of ultimate metaphysical solutions except by ethical postulates, but in his first book, *The Religious Aspect of Philosophy* (1885), he comes out as a full-fledged metaphysical idealist. This brilliant book at once made a profound impression, especially with the arguments that the very possibility of error cannot be formulated except in terms of an absolute truth or rational totality which requires an absolute knower. Like the parts of a sentence, all things find their condition and meaning in the final totality to which they belong. The world must thus be either through and through of the same nature as our mind, or else be utterly unknowable. But to affirm the unknowable is to involve one's self in contradictions. Royce delights in these sharp antitheses and the reduction of opposing arguments to contradictions.

In his next book, an unusually eloquent one entitled *The Spirit of Modern Philosophy* (1892), the element of will rather than knowledge receives the greater emphasis. The Berkeleian analysis of the world as composed of ideas is taken for granted, and the emphasis is rather on the nature of the World Mind or Logos. Following Schopenhauer, he points out that even in the idealistic view of the world there is an irrational element, namely, the brute existence of just this kind of world. The great and tragic fact of experience is the fact of effort and passionate toil which never finds complete satisfaction. This eternal frustration of our ideals or will is an essential part of spiritual life, and enriches it just as the shadows enrich the

[1] See Book III, Chap. x.

picture or certain discords bring about richer harmony. The Absolute himself suffers our daily crucifixion, but his triumphant spiritual nature asserts itself in us through that very suffering. This profoundly consoling argument, which both elevates us and sinks our individual sorrows in a great cosmic drama, is, of course, an expression of the historical Christian wisdom of the beatitude of suffering. But it offended the traditional individualism which finds its theologic and metaphysical expression in the doctrine of free will. If each individual is a part of the divine self, how can we censure the poor wretch who fails to live up to the proper standard?[1] It is significant of the unconventionality of Royce's thought that he never attached great importance to the question of blame or the free and intentional nature of sin. The evils uppermost in his mind are those resulting from ignorance, from the clumsiness of inexperience rather than from wilful misdeeds; and, unlike most American philosophers, he rightly saw that the religious conscience of mankind has always regarded sin as something which happens to us even against our will. Against the complacent belief of the comfortable that no one suffers or succeeds except through his own sins or virtues, Royce opposes the view of St. Paul that we are all members of each other's bodies and that "no man amongst us is wholly free from the consequences or from the degradation involved in the crimes of his less enlightened or less devoted neighbours, that the solidarity of mankind links the crimes of each to the sorrows of all."

For the elaboration of the social nature of our intellectual as well as of our moral concepts, Royce was largely indebted to suggestions from Peirce. In his earliest books we find no direct reference to Peirce. We can only conjecture that he owed to that man of genius the emphasis on the social nature of truth and the formulation of the ethical imperative: Live in the light of all possible consequences. But with the publication of the two volumes of *The World and the Individual* (1901), Royce's indebtedness to Peirce becomes explicit and steadily increases thereafter.

The main thesis of that book, the reconciliation of the existence of the Absolute Self with the genuine individuality of our

[1] See Howison in *The Conception of God*, by Royce, Le Conte, Howison, and Mezes.

particular selves, is effected by means of illustrations from the field of modern mathematics, especially by the use of the modern mathematical concept of the infinite as a collection of which a part may be similar to the whole. Peirce had done this before him in a remarkable article entitled *The Law of Mind*, in the second volume of *The Monist*. In generously acknowledging his obligation to Peirce, Royce rightly felt his fundamental idealistic position to be independent of that of Peirce; but it is noticeable that all Royce's references to the logic of mathematics are in full agreement with Peirce's view of the reality of abstract logical and mathematical universals, and it may well be questioned whether this can be harmonized with the nominalist or Berkeleian elements of Royce's idealism.

His subsequent work falls into two distinct groups, the mathematical-logical and the ethical-religious. Of the former group, his essay on logic in *The Encyclopædia of the Philosophical Sciences* is philosophically the most important. Logic is there presented not as primarily concerned with the laws of thought or even with methodology but after the manner of Peirce as the most general science of objective order. In this as in other of his mathematical-logical papers Royce still professes adherence to his idealism, but this adherence in no way affects any of the arguments which proceed on a perfectly realistic basis. In his religio-ethical works he follows Peirce even more, and the Mind or Spirit of the Community replaces the Absolute. In his last important book, *The Problem of Christianity* (1913), all the concepts of Pauline Christianity are interpreted in terms of a social psychology, the personality of Christ being entirely left out except as an embodiment of the spirit of the beloved community.

The World and the Individual is still, as regards sustained mastery of technical metaphysics, the nearest approach to a philosophic classic that America has as yet produced. Its publication was the high-water mark of the idealistic tide. Royce's previous monism had aroused the opposition of pluralistic idealists like Howison and Thomas Davidson.[1] But with the begin-

---

[1] Howison and Davidson both owed much of their impulse to philosophy to W. T. Harris. Howison proved one of the most successful and inspiring teachers of philosophy that America has as yet produced. Within a short period three of his pupils, Bakewell, McGilvary, and Lovejoy, were elected to the presidency of the American Philosophical Association. Davidson did not write much on

ning of the twentieth century idealism itself became the object of organized attack by two movements known as pragmatism and naïf- or neo-realism. The former was due to the work of James and Dewey; the latter to the spread of renewed and serious interest in scientific philosophy, especially in the renaissance of mathematical philosophy best represented by Bertrand Russell. It is, however, an historic fact that Royce contributed very largely to the effective spread of these new philosophies, to pragmatism by his ethical (as opposed to intellectual) idealism and by his emphasis on the practical aspect of ideas, and to neo-realism by his teaching and writing on mathematical logic. His profound and loyal devotion to the ethical interests of mankind did not prevent him from regarding the question of human immortality as "one for reason in precisely the same sense in which the properties of prime numbers and the kinetic theory of gases are matters for exact investigation." In this way he continued to represent, against the growing tide of anti-intellectualism, the old faith in the dignity and potency of reason which is the corner-stone of humanistic liberalism.

In William James (1842–1910) we meet a personality of such large proportions and of such powerful appeal to contemporaneous sentiment that we may well doubt whether the time has yet come when his work can be adequately estimated. There are many who claim that he has transformed the very substance of philosophy by bringing it down from the cold, transcendental heights to men's business and bosoms. But whether that be so or not, the width and depth of his sympathies and the irresistible magic of his words have undoubtedly transformed the tone and manner of American philosophic writing. Outside of America also his influence has been impressive and is steadily increasing.

It is instructive to note at the outset the judgment of orthodox philosophers, boldly expressed by Howison:

Emerson and James were both great men of letters, great writers, yes, great thinkers, if you will, but they do not belong in the strict

technical philosophy, confining himself for the most part to books on education. James called him a "knight errant of the intellectual life" (*Memories and Studies*). In a letter to the writer, Professor Höffding calls Davidson "one of the most beautiful figures in modern philosophy."

list of philosophers. Mastery in logic is the cardinal test of the true philosopher, and neither Emerson nor James possessed it. Both, on the contrary, did their best to discredit it.[1]

As a criticism this is hardly fair. James certainly elaborated definite doctrines as to the nature of mind, truth, and reality. In his *Radical Empiricism* and in *The Meaning of Truth* he even showed considerable dialectic skill. Moreover, it may well be maintained that he did not seek to discredit logic in general, but only the logic of "vicious intellectualism." Nevertheless, Howison's opinion is significant in calling attention to the distinction between philosophy as technique and philosophy as vision. From the professional point of view it is not sufficient that a man should believe in free will, absolute chance, or the survival of consciousness beyond death. To be worthy of being called a philosopher, one must have a logically reasoned basis for his belief. James was aware of the importance of technique, and was, in fact, extraordinarily well informed as to the substance and main tendencies of all the diverse technical schools. But he was wholly interested in philosophy as a religious vision of life, and he had the cultivated gentleman's aversion for pedantry. His thoughts ran in vivid pictures, and he could not trust logical demonstration as much as his intuitive suggestions. Hence his philosophic writings are extremely rich in the variety of concrete factual insight, but not in effective answers to the searching criticisms of men like Royce, Russell, and Bradley. James was aware of this and asked that his philosophy be judged generously in its large outlines; the elaboration of details might well be left to the future.

"The originality of William James," says one of his European admirers, "does not appear so much in his cardinal beliefs, which he took from the general current of Christian thought, as in the novel and audacious method by which he defended them against the learned philosophies of his day."[2] This, also, is not true without qualification. James took almost nothing from current Christian philosophy. Nor do any of the great historic Christian doctrines of sin and atonement or salvation find any echo in his thought. Orthodox Christianity would condemn James as a confessed pantheist who denied the omnipotence of

[1] *Philosophical Review*, vol. xxv, p. 241, May, 1916.
[2] Flournoy, *William James*, p. 16.

God. But though James is far from Christian theology, he gives vivid utterance to the ordinary popular Christianity which believes, not in a God who expresses himself in universal laws, but in a God to whom we can pray for help against our enemies, whom we can please and even help by our faith in Him. This is due to James's deep sympathy with common experience rather than with the problems of the reflective-minded. But the modern sophisticated intellect is certainly tickled by the sight of a most learned savant espousing the cause of popular as opposed to learned theology, and by the open confession of belief in piecemeal supernaturalism on the basis of spiritistic phenomena. James's antipathy to the Hegelian and Roycean attempts to prove the existence of the Absolute certainly plays a more prominent part in his writings than does his antipathy to popular unbelief. But the method of the absolutist he rejected, not only because of its insufferable pretension to finality of proof, but mainly because it is in the way of one who prefers an anthropomorphic universe that is tingling with life through and through and is constantly meeting with new adventures.

The union of religious mysticism with biologic and psychologic empiricism is characteristic of James's work from the very beginning. He grew up in a household characterized by liberal culture and mystic Swedenborgian piety.[1] The teacher who made the greatest impression upon him, Louis Agassiz, was a pious opponent of Darwin but a rare master in the art of observing significant details. More than one American naturalist caught the fire of his enthusiasm for fact. The companionship of Chauncey Wright and the writings of Renouvier weaned James from his father's religio-philosophical monism. The empirical way of thought of Hume and Mill proved most congenial to one who was par excellence a naturalist and delighted in the observation of significant detail.[2]

James began his career as a teacher of physiology and gradually drifted into psychology. His *Principles of Psychology* (2 vols., 1890) contains the substance of his philosophy. Having,

---

[1] His father, Henry James, Sr., was a Swedenborgian philosopher and a cultivated gentleman of ample means, who united to genuine originality of thought a remarkable insight into human character and a delightful freshness and pungency of language.

[2] James studied art and was a proficient draftsman before he finally decided to study medicine.

despite the influence of Agassiz, become converted to Darwinism, he was led to adopt as fundamental the view of Spencer that thought is something developed in the course of evolution and must, therefore, have a biologic function. The great idealistic argument against the old associationist psychology of Hume, Mill, Bain, and Spencer was to the effect that the sensational elements can at most account for the qualities of things, but not for their relations or connections; and when it was once granted that the relations between things were of a non-sensational or non-empirical character, very little of the world was left to the empiricist. James early became convinced of the force of this argument and, following certain suggestions of Peirce and possibly Hodgson, tried to save empiricism by making it more radical, by giving the connecting relations themselves a psychologic status on a par with the things they connect. Thus he thought to restore the fluidity and connectedness of our world without admitting the necessity for the idealist's transcendental glue to keep together the discrete elements of experience. Radical empiricism thus becomes a metaphysic which holds the whole world to be composed of a single stuff called pure experience. This sounds monistic enough, and James's adherence to the view of Bergson re-enforces this impression Nevertheless, James insisted that the world as experienced does not possess the degree of unity claimed for it by Royce and other monists, but that things are essentially many and their connections often external and accidental. At times James professes the dualistic realism of commonsense. "I start with two things, the objective facts and the claims." But ideas and things are both experiences taken in different contexts, so that his position has not inaptly been called neutral monism, and thus assimilated to the philosophy of Ernst Mach.

It has been claimed that this view eliminates most of the traditional problems of metaphysics, such as that of the relation of mind and body, and also eliminates the need for the Spencerian unknowable and Royce's or Bradley's absolute. But just exactly what experience is, James does not tell us, except that it is something to be lived rather than to be defined.

The exigencies of controversy as well as James's generous desire to give all possible credit to Peirce, have led the public to regard pragmatism and James's philosophy as identical terms. To James, however, pragmatism was but the method of philosophic discussion, the vestibule to his radical empiricism. The controversy, however, which arose about pragmatism enabled James to elaborate from different approaches his account of the nature of truth. The meaning of ideas is to be found in their particular experimental consequences. Abstract ideas are not copies of things but their substitutes or derivatives, evolved in the process of evolution to enable us to deal more adequately with the stream of immediate experience. An idea is, therefore, true if it enables us to deal satisfactorily with the concrete experiences at which it aims. An idea is said to work satisfactorily if it leads us to expected facts, if it harmonizes with other accepted ideas, if it releases our energies or satisfies emotional craving for elegance, peace, economy, or any kind of utility.

So anxious was James to overthrow the view that the truth of an idea consists in its being an inert copy of reality, so anxious to substitute for it the more activist view that an idea is true if it works or leads to certain results, that he neglected to indicate the relative importance of these results. This led to a great deal of misunderstanding and caused considerable scandal. Those brought up in the scientific tradition and trained to view the emotionally satisfactory consequences of ideas as having nothing to do with their scientific or theoretic value were scandalized by James's doctrine of the will or right to believe anything the acceptance of which made us more comfortable. This was in part a tragic misunderstanding. Most of James's life was a fight against accepting the monistic philosophy simply because of its æsthetic nobility. He rejected it precisely because it was "too buttoned up and white chockered, too clean-shaven a thing to speak for the vast slow-breeding, unconscious cosmos with its dread abysses and its unknown tides." It is true, however, that absorption in the psychologic factor, personal or æsthetic, which actually does make some people prefer a narrowly classic universe and others a generously romantic one, made him obscure the distinction between the causes of belief and the evidence for the truth which we believe. We may all start with a biassed or emotional preface, but that is neither evidence nor guaranty of our arriving at scientifi : truth.

Like other violent opponents of intellectualism, James himself falls into the intellectualistic assumption that we must either wholly believe or wholly disbelieve, just as one must either go to church or stay out. He ignores the scientific attitude of suspended judgment and the fact that men may be compelled to act without being constrained in judgment. We may vote for X or Y and yet know that owing to the absence of adequate information our choice has been little more than a blind guess. His interest in vital preferences and his impatience with the emotionally thin air of purely logical argumentation led James, towards the end of his life, to the acceptance of the extreme anti-logical view of Bergson that our logical and mathematical ideas are inherently incapable of revealing the real and changing world.

James's interest in philosophy was fundamentally restricted to the psychological aspect of things. He therefore never elaborated any systematic theory of morals, politics, or social organization. His temperamental preference for the novel, the unique, and the colourful re-enforced his traditional American liberalism and made him an extreme individualist. He attached scant value to the organized or fixed channels through which the fitful tides of ordinary human emotion find permanent expression. This shows itself best in his *Varieties of Religious Experience* (1902). He is interested only in the extreme variations of religious experiences, in the geniuses or aristocrats of the religious life. The religious experience of the great mass, or even of intellectual men like Chief Justice Marshall, who go to church without troubling much about matters of belief, seems to James "second-hand" and does not solicit his attention. Neither does the whole question of ritual or ceremony. He is interested in the beliefs of extraordinary and picturesque individuals. Hence his book on religion tells us almost nothing to explain the spread and the vitality of the great historic religions, Buddhism, Confucianism, Judaism, Islam, and Christianity. This extreme individualism, however, is connected with an extraordinary democratic openness and readiness to admit that it is only the blindness in human nature that prevents us from seeing the uniqueness of every individual. Unlike any other philosopher, William James was entirely devoid of the pride of the intellect. He was as willing as Jesus of Nazareth to associate with the intellectual publicans and sinners and learn from the denizens of the intellectual underworld.

James's position in the history of metaphysics is still a matter of debate, but as a seer or prophet he may fitly be put beside Emerson. Like Emerson, he preached and nobly exemplified faith in one's intuition and the duty of keeping one's oracular soul open. In spite of a note of obscurantism in his attitude to logic and "over beliefs," there is no doubt that the main effect of his work was to raise the American standard of intellectual honesty and courage: Let us stop this miserable pretence of having at last logically proved the comforting certainties of our inherited religion. Let us admit that we have no absolute assurance of the complete success of our ideals. But the fight is on. We can all take our part. Shame on the one who sulks and stays out.

The vital and arresting words in which James was able to put his thoughts were bound to attract large public attention. But it is doubtful whether he would have got a full hearing from American philosophers if it were not for the powerful support of John Dewey, the only American about whom has been formed a regular philosophic school. Dewey began his philosophic career under the influence of Harris, T. H. Green, and Bosanquet, and in his early writings, e.g., his *Psychology*, he showed himself a master of Hegelian dialectics. Reflection, however, led him to find an incurable incompatibility between the supernaturalism latent in idealism and the naturalistic account of the origin of human thought. He completely accepts James's view of the biologic function of thought, and brings to its service such a thorough mastery of philosophic technique as to compel attention from philosophers who, like other professionals, find it hard to admit the existence of good music where there is no obvious virtuosity. Despite his large debt to James's *Principles of Psychology*, Dewey is an independent ally rather than a disciple, and James was largely indebted in his later writings to Dewey's doctrine of the instrumental character of our ideas. It appears that pragmatism, like other successful human movements, can appeal to men of most diverse temperaments. While James is keenly alive to the claims of the traditional supernaturalism and uses pragmatism as a way of justifying it, Dewey uses pragmatism as a means of eliminating all theologic problems. Philosophic concepts, like God, Freedom, and Immortality, he tells us bluntly, have outlived their usefulness as sanctions, and the business of philosophy henceforth is to be with those ideas which will help us to transform the empirical world.[1] Despite the complexity of his sentences, which an austere regard for accuracy causes to be overloaded with qualifications, Dewey is essentially one of those philosophers who, like Spinoza, impress the world with their profound simplicity. He is entirely free from that human complexity which makes James banish the soul and even consciousness as psychologic entities and yet favour the subconscious mind, Fechner's earth spirits, and the like. Dewey is a thoroughgoing and consistent naturalist. He not only accepts the Darwinian account of the origin of the human faculty, but he also relies on the method of the Darwinian descriptive naturalist to build up the body of philosophic ideas. He makes no attempt to build up or deduce any part of the world on the basis of his fundamental assumption, but ideas are sought in their natural state and described just where, when, and how they function. This preference for naturalistic description rather than for systematic deduction as a philosophic method is not merely a matter of temperament; it also indicates the extent to which Darwin's work has so affected men's imagination as to cause natural history to replace mathematics and physics as the model of scientific method.

In the history of philosophy naturalism has been associated with the study of physics (generally atomic), with emphasis on the way our thoughts are controlled by our bodies or by the physical environment. Dewey has no physical theories. He is a psychologist, primarily interested in how and why men think and how their thoughts modify their experience. He is a professed realist in his belief that our thoughts alone do not constitute the nature of things but that there is a pre-existing world of which thought is an outgrowth and on which it reacts. But the continual emphasis on thought as efficient in transforming our world gives him the appearance of having remained

[1] Dewey's disciples like Moore and Bode are outspoken in their contempt for the view that philosophy may be a consolation for the irremediable evil growing out of our human limitations. Philosophy is to help us in our daily job and has nothing to do with vacations or holidays.

an idealist in spite of his conversion. Like the Hegelian idealists, he distrusts abstractions and prefers the "organic" point
of view to that which views things as composed of distinct
elements. He differs from the Hegelians in this respect only in
his contention that everything acquires its meaning by reference to a changing "situation" instead of by reference to an
all inclusive totality. Like the ethical idealists, also, Dewey
insists with Puritanic austerity on the serious responsibility of
philosophy. It must not be a merely æsthetic contemplation of
the world, nor a satisfaction of idle curiosity or wonder. It
must be a means for reforming or improving. Just what constitutes an improvement of man's estate we are not clearly told.
In his theory of education which forms the chief impetus and
application of his theoretic views the plasticity of human nature
is fully recognized; and he argues that intelligence not only
makes us more efficient in attaining given ends, but liberalizes
our ends. In the main, however, he emphasizes improved control over external nature rather than improved control over our
own passions and desires.

Judged by the ever-increasing number and contagious zeal
of his disciples, Dewey has proved to be the most influential
philosopher that America has as yet produced. This is all the
more remarkable when we remember that all his writings are
fragmentary, highly technical, and without any extraneous
graces of style to relieve the close-knitting of the arguments.
Clearly this triumph is due not only to rare personal qualities
as a teacher but also to the extent that his thought corresponds
to the prevailing American temper of the time. Dewey appeals
powerfully to the prevailing distrust of other-worldliness, a
distrust which permeates even our theology with its emphasis
on the social mission of the Church. The doctrine that all
ideas are and ought to be instruments for reforming the world
and making it a better place to live in, appeals at once to popular utilitarianism, to the worship of immediate practical results
of which Theodore Roosevelt was such a conspicuous representative. In a country where so many great deeds in the
conquest of nature are still to be performed, the practical man's
contempt for the contemplative and the visionary is re-enforced
by the Puritanic horror of idle play and of things which are
purely ornamental. A philosophy which views nature as

material to be transformed by our intelligence appeals to the pre-vailing light-hearted optimism which sees success as the constant reward of intelligent effort and finds no inherent obstacles to the establishment of a heaven on earth. Certainly Dewey nowhere calls to our attention the existence of incurable evil—the evil against which our only remedy is some form of wisely cultivated resignation.

In his zeal for making philosophy useful and responsible, a good deal of the traditional glory of philosophy is ignored, if not denied. The intellectual activity which we call theoretic science is subordinated to its practical application.[1] In eliminating the personal consolations of philosophy, he also eliminates the great saving experience which it affords us in making us spectators of a great cosmic drama in which solar systems are born and destroyed, a drama in which our part as actors is of infinitesimal significance. Yet historically the most significant feature of Dewey's thought is undoubtedly the fact that in an age of waning faith in human reason—witness the rapid spread of the romantic mysticism of Bergson—he has rallied those who still believe in the cause of liberalism based on faith in the value of intellectual enlightenment.

Similar to the view of James and Dewey in accepting the evolutionary philosophy as basic, and keeping even closer to Darwinian ideas, is the philosophy of J. Mark Baldwin. Baldwin began as a psychologist of the orthodox type; but availing himself of the views on social consciousness propounded by Royce in the early nineties, he produced a system of evolutionary social psychology with a very elaborate technical terminology and analytic scaffolding. This emphasis on technical apparatus makes his great three-volumed treatise on *Thoughts and Things* (1906–11) one of the most obscure books written in America, but for all that it seems to have met with appreciation in France and Germany, where it has been translated. An intelligible summary of his later views is to be found in his *Genetic Theory of Reality* (1915), in which he develops this theory of pan-

---

[1] Dewey insists with some justice that by practical he does not necessarily mean ends of the bread-and-butter type. But his illustrations of the process of knowledge are overwhelmingly of the type generally called useful and very seldom drawn from the experience of the mathematician or the philosopher himself, even if he is a pragmatist. He glorifies zeal for developing the applications of propositions rather than their implications.

calism, viz., that the æsthetic consciousness is primary.   In this
respect, as well as in his emphasis on the importance of the
play impulse, Baldwin is unique among American philosophers.

The philosophic temper of an age can be judged by the kind
of merit it neglects as well as by what it worships.   For this
reason as well as for the unique value of his work, no account
of American philosophy should omit a consideration of George
Santayana.[1]   If a European critic like Taine were to ask for an
American book on philosophy containing a distinct and comprehensive view of human life, its aims and diverse manifestations, we could not mention anything more appropriate than
Santayana's *Life of Reason* (5 vols., 1905–06).   Most American
philosophic works are either monographs on special topics or else
more or less elaborate controversial pamphlets on behalf of one
view or other.[2]   Santayana more than any other American since
Emerson has cultivated the ancient virtue of calm detachment
which distinguishes the philosopher from the partisan journalist
or the zealous missionary.   His zeal, if any, is that of the artist
freely picturing the whole of human experience as surveyed
retrospectively by one interested in the life of reason.   "The
unsolved problems of life and nature and the Babel of society
need not disturb the genial observer."   Dewey's anathemas
against the purely contemplative philosopher, the "otiose
observer," do not disturb one who holds that man's natural
dignity and joy—as manifested in art, pure science, and philosophy—consists "in representing many things without being
them; and in letting imagination, through sympathy, celebrate
and echo their life."   Man's proper happiness is constituted
by the interest and beauty of the mind's "inward landscape
rather than by any fortunes that await his body in the outer
world."[3]   Philosophy is not merely a means for improving the
conditions of common life, but is itself "a more intense sort of
experience than common life is, just as pure and subtle music
heard in retirement is something keener and more intense than
the howling of storms or the rumble of cities."[4]

[1] Another excuse for departing from the prudent policy of avoiding in history
any treatment of those still alive and active, is that at this date (1919) it does not
seem that Santayana's future career will belong to America.

[2] The conditions of academic life, in which nearly all of our philosophers are
placed, are certainly not favourable for sustained, deliberate, and thorough composition.   [3] *Winds of Doctrine*, p. 215.   [4] *Three Philosophic Poets*, p. 124.

That which distinguishes Santayana from all other modern philosophers is the way he combines thoroughgoing naturalism with profound appreciation of the wisdom commonly called idealism or other-worldliness. Completely free from all trace of supernaturalism in metaphysics, he is thoroughly Greek or humanistic in his valuation of those reasonable restraints which give order, dignity, and beauty to human life. Like Dewey, perhaps more than Dewey, Santayana is a thoroughgoing naturalist, believing that mind is the natural effect of bodily growth and organization. But unlike any other philosopher since Aristotle, Santayana holds fast to a sharp and clear distinction between the origin and the validity of our ideals. Though our ideals are of bodily origin they need not serve bodily needs, and above all they need no actual or sensible embodiment to justify their claims. There is no necessity for accepting the modern evolutionist's identification of the *best* with the *latest*. "Modern Greece is not exactly the crown of ancient Hellas." Other confusions between morality and physics, such as the Hegelian identification of the ideal and the real, of the desirable and the existent, are vehemently rejected as servile worship of brute power and treacherous to our ideal aspirations. Thus while naturalism is the only intelligible philosophy, the attempt of naturalists to look for all motives and sanctions in the material world always generates a profound melancholy from which mankind instinctively shrinks. The sensuous optimism called Greek or the industrial optimism called American are but "thin disguises for despair," against which the mind will always rebel and revert, in some form or other, to a cultus of the unseen. The explanation of this paradoxical fact Santayana finds in a Greek distinction between the form and the brute existence of things. The form and qualities of things are congenial to the mind's free activity, but "when an empirical philosophy calls us back from the irresponsible flights of the imagination to the shock of sense and tries to remind us that in this alone we touch existence,—we feel dispossessed of our nature and cramped in our life."[1] The true life of reason, however, is not to be found in wilful idealistic dreams, but in the logical activity which is docile to fact and illumines the actual world in which our bodies move.

[1] *Reason in Common Sense*, p. 191.

As a child of Latin and Catholic civilization, Santayana is profoundly devoted to those classic forms which enshrine the wisdom and happiness of the past. He abhors German philosophy for what he calls its romantic wilfulness, that protestant or rebellious spirit which regards the mere removal of restraints as a good. "The life of reason is a heritage and exists only through tradition."[1] Traditional forms may, indeed, cramp our life, and a vital mind like Shelley will revolt, but the end or good is not freedom but some more congenial form. Santayana holds in contempt the prevailing philosophy which glorifies striving and progress but in which there are no ends to be achieved and no ideal by which progress is to be measured.

The burden of his philosophy is the analysis of common sense, social institutions, religion, art, and science to show how reflection can distinguish the ideal from the physical embodiment in which traditional wisdom is delivered from generation to generation.

In his social philosophy he is essentially an aristocrat, valuing highly those historic institutions, cultivated forms, and reasonable restraints which impose order on our natural impulses. But he recognizes the shallowness of purely personal culture and admits that our emancipated, atheistic, international democracy is not only replacing the old order, but that "like every vital impulse [it] is pregnant with a morality of its own." Religion to Santayana is essentially a mode of emancipating man from worldliness and from merely personal limitations. But the wisdom which its dogmas, ritual forms, and prayers embody is not truth about existence but about those ideals which give us internal strength and peace. To regard God as an existence rather than an ideal leads to superstition. Religious superstitions, he admits, often debauch morality and impede science, but the errors of religion should be viewed with indulgent sympathy. Thus Catholic dogma is viewed as involving a reasonable deference to authority but leaving the mind essentially free. In his theory of art Santayana follows his master Aristotle closely in spirit though not in words. Art looks at life from above, and portraying our passions in their beauty makes them interesting and delightful, at the same time softening their vital compulsion. "Art is abstract and incon-

[1] *Winds of Doctrine*, p. 156.

sequential . . . nothing concerns it less than to influence the world"; but in revealing beauty it gives us the best hint of the ultimate good which life offers. Without this sight of beauty the soul would not continue its mortal toil. Perhaps the most characteristic of Santayana's views is his estimate of the value of modern science for the life of reason or civilization. He accords full recognition to mechanical science not merely as a source of useful insight but as a liberation of the human soul. But though the various parts of science are mutually illuminating, scientific achievement is fragmentary and a mechanical science like physiologic psychology may not give a man as much insight as does some poetic suggestion. Science grows out of common experience, but its power is new, comparatively feeble, and easily blighted. "The experience of the vanity of the world, of sin, of salvation, of miracle, of strange revelations, and of mystic loves, is a far deeper, more primitive, and therefore probably more lasting human possession than is that of clear historical or scientific ideas."[1]

Why, in spite of the incomparable distinction and modernity of his work, has Santayana received so little recognition? In part this is doubtless due to the unfortunate manner in which his principal book, *The Life of Reason,* is written—a manner which does not attract the public and repels the professional philosopher.[2] Despite unusual felicity of diction and a cadence which often reminds us of Walter Pater, his books are difficult reading. It is difficult to find the thought because of his preference for pithy and oracular epigrams rather than fully and clearly developed arguments. His abstract and distant view of the world unrolls itself without any vivid or passionate incidents to grip our attention. In the main, however, Santayana has failed to draw fire because few people are interested in a frankly speculative and detached philosophy that departs radically from the accepted traditions and makes no appeal to the partisan zeal of either conservatives or reformers. He does not aim to be edifying or scientifically informing. American philosophy has attracted two types of mind—those to whom

---

[1] *Winds of Doctrine,* p. 56.

[2] Not a single survey of American philosophy hitherto published mentions even the name of Santayana. See the works of Riley, Thilly, Perry, and McIntosh mentioned in the Bibliography.

philosophy is religion rationalized, and those (a smaller but perhaps growing number) to whom philosophy is a scientific method of dealing with certain general ideas. To the former a combination of atheistic catholicism and anti-puritanic, non-democratic, æsthetic morality, lacking withal in missionary enthusiasm, typifies almost all that is abhorrent. To the scientific group Santayana is just a speculative poet who may value science very highly but does so as a well-groomed gentleman who knows it at a polite distance, afraid to soil his hands with its grimy details.[1] These judgments illustrate the great tragedy of modern philosophy. In view of the enormous expansion of modern knowledge and the increased rigour of scientific accuracy, the philosopher can no longer pretend to universal knowledge and yet he cannot abandon the universe as his province. Genuinely devoted to philosophy's ancient and humanly indispensable task of drawing a picture or unified plan of the world in which we live, Santayana is willing to abandon the pretension to scientific accuracy and to face the problem as a poet or moralist. But whether because interest in a unified world view is weak and the possession of poetic faculty such as Santayana's uncommon, or whether because philosophy has been too long wedded to logical argumentation and scientific pretensions, the marked tendency is to make philosophy like one of the special sciences, dealing with a limited field and definitely solving problems. As philosophy is thus abandoning its old pretensions to be the sovereign and legislative science—it is no longer taught by the college president himself—all the fields of concrete information, physics, economics, politics, psychology, and even logic, are parcelled out among the special sciences and there is nothing left to the philosopher except the problem as to the nature of knowledge itself. On this problem Santayana has some suggestive hints, but no completely elaborated solution. Hence his essential loneliness. But perhaps every true philosopher, like the true poet, is essentially lonely.

The latest movement in American philosophy, opposing

[1] Santayana himself speaks of that virtual knowledge of physics which is enough for moral and poetic purposes (*Reason in Science*, pp. 303-304). Such virtual knowledge does not save him from absurd statements such as that Plato had no physics.

certain phases of pragmatism as well as of the older idealism, is the tendency known as the new realism. The common element in the diverse and often conflicting doctrines which constitute this general tendency is the opposition to the Lockian tradition that the objects of knowledge are always our own ideas. Realism maintains that the nature of objects is not determined by our knowing them. Unlike the older Scotch realism, it does not view the mind and nature as two distinct entities, but tends rather, like Santayana and Dewey, to conceive the mind in an Aristotelian fashion as the form or function of a natural organic body responding to its environment. The pioneers of this movement were Professors Woodbridge, Montague, Holt, and Perry.

Frederick J. E. Woodbridge is one of the very few Americans interested in metaphysics or the philosophy of nature rather than in psychology or epistemology. His sources are in Aristotle, Hobbes, and Spinoza rather than in Locke and Kant. He rejects the Lockian tradition that we must first examine the mind as the organ of knowledge before we can study the nature of existing things. For you cannot begin the epistemologic inquiry, how knowledge is possible, without assuming something already known; and we cannot know any mind entirely apart from nature. When the earth was a fiery mist there was no consciousness on it at all. Besides, the question how in general we come to know is irrelevant to the determination of any specific issue: as, for example, why the flowers bloom in the spring.

Studying mind not as a bare subject of knowledge, but as a natural manifestation in nature, we find it to be not an additional thing or term, but a relation between things, namely, the relation of meaning. Whenever through an organic body things come to stand in the relation of meaning to each other we have consciousness. From this distinctive view of mind and meaning, logic ceases to be a study of the laws of thinking and becomes a study of the laws of being.

For one reason or another, Professor Woodbridge has never fully elaborated his views, but has barely sketched them in occasional essays and papers. His personal influence, however, and the support of *The Journal of Philosophy, Psychology, and Scientific Method*, of which he is the editor, have undoubtedly helped to make the new realism a strong organized movement. Such it became with the publication of a volume of co-operative studies entitled *The New Realism* (1912) by Walter Taylor Marvin, Ralph Barton Perry, Edward Gleason Spaulding, W. P. Montague, Edwin Holt, and Walter B. Pitkin. The new realism began as an appeal to the naïve consciousness of reality; but relying naïvely as it does on modern physics, physiology, and experimental biology (as opposed to the field and speculative biology of the Darwinians) its doctrine necessarily becomes very technical and complicated. Its insistence on rigorous definitions and definitive intellectual solutions to specific problems has brought on it the charge of being a new scholasticism. But whatever the merits of scholasticism—the renaissance of logical studies has begun to reveal some of them —the new realism has certainly tried to avoid the tendency of philosophy to become a branch of apologetics or a brief in behalf of supposed valuable interests of humanity. In this a technical vocabulary and the ethically neutral symbols of mathematics are a great aid.

The period covered by the greater portion of this chapter is too near us to make a just appreciation of its achievement likely at this time. In the main it has been dominated by two interests, the theologic and the psychologic.[1] The development during this period has been to weaken the former and to deepen but narrow the latter and make it more and more technical. For this reason the philosophers covered in this chapter have as yet exerted little influence on the general thought of the country. The general current of American economic, political, and legal thought has until very recently been entirely dominated by our traditional eighteenth-century individualism or natural-law philosophy. Neither does our general literature, religious life, or current scientific procedure as yet show any distinctive influence of our professional philosophy. But it must be remembered that all our universities are comparatively young

---

[1] The history of philosophy has occupied a large portion of American philosophic instruction and writing. But apart from the books of Albee, Husik, Riley, and Salter (mentioned in the bibliography to this chapter) and articles by Lovejoy on Kant, and on the history of evolution, American philosophy has no noteworthy achievement to its credit—certainly nothing comparable to the historical works of Caird, Bosanquet, Benn, or Whittaker, not to mention the great German and French achievements in this field.

institutions and our university-trained men numerically an almost insignificant portion of our total population. In the field of education William T. Harris and after him Dewey have undoubtedly exerted potent influences, and it looks as if American legal thought is certain to be profoundly impressed by Roscoe Pound, who draws some of his inspiration from philosophic pragmatism as well as from Ward's social theories.

From the point of view of European culture, America has certainly not produced a philosopher as influential as was Willard Gibbs in the realm of physics or Lester Ward in the realms of sociology. Though Ward and even Gibbs may with some justice be claimed as philosophers, this can be done only by disregarding the unmistakable tendency to divorce technical philosophy entirely from physical and social theory. James, however, is undoubtedly a European force, and, in a lesser degree, Baldwin, Royce, and Dewey. Serious and competent students in Germany, Italy, and Great Britain have also recognized the permanent importance of C. S. Peirce's contribution to the field of logic. History frequently shows philosophers who receive no adequate recognition except from later generations, but it is hazardous to anticipate the judgment of posterity.

CHAPTER XVIII

The Drama, 1860-1918

FOR the ten years preceding the advent of Bronson Howard, the American drama settled upon staid and not very vigorous times. The Civil War was not conducive to original production at the time; and its influence was not great upon the character of the amusement in the American theatre. Only after many years had passed, and after local and national feeling had been allowed to cool, did the Civil War become a topic for the stage,—in such dramas as William Gillette's *Held by the Enemy* (Madison Square Theatre, 16 August, 1886),[1] *Shenandoah* (Star Theatre, 9 September, 1889) by Bronson Howard, *The Girl I Left Behind Me* (Empire Theatre, 25 January, 1893) by David Belasco and Franklyn Fyles, *The Heart of Maryland* (Herald Square Theatre, 22 October, 1895) by David Belasco, William Gillette's *Secret Service* (Garrick Theatre, 5 October, 1896), James A. Herne's *Griffith Davenport* (Washington, Lafayette Square Theatre, 16 January, 1899), *Barbara Frietchie* (Criterion Theatre, 24 October, 1899) by Clyde Fitch. No one dared to take the moral issue of the war and treat it seriously, Mrs. Stowe's *Uncle Tom's Cabin* (first played 24 August, 1852) having ante-dated the internecine struggle. Even today, the subject of the negro and his relation with the white is one warily handled by the American dramatist. Dion Boucicault's *The Octoroon* (Winter Garden, 5 December, 1859), was typical of the way that dramatist had of making hay out of the popular sunshine of others. William DeMille wanted to treat of the negro's social isolation, but compromised when he came to write *Strongheart* (Hudson Theatre, 30 January,

---

[1] Unless it is otherwise stated, the theatres and dates given with the titles of plays apply to initial New York productions.

1905) by making the hero an Indian; and he later fell into the conventional way of treating the war when he wrote *The Warrens of Virginia* (Belasco Theatre, 3 December, 1907). The more sensational aspects of the negro question, as treated by Thomas Dixon in *The Clansman* (Liberty Theatre, 8 January, 1906) were wisely softened and made into an elaborate record of the Civil War, in the panoramic moving picture, *The Birth of a Nation* (New York, 1915). Though Ridgely Torrence, in a series of one-act plays (*Granny Maumee, The Rider of Dreams, and Simon the Cyrenian*, Garden Theatre, 5 April, 1917), has sought poetically to exploit negro psychology, the only American dramatist who has approached the topic boldly, melodramatically, and effectively, thus far, has been Edward Sheldon, in *The Nigger* (New Theatre, 4 December, 1909).

It will be seen from this enumeration that during the period immediately preceding the Civil War the issues of the coming struggle were not treated for propaganda purposes, as were the issues of the Revolutionary War in our pre-national drama. The fact is, the features of the American theatre, and of the plays on the American stage, preceding the year 1870, were fairly well predetermined by the strong personalities among the managers and actors: by the distinct predilection, among theatre-going peoples, for plays to fit the temperaments of the reigning stage favourites, and by the styles and fashions that emanated from London and Paris. Neither the Wallacks, John Brougham, W. E. Burton, nor Augustin Daly showed, by their actual productions, that their tastes were native, although Brougham was led, through burlesque, to exercise his Irish wit on the land of his adoption, and Daly, as shown by his recent biographer, attempted to turn such literary workers as Bret Harte, Mark Twain, Henry James, and Howells to dramatic writing. Men expert in other literary forms have seldom fully grasped the demands of the theatre. Thomas Bailey Aldrich had his *Judith of Bethulia* produced (Boston, Tremont Theatre, 13 October, 1904) and his biographer says that in New York "it failed to take the taste of the large luxurious audiences that throng the Broadway theatres betwixt dinner and bedtime." But the poetic purple patches of Aldrich's verse might be another explanation for its short life on the stage.

When 1860 dawned, Dion Boucicault (1822–1890) and John Brougham (1810–1880) reigned supreme in American popularity, and they were both Irish. The former had yet to do his most popular and characteristic pieces, in which he won deserved success both as an actor and playwright: to read *Jessie Brown; or, The Relief of Lucknow* (Wallack's Theatre, 22 February, 1858) and *The Colleen Bawn* (Laura Keene's Theatre, 29 March, 1860), and to compare them with the later *Arrah-na-Pogue; or, The Wicklow Wedding* (London, 22 March, 1865) and *The Shaughraun* (Wallack's Theatre, 14 November, 1874), is to sound the genial depths of a flexible workman, who could find it as easy to shape a drama for Laura Keene as to re-fashion Charles Burke's version of Washington Irving's *Rip Van Winkle* for presentation by Jefferson (London, Adelphi, 4 September, 1865). One would say of Boucicault, as one would claim of John Brougham, that his local influence was due to local popularity rather than to any impetus he gave to native drama. While Brougham's *Po-ca-hon-tas; or, The Gentle Savage* (Burton's Lyceum, 24 December, 1855) and his *Columbus et Filibustero* (Burton's Lyceum, December, 1857) exhibited the good-nature of his irony; while his dramatizations of Dickens's *David Copperfield* and *Dombey and Son* were in accord with the popular taste that hailed W. E. Burton's *Cap'n Cuttle* —these dramatic products were exotic to the American drama, while reflecting the fashion of the American stage.

Yet nothing Boucicault enjoyed better than to descant on the future of the American stage. Like Palmer, like Daly, he was continually writing about the reasons for its poverty and the possibilities of its improvement. No one of these men, however, had any real faith in the American drama or in the native subject. Edwin Forrest (1806–1872) encouraged the Philadelphia group of writers,[1] but the topics chosen by Bird, Conrad, Stone, Smith, Miles, and Boker were largely in accord with English romantic models. Stone's *Metamora; or, The Last of the Wampanoags* spoke the language of James Sheridan Knowles; Boker's *Francesca da Rimini* reflected the accents of the Elizabethans. Forrest, therefore, encouraged the American drama indirectly. Charlotte Cushman (1816–1876) never even went so far, though her friendship with Bryant, R. H. Stod-

[1] See Book II, Chap. II.

dard, Sidney Lanier, together with the esteem in which she was held by all intellectual America, would show that she was not aloof from the life of the time. One looks in vain through the repertories of the great actors for that encouragement of the American drama which it most needed as an "infant industry." Edwin Booth (1833–1893) at the time the assassination of Lincoln by John Wilkes Booth, 14 April, 1865, drove him temporarily from the stage had built for himself a permanent reputation in Shakespeare, which he resumed and maintained until his last appearance as *Hamlet*, 4 April, 1891. Even as a manager, he chose English plays; and his close associate, Lawrence Barrett (1838–1891), was of the same mind, though he appeared in Boker's *Francesca da Rimini* (Chicago, 14 September, 1882) and W. D. Howells's version, from the Spanish, of *Yorick's Love* (Cleveland, 26 October, 1878).

Though as a family of managers the tradition of the Wallacks was distinctly English, Lester Wallack (1819–1888) romantically masked his old English comedy manner beneath local colour in *Central Park* (14 February, 1861); but his dash was happiest in such pieces, of his own concoction, as *The Romance of a Poor Young Man* (adapted by him 24 January, 1860) and *Rosedale* (produced 30 September, 1863). To the time of his last appearance (29 May, 1886), he was true to his English taste. To see Lester Wallack at his best, one had to see him as Shakespeare's Benedick or Mercutio; as Dumas's D'Artagnan, or in the social suavity of the Robertson and con-temporary French drama.

The British tradition seemed so natural to Lester Wallack [writes Brander Matthews], so inevitable, that when Bronson Howard, in his 'prentice days, took him a piece called *Drum-Taps*, —which was to supply more than one comedy-scene to the later *Shenandoah*,—the New York manager did not dare to risk a play on so American a theme as the Civil War. He returned it to the young author, saying, "Couldn't you make it the Crimea?"

In 1860, the comedian W. E. Burton died; his last appearance was as Micawber, 15 October, 1859—a fitting end, as he was in the forefront of the Dickens interpreters. Dramatizations of Dickens in America kept pace with those in England. It is well to emphasize Burton's stage career, because it brings to mind that the American theatre of that time was rich in comedians—all of them of the old school which looked for character parts to suit the old comedy style of acting. It was unfortunate for the American drama which began to develop after 1860 that it started just when the old-time stock company tradition passed from Burton and Brougham and Laura Keene to Mrs. John Drew (1820–1897), who assumed control of the Philadelphia Arch Street Theatre on 3 August, 1861—inaugurating a brilliant record which began to fade in 1877, just as Bronson Howard was gaining in his pioneer fight for the American dramatist, and just as the modern business of the theatre began to challenge consideration.

The reasons for the poverty of American plays in the decade 1860–1870 are thus readily suggested. Our modern native drama did not grow out of literature, as it did in England and in France; it grew out of the theatre, and so it had to bide its time until the theatre found a need for it.

Tradition, on the whole, is the element which most handicapped the American drama. Daly scanned the German horizon for adaptations, as Dunlap had done before him; A. M. Palmer was as eager for the French play as were the English managers abroad, who would complacently have kept T. W. Robertson and Tom Taylor literary hacks at ten pounds a play, if they had not rebelled. When one puts down the titles of dramas which Augustin Daly (1838–1899) actually had a literary hand in, it is surprising how far afield from the American spirit he could get; with him adaptation meant change of locality only, and though one can imagine what the scenic artist might do with his "flats" in picturing New York during the time opera reigned on Fourteenth Street, one can but reservedly call Boucicault's *The Poor of New York* (Wallack's Theatre, 8 December, 1857) or Daly's *Under the Gaslight* (The New York Theatre, 12 August, 1867) native dramas; they were domestic perversions of the same French source. The fact of the matter is that Bronson Howard, who came under the direct influence of the French drama of the time, felt, when he began to write such a comedy as *Saratoga* (Fifth Avenue Theatre, 21 December, 1870) that he must follow French convention; and when he reconstructed *The Banker's Daughter* on the ground-plan of *Lillian's Last Love* his originality was tied hand and foot. He was borrowing French villains, and making his American men exclaim "egad."

Daly adapted and wrote over four dozen plays. Among his so-called original attempts, this generation can recall only *Divorce* (Fifth Avenue Theatre, 5 September, 1871), *Horizon* (Olympic Theatre, 25 March, 1871), and *Pique* (Fifth Avenue Theatre, 14 December, 1875); among his adaptations, *Leah the Forsaken* (Niblo's Garden, 19 January, 1863), *Frou-Frou* (Fifth Avenue Theatre, 12 February, 1870), and *Article 47* (Fifth Avenue Theatre, 2 April, 1872). But in these, as in most of his attempts, he does not deserve any more claim to native originality than Matilda Heron does for her version of *Camille* (Wallack's Broome St. Theatre, 22 January, 1857), or A. M. Palmer for his productions of D'Ennery and Cormon's *A Celebrated Case*, adapted by A. R. Cazauran (Boston Museum, 28 January, 1878), and D'Ennery's *The Two Orphans*, adapted by Hart Jackson (Union Square Theatre, 21 December, 1874). What he did so successfully, and what Clyde Fitch did so well in later years, was to create rôles for the special qualities in his players: he wrote *Frou-Frou* for Agnes Ethel, *Article 47* for Clara Morris, and *Pique* for Fanny Davenport.

The emotional play went hand in hand with the emotional actress, and one fails to find Clara Morris showing a penchant for the American drama; her success in *Miss Multon*, a play built on a French version of *East Lynne* (Union Square Theatre, 20 November, 1876), and her Cora in *Article 47* measured her taste and training, rather than her Lucy Carter in Howard's *Saratoga*, which Daly produced. Palmer and Daly gave their players large doses of foreign drama or the classics. In such tradition Fanny Davenport flourished, and Ada Rehan was reared.

This was an unsettled period, therefore, of taste and managerial inclination; it is necessary to pick up the scant threads of American drama and hold them fast lest they be forgotten. Such a play as Densmore's pirated version of *The Gilded Age*, in which John T. Raymond made such a success during the early seventies, is scarcely known, even by Mark Twain's biographer; Benjamin Woolf's *The Mighty Dollar* (Park Theatre, 6 September, 1875), once the talk of the American theatre, is, so far as Woolf's family is concerned, non-existent.

Up to the time I started in 1870 [wrote Bronson Howard in 1906], American plays had been written only sporadically here and there by men and women who never met each other. . . . Except for Daly, I was practically alone; but he offered me the same opportunity and promise for the future that he gave to himself. From him developed a school of managers willing and eager to produce American plays on American subjects. . . . It was not until about 1890 that they [the writers] suddenly discovered themselves as a body of dramatists. This was at a private supper given . . . to the veteran playwright, Charles Gaylor.

It was on this occasion that Howard founded the American Dramatists Club.

At the same time other forces were preparing the way for the American drama, and these, viewed from a distance, are significant when one knows what actually followed them. In San Francisco, David Belasco was serving his novitiate as an actor, a playwright, a manager, and was coming into direct contact with the actors of the East, who travelled West for regular seasons. He was writing mining-camp melodrama, which was afterwards to flower into *The Girl of the Golden West*, and he was experimenting in all the subterfuges of stagecraft. The Frohman brothers were in their rough-and-tumble days, when Tony Pastor, Harrigan and Hart, the "Black Crook," and the Callender Minstrels were the ideals of managerial success. Close upon Charles and Daniel Frohman came David Belasco to New York in the later seventies. They arrived at a moment which was propitious, for Bronson Howard, rightly designated the Dean of American Drama, as Dunlap is called the Father of the American Theatre, had insisted on A. M. Palmer's advertising his play, *The Banker's Daughter*, as an American Comedy, and he stood for the rights of the native dramatist as opposed to the foreigner. It was a long time in the managerial careers of either Daniel or Charles Frohman before they could be brought to think that the word "American" was of commercial advantage; and this attitude of theirs is the first suggestion of the future estimate of the theatre as a commercial enterprise, against which all later native art has had to contend.

These days of the theatre have been chronicled by three critics: Laurence Hutton, Brander Matthews, and William

Winter. Winter[1] had a long perspective in theatre attendance, and left available a large body of journalistic reporting; it may be said that from 1854 to the time of his death in 1917 his pen was recording theatrical matters continually. But he was not concerned with the development of an American drama; his professional duty was to take the theatre as it came to him nightly; to estimate it as a presented thing, and to measure its acting value. His attitude, as becomes a dramatic critic for newspapers, was not concerned primarily with the literary side. Therefore, neither his *The Wallet of Time* nor his other voluminous works give one a comprehensive view of American drama. Laurence Hutton,[2] on the other hand, was interested in the appearance of American characteristics on the boards, and no more suggestive chapters can be read than in his *Curiosities of the American Theatre*. Certainly, his close friend and collaborator, Brander Matthews, must have had Hutton in mind when he compiled his essays *A Book About the Theatre*. It is to Professor Matthews—who has held the chair of Dramatic Literature at Columbia University since 1900, and who is the author of many poems, stories, and novels, as well as an essayist of wide range—that we must turn for estimates of American dramatists as distinct personalities in a native form of art. He has done for the American play what he has done for the subject of drama in general: popularized the philosophy of the theatre. That service is of inestimable worth. He has edited old texts, he helped to found The Players and The Dunlap Society; but, unfortunately, he has written no book on American drama. Yet his volumes of essays have full reference to the American theatre. He has a more organic sense of its development than either Hutton or Winter. In his reminiscences, *These Many Years* (1917), we not only have his love of the play well depicted, and his reflection of the New York, London, and Paris theatres during the period just sketched; but there is also the record of his own efforts as a dramatist—efforts coincident with those of Howells and Howard and James. One obtains fleeting glimpses of the managerial guilty conscience regarding the fate of American drama, in the efforts made by managers to engage the literary world in the interest of the theatre. In 1878 Professor Matthews wrote *Margery's Lovers*, produced in

[1] See also Book III, Chap. XIII.   [2] *Ibid.*

1887 at an author's matinée at the Madison Square Theatre, by A. M. Palmer, who likewise presented George Parsons Lathrop's *Elaine* and Howells's dramatization of *A Foregone Conclusion*. In similar fashion was *Decision of the Court* presented, 23 March, 1893, by the Theatre of Arts and Letters. This organization also offered Mary E. Wilkins's *Giles Corey*, Frank R. Stockton's *Squirrel Inn*, and Clyde Fitch's *Harvest* —which latter was afterwards evolved into *The Moth and the Flame*. Professor Matthews, as an American dramatist, has scarcely exhibited the qualities or won the fame which belong to him as a professor of Dramatic Literature.[1] The reason may be, as Bronson Howard declared after the experience they had together in collaboration over *Peter Stuyvesant* (2 October, 1899), that Professor Matthews, used to viewing the finished product in the theatre, was not used to the constant labour which always attends the writing and further re-writing of a play.

Bronson Howard (1842–1908) came to the theatre with a full journalistic career behind him. He had the serious mind of a student, the keen, polished culture of a man of the world. To play-writing he brought a convention typical of the day and a constructive ability which made him always an excellent workman but which often prompted him to sacrifice thoughtfulness for stage effectiveness and solid characterization for effervescent sprightliness. His style, so well contrasted in *Saratoga* (21 December, 1870), *The Banker's Daughter* (30 September, 1878), *The Young Mrs. Winthrop* (9 October, 1882), and *The Henrietta* (26 September, 1887), is limited by all the reticence, the lack of frankness which the seventies and eighties courted. In other words, he went on the supposition that so long as one was French one could be broad, but that Americans would never stand for too much latitude of morals from American characters. But, as a pioneer in the field of the drama of contemporary manners, Howard's plays are interesting and significant. His treatment of capital and labour, as shown in *Baron Rudolph* (25 October, 1887), his reflection of business stress, in *The Henrietta*,—these were, in their day, novel departures. But his plays were none of them organically close knit. It was easy to make *Saratoga* ready for consumption in

[1] For Professor Matthews's important writing on the short story see Book III, Chap. v.

London theatres by calling it *Brighton*. In 1886 Howard delivered a lecture before the students of Harvard University, illustrating the general laws of drama, and outlining the conventional traditions against which he worked. He was never able to escape them. *Shenandoah* (9 September, 1889) was more national than most of his work. To its preparation he brought that scholarly orderliness of mind which characterized the man in conversation.

The successes of those early days when Howard was knocking at the doors of Daly and Palmer, were fitful, and, though they are known by name today, their lack of a true note of reality and their stereotyped romanticism make them impossible either as reading dramas or as revivals. Joaquin Miller's *The Danites* (Broadway Theatre, 22 August, 1877), J. Cheever Goodwin's burlesque *Evangeline* (Niblo's Garden, 27 July, 1874), Bartley Campbell's *My Partner* (Union Square, 16 September, 1879), Wallack's *Rosedale* (Wallack's Theatre, 30 September, 1863), Olive Logan's *Surf* (Daly's Theatre, 12 January, 1870),—these were the types of native successes. None of them exploited deep-founded American characteristics, though they suggested the melodrama of American life. It was only by individualizing and localizing that the American drama, previous to 1860, became distinct. Only by these traditional marks could one recognize American drama of the early days. Until Howard's attempt at reality, New York "society" drama was either English or else crudely rustic, like Asa Trenchard in Taylor's *Our American Cousin* (Laura Keene's Theatre, 18 October, 1858). Over into this period of transition came the Yankee, the backwoodsman, the humorous lawyer of "flush times." As Howard said, writing of the American drama, the native dramatists were concerned with American character, hence Solon Shingle, Colonel Sellers, Judge Bardwell Slote, and Mose the fire-boy. Without them, we should not have had Joshua Whitcomb, Davy Crockett, and Pudd'nhead Wilson. Perhaps one of the most typically American pieces produced in this period of the seventies was Frank Murdock's *Davy Crockett* (New York, Niblo's Garden, 9 March, 1874), reminiscent in its colour of the elder Hackett's *Colonel Nimrod Wildfire*, and a romantic forerunner of Moody's *The Great Divide*. Mrs. Bateman's *Self* finds continuation in Howard's *Saratoga* and

Mrs. Logan's *Surf*, while these point the way to Langdon Mitchell's *The New York Idea*, written when dialogue for the theatre had grown in literary form and feeling, when a sense of atmosphere created an ironic response to fashionable manners and customs.

It is because of this isolated, accidental character of American drama that Bronson Howard's position was all the more remarkable in 1870, and thereafter. Yet his plays are dated. It may be that some day *Saratoga* can be made over into a costume play, though it was written as an up-to-date "society" comedy. But the difference between it and Mitchell's *The New York Idea* (19 November, 1906) is that the latter contains some of the universal depth that mere change in time and condition will not alter.

The theatre of the sixties and seventies was surfeited with the strong melodrama and romantic violences which suited a special robust acting. When David Belasco turned East, as stock dramatist for The Madison Square Theatre, a house to compete with the traditions of the Union Square and Daly's, there came into vogue a form of drama which allowed of a quiet, domestic atmosphere—in imitation of what Robertson, Byron, and their British contemporaries were striving for in London. The "milk and water" acting which was here introduced was what made of *The Young Mrs. Winthrop* (Madison Square Theatre, 9 October, 1882) such a phenomenal success. It was this tradition, not new but novel, which evolved into the present naturalistic method of acting. But the Madison Square Theatre gave impetus to something more than a school of acting. In its intimate management it furthered the dramatic writing of Steele MacKaye, whose *Hazel Kirke* (4 February, 1880) was written expressly for the stock company gathered there, and it brought Belasco and De Mille together in preparation for their later collaboration when, with Daniel Frohman, they went over to the Lyceum Theatre and in rapid succession wrote *The Wife* (1 November, 1887), *Lord Chumley* (21 August, 1888), *The Charity Ball* (19 November, 1889), *Men and Women* (21 October, 1890).

Steele MacKaye (1844–1894) while with the Madison Square management won popularity as a playwright, but none of his pieces is widely known to the theatre now, except by name. *Rose Michel* (23 November, 1875), *Hazel Kirke, Dakolar* (6 April, 1885), and *Paul Kauvar* (24 December, 1887) are among those that linger in memory as examples of picturesque melodrama created for a certain type of stage effect, with emotionalism of the Dumas kind. MacKaye once wrote: "The master playwright combines the constructive faculty of the mechanic and the analytical mind of the philosopher, with the æsthetic instinct of a poet, and the ethical ardour of an apostle." This is an all-inclusive definition, which MacKaye never encompassed in any of his plays, but which in himself was exemplified by the ardour of his temperament and the visionary character of his imagination. His son Percy might be said to have the same ideal, to which can be added a passion for civic art. He has tried to express this latter element in his pageants, but has never successfully done so. For Percy MacKaye is one of the most aristocratic of writers—farthest removed from a thorough realization of the emotions of the crowd. His poetic drama is academic in its scholarly allusions. One only has to read *Sappho and Phaon* (21 October, 1907) to realize this. As striking examples of the excellence of his dramatic force there are *The Scarecrow* (produced 17 January, 1911), *Jeanne d'Arc* (28 January, 1907), and *A Thousand Years Ago* (1 December, 1913). *The Scarecrow*, based on Hawthorne, ranks high among American plays. MacKaye's political philosophy, earnest but hazy, is seen in his *Mater* (25 September, 1908); his socio-scientific approach is measured in *To-Morrow* (31 October, 1913); his imaginative breadth and picturesque enthusiasm are evident in any one of his masques and pageants, *The Canterbury Pilgrims* (Gloucester, Mass., 3 August, 1909), *Sanctuary* (12 September, 1913), *Saint Louis* (St. Louis, 28 May, 1914), and *Caliban* (New York, 25 May, 1916). But all told, MacKaye has not reached the ideal he emphasizes in his essays on the theatre. If the civic theatre ever becomes a feature of American theatrical history, he will occupy, unless he changes his method of thought and character of technique, the peculiar position of being a pioneer believer in its efficacy, and of being unable in his plays to sound the true democratic note. The sense of American history is uppermost in his mind, but at present his use of materials is distinctly caviare to the popular theatregoer.

By the eighties there had been established in New York the nucleus of what was to be known as the modern American theatre. Daniel Frohman was at the Madison Square, his brother Charles was on the road with Wallack successes, and was thus early exhibiting his ability to pick plays and players by corralling Bronson Howard's *Shenandoah* (9 September, 1889)—his first real production in New York. William Gillette began his career as playwright in 1881; while it was 1889 before Augustus Thomas entered the field. The gradual rise of Richard Mansfield was identified with the names of Palmer and Wallack; and though he cannot be said to have been a patron of the American dramatist, his early appearances were in pieces like Hjalmar Boyesen's *Alpine Roses* (Madison Square Theatre, 31 January, 1884) and Henry Guy Carleton's *Victor Durand* (Wallack's Theatre, 18 December, 1884). But these were merely pieces of the theatre, like Cazauran's adaptation of a play by Octave Feuillet, called *A Parisian Romance*, in which Mansfield first attained prominent recognition (Union Square Theatre, 11 January, 1883). It was not until some while afterwards—in 1890, to be exact—that he offered Clyde Fitch the opportunity to collaborate with him in *Beau Brummell* (Madison Square Theatre, 17 May, 1890), and this may be accounted Fitch's beginning, followed directly afterward by a one-act sketch, *Frédéric Lemaître* (1 December, 1890), written for Henry Miller.

Up to the time of the appearance of these names in the history of American playwriting, it is difficult to give coherence to the development of American dramatic consciousness. The style in theatre management was "stock," until business combination began to assert itself. And such names as Bartley Campbell (1843–1888), Henry Guy Carlton (1856–1910), Edgar Fawcett (1847–1904) mean nothing in the way of native feeling for drama, however much Campbell's *My Partner* reflected Western melodrama. Even James A. Herne, who had a career as actor in San Francisco which presaged greater work to come, did not arrive in New York until later, though he had begun his playwriting when *Hearts of Oak* was given at Baldwin's Theatre, San Francisco, 9 September, 1879. And we are rightly inclined to regard Herne as our first exponent of reality in the sense of getting close to the soil. Edward Harrigan's (1845–1911) plays—the best of which were *Squatter Sovereignty* (Theatre Comique, 9 January, 1882), *Old Lavender* (Theatre Comique, 3 September, 1877), *The Mulligan Guard Ball* (Theatre Comique, 9 February, 1879)—were varied in their local colour, as were the farces of Charles Hoyt (1859–1900), who began playwriting with *A Bunch of Keys* (Newark, 13 December, 1883) and created such pieces of the political and social moment as *A Parlor Match, A Rag Baby, A Texas Steer; or, Money Makes the Mare Go, A Trip to Chinatown, A Milk White Flag,* and *A Temperance Town.*

By 1880 the modern period of American drama was in the bud: a journalistic sense had entered the American theatre, and entered to good purpose, for it had given Howard a sense of reality. It has stayed in the theatre and has deprived it, in later exponents, of a logical completeness of idea. It has in most cases kept our drama external.

Stage history must again be recalled, because the affairs of the theatre have so completely governed our playwrights. Howard, Herne, MacKaye, De Mille, Belasco, Gillette, Thomas, and Fitch—names which practically represent the American dramatist from 1888 until 1900—grew up, fought, and flourished under the increasing shadow of the commercial theatre. After Daniel Frohman left the Madison Square Theatre and opened his Lyceum (in May, 1885), and after his brother Charles (1860–1915) had opened the Empire Theatre (in January, 1893), with estimable stock companies, it became evident that two new elements confronted the American theatregoers. First, the interest in the play was largely centred in the personality of the player. Julia Marlowe, Edward H. Sothern, Otis Skinner, William Faversham, Henry Miller, Margaret Anglin, Maude Adams, James K. Hackett, Viola Allen,—all and many more came into prominence through the adoption of the "star" system—a system which was more firmly believed in by Charles Frohman than by his brother Daniel. But both of them began thus early to monopolize certain English dramatists, tying them up in "futures," as Pinero was tied, and as, later, the English playwrights J. M. Barrie, Jones, Carton, Marshall, Davies, and their generation were "signed up" by Charles Frohman on his yearly trips to London for material. The theatre was run on principles more

and more commercial, though both the Lyceum and the Empire
in these days gave agreeable artistic productions. It is true
that Daniel Frohman produced pieces by American playwrights
like Belasco, De Mille, Marguerite Merrington (*Captain Letter-
blair*, 16 August, 1892), Fitch (*An American Duchess*, 20
November, 1893; *The Moth and the Flame*, 11 April, 1898; *The
Girl and the Judge*, 4 December, 1901), Mrs. Frances Hodgson
Burnett (*The First Gentleman of Europe*, 25 January, 1897),
Madeleine Lucette Ryley (*The Mysterious Mr. Bugle*, 19 April,
1897; *Richard Savage*, 4 February, 1901), Grace Livingston
Furness and Abby Sage Richardson (*Colonial Girl*, 31 October,
1898; *Americans at Home*, 13 March, 1899). It is also true that
Charles Frohman, opening his Empire Theatre with the Belasco-
Fyles military drama, *The Girl I Left Behind Me* (25 January,
1893), figured largely in the development of Gillette, Fitch, and
Thomas. Nevertheless, it was not by their faith in the American playwright that the powerful position of the theatrical
managers was won, but rather through the astute manner in
which they watched the foreign market. They were sure of
foreign successes; they were not willing to risk the untried
American. Besides, with the end of the stock company fashion,
travelling companies began to increase in favour, and this
meant the growth of a system of "booking" which put into the
hands of a few the power of dictating what amusements the
theatregoing Americans, outside of large theatrical centres,
could have. The managers throttled the theatres by 1896,
when the Theatrical Trust was formed, and though actors
rebelled—men like Mansfield, Francis Wilson, Herne, and
Joseph Jefferson; though such actresses as Mrs. Fiske and Mme.
Bernhardt suffered from their enmity by being debarred from
places where the Trust owned the only available theatres—
still, the actors finally succumbed one by one, the playwrights
listened to their commercial dictators, managers of minor
theatres became their henchmen. In such an atmosphere,
while in time we got good plays, it was impossible for a serious
body of American dramaturgic art to develop. It was thought
that if the monopolistic power of the Trust could be broken, all
might be well again. And it was broken: there soon came two
combinations instead of one—with the same evils of "booking,"
the same paucity of good things because of commercial regula-

tions and measurements. Nothing could dispel this dull atmosphere but a complete reorganization of the theatre. It will later be seen that this break-up is now (1919) in process.

The only manager who, early in the nineties, seems to have had faith in the native product was David Belasco, and his belief was founded on faith in himself. His early training, as secretary to Dion Boucicault, as manager and stock-dramatist at the San Francisco Baldwin's Theatre; his ability to work over material supplied by others at the Madison Square Theatre—all served him to excellent account when he finally began for himself and fought against the Trust which did not care for his independence and grudged him his success. In his long and useful career we find his interest as a manager prompting his ability as a writer; we find his genius as a trainer of "stars" like Mrs. Leslie Carter, Blanche Bates, David Warfield, and Frances Starr regulating his selection of subjects for treatment as playwright. The advance from *The Heart of Maryland* (22 October, 1895) to the adaptation of *Zaza* (8 January, 1899) represented his discovery of increasing ability in the emotionalism of Mrs. Carter; and his successive presentation of her in such spectacular dramas as *Du Barry* (25 December, 1901) and *Adrea* (11 January, 1905) measured his belief in her histrionic power. In the same way, his faith in Blanche Bates prompted him to write many scenes in *Madame Butterfly* (5 March, 1900), *The Darling of the Gods* (3 December, 1902), and *The Girl of the Golden West* (14 November, 1905) for her. Taking Warfield from the Weber and Fields organization (a combination which produced about 1897–1900, by their burlesque of current American successes, a type of humour truly Aristophanean), Belasco had plays cut by himself and Charles Klein to fit Warfield's personality—and this impulse was back of *The Auctioneer* (23 September, 1901) and *The Music Master* (26 September, 1904). But there was something more behind Belasco's ability to create stage atmosphere by lighting and scene. His love of the West suggested *The Girl of the Golden West* and prompted his acceptance of Richard Walton Tully's *The Rose of the Rancho* (27 November, 1906)—a collaboration which left Tully with a love for the spectacular, apparent in his own independent dramas, *The Bird of Paradise* (Daly's Theatre, 8 January, 1912) and *Omar, the Tent Maker* (Lyric Theatre, 13 January

1914). In all of his productions, as a manager, Belasco has held the guiding hand. Though John Luther Long gave him the central materials for *Madame Butterfly*, *The Darling of the Gods*, and *Adrea*, the Belasco touch brought them to flower. This has been the invariable result of his collaboration. The one original play of his which best illustrates the mental interest of the man is *The Return of Peter Grimm* (2 January, 1911), which deals with the presence of the dead. A related subject of interest was dual personality, which prompted his acceptance of *The Case of Becky* (1 October, 1912) by Edward Locke and *The Secret* (23 December, 1913) by Henri Bernstein. The latter revealed the expertness of Belasco as an adapter far better than his work on Hermann Bahr's *The Concert* (3 October 1910) or on *The Lily* (23 December, 1909) by Wolff and Leroux. Had Belasco not been a manager, the effect on his own work might have been different. As it is, he has sought variety, he has followed the changing times. His interest in emotion, in picturesque situation, in unusual atmosphere, in modern realism, is evident in the long list of plays by himself, and in other dramas he has produced. Sentiment for the past encouraged him to further the career of William C. De Mille, son of his early associate, and while *The Warrens of Virginia* (Belasco Theatre, 3 December, 1907) and *The Woman* (Republic Theatre, 19 September, 1911)—both superior to *Strongheart*—show the younger De Mille an adept at the game of the theatre, there is no doubt that Belasco was an agent in the success of these two dramas.

The entire history of the American theatre within the past quarter of a century has been the continued struggle between the dramatist and the manager, resulting in the complete surrender of the former to the dictates of the latter. The native plays given us have been variously pruned and patched until, like fashion patterns, they have fitted a particular "star," or until the goods have become salable, dependent on box-office demand. When the play became a reading as well as an acting "thing," the dramatist first sensed that it was incumbent on him to turn out a literary product, enriched by style, and marked by conviction.

If, however, one reads the early dramas of Augustus Thomas and Clyde Fitch, it will be realized how dexterously the American playwright profited by the French technician in whom the commercial manager had faith. Considering the demands of the box-office, it is surprising that these dramatists developed so often along the lines of their own interests. Their plays are representative in part of the demands of the theatre of the time, but also they measure something more personal. Thomas at first wrote local dramas, like *Alabama* (1 April, 1891) and *Arizona* (Chicago, 12 June, 1899), which in content he never excelled; he showed his brilliancy of observation and terseness of dialogue in such pieces as *Mrs. Leffingwell's Boots* (11 January, 1905) and *The Other Girl* (29 December, 1903). Then he arrived at his serious period, where interest in psychic phenomena resulted in *The Witching Hour* (18 November, 1907), *The Harvest Moon* (18 October, 1909), and *As a Man Thinks* (13 March, 1911)—the latter extravagant in its use of several themes, excellent in its sheer talk. This development was not imposed on Thomas by commercial conditions.

But, like his contemporaries, Thomas was experimental in form; he was not moved by a body of philosophy in his dealing with character or theme. He was just as ready to write a farce like *The Earl of Pawtucket* (5 February, 1903) as he was to do a costume play like *Oliver Goldsmith* (19 March, 1900); just as willing to turn a series of cartoons into a play, like *The Education of Mr. Pipp* (20 February, 1905), as he was to dramatize popular novels of such different range as F. Hopkinson Smith's *Colonel Carter of Cartersville* (22 March, 1892) and Richard Harding Davis's *Soldiers of Fortune* (17 March, 1902). Thomas's observation of "things about town" is acute; one sees that to best advantage in *The Other Girl* and *The Witching Hour*. Most of his plays, as his introductions to the printed editions suggest, reveal his method of workmanship.

He has not the distinct literary flavour of Clyde Fitch; his stories are not so warmly human, his characters not so finished. Fitch (1865–1909) was as independent of the manager as Thomas, but he nearly always constructed his plays with a "star" in mind. He helped to increase the popularity of Julia Marlowe with *Barbara Frietchie* (24 October, 1899), Nat Goodwin with *Nathan Hale* (2 January, 1899), Mansfield with *Beau Brummell* (17 May, 1890), Maxine Elliott with *Her Great Match* (4 September, 1905), and Clara Bloodgood with *The Truth* (7 January, 1907) and *The Girl with the Green Eyes* (25 December, 1902). That is the superficial classification of Fitch. But there was a deeper sensitiveness and feeling in what he wrote. His appreciation of small details was a constant source of entertainment in his dramas; they rushed upon us with brilliant and rapid succession. To see a Fitch play was to become impressed with his facility in dialogue and ease of invention. But the fact is, Fitch's pen moved rapidly merely because he had pondered the plot, incident, and actual dialogue long before the transcribing began. And when he did write, it was a process of setting down from memory. For three years he studied over the psychology and situation of what he called his "jealousy" play, before he began *The Girl with the Green Eyes*.

Fitch, like Thomas, could do work for the commercial manager; and soon they both gained positions of confidence which allowed them to lead rather than be led. The mere fact that their dramas are readable measures something of their literary value. Thomas has always shown the limitation of not too clear thinking; Fitch often obtruded his smartness in places where sound characterization was needed. One noted this in a favourite piece of his, *A Happy Marriage* (12 April, 1909). But those who regarded Fitch's contribution to American drama as largely picturesque sentimentality, as in *Lovers' Lane* (6 February, 1901), *The Stubbornness of Geraldine* (3 November, 1902), and *Granny* (24 October, 1904); those who depreciate him by saying he spent his time flippantly in converting German farce to American taste, as in *The Blue Mouse* (30 November, 1908), should recall two of his dramas which compare favourably with the best of modern psychological pieces —*The Truth* and *The Girl with the Green Eyes*. He tried every form of comedy and farce; and while many of his stories, as plots, were slight and unworthy of him, he brought to the task always a radiant spirit which gave his dramas a distinctive tone. He could write melodrama too; *The Woman in the Case* (30 January, 1905) won recognition on the Continent. He could, through sheer strength of situation and fearlessness of attack, create something of the tragic, as in *The City* (22 December, 1909), written largely to refute the charge that he was solely a dramatist of the feminine. There was some of the bric-à-brac quality about Fitch. He caught the volatile in American life,—more especially in New York life,—and it is this quality which keeps so many of his plays still alive and fresh.

At the time Fitch and Thomas were gaining headway, another playwright came to the front, having attained beforehand a reputation for powerful acting and excellent stage management. This was James A. Herne (1839–1901). His distinctive gifts as a writer were clarity and simplicity, and his art of expression lay in the illumination he infused into homely things and simple people. Coming East from California with the traditions of florid melodrama which influenced Belasco (the two having worked together at the Baldwin Theatre), Herne fell under the influence of Darwin and Herbert Spencer, in philosophy, and of Henry George in economics. He arrived in Boston at the time W. D. Howells,[1] an exponent of realism in the novel, was the foremost writer of the day. All these forces prompted Herne to deal with the fundamentals of character in his dramatic work. He became interested, as Maeterlinck would say, in conditions of soul. His dialogue in *Margaret Fleming* (Lynn, Mass., 4 July, 1880), rang true, instinct with homely life; his *Griffith Davenport* (Washington, D. C., 16 January, 1899)—a drama of the Civil War based not on external action but on inward struggle—was filled with sincerity; his *Shore Acres* (Chicago, 23 May, 1892)—which, because of the précieuse success of *Margaret Fleming*, made concessions to the old-time melodrama, had passages of dominant realism, simple conversation warm with human meaning, which have not been surpassed by an American playwright thus far. The popular notion is that Herne wrote "by gosh" drama of the type of *The Vermont Wool-Dealer* and Denman Thompson's *Old Homestead* (Boston, 5 April, 1885). But that is farthest from a true comparison, for Herne's observation was based on profound appreciation of character and human relationship, and the Yankee-type drama was dependent on outward eccentricity.

The work in play-writing of William Gillette has been so closely identified with his peculiar technique as an actor that it is difficult to separate the two. Apart from his first collaboration with Mrs. Frances Hodgson Burnett in *Esmeralda* (29 October, 1881); apart from his dependence on French sources in *Too Much Johnson* (26 November, 1894) and *Because She Loved*

[1] See Book III, Chap. XI.

Him So (16 January, 1899), both of which showed the quickness of his farce spirit, one should judge him by the tenseness of his Civil War pieces, *Held by the Enemy* (16 August, 1886) and *Secret Service* (5 October, 1896); and by the refined melodrama of his *Sherlock Holmes* dramatization (6 November, 1899), which, for its success, was so dependent on the nervous quiet of his acting. As an actor, Gillette requires peculiar opportunities of hesitant firmness; only one dramatist outside of himself has recognized his special needs—J. M. Barrie in *The Admirable Crichton* (17 November, 1903). Gillette himself did not rightly estimate them when he wrote the sentimental comedy *Clarice* (16 October, 1906), nor did he, either as a technician or as a psychologist, create aright in such a piece as *Electricity* (31 October, 1910). As a dramatist he has remained undisturbed by the interest in modern ideas; his social conscience has not ruffled the even amusement tenor of his plays, which always arouse the observer to moods romantically tense, and depend on thoroughly legitimate situations rather than on ideas.

The American drama now began to show a greater sensitiveness to the social forces of the times. Herne's realism was not one of social condition, but expressed itself in human psychology. Charles Klein, however, tried to give newspaper crispness to business condition, which Bronson Howard had suggested in *The Henrietta*. In fact, the Dean of American Drama once said that in order to see how far American taste had advanced since his day, one had only to contrast the moral attitude of the heroine in Rachel Crothers's *The Three of Us* (Madison Square Theatre, 17 October, 1906) and the social fervour of the heroine in Klein's *The Lion and the Mouse* (20 November, 1905) with any of his own plays. The fact is that Charles Klein (1867–1915), from the moment he stopped writing librettos like *El Capitan*, had a strongly developed reportorial sense which was more theatrical than profound. None of his plays could bear close logical analysis; all of his plays had situations that were "actor-proof" and sure to get across on the emotional force of the moment. But his social and economic knowledge was incomplete. One feels this in contrasting his *Daughters of Men* (19 November, 1906) with George Bernard Shaw's *Widowers' Houses*. The fact is, Klein had no political vision, though none of his contemporaries could be more earnest in the handling of social materials. *The Third Degree* (1 February, 1909), *The Gamblers* (31 October, 1910), *Maggie Pepper* (31 August, 1911), are obviously built for effect; they have no organic growth. The truth is, Klein's solutions for the ills-of-America condition were all sentimental. He was much nearer his natural psychology in writing *The Music Master* (26 September, 1904) than in determining the outcome of social and economic problems.

In 1900 melodrama had a grip on the interest of the American middle class; it was the beau ideal of entertainment for the working people. Its violence accentuated the violences of American life, and Owen Davis and Theodore Kramer, the Thomas and Fitch of melodrama, flourished on half a dozen or more successes a year. The very names suggest their sentiment and colour: *Tony, the Bootblack; Nellie, the Beautiful Cloak Model; Bertha, the Sewing Machine Girl; Convict 999.* But soon, through the educational agency of the public libraries, the melodrama audiences began reading books more reserved in action, more logical in plot. While their eye would accept scenes of violence, their mind began to balk at repeated inconsistencies. Melodrama of this type began to fail, and the melodramatists were drawn towards work of a different kind. But the breathless stimulation, excitement, and variety of this special form of playwriting were taken over by the moving picture, which is based on restlessness, on kinetic motion.

Until 1900 the modern American drama advanced by fashions; managers followed like sheep in the wake of a popular success until the vein was exhausted. The dramatized novel went through its many phases of popular taste, beginning with Anthony Hope's *The Prisoner of Zenda*, Stanley Weyman's *Under the Red Robe*, and Mrs. Burnett's *The Lady of Quality*, and passing to Paul Leicester Ford's *Janice Meredith*, which as a novel competed with S. Weir Mitchell's *Hugh Wynne*.[1]

The manager thought there was certainty in a play based on a book which had sold into the thousands. The book market was full of literary successes and was drawn upon for the stage. Mary Johnston's *To Have and To Hold* and *Audrey;* Winston Churchill's *Richard Carvel* and *The Crisis;* Charles

[1] See Book III, Chap. XI.

Major's *When Knighthood was in Flower;* George W. Cable's *The Cavalier;* John Fox's *Trail of the Lonesome Pine;* Richard Harding Davis's *Soldiers of Fortune*—the list might be stretched to interminable length. Out of this type of playwriting the theatre gained certain striking successes. After the popularity of *Monsieur Beaucaire,* Booth Tarkington entered the dramatic ranks with his *The Man from Home* (in collaboration, Astor Theatre, 17 August, 1908), *Cameo Kirby* (Hackett Theatre, 20 December, 1909), *Your Humble Servant* (Garrick Theatre, 3 January, 1909), *The Country Cousin* (Gaiety Theatre, 3 September, 1917), *Penrod* (Globe Theatre, 2 September, 1918). Richard Harding Davis came from novel-writing to an occasional theatre piece like *The Galloper* (Garden Theatre, 22 February, 1906) and *The Yankee Consul* (Broadway Theatre, 22 February, 1904). Lorimer Stoddard, with his *Tess of the D'Urbervilles* (Miner's Fifth Avenue Theatre, 2 March, 1897) and Langdon Mitchell with his *Becky Sharp* likewise came into the theatre fold. Many American writers rushed in because it was a lucrative venture when successful; and coming in thus crudely and without preparation, they learned their technique at the expense of a theatre-going public.

It is a nondescript position taken by the novelist in his attitude towards the theatre. Rex Beach has had his novels turned into plays by others, and has written moving-picture scenarios. Alice Hegan Rice met with as great success in the dramatization of *Mrs. Wiggs of the Cabbage Patch* (3 September, 1904) as she did when the story ran into its million circulation as a book. Mrs. Kate Douglas Wiggin Riggs has tried time and time again to enter the magic realm, and did so with *Rebecca of Sunnybrook Farm* (Republic Theatre, 3 October, 1910). But the literary life of America has never, thus far, considered the theatre as anything more than a by-product of the novelist's art. Writers have, to use George Ade's phrase, "butted in" too easily, and they have had no appreciable influence on the craft.

Then, later on, the reverse process began. Though plays were being published and widely read by an audience trained in the special ability required—through a visualizing imagination—to get the most from the play form, it has been a long and arduous road to persuade American playwrights to publish their plays, even though they saw what good results followed the publication of British and Continental drama. Rather did they prefer to see their plays converted by some literary juggler into a novel, with the dialogue embedded in narrative and explanatory matter furnished by others. Long before any of the plays of Belasco, Broadhurst, Klein, Walter, and others were printed, they were thus "novelized" and read by a fiction public. But the custom is abating somewhat in favour of retaining the integrity of the play form.

The use of a college theme first undertaken by George Ade in *The College Widow* (20 September, 1904) was imitated by William De Mille in *Strongheart* (30 January, 1905) and by Rida Johnson Young in *Brown of Harvard* (26 February, 1906); and George Ade carried to the stage the newspaper humour which reflected so well the national characteristics celebrated by Eugene Field, Peter Finley Dunne, and Ade himself, the one humorist who builded in the theatre better than any of his brotherhood before him. For the kind of satirical fun one saw in *The Sultan of Sulu* (Wallack's Theatre, 29 December, 1902). *The County Chairman* (Wallack's Theatre, 24 November, 1903). *The Sho-Gun* (10 October, 1904), and *The College Widow* (20 September, 1904) had a national tang which transcended the local pride of the Indiana School. His humour bears the same relation toward social things that Mr. Dooley's political vein bears toward national politics.[1] In his generous modesty, Ade has always maintained that George M. Cohan, the many-handed wonder of Yankee-doodle-flag farces and *Over There* music, was more typically American than he. Cohan is the type of manager-playwright who has his pulse on the moment; he grows rich on local allusion. His *Little Johnny Jones* (7 November, 1904), *George Washington, Jr.* (12 February, 1906), *Forty-five Minutes from Broadway* (14 March, 1912), and *The Man Who Owns Broadway* (11 October, 1909) have the tang of the street about them. There is a quality to his music which has been brought nearer the psycho-state of a nervous crowd by Irving Berlin, with his jazz noises and his syncopated songs. But as a producer, in the sense that Belasco is a dramatist-producer, Cohan shows a genius more serious. His adaptation of Earl Biggers's story, *Seven Keys to Baldpate* (22 September, 1913), illustrated

[1] See Book III, Chap. IX

the more solid variety of his ability. All told, he reflects a nervousness which, while representative of the times, is not an enviable attribute in a nation, though its flexible humour indicates aliveness of mind and quick realization of national foibles. Mr. Dooley, Ade, and Cohan show, by the success they have had at the hands of the public, that as a people we are capable of enjoying humour, comic and trenchant, at our own expense.

The matter of popularity and permanence has confused the history of playwriting in America. There was a time when Joaquin Miller's *The Danites* held audiences spellbound; when Campbell's *My Partner* was considered as representative of America as Bret Harte's *The Luck of Roaring Camp*. *Way Down East* (7 February, 1898) and *In Old Kentucky* (27 April, 1897), by their extended acceptance, should place Lottie Blair Parker and Charles T. Dazey in the forefront of the theatre. But they are not widely known today. Nor is Martha Morton the significant figure she bid fair to be when she wrote *His Wife's Father* (Miner's Fifth Avenue Theatre, 25 February, 1895). Even the success of *Little Lord Fauntleroy* (10 September, 1888) did not make Frances Hodgson Burnett a dramatist, though she commanded the stage in several other plays for many years. The allurement held forth by large profits at first attracted the literary worker and then the layman in any field who thought playwriting lucrative. Colleges began offering courses in dramatic technique, and from the classes of Professor George P. Baker at Harvard and Professor Brander Matthews at Columbia commendable graduates have come to the theatre. The consequence is that the number of American writers of drama has increased largely, with not a commensurate increase of typically American plays.

The most notable examples of dramatic contributions within the past twenty years are William Vaughn Moody's *The Great Divide* (3 October, 1906), Josephine Preston Peabody's *The Piper* (New Theatre, 30 January, 1911), George C. Hazelton and J. H. Benrimo's *The Yellow Jacket* (Fulton Theatre, 4 November, 1912), Charles Kenyon's *Kindling* (Daly's Theatre, 3 December, 1911), and Eugene Walter's *The Easiest Way* (Belasco Theatre, 19 January, 1909). Moody,[1] whose untimely death cut short the future of a man who, with his literary sense,

[1] See Book III, Chap. x.

might have grown into theatre requirements because of an innate dramatic touch, in *The Great Divide* created something which in substance showed a deep feeling for native atmosphere and a broad understanding of human passion. However unsatisfying certain features of *The Great Divide*,—for instance, its lack of unity of scene, its mistakes in motive,—yet it gives one a comprehension of stern reality which makes Hawthorne's *The Scarlet Letter* so permanent a contribution to literature. But Moody's poetic sense, which was stronger and greater than his sense of drama, led him entirely astray in his *The Faith Healer* (Savoy Theatre, 19 January, 1910), with its mystical atmosphere where belief did not mix with reality, and conviction did not rise above picturesqueness. But in *The Great Divide* Moody caught the permanent passions of real people. This also may be said of Alice Brown's *Children of Earth* (12 January, 1915), which won a $10,000 prize offered by Winthrop Ames in the hope that competition would bring forth the American masterpieces which popular belief imagined were hid under a bushel by the ruthless hand of the managers of commerce. Miss Brown committed extravagances in her desire to reflect the New England life she knows so well—an atmosphere which relates her to the school of fiction ably represented by Sarah Orne Jewett, Mary E. Wilkins Freeman, and Mrs. Margaret Deland.[1] But *Children of Earth* failed because a narrative declaration of passion was substituted for the reality which would have made the heroine's moment of June madness grippingly convincing.

Mrs. Josephine Preston Peabody Marks, a poet with literary feeling, with an eye for the pictorial, won a prize offered by the English actor, Frank Benson, with *The Piper* (New Theatre, 30 January, 1911)—a charming resetting of the old Hamelin legend which has modern implication and application. Patches of poetry beautify the text but weight the acting quality. Its imaginative stretch was refreshing in the American theatre, however, and the production given by Winthrop Ames was distinctive. It possessed youthful spirit, and hints of dramatic tenseness. But Mrs. Marks has not yet added convincing proof that she is a dramatist above a poet, though her *Marlowe* furnishes a commendable example of poetic drama.

[1] See Book III, Chap. vi.

The fact is, American drama has always been so completely shadowing the newspaper on one hand or catering to Broadway on the other that any example of imaginative freshness with fanciful idea would appeal instantly to a sated public. It is on such psychology that Eleanor Gates's *The Poor Little Rich Girl* (Hudson Theatre, 21 January, 1913) succeeded—a literary feat in fantastic story-telling which possessed Barriësque qualities without Barrie's craftsmanship as a writer for the theatre. Is it fair to say that it was one of those happy accidents which so often happen in the theatre? For Miss Gates, in her next piece, *We Are Seven* (Maxine Elliott Theatre, 24 December, 1913), convinced the critics that she was happier as a storyteller than as a playwright. Her position in the theatre has yet to be won.

From the theatre direct, however, there has come a play which succeeded because of its universal dramatic and picturesque appeal and which, were the repertory idea again to become a fashion, should place it prominently in a list of permanent American products—George Hazelton and J. H. Benrimo's *The Yellow Jacket* (4 November, 1912), an imaginative creation of real worth, far exceeding anything that Hazelton had ever done before, and defying imitation by Benrimo, who built *The Willow Tree* (Cohan and Harris Theatre, 6 March, 1917) upon it. It convinces the most unhopeful critic that what the American theatre needs is not so much material as an intellectual, a spiritual unity about it which will encourage such writers as Hazelton, Austin Strong, whose *The Toymaker of Nüremburg* (1907) was simple and poetic, Edward Childs Carpenter, whose *The Cinderella Man* (17 January, 1916) was wholesome, and whose *The Pipes of Pan* (6 November, 1917) impressed one with its literary quality, to create rather than to build with an eye on what the manager conceives the public wants.

For it is this lack of guiding principle, this aloofness of dramatic effort, this isolation of the craft, which is quite as wrong as is the idea of a commercial theatre governing the art product. It is surprising, in view of these limitations, how excellently the American dramatist has progressed. We cannot, at present, put by the side of the school of British playwrights who grew in unity against the Censor, who grew in intellectual feeling under the impulse of Ibsen, who related themselves to a literary movement and to a social evolution, any such school of our own. We may be ashamed to claim that our theatre has produced a Broadway school of playwrights, of whom George Broadhurst (with his *Bought and Paid For*, Playhouse, 26 September, 1911) and Bayard Veiller (with his *Within the Law*, Eltinge Theatre, 11 September, 1912) are the typical examples. And the annoying feature of such a tradition is that here and there in the work done by these men there is some real flash, some real creative contribution, showing the inherent ability which purpose would have moulded into distinction. Now and then, out of such workmanship, the theatre gets a whole piece like Eugene Walter's *The Easiest Way* (19 January, 1909), which goes to the bone of realistic condition, cruel, ironic, relating it to a morbid type of emotionalism, of which Pinero's *Iris* is an example. Walter, by a feeling for character and situation, builds better than his contemporaries. His *Paid in Full* (25 February, 1908), barring certain evident situations on which uncertain suspense is built, has as much careful reproduction of average American life as Miss Baker's *Chains* has of English. And Walter's melodramatic sense, in *The Wolf* (Bijou Theatre, 18 April, 1908) and *The Knife* (Bijou Theatre, 12 April, 1917), is better than Veiller's trick method of suspense in such a piece of the theatre as *The 13th Chair* (48th Street Theatre, 20 November, 1917).

The American dramatist has always taken his logic secondhand; he has always allowed his theatrical sense to be a slave to managerial circumstance. The new drama of reality is not based on snap appreciation or judgment. Imagine John Galsworthy writing *Justice* after reading someone else's impression of the cell system of prison life. Yet Charles Klein wrote *The Lion and the Mouse* after reading Ida Tarbell's *History of the Standard Oil Trust*, and Edward Sheldon wrote his one political play, *The Boss* (30 January, 1911), after reading an editorial in *Collier's Weekly*. No drama can be built truly unless one feels deeply the materials used. Sheldon's *The Nigger* (New Theatre, 4 December, 1909) shows every evidence—however effective the situation—of the author's learning of the Southern problem from books read at Harvard University. It has none of the innate sincerity of Moody's *The Great Divide* or Alice

Brown's *Children of Earth*, written out of inherited feeling for spiritual yearnings and ancestral prejudices. Sheldon, cleverly alive to drama,—one of the many men who have come out of university courses specially dedicated to dramatic technique, like Professor Baker's Workshop at Harvard,—has always been entertaining, with a dexterity which might have gone far had he not, later in his youthful career, been swamped by managerial and actor demands—as when he dramatized Sudermann's *The Song of Songs* (Eltinge Theatre, 22 December, 1914). His first play, *Salvation Nell* (17 November, 1908), showed freshness of atmosphere; but it was brought to distinction by Mrs. Fiske, and it had none of the ironic intent of Shaw's *Major Barbara*. Even in the creating of atmosphere, Sheldon has not always been happy. His *Romance* (10 February, 1913) has none of the real New York flavour of Fitch's *Captain Jinks of the Horse Marines* (4 February, 1901).

With no philosophic body of ideas moving American drama, it is surprising what an excellent number of plays can be mentioned as illustrative of certain definite types of drama. It is not a dead creative field which can point to the high comedy of A. E. Thomas's *Her Husband's Wife* (9 May, 1910), Thompson Buchanan's *A Woman's Way* (22 February, 1909), Harry James Smith's *Mrs. Bumpstead Leigh* (Lyceum Theatre, 3 April, 1911), and Jesse Lynch Williams's *Why Marry?* (Astor Theatre, 25 December, 1917). Perhaps these examples are overtopped by Langdon Mitchell's *The New York Idea* (Lyric Theatre, 19 November, 1906), which has an irony of universal import—a tang of the Restoration drama, without its blatant vulgarity—a critical sense of manners at once timely and for ever true. This ability shown by Mitchell makes one deplore the time spent by him on dramatizations like *Becky Sharp* (12 September, 1899) and *Pendennis* (26 October, 1916).

We may point with just pride to examples of drama of social condition like Charles Kenyon's *Kindling* (Daly's Theatre, 3 December, 1911) and Medill Patterson's *Rebellion* (Maxine Elliott's Theatre, 3 October, 1911). And, even with its excrescences of bad taste, Louis K. Anspacher's *The Unchastened Woman* (9 October, 1915) possessed marked distinction of characterization. In the sphere of simple human comedy, Winchell Smith's *The Fortune Hunter* (4 September, 1909) and

J. Hartley Manners's *Peg o' My Heart* (Cort Theatre, 20 December, 1912), are typical; while Elmer Reizenstein's *On Trial* (31 August, 1914), with its "cut back" scenes, showed the direct influence of moving-picture technique on dramatic writing. There are hosts of American farces, true to type, racy with American foibles, like Rupert Hughes's *Excuse Me* (Gaiety Theatre, 13 February, 1911), Roi Cooper Megrue's *It Pays to Advertise* (Cohan Theatre, 8 September, 1914), Augustin McHugh's *Officer 666* (Gaiety Theatre, 12 August, 1912), Avery Hopwood and Mary Roberts Rinehart's *Seven Days* (Astor Theatre, 10 November, 1909).

One may point to Rachel Crothers's *The Three of Us* (17 October, 1906) and *A Man's World* (8 February, 1910) and say she is example of how a woman, anxious to show unity of purpose in her work, has been forced later into catering to popular demand. One may deplore that Margaret Mayo's cleverness of technique was used for the creation of such an advertising catch-piece as *Twin Beds*—which failed even to win the soldiers in cantonment or afield during the past war.[1] One may applaud the theatre atmosphere of James Forbes's *The Chorus Lady* (1 September, 1906), and yet see his limitations in the blind way he, like his contemporaries, gropes about for some external novelty.

The unfortunate thing is that the American drama has had

---

[1] It is too early to state what effect the entertainment of the soldier will have on the future theatre. When the Government mobilized men in cantonments it established a Liberty Theatre at each military centre. To this, entertainments were sent by an organized committee which drew upon the commercial theatre as well as upon the amateur. The draft army itself was so full of dramatic talent, so many writers and musicians found themselves in uniform, that in addition to professional entertainment sent to the camp, the soldiers created an army drama, rich in humour and local colour. Community interest centred itself in aiding the Government, whose sole desire was, both at home and abroad, to maintain the morale of men suddenly drawn by the draft from normal life and occupation. Community houses were established in towns nearest cantonments and embarkation points, and these community centres may give impulse to the community theatre. Certain it is that the Government has found amusement a "war necessity," and has determined, in peace times, to maintain Government theatres at military posts. If in war time the theatre has made itself necessary, does it not follow that some day the Government, regarding the theatre as a necessary social institution for the American people, will give it Congressional support in its artistic maintenance, and recognize its importance by having it represented in the Presidential Cabinet by a Secretary of Fine Arts? This might do much to give direction and purpose to future American playwriting.

many brilliant promises which have finally thinned out and never materialized. At the present moment we have every reason to believe that Clare Kummer (*Good Gracious, Annabelle*, Republic Theatre, 31 October, 1916, and *A Successful Calamity*, Booth Theatre, 5 February, 1917), Robert Housam (*The Gypsy Trail*, Plymouth Theatre, 4 December, 1917), the Hattons, W. J. Hurlbut, and Channing Pollock will contribute something to the future theatre.

The drama activity is constant, but uneven and fitful in quality. There is a depression somewhere, as there always has been in the theatre, and that depression has resulted, at times, in impetuous rebellion against the manner in which the theatre is run. While the democratic mass still supports musical comedy, which is as much our national art as goldenrod is our national flower; while the moving picture has deflected many pens into channels of scenario writing,—as it has deflected actors from the legitimate stage,—there still seems to be a public clamouring for a theatre of art and ideas. The spirit of secession, upon which the Shaw-Galsworthy-Barker school of playwrights flourished in England, seems at times to have flared up in America. We have had our Independent Theatres, our National Art Theatre Societies, our New Theatres, our Leagues for the support of the better drama. But these, while having some permanent effects, have not as yet changed the face of theatrical conditions. Even the New Theatre (which opened 6 November, 1909, and lasted nearly three years)—an institution begun on a money guarantee rather than on a body of ideas and a public that believed in them—was able to get from the drama market but one original American play for its repertory (Sheldon's *The Nigger*), unless we include Mary Austin's *The Arrow Maker* (27 February, 1911)—a thoughtful, accurate study of Indian life.

What, therefore, seems to be the salvation of the artist of the theatre? How will he gain his freedom from the dictates of the commercial manager? One way out was hailed by Percy MacKaye and others—the rise of the civic spirit, which caught hold of the idea begun in England by Louis N. Parker, who revived the conception of the mediæval guild pageant and applied it to local history. To the standard of this idea there flocked numberless enthusiasts: MacKaye, Thomas Wood Stevens, head of the Drama Department of the Carnegie School of Technology in Pittsburgh, William C. Langdon, of the Russell Sage Foundation. It became a social matter as well as an art matter. Towns, cities, localities dug deep into the public treasury, and spectacles—suggesting a community of interest like the New Orleans Mardi Gras, but actually based on a more self-conscious attempt at celebration—have encouraged a type of drama requiring special writing. But the pageant is not the popular form of drama which will satisfy democratic America. Nor has the pageant changed the face of the American theatre.

But what it did help to do was to awaken in communities an art consciousness. Individuals began to take pride in materials out of which local drama might be constructed. In addition this interest in pageantry, which called on the co-operation of the amateur spirit, made people all over the country feel that in the theatre they had heretofore possessed no participatory voice. For the public was coming more to understand the theatre and the drama, through the reading of plays, through books on the drama's history, through extension lectures on the theatre, through increasing numbers of courses in the practice and theory of the art of the theatre. And they began looking on the picture in their minds of the ideal theatre, and then on the actual commercial playhouse in their towns as run by the commercial manager; they compared the plays they liked to read with the plays they were forced by the Trust's system of "booking" to witness season in and season out. And the impression was not favourable to the old régime.

This critical attitude is behind the secession which is going on now (1919) in the theatre. Drama groups all through the country have sprung up, and whether it be in Boston, New York, Baltimore, Cleveland, Detroit, Chicago, and so on to the Pacific coast, the secession impulse is the same: a little theatre, managed by some radical artist, has sprung up. Apparently there is no compromise: the old theatre must go; the new theatre and the new art must reign instead. These theatres are independent of each other, though they exchange plays; they have no unifying idea which brings them close together; they are working in their separate ways, and upholding their own philosophies, which are not always philosophies in accord with the American spirit. Being secessionists, they fly far afield in their interpretation of American life; they are youthful. But their presence has already pointed a way to a more national unity in the art of the theatre. They have called forth scenic artists of their own, and in Robert Jones the regular manager has found a treasure from the amateur ranks. They have created schools of playwrights, like the Washington Square Players, the Provincetown Players, the Wisconsin Players. But if they ever expect to have real influence on the theatre as an institution they have yet to bring themselves out of amateur execution into the dignified ranks of the professional.

The little theatre, *per se*, is a misnomer; it has been carried too far. Art has often been cramped in a thimble. The amateur has built a small theatre because the large theatre was unwieldy for him. But the future salvation of the theatre has nothing to do with size. The little theatre has encouraged the one-act play, of which form George Middleton and Percival Wilde have been excellent exponents, and Theodore Dreiser, with his *Plays Natural and Supernatural*, a surprising one; but though the one-act play has great possibility it is not to be the reforming element in the theatre. What really matters is that the public taste is having a free outlet in its amusement. It is showing the manager that amusement governed by the cost of production is bound to debar from the theatre much that is good, much that the American dramatist would like to do which is of an experimental nature, but for which heretofore there has been no outlet. These little theatres bring to mind the possibilities of regional repertory and regional circuits; they point to less extravagance of material in the theatre, more dependence, in scene, plot, and literary expression, on the imaginative aliveness of audiences. It is in such atmosphere, which must sooner or later be recognized by the theatre at large, that the future American dramatist will work.

CHAPTER XIX

Later Magazines

IN an earlier volume of this history[1] will be found a record of the beginnings of periodical literature in America, and some account of the many ambitious attempts made by magazine editors and publishers before the middle of the nineteenth century. Since 1850 individual mistakes and failures have been more numerous than before, but there have been a few successes, and magazines as a class have attained a position of great importance. In fact, it is hardly an overstatement to say that the rise of the magazine has been the most significant phenomenon in the development of American publishing. The reading of magazines has come to be far more common than the reading of books. Thousands of persons who would resent the imputation that they are lacking in culture read almost no books at all; and thousands more read only those which they obtain at a public library. No home, however, in which there is pretence of intellectual interest is without magazines, which are usually read by all members of the family. This gain in the prestige of the magazine is due in part to the desire of many readers to be strictly up-to-date, in part to clubbing rates and special offers which are presented with an assiduity that book publishers rarely equal, but chiefly to the better reason that the magazines offer the writings of the best authors, artistically printed and often admirably illustrated, far cheaper than such work can be purchased elsewhere.

This generosity of offering on the part of the magazines is made possible by an illogically liberal postal policy and by the development of modern advertising. A century ago, and even much later, a magazine carried but a few pages of advertising

[1] Book II, Chap. xx.

mostly announcements of books and articles of stationery. The great development of advertising did not begin until some time after the Civil War, and it perhaps reached its climax about the close of the century. At that time many magazines printed more advertising pages than pages of text. In an earlier day the magazine had derived its revenue from its readers—from yearly subscriptions and from the sale of odd copies. In order to meet expenses the subscription price was placed high, and this price, in turn, kept the number of readers down. Moreover, the fear of alienating subscribers led the publisher to continue on his mailing list many persons who were hopelessly in arrears. The printer's bill often consumed the greater part of the total income, and both editorial salaries and payments to contributors were meagre. The addition of a large revenue from advertising made it possible to cut the subscription price to the amount that would secure the largest circulation; for advertising rates are determined chiefly by the circulation, and if they can be made to yield enough the receipts from subscriptions become an item of minor importance. It is said that in some states of the market the blank paper on which a successful magazine was printed has cost as much as the publisher received for the edition. Contributors, editorial and office expenses, printer's bills, and profits were all paid from advertising. The receipts from this source were so large as to make possible honorariums to authors far greater than had been usual before, and large enough to tempt into the pages of the more enterprising magazines almost any writer whom the editor might desire.

Short stories, which have proved so important a part of American literature during the last fifty years, have almost invariably made their appearance in magazines. By far the greater number of novels by writers of distinction have been published as serials before they were issued in book form. A considerable amount of poetry, many essays, and even historical writings of scholarly importance have found a place in the better popular magazines.

These changes have been accompanied by the good and the questionable effects that always accompany the democratization of culture. It has been well that the patron of the newsstand should be able to procure, sometimes for so small a sum as a dime, a periodical that contained work by the best living authors. It has been a misfortune that magazines which called themselves literary should be in the control of men who valued literature chiefly for its indirect effect on advertising receipts, and who mixed contributions signed by great names with others whose merit was a showy and specious appeal to the mass of readers. Nor has the offer of high pay to contributors been an unmixed blessing. The great author who was aware that the editor cared more for his name than for literary merit has been tempted to print work that he must have known was unworthy; and the young man or woman just coming into notice has been persuaded by an exploiting publisher to write too hastily. All the phenomena just mentioned can, however, best be traced in connection with a brief survey of some of the more important magazines.

It will be impossible, in the brief space allotted to this chapter, to discuss or even to name all the magazines with which the student of American literature may find himself concerned. There have been informational magazines, which made much of the timeliness of their articles; scientific and professional journals, popular, semi-popular, and technical; journals of sports; juveniles; and many others not easily classified. The changes of greatest importance have been the death or metamorphosis of the old-fashioned quarterlies and other heavy reviews, and the rise of two groups of popular magazines. One of these groups is represented by the *Atlantic*, *Harper's*, *Scribner's Monthly*, afterward the *Century*, and *Scribner's Magazine*, which all pride themselves on maintaining the highest practicable standard of literary and artistic excellence; the other and later group is represented by *The Ladies' Home Journal*, *McClure's*, *The American Magazine*, and a number more which frankly make an appeal to the widest possible constituency of fairly intelligent readers.

In 1850 the chief quarterlies and reviews in existence were *The North American Review*, *Brownson's Quarterly Review*, *The Christian Examiner*, *The New Englander*, *The Democratic Review*, *The American Whig Review*, *The Princeton Review*, *The Southern Literary Messenger*, and *The Southern Quarterly Review*. The decline of the quarterlies had already begun in England, and of the American list named above but one lived virtually unchanged through the Civil War. This was *The North Ameri-can Review*, which since its establishment in 1815 had been the leader in its class. In 1850 it was continuing its steady course under the editorship of Professor Francis Bowen. In the early fifties Professor Bowen was succeeded by Dr. Andrew Preston Peabody, who continued in control until after the Civil War had begun. During these years the *Review* maintained its original character as a sound, scholarly, if not a very virile journal, modelled as far as might be on the great English quarterlies. Its small circulation was distributed throughout the country, and when political and sectional animosities became strong it declined all controversial articles that might alienate subscribers. At last it reached the condition which Lowell described in a well-known letter to Motley: "It wanted three chief elements to be successful. It wasn't thoroughly, that is thick and thinly, loyal, it wasn't lively, and it had no particular opinions on any particular subject. It was an eminently safe periodical, and accordingly was in great danger of running aground." Lowell and Charles Eliot Norton became joint editors in 1864, and succeeded in giving the *Review* new force and character, though they naturally rendered it at the same time more provincial. About 1873 Henry Adams and Henry Cabot Lodge assumed the editorship. During the presidential campaign of 1876 these gentlemen found themselves at variance with the publishers regarding matters of editorial policy, and withdrew. The *Review* was then sold to Allen Thorndike Rice, who moved it from Boston to New York and made it first a bi-monthly, later a monthly. Since this time its character has still further changed, until current issues, with their short semi-popular and timely articles, bear slight resemblance to those of 1850. Since no other American magazine has lasted, even in name, for a hundred years, the centenary of the *North American* in 1915 attracted much attention.

The other New England reviews that were in existence in 1850 or that were established later had something of a theological cast. Orestes A. Brownson in *Brownson's Quarterly Review* (founded in 1844) continued to present his personal interpretation of the Roman Catholic faith until 1864, when he began a "National Series," announcing that the *Quarterly* "ceases to be a theological review" and "is to be rational and secular.

devoted to philosophy, science, politics, literature, and the general interests of civilization, especially American civilization." After one volume of this series the *Review* was abandoned for eight years. In 1873 the indefatigable editor renewed it for the purpose, as he said, of showing that he was still loyal to the church; and he again protested this loyalty when in 1875 he brought the venture to a final close. While Brownson was erratic in literary as well as in other judgments, he was an original thinker and a forceful personality, and the reviews of secular books in his quarterly are of constant value to the student of American literature and American thought.

The New Englander, founded at Yale College in 1843 to support evangelical Christianity though not avowedly a theological journal, passed through a variety of changes, and in time found itself devoted chiefly to history and economics. In 1885 it was known as *The New Englander and Yale Review*, and in 1892 it became *The Yale Review*. In 1896 it relinquished history to the newly founded *American Historical Review*, and when in 1911 the American Economic Association made plans for a journal of its own the occupation of the *Review* was gone. It then passed under the editorship of Wilbur L. Cross, who has continued it as a general literary magazine and review, printing poems, descriptive essays, and timely articles of moderate length, as well as more serious dissertations. For a time *The New Englander and Yale Review* tried the experiment of monthly and then of bi-monthly issue, but for the great part of its career the journal has been, as it is now, published quarterly.

The Christian Examiner (dating from 1824), a bi-monthly which bore something the same relation to the faculty of Harvard that *The New Englander* did to that of Yale, continued to 1869. It contained a large number of articles on purely literary topics, some of them fully the equal of those in the *North American*.

In connection with these semi-theological periodicals of New England may be conveniently mentioned *The Princeton Review*, which expressed the devotion of the faculty of Princeton College to conservative Presbyterianism, and was frankly a religious journal. It always contained, however, some articles of general literary interest. During its career from 1825 to 1884 it under-

went changes in name and in place and frequency of publication that need not be traced here.

New York was the centre for political rather than religious
reviews. *The Democratic Review*, founded in 1838, partook
somewhat of the nature of a general magazine. Among its
contributors were many of the most prominent American
authors, including the New Englanders; and it also accepted
contributions from relatively unknown writers, like Whitman
in his early period. The contents included a little poetry and
fiction, much on historical and political subjects, and some
literary criticism. For a time *The Democratic Review* was a
periodical of large relative importance, but it must have felt
keenly the competition of the popular illustrated *Harper's
Monthly*, and later of the *Atlantic*. Between 1853 and its death
in 1859 it adopted sundry changes of name, and tried experiments in monthly, weekly, and quarterly publication. *The
American Whig Review* had a briefer career, beginning in 1845
and coming to an end in 1852. It was a monthly, containing
some verse and fiction, and a considerable amount of general
literary criticism.

Among later attempts made to publish a review in New
York may be mentioned *The New York Quarterly*, which ran
from 1852 to 1855, *The National Quarterly Review*, 1860 to
1880, and *The International Review*, a bi-monthly, 1874 to 1883.
All these, and especially the two last mentioned, show distinguished names on the list of contributors, and contain
articles of value. Their successive deaths were doubtless due
to the fact that the form of periodical to which they belonged
had had its day. The latest venture, *The Unpartizan Review*
(until 1919 the *Unpopular Review*), established in 1914 by
Henry Holt and Company, and especially in charge of the
senior member of that firm, frankly makes an appeal to a
limited group of readers, and gives an opportunity for the
publication of clever and valuable essays that might not see the
light elsewhere.

The South, with its conservative tastes in literature, has
perhaps offered of late the best field for the quarterly. *The
Southern Quarterly Review*, published at Charleston and at
Columbia from 1842 to 1857, had distinction of the old-fashioned sort, and contained articles on science, law, philosophy,

and literature, and many brief book notices. *The Sewanee Review*, another quarterly, established in 1892, still continues. Though it is closely connected with the University of the South its contributors are not all local, and it has maintained its dignity and its literary tradition well. *The South Atlantic Quarterly*, edited at Trinity College, Durham, South Carolina, began publication in 1902, and has also kept to a uniformly high standard.

The most important popular magazines in existence in 1850 were the *Knickerbocker* in New York, *Godey's Lady's Book* and *Graham's* in Philadelphia, and *The Southern Literary Messenger* in Richmond. The *Knickerbocker* felt keenly the competition of the newer magazines, but it continued to be published through the Civil War, in its dying struggles adopting the name of *American Monthly*, with *Knickerbocker* as a sub-title, and in a final volume, January to June, 1865, dropping the old name altogether. Though never distinguished, the *Knickerbocker* had an honourable tradition, and offered a place of publication for many American writers. *Godey's Lady's Book* was continued to 1876, though it lost much of its popularity and almost all its literary prestige before its death. A magazine devoting much attention to the fashions and to fancy work never seems the most dignified medium of publication, but in the height of its glory *Godey's* was able to command original contributions from authors of the highest rank. *Graham's*, which during the editorship of Poe and for a few years thereafter had been the greatest of the Philadelphia magazines and one of the most honourable mediums of publication for authors all over the country, had deteriorated greatly by the mid-century, though it struggled on until 1859. *The Southern Literary Messenger* survived at Richmond, with better quality than might have been expected during the war, until 1864; but its period of greatest importance was earlier, and it has already been treated in another chapter.[1]

Of the four leading popular magazines of first rank the most important, though not the earliest in point of time, was *The Atlantic Monthly*. Emerson, Hawthorne, Longfellow, Whittier, and Holmes had been writing for more than twenty years, and Lowell for more than ten, before New England maintained a

[1] See Book II, Chap. xx.

general literary magazine of high grade. It was not till the stirring of political and sociological movements emphasized the need of an organ in which distinctly New England thought could find expression that the *Atlantic* was founded. The real father of the *Atlantic* was Francis H. Underwood, who projected a magazine as early as 1853 when he was in the offices of John P. Jewett and Co. of Boston. This firm had come into prominence as the publishers of *Uncle Tom's Cabin*, then at the height of its fame, and a serial story by Mrs. Stowe was to have been a feature of the new periodical. Financial considerations prevented the appearance of the magazine as planned. After the firm of Jewett failed, Underwood became connected with Phillips, Sampson and Co., and at length persuaded them to undertake the venture. According to a familiar story the plan was really launched at a dinner given by Phillips, the senior member of the firm, to Underwood, Cabot, Motley, Longfellow, Lowell, Holmes, and Emerson. Later, Lowell was decided upon as the first editor. To Holmes is given the credit of suggesting the name "Atlantic Monthly." Underwood went to England in the interest of the project, and elicited promises of support from some English writers. Later a number of manuscript offerings from these men were entrusted to Charles Eliot Norton, who was returning from Europe, and were mysteriously lost *en route*. New Englanders afterward felt a pious thankfulness for this accident, since it helped to make more certain that the *Atlantic* should be distinctly American.[1]

The first issue of the magazine, that for November, 1857, contained contributions from Emerson, Whittier, Lowell, C. E. Norton, J. T. Trowbridge, and others. The most notable feature was *The Autocrat of the Breakfast-Table*, which ran as a serial in the first twelve numbers, and was followed in successive years by *The Professor at the Breakfast-Table* and *The Professor's Story* [*Elsie Venner*]. With the failure of the publishers in 1859 the *Atlantic* passed to Ticknor and Fields, and a little later James T. Fields, the junior member of this firm, succeeded Lowell in editorial charge. Fields was one of the few publishers who have been regarded by most of their authors as

[1] See Dr. Edward Waldo Emerson's *The Early History of the Saturday Club*, 1918, Chap. II.

personal friends, and in many ways he made an ideal editor. No other magazine has come so near to comprehending the best that American writers had to offer as did the *Atlantic* during these early years. It was fortunate in having so many of its contributors within easy reach of Boston, and the dinners of the Atlantic Club—which seems never to have been a club—and of virtually the same group of men in the Saturday Club have often been celebrated in reminiscence and history. The jealous charge that only New Englanders were welcome to the pages of the *Atlantic* was probably never well founded, though it was natural that New England standards should be applied in judging contributions. It was the *Atlantic* which first recognized the value of Bret Harte's early tales, and drew the author from the West; and this is but one example of the reaching out of the magazine for what was best everywhere. A list of the contributors for the first fifty years would lack but few names of American writers of distinction, and these would in almost all cases be men who were committed to some other publisher. Yet perhaps after all the case is best put by Howells when he says: "The *Atlantic Monthly* . . . was distinctively a New England magazine, though from the first it has been characterized by what was more national, what was more universal, in the New England temperament."

Successive editors of *The Atlantic Monthly* have been James Russell Lowell (1857–61), James T. Fields (1861–71), William Dean Howells (1871–81), Thomas Bailey Aldrich (1881–90), Horace E. Scudder (1890–98), Walter Hines Page (1898–99), Bliss Perry (1899–1908), Ellery Sedgwick (1908–). While the development of the illustrated magazines during the seventies deprived the *Atlantic* of its conspicuous pre-eminence it long continued to maintain its high standard and its distinctive character. In 1908 it was sold by the Houghton Mifflin Company, the direct successors of Ticknor and Fields, to the Atlantic Publishing Company, of which Ellery Sedgwick is president, and under his editorship it has increased its circulation without becoming cheapened, though to conservative readers who recollect former days it seems to have departed sadly from its old traditions.

Harper's Monthly Magazine, the first of the greater illustrated magazines, was established in 1850 by Harper and

Brothers, publishers, of New York. It was founded, as a member of the firm said, as a "tender" to the publishing business. At first the contents were taken from English journals. The prospectus, issued in 1850, announced:

The Publishers of the *New Monthly Magazine* intend . . . to place everything of the periodical literature of the day, which has permanent value and commanding interest, in the hands of all who have the slightest desire to become acquainted with it. . . . The magazine will transfer to its pages as rapidly as they may be issued all the continuous tales of Dickens, Bulwer, Croly, Lever, Warren, and other distinguished contributors to British Periodicals: articles of commanding interest from all the leading Quarterly Reviews of both Great Britain and the United States: Critical Notices of the current publications of the day: Speeches and Addresses. . . . A carefully prepared Fashion Plate, and other pictorial illustrations will also accompany each number.

Borrowings were for a time credited to their original sources, but soon this credit was omitted. In a business way the venture was immediately successful, the circulation being given as fifty thousand after six months, and one hundred and thirty thousand after three years. Other magazines, especially those which published chiefly the work of American authors, resented this new competition and the attitude of Harper and Brothers toward international copyright. *The American Whig Review* for July, 1852, prints a long *Letter to the Publishers of Harper's Magazine* signed "An American Writer," which expresses with some show of temper sentiments that were not infrequently uttered. After asking, "Is such a publication calculated to benefit American literature? and secondly, is it just?" the writer continues:

Your publication, gentlemen, with all others of the same nature, is simply a monstrosity; and the more widely it is diffused, the more clearly is its moral ugliness revealed. It is an ever-present, ever-living insult to the brains of Americans, and its indignity is every day increasing in intensity. Heading a select band of English republications, it comes into our literary market month by month, offering a show of matter which no other magazine could present were it fairly paid for, and effectually shutting out the attempts of American publishers from even the chances of a sale. Its contents are often attractive, although, considering the unbounded range of your pillage, I have wondered that they were not better; it displays a large number of well-printed pages, and generally boasts a few thievings from *Punch* hardly up to the style of that very amusing sheet; and it pleases the economical tastes of its readers. As a scheme for making money, I cannot too highly commend your enterprise. It is a manifest improvement of the shopkeeper's maxim of buying in the cheapest market and selling in the dearest, for you do not buy in the market at all. You walk through the array of literary wares which the English nation spreads before you, taking what you please, and giving neither money nor thanks in return. You reproduce what you have so cheaply obtained, and are thus enabled to undersell your more scrupulous competitors. By this process of appropriation and sale, you prove your right to the enviable title of sharp business men, but you also show yourselves utterly destitute of regard for the literary talent of your own countrymen, and for those national opinions and sentiments which are only partially disseminated by the newspapers, and which it is the peculiar province of English literature to supplant and destroy.

In time *Harper's* came more and more to take the work of Americans, and it has long made a practice of printing only original contributions. If during its early career it sinned by ignoring and discouraging American authors, it seemed at a later date almost to sin in the opposite direction. At times it has published so many contributions from a young author of growing popularity as to raise the question whether it was not encouraging hasty and ill-considered writing. Among writers of tales whom it exploited in this way were Richard Harding Davis, Mary E. Wilkins, and Stephen Crane.

The first editor of *Harper's Monthly* was Henry J. Raymond. Henry M. Alden, his successor, was editor for fifty years (1869–1919). Fletcher Harper, a member of the firm, habitually contracted for the serials and for much other fiction, and had a great share in determining the contents of the magazine. Of the special departments which are distinctive of *Harper's Magazine* the most important is "The Editor's Easy Chair." George William Curtis assumed control of this in 1853, and his essays which appeared under this head are among the most delightful of his works. The most distinguished of Curtis's successors in the "Easy Chair" is its present occupant, William Dean Howells. Another department, "The Editor's

Study," has been conducted at different times by William Dean Howells and Charles Dudley Warner. Among the men in charge of "The Editor's Drawer" have been Lewis Gaylord Clark and John Kendrick Bangs.

The early numbers of *Harper's Monthly* each contained a few woodcuts, many of them portraits. The proprietors soon began to pay greater attention to illustration, and in 1856 started an engraving department of their own. Among well-known artists who have been upon the staff are C. S. Reinhart, E. A. Abbey, and A. B. Frost, while many others were frequent contributors of pictures. While *Harper's Magazine* may well claim to be the pioneer among high-class illustrated magazines in America, it was not spurred to its greatest exertions until the appearance of *Scribner's Monthly* in 1870. The rivalry between these two magazines, and later the triangular rivalry engaged in by *Harper's*, the *Century*, and *Scribner's Magazine*, has led to great improvements in the art of engraving and in the technique of printing illustrations. When wood engraving reached what was apparently its highest perfection, attention was turned to process engraving, and later to methods of colour reproduction; and though there have been some freakish and inartistic experiments the pictures in the better American magazines have been worthy accompaniments of the letterpress. The excellence of American illustrating attracted attention in Europe, and the three chief illustrated magazines have each maintained a London edition. That of *Harper's* was begun in 1880; Andrew Lang became editor in 1884.

The second of the greater illustrated periodicals in point of time, *Scribner's Monthly*, began publication in 1870, after *Harper's Magazine* had been in existence for twenty years. The editor and one of the proprietors was Josiah Gilbert Holland, who had made a wide appeal as author of commonplace works in prose and verse, and as successful editor of *The Springfield Republican*. Associated with Dr. Holland in the ownership of the magazine were Roswell Smith and Charles Scribner, head of the well-known firm of book publishers. After the death of Charles Scribner differences arose between the management and the publishing firm of Charles Scribner's Sons, which resulted in the withdrawal of the Scribner interests and a change of name to *The Century Magazine* in 1881. Dr. Holland was to have continued in the editorship, but before the appearance of the first issue of the *Century* he died and was succeeded by Richard Watson Gilder, who from the first had been associate editor. The change of name brought no radical change in scope or policy, and *Scribner's Monthly* and the *Century* constitute virtually an unbroken series from 1870 to the present time.

Dr. Holland was a clever editor who knew what the public wanted. From the first he secured well-known contributors of high rank. A "Publisher's Department," with "A word to our readers," or "A talk with our readers," though relegated to the advertising pages, continued the methods of the old-fashioned personal journalist. Richard Watson Gilder was a man of greater literary ability and finer taste, and though he could hardly have gained initial success for the venture as well as did Holland it is to him that the high rank of the *Century* is largely due. *Scribner's Monthly* at first printed serials by English writers, but later made much of the fact that its longer selections in fiction were all of American origin. Howells's *A Modern Instance* was made a feature of the first volume after the change of name. The *Century* has always given much space to illustrated articles on history. There was something a trifle "journalistic" in a series of articles on the Civil War by Northern and Southern generals, yet even in these the editorial control was such as to insure a reasonable standard of excellence. The *Life of Lincoln* by Nicolay and Hay, large parts of which appeared serially in the *Century*, was of higher grade. In literary criticism E. C. Stedman had, even in the days of *Scribner's Monthly*, contributed articles on the American poets. Without neglecting fiction, poetry, and other general literature the magazine has devoted rather more attention than has *Harper's* to matters of timely, though not of temporary, interest. From the first *Scribner's Monthly* made much of its illustrations, and both directly and by the effect on its competitors its advent had much to do with the improvement of American engraving and printing. It claims credit for originating, in the mechanical department, several practical innovations of value, such as the dry printing of engravings.

Scribner's Magazine (always to be distinguished from *Scribner's Monthly*), published by Charles Scribner's Sons and edited continuously until 1914 by Edward L. Burlingame, first appeared in January, 1887. Like *Harper's Magazine* it is closely associated with a great publishing house, but unlike *Harper's* in the early years it was never a mere "tender to the business." Though announced by a rather conventional prospectus it began auspiciously. Among the earliest contributors were William James, Robert Louis Stevenson, Sarah Orne Jewett, Thomas Nelson Page, Elizabeth Akers, H. C. Bunner, Andrew Lang, Austin Dobson, Charles Edwin Markham, Edith Thomas, Percival Lowell, A. S. Hill, and Thomas A. Janvier; and it has since kept up the high quality and the diversity of material suggested by these names. Like its chief rivals it maintains an English edition.

It is not easy to characterize the distinctions between *Harper's Magazine*, the *Century*, and *Scribner's Magazine* as these have existed for the last thirty years. The long editorships of Alden, Gilder, and Burlingame tended, fortunately, to produce stability and to develop an individuality of tone in the periodicals with which these men were respectively associated. The difference is, however, one of tone merely, and is too subtle to be readily analyzed or phrased. As has been said, the *Century* is distinguished by special attention to history and timely articles, but in fiction, verse, and general essays they are much the same. None has been supported by a clique, party, or school. Most of the greater American writers of the last generation have contributed to at least two, many to all three of these magazines. None of them has had a monopoly of the work of any distinctive and distinguished writer as the *Knickerbocker* had a monopoly of Irving and the *Atlantic* had a monopoly of, for example, Holmes.

Before the middle of the nineteenth century the better magazines had mostly refrained from illustrations, except, perhaps, occasional full-page inserted plates. It was for *Harper's Magazine* and *Scribner's Monthly* to show that pictures in the text were not incompatible with literary dignity and excellence; and they did this by securing the best available literary material, and developing illustrations that were not unworthy to accompany it. In so doing they indirectly and unconsciously helped to prepare the way for the cheaper magazines which sprang into such prominence a few years later.

Among the less successful attempts at a literary magazine were three which bore the name of another distinguished New York publishing house. *Putnam's Monthly Magazine* first appeared in January, 1853, with C. F. Briggs as editor and George William Curtis and Parke Godwin as assistant editors. In introducing itself it said, with an evident glance at *Harper's*, then so conspicuous and so irritating a figure in the magazine world:

A man buys a Magazine to be amused—to be instructed, if you please, but the lesson must be made amusing. He buys it to read in the cars, in his leisure hours at home—in the hotel, at all chance moments. It makes very little difference to him whether the article date from Greece or Guinea if it only interest him. He does not read upon principle, and troubles himself little about copyright and justice to authors. If a man goes to Timbuctoo and describes his visit picturesquely and well, the reader devours the story, and is not at all concerned because the publisher may have broken the author's head or heart, to obtain the manuscript. A popular Magazine must amuse, interest, and instruct, or the public will pass by upon the other side. Nor will it be persuaded to "come over and help us" by any consideration of abstract right. It says, very justly, "if you had no legs, why did you try to walk?"

It is because we are confident that neither Greece nor Guinea can offer the American reader a richer variety of instruction and amusement in every kind, than the country whose pulses throb with his, and whose every interest is his own, that this magazine presents itself today.

This opinion, that for interest American writings could hold their own with those that might be purloined anywhere in the world, must have been pleasing to American authors. The editors gave evidence of their sincerity by preserving the anonymity of articles, letting each stand on its merits. The first volume contained poems by Longfellow and Lowell, and others of the New England group wrote for the magazine. Curtis contributed his *Potiphar Papers* and *Prue and I*, Lowell his *Fireside Travels* and *Moosehead Journal*, and Thoreau his *Cape Cod Papers*. It would seem that a journal so edited and so supported ought at this time to have succeeded, even though in mechanical appearance it was somewhat heavy and unattractive. For reasons not fully explained, but supposedly financial, the house of Putnam sold it after two years, and after three years of deterioration under another management it was merged with *Emerson's Magazine*, which itself died soon after.

Putnam's Magazine, sometimes referred to as a revival of the older *Putnam's Monthly Magazine*, began publication in January, 1868. R. H. Stoddard, E. C. Stedman, and Bayard Taylor were connected with the editorial staff, but the list of contributors was hardly as impressive as that of the former *Putnam's*. According to the frank statement of the publishers this magazine did not pay, and after three years it was merged with the newly founded *Scribner's Monthly*. In 1906 a third *Putnam's* made its appearance, this time *Putnam's Monthly and The Critic*. The last half of the title was retained from an older periodical which was merged in the new. It was a semi-popular, illustrated, bookish journal which lasted with some changes of name until 1910.

The *Galaxy, an Illustrated Magazine of Entertaining Reading* was published in New York from 1866 to 1878. Among contributors to the first volume were William Dean Howells, Henry James, Stedman, Stoddard, Bayard Taylor, Anthony Trollope, William Winter, Phœbe Cary, and C. G. Leland. As might be inferred from the subtitle, the *Galaxy* devoted much space to fiction, yet its quality may be indicated by the fact that when it died its subscription list went to *The Atlantic Monthly*.

In Philadelphia, *Sartain's Union Magazine of Literature and Art* ran its brief course from 1849 to 1852. The proprietor, John Sartain, was one of the greatest of American mezzotint engravers, and the artistic excellence of the plates issued with the magazine may have helped to arouse interest in periodical illustrations of high grade; but the development of later magazine illustration did not lie in the direction of mezzotints. *Lippincott's Magazine of Literature, Science, and Education*, founded in 1868, was at first a fairly solid general magazine, without illustrations. In the competition toward the close of the century it adopted a popular form, with many pictures and a complete novelette in each issue, and boasted in its prospectus: "It offers no problems to solve, has no continued stories to hinder, and appeals to you just when you want it."

Many cities of the South and of the West have had their

literary journals, the brief careers of which are duly chronicled in local histories, but they can hardly claim space in a more general survey. The one exception is *The Overland Monthly*, which began publication at San Francisco in 1868, with Bret Harte as the first editor. An earlier chapter of this history[1] remarks on the number of creditable literary periodicals that were developed in the Ohio Valley while difficulties of communication isolated communities in which there were many persons of intellectual interests. By 1850 the Alleghanies were no longer a serious hindrance to intercourse with Eastern cities, and the magazines of Kentucky, Ohio, and Illinois had lost their chief reason for existence. Soon after the discovery of gold the Pacific slope offered another example of an isolated community with a civilization of its own. The *Overland* was not the first attempt at a literary magazine in San Francisco; and though it had considerable real merit it owes its fame chiefly to Bret Harte. With the completion of the trans-continental railroads the culture of the West was free to merge in that of the nation. The *Overland* ceased publication in 1875. A successor, bearing the same name and established in 1883, is still, however, one of the best of the frankly provincial literary periodicals.

Among the magazines of a more recent generation is *The Ladies' Home Journal*, a periodical of a sort which has always flourished in Philadelphia. This had a small beginning in 1883, and entered on its period of rapid growth with the accession of Edward W. Bok to the editorship in 1889. Bok adopted some of the methods of personal journalism, and thousands of readers who could have named no other magazine editor knew of him, and rejoiced that his career was in outline that of the traditional industrious apprentice. Even more than its predecessor, *Godey's Lady's Book*, *The Ladies' Home Journal* is devoted to household arts, but it has always laid emphasis on the stories, essays, and poems that it published. Many of these make a specious sentimental appeal, but from time to time the *Journal* has contained noteworthy contributions from men of the rank of Kipling and Howells. Many of the million readers which it long boasted firmly believed it to be a literary magazine, and its influence on popular taste must have been considerable.

The most significant group of later popular magazines had

[1] See Book II. Chap. xx.

its phenomenal development in New York during the last de
cade of the nineteenth century and the earlier years of the
twentieth. The most conspicuous members of this group, with
the dates of their establishment were: *The Cosmopolitan* (1886,
founded in Rochester but removed to New York in 1887),
Munsey's (1891), *McClure's* (1893), *Everybody's* (1899), *The
American* (1906), *Hampton's* (1908). All of these were profusely
illustrated, mostly with half-tone engravings; all of them were
supported chiefly by the advertising pages—the improvement
of the half-tone process and the development of advertising
being the two things that made them economically possible.
All of them were planned as business enterprises, rather than as
mediums for the literary expression of certain communities or
groups of authors. All of them sold for some years, as a result
of competition, at the surprisingly low rate of ten cents a copy
or one dollar a year. All of them attained large circulations,
estimated in several instances as nearly three-fourths of a
million copies of each issue.

Of those mentioned, *McClure's* may be taken as a type, and
as most interesting to the student of literature, though it was
not the earliest in the field, it did not attain the greatest circulation, and in recent years it has suffered a more serious decline
than some of its rivals. S. S. McClure, the projector and editor,
had established a syndicate which bought the work of prominent authors and sold the rights of publication to newspapers.
He was thus able to pay sums which obtained manuscripts from
the more distinguished writers of the day, English and American. Among those who contributed, often of their very best
work, to the early volumes of the magazine were Stevenson,
Kipling, Thomas Hardy, Andrew Lang, Conan Doyle, William
Dean Howells, Joel Chandler Harris, F. Marion Crawford,
Edward Everett Hale, George W. Cable, and others of similar
rank. It is not, however, great names or even meritorious
articles bought and inserted at random which give character
to a literary periodical. In its best days *McClure's* was in no
sense a rival of the *Atlantic*, *Harper's*, the *Century*, or *Scribner's*, though at times these could hardly boast more impressive
lists of contributors. It did not even equal in popularity some
of the other magazines of its own class. Its greatest success
was due, not to the work of the well-known writers named

above, but to articles of a sensational and timely nature—the so-called "literature of exposure." The formula for these articles was simple. It consisted in adhering strictly to the literal truth, but in so arranging and proportioning statements of fact as to show most disadvantageously some person, corporation, or other organization of which the public mind was predisposed to believe the worst. Although the formula was simple, the technique attained was in its way masterly. The writers were mostly persons of journalistic instincts and practical newspaper training who on giving evidence of unusual aptitude for this kind of writing were regularly employed on the staff of the magazine. Ida Tarbell, who had previously compiled a life of Napoleon and a popular life of Lincoln, prepared a hostile history of the Standard Oil Company. Ray Stannard Baker also wrote sensationally on economic questions, and attacked other corporations. Lincoln Steffens confined himself especially to political corruption. These flourished in *McClure's* from 1902 or earlier until 1906, when they associated themselves with the newly-established *American Magazine*, and *McClure's* developed a new staff of workers according to the same models. In 1906 President Roosevelt in a famous address expressed his disapproval of this kind of writing, and applied to its authors the term "muck-rakers," which with the derivative "muck-raking" has since been accepted as a fitting designation. Popular judgment agreed on the whole with the President, and while this type of writing is not even now extinct, it gradually lost its vogue. Though it may fairly be said to have begun with *McClure's Magazine*, it was really symptomatic of a tendency of the time, and most other popular magazines with the exception of *Munsey's* indulged in it. One of the most famous series of muck-raking articles, in some ways more sensational than anything in *McClure's*, was *Frenzied Finance*, by Thomas W. Lawson, published in *Everybody's*.

Most of the magazines named above are still issued though in most instances with change of format, and at an increased price; but they no longer exert so great an influence. It is too early to comment with certainty on their significance; yet they cannot be ignored in a study of nineteenth century literature, even if they reached their culmination just after 1900. Indeed, it may appear that many of the literary tendencies that developed during the nineteenth century were concentrated and delivered to the twentieth century through this peculiar development of periodical literature. If irresistible forces are making toward the democratization of literature, then the rise of these magazines marks an important step in the movement. They brought writers who were unquestionably the best of their time to a great number of readers who might not otherwise have known them. On the other hand, they brought into magazine writing some of the qualities that had been developed by the modern journalist. Bad as the muck-raking articles were in content and temper, they showed forth methods of popular exposition that later essayists, even the most conservative, are now adopting. Nor have the older magazines escaped the influence of their younger rivals. *The Atlantic Monthly*, long the exponent of the most reserved and bookish tradition, has for its present editor a man who received his training with *Frank Leslie's Monthly, The American Magazine*, and *McClure's;* and while old-fashioned readers may now and then regret the resulting change of tone, it would be rash to say that the change was all for the worse, or to feel that the outlook for periodical literature today was not as bright as it has been at any period of our national life.

CHAPTER XX

Newspapers Since 1860

WHEN the sudden beginning of the Civil War changed the whole current of national life, the newspapers of the country were in many respects prepared to report and interpret the great event. Had the war been clearly foreseen for a decade, more adequate preparation could hardly have been made to adjust the service to the momentous changes which came so swiftly. Ingenuity and aggressiveness in the gathering of news, the rise and growth of which has been sketched in another chapter,[1] had quickened the whole profession. The telegraph, which was little more than an experiment when the Mexican War came on, had by 1860 been extended to all parts of the country directly affected by the war. The revolution thereby created in methods of gathering, transmitting, and vending news had been accomplished in the interval of twelve or fifteen years, and journalism was becoming accustomed to the new order. The growing use and expensiveness of the telegraph had already led to the formation of press associations. And at almost the same time the invention of the modern *papier maché* process of stereotyping, together with improvements in printing presses, removed mechanical obstructions which until 1861 had curbed the production of newspapers. With all these general developments there had been, until a few weeks before hostilities began, little detailed preparation to meet the actual crisis; the press was not on a war footing; there were no experienced war correspondents.

Newspapers had spread over the whole country, flowing into the Central valleys and plains and down the Western slopes

[1] See Book II, Chap. XXI.

along with the most enterprising of the early settlers. When Lincoln read his first inaugural, only four states or territories in the Union were without newspapers to report it; twelve years later, not one was without a newspaper to chronicle the defeat and death of the great journalist who sought the Presidency. News style had taken essentially the form still to be found in the more conservative papers of the country; headlines were still inconspicuous, never more than one column wide, and seldom revealing the news they topped. The custom among many papers of sending correspondents throughout the South and the Far West to report conditions and events was now to prove useful preparation for the period when the South became the greatest source of news in the world. Foreign correspondence after its rapid spread in the forties had been somewhat more fully organized, although it was no more ably conducted. The pressure of domestic events led to some neglect of the foreign field, just before and during the war, and it was not until the short Franco-Prussian conflict that European affairs again received much attention from the American press.

Never before was a war so well reported as was the American Civil War—so fully, promptly, and accurately. Although it is generally believed that Englishmen in the Crimea virtually created modern war correspondence, its real beginnings had been made years before by American reporters in the war with Mexico, and the whole system of reporting the progress of war and presenting it fully and promptly to the public was developed very nearly to perfection by American journalistic enterprise in the Civil War. The problems confronting the newspapers when the war began were the greatest ever faced by journalists. The size of country to be covered, the number of armies and of widely separated actions, and the still primitive means of communication tested the valour and ingenuity that sought to overcome them. When the first gun was fired no paper had a system for reporting from the front, though in the weeks before that event several of them had begun to send men to important places by way of precaution. Before Sumter fell, the New York *Herald* had received enough papers from its correspondents to furnish a roster of the Southern army which convinced the leaders that there was a spy in the Confederate war office, and in a short time after Sumter a net of reporters was spread all over the South, placed at every important point, and sent with every army. The *Herald* quickly built a great news-gathering organization, with the *Tribune* and the *Times* following as close competitors, while every important paper in the country sent at least one correspondent to Washington or to the front. These men, nearly all inexperienced in their special duties, but called upon to report a more rapid and long-continued series of military movements than had ever before been recorded, not only accomplished a remarkable series of individual achievements but set a new standard in that type of journalism.

The task of organizing such corps of correspondents as were sent out by the *Herald*, *Tribune*, and *Times*, of New York, of discharging the normal functions of the papers, and of supplying the unprecedented demand for newspapers, extraordinary as it was, did not lead to many important advances in journalistic practice. The changes due to the war were mainly economic. In the South, which had depended almost entirely on the North for its supplies, the lack of paper was soon felt and before peace came had caused the suspension of many papers. Many others were suppressed by Northern military authorities. The press of the South, indeed, lost much and gained little or nothing by the war. A rigid government censorship and news bureau deprived those papers even of such opportunities as other circumstances might have permitted. Less enterprise was manifest in news-gathering than in printing official communications and editorials. But it may be said that, although before the war began there was much difference of Southern editorial opinion regarding the advisability of secession, after the decision was made, a united press supported the Confederate authorities.

Censorship in the North was unorganized, spasmodic, sometimes oppressive, and generally ineffectual. The Post Office Department then, as more recently, denied the privilege of the mails to papers adjudged to be treasonable, even to some which criticized the use of force against the seceding states. Correspondents were in some cases welcomed and trusted by the military authorities; in others they were excluded. Early in the war a censor was placed in the telegraph office at Washington; but official oversuppression finally brought about a reaction which led to a more liberal policy. The natural desire of the authorities to prevent the circulation of information that might be useful to the enemy, and the nervousness caused by the many Copperhead papers opposed to the war, friendly to the South, or unfriendly to the government, led to much official criticism of mere news enterprise and to acts of suppression by the authorities. For instance General McClellan requested the War Department to suppress the New York *Times* for printing a map of the works and a statement of forces beyond the Potomac, no part of which had, in fact, come from other than public sources. The New York *World* and *Journal of Commerce* were suspended for several days because they unsuspectingly published a bogus presidential proclamation. The Chicago *Times*, a leading Copperhead paper, was forced to suspend publication for a short time because of disloyal utterances. The strong feeling engendered by the conflict led to many acts of mob violence against newspapers, most of them in smaller towns, and in the aggregate, scores of them were as a result suspended or destroyed, though relatively fewer fatalities resulted than from the earlier acts of violence against the abolitionist press. The most important mob attack on a great city paper was directed against the New York *Tribune* during the draft riots on 13 July, 1863.

It was not mere editorial arrogance or vanity that James Gordon Bennett displayed when at the outbreak of the war he assured President Lincoln of the support of the New York *Herald*. Lincoln's subsequent offer of the French mission to the erratic journalist vouches for that. For editorial influence was then at its greatest, and the power wielded by the leaders in the great era of personal journalism—such men as Greeley Bennett, Bowles, Raymond, Bryant, Schouler—made government by newspapers something more than a phrase. The country was accustomed to a journalistic leadership in which it had faith. Not a few editors felt competent to instruct the government in both political and military affairs, and some undertook to do so, notably Horace Greeley, in the New York *Tribune*, to the clamour of which paper is attributed the ill-advised aggression which led to the defeat at Bull Run. Of all the editorials written during the war, Greeley's "The Prayer of Twenty Millions," printed in the *Tribune* on 20 August, 1862, is probably the most significant, not only because it indicates the tone assumed in many papers, but especially because it drew from President Lincoln a reply which defined more clearly than ever before his position on the question of slavery and made unmistakable the relative positions of President and editor. There is a resemblance between this encounter and an earlier and less public one between Lincoln and Seward, and the two events are not incomparable in importance. After that exchange of ideas the newspapers of the North supported the President more completely than before. As the war progressed, however, the editorial gradually came to occupy a less important place than news, and by the close of the conflict the authority and influence of the great personalities of journalism had appreciably declined.

The war produced one immediate economic change which proved the beginning of a revolution still going on. The great demand for news brought a tremendous increase in circulation to those papers able to furnish the fullest accounts of the war, and contributed to the prosperity of the larger papers at the expense of the smaller ones. Although great numbers of papers were set up to meet the demand for war news, still more suffered extinction, with the result that in many states there were fewer in 1865 than in 1861. In Illinois, for instance, 144 papers were begun, and 155 were discontinued in the four years. Part of the decrease was due to lack of labour, a condition which led to the invention of the "patent insides." Contrived as a means of economy, this device led to important developments in country journalism in later decades by reducing the cost of printing.

Reconstruction was accompanied by still further mechanical improvements in stereotyping and in presses which made possible great growth in the industry. The extension of co-operative news-gathering was rapid after 1865, when the Western Associated Press was formed, largely through the initiative of Joseph Medill of the Chicago *Tribune*. This association, co-ordinated with that of New York, greatly broadened the news resources of both Western and Eastern papers. The rapid growth to the West and in the great Central valleys continued, accelerated by a decrease in the price of paper towards the end of the period, as well as by the increase in population. In the South, where the business had suffered most, the dozen years following the war were a time of restoration, as well as of extension. Many of the leading papers had survived—in Louisville, Memphis, Nashville, Richmond, Atlanta, New Orleans—and these laboured energetically, in the face of appalling difficulties, political as well as material, to hasten the revival of the country. Many suspended papers were restored, and many new ones of stability were begun. There were other new ones, also, ephemeral but troublesome, set up to support the carpet-baggers and others who delayed the healing of old sectional wounds. Twenty years passed before the newspapers of the South recovered from the injury wrought by the war.

The war had accustomed publishers to lavish expenditure of money in gathering news and had created many new readers who could not be retained by editorial discussion or heavy style. They had been attracted by lists of killed and wounded, narratives of vivid fact, rather than by discussion; it was necessary to find a substitute for the absorbing accounts of war. One result of this effort to avert a return to the earlier heaviness, perhaps, was the development of a new journalistic technique, the cultivation of an artistic narrative style. It was Charles A. Dana, through the New York *Sun*, who set the new pattern that was followed by the American press generally for two decades. His idea was merely to apply the art of literary craftsmanship to the choosing and the telling of the varied stories of the day's events. Human interest, not importance of meaning or consequences, governed the choice of topics. This new style possessed simplicity and clearness; it abounded in details chosen for artistic effectiveness rather than for intrinsic news value. It added grace, without losing force; the deft touch replaced the heavy or awkward stroke. Dana had begun his journalistic career on the New York *Tribune* under Greeley, where he was managing editor and a most important figure until 1862. He became editor of the *Sun* early in 1868. What he meant to do, and did, Dana announced thus: "The *Sun* . . . will study condensation, clearness, point, and will endeavour to present its daily photograph of the whole world's doings in the most luminous and lively manner."

In certain other respects, also, Dana and the *Sun* were characteristic of the new era. The great majority of papers were still servile party organs; political discussion was as bitter as ever, and nowhere more so than in the *Sun;* vigorously expressed personalities enlivened the editorial columns. The rancour displayed in the presidential campaign of 1872 was unparalleled. But in the midst of bitter party controversy, independent journalism was growing apace; the editor and the politician were becoming more and more disentangled. The politician kept political power and the editor looked elsewhere for his influence—in a variety of interests, social, literary, and commercial. The influential editors throughout the country who were taking the place of the giants of the preceding era were following the precept of Bowles in learning to control what they seemed only to transcribe and narrate. They no longer preached or laid down the law. It was the publishing and depicting of facts, not the invective of editorial attack, that achieved results in the exposure of the Tweed ring by the New York *Times* and *Harper's Weekly* in 1871 and of the "Whiskey Ring" by the St. Louis *Globe-Democrat*. Exploits like these had never been attempted before; though they have never since been equalled in daring or in results obtained, they were progenitors of the sensational press characteristic of a later period.

Independent political thought and discussion were greatly strengthened by the growth of weekly papers which were established or which became prominent just after the war. The *Independent*, founded as a progressive and liberal religious journal in 1848, had been a powerful anti-slavery force, a leading journal of political, literary, and social, as well as of religious discussion. When Henry Ward Beecher took the editorship in 1861 he said he "would assume the liberty of meddling with every question which agitated the civil or Christian community," and in doing so he wrote, in this weekly newspaper, and in the *Christian Union*, now the *Outlook*, of which he became editor in 1870, some of the strongest editorials in the American press. "It is the aim of the *Christian Union* to gospelize all the industrial functions of life," Beecher wrote. These two are but the most conspicuous of a large class of religious journals, more nearly newspapers than magazines, which had much popularity and influence as organs of general discussion through the years of Reconstruction.

When the New York *Times* attacked the Tweed ring, its most effective ally was *Harper's Weekly*, an illustrated paper established in 1857, which partly through its remarkable use of illustrations and its sound editorial policy under George William

Curtis[1] had become popular and influential. The illustrations and cartoons of Thomas Nast in this paper were one of the striking features of the journalism of the war, and in the years following became a national force—the artist was declared by General Grant to be the foremost figure in civil life developed by the war. His power as a cartoonist was still growing when in 1870 the *Times* began its great exposure, and Nast, who in *Harper's Weekly* had already begun the fight, collaborated with a series of cartoons which still rank with the greatest, both in conception and in effect, ever published. At the same time Curtis, who became political editor in 1863 and editor three years later, made the paper a telling force in independent journalism, notably during the following decade in advocating civil service reform and similar movements for the cleansing of politics.

A more potent force in the movement towards independence was another weekly, the *Nation*, established under the editorship of Edwin Lawrence Godkin in 1865, which in the course of a few years set a new standard of free and intelligent criticism of public affairs. Godkin had begun serious work in journalism when in 1853, at the age of twenty-two, he had gone to the Crimea for the London *Daily News*. He had come to the United States in 1856, had become a keen student of American life, politics, and journalism, and during the war had done the country great service by telling Englishmen, through the *Daily News*, the truth concerning American conditions. He felt that the American press did not fairly represent the thought and opinions of educated men. He wanted to "see whether the best writers in America cannot get a fair hearing from the American public on questions of politics, art, and literature through a newspaper." Within a year after the *Nation* was established a discerning observer said that "it will do much to raise the reputation of American journalism in Europe and by its example to raise the tone of our other newspapers," and twenty years later an eminent English editor called it the best periodical in the world. It has been said that all the problems of democracy had a fascination for Godkin, and into the discussion of them he flung himself with enthusiasm and vigour equalled only by his breadth and keenness of understanding

[1] See Book III, Chap. XIII.

and the clear, pungent attractiveness of his style. He soon made the *Nation* a source of intellectual and political inspiration for that somewhat limited number to whom intellectual journalism could appeal. Best known for the long struggle of the *Nation* for civil service reform, and for a prolonged and finally successful fight against Tammany, through the *Evening Post*, of which he became editor in 1881, and for other great combats in which popularity was never considered, Godkin was probably the greatest single force for better government in the thirty years following the war. And although never read by the people generally, he profoundly affected the leaders of thought and of journalism, and through them exerted an influence no less wide, and, certainly no less vital to the health of the finer type of democracy, than that of men whose service to journalism is more frequently mentioned and imitated.

But the strongest tendency of the newspapers was not indicated by the independence of a Bowles or a Godkin, nor by any apparent revival of the idea that editorial discussion was an important function of the newspaper. Successors of the early editorial giants were found in Prentice, Medill, Grady, Rhett, Gay, Young, Halstead, McCullagh, the second Samuel Bowles, Rublee, McKelway, Hemphill, and Watterson, to mention only a few of many; personality continued to make itself felt, as it has done in Henry Watterson,—who carried into the new century traits of a journalism fifty years old,—in Scripps, Otis, Nelson, Scott, and scores of others; but by the early eighties the name of the editor had become relatively unimportant along with the editorial.

The principal features in journalistic development after the close of the era of Reconstruction were the transformation of the larger papers into great business concerns closely connected with the manifold increase in the amount of advertising printed, the extension and minute organization of news service, the development of variety in subject matter, and the growth of sensationalism in the treatment of news. The tremendous growth of advertising, which by 1890 had become the principal source of income, and which has gained greatly since then, transferred the controlling interest in newspaper policy from the editorial office to the business office, from politics to salesmanship. Circulation was stimulated to furnish an outlet for advertising rather than, as in earlier times, for its own sake as a source of income and power.

The largest single factor in building the machinery for news-gathering was the press association. After a period of change and struggle beginning in the forties, the Associated Press gradually acquired a dominant position, taking its present form in 1900, and growing in prestige ever since. For years it dealt only with routine events reported by its clients, but in later years it has formed a staff of experienced journalists of its own, has established its bureaus in all leading cities in this country, in the capitals and the larger cities of Europe, and in Central and, more recently, South America. Except that the leading papers maintain special correspondents in Washington, all papers obtain most of their news, except that of local affairs, from the Associated Press or one of its two chief competitors. This news is written in full, and printed, usually, as served. Consequently the press association has had a great influence not only in establishing the tenor of news and the point of view in reporting, but in developing a uniform style in news-writing as well. The influence has been one of restraint, conservative and sound, and for thirty years has tended to improve the tone, as well as the news quality, of American newspapers. The art of reporting and interviewing was assiduously cultivated; the practice of correspondence declined, and along with it the attention paid to foreign news. Although the Associated Press and several newspapers had European bureaus, that field was but superficially covered between the Civil War and 1898, except for a few exploits during the Franco-Prussian war. The war with Spain gave occasion for some of the most brilliant feats of individual reporting yet achieved, and in its sequel served to stimulate interest in events beyond our borders. Several papers, notably the Chicago *Daily News*, built up staffs in the foreign field exceeding in scope and effectiveness those of any other newspapers in the world. But in general the foreign news service languished.

The most conspicuous and pervasive influence was the sensationalism introduced about 1880 and reaching its climax early in the present century. It was compounded of the practices first exemplified by Bennett and of all subsequent methods capable of appealing to popular curiosity and emotion, all carried to extremes. The example was set by Joseph Pulitzer, a brilliant journalist of Hungarian birth who in 1878 bought the St. Louis *Post-Dispatch*, put his methods into effect with marked success, and in 1883 carried his idea to New York, where he bought the moribund *World* from Jay Gould and in a few years made it the most profitable and the most widely imitated newspaper in the country. In the hands of Pulitzer the new journalism was much more than merely sensational. His purpose was to make his paper an organ for the expression of popular opinion, in order to achieve social and political reforms through giving expression to the democratic will. The programme he laid down in 1883 and followed vigorously was to advocate a tax on incomes, inheritances, luxuries, monopolies, and privileges, to reform the civil service, punish corruption, and otherwise equalize the distribution of opportunities and advantages. To that end he produced one of the most brilliant and forcible editorial pages in the country.

Journalistic practice was less influenced by the example of the editorial page of the *World*, however, than by the sensational selection and treatment of news. The tone of the paper was brisk and vivacious, the subject matter appealed to the emotions and interests of the largest number of people in the middle and lower classes. Wrongs of all sorts from which the people suffered were to be corrected by the exposure of startling examples. Naturally, having found the way to make a startling appeal through the recital of evil and misfortune, it was discovered that a similar appeal to any emotions produced much the same result, and yellow journalism was the inevitable sequel. The many papers which followed the example of Pulitzer lacked the fine purpose and the genius of their model, and therefore imitated only the blatancy, the vulgarity, the lack of restraint and of scruple which became an invariable part of the method.

The greatest of all the followers of Pulitzer was William Randolph Hearst, who, beginning with the San Francisco *Examiner* in the middle eighties, by the use of methods much the same as those of Pulitzer soon surpassed the elder sensationalist because he was untrammelled by other journalistic purposes than the most profitable news-vending. Hearst's task, as has been said, was to cheapen the newspaper until it sold at the coin of the gutter and the streets. So he rejected news which "did not contain that thrill of sensation loved by the man on the street and the woman in the kitchen. He trained his men to look for the one sensational picturesque fact in every occurrence, and to twist that fact to the fore." In 1895 he went to New York, where he bought the *Journal*, and contested with Pulitzer for the palm of "yellow" sensationalism. He won, for by the close of the century the *World* had begun to moderate its tone and methods, while Hearst had only fairly begun the career which has strung a series of his papers from coast to coast and tainted the whole of American journalism with cheap and flashy emotionalism.

The changes which the example of these leaders brought into the newspapers at large were various, and not all undesirable. The militant journalists exposed abuses and accomplished many reforms and undoubtedly made themselves feared by many wrongdoers. And in doing so they gained in boldness and independence, especially so far as politics was concerned. Not only have Pulitzer and Hearst attacked some of the oldest and worst abuses of intrenched privilege; they have been the example for many other journalists, who, in spite of extravagances and mistakes, have helped to cure many an evil by exposing it to the light. They reached an ever increasing proportion of the population, vastly added to the sum of general knowledge among the least literate elements of the population, and appealed to a greater variety of interests than had before been touched by the newspapers. More attention was given to amusements, to sports, to the special domains of women and children. The perfecting of mechanical engraving made the use of illustrations convenient and cheap, and the possibilities in this field were promptly exploited. There had been but a slight increase in the use of cartoons in the daily newspapers, even after the great battle of pictures in the campaign of 1872, until the *World* during the eighties developed that feature into a leading characteristic of popular daily journalism. Its popularity and its utility, both as a source of entertainment and as a ready and effective substitute for the editorial, have never decreased.

Closely related to this aspect of growth is the rise of the Sunday supplement. Sunday newspapers had occasionally vexed the pious all through the nineteenth century, and Sunday issues of daily newspapers, containing some news, but mainly fiction, features, and pictures, had gradually found a place, especially during and after the Civil War, when seven issues a week were deemed a necessity. But the old-fashioned journalists were unfriendly to the idea. Greeley in the later fifties had no sympathy with the proposal of Dana, then his managing editor, to issue a Sunday "picture paper." The essence of the modern Sunday supplement is that it is made of pictures, light or sensational fiction, accounts of the strange, mysterious, or queer, gossip about persons of interest or notoriety—the frothiest part of the journalism of sensation. Its popularity has been due in great measure not merely to the lightness of tone but to the "comics" and the coloured pages, which interest the uneducated and the very young without making any demand on the intelligence. Only a small number of papers have been able to sustain, against the demand for the sensational, a Sunday supplement of real literary or pictorial worth.

Although sensationalism has contributed much of value to journalism, much that is undesirable must be charged against it. One of its staple commodities is gossip, scandal, crime, the whole miserable calendar of misery and ugliness of life, served with a flavor of sentimentalism. This aspect of life was kept to the fore in the leading mongers of sensation, and, although the worst of them have gradually modified their tone since the closing decade of the last century, and a relatively small number of papers went to extremes at any time, the effect has been general and lasting. The demand for gossip led to ruthless trespassing on the right of privacy; the taste for exciting details led to distortion of facts or deliberate falsification; the appetite for the personal and concrete induced rank abuses of the otherwise admirable development of the interview. The inevitable effect of this emphasizing of the superficial and mere tricious was a decline in the more substantial content of the papers. Instead of what a speaker said, appeared light-hearted chatter about his appearance, the audience, an interruption. Instead of the substance of discussions on public questions, in Congress or elsewhere, brief, inconsequential résumés were provided by writers of no authority. Against this tendency the most substantial press associations have exerted a constant and helpful influence, and a growing number of papers, great and small, have steadily maintained and improved many of the

better characteristics of journalism; but these have not altered
the general drift. The quality of editorial discussion has declined along with that of the news. Discussion and criticism
of literature, drama, and art has almost disappeared in a flood
of gossip about writers, actors, and artists. These important
matters, which were once a leading occupation of the daily
press, have been driven to find other journalistic lodgment.

The period embraced in the first twenty years of the present
century may not inappropriately be characterized as one of
transition and specialization. The older journalism has passed
away and the newer has not yet found a medium of control
satisfactory to the press itself and to society. The decay of
old political and social definitions in society itself has aggra-
vated and prolonged the process. As additional sources of news
have been developed and the machinery for gathering and distributing the product has been improved, the problem of what
to do with the available material has become increasingly difficult and important. In so far as a solution has been found, it
has been in the selection of news and in the growth of innumerable papers having special interests. The all-round newspaper
has become so huge an undertaking, entirely dependent on the
more or less uncertain whim of popular favour, that the organs
of special interests have usually taken some other form.

The necessity of selecting for publication only a small part
of the available wealth of daily news has made of the news
editor the judge of what aspect of the world's activity should be
presented to the readers, who must see the world through his
eyes, if at all, and has placed in his hands incalculable power in
moulding public opinion, in establishing in countless ways the
levels and proportions of daily thought and life. This has always
been true in some measure of course, and so long as newspapers
were predominantly political the bias of the editor was understood and discounted. When they were no longer mainly concerned with politics, and the lines of cleavage in public affairs
became uncertain, shifting from the political to the social and
economic, the point of view of the editor became not only increasingly important to the reader who sought the light of truth but
also increasingly difficult to ascertain. In such measure as the line
of cleavage has been established between the two chief economic
elements in society, self-interest, if nothing else, would naturally

have led the greatly capitalized newspapers to look at life from the point of view of property interest. Enough of such a bias has been perceptible to arouse a profound distrust of the daily press as an institution in which the point of view, the purposes, and aspirations of large classes were sure of adequate or sympathetic representation. A similar distrust of the Associated Press has arisen for precisely the same reasons. It has been the avowed aim of that association to render its members a service entirely uncoloured by prejudice, and so long as political bias was the only one to be taken into account it succeeded admirably. Whether justified in doing so or not, the leaders and sympathizers in labour movements and other manifestations of new social and industrial forces have come to believe that the press associations have the same restricted outlook as the "capitalistic" press, and that the world they picture day by day is but a partial world. An equally widespread possibility of control of opinion through the purposeful selection or modification of intelligence has been perceived in the "plate matter" furnished to thousands of smaller papers throughout the country by the Western Newspaper Union.

The editorial page of the daily newspaper has in recent years become a receptacle for humour, health hints, religious tidbits, questions and answers, social pleasantries, and other miscellany, crowding the early solid area of discussion and debate into a column or two of uncertain significance or value. There are striking exceptions to this, but generally, thoughtful editorial discussion has gone from the daily papers to the weeklies. The inadequacy of American newspapers in discussing the problems produced by the World War is a sobering manifestation of present journalistic limitations. No errors of the administration during the latest war have been charged to the compelling leaders of the Greeleys of today.

Such papers as the *Outlook*, the *Independent*, the *Nation*, and other survivors from an earlier period have come to have a place of increased importance in the journalistic scheme, and have been joined by many later comers, like *Collier's*, the *Survey*, the *New Republic*, the *Review*, the *Liberator* (formerly the *Masses*), *Reedy's Mirror*, the *Dial*, the *Bellman* (some of which have already run their course and died), and a number of others to which the thinking public must turn for much important but unexciting news and well-considered discussion of matters of current interest. There have also arisen a number of party or individual organs, like Bryan's *Commoner*, *La Follette's*, and *Harvey's Weekly*, which seek to preserve the personality and individuality now almost wholly gone from the daily press.

Enterprises in social service have become an established activity of the newspapers. From lending aid to police officials in investigating crime and detecting criminals, reporters have proceeded on behalf of their papers and the public to many notable exploits of this kind. These have been in large measure, like Stanley's search for Livingstone, undertaken to create sensational news. Related to this conception of the uses of a newspaper go the departments of personal aid, giving advice in matters of health, courtship, manners, law, greatly helpful, though sometimes reminiscent of the *Athenian Mercury*. More ambitious have been such undertakings as the long-continued campaign carried on by the Chicago *Tribune* for a "sane Fourth" and the Good Fellow movement at Christmas time, the series of free lectures and other educational endeavours of the Chicago *Daily News*, the municipal projects of the Kansas City *Star*, the fresh air funds, ice funds, pure milk funds, and other philanthropic projects supported by many papers. These had become an established function of American newspapers long before the calamities of Europe made of them the wonderful collectors of charitable gifts they have been throughout and since the war. The newspapers have made efforts to prevent swindling by excluding questionable advertising and exposing frauds. Some have gone so far as to guarantee their advertisements. Others have established "bureaus of accuracy and fair play" and made systematic plans to publish corrections of their mistakes.

While the newspapers have been finding new ways in which to serve the public, the public through state and Federal laws has been manifesting a similar interest. In 1900 the Associated Press gave up its charter in Illinois and secured a new one in New York because the Illinois Supreme Court held that it had "devoted its property to a public use . . . in effect, granted to the public such an interest in its use that it must submit to be controlled by the public, for the common good, to the extent of the interest it has thus created in the public in its private property." In somewhat this spirit, laws have been enacted within the present century requiring the publication of ownership and circulation of newspapers, stipulating that all advertisements shall be labelled, and in various states curtailing the right of papers to emphasize the evil exposed in divorce and other trials.

These manifestations of a desire to make the newspapers as clean and useful as possible are in part a development of, in part a reaction from, the era of sensationalism. The excesses of that era, together with the growing wealth of the larger papers, and a clarifying realization of the vital need for honest newspapers with more than a commercial purpose, are beginning to show secondary consequences.

The principal journalistic result of the World War was the elimination of the war correspondent, in the character displayed in previous wars. Scores of correspondents went to Europe, and the burden of expense laid upon the newspapers by the enormous conflict and the excessive cable tolls was unprecedented. But the correspondents were rigorously restricted in their movements and their reports censored so thoroughly that, although a vast quantity of matter was transmitted, for the first time the news of a great war was under practically complete governmental control. In addition to being subject to the trans-Atlantic official censorship of European news, our newspapers united in a voluntary censorship of domestic news, suggested by the Committee on Public Information. Restrictions were laid on the press by the Espionage and other laws which led to considerable suppression, principally through denial of mailing privileges, and brought up for consideration the perennial question of the freedom of the press.

The great advance during and since the World War accelerated an already considerable decrease in the number of weeklies and smaller dailies and led to the disappearance of many larger papers, including some of the oldest and best known in the country. War-time conditions served also to diminish greatly the number of papers printed in the German language, and brought sharply to public notice the great number and influence of the foreign-language papers.

American newspapers surpass in number the papers of all other countries; they have steadily for many decades led in the development of energy and resourcefulness in collecting and dispensing news, as well as in adroitness in perceiving and satisfying popular tastes and demands for information and entertainment. Unsettled as are now the foundations on which the institution of journalism lies, its desire and ability to serve what it considers the best public interests are on the whole remarkable. The extravagances of sensationalism are passing out of fashion; newspaper style, despite the argot of sports and the extravagances due to overzealous pursuit of brightness and catchiness of phrase, is gaining in effectiveness and finish; barring the spectacular sheets, no other newspapers in the world show such typographical beauty. Within the present century men with college education have rapidly replaced the earlier type of journalist, and multiplying schools of journalism are making a profession of the trade.

CHAPTER XXI

Political Writing Since 1850

THE year 1850 was a landmark in American political history. In September the Great Compromise was enacted. It tempered the slavery controversy and checked impending secession. To abide by the measure or to reject it was the issue in state campaigns, especially in the cotton states, during 1851. There, and also in the North and the West, the Whigs worked intensely for popular support of the compromise. In fact, they seem to have spent their strength in the cause, and when the country accepted "the finality of the compromise" they were unable to raise a new issue, and their organization rapidly went to pieces after 1852. In the meantime a change was taking place in the personnel of political leadership. Calhoun[1] died before the compromise bill became a law, Clay[2] and Webster[3] in 1852. A number of men of less distinction but of invaluable service retired from politics about the same time: Van Buren in 1848, likewise Benton, Winthrop of Massachusetts, Ewing of Ohio, Foote of Mississippi, and Berrien of Georgia in 1851. With the death or retirement of these men the sentiment for union which they had fostered, declined. Among those who took their places partizanship was supreme, and until the advent of Lincoln originality and sincerity were almost totally lacking. It is not surprising, therefore, that for two decades after 1850 political thought and discussion centred around inherited issues relating to sectionalism and nationality.

In the South the philosophy and defence of slavery and of a society based on inequalities among its members became the dominating theme. The discussion had begun a generation earlier with the memorable debates in the Virginia Legislature

[1] See Book II, Chap. xv.   [2] *Ibid.*   [3] See Book II, Chap. xvi.

of 1831. To a committee was referred a number of petitions and memorials requesting emancipation or colonization of slaves and the removal of free negroes from the state. These furnished the cue for one of the really notable books in the history of American political thought, Thomas R. Dew's *Review of the Debates in the Virginia Legislature* (1833). The author, after graduation from William and Mary at the early age of twenty, travelled and studied in Europe; then in 1827 became Professor of History, Metaphysics, Natural and National Law, Government and Political Science at his Alma Mater, and in 1836 was made president of the institution. His writing and teaching marked the beginning of the transition in the South from the political philosophy of the Revolution and the early nineteenth century, of which Jefferson was the ablest exponent, to that which dominated that section in the fifties. He argued against emancipation or colonization. His reasons were based on history, religion, and economics. Slavery was a characteristic of classical civilization; it was approved by the Scriptures; and in America the slave-holding states produced most of the country's wealth—in fact, in Virginia the sale of surplus slaves equalled each year the value of the tobacco crop. Moreover, emancipation and deportation were impractical and the condition of the negro slave in the South was far better than that of the native African. Professor Dew publicly stated what many were privately thinking. His book therefore had a wide circulation and was reprinted in 1852 by William Gilmore Simms[1] in his collection entitled *Pro-Slavery Argument*.

Dew's defence of slavery was based on things practical; others sought to justify it through political and social philosophy. Consequently the theories of social contract, equality, and inalienable rights, immortalized by Jefferson, were subjected to rigorous criticism. One of the pioneers in this task was Chancellor Harper of South Carolina. His *Memoir on Slavery*, published in 1838, was likewise reprinted in Simms's collection. In contrast to the dictum of Jefferson that "all men are created free and equal" Harper declared that "man is born to subjection—as he is born to sin and ignorance." The proclivity of the natural man is to dominate or to be subservient, not to make social compacts. Civil liberty is therefore an artificial

[1] See Book II. Chap. VII.

product, and the inalienable rights of life, liberty, and the pursuit of happiness are merely unmeaning verbiage. There is no place for contract as the basis of government, since it is "the order of nature and of God that the beings of superior faculties and knowledge, and superior power, should control and dispose of those who are inferior." It is therefore as much in the order of nature that "men should enslave each other, as that animals should prey upon each other."

Yet Harper's book is more of a defence of Southern society than an attack on existing political theories. Such an attack was more definitely the aim of Albert T. Bledsoe, Professor of Mathematics in the University of Virginia, in his *Liberty and Slavery* (1856). He boldly rejected the traditional conceptions of natural liberty and the origin of government. Public order and private liberty, he held, are non-antagonistic. Civil society is "not a thing of compacts, bound together by promises and paper, but is itself a law of nature as irreversible as any other." The only inalienable rights are those coupled with duty, and they do not include life and liberty. Another teacher, William A. Smith, President of Randolph Macon College, gave to the public the arguments already presented to his classes in his *Lectures on the Philosophy and Practice of Slavery* (1856). Two aims inspired his work: to show "that the philosophy of Jefferson is false, and that the opposite is true, namely, that the great abstract principle of domestic slavery is, *per se* right," and that "we should have a Southern literature," especially textbooks in which there should be no poison of untruth. The books of these two teachers were widely circulated; Bledsoe's was especially well-known, finding its way into many private libraries of the age.

Not only were Jefferson's ideals combatted, but in society as organized there was also found a basis for the defence of slavery. In Europe the industrial revolution had brought in its train poverty, child labour, distress, new social philosophies, and revolt. In contrast was the South with its contented labourers, its planters who had a personal interest in the welfare of those dependent on them, its wealth, its conservatism, and its spirit of chivalry. Here lay the theme of George Fitzhugh's *Sociology for the South* (1854). In Europe, he pointed out, free labour had resulted in exploitation of the workers by the capitalists. There

actual conditions demonstrated the failure of the *laissez faire*
theory of economics and politics. The remedy was a proper
stratification of society through a strong-armed government.
Let the state see that men, women, and children have employment and support. To this end let the English Government subordinate the mill owners to the state, and let the state furnish
them employees who will be compelled to labour by the government at wages fixed by the state, which will insure a decent
living. Thus only can strife and poverty be abolished in England. In our own country, let the government make over the
public lands to responsible men, to be entailed to their eldest
sons; let the landless and idle population of the Eastern states
be attached to these vast tracts of land as tenants for life. By
such a process peace and order will be established. "Make the
man who owns a thousand dollars of capital the guardian (the
term master is objectionable) of one white pauper of average
value; give a man who is worth ten thousand dollars ten pau-
pers, and the millionaire a thousand. This would be an act of
simple justice and mercy; for the capitalists now live by the proceeds of poor men's labour, which capital enables them to command; and they command and enjoy it in almost the exact
proportions which we have designated." Undoubtedly this programme of rigid state control was not acceptable to the South;
but Fitzhugh's attack on free society and its political philosophy was approved, and his work in revised form was republished in 1857 under the title *Cannibals All! or Slaves Without
Masters.* It should also be noted that Fitzhugh was an admirer
of Thomas Carlyle, with whom he corresponded, and that his
style shows unmistakable evidences of the great Scotchman's
influence.

Pro-slavery propaganda was not confined to teachers and
publicists. The clergy also made their contribution. Dr. Thorn-
ton Stringfellow of Virginia wrote *The Bible Argument against
Slavery in the Light of Divine Revelation* (1850). The Rev. Fred
A. Ross of Alabama in his *Slavery Ordained of God* (1857) maintained that "Slavery is part of a government ordained to certain conditions of fallen mankind." Charles Hodge[1] of Princeton
with learned erudition criticized the religious argument against
slavery. "Parson" W. G. Brownlow of Tennessee, in a memor-

[1] See Book III, Chap. xvi.

able debate with Abram Prynne, portrayed the advantages of Southern society over that of the North. Political economists also wrote in the defence. Edmund Ruffin of Virginia, successful planter, pioneer in scientific farming, and editor of agricultural journals, in his *Political Economy of Slavery* (1857) claimed blessings for the existing relation of master and slave. David Christy of Cincinnati in *Cotton is King* (1855) showed the place of the plantation system in the wealth of the nation and pointed out the need of more territory for slavery and the cultivation of cotton.

These writings and others of minor importance are the record of a change in Southern opinion, the passing of the conviction that slavery is inherently wrong, to be abolished in the future, to as strong a conviction that slavery is right *per se;* they also mark the declining influence of Jefferson's political ideas. The constitutional theories of states' rights and secession, to which the protagonists of slavery looked for ultimate defence, were likewise the subject of discussion. Calhoun's *Disquisition on Government* and *Discourse on the Constitution* were posthumously published in 1851. Politics gave an opportunity to carry to the people the constitutional conceptions of the great theorist. This was notably true just after the compromise of 1850 was enacted, when a definite movement was inaugurated in the cotton states to reject the compromise and bring about secession. Typical was the trend of argument and appeal in South Carolina. Edward B. Bryan, in advocating immediate secession, anticipated one of Lincoln's themes when he wrote: "The cement is broken; the house is divided against itself. It must fall." William Henry Trescott, about to begin a long career in diplomatic service, likewise wrote; "The only safety for the South is the establishment of a political centre within itself; in simpler words, the formation of an independent nation." The aged Langdon Cheves wrote the following call to the Southern people: "Unite, and you shall form one of the most splendid empires on which the sun ever shone, of the most homogeneous population, all of the same blood and lineage, in soil most fruitful, and in climate most fruitful. But submit—submit! The very sound curdles the blood in my veins. But, Oh, Great God, unite us, and a tale of submission shall never be told."

Against this rabid sectionalism there were a few notable

protests. William J. Grayson, Collector of the Port of Charleston, and a lifelong champion of slavery, boldly opposed the secession movement in his state. So too did Benjamin F. Perry, an up-country editor, and Bishop Ellison Capers of the Protestant Episcopal Church. It is also a strange coincidence that a nationalistic philosophy, as radical as that of the secessionists when compared with the thought of earlier days, also emanated from South Carolina. Its author was Francis Lieber, a German liberal who, persecuted in his native land, sought refuge in America and became Professor of Political Economy in South Carolina College—a position he held from 1835 to 1857, when he went to New York to join the faculty of Columbia College. Like contemporary Southerners, he rejected the social compact theory; he could assign no definite explanation for the origin of the state, but found it to be in the institutional forces of human nature. Most significant was the distinction he drew between the *people* and the *nation*. The former signifies "the aggregate of the inhabitants of a territory without any additional idea"; the latter implies a homogeneous population having "an organic unity with one another as well as being conscious of a common destiny." In other words, the nation is organic, not contractual, in nature. In it, not in the individual states, lies sovereignty, which is one and indivisible. Such was the elemental thought in Lieber's *Political Ethics* (1838) and *Civil Liberty and Self Government* (1853), books which in time profoundly influenced political science in the United States. That Lieber, holding such views and also having no sympathy for slavery, could live so long in the very heart of the cotton kingdom, is remarkable. While his son lost his life in the Confederate Army, Lieber became legal advisor to President Lincoln and was the author of *Instructions for the Government of the Armies of the United States in the Field*, which was a starting point for more humane rules of warfare, both in this country and abroad.

Against slavery there were a few notable protests in the South. They were made, however, in the interest of the white man rather than of the negro. Daniel Reaves Goodloe, a North Carolinian, and editor of newspapers in his native state and Washington, published in 1846 a pamphlet in which he concluded that "capital invested in slaves is unproductive in that it only serves to appropriate the wages of the labourer." In 1858 he also issued his *Southern Platform*, a digest of the opinions of "the most eminent southern Revolutionary characters" upon the subject of slavery, which was widely circulated. In Virginia, Dr. Henry Ruffner, President of Washington College, the present Washington and Lee University, advocated in 1847 the gradual emancipation of slaves in the western counties of the state, on the ground that slavery was destructive to the best interests of the white people. After a lengthy demonstration of the evils induced by slave labour, he declared: "Delay not, then, we beseech you, to raise a barrier against this Stygian inundation—to stand at the Blue Ridge, and with sovereign energy say to this Black Son of misery; 'Hitherto shalt thou come, and no farther!'" But the Southern protest *par excellence* was *The Impending Crisis of the South* (1859), the work of Hinton Rowan Helper of North Carolina. With the moral aspect of slavery he had no interest; that he left to Northern writers, especially to "Yankee wives" who have "written the most popular anti-slavery literature of the day. Against this I have nothing to say; it is all well enough for women to give the fictions of slavery; men should give the facts." These facts were suggested to him by a visit to the free states of the West. Their wealth and prosperity, as compared with conditions in the home country, made a deep impression upon him. He thereupon made a study of the comparative resources and development of the slave and free states. His conclusion was that slavery was a positive evil to the white men of the South. Notable was the distinction he drew between the slaveholders who were numerically in the minority, but shaped the public policy, and the non-slaveholders, numerically in the majority, but having little political power. Let the latter organize, take over the government, exclude the slavocracy from office holding, and abolish the institution which sapped the strength of the country. The book, published after some difficulty, became exceedingly popular in the North, and was reprinted in 1859 as a campaign document. In the South it was regarded as incendiary literature; agents who distributed it were imprisoned and fined, and any one possessing a copy was regarded as a traitor to his country. Among those who had commended the book was John Sherman, candidate for the speakership of the House of Representatives in 1859. During the contest this fact was brought into the discussion. Thereupon a Virginia congressman declared that "one who consciously, deliberately, and of purpose lends his name and influence to the propagation of such writing is not only not fit to be Speaker, but he is not fit to live." Yet, strange to say, the particular passage which called forth this remark was a quotation from the Virginia Debates of 1831.

Between the extremes represented by Helper and Thomas Dew, there existed a moderate school of thought, which acknowledged the evils of slavery, especially the burden it imposed upon the whites, but deprecated any artificial attempt toward its abolition. This, it was held, time and natural causes would bring about. Such a writer was J. H. Hammond, of South Carolina. In his *Letters on Slavery*, written in reply to the criticisms of Thomas Clarkson, he conceded that slavery was more expensive than free labour, but that the remedy lay not in immediate abolition but in an increase in the density of the population, which would make the supply of free labour more available. Likewise George M. Weston, a native of Maine, who lived in Washington, pointed out, in his *Progress of Slavery in the United States* (1857), the steady encroachment of free labour upon slave labour along the border of the South, the ultimate advantage in the continuance of this process, and the purely political character of the demand for the extension of slavery into the territories of the Northwest. Such undoubtedly were the convictions of thousands; but they smacked too much of compromise in a decade when an increasing number of radicals, North and South, would yield not one jot or one tittle from their respective positions.

While Southern thought was being moulded into the unity of conservation, opposite tendencies were at work in the North and West. Trade-unionism took on new life about 1850, and William H. Sylvis, the first great figure in the American labour movement, began his agitation. Wilhelm Weitling, a German immigrant, introduced the ideas of Marxian socialism. In the demand for suffrage and broader legal rights for women, Thomas Wentworth Higginson, William Lloyd Garrison, Joseph Sayers, Henry Ward Beecher, and Elizabeth Cady Stanton were leaders. Traditional political alignment was threatened by the American or Know Nothing movement, which sought to capitalize the prejudice against those of foreign birth and the Catholic faith. Among its propagandists were S. F. B. Morse, whose *Foreign Conspiracies Against the Liberties of the United States* (1852) ran through seven editions, and Thomas R. Whitney, author of a *Defense of American Policy as Opposed to the Encroachment of Foreign Influence* (1856). These issues, also the industrial development and commercial expansion, tended to divert attention from the slavery question. Indeed, the capitalists of the Northeast and the large planters of the cotton states drifted toward a *rapprochement*. Noteworthy also was the fact that many defenders of slavery were found among the clergy of the North, and that silence on the issue because of the policy of the churches. The Rev. Nehemiah Adams won notoriety by his favorable *South Side View of Slavery* (1854), as did also Nathan Lord, President of Dartmouth College, the Rev. Samuel Seabury of the Episcopal Church, Moses Stuart, Professor of Hebrew at Andover, and John Henry Hopkins, Episcopal Bishop of Vermont, for their various defences of slavery.

Three factors, however, kept alive and stimulated the moral interest in human bondage. One of these was the Federal Fugitive Slave Law, a part of the Great Compromise. There was considerable violence in resisting its enforcement, but its greatest contribution was to inspire a novel—Harriet Beecher Stowe's *Uncle Tom's Cabin* (1852), a book which the author declared to be "a collection and arrangement of real incidents, of actions really performed, of words and expressions really uttered, grouped together with reference to a general result, in the manner that a mosaic artist groups his fragments of various stones into one general picture." The political significance of the book was that it made the people of the North and the West ponder questions which the Great Compromise, it was generally said, had settled. Very significant was its influence on the rising generation. Says James Ford Rhodes:

The mothers' opinion was a potent factor in politics between 1852 and 1860, and boys in their teens in the one year were voters in the other. It is often remarked that previous to the war the Republican party attracted the great majority of schoolboys, and that the first voters were an important factor in the final success . . . the youth of America whose first ideas on slavery were formed by reading *Uncle Tom's Cabin*, were ready to vote with the party whose existence was based on opposition to the extension of the great evil.

Abroad, the book made a deep impression. It was translated into twenty-three languages, and over a million copies were sold in the British Empire. [1]

A second factor in stimulating interest in the slavery issue was the Kansas Nebraska Act of 1854, by which more territory was opened to the slave system. The moral revolt which *Uncle Tom's Cabin* had kindled took the form of political action in the organization of the Republican party. A new group of leaders sought to arouse the conscience of the country. Among them was Charles Sumner, of Massachusetts, member of the Senate from 1851 to 1874. In the movement against slavery he is the logical successor of John Quincy Adams, [2] with the exception that his opposition was moral as well as political. His pamphlets, *Crime against Kansas* (1856) and *Barbarism of Slavery* (1860) were circulated by the million. Not the equal of Webster as a constitutional lawyer, and too often extremely personal in his discussion of Southern policies, he was a most skilful and resourceful special pleader in a great cause. With him should be mentioned William H. Seward, a noted politician of New York and chief figure in the Republican party in the East. His presentation of the "irrepressible conflict" which would make the United States "a slave-holding nation or a free labour nation" did much to crystallize opinion in the East. The crisis also brought forth Abraham Lincoln, who re-interpreted the American theory of democracy. As the author of political phrases and aphorisms, he is equalled only by Jefferson. "No man is good enough to govern another man without that other's consent" applies the principle of democracy to the fact of slavery. "When the white man governs himself, that is self-government; but when he governs himself and also governs another man, that is more than self-government—that is despotism." Finally, the Dred Scott case brought the slavery issue to a climax, for in that decision it was evident that the Supreme Court was pro-slavery. Shortly followed the Lincoln-Douglas debates, in which Lincoln pointed out the antithesis between popular sovereignty and the Dred

[1] See also Book III, Chap. xi.   [2] See Book II, Chap. xv.

Scott decision.   Thereafter his leadership in the West was unquestioned.[1]

The advent of war forced the nationalists to re-shape their political theories.   The legal and constitutional proofs that the United States was a nation, advanced by Webster and his school, had not counteracted sectionalism; the conflict of arms threatened to demonstrate how baseless they were.   Moreover the conduct of the war brought about a certain disregard, on the part of the government, of various limitations, rights, and liberties set forth in the Constitution.   It is not strange, therefore, that a new basis for nationality was sought, not in the Constitution or the old political formulas, but in the hard school of necessity.   Thus President Lincoln declared that "measures otherwise unconstitutional might become lawful by becoming indispensable to the preservation of the constitution through the preservation of the Nation."   Pertinent also were the words of Sydney George Fisher written in 1852: "If the Union and the Government cannot be saved out of this terrible shock of war constitutionally, *a* Union and *a* government must be saved unconstitutionally."   The pathway for the new thought had already been indicated by Francis Lieber, and soon the organic theory, with sovereignty in the nation rather than the states, was well under way.   Very significant was the effort to distinguish between the written and the unwritten constitution.   Thus J. A. Jameson, eminent jurist and exponent of the new school, divided constitutions into two classes; those which are organic growths, the products of social and political forces, and those which are "instruments of evidence," the results of attempts to express in language the sense of organic growth.   Likewise Orestes A. Brownson,[2] a devoted Catholic, who found in the church fathers and the traditions of early Christianity the principles of democracy, distinguished between the constitution of the state or nation and the constitution of the government.   In the same vein was the declaration of John C. Hurd, that "sovereignty cannot be an attribute of law because by the nature of things, law must proceed from sovereignty," and consequently the Constitution of the United States cannot be cited as evidence for the sovereignty of the states or the nation.

[1] See also Book III, Chap. xxii.
[2] See also Book II, Chap. viii and Book III, Chap. xix.

Naturally, by such writers sovereignty is conceived as undivided and as being in the nation, and the social compact and related political theories are rejected. With the passing of years their views have predominated. Thus the war which "joined with bayonets" the Union, like the defence of slavery, caused a decline of the political theory of the Revolutionary and federal periods.

Among the practical problems in the preservation of nationality were certain measures taken to preserve unity behind the military lines, the treatment of conquered enemies and their property, and the relations between the South and the national government. States' rights ideas were widely disseminated in the North and West and there was also much sympathy with secession. Consequently the executive authority expanded; particularly military arrests and the denial of the writ of *habeas corpus* were frequent. Captured Confederates were not executed as traitors, yet Confederate property was confiscated. These matters, and the kindred question of emancipation and conscription, were the subject of extensive legal and constitutional discussion, of which Whiting's *War Powers* (1862 *et seq.*) was the most comprehensive. The eclipse of constitutional rights enjoyed in time of peace and the supremacy of the war powers became the chief issue in politics. "The Constitution as it is, and the Union as it was" became the slogan of the opposition. In New York the Society for the Diffusion of Political Knowledge, with S. F. B. Morse as president, was active in the publication of pamphlets criticizing the measures of the administration. Its objects were to popularize the principles of constitutional liberty "to the end that usurpation may be prevented, that arbitrary and unconstitutional measures may be checked, that the Constitution may be preserved, that the Union may be restored, and that the blessings of free institutions and public order may be kept by ourselves and be transmitted to our Posterity." Among the contributors to its pamphlets were Morse, Samuel J. Tilden, and George Ticknor Curtis. Likewise, in the defence of the administration, the Loyal Publication Society was organized, and among the writers for its publications were Francis Lieber, Robert Dale Owen, and Peter Cooper. Much of the literature in criticism of the government has been lost. Of that which survives, D. A.

Mahoney's *Prisoner of State* (1863), the recital by an Iowa editor of his own imprisonment and that of others, is illustrative. The author's theme is summarized in the following sentence from the dedication:

> To you, then, far beyond and above all others of the monsters which have been begotten by the demon of fanaticism which is causing our country to be desolated, belongs the distinction of connecting your name with this work, not only to live in the memory of the deeds which you have caused to be committed, but to be kept forever present in the American mind whenever it recurs in time to come to that period in American history when the Constitution of the United States was first abrogated, when the Government of the Union was subverted, and when the rights and liberties of the American People were trampled like dust beneath the feet of a person clothed in a little brief authority which is used to subvert and destroy that which it should preserve, protect and defend, and who uses as the heel of his despotism, you, Edwin M. Stanton.

More widely known was the case of Clement L. Vallandingham. A member of Congress and actively engaged in campaigning against the administration in 1863, he was arrested by military authority, tried by court martial, and sentenced to imprisonment. The sentence was commuted by President Lincoln to exile within the Confederate lines. The episode led to the writing of Edward Everett Hale's short story, *A Man Without a Country* (1863), of which five hundred thousand copies were sold within thirteen years.

The relation of the South to the Union became the subject of discussion with the first signs of Federal victory, and grew acute with the close of hostilities. If secession, as the Lincoln administration had claimed, was unconstitutional and the Southern states had never been out of the Union, it seemed logical for those states to resume their functions under the Constitution, by participating in Federal elections, by sending representatives to Congress, and by exercising other rights generally guaranteed to the states. Such a policy was in harmony with antebellum nationalism, and it was advocated by leading Southerners. But such a procedure did not harmonize with the new sense of nationality; it made no guarantee against another experiment in secession; and it might also restore to political authority in the South the very class that had been in power in 1860. For these reasons four contrary theories were evolved. They were given the names Presidential, State Suicide, Conquered Province, and Forfeited Rights. According to the Presidential theory, the Southern states, though they had never been out of the Union, no longer had constitutional governments. To establish such governments, representative in form and loyal to the Union, the President proposed to lend aid, and even to exercise a certain amount of control. This theory was formulated by Lincoln and was notable for its liberal conditions, which the Southerners might easily fulfil. Application was attempted in Louisiana, Arkansas, and Tennessee. But the Presidential plan was too lenient for the leaders of Congress, even under the stricter terms imposed by Andrew Johnson. Hence Charles Sumner advanced the theory of State Suicide Although the states had not been out of the Union, the adoption of ordinances of secession had caused them to commit *felo de se*, and they were, therefore, in the status of territories, for which Congress should prescribe rules and regulations. More extreme was the Conquered Province theory of Thaddeus Stevens, of Pennsylvania, which held that the states in question had lost all their rights under the Constitution, and were merely so much conquered territory, possessing only the rights they might claim under international law. Finally, by the Forfeited Rights theory, the states had never been out of the Union, but had forfeited certain rights under the Constitution, which could be restored only through the direction of Congress. These theories, the controversies, the violence, and the bitterness which developed over their adoption or rejection, were but the birth pangs of a new political and constitutional order. For the ultimate result, the theory of the Supreme Court in *Texas vs. White* is also pertinent; that the Constitution, in all its provisions, looks to "an indestructible Union, composed of indestructible states." The great monuments of the new sense of nationality, the thirteenth, fourteenth, and fifteenth amendments, likewise precipitated questions which have enriched legal literature. What is involuntary servitude? How inclusive are rights and liberties? What is due process of law? When does a state deny suffrage on the ground of race, colour, or previous condition of servitude? Meanwhile, the view of the

Union which had made secession possible was given able and sympathetic defence by Alexander H. Stephens in his *War Between the States* (1868), by Jefferson Davis in the *Rise and Fall of the Confederate States* (1881), and by Bernard J. Sage's *Republic of Republics* (1865).

One of the characteristics of literature in America since the war has been the increasing number of personal narratives, autobiographies, memoirs, and diaries. Many of these arise from a desire to tell one's relation, however humble, to the great conflict and its heroes—a desire which possessed all classes and conditions from the commanders of armies to Mrs. Keckley, the coloured serving woman of Mrs. Lincoln. Others have an aim primarily political, to recount policies and movements in which the authors participated. In the latter class a few have preeminence. Hugh McCulloch's *Men and Measures of Half a Century* (1888) is invaluable for financial history and its sketches of conditions in the West. John Sherman's *Recollections of Forty Years* (1895) is likewise important for financial measures, and is also an uncommonly good revelation of political opportunism. S. S. Cox's *Three Decades of Federal Legislation* (1885) is notable for a lengthy account of reconstruction in the Southern states, which was written by Daniel Reaves Goodloe and inserted without explanation of authorship. G. S. Boutwell's *Sixty Years in Public Affairs* (1902) is entertaining for its sketches of public men, and is also illustrative of the limitations of mind and training in the average American politician. Inimitable are the *Reminiscences* of Benjamin Perley Poore, with their intimate sketches of men and events around Washington for half a century. The *Autobiography* of G. F. Hoar (1903) reveals a blind devotion to party in a soul of unquestioned integrity. Surpassing all other narratives by contemporaries is the *Diary* of Gideon Welles (1911), Secretary of the Navy under Lincoln, rich for the light it throws on personalities and animosities in the cabinet and on political conditions in 1866, and revolutionary in its interpretation of Andrew Johnson.

While Northern politicians vied with each other to tell their story, the leaders of the South, with the exception of the military men, were singularly silent, Alexander H. Stephens's *Prison Diary* and John H. Reagan's *Memoirs* (1906) being the only intimately personal accounts by the political leaders of the Confederacy. But so personal in tone as to make them almost autobiographical are Fielder's *Life and Times of Joseph E. Brown* and Dowd's *Life of Zeb Vance*, and the writings of E. A. Pollard, a Richmond editor during war time.[1] Humorous, but accurately portraying certain types of Southern character, is Charles H. Smith's *Bill Arp So Called*, a book which in a period of economic depression and political disappointment had the power to make Southerners laugh. Among the Southern malcontents who had no sympathy for secession, two left accounts of their opinions and experiences. "Parson" Brownlow, who was expelled from Tennessee early in the war, published in 1862 his *Sketches of the Rise and Progress of Secession*, replete with quotations from the contemporary Southern press. A few years later a Virginian, John M. Botts, made Southern policies the subject of denunciation in his *Great Rebellion* (1866) and started a memorable historical controversy by declaring that Lincoln had offered to surrender Fort Sumter provided that the Virginia convention of 1861 would adjourn without taking action on secession.

Closely related to the autobiography were the reports of newspaper correspondents and tourists. These were especially noticeable between 1865 and 1876 when the economic and social upheaval in the South was a subject of general interest. Of this literature, some was "inspired," notably the reports made to President Johnson in 1866 by B. C. Truman, Carl Schurz, and General Grant. Other contributions to this class of writing were Whitelaw Reid's *After the War*, Sidney Andrew's *The South Since the War*, and J. T. Trowbridge's *The South*, all published in 1866. More notable were the books of two former abolitionists, J. S. Pike and Charles Nordhoff; the former left a memorable description of the barbarism of negro rule in South Carolina in his *Prostrate State* (1874), and the latter gave a valuable account of Southern conditions in his *Cotton States in 1875*. The personal experiences of a Northerner during his residence in the South were the basis for the novels of A. W. Tourgee,[2] and of similar character is A. T. Morgan's *Yazoo, or On the Picket Line of Freedom in the South*.

Hardly had the Civil War ended when other questions, in

[1] For other memoirs, see also Book III, Chap. xv.
[2] See Book II, Chap. xi.

addition to those involving theories with respect to the nature of the nation, claimed public attention. Of these four were of primary importance and were productive of a new trend in political thought: civil service reform, tariff reform, the currency, and the farmer's movement.

The spoils system had long characterized office holding in the United States. Shortly after 1865 certain general influences made possible the agitation for efficiency and merit in the patronage. Among these were the revelations of inefficiency in the conduct of the war, the conflict between Andrew Johnson and Congress over control of the patronage, and examples of corruption in contemporary life. Especially did the activities of the Tweed Ring, ridiculed in the celebrated cartoons of Thomas Nast, create a sense of revolt against the existing order. The pioneer in the movement for new standards in the public service was Thomas A. Jenckes of Rhode Island. A lawyer, a man of wealth, and a congressman, he secured the reference of the appointing system to the committee on retrenchment in 1866. The resulting report, submitted in 1868, is "the effective starting point" in the modern movement for civil service reform in this country. Yet there was at first little interest in the cause. Mr. Jenckes was aptly compared to "Paul at Athens, declaring the unknown God." The average citizen regarded corruption as an unavoidable evil. The professional politician had only sneers for the reformer. Said Roscoe Conkling: "When Dr. Johnson defined patriotism as the last refuge of a scoundrel, he was then unconscious of the then undeveloped capabilities of the word 'reform.'"

In a few years recruits were gathered from the intellectual and literary class. George William Curtis,[1] editor and essayist, was chairman of the first commission to draft rules for the civil service. After Congress failed to provide an appropriation and also after a period of flirtation with the issue by political parties, Curtis became, in 1881, the first president of the National Civil Service League. For ten years he was "the intellectual head, the guiding force, and the moral inspiration of the Civil Service movement. The addresses he delivered at the annual meetings of the League were like milestones in the progress of the work—he reported to the country what had been done and

[1] See Book III, Chap. XIII.

what was still to be done, enlightening public sentiment, encouraging his fellow-labourers and distributing with even-handed justice, praise and reproof among the political parties as they deserved it." Other early leaders of the cause were Dorman B. Eaton, whose *Civil Government in Great Britain* (1880) ranks with Jenckes's report in the literature of the reform movement; Carl Schurz, Curtis's successor as head of the Civil Service Reform League and champion of the movement in the President's cabinet; Andrew D. White[1] and Charles W. Eliot, presidents of Cornell and Harvard; and a group of young politicians, among whom were Theodore Roosevelt and Henry Cabot Lodge. Soon the attitude toward civil service reform became the test of executive independence.

Hayes was notable for the aid he rendered it, while Cleveland's declaration "Public office is a public trust" won for him wide popularity. The principle involved, that efficiency and merit rather than party loyalty should be the standard for public office, aroused the interest of the intellectual class as had no other issue except that of slavery. It caused thousands to break party lines and played a great part in the rise to power of the independent vote.

The movement for tariff reform paralleled and, in many respects, was similar to that for civil service reform. Just as the existing political machines were wedded to the spoils system, the Republican party was identified with the policy of protection. It had won the election of 1860 very largely on that issue, had put the policy into practice during the war, and after the conflict continued it. The result was a period of exploitation of natural resources, great increase in manufacturing, alternating periods of speculation and trade depression due to displacement of capital, and special privileges for special interests. Leadership and protest came to a large extent from the class from which came the early agitation for civil service reform—the intellectuals. The pioneer was David A. Wells,[2] chairman of the Revenue Commission which made recommendations for a readjustment of national finances from a war to a peace basis. His examination of conditions in the United States caused a radical reaction in his views; from a protectionist he became a violent anti-protectionist. His report to Congress in 1870 was

[1] See Book III, Chap. xv. [2] See Book III, Chap. xxiv.

extremely free trade in tone, and deserves a place with that of Jenckes on the civil service as indicating the dawn of a new political thought, while his *Creed of a Free Trader* (1875) more definitely set forth his convictions.

Equally notable was the influence of William G. Sumner,[1] Professor of Political and Social Science in Yale College. In classroom and before the public, by lecture, pamphlet, and book, he assailed the protectionist system as "an arrant piece of economic quackery," masquerading "under such an air of learning and philosophy" as deserved only "contempt and scorn, satire and ridicule." No one did more than he to lay the basis of new thought concerning our national economy. To the manufacturing and commercial classes protectionism was a fetish, essential to American prosperity; and whoever rejected it or even questioned it could not be a patriot. It is not surprising, therefore, that Wells was accused of sympathy for the "lost cause" of the Confederacy, even of being bribed by British gold to advance free trade principles, and that there was a demand that Professor Sumner be removed from his position at Yale. However, the increasing surplus in the national treasury and the demand for tariff reform by the Democratic party relieved anti-protectionism of its opprobrium. The campaign of 1888 was notable, for both political parties sought to inform the voter on the tariff issue by book and pamphlet, as well as by speech and editorial. Wells, in his *Relation of Tariff to Wages*, pointed out that higher wages in the United States are the results of the productiveness of labour rather than of the protectionist policy. Sumner's *Protectionism* answered in simple but bellicose language the stock arguments of the protectionists. Half a dozen other works, about equally divided in defence and criticism of the existing tariff policy, were issued during the campaign, and the presidential campaign four years later was also notable for a similar tariff literature. The results on public opinion were favourable to the anti-protectionists; ever since the criticism of protection has steadily increased and the more scholarly writings on the tariff have been with a few exceptions unsympathetic toward the principle of protection.

Agitation for civil service reform and revision of the tariff centred in the East. On the other hand, the agrarian agita-

[1] See Book III, Chap. XXIV.

tion and the demand for more liberal coinage of silver were Western movements. Rapid settlement and the exploitation of the
West with borrowed capital, insufficient commercial facilities
and high rates of interest, and speculation in railway construction created economic depression in that region. For relief, the
farmers in the seventies organized the "Grange" or "Patrons
of Husbandry," a secret society. Among its objects were
co-operation in business and state-regulation of public utilities.
The grievances and purposes of the organization were reflected
in scores of periodicals; also in three widely circulated books,
Jonathan Perriam's *Groundswell*, E. W. Martin's *History of the
Granger Movement*, and O. H. Kelley's *Origin and Progress of the
Patrons of Husbandry*.

Now the prevailing doctrine was that of economic individualism, which emphasized the sanctity of private property, the development of natural resources under private direction only,
and the *laissez faire* theory of economics. With this the agrarian
experiments in co-operation and the demand for state control
were at variance. The conflict of ideals deeply influenced
jurisprudence, for it raised the question of public regulation
of railroads and other utilities versus the rights of property
guaranteed by the Constitution. Undoubtedly one purpose of
the fourteenth amendment was to afford protection to property
interests against hostile legislation; but the Supreme Court of
the United States was not prone to extend the scope of Federal
supervision, and in 1876 it upheld an Illinois statute regulating
grain elevators. "For protection against abuses by legislatures the people must resort to the polls, not to the courts."
Twelve years later, however, in the celebrated Minnesota
Rate Case the court took the opposite opinion, holding that
the reasonableness of railroad rates was a question for judicial review.

The question of the reasonableness of the rate of charge for
transportation by the railroad company, involving as it does the element of reasonableness both as regards the company, and as regards
the public, is eminently a question for judicial determination. If
the company is deprived of the power of charging reasonable rates
for the use of its property, and such deprivation takes place in the
absence of the investigation by judicial machinery, it is deprived of
the lawful use of its property, and thus in substance and effect, of

the property itself without due process of the law and in violation of the Constitution of the United States.

Deep was the significance of this decision; property interests now found protection against public regulations, and naturally the courts became the object of increasing criticism by those who were discontented with the existing social and economic order.

The Grange and the minor political parties identified with it declined, but a second wave of discontent in the eighties was the background for the Farmers' Alliance and the Populist party of the early nineties. In the whole range of American political literature no document is more remarkable than the Populist platform of 1892; it summarized the existing discontent and recommended remedies which, generally regarded at the time as too radical ever to be applied, today are a part of our orthodox political system. Most of the literature relating to Populism is ephemeral; but of real artistic merit is *The Kansas Bandit, or the Fall of Ingalls*, a dramatic dialogue inspired by the defeat of Senator Ingalls of Kansas in his contest for re-election to the United States Senate.

Parallel with the agrarian movement was the demand for bimetallism; indeed Senator Peffer in his *Farmers' Side* urged free silver as a remedy for the grievances of the farmers. The "battle of the standards" became the all absorbing political issue between 1888 and 1896. Most of the economists favoured the gold standard, notably Professor J. Laurence Laughlin of the University of Chicago. His *History of Bimetallism in the United States* was more than a history; it was also a defence of monometallism, and was widely quoted throughout the silver agitation. The minority of the economists, who defended bimetallism, was best represented by E. Benjamin Andrews, President of Brown University, in his *An Honest Dollar*. So strongly was the monometallic theory favoured among the conservative classes of the East that President Andrews's contrary views were one cause of his resignation from Brown in 1897. But the *pièce de resistance* in the whole agitation was W. H. Harvey's *Coin's Financial School* (1894), a little book, simple in style, graphic in illustration, which, reprinted during the campaign of 1896, enjoyed a circulation similar to that of the

Impending Crisis in 1860. A reply to his arguments, in imitative style, was made by Horace White in *Coin's Financial Fool*.

In the meantime, whatever complacency the average man of business between 1875 and 1890 possessed was rudely shaken by three phenomena: the rapid organization of labour, the trust movement, and the disfranchisement of the negro. The Knights of Labour, the first extensive labour organization in the United States, disturbed the balance of American temper. Said Francis Walker,[1] the economist: "Rarely has the sceptical, practical, compromising spirit of our people, which leads them to avoid extremes, to distrust large expectations and to take all they can get, 'down,' for anything they have in hand, however promising, so far lost control of our acts and thoughts and feelings." The nascent consciousness of labour was well reflected in Powderley's *Thirty Years of Labour*, the author being official head of the Knights.

The tendency towards combination in industry was the subject of many investigations by Congress and state legislatures. These disclosed notorious methods of competition and sinister activities in politics. Here was the subject matter of Henry Demorest Lloyd's *Wealth vs. Commonwealth* (1894), a popular presentation of the methods and policies of the Standard Oil Company. Startling facts concealed in the masses of legislative documents and court proceedings were dramatically marshalled. In shaping public opinion the book has a place not unsimilar to that of *Uncle Tom's Cabin*. Finally, in spite of the guarantees of the fourteenth and fifteenth amendments, negroes in the South endured discrimination in "Jim Crow car laws" and police regulations, and in 1890 and after they were practically disfranchised in seven of the Southern states. Convictions born of race proved superior to the mandates of government.

Contemporary with political agitation went a transformation in economic thought and the philosophy of government. Its immediate cause was a remarkable growth of industrialism with its attendant concentration of wealth, poverty, and inequality in the enjoyment of luxuries.

Criticism was started by Henry George[2] in his *Progress and Poverty* (1879):

[1] See Book III, Chap. xxiv.   [2] *Ibid.*

So long as all the increased wealth which modern progress brings goes but to build up great fortunes, to increase luxury and make sharper the contrast between the House of Have and the House of Want, progress is not real and cannot be permanent. The reaction must come. The tower leans from its foundations, and every new story but hastens the final catastrophe. To educate men who must be condemned to poverty, is but to make them restive; to base on a state of most glaring social inequality political institutions under which men are theoretically equal, is to stand a pyramid on its apex.

The remedy was an application of the physiocratic doctrine of the eighteenth century. The land of each country belongs to all of its people but it is occupied or used by individuals. Therefore all land rents, or taxes on rents, should be used for the common good, thus removing all existing revenues. Thus abolishing taxes on labour and production would stimulate wages and profits. Land values would decline and land held for speculation would be thrown in the market. This argument won great popularity and George suddenly became the leader of a new movement—the single tax. It had much popularity and influence abroad; it contributed to the introduction of increment taxes in Germany and Australia; in England it was well received on account of the Irish situation. In the United States it has had less practical results, but one of the attendant theories—that wages are paid out of the value created by labour, not out of capital—has had a wide acceptance. Gradually, also, all types of economist emphasized questions of distribution and the ground of the older individualistic *laissez faire* school was abandoned. The great question of taxation was subjected to analysis and new sources of revenue were defended in Max West's *Inheritance Tax* and E. R. A. Seligman's *Essays on the Income Tax*. Thus within fifteen years after the publication of George's work the revision of America's tax systems was well under way. Reform was openly advocated by liberals and bitterly opposed by conservatives. Illustrative of the conservative view were the words of Justice Field in the decision by which the Federal income tax law of 1894 was declared unconstitutional: "The present assault upon capital is but the beginning. It will be but the stepping-stone to others larger and more sweeping till our political conditions will become a war of the poor against the rich; a war growing in intensity and bitterness." In contrast was the more liberal spirit in Justice Harlan's dissenting opinion:

> The practical effect of the decision today is to give certain kinds of property a position of favouritism and advantage inconsistent with the fundamental principles of our social organization, and to invest them with power and influence that may be perilous to that portion of the American people upon whom rests the larger part of the burdens of the Government and who ought not to be subjected to the dominion of aggregated wealth any more than the property of the country should be at the mercy of the lawless.

In the meantime a vision of a new and radically different social and industrial order was popularized in 1888 in Edward Bellamy's *Looking Backward*.[1] The book was a romance in which the hero, after going to sleep in 1887, awakes in the year 2000 to find vast changes. He learned that

> there were no longer any who were or could be richer or poorer than others, but that all were economic equals. He learned that no one any longer worked for another, either by compulsion or for hire, but that all alike were in the service of the nation working for the common fund, which all equally shared, and even necessary personal attendance, as of the physician, was rendered as to the state, like that of a military surgeon. All these wonders, it was explained, had very simply come about as the results of replacing private capitalism by public capitalism, and organizing the machinery of production and distribution, like the political government, as business of general concern to be carried on for the public benefit instead of private gain.

The book was extremely popular for a few years. Bellamy Clubs were organized to discuss the questions it suggested, and it became the confession of faith of the Nationalist party.

Equally important was the new criticism of the operation of government and its purposes. This began with Woodrow Wilson's *Congressional Government* (1885), which pointed out the evil results in the existing relations of the executive and the legislature, notably the irresponsibility in legislation and the lack of leadership in Congress, which his own administration has since so well illustrated. A few years later Frank J. Good-

---

[1] See also Book III. Chap. XI.

now pointed out the defects in the American theory of the separation of powers; indeed his *Comparative Administrative Law* (1893) was the first work in English on administrative as distinct from constitutional law. John R. Commons in his *Proportional Representation* (1896) advanced a substitute for the existing unjust methods of representation. Municipal government also became the subject of criticism. A supplementary chapter to Bryce's *American Commonwealth* on the Tweed Ring caused the whole first edition of that excellent book to be suppressed. E. L. Godkin pointed out the weaknesses in the government of our large cities in his *Unforeseen Tendencies of Democracy*, while Albert Shaw showed the superiority in municipal ideals and forms of government of English and Continental cities as compared with those of the United States. Finally, the function of the state was re-examined. The early conception, born in the days of the Revolution, that the function of the state is confined to the protection of life, liberty, and property yielded to one more comprehensive. Thus Woolsey declares that "the sphere of the State may reach as far as nature and the needs of men reach." Woodrow Wilson in his *The State* advocated state regulation in industrial matters. W. W. Willoughby makes the economic, industrial, and moral interests of the people "one of the essential concerns of the state"; and John W. Burgess, working under the influence of German rather than American ideals, makes the ultimate aim of the state "the perfection of humanity, the civilization of the world; the perfect development of human reason and its attainment to universal command over individualism; the apotheosis of man."

The changes in the viewpoint of the leaders of thought came as a shock to the pillars of conservatism. Not infrequently the writings and influence of teachers cost them their positions in colleges and universities

In the meantime a startling change took place in foreign policy. From the close of the Civil War to 1898 the native mania for territorial expansion was held in restraint. Alaska, it is true, had been acquired, but an excuse was found in a desire to accommodate Russia. The offer by Denmark and Sweden of their West Indian possessions was rejected. Instead of annexing Hawaii in 1894 the sovereignty of a native queen was openly supported. With this sort of background came the Spanish-American War of 1898, and with it the annexation of Hawaii, and in its train the establishment of a protectorate over Porto Rico and the acquisition of the Philippines. For this sudden shift to a policy of territorial expansion economic conditions were largely responsible. By 1890 more manufactured goods were produced than were necessary for home consumption and the nation began to compete with European countries in the markets of the world. By 1898 the country was filled with capital, production was greater than consumption, and interest rates were falling. The leaders of industry were alarmed over the unrest in labour and intellectual circles; to them the remedy seemed to lie in a foreign policy which would encourage trade expansion. The argument for such a policy was ably presented by Charles A. Conant:

There are three important solutions of this enormous congestion of capital in excess of legitimate demand. One of these is the socialistic solution of the abandonment of saving, the application of the whole earnings of the labourer to current consumption, and the support of old age out of taxes levied upon production of the community. It will be long before this solution will be accepted in a comprehensive form in any modern civilized state. The second solution is the creation of new demands at home for the absorption of capital. This has occurred at several previous stages of the world's history, and is likely to continue as long as human desires continue expansible. But there has never been a time before when the proportion of capital to be absorbed was so great in proportion to possible new demands.

Aside from the waste of capital in war, which is only a form of consumption, there remains, therefore, as the final resource, the equipment of new countries with the means of production and exchange. Such countries have yet to be equipped with the mechanism of production and of luxuries which has been created in the progressive countries of recent generations. They have not only to obtain buildings and machinery—the necessary elements in producing machine-made goods—but they have to build their roads, drain their marshes, dam their rivers, build aqueducts for water supplies, and sewers for their towns and cities.

The United States cannot afford to adhere to a policy of isolation while other nations are reaching out for the commerce of these new markets. . . . The interest rates have greatly declined here during the last five years. New markets and new ports must, therefore, be found if surplus capital is to be profitably employed.[']

The argument for foreign territory met vigorous opposition. Prominent among its critics were those who had been identified with the abolition of slavery, notably George S. Boutwell, George F. Hoar, George F. Edmunds, Samuel Bowles, John Sherman, Charles Francis Adams, and Carl Schurz. Illustrative of the sentiments of these men is the following passage from the *Autobiography* of George F. Hoar upon the conquest of the Philippines:

When I think of my party, whose glory and whose service to Liberty are the guide of my life, crushing out this people in their effort to establish a republic, and hear people talking about giving them good government and that they are better off than they ever were under Spain, I feel very much as if I had learned that my father or some other honoured ancestor had been a slave trader in his time and had boasted that he had introduced a new and easier kind of handcuffs or fetters to be worn by the slaves during the horrors of the middle passage.

Co-operating with this group were Samuel Gompers, the labour leader, Edward Atkinson, statistician, Professor Sumner, David Starr Jordan, President of Leland Stanford University, and Andrew Carnegie. As an organ for propaganda the New England Anti-Imperialistic League was formed at Boston in 1899, and about one hundred subsidiary branches were established. A notable episode was the exclusion from the mails by the postmaster at San Francisco of three pamphlets addressed to members of the Philippine Commission, written by Edward Atkinson. These were entitled *The Cost of a National Crime*, *The Hell of War and Its Penalties*, and *Criminal Aggression; By Whom Committed*. They pointed out the cost of imperialism, its "moral, physical, and social degradation," and the responsibility of President McKinley for the annexation of the Philippines. Not daunted by the action of the government Atkinson promptly reprinted the pamphlets and gave them a wide circulation in his serial publication, *The Anti-Imperialist*. Other noteworthy pamphlets were Sumner's *Conquest of the*

[']*Economic Basis of Imperialism in the United States and the Orient*

United States by Spain (1898), Schurz's *American Imperialist* (1899), and Hoar's *No Power to Conquer Foreign Nations* (1899).

These protests were ineffectual. The triumph of the manufacturing and commercial interests in shaping public policy was well illustrated by two practical problems: Did the Constitution and the laws of the United States apply to conquered territory without special legislation by Congress? Was Congress bound by all of the principles of the Constitution in legislating for the territories? Regarding the first of these the policy of the President was negative, and Congress took a similar position in regard to the second. The issue involved was the application of tariff duties to goods coming from the newly acquired territories, the beet sugar and other trade interests opposing free competition and demanding the application of tariff duties to Porto Rican and Philippine products. The position of the executive and the legislature was upheld by the Supreme Court in the celebrated Insular Cases, but the reasoning of the majority opinions was notoriously confusing and unsatisfactory from the standpoint of constitutional law.

Imperialism did not allay criticism of the existing order. Gradually public opinion concerning the scope and purpose of government in its relation to the general welfare underwent a transformation. The view which had long been dominant was that national prosperity depended upon the prosperity of the manufacturing and commercial classes of the country; when they flourished the labourer would enjoy a "full dinner pail," the shopkeeper a good trade, the farmers high markets, and the professional classes would collect their fees; consequently it was only right that such important matters as the tariff and monetary standards should be determined according to the ideals of the great business interests of the country. The new view was that the object of legislation should be to aid all citizens with no special privilege or regard to any one class. Its birth was in the Granger movement. It was more widely disseminated by Populism, but its ablest presentation was by William Jennings Bryan, notably in his speech before the Democratic Convention in Chicago in 1896:

You have made the definition of a business man too limited in its application. A man who is employed for wages is as much a business man as his employer. The attorney in a country town is as much a business man as the corporation counsel in a great metropolis. The merchant at the crossroads store is as much a business man as a merchant of New York. The farmer who goes forth in the morning and toils all day—who begins in the spring and toils all summer—and who, by the application of brain and muscle to the natural resources of the country, creates wealth, is as much a business man as the man who goes upon the Board of Trade and bets upon the price of grain. The miners who go down a thousand feet into the earth, or climb two thousand feet upon the cliffs and bring forth from their hiding place the precious metals to be poured into the channels of trade, are as much business men as the few financial magnates, who, in a back room, corner the money of the world. We come to speak for this broader class of business men.

This ideal, rejected by the dominant political parties, led to a revolt. Elaborated into a definite programme with definite methods, it became known as Progressivism, possessing three aims: to remove special, minority, or corrupt influences in the government and to revise the political machinery; to enlarge the functions of government by exercising greater authority over individual and corporate activities; and to provide measures of relief for the less fortunate citizens. The first triumphs of its origins and conflicts, in Wisconsin, are well told in Robert M. La Follette's *Autobiography* (1911) and its definite programme in the same State in McCarthy's *The Wisconsin Idea* (1912); while progressive achievements along the Pacific coast are described in Hichborn's *Story of the California Legislature of 1911* and Barnett's *Oregon Plan*. In municipal affairs the Progressives looked to stricter control of franchises and the commission and managerial forms of government; in the literature of this phase of the movement, Tom L. Johnson's *My Story* (1913) is pre-eminent. In national government it brought about stricter Federal control of railways, a definition of restraint of trade, a more democratic banking system, and efforts toward conservation of natural resources. Progressivism was the dominant issue in the presidential campaign of 1912. Its arguments as set forth at that time may be found in Theodore Roosevelt's *New Nationalism* and Woodrow Wilson's *New Freedom*. Less popular but more profound presentation of its philosophy is given in the writings of Walter Weyl and Herbert Croly.

Aside from its practical merits and achievements, Progressivism marked something of a revolution in American political ideals. Representative government, as understood by the old schools of thought, was to be replaced by direct government; the supremacy of the judiciary was to be questioned if not overthrown; the last limits of government interference in private rights and property were to be removed; and with the breaking of the alliance of business interests with the government, a new type of leader and public servant was to appear upon the scene. The World War, however, so greatly confused the issues and involved the policies of the nation that at the moment Progressivism appears under very different colours from those it wore even two or three years ago, and judgment upon the movement cannot safely be passed.

CHAPTER XXII

Lincoln

THE man of many minds who upon the surface, at least, is variable is not thought of ordinarily as a great leader. And yet in some of the greatest of men a surface variableness has not in the long run prevented a consummate achievement. There is Cæsar, to be pondered upon by all who consider such men second rate. And in American history, there is Lincoln. His life as man of action brings this out well enough. He wavered during many years, hesitating between politics and law, not drivingly conscious of his main bent. Still more clearly is this brought out by his personal life and by those literary and mystical phases that are linked so intimately with the personal. The changes of his mood are at times bewildering. He is often like a wayfarer passing through successive strata of light and darkness, the existence of which does not seem to be explained by circumstance, of whose causes neither he nor his observers have explanation. Did they arise from obscure powers within? Were they the reaction of an ultra-sensitive nature to things without that most people were not able to perceive? He speaks of himself in one of his letters as superstitious. Should the word give us a hint? Whatever theory of him shall eventually prevail, it is sure to rest on this fact: he was a shrouded and a mysterious character, a man apart, intensely reticent, very little of whose inner life has been opened to the world.

It is significant that he was not precocious. The touching picture, preserved in several memories—the lonely, illiterate boy with a passion for reading, indulging the passion at night by a cabin fire—this picture has nothing of early cleverness. Of the qualities that appear after his advent, it is the moral not the mental ones that were clearly foreshadowed in his youth. The simplicity, the kindliness, the courage, the moderation of the matured man have their evident beginnings in the boy. His purely mental characteristics appeared so gradually, so unostentatiously, that his neighbours did not note their coming. Today, seen in the perspective of his career, their approach is more discernible. To one who goes carefully through the twelve volumes of the chronological edition of Lincoln's writings, though the transition from characterlessness to individuality is nowhere sudden, the consciousness of a steady progress in mental power, of a subtle evolution of the literary sense, is unmistakable. The revelation gains in celerity as one proceeds. But there is no sunburst, no sudden change of direction. And yet, for all the equivocality of the early years, one ends by wondering why the process has seemed vague. It is like that type of play whose secret is not disclosed until just before the curtain but which, once disclosed, brings all preceding it into harmony.

So of the literary Lincoln. Looking back from the few great performances of his fruition, why did we not earlier foresee them? There are gleams all along that now strike us as the careless hints of a great unseen power that was approaching. But why—considering the greatness of the final achievement— were they no more than gleams?

Here is an original literary artist who never did any deliberate literary work, who enriched English style in spite of himself under pressure of circumstances. His style is but the flexibility with which his expression follows the movements of a peculiar mind. And as the mind slowly unfolds, becomes overcast, recedes, advances, so, in the main, does the style. The usual symptoms of the literary impulse are all to seek. He is wholly preoccupied with the thing behind the style. Again the idea of a nature shrouded, withdrawn, that dwells within, that emerges mysteriously. His youth, indeed, has a scattered, unemphatic intimation of something else. What might be called the juvenilia of this inscrutable mind include some attempts at verse. They have no literary value. More significant than his own attempts is the fact that verse early laid a strong hold upon him. Years later, when the period of his juvenilia may be counted in the past, as late as 1846, in denying the authorship of a newspaper poem he added: "I would give all I am worth and go in debt to be able to write so fine a piece." Even in the first period of his maturity he could still lapse into verse. A visit to his former home in 1844 called forth two poems that have survived. One was a reverie in the vein of

> O Memory! thou midway world
>   Twixt earth and Paradise,
> Where things decayed and loved ones lost
>   In dreamy shadows rise.

The other was a description of an idiot, long a familiar village figure. Commenting on this poem, Lincoln refers to his "poetizing mood." His official biographers tell us that his favourite poets were Shakespeare, Burns, Byron, and Tom Hood, and add that his taste was "rather morbid." Byron's *Dream* was one of his favourites. It is a commonplace that he never tired of the trivial stanzas beginning

> Oh why should the spirit of mortal be proud.

When his writings come to be edited as literary remains— not merely as historical data—the period of his juvenilia will close with the year 1842. The first period of his maturity will extend to the close of his one term in Congress. Or, it may be, these two periods will be run together. To repeat, there are no sharp dividing lines across this part of his life. He was thirty-three in 1842; forty when he retired from Congress. Either age, in such a connection, is strangely removed from the precocious. In his writings before the end of his thirty-third year there is nothing that would have kept his name alive. However, even as early as twenty-three, in an address to the "People of Sangamon County" submitting himself as a candidate for the legislature, Lincoln revealed two, at least, of the characteristics of his eventual style—its lucidity and its sense of rhythm. Boy as he was, he was little touched by the bombastic rhetoricality of his day. On this side, from the first, he had purity of taste. His sense of rhythm—faintly to be sure—was also beginning to assert itself in 1832. Lincoln's sense of rhythm was far deeper, far more subtle, than mere cadence. In time it became a marvellous power for arranging ideas in patterns so firmly, so clearly, with such unfaltering disposition of emphasis that it is impossible to read them into confusion—as is so easy to do with the idea-patterns of ordinary writers. And with this sense of the idea-pattern grew up at last a sense of cadence most delicately and beautifully accompanying, and reinforcing, the movement of the ideas. In 1832 there were but gleams of all this—but genuine gleams.

The ten years following, sterile from the point of view of production, are none the less to the student of Lincoln's mind most important. As to literary workmanship in these years, what he did to develop his power of expression—in all but the vaguest outline the story is gone. That he read insatiably, that he studied and practised law, that he won local fame as an oral story-teller and as an impromptu debater, these details are preserved. With these is another tradition borne out by his writing. He was a constant reader of the Bible. This introduces the most perplexing question of his inner life. What was his religion? The later Lincoln—the one to whom, perhaps, we get the clue in these ten years between twenty-three and thirty-three—is invariably thought of in popular local tradition as a man of piety. But on this point what do we know? Lincoln has left us no self revelation. His letters, with the exception of one group, are not intimate. His native taciturnity, in this respect, was unconquerable.

Though born in a family of Baptists, he never became a member of the Baptist or of any church. Except for one amazing fragment he has left no writings that are not more or less obscure where they touch on religious themes. It is a curious fact that in the index to the voluminous official *Life* the word religion does not occur. As against this singular negative evidence there are anecdotes of a religious attitude. But the historian learns to question the value of all anecdotes. Nevertheless the tradition of Lincoln's piety—of his essentially religious nature —will not down. A rooted tradition, almost contemporary, is more significant than anecdotes, less susceptible of that constant dramatic heightening which makes the anecdote in retelling more and more positive. Now, the traditional Lincoln is a man overshadowed, a man of infinite gentleness whose pity seems to be more than mere friendliness or generosity. His own world, though uninformed as to his specific beliefs, persistently conceived of him as a mystic, as a walker apart with God. For evidence to support this impression we naturally look to his intimate letters. If we may judge by the surviving correspondence, this man, of whose friendliness ten thousand authentic instances testify, seems none the less to have lived and died solitary. The one mitigating experience appears in his early friendship for Joshua F. Speed. Cordial, trustful, sympathetic he was with many friends. The group of letters written to Speed in 1842 are in a vein that sets them apart. Both men had suffered through their emotions, and each in an analytical, self-torturing way. Upon Lincoln the sudden death of Ann Rutledge, with whom he thought himself in love at twenty-three, is supposed to have had, for the time at least, a deeply saddening effect. A second love affair was lukewarm and ended happily in divergence. The serious matter, his engagement to Miss Mary Todd, led to such acute questioning of himself, such painful analysis of his feeling, such doubt of his ability to make her happy, that the engagement was broken off. Within a month he had written: "I am now the most miserable man living. If what I feel were equally distributed to the whole human family, there would not be one cheerful face on earth." (23 January, 1841.) Two years were to elapse before the harm· was repaired and Lincoln and Miss Todd married. Meanwhile Speed, becoming engaged, suffered a similar ordeal of introspection, of pitiless self-analysis. He too doubted the reality of his feeling, feared that he would be wronging the woman he loved by marrying her. Lincoln's letters to his unhappy friend are the most intimate utterances he has left. Sane, cheerful,—except for passing references to his own misfortune,—thoughtful, they helped to pull Speed out of the Slough of Despond.

As nothing in these letters has the least hint of the perfunctory their reverent phrases must be accepted at face value. That a belief in God, even in God's personal direction of human affairs, lies back of these letters, is not to be doubted. Nevertheless the subject remains vague. Lincoln's approach to it is almost timid. There is no hint of dogma. But the fact that he here calls himself superstitious sends us back to his earliest days, to his formative environment, seeking for clues to the religious life he may have inherited.

Loneliness was the all-pervading characteristic of that life. The pioneer cabin, whether in Kentucky, Indiana, or Illinois, was an island in a wilderness. The pioneer village was merely a slightly larger island. Both for cabin and for village, the near horizon encircled it with the primeval. This close boundary, the shadow of the old gods, is a mighty, neglected factor in all the psychological history of the American people. In the lives of the pioneers, scattered over the lonely West, it is of first magnitude. It bore in upon them from every point of the compass, the consciousness of a world mightier than their own, the world of natural force. To a sensitive, poetic spirit, temperamentally melancholy, that encircling shadow must have had the effect of the night on Browning's David, though without producing the elation of David. That the mysticism of the primitive should have developed to full strength in a dreamer of these spiritual islands, but that it should not have risen victorious out of the primeval shadow, is explicable, perhaps, by two things—by the extreme hardness of pioneer life and by the lack of mental fecundity in these men whose primitive estate was a reversion not a development. While their sensibilities had recovered the primitive emotions, their minds, like stalled engines, merely came to a pause. Except for its emotional sensing of the vast unseen, the religious life of the pioneer islands lay most of the time dormant. It is a fact of much significance that the Western pioneers were not accompanied by ministers of religion—which is one detail of the wider fact that their migration was singly, by families, not communal. What a vast difference between the settlement of a colonial community, bringing with it organized religion, and these isolated, almost vagrant, movements into the West with organized religion left behind! Most of the time, in the places where Lincoln's boyhood was passed, there were no public religious services. Periodically a circuit-rider appeared. And then, in a terrific prodigality, the pent-up religious emotion burst forth. The student of Dionysus who would glimpse the psychology of the wild women of the Ecstasies, if he is equal to translating human nature through widely differing externals, may get hints from the religious passion of the pioneer revival. Conversely, Dionysus will help him to understand the West. That there was not much Christianity in all this goes without saying. It was older, simpler, more elemental. But it was fettered mentally in a Christian phraseology. Out of this contradiction grew its incoherency, its mean-

inglessness. With the passing of one of these seasons of storm-
ful ecstasy, there was left in its wake often a great recharge of
natural piety but nothing—or hardly anything—of spiritual
understanding.

And out of these conditions grew the spiritual life of Lincoln.
He absorbed to the full its one great quality, the mystical
consciousness of a world transcending the world of matter. He
has no more doubt of this than all the other supreme men have
had, whether good or bad; than Napoleon with his impatient
gesture toward the stars, that night on shipboard, and his
words, "There must be a God." But when it comes to giving
form to what he feels encompassing him, then Lincoln's lucid
mind asserts itself, and what has imposed on his fellow-villagers,
as a formulation, fades into nothing. And here is revealed a
characteristic that forms a basal clue. His mind has no bent
toward this sort of thinking. Before the task of formulating
his religion he stands quite powerless. His feeling for it is
closer than hands or feet. But just what it is that he feels im-
pinging on him from every side—even he does not know. He
is like a sensitive man who is neither a scientist nor a poet in
the midst of a night of stars. The reality of his experience
gives him no power either to explain or to express it.

Long afterward, in one of his most remarkable fragments,
the reality of his faith, along with the futility of his religious
thinking, is wonderfully preserved. It was written in September, 1862. The previous February the death of one of his
children had produced an emotional crisis. For a time he was
scarcely able to discharge his official duties. This was followed
by renewed interest in religion, expressing itself chiefly by constant reading of Scripture. Whether any new light came to him
we do not know. But in the autumn he wrote this:

The will of God prevails. In great contests, each party claims
to act in accordance with the will of God. Both may be, and one
must be wrong. God cannot be for and against the same thing at
the same time. In the present Civil War it is quite possible that
God's purpose is something quite different from the purpose of
either party; and yet the human instrumentalities working just as
they do, are the best adaptation to effect His purpose. I am almost
ready to say that this is probably true; that God wills this contest
and wills that it shall not end yet. By His mere great power on the

minds of the now contestants, He could either have saved or ae-
stroyed the Union without a human contest. Yet the contest began. And, having begun, He could give the final victory to either
side any day. Yet the contest proceeds.

Six months later one of the great pages of his prose called
the nation to observe a day of "national humiliation, fasting,
and prayer." That the Dionysian and circuit-riding philosophy
had made no impression on his mind is evinced by the silences
of this singular document. Not a word upon victory over enemies—eagerly though, at the moment, he was hoping for it—
but all in the vein of this question:

And insomuch as we know that by His divine law nations, like
individuals, are subjected to punishment and chastisement in this
world, may we not justly fear that the awful calamity of civil war
which now desolates the land may be a punishment inflicted upon
us for our presumptuous sins, to the needful end of our national
reformation as a whole people?

The context shows that he was not—as the abolitionists wished
him to do—merely hitting at slavery over the Lord's shoulder.
The proclamation continues the fragment. This great mystic,
pondering what is wrong with the world, wonders whether all
the values, in God's eyes, are not different from what they seem
to be in the eyes of men. And yet he goes on steadfast in the
immediate task as it has been given him to understand that
task. So it was to him always—the inscrutable shadow of the
Almighty for ever round about him; the understanding of His
ways for ever an insistent mystery.

To return to Lincoln's thirty-third year. Is it fanciful to
find a connection between the way in which his mysticism develops—its atmospheric, non-dogmatic pervasiveness—and the
way in which his style develops? Certainly the literary part of
him works into all the portions of his utterance with the grad-
ualness of the daylight through a shadowy wood. Those seven
years following 1842 show a gradual change; but it is extremely
gradual. And it is to be noted that the literary quality, so far
as there is any during these years—for it comes and goes—is
never incisive. It is of the whole, not of the detail. It does not
appear as a gift of phrases. Rather it is the slow unfolding of

those two original characteristics, taste and rhythm. What is growing is the degree of both things. The man is becoming deeper, and as he does so he imposes himself, in this atmospheric way, more steadily on his language.

Curiously enough it is to this period that his only comic writings belong. Too much has been said about Lincoln's humour. Almost none of it has survived. Apparently it was neither better nor worse than the typical American humour of the period. Humorously, Lincoln illustrated as an individual that riotous rebound which so often distinguishes the nature predominantly melancholy; and as a type, he illustrates the American contentment with the externals of humour, with bad grammar, buffoonery, and ironic impudence. His sure taste as a serious writer deserts him at times as a reader. He shared the illusions of his day about Artemus Ward. When he tried to write humorously he did somewhat the same sort of thing—he was of the school of Artemus.

A speech which he made in Congress, a landmark in his development. shows the quality of his humour, and shows also that he was altogether a man of his period, not superior in many small ways to the standards of his period. The Congress of the United States has never been distinguished for a scrupulous use of its time; today, however, even the worst of Congresses would hardly pervert its function, neglect business, and transform itself into an electioneering forum, with the brazenness of the Congresses of the middle of the last century. In the summer of 1848, with Zachary Taylor before the country as the Whig nominee for president, Lincoln went the way of all flesh political, squandering the time of the House in a jocose electioneering speech, nominally on a point before the House, really having no connection with it—in fact, a romping burlesque of the Democratic candidate, Cass. As such things went at that day, it was capital. It was better than most such speeches because, granting the commonplace thing he had set out to do, Lincoln's better sense of language gave even to his romp a quality the others did not have.

We come now to the year 1849, to Lincoln's fortieth birthday, and probably to another obscure crisis in his career. For thirteen years at least, politics had appeared to contain his dominant ambition. Amid bursts of melancholy of the most

intense sort, in spite, it would seem, of occasional fits of idleness, he seems in the main to have worked hard; he had made
headway both in politics and in law; he had risen from grinding
poverty to what relatively was ease. Now, he made the surprising decision to abandon politics. The reasons remain obscure. However, he carried his decision into effect. What the
literary student might call his second period extends from his
abandonment of politics to his return, from 1849 to 1855—or
perhaps through the famous Douglas controversy in 1858.

It was a period of slight literary production—even including
the speeches against Douglas—but of increasingly rapid literary development. One curious detail perhaps affords a clue
worth following up. Shortly after his return from Congress
Lincoln, with several other middle-aged men, formed a class
that met in his law office for the study of German. Was this an
evidence that his two years in the East had given him a new
point of view? Was this restless mind, superficially changeable,
sensitive to its surroundings, was it impressed—perhaps for the
moment, overawed—by that Eastern culture of the mid-century, of the time—so utterly remote it seems today!—when
German was the soul's language in New England? Lincoln had
visited New England, on a speech-making invitation, as a consequence of his romp against Cass. He was made much of by
the New England Whigs—perhaps for what he was, perhaps
as a Western prodigy uncouth but entertaining. From New
England, and from his two years in Congress, he came home to
forsake politics, to apply himself with immense zeal to the law,
to apply himself to the acquisition of culture. The latter purpose appears before long to have burned itself out. There was
a certain laziness in Lincoln alongside his titanic energy. It
would seem that the question whether he could keep steadily
at a thing depended not on his own will but on the nature of
the task. With those things that struck deep into the parts of
him that were permanent he was proof against weariness. But
with anything that was grounded on the surface part of him,
especially on his own reactions to the moment, it was hit or
miss how long he would keep going. Whatever it was that
started him after formal education in 1849, it had no result.
In the rapid development of the next few years his new-found
enthusiasm disappears. It is the native Lincoln moving still

upon his original bent, though with swiftly increasing mentality, who goes steadily forward from the able buffoonery of the speech against Cass to the splendid directness of the speeches against Douglas.

In these years he became a very busy man. At their close he was one of the leading lawyers of the state. Two things grew upon him. The first was his understanding of men, the generality of men. He always seemed to have known men's hearts. This was the gift of his mysticism—the gift which mysticism has often bestowed upon natures predisposed to kindness. Almost inevitably this gift produces sadness. Lincoln did not form an exception. The pity of men's burdens, the vision of the tears of the world falling for ever behind its silences, was as real in this peasant dreamer of our rude West as in that clerkly mediæval dreamer whom Walter Pater has staged so magically in the choir at Amiens. But the exquisite melancholy of the singer in the high church with its glorious windows can easily slide down smooth reaches of artistic contemplation into egoism. The rough, hard world of the West, having less of refuge for the dreamer, made the descent less likely. Nevertheless its equivalent was possible. To stifle compassion, or to be made unstable by compassion, was a possible alternative before the rapidly changing Lincoln of the early years of this period. What delivered him from that alternative, what forced him completely around, turning him permanently from all the perils of mysticism while he retained its great gift, may well have been his years of hard work, not in contemplating men but in serving them. The law absorbed his compassion; it became for him a spiritual enthusiasm. To lift men's burdens became in his eyes its aim. The man who serves is the one who comes to understand other men. It is not strange, having such native equipment for the result, that Lincoln emerged from this period all but uncannily sure in his insight into his fellows.

The other thing that grew upon him was his power to reach and influence them through words. The court room was his finishing academy. The faculty that had been with him from the start—directness, freedom from rhetoric—was seized upon in the life-and-death-ness of the legal battle, and given an edge, so to speak, that was incomparable. The distinction between pure and applied art, like the distinction between pure and applied mathematics, is never to be forgotten. Applied art, the art that must be kept in hand, steadily incidental to an ulterior purpose, affords, in a way, the sharpest test of artisticality. Many a mere writer who might infuse himself into an imaginative fantasy would fail miserably to infuse himself into a statement of fact. To attend strictly to business, and yet to be entirely individual—this is a thrilling triumph of intellectual assimilation. This is what Lincoln in these years of his second period acquired the power to do. When he emerges at its close in the speeches against Douglas, at last he has his second manner, a manner quite his own. It is not his final manner, the one that was to give him his assured place in literature. However, in a wonderful blend of simplicity, directness, candour, joined with a clearness beyond praise, and a delightful cadence, it has outstripped every other politician of the hour. And back of its words, subtly affecting its phrases, echoing with the dreaminess of a distant sound through all its cadences, is that brooding sadness which was to be with him to the end.

Another period in Lincoln's literary life extends from his return to politics to the First Inaugural. Of all parts of his personal experience it is the most problematic. At its opening there rises the question why he returned to politics. Was there a crisis of some sort about 1855 as, surely, there was about 1849? His official biographers are unsatisfying. Their Lincoln is exasperatingly conventional—always the saint and the hero, as saint-heroes were conceived by the average American in the days when it was a supreme virtue to be "self-made." That there was some sort of failure of courage in the Lincoln who gave up politics in 1849 is of course too much for official biography to be expected to consider. But it might perceive something besides pure devotion to the public weal in Lincoln's return. That this successful provincial lawyer who had made a name for conscientiousness should be deeply stirred when politics took a turn that seemed to him wicked, was of course quite what one would expect. And yet, was the Lincoln who returned to the political arena the same who had withdrawn from it? Was there not power in him in 1855 that was not in him in 1849? May it not be that he had fled from his ambition in an excess of self-distrust, just as in his love affair doubt of

himself had led him for a time to forsake what he most desired?
And may not the new strength that had come to him have
revived the old ambition, blended it with his zeal for service,
and thus in a less explicit way than his biographers would have
us think, faced him back toward politics. Be that as it may,
his literary power, which took a bound forward in the excitement following the Nebraska Bill, holds itself at a high level for
several years, and then suddenly enters into eclipse. Beginning
with the speech at Springfield on the Dred Scott case, including
the "house divided" speech, the Douglas speeches, and closing
with the Cooper Union speech in February, 1860, there are a
dozen pieces of prose in this second manner of Lincoln's that
are all masterly. If they had closed his literary career we
should not, to be sure, particularly remember him today. In
his writing as in his statesmanship it was what he did after
fifty—the age he reached 12 February, 1859—that secures his
position. None the less for surety of touch, for boldness, for
an austere serenity with no hint of self-distrust, these speeches
have no superiors among all his utterances, not even among the
few supreme examples of his final manner. Reading these
speeches it is hard to believe that this man in other moods had
tasted the very dregs of self-distrust, had known the bitterest
of all fear—that which rushes upon the dreamer from within,
that snatches him back from his opportunity because he doubts
his ability to live up to it.

The confident tone of these speeches makes all the more
bewildering the sudden eclipse in which this period ends. The
observer who reaches this point in Lincoln's career, having pondered upon his previous hesitation, naturally watches the year
1860 with curious eyes, wondering whether 1841 and 1849 will
be repeated, whether the man of many minds will waver, turn
into himself, become painfully analytical, morbidly fearful, on
the verge of a possible nomination for the Presidency. But the
doubtfulness of the mystics—who, like Du Maurier's artists,
"live so many lives besides their own, and die so many deaths
before they die"—is not the same thing as the timidity of the
man afraid of his fate. Hamlet was not a coward. The impression which Lincoln had recently made upon the country was
a true impression—that he was a strong man. However, not
his policies, not his course of action, had won for Lincoln his

commanding position in his party in 1860, but his way of saying
things. In every revolution, there is a moment when the man
who can phrase it can lead it. Witness Robespierre. If the
phraser is only a man of letters unable to convert literature
into authority, heaven help him. Again witness Robespierre.
Although if we conclude that the average American in the
spring of 1860 was able to read through Lincoln's way of handling words deep enough into his character to perceive his power
to handle men, we impute to the average American an insight
not justified by history, yet that average man was quite right
in hearing such an accent in those speeches of the second manner as indicated behind the literary person a character that was
void of fear—at least, of what we mean by fear when thinking
of men of action. That Lincoln wanted the nomination, welcomed it, fought hard for his election, only the sentimental
devotees of the saint-hero object to admitting. Nor did his
boldness stop at that. Between the election and New Year's
Day, the secession of South Carolina and the debates in Congress forced the Republicans to define their policy. The President-elect, of course, was the determining factor. Peace or war
was the issue. There is no greater boldness in American history
than Lincoln's calm but inflexible insistence on conditions that
pointed toward war. No amiable pacifism, no ordinary dread
of an issue, animated the man of the hour at the close of 1860.

Then, in the later winter, between his determination of the
new policy and his inauguration, came the eclipse. All the
questions roused in the past by his seasons of shadow, recur.
Was it superstition? Was it mystical premonition? Was there
something here akin to those periods of intense gloom that
overtook the Puritans of the seventeenth century? In a few
respects there are points of likeness between Lincoln and Cromwell. In most respects, the two men are widely dissimilar.
But in their susceptibility to periodic and inexplicable over-
shadowing they are alike. With Cromwell, besides his mysticism, there was a definite, an appalling dogma. Though Lincoln
did not carry the weight of Cromwell's dogma, perhaps the
essential thing was the same in both—the overwhelming, encompassing sense that, God being just and our Father, human
suffering must somehow be the consequence of our human sins.
Endow Cromwell with Lincoln's power of expression, and we

can imagine him in one of his grand moments writing that piece of superb humility, the Fast Day Proclamation. Again, was it superstition, was it premonition, that created in Lincoln, as he faced toward Washington, a personal unhappiness? No recollection of Lincoln is more singular than one preserved by his law partner with regard to this period of eclipse. He tells of Lincoln's insistence that their sign should continue to hang over the office door; of his sad eagerness to have everyone understand that his departure was not final; of his reiteration that some day he would come back, that his business would be resumed in the plain old office just as if nothing had happened.

Lincoln was so absolutely the reverse of the rhetorician that when he had nothing to say he could not cover up his emptiness with a lacquer of images. Never his the florid vacuousness of the popular orators of his day. When his vision deserted him, his style deserted him. It is confidently asserted that he never was able to press a law case unless he wholly believed in it. Strong evidence for the truth of the tradition is the obedience of his style to the same law. It behaved in this way, the eclipse being still upon him, when he was subjected to the misfortune of having to speak out of the shadow, in February, 1861, on his way to the inauguration. He could not escape this misfortune. The notions of the time required the President-elect to talk all the way from his home to the White House. This group of speeches forms an interlude in Lincoln's development so strange that the most psychological biographer might well hesitate to attack its problem. As statecraft the speeches were ruinously inopportune. Their matter was a fatuous assurance to the country that the crisis was not really acute. As literature, his utterances have little character. The force, the courage, the confident note of the second manner had left him. His partisans were appalled. One of the most sincere among them wrote angrily "Lincoln is a Simple Susan."

And then, lightning-like, both as statecraft and as literature, came the First Inaugural. Richard was himself again. He was much more, he was a new Richard. The final manner appeared in the First Inaugural. All the confident qualities of the second manner are there, and with them something else. Now, at last, reading him, we are conscious of beauty. Now we see what the second manner lacked. Keen, powerful, full of char acter, melodious, impressive, nevertheless it had not that sublimation of all these, and with that the power to awaken the imagination which, in argumentative prose, is beauty.

Lincoln had apparently passed through one of those indescribable inward experiences—always, it seems, accompanied by deep gloom—which in mystical natures so often precede a rebirth of the mind. Psychology has not yet analyzed and classified them. But history is familiar with a sufficient number to be sure of their reality. From Saul agonizing in his tent to Luther throwing his inkpot at the devil; from Cromwell wrestling with the Lord to Lincoln striving to be vocal when his mind was dumb—in a hundred instances there is the same range of phenomena, the same spiritual night, the same amazing dawn.

And now the most interesting of the literary questions concerning Lincoln presents itself. It is to be borne in mind that he was essentially non-rhetorical. He towers out of the literary murk of his day through his freedom from rhetoric. And yet, pernicious as it is, mere rhetoricity has its base in genuine artistic impulse. It is art perverted and made unreal, just as sentimentality is sentiment perverted and made unreal. And just as the vision of conduct which sentimentality perceives—and spoils—is an essential to noble living, so the vision of word-use which rhetoric perceives and spoils is essential to literature. Hitherto Lincoln had been ultra-sensitive to the spoiling done by rhetoricality. Had he been duly sensitive to the vision which the word-jobbers of his day had degraded to their own measure? It may be fairly doubted. But hereafter, in the literary richness of the final manner, no one can doubt the fulness and the range of his vision as an imaginative artificer in words. Had any new influence, purely literary entered into his life? One hesitates to say, and yet there is the following to consider. Lincoln submitted his First Inaugural to Seward. Several of Seward's criticisms he accepted. But Seward, never doubting that he was worth a dozen of the President in a literary way, did not confine himself to criticism. He graciously submitted a wholly new paragraph which Mr. Lincoln might, if he cared to, use as peroration. It read:

I close. We are not, we must not be, aliens or enemies, but fellow countrymen and brethren. Although passion has strained our bonds of affection too hardly, they must not, I am sure they will not, be broken. The mystic chords which, proceeding from so many battlefields and so many patriotic graves, pass through all the hearts and all hearths in this broad continent of ours, will yet again harmonize in their ancient music when breathed upon by the guardian angel of the nation.

One of the most precious pages in the sealed story of Lincoln's inner life would contain his reflections as he pondered this paragraph. Deeply as he knew the hearts of men, here—in spite of its lack of weight—was something that hitherto he had not been able to use. The power of it in affecting men he must have understood. If it could be brought within his own instrument, assimilated to his own attitude, a new range would be given to his effectiveness. Was he capable of assimilating it? We do not know how he reasoned in this last artistic crisis; but we do know what he did. He made Seward's paragraph his own. Into the graceful but not masterly—the half-way rhetorical—words of Seward he infused his own quality. He reorganized their feeble pattern by means of his own incomparable sense of rhythm. The result was the concluding paragraph of the First Inaugural:

I am loath to close. We are not enemies, but friends. We must not be enemies. Though passion may have strained, it must not break our bonds of affection. The mystic chords of memory, stretching from every battlefield and every patriot grave to every living heart and hearthstone all over this broad land, will yet swell the chorus of the Union when again touched as surely they will be, by the better angels of our nature.

The final Lincoln, in the literary sense, had arrived. Though an ultra-delicate critic might find a subdivision of this final period in the year 1862, the point is minute and hardly worth making. During the four years remaining in his life, his style has always the same qualities: flexibility, directness, pregnancy, wealth. It is always applied art, never for an instant unfaithful to the business in hand. Never for an instant does it incrust the business,—as the rhetorician would do,—nor ever overlay it with decoration. At the same time it contrives always to compel the business to transact itself in an atmosphere that is the writer's own creation; an atmosphere in which great thoughts are enriched by golden lustres, while ordinary thoughts bear themselves as do poor souls transfigured, raised momentarily to a level with the great by a passionate vision of great things

CHAPTER XXIII

Education

THE contribution of America to education is in the realm of practical ideas and institutional organization, not in that of philosophical theory or of literature. Even an adequate literary expression of the practical ideals which have dominated in varying form from decade to decade, or of the institutions which sprang therefrom, is rarely found. For the most part the literature has been ephemeral, serving the purposes of its own generation but carrying no great message to subsequent ones; or incidental, forming but a minor interpolated part of some other type of literature. Not until our own generation has there arisen a philosopher to give vitalizing expression to the dominant progressive ideas of America, or scientists to apply in literary form their instruments and methods to the problems of education.

The colonists of the seventeenth century transplanted to a virgin soil the old institutions of Europe. Some, as those of the South or of New Netherland, sought a new home merely to better their economic condition—not to modify a social system with which they were otherwise well satisfied. Some, chiefly of the Middle Colonies, sought to escape from persecution and thus to preserve cherished institutions. Only those of New England were beckoned by the vision of new institutions and customs in conformity with ideals cherished in the home land but not to be realized there.

Of the first type, Berkeley, the testy governor of Virginia, is the best spokesman. Replying in 1672 to the inquiry of the home government as to what policy was pursued in the colony regarding the religious training and education of the youth and of the heathen, he wrote: "The same course that is taken in

England, out of towns, every man according to his ability instructing his children." This represents accurately the condition of a colony where the largest town numbered not over twenty families, and the total population, no greater than that of a London parish, was scattered over a region larger than all England. While this part of the Governor's reply is seldom quoted, the latter part of it, probably inaccurate, certainly misleading, is often given. It continues:

> But I thank God there are no free schools or printing, and I hope we shall not have them these hundred years; for learning has brought disobedience and heresy and sects into the world and printing has divulged them and libels against the best of governments. God keep us from both.

Much of the scanty educational writings of colonial Virginia concerns the founding and the early work of its university, William and Mary, founded in 1693 through the efforts of the Rev. William Blair, a Scotch cleric, the head of the Established Church in the colony. Of this body of material, one bit is of more than ephemeral value. For when the persuasive Blair pleaded for the chartering and endowment of the college by the monarchs on the grounds that the colonists, as well as the people at home, had souls to save, the testy Seymour replied, with more force than elegance, "Damn your souls! Make tobacco!"

The fullest account of Southern colonial education, in fact of Southern colonial life, is Hugh Jones's *Present State of Virginia* (1724). He pays his compliments to the prevailing type of education in the following description of an important educational custom of the colonial period:

> As for education, several are sent to England for it, though the Virginians, being naturally of good parts (as I have already hinted) neither require nor admire as much learning as we do in Britain; yet more would be sent over were they not afraid of the smallpox, which most commonly proves fatal to them. But indeed, when they come to England they are generally put to learn to persons that know little of their temper, who keep them drudging on in what is of little use to them, in pedantic methods, too tedious for their volatile genius. For grammar learning, taught after the common

round-about way, is not much beneficial nor delightful to them; so that they are noted to be more apt to spoil their schoolfellows than improve themselves; because they are imprisoned and enslaved to what they hate and think useless, and have not peculiar management proper for their humour and occasion.

From the harassed Quakers of Penn's colony came a far more radical and forward-looking statement of the social theory of education, as befitted those persecuted for their ideals. It is obvious, however, from later records that little more was actually accomplished in Pennsylvania than in the South. The Frame of Government of 1682, with greater precision than any other colonial document, required that "to the end that the poor as well as rich may be instructed in good and commendable learning which is to be preferred before wealth" all children should be instructed "that they may be able at least to read the Scriptures and write by the time they attain to twelve years of age." Then that there should be neither failure to provide the fundamental practical training nor failure to perceive the social theory underlying it, these makers of society add "and that they [all children] be taught some useful trade and skill, that the poor may work to live, and the rich if they become poor may not want." But in order to meet the wishes of a heterogeneous population, Pennsylvania within a generation adopted the policy of giving to each religious sect the control of the education of its own youth. This plan remained in force until near the middle of the nineteenth century.

Throughout its history the Dutch colony of New Netherland was little more than the trading outpost of a commercial company. The career of the earliest schoolmaster we learn through the unsavoury record of the police court; those of his successors through the tedious records of the church, examining, licensing, and supervising, and through those more sordid though more human documents, the records of the commercial company, providing, under greater or less protest, the meagre salary.

It was the colonists of New England, particularly those of Massachusetts, who had visions of a new education in a new society and who left us abundant written records of their purposes and achievements. As specific as the Pennsylvania formulation and far more effective was the often quoted statement of the Massachusetts law of 1647:

It being one chief point of that old deluder, Satan, to keep men from the knowledge of Scriptures, as in former times, by keeping them in an unknown tongue, so in these latter times, by persuading them from the use of tongues that so at last the true sense and meaning of the original might be clouded by false glosses of saint-seeming deceivers, that learning might not be buried in the graves of our fathers, in church and commonwealth, the Lord assisting our endeavours,—it is therefore ordered. . . .

From this law came the establishment of schools in every town, elementary schools only in towns of fifty families, secondary or Latin grammar schools also in towns of over one hundred families. Within the century, through the provision of the law and the experience of a free people, these schools became free. Consequently this statute of 1647 constitutes the Magna Charta of the American public school system. The theory of education expounded may now seem narrow, but it was at least far more concrete, definite, and vitally connected with the life of the times than the worn-out theories used by later generations to justify the same narrow linguistic education.

Specific literary education was supplemented by, or rather was supplemental to, a broader social training provided for by a law enacted five years previously which related to the training of all children "in learning, labour, and other employments which may be profitable to the commonwealth," and provided adequate machinery to see that its provisions were applied to every child. Local records of the towns afford abundant evidence that these laws were carried out with fidelity throughout the seventeenth and most of the eighteenth centuries. Education in handicraft or some form of industry through the apprentice system constituted, indeed, the most important aspect of education throughout the colonial period; and those who are content to form their picture of educational conditions in the colonies from the laws or documents concerning the schools or more particularly the colleges—which affected but the few—overlook the most substantial and far-reaching part of the educational system. Many legislative enactments refer to it though as a matter of fact it was not actually necessary to legalize English customs in English colonies.

The fullest account of the apprentice system, especially as it was applied to the adult labourer, is given in the diary of John Harrower, a Scotchman, who, having indentured himself for some years to pay for his passage, landed in Virginia in 1774. Like many others he was sold as a schoolmaster; but unlike the many known only through newspaper advertisements, he left a long detailed record of his experience. A good account of the apprentice system as a scheme of education is found in the *Autobiography* of Benjamin Franklin. Franklin speaks of his father's desire to give him an academic education and of the unattractiveness of the Latin grammar school. That this disinclination to acquire the prevailing literary education was not due to lack of genuine interest in books is indicated by the fact that after other ventures the boy was finally apprenticed to the printer's trade on account of his "bookish inclination." Custom and finally statute in most of the colonies required that all such apprentices should be taught to read and write, as the early Massachusetts and Pennsylvania laws had dictated from the first.

The colonial elementary school received little attention in written records except in the minutes of ecclesiastical bodies and in town records. In these references the records of Massachusetts towns are particularly rich. The town of Salem ordered in 1644 "that a rate be published on next lecture day that such as have children to be kept at school would bring in their names and what they will give for one whole year, and also that if any poor body hath children, or a child, that the town will pay for it by rate." The first part of this town order indicates the method by which the earliest schools were generally supported—that of voluntary contribution. The last clause of the entry constitutes probably the first instance in America of legal provision for free education by state support. From these conditions and within a generation free public education in the Massachusetts towns developed.

It was, however, the Latin grammar school, found in all the colonies, that received the greatest attention, attaining at times the dignity of a newspaper or pamphlet agitation. Cotton Mather has left us the petition which John Eliot offered repeatedly at the synod of churches: "Lord, for schools everywhere amongst us! That our schools may flourish! That every member of this assembly go home and procure a good school to be encouraged by the town where he lives! That before we die we may be so happy as to see a good school encouraged by every plantation in the country!" Such zeal was not an isolated phenomenon and could not but bear fruit. The enthusiasm of America for education and the great public school system of subsequent days are but the legitimate results of such early devotion.

The outstanding figure in the conduct of the Latin school, as well as the chief representative of the colonial schoolmaster, is Ezekiel Cheever, who taught for seventy years, the last thirty-eight of them as master of the Boston Grammar School. Cheever himself contributed little to literature except a Latin *Accidence*, probably the earliest American school book, entitled *A Short Introduction to the Latin Tongue* (before 1650). This in itself was no more voluminous than the poetic tribute paid after his death by one of his pupils, Cotton Mather. With better motive perhaps than metre he thus records his esteem:

> A mighty tribe of well instructed youth
> Tell what they owe to him and tell with truth,
> All the eight parts of speech he taught to them
> They now employ to trumpet his esteem.
>
> .   .   .   .   .
>
> Ink is too vile a liquor; liquid gold
> Should fill the pen by which such things are told.

Another of Cheever's pupils was Judge Sewall, who has left us in his diary some details of the schooling of his children. After hearing Mather's funeral oration upon Cheever, Sewall made in this diary but one brief entry about their departed master: "He abominated periwigs."

Of the other colonial schoolmasters who contributed to literature the German pedagogue of Pennsylvania, Christopher Dock, has left the most substantial literary product. Besides a text or treatise he wrote an elaborate set of rules, one hundred in number, which portray in great detail the conduct of schools of the time, but which after all reveal merely transplanted European customs. Methods were extremely practical; although they indicate considerable empirical knowledge of human nature they show no scientific or philosophical knowledge of education. "When he can say his A B C's and point out each letter with his index finger, he is put into the A, b, abs. When he reaches this class his father owes him a penny and his mother must fry him two eggs for his diligence." One of the most fundamental of modern educational principles is indeed recognized: "Different children need different treatment." But how typical of the times is the interpretation, for he goes on to say: "That is because the wickedness of youth exhibits itself in so many ways." This most elaborate of colonial pedagogical works is similar in form and purpose to the numerous books on behaviour produced in all European countries during the seventeenth and eighteenth centuries, but it has little of the penetration or urbanity and none of the literary grace of Castiglione or of Chesterfield, or of the good Bishop de la Casa.

The most influential as well as most characteristic textbook of the colonial period was *The New England Primer*,[1] first issued about 1690 by a Boston printer. Constructed on principles borrowed from Comenius's *Orbis Pictus* and from the *Protestant Tutor*, it was used quite generally throughout the colonies and universally in New England. Countless youth made their way through the alphabet from "In Adam's Fall We Sinned All" to "Zaccheus he Did Climb the Tree, Our Lord to See." To its sombre interpretation of life was given a touch of human interest by the vivid description and illustrations of the martyrdom of Mr. John Rogers in the presence of his wife and nine small children "and one at the Breast." This little volume, no larger than the palm of a child's hand, was spelling book, reader, and text in religion, morals, and history. It culminated in the shorter catechism, but no part of it was without its religious phase, for the achievement in spelling extended to "abomination" and "justification." From the seed of this little volume sprang the notable harvest of schoolbooks, one of the most practical as well as most substantial of American achievements in education. A maturer companion piece to *The New England Primer* was Wigglesworth's *The Day of Doom* (1662). Though it was used perhaps more for home reading than for schools, few Puritan

[1] See also Book II, Chap. VII.

children escaped the task of memorizing its description of the last judgment.[1]

More voluminous than the literature of the lower schools is that relating to the colleges. One of the earliest literary productions of the colonists, the anonymous *New England's First Fruits* published in 1643, gives a full description of Harvard with its charter, curriculum, and rules governing student conduct. It reflects the spirit of the times, revealing the conception of education and the devotion of the people.

After God had carried us safe to New England, and we had builded our houses, provided necessaries for our livelihood, named convenient places for God's worship and settled the civil government, one of the next things we longed for and looked after was to advance learning and perpetuate it to posterity, dreading to leave an illiterate ministry to the churches when our present ministry shall be in the dust.

At the close of the century Cotton Mather in his *Magnalia* gave an elaborate history of the college, with accounts of its later rules and its chief dignitaries. Such charters and codes of rules are to be found for all the colonial colleges. These include Harvard, founded in 1636, named two years later, opened in 1639, and graduating its first class in 1642; William and Mary, founded in 1693 but for a generation perhaps little more than a grammar school; Yale, founded in 1701 but migratory for sixteen years; the college of New Jersey, more popularly called Princeton, founded in 1746; Pennsylvania, founded as an academy by Franklin in 1746 but chartered as a "college, academy and charitable school" in 1756; King's, now Columbia, founded in 1754; Brown, founded in Rhode Island by the Baptists in 1764; Queen's, now Rutgers, founded by the Dutch Reformed Church in 1766; and Dartmouth, founded as an Indian charity school in 1754 and chartered as a college in 1785. The first six were the achievements of entire colonies in which the sectarian motive was strong and the early population unified by belief. Two were direct outgrowths of religious sects. The last was a philanthropic venture. Benefactors gave their names to three; colonies to two; loyalty to reigning monarchs to three; Franklin was largely instrumental in the creation of Pennsyl-

[1] See Book I, Chap. IX.

vania. Dartmouth alone was "the lengthened shadow of a man," Eleazar Wheelock.

Each institution developed a mass of literature, in some cases controversial, but for the most part merely descriptive or apologetic. With the middle of the eighteenth century there appeared an educational literature revolutionary in character. Benjamin Franklin was the protagonist of these writers, and in truth colonial America's greatest educational leader. No one more clearly portrayed or did more to formulate the practical temper of American education for the half century succeeding the achievement of political maturity as well as for the half century preceding. Through the pages of *Poor Richard's Almanac* and by his own philanthropic activities he instilled the practical wisdom of economy, industry, thrift, virtue, into the receptive minds of his fellow colonists. He set up models of self-education in his *Plan of Daily Examinations in Moral Virtues* and in *Father Abraham's Speech*, which was a condensation of the wisdom of *Poor Richard*. His educational ideals, realized only fragmentarily in his own lifetime but more fully in succeeding generations, he formulated in his *Proposals Relating to the Education of the Youth of Pennsylvania* and in his *Sketch of an English School*. The former led ultimately to the establishment of the University of Pennsylvania.

The scheme for an English classical school or academy was the first effective revolt against the traditional education. While this portion of the school thrived not at all and persisted only under great difficulties, yet the idea survived and effected reform in the college from time to time. The same practical ideas appear in the announcement of King's College in 1754. The first president outlined his curriculum as follows:

And lastly, a serious, virtuous, and industrious course of life being first provided for, it is further the design of this college to instruct and perfect the youth in the learned languages, and in the arts of reasoning exactly, of writing correctly, and speaking eloquently; and in the arts of numbering and measuring, of surveying and navigation, of geography and history, of husbandry, commerce, and government, and in the knowledge of all nature in the heavens above us, and in the air, water, and earth around us, and the various kinds of meteors, stones, mines and minerals, plants and animals, and of everything useful for the comfort, the conven-

ience, and elegance of life; in the chief manufactures relating to
any of these things, and finally to lead them from the study of
nature to the knowledge of themselves and of the God of nature,
their duty to Him, themselves and one another and everything that
car constitute to their true happiness, both here and hereafter.

Though this programme was set forth by President Johnson,
the chief advocate of these views before the public was Dr.
William Smith, who was largely instrumental in the founding
of King's and who became the first provost of Pennsylvania.   In
1753 he published his *College of Mirania*, a Utopian educational
scheme containing the ideas advanced in the curriculum given
above and in fact the germ of a reformed higher education.
The underlying principle of Smith's proposed reforms is one
which has been repeated by educational innovators of many
generations, the realization of which must be attained anew by
each generation.   "The knowledge of what tends neither directly nor indirectly to make better men and better citizens is
but a knowledge of trifles.   It is not learning but a specious and
ingenious sort of idleness."   The most revolutionary part of his
scheme was the proposal of a mechanics' academy, as a counterpart of the collegiate school for the learned professions.   This
academy was to formulate an education for those "designed for
the mechanic professions and all the remaining people of the
country."   The essential features of the curriculum of this type
of schools are what in present times we should call the sciences,
theoretical and applied.   Franklin's scheme in the English academy was essentially the same.

But the dawning of political revolution eclipsed the rising
educational one, the new colleges fell back into the easier ways
of the old, and educational advance awaited a new nation, a
new century, and a new vision.

Problems of political construction, of economic development,
of national expansion and protection thoroughly absorbed the
interests and energies of the Americans for the first half century
of their national existence.   Education was left to individual
initiative or to quasi-public philanthropic interests.   During
this period there is no literature which may be termed educational except by loosest interpretation, and the references to
education in such literature as was produced are few.

Our national constitution, the great political document of the era, does not mention the subject. Of the sixteen state constitutions adopted during the eighteenth century, only five treat of it, and these, with one exception, in the most general manner. Thus it would seem that our forefathers looked upon education, at least of the elementary type, as a matter of individual concern, or as of local interest only. Two enactments of the national legislature had profound influence on the subsequent development of education and represent all that the national government did for public education until the Civil War period. The third article of the famous ordinance of 1787 reads: "Religion, morality, and knowledge being necessary to good government and the happiness of mankind, schools and means of education shall be encouraged." Two years previously, however, Congress had passed the Land Ordinance of 1785 by which the sixteenth section in each township was set aside for educational and gospel purposes. These two ordinances, together with subsequent modifications, ultimately gave as an endowment for public education a domain about as large as the Netherlands or Belgium or Denmark.

The local legislation of this period was chiefly permissive, and outside of New York and New England of little significance. In these states as elsewhere legislation was directed to the establishment of a district system of elementary schools. Such a system was the expression in educational terms of the most extreme principle of democracy. For it gave to the smallest unit which had or could have political organization and which could utilize a school, complete determination and control of the method of its support, the length of term, the character and equipment of teachers, the curriculum, and the textbooks. In time this system performed the great service of educating the American democracy to an interest in education, a belief in publicly supported schools, and an educated citizenship. Yet it also greatly limited that education and retarded educational development in other respects, in that the poorest teacher and the briefest term meant economy for the taxpayer, as irregular attendance and cheap textbooks did for the parent; while a restricted curriculum accomplished the same result for both these and the pupil as well. Such a system was destructive of professional interest and injurious to public spirit; but such no doubt was the necessary path to a broader and freer education if worked out in the democratic way. This explains largely the dearth of educational literature during this period, or its limitation to casual interpolations, private letters, legislative matter, or advertisement. One such advertisement contains in itself a further explanation of the indifferent status of education:

Wanted—a person qualified to teach school, and as an amanuensis to write grammatically for the press the composition of an old invalid. He must be a proper judge of securities for cash; draw leases; make wills; and undertake the clerkship of a large Benefit Society, with whom he must, by their articles, pray extempore and give them lectures. He ought to be able to sing and play different instruments of music, to teach his pupils to dance, and to shave and dress a few gentlemen in the neighborhood. Bleeding, drawing of teeth, and curing fire-legs, agues, and chilblains in children, will be considered as extra qualifications.

During this period communication was slow, travel most difficult, publication costly. As bespeaks an age of relative leisure, much of the literature was epistolary in character. The subject of education often entered into the correspondence of our forefathers, and sometimes found its way into the public press of the day. But on the whole the amount of such writing is surprisingly small; the interest in education of the generation that founded our government and put it into operation was slight and lacking in penetration.

Washington believed in a national university and wrote frequently on that subject. His outlook here, as on other aspects of education, was that of a Virginian or an English country gentleman—that educators were necessary but that the means to this end were a matter chiefly of individual concern. John Adams wrote his views into the first state constitution of Massachusetts, but they were the traditional views of colonial Massachusetts. He also left a diary or fragmentary autobiography which covers his experience as a district school teacher, without revealing more than a passing interest in education. James Madison held a broad conception of education, expressed frequently in his correspondence, but not at length. "A popular government, without popular information or the means of acquiring it, is but a prologue to a farce or a tragedy or perhaps both." Though probably the most widely informed man of his time, he did little more for education than occasionally to express such views.

Of all the national leaders, Thomas Jefferson alone took a vital interest in education, held broad and progressive views upon the subject, laboured incessantly for their realization, and left a literary record of them. The two most elaborate presentations of these views are in proposed laws or codes, one of 1779, the other of 1816. The first, a bill for the general diffusion of knowledge, proposed for Virginia a reproduction with elaborations of the essential features of the New England school system which was never realized; the second eventuated in the University of Virginia, the first of the state institutions, now so characteristic of America, to achieve material form. Much of the voluminous correspondence of Jefferson relates to these projects. He wrote often to his friend and political and legislative representative, George Cabell, advancing arguments, answering objections. His correspondence with Professor Ticknor of Harvard, lately returned from European universities, reveals his interest in and knowledge of foreign institutions. From this source no doubt came the innovations regarding freedom of choice of studies, the divorce of these from degrees, the lack of a permanent administrative head, the democratic government of both students and faculties, and other features which made the University of Virginia unique among American universities.

Jefferson's influence on education was local, not national. Only one other local or state leader of this generation was comparable to Jefferson: Governor De Witt Clinton of New York. Clinton, an organizer and a promoter of all movements for social betterment, left numerous addresses on various phases of the quasi-public educational endeavours of his time. Scientific societies, libraries, mechanics' institutes, hospitals, societies for the relief of the poor, infant school societies, Lancasterian societies, all held his interest and called forth statements of his democratic views. These, together with his messages to the legislature commending educational reforms, constitute the most considerable body of educational materials of the times. It was particularly the mechanical and temporarily successful Lancasterian system which aroused his greatest

enthusiasm. While Mayor of New York City he was instrumental in organizing (1805) the Free School Society of which
he was president until his death. For thirty-eight years this
society was the sole public or quasi-public educational agency
for the children of the metropolis, and for ten years longer it
continued a potent factor in competition with the growing public school system. As Governor of the state (1817–22 and
1824–28) Clinton continued an ardent advocate of this system
through public address and official paper.

The chief literary as well as practical exponent of the system
was John Griscom (1774–1852), a New York Quaker. In 1819
he published his observations on a visit to European countries,
as *A Year in Europe*. In this he records his impressions of all
types of European educational, philanthropic, and reformatory
efforts, thus giving to his countrymen in this direction a great
stimulus to endeavour. Of this work Henry Barnard later declared: "No one volume in the first half of the nineteenth century had so wide an influence on our educational, reformatory,
and preventive measures, directly and indirectly, as this."
Griscom's *Recollections* gives an intimate account of his services as teacher, administrator, educational innovator, and public-spirited citizen, covering a period of more than half a century.

The Lancasterian system had run its course before the death
of Griscom. Its mechanical scheme of organization made it
possible at least to attempt the education of children in large
groups. Lancaster claimed that one teacher, by using the older
pupils as monitors, could teach one thousand pupils. This ideal
was beyond the reach of his followers, though he himself is said
to have demonstrated its feasibility. The early New York
schoolrooms were built for five hundred pupils. Economically the scheme claimed to educate the child at an expense of
one dollar a year. Thus it put within the realm of possibility
the education of all the children of a community on the basis
of philanthropic and later of public support. To communities
not yet accustomed to taxation for police or fire protection, for
means of communication, care of streets, or sanitary provisions,
experience with the Lancasterian plan was an essential factor
in the evolution of schools. But the superficiality of the method
and its meagre intellectual results, its repressive disciplinary
measures, its false conception of child nature, its low moral

plane resulting from dependence on motives of reward and punishment, and the formality of its religious instruction brought about its final rejection.

Meanwhile a European educational influence of quite different character was being exerted through literary channels. This was the Pestalozzian movement in Switzerland and Germany, destined in later decades to have a powerful effect on American education. In 1806 William McClure, a Scotch philanthropist recently settled in Philadelphia, returned from Paris whither he had been sent as a commissioner to settle the French war claims. While there he had gone on an occasion to see the great Emperor, when it had been announced that Napoleon was to visit an experimental school kept by one of his old soldiers, Neef by name. Napoleon rejected the Pestalozzian ideas urged on him by Neef, while McClure accepted them, as did also the Prussian government.

Through various articles McClure was the first to introduce the Pestalozzian conception of education into America; later he induced Neef to remove to America, and in Philadelphia in 1808 Neef issued his *Plan and Method of Education*, the first distinctly pedagogical work published in the United States. The work of Neef in his first school was briefly described in later years in the memoirs of his most distinguished pupil, Admiral Farragut. Subsequently McClure and Neef both joined in the communistic and educational scheme which Robert Owen established at New Harmony, Indiana, in 1825. Owen had published in 1813 his *New Views of Society*, which was widely circulated in America as a means of educational and social propaganda. The substance of this dissertation was delivered by invitation before the American Congress, of which Owen's son, Robert Dale Owen, was later a member. The son also issued his *Outline of the System of Education at New Lanark, Scotland*, as a part of the American propaganda. The New Harmony experiment was a failure (1828), and the literary propaganda aroused intense opposition upon the part of the conservative elements in American society, particularly the religious, which then dominated the traditional education. The general triumph of the Pestalozzian ideas did not come until after the Civil War.

One great factor in the secularization of American education was formulated during this early national period—the school textbook. A second factor in this process was the change of dominant profession. During the colonial period, in education as in social and political life, this was the ministry. Immediately preceding and following the Revolutionary War leadership was largely assumed by the legal profession. The practical bent given to education by such men as Franklin and by the actual conditions of American life constituted a third factor. The three together resulted during the middle national period in the complete secularization of education at least in the elementary field. This change was accomplished in the United States long before it came about in any European country.

The textbooks of the colonial period were almost exclusively religious in character and content. From the close of the Revolution a distinct type of American textbook began to appear. Political material in the form of orations, patriotic appeals, and more or less exaggerated or distorted descriptions progressively replaced the sombre religious contents of the earlier books. Undoubtedly the bombastic oratory, exaggerated style of speech, and rather flamboyant views and claims of the American citizens of these and succeeding generations were largely due to this change. However, this was one of the means, perhaps a necessary one, by which provincialism vindicated itself, maintained its independence of "effete" European society, and developed in time a strong nationalism.

The earliest and most influential of these textbook writers was Noah Webster (1758–1843), whose fame as a lexicographer has long outlived his fame as textbook writer. In explanation of his work he wrote: "In 1782, while the American army was lying on the banks of the Hudson, I kept a classical school at Goshen, N. Y. The country was impoverished; intercourse with Great Britain was interrupted, and schoolbooks were scarce and hardly attainable." Accordingly, in 1783 he issued the first part of his *Grammatical Institute of the English Language, Comprising an Easy, Concise, and Systematic Method of Education Designed for the Use of English Schools in America.* This was a combination speller, reader, and grammar, which had patriotic as well as educational aims. Out of it grew various modifications, the most noted of which was *The American Speller*. This is the premier American textbook, of which more than seventy-five million copies have been sold and which still nas its devotees. In 1806 appeared his *Compendious Dictionary of the English Language*, which in its school or in its unabridged form has ever since been a familiar and popular work of reference.

The only rival to Webster in popularity and fame was Lindley Murray (1745–1826), a Quaker educator of New York and New Jersey. In 1795 he published his *English Grammar*, in 1797 his *English Reader*, and in 1804 his *Spelling Book*. These, somewhat more scholarly than those of Webster, and, as became an author English-born, somewhat less narrowly nationalistic, were also extremely popular, widely used, and greatly influential. In 1784 Jedidiah Morse issued his *Geography Made Easy*, the first American text on this subject. This was followed in 1789 by *American Geography, or a View of the Present Situation of the United States*, which was even more distinctly a means of political and nationalistic propaganda. In 1797 he published his *Elements of Geography*, and in 1814 his *Universal Geography*. The *New and Complete System of Arithmetic* by Nicholas Pike, avowedly a patriotic or nationalistic endeavour, came from the press in 1788. In its original form, too bulky for simple school use, or in numerous simpler offspring it dominated American schools for half a century.

There followed a deluge of school texts, as might be expected of an independent people blessed with initiative and groping for a democratic education. Many of these attempted the synthesis of the old and the new. There were those which began geographical studies with the exploration by Moses of the Red Sea; or the study of ichthyology with Jonah. Many still used the old catechetical form. Most included material of religious character, some of it in violently controversial form. Some adopted Biblical phraseology, hoping that the form would make alive, even if the spirit were gone. All were intensely nationalistic.

In the field of higher education, the outstanding change during this period was the development of the professional schools of medicine and law. The creation of a professional literature followed. The old colonial government was superseded by national and state governments based on written constitutions, "a government of law, not of men." Law reports began to appear in 1789, with Kirby's Connecticut Reports, and a book of practice was published as early as 1802. Courses in law were offered as early as 1773 at King's, now Columbia; at William and Mary, Yale, and Princeton before 1795. In 1793 James Kent was appointed lecturer in law at Columbia and served for three years. After twenty-five years at the bar and on the bench he returned to the academic position and delivered the series of lectures which forms the basis of American legal literature, his *Commentaries on American Law*.[1]

Medical education, like legal education, had been given during the colonial period chiefly by the apprentice system. Transition from this occurred through proprietary schools. While these schools persisted for the most part until the middle of the nineteenth century, yet university affiliation was found as early as 1767 at King's, now Columbia. More noted, however, was the proprietary school in Philadelphia from which the patriot physician Benjamin Rush laid the foundation of American medical literature.

The literature of science and philosophy stimulated in England and France chiefly through the quasi-public academies and in the Teutonic countries chiefly through state-controlled universities, found its chief encouragement in America through privately organized societies. The earliest of these was the famous Junto of Benjamin Franklin, organized in 1743. In 1780 this developed into the American Philosophical Society at Philadelphia. The same year the American Academy of Arts and Sciences was organized at Boston. This institution was chiefly under English influences, as the former was under French. Under the auspices of these two organizations most of the early scientific and philosophical publications of Americans were produced. Much of this literature was of very practical character, relating to agriculture, climatology, applied sciences, industry. Before 1820 eight or ten such societies were organized. After that period the number of such societies increased rapidly; but with growth in numbers came increased specialization. The development of the natural sciences brought about a less popular character of publication. Finally the literature of these societies became so technical as to fall out of the field of general educational literature.

As has been indicated, almost half a century of national

[1] See Book II, Chap. xv.

life had passed before the masses or even the leaders came to any general realization of the importance of public education to the new nation. During the second half century (1825–1875), which may be termed the middle national period, education was nationalized, democratized, and made free. This necessitated the education of the masses of the new democracy to the significance of education in its political and social bearing; the conversion of the professional teacher to a revised form of schooling less aristocratic in control, content, and method; and the persuasion of the hard-headed, not to say close-fisted, taxpayer that the expense was a legitimate object of government, not simply a matter of individual inclination and ambition. Each was a difficult task, and each produced its own type of literature.

Periodical publications devoted to education made their appearance. In 1818–19 there was published in New York *The Academician*, the first American educational periodical. Its standard was high, its appeal was made in no pettifogging spirit:

> O ye, whom science choose to guide
> Her unpolluted stream along,
> Adorn with flowers its cultured side
> And to its taste allure the young.

This was followed by *The American Journal of Education* (1826–30), making its appeal to the cultured classes and aiming to inform them on the subject of education and to persuade them of its fundamental importance. In the broadest social sense, not in the narrow technical one, it aimed to be educative. It proposed to diffuse enlarged and liberal views of education, to lay emphasis on physical education, moral education, domestic education, and personal education. Above all it considered the subject of "female education to be unspeakably important." The *Journal* was continued in *The American Annals of Education* (1831–39), the editors of which were William C. Woodbridge and A. Bronson Alcott. Alcott's other contribution to educational literature, *The Records of a School*, aroused to violent reaction the conservatives of his time, for in it were set forth educational doctrines which were not only radical after the type of Pestalozzi but revolutionary in the sense of the "modern chools" of Ferrer and other more recent radicals. From Alcott's school Louisa M. Alcott is said to have chosen the characters for some of her stories for the young. The *Journal* and the *Annals* were as worthy educational publications as any that we have in our own time, and appealed to the interests of the entire educated class instead of to the teaching profession, which indeed can hardly be said to have existed then.

Similar to these, in content at least, was the first educational periodical of the Middle West, *The Western Literary Magazine and Institute of Instruction*, published in Cincinnati (1835–39). The quality of this journal is a surprising comment on the high character of the interests of the frontier region. Its efforts were largely directed toward the development of free public schools and the higher education of women.

These were succeeded by a number of other magazines whose interests were localized in particular states, whose appeal was to the teaching profession alone, and whose objects were merely the development of a particular school system and of the technique of teaching. By the close of this period practically every state had one or more such publication. Only one of these, the first and the most influential, need be mentioned. This was *The Common School Journal* of Massachusetts, founded and for ten years edited by Horace Mann. It became the channel of official report and leadership, the source of professional training and stimulation, and the chief means by which Mann carried on his prolonged struggle for the reform and betterment of popular education. Yet this journal, like all of its type, was distinctly below the grade of the group of magazines first mentioned.

In magnitude, scope, and quality, however, all were outclassed by one great publication, Henry Barnard's *American Journal of Education* (1856–82). No other educational periodical so voluminous and exhaustive has issued from either private or public sources. It will ever constitute a mine of information concerning this and earlier periods in both Europe and America. Through this and his other publications, as well as through his position as first Commissioner of Education at the head of the National Bureau (founded 1867), Barnard exerted widespread influence on the developing educational interests of America. So valuable are the volumes of this magazine that when in subsequent years it was proposed to destroy the plates from which they were printed, a private subscription by appreciative friends of education in England saved them.

During the third, fourth, and fifth decades of the century another class of periodicals disseminated much material on education and exerted a peculiar influence on the developing ideas of the new democracy. These were the labour publications, particularly *The Workingman's Advocate*, *The Daily Sentinel*, and *The Young American*. Those enumerated were all issued in New York, but similar publications appeared in Boston, Philadelphia, Baltimore, and Cincinnati. The labour element, which during this period came into self-consciousness and achieved organization, took greater interest in education than at any subsequent time, but was peculiarly interested in the establishment of free public education of democratic character.

The most succinct and effective of the statements of labour on education is found in a series of six articles first issued in 1830 and republished subsequently in a number of publications. The first essay addressed itself to the question "What sort of an education is befitting a republic?" and answered "One that is open and free to all." An education, such as then prevailed, which shut the book of knowledge to one and opened it to another, was undemocratic. The second essay discussed the source of support, and asserted that it should be "from the Government," because education was in reality a form of legislation and if wisely cared for might to a great extent supersede the necessity and save the expense of criminal law, jails, and almshouses. The third essay considered the question "What sort of an education should the people have?" and answered "Whatever is good enough for human beings." The current aristocratic education "of adornment" was rejected, "not because Hebrew and velvet painting are good only for the rich and privileged, but only because we think them useless for any one." The purpose of education is to make men "not fractions of human beings, sometimes mere producing machines, sometimes mere consuming drones, but an integral republic, at once the creators and employers of industry, at once master and servant, governor and governed." The specific scheme recommended was a combination of industrial and agricultural train-

ing with a more practical literary education than that in vogue
at the time.

These educational demands of labour were combined with
many other calls for social reform. Some of these, long since
attained, such as free access to public lands, abolition of imprisonment for debt, adoption of general bankruptcy laws, removal
of property qualification for voting, have an antiquated sound
at present. Some, such as abolition of monopolies, shorter
working hours, equal rights for women with men in all respects,
are still familiar slogans; some, such as the abolition of all laws
for the collection of debts, the housing of all children in barracks
for educational purposes, possess a radicalism which puts them
in the realm of Utopias, desired or undesired.

With the substantial achievement of free public education,
at least in theory, by the middle of the century, the labour groups
lost their interest in education and in large public questions in
general, and transferred it to the economic problems in which
they were interested.

During this period America was peculiarly conscious of its
growth in national independence and sensitive as to its provincialism. This sensitiveness was not rendered less acute by the
comments of friendly visitors such as Miss Martineau (*Society
in America*, 1837) and Charles Dickens (*American Notes*, 1842),
guests not inclined to "see Americans first." Some of these
foreign commentators on educational America were more generous in appreciation. George Combe, the celebrated phrenologist, in his three volumes of *Notes on the United States of
America* (1841), makes frequent reference to educational affairs
in which he was much interested; the Swede, Siljestrom, published in 1853 *The Educational Institutions of the United States*,
the most elaborate description and most favourable commentary
of all.

The educational leaders of America, however, and to a less
extent the educated public, were keenly alive to the technical
superiority of European education and to the value of some of
the novel European experiments. The two most important of
these have been mentioned. The mechanical English Lancasterianism reached the zenith of its popularity before the middle
of the century and disappeared before the close of this middle
national period. The Swiss Pestalozzianism, especially in its

systematized German form, greatly increased in influence. Because of its liberal and more accurate interpretation of human nature, its kindly sentiment, its democratic bearing, and the social significance which it gave to education, it fitted into the American environment. School method was greatly modified and in time shaped by a more psychologically accurate interpretation of the child mind, as school management was by a more human conception of the educational process. Both Lancasterianism and Pestalozzianism occasioned a mass of publications, in pamphlets, newspapers, periodicals, books, and special reports. The infant school, borrowed from England, though it had a briefer vogue than Lancasterianism, contributed to the development of our primary schools.

The Fellenberg experiment in Switzerland (1809–44) exerted, according to Barnard, a greater influence in America than any other single educational institution ever did. Its fundamental idea was the unifying of an academic and a practical industrial or agricultural education as this union is now achieved by such an institution as Hampton. Scarcely an American college and few academies founded between 1825 and the middle of the century but sought to embody this idea. Consequently early collegiate literature is saturated with this suggestion. Suggestion only, however, it proved to be, for few followed the experiment long and none actually understood the fundamental educational principles involved. The plan commended itself to provincial America, since it made collegiate education feasible to many to whom it were otherwise impossible because of financial limitations. It met with approval also because it promoted the physical health so much needed by students who were yet living under the ideals of a religious asceticism tempered only by occasional relapse. There were good souls who justified this type of education by recalling that Samson was a man of strength, David was ruddy of countenance, and that Moses must have been of strong physique to judge by certain incidents in his early manhood.

European endeavour and achievement in education became the subject of much study by American educators and occasioned a few outstanding reports. Some of these reports were personal only, as that on the Fellenberg plan (1831–32) by William C. Woodbridge, who taught for a year in the parent institution. Others were official, as that made by Professor Calvin E. Stowe on the Prussian school system to the Ohio legislature in 1837. This brief volume, admirable in conciseness, temper, and insight, had wide influence and was republished by many state legislatures. So also was the report of the French philosopher Cousin, *On the State of Public Instruction in Germany, Particularly in Prussia* (1831). This, indeed, because of its wide influence came to be considered a part of American educational literature.

More ponderous and less influential was the exhaustive report of Alexander Dallas Bache (1839), the first president of Girard College. Authorized by the trustees to gather information concerning the education of orphans, he included an elaborate study of school systems of most European countries. The influence of all these reports was focussed by Horace Mann in his *Seventh Annual Report* (1844) as Secretary of the Massachusetts Board of Education.

Mann was an ardent patriot, an experienced politician and public administrator, a keen observer, an energetic reformer, and the wielder of a trenchant pen. His forceful statement was followed up by yet more forceful practical endeavour. The abolition of corporal punishment, the introduction of an enriched curriculum, the training of teachers, the adoption of methods based on a scientific knowledge of the human mind, the proper classification of school children, the elaboration of the public school system to include many if not all of the quasi-public organizations so numerous in America—these were his demands. The effect of all of the efforts to borrow lessons from European, particularly German, experience was thoroughly in evidence.

One other of these observers of European experiment has already been mentioned,—Henry Barnard (1811–1900),—the record of whose observations exceeds in bulk the work of all the others. In 1852 Barnard issued a volume of *School Architecture* placing that phase of educational activity on the most advanced plane, where it has since been maintained. In 1851 he published an extensive volume on *Normal Schools*, and in 1854 one on *National Education*. These activities were continued in the serial publication of the *American Journal of Education*.

Horace Mann's activities were directed pointedly against local evils and produced violent reaction. The controversy in magazine and newspaper was prolonged and became of national interest. So it happened that the great educational reforms of the fourth, fifth, and sixth decades of the century, in which Barnard and many others laboured no less effectively than Mann, became generally connected with Mann's name

In this period official educational reports appeared in great quantities. Such documents actually began as early as 1789 with the Reports of the Regents of the State of New York to the legislature. This series, still continued, gives us the longest survey of education to be found in state or nation. Reports of state superintendents of education began with the establishment of such an office in the State of New York in 1812. These two series were the only ones, however, before the appointment of Mann in Massachusetts in 1837 and of Barnard in Connecticut in 1838. The reports of Horace Mann are to this day outstanding documents and reveal in detail the accomplishments as well as the needs of education in his time. Others of importance were those of Lewis of Ohio, Pierce of Michigan, and Gilman of Connecticut, later the first president of Johns Hopkins University. While none of these documentary reports possess the literary quality of those of Mann and Barnard, and perhaps gain their classification as literature merely because they appear in print and cumber the shelves of our libraries, yet in them one can discover the educational achievements and aspirations of the period.

Technical professional literature began to appear towards the middle of the century, with the founding of the normal schools. Omitting the short production of Neef, the earliest and undoubtedly the most popular and influential through all of this period was *The Theory and Practice of Teaching* (1847) by David T. Page, principal of the first New York normal school.

Popular educational discussion was largely if not wholly directed to the question of free public schools as opposed to the traditional private, church, or quasi-public schools supported by tuition fees or rates. It is difficult for Americans of the present generation to realize that little more than half a century ago free public schools were frequently attacked as having

dangerous socialistic tendencies, as being atheistic, or as devices
of the evil one. Even political radicals could resolve "that all
compulsory school establishments are as oppressive as church
establishments and no reasoning, no arguments, can be offered
in support of the former which are not equally applicable to
the latter." The conservatives, represented by the most influential *National Gazette* (1830), argued: "It is our strong inclination and our obvious interest that literary education should
be universal; but we should be guilty of imposture if we professed to believe in the possibility of that consummation . . . .
The 'peasant' must labour during those hours of the day which
his wealthy neighbour can give to the abstract culture of the
mind." The ecclesiastical representative arguing for the repeal
of the free school act in New York (1850) claimed that "it
will at least give us hope that if the people of the State shall be
delivered from this odious act, the people of this city will soon
follow in demanding freedom from schools that are a moral
nuisance, and have no kind of claim upon the confidence of the
public." The views of the aristocratic class may be represented
in a sentence or two from John C. Calhoun (1834):

> The poor and uneducated are increasing; there is no power in a
> republican government to repress them; the number and disor-
> derly tempers will make them the efficient enemies and the ruin of
> property . . . . Education will do nothing for them; they will
> not give it to their children; it will do them no good if you do. . . .
> Slavery is indispensable to a republican government.

To counteract and destroy such views was not an easy or a
brief task. The controversy was prolonged through years of
public discussion and debate. The most important of the arguments for the free school which found permanent form were the
Essays on Popular Education (1824) by James T. Carter of
Massachusetts; the address of Thaddeus Stevens on *Free
Schools vs. Charity or Pauper Schools* before the legislature of
Pennsylvania in 1835; the *Tenth Annual Report* of Horace Mann
in 1846; and finally the address of James A. Garfield, then congressman, later President, on the establishment of a national
bureau of education in 1867. Surprising as it now seems, the
controversy terminated only after the Civil War. The free

school system was not finally established in New York until 1867, in New Jersey until 1869; in actual practice it was not in operation in a number of the Middle Western states until after 1870, and in some of the Southern states a decade or so later.

As *The Journal of Education* said, during this period the problem of "female education" was "unspeakably important." In the successful agitation of that subject America made one of her great contributions to education. Undoubtedly the prevalent view was that "education renders females less contented with the lot assigned them by God and by the customs of society; that it tends to withdraw them from their appropriate domestic duties, and thus make them less happy and less useful." The first effective protest against this view was made by Mrs. Emma Hart Willard (1787–1870). After a teaching experience which began at the age of seventeen, she drew up in 1816 an *Address to the Public, Particularly to the Legislature of New York, Proposing a Plan for Improving Female Education.* At the urgent advice of Governor Clinton the legislature voted (1819) that the academy which Mrs. Willard had founded should be entitled to share in the state funds. Though these funds were probably never granted by the regents and consequently never became available, the institution has the credit of being the first institution, in America at least, for the higher education of women to which state aid was voted. Mrs. Willard wrote many textbooks and was credited by her generation with opening to women the "masculine subjects" of mathematics and the descriptive sciences.

The pioneer work of Mrs. Willard in founding the Troy Academy was followed by that of Mary Lyon in the founding of Mount Holyoke Seminary (1837). Miss Lyon's one contribution to literature, aside from the circular of the institution, was *Female Education* (1839), which was but an enlarged prospectus of the Seminary and a defence of the type of education then offered to girls. By a narrow margin the institution escaped being labelled "The Pangynaikean Seminary," and by a margin quite as narrow did the education offered vary from the traditional formal education of young men. The tendency to make women's newly won privilege a mere copy of the formal education offered to men is revealed in a yet more extreme form in the next step, the establishment of the first women's college, Vassar, in 1861. Nevertheless the literary documents produced by these foundations are far more radical than the views prevalent and reveal a greater independence of thought than do the institutions in their practice.

The literary discussions called forth by this subject during this entire period while voluminous in quantity have only historical interest; nor had the cause any advocates who can compare in literary skill or influence with Hannah More or Maria Edgeworth.

In the field of higher education the middle half-century was one of great activity and advance. The Dartmouth College Case by its decision (1819) that the state could have no part in determining the character or activities of denominational institutions once chartered, stimulated both secular authorities and sectarian religious interests to renewed activity in fostering such institutions. Beginning with the University of Virginia, opened in 1824, and led particularly by the University of Michigan, opened in 1841, such secular institutions multiplied and flourished. Similar to these were Wisconsin, 1848, Minnesota, 1864, Illinois, 1867, California, 1873—to name only the largest and most widely known of the state universities; and of privately endowed institutions, the Johns Hopkins University, 1876, and Leland Stanford, Jr., University, 1891. In the case of denominational foundations the situation was similar. While eleven colleges were established previous to the Revolution and thirty-four in the following half century, no less than 285 such institutions, of acknowledged standing and still in existence, originated during the middle half-century. The University of Chicago, established in 1892, is the most famous.

Each institution produced certain literary efforts in the form of propaganda, report, and product. Undergraduate journalism originated and flourished. Sectarian propaganda was stimulated. College officials in time ceased to regard student instruction and discipline as their only function and began to attend to larger and more impersonal educational problems. The two most important products of these new interests were reports, one by the faculty of Amherst College in 1827, the other by the faculty of Yale College in 1829. It is an indication either of the progessiveness of that period or of the non-progressiveness of the century intervening between then and now, or perhaps of the traditional character of educational ideas in general, that the problems discussed in these pamphlets are much the same as those of the present day, and that the arguments then offered differ but little from those now heard. A paragraph from the Amherst report states the problem clearly:

Why, it is demanded, such reluctance to admit modern improvements and modern literature? Why so little attention to the natural, civil, and political history of our own country and to the genius of our government? Why so little regard to the French and Spanish languages, especially considering the commercial relations which are now so rapidly forming, and which bid fair to be indefinitely extended between the United States and all the great Southern republics? Why should my son, who is to be a merchant at home, or an agent in some foreign port; or why, if he is to inherit my fortune, and wishes to qualify himself for the duties and standing of a private gentleman, or a scientific farmer—why, in either case, should he be compelled to spend nearly four years out of six in the study of the dead languages, for which he has no taste, from which he expects to derive no material advantage, and for which he will in fact have but very little use after his senior examination?

This quotation indicates the tenor of the Amherst reply; it was favourable to a progressive, even radical, solution. On the other hand the very elaborate Yale discussion of the same subject, the product of prolonged faculty deliberation, is the fullest statement of the traditional "disciplinary" view of collegiate education.

The best literary presentation of the period of conflict is President Wayland's *Thoughts on the Present Collegiate System in the United States* (1842). This discussion, as also President Wayland's various annual reports, emphasized the need of radical reform in the collegiate system.

The middle decades of the century were characterized by the prominence of a few influential college presidents whose personality dominated the period and whose writings and official reports gave character to the literature relating to higher education. Among these were Eliphalet Nott (1804–66) of Union, Francis Wayland (1827–55) of Brown, Mark Hopkins (1836–72) of Williams, Frederick A. P. Barnard (1864–89) of Columbia. Nott for more than half a century gave his impress to the independent non-sectarian type of institution; Wayland directed the transformation of a small denominational college into an institution with broad outlook, efficiently serving the whole community; Hopkins[1] represents the entire conception of collegiate education as the moulding of the character of youth, as witnessed by the proverbial collegiate log with Hopkins at one end and the future President, Garfield, at the other; Barnard first caught the vision of the future university, growing out of the traditional college, and led the way to the threshold of a new day. Whether the curriculum should be reformed by the introduction of modern subjects; whether there should be a choice of these, when introduced, to the exclusion of the traditional classics; whether technical subjects, preparatory to the new professions of engineering, medicine, industry, and business should find a place—these became the subjects of continued discussion. The sectarian and hortatory discussions which prevailed before the Civil War gave way rather definitely after that conflict to such as these.

An important phase of the public education movement of the early half of the century has almost faded from our conception of education. To these generations, to whom the new, broader democratic views appealed because of the social, political, and economic benefits to the contemporary generation, the problem of adult education was of far more significance than it is today. This adult education was given through the medium of mechanics' institutes, debating clubs, "Ciceronian associations," and, most numerous of all, lyceums. A national convention of 1831 enumerated almost a thousand such organizations. The Massachusetts Report of 1840 lists eight mechanics' institutes and 137 lyceums. The lyceum organization, launched in Boston in 1829, included the town lyceum, and country, state, and national organizations. In reality the scheme never arrived at such complete general organization; however, it did attain universal popularity, very general distribution, and in some sections effective state as well as local organization. As the epistolary form of literary composition was the most popular in the preceding period, the lecture or address was during this period the dominant form of expression, even in the field of education. The leaders of thought in every walk of life

[1] See also Book II, Chap. XXII.

participated in this adult form of education, and much of the most important literary expression of the period was originally published through this channel. De Witt Clinton, Edward Everett, Ralph Waldo Emerson, Wendell Phillips, William Lloyd Garrison, Bronson Alcott, George William Curtis, William Cullen Bryant, Henry David Thoreau, James Russell Lowell, Edward Everett Hale; such political leaders as Sumner, Douglas, Greeley; women leaders, as Julia Ward Howe, Susan B. Anthony, Emma Willard; foreign visitors; and almost every man of literary prominence made contributions to this form of literature, more or less permanent, and more or less educational in character.

The most important contributor to the lyceum type of education and its chief adornment was Emerson,[1] an essayist because he was a lecturer, rather than a lecturer because he was an essayist. His livelihood for a considerable period depended upon his professional activity upon the platform. Though the remuneration of these lecturers seems absurdly small when compared with the extravagant earnings of Chautauqua favourites, yet they were sufficient for the simple life of that period. The lecture had to be adapted to a mixed audience; it had to be limited to an hour's time; it had to be varied and stimulating; and it had to conform to certain literary or technical forms. Nevertheless there was a freedom in this literature given for the occasion and the people which bespeaks the educational character. Emerson himself said: "I preach in the lecture room, and there it tells, for there is no prescription. You may laugh, weep, reason, sing, sneer, or pray, according to your genius." The stimulating and illuminating idealism of Emerson's essays is an indication of the high purpose, if not an index of the normal attainment, of the adult educational endeavour of this generation. For his *Self Reliance, Compensation, Prudence, Intellect, The Over-Soul* not so much moulded the beliefs of his generation as expressed the unformulated thought and the highest aspiration of the New England Puritanism of his day.

Of literature presided over by the muses, there is little which relates to education. In this group Irving's *Legend of Sleepy Hollow* (1819) undoubtedly takes first place. If the delineation of Ichabod Crane is a caricature, that of the school is not, nor

[1] See Book II, Chap. IX.

is the "half itinerant life" of the master. No other account of the old district school approaches this one in charm. Nathaniel Hawthorne's *Grandfather's Chair* retells the story of Ezekiel Cheever; and *Daffy-down-Dilly* and other stories draw on the rich experience of the district school. Henry Ward Beecher's *Norwood* (1868) is a tale, or rather a series of sketches, of New England life in which the New England academy finds a place, as it properly should, since no institution or phase of life was more characteristic of this period. In a more humorous vein is Oliver Wendell Holmes's description of the Apollinean Female Institute in *Elsie Venner*. At a later day and in more attractive form the New England private school receives probably the most attractive treatment given to a school in American literature in J. G. Holland's *Arthur Bonnicastle* (1873).

If American literature is not rich in materials chosen from the schools, probably no other literature is so enriched by casual references to the school. Perhaps no evidence of the practical efficiency and worth of the American public schools is more significant than the frequent reference in public speech, in the daily press, in ephemeral or permanent literature, to "the little red schoolhouse." This conventional phrase typifies the simple and somewhat forbidding form of our education of the past, and at the same time the sturdy activities and high ideals of our moral life from which the generations of the past have drawn their sustenance. If our theme were the contribution of educators to literature a most fruitful subject would here be presented. For the mid-century productive period in American literature was closely associated with college life, particularly in New England. The period when Longfellow, Holmes, Lowell, and Agassiz were members of the Harvard faculty was an epoch-making one in our American literature. Holmes's *Professor at the Breakfast Table* and Longfellow's *Outre-Mer* give the flavour of this life and make the nearest approach to the subject of the technical educator; perhaps by the same measure they fall below the literary standard of the other writings of these professors.

The one ambitious attempt to draw the materials of fiction from the life of the school is found in *Locke Amsden, or the Schoolmaster* (1847),[1] by Daniel Pierce Thompson. The old

[1] See Book II, Chap. VII.

district school finds here its fullest literary presentation. Though the mid-century popularity of this book was sufficient to call forth many editions, it is now nearly forgotten, and its author is remembered, if at all, by his more stirring *Green Mountain Boys*. At the close of this period, but drawing its inspiration from the frontier conditions of the early portion of this period in the Middle West, appeared Edward Eggleston's *The Hoosier Schoolmaster* (1871).[1] This racy narrative is the liveliest account of the pioneer schoolmaster to be found, and as a delineation of frontier life will compare favourably with the best in its sort. Eggleston's later work, *The Hoosier Schoolboy* (1883), is in similar vein. His *Schoolmaster in Literature* (1892) adds nothing to his repute and little to our subject.

A characteristic feature of American life is its tendency to voluntary organization. Perhaps as a substitute for the pomp and ceremony of an aristocratic society the tendency reveals itself in the many secret societies with their elaborate ceremonials. This national characteristic shows itself in American college life in the numerous Greek letter societies or fraternities. Only the earliest of these, founded as an honour society with political purposes also, has furnished occasion for a considerable literary product, much of it of superior quality. The Phi Beta Kappa was organized at the College of William and Mary in 1776 with membership based on scholarly attainments. Chapters were soon to be found in the leading institutions of the country. The annual meetings of these constituent chapters have been the occasion of many notable addresses or poems. Emerson's *The American Scholar* was written for such an occasion (1837). The list of these productions is a long one, most of them having an academic significance. As illustrative of this type may be mentioned: *The American Doctrine of Liberty*, by George William Curtis; *The Scholar of the Republic* by Wendell Phillips; *Academic Freedom* by Charles W. Eliot; *What is Vital in Christianity?* by Josiah Royce; *The Mystery of Education* by Barrett Wendell; *The Spirit of Learning* by Woodrow Wilson. These with many others of similar excellence are scattered throughout the century.

One other type of literary production having incidental educational importance is found in the reminiscences or memoirs of

[1] See Book III, Chap. XI.

the men of this period. None of these writers, however, enter seriously enough into their earlier experiences to make the accounts of any value except that of personal testimony as to existing conditions. The best of these are from Edward Everett, Samuel G. Goodrich, and Noah Webster. Similar to these, though much fuller and of no great literary merit, was *The District School As It Was* by the Rev. Warren Burton, depicting conditions at the opening of the century.

No phase of informal education is more important than the moulding of the character of children by their choice of interests and activities out of school, particularly as determined through their reading. In another chapter[1] of this history will be found an account of American books for children; here it is sufficient to note the steady trend away from moralizing and religious disquisition to wholesome amusement and secular instruction.

The last three or four decades have witnessed a marked change in the character of the literature relating to education. As in other phases of thought and action, the dominating influence has been that of science. Educational literature characteristic of the period is scientific, either psychological, experimental, or statistical; consequently it has become far more technical.

Old types continue, perhaps still dominating in mere quantity; but they are no longer characteristic. School publications of advice and device yet flourish, but the scientific educational journal now receives the support of a definite and daily enlarging clientèle. Official reports multiply with an annual certainty which sets at naught any Malthusian law in the world of books. But accurate statistical method is making an impression on the content, providing these forbidding tomes with an enhanced value; while the school survey has furnished an entirely new type. Works on pedagogy, addressed to the profession, have become so numerous as to preclude even comparison with those of the preceding period; yet the nascent sciences of psychology and sociology have given to many of these a substantial character which justifies a large allotment of space in libraries and bibliographies.

While there has been much of note along scientific and philosophical lines, literature as an art has paid little heed to

[1] See Book III, Chap. VII.

the schoolmaster or his need. Professor William James [1] "wrote psychology which reads like a novel," and Henry James [2] added to his novels the autobiographical volumes *A Small Boy and Others* and *Notes of a Son and a Brother* which contain much material of interest relating to the educational experience of the two brothers. Howells, [3] Aldrich, [4] and Hamlin Garland [5] in their autobiographical volumes adorn the schoolday tales of their youth with the grace of the life of the imagination; but no Kipling dramatizes fully the incidents of school life and no Wells makes the novel the instrument of educational reform. The nearest approach to this standard is that of a few educational romances, whose appeal does not carry beyond the teachers' circle. Chief among these is William Hawley Smith's *Evolution of Dodd*, remarkable for its early failure due to the prejudice against the title, its later success, and the fact that though over a million copies have been sold the author received not a penny.

A number of volumes of memoirs furnish valuable literary materials of education. The works of Henry James have been mentioned. The reminiscences of Senator Hoar and of Senator Lodge give illuminating accounts of mid-century New England education. More recently and at greater length, Professor Brander Matthews has performed a similar service for New York. Most important of all is the recent volume entitled *The Education of Henry Adams* (1908, 1916). More frankly devoted to the educational aspect of experience than any other autobiographical work, vying with them all in literary charm, this study by one of the most reflective students and keenest observers of the generation just passing holds an outstanding place in this type of literature, and in educational literature is unique. [6]

Children's literature, as fits a "children's century," has become most varied and attractive. No longer is it the formal piety of the adult reduced to the priggishness of the child; nor, on the other hand, the extravagant tale for surreptitious enjoyment. Child life depicted for the enjoyment of the adult; adult life brought within the interest and comprehension of the child through the new knowledge of psychology; animal life personi-

---

[1] See Book III, Chap. XVII. [2] *Ibid.*, Chap. XII.
[3] *Ibid.*, Chap. XI. [4] *Ibid.*, Chaps. VI, VII, and X.
[5] *Ibid.*, Chap. VI. [6] *Ibid.*, Chap. XV.

fied; science humanized, so that the child can live in an environment of reality, tenanted by the creatures of his imagination—-
into such classes do the books for children now chiefly fall.
Most of these assist in the real education of the child in accordance with principles which were anathema to our fathers.
Some of them, as George Madden Martin's *Emmy Lou*, belong
to the school. Myra Kelly's stories of the East Side New York
schoolchild, *Little Citizens* and *Aliens*, have introduced to literature a new type, the children of the immigrant, with their
humour, pathos, promise. In Lucy Pratt's *Ezekiel* the negro
schoolchild of the South finds utterance. On the borderland
of the literature of the school are the stories *Seventeen* and *Penrod*, by Booth Tarkington, revealing the experience of the adolescent schoolboy and girl on its obverse and reverse side—its
tragic seriousness to them, its humour and irritation to the adult.
Literature for children has now become so voluminous in quantity, so varied in character, so rich in content, that it can no
longer be considered merely as a class of educational literature.
However, it performs more efficiently than ever before a genuine
educational function through the happy union of humanitarian
sentiment, scientific psychological knowledge, and attractive
literary form.

One type of literature is peculiar to America, the literature
of the immigrant. Much of this is educational, for the whole
process of making the immigrant into the citizen of the adopted
country is an educational one of scarcely realized importance.
Of fascinating interest also are the literary accounts of the
process. First among these was *The Making of an American*
(1901) by Jacob Riis, a newspaper reporter and social reformer,
of Danish birth. *The Reminiscences* (1907) of Carl Schurz, the
soldier, statesman, and liberal political leader, of German birth,
are quite the most voluminous and important of these books
from the general, though not from the educational, point of
view. The numerous volumes of Edward A. Steiner, of Bohemian origin, cover the experience of a successful educator, lecturer, and sociologist in a variety of phases of American life.
Chief among his works are *From Alien to Citizen* and *Confessions
of a Hyphenated American*. Mary Antin's *Promised Land*
(1912) contains much that is of interest to the educator, for it
gives a detached and yet intimate or personal view of many of

our customs and institutions, including the school, into all of which the native so gradually grows that he never becomes reflectively conscious of them. This conscious reaction to the new environment by one foreign to it and acute enough to observe, constitutes in fact the real educative influence of a society. More recently a Syrian, Abraham M. Rihbany, has given an account from a new angle; while the latest, and from the formal educational point of view the fullest, account is *An American in the Making*, by M. E. Ravage, of Rumanian origin. This latter gives quite the best description of the life and spirit of a Mid-Western university that is to be found. No other part of the recent educational literature of America deserves greater attention than the volumes of this group or possesses anything like their charm, originality, or significance.

With the increasingly technical character and appeal of scientific and philosophical literature—particularly the former—has gone a similar technical development of the literature of education. This has been of profound significance, for a sort of cross-fertilization has taken place, resulting in two new species— a genuinely scientific and a genuinely philosophical type of educational writings. Both groups sprang originally from the new science of psychology and the less accurate one of sociology, or more specifically from the methods of measurement, whether experimental or statistical, developed in connection with psychology and sociology. Even though the results obtained are, as some maintain, "the vociferous reiteration of the obvious," yet there is much to be gained through a scientific interpretation of the obvious. The application of the same methods to problems where conclusions are not obvious results in profoundly important, if gradual, advance. The two-volume *Principles of Psychology* (1890) of William James,[1] probably the most fascinating presentation of scientific material in literature, is the most important, though not the earliest manifestation of this progress. His brief popular application of these principles to the problems of education, *Talks to Teachers*, is yet the most widely circulated of books for teachers. Since those days, the literature of psychology in its application to education has become most voluminous. Numerous university departments have perfected the technique of such work; several scientific

[1] See Book III, Chap. XVII.

magazines devoted to this field afford channels of publication. Of this literature the features of two distinct types may be mentioned.

The field of child and adolescent psychology was developed by President G. Stanley Hall; none of the numerous investigations or publications in these fields but bear the distinct impress of the work of this pioneer, or at least owe a great debt to him. His *Adolescence* (1904), with its great store of accumulated data and its vast range of observation, represents, though often in an ill-digested form, the results of several decades of research of this entire school of investigation.

In the later development of scientific method, that of exact quantitative measurement, particularly as applied to groups, the methods of Galton have been applied in the field of education. The chief exponent of this work has been Professor Edward L. Thorndike. His *Educational Measurements* and *Principles of Psychology* laid the foundation for this type of educational literature. A new type of literature, rapidly expanding, has been produced. Much of this, fostered by educational endowments, university departments, and the national Bureau of Education, has appeared in the form of school or institutional surveys. Such surveys attempt to measure by accurate scientific standards the efficiency of organization, the character of instruction, the value of specific methods, the amount of acceleration and of retardation of pupils, the practical value of the school plant, and a variety of phases of school work hardly thought of previously in any definite quantitative way. All of this promises a new era of scientific progress in education.

On the philosophical side, modern science has given to education a more pragmatic and realistic interpretation. Many volumes of exposition, logical or sociological in character, have appeared. The closing decades of the century witnessed a revival of interest in this field, chiefly under the leadership of Dr. William T. Harris,[1] United States Commissioner of Education from 1889 to 1906. Through official reports, public addresses, and published volumes he was chiefly responsible for the popularity of German philosophical interpretation, particularly of the Hegelian character. In a more general field President

[1] See also Book III, Chap. XVII.

Butler, through his *Meaning of Education* and other essays, has given more popular interpretation of educational principles. In this field of philosophical interpretation the writings of one man, John Dewey,[1] transcend all others in American educational literature. In fact it may be said that in the field of strictly technical literature Professor Dewey has made the one great American contribution. While most of these writings have appeared in monographic form, such as his *School and Society* (1890), *Interest as Related to Effort* (1896), *Child and the Curriculum* (1902), *How We Think* (1911), his *Democracy and Education* (1917) is a complete logical scheme of educational interpretation, the only one ever worked out by an American, and the one most representative of present world thought and modern science.

In the literature of appreciation some contributions have been made. Professor Barrett Wendell's *Universities in France* uses the foil of French customs and institutions to reveal American light and shade. Professor Gayley's *Idols*, as well as occasional essays from a number of pens, reminds us of the inexhaustible field for appreciation or for criticism of the teacher's experience or of the teacher's problems. Effective and delightful in its form is Professor Francis G. Peabody's *Education for Life* (1918), an appreciation of one of America's most significant educational experiments, Hampton Institute.

Foreign observers, with either greater detachment or more scientific attitude, have rendered their tribute of comment. Some of these, as the Moseley Commission from England, offer comments valuable to both observed and observer. Perhaps the chief defect to be noted in these foreign comments is the failure to perceive that the "feminization" of American education does not necessarily mean its "effeminization."

On the whole, the literature of American education is typical of that education. In the past when education was a subordinate thing, a concern of the church or of the family or of the individual, the literature was fragmentary and interpolated. When education became general and technical in a crude way, a technical literature having similar crudities developed. With the fresh substance for literary creation at hand, furnished by savages, by frontier life, by the new life of freedom, with its new

[1] See also Book III, Chap. XVII.

institutions, by ingenious conquest of the nation's boundless wealth, the literary creator had no need to turn for materials for the imagination to the slightly stimulating and highly conventional life of the school taskmaster. Still is much of the present educational literature characterized too often by superficiality, as is our education; still is it inaccurate, as our educative processes are inexact; practical, as the demands of our lives are practical; still does it deal with immediate problems, as our education and our social organization are bound to do. On the other hand, much of it has attained a scientific character unknown in any preceding period; some of it possesses a philosophical penetration and reveals a form of exposition worthy of the best of any period. Much of it is rich in the promise of the future. In some respects even the practical working idealism of American life, usually concealed under a materialistic exterior, finds expression in literary forms worthy of its conscious, though usually unexpressed, purposes.

CHAPTER XXIV

Economists

ECONOMICS as a science is due to the analysis of the modern economic organization which was beginning to take shape in Great Britain at the time of Adam Smith and in France at the time of the Physiocrats. In the United States the economic transition occurred much later. There, as in Europe, the formulation of systematic thought was preceded by a series of unsystematic discussions and by a groping after true principles. These discussions were the outgrowth of dissatisfaction with existing conditions and centred about definite practical problems. Moreover, in almost all cases, the discussion took the form of a pamphlet literature which, in not a few instances, developed into a wordy warfare. In the pre-Revolutionary period in America there were only a few economic topics that attracted any attention. These were agriculture, trade, taxation, and currency, of which the most important, as well as the most contentious, was the last.

As in every primitive society, the currency problem involved the means of payment, public and private, and always loomed large in popular interest. Since it was almost impossible, for well-known reasons, to retain in the colonies an adequate circulation of coin, the gap was filled by the issue of paper money. Banking and currency problems therefore early engrossed the attention of colonial thinkers.

The first, and the only, economic pamphlets of the seventeenth century that have been preserved are *Severals Relating to the Fund* (1682), *A Discussion and Explanation of the Bank of Credit* (1687), and *Some Considerations on the Bills of Credit now passing in New England* (1691). These were anonymous

Massachusetts publications of ephemeral merit. In the eighteenth century there were several well-defined periods of active discussion in Massachusetts, centring respectively about the years 1714, 1720, and 1740.[1] Among the disputants were men like John Wise, John Colman, Hugh Vance, and Richard Frye—clergymen, business men, and visionaries. Far and away the ablest was the learned physician, Dr. William Douglass (1692–1742), who wrote *An Essay Concerning Silver and Paper More Especially with Regards to the British Colonies in New England* (1738) and a *Discourse Concerning the Currencies of the British Plantations in America, Especially with Regard to Their Paper Money* (1740).

The currency debate was not confined to Massachusetts. In 1729 there appeared in Philadelphia Benjamin Franklin's *A Modest Inquiry into the Nature and Necessity of Paper Currency*. This was a well-reasoned defence of the government notes issued by Pennsylvania on land security and in reference to which the distinguished author later wrote in his *Autobiography:* "My friends, who considered I had been of some service, thought fit to reward me by employing me in printing the money, a most profitable job and a great help to me." In 1734 there was published in Charleston the first Southern tract on the subject, an *Essay on Currency* of some merit. In 1737 a New York pamphlet appeared, under the title *Scheme (by Striking 20,000 Pounds of Paper Money) to Encourage Raising of Hemp and the Manufacture of Iron in the Province of New York*. This was followed in the ensuing decade by two tracts, *A Discourse Concerning Paper Money in which its Principles are Laid Open* (Philadelphia, 1743), by John Webbe, and *An Address to the Inhabitants of North Carolina on the Want of a Medium in Lieu of Money* (Williamsburg, 1746).

With the prohibition, in 1751, of the further emission in the New England colonies of any paper money the discussion was transferred to coinage problems. Two Boston tracts of 1762 are here to be noted: Thomas Hutchinson's *A Projection for Regulating the Value of Gold and Silver Coins* and Oxenbridge Thatcher's *Considerations on Lowering the Value of Gold Coins within the Province of Massachusetts Bay*. An echo of the

[1] These pamphlets were reprinted in four volumes in 1911 by the Prince Society of Boston under the editorship of McFarland Davis.

older discussions is found in Roger Sherman's *A Caveat against Injustice or an Enquiry into the Evil Consequences of a Fluctuating Medium of Exchange*, published at New York in 1752 under the name of Philoeunomos; R. T.'s *A Letter to the Common People of the Colony of Rhode Island Concerning the Unjust Designs . . . of a Number of Misers and Money Jobbers* (Providence, 1763); and a *Letter from a Gentleman in Connecticut relative to Paper Currency* (Boston, 1766). The ablest of the pamphlets of this period was *Considerations on a Paper Currency* by Tench Francis, of Pennsylvania, in 1765.

While the currency question attracted the greatest attention, we find a few discussions of trade and tax problems. Among these tracts worthy of mention are *Proposals for Traffic and Commerce or Foreign Trade in New Jersey* by "Amicus patriæ" (Philadelphia, 1718); *Observations on the Act for Granting an Excise on Wine* (Boston, 1720); Francis Rawle's *Some Remedies Proposed for Restoring the Sunk Credit of the Province of Pennsylvania with Some Remarks on Its Trade* (Philadelphia, 1721); and the anonymous *The Interest of the Country in laying Duties: or a Discourse shewing how Duties on some Sorts of Merchandize may make the Province of New York richer than it would be without them* (New York, n. d. [1726]). To the last tract two replies were published in the same year. It was not until the middle of the century that we again find any discussion of taxation in *Some Observations on the Bill Intitled An Act for Granting to His Majesty an Excise upon Wines and on Spirits Distilled* (Boston, 1754).

The writings on agriculture, on the other hand, began a little later. The well-known clergyman, Jared Eliot, published his *Essays upon Field Husbandry in New England as it is or may be Ordered*, in six parts from 1748 to 1759 in New London, New York, and New Haven. The interest engendered in the problem led to the publication of *Extracts from the Essays of the Dublin Society Relating to the Culture and Manufacture of Flax* (Annapolis, 1748) and to Charles Woodmaston's *A Letter from a Gentleman from South Carolina on the Cultivation of Indico* (Charleston, 1754).

With the enactment of the Molasses Act of 1763 there ensued a discussion of the economic aspects of the problem. Among the pamphlets three deserve mention: *Considerations upon the Act of Parliament whereby a Duty is Laid of 6d. Sterᐟ ing per Gallon on Molasses, etc., Shewing some of the many Inconveniences Necessarily Resulting from the Operation of the said Act* (Boston, 1764); *Reasons Against the Renewal of the Sugar Act as it will be Prejudicial to the Trade not only of the Northern Colonies but to those of Great Britain also* (Boston, 1764); and Thomas Fitch's *Reasons why the British Colonies in America should not be Charged with Internal Taxes* (New Haven, 1764). In fact, the only tract of this period not directly connected with taxation was *The Commercial Conduct of the Province of New York Considered* by "A Linen Draper" (New York, 1767), which consisted of a plea to establish manufactures. With the imposition of the stamp taxes by the mother country in the following years there came a flood of controversial literature which was, however, so overwhelmingly political in character as to call for no detailed comment here.

In the pre-Revolutionary literature there stands out only one prominent name in American economic discussion, Benjamin Franklin.[1] His contributions represent the common-sense reactions of a powerful mind to the problems of the day, reinforced later on by general reflections suggested by the Physiocrats and Adam Smith. In his first work on paper currency, referred to above, Franklin was influenced by Petty in selecting labour, rather than silver, as the best measure of value. In his *Observations Concerning the Increase of Mankind* (1751) he shows himself a forerunner of Malthus, and incidentally points out why wages must continue to be high in a country where there is an abundance of free land. In *The Interest of Great Britain Considered with Regard to her Colonies and the Acquisition of Canada and Guadaloupe* (1760) he emphasizes the principle of division of labour, and explains why manufacturing industry is difficult to introduce where the profits of agriculture are high. In *On the Price of Corn and Management of the Poor* (1767) he elucidates the reasons why export taxes are injurious and contends that "The best way to do good to the poor is not making them easy in poverty, but leading or driving them out of it." In his *Positions to be Examined Concerning National Wealth* (1769) he considers, and gives partial adherence to, the Physiocratic doctrine. In his *Reflections on the Augmentation of Wages which will be Occa-*

[1] See, also, Book I, Chap. VI.

sioned in Europe by the American Revolution (1788) he virtually develops the modern theory of the economy of high wages. Finally, in his *Wail of a Protected Manufacturer* (1789) he punctures some of the selfish arguments of a favoured class.

With the outbreak of the Revolution a new chapter in economic discussion is initiated. The fiscal difficulties of the Revolution and the economic distress under the Confederation engendered much debate. Far and away the two ablest writers were Pelatiah Webster and S. Gale. Webster began in 1776, and continued for a decade, to expound, in consonance with the most modern principles, the currency evils of the time. These tracts were collected, with some additions, in a volume entitled *Political Essays on the Nature and Operation of Money, Public Finances, and Other Subjects* (Philadelphia, 1791). Gale, a native of South Carolina, published in three volumes four *Essays on the Nature and Principles of Public Credit* (1784–1786), which have, moreover, the distinction of being the earliest effort to illustrate economic problems by mathematical symbols. Other substantial contributions were made to the discussion, notably in *An Essay on the Causes of the Decline of Foreign Trade* (Philadelphia, 1784); James Swan's *A National Arithmetic or Observations on the Finances of Massachusetts* (1786); William Barton's *The True Interest of the United States and Particularly of Pennsylvania Considered* (Philadelphia, 1786); the anonymous *Reflections on the Policy and Necessity of Encouraging the Commerce of the Citizens of the United States* (Richmond, 1786); Matthew McConnell's *An Essay on the Domestic Debts of the United States* (Philadelphia, 1787); and the anonymous *Observations on the Agriculture, Manufactures, and Commerce of the United States by a Citizen of the United States* (New York, 1789).

With the adoption of the new Constitution the economic questions were put in the forefront of the battle and engaged the attention of the leading statesmen. Of these only a very few were pre-eminent as economic thinkers. Jefferson never pretended to grasp economic problems, his only contributions to the subject being found in his *Notes on Virginia* (1786), which disclose a striking incapacity to foretell the future industrial development of the country. Many years later Jefferson, as he tells us himself, "carefully revised and corrected" Destutt

Tracy's *A Treatise on Political Economy* (Georgetown, D. C., 1817), which was translated from the unpublished French original. There is, however, no evidence that Jefferson profited from its perusal. On the other hand, Hamilton showed in his great state papers and notably in his two *Reports on Public Credit* (1790, 1795), as well as in his *Report on Manufactures* (1791), that he possessed a remarkable acquaintance with economic principles as then understood. There is in fact no statesman of the eighteenth century, with the exception of Turgot, who combined more successfully the perspicacity of a great leader of men with the ability to present powerful and sustained reasoning on economic problems. The only other American statesman who can even remotely be compared to Hamilton is Gallatin, who even proved himself the superior of Hamilton as a technical financier. His principal contribution to fiscal science was the proof, long before it was recognized by the British economists, of the fallacy underlying the sinking fund. The chief of his earlier writings was the *Sketch of the Finances of the United States* (1796) and the most important of his later contributions were his *Considerations on the Currency and Banking System of the United States* (1831) and the *Memorial of the Committee of the Free Trade Convention* (1831). Worthy of note also is Secretary Wolcott's *Report on Direct Taxes* (1796).

The last decade of the eighteenth century witnessed an increasing attention paid to commercial and financial questions. In 1791 there appeared *A Brief Examination of Lord Sheffield's Observations on the Commerce of the United States* and in 1795 a translation of Brissot de Warville's *The Commerce of America with Europe*. Prominent in the financial discussion were Governor James Sullivan's *The Path to Riches. An Inquiry into the Origin and the Use of Money* (Boston, 1792); *The Shepherd's Contemplation, or an Essay on Ways and Means to Pay the Public Debt* (Philadelphia, 1794); and William Findley's *Review of the Revenue System Adopted by the First Congress* (Philadelphia, 1794). Works on agronomy now multiplied. The field had up to that time largely been occupied by the two-volume work on *American Husbandry. By an American* (1775). Now there appeared in rapid succession Samuel Deane's *The New England Farmer* (Worcester, 1790); the *Sketches on Rotations of Crops* (Philadelphia, 1792); John Spurrier's *The Practical*

Farmer (Wilmington, 1793); and J. B. Bordley's *Essays and Notes on Husbandry* (Philadelphia, 1799). This period also witnessed the beginnings of statistical investigation, as notably Jedidiah Morse's *The American Geographer* (Elizabethtown, 1789); and *A View of the United States* (Philadelphia, 1794) by Tench Coxe, who was also responsible for a number of other memoirs on economic topics.

The first quarter of the nineteenth century saw but little change in the general character of economic discussion. The United States continued to be overwhelmingly an agricultural country and it was only toward the end of this period that New England was beginning to be affected by the industrial transition which was responsible for the growth of economic science in Great Britain. Adam Smith's *Wealth of Nations*, of which the first American edition had appeared in 1789, was now reprinted in 1811 and 1818; Ricardo's *Principles* appeared in an American edition in 1819, and J. B. Say's *Treatise on Political Economy* was translated in 1821. None of these, however, seems to have aroused much attention or interest. The first American work with an independent title was *An Essay on the Principles of Political Economy* (1805), which was a rather insignificant treatise on banking and public revenue. Somewhat similar were L. Baldwin's *Thoughts on the Study of Political Economy as Connected with the Population, Industry, and Paper Currency of the United States* (Cambridge, 1809) and A. V. Johnson's *Inquiry into the Nature of Value and Capital* (New York, 1813). More significant was Daniel Raymond's *The Elements of Political Economy* (1820), which disclosed an acquaintance with the English writers and which laid the foundations for the defence of the protective system, afterwards elaborated by List. The influence of Malthus is perceptible in A. H. Everett's *New Ideas on Population* (1823), in which the invincibly optimistic attitude of youthful America is revealed.

The chief lines of discussion were therefore largely a continuation of the preceding period. The interest temporarily manifested in industry is attested by George Logan's *A Letter to the Citizens of Pennsylvania on the Necessity of Promoting Agriculture, Manufactures and the Useful Arts* (1800) and the *Essay on the Manufacturing Interests of the United States* (Philadelphia, 1804). Agricultural problems were treated by

Thomas Moore in *The Great Error of American Agriculture Exposed* (Baltimore, 1801); James Humphrey's *Gleanings on Husbandry* (Philadelphia, 1803); John Roberts's *The Pennsylvania Farmer* (Philadelphia, 1804); and, above all, by John Taylor's *Arator* (Georgetown, 1814) and J. S. Skinner's *The American Farmer* (Baltimore, 1820). Colonel Taylor, of Virginia, is also to be noted for his earlier *Enquiry into the Principles and Tendencies of Certain Public Measures* (Philadelphia, 1794) and his later *Tyranny Unmasked* (1822). A growing interest was now taken in statistical presentation. Worthy of notice are S. Blodgett, Jr.'s *Thoughts on the Increasing Wealth and Natural Economy of the United States* (1801) and *Economica* (1806); Timothy Dwight's *Statistical Account of Connecticut* (1811); R. Dickinson's *A Geographical and Statistical Review of Massachusetts* (1813); and Moses Greenleaf's *Statistical View of Maine* (1816). Widely read were Adam Seybert's *Statistical Annals* (1818), D. B. Warden's *Statistical, Political, and Historical Account of the United States* (3 vols., 1819), John Bristed's *Resources of the United States* (1818), and William Darby's *Universal Gazetteer* (1827) and *View of the United States, Historical, Geographical, and Statistical* (1828). We may also mention that the discussion on the recharter of the bank was responsible for Dr. Erick Bollman's *Paragraphs on Banks* (Philadelphia, 1810) and the *Letters of Common Sense Respecting the State Bank and Paper Currency* (Raleigh, 1811).

There is only one author of prominence during this period and he was in many respects an amateur economist whose chief reputation was earned in other fields. Mathew Carey (1760–1839) of Philadelphia diverted such leisure as he could take from his publishing business to a consideration of economic questions. In the earlier period he was interested in banking topics, as is shown by his *Memorials Praying a Repeal or Suspension of the Law Annulling the Charter of the Bank* (1786), his *Letters to Adam Seybert on the Bank* (1811), and his *Essays on Banking* (1816). In the meantime he had issued *The Olive Branch* (1814), devoted to some of the economic and political questions growing out of the war, which rapidly ran through many editions. Beginning in the twenties, however, he devoted most of his efforts to a defence of the protective system, as is evidenced by his *Essays on Political Economy* (1822), *An*

Appeal to Common Sense (1823), *The Crisis* (1823), *The Political Economist* (1824), *Prospects on and beyond the Rubicon* (1830), and an *Appeal to the Wealthy of the Land* (1836). Carey was primarily a controversial pamphleteer, and his contributions, although exerting considerable influence at the time, were not of lasting note.

The second and third quarters of the nineteenth century were marked by two significant facts. The industrial transition in the East, together with the immigration to the West and South, brought into the forefront of political discussion four economic problems. These were the labour question, the land question, the money question, and the free trade controversy.[1] Each of these gave rise to a vast pamphlet literature. The other important fact is the emergence of some interest in political economy as a science and the institution of college chairs devoted to the subject.

Taking up first the general economic discussion, two prominent names deserve attention. The Rev. John McVickar (1787–1868) occupied from 1817 at Columbia College the chair of philosophy, to the title of which there was added shortly thereafter that of political economy. Having already made a contribution to the banking system in New York under the pseudonym of Junius, he published, in 1825, his *Outlines of Political Economy*, followed a decade later by his *First Lessons in Political Economy* (1835). The *Outlines* were a reprint of McCulloch's article in the Encyclopedia Britannica, but McVickar added what is described on the title page as *Notes Explanatory and Critical and a Summary of the Science*. Thomas Cooper (1759–1840) was president of South Carolina College at Columbia, and from 1824 professor of chemistry and political economy. Having previously (1823) written *Two Tracts on the Proposed Alteration of the Tariff*, he published in 1826 his *Lectures on the Elements of Political Economy*, which ran through several editions and which devoted some attention to the views of the socialists in New York. Cooper followed this by a *Manual of Political Economy* (1834). Neither McVickar nor Cooper departed materially from the position of the nascent political economy in England. A keener writer was the Southern editor, J. N. Cardozo, whose *Notes on Political Economy* (1826) dis-

[1] See also Book III, Chap. XXI.

closed opposition to the Ricardian law of rent, but whose book culminated in a defence of free trade. The only other contribution of the decade was the *Outline of Political Economy* (1828) by William Jennison.

The next decade showed more activity. Beginning with the fugitive writings of William Beach Lawrence, *Two Lectures on Political Economy* (1832), W. H. Hale's *Useful Knowledge for the Producers of Wealth* (1833), and *An Essay on the Principles of Political Economy Designed as a Manual for Practical Men by an American* (1837), we come to more formal works: S. P. Newman's *Elements of Political Economy* (1835); President Francis Wayland's *Elements of Political Economy* (1837); and Theodore Sedgwick's *Public and Private Economy*, in three parts (1836–39). Professor H. Vethake, of the University of Pennsylvania, who had published several *Introductory Lectures on Political Economy* in 1831 and 1833, now issued his *Principles of Political Economy* (1838), containing the substance of the courses given since 1822. Professor George Tucker, of the University of Virginia, published in 1837 *The Laws of Wages, Profits, and Rent Investigated* and followed this by *The Theory of Money and Banks Investigated* (1839). Worthy of notice also is the work by the engineer Charles Ellet, Jr., *An Essay on the Laws of Trade in Reference to the Works of Internal Improvement* (1839).

The only book of this period which manifested any originality was John Rae's *Statement of New Principles on the Subject of Political Economy* (Boston, 1834). Rae, a Canadian, took issue with the prevalent English school in two points. He made a distinct contribution to the theory of capital and he laid a more solid foundation for the defence of the protective system. Rae is the only American writer of this period who attracted the notice of John Stuart Mill and whose contributions have received much attention in recent times.

During the forties the interest in political economy seemed to slacken. Only four books are to be recorded. Professor A. Potter's *Political Economy, Its Objects, Uses and Principles* (1840), which was largely an adaptation of Poulett Scrope; the *Notes on Political Economy* (1844) by "a Southern planter" (N. A. Ware); E. C. Seaman's *Essays on the Progress of Nations in Productive Industry, Civilization, and Wealth* (1846); and

Calvin Colton's *Public Economy for the United States* (1848). Much the same is true of the fifties, with the appearance of G. Opdyke's *A Treatise on Political Economy* (1851); Professor Francis Bowen's *The Principles of Political Economy* (1856); and Professor John Bascom's *Political Economy* (1859). Most of these were textbooks exerting comparatively little influence outside the colleges. More widely read were the *Elements of Political Economy* (1865) by Professor A. L. Perry, of Williams College, which ran through many editions, and *The Science of Wealth; a Manual of Political Economy* (1866) by Professor Amasa Walker, of Amherst. Less important were E. Lawton's *Lectures on Science, Politics, Morals, and Society* (1862) and President J. T. Champlin's *Lessons on Political Economy* (1868).

All of these were cast into the shade by the one American author who soon acquired an international reputation. Henry C. Carey (1793–1879), the son of Mathew Carey, was well in the forties before he commenced to write. Beginning in 1835 with his *Essay on the Rate of Wages* he published in rapid succession a flood of pamphlets as well as a series of volumes. Chief among the latter are the *Principles of Political Economy* (3 vols., 1837–40); *The Past, the Present, the Future* (1848); *The Harmony of Interests* (1850); *The Slave Trade* (1853); *Principles of Social Science* (3 vols., 1858–59); and *The Unity of Law* (1872). Carey started out as a free trader, but soon became an ardent protectionist and took issue at almost every point with the doctrines of the classical school. He opposed Adam Smith on the theory of productive labour; he objected to the Ricardian theories of rent and wages; he criticized the Malthusian theory of population; he laid stress on his own law of value and utility; and he elaborated, on original but none the less secure foundations, a whole structure of economic thought. At a time when the field was occupied by the American imitators of British classical political economy and by the widely read translations of Bastiat, the French free trader, Carey heartened all those both at home and abroad who were seeking some economic basis for the newer nationalism with its policy of protection. Great as was the influence that he exercised at the time, later generations have found but little of enduring value in his contributions to economic science; and toward the end of his career he weakened his influence by espousing the inflationist currency arguments. At the time, however, Carey formed a school which counted among its adherents thinkers like Dühring in Germany and Ferrara in Italy, and which included at home three Pennsylvania publicists: William Elder, who wrote *Questions of the Day, Economic and Social* (1871); E. Peshine Smith, *A Manual of Political Economy* (1873); and Robert Ellis Thompson, *Social Science and National Economy* (1875) as well as several other works on protection. Belonging in part to the same school is Stephen Colwell's *A Preliminary Essay to the Translation of List's National System of Political Economy* (1856), with a good historical sketch of the science in which he declared his variance at some points from Carey. Colwell also wrote *Ways and Means of Payment: a Full Analysis of the Credit System* (1859).

Side by side with this development of the general theory of economics, there proceeded, as mentioned above, a heated discussion on practical economic problems. Most of this pamphlet literature, interesting as showing the current of popular thought, was of only temporary interest and must be passed over in this brief sketch. A few books are deserving of mention. In the workingman's movement which developed in the third decade in New York, three authors exerted more than a passing influence. L. Byllesby's *Observations on the Source and Effects of Unequal Wealth* (1826) and Thomas Skidmore's *The Rights of Man to Property* (1829) furnished the basis for the new and short-lived socialist movement. Frances Wright, the eloquent and attractive apostle of freedom for women and negroes, exerted a great influence by her *Course of Popular Lectures* (1829) and by *The New Harmony Gazette* (1825–35) which she edited in co-operation with Robert Dale Owen, a son of Robert Owen. Interesting discussions of the principles of the labour movement are found in *The Journeyman Mechanic's Advocate* (1827), which has the distinction of being the first labour paper in the world; *The Mechanics' Free Press* (from 1828–1831); and *The Workingmen's Advocate*, edited by G. H. Evans (1829–36).

For the next few years the interest in the question was maintained by William Maclure's *Opinions on Various Subjects Dedicated to the Industrious Producers* (1831), Stephen Simpson's *Workingman's Manual, a New Theory of Political Economy* (1831), and Seth Luther's *An Address to the Workingmen of New England* (1833), as well as by the labour periodicals of which the most important were *The Man* (1834-35), *The National Labourer* (1836-7), Thomas Brothers's *The Radical Reformer* (1836), and Ely Moore's *The National Trades-Union* (1836-37).

The labour movement was succeeded in the forties by a wave of Fourierism and Associationism. The chief advocate of this was Albert Brisbane, with his *Social Destiny of Man* (1840), *Association* (1843), various translations of Fourier, and *The Phalanx; or Journal of Social Science* (1843-5). He was followed by Parke Godwin in his *Popular View of the Doctrines of Fourier* (1844) and by Horace Greeley in *Association Discussed* (1847). Greeley, who for a time opened the influential columns of the *Tribune* to this movement, showed his interest in the general subject by writing an introduction to Atkinson's *Principles of Political Economy* (1843). He soon became more interested in the problems of protection and free land, editing, in 1843, *The American Laborer* and publishing toward the end of his career the *Essays Designed to Elucidate the Science of Political Economy* (1869), devoted to the same topics.

The interest in the Communist movement was carried on in *The Harbinger* (1845-47), of the Brook Farm phalanx; J. M. Horner's *The Herald of the New-Found World* (1841-42); *The Communitist* (1844); and J. A. Collins's *The Social Pioneer* (1844). The general theories of the labour movement are reflected in Robert McFarlane's *Mechanics' Mirror* (1846). This period is also marked by the advent of three original thinkers who emphasized individualism to the very extreme of anarchism: Josiah Warren in *Equitable Commerce* (1846) and *True Civilization* (1846); Stephen Pearl Andrews in *The True Constitution of Government in the Sovereignty of the Individual* (1851) and *Cost the Limit of Price* (1851); and Lysander Spooner in *Poverty: Its Alleged Causes and Legal Cure* (1846). Less important were J. Pickering's *The Workingman's Political Economy* (1847), J. Campbell's *A Theory of Equality* (1848), and E. Kellogg's *Labor and Other Capital* (1849). The next decade, with its period of prosperity, is marked by only two noteworthy books: Adin Ballou's *Practical Christian Socialism* (1854) and H. Hughes's *Treatise on Sociology* (1854).

With the end of the Civil War the falling prices brought a renewed interest in the labour question. The two national periodicals were Fincher's *Trades Review* (Philadelphia) and *The Workingmen's Advocate* (Chicago). The philosophy of the labour agitation was expounded by Ira Steward in *The Eight Hour Movement* (1865) and *Poverty* (1873); by William Dealtry in *The Laborer* (1869); and by E. H. Haywood in *Yours and Mine* (1869); while the Communist movement was best represented by Alexander Longley in *The Communist* (1868–79). During the early seventies there are to be noted H. B. Wright's *Practical Treatise on Labor* (1871), W. Brown's *The Labor Question* (1872), W. B. Greene's *Socialistic, Communistic, Mutualistic, and Financial Fragments* (1875), and L. Masquerier's *Sociology or The Reconstruction of Society* (1877).

The tariff controversies elicited but few works of importance. In the earlier period, in the contest centring around the Bill of Abominations of 1828 and its immediate successors, we have to note, in addition to the works of Lee and Gallatin referred to above, T. R. Dew's *Lectures on the Restrictive System* (1829) and Hezekiah Niles's *Journal of the Meeting of the Friends of Domestic Industry* (1831). Perhaps the most outstanding figure of this period was Condy Raguet, author of *The Principles of Free Trade* (1835) and *The Examiner and Journal of Political Economy* (1834–35). In the later period, immediately after the Civil War, we need mention only W. M. Grosvenor's *Does Protection Protect?* (1871) and the numerous publications of E. B. Bigelow.

Much the same may be said about the controversies on the currency, which produced only a few works of more than passing interest. Worthy of mention are E. Lord's *Principles of Currency* (1829), W. M. Gouge's *A Short History of Paper Money and Banking* (1833) and *The Fiscal History of Texas* (1852), W. Beck's *Money and Banking* (1839), R. Hildreth's *Banks, Banking, and Paper Currencies* (1840), and Dunscombe's *Free Banking* (1841). In the later period we may call attention to J. A. Ferris's *The Financial Economy of the United States* (1867).

This period is also marked by a more systematic study of statistics as evidenced by A. Russell's *Principles of Statistical Inquiry* (1839), Professor G. Tucker's *Progress of the United States* (1843), and J. D. B. De Bow's *The Industrial Resources of the Southern and Western States*. In 1839, moreover, was founded the American Statistical Association, whose first secretary, J. B. Felt, published a variety of historical and statistical works on population and finance; while the subject of vital statistics was cultivated especially by L. Shattuck and by Dr. Edward Jarvis, for thirty-one years the president of the Association.

The last quarter of the nineteenth century witnessed a marked change in economic conditions. The two fundamental facts were the industrial transition with the advent of modern capitalism, which completely transformed the East and which was fast spreading inland; and, on the other hand, the gradual disappearance of the free lands in the West. These facts were responsible for the emergence of the labour problem in its modern setting. Moreover, the rapid growth of the railway system brought that subject to the front, and the fall in prices coupled with the growing pressure of taxation attracted attention to the silver problem and the general fiscal situation. In short, the United States now reached its own as a more or less fully developed modern economic community and was confronted by a multiplicity of difficult economic questions. The great strike of 1877 sounded the first note of the newer and modern campaign. Almost simultaneously a number of young and enthusiastic scholars went abroad to seek on the Continent an economic training which could not be obtained at home. It was these younger men who on their return at the end of the seventies and in the early eighties founded the modern scientific study of economics in the United States. Before speaking of them, it may be well to mention a few of the more distinguished representatives of the older school who had grown up amid the former conditions.

David A. Wells (1828-98) was a chemist who had sprung into prominence by a pamphlet *Our Burden and Our Strength* (1864), which contributed not a little to increase the confidence of the North in ultimate victory. He now addressed himself to fiscal problems and became the special commissioner on internal revenue. Having been converted from protectionism to free trade, he issued in rapid succession a number of important books. Among these we may mention, in addition to his official reports, *The Relation of the Government to the Telegraph* (1873), *Robinson Crusoe's Money* (1876), *Practical Economics* (1885), *Recent Economic Changes* (1890), and *The*

Theory and Practice of Taxation (1900). Wells had a remarkable faculty for marshalling economic facts and exerted a great influence on public opinion and legislation. But he was far stronger in explaining facts than in elucidating economic principles, and his extreme advocacy of individualism and free trade, together with a lack of acquaintance with the history of economic literature, conspired to limit his influence within narrow circles. Much the same may be said of Edward Atkinson (1827–1905), whose chief contributions were a *Report on the Cotton Manufacture* (1863), *Revenue Reform* (1871), *The Distribution of Products* (1885), *The Margin of Profits* (1887), and *The Industrial Progress of the Nation* (1890), together with innumerable pamphlets. Belonging to the same group was Horace White, who specialized on the currency problem in *The Silver Question* (1876) and *Money and Banking* (1895), as well as J. Schoenhof, who wrote *The Destructive Influence of the Tariff* (1883), *A History of Money and Prices* (1885), and *The Economy of High Wages* (1893). Somewhat more academic were Professor W. G. Sumner (1840–1910), with his *Lectures on the History of Protection* (1877), *A History of American Currency* (1878), *Problems in Political Economy* (1885), and *What Social Classes Owe to Each Other* (1883), and Professor C. F. Dunbar (1830–1900) with his *Chapters on the Theory and History of Banking* (1891) and *Economic Essays* (1904). A more original mind was the astronomer Simon Newcomb (1835–1919), who after devoting some attention to financial policy made his chief contribution in *Principles of Political Economy* (1886). Worthy of mention as writers on money are S. Dana Horton, *Silver and Gold* (1876), *The Monetary Situation* (1878), *The Silver Pound* (1887); John J. Knox, *United States Notes* (1884); A. Del Mar, *A History of the Precious Metals* (1880) and *Money and Civilization* (1886); and C. A. Conant, *A History of Modern Banks of Issue* (1886) and *The Principles of Money and Banking* (1905).

Far and away the most prominent figure of the period was Francis A. Walker (1840–97), who was the first lecturer on economics at Johns Hopkins in 1876. Although not acquainted with much of the newer Continental literature in economics, General Walker possessed a powerful intellect and was so hospitable to the newer ideas that he lent his weighty support to the efforts of the younger men to put economic study on a scientific basis. He became the first president of the American Economic Association. His chief works, each marked by vigour and independence of thought, are *The Wages Question* (1876), *Money* (1878), *Land and its Rent* (1881), *Political Economy* (1883), *International Bimetallism* (1896), and *Discussions in Economics and Statistics* (1899). Walker helped to give the *coup de grâce* to the wages fund doctrine, and his theory of distribution has come to be known as the residual theory. Not only did he exert a great influence on economic thought but his contributions to statistics as Superintendent of the Ninth and Tenth Census were scarcely less pronounced.

Another important milestone in the progress of economic science is marked by Henry George (1839–97). George, living in California at a time when everything seemed to point to the rapid growth of bonanza farms, came to the conclusion that the solution of the modern social problem lay in the nationalization of land, through the medium of the single tax. Beginning with *Our Land and Land Policy* (1871), he elaborated his general theory in *Progress and Poverty* (1879), which ran through countless editions. The same ideas with further applications were repeated in *Social Problems* (1884), *Protection or Free Trade* (1891), *A Perplexed Philosopher* (1892), and *The Science of Political Economy* (1898). In all other respects an extreme individualist, Henry George carried to its logical extreme John Stuart Mill's theory of the unearned increment. One-sided as his doctrine has come to be considered, he contributed two important points to the progress of economic thought in the United States. The one was his theory of privilege—even though he was extreme in limiting this to land; the other was the theory that wages are fixed by the product of rentless land, which started the thinking of Professor Clark.

The real beginning of the modern science of economics is to be found in that group of younger men, all of them, with one exception, still living, who founded at Saratoga in 1883 the American Economic Association. This has now become one of the most influential scientific organizations in the country. The underlying principles of this group of younger thinkers, almost all of whom had studied in Germany, appeared in 1886 in a volume entitled *Science Economic Discussion*. The most eminent of the group is John Bates Clark (1847–   ), whose chief contributions are found in the *Philosophy of Wealth* (1886), *The Distribution of Wealth* (1899), *The Control of Trusts* (1901), and *Essentials of Economic Theory* (1907). Professor Clark worked out independently the marginal-utility theory of value as expounded by Jevons, Menger, and Walras, and is to be noted for the elaboration of the doctrine of specific productivity as applied to the shares of distribution. This doctrine, in connection with his theory of capital and his distinction between static and dynamic economics, has shed a flood of light on the recesses of economic life and has been the starting point of much modern discussion. Henry C. Adams (1851–) published in 1886 his *Outline of Lectures upon Political Economy* as well as *A Study of the Principles that Should Control the Interference of the State in Industries*, in which issue was squarely taken with the philosophy of *laissez-faire*. Later his *Public Debts* (1887) and the *Science of Finance* (1898) proved to be the pioneer American works in those fields. Richmond Mayo-Smith (1854–1901) chose the field of statistics, which he treated from the modern and comparative point of view in *Statistics and Economics* (1888) and *Statistics and Sociology* (1895), as he was also the first to make a scientific study of the immigrant problem in *Emigration and Immigration* (1890). Richard T. Ely (1854–), the first secretary of the American Economic Association, did perhaps more than any of the others in breaking into new fields and in popularizing the modern concepts of economics. Among his contributions may be mentioned *French and German Socialism* (1883), *Taxation in American States and Cities* (1888), *Monopolies and Trusts* (1900), *Outlines of Economics* (1893), *Studies in the Evolution of Industrial Society* (1903), and *Property and Contract* (1914). Simon N. Patten (1852–), in many ways the most original thinker of the group, made a series of notable contributions in *The Premises of Political Economy* (1885), *The Economic Basis of Protection* (1886), *The Development of English Thought* (1889), *The Theory of Prosperity* (1902), and *The New Basis of Civilization* (1907). President A. T. Hadley (1856–) won his spurs by a scientific study of the railroad problem in *Railroad Transportation* (1885), and followed this by an attempt to sum up in one volume the present state of modern thought in *Economics* (1896). F. W. Taussig (1859–) started with *Protection to Young Industries* (1883) and followed this with *The Silver Situation* (1893), *Wages and Capital* (1896), *The Principles of Economics* (1911), *Investors and Money Makers* (1915), and a series of collected essays on the tariff problem. The author of the present sketch (1861–) is responsible for *Railway Tariffs* (1887), *Progressive Taxation* (1892), *The Shifting and Incidence of Taxation* (1894), *Essays in Taxation* (1895), *The Economic Interpretation of History* (1902), *The Principles of Economics* (1905), and *The Income Tax* (1911). Among the economists who studied abroad but who have since died may be mentioned President E. B. Andrews of Brown (1844–1917), a student of Helfferich, best known by his *Institutes of Economics* (1889), and J. C. Schwab (1865–1916) of Yale, a student of Gustav Cohn, whose chief contribution was *A Financial and Industrial History of the South during the Civil War* (1901).

From the advent of this group of writers may be marked the rapid progress of economic thought in the United States. Beginning in the early eighties the chairs of political economy multiplied, and an opportunity was given to our university students for advanced study of economics at home. With the beginning of the present century the output of scientific literature in economics multiplied rapidly, with the result that the United States counts today a body of economic thinkers superior in numbers and not inferior in quality to those of any other country, who are devoting themselves with conspicuous success and from many different points of view to the elucidation of the complex principles that underlie modern economic life.

NOTE.—On page 427 the four following important tracts were omitted: Francis Rawles's *Ways and Means for the Inhabitants of Delaware to become Rich* (Philadelphia, 1725); a reply to the same by James Logan, *A Dialogue shewing What's therein to be found. A Motto being Modish for Want of good Latin, are put English Quotations* (n. p., 1725); Cadwallader Colden, *Papers relating to an Act of Assembly of the Province of New York, for Encouragement of the Indian Trade, etc. and for Prohibiting the Selling of Indian Goods to the French, viz. of Canada* (New York, 1724); Joseph Morgan, *The Nature of Riches, shewed from the Natural Reasons of the Use and Effects thereof* (Philadelphia, 1732).

CHAPTER XXV

Scholars

THERE seem to be three external modes conditioning the production of our scholarly literature. Until the Revolution, it was produced by scattered individuals. Thereafter literary coteries and learned societies supervened upon individual production, which continued, but with a more definite tone and focus. Finally, with the nineteenth century in its second quarter, the universities supervened upon the other two modes, and were added to them, as stimulus and audience, outlet and patron. Then all three modes continued together, and were compounded. Speaking generally and tentatively, the individualism of the first mode may be called British; the urbane social tone of the second, French; the organized institutionalism of the third, German.

With the exception of a monstrous accretion like the learning of Cotton Mather,[1] a leviathan of the seventeenth-century type, such learning as the eighteenth century could muster in this country was on the one hand rather elegant than professedly scholarly, for a gentleman must not be too much of a specialist; and on the other hand, distinctly didactic, for a cultivated citizen of a new country must endeavour to teach and improve its uncultivated masses. What the eighteenth century offers is a clerical and gentlemanly cultivation of Hebrew and the classics, a missionary concern with the languages of the American Indians, a somewhat schoolmasterly interest in English grammar and lexicography, and an elegant trifling with the modern and the Oriental languages. Ezekiel Cheever's *Short Introduction to the Latin Tongue . . . being Accidence Abridged* was published in 1709. A mock-heroic Latin poem, *Muscipula:*

[1] See Book I, Chap. III.

444

The Mousetrap, by Edward Holdsworth, translated into English by Richard Lewis, was published at Annapolis in 1728; and the next year Samuel Keimer printed at Philadelphia a translation of the *Morals* of Epictetus in a "second edition," possibly after a first edition published in Europe. William Logan, Chief Justice of Pennsylvania, William Penn's friend, business agent, and deputy governor, collected books, founded in 1745 the Loganian Library,[1] conducted an extensive correspondence with scholars, and published Latin treatises and translations. His translation of Dionysius Cato's *Moral Distichs* (1735) and of Cicero's *Cato Major* (1744) were both of them printed by Benjamin Franklin. Another public man, James Otis,[2] found leisure to publish at Boston in 1760 the *Rudiments of Latin Prosody*, which is said to have been used as a text book at Harvard. Samuel Sewall the younger (grandnephew of Judge Sewall), who in 1762 was librarian and instructor in Hebrew at Harvard, published a Hebrew grammar (1763), a Latin version of the first book of Young's *Night Thoughts* (1780), as well as several poems and orations in Greek and Latin. "A native of America," namely John Park,[3] lieutenant-colonel in the army of General Washington, dedicated to his chief the *Lyrick Works of Horace translated into English Verse* (Philadelphia, 1786). In 1804 Sallust's complete works—an edition based upon Crispinus's Delphin—appeared in Philadelphia, and in 1805, at Salem, Sallust's history of the Catilinarian and Jugurthine wars—the latter "the first edition of an ancient classic ever published in the United States, which was not a professed reimpression of some former and foreign edition."[4] The omniscient Dr. Samuel Latham Mitchill,[5] when he was United States Senator from New York, had a song on war "in the Osage tongue" and two Cherokee songs of friendship, which were sung at his house in Washington, translated into French "by an interpreter and rendered into English immediately, January 1, 1806."[6] From the Latin Mitchill also translated into sober English verse the third and the

---

[1] Annexed in 1792 to the library of the Library Company of Philadelphia.
[2] See Book I, Chap. VIII.
[3] Sandys's *History of Classical Scholarship*, III, 451.
[4] J. S. Buckminster, *Monthly Anthology*, II, 549 (1805).
[5] See Book II, Chap. III.
[6] American Antiquarian Society, *Transactions*, I, 313 (1820)

fifth of Sannazaro's *Piscatory Eclogues* (1815); and, from the Italian, Lancisi *On the Fens and Marshes of Rome*. Not only Lindley Murray's *Grammar* (1795), and Noah Webster's *Compendious Dictionary* (1806) and *Philosophical and Practical Grammar of the English Language* (1807), but also Webster's great *Dictionary* of 1828, though it represents twenty years of additional work and even some study abroad, belong essentially to this epoch of individual production.[1] Joel Barlow translated Volney's *Ruins*. Richard Alsop, one of the Hartford Wits, made translations from the French and the Italian. In *The Monthly Anthology* in 1805 was reprinted Sir William Jones's translation of *Sacontalà . . . from the Sanscrit of Calidas*.

Thus the utilitarian and the dilettante production went sporadically on, continuing, as has been indicated, long after the new forces had begun to work. The signs of these were not wanting. During and shortly after the Revolution American learning became self-conscious, and took account of itself. In 1794 Mitchill, then professor of chemistry and botany in Columbia College, made a report to the Senatus Academicus on "the present state of learning in the College of New York" (*i. e.* Columbia College); and Ezra Stiles, in his Latin Inaugural Oration upon his induction as president of Yale in 1778, offered a prospectus of much the same kind, which is notable as showing the relative values that a highly estimable scholar then attached to the various disciplines. Stiles would have his ideal pupil study the vernacular with a view to rendering materials from other languages available in it, and for practice in writing and public speaking. Latin and Greek, Hebrew, Syriac, and Arabic he is also to study; but arithmetic, algebra, geometry, geography, logic, and rhetoric are mentioned only to be dismissed as *leviora studia*. Let the youth pass onward to the higher mathematics, natural philosophy, and astronomy. Astronomy will lead him to the heavenly hierarchy, this to metaphysics and ontology, and thence to ethics and moral philosophy—the latter chiefly mystical and concerned with the Divine Love. He is to study human history too; and at odd times (*subsecivis horis*), music, poetry, drama, and polite and belles lettres. The programme is closed with the professional

[1] For early school books see Book III, Chap. XXIII.

studies: medicine; theology, which Stiles analyzes in some detail as doctrinal, historical, etc.; and law, for which he lays out a course in considerable detail. Notable especially are the slighting mention and the small space (only a little more than four pages out of his forty) and with which Stiles dismisses the humanistic studies.[1]

The time, ripe for change, soon began to feel new tendencies away from English and toward Continental culture. As early as 1778, the Chevalier Quesnay de Beaurepaire was encouraged by John Page, Lieutenant-Governor of Virginia, to establish at Richmond a French Academy of the Arts and Sciences, and by 1786 he had obtained from a number of prominent Virginians and Baltimoreans a subscription amounting to sixty thousand francs. Quesnay had in mind the highest special training of American students in the arts and sciences; he planned "solely for the completion of the education of young men after they have graduated from college."[2] Among the supporters of this proposal for the first graduate school in America was Thomas Jefferson, then resident in Paris; it is contemporaneous with his own plan (1779) to develop William and Mary College into a true university by modernizing its curriculum. The Academy proposed to institute "schools" in foreign languages, design, architecture, painting, sculpture, and engraving, as well as in the natural sciences; similarly, of the eight professorships proposed by Jefferson for the expanded William and Mary College, four were distinctly humanistic.

Quesnay's plan for the Academy fell through because the French Revolution withdrew from it his country's attention and support; Jefferson's plan for the extension of William and Mary developed at length into his foundation of the University of Virginia; and the curriculums proposed for these earlier schools became the basis of the genuinely humanistic curriculum and the advanced university organization of that institution. Moreover, the organization by "schools" or subjects instead of by college classes is believed by historians of education to have suggested to George Ticknor the idea of the departmental and

---

[1] Stiles's *Literary Diary* and *Itineraries* are an unworked mine of material upon the state of learning in the eighteenth century.

[2] See Benjamin Rush's scheme of a national university (1788), *American Museum*, IV. 442 ff. (so G. W. Spindler, *Karl Follen*, 94 and note).

of the elective system, so far as he was able to introduce them at Harvard.

Meanwhile there had arrived in this country several other bearers of influence from Latin countries. Peter Stephen DuPonceau (1760–1844) at the house of Beaumarchais in Paris met Baron Steuben, and came to America with him as secretary and aide de camp. Arriving in 1777, he received a captaincy in the American army and served until 1780, when bad health obliged him to give up active campaigning. For a while he was secretary to Robert Livingston, then in charge of the Department of Foreign Affairs, and after studying law he was in June, 1785, admitted to the bar in Pennsylvania, where he had become a citizen. He rose to such eminence in his profession that he afterwards declined Jefferson's offer to appoint him Chief Justice of Louisiana and was able to retire early in life and devote himself to linguistics. From 1791 he was a member of the American Philosophical Society, to whose interests he gave much time and energy, and to which he communicated his papers, for example, his *English Phonology* (1817) and his report on *The Structure of the Indian Languages* (1819). His memoir on *The Indian Languages of North America* brought him the Volney prize awarded for linguistics by the Academy of Inscriptions of the French Institute. DuPonceau is notable also for his broad conception of the future of American literature, which he wished to emancipate from provincialism by bringing it into the great Continental European tradition. His discourse *On the Necessity and Means of Making our National Literature Independent of That of Great Britain* (1834) is one of the earliest American documents to exhibit a comparative study of literature.

Closely associated with DuPonceau both by personal friendship and by the broad humanism of his work was John Pickering (1777–1846), a son of the more celebrated Timothy Pickering. In Salem and in Boston John Pickering continued his literary studies, becoming by 1806 "an adept in the Hebrew and probably in one or two Semitic tongues beside," but declining an appointment as Hancock Professor of Hebrew and other Oriental Languages at Harvard. He likewise declined (1814) the newly established Eliot Professorship of Greek Literature, of which Edward Everett thereupon became the first incumbent. Pickering's *Greek and English Lexicon* (1826)—a translation of Schrevelius projected and partly executed in 1814—just misses being the earliest of all the Greek-English lexicons. Acquainted with Oriental languages, including Chinese and a number of African and Pacific dialects, Pickering was one of the founders and was the first president of the American Oriental Society. He was deeply versed as well in the American Indian languages, and his treatise *On the Adoption of a Uniform Orthography for the Indian Languages of North America* (*Memoirs of the American Academy*) excited much interest abroad. He lectured to popular audiences upon Champollion's discoveries concerning the hieroglyphic language of Egypt. Today he is best remembered by his work on Americanisms, as presented to the American Academy in 1815 and published the next year in enlarged form—an invaluable record of American speech in the first quarter of the nineteenth century.

Another of the notable transmitters of Latin culture was Lorenzo Da Ponte (1749–1838), a genuine celebrity, and, as the librettist of Mozart's *Nozze di Figaro*, *Don Giovanni*, and *Cosi Fan Tutte*, one of the lesser immortals. A converted Jew, he was educated and he taught in a church seminary, and actually became an Abate. He mingled freely in the gay and the learned society of Venice, carrying on numerous love intrigues and supporting himself by private teaching. One of his sonnets having given offence, in 1777 he left Italy to wander over Europe. At Dresden he made translations and redactions of plays for the Electoral Theatre; thence he removed to Vienna, where he became acquainted with Mozart, and wrote the libretti for *Figaro* (1786) and *Don Giovanni* (1787), produced with brilliant success. Driven away by court intrigues Da Ponte in 1793 went with his young English wife to London, and there made his headquarters for some twelve years, writing for the Italian theatre, touring the Continent to engage singers, opening an Italian book shop, and always more or less retreating from his creditors, from whom, indeed, he retreated to Philadelphia in 1805. Again he moved about erratically, but he settled finally in New York in 1819, gave Italian lessons (Fitz-Greene Halleck was one of his pupils), again opened a book shop, and helped in 1825 to bring over Garcia's troupe, which introduced Italian opera to New York. His own *Don Giovanni* was performed with great éclat. He published several volumes of Italian verse, gave lectures and conversazioni upon Italian literature; read and expounded Alfieri, Metastasio, Tasso, and Dante to his pupils, and in 1825 published in *The New York Review* interpretative notes upon several passages of the *Inferno*. This was the first time Dante had been taught or commented upon in America; Ticknor's classes in Dante did not begin until 1831. In 1829, upon Da Ponte's offer to give instruction in Italian gratis at Columbia College, he was named professor—*inane munus*, for he had neither salary nor fees nor pupils. Two months before his death in 1838 he wrote in a piteous letter to a friend in Paris; "The author of thirty-six dramas; the poet of Joseph II, of Salieri, of Martini, and of Mozart; after having given to America the Italian language, literature, and music; after having taught about three thousand pupils, imported thirty thousand volumes of precious treasures; established libraries, public and private; formed professors; given to the college three hundred volumes of classic verse; having finally reached the age of eighty-nine years, and lavished away all he had in the world; now remains deserted, neglected, and forgotten, as if his voice had never been heard, or as if he were a fugitive escaped from the galleys."

Da Ponte's fatal facility in verse—for he was an improvisatore of the old stripe—of course prevented his ever becoming a poet, yet the writer of *Batti batti* and of *La ci darem la mano* ought surely not be forgotten. His *Memoirs*, published in New York in 1823, also belong in the great Venetian eighteenth-century tradition with those of Goldoni and Carlo Gozzi, and bring back the merry time of *ridotti* and *cicisbei*, of *petits abbés*, theatrical cliques and claques, and wandering adventurers. How this echo of the days of Cagliostro and Casti and Casanova happened to be first heard in the New York of 1823 is one of the curiosities of literature. That American scholarship owes Da Ponte no great debt is not his fault. The time and the ground were not prepared for him. He is significant rather as the most brilliant of the group which transmitted to America the traditions of an urbane—a humane—Latin culture.

After 1815 the stream of Romanic culture seems not to have

received new affluents; as it had been headed toward America by the political disturbances of the American and the French Revolutions, so, apparently, it ceased with the Revolutionary period, though Du Ponceau and Pickering continued to produce works of genuine scholarship, and the initial impulse imparted by Jefferson's French ideas reached a ripe issue in the opening of the University of Virginia in 1825.

German scholarship did not come to these shores until after Americans had gone abroad to get it. The German immigration to New York and Pennsylvania in the eighteenth century brought few scholars. It was not until 1824 that the pioneers of the riper German culture, Karl Beck (1798–1866) and Karl Follen (1785–1840), arrived, at a time when Everett, Ticknor, Cogswell, and Bancroft had all returned from their studies in Germany. Follen and Beck, like Pietro Bachi, who came a year later, emigrated in consequence of the disturbances that attended the end of the Napoleonic régime. Follen had taken part in the war of liberation and had been one of the founders of the Burschenschaften. Charged with complicity in the assassination of Kotzebue, he made his escape to Switzerland, and then to Paris. There he fell in with his friend Karl Beck, likewise a refugee, and the two together came to America. Upon the recommendation of Ticknor, Beck was appointed teacher of Latin and gymnastics in the Round Hill School at Northampton, Massachusetts. In 1832 he became professor of Latin at Harvard, where he remained until his death in 1866. Upon Ticknor's recommendation, too, Follen was appointed instructor in German at Harvard—the first to teach that subject there. He soon became a citizen, was highly esteemed among the Boston liberals, was a friend of W. E. Channing and of James Freeman Clarke, and himself entered the Unitarian ministry. In 1830 he was advanced to a full professorship of the German Language and Literature, which, however, was endowed for a period of five years only. He published a German reader (1826) and a German grammar (1828). His loss of his Harvard position is thought to have been due to his anti-slavery propaganda; and thenceforth he threw himself still more enthusiastically into speechmaking and preaching.

With the return of Edward Everett (1794–1865), George Ticknor (1791–1871), Joseph Green Cogswell (1786–1871), and

George Bancroft[1] from Germany, the German influence in American scholarship becomes palpable. Bancroft and Cogswell established the Round Hill School, which in some ways was modelled upon the German *gymnasium*, and which sent out many boys who afterwards became distinguished. Bancroft left it in 1829. Cogswell, who remained till 1834, was a rolling stone and did not really find himself until past fifty. In New York in 1838 he became acquainted with John Jacob Astor, and led him to establish the Astor Library, of which, after Astor's death in 1848, Cogswell was appointed superintendent. His only important literary monument is the Astor Library Catalogue (1857–66).

Everett, after his election to the Eliot Professorship of Greek Literature at Harvard, had gone abroad in 1815 and had achieved the doctorate at Göttingen in 1817. Thereafter he went alone on the Greek tour which for a while Cogswell and Ticknor had been planning to take with him, and became acquainted with Adamantios Koraës just before the outbreak of the Greek war for independence. Returning in 1820 full of enthusiasm for learning and for Greece, he gave lectures which must have been inspiring, else Emerson would not have praised him so highly.[2] But "what avails thorough preparation of the college teacher, if his pupils are unprepared? We need to reform our secondary schools," Everett had written from Göttingen; and the want of adequate preparation on the part of his pupils may help explain why he left no school. Moreover, he soon resigned his professorship and his editorship of *The North American Review*, to enter public life; and though he was afterward president of Harvard College, he is known no more as an American scholar. His writings show him rather in the attitude of a Roman orator, draped in a toga which to modern taste seems less *virilis* than *prætexta*.[3]

Of the Göttingen group there remains that one who was on the whole the soundest scholar, and who in time became the first American scholar to achieve a permanent international reputation. George Ticknor was born in Boston in 1791, of parents who were both teachers. Having graduated from Dart-

[1] See Book II, Chap. XVII.
[2] *Historic Notes of Life and Letters in New England.*
[3] See also Book II, Chap. XV.

mouth in 1807, he read Greek and Latin authors for three years with the rector of Trinity Church, Boston, a pupil of Samuel Parr. From 1810 Ticknor read law and in 1813 was admitted to the bar, but he gave up practice in a year. The country, he thought, "would never be without good lawyers," but would urgently need "scholars, teachers, and men of letters." From Madame de Staël's *De l'Allemagne* (1813) Ticknor had got an intimation of the intellectual mastery of the Germans; he elected therefore to study in Germany, and particularly at Göttingen. Through the summer and autumn of 1814 he worked hard at German, borrowing a grammar from Edward Everett, sending to New Hampshire, where he "knew there was a German dictionary," and translating *Werther* from John Quincy Adams's copy, stored at the Athenæum.

Before going abroad, though, he must make the American grand tour to Washington and Virginia. During the winter of 1814–15 he travelled by slow stages and sometimes under difficulties as far as Richmond, everywhere supplied with introductions to and from eminent persons such as John Adams, President Madison, and Thomas Jefferson. He met, among others, Eli Whitney, Robert Lenox, John Randolph, and Charles Carroll of Carrollton; attended the Hartford Convention; saw the ruins of Washington, then recently burned by the British; and at Monticello got the news of their defeat at New Orleans. Already he was exhibiting the social gifts which later distinguished him—a power of holding substantial conversation when that was in order; a tact that kept him wisely and quizzically silent during an outburst of bad temper on the part of Adams, and in the presence of Jefferson's philosophical oddities; together with a cool sub-acid judgment in estimating and reporting such phenomena as these and the ways of men in general. He made an especially favourable impression upon Jefferson, who twice—in 1818 and again in 1820—invited him to a chair at the University of Virginia.

In April, 1815, Ticknor sailed for Liverpool with Edward Everett and several other friends. At Liverpool and on the way to London he paid his respects to Roscoe and to Dr. Parr. In London he met Hallam, and various lesser scholars. At Göttingen Ticknor settled down to a monastic regimen of study, specializing in Greek. He met the Homeric Wolf, "coryphæus of German philologists," then on a visit to Göttingen; and, during an eight weeks' holiday trip across Germany, Gesenius and Goethe. For a full year he continued his classical studies without any notion that his field was to lie elsewhere. From Byron in London he had got hints for a tour in Greece, and he was preparing to make it, when late in 1816 Harvard offered him the College Professorship of the Belles Lettres and the Smith Professorship of the French and Spanish Languages and Literatures, then just established upon the death of its founder Abiel Smith. Accordingly Ticknor gave up his Greek tour, and after a few months in Göttingen began in the spring of 1817 an extensive course of travel and study in the Latin countries. In Paris he worked with great diligence at French and Italian. In Rome by November he studied Italian and archæology. Leaving Rome late in March of 1818, he made his way slowly to Spain via Italy and southern France. In Madrid he at once settled into his habitual studious ways. During the summer and autumn of 1818 he made several excursions and a considerable journey in Spain and Portugal; whence in November he went via England to Paris again. Here he privately studied Spanish literature, Portuguese, and Provençal. In London in January, 1819, he dropped study for awhile, and was taken up by the great Whigs—Lord Holland, Sir James Mackintosh, Richard Heber, Hookham Frere, Lord John Russell, and Sydney Smith. He visited the Marquis of Salisbury at Hatfield House and the Duke of Bedford at Woburn Abbey; again touched classical studies in a sojourn at Cambridge; and before February reached Edinburgh. Picking out, as was usual with him, a specialist to help him in his studies, he read Scotch poetry. Here he frequented the Tory circle of Mrs. Grant of Laggan, and made the acquaintance of Scott, whom he visited at Abbotsford for a few days; proceeding thence to Southey at Keswick and to Wordsworth at Rydal Mount. At Hatton he saw old Dr. Parr once more, who condemned everything contemporary but gave Ticknor his blessing.

In London again, early in April, Ticknor went with Irving to the "damning of a play" and afterwards to the Lord Mayor's ball, which he also damns in a series of contemptuous remarks about the "City crowd." Though he had already disparaged Godwin as the "notorious William Godwin," he dined at his house; and then proceeded to disparage him further, together with the company he met there, including Hazlitt, Hunt, and Lamb. Ticknor was as much at home with the "big Whigs" as with the grand Tories, especially the great Tory of Abbotsford; *Whig Toriusve mihi nullo discrimine agetur*, he might have said; but he could not abide a Philistine or a Bohemian.

At the end of April, 1819, after a brief visit to Roscoe in Liverpool, he sailed for home, and reached Boston early in June, with an equipment far beyond that of any previous American student. His teaching at Harvard began in the same year and continued until he resigned in 1835. Like Everett's, it was so far in advance of his time and of the training his students brought to it that he founded no school of research and made no disciples in advanced scholarship. But he greatly improved elementary instruction in the modern languages, and could find sometimes (as in 1831) a class that would read Dante with him; he established for his own subjects a departmental system, with considerable freedom of election, and with promotion and grouping according to proficiency; and he went as far as the college authorities would allow in establishing an elective system within his own jurisdiction. These reforms being opposed, actively by some other members of the faculty, passively by President Kirkland, Ticknor felt, after sixteen years of service, that he had done all the missionary work that could reasonably be expected of him. He resigned his professorship, and made a second sojourn in Europe (1835–38), Longfellow having been chosen to be his successor.

This second residence in Europe Ticknor undertook not primarily as a student but as a ripe scholar; and although he had as yet produced no great work, he was everywhere received as one whose standing was assured. The acquaintances he formed or renewed are too numerous to be even catalogued in full. In England he saw a good deal of the scientific men. At Dresden he examined Ludwig Tieck's collection of Spanish books, and he joined the scholarly circle of Prince John of Saxony. In Berlin in the spring of 1836 Ticknor visited the church historian Neander, and saw Alexander von Humboldt frequently. In Vienna, in June, he examined the old Spanish books in the Imperial Library. After a summer in Switzerland and southern Germany, he moved towards Rome, which he reached in

December, and in which he remained until May of 1837. He
went north for the summer again, to Venice, Innsbruck, and
Heidelberg, and to Paris for the winter, where he looked over the
Spanish library of Ternaux-Compans and frequented the study
of Augustin Thierry. By March, 1838, Ticknor was in England again, having long talks with Hallam. He once more
visited Southey and Wordsworth at Keswick; was disappointed
in the Spanish collection at the Bodleian; met at breakfast "a
Mr. Ruskin," who had a most beautiful collection "of sketches,
made by himself, from nature, on the Continent"; and heard
Carlyle lecture.

Arriving at home in June, 1838, Ticknor settled down to
research, to extensive correspondence with many friends, both
European and American, to the collecting of Spanish books, and
to the writing of his *History of Spanish Literature*, which was
published in 1849 and was at once recognized as a work of
international standing. He found time also to work hard for
the Boston Public Library, of which he was a trustee; doing for
it what his friends Buckminster and Cogswell had done respectively for the Athenæum and the Astor. Upon the third
and last of his European tours, undertaken in 1856–57 for
the sake of the library, he had little time for his own studies,
but he was lionized—being now the author of a famous book—
as never before, and moved in the most brilliant society. At
home again from September, 1857, Ticknor took up once more
his life of study and business, serving the library until 1866,
revising the *History of Spanish Literature* for its third and its
fourth editions, maintaining a voluminous correspondence, and,
after the death of Prescott in 1859, writing his *Life* (1864). At
this time, too, Ticknor resumed his active interest in Harvard.
He died in 1871.

Ticknor's life, as recorded in his *Life, Letters and Journals*,
is that of a great man of business, a great social talent, almost
a *grand seigneur*, who stood before kings, or rather sat down
with them,—and who was incidentally a scholar. It is necessary, in an account of his works, to distribute the emphasis in
this way, partly because the *Life*, considered as one of them,
depends decisively upon his social powers, which elicited
characteristic attitudes and utterances from the persons he met,
and partly because these powers gave a characteristic turn

even to the *History of Spanish Literature*. The *Life*, a treasury of anecdote and portraiture, which it costs an effort not to quote, would, if well annotated, be found to be also a compendium of European history in its social and literary aspects during the first half of the nineteenth century. The English great houses, the Paris salons, the German courts and scholars, the international social complex at Rome and Florence—Ticknor saw more of these than any other American, and than any but a few of the most highly placed Europeans. His *Life* is, emphatically, good reading, and can only increase in interest with time.

His *History of Spanish Literature* has so impressed critics by its great reputation and by its great conception, scope, and bulk, that they have given it rather praise than appraisal. The claim made by the editors, in their preface to the fourth edition, represents the current opinion of its merits. "So far as the past is concerned, the history of Spanish literature need not be written anew, and the scholars who may hereafter labour in this field of letters will have little else to do than to continue the structure which Mr. Ticknor has reared." Now it is true that Ticknor is strong in his sense of fact, in his feeling for evidence, and in the sanity of his opinions. Very few indeed of his attributions need revision in the light even of the acutest later scholarship. His very comprehensive bibliography, universally praised by his critics, is a second consequence of his strength. He had probably handled and read more Spanish books than had anybody else in his time. His thoroughness extends also to a pretty full use of existing authorities, Spanish, German, French, and English. His combination of their results with those of his own bibliographical research constitutes his title to be considered a pioneer. Still, pioneer work is one thing; definitive work is another. In many fields of Spanish literature it was Ticknor's task actually to find and identify the works he describes. For such work—the primary dealings with raw material—his mind was well fitted. But the later regroupings and higher generalizations of the inductive process, the perception of broad differences, resemblances, connections, and tendencies, the framing of comprehensive concepts, and, in general, the freedom of movement in the conceptual world—these things require a mind set free from the pedestrian tasks to which Ticknor willingly committed himself, and another strength than the one he had. There were temperamental reasons, too, why Ticknor could never have made such a higher synthesis. He belongs essentially to the hard-headed group of American writers who, like Andrews Norton, stopped short of transcendentalism. Ticknor's German training had taught him what much of the British scholarship of his time sorely needed to learn—the need of the broadest possible basis in facts; from that point onward, however, his scholarship remained essentially British in its distrust of ideas. The *History of Spanish Literature* is much more like Warton's *History of English Poetry* and Hallam's *Middle Ages* than it is like anything German. More serious temperamental defects are still to be mentioned. The plain fact is that Ticknor did not possess certain of the indispensable organs of literary scholarship. He lacked *ordonnance;* he was blind to the French literature of the Middle Ages and of the Renaissance; and he wanted ear—especially for verse. His lack of the sense for sequence, arrangement, and emphatic or conspicuous position appears even in the unworkmanlike construction of many of his sentences, and in the misplacement of matter (especially in footnotes) just at the point where random association happened to make him think of it. In his references to French literature, which in the Middle Ages and the Renaissance was so closely connected with Spanish, he disparages Ronsard and misassigns him with the decadents; he has not a word about Du Bellay; and, almost incredibly, he seems not even to have known of the *Chanson de Roland*. His want of ear and want of the sense of arrangement make his history difficult reading. Only occasionally does it attain anything worthy of the name of style.

Ticknor, as has been intimated, left no school; though American scholars have since studied *cosas de España*, they do not take him for their point of departure, and his work ends rather than begins an era. While it was Ticknor who turned the attention of Prescott to Spanish history, yet Ticknor's own *History* did not appear until after Prescott's *Ferdinand and Isabella*, *Conquest of Mexico*, and *Conquest of Peru*. It belongs in fact rather with the discursive historical work of Irving and of Prescott than with the minute textual studies and editions which have been the chief task of later Spanish scholarship in this country.[1] Similarly, a direct connection between Ticknor's teaching and the later teaching of modern languages and literatures would be difficult to trace. Longfellow never studied under him, and took his own scholarship according to his own poetic temper. Ticknor retired from Harvard when Lowell was a sophomore; and there was no sympathetic contact between the two in later years. Charles Eliot Norton came to Harvard after his "Uncle Ticknor" had gone, and his studies in Dante give no sign of contact with those of his kinsman.

The impulse after 1850 toward the study of the modern languages and literatures was due rather to the immigration which had been set up by the European troubles of 1848, and which brought many cultivated Germans and Frenchmen to the United States. Hindered by our own political disturbances during the fifties and sixties, and helped by the "scientific" and utilitarian opposition to the classics, it reached self-consciousness and scholarship in the seventies, with the foundation of the Johns Hopkins University (1876), which proposed a scientific philology, impartial whether ancient or modern. Professor Gildersleeve having founded the American Journal of Philology in 1880, his colleague A. Marshall Elliott (1844–1910) soon interested a sufficient number of advanced teachers of the modern languages to found in 1883 the Modern Language Association of America,[2] of which he was the first secretary, and of whose *Publications*, also suggested by him, he was the first editor (1884–92). For twenty-five years, also, until his death, he edited *Modern Language Notes*, now continued by his former colleague, James Wilson Bright. The progress of "modern philology" in America thus belongs to the university era, and is detached from Ticknor.

University production obtained its other great successes in the philology of the classics, of general linguistics, of English, and of the fine arts.

The University of Virginia opened with several foreign teachers whom Jefferson's friend Francis W. Gilmer had engaged abroad. Its first professor of the Ancient Languages (1825–28) was George Long, who is best known for his transla-

---

[1] See Romera-Navarro, 135.

[2] Charles Francis Adams's address, *A College Fetich*, delivered at Harvard in June, 1883, independently excited public interest in the subject.

tions of Marcus Aurelius (1826) and of Epictetus (1877). Upon his recall in 1828 to the chair of Greek at the newly established University College, London, he named as his successor his pupil Gessner Harrison (1807-62), with whom he remained in correspondence and to whom he sent copies of the earlier portions of Bopp's *Comparative Grammar* as they appeared from 1833 onward. Harrison thereupon applied the comparative method to his own studies and teaching long before it had been practised elsewhere in America, or in England, or had been generally accepted even in Germany

Among classical scholars in America as elsewhere two types are distinguishable; the one indulging its æsthetic appreciation, historical and archæological associations, and a philosophical discursiveness about the ancients, and the reconstitution of antiquity as a whole—Boeckh's ideal of *Altertumswissenschaft;* the other inclining towards minute grammatical, textual, and metrical investigations—the ideals rather of Hermann and Curtius. Two scholars of the first type are Cornelius Conway Felton and Theodore Dwight Woolsey.

Felton (1807-62), like Harrison, his exact contemporary, received all his training in this country. Seven years after his graduation from Harvard he became in 1834 Eliot Professor of Greek Literature, made his first journey abroad in 1853-54, spending several months in Greece, and became president of Harvard two years before his death. The close friend of Longfellow, Felton, was a genial soul, enthusiastic for antiquity, who rather deprecated minute grammatical study and overmuch concern with choric metres and textual readings and emendations. These things he thought dried up the springs of human feeling in the student. He favoured instead the appreciative study of ancient and modern literatures together, paralleling Æschylus with Shakespeare and Milton, comparing Sophocles and Euripides with Alfieri, Schiller, and Goethe, and contrasting Greek with French drama. He published (1834) Wolf's text of the *Iliad* with Flaxman's illustrations and his own notes; and made college editions of *The Clouds, The Birds,* and the *Agamemnon,* and of the *Panegyricus* of Isocrates. The fruits of his journey were his *Selections from Modern Greek Writers* (1856) and several series of Lowell Institute lectures, published posthumously as *Greece, Ancient and Modern.*

Theodore Dwight Woolsey (1801–89), who graduated at Yale in 1820, was in Germany and France from 1827 to 1830, studying with Welcker, and with both Hermann and Boeckh. In 1830 he was present at the "Literary Convention" held in New York, which was the first important American assemblage of professional educators, and was associated with the founding of New York University. Woolsey and others—among them, Francis Lieber—addressed the convention in defence of liberal studies. At Yale he was professor of Greek from 1831 to 1846, and president from 1846 till he resigned in 1871. He edited the *Alcestis* (1834), the *Antigone*, and the *Electra* (1835–37), the *Prometheus* (1837), and the *Gorgias* (1842). Like Felton, Woolsey did not train professional philologists, but did much to induct American youth into a liberal education. He exhibits the Yale sobriety and lucidity that is characteristic of his uncle, Timothy Dwight, and of his younger contemporaries, James Hadley and William Dwight Whitney; and like Lieber and Hadley he turned from the classics to political science and law.

Others of this generation worked at lexicography. John Pickering's *Lexicon* has already been mentioned. Evangelinus Apostolides Sophocles (1807–83), born in Thessaly, taught Greek at Yale from 1837 to 1840, and thenceforth at Harvard, where from 1860 he was professor of Ancient, Byzantine, and Modern Greek. He published a *Greek Grammar* in 1838, but what makes him memorable is his compilation of the Greek Ducange, his great *Greek Lexicon of the Roman and Byzantine Periods* (1870). To Henry Drisler (1818–97) are due most of the emendations in the second edition (1887) of Sophocles's *Lexicon*. Drisler, who was a professor of Greek in Columbia College, also prepared American editions of Liddell and Scott (1851) and of Yonge's *English-Greek Lexicon* (1858). With Howard Crosby (1826–91), he founded in 1857 the "Greek Club" which ended with his life. Forcellini's *Latin Lexicon*, abridged by Wilhelm Freund (1834–35), was the foundation of a Latin Dictionary (1850) by E. A. Andrews (1787–1858); which in turn was revised and re-edited in 1879 by Charlton Thomas Lewis (1834–1904), an ex-professor of Greek who at the time was practising law in New York, and Charles Lancaster Short (1821–86), professor of Latin in Columbia College.

The next generation turns somewhat decisively to the ideals

of Hermann. James Hadley (1821–72), before he entered Yale as a junior in 1840, had "read as much Greek and Latin as Macaulay had read during his whole school and university life." By 1851 he had become professor of the Greek Language and Literature at Yale. Meanwhile, with his friend William Dwight Whitney, he had been studying Sanskrit under Edward Elbridge Salisbury (1814–1901), then our only trained Oriental scholar, who had but two pupils in Sanskrit—Hadley and Whitney, *duos sed leones*. Whitney went abroad to continue his studies; Hadley married and settled in New Haven, where he remained until his death. When Hadley decided to become a philologist, Benjamin Peirce said that one of the finest mathematical minds of his generation was lost; in fact, Hadley's work produces an irresistible impression of sheer all-round power. The day of narrow specialization had not come, and Hadley could write with equal authority a *Greek Grammar* (1860); a *Brief History of the English Language;* and *Lectures on Roman Law* (1873). The *Greek Grammar*, as revised by Frederic De Forest Allen in 1884, and the *Brief History of the English Language*, as revised by G. L. Kittredge, are still in use. The *Lectures on Roman Law* were said as recently as 1904 to be "in some respects the best elementary exposition of the system of Gaius and Justinian." Hadley's shorter papers were edited after his death by Whitney (*Essays Philological and Critical*, 1873). They discuss, among much else, Ernst Curtius's theory that the migrating Ionians were only going back to their home land in Asia; the Byzantine Greek pronunciation of the tenth century; and the origin of the English possessive case. They review Ellis's *Early English Pronunciation*, and wittily demolish Ludwig Ross's *Italiker und Gräken*. They contain, finally, perhaps the ripest and best known of Hadley's memoirs, that *On the Nature and Theory of the Greek Accent*. In the light of such work, Whitney's opinion that Hadley was "America's best and soundest philologist" is not a friendly exaggeration, but an expert's cool appraisal.

George Martin Lane (1823–97), a pupil of Karl Beck, in 1847 resumed the Harvard tradition of study in Germany, which for a long period after the return of the Göttingen group had been almost intermitted. Working at Göttingen, Berlin, Bonn, and Heidelberg under K. F. Hermann, Welcker, Heyse,

Ernst Curtius, and others, Lane received his degree at Göttingen in 1851 for a dissertation which has remained an authority upon the history of the city of Smyrna. In the same year he succeeded Beck as professor of Latin, and served until 1894, promoting the work of the graduate school of research, and offering courses more and more advanced. The soundness and the brilliancy of his teaching are still proverbial, and his publications, though few, are influential. *Latin Pronunciation* (1871) is said to have "worked a revolution in exterminating the English pronunciation of Latin in this country—a revolution which even the weight and learning of a Munro could never even begin in England."[1] Lane assisted Charlton T. Lewis in producing the large *Harper's Latin Dictionary* (Lewis and Short), but contributed more vitally to the smaller or *School Lexicon*, "by far the more original and trustworthy book." Chief of his works is the *Latin Grammar*, for which he had been collecting material since 1869, but which was just approaching completion when he died. Lane wore his learning lightly and was remarkable for his wit. At the Newport Town and Country Club, presided over by Julia Ward Howe, he presented in Latin a burlesque Harvard Commencement programme; upon an adventure of his own he composed the far-famed ballad of "The Lone Fish Ball."

The brothers Joseph Henry Allen (1820–98) and William Francis Allen (1830–89) together edited Virgil (1880), and with James Bradstreet Greenough (1833–1901) produced the well-known "Allen and Greenough" Latin texts, which included Cæsar, Sallust, Ovid, and Cicero. J. H. Allen with Greenough wrote the Allen and Greenough *Latin Grammar*, published 1872, and an *Elementary Latin Composition*, published 1876. W. F. Allen contributed the historical and archæological material to the Allen and Greenough series, and later edited Tacitus. Greenough in 1865 was appointed to a Latin tutorship at Harvard, and was professor of Latin from 1883 until the year of his death. He taught himself Sanskrit, became interested from the first in comparative grammar and general linguistics,

---

[1] It is said, however, that "Washington and Lee University was the first institution in this country to adopt the Roman pronunciation of Latin"—it was introduced there in 1868 by Milton W. Humphreys, later (1887) professor of Greek at the University of Virginia.

an interest stimulated by Goodwin's *Greek Moods and Tenses* (1860), and applied these methods to the Latin verb in his *Analysis of the Latin Subjunctive* (1870). The principles here laid down and followed seem to show that Greenough was strongly influenced not only by the German originators of the comparative linguistic method, and by Goodwin, but by W. D. Whitney as well, whose *Language and the Study of Language* had appeared at the very time (1867) when Greenough was undertaking his researches. Greenough introduced the teaching of Sanskrit and comparative philology at Harvard, and gave courses in them from 1872 until the appointment of C. R. Lanman as professor of Sanskrit in 1880. In 1872, likewise, he published with Joseph Henry Allen a *Latin Grammar for Schools and Colleges, founded on Comparative Grammar*, in which he applied the methods and amplified the results of the *Analysis*. This, though in name only a schoolbook, contains in its successive editions the results of Greenough's research, and has been widely influential upon the subsequent study of Latin syntax. The issues of his investigation in other fields quietly appear in the same way in the volumes of the Allen and Greenough series. *Words and their Ways in English Speech* (1901), which Greenough and G. L. Kittredge prepared together, presents in racy and readable form the substance of much solid scholarship. Greenough was active in the development of the Harvard Graduate School; established in 1889 the *Harvard Studies in Classical Philology;* introduced reading at sight into American classical teaching; promoted the collegiate instruction of women; wrote excellent Latin verse and prose; and, like Lane and Child and Goodwin, delighted in learned fun.

Frederic DeForest Allen (1844–97) in 1879 was appointed Hadley's successor at Yale, and in 1880 was called to Harvard as the first professor of Classical Philology, where he remained until his death. Those who could best judge his work found in him a tireless questioner of traditions, an essential investigator; and what he investigated was the life of the ancients. He considered classical learning to be "a great branch of anthropology, giving insight, when rightly studied, into the mental operations and intellectual and moral growth of ancient peoples. To him, literature and monuments were records of life, and they were to be interpreted by it and in turn were themselves to interpret it." His only volumes are an edition of the *Medea* (1876), a collection of *Remnants of Early Latin* (1879), Hadley's *Greek Grammar*, revised and in part rewritten (1884), and a translation of the *Prometheus Bound* (1891); but he published many short papers, chiefly upon etymologies, inscriptions, and ancient music and metres. In 1885 and 1886 he had charge of the American School at Athens, and had, at his death, gathered materials for an edition, never finished, of the *scholia* of Plato.

William Watson Goodwin (1831–1912), after his graduation at Harvard in 1851, studied at Göttingen, returned in 1856 as tutor in Greek, and was Eliot Professor of Greek from 1860 until his resignation in 1901. His *Syntax of the Moods and Tenses of the Greek Verb* (1860) has passed through many editions and revisions, and still holds the field as an epitome of classical usage. Its lucid analysis and arrangement and copious citations of its basic material make it both a reference book and a thesaurus. Its results enter more briefly into the *Greek Grammar* of 1870, which like *Moods and Tenses* remains in current use after a good half-century. Goodwin also revised Felton's edition of the *Panegyricus* of Isocrates (1864), and edited *The Clouds* (1873) and the collected translation of Plutarch's *Morals*, by several hands (1871). The *Agamemnon*, in his text, was performed at Harvard in 1906. His greatest editions are those of Demosthenes *On the Crown* (1901) and *Against Midias* (1906).

Basil Lanneau Gildersleeve, still living as the dean of American philologists, was born in 1831 at Charleston, South Carolina. After his graduation at Princeton in 1849, he studied under Boeckh, Schneidewin, and Ritschl at Berlin, Bonn, and Göttingen, where he achieved the doctorate in 1853 with a dissertation upon Porphyry's Homeric studies. At the University of Virginia he was from 1856 to 1876 professor of Greek, and from 1861 to 1866, professor of Latin. Upon the establishment of the Johns Hopkins University in 1876 he was appointed to its first professorship, that of Greek, which, as Emeritus, he still holds. He gave powerful aid in making the university a true school of research and his own department a training ground for philologists.[1] In 1880 Gildersleeve established the

---

[1] Among his pupils was Thomas Randolph Price, exemplar of the essential oneness of the humanities, who both at Randolph-Macon and at the University of

American Journal of Philology, which from the first took high
rank as a repository of solid contributions to philology modern
as well as classical, and which published from time to time the
results of his own research, both *in extenso* and in the notes and
short reviews which filled his special department, "Brief Mention." Gildersleeve's great power of literary appreciation and
expression is grounded upon endless interest in the minutiæ of
syntax and metre. His *Latin Grammar* (1867) had already
reached a stage of induction which enabled its analysis to stand
as the method of the *Syntax of Classical Greek* (1900, 1911)
still in course of publication. The edition of *Persius* (1875)
shows the combination of these qualities, its Introduction
taking high rank as a literary and historical essay, and its notes
guiding the student through the intricacies of Persius's language and allusion. Professor Gildersleeve himself confesses
that he used his edition of the *Apologies* of Justin Martyr (1877)
and his edition of Pindar (1885) chiefly as a repository of his
syntactical theories—an assertion doubtless flavoured with
Socratic irony. His *Syntax* has recorded and explicated usage
without resort to metaphysics. Through his publications he
has exercised a very great influence upon many scholars who
were not his students, but who acknowledge that they "have
all been to school to Gildersleeve."

The technical content of most of Professor Gildersleeve's
writings has perhaps kept the larger public from appreciating
his literary merit. Nor can even so much of his work as might
be open to popular appreciation, like the collected *Essays and
Studies* (1890), hope for a very numerous reading public. For
it is a work of disillusionment. Just as in his own professional
field Professor Gildersleeve has witnessed and partly undergone "The Oscillations and Nutations of Philological Studies,"
so he looks upon the general human scene with the eyes of
Ecclesiastes. Like that other veteran Hellenist, Professor
Mahaffy, he seems to grow weary of the high and central
classics (his *Pindar* is his only edition of any one of them), and
to turn with a certain relief to secondary writers, like Persius

Virginia, where he followed Gildersleeve as professor of Greek, wove classical studies and English together, considering the study of English partly "as an Introduction to the Study of Latin and Greek" (1877). He later was professor of English
at Columbia University.

and Lucian and Platen, who hold life at arm's length for satirical comment. But his disillusionment brings with it no impairment of his wit, and this, despite the irrelevancies into which it often leads him, is both brilliant and profound. Everywhere his essential *esprit* and intellectual energy, when they do not bewilder the reader and leave him far behind, delight and stimulate him. A literary satirist, Gildersleeve should have written a History of Literary Satire; and one who would form an anthology of the less technical sayings from "Brief Mention" would find that he had gathered many of the materials for such a work. Upon Gildersleeve all the ends of the world are come; he has lamented the old Germany that died with the Franco-Prussian war, and the old South that died with the Civil War; and, having witnessed the passing of two civilizations and the unending vicissitudes of mankind, he is still gathering his multiform experience into writing, and γηράσκει αἰεὶ πολλὰ διδασκόμενος.

The greatest English-speaking student of general linguistics and of the science of language, William Dwight Whitney (1827–1894), was born at Northampton, to a fine local and family tradition of manners, character, and scholarship. Having graduated in 1845 at Williams College, he later became an assistant to his brother Josiah, who in 1849 was conducting the United States survey of the Lake Superior region; and he wrote for the report of the expedition the chapter on botany. Meanwhile he had become interested in Sanskrit; he studied it in his leisure time during the survey, and immediately afterward went to Yale for graduate study in the Department of Philosophy and the Arts, which Professor Salisbury had been active in organizing (1846–48), and which was the first graduate school of genuine university rank in the United States.

From 1850 to 1853 Whitney studied in Berlin under Weber, Bopp, and Lepsius, and at Tübingen under Roth. Returning to the United States in 1853, he was next year appointed Salisbury's successor in the chair of Sanskrit, his duties including instruction in the modern languages. He was not released from undergraduate teaching until 1869, when Salisbury increased the endowment of Whitney's Yale professorship, and Whitney became "the only 'university professor' . . . in the whole country." He was now enabled to organize fully a graduate school of philology, which very soon attracted able students, among them Charles R. Lanman, Irving Manatt, Bernadotte Perrin, A. H. Edgren, and William Rainey Harper, who well represent the variety of interests arising from the studies which Whitney directed. From 1850 Whitney had been a member of the American Oriental Society, and he became successively its corresponding secretary, its librarian, and its president. From 1857 to 1885 more than half of the Society's *Journal* came from his busy pen. He was also one of the founders and was the first president of the American Philological Association.

Whitney produced a large volume of work, and left his mark upon many different departments of scholarship. His important achievements in his particular field of Indology can be truly evaluated only by Indologists. His first large work in Indian scholarship was his edition, with Roth, of the *Atharva-Veda-Sanhitā* (1855–56), and his very last was the translation of the same Veda, edited after his death by Charles R. Lanman (1905). Whitney edited in 1862 the *Atharva-Veda-Prātiçākhya* with a translation and notes, and in 1871 the *Taittirīya Prāti-çākhya*. "The Prātiçākhyas are the phonetico-grammatical treatises upon the texts of the Vedas, and are of prime importance for the establishment of the text. Their distinguishing feature is minutiæ of marvellous exactness, but presented in such a form that no one with aught less than a tropical Oriental contempt for the value of time can make anything out of them as they stand. Whitney not only out-Hindus the Hindu for minutiæ, but also, such is his command of form, actually recasts the whole so that it becomes a book of easy reference."[1] These intensive studies of the Hindu grammarians and of the Sanskrit texts gave Whitney the material for his great Sanskrit *Grammar* (1879), with its supplement, *The Roots, Verb-forms, and Primary Derivatives of the Sanskrit Language* (1885), which together form "the crowning achievement" of his work as a Sanskrit scholar. Whitney's book goes behind the Hindu grammarians and rests upon direct induction from the texts. Beginning thus with the phenomena, Whitney might not be too severely condemned if, like Ticknor in the *Spanish Literature*, he had failed to rise much above their merely factual level.

[1] C. R. Lanman: *Memorial Address*, in Whitney Memorial Volume.

But his induction is complete; there are none of those confused categories or obscure arrangements that betoken failure to reach illuminating concepts. Whitney has thus left for the use of students in Indo-European linguistics an organon that is not likely to be soon discarded.

Whitney's works upon the general science of language— *Language and the Study of Language* (1867), *The Life and Growth of Language* (1875), etc., might perhaps never have been written if he "had not been driven to it by . . . the necessity of counteracting as far as possible the influence" of Max Müller's views. Against the idealism, transcendentalism, and logical fallacies of Müller, Whitney takes a distinctly common-sense and almost pragmatic view. Language is for him a human institution, an instrument made by man to meet human needs, and at no time beyond human control. It has to be acquired afresh by every speaker, for it is not a self-subsisting entity that can be transmitted through the body or the mind of race or individual. Whitney thus decisively ranges himself against all absolutist and determinist theories of the nature of language. Upon the origins of language, though he declined to commit himself, as feeling that the evidence warranted no positive assertion, he yet felt equally certain that the evidence did *not* warrant Müller's assertion of a multiple origin—languages springing up here, there, and everywhere upon the surface of the earth. The trend of Whitney's opinion, though he asserts nothing positively, is towards a single primal language.

As in Indology, so in general linguistics, Whitney left a school, represented in Germany by the so-called Jung-Grammatiker, who include Osthoff, Brugmann, Leskien, Fick, and Paul, and in the United States by Professor Hanns Oertel and other disciples. They emphasize the importance of analogy and of phonetic economy, as chief among the psychic factors that must be added to the physical in order to account fully for linguistic change. All Whitney's modes of thinking tended away from those integrations which take the investigator back towards undifferentiated origins, and worked forward among the differentiations that account for linguistic progress towards the present and the future. Whitney is much more interested in the processes of linguistic change than in the evidences of linguistic unity.

The forward look is equally characteristic of his work in orthography and lexicography, which assumed that neither in meaning nor in form is language to be dominated by its past. He consistently and lucidly favoured a reformed spelling, but here too his common sense and regard for present actualities controlled his doctrine, and he never made among the lay public any propaganda looking to the adoption of a phonetic system. In the same way, when he came to the making of *The Century Dictionary*, he conceived it as bound to offer, not a standard of "correctness" derived from classical periods in the past, but a compendium of the actual use and movement of the word throughout its history. Together with this kinetic conception both of the vocabulary and of the semantics of his *Dictionary*, Whitney gave the most minute attention to his etymologies and definitions. Among the editors of Webster's *Dictionary* in 1864, Whitney and Daniel Coit Gilman had had special charge of the revision of the definitions; for the *Century* Whitney obtained the assistance of his brother Josiah in defining the technological words, and the assistance of other experts in their special fields. The result was an extensive vocabulary intensively defined. The etymologies are brought up to the state of knowledge in 1891. The quotations (undated) illustrate rather than fully set forth the semantic history of the word; the *Century* in this respect is surpassed by the Oxford Dictionary, to which alone among English dictionaries it is in any respect second.

Whitney's own writing is a model of lucid exposition. It neither has nor needs adventitious ornament; it does not even need the play of humour to make his most technical essays readable. There are to be sure, flashes of a polemic wit, but what keeps the text alive and at work is the reader's sense that he is in powerful hands that bear him surely along. Whitney seems to divine that particular analysis of his material which will carry the reader cleanly through it. The ultimate impression left by his writings is that of a powerful intellect controlling enormous masses of fact and moving among them as their master. To be interesting, such power needs no play other than its own.

English philology of the nineteenth century in America began with old-fashioned descriptive rhetoric and with increasingly scholarly lexicography; it passed through a middle stage in which it studied Old English and the history of the English language, and amassed solid materials for inferences about English usage; and it emerged at length into distinctly literary studies and editions of great authors or great literary types—Chaucer, Shakespeare, the ballad.

The beginnings were meagre. The low estate of belles lettres and liberal studies in general at Yale in 1778 has been indicated in President Stiles's *Inaugural Oration*. Almost at the same time (1776) Timothy Dwight, then a tutor, "gave a course of lectures on style and composition similar in plan to the lectures of Blair," then not yet published. During his presidency Dwight resumed the teaching of belles lettres, probably with the same scope as that of Blair's rhetoric—the study of diction and style in the narrower sense. Rhetoric at Yale, however, was until a late period generally rather a step-child in the family of the arts. At Harvard, rhetoric has been taught continuously and systematically. The sum left by Nicholas Boylston (1771) for the foundation of a professorship of Rhetoric and Oratory having accumulated until 1806, John Quincy Adams was installed and held the chair until 1809. His *Lectures on Rhetoric and Oratory* (1810), to the number of thirty-six, begin with the regular defence of rhetoric against its maligners; move historically through Greece and Rome down to Quintilian, with, however, only the barest mention of Aristotle; and thence build upon a combination of Cicero's analysis (invention, disposition, elocution, memory, and pronunciation or action) with Aristotle's classification of all oratory as demonstrative, deliberative, and judicial, adding a modern class, "eloquence of the pulpit." The discussion throughout is illustrated by excellently chosen examples from the orators and the poets, modern as well as ancient. It is doubtful whether anybody wrote or spoke the better for having listened to these lectures, substantial and sensible as they are, but that fact does not prevent them from being an exceedingly interesting account of rhetoric as understood early in the nineteenth century.

The Boylston Professorship was held from 1819 to 1851 by Edward Tyrrel Channing (1790–1856), a younger brother of William Ellery Channing. His *Lectures*, published immediately after his death, obviously owe much to Adams's. From a comparison of the orator's opportunity in ancient and in modern times, they proceed through the usual apology for rhetoric to the usual division into demonstrative, deliberative, judicial. and pulpit oratory. They omit the discussion of composition itself in its parts and phases, and treat instead the standards and the forms of criticism, with what looks like a distinct plea in defence of the cryptic and Orphic utterances of the transcendentalists. Channing, like Adams, is descriptive and critical rather than practical; he gives a student standards by which to judge existing discourse rather than assistance in producing his own. Such assistance he seems to have reserved for the personal conferences which he held with his students over their themes. There is general agreement that he was a most successful teacher of the art of writing, and that, as Colonel Higginson says, Channing "turned out more good writers than any half-dozen other rhetoric teachers in America." Among his pupils were Emerson, Edward Everett Hale, Thomas Wentworth Higginson, Holmes, Lowell, Motley, Parkman, George Ripley, W. L. Furness, and Andrew Preston Peabody, the last of whom considers Channing's appointment as "perhaps the most important ever made in the interest of American literature."

Channing's personal conferences with students over their written work foreshadowed the changes which the nineteenth century wrought in the philology of rhetoric. Rhetoric has moved from oratory and public speaking to writing, and to speaking as a preparation for writing. It has moved from rhetorical history, precept, and theory, to practice. It has moved from the study of diction and style to the study of development and structure. It has moved from rules, through logic, to psychology.

Meanwhile, in the fifties and sixties, just when rhetoric was turning from diction to invention, there arose a new group of writers on diction. These seldom deal with linguistic groups larger than the phrase, and never with the sentence; they are interested for the most part in the history of words and locutions; and they all sooner or later discuss Americanisms as an exceedingly interesting phase of this history. Though they all more or less tell the reader what to say and not to say, they are distinguished from mere writers of textbooks by their much higher degree of historic purpose and objectivity.

The first of this group seems to have been George Perkins Marsh (1801–82). At Dartmouth College he read Latin and Greek far beyond the requirements of the curriculum, and taught himself to read fluently French, German, Spanish, Portuguese, and Italian.[1] He then turned to the Scandinavian languages; from 1832 onward kept up a correspondence "indifferently in English and Danish" with C. C. Rafn of Copenhagen; and in 1838 printed an Icelandic grammar. His appointment in 1849 as minister to Turkey enabled him to travel extensively, and nourished still further his somewhat exotic powers. In 1852 he went to Athens as special minister to Greece. It was in 1858–59 that he delivered at Columbia College, as one of the "Post-graduate" courses of instruction (organized 1858), his *Lectures on the English Language.* Of the thirty lectures, seven deal with the sources, composition, and vocabulary of the language, six with parts of speech and grammatical inflections, three with English as affected by the art of printing, three with rhyme, alliteration, and assonance, and others with pronunciation, synonyms, the principles of translation, the English Bible, corruptions of English, and the English Language in America. Marsh's Lowell Institute lectures of 1860–61, *The Origin and History of the English Language* (1862), were much more distinctly historical. They come down chronologically from "Origin and Composition of the Anglo-Saxon People and Their Language" to "The English Language and Literature during the Reign of Elizabeth." Marsh's last and greatest foreign venture was his mission as our first minister to the Kingdom of Italy, to which he was appointed by Lincoln in 1861. He died in Italy. Marsh was an early and frequent contributor to *The Nation;* prepared a number of articles, chiefly on Spanish, Catalan, and Italian literature, for Johnson's Cyclopædia; and wrote monographs on *The Camel* (1856) and on *Man and Nature* (1865; afterwards issued as *The Earth as Modified by Human Action*, 1874). His philological work is spoken of with respect by the other members of the group, even by Fitzedward Hall.

Richard Grant White (1821–85), who will demand attention later as one of the outstanding American editors of Shakespeare.

[1] At some time he was a pupil of Lorenzo Da Ponte.

having in the late sixties contributed to a periodical a number of articles on English usage, published them in a volume as *Words and Their Uses* (1870). A second series, *Every Day English*, appeared in 1880. In these books, White, of New England Brahmin stock, made up for having been accidentally born in New York by exhibiting all the linguistic and racial prejudices of Boston. He attached to English usage an alluring and a threatening social sanction, which helps partly to explain his popularity. His prohibition of certain forms of speech is "exclusiveness" in linguistic disguise; and the uninstructed reader felt—for White told him so—that he should probably be beyond the social pale even if he obeyed White, but should certainly be if he did not. Social distinction was thus the prize which White offered, with a precariousness that rendered it only the more attractive. It soon became evident that he had not sufficiently studied the history of some of the locutions which he condemned—"had rather," "reliable," and "is being built," for example; but when taken to task for setting up personal preferences as if they were established by weight of usage, he would amiably deprecate authority, delicately implying that his opponent was of course learned, but a pedant. White's more relevant defence was that historical usage afforded after all only the raw material from which present writers and speakers might choose, exercising by way of principles of selection both taste—especially in the direction of simplicity—and reason, to which White thought usage tended continually to approach.

His chief opponent was the incomparably more scholarly Fitzedward Hall (1825–1901). Hall, of the Harvard class of 1846, just before graduation left college to search for a runaway brother in India. There in time he became tutor and professor of Sanskrit and English in the Government College at Benares, and in 1862 he was appointed professor of Sanskrit, Hindustani, and Indian Jurisprudence in King's College, London. In the fifties and sixties he edited a number of Sanskrit texts, as well as a Hindi grammar and reader, but in the seventies and the eighties his publications dealt chiefly with English usage, to the elucidation of which he brought vast accumulations derived from his enormous reading. His *Recent Exemplifications of False Philology* (1872), though it incidentally bowls over Landor.

Coleridge, and De Quincy, fulminates chiefly against Richard Grant White, and his *Modern English* (1873) returns to the attack, once more leading up to White through Cicero, Sir John Cheke, Bentley, Swift, Dr. Johnson, and others who have laboured under the delusion that usage needs to be fixed in order to save a language from corruption. Wherever Hall attacks White he routs him. Yet the actual influence of White has probably been greater, and this not without reason. Hall often adopts a tone of personal vituperation which antagonizes while it amuses. His own crabbed sentences go far to exasperate even a reader who must needs respect his scholarship. White, though he tried to schoolmaster the language, did generally prefer the things which are of good report; and his precepts, apart from certain easily exploded pedantries, made in general against affectation and for simplicity. The solid masses of Hall's erudition have needed to be diluted for popular consumption, and it is this dilution that Professor Lounsbury performed in some of his less weighty works, for example, *The Standard of Usage in English.*

The Harvard achievement in rhetoric is matched by the Yale achievement in lexicography. Webster and Worcester were Yale men; Whitney is closely associated with Yale; and the first American dictionary, that of Samuel Johnson, Jr. (1757–1836), grandnephew of the Samuel Johnson who was the first president of King's College, was published (1798) in New Haven.

Noah Webster (1758–1843), a Connecticut farmer's boy, graduated at Yale in 1778, and after studying law and teaching school in several Connecticut towns, compiled in the years following 1782 his *Grammatical Institute of the English Language,* in three parts: (I) his celebrated *Spelling Book* (1783), of which "more than eighty million copies are said to have been sold before 1880"; (II) a *Plain and Comprehensive Grammar* (1784); (III) a *Reader* (1785). His first dictionary, the *Compendious Dictionary* of 1806, at once takes independent Yankee ground. Webster was not to be imposed upon by even the authority of the English Johnson; the locution "never so wise," opposed by Johnson, he favoured on historical grounds; "skeptic," proposed by Johnson, he opposed on grounds of analogy. In fact, Webster had taught himself some Anglo-Saxon, and, however imperfectly acquainted with it, had acquired a true and sensible feeling for historical method and for the weight of analogy in deciding points where usage is doubtful. In these respects his *Dictionary* anticipates the methods of the larger *American Dictionary of the English Language* of 1828, in the preparation of which he spent the next twenty years.

Meanwhile there should be noted the appearance of a dictionary by Burgiss Allison: *The American Standard of Orthography and Pronunciation, and Modern Dictionary of the English Language* (1815). This is an abridged form of material which Allison promised to issue soon without abridgment; but whether he did so is not certain. What distinguishes his work is that he aimed not merely at utility, as Webster did, but at "fixing a standard," and that he had enlisted the interest of "many distinguished Characters, and Seminaries. . . . The reception of their collective observations, and through them of the literati in general, must eventually furnish a highly perfected dictionary."

Webster's studies were without any such guidance. He applied himself to etymology; undertook a comparative study of the "principal words in twenty languages, arranged in classes under their primary elements or letters"; and of these made a *Synopsis* which gave him "what appeared to be the general principle on which these languages were constructed." Thereupon he spent a year abroad, studying chiefly "the pronunciation of the language in England . . . and incidental points in pronunciation and grammatical construction." The book, finished at Cambridge early in 1825, was issued in 1828. Webster lived to make one revision (for the edition of 1840), and was engaged upon another when he died. It was unfortunate that Webster did not come into contact with the "literati," for they would have enabled him before his second edition, and all the more before his third, to correct his work by means of the comparative method which had been elaborated in Germany. Yet even had the complete method of Grimm and Bopp been accessible to him in 1828, Webster, then seventy years old, could hardly have been censured for not acquiring at that age a new set of highly inflected languages with complex inter-relations, or even for not realizing that the new method would kill his old etymologies. But the fact seems to be that he was simply unaware of the new movement. It was not until 1833 that Gessner Harrison received his materials upon it from George Long; not until 1839 that Salisbury brought it to Yale, where Webster might have had a chance to hear of it.

Webster much enlarged Johnson's vocabulary, admitting a large number of technical terms which Johnson considered outside the classic pale. In this respect Webster's broad personal experience as farmer, lawyer, teacher, editor, and pamphleteer served him well. He was open-minded and meant his book to be serviceable to the common man. In spelling, though his fondness for analogy tended toward a logical schematism, he yet guarded his reforms in most cases by consulting usage, *logic* not *logick*, *meter* not *metre*, *honor* not *honour*, *symbolize* not *symbolise*. Webster's definitions are admittedly his forte. They are untinged with personal bias; they are proportioned in space to the importance of the word and the number of its meanings; and they are so phrased that generally they can be substituted for the word itself. Quotations it was Webster's policy to employ only "to illustrate those definitions that are not entirely evident in sense" without them.

Though in England Webster's *Dictionary* has not superseded Johnson's, it soon became the standard in the United States. The revision of 1847, conducted by Chauncey A. Goodrich, was authoritative. After the fourth edition, the so-called *Pictorial*, further revised by Goodrich but considered only provisional (1859), there appeared in 1864 the fifth edition, the first to be known as the *Unabridged*, a thorough recension by Goodrich (who died in 1860) and by Noah Porter, with a staff which included C. A. F. Mahn of Berlin (who revised the etymologies), W. D. Whitney, James Dwight Dana, Daniel Coit Gilman, and James Hadley. This has been the basis of later revisions, gradually getting rid of some of its defects; for instance, its unscholarly treatment of locutions like "had better," "had rather," and its derivation of "gonoph" from "gone off"! The sixth edition (1890)—the *International*—was the result of the most "extensive and exhaustive revision that the *Dictionary* had received." In 1900 there was added a *Supplement*, still edited by Noah Porter, who had now associated with himself William Torrey Harris; and in 1909 the seventh edition—the *New International*—"entirely remade," was published by Harris as editor-in-chief, and F. Sturges Allen who had been on the staff of the original *International*, as general editor.

Joseph Emerson Worcester (1784–1865), a graduate of Yale in 1811 and Hawthorne's schoolmaster at Salem in 1813, afterward removed to Cambridge, where he came to be numbered among the eccentric characters of the place, and produced school books and books of reference in history and geography. His series of dictionaries (1828, 1830, 1846, 1855) brought on the "War of the Dictionaries" with Webster and his adherents. Apart from irrelevant personalities, the controversy is reducible to one between a retiring and conservative scholar, willing to record the actualities of usage, and a brisk business man and linguistic reformer. Worcester's large *Dictionary of the English Language* (1860) for a few years rivalled the *Pictorial* Webster of 1859, especially in England and in New England; but after the *Unabridged* of 1864 it lost popularity and authority.

For the beginnings of Old English philology in America we must look once more to Thomas Jefferson. As has been noted, Jefferson favoured the study of the Germanic languages in general, and gave them a place in the proposed curriculum of William and Mary College and of the University of Virginia. Though he made no independent research into any of these languages, he had diligently studied and annotated several Anglo-Saxon grammars; he read Old English "with his feet on the fender"; and in the course of his works he expressed many ideas on English philology, some erroneous but all interesting. He favoured neologisms as a sign of a language's vitality; he urged the systematic study of dialects because these often preserved racy and primitive forms which the literary language had lost; he felt that Anglo-Saxon was merely "old English"; he deprecated the treatment of Germanic grammar, old or new, as if it were Latin grammar; and he definitely recognized the connection of "the ancient languages and literature of the North . . . with our own language, laws, customs, and history."

To teach Germanic philology Jefferson appointed George Blaetterman, a German then resident in London, to the first professorship of Modern Languages in the University of Virginia, a post which he held from 1825 to 1840. He is said to have "found peculiar pleasure" in comparative philology and to have contributed, with George Long, to a *Comparative Grammar*. Blaetterman was succeeded by Charles Kraitsir, who published among other works a *Glossology: Being a Treatise on the Nature of Language and on the Language of Nature* (New York, 1852). The third incumbent was Maximilian Schele DeVere, who published several works upon French, Spanish, and English, as well as two upon Americanisms. Probably the first Anglo-Saxon texts and grammar to be published in America were those edited by Louis F. Klipstein, a native of Virginia and a graduate of Hampden-Sidney College, who also studied at Giessen. In 1844 he edited in Charleston the *Polyglott*, a monthly magazine "devoted to the French, German, Spanish, and Italian Languages." His *Grammar of the Anglo-Saxon Language* and *Analecta Anglo-Saxonica—Selections in Prose and Verse from the Anglo-Saxon Literature* (two volumes), both indebted to Thorpe, were much used as text books and went through several editions. He wrote and edited other books dealing with Anglo-Saxon, and planned still more, all of them deriving not from the German scholarship of his day but from English models.

Old English, thus first cultivated in Virginia, was taught from 1839 to 1842 at Randolph-Macon College, Virginia, by Edward Dromgoole Simms. At Amherst it was taught as early as 1841, if not before, by William Chauncey Fowler, Noah Webster's son-in-law. In 1851 Child introduced it at Harvard. In 1856 it reached Lafayette; in 1867, Haverford; in 1868, St. John's College; in 1871, Cornell; and by 1875 it was read at Columbia and the University of Wisconsin, and at Yale in the Sheffield Scientific School and the Post-Graduate Department.

Fowler by his teaching and Webster through his writings are said to have "exercised a dominant influence" on the mind of Francis Andrew March (1825–1911), a graduate of Amherst and after 1855 a professor at Lafayette College. March there taught Latin and Greek, French and German, botany, law, political economy, "mental philosophy," and the Constitution of the United States—all this as professor of the English Language and Comparative Philology. "Teaching English classics like the Greek and Latin" became his characteristic. As English gradually gained a place in the curriculum beside the ancient classics or in their stead, it was challenged to furnish an equivalent discipline. For this process March's method was admirably fitted. It is fully set forth in his *Method of Philological Study of the English Language* (1865), which is modelled upon the *Method of Classical Study* (1861) by Samuel Harvey Taylor, principal of Phillips Andover Academy. These books gave a minimum of text and a maximum of questions and notes on grammar, syntax, and etymology. As a classical scholar himself, March undertook the general editorship (1874–77) of the Douglass Series of Christian Greek and Latin writers, in which the two principal volumes were March's *Latin Hymns* and Gildersleeve's *Justin Martyr*.

March's chief work, however, lay in English philology. His *Comparative Grammar of the Anglo-Saxon Language* (1870) was the first attempt anywhere to concentrate upon Old English the results of general Indo-European linguistic study. It focusses upon the illustration of Old English forms a collection of the forms of "Sanskrit, Greek, Latin, Gothic, Old Saxon, Old Friesic, Old Norse, and Old High German." According to a competent critic "the *Grammar* 'marked an epoch,'" and "revealed the author's full stature as a commanding figure in the world of philological scholarship."[1] March was "controlled by the noblest philosophic conception of the science of grammar"—the conception that the "facts and laws of language are seen to be facts and laws of mind and of the history of man." He was profoundly interested in spelling reform, which he actively urged upon both the learned and the unlearned. His work in lexicography is also notable. For several years he cooperated with the Oxford Dictionary by selecting and directing its American readers (1879–82). As consulting editor he planned the *Standard Dictionary* (1890–95). The *Thesaurus Dictionary of the English Language* (1902), said to have been "prepared under the supervision of Francis Andrew March," is really a recension of Roget, for which March "did little more than read printers' proofs and contribute a 'Foreword.'"

American editions of Shakespeare,[2] from 1795, when the first one, edited anonymously, was published in Philadelphia,

---

[1] J. W. Bright. *Mod. Lang. Ass. Pub.*, XXIX, cxxix.

[2] For a full account, see Jane Sherzer's valuable article, *Mod. Lang. Ass. Pub.*, XXII, 633–96.

down to 1836, have considerable bibliographical interest, but bibliographical interest almost exclusively. They are all derived, with a minimum of editorial work, from contemporary English editions. The possible exception is the Philadelphia edition of 1805-9, anonymous but pretty surely edited by Joseph Dennie, who, adopting Reed's text of 1803, made a few changes after the text of Ayscough (Dublin, 1791), suggested some conjectural emendations of his own, generally needless, and added a large number of original notes, mostly verbal. The Boston edition of 1836, edited anonymously by Oliver William Bourn Peabody (1799-1848), at that time an editor of *The North American Review*, is the first American Shakespeare which at least professes to base its text independently upon the Folio of 1623. In point of fact, Peabody's text is mainly that of Singer; there are very few avowed textual emendations; and of these about one-third "do not follow the Folio, although they would better have done so." Peabody's few notes deal with the text as such. It is his distinction to have been the first American textual critic of Shakespeare, and to have set before himself at least as an ideal the constitution of a text upon the early authorities.

Gulian Crommelin Verplanck (1786-1870) issued under his own name an edition published in New York in 1847. He based his text upon Collier's, departing from it in several places by reason of his preference for the Folio; he believed that the Quartos represent Shakespeare's early or unrevised work, while the Folios contain his work matured and revised. This in turn is linked with Verplanck's theory of the growth of Shakespeare's genius—a theory which Verplanck took as the basis of almost his entire conception of Shakespearian editorship. It is according to this theory that he attempts to fix the chronology of the plays, and prints them in supposed chronological sequence within their generic division into Comedies, Histories, and Tragedies. With Verplanck the subjective and æsthetic criticism of the Romantic School avowedly enters American Shakespearian scholarship, coinciding rather closely with transcendentalism in general, which had no Shakespearian scholar.

The romantic treatment of Shakespeare reaches its culmination in the essays and the editions of Henry Norman Hudson (1814-86), whose edition (1851-56) is distinctly popular rather than scholarly.   It makes many needless textual changes, some of them rather wild conjectural emendations of his own, but most of them adopted from other editors.   His notes are very full and often obvious.   His Introductions and Commentary in general, like the *Lectures* (1848) which preceded the edition and which are largely embodied in its Introductions, belong to the Coleridgean type of criticism—the type of criticism which endeavours to set forth Shakespeare's inwardness, and pays comparatively little attention to his outwardness.   The plays are made from within; the characters grow like a tree, by successive natural accretions; the whole effect is like that produced by a work of Nature; nature, in fact, is the essential quality of Shakespeare; and each play and each character in each play is, like Nature, the superlative embodiment of some essential and archetypal idea.   This mode of disquisition, together with the treatment of Shakespeare's "alleged immorality," and "alleged want of taste," naturally sentences itself to swift obsolescence.

Richard Grant White's *Shakespeare's Scholar* (1854) criticized acutely the manuscript "corrections" in J. P. Collier's then famous and afterward notorious "Perkins Folio."   White did not at first believe that these had been forged by Collier, and he considered that many of them had intrinsic merit; but he demonstrated that they were not early emendations, and were wholly without authority as such.   His edition of Shakespeare (1857–66) and his later *Studies in Shakespeare* (1885), though they retain certain characteristics of the Romantic School, exhibit on the whole a healthy reaction against it such as became the friend of Lowell and of Norton.   White is romantically inclined to a personal interpretation of Shakespeare's *Sonnets* and of many of the speeches in the plays, believing in particular that Ulysses in *Troilus and Cressida* is Shakespeare's own mouthpiece.   On the other hand, he anticipates the later non-idealistic school in regarding Shakespeare as intent simply on writing plays that will pay, and as having "no system of dramatic art."   White's text is based upon a careful examination of the Folios and Quartos, accepting the first Folio as generally authentic.   In the matter of emendations he is exceedingly cautious—too cautious to suit Lowell.[1]   White's notes and commentary in general endeavour

---

[1] Lowell's anonymous review (*Atlantic Monthly*, Jan.–Feb., 1857) deserves to be reprinted.

simply to put the reader face to face with Shakespeare, and his edition as a whole is justly recognized as combining scholarship with attention to the needs of the general reader.

The *New Variorum Shakespeare*, edited by Horace Howard Furness (1833–1912), began appearing in 1871. Furness was a member of the Shakespeare Society of Philadelphia (established 1851 and the oldest Shakespeare society in existence); under its influence he is said to have begun about 1862 a variorum text of *Hamlet*, and it may be that the plan for the *New Variorum* originated among the members of this Society. In any case, though Furness was a Harvard graduate, his undertaking belongs less to any university than to the social and urbane scholarship cultivated among *Privat gelehrten* during the period of learned societies. He conceived the immediate need for his edition to be that the Cambridge edition of 1866 "did not give the history of variant readings in the hands of successive editors, and that it also neglected to record the first editor to adopt a generally accepted reading."[1] These deficiencies the *Variorum* supplies. After the first three volumes, whose text is composite, Furness in *King Lear*, his fourth volume, virtually followed the first Folio, and beginning with the fifth, *Othello*, printed the first Folio text itself, with all variants and emendations in the textual notes. Besides these there are notes explanatory and interpretative, as well as prefatory and appended editorial matter of various kinds, including much æsthetic criticism. Furness in fact was primarily interested, very much as Hudson was, in each play as a self-subsisting entity. Preoccupied thus with the inwardness of Shakespeare, he neglected some material that a variorum edition ought to include—much of the later criticism that deals with Shakespeare's outwardness; with matters like chronology, verse tests, attributions, and types of personage, incident, and dramatic structure common to Shakespeare and his contemporaries. Matter of this kind is being supplied in the later volumes edited by Horace Howard Furness, Jr. Even without it, the *New Variorum* is indispensable. Its special "note" is that it combines all the scientific apparatus that is necessary for the student with all kinds of criticism, which Furness's humour and good judgment hold in clear solution.

[1] Steeves, *American Editors of Shakespeare*, p. 362.

Francis James Child (1825–96), who graduated at Harvard in 1846, spent the remainder of his life in the service of the University. In 1851, when he returned from two years' study of Germanic philology at Göttingen and Berlin, he succeeded E. T. Channing as Boylston Professor of Rhetoric and Oratory, and in 1876 became professor of English. His critical annotated edition of *Four Old Plays* (1848) was the first of the kind to be produced in America. From 1853 onward, as general editor of a series of the British poets, he studied especially Spenser, Chaucer, and the English and Scottish ballads, himself editing Spenser (1855) and the *Ballads* (1857–58). His Spenser, according to Professor Kittredge, "remained after forty years the best edition of Spenser in existence." Child was to have edited Chaucer, too, but he felt that the state of the text and of Chaucerian scholarship generally was not such as to make possible a satisfactory edition. Instead, he proceeded to help make a critical edition possible. His *Observations on the Language of Chaucer* (1863) put definitely out of date the random and arbitrary opinions—favourable or unfavourable, untrue or accidentally true—which critics had ever since the Renaissance been pronouncing upon Chaucer's versification, and placed the matter henceforth upon a basis of exact knowledge. Child's work has not had to be done over again; it has been the point of departure for later research, and remains the classic memoir in this field.

The *Ballads* of 1857, though it easily superseded all other collections, was for Child only a *coup d'essai*, its material mostly from printed sources. The great *English and Scottish Popular Ballads* of 1882–98 is based as much as possible upon manuscript sources, especially the Percy Folio manuscript and Sir Walter Scott's collections at Abbotsford. Child had decided "not to print a line . . . till he had exhausted every effort to get hold of whatever manuscript material might be in existence." With this material Child did not attempt to constitute for each ballad a single critical text, but, recognizing implicit differences between "popular" and "artistic" production, admitted the right of every traditional version to a place in his canon, and, by printing all obtainable versions, offered the broadest possible basis for comparison. His own *Introductions* and *Notes* enrich this material still further by bringing in all the obtainable foreign versions of each ballad theme. His collection is thus both a definitive *corpus* of English ballad material[1] and a notable exemplar of the comparative study of literature.

In both his fields of scholarship—Chaucer and the ballad—Child left numerous disciples; and besides the legacy of a fixed body of material ready to be taken as a point of departure, he left the materials for a very lively and still very active controversy upon ballad origins, into which, however, it is impossible to go here. Child himself died before completing the last volume of his *Ballads*, which was to have contained a general preface or introduction that would in all probability have given his view upon the mooted topics. The animation and playfulness of Child's learning must not go unmentioned. His humour everywhere leavens and feeds the very substance of his work—a humour which, playing with the solid materials of his scholarship, would have made him the ideal editor of those sane, humane, and playful persons, Chaucer and Shakespeare. Among the unwritten works, *valde desiderata*, of American scholarship, books like Norton's On the European Power of Italy, and Gildersleeve's History of Literary Satire, there must surely be counted the Shakespearian and Chaucerian texts and studies which Child did not produce.

It was the fortune of Thomas Raynesford Lounsbury (1838–1915) to produce studies of both Chaucer and of Shakespeare. In 1870 he was appointed instructor in English in the newly established Sheffield Scientific School at Yale, and in 1871 became professor in charge of the English department. The first fruit of his work in Chaucer was an edition of the *Parlement of Foules* in 1877. His *History of the English Language* (1879) has gone through many editions and still holds its place as a standard textbook. It was in 1892 that he published the ripe results of his labors upon Chaucer. *The Studies in Chaucer* comprise eight monographs. The first two present Chaucer's biography—one the biography as far as it is established by evidence and duly guarded inference from the documents, the other the mythical biography or "Chaucer Legend." This simple and profitable distinction Lounsbury seems to have been the first to make, and the effect is comparable to that of

---

[1] The quarter of a century since Child's death has added almost no genuine ballads to his three hundred and five.

Observations on the Language of Chaucer. Slight errors in detail did not prevent this account of Chaucer's life from being the most accurate which had yet been written. The third monograph, that on Chaucer's text, is an admirable popular account of the method of textual criticism. The fourth presents Lounsbury's canon of Chaucer's work. The fifth, that on Chaucer's learning, is admirable again in its comprehensive view of Chaucer's sources and of the use he made of them. The sixth consists of two sections, one on Chaucer's language, and the other on his religion. The seventh and the eighth, perhaps the most valuable of all, treat respectively Chaucer's "fortunes"— *Chaucer in Literary History*—and his craftsmanship—*Chaucer as a Literary Artist.* The *Studies* are exceedingly diffuse. They suffer from occasional paradox. Their arguments (Chapter VII) that Chaucer's spelling and pronunciation should be modernized, can surely not be allowed. Yet, volume for volume, it would not be easy to find anywhere a set of more solidly valuable literary studies. They have served to give body and weight to many a student's vague conceptions of Chaucer, and, as their style is popular, they must also have carried their substantial materials to many "general" readers.

The three volumes of *Shakespearean Wars* (1901–06) began as a study of Shakespeare's text. Soon it appeared that the treatment accorded the text by editors and critics depended in great measure upon their conception of Shakespeare's art; hence Lounsbury, in much the same way in which he had studied the "fortunes" of Chaucer, was led to study the "fortunes" of Shakespeare. These, as might have been expected, proved to be deeply involved in the general opposition of romanticists to classicists; and of the latter Voltaire emerged as the international champion. Thus finally Lounsbury's studies took shape in a volume on *Shakespeare as a Dramatic Artist*, a volume on *Shakespeare and Voltaire*, and a volume on *The Text of Shakespeare.* The first traces to the end of the eighteenth century the course of English opinion about dramatic matters. It shows, what had perhaps been only suspected or inferred, that Shakespeare was, throughout, an encouragement to the more "romantic" party in the controversies; contrary to an opinion rather generally credited, it shows, too, that Shakespeare was esteemed at all times, and esteemed highly even by "classical" opponents of his practice, who, while they lamented his want of art, admitted that they were pleased by his wildness and nature. With the volume on Voltaire the field of controversy becomes international: Voltaire's exile and return; his initial appreciation of Shakespeare and later recoil from its revolutionary consequences; his belief in the dangers of a barbaric romanticism; his wrath at Letourneur; his controversial relations with Kames, Walpole, Johnson, and Garrick, and the retroactive effect upon his own reputation in England; finally the persistence of his authority as literary arbiter upon the Continent even to the day of *Goetz von Berlichingen*, when the Mede was at the gate and the handwriting clear upon the wall. The third volume centres upon Pope's and Theobald's editions of Shakespeare; the meannesses of Pope and the significance of the first version of the *Dunciad* as a piece of Shakespearean controversy; Bentley's emendations of *Paradise Lost* and the discredit they brought upon all verbal criticism, including the prospective criticism of Theobald—the history, in a word, of the means by which one of the ablest of all the editors of Shakespeare has been pilloried for posterity as "piddling Tibbald."

It will be seen that compared with the *Studies in Chaucer* the *Shakespearean Wars* occupied a much smaller portion of a much larger field; that even this portion had been cultivated before, though never so intensively; that, of course, it was needless to do for Shakespeare what the earlier studies had done for Chaucer; and that for all these reasons the later studies are distinctly less important than the earlier. The same remark applies to Lounsbury's still later works on usage—in diction, in spelling, and in pronunciation, where his diffuseness has come dangerously near prolixity; and to his studies of Tennyson and of Browning, interesting and appreciative though these are. Lounsbury will, it is safe to say, be remembered partly as a scholar who elucidated the attitude of the eighteenth century toward Shakespeare, but chiefly as the scholar whose book made Chaucer a reality beyond the circle of specialists.

It would be an agreeable task to treat in detail the American writers upon art, and to determine whether any definite tendency underlies the work of William Dunlap, Washington Allston, William Wetmore Story, Henry Theodore Tuckerman, W. J. Stillman, and the rest. It will be possible, however, to treat only the most important member of the group. Charles Eliot Norton[1] (1827–1908), the son of Andrews Norton, graduated at Harvard in 1846, spent five years in business and travel in India and in Europe, was abroad again in England and Italy in 1855–57, and after his return busied himself with writing for the newly established *Atlantic Monthly* and with bringing out certain books of his own. The Civil War gave to his political opinions a stamp which they never lost. From 1864 to 1868 he edited, jointly with Lowell, *The North American Review*, and in 1865, with Frederick Law Olmsted, James Miller McKim, and Edward Lawrence Godkin, he helped to found *The Nation*, to which he contributed generously, and the success of which Godkin credited largely to him. From 1868 to 1873 he was in Europe again. From 1875 to 1898, when he became Emeritus, he held at Harvard the professorship of the History of Art.

During his sojourns abroad, he formed lifelong friendships with Carlyle, Ruskin, FitzGerald, and Leslie Stephen. These men, as well as his American friends, Lowell, Longfellow, Emerson, George William Curtis, and others, found in him a remarkably receptive and interpretative mind, together with an uncompromising rectitude and independence of judgment—traits which made him an admirable friend to men of gifts more conspicuous than his own, and eminently qualified him for his literary executorships and editorships. He brought out, for example, various portions of Carlyle's correspondence and reminiscences—the correspondence with Emerson (1883) and with Goethe (1887), *Reminiscences* (1887), and letters (1886 and 1889); the letters of Lowell (1893), George William Curtis's *Orations and Addresses* (1894), further Emerson letters (those to Samuel G. Ward, 1899), and Ruskin's letters to Norton himself (1904).

A volume of *Notes of Travel and Study in Italy* (1860), a portion of which appeared in *The Crayon*[2] during 1856, contains the beginnings, or more than the beginnings, of his accomplishment in the two other fields of scholarship for which he is notable—the fine arts and Dante. Norton presents the extensive studies he has already begun in Dante's works: gathering from the *Commedia*, the *Convito*, and the *De Vulgari Eloquentia* the

[1] See also Book III, Chap. XIII.
[2] The first magazine of art in America; it was edited by W. J. Stillman.

passages that are concerned with Dante's relation to Rome; studying the interchange of eclogues between Dante and Giovanni del Virgilio; and citing passages from the *Inferno* as probably the literary originals of some of the sculptures on one of the piers of the cathedral at Orvieto. Of the building of this cathedral he gives a detailed account which anticipates in many ways the method and content of his later *Historical Studies of Church Building in the Middle Ages*.

Norton's judgment of painting and architecture at this time suffers severely from the despotism of Ruskin, the Ruskin of *Modern Painters*, whom Norton had first met in 1855. Like Ruskin, he can find little to praise after 1500; and even the fifteenth century comes in for some rather severe reflections. Nothing is worth while but Gothic, and the merits of Gothic consist in its being like nature and at the same time (Norton did not trouble to explain how) an expression of the deepest and highest religious aspirations of man. Norton even imitates some of Ruskin's stylistic mannerisms, though occasionally he finds a sturdier model in Gibbon. A certain banal moralism, when he speaks of retribution in the affairs of nations, is rather in the vein of Carlyle; while on the other hand the following passage, dated "Rome, 20th January, 1857." shows a remarkable coincidence with several passages in *The Marble Faun*[1]: "There is many a wall in Rome made of old materials strikingly joined together,—bits of ancient bricks stamped with a consular date, pieces of the shaft of some marble column, fragments of serpentine, or even of giallo antico, that once made part of the polished pavement of a palace,—now all combined in one strange harmony by Nature, who seems to love these walls and to reclaim them to herself by tinting their various blocks with every hue of weather stain, and hanging over them her loveliest draperies of wall flower and mosses."

Norton continued his work on Dante with a translation of the *Vita Nuova*, first published in 1859. From September, 1865, to May, 1867, he and Lowell, and occasionally George W. Greene, James T. Fields, William Dean Howells, and others, used to gather on Wednesday evenings at Longfellow's house to offer their suggestions and criticisms upon Longfellow's trans-

---

[1] Hawthorne arrived in Rome 20 January, 1858, began *The Marble Faun* there in the winter of 1859, and finished it in England in March, 1860.

lation of the *Divina Commedia*. This informal Dante Club was the precursor of the Cambridge Dante Society, the foundation of which Norton suggested to some members of his Dante class at Harvard in 1880. These students offered to support the plan, and when Longfellow consented to take the presidency of the club, it was actually inaugurated (1881). Its second president was Lowell; its third, Norton. The Society issues annual reports, accompanied by valuable papers, usually bibliographical, upon various points in Dante scholarship; it has contributed to the assembling in the Harvard library of a large Dante collection; it offers an annual prize for an essay upon a topic relating to Dante; and it has supported and encouraged the publication of the valuable *Concordance* of the *Divina Commedia* by Edward Allen Fay (1888) and of other works.

Norton published his own translation of the *Commedia* in 1891–92—a prose translation, and, needless to say, a faithful one. Compared with a prose masterpiece like Andrew Lang's version of Theocritus, it seems rather dry, and wanting in such rhythmic beauty as is well within the reach of prose. Here the austerity of Dante seems to have fused with the austerity of the Norton stock to produce something more austere than either. Norton's version holds its own, however, with other prose versions of Dante.

Norton's teaching and writing about the fine arts soon became emancipated from the extreme of Ruskin's influence; the relation was reversed; and Ruskin rather looked upon his younger friend as his "tutor," recognizing in him a mental balance and a steadfastness that he knew to be wanting in himself. Norton, to be sure, retained the strongly ethical trend of his early days. He never achieved the economic precision of Henry Adams, who considers Chartres as releasing a certain quantity of force, like a railway just built, or a new coal mine. He never reached the degree of æsthetic detachment since attained by Bernard Berenson, who, when he is responding to spatial stimuli in a domed church, is inclined to ask "Why drag in religion?" For Norton the determining consideration is never just the effect of the work of art upon the percipient. What concerns him is the spirit of the artist, together with the spirit of national or civic movements which have produced great art; consequently his approach is historical and ethical:

and with Ruskin and Carlyle, he never ceases to be interested in the moral forces which they all believed to be at work in the rise and fall of states. This is the characteristic interest of his *Historical Studies of Church Building in the Middle Ages: Venice, Siena, Florence* (1880).

On the other hand, Norton's emancipation from Ruskin's naturalism was absolute. Humanism is the note of all his later thought and of his influence upon his pupils. It has actuated in several ways a number of men now writing, a group which may perhaps be called "the new humanists," and which includes Paul Elmer More, Irving Babbitt, John Jay Chapman, and George Edward Woodberry. These all attend to one or another phase of the cleavage between man's way and nature's way—a dualism which, whether it cut between man and external nature, or between the "natural man" and the "spiritual man" within; whether it emphasize the "inner check" in any of its various modes, or, as against the naturalistic "education of the senses," commend to man the study of his own humane tradition,[1] and summon him to take up the racial torch and hand it on,—in any case places man's hope not upon what nature, whether within or without, may do for him, but upon his making himself more completely man.

[1] Norton was one of the founders (1879) of the Archæological Institute of America, which in turn established the American Schools of Classical Studies at Athens (1881) and at Rome (1895) and which publishes *Bulletins* and the *American Journal of Archæology*. James Loeb, founder of the Loeb Classical Library, was a pupil of Norton.

CHAPTER XXVI

Patriotic Songs and Hymns

ALTHOUGH Americans have been a relatively untuneful people, popular song has never been inaudible since the beginning of our national life. Out of the steady succession of jaunty or sentimental melodies a few have been saved through their appropriation for patriotic ends. A larger body of hymns has survived in the traditions of public worship and through the conserving influence of the hymnals. A common religious feeling makes the appeal for the religious lyric; the corresponding motive for secular song is a wave of community enthusiasm; and patriotic zeal seldom becomes vocal except in times of actual or imminent national danger. A brief account of this double theme must be limited to the interpretation of established facts about songs that are sung, and must omit all purely literary lyrics; and where the facts as to origins of texts and melodies are in debate, the apparently best findings must be given without much argument.

Considered as expressions of popular feeling, patriotic songs are full of varied significance. The origin of the tunes is interesting; the question of a previous vogue and how it was attained; the question as to whether they were written for the words, or merely combined with them; the relation of the tunes to their musical periods; and their vocal quality. Corresponding points arise with reference to the words: in particular whether they were inspired by some occasion, or written on request; the circumstances in which they were produced; when and how they achieved national favour; and how far they have held it. The answers to these questions do not supply the material for any compact formula; they prove rather that the ages do not exhaust, nor custom limit, the variety of ways for satisfying popular taste.

Yankee Doodle, for example, is full of surprises, inconsistencies, paradoxes in its career. It is not really a song, but it is a band tune which no existing adult audience has ever sung together. The single stanza known to everyone is not a part of the Revolutionary War ballad, but belongs to an earlier period in its history. The music is unheroic; the title ("a New England Noodle") is derogatory to the people who adopted it in spite of its ridicule. And yet it has become a piece of jovial defiance as stirring as *The Campbells Are Coming*. The melody, as has often been the case, was generally known for several years before it was turned to patriotic account. As early as 1764 the familiar quatrain was current in England, and by 1767 the tune was familiar enough in America to be cited in Barton's (or Colonel Forrest's) comic opera, *Disappointment, or The Force of Credulity*. In derision of the foolish Yankee there soon began to multiply variants, most of which have come down by hearsay, and are very vague as to date; but one was a broadside and attests in the title to its currency before April, 1775: *Yankee Doodle; or, (as now christened by the Saints of New England) the Lexington March. N.B. The Words to be Sung throu' the Nose, & in the West Country drawl and dialect.* The text of *The Yankee's Return from Camp*—the famous but forgotten version—is attributed to Edward Bangs, a Harvard student, and was written in 1775 or 1776. Tory derision did not cease with its appearance, and between the accumulating stanzas in rejoinder and those in supplement gave ground for the speech of "Jonathan" in Tyler's *The Contrast* of 1787: "Some other time, when you and I are better acquainted, I'll sing the whole of it—no, no, that's a fib—I can't sing but a hundred and ninety verses; our Tabitha at home can sing it all." In time, however, the words lost interest for all but antiquarians, so that the stanza in *The Songster's Museum* was literally true in 1826 as it is to-day:

> Yankee Doodle is the *tune*
>   Americans delight in.
> 'Twill do to whistle, sing or play,
>   And just the thing for fighting.

The story of *Hail Columbia* is an almost complete contrast with that of *Yankee Doodle*, the chief point in common being that the music preceded the words. *The President's March*, probably composed by Philip Phile, a Philadelphia violinist, was popular in 1794 within a year of its production. In 1798 an actor, Gilbert Fox, applied to Joseph Hopkinson, accomplished son of the talented Francis, for a patriotic song adapted to *The President's March*, to be sung by Fox at a personal benefit performance, for which the prospects of a good house were discouraging. Hopkinson wrote in behalf of a unified country at a moment when, according to Freneau's *The Rival Suitors for America*, party claims were creating a dangerous rift through conflicting sympathies with France and England. *Hail Columbia*, as introduced by Fox, was a favourite from the start. It was encored a dozen times. It was repeated at other theatres, and on "circus nights." It was printed in *The Porcupine Gazette* three days later, 28 April, in the May number of *The Philadelphia Magazine*, in *The Connecticut Courant* of 7 May. "Soon no public entertainment was considered satisfactory without it"; and it has continued in use without textual change until the present day.

We owe *The Star Spangled Banner* to the existence of a long-popular melody and to the inspiration of a thrilling event—the British attack on Fort McHenry, 13 April, 1814. Words and music of *To Anacreon in Heaven*, constitutional song of the Anacreontic Society in London, were published in 1771. They became so beloved of all convivial souls that the words (with or without the music) were reprinted in twenty-one known magazines and song collections in England between 1780 and 1804, and the melody (with the original or adapted words) was printed no less than thirty times in America between 1796 and 1813. For this tune, in the thrill of the moment of discovery that "the flag was still there," Francis Scott Key began his version of the song "in the dawn's early light," sketched out the remainder on the way to land, copied it on arrival at his Baltimore hotel, and saw it in circulation as a broadside on the next day. At the outset it met with only moderate popularity, being omitted, as a universal favourite never could have been, from many important song books during the next twenty years. Not until the Civil War was it widely accepted as a national anthem, and then came two more paraphrases in St. George Tucker's attempt to requisition it for the Confederacy in *The Southern Cross* and in Oliver Wendell Holmes's added stanza.

Here are three types, the common factor being that the music always provided the pattern for the words. *Yankee Doodle* was a sort of ballad, loaded on a music vehicle which has rolled through the decades without its burden. *Hail Columbia*, written for a march tune, was made public in propitious circumstances and achieved an immediate vogue, but is seldom sung today except to fill out a program. *The Star Spangled Banner*, set to an old convivial song, with a range that demands the exhilaration of the cup, has been granted long life on account of its official recognition; yet it successfully defies vocal assault by any mixed group. *America*, the fourth permanently national song, casually written in 1832 by the youthful S. F. Smith, was set to an English tune of ninety years' standing encountered in a German song book lent him by Lowell Mason. This, therefore, though simple and popular, was no more indigenous than *Yankee Doodle* or *The Star Spangled Banner*. In recognition of these facts an attempt was made in 1861 to elicit a national hymn by means of a public competition for a substantial prize. The committee of award accepted their duty with misgivings, reluctant "to assume the function of deciding for their fellow-citizens a question which it seemed to them could really be settled only by general consent and the lapse of time." Their fears were realized, and they exercised the right they had reserved to make no award.

In the meanwhile general consent was being given to a song and to a hymn which are more and more popular with the lapse of time. These are *Dixie* and *The Battle Hymn of the Republic*. The original *Dixie* was composed on forty-eight hours' notice by Dan D. Emmett in September, 1859. He was then under contract with Bryant's Minstrels, New York, as musician and composer of "negro melodies and plantation walk-arounds." On a bleak northern Sunday he composed this "rush order" around the showman's autumnal and winter saying, "I wish I was in Dixie." The rollicking measure scored a natural success with every audience, and the sentiment reinforced its appeal in the South. Sung late in 1860 and early in 1861 at New Orleans, it made an especially sensational "hit" and soon all the Confederate states rang with it.[1] On 30 April of that year *The Natchez Courier* printed Albert B. Pike's "Southrons, hear your country call you," a stirring lyric itself, but only a temporary substitute for the Emmett words, "I wish I was in de land ob cotton," the first stanza of which is known everywhere in America. Fanny J. Crosby's attempt to regain the tune for the North with her "On ye patriots to the battle" was wholly unsuccessful; the other Southern variants died away; Pike's version is now a literary memory; but Emmett's original words and music still bring people to their feet as no other song in America does. They stand in deference to the tradition of *The Star Spangled Banner*, but they rise to *Dixie* itself.

The melody for *The Battle Hymn of the Republic* has had quite the most varied career in the history of American patriotic song. It came into being as a Southern camp-meeting song early enough to have been included in Henry Ward Beecher's *Plymouth Collection* of 1852. With the organization of the 12th Massachusetts Infantry in 1861 two Maine men in the second battalion introduced to camp "Say brothers, will you meet us, On Canaan's happy shore?" To this melody the glee club of the unit evolved a set of verses half applied to one of their own members, a Scotch John Brown. When these words became the characteristic song of the regiment, the officers tried in vain to have the words applied to Ellsworth, the first Northern commissioned officer who had fallen in the War. Inevitably many new versions were composed on John Brown of Ossawatomie—by H. H. Brownell, Edna Dean Proctor, Charles Sprague Hall, and anonymous writers; and from these developed variants beyond recall. The hymn had become a war ballad of widest popularity; but the ballad was to be rehabilitated as a hymn again. This occurred when Julia Ward Howe, one of a party to visit the Army of the Potomac in December, 1861, was urged by James Freeman Clarke to dignify the chant with adequate words. Her attempt was christened by James T. Fields and appeared in the *Atlantic*, February, 1862, as *The Battle Hymn of the Republic*. The marked differences between these three lyrics show how vital

[1] See, also, Book III, Chap. III.

is the relation between words and music. The colourless, seven-syllabled, thrice-repeated line, "Say brothers, will you meet us," is plaintive, if not dreary, in effect. The eleven syllables of "John Brown's body lies a-mouldering in the grave," with their stronger vocal quality and their sinister suggestiveness, have a primitive folk-quality and a martial vigour. The iambic heptameters of "Mine eyes have seen the glory of the coming of the Lord" rise to the elevation of a religious processional.

From the Civil War period the lapse of time and popular consent have elected to preserve a few other melodies, and incidentally the words attached to them, unless these have been displaced by later versions. George F. Root's *Battle Cry of Freedom* and *Tramp, Tramp, Tramp, the Boys Are Marching*, Henry Clay Work's *Marching through Georgia*, and Patrick S. Gilmore's *When Johnny Comes Marching Home* are examples of original words and music[1]; and James R. Randall's *Maryland*,[2] of the successful setting of words to a favourite melody—this time the German *Tannenbaum*. But they are not genuinely national songs. *Maryland* belongs, of course, to a state; the others are all marching songs, widely played by bands, occasionally resorted to at "patriotic exercises," and kept alive chiefly by their use with special words in colleges, fraternities, and other social groups.

Since the Civil War there has been no significant addition to the anthology of patriotic song. The depressing years of Reconstruction, the general trend of industrial development, the tiding in of an enormous immigrant population, and the relaxing effect of the "magnificent isolation" and the "manifest destiny" illusions, were all disintegrating rather than unifying influences; and songs thrive only with group feeling. Even the Spanish War failed to inspire a lasting song, a fact which is intelligible in the light of the two most insistent memories from that conflict—resentment at the maladministration of the War Department and perplexity before the ominous problems of imperialism.

There is a temptation to generalize on the passing favourite song of the World War—*Over There*. It does not contain great music or any kind of poetry. It meets only one of the requirements laid down for the fruitless competition of 1861; it is

[1] See, also, Book III. Chap. II.   [2] See. also. Book III, Chap. III.

"of the simplest form and most marked rhythm, the words easy to be retained by the popular memory, and the melody and harmony such as may be readily sung by ordinary voices." In this respect George M. Cohan met the situation as Root and Work and Gilmore did fifty years ago, and, like them, he wrote music of the day. It belongs to the same public that delights in O. Henry, Walt Mason, Irvin S. Cobb, and Wallace Irwin, all in the main sane, wholesome, obvious people. It comes from Broadway, which supplies the populace with much of their fun. On the other hand *The Star Spangled Banner* belonged to the public of Francis and Joseph Hopkinson and John Copley and Gilbert Stuart. The artistic work of that day was well-turned and graceful; poetry and music lent themselves to dashes of magniloquent heroism and tender sentiment. The courtly traditions of manly strength, feminine grace, the cheering influence of the social glass, and a traditionally aristocratic point of view, were all implicit in them. What John Howard Payne's patron called "the desolating effects of democracy" he would say were registered in the loss of these echoed gentilities. The same loss is apparent in the course of American hymnology; but there is no reason for considering it more than a cheap and temporary price for benefits received and in store.

For various reasons no selection of American hymns can quite compare in certainty with the choice of patriotic songs. As expressions of religious feeling hymns belong to an unnational language, and the most excellent are sung without regard to authorship. The best American hymns have, therefore, to meet the challenge of the best from every other Christian source, and the process of grouping them together is arbitrary and local rather than logical. Moreover, the traditions of worship have been responsible for the iteration of a great deal of bathos, since the convenience of public worship has made the hymnal far more of an instrument than the song book in conserving words and music that ought to have gone to oblivion. Yet though the fields of secular and religious song are very different, the outstanding types and the drift of development are quite comparable.

Three hymns of Timothy Dwight, Ray Palmer, and Oliver

Wendell Holmes are broadly representative of tendencies up to 1860. Dwight's contribution, *I Love Thy Kingdom Lord*, belongs to the period of *Hail Columbia* (which is sometimes wrongly ascribed to him), and is involved in the theology of Jonathan Edwards, Dwight's grandfather. After the confusion of the second stanza,

> Her walls before Thee stand,
> Dear as the apple of Thine eye,
> And graven on Thy hand,

and after the Calvinistic prospect of death in the third, it rises to a tone of solemn and hopeful self-dedication; and, set to the eighteenth-century tune "St. Thomas," it becomes an austere but not unlovely choral. Palmer's *My Faith Looks up to Thee* (1830) is strictly orthodox in its theology, representing life as a vale of tears, a period of durance before an ultimate ransom; but in its way it has reinforced the faith of millions who are no less indebted to its sentiments than to Lowell Mason's rather sentimental "Olivet," which he composed for it and which perfectly fits it. Holmes's *Sun-Day Hymn*, better known as *Lord of All Being Throned Afar* (1859), is very properly described by one hymnologist as "always a favourite in gatherings . . . of different denominations and creeds" since it "admits of the widest doctrinal divergencies." The Professor at the Breakfast Table composed with this intent, prefacing his hymn with the hope that men would "forget for the moment the difference in the hues of truth we look at through our human prisms, and join in singing (inwardly) this hymn to the Source of the light we all need to lead us, and the warmth which alone can make us all brothers." And his hope has been more than fulfilled, for the hymn has not only found its adequate melody, but has transformed "Louvan" from the utterly saccharine thing it was when set to Bowring's *How Sweetly Flowed the Gospel Sound*. *The Sun-Day Hymn* belongs to the slender anthology of sacred songs that are indubitable poetry.

The theme of *My Faith Looks up to Thee* is the theme of Phœbe Cary's *One Sweetly Solemn Thought* (1852), which deserves far less congregational attention than it receives, as

Mrs. Stowe's beautiful *Still, Still with Thee, When Purple Morning Breaketh* (1855) deserves far more. Mrs. Stowe shook off the spell of the mortuary muse so that, though mindful of death, she was first concerned with a living faith. This faith is the burden, too, of Whittier's *Our Master* (1866), a devotional poem from which several hymns have been excerpted, the best known of which is the passage beginning

> We may not climb the heavenly steeps,
> To bring the Lord Christ down.

With this mid-century group arrived a new set of composers, such as Barnby and Dykes and Bradbury, whose music is a departure from the sturdy four-four rhythms of Lowell Mason's "Laban" or "Uxbridge" or "Hamburg." Their newer melodies tend to the use of three-four and six-four measures, and to consequent sweetness rather than vigour. They are attuned to the emotional appeals of the non-conformist pulpit rather than to the stately traditions of Rome or England. They mark the difference between Longfellow and Newman, or between Calkin's "Waltham" for Bishop Doane's *Fling out the Banner* and Sherwin's "Chautauqua" for Mary A. Lathbury's *Day is Dying in the West*, each a high example of its kind in the seventies. In other words, the new hymns, both text and music, were at one with the theology and the secular poetry of the day—fervent, aspiring, confident. The period could produce such triumphant songs as the Doane-Calkin *Fling out the Banner* or the Baring-Gould-Sullivan *Onward, Christian Soldiers* (the latter, of course, English), and such hymns of tenderness and serenity as those of Whittier and Lathbury already alluded to; but the pursuit of these inclinations led to the edge of a precipice.

For, unhappily, the influences at work in uniting the breadth and dignity of older song with the warmth and colour of the later generation led very easily from sentimental ornateness to tawdry sensationalism. The decline in hymn-writing from Bernard of Clairvaux by way of the Wesleys to Phœbe Cary, and in composition from the Gregorian chants via Lowell Mason and Bradbury to P. P. Bliss, reached the popular *descensus Averni* in the Moody and Sankey "gospel hymns." The banalities of evangelistic song have not been offset by a corresponding output of finer and purer music; they have only been held in partial check by the restraining influence of the more excellent recent collections of "standard hymns" for public worship. Here the matter rests, and here it may rest until the influence of some great religious awakening leads to a new upwelling of religious song.

CHAPTER XXVII

Oral Literature

BOTH literary and historical interest attaches to the songs and rhymes which pass from region to region and from generation to generation in oral tradition. They have value as social documents. They reflect not only the fading life of the past, its events, its scenes, and its heroes, but the life of the society which inherits and so often transforms them. The great body of this floating literature consists of old ballads and songs, nursery jingles, game songs, and popular satires and sentimentalities. Occasionally such material exhibits a touch of real literary genius or of illuminating imagination; and these flashes of quality are eagerly sought for by the lover of poetry. Especially, such material affords opportunity to the critical student to study the literary instinct in its elementary expression. The main interest of oral literature is historical. From it may be seen how songs and verse tales develop, how themes and styles are transmitted from generation to generation, and from one region or land to another.

The mediæval ballads of England and Scotland have for their matter the adventures of lord or lady, the incidents of the hunt, clan feuds, the love affairs of the nobly born. They are frankly aristocratic. In later British balladry, these are succeeded by less ambitious pieces. Commonplace characters replace the aristocrats, paralleling the democratization of fiction and of the drama; and other styles succeed the minstrel style— much as Defoe's plebeian narratives, in homely setting, succeeded romances of knight errantry. Both types of song have been brought to America from the mother country; but alongside this imported material, types of indigenous song have developed. A rough classification of the poetic literature orally current in the United States includes many groups. There are English and Scottish traditional ballads and songs, and Irish and pseudo-Irish ballads and songs. There are songs of the tragic death of the true love, and dying messages and confessions, some of these imported and some not. There are picturesque songs of pioneer and Western life, songs of criminals and outlaws, of soldiers and wars, of tragedies and disasters, and even of the lost at sea. Sentimental songs play an important rôle; and religious and moralizing songs, political campaign songs, humorous songs, negro and pseudo-negro and Indian songs, appear. And, finally there are sequence songs and rhymes, singing games, movement songs, nursery rhymes, and the like. All these belong to "folk-song." For songs are folk-songs if the people have liked them and preserved them—if they have "lived in the folk-mouth"—and if they have persisted in oral currency through a fair period of years. Questions of origin, quality, technique, or style, are secondary. Attempts at differentiating traditional songs into "popular songs," or songs made *for* the people, and "folk-songs," or songs made *by* the people, based on some hypothetical manner of origin or on the continuation of a mediæval style are undependable and unsafe. This has been demonstrated many times, when the origin of any body of folk-songs is subjected to study. Whatever has commended itself to the folk-consciousness and has established currency for itself apart from written sources is genuine folk-literature.

An early mention of popular song in America occurs in an entry in the diary of Cotton Mather for 27 September, 1713:

"I am informed, that the Minds and Manners of many people about the Countrey are much corrupted by foolish Songs and Ballads, which the Hawkers and Peddlars carry into all parts of the Countrey. By way of antidote, I would procure poetical Composures full of Piety, and such as may have a Tendency to advance Truth and Goodness, to be published, and scattered into all Corners of the Land. There may be an extract of some, from the excellent *Watt's* Hymns."

Doubtless many legendary and romantic ballads were brought from England by the colonists, but probably Mather's "foolish songs and ballads" did not refer to these but rather to convivial, sentimental, or humorous ditties, the street pieces or broadsides popular in the mother country. These he would like to see replaced by religious and moralizing songs. Most songs, of either type, in the period before the Revolution, were probably imported, either orally or in broadside versions; but there were also historical pieces that were indigenous. Professor Tyler, writing in 1878, mentions as ballads popular in New England *The Gallant Church*, *Smith's Affair at Sidelong Hill*, and *The Godless French Soldier*. These pieces do not appear in printed collections, however, and, in general, little has been done in the way of an attempt to recover songs from the period before the Revolution. The oldest remaining historical ballad composed in America of which texts are available is *Lovewell's Fight*, recording a struggle with the Indians in Maine, 8 May, 1725. It was composed not long after the event, and was long popular in New England. A text reduced to print almost a century later begins:

> What time the noble Lovewell came,
> With fifty men from Dunstable,
> The cruel Pequa'tt tribe to tame
> With arms and bloodshed terrible.

Longfellow chose the same subject for his early poem *The Battle of Lovell's Pond*.

Greater effort has been made toward collecting songs and ballads of the Revolution, though the work should be done again more exhaustively and more critically. Frank Moore printed in 1856 a collection of verse, brought together from newspapers, periodicals, broadsides, and from the memory of surviving soldiers. Most of these pieces are semi-literary in character, to be sung to familiar tunes imported from England. That oftenest quoted as having the best poetical quality is *Nathan Hale*.[1] Many express the discontent of the colonists, and many are burlesques. Sometimes they were based on older pieces, as Major André's *The Cow Chace*, which is built on *The Chevy Chase*. Of better quality is *A Song for the Red-coats*, on the defeat of Burgoyne.

> Give ear unto my story,
> And I the truth will tell
> Concerning many a soldier
> Who for his country fell.

[1] See Book I, Chap. ix.

Some of the most popular pieces of the Revolutionary period, mostly satirical verses by known authors, have been treated in an earlier chapter.[1]

From the War of 1812 remain *James Bird*, a ballad of a hero shot for desertion, texts of which have drifted as far inland as the Central states, and a camp song in ridicule of General Packingham.   Some verses beginning

> Then you sent out your Boxer to beat us all about;
> We had an enterprising Brig to beat the Boxer out,

and some stanzas preserved as a marching song for children—

> We're marching down to old Quebec
> While the drums are loudly beating—

may also date back this far.   *The Texas Rangers*, widely current through the South and the West, and modelled on the British *Nancy of Yarmouth*, sounds like an echo of the fight with the Mexicans at the Alamo in 1835.

Songs surviving from the Civil War are frequently sentimental in character, like *When this Cruel War is Over* and *The Blue and the Gray*.[2]   These are of traceable origin, yet they have passed widely into oral tradition.   There were numerous camp songs on sieges or battles, but these have not shown vitality.   Best remembered in popular literature from the time of the Civil War are many negro, or rather pseudo-negro songs, given diffusion by the old-time itinerant negro minstrels.   Many are the work of composers like Stephen C. Foster[3] or Henry C. Work.[4]   These persist in popular memory side by side with songs like *Juanita* or *Lorena*, or the later *After the Ball*.   Every collector of folk-song comes upon pieces of this type far oftener than upon songs commemorating battles or political events.   In similar manner, the popular song given currency by the Cuban War, *A Hot Time in the Old Town To-night*, modelled on a Creole song, does not reflect directly the war that "floated" it.   Nor do the songs universalized for England and America by the war of 1914—*Tipperary*, *Keep the Home Fires Burning*, *Over There*, *The Long, Long Trail*—commemorate its leading events.

---

[1] See Book I, Chap. IX.   [2] See Book III, Chaps. II. and III.
[3] See Book III, Chap. V.   [4] See Book III, Chap. II.

In general, as over against sentimental, romantic, or adventure pieces, ballads dealing with historical events or important movements occupy but a small corner in American popular song. *Captain Kidd* has retained currency in New England and in the West, and the collector still comes at times upon ballads of the British highwayman, Dick Turpin. Some widely diffused songs, their authorship and origin now lost, which reflect emigrant and frontier life, especially the rush for gold in 1849, are *Joe Bowers*, *Betsy from Pike*, and *The Days of Forty-Nine*. *Pretty Maumee* possibly echoes relations with the Miami Indians. *The Dreary Black Hills* reflects the mining fever of one period of Western history; and there are other sectional satires, like *Cheyenne Boys*, *Mississippi Girls*, or humorous narratives or complaints, like *Starving to Death on a Government Claim*. The best-known pieces reflecting pioneer or prairie life are *O Bury Me not on the Lone Prairie*, and *The Dying Cowboy*, or *The Cowboy's Lament*, both of which are adaptations. The latter especially has roamed very far, as will be seen later, and exists in many varying texts, with changed localizations. These pieces have currency chiefly in the Far West and in the Central West. Nor are political campaign songs long-lived; like historical songs, songs mirroring transient phases of national life are likely to fade early.

Interest in orally preserved verse in the United States has centred hitherto mostly in English and Scottish romantic and legendary narrative pieces, or traditional ballads, emigrants from the Old World. Imported songs of other character and verse stories indigenous to America have had less attention. Here, as in England, the pieces which have been singled out as worthy of recovery and study are chiefly those of the type collected and preserved in Professor Child's *English and Scottish Popular Ballads*. They are likely to have the longer history, and, in their Old World form, higher poetical quality; and there is more mystery concerning their origin. Attempts have been made to register the number emigrating to, and surviving in America, to note their geographical distribution, and to watch what has happened to them.

Some narrative poems or songs of the type collected by Professor Child were no doubt brought over in the colonial period by emigrants, or by sailors, or returned travellers, and the process of importation from England has not yet entirely ceased. In almost any community some new arrival from the Old World may bring over an old song; though as time passes the chance for survival grows less. The communities richest in these pieces are, as might be anticipated, the North Atlantic and the Southern; that is, the older, not the more newly settled sections of our country. At present, representatives of nearly eighty of the three hundred and five ballads, or lyric-tales, included in the collection of Old World pieces by Professor Child have been salvaged in the United States, besides many not included in his collection, some of which he may not have known. They come from New England, from the Middle Atlantic, North Central, Western, and Southwestern states, and from the Southern mountains. Some of the most popular of these traditional pieces, their popularity varying in varying regions, are *Barbara Allen's Cruelty,* which leads in geographical distribution and in number of variants, *Lord Lovel, The Two Sisters, The Two Brothers, The House Carpenter, Young Beichan, The Wife of Usher's Well,* and *Lord Randal*—who appears as Johnny Randall in Colorado, Jimmy Randall in Illinois, Jimmy Ransing in Indiana, Johnny Ramble in Ohio, and Jimmy Randolph in North Carolina. Sentimental ballads are well represented, among these emigrants from the Old World, and ballads of romantic tragedy and adventure. A riddle ballad remains, *The Cambric Shirt,* deriving from *The Elfin Knight,* and in *Little Harry Hughes,* from the Old World *Sir Hugh,* a relic of the mediæval superstitions concerning the Jews; and there are some sea narratives. Heroic ballads, or local or border ballads, have not found diffusion in the New World.

These traditional pieces find their best chance for survival in outlying, isolated, or secluded regions, those least invaded by modern songs or song modes. Sometimes city dwellers remember and hand them on; but for the most part they are best sought for in mountain districts or in rural communities in the South and East, and on isolated farms or ranches in the West. The Southern Appalachians are peculiarly rich in the preservation of Old World ballads. Sometimes traditional ballads remain, in degenerate form, as nursery songs, where adults have no longer cared to preserve them; examples are *Lamkin, Lord Randal, The Two Brothers.* Usually these transplanted pieces are sung to a variety of tunes. The text and the melody brought from the Old World occasionally survive together; but, on the whole, one text holds to one air with little regularity. Despite its fluctuations and the variant forms it assumes, the text of a ballad remains more constant and is more easily identified than the air. Nevertheless it is the singing which tends to keep ballads alive. The words and the music are recalled together by the singers. The music and the text help to preserve each other. Where comparison is possible between the melodies of the American pieces and their Old World originals, it shows that the tendency is constantly toward greater simplicity in the New World derivatives. This is true also when ephemeral popular airs of the day are taken up by the people and persist in folk-song. Like the songs which are emigrants they tend toward simplification in transmission.

Many Old World songs and ballads now having oral currency in the United States have passed through the medium of print, and owe something of their diffusion to broadsides and songbooks, or to rural newspapers. When ballads are reduced to print, they are not "killed" but have a better chance to survive; and the same is true when they have been transcribed in manuscript books. Most of the ballads included in the Child collection were preserved in broadsides or printed sources, or in manuscripts, and the same agencies have helped to perpetuate these songs when they reach the New World. The life of ballads is not ended by their reduction to print or to writing, but they are likely to receive new tenure therefrom.

Various things happen in America to these Old World emigrants. Occasionally they are preserved pretty exactly. A few lose compactness and are lengthened by repetition, iteration, or garrulous protraction, sometimes from the example of other songs, or they cross outright with other songs. More often they are shortened. Passages are forgotten until hardly recognizable fragments remain. Moralizing banalities drop out. Frequently ballads become disordered, one well-known piece blending with another; and a new amalgam song may arise. And sometimes they cross with songs of recent origin, lending a few stanzas to assimilated street songs of unmistakably modern composition. The more vulgar and repugnant elements tend to disappear, and also the supernatural elements. In *The House Carpenter*, the returned lover becomes a living lover, not a ghost; and in some versions of *The Farmer's Curst Wife*, the devil disappears. Characteristically they take on modern elements, substituting the known for the unknown, and accommodating their personal names, and their localizations. One, *The Farmer's Curst Wife*, just mentioned, has drifted to Texas, and has taken to itself classification as a cowboy song. *The Two Brothers*, in a Nebraska version, seems well on the way toward becoming a Western song.

> " O what shall I tell your true love, John,
>   If she inquires for you?"
> " O tell her I'm dead and lying in my grave,
>   Way out in Idaho."

Popular tradition dims the romantic elements. Lords lose their nobility and become ordinary citizens. Kings and princesses and ghosts are made over into the singer's own kind of people. The narrative loses its reflection of the original surroundings, and assumes altered character. And, in both imported and indigenous pieces, serious events or sentiments are often vulgarized or made commonplace, till the originally earnest survives only in farce.

The general trend is toward degradation, not improvement, by the process of oral preservation and transmission. This may be seen when there is comparison of a body of New World texts *en masse* with the texts printed by Professor Child. There is no improvement in the narrative element—though some theorists hold that communal preservation brings epic development—nor are artistic sequences and climaxes evolved, unless where an inferior piece crosses with a better. In communities where the style of English and Scottish pieces has best maintained itself, new songs assimilate themselves to this style, in rare instances, and assume some of the mannerisms of the English and Scottish ballads, like the "legacy" motive, or the "climax of relatives"—mannerisms, on the whole, of the later Old World ballads rather than the earlier. More often, however, these distinctive mannerisms, when inherited, become lost. Communal preservation and re-creation, in the New World, tends, not to improve inherited ballads or to increase the presence of these ballad mannerisms, but to obscure or obliterate them

The Old World songs having on the whole the best chance to survive are those which tell some tragic story, or contain some strongly marked formula. The same is true of parallel indigenous verse. The short song telling a story, in particular a tragic story, has the best chance of vitality. Whatever else drops out, the death, or the immediate event bringing it, lingers in the memory. The moving or the striking in subject matter, and the familiar or conventional in style, are likeliest to persist.

Beside the imported romantic and legendary ballads, many songs and song-tales on the themes of broadside balladry of the last two centuries in England have currency in the United States, often in such disguised or modified form that their origin is no longer recognizable. Of this character is *The Butcher Boy*, whose forsaken sweetheart hangs herself—a ballad related to the British *A Brisk Young Lover;* also *The Boston Burglar*, or *Charlie's Town*—related to *The Sheffield Apprentice*. To this same group belongs probably the "confessions" of *Young McAffie*, who poisoned his wife and her baby. *The Dying Cowboy*, despite its name, is ultimately imported. Still older is the ballad of the maidservant *Betsy Brown*, who is "sold to Verginny" by her mistress. An instructive instance of the migration of a song is offered by *The Romish Lady*, a story of a Protestant martyr, having considerable currency in the Central West.

> There lived a Romish lady
> Brought up in proper array.
> Her mother oft times told her
> She must the priest obey.

This is the Elizabethan ballad "It was a lady's daughter, of Paris properly," introduced into Fletcher's *Knight of the Burning Pestle*. It was reprinted in the reign of Charles II, and is to be found among the *Roxburgh Ballads*.

> It was a lady's daughter,
> of Paris properly;
> Her mother her commanded
> to Mass that she should hie.

The American texts show simplification in transmission, but remain strikingly faithful to the original narrative.

Most of the later imported pieces show, like the earlier,

inclination for romantic pathos or tragedy, or for sentimental story. Several tell of the return of a lover, as *The Banks of Claudy*, or of a girl who follows her lover. Others tell of a girl whom her lover lures away and kills. A striking piece of wide diffusion and of Old World provenance is *The Drowsy Sleeper*, known as *The Bedroom Window, Willie and Mary*, etc.

> "O Mary dear, go ask your father
> If you my wedded bride may be;
> And if he says nay then come and tell me,
> And I no more will trouble thee."

> "O Willie dear, I dare not ask him,
> For he is on his bed of rest,
> And by his side there lies a dagger
> To pierce the one that I love best."

Robbin, Bobbin, Richard, and John, or *The Wren Shooting* is a St. Stephen's Day song, from the Isle of Man. Other pieces connected with British folk-song, some of them lingering only as songs for children, are *Father Grumble*, or *Old Grumbly*, etc., who thinks "he can do more work in a day than his wife can do in three," *The Children in the Wood, Billy Boy, The Frog and the Mouse*, and many nursery rhymes. Of modern importation and widely current because used as a party song is the Irish *William Reilly* or *The Coolen Bawn*. Ritual songs hardly occur in the United States; for instance Harvest Home songs, carols, springtime and Mayday songs. Ritual observances have not been transplanted.

Aside from the historical pieces enumerated earlier, there are now many short narrative pieces, orally preserved, and apparently authorless, which may fairly be called indigenous ballads. Already, they are marked, to an instructive degree, by fluctuation of text, variant versions, and local modifications and additions. Most of them have a direct unsophisticated note, and some show traces of rude power. An example of an indigenous ballad is *Young Charlotte*, who was frozen to death at her lover's side, on her way to a ball.

> Spoke Charles, " How fast the freezing ice
> Is gathering on my brow."
> Young Charlottie then feebly said
> " I'm growing warmer now."

This ballad is current through the Middle West, and has been recovered as far southwest as Texas, owing, apparently, nothing of its circulation to print. Phillips Barry has shown that it was composed at Bensontown, Vermont, as far back as 1835. Another piece which has roamed everywhere is *Springfield Mountain*, the story of a young man mowing hay who was "bitten by a pizen serpent" and died. W. W. Newell was able to trace the history of this piece to New England composition in the late eighteenth century. Of unknown origin but of equally wide diffusion is *Poor Lorella*, who was killed by her lover, and lies down under the weeping willow:

> Down on her knees before him
> She pleaded for her life;
> But deep into her bosom
> He plunged the fatal knife.

This is known also as *The Weeping Willow*, *Poor Floella*, *Floe Ella*, *Lurella*, *Lorla*, *Loretta*, *The Jealous Lover*, *Pearl Bryn*, etc. Also of unknown origin and also tragic is *The Silver Dagger*. *Jesse James* claims sympathy for its outlaw hero, an American Robin Hood. *The Death of Garfield* reflects moralizing delight in a criminal's repentance, a stock motive. *Fuller and Warren* tells of a fatal quarrel between rival lovers; *Casey Jones* of a fatal railroad run. From the standpoint of the New World, ballad-making is not a "closed account." Probably there will always be a body of short narrative pieces, their authorship and origin lost, preserved in outlying regions. They will shift in style, for there is a history of taste for folk-poetry as there is for book-poetry; but they will ever be behind contemporary song-modes by a generation or more. These are genuine ballads—unless there is insistence on some communal-mystic origin for what may be termed a ballad, or on the preservation of a mediæval song style. The mediæval song style is the more memorable, because it dated from a time when singing was nearly universal, and when songs were composed for the ear, not for the eye; but it may not logically be insisted upon as a test of what is genuine balladry and what is not.

There have been many helps to diffusion of popular pieces in this country as in England. Fairs or circuses at which broadsides or sheet music were offered for sale have served as agencies of diffusion, and so have itinerant vendors and entertainers of all kinds. Songs learned at school and in childhood stay in the memory with especial tenacity. Country newspapers have reprinted many well-cherished pieces, later pasted into scrapbooks. Even city newspapers like the Boston *Transcript* and the Boston *Globe* have "folk exchanges" which have preserved many good texts. And now, as before the days when print was so common, song lovers copy their favourite texts into manuscript books. Pepys testified to his pleasure at hearing an actress, Mrs. Knipp, sing "her little Scotch song of Barbara Allen"—perhaps the début of this song; and the stage star still remains a great agent in popularization. So do wandering concert troups and minor singers of many types. The once popular negro minstrels helped to universalize many pseudo-negro songs, and real negro singers, like the Jubilee singers and the Hampton Institute singers, have kept alive many songs. A striking text or a tuneful melody, given some impetus in diffusion, lingers when its history has been forgotten. *After the Ball* and *Two Little Girls in Blue*, popular stage songs of the 1890's—the first sung all over the country in the farce *A Trip to China Town*—are heard no longer in the cities, but they are still vigorous in village communities and on Western ranches.

The name "American ballads" is now often applied to a body of cowboy, lumbermen, and negro songs, recovered, chiefly by John A. Lomax, in Texas, New Mexico, Montana, and other States. These make when brought together an interesting and picturesque display. They reflect the life, tastes, narrative themes, and metrical modes of the singers. Cowboy life is "communal," and it is vivid, full of incident, and exciting. The cowboy pieces, despite their prevailing crudity, have a certain force and breeziness.

> I'm a rowdy cowboy just off the stormy plains,
> My trade is girting saddles and pulling bridle reins.
> O I can tip the lasso, it is with graceful ease;
> I can rope a streak of lightning, and ride it where I please.

The mass of cowboy songs, so-called, including probably that just quoted, is not, however, of cowboy creation, the result of group improvisation. but rather of cowboy adoption or adaptation, homogeneous as they seem. The few indigenous pieces, attested as of cowboy origin, are the most negligible and the weakest. They have little or no narrative element, are songs rather than ballads, have won no diffusion, and hold no promise of reaching better form or of assuming real ballad structure. The majority of the songs represent assimilated material, made over until the characters and the events conform to the horizon of the singers. In general, material from all sources, once in the stream of popular tradition, tends to accommodate itself to the modes and the tastes of the community that preserves it. It is instructive to analyse the cowboy pieces, as a group, for the light that is thrown on the songs of a new community and on the processes of folk-song.

Young Charlotte has been referred to as composed early in the nineteenth century in New England. *Rattlesnake—A Ranch-Haying Song* is a stuttering farce version of the New England *Springfield Mountain*. *The Cowboy's Lament*, known also as *The Dying Cowboy*, is a plainsman's adaptation of *An Unfortunate Rake*, current in Ireland as early as 1790. Its origin is reflected in the absurd request for a military funeral retained in the chorus:

> O beat the drum slowly and play the fife lowly,
>   Play the Dead March as you carry me along;
> Take me to the graveyard, there lay the sod o'er me,
>   For I'm a young cowboy and I know I've done wrong.

Bury Me not on the Lone Prairie is an adaptation of *Ocean Burial*, by W. H. Saunders. *The Little Old Sod Shanty on My Claim* is an adaptation of Will S. Hays's *The Little Old Log Cabin in the Lane*. *Bonnie Black Bess*, *Fair Fannie Moore*, *Rosin the Bow*, *The Wars of Germany* are from the Old World. *The Old Man under the Hill* is a Child piece. *The Railroad Corral* was composed by J. M. Hanson, and originally published in an Eastern periodical. *The Ride of Billy Venero* is made over from Eben E. Rexford's *Ride of Paul Venarez*, first published in *The Youth's Companion*, and once a popular declaiming piece. *Home on the Range* was a popular parlour song, while *From Markentura's Flowery Marge* reflects the flowery sentimental day of American poetry. *The Boston Burglar* and *McAffie's Confession* are derivatives of Old World ballads; and *Jesse James*,

Betsy from Pike, The Days of Forty-nine, Fuller and Warren are not of cowboy origin but immigrated from other States. *I'm a Good Old Rebel* is *Unreconstructed*, the composition of Innes Randolph, who wrote for *The Baltimore American*. Even the few rough improvisations which seem to have come from the cowboys themselves are largely built on or reminiscent of some well-known model and are fitted to some well-known melody. They are creations in a qualified sense only. For instance, *Whoopee-Ti-Yi-Yo, Git along Little Dogies* owes its form to *The Cowboy's Lament*, the origin of which has been mentioned, and it is sung to the same melody as its Old World original. The influence of Irish "Come-all-ye's" and of death-bed confession pieces is pretty strong on the cowboy songs as a whole.

The term "American ballads" is better applied, not to the small, structureless and nearly characterless group of cowboy songs which may be genuinely of cowboy improvisation, but to ballads of the type exemplified by *Springfield Mountain, Young Charlotte, Poor Florella, The Young Man who Wouldn't Hoe Corn, Jesse James*. It is these which form the truer analogues of the oral legendary and romantic song-tales of England and Scotland.

Still another type of orally preserved verse appears in ring games, on the grass or in the parlour, "Play-party" songs, so-called, and in the singing games of children. The latter are now assuming a certain degree of stability or uniformity, owing to the printing of traditional songs for children in books of games, from which they are taught to pupils in the primary grades at school. "Play-party" games of young people are not yet quite extinct, though they are becoming so. They are typically dances, except that the participants move to the rhythm of singing, not to the accompaniment of some musical instrument. The words of the texts are more unstable, and the songs more structureless than in songs and ballads proper, and they are even more subject to local changes and improvisations. Game-songs with strong formulæ of some kind are likeliest to retain vitality, because most easily remembered; the formula remains constant if nothing more. Collection of such songs has been made by W. W. Newell for New England, and by many collectors for the Central West. Some well-known examples of game-songs, most of them imported from the Old World, are *Weevilly Wheat, Juniper Tree, Skip to My Lou, The Needle's Eye, Happy is the Miller, We're Marching Round the Levy;* some favourite game-songs of the Central West are *Bounce Around, We'll All Go Down to Rowser's, Pig in the Parlour.* Beside traditional pieces and those of obscure origin, modern songs of all kinds have been utilized in play-party games: minstrel songs—as *Old Dan Tucker, Angelina Baker, Jim Along Jo, Buffalo Gals*—and the popular street songs, *Nelly Gray, Little Brown Jug, John Brown's Body, Captain Jinks of the Horse Marines.* The modern pieces are likeliest to escape mutilation, at least so long as they retain currency as separate songs. Even hymns, scraps of glee club songs, and Mother Goose rhymes are sometimes utilized to form accompaniments to dances. New stanzas are welcomed, and local adaptations, irrelevant or facetious. Judging from recorded material, communal utilization and preservation of a song as a dance song does not bring improvement, nor does it bring development of a narrative element. The refrain formula, that element which shows greatest fluctuation in traditional ballads like the Child ballads, is the most stable element in traditional dance songs.

Other "floating" matter entering obviously by immigration like so many folk-songs and dance songs, and owing its existence to oral tradition, includes counting-out rhymes, flower oracles, skipping-rope rhymes, rhyming proverbs, or aphorisms, saws, weather lore, plant and animal lore, and good and bad luck signs. These belong, however, rather to folk-lore than to literature.

CHAPTER XXVIII

Two New Religions

I. THE BOOK OF MORMON

THE Book of Mormon is a curiosity of literature. It is evidently an effort to reconstruct in archaic language the Hebraic age and to project by a special process some of its characters into nineteenth-century life, as well as to place the civilization they represent in an American setting. Just as Chatterton appealed to those interested in a Gothic revival, Joseph Smith, for whom the claim is made that the Book of Mormon was revealed to him in 1827, assumed a permanence of interest in the verbalism of the Old Testament. He also appealed to those who were curious about American antiquities, speculative about the lost Ten Tribes reported by tradition to have found their way to the New World, and eager both to excavate prehistoric mounds and to decipher the picture writings of the Aborigines.

Without professing that the Book is a substitute for the Bible, such authoritative interpreters as Professor James E. Talmage, one of the Twelve Apostles of the Mormon Church, does call it "a parallel volume of Scripture," and claims that "the Nephite and the Jewish Scriptures are found to agree in all matters of tradition, history, doctrine, and prophecy upon which both the separate records treat." It is distinctly stated that "America was settled by the Jaredites, who came direct from the scenes of Babel," that the Aborigines also came from the East, and were followed by peoples at least closely allied to the Israelites, that the existing native races of America were born of a common stock, and that the so-called historical part of the Book of Mormon has adequate testimony to its claims.

The Jaredites, extinct by 590 B.C., are thus reported to have occupied both North and South America for about 1850 years. Then came Lehi and his company to this continent to develop into segregated nations, Nephites and Lemanites; the former disappearing about 385 A.D., the latter degenerating into the Indians of a century ago.

In consequence the Book of Mormon becomes an effort to transplant Hebraic traditions, though scholarship takes no such hegira seriously, and the volume depends for its validity on evidence and assertion presented by itself and accepted only by those convinced by the same. To "Gentiles" objecting to any new revelation beyond the Bible. the Book of Mormon, offering itself as proof that it is valid, reports Jesus as saying, "Wherefore murmur ye, because that ye shall receive more of my word?"

The Book was launched at a moment favorable to its acceptance by a certain type of the well-meaning but unschooled. The modern interpretation of the Bible had not begun. Literalism was still in the saddle. Books such as *Lux Mundi* had not appeared. Matthew Arnold was not yet startling the conventional with his counsel to rest heavily on some things in the Bible, on others lightly. The revisers of the King James version, were still a half century from their work which was to be followed by successive revisions until every little while sees a new translation of at least the New Testament. It is with such a background that the man of modern training approaches the Bible, and to him the Book of Mormon seems something born out of due season.

Again, when Joseph Smith received in 1827—as the Book affirms—the "Golden Plates" first published in 1830, the New World, particularly west of the Alleghanies, was plunging into various religious extravagances, the wonders which the withdrawing frontier spread before the pioneer were on many a tongue, the origin of the Indians was a live issue, and wiseacres here and there identified them with the lost tribes. It was a day when men still dreamed of and dug for treasures buried by Spaniards or by Kidd. The Masonic-Morgan mystery and the Fox sisters found in Western New York a local habitation and people were still alive there who recalled the "Jerusalem" of Jemima Wilkinson. Mesmerism and the miraculous were of common interest, and here and there community of property and even person was a mooted topic.

In the Book of Mormon we shall look in vain for more than is already found, at least in spirit, in the Scriptures. Its teachings are in general in surprisingly close accord with the outstanding teachings of the Bible. The doctrines both of pre-existence and of perfection are reiterated, if not emphasized. Continuity beyond the grave of relationships begun here is preached. No suggestion is made of polytheism, and polygamy is expressly forbidden. Stress is laid on the second coming of the Lord, which the Millerites, in their white robes by thousands, gathered one day on the banks of the Schuylkill to witness only to be disappointed and chagrined. "No idea was so absurd," as Schouler, the historian, writing of the time has said, "or so visionary that one might not hope to found a school or sect upon it in this new American society, if only he seemed to be in earnest."

To understand today the Book of Mormon one must take into account the environment in which it came to light, the type of men responsible for its origin and for the organization created in its name, and the accretions, interpretations, and history soon to follow its publication.

Joseph Smith, sprung of parents reported to be specially responsive to local conditions, said in 1838 that on the night of September 21, 1823, at his home in Manchester, near Canandaigua, New York, the angel Moroni three times appeared to him with a revelation of "Golden Plates" buried on Cumorah Hill, and that on September 22, 1827, in accordance with instructions, he dug up the same, and found them covered with small, mystic characters "of the Reformed Egyptian style"—as Professor Talmage hints. It was a time when people were still talking of the Rosetta Stone, when travelling showmen were exhibiting mummies, and when the Egyptian style was affecting the public taste, even in some housebuilding.

With the aid of a pair of crystal spectacles, his "Urim and Thummim," which Smith said he found, and with the co-operation of certain kindred spirits, Martin Harris, Oliver Cowdery, and David Whitmer by name, whose services were the more **valuable** because Smith seemed expert neither in reading nor in writing, in 1830 the Book of Mormon was published, and the angel Moroni, according to the narrative, then took away the "Golden Plates." This is the story the Mormons tell of the origin of their Book, and those will accept its authenticity who without challenge are willing to accept the testimony of the four witnesses supplemented in part by the testimony of eight more, three of whom were Smiths, not including Mrs. Joseph Smith, who opposed the publication of the Book. By those accustomed to consider historical evidence it will perhaps be kept in mind that of only Joseph Smith have we more important knowledge than the mention of their names, and that he was the party most concerned.

From such a questionable beginning Mormonism has grown —as a standard historian admits—into "an extraordinary force." The latest report, dated May 3, 1921, from the official headquarters in Salt Lake City, states that there are now 900 Latter Day settlements, many of importance, that representatives of the faith have made a world-wide reputation as superior colonizers of good character, that great progress has been made in education, that 1933 of their missionaries are now carrying the message at their own expense to many quarters of the globe, that their book, now published in fifteen languages, has run into "the hundreds of thousands," and that they are represented in Congress and for their good works have been recognized abroad.

Although no sect in all our history has had so much conscientious, determined, and intelligent opposition, to plead that they are persecuted is no final word with which the Mormons can close controversy. The fault is not altogether with the Book, which undeniably teaches much that is definitely Christian, supplemented, unhappily, by other things that later gave immediate offence and still keep many an honest judgment in suspense.

Joseph Smith could not let well enough alone. After claiming that Moroni, God, Christ, John the Baptist, Elijah, and others in their very person appeared before him to confirm his amazing revelation, he was unwise enough to add to it, in 1843, a revelation, published officially in 1852, of polygamy. This aroused public opinion everywhere against the sect, which, also because of other difficulties, was kept wandering in frequent collision with neighbours and others till the final settlement in Utah.

The story of these successive clashes with "Gentiles" and the Government has significance in interpretation of the Book of Mormon only as it indicates the exercise of a power which the Book itself at least allows and the growing determination of the American people to have done with polygamy. Finally in the constitution of the State of Utah, dated 1896, it was stipulated that "polygamous or plural marriages are forever prohibited." Charges have since been made in reputable journals that good faith has not been kept, but even Ex-Senator Cannon, sometime high in Latter Day Councils writing a few years ago, says it is the leaders who were guilty, not the Mormon people, whom he describes "as gentle as the Quakers, as staunch as the Jews."

The Book itself provides for a complicated hierarchy with a President—"Seer, Translator, Prophet"—having great authority and supported by two counsellors, the three regarded as successors to "Peter, James, and John," symbolizing the Trinity and perpetuating the priesthood of Melchizedek. There are besides a patriarch and twelve apostles, forming an itinerant high council, and authorized to ordain elders, priests and deacons, to conduct religious meetings and to administer the sacraments. There are also "Seventies" who serve as missionaries and propagandists, "high priests" to take the places when necessary of those above them, and below all such of the order of Melchizedek there is the Aaronic priesthood usually occupied with temporal concerns.

Not to the Book of Mormon providing this elaborate hierarchy, but to the hierarchy itself which has not always recognized that

"New occasions teach new duties,"

is due much that affronts "Gentiles."

The Book differs in its spirit little from the Bible. The Latter Day Saints, in or out of the hierarchy, who in great numbers try to live up to the teachings of the Bible and the Book, live simple, godly lives of love and faith and hope. But they are themselves an argument against their Book. By their daily conduct they testify that there is no need for their volume. The spirit the Bible inculcates meets human needs wherever there are human souls. To reveal a special Bible for each people in the world would seem to deny the unity of human experience and the universality of human brotherhood.

With Christians, in spite of the same Bible divided into sects agreeing about the essentials, differing only in details of doubtful exegesis or of organization, to see the Latter Day Saints— a half million strong—both using a new Book they claim to be revealed besides the Bible, and in a democratic age evolving a hierarchy projected by a special revelation, harking back to ancient times, in no sense born of modern experience in Church or State, diverts attention from the common interest of Christendom, makes co-operation difficult with those who think no special Bible needed for the western world, and tends to postpone the coming of that day when world peace will be secured by "one holy bond of truth and peace, of faith and charity."

II. Science and Health with Key to the Scriptures

As the Book of Mormon describes the hegira of an adventurous folk moving by successive stages from the East to the Salt Lake Valley, so *Science and Health with Key to the Scriptures* by Mary Baker Eddy, marks the pilgrimage of a group of seekers after health and truth from an idealism, at first indeterminate and amorphous, up to a unique religiousness challenging modern medicine, and that *odium theologicum* which is largely responsible for the multiplication of denominations dividing Christendom, at a time when in union only is there strength.

Napoleon had gone at last beyond ambition's lure, and family talk in many a New England home was turning toward the slavery issue just emerging above the horizon, when Mary Morse Baker was born to Mark and Abigail Ambrose Baker on July 16, 1821, at Bow, New Hampshire. Mary Baker's parentage was New England to the backbone, substantial, intelligent, and very religious. She began her church going when as a little girl she was taken by her parents every Sunday to the First Congregational Church at Concord. She joined the Tilton Congregational Church when she was seventeen years old. A family of consequence, the Bakers read the papers of the day, particularly the "New Hampshire Patriot and State Gazette," and talked over what they read in the living room. Mary listened in and also joined in. Evidence abounds that from the first her mind was quick and active.

In 1843, the Christmas spirit was already in the air when Mary Baker was given in marriage to George Washington Glover on Tuesday, December 12. The wedding night was spent at Concord, and the next day the bride and groom drove up to Bow for a fitting farewell to the birthplace of the bride. Then Mr. and Mrs. George W. Glover set sail from Boston for their new home in the South. June of 1844 found her accompanying him on a business trip to Wilmington, North Carolina, where an epidemic of yellow fever was then in full swing. George Glover was at once laid low by it. His brother Masons —for he ranked high in Masonry—attended his sick bed, where Mrs. Glover also would have been, but that both the doctor and the Masons forbade her, realizing that she was soon to become a mother.

The dying man's last words were a pathetic plea to his brother Masons to see his wife safe to her home in the North. Faithful to their trust, they laid their brother's form to rest with the full Masonic ritual in the cemetery of St. John's Episcopal Church at Wilmington. During the weeks that followed they gave the grieving widow tender care while, with their counsel, she salvaged what she could of her husband's estate, informally allowed the slaves, now hers alone, to go free, and under Masonic escort made the journey to New York where her brother, George, was waiting to greet her. In August Mrs. Glover was once more under the Baker roof.

Born September 11, 1844, her son was named George Washington Glover II, for his father. Childbirth all but plucked life from her body. For a time her family gravely doubted whether she would survive. Not even her stout-hearted father thought she would ever regain strength enough to nurse her child and bring him up. Through the long nine years that followed, she suffered from ill health, which persisted almost unbroken until she was in middle life. The symptoms were different from earlier adolescent disturbances.

Seldom after George was born can she be said to have rested well. She suffered from pangs of indigestion traceable to the stomach, as well as to the intestinal tract. But it was the persistent pain she habitually located in her spine which indicated that something may have gone wrong when George was born.

On June 21, 1853, she married Dr. Daniel Patterson, a New Hampshire dentist. But this marriage was not to last. Early in the Civil War, he went off to Washington, commissioned by the Governor of New Hampshire to collect a fund for distribution among Union sympathizers in the South. He left his wife without money, and also without food. With customary carelessness, straying in March, 1862, too near the Confederate lines, he was captured and sent to Libby prison. After his release he failed to reestablish a home, eloped with the wife of another man and in 1873 was divorced for his unfaithfulness.

When Mrs. Patterson came to P. P. Quimby's office in the International Hotel at Portland, in October, 1862, she showed evidence of unmistakable frailness and poverty. The young George Quimby—he told the author so himself in 1907—helped her up the stairs. "She was too feeble," wrote her sister-in-law, Mrs. Mary A. Baker, who went with her, "to go unattended." P. P. Quimby was her last hope. She had heard of him a year before, for stories were in wide circulation of his magic cures. People reported that he used no medicine and was particularly helpful in afflictions of long standing. As with kindly eyes and sympathetic heart, Quimby looked into that wan, worn face, his friendly understanding went out to her in a consuming desire to do all he could for her. His diagnosis in itself increased her faith. He told her that she was "held in bondage by the opinion of her family and physicians," and "her animal spirit was reflecting its grief upon her body and calling it spinal disease." His assurance that she would soon be well was accompanied by his usual manipulation of the head to generate the flow of healthy electricity, on which he laid great stress.

Encouragement to expect recovery was furnished with persuasive forcefulness. With her flaming faith the patient helped herself while she thought she was only helping Quimby to help her. The change was instantaneous. Her pain and weakness disappeared. A sense of comfort and well-being stepped into their place. Within a week she says that without help she climbed the one hundred eighty-two steps to the dome of the City Hall. And in this whole experience she furnished, though she was not to realize it until 1866, a new illustration of the words Jesus spoke to the woman healed after twelve years' illness, "Thy faith hath made thee whole." At last the prayers of years seemed to be answered. Though her healing was not permanent and she soon suffered a relapse, she told others of the change that had come over her.

This, then, was Mrs. Eddy at the age of forty-three, her health improved but not yet all it should be; somewhat better friended than before, but still hard pressed to make a living; overrating in a grateful woman's way what she owed to Quimby, and looking vainly for a man to carry on his work,—and, when none appeared, carrying on herself till the hour struck when she could write with truth: "In the year 1866, I discovered the Christ Science." She, who in childhood at her mother's knee, had listened with joy to the Bible stories about the healing of the sick, was now promising God that if He would raise her up to health she would give her life to the help of the sick.

Starting from her home in Swampscott, Massachusetts, anticipating a happy evening at a temperance meeting in nearby Lynn, on Thursday, February 1, 1866, she had a hard fall on the ice, of which this account appeared the next Saturday in the Lynn Reporter:

Mrs. Mary Patterson of Swampscott fell upon the ice near the corner of Market and Oxford streets on Thursday evening and was severely injured. . . . Dr. Cushing, who was called, found her injuries to be internal and of a severe nature, inducing spasms and internal suffering. She was removed to her home in Swampscott yesterday afternoon, though in a very critical condition.

The Sunday following the fall, still prostrate in her Swampscott home from the accident, as she was reading the Bible narrative of how Jesus healed the palsied man, she experienced one of those rare visitations reserved for the religious discoverers of the race. Her consciousness of God's power to heal, which had been ever growing brighter with the years, and had been enhanced by the idealizing faith which for a while she honestly believed that Quimby also had, was now at its full.

The way began to clear for that complete concentration on her life work which was essential if the goal she set before her was ever to be reached. She now began to build her book. However, the truth pressed home that she could never hope to do this until she had first acquired an income on which to live; a sum at least above the margin of actual want. To this grilling task she set her hand while her spirit ranged the skies. If she was to write, she had to have a roof over her head, and food to eat.

In those dark days when, with the odds against her, she learned to make a living, she demonstrated that those who, in singleness of mind, seek the kingdom receive all the human things of which they have real need. The spring before the book appeared, Mrs. Eddy was living in a boarding house at Number 9, Broad Street, Lynn. Leaning one day from her window, she observed a sign "For Sale," fastened on the two-story frame house, with attic, at Number 8, across the street. She resolved that this should be her haven and on March 31, 1875, she bought the place for five thousand six hundred and fifty dollars.

Certain phrases used by Emerson are in accord with *Science and Health*. Those were the days when he was telling lecture audiences: "Mind is supreme, eternal, and one. . . . The universe is the result of mind." But we have Mrs. Eddy's own word dictated to a secretary that she never read Emerson till after her book was published. Between Emerson and Mrs. Eddy there was a great gulf fixed. He was all for thought, and she was for demonstration. He never fired her imagination, or awakened her enthusiasm. But to Whittier she turned instinctively. He was more approachable and more responsive. Eight of his poems, with her approval, were put into the *Christian Science Hymnal*, and to the end it was a joy to her to hear people sing:

> The healing of his seamless dress
> Is by our beds of pain;
> We touch him in life's throng and press,
> And we are whole again.

At a time in life when many a fecund writer has said farewell to his creative power, Mrs. Eddy, in 1875, put the last touch on the first edition of *Science and Health*. To manufacture the book would cost more than fifteen hundred dollars. Two of her friends advanced the required amount, and the first edition of one thousand copies appeared on October 30, 1875. No sooner was it off the press than Mrs. Eddy was visualizing, in a letter written to a student, a new edition. If the first edition bears some of the marks of a first book, she at once began to remove them and continued to improve the successive editions till at last *Science and Health* became, next to the Bible, a "best seller" among serious books. Like the Bible it was published—as Mrs. Eddy wrote in her first preface —"to do good to the upright in heart, and to bless them that curse us, and bear to the sorrowing and the sick consolation and healing." The style is well adapted to the end in view. Without sacrificing dignity, the language is often conversational. Developing out of her rich experience among the plain people, the *Science and Health* of 1875, like the King James Version of the Bible, is easily "understanded of the people."

Never was Mrs. Eddy satisfied with anything she wrote. The publication of each edition of *Science and Health* was simply a new challenge to make the next edition better. Between the table of contents of that first edition of 1875 and the latest of 1910, there is not merely a wide difference but also a complete reordering. All the way through the thirty-five years which elapsed between the first edition and the last, she was consumed with a desire to make her book more accurately express her meaning, more perfectly disclose the revelation she never doubted God had given her. Into the expanding life of this unusual woman Asa Gilbert Eddy came unobtrusively. On New Year's Day, 1877, they were married, and a satisfying home was now hers which all her life she had been craving and sometimes seemed destined never to possess.

It was not long before Mrs. Eddy entered into those business arrangements which were to continue for many a year with John Wilson, head of the Cambridge University Press, the artistic craftsmanship of whose books has in all the years been matched by their intrinsic worth. With the entire firm her relations remained until the end both friendly and agreeable

Indeed, the story of the successive editions of *Science and Health* can be traced in detail from the letters and the memoranda of such representatives of the University Press as John Wilson, William Dana Orcutt, and William B. Reid. They are used here the more lavishly because they dismiss much idle speculation—including Mark Twain's—about the originality and the orderly development of Mrs. Eddy's thinking, as revealed from year to year in *Science and Health*.

From the first, Mrs. Eddy made on these substantial men a profound impression, which they saw no reason to change in a business and personal relationship lasting through an entire generation. To them she seemed a high-bred gentlewoman, sure of herself and her ideas, yet considerate and courteous to all. Upon every detail they indicate Mary Baker Eddy lavished care constant and untiring. From the head of the firm down to the youngest office boy, she knew them all. She earned the respect they freely gave her; and increasingly their personal affection.

When she inquired where she could obtain the services of a trained editor, the Reverend James Henry Wiggin, staff reader for the University Press, was "detailed to the work (punctuation, capitalization and general smoothing out as to construction of sentences); and, as he did this on his own time, the payment for these services was made by Mrs. Eddy. This was well known to those in our office," says Mr. Reid, "as well as in our proof reading department, and caused many a smile among us when we read, from time to time, the repeated assertion that Mr. Wiggin had written the book, and it tickled him, more than perhaps anyone else to read that he was the *author*. In later years, Mr. Wiggin once remarked to Mr. Wilson: "Wouldn't it have been fine if I had?"

With or without help, she pressed forward through the years, endeavoring to make her leading idea, increasingly to her a solemn revelation, as clear to others as it was to her. Not a day passed even in her latest years—it is credibly reported—that she did not put some touch upon the book. Not even Lincoln surpassed her in the patient effort to express her ideas more clearly. Her thought was on a single track, but to her apprehension and to that of many others the track led heavenward.

Like all great teachers, she developed for herself in her voluminous writings a vocabulary of some 18,000 words. *Science and Health* is written in very original language whose style has been both highly commended and adversely criticized. Judgment of style is sometimes influenced by the reader's belief in the context, and, after all, in such a revolutionary book as *Science and Health* it is its teaching which is basic.

Mrs. Eddy's best qualities seem to be illustrated in the following quotations which are believed specially to have commended themselves to Christian Scientists:

"Truth's immortal idea is sweeping down the centuries, gathering beneath its wings the sick and sinning. My weary hope tries to realize that happy day, when man shall recognize the Science of Christ and love his neighbor as himself,—when he shall realize God's omnipotence and the healing power of the divine Love in what it has done and is doing for mankind. The promises will be fulfilled. The time for the reappearing of the divine healing is throughout all time; and whosoever layeth his earthly all on the altar of divine Science, drinketh of Christ's cup now, and is endued with the spirit and power of Christian healing." (*Science and Health*, p. 55.)

"The divine Love, which made harmless the poisonous viper, which delivered men from the boiling oil, from the fiery furnace, from the jaws of the lion, can heal the sick in every age and triumph over sin and death. It crowned the demonstrations of Jesus with unsurpassed power and love. But the same 'Mind . . . which was also in Christ Jesus' must always accompany the letter of Science in order to confirm and repeat the ancient demonstrations of prophets and apostles." (*Science and Health*, p. 243.)

"The time for thinkers has come. Truth, independent of doctrines and time-honored systems, knocks at the portal of humanity. Contentment with the past and the cold conventionality of materialism are crumbling away. Ignorance of God is no longer the stepping-stone to faith." (*Science and Health*, Preface, p. vii.)

"Christian Science exterminates the drug, and rests on Mind alone as the curative Principle, acknowledging that the divine Mind has all power." (*Science and Health*, p. 157.)

"The divine Principle of the First Commandment bases the

Science of being, by which man demonstrates health, holiness, and life eternal. One infinite God, good, unifies men and nations; constitutes the brotherhood of man; ends wars; fulfils the Scripture, 'Love thy neighbor as thyself;' annihilates pagan and Christian idolatry,—whatever is wrong in social, civil, criminal, political, and religious codes; equalizes the sexes; annuls the curse on man, and leaves nothing that can sin, suffer, be punished or destroyed." (*Science and Health*, p. 340.)

"No human pen nor tongue taught me the Science contained in this book, SCIENCE AND HEALTH: and neither tongue nor pen can overthrow it." (*Science and Health*, p. 110.)

"Only as we rise above all material sensuousness and sin, can we reach the heaven-born aspiration and spiritual consciousness, which is indicated in the Lord's Prayer and which instantaneously heals the sick.

"Here let me give what I understand to be the spiritual sense of the Lord's Prayer:

Our Father which art in heaven,
    Our Father-Mother God, all-harmonious,

Hallowed be Thy name.
    Adorable One.

Thy kingdom come.
    Thy kingdom is come; Thou art ever-present.

Thy will be done in earth, as it is in heaven.
    Enable us to know,—as in heaven, so on earth,—God is omnipotent, supreme.

Give us this day our daily bread;
    Give us grace for to-day; feed the famished affections;

And forgive us our debts, as we forgive our debtors.
    And Love is reflected in love;

And lead us not into temptation, but deliver us from evil;
    And God leadeth us not into temptation, but delivereth us from sin, disease, and death.

For Thine is the kingdom, and the power, and the glory, forever.
    For God is infinite, all-power, all Life, Truth, Love, over all, and All."

(*Science and Health*, pp. 16, 17)

Critics have studied *Science and Health* with varying results. Some see nothing good in book or author. That is understandable, but it must also be admitted that under criticism many Christian Scientists have kept a silence usually as wise as it is Christian. Others, in a purely scientific spirit, have dissected the book without bias and the author's career with no more bitterness than the trained historian brings to the consideration of Mahomet or Queen Elizabeth. Mrs. Eddy staked the value of her *magnum opus* upon the therapeutics which it taught. Her followers have done the same. Results have been shown in the many cures reported in the Wednesday evening testimony meeting, so well attended, in some places regularly by thousands, that the mid-week service, to most denominations a problem, and to many a farce, must be reckoned with by those who study *Science and Health* from any point of view.

Through her book Mrs. Eddy has achieved results, having made effective a recognized principle. On a smaller scale others too have obtained results. Drugless healing has been everywhere subjected to scientific study. Professor Goddard's only interest is psychological, and he reports that the cases he has studied cover almost the whole field of pathology. Of the patients thirty-three per cent. claimed instantaneous healing, fifty per cent. a gradual cure, and seventeen per cent. incomplete. Parkyn, Van Rhenterghem, Cabot, and others have made analogous studies and make similar reports. Christian Science submits to no such tests. It admits practically no limitations to its possibility of cures. Percentages are therefore not scientifically ascertainable in Christian Science. But the average man has perhaps little interest in scientific percentages.

In these days when suffering is more general and more intense, many honestly report that they find in *Science and Health* what Ex-President Crowell calls "a remarkable personal narrative, combining the contemplative and the practical in the field of Christian teaching." There are (as in the chapter on prayer, where in spite of the discouragement of petition and of audible expression there is a deeply religious spirit) passages which would seem to be helpful in spiritual distress. The general effect of the book has been to encourage daily Bible reading until today Christian Scientists are probably the most numerous and most faithful Bible readers in the world. Dean Charles Reynolds Brown of Yale University is convinced that Christian Scientists, with this book before them, as "a class are upright and clean." With allowance for those in every religion who do not try to live up to its highest teachings, they measurably avoid friction and irritation and preserve considerable serenity amid worldliness and temptations which many of us seem unable to resist. They have to their credit a widely read daily paper which for editorial ability as well as excellent news service ranks among the best journals in the country. Finally, as the years go by, it is thought by many that Christian Scientists seem to be increasingly disposed to emphasize the outstanding virtues which their book teaches, and in consequence to bring forth "the fruit of the spirit—love, joy, peace, long-suffering, gentleness, goodness, faith, meekness, temperance; against such there is no law."

CHAPTER XXIX

Book Publishers and Publishing

THE history of book publishing in British North America begins with 1640, when Stephen Daye printed at Cambridge *The Bay Psalm Book*, the first real book to issue from a press north of Mexico. Daye continued to print for only about seven or eight years, when he was succeeded by Samuel Green, for causes known only to the authorities of Harvard College, under whose direction this first American press was operated. Back of Harvard stood the more or less arbitrary authority cf the Crown, exercised against publication in more than one colony through some ultra-conservative governor or council. In fact not until about twenty-one years before the Revolution were legal restrictions removed from publishing in the colony where it was born.

These restrictions, in the case of Massachusetts, were largely motivated by religion; and the early issues of the press were almost entirely religious in character. The first monument of American scholarship and printing ability, for instance, is *The Holy Bible . . . Translated into the Indian Language*, Cambridge, 1663. Six years later from the same press appeared what seems to be our first original book not strictly religious in character, Nathaniel Morton's *New England's Memorial*. Moreover this work announces that it is "Printed for H. Usher of Boston." Urian Oakes's *Elegie Upon the Death of the Reverend Mr. Thomas Shepard*,[1] in some respects the best poem produced in the colonies before the eighteenth century, dates from 1677. As early as 1693, at least, book dealers had begun to sell private libraries, for in that year appeared *The Library of the Late Reverend and Learned Mr. Samuel Lee . . .*

[1] See Book I, Chap. IX.

532

Exposed . . . to sale, by Duncan Campbell, Boston. At Boston also was issued in 1717 *A Catalogue of curious and valuable books, belonging to the late Reverend & learned Mr. Ebenezer Pemberton . . . To be sold by Auction, at the Brown Coffee-House in Boston, the second day of July, 1717*, which is held to be our first auction sale catalogue of books.

With these dates, involving as they do scholarly activity, press work of some note, printer and publisher, adumbrations at least of literary genius, and the circulation of books through carefully formulated advertisement, the history of American publishers and publication may truly be said to be under head-way.   In these early days, as well, even in the stronghold of the Puritans, there were attempts at something above mere utilitarianism in books, for about 1671 John Foster, the earliest American engraver and the first person to set up a press in Boston (in 1675), had published an engraved portrait of Richard Mather.   In the same town in 1731 appeared what is regarded as our first portrait engraved on copper plate.

Clearly the pioneer position in American publication belongs to Cambridge and Boston, and the latter city was to hold first place as a publishing centre until about 1765, when Philadelphia was to eclipse it, an eclipse from which it was not to emerge until about the fourth decade of the nine-teenth century.   William Bradford in 1682 landed in Pennsyl-vania, and by 1685 was printer and publisher of *The Kalen-darium Pennsilvaniense*.   Bradford's career in Pennsylvania was far from happy, however.   Twice he was summoned before the governor, once put under heavy bond, and once thrown into jail; so that in 1693 he departed in wrath for New York.   For the next six years there appears to be no record of printing in the colony.

But Philadelphia was too highly favoured in the eighteenth century by geographical situation and by political, financial, and social currents not to begin soon to assert herself.   Already as early as 1740 a would-be magazine publisher had stated in a few words the dominant reasons for the leadership of Phila-delphia during its some sixty years of hegemony:

As the City of *Philadelphia* lies in the *Center* of the *British* Plantations, and is the *Middle* Stage of the Post, from *Boston* in *New England* Northwards, down to *Charlestown* in *Carolina* Southwards, and as that City, besides its frequent Intercourse with *Europe*, derives a continued Trade with the *West India Islands*, and also has a considerable Commerce with the rest of the Colonies on the Continent; We *Therefore* fixed upon it as the properest Place, and more commodiously situated than any other, for carrying on the various correspondences, which the Nature of the Work renders necessary.[1]

What the writer says of magazines applies equally well to books at an early period, even in the reference to the West Indies, which in colonial days received a considerable part of their publications from this country.

Bradford, then, was succeeded by a long line of illustrious printers and publishers; for after the famous trial of Peter Zenger at New York in 1734–35 (the *Brief Narrative* of which became the most famous publication issued in America before the *Farmer's Letters*), a trial which virtually decided the freedom of the press in America, there was no more necessity for such cases as his. By 1770 Robert Bell had gained the reputation of being the most progressive publisher in the colonies. Then came the Revolution, the sum total of its effects being a powerful factor in the rise to leadership of Philadelphia. Bell was ably succeeded by Robert Aitken. When Jeremy Belknap of Massachusetts was seeking a publisher in 1782, Ebenezer Hazard, an authority for the period, pronounced Aitken the best publisher in America. He was followed by Mathew Carey, one of the greatest publishers, all things considered in their true historical perspective, yet produced by this country.

But while Philadelphia was thus climbing to pre-eminence and weathering the Revolution, with its marked emphasis on publications of a purely utilitarian and controversial nature, other printing centres were springing up over the country. New York had received the disgruntled Bradford, who in 1694 issued Keith's *Truth Advanced*, according to Hildeburn the first book to appear in that city. Both New York and Philadelphia were, in one respect, at a disadvantage as compared to Boston in the circulation of their publications, in that the population they supplied was much less homogeneous. As early as 1708, at least, a Dutch book, Falckner's *Grondlycke*

---

[1] *The American Weekly Mercury*, 6 Nov., 1740.

Onderricht, had appeared in New York. Yet while thirty Dutch publications were issued between 1730 and 1764, the influence of that language as a publishing medium was practically dead by 1800, although it was revived much later at Grand Rapids, Michigan.

With the German language, however, the case was far different. Andrew Bradford printed Conrad Beissel's *Das Büchlein vom Sabbath* in 1728, ushering in German printing in this country. In 1738 Christopher Saur or Sower established at Germantown what is the oldest extant publishing firm in the United States. Sower won his place in publishing annals by his three editions of the Bible, in 1743, 1762, and 1776. Not until 1782 was our first Bible in English published, by Robert Aitken at Philadelphia. But even more remarkable than Sower's editions of the Bible was the issue of Van Bragt's *Martyr Book* by the Ephrata brethren in 1748 and 1749, which, in an edition of about 1300 copies of a massive folio of 1512 pages on thick paper, was the largest book until after the Revolution. Up to 1830 German printing was carried on in some 47 places, and of these at least 31 were in Pennsylvania, while in actual output and in intellectual stirring the balance was even greater in favour of that colony than these figures would indicate. Moreover, Germantown was the first place to gain wide recognition for itself as a paper manufacturing centre.

Of book publication in other languages during this period, little account need be taken, though there were a few French issues. When one turns, however, to the more subtle and pervasive influence of cultural infiltration, something more must be said for French. The intensely interesting catalogue of Moreau de St. Mery & Company's Store, Philadelphia, 1795, with some 920 entries of French books, together with other evidence, shows that book dealers must have reckoned directly and publishers indirectly with French influence. Moreover, this catalogue, with its list of Latin, Italian, Spanish, German, and Dutch works gives eloquent testimony to the cultivation of our cosmopolitan capital. In no wise accidentally, as in large measure is to be said of Boston at a later period, was Philadelphia our chief centre of publication as the Republic began its political career.

In the meanwhile in this germinal eighteenth century

other colonies had been making a beginning. One of the most influential of these, Virginia, had possibly seen an issue from her press as early as 1682, but at any rate it is fully authenticated that from 1730 to 1737 William Parks was under contract by the governments of Virginia and Maryland to maintain printing presses at Annapolis and at Williamsburg. The dates for the establishment of presses in other colonies and states most noteworthy in the annals of our early publishing are, according to the best authorities, Connecticut, 1709; Rhode Island, 1727; South Carolina, 1732; Kentucky, 1787[1]; and Ohio, 1793.

Under modern conditions these dates would mean little or nothing, save perhaps that some venturesome printer saw an opening for a newspaper and job printing. But in the eighteenth century specialization and concentration in publication had not yet taken place, nor is it fully visible until the beginning of the second quarter of the next; for even as late as 1837 the Harpers did printing for any one who would bring it in to them, and James and Thomas Swords were pronounced as being in about 1815 the first New York bookmakers who were distinctively publishers. So in these early days, when a press was set up usually a few books were soon issued. It was a period of cheap apprentice labour, of widespread religious activity, of the formulating of new laws, and of purveying to a scattered population elementary books of an educational character. Communication was difficult, and the publisher of a book was not likely to fail to sell it because some highly organized firm at a distance might supply his limited territory. Moreover, quite frequently in a costly undertaking the publisher's risks were minimized by the fact that the work was not put to press until he thought such a number of subscribers had been obtained as would insure him against financial loss. After the middle of the century one marked phenomenon, interrupted only during the Revolution, was the increasingly large output of classic reprints from American presses.

Therefore there sprang up towards the end of the eighteenth and at the beginning of the nineteenth century a large number of publishing centres that until the period of centralization began had fairly noteworthy careers. Reading,

[1] Thomas says 1786.

Lancaster, and Germantown in Pennsylvania; Brattleboro, Vermont; Hartford, Connecticut; Burlington, New Jersey; Charleston, South Carolina; Lexington, Kentucky; and Newport, Rhode Island, were early of some note, while in 1834 Hartford was said to be our largest school-book publishing centre.

The reprinting of standard literature referred to above first begins to make itself noticed about 1744. In that year was published Cicero's *Cato Major*, while New York, Philadelphia, and Boston each issued an edition of Richardson's *Pamela or Virtue Rewarded*, the sub-title of which, together with its British reputation for unimpeachable piety, caused thus early even a Boston publisher to risk bringing it out. As late as 1800 Mathew Carey's printer wrote to him "if you can think of printing a Novel."

Very early, however, graceless New York had found, in the person of Hugh Gaine, one of the most interesting of all American publishers, a producer not only of novels but of what north of Virginia at least was usually looked upon with even greater disfavour, that is, plays. In the one year of 1761 alone he put out not less than twenty-two plays, more than one of which was by a Restoration dramatist. The decorous publishers of Philadelphia and Boston followed less radical paths, reading aright the comparative conservatism of their public. Moreover, it is risking little to say that the trouble which befell Gaine during the Revolution was not all political but was acidulated by Puritan rancour over the class of his publications. Within a few years of 1761 Andrew Stewart, of Philadelphia, issued two or three plays; but in general the press of that city reflected a staid psychology, while Boston contented itself with the Puritan tenor of *The Messiah*, *Night Thoughts*, and *The Day of Doom*, a tenor which was not to be changed materially until the last decade of the eighteenth century.

The Revolutionary period was quite different from any that had preceded it. Before the war, although the issues of the American press showed, as noted, a sprinkling of non-theological works, they were nevertheless overwhelmingly religious in character. But now politics becomes of first importance, and we pass from dominant figures to the frequent anonymity of dangerous discussion. There was great difficulty in obtaining paper during and just before the war, and as pamphlets were too expensive, not to say books, broadsides became the prevailing form of publication. Rags were regularly advertised for by the publishers. Yet although American publishing bears eloquent witness to the all-obsessing nature of the stern struggle, coming as it did at a time when our publishing facilities were not materially far enough advanced to absorb the blow, nevertheless the love of literature was not dead. The opening years of the Revolution saw, in addition to Brackenridge,[1] Trumbull,[2] Freneau,[3] and Hopkinson,[4] who of course would be issued regardless of conditions, works issued of Alsop,[5] Defoe, Falconer, Garrick, Milton, Pope, Sterne, Thomson, Voltaire, and Young.

Back of all publication, and in the final analysis dominating it, stands of course the psychology of the reading public. And especially as we approach the present century does it become more and more evident that the great publisher must be a psychological expert in public literary tastes and interests. Somewhere, then, about the fourth quarter of the eighteenth century American publishers began to sense the fact that the people of the country, having won some slight measure of victory over the imperious necessities of mere material existence, and having to some degree slowly broadened down to a mellowness where life was no longer solely a struggle with the flesh and the devil, were beginning to demand real literature.

After the Revolution, which had temporarily dammed back this current of our culture, the recovery, considering the prostration of our material resources, was little short of marvellous. Now for the first time in our bibliographies it becomes necessary to divide our literary output into genres. Evans, for instance, for the period from 1786 to 1789 gives drama, 38; fables, 8; fiction, 43; juvenile, 104; poetry, 130; and miscellany, 12.

Probably the best domestic seller of 1786 was James Buckland's *An Account of the Discovery of a Hermit, Who Lived about 200 Years in a Cave at the Foot of a Hill, 73 Days Journey*

---

[1] See Book II, Chap. VI.   [2] See Book I, Chap. IX.   [3] *Ibid.*
[4] See Book I, Chap. IX, and Book II, Chap. II.
[5] See Book I, Chap. IX.

Westward of the Great Alleghany Mountains, which appeared in that year at Pittsburg, Portsmouth, Middletown, New Haven, Norwich, and Boston, and which went through several myth-adding editions in the next few years. Its vogue is noted here merely to emphasize the fact that the American public was becoming prepared for that literary enfranchisement noticeable in the last years of the eighteenth century. True enough, until within the days of Hay[1] and Eggleston[2] the publishers could have noted an opposition to the novel, but it was even after the beginning of the nineteenth century one that, save in some districts, they need not note as prohibitive.[3] The South, even before the Revolution, was obtaining by direct importation, through book dealers, and from American publishers large quantities of belles-lettres, especially novels.

One aspect of the book business disconcerting to the American publisher existed for some time after the Revolution, however, and that was the publication in England of books by our authors. Roughly speaking the dominant centres of publication for American books during the period from 1765 to 1783 were, in the order of their importance, Philadelphia, London, Boston, New York, Charleston, Newport, and New Haven. For several years after the war any American book published in London had acquired a noteworthy prestige at home and had materially increased its chances for sales on both sides of the Atlantic. In some few cases, in fact, where presswork offered unusual difficulties, or where, especially, illustrations were numerous and costly, it was best that the work be published abroad. Moreover, American authors first obtained really commanding international standing through books of information concerning this country, and it was but natural that such works should obtain wide circulation in Europe with its ever-pressing problem of emigration.[4]

In the last two decades of the eighteenth century, signs

---

[1] See Book III, Chaps. x and xv.   [2] See Book III, Chap. xi.

[3] For a discussion of this phase of American psychology, see *Some Aspects of the Early American Novel, The Texas Review*, April, 1918. The publication of the works of Darwin, Spencer, Huxley, and Tyndall was at first bitterly opposed in this country by an influential class.

[4] Any one interested in this phase of American publication should study the lives of Major Robert Rogers, William Bartram, Audubon, and, especially, Captain Jonathan Carver. [See Book II, Chap. i, and bibliography.]

begin to accumulate in our publishing life of the awakening of an American nationality. For instance, the reason why the president of Harvard and two of his professors, together with a governor, recommended Nicholas Pike's *Complete System of Arithmetic* in 1786, is that it is "*Wholly American*" in both "Work and Execution" and will keep much money in this country. Moreover, though to most Americans the works of Noah Webster[1] have even yet a dim aura of classicism, they little realize how he had to fight to overcome the conservatism and the pro-British tendencies of his public. In 1807 he writes:

But there is another evil resulting from this dependence [upon Great Britain] which is little considered; this is, that it *checks improvement*. No one man in a thousand—not even the violent political opposers of Great Britain—reflects upon this influence. Our people look to English books as the standard of truth on all subjects, and this confidence in English opinions puts *an end to inquiry*. . . . We have opposed to us [in introducing American books] the publishers of most of the popular periodical works in our large towns.[2]

Webster further says that the educated men of the smaller towns and the professors of the Northern colleges generally are favourable to American publications, but that the large cities are strongholds of British subserviency.

Thus American scholarship began to assert itself during the opening decades of the nineteenth century with more real vigour than did American belles-lettres, for against the popularity of Mackenzie, Mrs. Radcliffe, Mrs. Roche, Hannah More, Jane Porter, Mrs. Smith, Mrs. Chapone, Miss Williams, Mrs. Rowson[3] (in part, however, to be claimed as American), and later of Scott, 500,000 volumes of whose novels were issued from the American press in the nine years ending with 1823, the struggle was desperate. There were no restraints, either legal or ethical, at this period to prohibit the publication of these authors; and the publishers issued them in large numbers, sometimes in chap-books as low as five cents. Moreover,

---

[1] See Book III, Chaps. XXIII and XXV.
[2] Todd, C. B., *Life and Letters of Joel Barlow*, p. 247. The entire letter, pp. 247–252, is worthy the careful study of the student of our early literature.
[3] See Book II, Chap. VI.

during the three decades before Scott's novels appeared, there were frequent republications or importations of, especially, Bunyan, Milton, Defoe, Pope, Addison, Thomson, Young, Darwin, Lewis, Johnson, and Goldsmith. The publishers of Trumbull, Barlow,[1] Dwight,[2] and Brown,[3] while receiving apparently fair returns from these men of popularity or near popularity, must have been, as a whole, keenly aware what a tiny rill was flowing into their coffers from their publications by American authors of belles-lettres.

Simms,[4] in 1844, thought that American literature really began with the War of 1812; and viewing the matter, as he appears temporarily to be doing, in the light of the publisher, there is some truth in his argument. He overstates his side of the question, however, when he says that prior to 1815 the issues from American presses were not only reprints wholly from foreign sources but were confined chiefly to works of science and education. There were too many reprints of belles-lettres, too much cultural striving, for the latter part of this to hold good. He is, however, quite correct when he calls attention to the small chance the American poet had in publishing in those days, and equally correct when he notes an awakening in the publication of "school and classical books." American intellectual freedom was voicing itself through its publications, and soon it was to become pathetically and perennially vocal in its cry for an American literature.

In 1820 about thirty per cent. of our publications were by our own authors; by 1840 it was approximately half, though the large increase in school books during the thirties had much to do with the rise. In 1856 the proportion had risen to about eighty per cent.[5] The vast bulk of the remaining portion is, in each case, composed of British productions. If to this be added the fact that sometime in the late forties the rage for Americana became pronounced, the middle of the nineteenth century may be taken as the turning point of nationalism in our publishing history.

---

[1] See Book I, Chap. IX.
[2] See Book I, Chap. IX., and Book II, Chap. XXII.
[3] See Book II, Chap. VI.　　　　[4] See Book II, Chap. VII.
[5] Two authorities, one British and the other American, reach practically the same conclusion for these periods, though each worked independently of the other.

Besides the beginnings in the reflection of American consciousness of nationalism and the noteworthy increase in school books of our own authorship and manufacture, the period immediately after 1812 was made notable by the many mechanical improvements introduced. In 1813 stereotyping was first employed. Iron presses began to replace the old wooden ones about 1817; in 1819 our first lithograph appeared, though about 1802 Mathew Carey had corresponded with Didot concerning his method of lithographing; while about 1825 bindings were cheapened by the use of muslin. Type casting had been attempted as early as 1768 and made a success of but a few years later. Therefore, though as late as 1834 Audubon was publishing in Edinburgh, primarily for mechanical reasons apparently, and though even in 1835 Harper & Brothers printed all their books on hand presses, yet by the end of the first quarter of the nineteenth century, American publication may be said to have passed through the period of mechanical adolescence.

At the very end of this period the annuals began to appear. Through their profusion of illustrations they notably raised the standard of the publisher's art all over the civilized world. The year 1843 was distinguished by the publication of Harper's *Pictorial Bible* and the Verplanck *Shakespeare*, which, containing as they did over 2500 pictures, strikingly emphasized the development of wood engraving; while, says Major G. H. Putnam, "beginning with 1869 the art of printing with the best possible artistic effects large impressions of carefully made illustrations was developed in the United States to an extent that has never been equalled in any other country."[1]

This constant mechanical improvement had, of course, the inevitable effect of cheapening the price of books, especially when reinforced by conditions growing out of the lack of an international copyright law. Accordingly, a little while after it became clear that stereotyping was a success, there was a noticeable lessening in price. Before this period, though there were no heavy advertising bills as at present, books, because of the cost of mechanical production and of carrying charges, especially of overland transportation, were markedly higher than they are today, measured in terms of labour and its pro-

[1] Putnam, G. H., *George Palmer Putnam: A Memoir*, p. 364.

ducts. In fact, they may be said to have been anywhere from two to two and one half times more costly. The constant tendency towards less bulky volumes seems to have received its first impetus from the fact that at an early date books were charged for at circulating libraries according to size; but of course weight in the hand and improvement in paper and type have had most to do with it.

During these opening decades of the nineteenth century, Philadelphia had been retaining her position as our foremost publishing centre. Two encyclopædias in twenty-one and in forty-seven volumes, one of them representing an investment of $500,000, had been completed there by 1824, works that would have probably overtaxed the publishing facilities of any other of our printing centres. Philadelphia has to her credit, too, the first American edition of Shakespeare and the first American anthology,[1] though one had been projected previously at New York. The final word was said as to the reality of her supremacy when Barlow, a New England man, published there, in 1807, his *Columbiad*, "in all respects the finest specimen of book making ever produced [up to that time] by an American press." Though Carey and Hart were ten years after their foundation in 1829 regarded as the leading publishers of belles-lettres in America, their place in this respect was soon to be taken by Ticknor and Fields of Boston. And while Philadelphia holds to the present day supremacy in the publication of medical literature, the foundation of her primacy running back well into the eighteenth century, the rising greatness of New York began somewhere about 1820 to relegate her, as a whole, to second place.

Perhaps the dominant reason for this change was the fact that during the period of bitterly intense rivalry to secure the latest European success for reprinting, the port of New York won a publishing victory over that of Philadelphia. One does not, however, have any too comfortable a feeling in asserting that primacy ever did belong to New York until the sixties. Philadelphia declined slowly; and up to the Civil War it, conserva-

[1] *Beauties of Poetry, British and American* (1791). Nineteen American writers are represented. The first of a proposed series of volumes of *American Poems Selected and Original*, printed at Litchfield, Connecticut, in 1793 is usually given as our earliest anthology

tive and neutral, was the chief distributing centre for the South and, to a considerable extent, for the West.[1] Moreover, evidence is not clear as to when Boston, for the second time, began to lead, though we may say probably some time in the early forties.

During the prolific period between the establishment of the house of Harper in 1817 and that of Scribner in 1846, New York saw the birth of many houses that were and are destined to loom large in the history of American publishing. In 1825 the house of Appleton was founded; in 1832 appeared John Wiley & Sons; John F. Trow, and Wiley, Long & Putnam were established in 1836, to be followed three years later by Dodd, Mead & Company. Of a much later period are the firms of McClure and Company, Doubleday, Page and Co., The Century Co., and Henry Holt and Company. The successful booksellers and publishers of the first quarter of the century, Small, Carey, Thomas, and Warner of Philadelphia; Duyckinck, Reed, Campbell, Kirk & Mercein, Whiting & Watson, of New York; West & Richardson, Cummings & Hilliard, R. P. & C. Williams, Wells & Lilly, and S. T. Armstrong, of Boston; Beers & Howe, of New Haven; and P. D. Cooke, of Hartford, who had, in almost every case, won success as mere reproducers of British works or of purely utilitarian American ones, were being replaced, in all these cities save the last two, by firms whose names are now familiar wherever the English language is read. Almost inevitably the average reader will underestimate the profound influence of our old publishers in bringing sweetness and light into the sombre, narrow lives of our forefathers, in spreading education, and, above all, in helping to inculcate the national consciousness without which a literature cannot exist; though of course the two wars with Great Britain were the all-enveloping factors which make a history of purely American publication possible.

But the great outstanding factor in the history of our publishing in the nineteenth century is the absence of and the struggle for an international copyright law. Much of the development of the short story in America,[2] the rise to

---

[1] See Brotherhead, W., *Forty Years among the Old Booksellers of Philadelphia*, p. 27. Brotherhead also has an interesting discussion of the beginnings of the vogue for Americana.   [2] See Book III, Chap. VI.

commanding position of the American magazine, [1] the stifling
of the American playwright for three quarters of a century, [2]
and the desperate struggle of all save our greatest novelists
against grave difficulties until 1891 [3] may be traced to the want
of such a law.

In 1790 Congress passed a national law for the protection
of literary property; and in those days of non-professional
authorship and of dependence upon Europe, it no doubt
thought that the situation had been fully met, even though as
early as 1782 Jeremy Belknap [4] was gathering advice as to how
he might prevent himself being pirated in London. But
when professional authorship began in America with Morse, [5]
the geographer, Webster, and Brown, a new influence was introduced, for the rewards of American authorship, in fact,
the possibility of American authorship in some cases, and the
tenor of American publications are inextricably inwoven with
the international copyright law.

Beginning with Scott's novels, the American publishers,
who before had not been numerous enough to interfere seriously
with each other or able to supply the demands for British
classics, entered on an absorbing race in speed of publications
and in underselling powers. In 1823 Carey & Lea of Philadelphia received advance copies of cantos eleven and thirteen
of Byron's *Don Juan*. It was immediately given out to thirty-
five or forty compositors, and within thirty-six hours an
American edition was on sale. Later equally marvellous
tales come down to us of speed in translating the last French
success.

When in 1838 the *Great Western* and the *Sirius*, the first
vessels to cross the Atlantic entirely by steam, arrived at
New York, the great idea dawned upon a certain class
of publishers that with this close connection journalism
might be made of literature. Accordingly there sprang
up a large number of mammoth weeklies for the republication in cheap form of whatever, in this eager age of
reading, promised to be popular as it issued from the European
press. For instance, *Zanoni* was published in the spring of 1842

---

[1] See Book III, Chap. XIX.
[3] See Book III, Chap. XI.
[5] See Book II, Chaps. I and XVII.

[2] See Book III, Chap. XVII.
[4] See Book II, Chap. XVII.

by the Harpers, and in *The New World*, and in *Brother Jonathan*, and the price went as low as six cents. The better class of publishers on both sides of the Atlantic tried to do at least a nominal justice to the authors they republished, and instituted a system of payment for advance sheets or copies.[1] Such luxuries of conscience, however, were not indulged in by many; and as soon as a reputable American publisher had issued a book that held the promise of a sale, the pirates rushed out an edition. Sometimes owing to the uncertainty of the ocean transit they were even able to get out the first one. In self-defence the respectable firms began a retaliatory war of under-selling; and having a sounder financial basis, they won in the contest. Then ensued an arrangement, more or less irritatingly defective, known as trade courtesy, whereby an understanding with an overseas author was respected. But after the Civil War, under the stress of economic readjustment chaos came again.

In 1837 the first recorded movement in the United States was taken towards international copyright. In the next five years numerous petitions for a law, signed by many prominent authors on both sides of the Atlantic, were presented to Congress. Some of the publishers soon became interested in the movement, one of the first and most aggressive being G. P. Putnam. Opposed to it for some time were, most prominently, the Harpers; but the chief centre of opposition was Philadelphia. For a while, ending with 1850, the British laws had been interpreted so as to protect American interests, but the golden opportunity was allowed to pass. On the part of the opponents of the law there was a tendency to confuse it with the protective tariff; and above all did they contend that American education would be injured by the increased price of books and by the fact that European works could not be adapted to our needs. Through the American Copyright League founded in 1883 and the American Publishers' Copyright League (1887) especially was the struggle finally brought to a victorious close in 1891. The chief effects up to the present of the law seem to be threefold. There has been a tremendous and immediate widening of the circle of readers the average author may address. Branch

[1] For the relative value of British authors to American publishers see J. H. Harper's *The House of Harper*, p. 115, and E. L. Bradsher's *Mathew Carey*, pp. 93–94.

houses have been established on both sides of the Atlantic, and existing houses have been enabled to broaden greatly their appeal to the reading public.   Chief among such firms in America are The Macmillan Company, Longmans, Green and Co., G. P. Putnam's Sons, The Oxford University Press, Charles Scribner's Sons, and E. P. Dutton and Company.   But, above all, there has resulted an immense stimulus to the possibilities of American literature through the securing of adequate returns to our authors.

The three professional authors already referred to were fortunate in that in two cases they published works of such nature that American superiority of domestic information or a growing feeling of nationalism could be enlisted in their behalf.   Brown came before closeness of communication and the latest great success could unite to rob him of even his slender gains, for though Morse and Webster and, later, Barnes, Andrews, Anthon, and Stephens made fortunes through the authorship of school books, belles-lettres were but a sorry crutch indeed until well within the nineteenth century.   European, especially British, supplies were too cheap and plentiful.

Goodrich, speaking of the time about 1820, says that " it was positively injurious to the commercial credit of a bookseller to undertake American works unless they might be Morse's Geographies, classical books, Watts's Psalms and Hymns, or something of that class."   Hawthorne's *The Devil in Manuscript* has a passage of like tenor; and as late as 1886 Dana Estes of Boston testified before the Senate Committee on Patents:

For two years past though I belong to a publishing house that emits nearly $1,000,000 worth of books per year, I have absolutely refused to entertain the idea of publishing an American manuscript. I have returned scores, if not hundreds, of manuscripts of American authors, unopened even, simply from the fact that it is impossible to make the books of most American authors pay, unless they are first published and acquire recognition through the columns of the magazines.

Against such an adverse current, American authorship was slowly winning its way. In 1829, it is asserted no author

of belles-lettres was living by his pen in New York.   The lives
of Richard Dabney, Percival,[1] and Halleck[2] throw a strong
light upon the rewards of authorship during the first four
decades of the century.   The first two men, though possessed of a thin strain of genius, were constantly in desperate
straits on Grub Street.   Halleck, in spite of some aspects
of popularity, received for the entire labours of a literary
lifetime but $17,500, or approximately $364 a year.   Irving[3]
and Cooper[4] had other financial resources than authorship,
but according to Longfellow, Professor Ingraham's bad
novels[5] were rewarding him richly in the thirties.

Simms affirms that up to the year 1834 American literature
was with a few exceptions the diversion of the amateur but
that about that time it began to assume the aspect of a business; while as late as 1842 Channing[6] ventured the (mistaken) opinion that Hawthorne[7] was the only American who
supported himself by authorship.   Yet the remark of such a man
shows how few were our temerarious professional authors.
By 1842 a man of great ability, unless divided against himself
like Poe,[8] could find support in literature in most fields of prose,
for one must always remember Bryant's remark implying that
poetry and a full stomach did not go together.   In a large
measure both Longfellow[9] and Whittier[10] must have felt likewise, for the latter, who had little to fall back upon, was in
straitened circumstances until the publication of *Snow-Bound*.
Lowell[11] had to superintend his own publications for a time, but
in 1870 he was able to say that he had lately declined $4000 a
year to write four pages monthly for a magazine.   One striking
exception to poor pay for poetry is, however, found in Willis,[12]
but even his magazine receipts of $4800 a year about 1842 were
largely from prose.

The magazines were indeed a saving influence in the life
of the hard-pressed American author.   "The burst on author-
land of Graham's and Godey's liberal prices," Willis said,
"was like a sunrise without a dawn."   *Graham's Magazine*,[13]

[1] See Book II, Chap. v.   [2] *Ibid.*   [3] See Book II, Chap. iv.
[4] See Book II, Chap. vi.   [5] See Book III, Chap. xi.
[6] See Book II, Chap. viii.   [7] See Book II, Chap. xi.
[8] See Book II, Chap. xiv.   [9] See Book II, Chap. xii.
[10] See Book II, Chap. xiii.   [11] See Book II, Chap. xxiv.
[12] See Book II, Chap. iii.   [13] See Book II, Chap. xx.

established in 1841, was especially liberal in its payments, particularly to Cooper and Hawthorne. It must have been largely of the aid of the magazines that Goodrich was thinking when he said in 1856 that nothing was more remarkable than good writing, though he truly adds that authorship does not rank financially with other professions.

History of good quality has apparently always paid. Before Mrs. Stowe's great success in *Uncle Tom's Cabin*,[1] Prescott[2] was probably the best rewarded of our classic writers. As early as 1846 he says that his copyrights were considered by his publishers as worth $25,000 each, and that on his two histories he had already received about $30,000; and even better things could be reported of the next two histories. Against this must be balanced the fact that the proceeds of Emerson's[3] literary life were little more than $30,000.

Since 1891 both the playwright and the novelist have flourished. While there are striking instances of financial success for both before that period, the former was especially hard hit by the constant stream of plays flowing in, copyright free, from Europe. Kotzebue and Scribe especially figured constantly in this retarding of the American playwright. But as a class the novelists have won the most spectacular monetary rewards of our time. Just what these returns are, it is not possible to ascertain nor perhaps advisable to reveal if it were. In attempting to find them out, one becomes hopelessly involved in guesses and in interested gossip. However, one prominent publisher of our century has committed himself to the assertion that Mary Johnston must have made from $60,000 to $70,000 on *To Have and to Hold*, which statement may be taken as some fair gauge of the returns of a modern best seller.

But as we go backwards to our classic novelists, it becomes strikingly apparent that, save in one or two instances, they got no such rewards. The reason lies in the unending flow of European fiction reproduced in the mammoth weekly for five cents, and by the best publishers, usually, in Cooper's time for $1.50, while American novels were $2. Then, to catch all classes of buyers, between these two came the cheap series so popular even a generation ago. Harper's Library of Select

[1] See Book III, Chap. XI.   [2] See Book II, Chap. XVIII.
[3] See Book II, Chap. IX.

Novels in brown paper covers began in 1842, reaching 615 volumes, all of them save some half dozen being foreign authors, in part contemporary ones. This is but a type of what publishers were doing, or trying to do, all over the country. After the Civil War, when trade courtesy died, this deluge of cheap literature began again, the Seaside Library being especially noteworthy, though scarcely less so than the Lakeside Series from Chicago, both selling as low as ten cents. Both were births of the end of the seventies. Meanwhile, if the European author was being robbed directly and the American author indirectly in this country, the latter was receiving little from Europe. As early as 1793 Germany was pirating our authors; and Cooper was but a type when he remarked after his residence in France that the return to him from the sales of his books in France did not pay his French taxes; and he was highly popular there at that time, too. The British pirate was not handicapped by the necessity of translation.

A few words must yet be said upon the concentration of American publishing. In 1858 Simms wrote: "We have not a single publisher in the whole South, from the Chesapeake to the Rio Grande. We have book sellers and printers, who occasionally issue books originally from the press but who . . . rarely succeed in selling them."[1] Concentration of population and facility of communication, both largely lacking, were, he thought, the two secrets of success. The Southern city which came nearest being a publishing centre at this period was Richmond, while Mobile had one firm of some local prominence; but the favourite publishers of Southern writers for a generation before the war were the Harpers, the Appletons, Jewett & Company, Derby & Jackson, and the Lippincotts. But if the South was not active in publication, the evidence is overwhelming that it was an unusually large buyer of fine books.[2]

In the Middle West, to an eminent degree Cincinnati had facility of communication through her strategic position on the Ohio in days of slow overland communication; and for two decades or more before the war it was a great publishing

---

[1] *Literary Prospects of the South, Russell's Magazine*, June, 1858, p. 202. There is a possibility that Simms did not write this unsigned article

[2] New Orleans, Nashville, and Charleston were especially noteworthy in this regard.

factor along the Ohio, the Mississippi, and westward through Texas. Later came the period of rapid and cheap overland shipments and of great publishing houses with a far-flung corps of salesmen and all-pervading methods of advertising; and Cincinnati relatively lost its bright promise, being therein but a type of what, broadly speaking, took place outside of three or four great cities.

Perhaps the most illuminative document of this century is the figures of the United States Census giving the total value of book and job printing for 1905. In the nearest million dollars it runs: New York 44, Chicago 26, Philadelphia 14, St. Louis 8, Boston 7, San Francisco 4, and Cincinnati 4.

Unfortunately, as we are concerned primarily with the publication of notable literature, these figures are somewhat misleading but possibly prophetic of the future. Boston, for instance, which found itself in the forties forced once more into leadership through the race of great writers that sprang up in New England, though it lost its primacy to New York in the sixties, yet has in Houghton Mifflin Company the publishing house that issues a larger number of truly great literary works by American authors than any other house in the country; while the firm of Little, Brown and Company holds an honourable place in the development of our literature. Boston has, too, in D. C. Heath & Co. and in Ginn and Company text-book firms of commanding importance. One of the most prominent publishers of Chicago, writing in the year 1918 says: "Publishing in the west is attended by many difficulties. **The principal** book market is east of the Alleghenies, and the natural source of supply is the eastern cities." So, if from the standpoint of pure literature one should attempt a rearrangement of this table it would probably run relatively, New York, Boston, Philadelphia, and Chicago. St. Louis is a medical book publishing centre of importance, and San Francisco has some standing for her finely printed books. Cleveland, Louisville, Springfield (Mass.), St. Paul, and Indianapolis have firms of note.

Some of the most striking phases of publication within the last two decades are the increased stress upon juvenile literature,[1] the emphasis thrown upon a few best sellers by insistent

[1] Goodrich says that in 1827 juvenile literature received little consideration from the publishers (vol. ii, pp. 279–80), but he coincides with the writer of *The*

advertising and especially by the sales methods of department stores, the springing up of a large number of publishing firms connected with the best-known universities, and the appearance of small firms that turn out books, usually reprints, that strive to reach perfection in every detail that is conducive to beauty in the finished book. But according to the president of The Macmillan Company the most inclusive new feature of the century seems to be the tendency of our larger publishers to widen the class of their publications so as to include school, technical, and medical books. For in such books and in magazines rather than in miscellaneous publications seem to lie at present the surest financial rewards of the publisher.

New Literature (*Southern Literary Messenger*, April, 1854) in noting a marked emphasis upon it in the early fifties. [See, in this history, Book III, Chap. VII.]

CHAPTER XXX

The English Language in America

O N 22 February, 1917, the American Academy of Arts and Letters sat to consider its duty toward the English language in America. The published reports of the session proclaim its "academic" character in that nothing resembling a plan of action was proposed. It was less to be expected, perhaps, that no problem should be clearly formulated, but this may be accounted for partly by reason of the fact that much of the discussion turned not on the problem itself but on the duty of the Academy in the face of a problem of which everyone more or less definitely assumed the existence without attempting to state it, and partly because the company contained among many skilful users of the English language hardly more than one qualified to speak from any extended study of the problem, a lack which was expressly noted. It is not so surprising that to the mind of an assembly of this sort English as written was more constantly present than English as spoken. But from so many men of accomplishment in various forms of artistic expression there could hardly fail to emerge various points of view, prejudices, agreements and disagreements, which further discussion of the subject would do well to begin by taking into account.

To the reader of these proceedings it is made abundantly plain, taking what was said with what was implied, that in the minds of an overwhelming majority of the members, though not of all, the English language in America is in a very bad way. That this should have been their opinion might easily have been predicted. English is the most bewept of the tongues. From the days of Caxton its uncertain syntax, its perplexing variety of forms, its exotic and luxuriant vocabulary have brought distress to most of those who have taken thought of it. Compunctious visitings of an idealized Latinity have caused some to strive to regulate an apparent chaos, but all, or nearly all, to despair of stopping a heedless journey to destruction. Historically, the question turned first on matters of vocabulary, later on points of form and meaning, and at present, though the other questions are not forgotten, alarm is felt chiefly, as Henry James puts it, on account of "those influences around us that make for the imperfect disengagement of the human side of vowel sound, that make for the confused, the ugly, the flat, the thin, the mean, the helpless, that reduce articulation to an ignoble minimum . . . a mere helpless slobber of disconnected vowel noises." It is because of a growing slovenliness in uttering the unstressed vowels that the British poet-laureate, Robert Bridges, is inclined to believe that English pronunciation, even in Britain, is on the road to ruin.

It seems impossible for a student of language to refuse to be stampeded by these alarms, to maintain a certain serenity before so doleful a picture of things, pending some effort to assure himself that the picture is drawn to scale, without being accused in his turn of proclaiming with a sort of blatant cheerfulness that whatever is, linguistically, is right. Such extremes of optimism and pessimism are, of course, absurd. If they seem to exist, it must be because people are talking from different points of view about different sets of facts. To attempt to steer a rational middle course between these extremes, however, demands for its success some rehearsal of the facts. And at once, to show the existence of a middle ground, over against centuries of forebodings may be placed the fact that since Chaucer's day there has been continuously evolving, step by step with the widening experience of men, an English in which men of education everywhere in the far-flung English-speaking world could write and converse together in a way highly agreeable to any but a most inflexibly provincial taste. Amid much confusing detail it is as well not to lose sight of this central fact, that the thing we all are talking about exists. But where, and in what form?

Variety is of the essence of language. Uniformity and consistency are inventions of philosophical grammarians whose efforts are most successful when they deal with a language no longer used to satisfy elementary social needs. A living language is one of the *mores* of a social group; it is neither a biological growth unaffected by human intervention nor a work of art given its form for all time by a single act of human creation. Consequently it will vary within the group somewhat according to the variation in other respects to be found in the individuals comprising it, and between groups it will vary still more. Like other *mores* it will be subject to modification by time. But the necessity for mutual intelligibility within the group will greatly restrict the play of individual whim; between groups this force will operate somehow in proportion to the immediacy of their contacts. In a cultured city like ancient Rome or mediæval Florence a group of people might raise and maintain a literary standard around which literary people of other groups would rally. Or, again, a convenient dialect might be somewhat arbitrarily chosen for a particular literary task, as Luther chose the dialect of the Saxon chancellary for his translation of the Bible, and this dialect, with more or less conscious modification from time to time, might remain the standard literary language. In all these cases the great mass of people, not wholly uninfluenced by the literary language perhaps, would go on speaking their own dialects, just as the Romans did until their language of the street, of the camp, and of the provinces broke up into the larger groups, such as French, Spanish, and the rest, each containing within itself many smaller groups; or just as the Italians and the Germans have gone on speaking their dialects to the present day, learning their literary language as best they can besides.

The history of English is somewhat different from any of these. In origin, Modern English, as it appears everywhere in books and as it falls from the lips of the vast majority of speakers, is the dialect of a city, London. But unlike the case of Rome, there was at the outset presumably no great difference between the language of literature and the language of every day, and, unlike Florence, London was the chief city of a steadily unifying country. With the changing language of the city, its gradual loss of Southern, or Saxon, forms and its gradual acquirement of Northern, or Anglian, forms, the language of literature kept closely in touch. By the early sixteenth century, though details are shifting, the outlines of

Modern English are fairly clear. Then came a period of great expansion. The language was carried, farther than the Roman legionaries carried theirs, into the remotest parts of the world; it came to be spoken by more people than ever before in the history of the world could hold comfortable converse together. The really surprising thing is not that the result exhibits some variety but that, when the lapse of time afforded opportunity for, and indeed effected, so much change, when groups widely scattered might so easily have completely lost contact when there was so little external compulsion of any kind to keep even the literary language true to itself, there should have resulted a literary language that is almost uniform and a number of spoken dialects which never become unintelligible one to all the rest. In 1789 Noah Webster prophesied that there would develop, "in a course of time, a language in North America, as different from the future language of England, as modern Dutch, Danish, and Swedish are from German or from one another." When it was made this was not a foolish guess; all analogy supported it. That it has not come about, that every passing day adds to the unlikelihood of its realization, is one of the things that the observer of the ways of language thinks about when he is invited to be very miserable. Clearly, matters are not so bad as they quite easily might have been.

But this is speaking in the large. What of details? Excellence is largely a matter of details. A literary language "almost uniform"—why not entirely so? "A number of spoken dialects"—why any dialects at all? Confronted with a demand for perfect uniformity—one of our academicians very expressly makes it and deplores the fact that Americans use "back of" and "toward" and "spool of thread" instead of British "behind" and "towards" and "reel of cotton"—what can we say? Obviously, such a demand more nearly concerns the literary English of books than the vernacular of daily intercourse; no one seriously hopes to see us all regimented into speaking exactly alike. But even in the former case it is proper to ask not only how far uniformity may be possible, but also how far an absolute uniformity, as opposed to something fairly close to it, is really desirable. On what ground shall this agreement be effected? Few would now feel, as some did in

[1] *Dissertations*, pp. 22–23.

the early days of the Republic, that the dignity of the nation requires that it should have a language entirely its own.   More would be ready to assent to the implication of one of our academicians that American usage conform itself as far as possible to the practice of British writers.   It is an old notion; Franklin and Webster both gave reverent expression to it, but neither, it should be noted, made any special effort to live up to it, and Webster at other times professed quite a different ideal.   They made no more effort, that is, than any educated man does who allows his best reading to be reflected in his best writing.   The simple fact is that such differences as exist between English in America and English in Britain are not mainly due to ignorance or perversity.   The days are long past when the British reviewer branded as an "Americanism" every word and every construction which, during a period of enormous growth in the demands made upon the language, he could not remember having met with before.   Such differences as there are, it is now well recognized, are due to the historical evolution of the language.   It will be well to look at this for a moment before casting up the losses and gains and before pointing out a possible, indeed a very real, danger involved in attempting to alter too drastically the record with which history presents us.

The literary dialect of London never, as has been said, got wholly out of touch with the other dialects of the island. They continued to affect it in many ways; it was a "natural" growth in that it was not consciously regulated by groups of literary men in the way that German or French has been regulated.   In company with the British Constitution it muddled along, obtaining surprisingly good results, all things considered.   Of the spoken language, apart from many rustic dialects of a pedigree as honourable as it is ancient, there are at least two recognized standards in England, a Northern British and a Southern British, and, in addition, educated Scots and Irishmen and Welshmen have ways of speaking that are quite distinctly their own.   The farther one travels from London the less noticeable becomes the difference between British English and American.   If it be urged that the literary language is largely uniform throughout the British Isles—leaving out works that are frankly in dialect—this can in great part be accounted for by the fact that political and literary life centre in the great commercial city of London. But the varieties that characterize spoken English today were probably even greater—less subdued to a literary medium—in the seventeenth century when the language was transplanted to America. And American authors have seldom written with an eye to the London book market. It is not, therefore, surprising that the English in America, cut off from the British at home by an estranging sea and feeling for them an affectionate regard in about the same degree as it was accorded, should not have followed precisely the same lines of change. Some of the resulting differences it will help matters to glance at.

The early colonists in America brought their English with them. They were for the most part plain people and their language must have had all the characteristics of the several dialects which they spoke at home. How far their original dialectical peculiarities are reflected in later American speech it might be hard to determine; probably so far as the later educated speech goes, not much. But the old New England plural *housen*, *clever = good*, *mad = angry*, *I be, you be, they be*, *shet* (*shut*), *becase* (*because*), *sich* (*such*), *wrastle*, *mought* (*might*), *ax* (*ask*), *ketch* (*catch*),[1] *guess = suppose*, and many others more certainly came over in the *Mayflower* than much else reputed a part of that seemingly miraculous cargo. Some of these forms are not often heard today, though *guess* has become a sort of shibboleth.[2] If they were once more common, it should be remembered that the situation in America was not wholly unlike that of England after the Norman Conquest; with the relaxation of literary standards, dialect forms, no longer repressed, gained recognition they could not have had in conflict with a strong literary tradition.

But it is not chiefly here that we are to look for the causes of such differences as gradually separated American and British speech. New conditions of life, to be sure, called for new words: *wigwam, tomahawk, squaw, papoose, prairie, canyon,*

---

[1] *Ketch*, Spenser's form of the word, is, to many educated people, the only natural pronunciation, and *catch* a purely literary affectation. There is a certain pleasant irony in the fact that in the strictly analogous word *keg* it is the pronunciation *kag* that is regarded as a vulgarism.

[2] The real objection to such expressions as *guess* and *right away*, as to *quite so* and *I mean to say*, lies not in themselves but in their monotonous employment as catch-words.

and all the others that have become a part of the general stock of English. *Stores* in the Western world (the usage is not confined to the United States) really were stores and not shops. Our most common *corn* was maize, and it naturally became *corn* par excellence. *Fall* (*autumn*) and *rare* (*underdone*) are "Americanisms" only in the sense that they have retained a vitality here which even in England they have not wholly lost. Political life, sport, changed economic conditions, have all furnished the language with new words, or old words in new senses. The most striking differences, however, have come about, not through the retention of dialect words or the introduction of new words for new ideas, but because American English, in its comparative isolation, has not followed step by step the many changes that have occurred in British English since the seventeenth century. American English is in some respects archaic. It has never developed, for example, the swooping diphthongs that, since the end of the eighteenth century at least, have characterized the British pronunciation of *ē, ī, ō, ū,*[1] to represent which the British phoneticians write *say, be, boat,* and *do* [sei], [bij], [bout], [duw]. The American diphthongs, so far as they exist, are much less noticeable. The characteristic American unrounding of [o] to [a], *got, not* [gat], [nat], occurs in some of the British dialects and was an elegant affectation in the days of Charles II. The palatal *g* and *c* still sometimes heard in the Virginia pronunciation of *garden* and *card* (written "gyarden," "cyard") were held by many in eighteenth-century England to be the height of refinement. The old distinction between *hoarse* (vowel of *no*) and *horse* (vowel of *law*) is still preserved by many Americans, especially outside the Middle States. Elizabethan *gotten* and the old preterite *ate* are heard oftener in America than in Britain. Americans, indeed, look on a pronunciation "et" as vulgar. They have either never lost or have, for the most part, successfully recovered the ancient distinction between the voiceless initial in *which* and the voiced in *witch*, where the South Briton pronounces them both *witch*.

Finally, the so-called broad or Italian *a*, which began to be fashionable in England near the close of the eighteenth century, never established itself outside of New England and, to some

[1] In phonetic notation vowels should be given their Continental sounds.

extent, in Virginia, except in *father*, before *r* (*car, arm*), and somewhat uncertainly before *lm* (*calm, psalm*). The American, then, who pronounces *pass, dance, aunt*, with the vowel of *hand* does only what all the authorities before the last quarter of the eighteenth century told him to do, and what apparently everybody in England did do who wished to avoid an appearance of vulgarity.

Certain anomalous British forms, of comparatively recent origin, have never become established in America. The pronunciation of *wrath* as if *wroth*, and the occasional pronunciation of the latter with long ō, are seldom (one dare not say never) heard in America. *Wrath* (with the vowel of *law*) does not seem to be older than the end of the eighteenth century, and *wroth* (with the vowel of *no*) is a recent attempt to distinguish anew between the words. Another anomaly is *schedule*, commonly pronounced by the British with *sh*. The earlier pronunciation of this French word was *sedyul*, and it might have retained this pronunciation in spite of its classical spelling, just as *schism* has done. But the spelling suggests other classical analogies like *scholar* and *scheme*, and this pronunciation followed by American English seems to offer the only reasonable alternative to *sedyul*. What analogy the British pronunciation follows is not easy to see; one hesitates now to urge afresh the old suggestion that in this word, as in *schist*, the determining influence is German.

The pronunciation of *either, neither*, with the diphthong of *eye*, which is not recorded before the eighteenth century, has met with better reception in America. It was Franklin's pronunciation. But with many of the persons who use it it is a conscious affectation. The Elizabethan pronunciations, it may be noted, were "ayther," "nayther," just as the Irishman still says it, and "ether," "nether," to rhyme with *leather*. The ordinary American pronunciation is the representative of the former type; the latter seems to have left no modern descendants.

Besides being in some respects more conservative, American English has in still other respects grown apart from British English through following different analogies. The question how an English word shall be pronounced breaks up at once into a whole set of queries. Shall it be pronounced as a Latin word, a French word, or as a more or less domesticated form of either? What other word is it like? Shall the spelling be allowed full weight? In general, of two forms already in existence which shall be preferred? To such questions it is only to be expected that the two countries should in many instances make different responses.

British English frequently makes more effort to imitate a modern French pronunciation in *trait, chamois, turquoise, charade, imbecile,* and *vase,* where Americans frankly accept them as native words. It is, however, the French tradition rather than the Latin which Americans follow in preferring [i] to [ai] forms in the terminations *-ide,-ine,-itis,-ique.*

Dr. Johnson's spelling has undergone some simplification in both countries: *almanack, musick, errour, horrour, interiour, successour, emperour, oratour,* have everywhere dropped unnecessary letters. The abandonment of the French *-our* for Latin *-or* has gone a little further in the American printing-houses; *honour, humour, vigour, harbour, labour, neighbour, valour, clamour, clangour, saviour,* and a few others have joined the overwhelming majority of *-or* words. British men of letters could be cited who have employed the same simplification. Other French spellings like *theatre* and *centre* are less common in America than in England. Parallel to the simplification of *almanac(k)* are *wag(g)on, travel(l)er.* Of the British attempts to distinguish by the spelling *story,* narrative (plural *stories*), from *storey,* floor (pl. *storeys*), and *curb* (bit) from *kerb* (stone), the first has some etymological argument in its favour, but neither has commended itself to American usage. Britons themselves are quite as likely to spell *cider* and *pajamas* in the fashion always employed in America as they are to write *cyder* and *pyjamas.*[1]

The spelling book has exerted a powerful influence in America, where so many speakers have learned their language in the school and looked to it as a more compelling authority than the sometimes uncertain tradition of the home. The notion that all the letters of a word are entitled to a certain respect, reinforced by the native slowness of utterance, has led to the retention of unstressed vowels in *tapestry, medicine, venison,* and

[1] The spelling used in this chapter, as of this history in general, conforms ordinarily to British usage.

produced a secondary stress in such words as *secretary, extraordinary*. The eighteenth-century refinement of "dropping the *g*" in *going, seeing*, which still persists as a "smart" pronunciation in England, almost all Americans, though they use it oftener than they could be got to confess, would regard with horror because it violates what seems to them the obvious principle that all the letters should be pronounced. The same state of mind leads to the retention of *h* in *hotel, hostler*, reinforces the distinction between *w* and *wh*, and induces many to persist in pronouncing an *r* final and before consonants, in spite of the frankly expressed disgust even of their own countrymen of the East and South. *Figure* has lost its fine old pronunciation ("figger") for a spelling pronunciation "figyure." As for *lieutenant*, Coxe (1813, p. 36) notes that "*lef-tenant* prevails most generally, but *lew-tenant* appears to be becoming more popular"; spelling has now completely carried the day. Out of deference to spelling Americans pronounce a *g* in *physiognomy, recognizance*, and sometimes even in *suggest*.

Enough has been offered in support and illustration of the contention that the roots of American speech lie deep in history. The same might be done for less literary speech. Lowell established the antiquity of much in the Yankee dialect of his Hosea Biglow, and it is to be presumed that research, of which there has been far too little in this field, may establish the antiquity, if nothing more, of many other dialectical peculiarities.[1] There is not an oddity in the "coarse, uncouth dialect" of the Deerslayer and Hurry Harry (*The Deerslayer*, 1841) that has not its root deep in the soil of the eighteenth and preceding centuries.[2] Cooper has Noah Webster's own *creatur', ventur', f'erce. Sarpint, desarted, vartue, larned, s'ile, app'inted, expl'ite* can all be found recommended in grammars of the eighteenth century. *The Oxford Spelling Book* (1726) says that *sigh* is pronounced *sithe* "according to the common way of speaking," just as Natty Bumppo pronounces it. His *ven'son* is still good English. His *consait* (*conceit*), *ginerous, fri'nd, 'arth* sound Irish, but that is as much as to say that they belong to the old,

---

[1] For the literary use of American dialects see Book III, Chap. v.

[2] An interesting list of "vulgar errors" may be found in Elliot and Johnson's *A Selected Pronouncing and Accented Dictionary*, Suffield [Conn.], 1800, p. 16.

authentic vernacular; they cannot be made to serve as illustrations of any wanton perversity on the part of Americans.

But cannot all these historical reasons for American English being what it is be granted (and they pretty generally are) and still leave us facing a very desperate situation about which something should be done?   History, after all, brings no solution to the problem which it helps to define.   It does not furnish a standard, it can only show us the steps by which all present English has gone very badly astray.   But a standard is precisely what is wanted; lack of standard, our academy was quite persuaded, is what ails American English.   Enough has been said already to suggest the hopelessness of finding such a standard in literary South British.   Just what sort of folly that leads to may be seen in the case of the academician who lamented that Americans wrote *toward* when an Englishman, "following the established usage of prose," wrote *towards*.   *Towards* is not the established usage of prose, and quite as many Englishmen write *toward* as *towards*.   All that the academician can mean is that he personally prefers *towards*.   No one could deny him the privilege of choosing, but no one would attach the slightest significance to his choice either way.   Much the same can be said of most of the differences of detail between literary English in America and the same thing in England; they are too trivial to be worth much trouble in trying to remove them.

But even the attempt to remove these peculiarities of American English in deference to some standard outside itself may work harm vastly greater than it is proposed to help.   If English had remained the literary language of a small homogeneous group, who like the Athenians could consent instantly in the pleasure of jeering a misplaced accent, the single and precise kind of standard which some critics of English seem to have in mind might have been successfully applied to it. But English has become the common possession of many scattered peoples.   It is quite possible that this involves some sacrifice with some gain.   English can hardly become the adequate expression of so varied a human experience, the medium of so many diverse men, without losing something in the direction of perfect uniformity as against its gains in range. This expansion has its too evident dangers, but to try to correct them by a single narrow standard is not only impossible; it is harmful in its results just so far as it breeds in the mind of speakers and writers an uneasy feeling that really good English is something vaguely and beautifully beyond them, something they can never hope to attain to, something so high and delicate that they would not care to use it if they could get it, certainly not for even the best moments of every day.

This brings us to the very centre of the problem. The trouble with American English, it might reasonably be urged, is that it has been so constantly disparaged in comparison with a standard so vague, so remote, so "superior," but of so little practical guidance, that the fine sense of possession, the feeling that the way one goes about one's *mores* is inevitably the right way, has been in many cases completely lost. "I say 'dawg,'" said an American teacher of English, "but I know 'dahg' is correct and I make my pupils say it." We can be sure that her pupils do not say "dahg" outside the classroom, and carry away with them only a conviction that "good English" is something with which they can and will have nothing to do.

"All this is very different in English English," says another of our academicians. "They believe in English and have the ideal of good usage." But the standard, it should be noted, is a native standard; it is fairly well defined; it is not impossible of attainment; and it is not flagrantly at variance with the practice of the linguistic environment in which the fortunate young Britisher is being fitted by governesses, tutors, and public-school masters to take his place. Conditions so favourable must be somewhat limited in their occurrence even in England. In America those who inherit a sound native tradition in their homes are more than likely to spend large parts of their lives in regions of quite other language habits. In school they will encounter many who have been brought up in an environment distinctly foreign, the teacher even may have an unsure control of the language, and he—or more generally she—is sure to have some very extravagant and ill-informed notions of what constitutes good English. In the university they may learn a good deal about correctness in composition but will encounter no very definite standards of speech, for both teachers and students are usually drawn from all parts of the country and represent every sort of social opportunity.

All this sounds much worse than it actually turns out to be.

For English is the authentic speech of free peoples and it is endowed with an innate energy for getting along, going into strange places on strange errands, but never quite losing its sense of identity.   It breeds surprisingly true, in the main, even amid the most unpromising conditions.   Franklin, the cosmopolitan, said "air" for *are;* "hev" and "hez"; sounded the *l* in *would* and *calm,* and in the latter used the vowel of *hat;* uttered *new* with the vowel of *too,* and *bosom* as who should write "buzzum." Noah Webster, father of American lexicography, advocated the pronunciations "creatur," "natur," "raptur"; *angel* with the vowel of *hat, chamber* with that of *father; fierce* and *pierce* were to rhyme with *verse, beard* with *third,* and *deaf* with *thief;* the present pronunciation of *heard* and *wound* he regarded as new and objectionable.   With such a start what might not American English have become?   Without any external compulsion, without any very clearly expressed ideals, however, American English has kept pace step by step in these particulars with the development of British English.

The problem of American English resides, then, not in its differences from British English, nor yet in its own infinite variety—here history is both enlightening and consoling—but in the attitude which it adopts toward itself.   It is not as good as it might be—no language is so in its entirety, because people are not so wise and well-bred, so sensitively in touch with the best of literature and of life as they might be—but to make itself better it has no reasonable standards to look to.   It has held up to it silly ideals, impossible ideals, ignorant dogmatisms, and for the most part it wisely repudiates them all. But in so doing it is left with a diminished self-respect.   Excellence is not for it.   Why bother about the impossible? We shall get along.   Not thus, however, is bred that subtle atmosphere of linguistic authenticity, the inevitableness of the thing rightly said, which is the peasant's by inheritance and to which the man of letters attains by giving his toilsome nights to much else beside Addison.   The great mass of men lies between, the many who write and are not great writers, the many who talk not so well as they might; where in irritation and bewilderment may they look?

"All this is very different in English English."   Here, quite possibly, is a hint of some value.   One can hardly

suppose that there is any very determined effort to make
Scottish boys and girls acquire what Arnold Bennett calls a
Kensingtonian accent. There is a distinct and well recognized
standard of North British, as well as South British. American
English has a history that entitles it to consideration. It has
certain peculiarities of vocabulary. Let them be kept; half
of them will be adopted by the rest of the English-speaking
world, the other half will be liked by them if the American who
uses them is otherwise likable, and above all if he uses them as
if they were authentically his. The well of English has never
mistaken increase for defilement. The American is traditionally supposed to have a "nasal twang." If any allow air to
leak through the nasal passage when it should be closed (a
characteristic of unrefined English outside of America); if any
speak with a certain constriction of the muscles of the nose
and upper lip, with a certain shrillness and thinness of voice
(and many do), let them be taught not to do it. That is something worth making a fight for. But let them not give up the
cool, deliberate, level tone, with half a laugh in it, which shall
be the mark of the American in whatever part of the world
his destiny calls him. Let his restrained speech keep to the
unemphatic forms of the verb *to be* which it has instinctively
preferred. *Were* ("wear") and *been* ("bean") are emphatic
forms that sort well with the highly energized speech of South
Britain, with its sudden changes of speed and pitch, its great
expenditure of breath.

American English is not uniform. But neither is British
English uniform. Only a dead language, or the language of a
highly centralized country, or a more or less artificial literary
language, can approach uniformity. But American English
falls into clearly recognizable groups that are not too many to
handle in the sensible way in which the British regard the several
types of English of their own islands. By all means recognize
an English of New England, an English of the Middle States,
of the South, and of the West. To attempt to harmonize them
in an impossible unity is only to confirm them in their several
peculiarities. It would be wiser to direct the attack against
those peculiarities which are a little too peculiar. If the New
Englander shortens his long *o*'s, if the New Yorker confuses
voice and *verse* in an absurd diphthong that both misleads and

offends, if the Southerner loops and curls the diphthong of *cow*, if the Westerner in pronouncing *r* retorts the tongue so far back upon itself that no clear vowel can be made before it, each can be told, with some hope of affecting both his belief and his practice, that such extremes have no appropriateness, are not indulged in, indeed, by the best speakers of his own region. If many Americans tend to lengthen the vowel in *frost* and *long*, that is something that can be effectively discouraged without resorting to the equally objectionable extreme of saying "frahst" and "lahng." But it is just as useless to tell a Westerner that he must not use an *r* as to tell a New Englander that he must furnish himself with one.

It is, then, not a question of one standard that does not exist against no standards at all; it is a question of sensibly recognizing several standards that do exist and making the best of them, criticizing the language of each main group according to its own standard, and not on grounds of right and wrong but on grounds of what may be regarded as appropriate. The peasant and the pedant, though one talks like a man and the other like a book, are alike in that each speaks his language in only one way; the educated man knows and employs his language in three or four ways. He has only an enlightened sense of appropriateness to guide him. But it is enough.

How to get such a sense of appropriateness widely diffused among people of widely various opportunities, is the problem of American English. It is a serious problem. With Italian-American, Yiddish-American, Scandinavian-American, German-American yammering in our ears, it is not a time for academicians to regret that we write *toward* and not *towards*, or for teachers of "oral" English to endeavour to make broad our *a*'s. Such scribal pharisaism, if it were harmless, would be amusing. But it is chiefly owing to such folly that sound and reasonable standards for American English have never come into recognition. What is needed is some knowledge of the facts, a willingness to face them with a sympathetic and rational criticism, and above all a belief that life as lived in America has a value and an atmosphere of its own. It is distinctly to be desired that British authors should write *whilst* and *different to;* we rejoice when the hero begins his dinner with "an" oyster, talks about "coals," takes "in" the *Times*, says "directly" and "expect,"[1] and knows exactly what he means when he says "sick" and "bug," or rather knows exactly why he does not say them. We should be "very disappointed" if he did not do these things; it is all part of the British atmosphere; it goes with the very smell of the book. These things are not good or bad, right or wrong, in themselves; they are merely appropriate, or the reverse. And Americans will generally speak well when they are taught to look for the best in the speech of their neighbours, pruning the more luxuriant growths of dialect and tempering their speech in the glowing heat of the common literary tradition; no longer reluctant to speak well because "good" English is unnatural and unattainable, but conscious that a really good English, such as the world will value according to their worth as individuals and as a nation, is their rightful heritage to enter upon and enjoy.

Great things have been expected of American English in the past. A Frenchman, Roland de la Platière (1791), saw in America, a land so fortunately situated, so happily governed, with a people so constituted that they "fraternized with the universe" and presumably to be trusted to benefit by association with the primitive virtues of Indians and negroes, the country which was most likely to develop its speech into a universal language. Whitman, in the notes published as *An American Primer*, dug deep in the recesses of language for a word-hoard that should be distinctly American, and rolled the aboriginal names—Monongahela—with venison richness upon his palate. He saw an America cleared of all names that smack of Europe, an American vocabulary enriched with many words not in the print of dictionaries.

American writers are to show far more freedom in the use of words. . . . Ten thousand native idiomatic words are growing, or are today already grown, out of which vast numbers could be used by American writers, with meaning and effect—words that would be welcomed by the nation, being of the national blood— words that would give that taste of identity and locality which is so dear in literature.

No such drastic Americanization of the language as was prophesied has come to pass, or is likely to come to pass. The

[1] In the senses of *as soon as* and *suppose*, not unheard, indeed, in America.

old dream of an America *penitùs divisa* was grievously troubled
at Manila Bay and ended for ever at Château Thierry.   A literary America apart was never even a possibility.   Hencefor.
ward there is less excuse—if there ever was any—for emphasizing differences merely as differences.   The burden of this
chapter has been to crave a certain intelligent respect for what
exists.   And it is directed mainly, perhaps, at the theorizings
of men of letters, of all amateur critics of language, and at the
practice of most school teachers, who so peculiarly hold the
destinies of American speech in their hands.   American writers
have generally been bold enough.   Emerson, Whitman, Mark
Twain—but that is the subject of this whole work and needs
no recapitulation in a final chapter.   The wish to see things
afresh and for himself is indeed so characteristic of the American that neither in his speech nor his most considered writing
does he need any urging to seek out ways of his own.   He
refuses to carry on his verbal traffic with the well-worn coun-
ters; he will always be new-minting them.   He is on the lookout for words that say something; he has "a sort of remorseless
and scientific efficiency in the choice of epithets," which the hy-
percritical authors of the "King's English" ascribe to Kipling,
who is "americanizing us."   The American's slang is not made
up of words that look like words, as is the case with much British slang, but words that are things, images; grotesque, preposterous, perhaps, but born of a quick fancy.   He has an
Elizabethan love of exuberant language.   The highfalutin'
spread-eagleism of the old-fashioned Fourth of July oration, the
epistolary style of Lorenzo Altisonant in his *Letters of Squire
Pedant*, who "merged his plumous implement of chirography
into the atramented fluid," the sort of polysyllabic eloquence
of which Holmes and Lowell made such excellent fun, now
linger perhaps only in the columns of the rural weekly newspaper and in a Congressional speech which is delivered to be
heard a long way off.

There is in this view of the American speech a good deal of
carefully cherished tradition.   No American writer has perhaps played with words as daringly as Meredith or expressed
himself as whimsically as Carlyle.   There is in American speech
and writing a good deal of timidity, as well as audacity, quite
as much colourlessness as picturesqueness.   A British critic

wrote somewhere the other day of the "whitey-brown" style of American college professors. Such a charge is not directed against too great linguistic daring. A lack of pith, of raciness, an insecure hold on idiom in some of its more slippery turns might very properly be remarked in not a little American writing; in short, an anxiety to play safe in a dangerous game. There is nothing unnatural in an association of boldness and timidity. Both, however, represent excess. The discovery of the mean is the problem, and that will move toward a solution as the standards which express it are more zealously and intelligently sought within the history and present practice of American English itself.

CHAPTER XXXI

Non-English Writings I

GERMAN, FRENCH, YIDDISH[1]

I. German

THE memoirs, poems, and essays, the books of travel, fiction, and science that have been written in the German language in the United States, are of greater historical than literary interest. Their value consists in their record of human experience, mainly that of pioneers whose labours were devoted to the present, whose hopes lay in the future, yet whose meditations lingered fondly with the past. Three periods can readily be distinguished: that of the eighteenth century, in which religious writing predominated; that of the nineteenth century before 1860, the period of political idealism; and lastly, continuous from 1860, what may be called the period of opportunity. The two later periods in many instances overlap.

The name Francis Daniel Pastorius (1651–1719) begins the literary as well as the historical annals of the Germans in America. Pastorius, in 1683 founder of the first German settlement at Germantown, Pennsylvania, was a thorough scholar, a university man, trained in theology and law. Mortified that Latin provided a very inadequate preparation for the pioneer, he turned into service even the meanest of his accomplishments, his clean and stately handwriting, which appears in most of the documents of the new colony and most nobly in the first public

[1] The language of the people of the United States has been English even more prevailingly than their institutions and their culture. Practically every written tongue, however, is represented by newspapers designed for the use and pleasure of the various language-groups among Americans, although only German, French, and Yiddish may be said to show something like a special literature of their own.—THE EDITORS.

protest against negro slavery on record in America, made by the German Quakers of Germantown in 1688. Pastorius's familiarity with ancient and modern languages is seen in his *Hive or Beestock* (*Bienenstock, Melliotrophium*), his scrap-book of encyclopædic learning, in which historical, statistical, and geographical materials are mingled with epigrams and verses in many languages. More valuable is his description of Pennsylvania (*Umständige geographische Beschreibung der zu allerletzt erfundenen Provintz Pennsylvania, etc.*), a collection of letters and reports sent to his father and published by the latter in book form.[1] The manuscript verse-collections, *Voluptates Apianæ* and *Deliciæ Hortenses* reveal Pastorius as a cultivator of bees and flowers. "He who never has a garden, and knows naught of flowers, and never looks back into the earthly paradise,—he is but a slave and serf of the plough, and is accursed," said Pastorius the teacher, caring not solely for the progress of his pupils in the three R's or even in Latin, and fearing the engrossing materialism of the pioneer's existence.

Contemporary with Pastorius, most quaint and curious, are the odes and theosophical writings of John Kelpius and his mystic brotherhood, called *The Woman in the Wilderness.* Yet more impressive still is their act of awaiting in the American forest the end of the world, forecast to come at the close of the century by the mystic astronomer Zimmermann, who died on the eve of embarkation for the New World in 1693. No hermit in the African desert was ever more sincere in his flight from the world's temptations or more devout in his communion with the Divine Spirit than Kelpius in his dingy cavern by the banks of the Wissahickon, then beyond the area of settlement. His anxious soul, shedding a mystic brightness upon the gloom of the wilderness, long pleaded in vain to be released from the bonds of the flesh:

> Tormenting love, O sweetest pain, delay,
> O delay not longer the blessed day!
> Speed on the time, let the hour come!
> Remember the covenant graciously sealed,
> In faith, to the whole world be it revealed![2]

[1] See Bibliography.
[2] Ode IX. *Ein verliebtes Girren der trostlosen Seele in der Morgendämmerung.*

There followed the hymns of the monks and nuns of the Ephrata cloister, led by Conrad Beissel, the seceding Dunker. His monastery, near the Cocalico in Lancaster County, Pennsylvania, remains to this day the most interesting architectural relic of eighteenth-century sectarianism. Beissel wrote a treatise on harmony, the first crude attempt made in America to compose sacred music, a quarter of a century before William Billings published his *New England Psalm Singer*. The chorus singing of the brothers and sisters at Ephrata was well reputed in colonial times, visitors commenting on "the impressive cadence of the chorals and hymns of the combined choirs," and "the peculiar sweetness and weird beauty of the song of the sisterhood." Hymn books were printed for them by Franklin in 1730, 1732, and 1736, by Saur in 1739, and subsequently by their own Ephrata press, the most complete edition being that of 1766, entitled *Das Paradisische Wunderspiel*. The hymn book of 1739 (*Zionitischer Weyrauch-Hügel oder Myrrhen-Berg*) had already been a stupendous collection consisting of 654 songs and an appendix with 38 more, 820 pages in all. The edition of 1766 was even larger, with 441 songs by Beissel alone, and an equal number by others, divided into songs by the brothers, the sisters, and the laity. All were asserted to have been written in America for the Ephrata monastery, though the models for them can be found in the German hymns of the seventeenth century. The theme of the amorous soul awaiting the coming bridegroom, and the rhetoric of the sentimental pastorals of the Silesian poets, reappear in these crude though well-intentioned lyrical effusions. Many other collections were published, as the hymns of the Schwenkfelders, Moravians, and of other sects or individuals, but in form and content not differing essentially from the types described.

The most noted German press during colonial times was that of Christopher Saur, established in 1738 and continuing for forty years, the son of the same name succeeding his father. In the first year there appeared a High German Calendar, which became a very popular and useful institution, published annually. The greatest achievement of the Saur press was the Lutheran Bible, both Testaments complete, issued in 1743.[1] As the preface stated, this was the first time in the Western

[1] See also Book III, Chap. xxix.

Hemisphere that the Scriptures had been printed in a European language; the Bible of John Eliot (Cambridge, 1661–1663) had been a translation and adaptation in the language of one of the North American Indian tribes. Saur's Bible, containing 1272 pages, was printed in quarto form, on paper manufactured in Germantown and with German types imported from Frankfort-on-the-Main. The second edition appeared in 1763, and a third in 1776. Saur also printed the New Testament and Psalter in separate editions, a large number of hymn-books for various sects, and some hundred and fifty books and pamphlets on a variety of subjects. His most influential serial publication was his newspaper, *Der Hoch-Deutsch Pennsylvanische Geschicht-Schreiber, oder Sammlung wichtiger Nachrichten aus dem Natur- und Kirchen-Reich*, at first a monthly, finally a weekly. The changes in the title to *Berichte*, and to *Sammlung "wahrscheinlicher" Nachrichten*, bear witness to Saur's sense of responsibility and his love of truth. In 1753 the paper had four thousand readers, spread over all the areas of German settlements, from Pennsylvania to Georgia.

The only worthy rival of Saur's Germantown newspaper was that published by Henry Miller in Philadelphia, *Der Wöchentliche Philadelphische Staatsbote*, founded in 1762 and continuing to 1779. Miller had had an exceptionally wide experience in Europe, having plied his trade in Hamburg, Basel, Paris, and London, and sojourned and laboured in numerous other European centres. Naturally his horizon was larger, and his attitude more objective and progressive than could be expected of the younger Saur, whose views were narrowed by provincial and sectarian conditions, in which he had spent all his life. Nevertheless the personality of Saur, as it appears in his paper, was more impressive, his manner more intensely serious, his attitude toward the daily life and customs of the Pennsylvania German farmers more deeply sympathetic. Being the conservative guardian of their language and religion, he opposed the free public schools as too powerful an assimilating agent; being a member of the non-resistant Dunker sect and the spokesman for the sectarian doctrines in general, he was, when the revolutionary agitation arose, a pacifist, though not a Tory. Henry Miller, on the other hand, was from the beginning an aggressive agitator for the cause of independence and armed resistance, as he had been an earnest advocate of the free public schools. His paper circulated not among the sectarians, but among the much larger bodies of Lutheran, Reformed, and Moravian Germans of Pennsylvania and neighbouring colonies. During the stormy period preceding the Revolution Miller's *Staatsbote* was unquestionably by far the most influential German newspaper, while Saur's *Germantowner Zeitung* de-~lined hopelessly.

As many as thirty-eight newspapers printed in the German language appeared between the years 1732 and 1801. Many of them had a very short life, among them the first attempt, the fortnightly *Philadelphische Zeitung*, a German edition of Benjamin Franklin's *Pennsylvania Gazette*. Copies of twenty-five of the thirty-eight German newspapers of the eighteenth century have come down to us, and of the six most important among them an abundant supply has survived to testify to their character and circulation. Of Saur's paper about 350 issues are available, between 1739 and 1777; of Miller's *Staatsbote* about 900, published between 1762 and 1779; of the *Philadelphische Correspondenz* more than 950, between 1781 and 1800; of the *Germantauner Zeitung* (not Saur's) 246, between 1785 and 1793; of the *Neue Unpartheyische Lancäster Zeitung* 465, between 1787 and 1800; of the *Neue Unpartheyische Readinger Zeitung* about 600, between 1789 and 1800. To this list of leading papers there should be added one born very near the end of the century, the *Reading Adler*, which lasted for more than a century, from 1796 to 1917, and of which complete files exist.[1]

Postbellum newspapers in German were more numerous than German papers before 1780, and especially toward the end of the century, during the party strife between Federalists and Republicans, was there an acceleration of newspaper production in the German language. *Facile princeps* among them was the *Philadelphische Correspondenz*, established in 1781. It lived for more than thirty years, though with many vicissitudes. Its best period was the first decade of its career, when its publisher, Steiner, secured as editors the two Lutheran ministers the Rev. J. C. Kunze and the Rev. J. H. C. Helmuth,

---

[1] The statistics in the above paragraph are taken from the investigations of James O. Knauss. See Bibliography.

also well known as professors at the Philadelphia Academy, the parent of the University of Pennsylvania. In 1782 English papers published translations from its news columns, and in 1788 the paper had a considerable number of readers in Germany, facts which support the reputation of the editors Kunze and Helmuth for having established a good news service, and for having written the paper in a good German style, which the native German recognized as his own language.

To the literature of the eighteenth century belong the extensive reports and letters by Lutheran ministers in America to the church's fathers at home. Thus the *Hallesche Nachrichten*, addressed to the Lutheran ministerium in Halle, carefully written with minute details by the Rev. Heinrich Melchior Mühlenberg, patriarch of the Lutheran church in America, and by other Lutheran ministers, give us an authentic picture not only of the beginnings and growth of the Lutheran Church in America but also of pioneer conditions in many of the colonies. Similarly the *Urlsperger Nachrichten*, addressed to the Rev. Dr. Samuel Urlsperger at Augsburg, give us an intimate view of the Salzburgers of Georgia and the beginnings of the Lutheran church in the South. The *Diaries of Moravian Missionaries* (Brothers Schnell, Gottschalk, and Spangenberg), who visited the frontier settlements, travelling mostly on foot, from Western Pennsylvania, to the Valley of Virginia, and through trackless wastes to the western settlements of North Carolina, thence to the coast, in 1743–1748, are a wonderful record of modest courage and splendid sacrifice. Dark in colouring is the picture drawn by Gottlieb Mittelberger in his *Reise nach Pennsylvanien im Jahr 1750 und Rückreise 1754*, in which the misfortunes of immigrants on the sea and their slavery on land is painted with terrifying realism. More judicial is Achenwall in his *Anmerkungen über Nordamerika* (1769), or J. D. Schöpf in his *Reise durch einige der mittlern und südlichen vereinigten Staaten . . . in den Jahren 1783 und 1784*. Very interesting are the letters of Hessian soldiers, who fought for the English king, found in Eelking, Schlözer's *Briefwechsel*, and elsewhere,[1] or the letters of the Baroness von Riedesel, the wife of the Brunswick general who was captured with Burgoyne at Saratoga. Her letters describe the whole of the disastrous British cam-

[1] See Bibliography.

paign, and subsequent to that the journey from Canada to Virginia, and thence several times back and forth to New York in the expectation of release from captivity. Among the mercenary soldiers stationed in Canada was the German poet J. G. Seume, who had been kidnapped by recruiting officers and forced into foreign military service against his will. Seume's autobiography, *Mein Leben*, records his experiences in America closing with 1784, and many of his best poems were inspired during this period, among them the ballad *Der Wilde*, which contains the oft-quoted phrase *Europas übertünchte Höflichkeit*, in antithesis to the blunt simplicity but genuine hospitality of nature's children.

Newspapers in the German language declined in quality in the early nineteenth century until the coming of the political refugees of the thirties and forties, when increasing numbers of German immigrants created a demand for newspapers in their own language. Among the early foundations which extended their influence beyond the close of the nineteenth century were the *New Yorker Staats-Zeitung*, founded in 1834; the *Anzeiger des Westens* (St. Louis), in 1835; and the *Cincinnati Volksblatt*, in 1836. The years succeeding the German revolution of 1848–1849 brought a large number of liberal leaders to the United States, who founded new journals or infused new life into the old, and aided in shaping public opinion in favour of abolition and union.

German travellers in the United States became more frequent in the second decade of the nineteenth century, and their books and stories were instrumental in accelerating and directing the tide of German immigration. Thus Duden's *Berichte über eine Reise nach den westlichen Staaten Nordamerikas und einen mehrjährigen Aufenthalt am Missouri, 1824–27*, started the great mass of German settlements on both banks of the Missouri River. Subsequently pamphlets and books on Texas and Wisconsin directed immigration to those states. To the travel literature[1] of the earlier periods belong the books of Fürstenwärther (1818), Gall (1822), Bernhard von Sachsen Weimar (1828), Duden (1829, etc.), Von Raumer (1845) Büttner (1845), Löher (1847), Fröbel (1853–58), and Busch (1854). Since then a host of others have appeared, ranging

[1] See Bibliography for titles.

from the scientific and critical works of Ratzel (*Kultur-geographie der Vereinigten Staaten*), Polenz (*Das Land der Zukunft*), Goldberger (*Das Land der unbegrenzten Möglichkeiten*), von Skal (*Das amerikanische Volk*), to the popular pictorial books of Karl Knortz and Rudolf Cronau.

Contemporaneous with travel literature and the ever present *Ratgeber*, or counsellor for immigrants, there appeared a growing array of romances and literary sketches by German writers who had travelled in America, by some also who had not. The latter were severely critical, as Kürnberger in his *Amerikamüde* (1855), a title antithetic to Willkomm's *Europamüde* (1838), with a plot based in part on the poet Lenau's unfortunate experiences in America. The former placed a romantic halo about life in the New World, painting the noble red man in the manner of Chateaubriand and Cooper, and portraying types of frontier and pioneer life that compare not unfavourably with what was done in this department by American writers. Foremost among them was the Austrian Charles Sealsfield ("Karl Postl"), proud to call himself "Bürger von Nordamerika," who held up to view virile, reckless, self-reliant types of American manhood as objects for emulation to enthralled Europeans. Longfellow was especially fond of Sealsfield's depictions of the Red River country and its Creole inhabitants. The *Cabin Book* (*Das Cajütenbuch*) has for its historical setting the Texan war of independence against Mexican misrule. *Morton oder die grosse Tour* presents a view of Stephen Girard's money-power and personal eccentricities. *Lebensbilder aus der westlichen Hemisphäre* introduces the lure of pioneer life, with its gallery of Southern planters, hot-tempered Kentuckians, Eastern belles and dandies, alcaldes, squatters and desperadoes, American types as they appeared between 1820–1840. Sealsfield's Mexican stories (*Virey*, *Nord und Süd*) contain nature pictures in wonderful colours, a striking instance of which is found also in the *Cabin Book*, in the chapter called "The Prairie of St. Jacinto."

Second to Sealsfield is Friedrich Gerstäcker, a great traveller and hunter in both North and South America. Ready to take up his gun and depend upon it for his daily subsistence where nature was wildest and game most plentiful anywhere from the Missouri to the Amazon and beyond, he spent many years roaming about aimlessly before he discovered his ability with the pen. He found friends interested in his *Streif und Jagdzüge durch die Vereinigten Staaten Nordamerikas* (1844), and he turned to fiction. There followed rapidly upon one another *Die Regulatoren von Arkansas* (*1845*); *Die Flusspiraten des Mississippi*, and other Mississippi pictures (1847–1848); *Gold, Ein Californisches Lebensbild* (*1856*)—all blending fiction and actual experience. His most popular work and in many respects his best, *Nach Amerika! Ein Volksbuch* (1855), describes the fortunes of a shipload of German immigrants landing at New Orleans and making their way up the Mississippi for permanent settlement. Industry and honesty, after learning to adapt themselves to new conditions, succeed in Gerstäcker's works, while unsteady character and indolence are given stern justice. Gerstäcker cannot be accused of arousing false hopes, for he draws with a realistic pen, and does not fail to emphasize the hardships and disappointments of frontier life. His heart is with the immigrant rather than with the older settler, against whom he warns repeatedly. Similarly Otto Ruppius in his *Der Pedlar* (1857) and its sequel *Das Vermächtnis des Pedlars* (1859) aims to give a just view of the German immigrant and refugee in America, and his books deserved their popularity. Friedrich Strubberg, who wrote under the pen-name Armand, was a voluminous writer whose best works are those descriptive of the German frontier settlements in Texas, e. g. *Friedrichsburg, die Kolonie des deutschen Fürstenvereins in Texas* (1867), for he had lived there for many years, on the vanguard of civilization. His *Carl Scharnhorst, Abenteuer eines deutschen Knaben in Amerika* (1863) remains one of the most popular German stories for boys, while many of his other works stray widely in the realm of fiction without Baron Münchhausen's saving grace of humour. Balduin Möllhausen, the last of the popular writers of exotic romances, was employed on several United States Government exploring expeditions in the Far West as artist and topographer, and during this time he learned to know the Western Indians well and became an authority on the physiography of sparsely settled areas. His first account of his travels in 1858 was introduced by Alexander von Humboldt, his second, three years later, was also of scientific merit, *Reisen in die Felsengebirge Nord Amer-*

ikas bis zum Hoch-Plateau von Neu-Mexiko. Then he turned to fiction, fully able to give his countless stories a setting in Western American life but handicapped by a fatal facility both in sketching characters and weaving entertaining plots. *The Halbindianer*, his first novel, compares favourably with his later work. *Die Familie Neville* is a three-volume novel with the background of the Civil War. *Das Mormonenmädchen* (1864) was a timely warning for European girls against the practices of Mormon missionaries in Germany and Switzerland before governments intervened.

Throughout the nineteenth century a great mass of lyrics were written by cultivated Germans in the United States. They are scattered in journals and booklets and have only in part become accessible in anthologies.[1] They sang the praises of America, her political freedom, resources, and natural beauties; they also voiced a love of the German mother-tongue, the language of poetry. To the rich and abundant harvest of song in German literature they contributed nothing new, except it be an occasional note of homesickness, the melancholy of expatriation. The following may serve as illustrations: Franz Lieber (*Der Niagara*), K. H. Schnauffer (*Turnermarsch*), E. Dorsch (*Californien*, 1849), J. Dresel (*Auswanderers Schicksal*), J. Gugler (*Vaterlandslos*), H. A. Rattermann ("Reimmund," *Aphorismen und Agrionien*), Konrad Krez (*An mein Vaterland*, the best of the songs of this type), B. Brühl ("Kara Giorg," *Poesien des Urwalds*), T. Kirchoff (*California, Das Stille Meer*), F. C. Castelhuhn (*Zweihundertjährige Jubelfeier der deutschen Einwanderung, den 6. Oktober*, 1883). Recent contributors, and more modern in spirit are: Martin Drescher (*Gedichte*), Fernande Richter ("Edna Fern," *Gedichte und Erzählungen*), Konrad Nies (*Funken Auswestlichen Weiten*), a master of form, though not surpassing G. S. Viereck, whose poems (*Niniveh und andre Gedichte*) and prose works (*The House of the Vampire, A Game of Love and other Plays*, etc.) were well rendered into English by himself.

Excellent translations of American authors were furnished by the poet Udo Brachvogel, who translated the works of Bret Harte and Aldrich; by Franz Siller, of Longfellow's poems; by Eduard Leyh, of Joaquin Miller's *Arizonian*. Some original dramas performed in German theatres of this country were

Udo Brachvogel's *Narciss;* E. A. Zündt's *Jugurtha;* Mathilde
Giesler-Anneke's *Oithono;* P. J. Reusz's *Tippo Saib, and others;*
K. Lorenz's *Das Schandmal* (a tragedy based on Hawthorne's
Scarlet Letter); V. Precht's *Jakob Leisler;* A. Schafmeyer's
Ehrliche Menschen; Wilhelm Müller's *Festspiel, Im gelobten
Lande Amerika*, and *Ein lateinischer Bauer.*

Among writers of novels Reinhold Solger gave great promise in his *Anton in Amerika*, but an early death ended his
career. L. A. Wollenweber, for a long time editor of the
Philadelphia Demokrat, wrote sketches of Pennsylvania German life. Udo Brachvogel's *König Korn* is a picture of Western farm life. Mediocre sketches such as those of Stürenburg
(*Klein Deutschland*) or J. Rittig (*Federzeichnungen aus dem ameri-
kanischen Stadtleben*) appeared in great numbers. Max Arlberg
wrote a socialistic novel called *Joseph Freifeld.* R. Puchner's
Anna Ruland and H. Bertsch's *Die Geschwister*, or *Bob der Son-
derling*, are worthy of mention in a list that might be prolonged.
Among very recent works Bernhard Kellermann's *Der Tunnel*
(1913), a fantastic dream of tunnelling the Atlantic, seems to
indicate some experience or residence in the United States.

The distinction of having been the master of German prose
in America belongs to the brilliant Robert Reitzel (1849–1898).
He is of the type of the lyrical poets and essayists who arose
in Germany during the eighties, like the brothers Hart, Arno
Holz, and Karl Henckell, the last of whom Reitzel often mentions as his personal friend. Like these modern "Stu mer und
Dränger," Reitzel defies arbitrary power, loves truth even to
a pose; he is the herald of a new socialistic age, a spokesman
for the submerged class, the proletariat. Yet the most fascinating subject of his clear and sparkling prose is his own ego-
centric personality, a characteristic of the poet Heine, whose
influence upon Reitzel is obvious. Reitzel's self-portraiture is
seen to best advantage in his *Abenteuer eines Grünen*, the story
of his life, including his initial hardships in America, when the
grinding wheel of fortune made a tramp of him. But even as
an outcast he keenly felt the poetry of existence:

> Ich lobe mir das Leben,
> juhei! als Vagabund,
> Mich drücken keine Sorgen;
> Frei bin ich alle Stund;

Die Erde ist mein Lager,
Der Himmel ist mein Dach,
Und mit den Vög'lein werd' ich
Des morgens wieder wach.

Rescued from despair by a German minister in Baltimore, he completed a course of study for the ministry already begun abroad, and he soon accepted a charge. But fortune again turned against him, when the congregation recognized in him a freethinker. Once more a wanderer, he lectured for some years and in many places, until he finally found liberal friends in Detroit who supplied the means in 1884 for his favourite wish, a weekly literary paper. This he named *Der arme Teufel*, and into it he poured his soul for the remaining fourteen years of his life. A kindred spirit, the poet Martin Drescher, collected some of his writings in *Mein Buch* (1900); a larger collection was published in a limited edition soon after by the Reitzel Club of Detroit, under the title *Des armen Teufel gesammelte Schriften*. Reitzel's poems are hardly less noteworthy for their form than his prose. They betray an influence of Heine and Nietzsche, though not sufficient to obscure a style of his own.

Dialect literature has been popular with Germans in America for its humorous element mainly. We find low German dialects in the works of Lafrentz and Bornemann, but the most successful imitation of Plattdeutsch in Carl Münter's *Nu sünd wi in Amerika*. Dietzsch, Heerbrandt, and Bürkle have imitated high German dialects, the first-named that of the Palatinate, the latter two the Swabian speech. The Hessian dialect appears in a most amusing little book by Georg Asmus, called *Amerikanisches Skizzebüchelche, Eine Epistel in Versen* in which an immigrant of little cultivation but considerable native wit writes home to his uncle about the strange things that happened to him in America (1874). The method of mingling broken English with German dialect to heighten the comical effect was used by Asmus and also by Karl Adler (*Mundartlich Heiteres*), but the greatest popular success in this department was achieved by the American writer Charles Godfrey Leland[1] in his *Hans Breitmann's Ballads*, a caricature that has often been wrongly taken as a truthful picture of existing conditions—just as Ir-

[1] See Book III, Chap. IX.

ving's *Knickerbocker History* has been of Dutch New York. Sometimes *Breitmann's Ballads* are erroneously placed under the head of Pennsylvania German dialect literature.

The so-called Pennsylvania German (or Dutch) dialect is a speech-form based upon South-German dialects of the eighteenth century, upon which English speech-forms were grafted. Since the German immigrants of the eighteenth century came mostly from the Palatinate and the Upper Rhine country, the dialect of those sections prevailed in their daily intercourse among the Germans of Pennsylvania and neighbouring provinces. Being in constant contact also with English-speaking people, an English word-stock, especially of objects and affairs new to them, was imposed upon their dialect, while contact with modern literary German of the nineteenth century practically ceased. Pennsylvania German, being isolated, had an independent growth, which is exceedingly interesting to the philologist.[1] Its tendency, as time goes on, is to come nearer and nearer the English language until German disappears. Though the Pennsylvania German dialect undoubtedly assumed definite form much earlier, written records of it did not appear before the last half of the nineteenth century. The most prominent name among the poets who wrote in the dialect is that of Henry Harbaugh, a collection of whose poems was published posthumously in 1870, under the title *Harbaugh's Harfe*. Most of his poems appeared also in English translations by the poet, such as his much appreciated verses on *The Old School house on the Creek*, beginning:

> Today it is just twenty years
> Since I began to roam:
> Now, safely back, I stand once more,
> Before the quaint old school-house door,
> Close by my father's home.

In Pennsylvania German:

> Heit is's 'xäctly zwanzig Johr,
> Dasz ich bin owwe naus:
> Nau bin ich widder lewig z'rick
> Un schteh am Schulhaus an d'r Krick,
> Iuscht neekscht an's Dady Haus.

See Bibliography for grammars and literature of the dialect.

The elegiac note also prevails in the poems *Heemweh, Der alte Feierheerd, Die alt Miehl*. We are reminded of the homely simplicity and tender pathos of the dialect poet of the Black Forest, J. P. Hebel (*Alemannische Gedichte*), as we listen to Harbaugh's *Das Krischkindel* (Santa Claus), *Busch und Schtedel* (Town and Country), *Der Kerchegang in alter Zeit* (Going to church in the old time), *Will widder Buwele sei* (I want to be a boy again). Two collections of Pennsylvania German folksongs were published by Henry L. Fisher, entitled: *'s alt Marik-Haus mittes in d'r Schtadt*, and *Kurzweil und Zeitfertreib odder Pennsylfanisch-deutsche Folkslieder*. This anthology and the more recent collection of prose and verse in two volumes by Daniel Miller furnish pleasing pictures of country life, joyful frolics, huskings, apple-butter and quilting parties; they playfully ridicule ministerial plights and difficulties, and the follies of superstition. Some of the prose tales are traceable to sources many generations back in Swabia and the Rhineland, but in the new setting they receive a renewed charm. The Pennsylvania German dialect literature is undoubtedly the most quaint and original contribution of the older German immigrations, and it is unfortunate that no comprehensive anthology has as yet appeared. The stories in English by Elsie Singmaster Lewars are far more artistic and trustworthy depictions of the Pennsylvania Germans than the pseudo-realistic fictions of Helen Reimensnyder Martin.

The most valuable writing done by Germans in the United States has been their scholarly work, historical, autobiographical, and scientific. Works of this class have generally been published in English and therefore do not properly belong to a sketch of the literature written in German. They are books of specialists: E. W. Hilgard on soils, A. A. Michelson (Nobel prize winner) in physics, Paul Haupt and F. Hirth on Oriental languages, Drs. Jacobi and Meyer in medical research, B. E. Fernow on scientific forestry, Paul Carus as editor of *The Open Court* and *The Monist*, Kuno Francke in German literature, and a group of other scholars born in Germany who held chairs in American universities and gained a wider hearing through the use of the English language in their books. Two of the ablest Germans who came to this country before 1830, Karl Follen and Francis Lieber, in their mature works used the language of their adopted country, Follen in his essays and sermons, Lieber in his literary essays and books on political science. We can observe this tendency even earlier, in Baron Steuben's *Regulations for the Order and Discipline of the Troops of the United States*, published in 1779 and reprinted many times for use at West Point. Others published in both languages, notably Carl Schurz, whose widely-read *Reminiscences* were first written in German, but whose speeches (with many exceptions), reports, and essays appeared mostly in English.[1] The *Memoirs* of Gustav Koerner are a fit companion piece to the autobiography of Carl Schurz, since they amplify the account of conditions in the Middle West between 1835 and 1865, and particularly the rise of the Republican party. In the historical field the crown of achievement belongs to Hermann von Holst, whose work on the constitutional and political history of the United States is generally conceded to be authoritative. It was written during the period of his professorship in the University of Chicago, and published in sections under the general title *Verfassung und Demokratie der Vereinigten Staaten von Amerika*. Unfortunately the English translation is too literal and by no means does justice to the virile style of the original. Hugo Münsterberg in his *Die Amerikaner* (*American Traits*, etc.), gave a view of America from the psychologist's standpoint, a book comparable to the works of De Tocqueville and Bryce for its critical and sympathetic treatment. An historical work of merit, though little known (the poor translation is perhaps partly responsible), is that of Therese von Jakob ("Talvj"), the wife of the American Orientalist Edward Robinson, entitled *Geschichte der Colonisation von Neu-England, 1607–1692. Nach den Quellen bearbeitet.* In its wisely restricted field it is not surpassed. Among the many valuable memoirs that have been written by Germans in the United States, some of which have already been mentioned, we should not forget the reminiscences of Hans Kudlich, the emancipator of the serfs in Austria, and a secretary in the provisional revolutionary government of 1849 in the Palatinate. Others of interest are *Aus zwei Weltteilen*, by Marie Hansen-Taylor (wife of Bayard Taylor[2]); *Memoiren einer*

[1] See Bibliography for exact references to biographical works.
[2] See Book III, Chap. x.

Frau aus dem badisch-pfälzischen Feldzuge by Mathilde Giesler-Anneke, the ardent woman suffragist; *Länger als ein Menschenleben in Missouri,* by Gert Göbel; and similarly autobiographical writings of Friedrich Münch, Philip Schaff, H. Börnstein, and Carl Heinzen. Pioneers in the search for historical records of the Germans in the United States were Friedrich Kapp, Oswald Seidensticker, and H. A. Rattermann, the authors of many instructive monographs.

A concluding paragraph may well be devoted to the institution which in German-speaking communities upholds the standard of the spoken language—the theatre. The German drama has been performed in the original language continuously in New York City since 1853, though the beginnings go back as far as 1840 or earlier. When in 1866 Dawison, the greatest German actor of his day, came to the United States he received offers from two rival German theatres in New York. He accepted an extraordinarily liberal inducement from the manager of the Stadttheater, Otto Hoym, who for ten years was the leader in German theatrical ventures. Dawison's great rôles were Wallenstein, Franz Moor, Othello, Shylock, and Hamlet, and the reputation that he established was not clouded by the successes of many subsequent visiting stars. After Hoym's retirement Adolf Neuendorff, a man of high ideals, founded the Germania Theater, beginning in 1872. He imported a stock company of superior talent, including Heinrich Conried, Leon Wachsner, and Mathilde Cottrelly, all three destined to become prominent also as managers. Conried had a period of very great popularity in the rôles of Franz Moor, Mortimer, Just, Gringoire, and Dr. Klaus. In 1879–1880 the Thalia Theater was opened as a rival to the Germania, and for a number of years both theatres played to crowded houses, thanks to the high tide of German immigration in the early eighties. No expense was spared by the rivals in their efforts to offer superior attractions. Karl Sontag was the star of first magnitude at the Germania, Marie Geistinger at the Thalia. At this period the classical German drama, the comedy, the farce, the operetta were all performed with popular and artistic success. Then Neuendorff ventured too far. He left a theatre with a seating capacity of three thousand and leased Wallack's on Broadway, then the largest and finest theatre available.

He also entered into an expensive contract with the actor Haase, who proved a disappointment on this his second visit. Moreover, the popularity of Marie Geistinger stood in his way. Never before or after was there such a favourite in the German theatres. Her versatility was marvellous. She could fascinate with her singing in light operas, *Der Seekadet* or *Die schöne Galatee*, and on a succeeding night thrill an audience with her *Kameliendama* or some other tragic rôle. Neuendorff deplored the fact that she was too willing to yield to the popular taste for musical comedy, and that her great influence was leading New York audiences away from the classical drama. But the impending failure of Neuendorff was also in part his own fault, for he and the rival Thalia Theater had perverted the taste and increased the expectations of theatre-goers with an extravagant array of stars, speculating upon their curiosity and eagerness for the new and sensational. Both theatres were obliged to close their doors in spite of many striking successes. The next leader among theatrical managers was Gustav Amberg, who took over the Thalia, and subsequently in 1888 founded what was long the home of the German drama in New York, the Irving Place Theatre. Amberg started with a stock company of very indifferent merit. They could not play up to the stars (Gäste) whom he occasionally invited. Nevertheless, at the close of the season of 1887–1888 he presented a "Gastspiel" which has probably not been surpassed in the history of the German stage in America. It was the double-star cast of Barnay and Possart, when Barnay appeared in the rôles of Hamlet, Uriel Acosta, Karl Moor, Wallenstein, Tell, and Bolz with Possart as Polonius, De Sylva, Franz Moor, Buttler, Gessler, and Schmock.

A step forward was made in the history of the German stage in New York when Heinrich Conried in 1893, on the invitation of Henry Steinway, assumed control of the Irving Place Theatre. Deeply impressed with the failures, both financial and artistic, which the starring system had produced, and an interested witness of the reforms which the *Meininger* company of players had brought about in Germany, Conried proceeded to build up a well-matched company of resident players, whose aim was not individual display of talent but an harmonious ensemble with the purpose of interpreting the genius of the dramatic poet. It was several seasons before he had a company that could play together well enough to satisfy him, and one large or versatile enough to vary classical drama with comedy and farce and even operetta in order to guard against annual deficits. A place had to be won also for the modern drama, which was obstructed not, as in the case of the classical drama, by the indifference but by the hostility of the general public. Conried's theatre for many years remained an example and inspiration for all the German theatres of the United States, and its influence did not stop there. It was used by critics of the American stage as an object lesson for the propagation oi certain reforms, particularly against the starring system. It is well-known that Conried's success with the Irving Place Theatre brought him the appointment to the managership of the Metropolitan Opera, but this was not his greatest ambition. We learn from Winthrop Ames in his account of the New Theatre,[1] that it was Conried's great aim to help in the founding of a national American theatre, based upon the principle of the resident stock company, and that if he had lived he would have been logically its first manager. With the Metropolitan Opera on his hands, Conried was obliged to neglect his German theatre company, and as a result it declined steadily until he gave it up in 1907. There followed a meteoric rise under the management of Maurice Baumfeld, and then varying fortunes under different heads, but the Irving Place Theatre never regained its important position of influence.

Second to New York was the German theatre of Milwaukee. Beginning in the fifties with amateurish performances, good traditions were established with the Stadttheater in 1868. The same struggle to maintain the classical drama along with the more popular and financially more successful comedy and farce is also to be observed in the history of the Milwaukee German theatre. Later the engagement of too many stars here also brought about an overstimulation and a perversion of taste. The stock company system rescued the situation under the management of Richard, Welb, and Wachsner, 1884–1890. Richard subsequently managed a German theatre in Chicago, Welb in St. Louis. A new home was provided in Milwaukee in 1895 by F. Papst, and in this well-equipped play-

[1] See Bibliography.

house, under the able management of Leon Wachsner, the
stock company developed an artistic ensemble during some
seasons not inferior to Conried's best.   As at the Irving Place
Theatre, stars were not altogether banished, and visits were
welcomed from Sonnenthal, Kainz, and Agnes Sorma, but they
were introduced toward the end of the season.   A just local
pride has been felt by Milwaukians in their German theatre,
as is shown by the payment of heavy annual deficits incurred
to keep the standard high.   Many other cities with large German populations, Philadelphia, St. Louis, Chicago, and Cincinnati, have had German theatres intermittently, with the
same history: early amateur beginnings, then professional players and the star system until some skilful manager brought
together a company of resident actors.   A very promising
foundation was the Deutsches Theater of Philadelphia, for
which a handsome home was built in 1906 and successfully
maintained for several seasons, until it yielded, like so many
other noble theatrical ventures, to the pressure of deficits inevitable in the history of high-class theatres.

II.   *French*

To furnish an account of the French literature of Louisiana
is not a simple task.   The facts that are known concerning the
lives of many of the writers, particularly in the early periods,
are few or none.   Nor is there any complete collection of the
works which comprise this literature; unique copies of important books repose in private libraries, or lie moulding in the
cellars of old Creole homes.

The beginnings of Louisiana were wholly French.   The
colony was founded by Iberville at Biloxi, in 1699.   The immigrants during the following century were for the most part
well-bred, and spoke the best French; during that century it
was customary for the more favoured sons to return to France
for their education, so that the colony kept fairly abreast of
the parent civilization.   Louisiana was ceded to Spain in 1762,
and although Spanish thus became the official tongue, French
continued as the language of society.   When the territory
was purchased by the United States in 1803, French was
still almost universally spoken.   Not until the middle of

the nineteenth century was English the more generally employed.

Under French rule the only literature produced consisted of official accounts like the journal of Penicault, or the *Mémoire des négociants et habitants de la Louisiane sur l'événement du 29 octobre, 1768*, by Lafrénière et Caresse, of interest chiefly to historians. Under the Spaniards only a few pieces of any significance were written, and they uninspired, being altogether in the prevailing French mode. Julien Poydras, a wealthy planter, published at New Orleans in 1779 an epic poem on *La Prise du Morne du Bâton-Rouge par Monseigneur de Galvez*. Berquin Duvallon, a refugee from Santo Domingo, offered in 1801 a *Recueil de Poésies d'un Colon de Saint-Domingue*, of which *Le Colon Voyageur* is the best specimen.

It was not until after the War of 1812 that letters really flourished in French Louisiana. The contentment and prosperity that filled the forty years between 1820 and 1860 encouraged the growth of a vigorous and in some respects a native literature, comprising plays, novels, and poems.

The first drama written in Louisiana took a native theme. *Poucha-Houmma* was composed by Le Blanc de Villeneufve at the age of seventy-eight, being based upon an Indian story he had heard fifty years before while in the employ of the government among the Tchactas (Choctaws). It is a tragedy in the familiar Alexandrines, and it observes the unities. It was written, says the author, to vindicate the noble character of the Indian. The manner is that of Corneille; indeed, the play might well be called a Louisiana *Cid*. The old chief addresses his warriors thus:

> Augustes descendants d'un peuple sans pareil,
> Très illustres enfants des enfants du Soleil.

The best dramatist produced by Louisiana was Placide Canonge, who wrote between 1839 and 1860. He was educated in New Orleans, and was a frequent visitor in Paris. He was a director of opera and a journalist of some note; he edited *La Lorgnette, L'Entr'acte, Courrier, L'Impartial, Le Courrier Français, Le Sud, La Renaissance, L'Époque,* and *L'Abeille*, the last-named, founded in 1827, being the first French daily news paper published in the United States. His plays followed the French romantic tradition, and were extremely popular because of their gaiety and enthusiasm. The best known are *Qui perd gagne* (1849), *Le Comte de Carmagnola* (1856), *Grand d'Espagne*, *Gaston de Saint-Elme* (1840), *Le Maudit Passeport* (1839), *Don Juan ou une histoire sous Charles-Quint* (1849), *Le Comte de Monte Christo* (1848), and *L'Ambassadeur d'Autriche*.

Canonge shares with Lussan, Dugué, Testut, and others the honour of creating an indigenous drama based on local history and manners. Both he and Lussan treated a famous crisis in colonial history, the Revolution of 1768, in which leading French colonists unsuccessfully opposed the accession of the new Spanish governor and were led to execution. Plays on this and kindred subjects found eager audiences from about 1840 on to the Civil War. In 1836 Charles Gayarré had published his *Essai Historique*, which was widely read and which led the imaginations of many back to the past. A. Lussan based his play, *Les Martyrs de la Louisiane* (1839), directly upon the account of the Revolution which Gayarré had so dramatically rendered. The play is conceived somewhat in the spirit of Victor Hugo; it is in verse, in five acts, and is dedicated to the martyrs of 1769. Very little is known of Lussan's life. Canonge's play on the Revolution of 1768, *France et Espagne* (1850), follows history less closely, new romantic characters being introduced to heighten and complicate the effect. It is based not on Gayarré's book but on a novel, *Louisiana*, written by Garreau and published in *La Revue Louisianaise* in 1845. The play is in prose, in four acts.

Oscar Dugué wrote in 1852 a tragedy called *Mila ou la Mort de La Salle*. The action takes place in Texas, and the chief characters are La Salle, his Indian bride Mila, and their murderous adversary, Liotot. It is not known whether the piece was ever staged. It is a tragedy in the manner of Voltaire, written in regular verse, and furnished with a chorus. The author was born in New Orleans in 1821. He studied in Paris, returning to Louisiana in 1846. He edited *L'Orléanais* for a while, and for a period was president of Jefferson College, in Saint-Jacques parish. He wrote one other historical drama, *Cygne ou Mingo*, highly praised in its day. P. Pérennes, whose tragedy in verse, *Guatimozin ou le Dernier Jour de l'Empire*

Mexicain (1859), dealt with the conquest of Mexico by the Spaniards, claimed to have been inspired to write his play during a sojourn among certain venerable ruins in Mexico; in reality he was only making over the *Guatimozin* of M. Madrid, which had appeared on the French stage as early as 1828. *L'Hermite du Niagara* (1842), a *mystère* by the novelist Alfred Mercier, should be mentioned here. Victor Sejour, the dramatist, though born in Louisiana, does not call for treatment, since he left the United States at an early age.

The novel owed its prosperity between 1845 and the Civil War chiefly to popular magazines like *La Revue Louisianaise*, *Les Veillées Louisianaises*, *La Violette*, and *L'Echo National*, whose feuilletons are now an interesting mine. In this period there was a demand for historical tales and stories of Louisiana life; as witness the following titles, announced by *La Revue Louisianaise: Histoire de toutes des rues de la Nouvelle-Orléans, par un Vieux Magistrat; Une Famille Créole; Or et Fange*, *mystères* of New Orleans. Garreau's *Louisiana*, the source of Canonge's *France et Espagne*, appeared in *Les Veillées Louisianaises* in 1845. It is long and formless, though the style is clear and the history fairly faithful. Garreau was virtually the first novelist to attempt a re-creation of colonial Louisiana.

Charles Testut, one of the most prolific of writers, author of *Portraits Littéraires de la Nouvelle-Orléans*, and of several volumes of poems, and editor-in-chief of *Les Veillées Louisianaises*, wrote three historical novels, *Saint-Denis*, *Calisto*, and *Le Vieux Salomon*. They were produced to fill space in his magazines; they are long, loosely composed, and often forced in language and sentiment. Yet they are eloquent, and rich in Louisiana lore. Whole pages are borrowed from Gayarré; in *Calisto* a long digression begins with the words "Comme le disait Charles Gayarré." *Saint-Denis* (1845) recounts the adventures of the Chevalier Juchereau de Saint-Denis in New Mexico, whither he has been sent by Governor Cadillac of Louisiana to open up new channels of trade, and where he falls in love with Angela, the governor's daughter, and fights a duel for her. *Calisto* (1849) is an extraordinary tale. The scene is laid at Carrolton, now a part of New Orleans. Sophie de Wolfenbuttel, a German princess, is brutally treated by her husband Alexis, a Russian prince. He struck her one day, and believes he has killed her. She smuggles herself out of the palace and comes to Louisiana under the name of Calisto. She hears of the death of Alexis, and marries a young Frenchman, the Chevalier D'Olban. Returning to Paris with D'Olban and a daughter Caroline, she is recognized and forced to retire to the country, where her husband and daughter die, and where she ends her days in a convent. The novel contains, in addition to this train of events, notable descriptions of the huge Louisiana forests, and of a violent hurricane on the Mississippi. Testut's third novel, *Le Vieux Salomon* (written 1858, not published until 1877), deals at great length with slavery in Louisiana, and is virtually a second *Uncle Tom's Cabin*, with a second Simon Legree for its principal character. The other side of the picture was given in 1881, in Dr. Alfred Mercier's *Habitation St. Ybars*, where the relation between master and slave is a happy one and the old Louisiana life is almost idyllic.

Alexandre Barde wrote *Michel Peyroux ou l'Histoire des Pirates en Amérique* in 1848. The story began serially in *La Revue Louisianaise*, but was never completed because the manuscript was lost by the printers. It is an account, as far as it goes, of the band of pirates who were led by the famous Lafitte. The novel begins well, and the loss of the manuscript must be considered a real misfortune; the French is excellent.

Le Soulier Rouge (1849), by D'Artlys, is an Indian story with a considerable historical basis. Governor Vaudreuil sends Aubry to negotiate with Soulier Rouge, who is chief of the Choctaws. Aubry's guide through the Louisiana forests has a niece, whom Aubry marries. The negotiations are not successful, and Aubry kills Soulier Rouge, who had killed his father. Aubry appears in Gayarré's history, from which D'Artlys borrowed. The story is only moderately long and is excellently written. The numerous descriptions of savage ceremonies make it an interesting document. D'Artlys had a nimble pen. He contributed regularly to *La Violette*, in the department called *Revue de la Semaine*. He retailed there the news from Europe, discussing the latest nothings with finesse and spirit. He was editor for a short time of *La Presse des Deux-Mondes*.

Between 1860 and 1870 no novels were published in Louisiana, because with the coming of the Civil War the popular magazines went out of existence. Thereafter novels in French were not numerous. *Les Amours d'Hélène*, by Jacques de Roquigny, and *Rodolphe de Branchelièvre* by Charles Lemaître, should at least be mentioned. The works of Dr. Alfred Mercier and Adrien Rouquette were more important. In addition to his *Habitation de St. Ybars*, Dr. Mercier, who spent a large portion of his life in Paris as lawyer, physician, and man of letters, wrote *Hénoch Jédésias; Lidia*, a charming Italian idyl; *Le fou de Palerme* (1873), a touching Italian love story; *La Fille du Prêtre* (1877), an attack against the celibacy of priests; and *Johnelle* (1892). Dr. Mercier handled the Creole patois skilfully, and was altogether highly successful in his fiction. Adrien Rouquette's *La Nouvelle Atala* (1879), it is hardly necessary to say, is an echo of Chateaubriand. The author was a priest who lived among the Indians of Saint-Tammany parish, reading Ossian, Young's *Night Thoughts*, various French books, and the Bible. Atala is a young girl who loves solitude and retires to the forests, where she has subtle spiritual adventures, and dies swooning. There are numerous mystical digressions in *La Nouvelle Atala;* Nature, as the guardian of Atala, is handled with all the superstitious reverence of Chateaubriand himself, and often with genuine eloquence.

Louisiana, with its luxurious vegetation, its bayous bordered with ancient oaks, its picturesque gulf coast, and its proud race of people, has made many poets, the most fecund of whom, and the most popular, if not the greatest, is Dominique Rouquette, brother of Adrien Rouquette. Dominique went to be educated in Paris; upon his return he took up the life of a hermit, writing sentimental verses, dreaming, and bothering very little about his daily bread. He was a picturesque figure on the streets of New Orleans as he strolled along with a great cudgel in one hand and a bouquet of flowers in the other, singing his verses at the top of his voice. His poetry was well received in France, notably by Hugo; it was said that Béranger and Deschamps learned some of his lines by heart. He published two volumes, *Les Meschacébéennes* and *Fleurs d'Amérique*. The following is from the *Fleurs:*

LE SOIR

Déjà dans les buissons dort la grive bâtarde:
La voix du bûcheron, qui dans les bois s'attarde,

> A travers les grands pins se fait entendre au loin;
> Aux bœufs libres du joug ayant donné le foin,
> Sifflant une chanson, le charretier regagne
> Sa cabane où l'attend une noire compagne,
> Et fume taciturne, accroupi sur un banc,
> Sa pipe, au longs reflets du mélèze flambant.

Adrien Rouquette wrote in a similar strain. His *Antoniade ou la Solitude avec Dieu* (1860) is a long eremitic poem on what had been one of the most popular subjects in Europe or America, solitude. *Les Savanes* (1841) is a collection of his shorter pieces. Tullius Saint-Céran wrote *Rien ou Moi* in 1837, and *Mil huit cent quatorze et Mil huit cent quinze* in 1838. The latter celebrates the battle of New Orleans, as does an epic in ten cantos by Urbain David, of Cette, entitled *Les Anglais à la Louisiane en 1814 et 1815* (1845). Lussan, the author of *Les Martyrs de la Louisiane*, produced in 1841 *Les Impériales*, a volume of homage to Napoleon in the style of Hugo. Felix de Courmont began in 1866 a poetical daily, in which he printed his own mediocre verse, chiefly satirical. Constant Lepouzé, the best Latin scholar of Louisiana, gracefully translated the odes of Horace in *Poésies Diverses* (1838). In 1845 Armand Lanusse published *Les Cenelles*, a very interesting volume of poems by Boise, Dalcour, Liotau, Valcour, Thierry, and others, inspired evidently by Hugo and Béranger, but striking at times a note of independence and jocularity. The following, from Thierry, was first printed in Paris:

> Parle toujours. j'aime à t'entendre,
> Ta douce voix me fait comprendre
> Que je dois encore au bonheur
>   Prétendre
> Car j'ai pour chasser le malheur
>   Ton cœur.

Oscar Dugué, the dramatist, published *Essais Poétiques* in 1847. The poems are formal and without variety, and cultivate melancholy. His *Homo*, a didactic poem, is not very interesting.

Alexandre Latil, in his *Éphémères* (1841), a protest against the modern school, produced verses of delicacy and felicity which make him seem, on the whole, one of the most memorable

as well as the most pathetic of the Louisiana poets. A lifelong
invalid, he addressed to his father and mother a tender lament
from which a few lines should be quoted as an illustration of
the elegiac verse in which his state has done perhaps its finest
work :

> Encore un dernier cnant, et ma lyre éphémère
> S'échappe de mes mains, et s'éteint en ce jour,
> Mais que ces sons mourants, ô mon père, ma mère,
> Soient exhalés pour vous, objets de mon amour.
> De cet hymne d'adieu si la note plaintive
> S'envole tristement pour ne plus revenir,
> Vous ne l'oublîrez pas : votre oreille attentive
> L'empreindra pour jamais dans votre souvenir.

Dr. Mercier and Charles Testut, the novelists, both turned
their hands to poetry. Mercier's *Rose de Smyrne* and *Erato*
were printed in Paris in 1842 : the first is an Oriental tale; the
second a collection of pleasant pieces in praise of love and
Louisiana. The merest mention can be made here of Barde,
Guirot, Calogne, and of Madame Emilie Evershed, the only
poetess produced by French Louisiana.

The English-speaking United States knows Louisiana largely
through the graceful and charming, though not all equally accurate, stories and essays of G. W. Cable,[1] Kate Chopin,[2] and
Grace Elizabeth King. Louisianians themselves, and indeed
these writers, are under a particular and special indebtedness
to a man whose name has often been mentioned in this chapter
—Charles Étienne Arthur Gayarré (1805–95). That Louisiana,
says Miss King,

lives at all in that best of living worlds, the world of history, romance, and poetry, she owes to him. . . . As a youth, he consecrated his first ambitions to her; through manhood, he devoted his
pen to her; old, suffering, bereft by misfortune of his ancestral heritage, and the fruit of his prime's vigour and industry, he yet stood
ever her courageous knight. . . . He held her archives not only
in his memory but in his heart, and while he lived, none dared make
public aught about her history except with his vigilant form in the
line of vision.

Too great a stress, however, need not be laid upon Gayarré's
passionate provincialism. It is enough to say that in his

[1] See Book III. Chap. VI.   [2] *Ibid.*

many historical writings, both French and English, he displayed to a friendly public not only the ascertained facts of those portions of Louisiana history which he investigated but the many charming traditions and romantic legends upon which he came, and which he embedded in his narrative somewhat after the manner of Barante's *Ducs de Bourgogne.* Of American authors he most nearly suggests Prescott, whose own cycle of studies indeed he touched upon in his life of Philip II of Spain (1866). Besides histories, addresses, and articles he produced comedies—*The School of Politics* (1854) and *Dr. Bluff, or the American Doctor in Russia* (1869)—and novels—*Fernando de Lemos, Truth and Fiction* (1872) and its sequel *Aubert Dubayet.* The novels contain some excellent descriptions of New Orleans.

For a generation nearly all that has been written in French in Louisiana may be found within the volumes of *Comptes Rendus* of L'Athénée Louisianais, a society for the encouragement of the French language and literature. Much of it is amateur and dilettante; much of it also is carefully considered and well written. Poems, essays, antiquarian researches, stories, discussions of many sorts—these indicate the taste of the contributors and readers. Dr. Mercier, founder of the society in 1876, was one of the most voluminous of these pleasant writers; another was Professor Alcée Fortier (1856–1914) of Tulane University, active and learned, the author of numerous studies of the language and folk-lore of his state, and of the elaborate *History of Louisiana* in four volumes which crowned his labours in 1904. His *Louisiana Studies* (1894) forms the basis of all our knowledge of the French literature of Louisiana.

III. Yiddish

It is very difficult to set geographical limits to Yiddish literature. American Yiddish authors were all born in Europe, and it is quite natural for them to revert to themes of the old home. The constant intercourse among Jewish authors in both hemispheres and the mutual influence exerted render geographical divisions still more artificial. Yet it's necessary, in the interests of orientation, to omit authors only indirectly related to American Yiddish literature and to dwell only on those who have settled permanently in the United States and whose works reflect the life of the Jewish immigrants.

Judæo-German, now known as Yiddish, branched out from the German during the latter half of the sixteenth century when German Jews settled in compact masses in the Slavic countries. The vernacular developed by the Jews there gradually departed from the original dialect and became distinct from it, and to· day idiomatic Yiddish bears only a remote resemblance to the German. Many Hebrew words ingrained in the body of Yiddish, together with numerous words and expressions borrowed from contiguous Slavic vernaculars and thoroughly assimilated, make Yiddish a distinct linguistic unit. The Yiddish vernacular in America, retaining to a degree the characteristics of its several European sub-dialects, has also absorbed a great number of English words and turns of speech, which either have no Yiddish equivalents common to all dialects or represent conceptions that are new to the immigrant. Literary Yiddish in America is, however, relatively free from these Anglicisms.

Yiddish literature in the United States is less than half a century old. The first Yiddish periodical in America, the *Yiddische Neues*, was founded in New York in 1871. But it was a decade or so later before Yiddish received a real impetus in this country from the arrival of large numbers of Russian Jews fleeing the wave of persecutions and massacres at home. The intellectual immigrants who came with the masses brought with them the radical doctrines and ideals of socialism, anarchism, and other political and social tendencies current among the enlightened Russian and Jewish classes of the time. The vernacular of the immigrants was the only medium of appeal which would reach them, and although many of the educated American Jewish pioneers were averse to the use of Yiddish as a literary instrument they resorted to it as a matter of expediency. The growth of Yiddish literature in this country has been commensurable and co-extensive with the growth of Jewish immigration to the New World. The widening out of the spiritual interests of the older immigrants as well as the ever-increasing number of the new immigrants naturally created a larger and more diversified demand for printed Yiddish. The undifferentiated weeklies and miscellanies of the early eighties developed into a literature with all modern ramifications.

Periodicals for a long time remained the only carriers of printed Yiddish. The intellectuals were quick to seize the opportunities of free speech and to make liberal use of them for the spread of radical doctrines. The *Yiddische Gazetten*, started as early as 1874, was typical of the inferior kind of Yiddish periodicals. A semi-rabbinical, vulgar makeshift, printed in a jargon abounding in Talmudical Hebrew and spurious German, it had no programme, no spiritual physiognomy, and ministered to the coarser tastes of the masses. The *Arbeiter Zeitung* was representative of the better class. It was a strictly socialist organ and stood unflinchingly by its ideals. Launched as a weekly in 1890 by a number of Jewish workmen-socialists under the editorship of J. Rombro (Philip Krantz) and a year later taken under the direction of the gifted and versatile Abraham Cahan, it at once became the rallying point for the best intellectual forces the Jewish immigrants had in America. Names now illustrious in Yiddish literature— Abraham Cahan, Philip Krantz, David Pinski, Z. Libin, L. Kobrin, B. Gorin, Morris Rosenfeld, and others—are intimately connected with the history of the *Arbeiter Zeitung* and later with the daily *Abend Blatt* and the monthly *Zukunft*.

Financially these periodicals, and their editors, led a hand-to-mouth existence, but they carried their banner high.[1] Although the avowed purpose of such periodicals was to carry socialism to the masses, the necessity of a wider scope was soon recognized, and men like Abraham Cahan and Philip Krantz forced a widening of the field of interest and discussion. In the first issue of the *Zukunft* (January, 1892), the leading article avowed that "we can really express our programme in three words: we are Social Democrats." But . . . "we shall also give stories, poems, and art criticism; for we hold that art educates and refines the man, and we shall combine, so to speak, the pleasant with the useful." The issue contained *A Biography of Karl Marx* by Morris Hillquit; *God, Religion, and Morality* by Philip Krantz; *The Growth of the Proletariat in America* by Prof. Daniel De Leon; *Elections in Germany* by Herman Schlüter; the first of a series of articles on *Darwinism* by Abra-

---

[1] Krantz as editor of the *Arbeiter Zeitung* had a salary of six dollars a week.

ham Cahan; *Malthusianism and Capitalism* by Philip Krantz.
Of belles-lettres we find only *The Swimming Coffin*, a fantasy
by Jacob Gordin. The evolution of this magazine, still the
only serious American Yiddish monthly, may be judged
from the table of contents of any issue of recent date. We
now find fiction and poetry predominating, and topics of the
times treated without academic pretension. This evolution
is characteristic of all Yiddish-American journalism. There
has been a levelling up and a levelling down in Yiddish periodicals which have put them on a sound financial basis and have
removed both hyper-intellectual and vulgar elements. The
editors and contributors of Jewish newspapers now realize that
their readers are live men and women. Having adopted the
features of American journalism "which make a paper go,"
they have also retained the traditional elements of definite
social and political policies in both general and specifically
Jewish matters.

The Jewish Daily Forward (founded in 1897), which harbors
practically the entire *Arbeiter Zeitung* group, with Abraham
Cahan as editor-in-chief, B. Feigenbaum, Philip Krantz, Z.
Libin, and others as contributors, has become a potent force
with the Jews of America. It is committed to socialism, but
its socialism no longer hangs out of joint with its actual
environment, and it undoubtedly makes for better citizenship among the immigrants. It is the largest Yiddish newspaper in America, and, indeed, in the world. Several other
Yiddish dailies have attained the proportions of metropolitan
newspapers. Of these *The Day* is the more influential and
widely read. *The Jewish Morning Journal*, *The Warheit*
(now merged with *The Day*), *The Jewish Daily News*, all published in New York, have each their following, and have to a
large extent freed themselves from objectionable features.
Though the Yiddish book market is becoming stabilized and
several publishing houses operate on a business basis, the daily
newspaper is still the vehicle of the best fiction produced.

The Jew is known for his love of the song, and the sadder the
song the more intense the response. The *badchen*, the wedding
bard, with his mournful singsong and his opening formula
"Weep, bride, oh weep!" is a traditional figure of the Ghetto.
The modern composer of literary verse is known among the

masses, if at all, by poems that have been set to music, and every Jewish poet of repute has many such to his credit. Frug, the celebrated Jewish-Russian poet, is sung perhaps more than read. Reisin's *Mai Kamashmalon*, that groan of the Ghetto, and the same author's portentous *Huliet, Huliet, Boese Winten* have become national lyrics.

The Jewish immigrant in America found his sorrows and sufferings voiced in the songs[1] of one of the foremost Yiddish poets, Morris Rosenfeld, who in echoing the agonies of his brethren in the foreign land also echoed his own, for he was as much as they a victim of the infamous industrial plague known as the sweat shop. He was born in Russian Poland in 1862. His early education was religious and Talmudical with a smattering of the Polish and the German languages. In 1882 he left his native village of Boksha, in the province of Suvalki, for Amsterdam. He came to New York in 1883, left again for Russia, and in 1886 settled permanently in New York. His début in America was with a poem called *The Year 1886* printed in the *New Yorker Yiddische Folkszeitung*. His talent was quickly recognized and his verse soon appeared in practically every Yiddish periodical. But for twelve years he was forced to support himself in the sweat shop. Only when Professor Leo Wiener brought him to the attention of the American public through a volume of his poems, transliterated and translated, was Rosenfeld able to take eager leave of the cheerless toil that had so long been his nightmare.

Rosenfeld wrote in many genres. His satires were as deadly as his lyrics were moving. Resourceful in his vocabulary, happy in his sense of rhythm, rich in his colouring, sincere in his wrath, he brought in his Ghetto poems burning accusations against the order of things that made this hell on earth possible. He immortalized the sweat shop in many songs and poems. His *Die Sweat Shop, Mein Yüngele, Verzweiflung, Der Bleicher Apreitor*, and *A Trer auf'n Eisen* are some of the most dreadful testimonies of a soul's agony and the most damaging arraignment of social injustice. Future generations reading Rosenfeld will see in him a poet of high merit; but in his time he was more than a poet—he was the great accuser, the great champion of his fellow-slaves, the great mourner of his

[1] Yiddish poets generally call their productions "lieder" and not "gedichte"

fellow-Jews. In his nationalistic poems he sings the sorrows of the Jew as Jew, and in these, too, one can feel the throbbing of the aching heart of the eternally persecuted people. Rosenfeld knew how to reconcile his socialist views with his nationalist tendencies. He knew how to sing for the world of the oppressed, and he found in his heart special melodies for his suffering race.

Morris Winchevsky (born in Russia in 1856) is of a kind with Rosenfeld in his themes but quite inferior as a poet. His songs are all coloured with propaganda, though some of them, by virtue of correct versification and essential sincerity, are of decided poetic merit. An old man, he is now more or less reposing on his laurels, and these are not few. Successful translator of Hugo's *Les Miserables*, Ibsen's *Doll's House*, and Hood's *The Song of the Shirt*, he was also tireless as a disseminator of radical doctrines. He is still revered by the radical masses, who fondly know him as the "grandfather of Yiddish socialism."

Rosenfeld and Winchevsky are the two Ghetto poets of magnitude. David Edelstadt (1866–1892), the official poet of the anarchist group, was popular in his days, when radicalism as such was at a premium. His poetry, however, hardly deserves the name. Of the lesser Ghetto poets, Michael Kaplan is worth noting. His *Ghetto Klangen* are rich in original, homely plaint. His poetic adaptation of the American-Yiddish vernacular abounding in· Anglicisms is decidedly novel. Kaplan in his poetry is the immigrant who is destined to live on a foreign soil without striking root, and his songs fall on sympathetic ears.

S. Blumgarten (born in Russia in 1870), known by his pen name of Yehoush, is a poet of high rank, who would be a credit to a literature less obscure and local than Yiddish, perhaps even to a world literature. In this he marks a departure from the older Yiddish tradition. Finding Yiddish inadequate for his new concepts, he introduced a number of foreign words, happy in most cases, but not always adapted to the idiom. He began his literary effort in Russia, but it was in America, after ten years of business pursuits, that his talent found expression. He wrote in many styles and in all of them emphasized ideas rather than poetic modes; with the exception, perhaps, of his nature poems, where he stands supreme among Yiddish poets in his fine sense of landscape. His translation of *Hiawatha* would be excellent were it not for the occasional dissonance of foreign words. His Jewish themes are permeated with a romantic charm. Yehoush also made valuable contributions to the study of Yiddish. His Yiddish dictionary is a helpful volume to all who write the dialect.

That Yiddish poetry has a future is strongly contended by the "young," as the rebels of Yiddish rhyme like to style themselves. The conservative Yiddish reader frowns at them; to the Ghetto writer they are anathema; but they are fascinating, like all rebels. The time is not yet ripe to give a just estimate of the individual representatives of this promising school: Mani Leib, M. L. Halpern, Joseph Rolnik, for example. Speaking of Mani Leib the "young" critic Noah Steinberg says that he shook off all proletarian and nationalistic traditions. This they all did. Whether they are proselytes or mere renegades remains to be seen. They are still in the ferment.[1]

The short story or "Skitze" is the prevalent form of Yiddish fiction. It owes its continued existence not so much to choice as to the exigencies of Yiddish literature in America. In the absence of a book market to speak of—until very recently at any rate—practically all Yiddish literature produced in the United States was first printed in the dailies and weeklies. This circumstance, together with the fact that most of the Yiddish writers until lately have had to lead a precarious existence without leisure for longer works, has fostered the short story form, ill-suited as it is to the talents of some of its users.

Z. Libin (Israel Hurowits, born in Russia in 1872) occupies in American Yiddish fiction the place that Rosenfeld occupies in poetry, though much less talented and relatively free from nationalistic themes. His realism was inspired by the Russian masters at whose altar most of the Yiddish-American writers still worship, but his themes are predominantly local. He writes of the Jewish workman in the sweat shop, in the pestiferous tenement house, in the slums of the summer resorts. He treats of poverty, unemployment, misery, disease, the "white plague," and all the agonies of soul that these

[1] As this chapter was written in 1918 it does not chronicle the interesting development of these "young" writers during the past two years.

generate. He does not protest, accuse, or denounce, as does his brother poet; he is simply a recorder of the multiform hell of the Ghetto. His genuine pathos lies in the simplicity and accuracy of his tales. "The life of the Jewish workmen in New York is the life I know best," he writes in his autobiography. "My Muse was born in the dark sweat shop, her first painful cry resounded near the Singer machine, she was brought up in the tenement tombs." In his later years, when the more objectionable aspects of the sweat shop were gradually becoming extinct, Libin relaxed somewhat, and admitted a little humour to his stories. But essentially he remained the Ghetto writer, with a talent for the cheerless, the desolate. Z. Levin is another of the realistic "skitze" writers. Many of his stories are meritorious, but with all the correctness of his realism, with all his insight into human motives, he leaves the reader cold. Only the worshippers of realism as a cult enjoy him.

Of much bigger calibre is Leon Kobrin (born in Russia in 1872). His literary début was in Russian, and when he came to New York in 1892 he was surprised to hear that there was such a thing as literature in Yiddish or "jargon," as the vernacular was contemptuously called in Russia. Nevertheless he joined hands with the inspired band of intellectuals and propagandists led by Abraham Cahan, Philip Krantz, and Benjamin Feigenbaum, and began contributing to the socialist publications in the vernacular, shelving his squeamishness and wielding his pen from right to left as best he could. In 1894 he published his first story, *A Moerder aus Liebe*. It attracted universal attention, and Kobrin became a Yiddish writer.

Kobrin is a realist but he is more than that. He knows the value of artistic selection and arrangement, and is something of a virtuoso of the short story. His subjects are not all of American life. He still dwells caressingly on places and characters of the old home. In his *Litwisch Staedtel*, written in 1914 and "dedicated to my old father and mother," the obscure town in the Lithuanian Ghetto is treated with a love and a reminiscential tenderness worthy of a better place. In his stories of Jewish life in America he gives us vivid pictures of the life of the poor, though he does not emphasize the sombre colours. The dramatic quality of his talent is manifest in many of his tales, of which some were adapted by the author for the stage. The conflict between the older generation of immigrants and their offspring, who are as a rule out of sympathy with the uncouth "old folks," is a favourite theme with Kobrin, and he portrays masterfully the mute tragedies of the uprooted refugees who find in America a measure of material comfort but who are agonized by new customs deeply offensive to their traditions. Of these stories the *Versterter Sabath* and *Thier Numer 1* of the series *A Tenement House* are among the best.

During the fifteen years of his literary career Kobrin wrote a great deal of fiction, and with the death of Jacob Gordin became one of the principal American-Yiddish playwrights. He also enriched Yiddish fiction by creditable translations from Maupassant, Zola, Gorki, Tolstoy, Dostoevski, Chekhov, and others.

Within the last decade numerous lesser short story writers have arisen. Some of them display qualities that justify hopeful expectations. Proletarian tendencies do not appear in their work. B. Botwinik, though crude in style at times, is arresting and thoughtful. Yenta Serdatsky has written a number of stories concerning the deracination of the later Jewish-Russian intellectuals who have become a cross between complacent bourgeois and spiritual malcontent. M. Osherowitz is another of the "skitze" writers whose heroes are exclusively of this new type, perhaps the most piteous among all the immigrants.

The school of the "young" is also strongly represented in fiction. Its followers have ushered in the longer story and the novel. I. Opatoshu is not a traditional Ghetto writer, for erotic passion is his main subject. His *Polische Welder*, however, is less open to objections on the part of the conservative critic. He has been called the originator of the Yiddish historical novel. David Ignatov is a "young" novelist who likes to write of men of indomitable will moving in an atmosphere of the elemental and the infinite, quite out of the Yiddish realistic tradition.

At the risk of being facetious it may be said here that the best Yiddish novel is one written in English. Abraham Cahan's *The Rise of David Levinsky* is a better reflection of Jewish life in American surroundings than all American-Yiddish fiction put together. The book is especially interesting to Americans, since the author sets out with the manifest purpose of taking the American reader by the hand and showing him through all the nooks of the Ghetto. This motive, with the author's genuine literary talent, a most felicitous style, a realistic treatment that is both engaging and convincing, makes *The Rise of David Levinsky* a monumental work, and surely the most remarkable contribution by an immigrant to the American novel. Cahan's work as editor of *The Jewish Daily Forward* and as literary critic, his novel, and his subsequent attack upon American fiction constitute a bold challenge to American novelists.

The Yiddish drama in America has always been trammelled by the immediate requirements of the playhouses, has been dictated mainly by box-office considerations, and, as a result of this, is of a decidedly inferior nature.[1]

At first the American Jewish theatre ministered to the crude wants of the coarser elements among the immigrants, who sought diversion rather than art. The actor as a professional was hardly yet differentiated, and the performers on the stage were of a kind with the hearers. The public did not value the labours of the dramatist, taking the actors to be the improvisors of the songs and the "prose."[2] But the actors regarded the playwright as the chieftain of their tribe. The institution of the "retained" author at the theatre became firmly established, and outsiders could not get a hearing with the theatrical managers. The names of A. Goldfaden, I. Shaikewitz, J. Lateiner, and M. Hurwitch are worth mentioning in connection with the beginnings of the Yiddish drama in America. Goldfaden is considered the founder of the Yiddish theatre. All of them had been practised in their craft before they came here. They knew their audience from the old Ghetto and understood perfectly well how to suit its tastes. Their plays were mostly adaptations from the inferior European stage. The most preposterous plots, a few songs of the salacious and sentimental pseudo-nationalistic kind, a comedian for the display of whose "stunts" the action was frequently and arbitrarily suspended

---

[1] The Jewish Art Theatre, established in 1919, bids fair to make an important contribution of a higher sort.

[2] Z. Libin is authority for the story that only some ten years ago he had great difficulty in explaining to a Jewish audience in a country town that he was a playwright. "Why should you write the words after the actors have said them?" he was asked.

—these were the elements of which a Yiddish "show" was concocted. Pseudo-biblical plots were greatly in vogue, the material of these also being handled quite unceremoniously. It must be said, however, in justice to Goldfaden, that his "historical operettes" *Bar Kochba*, *Doctor Almosado*, and particularly *Sulamith* are imbued with a genuine folk-spirit, and the songs in these plays are of a tender plaintiveness that is characteristic of the best Jewish folk-songs. Goldfaden composed both music and text.

Yiddish drama took a decided turn for the better with the appearance of the first play (*Siberia*) by Jacob Gordin (1853–1909), the acknowledged reformer of the Yiddish stage. Born in Russia, he received a liberal though irregular education. When he came to New York in 1892 he was already a reformer and a fairly well recognized Russian writer. His acquaintance-ship with the noted Jewish actors Adler and Mogulesko prompted him to try his hand at play-writing. His first play met with success and it laid the foundation of his career as Yiddish playwright. Gordin took the Yiddish drama in America from the realm of the preposterous and put a living soul into it. The methods of Goldfaden, Hurwitch, and Lateiner were not entirely abandoned; dancing and songs unrelated to the plot still occupied a prominent part in the play. But the plots were no longer of the blood-curdling, impossible kind, and the characters were living persons. Under the influence of his plays, Jewish actors began to regard their profession as one which calls for study and an earnest attitude. But while his achievements are invaluable as those of a reformer, his work is not intrinsically great. With all the realism of his situations, with all the genuineness of his characters, he was rather a pro-ducer of plays for a particular theatrical troupe than a writer of drama. That his comic characters generally stand in organic relation to the play is one of his chief merits. Of his many pieces (about 70 or 80) only a score or so have been published, and some of these are worthless as literature. *Mirele Efros*, *Gott Mensch un Teufel*, and *Der Unbekanter* are among the best of them.

Gordin's successors and disciples have not advanced the Yiddish stage beyond realistic melodrama. The two better play-wrights supplying it, Leon Kobrin and Z. Libin, both display a

knowledge of theatrical and histrionic requirements, but as literature their dramatic productions are inferior or at best mediocre.
In the case of Kobrin one may observe a struggle between the
writer of temperament and the producer of melodramas "made
to order." Even in his "problem plays" the melodramatic
elements prevail.

The standards of the Yiddish stage in America have not
permitted David Pinski (born in Russia in 1873) to attain the
distinction that is due him as a playwright. He is known
among the Gentile lovers of the drama better than among his
own kin. His plays have none of the vices of the regulation
Yiddish play, and this may explain the fact that many of them
were produced for the first time only several years after their
publication. Nevertheless, he is a dramatist of high order.
There is intensity and vigour in his plots, which are raised above
the accidental configuration of circumstances. His characters, too, are broad and significant. His dynamic quality
reveals itself in the themes he essays as well as in his characters.
Clash and struggle are Pinski's elements. The conflict of
social forces is best brought out in his *Isaac Sheftel, an Arbeiter
Drama;* and his *Familie Zwi, Tragedie vun dem einzigen Yidden*
reveals the powerful cross-currents in Jewish life, the grapple
of the old and the new. His plays should easily outlive their
run on the stage, and remain permanently valuable as literature

CHAPTER XXXII

Non-English Writings II

ABORIGINAL

PROBABLY never before has a people risen to need a history of its national literature with so little conscious relation to its own aboriginal literature. Yet if we extend the term America to include the geographical and racial continuity of the continent, unbroken at its discovery, we have here the richest field of unexploited aboriginal literature it is possible to discover anywhere in the world.

It begins in the archaic and nearly inarticulate cry of awakening consciousness, and carries us to about the point at which Greek literature began to exhibit continuity of thought and style. Only in America we have the advantage of having all these literary patterns developed on a consistent warp of language, and with the woof of an unmixed racial psychology. Varied as all its tribal manifestations were, from Aleut to Fuegian, the aboriginal American was of one uncontaminated strain.

Something more than a scholarly interest attaches to this unparalleled opportunity for the study of a single racial genius. To the American it is also a study of what the land he loves and lives in may do to the literature by which the American spirit is expressed. These early Amerinds had been subjected to the American environment for from five to ten thousand years. This had given them time to develop certain characteristic Americanisms. They had become intensely democratic, deeply religious, idealistic, communistic in their control of public utilities, and with a strong bias toward representative government. The problem of the political ring, and the excessive accumulation of private property, had already made its appearance within the territory that is now the United States. And along with these things had developed all the varieties of literary expression natural to that temperament and that state of society—oratory, epigram, lyrics, ritual-drama, folk-tale, and epic.

In any competent account of this aboriginal literature of ours it will be necessary to refer to the points, in Mexico and Peru, where the racial genius that produced it reached its highest expression. But between the St. Lawrence and the Rio Grande the one item which primarily conditioned all literary form was complete democracy of thinking and speaking.

Such education as the aboriginal Americans had was "free" in the sense that there were no special advantages for particular classes. Their scholars were wise in life only; there were no "intellectuals." The language being native, there were no words in it derived from scholastic sources, no words that were not used all the time by all the people. It was not even possible for poet or orator to talk "over the heads" of his audiences. There was a kind of sacred patter used by the initiates of certain mysteries, but the language of literature was the common vehicle of daily life.

This made for a state of things for which we are now vaguely striving in America, in which all the literature will be the possession of all the people, and the distinction between "popular" and real literature will cease to exist. And in aboriginal literature we have interesting examples of how this democracy of content modifies the form of what is written.

The controlling factor in the form of aboriginal literature was its need of being rememberable. Transmitted as it was by word of mouth, every song and story had to shape itself, as naturally as a river to its bed, to the retentive faculty of the mind. Ceremonies occupying several days for their performance must be passed, letter-perfect, from generation to generation. It was etiquette in Indian assemblies for a speaker, on rising, to repeat all that had been said by previous speakers on that subject. Under these circumstances remembering became a profession. Individuals with exceptional endowment became the custodians of tribal history. "Keeper of the Wampum" grew to be a title of distinction, and it is related of one of these keepers among the Five Nations that he was able to repeat all the details of public transaction connected with every one of the five hundred belts entrusted to his care.

Other aids to memory were occasionally employed, bundles of notched sticks, the painted skins of the Plainsman's Summer and Winter counts. These were in the nature of public documents. Chippewa (Ojibway) tribes had "board plates" on which between straight lines were painted or incised ideographic symbols indicating the song sequences of their rituals. But these could be read only by members of the societies to which they pertained. In the whole of what is now the United States there was but one native record that could be called, in our fashion, a book. It consisted of a number of birch-bark plates, incised and painted red, the *Walam Olum*, the Red Score of the Lenni Lenape. For the rest, the record of the Amerind soul was committed to the mind and the heart.

This is only another way of saying that all Amerind literature was rhythmic. It was true of all those forms we are accustomed to think of as prose, oratory, epigram, and tribal history, as well as of lyric and epic. But, though the Indian had no names for them, there was always a distinction in his choice of rhythms to be used. The difference was in their psychological relation to himself. The thing that came out of the Amerind heart was poetry, but if it came out of his head it was prose. This is a distinction to be borne in mind, for in the present state of our knowledge it is the only possible classification of aboriginal literary modes.

If utterance was out of the Indian heart, it could be sung or danced. But all Indian life was so intensely democratic that there was very little to be danced and sung which had not to be danced and sung in common, by the group or the tribe. When literature is danced or chanted in common there must be some common measure, some time-keeper. Among the Indians this was the drum, that "breathing mouth of wood," the hollow log or hoop with a stretched skin. All Amerind literature is of these two classes: it can be drummed to, or it cannot.

Of the literature which came out of the Indian's head, too little has been preserved to us, and that little by ethnologists rather than literary specialists. Translators have been chiefly interested in mythology, in language, in anything except literary form.

Sir William Johnson, the earliest observer of oratory among the Five Nations, that original American centre of political corruption and senatorial sabotage, was impressed by the "Attic elegance" of diction and the compelling rhythm of their orators. The necessity for a unanimous vote on all important measures in Indian councils made the man who could weld the assembly with his voice the great man among them. The exercise of a gift for speech-making was not confined to the formal assembly, however. If a man "felt in his heart" that he had anything to say, he went from village to village claiming an audience, preceded by an advance agent who made all the necessary arrangements. There were prophets in those days, religious enthusiasts and reformers as well as politicians, and successful "spellbinders" who did not decline to teach their art to neophytes. Effects were studied. Apt illustrations and figures of speech would be remembered and appropriated by other orators. The flowing and meaningless gestures, so dear to our own early republican orators, did not enter into Indian speech. Descriptive pantomime and mimicry were used with profound and dramatic effect, as when the Wichita chief, standing before a commission which would have made windy terms with him, stooped, gathered a handful of dust, and tossing it lightly in the air replied: "There are as many ways as that to cheat an Indian." So seriously was the business of speech-making undertaken, that Powhatan is reported to have instantly slain one of his young men who interrupted him. And, so the chronicler relates, the only interruption to the speech was the carrying out of the body.

Examples in translation from the speeches of Logan, Red Jacket, and the Seneca chief who was called Farmer's Brother show traces of that balanced and flowing sentence structure which we associate with the Old Testament prophets. Direct observation of Indian speech-making leads the writer to conclude that the aboriginal orator composed his speech in units, the order and arrangement of which were varied to meet the special audience. This, if true,—and the decline of tribal life has occasioned such a decline in the art of speech-making that this is only an inference,—would relate the art of oratory to drama and cover one of the two or three gaps in the development of stanza form. Oratory had, however, an important function in relating literary composition to the audience, for it was the only art practised wholly for the purpose of affecting the decisions of the tribe.

There was something akin to oratory, and in the nature of sermonizing, which occurred in connection with the initiation of youth into tribal responsibility. Certain of the Elders, regarded as the repositories of tribal wisdom, were required to expound it from time to time, but always in connection with tribal mysteries, so that there is very little of it accessible in its original form. It probably tended to fall into aphoristic balance like the Wisdom of Solomon and the Almanac of Poor Richard.

> Would you choose a councillor,
> Watch him with his neighbour's children.
>
> *Sioux.*

> Do not stand wishing for the fish in the water,
> Go home and make a spear.
>
> *Puget Sound.*

Something of the high simplicity and clarity of aboriginal moralizing can be gathered in the writings of a man of such pure Indian stock as Charles Eastman. No one can associate intimately with Indians without continually surprising from them such apt and balanced utterances as this, from the last of the Catalinans:

I always remember what the old men told me: that the world is God.

Literary allusion, drawn from their folk or hero-tales, is part of the Amerind daily speech. Of an affair which makes a great stir without getting forward the Micmac will say: "It goes like the canoe that the Partridge made." The point of the comparison is in the fable of the Partridge who, observing that a canoe goes faster when the ends are well rounded, conceived the brilliant idea of a canoe which should be rounded on the sides also. The result was a bowl-shaped structure which went round and round without progress.

There was an apt anecdote like that for every occasion, or if there was not, somebody made one on the spot. This quick facility for noting resemblances, and the play of humour, has given us a body of folk-tale and fable not surpassed by any country in the world, folk-tale and fable which would illustrate our common American life with far more point than the things we derive from Europe.

Unfortunately, writers who have undertaken to utilize this material have missed its native quality, and attempted to crowd it into the mould of European fairy-tales, though in fact both the mood and the method of Amerind folk-tales are as distinctively American as the work of Mark Twain. In some respects Mark Twain in his shorter anecdotes, and Edgar Lee Masters in the *Spoon River Anthology*, have come nearer the mark of Amerind humour than any direct translation or interpretation. The one really notable success at transcription of the Amerind mode seems to have been accident, that sort of divine accident that one wishes might happen oftener. It appears that Joel Chandler Harris did not himself know, when he wrote them, that his Br'er Rabbit and Br'er Fox were original Cherokee inventions. In the reports of the Bureau of Ethnology, where you will find their Amerind forebears, the tales have a grim quality, a *Spoon River* quality, which to our understanding misses the humouresque which they had to the Indian. Coming to Harris as they did through the modified primitiveness of the negro, their essential frolicsomeness is transmitted with surprisingly few African interpolations. Undoubtedly there were exchanges between Indian and Negro slaves and assimilations took place at all their points of contact. But for the Americanness of the Uncle Remus stories, one has only to point to that other so popular folk hero, Get-Rich-Quick Wallingford, the Br'er Fox of the current hour.

One other supreme achievement in the adaptation of Amerind folk-tales is Frank Hamilton Cushing's *Zuñi Folk Tales*, almost the only convincing rendition of the non-sacred stories of the South-west. Particularly illuminating of the Amerind story method is the Zuñi version of the story of the Cock and the Mouse, and the adventure of the Twins of War and Chance among the Unborn Men of the Underworld, one of the few examples of pure Amerind prose.

All our conclusions about aboriginal prose style are more or less conjectural. Because of the necessity of carrying it wholly in mind, sacred matter was committed almost wholly to song and symbolic ritual. Explanation and narration of the story, necessary for the carrying out of these rites, took place only before the novitiates. When the rites themselves were made public, the story on which they were strung was sketchily the common possession. In the kiva or earth-lodge, in whatever sacred privacy they were rehearsed, the story was a solemn narrative, developed by repetition to explicit form. Beginning as informal prose, such a narrative tended to become more and more rhythmic, until it made a matrix within which the lyric and symbolic elements were enclosed. Tribal ceremonies in all stages of this logical development can be found among the American tribes, well on their way to becoming epic and drama.

In the descriptive and explanatory matter of Frances Dinsmore's *Sun Dance*, and in the prose intervals of the Hako Ritual as recorded by Alice Fletcher, one sees this process going on; and, incidentally, for the student of drama there is much light thrown on the office and evolution of the Greek chorus. For not the least advantage of the study of our own aboriginal literature is the place it fills in the evolution of form.

Amerind prose, and prose becoming poetized by growing important, has the first consideration, because this is the nearest point of contact. The earliest forms as well as the preponderant forms are all well within our own definition of poetry. That is to say, they have definite, repetitive rhythm pattern. They have sonority, assonance, and in some instances even alliteration and rhyme.

Over and above the quality of rememberability which every aboriginal composition was obliged to have, the instinctive choice of poetry as a medium of intimate expression had to do with the Indian's religion. He began by being convinced of unity and continuity of life. Earth, ant-heap, beast, and stone were permeated with the same Essence which was in himself, for which we may adopt the ethnologist's term Wakonda. To put himself in touch with the Wakonda of whatever item of creation held his interest of the moment, was the serious business of the Indian's days. He thought of the animals as nearer to the Cause of Causes than men were, and of the forces of nature as still nearer, being so much more mysterious. At all times and continuously he thought of the necessity of keeping himself in harmony with these.

First of all he hit upon the idea of rhythm, vibration, as being the secret of such harmony, the ululating voice, the cry beaten into rhythm with the hand, then the hollow log, the pebbled gourd. Then words began to rise like bubbles through the cry, mere syllables, unrelated words, a shorthand note to the emotions involved, all arranged around the emotional impulse which set them in motion, annotating the experience, but not until a much later stage describing it.

The process of raising annals, incident, and law to the point at which they became precious enough to require remembering, in other words, to the point at which they could be called literature, was obvious and slow. But spiritual and emotional experiences were literary in their mode from their very inception. That is to say, they could be drummed, if no more than on the singer's breast. Single personal experiences gave rise to the love song, the death song, the cradle song. Where a succession of incidents was required to complete the experience, the song sequence arose. Out of such sequences developed, with the help of the sustaining narrative, all epic and drama.

In this stage the poetic art admitted no aristocracy of talent. Any Indian who had a poetic experience could make a song of it, and apparently every Indian did. It is no uncommon thing even today to find a singer with a repertory of two hundred or more songs. Some of these will be found to be fragments of ceremonial sequences, but most of them will be personal expressions.

> I did not make my looks,
> Why blame me if the women fall in love with me?[1]

sings the Omaha beau;

Setting out on the war trail, the Pawnee sings

> Let us see is it real,
> This life that I am living.[2]

Thus the north coast lover:

> Even from a house of strong drink
> Men get away,
> But not from you,
> Raven woman.[3]

Alice Fletcher.   [2] Frances Dinsmore.   [3] Franz Boas.

Almost all personal songs are of this stenographic character so far as they are concerned with mere words. It is even possible to dispense with words altogether, but the translator will go astray who contents himself with the words and does not put into his work the rhythm pattern and the emotion of the melodic intervals. Music is to the highest degree literary with the aboriginal.

Even with these aids the meaning of Amerind verse is obscure unless one understands that the genius of the language is holophrastic. This is to say, there is an effort to express the relationship of several ideas by combining them into one word. In the Quicha tongue it is possible to say in a single word, "the-essence-of-being-as-existent-in-humanity." There is a Chippewa word, which means "I-laugh-in-my-thoughts," and an Algonkin word which an unliterary translator might render correctly as dawn, actually means "hither-whiteness-comes-walking."

Another difficulty encountered by the student of aboriginal American verse who is not also a student of aboriginals is the relationship of ideas. When the Paiute Ghost dancer sings

> The cottonwoods are growing tall,
> They are growing tall and green,

or the Ojibway,

> All night on the river I keep awake,

the first is not describing the spring landscape, but a vision of spiritual regeneration and resurrection from the dead. Nor has the latter lost his sweetheart: he speaks of the search of the soul for mystic completion.

As tribal culture advances, the stanza form makes its appearance, assonance, measure, and in descriptive passages an instinctive attempt to make the rhythms suggestive if not actually imitative.

Two or three distinct stanza forms with refrain can be found in the songs of the house-dwelling tribes of the South-west. Garcilasso de la Vega says that the Incas were proficient in the quatrain in which the first line rhymed with the last and the second with the third. Among our own tribes a very competent blank verse had developed, capable of carrying long narrative and susceptible of variation to meet the demands of dialogue.

In one or another of these forms all that was really important to the aboriginal American was stated. Longfellow, had he been more of an American and less of an academician, could have easily found native measures for his Hiawatha cycle without borrowing from the Finnish, although he showed more discrimination than most writers who have attempted to render Indian epics, in choosing a form that was very closely akin to the Amerind.

It is possible that the literary mode of the Amerind epics has been influenced by the native choice of story interest. While all of the longer poems begin with the creation of the world and purport to record the early wanderings of the tribe and its subsequent history, there is a notable lack of the warrior themes that occupy the epics of the old world. The Amerind hero is a culture hero, introducer of agriculture, of irrigation, and of improved house-building. Hiawatha, not Longfellow's Ojibway composite, but the original Haion 'hwa'tha of the Mohawks, was a statesman, a reformer, and a prophet. His very name ("he makes rivers") refers to his establishment of canoe routes among the Five Nations and with the peoples along the headwaters of the Ohio River. In company with Dekanawida, an Onondaga coadjutor, he formed the original League of Nations with the object of "abolishing the wasting evils of inter-tribal blood feuds."

We may select for analysis two of the best and best known of these culture epics, the *Walam Olum* already mentioned as the earliest American book, and the Zuñi Creation Myth as it has been made known to us through the labours of Frank Cushing.

The record of the Red Score was obtained by Constantine Samuel Rafinesque while he was holding the chair of Historical and Natural Science in the Transylvania University of Kentucky, and a translation was printed by him in 1836. The original copy was a collection of the before-mentioned bark or "board plates," incised and painted with the picture writings of the Lenni Lenape. The words, found somewhat later by Professor Rafinesque, have been pronounced by Daniel Brinton to be a genuine oral tradition written down by one not very familiar with the language.

The text consisted of a series of ideographic writings, each one representing a verse, obviously metrical, with syllabic and accentual rhythm, and occasional alliteration. That the syllabic arrangement is not accidental, but studied, is shown by the frequent sacrifice of the correct form of the word to secure it. The tendency to rhyme, especially to what is known today as internal rhyme, is noticeable, but Brinton thinks it possible that this may have been owed to influences of Christian hymns, with which the Lenni Lenape had been familiar for two generations. This seems hardly likely. It is as unlikely as that the Psalms of David should be affected by modern revivalism.

Two examples of the ideograph and accompanying verse from the *Walam Olum* are here given, those two which are probably of most interest to Americans of today, the advent of the first Tammany chief (Tamenend) and the coming of the Discoverers.

PLATE I

Weninitis Tamenend sakimanep
nekohatami
All being friendly, The Affable
was chief, the first of that name.

Wonwihil wapekunchi wapsıpsyat
At this time Whites came on the
eastern sea.

The Red Score begins with creation, when "On the earth there was an extended fog . . . at first, for ever, lost in space, there the Great Manitou was. . . ." After the creation, began the rise of the Lenni Lenape in a land which has been identified as north of the St. Lawrence, toward the east.

> The Lenape of the Turtle were close together
> In hollow houses, living together there.
> It freezes where they abode:
> It snows where they abode:
> It storms where they abode:
> It is cold where they abode.
> At this northern place they speak favourably
> Of mild, cool lands,
> With many deer and buffaloes.

Accordingly they set out for that land, but found their way blocked by the Tallegewi, generally conceded to be the Mound

Builders, who in turn are supposed to be the forebears of the present Cherokees. At first the Lenape made a treaty by which they were to be permitted to cross toward the south and east, but treachery arose. The Lenape retreated across Fish River, which was probably the Detroit crossing of the St. Lawrence, and, making an alliance with the Mingwe, the originals of the Five Nations, they descended on the Mound Builders and, after a hundred years' war, drove them south of the Ohio.

The Red Score relates further how the descending northern peoples distributed themselves in the region south of the Great Lakes, and the Lenni Lenape finally separated themselves from their allies, going toward the East River, the Delaware, where the English found them. The record ends practically with the beginning of white settlements, and there is no reason to believe that the epic as a whole is anything other than a fairly accurate traditional account of actual tribal movements.

The Zuñi creation epic, though never committed to writing, is several literary stages in advance of the *Walam Olum*. The Zuñi are a sedentary people living in the high valleys of what is now New Mexico. When Coronado discovered them in 1540 they were distributed among the Seven Cities of Cibola, subsisting on agriculture and an extensive trade with adjacent tribes in blankets, salt, cotton, and silver and turquoise jewelry. Like the *Walam Olum* their Creation Myth purports to give a history of the tribe from the creation of the world to its settlement in its present location. The manner in which it is preserved in entirety is exceedingly interesting. It is serial in composition, and the various parts are each committed to one of the priestly orders called the Midmost, whose office is hereditary in a single clan, outranking all other clans and priesthoods as "Masters of the House of Houses." Each division of the Epic is called a "Talk," but the completed serial is known as "The Speech." When performed in order accompanied by dance and symbolic rites, it constitutes the most interesting literary survival in the New World.

In structure the parts of the Zuñi myth indicate development from primitive song sequences, the narrative parts of which have been shaped, as already suggested, out of prose, into a blank verse matrix. Within this the speeches of the Uanami, or Beloved Gods, which were naturally the first parts to take permanent literary form, are enclosed. These speeches are more lyric in feeling than the narrative parts, and, says Cushing, "are almost always in faultless blank verse measure, and are often grandly poetic," an observation which is borne out by his own incompleted translations. See the following speech of the Beloved Gods, taking counsel how they will prepare the earth for men:

Let us shelter the land where our children are resting.
Yea, the depths and the valleys beyond shall be sheltered
By the shade of our cloud shield.
                              Let us lay to its circle
Our firebolts of thunder, to all the four quarters
Then smite with our arrows of lightning from under!
Lo the earth shall heave upward and downward with thunder!
Lo the fire shall belch outward and burn the world over
And floods of hot water shall seethe swift before it!
Lo, smoke of earth stenches shall blacken the daylight
And deaden the sense of them else escaping
And lessen the number of fierce preying monsters
That the earth be made safer for men and more stable.

Or later, in another measure, Pautiwa, the "cloud sender and sun priest of souls," speaks in the councils of the gods to the K'yah'he:

As a woman with children
Is loved for her power
Of keeping unbroken
The life line of kinsfolk,
So shalt thou, tireless hearer,
Be cherished among us
And worshipped of mortals
For keeping unbroken
The tale of Creation.

The prose portions of the tale relate how Awonawilona, the All-Father, was "conceived within himself and thought outward in space; whereby mists of increase, steams potent of growth, were evolved and uplifted." By this process of out-thinking he concentrated himself in the form of the Sun, forming out of his own substance the Fourfold-Containing Earth Mother and the All-Covering Father Sky. The world of men were the offspring of these two.

In the beginning men existed in an unfinished state in the lowest of the four cave wombs of the Earth, groping in darkness. Then appeared the first saviour who by virtue of his innate "wisdom-knowledge" made his way to the upper world. At his entreaty the Sun Father impregnated with his beam the Foam Cap of the sea, from which were brought forth the Beloved Twain, twin gods of Fate and Chance, who figure in all pueblo folk-lore, "like to question and answer in deciding and doing." In one of their metamorphoses they are described:

> Strong were they Twain,
>   Strong and hard favoured.
> Enduringly thoughtful were they Twain
>   Enduring of will.
> Unyieldingly thoughtful were they Twain
>   Unyielding of will.
> Swiftly thoughtful were they Twain
>   Swift of will.

The rest of the story, dealing with the rescue of men by the Beloved Twain, the rendering of the earth stable and safe, and the teaching of the arts of war and peace, is too involved for recapitulation. Tribal history is indicated, but in a mythological, mystical manner. The Zuñi are by temperament disposed toward symbols and abstractions, for which their language is well adapted.

The following description of the creation of the twin gods is an excellent example of the rhythmic, unmeasured matrix:

To them the Sun Father imparted, still retaining, control-thought and his own knowledge-wisdom, even as to the offspring of wise parents their knowingness is imparted, and as to his right hand and his left hand a skilful man gives craft, freely, not surrendering his knowledge.

In presentation, the Zuñi Creation Myth is dramatized. This is true so far as discoverable—for we do not know exactly how the *Walam Olum* was recited—of all the tribal cycles. But in dealing with Amerind drama we must distinguish between dramaturgic recapitulation of creative episodes, and drama as literary form. It has occurred to the primitive mind everywhere that the gods are influenced by representations of their supposed acts. The Shaman brings thunder by mimic thunder of his drum; he secures the return of summer by enacting the annual victory of heat and light over cold and darkness; he increases the fertility of the earth by performing reproductive acts amid solemn ceremonies.

It is possible that some such notion of promoting the welfare of the tribe may have been at the bottom of the performance at stated intervals of the pageant play of tribal history. But in most cases it has been superseded by motives of festivity and commemoration, and in part by those appetites for æsthetic enjoyment which we satisfy in modern drama.

The Indian is an excellent actor. Mirth-provoking mimicry and impromptu pantomime are the universal accompaniments of tribal leisure. Commemorative festivals frequently take the form of the Italian *commedia dell' arte*, in which an old story is played anew with traditional "business" and improvised lines.

In the history of one of the pueblos of the Rio Grande valley, there used to be celebrated a periodic community drama, which, given time to develop, might have resulted in a farce comedy of the sort which undoubtedly gave rise to, or at least suggested, the comedies of Aristophanes. The story relates that on an occasion when all the men of the pueblo were away on a buffalo hunt the women discovered an enemy party approaching. Hastily dressing themselves as men, the women stole upon their foes while they were still some distance from the pueblo, and by a show of force frightened them away. At the festival of this event, men and women change places for the whole of that day, wearing one another's clothes, assuming one another's duties, men at the ovens and women flourishing weapons. At some point in the day's events there is a re-enactment of the incident that gave rise to the celebration, in excellent pantomime, enriched by recollected "hits" of other days.

This sort of thing was usual throughout tribal life, and there is reason to believe that in the more advanced cultures it gave rise to more or less fixed comedy forms, some of which may yet be recovered in Mexico and Peru. Among our own Navaho Indians, parts of the Night Chant seem to be of this character. Unfortunately, however, the quality of the humour is such that it cannot be offered here. That such comedy, popular and universal as it was, did not receive what may be called literary form, is probably partly owing to the nature of comedy, which demands spontaneity as its chief concomitant, and in part to the lower esteem in which it was held. Comedy had little to do with making the world work well together, which was the primary object of Amerind literature.

What appears as a single exception to the seriousness of formal drama among American aborigines is the institution known among the pueblos of the South-west as the society of the Koshare, the Delight Makers. The function of this group is differently understood by ethnologists. Bandelier interprets it chiefly as social corrective through the whips of laughter. Originally it seems to have personated the Spirits of the Ancestors, in connection with ritual dancers, cheering the tribe with the assurance of interest uninterrupted by death. Always the Koshare are supposed to be invisible, so their quips cannot be resented. But there is no doubt also that there is symbolic association of their function with the fertility-inducing thunderstorms of early summer, and with the idea of laughter and good nature as mystically beneficial to both the tribe and the crops. Their black and white makeup, such as clowns have immemorially worn, and their antic behaviour, is the sole tribute of the Amerind mind to the æsthetic use of the Comic Spirit.

For the basis of serious drama we have to fall back on the song sequence, which we have just seen is also the source of epic. There is no tribe without a number of such sequences arranged around either a story or a dramaturgic presentation of a saving act. Not until this material is all collected and compared can we be certain at what point the untutored literary instinct of the aboriginal turned to one form or the other. At present it seems unsafe to conclude that a ritual of acts will invariably produce the dramatic form, or a sequence of episodes an epic. The most that we can say is that it is easier, on the whole, to trace the song sequence under what is left to us of even the most sophisticated Amerind drama.

In the *Ollantay Tambo*, the best example of Inca drama, reduced to Spanish by Don Antonio Valdez, the Cura of Tinto, some five years before all Inca drama was forbidden, the dialogue still breaks into lyric quatrains at the high moments. The story dialogue is carried in very good octosyllabic blank verse, but every important speech is cast in such verse as this quotation from the speech of Ollantay, the hero, when he goes to ask the hand of his daughter from the Inca Pachacuti:

> 'Twas I that struck the fatal blow
> When warlike Huncavila rose
> Disturbing thy august repose,
> And laid the mighty traitor low.[1]

Earlier in the play the friends of Ollantay warn him that his too ambitious passion for the Inca's daughter has been discovered; the warning is given in a song purporting to be addressed to the little field finch, in what appears to have been a favourite song measure:

> Thou must not feed,
> O Tuyallay,
> In Nusta's field,
> O Tuyallay,
> Thou must not rob,
> O Tuyallay,
> The harvest maize,
> O Tuyallay.

Let us select three of the many song sequences which are available for study, presenting three characteristic stages of literary development: the Songs of the Midé Brethren, a simple song ritual; the Hako, which might be described as a morality play or masque; and the Night Chant of the Navaho, which tends toward a generic American dramatic method.

The Midé Wiwin, or society of Shamans, is a secret organization of the Ojibway, including both men and women, and has for its object the attainment of mastery over the means of life, health, and subsistence, through communion with Spirit Power. Its chief interests to the literary student are the facts that it is one of the few literary enterprises which make use of "song boards," or "board plates," in which between straight lines are incised or painted mnemonic keys to the songs, and that the forms of those songs closely resemble the modern poetic mode which goes by the name of Imagism.

[1] Sir Clements Markham.

The Midé ritual is divided into four parts, each representing a degree of spiritual progress in the initiate, who must be letter-perfect in the songs. Each sequence is introduced by a recitative of instruction. Each song consists of a single sentence of recognizable poetic measure, repeated as many times as is necessary to complete the appropriate rhythm, with slight melodic variations.

When we say that the form of the Midé songs is Imagistic, we mean that each one of them states a thing apprehended through the external sense; something seen, heard, or done, enclosing a spiritual experience as in the thin film of a bubble. Thus, the literal Midé song says:

> The sky
> We have lost it.

But the shape of the song determined by the drum is as follows:

PLATE II

the words and additional meaningless syllables being repeated as often as necessary to complete it. The full content of this combination of words and rhythm, which is directed toward the acquirement of magic power over the weather, would be something like this:

> Darkness devours our sky!
> Toward its obscuring clouds
> We extend our hands
> For the favour of clear weather.
> By our power we attain it!

Though the idea of reaching toward the sky is not to be found in the words, it is plainly indicated in the ideographic key by a hand extended toward a cloud.

If we assume that the office of the drum in this song is merely to unify, an office that in our sort of verse is served by the conventions of the printed page, we may safely discard the drum measure in translating, as is here done. It would also be entirely within the province of faithful translation to express all the subtleties of Indian thought in this connection, the Indian's sense of the forces of nature, cloud, wind, and rain as being nearer to God than he is, and of his power over them through the attainment of mystic purity of heart and oneness of thought. The one convention of Indian verse which must not be broken is also the convention of Imagism, that the descriptive phrases must not merely describe, but must witness to something that has occurred in the soul of the singer. A little later in this same sequence this is even more clearly indicated. The women sing

> We are using our hearts,

meaning in full:

> With deep sincerity
> We join our hearts
> To the hearts of the Midé Brethren
>   To find our sky again.
> With our hearts
> Made pure by singing
> We uphold the hearts
>   Of our Midé Brethren
>   Seeking our sky.

Any number of interesting observations of the co-ordinate development of writing and poetry could be made from the study of this single ceremony, and the relation of both to their forest environment. In both there is that tendency, always so clearly marked in a complicated environment, to take the part for the whole, the leaf for the tree, the track of the bear's foot for the bear, the reaching hand for the aspiring spirit of man.

It is this suggested relation between literary form and the land which produced it, which gives point to a choice of the Hako ceremony of the Pawnees for analysis. Also, thanks to Alice Fletcher,[1] it is the best studied of Amerind rituals. The word Hako refers to the pulsating voice of the drum, the voice not only of the singers but the voice of all things, the corn, the eagle, the feathered stems, everything that partakes of the sacred function.

[1] See Bibliography.

The requisites of the Hako were such that only the well-to-do and important members of the tribe could assume responsibility for its performance. Two groups were required, who must not be of the same clan, and might even be of different tribes, for it was essentially a social drama, designed to insure friendship and peace between social groups, and to benefit society as a whole by bringing children to individuals.

Ritualistic in structure, the Hako exhibits a compactness and progressive unity that could be studied to advantage by modern writers of community masques and pageants. Miss Fletcher's analysis of the ceremony as a whole is so masterly that it would be as unfair to her as to the reader to abridge it. But there are some features that distinguish it as a literary production, which must be mentioned. Each movement is complete in itself, but indispensable. There is a closer relation between the emotional episodes and the rhythm, a finer web of words. Progressive stanza structure characterizes every movement. The verse forms are dramatically logical and rhythmically descriptive, the action leading and largely determining the form. To a very remarkable degree the verse contours conform to the contours of the country traversed, either actually or imaginatively, throughout the performance.

It is probable that this correspondence of form is unconscious on the part of the Pawnee authors, for, as with most folk-drama, many minds must have gone to the making of it. The Pawnees and cognate tribes who use the Hako have lived so long exposed to the influence of the open country about the Platte River that their songs unconsciously take the shape of its long undulations. Miss Fletcher has not always been successful in preserving the poetic quality of the songs, but their rhythms are most faithfully worked out, as in the following, one of a series of songs describing the journey of the Father group to the group called The Children:

> Dark against the sky yonder distant line
> Runs before, trees we see, long the line of trees
> Bending, swaying in the breeze,

which accurately represents the jog trot of journey across the rolling prairie. A little later comes the crowding of ponies on the river bank:

> Behold upon the river's bank we stand,
> River we must cross.
> Oh Kawas come, to thee we call,
> Oh come and thy permission give
> Into the stream to wade and forward go.

Finally, on the other side, after stanzas representing every stage of the crossing, there is the flick of the ponies' tails as the wind dries them.

> Hither winds, come to us, touch where water
> O'er us flowed when we waded,
> Come, O winds, come!

Again, as the visiting party draws up from the lowlands about the river, we have this finely descriptive rhythm:

The mesa see, it's flat top like a straight line cuts across the sky,
It blocks our path, and we must climb, the mesa climb.

What work in any language more obviously illustrates the influence of environment on literary form? Other examples there are of much subtler and more discriminating rhythms, but they only announce themselves after long intimacy with the land in which they develop. The homogeneity of the Amerind race makes it possible to detect environmental influences with a precision not possible among the mixed races of Europe.

In the Mountain Chant, the *Dislyidje qacal* of the Navaho, we have the Odyssey of a nomadic people, of great practical efficiency, wandering for generations in such a country as produced the earlier books of the Old Testament. It is notable that while the epics of their town-building neighbours, the Zuñi, Hopi, and Tewa peoples, are tribal, the chief literary product of the wandering Diné, like the story of Abraham, is the personal adventure of one man with the gods.

The full ceremony of the Night Chant is a nine days' performance of symbolic rites, song sequences, and dramatic dances. The final act of all, performed in public as a sort of tribal festival, at night, within a corral of juniper boughs, takes a special name, *Ilnasjingo qacal*, "chant within the dark circle of branches." This is the only part of the ceremony witnessed by whites, and conforms more nearly to our idea of dramatic entertainment.

The hero of the *Dislyidje qacal* is a Navaho, reared in the neighbourhood of the Carrizo Mountains, Arizona, from which he later takes his name, Dislyi Neyani, "Reared-within-the-Mountains." Having disregarded the instruction of his father while out hunting one day, he is taken captive by the Utes and carried to their country. Here the gods, in the shape of an old woman and an owl, the little burrow-nesting owl, signify their intention of befriending him, calling him very much as Abraham was called out of Ur of the Chaldees, and setting him, under their tutelage, on the trail toward his home.

The rest of the story is taken up with his adventures, all of a supernatural character, and all directed toward the Indian's great desideratum, the acquirement of mystical knowledge and power. The itinerary of this journey is mapped across the Navaho country as was the voyage of Ulysses along the coasts of the Mediterranean, with the addition of a number of places belonging exclusively to Navaho cosmogony, the House of the Dew, the House of the Lightning, and the House of the Rock Crystal.

Reaching his old home at the end of these adventures, Reared-within-the-Mountains discovers that even after he has been washed and dried with cornmeal according to the Navaho custom, the odours of his people and their lodges are intolerable to him. Finally the difficulty is remedied by performing over him the ceremony of the *Dislyidje qacal*, recapitulating his adventures, and his people become tolerable to him once more.

Not long after this ceremonial purification, Reared-within-the-Mountains is out hunting with his younger brother on Black Mountain. Suddenly he speaks and says: "Younger Brother, behold the Holy Ones." But his brother sees nothing. Then Dislyi Neyani speaks again:

Farewell, Younger Brother. From the holy places the gods come for me. You will never see me again, but when the showers pass and the thunders peal, "There," you will say, "is the voice of my Elder Brother." And when the harvest comes, of the beautiful birds and grasshoppers, you will say, "There is the ordering of my Elder Brother."

And with these words he vanished.

This incident of the passing of Dislyi Neyani is referred to in the Songs of the Thunder, of which the opening stanza of the first and the second stanza of the twelfth follow:

I

Thonah, Thonah!
There is a voice above,
The voice of the Thunder,
Within the dark cloud
Again and again it sounds!
Thonah, Thonah!

12

The voice that beautifies the land,
The voice above,
The voice of the grasshopper,
Among the plants.
Again and again it sounds,—
The voice that beautifies the land.

The ostensible purpose of any given presentation of the Night Chant is to cure sickness, but it is made the occasion of invoking the Unseen Powers on behalf of the people at large. The first four days are by way of preparation and purification, four being the sacred Navaho number, the number of the four quarters. The other five are essentially dramatic, beginning on the fifth day with an attempt to create the *mise-en-scène* with dry sand paintings on the floor of the Medicine Lodge.

Heretofore all pictorial designs of this sort have been studied wholly from the point of view of their relation to the religious significance of the rite. If the sand paintings, reproductions of which are to be found in reports of the Bureau of Ethnology, instead of being spread out flat, and the ritual performed around them, were stood up on edge with the ritual performed in front, we should quickly discover what seems clearly indicated, the operation of the dramatic instinct. Disciples of Gordon Craig and the symbolists would require very little assistance from the ethnologist to make out the relevance of the sand paintings to the action going on around them.

Nor is this the only green twig of modern stagecraft which may be observed at the Night Chant. The legerdemain of the

Hoshkwan dance, in which the yucca is made to appear as growing from the newly planted root to flower and fruit in about the space of an hour, is the forerunner of the theatrical "transformation scene" still so dear to popular taste. All these things will bear study from the theatrical point of view. For the literary rendering of the lines, from which quotations have been given, we are indebted to Washington Matthews, as well as for all we know as a whole of the Night Chant, or, as it is otherwise known, the Mountain Chant.

Like the Hako, the Navaho chant is based on a song sequence; the logical relation is scarcely discoverable without the accompanying action. Taken together, the songs, dances, and interpolated comedy of the last night's performance, within the dark circle of branches, is akin to that most American and popular variety of entertainment, the musical comedy. The same can be said of many of the South-west ceremonials, where the social character is evident, modifying the element of religious observance.

There is a disposition among ethnologists to regard the loosened structure of tribal performances as indicating the breaking down of religious significance. It seems perhaps rather the breaking in of the literary instinct; the unconscious movement of a people to utilize a philosophy already thoroughly assimilated and familiar as a medium of social expression.

It is not, however, the significance of Amerind literature to the social life of the people which interests us. That life is rapidly passing away and must presently be known to us only by tradition and history. The permanent worth of song and epic, folk-tale and drama, aside from its intrinsic literary quality, is its revelation of the power of the American landscape to influence form, and the expressiveness of democratic living in native measures. We have seen how easily some of our outstanding writers have grafted their genius to the Amerind stock, producing work that passes at once into the category of literature. And in this there has nothing happened that has not happened already in every country in the world, where the really great literature is found to have developed on some deep rooted aboriginal stock. The earlier, then, we leave off thinking of our own aboriginal literary sources as the product of an alien and conquered people, and begin to think of them as the inevitable outgrowth of the American environment, the more readily shall we come into full use of it: such use as has in other lands produced out of just such material the plays of Shakespeare, the epics of Homer, the operas of Wagner, the fables of Æsop, the hymns of David, the tales of Andersen, and the Arabian Nights.

Perhaps the nearest and best use we can make of it is the mere contemplation of its content and quality, its variety and extent, to rid ourselves of the incubus of European influence and the ever-present obsession of New York. For we cannot take even this cursory view of it without realizing that there is no quarter of our land that has not spoken with distinct and equal voice, none that is not able, without outside influence, to produce in its people an adequate and characteristic literary medium and form.

INDEX

Please note that this edition of "The Cambridge History of American Literature" consists of three volumes in one, and that this is the index only for Volume III. The indexes for Volumes I and II will be found toward the front of this edition.

Index

Index

Index 673